THE PAPERS OF

Andrew Jackson

•

DANIEL FELLER
EDITOR-IN-CHIEF

THE PAPERS OF

VOLUME VIII, 1830

DANIEL FELLER

THOMAS COENS

LAURA-EVE MOSS

EDITORS

•

Ed Speer, Erik B. Alexander, Vicki Rozema
Assistants

•

THE UNIVERSITY OF TENNESSEE PRESS
KNOXVILLE

Frontispiece: Andrew Jackson, 1830. Lithograph (detail).
Copy by Albert Newsam after William James Hubard. Courtesy of
National Portrait Gallery, Smithsonian Institution.

This book is printed on acid-free paper.

Library of Congress Cataloging in Publication Data
(Revised for vol. 8)

Jackson, Andrew, 1767–1845.
The papers of Andrew Jackson.
Vol. 2 edited by Harold D. Moser and Sharon MacPherson.
Vol. 6 edited by Harold D. Moser and J Clint Clifft.
Vol. 7 edited by Daniel Feller, Harold D. Moser, Laura-Eve Moss,
and Thomas Coens.
Vol. 8 edited by Daniel Feller, Thomas Coens, and Laura-Eve Moss.

Includes bibliographical references and indexes.
Contents: v.1. 1770–1803.—v.2. 1804–1813—[etc.]
—v.6. 1825–1828.—v.7. 1829.—v.8. 1830.
1. Jackson, Andrew, 1767–1845.
2. United States—Politics and government—1829–1837—Sources.
3. Presidents—United States—Correspondence
I. Smith, Sam B., 1929–.
II. Owsley, Harriet Fason Chappell.
III. Moser, Harold D.
IV. Feller, Daniel.
V. Title.

ISBN 0-87049-219-5 (v. 1: cl.: alk. paper)
ISBN 0-87049-441-4 (v. 2: cl.: alk. paper)
ISBN 0-87049-650-6 (v. 3: cl.: alk. paper)
ISBN 0-87049-778-2 (v. 4: cl.: alk. paper)
ISBN 0-87049-897-5 (v. 5: cl.: alk. paper)
ISBN 1-87049-174-7 (v. 6: cl.: alk. paper)
ISBN 978-1-57233-593-6 (v. 7: cl.: alk. paper)
ISBN 978-1-57233-715-2 (v. 8: cl.: alk. paper)

Publication of this volume was assisted by a subvention grant from
the National Historical Publication and Records Commission.

*Publication of
The Papers of Andrew Jackson
was supported by funding from*

THE COLLEGE OF ARTS AND SCIENCES OF
THE UNIVERSITY OF TENNESSEE, KNOXVILLE

THE NATIONAL HISTORICAL PUBLICATIONS
AND RECORDS COMMISSION

THE LADIES' HERMITAGE ASSOCIATION

THE TENNESSEE HISTORICAL COMMISSION
and

THE NATIONAL ENDOWMENT FOR THE HUMANITIES
a "We the People" project

Contents

For the page number on which each document
of The Papers begins, see the Calendar.

How to Use This Volume

HISTORY AND SCOPE OF THE PROJECT

This eighth volume of *The Papers of Andrew Jackson* is the second of Jackson's presidency and also the second produced by the team of chief editor Daniel Feller and associate editors Laura-Eve Moss and Thomas Coens. Our editorial policies, here briefly explained, continue unchanged from the previous volume.

Our aim is to systematically present Andrew Jackson's full extant literary remains. We define "papers" broadly, to mean everything written to, by, or for Jackson, or annotated by him—every piece of paper, so to speak, on which Jackson left his DNA. This includes incoming as well as outgoing correspondence, official documents, drafts, memoranda, and financial and legal records. (For a fuller definition, including some exclusions particular to Jackson's presidency, see "What is a Jackson Document?" below.)

The project began several decades ago with a worldwide canvass for Jackson papers. The search yielded photocopies of some 100,000 documents held by hundreds of libraries, archives, and private owners. The two largest holdings are in Washington, D.C. The bulk of Jackson's surviving retained personal papers are in the Library of Congress, while the National Archives has many Jackson documents scattered through its holdings of official records of the various branches of the federal government. In 1967 the Library of Congress microfilmed its entire Andrew Jackson Papers collection on 78 reels. The National Archives has also filmed many Jackson documents on its M and T series microfilms of government records. In 1987, when our project's initial document search was complete, we produced a 39-reel Microfilm Supplement containing all Jackson items that were not already on the National Archives or Library of Congress films. (We also refilmed some Library of Congress documents that were misdated or otherwise unfindable on the Library's own film.) As of 1987, then, every known Jackson document had been microfilmed by the Library, the Archives, or us. To provide unified access to them all, our project published *The Papers of Andrew Jackson: Guide and Index to the Microfilm Editions* (Scholarly Resources, Inc., 1987), which listed every document alphabetically by name of author or recipient, with the microfilm location for each. (For a full listing of microfilms pertinent to this volume, see "Microfilm Series" below.)

Meanwhile our project embarked on its plan to publish a carefully chosen selection of Jackson's papers in sixteen chronological volumes: six pre-presidential, one for each of the eight presidential years, and two post-presidential. This volume is part of that series. Presenting the most significant documents in full annotated text, and summarizing the rest in calendar form, the volumes are designed both to stand on their own as a compilation of Jackson's most important papers and to offer to those who wish to delve further an easy window into the full corpus of papers available on microfilm.

Although our initial search for Jackson's papers was painstakingly thorough, new documents continue to surface at a surprising rate. Those discovered in time are incorporated into the chronological volumes, including this one, as they appear. We also plan to gather images of all the documents found since 1987, and therefore absent from the existing microfilms, in a concluding digital supplement when the volume series is complete.

WHAT IS A JACKSON DOCUMENT?

The following types of papers lie within our corpus:

Documents written or signed by Jackson, except those excluded below.

Documents composed for Jackson, such as drafts of his messages.

Documents addressed, written, or delivered to Jackson.

Documents annotated, inscribed, or endorsed by Jackson.

All documents in the Library of Congress Jackson Papers. These were, with few if any exceptions, papers received and kept by Jackson even if not addressed to him.

Other items that were microfilmed and included in our *Guide and Index*, especially some civil commissions signed by Jackson and job applications and recommendations addressed to his private secretary, Andrew Jackson Donelson. Even if these do not meet our present definition of Jackson documents, they are retained herein to preserve, as much as possible, a one-to-one correspondence between the listings in the *Guide and Index* and the volume. On the other hand, a very few items that were included as Jackson documents in the microfilm and the *Guide and Index* not by a variant definition but by simple mistake have been omitted.

We exclude the following:

Routine official documents bearing Jackson's signature as president (unless appearing in the microfilm and *Guide and Index*, as above). These are often printed forms with handwritten insertions. They include civil and military commissions, land patents, proclamations of federal land sales, diplomatic credentials, consular exequaturs, and ship passes.

Reported utterances, conversations, or remarks by Jackson, unless made from a written text.

Communications made by others in Jackson's name, such as a letter from a government official beginning "the president directs me to say...."

Published materials ostensibly addressed or inscribed to Jackson or to the president, unless known to be sent to him or seen by him.

Spurious documents, either faked, forged, or misattributed. We have encountered no prominent spurious documents for 1830.

ORGANIZATION AND PRESENTATION

Like its predecessors, this volume contains three parts. The main body presents full texts of Andrew Jackson's most significant papers from 1830 with explanatory notes. Following the text is a calendar—a chronological listing of *all* the papers, with a brief content synopsis for each item not printed in full. Together, the text and calendar account for every 1830 Jackson document falling within our definition of his papers. The index at the back provides full coverage of document authors, recipients, and contents for both text and calendar.

The volume text, calendar, and index can be used in tandem with each other and with the microfilms and microfilm *Guide and Index* to pursue almost any kind of research inquiry. If the subject is a person, say John Doe, the *Guide and Index* will give dates and microfilm locations for all letters he wrote to, or received from, Jackson. Each letter will also be either printed in the appropriate volume or summarized in its calendar. If Doe is mentioned in a letter by someone else, that mention will appear in the volume index. Reaping the full benefit of a volume requires consulting calendar as well as main text, and using the index as a guide to both.

Selection of Documents for Printing

Nearly one-third of Jackson's 1830 papers are presented here in full text; the rest are calendared. We have selected for printing what we judge to be the most significant papers, defining significance by the widest possible criteria: those documents that most illuminate Jackson, his presidency, his country, and his times. In general we have made our decision to print a document regardless of whether it has been previously published. However, Jackson's public papers—his official presidential addresses, messages, and proclamations—constitute a special case.

Jackson's Official Papers

Jackson's presidential public papers in 1830 include his second annual message to Congress, two vetoes, several proclamations, messages to the Senate conveying nominations for office or submitting treaties for ratification, and various special messages to one or both houses of Congress, often transmitting documents or reports. Nearly all these papers have been published in one or more of three official series. First, many messages to Congress with their attachments were immediately printed by order of the House or Senate and included in the consecutively numbered volumes of congressional documents known as the Serial Set. Secondly, messages concerning nominations and treaties, received by the Senate in executive session, were later collected and published in Volume IV of the *Journal of the Executive Proceedings of the Senate of the United States of America.* Lastly, at the end of the nineteenth century James D. Richardson published under congressional authorization *A Compilation of the Messages and Papers of the Presidents 1789–1897* in ten volumes, the second and third of which included Jackson's presidency. Richardson's compilation was itself included in the Serial Set (*House Miscellaneous Document* 210, 53d Congress, 2d session, Serial 3265) and was reissued in several later editions. (These editions were variously repaginated. All page citations herein are to the original, official Serial Set version.)

Today all three publications are widely available, not only in print but through electronic media. (As of this writing, the *Senate Executive Proceedings* and portions of the Serial Set have been posted to the Library of Congress website entitled American Memory: A Century of Lawmaking for a New Nation.) Their texts are reliable and authoritative. There seems no point to reproduce in this volume previously published documents that readers can find at their fingertips; and to do so would consume much precious space. Accordingly we have determined not to print the final, official texts of any presidential papers that appeared in the Serial Set, the *Senate Executive Proceedings,* or Richardson. The manuscript originals of these documents, residing now generally in the National Archives, were microfilmed by our project and listed in the *Guide and Index;* they are calendared here, and their publication in official series is uniformly noted. But they are not printed. However, we do print the rare presidential message that escaped official publication and we also print drafts, where such exist and differ significantly from the final versions. Readers may track the evolution of, for instance, Jackson's Maysville Road veto or his second annual message to Congress by comparing the drafts in this volume to the final texts in the Serial Set or Richardson.

For a full listing of Jackson's 1830 public papers with their official publication history, see the table "Jackson's Presidential Public Papers" below.

Ordering of Documents

The general order of documents, both in text and calendar, is chronological. Inferred dates are given in brackets; estimated ones are preceded by c (*circa*). Items within a month, or within the year 1830, that cannot be dated more precisely go at the end of the month or year respectively. Documents with spread dates, such as running financial accounts, are placed at their opening date. Within each day, letters from Jackson, arranged alphabetically by recipient, come first, followed by letters to Jackson alphabetically by author, then other Jackson documents, and lastly third-party correspondence. However, where a chronology can be established within a day—an exchange of notes back and forth, for instance—the documents composing it are grouped in sequence.

A special case concerns the private memorandum book Jackson began keeping in 1829. It contains a sequential series of entries, mostly short and undated, and some longer memoranda at the back. To preserve the book's distinctive character, we have not broken up the 1830 sequential entries into individual items but printed them in two groups, close to their likely time of composition, at the end of March and beginning of November.

Transcription

Each document printed here is presented in full, including all endorsements or notations by Jackson on documents written by others. The originals of most documents are handwritten. Where the original is a printed text, for instance a letter published in a contemporary newspaper, its appearance and typography have been replicated as closely as possible.

Converting handwriting to print is an inexact process. It requires rendering a nearly limitless array of pen markings into a finite set of typographic characters. In Jackson's era, even polished writers often punctuated sentences with marks that lay somewhere between clear dashes, periods, commas, or semicolons; and they formed letters such as *c, m,* and *s* not simply in upper or lower case but in a variety of styles and gradations of size. Jackson, for instance, had at least three, not two, distinct ways of making an *a* and a *t*.

That said, within the limits of the medium, our policy is to reproduce the original text as closely as possible, retaining its peculiarities of grammar, spelling, capitalization, and punctuation. When Jackson reversed "the" and "they," as he sometimes did, we have transcribed just what he wrote, without comment or [*sic*]. The following are exceptions and clarifications. Inadvertent word repetitions ("and and"), nonfunctional dashes following other punctuation, and addressees' names at the end of a document have been omitted. Superscript characters have been brought down to the main line. Dates placed at the bottom of a document have been moved up to the top, and interlined or marginal additions have been inserted in the text at the spot marked by the writer. Cross-outs, where decipherable, are represented by lined-through text. Interpolated readings of missing or obscured text are bracketed; where conjectural, they are also italicized. Complimentary closings to letters ("your obedient servant") have been run onto the preceding text. Implied but unpunctuated sentence breaks, as at the end of a line, are represented by elongated spacing.

Annotation

Each printed document is followed by a source note that identifies its type, its repository or owner, its location on microfilm (in parentheses), and whether it has been previously published, as shown in the example below. Where more than one version of a document exists, the one we print is listed first.

> ALS, DNA-RG 59 (M179-68). AL draft, THi (12-1456); LC, DLC (60). *Niles,* January 18, 1830; *Doe Papers,* 18:243.

In this sample case, our printed text is from an Autograph Letter Signed (ALS)—a letter handwritten and signed by its sender—housed in Record Group 59 of the National Archives (DNA-RG 59) and filmed on Reel 68 of National Archives microfilm series M179 (M179-68). There is also an unsigned draft of the letter in the sender's hand (AL draft) in the Tennessee Historical Society (THi) and filmed on Reel 12, frame 1456, of the Microfilm Supplement produced by this project; and also a letterbook copy (LC) held by the Library of Congress (DLC) and filmed on Reel 60 of the Library's Jackson Papers microfilm. The letter was published contemporaneously in *Niles' Weekly Register* and again in the modern *Papers of John Doe.*

For lists and explanations of document types, repositories, microfilm series, and publication titles, see "Codes and Symbols" below. Our general policy in noting previous publication of a document is to cite the first or earliest known contemporary printing and the most authoritative modern one. For items we print, we do not cite previous appearance in John Spencer Bassett's *Correspondence of Andrew Jackson,* which our series supersedes.

The source note also presents information germane to or explanatory of the document as a whole. Numbered footnotes, keyed to callouts in the text, give further information on particular points. Our aim is to offer only what facts are necessary to make a document intelligible and to place it in immediate context, leaving the rest to the reader.

We have tried to briefly identify, with full name and dates, each person named in the text at the point of his or her first significant appearance. A caution is however in order. Systematic government recording of births, deaths, and legal names began long after 1830. In the absence of official records, family researchers have assembled a plethora of genealogical data of highly variable provenance and quality. We have used such information only with extreme care. Still, readers should be aware that dates and full names for many people appearing in this volume are less than certain.

We have not routinely employed cross-referencing footnotes to link up related documents within the volume, as these may be located by using the index and calendar. When Jackson writes to Smith, "I have received yours of the 17th instant," that letter, if extant, will appear in the calendar at its proper date ("instant" means this month; "ultimo" means last month) and it, with all other mentions of Smith, will be indexed under his name. Likewise we have not noted "not found" for Smith's letter if it is not extant or not known to us. The calendar includes all found documents. Any letter not listed in it was not found.

Calendar

In the calendar, each entry for a document printed in the volume is italicized, with a page number. The calendar thus also serves as a table of contents for the main text. For a document not printed in the volume, the calendar entry presents the same identifying and locating information as a text source note (see Annotation above), followed by a brief synopsis of contents. To save space, we have in a very few cases merged the entries for substantively identical documents of the same date—for instance, multiple copies of a printed petition. Routine Jackson notations on incoming documents—for instance, referring a letter to one of the executive departments—are not mentioned in the calendar. However, we have noted substantive Jackson endorsements, and also those on third-party letters where the endorsement is what makes the item a Jackson document.

Codes and Symbols

DOCUMENT TYPES

Abbreviations

A   Autograph—written in the author's hand
D   Document—a manuscript document other than a note or letter
L   Letter—a manuscript letter
LC   Letterbook copy—a handwritten copy recorded in a letterbook
N   Note—a brief informal manuscript message or memorandum
S   Signed—bearing the author's signature

Other Notations

Abstract   A précis of a document
Copy   A handwritten copy
Draft   A handwritten draft
Duplicate   A document created in identical multiple versions
Extract   A copied or printed excerpt from a document
Facsimile   A pictorial image of a manuscript document
Fragment   A partial document
Printed   A printed document

Sample Combinations

AL   Autograph Letter—an unsigned sent letter, written by the sender
ALS   Autograph Letter Signed—a sent letter, written and signed by the sender
ALS copy   Autograph Letter Signed copy—a copy of a sent letter, written and signed by the sender
ALS draft   Autograph Letter Signed draft—a draft of a sent letter, written and signed by the sender
LS   Letter Signed—a sent letter, signed by the sender but written in another hand

REPOSITORIES

A-Ar	Alabama Department of Archives and History, Montgomery
ArU	University of Arkansas, Fayetteville
CLjC	James S. Copley Library, La Jolla, Calif.
CSmH	Henry E. Huntington Library, San Marino, Calif.
CSt	Stanford University, Stanford, Calif.
CtHi	Connecticut Historical Society, Hartford
CtY	Yale University, New Haven, Conn.
CU-BANC	Bancroft Library, University of California, Berkeley
DCU	Catholic University of America, Washington, D.C.
DLC	Library of Congress, Washington, D.C.
DNA	National Archives, Washington, D.C.
	RG 11, General Records of the United States Government
	RG 15, Records of the Department of Veterans Affairs
	RG 26, Records of the United States Coast Guard
	RG 28, Records of the Post Office Department
	RG 45, Naval Records Collection of the Office of Naval Records and Library
	RG 46, Records of the United States Senate
	RG 49, Records of the Bureau of Land Management
	RG 50, Records of the Treasurer of the United States
	RG 56, General Records of the Department of the Treasury
	RG 59, General Records of the Department of State
	RG 60, General Records of the Department of Justice
	RG 75, Records of the Bureau of Indian Affairs
	RG 76, Records of Boundary and Claims Commissions and Arbitrations
	RG 77, Records of the Office of the Chief of Engineers
	RG 80, General Records of the Department of the Navy
	RG 84, Records of the Foreign Service Posts of the Department of State
	RG 92, Records of the Office of the Quartermaster General
	RG 94, Records of the Adjutant General's Office
	RG 104, Records of the U.S. Mint
	RG 107, Records of the Office of the Secretary of War
	RG 108, Records of the Headquarters of the Army
	RG 125, Records of the Office of the Judge Advocate General (Navy)
	RG 127, Records of the United States Marine Corps
	RG 153, Records of the Office of the Judge Advocate General (Army)

	RG 156, Records of the Office of the Chief of Ordnance
	RG 192, Records of the Office of the Commissary General of Subsistence
	RG 206, Records of the Solicitor of the Treasury
	RG 217, Records of the Accounting Officers of the Department of the Treasury
	RG 233, Records of the United States House of Representatives
	RG 393, Records of the United States Army Continental Commands
F	Florida State Library, Tallahassee
FrPMAE	Archives du Ministère des Affaires Étrangères, Paris
G-Ar	Georgia State Department of Archives and History, Atlanta
GHi	Georgia Historical Society, Savannah
ICHi	Chicago Historical Society, Chicago, Ill.
InU	Indiana University, Bloomington
KHi	Kansas State Historical Society, Topeka
LNHiC	Historic New Orleans Collection, New Orleans, La.
LNT	Tulane University, New Orleans, La.
MB	Boston Public Library, Boston, Mass.
MdHi	Maryland Historical Society, Baltimore
MeB	Bowdoin College, Brunswick, Maine
MH-H	Houghton Library, Harvard University, Cambridge, Mass.
MHi	Massachusetts Historical Society, Boston
MiDbEI	Edison Institute, Henry Ford Museum, and Greenfield Village Library, Dearborn, Mich.
MiU-C	William L. Clements Library, University of Michigan, Ann Arbor
MMHi	Milton Historical Society, Milton, Mass.
MNS	Smith College, Northampton, Mass.
Ms-Ar	Mississippi Department of Archives and History, Jackson
MWiW-C	Chapin Library, Williams College, Williamstown, Mass.
NBuHi	Buffalo and Erie County Historical Society, Buffalo, N.Y.
NcD	Duke University, Durham, N.C.
NcU	University of North Carolina, Chapel Hill
NHi	New-York Historical Society, New York, N.Y.
NIC	Cornell University, Ithaca, N.Y.
NjHi	New Jersey Historical Society, Newark
NjMoHP	Morristown National Historical Park, Morristown, N.J.
NjP	Princeton University, Princeton, N.J.
NN	New York Public Library, New York, N.Y.
NNPM	Pierpont Morgan Library, New York, N.Y.
NWM	United States Military Academy, West Point, N.Y.
OCX	Xavier University, Cincinnati, Ohio

OHi	Ohio Historical Society, Columbus
PHi	Historical Society of Pennsylvania, Philadelphia
PP	Free Library of Philadelphia, Philadelphia, Pa.
PPPM	Philadelphia Museum of Art, Philadelphia, Pa.
PPRF	Rosenbach Foundation, Philadelphia, Pa.
PPT	Temple University, Philadelphia, Pa.
PU	University of Pennsylvania, Philadelphia
RPB	Brown University, Providence, R.I.
RPB-JH	John Hay Library of Rare Books and Special Collections, Brown University, Providence, R.I.
ScU	University of South Carolina, Columbia
T	Tennessee State Library and Archives, Nashville
THer	Ladies' Hermitage Association, Hermitage, Tenn.
THi	Tennessee Historical Society, Nashville
TLWil	Wilson County Archives, Lebanon, Tenn.
TNDa	Davidson County Archives, Davidson County Court, Nashville, Tenn.
TNJ	Vanderbilt University, Nashville, Tenn.
TU	University of Tennessee, Knoxville
Tx	Texas State Library and Historical Commission, Austin
TxU	University of Texas, Austin
Uk	British Library, London
UkOxU-As	Oxford University, All Soul's College, Oxford, England
UPB	Harold B. Lee Library, Brigham Young University, Provo, Utah
Vi	Virginia State Library, Richmond
ViFreM	University of Mary Washington, Fredericksburg, Va.
ViHi	Virginia Historical Society, Richmond
ViLeTBL	Thomas Balch Library, Leesburg, Va.
ViU	University of Virginia, Charlottesville
ViW	College of William and Mary, Williamsburg, Va.
WHi	Wisconsin Historical Society, Madison

MICROFILM SERIES

Microfilm citations (in parentheses) are of four types:

37	The Library of Congress Andrew Jackson Papers microfilm, listed by reel number (reel 37). For contents of reels cited in this volume, see below.
M179-68 or T967-1	National Archives microfilms, listed by publication series and reel number (series M179, reel 68, or series T967, reel 1). For series titles cited in this volume, see below.
12-1456	*The Papers of Andrew Jackson* Microfilm Supplement, listed by reel and frame number (reel 12, frame 1456).
mAJs	Items acquired since 1987 and therefore not included on the Library of Congress, National Archives, or project microfilms. These will be collected in an addendum at the project's conclusion.

Library of Congress Andrew Jackson Papers Reels, 1830

37–38	General correspondence
58–59	Undated correspondence
60	Undated correspondence & letterbook
64	Memorandum book
72–73	Correspondence
75	Correspondence and a volume of copied 1829 letters regarding the Eaton affair
76	Presidential message drafts

National Archives Microfilms

M6	RG 107: Letters Sent by the Secretary of War Relating to Military Affairs, 1800–1889
M9	RG 59: Despatches from U.S. Consuls in Cap Haitien, Haiti, 1797–1906
M15	RG 75: Letters Sent by the Secretary of War Relating to Indian Affairs, 1800–1824
M18	RG 75: Register of Letters Received by the Office of Indian Affairs, 1824–1880
M21	RG 75: Letters Sent by the Office of Indian Affairs, 1824–1881
M22	RG 107: Registers of Letters Received by the Office of the Secretary of War, Main Series, 1800–1870

M25 RG 49: Miscellaneous Letters Sent by the General Land Office, 1796–1889

M30 RG 59: Despatches from U.S. Ministers to Great Britain, 1791–1906

M34 RG 59: Despatches from U.S. Ministers to France, 1789–1906

M40 RG 59: Domestic Letters of the Department of State, 1784–1906

M46 RG 59: Despatches from U.S. Ministers to Turkey, 1818–1906

M50 RG 59: Notes From the British Legation in the United States to the Department of State, 1791–1906

M52 RG 59: Notes From the Danish Legation in the United States to the Department of State, 1801–1906

M53 RG 59: Notes From the French Legation in the United States to the Department of State, 1789–1906

M54 RG 59: Notes From the Mexican Legation in the United States to the Department of State, 1821–1906

M55 RG 59: Notes From the Kingdom of the Two Sicilies Legation in the United States to the Department of State, 1826–1860

M57 RG 59: Notes From the Portuguese Legation in the United States to the Department of State, 1796–1906

M60 RG 59: Notes From the Swedish Legation in the United States to the Department of State, 1813–1906

M65 RG 77: Letters Sent by the Office of the Chief of Engineers Relating to Internal Improvements, 1824–1830

M77 RG 59: Diplomatic Instructions of the Department of State, 1801–1906

M97 RG 59: Despatches from U.S. Ministers to Mexico, 1823–1906

M124 RG 45: Letters Received by the Secretary of the Navy: Miscellaneous Letters, 1801–1884

M125 RG 45: Letters Received by the Secretary of the Navy: Captains' Letters, 1805–1861

M127 RG 107: Letters Sent to the President by the Secretary of War, 1800–1863

M148 RG 45: Letters Received by the Secretary of the Navy from Officers Below the Rank of Commander, 1802–1884

M149 RG 45: Letters Sent by the Secretary of the Navy to Officers, 1798–1868

M178 RG 56: Correspondence of the Secretary of the Treasury with Collectors of Customs, 1789–1833

M179	RG 59: Miscellaneous Letters of the Department of State, 1789–1906
M205	RG 45: Correspondence of the Secretary of the Navy Relating to African Colonization, 1819–1844
M209	RG 45: Miscellaneous Letters Sent by the Secretary of the Navy, 1798–1886
M221	RG 107: Letters Received by the Secretary of War, Registered Series, 1801–1870
M222	RG 107: Letters Received by the Secretary of War, Unregistered Series, 1789–1861
M234	RG 75: Letters Received by the Office of Indian Affairs, 1824–1881
M235	RG 217: Miscellaneous Treasury Accounts of the First Auditor (Formerly The Auditor) of the Treasury Department, 1790–1840
M273	RG 125: Records of General Courts-Martial and Courts of Inquiry of the Navy Department, 1799–1867
M472	RG 45: Letters Sent by the Secretary of the Navy to the President and Executive Agencies, 1821–1886
M477	RG 49: Letters Sent by the Surveyor General of the Territory Northwest of the Ohio River, 1797–1854
M478	RG 49: Letters Received by the Secretary of the Treasury and the Commissioner of the General Land Office From the Surveyor General of the Territory Northwest of the River Ohio, 1797–1849
M531	RG 59: Letters of Application and Recommendation During the Administration of John Quincy Adams, 1825–1829
M567	RG 94: Letters Received by the Office of the Adjutant General (Main Series), 1822–1860
M601	RG 28: Letters Sent by the Postmaster General, 1789–1836
M625	RG 45: Area File of the Naval Records Collection, 1775–1910
M639	RG 59: Letters of Application and Recommendation During the Administration of Andrew Jackson, 1829–1837
M668	RG 11: Ratified Indian Treaties, 1722–1869
M688	RG 94: U.S. Military Academy Cadet Application Papers, 1805–1866
M699	RG 60: Letters Sent by the Department of Justice: General and Miscellaneous, 1818–1904
M735	RG 56: Circular Letters of the Secretary of the Treasury ('T' Series), 1789–1878

M804   RG 15: Revolutionary War Pension and Bounty-Land
         Warrant Application Files
M857   RG 108: Letters Sent by the Headquarters of the Army
         (Main Series), 1828–1903
M899   RG 59: Despatches From U.S. Consuls in Havana, Cuba,
         1783–1906
M977   RG 80: Navy Department General Orders and Circulars,
         1798–1862
M1113   RG 77: Letters Sent by the Chief of Engineers, 1812–1869
M1329   RG 49: Letters Received by the Secretary of the Treasury
         and the General Land Office from the Surveyor
         General for Mississippi, 1803–1831
T1   RG 59: Despatches From U.S. Consuls in Paris, France,
         1790–1906
T33   RG 59: Despatches From U.S. Ministers to Colombia,
         1820–1906
T34   RG 59: Notes From Central American Legations in the
         United States to the Department of State, 1823–1906
T203   RG 59: Despatches from U.S. Consuls in Fayal, Azores,
         Portugal, 1795–1897
T215   RG 59: Despatches from U.S. Consuls in Leipzig,
         Germany, 1826–1906
T239   RG 59: Despatches from U.S. Consuls in Southampton,
         England, 1790–1906
T412   RG 60: Opinions of the Attorney General, 1817–1832
T431   RG 59: Despatches from U.S. Consuls in St. Pierre,
         Martinique, French West Indies, 1790–1906
T494   RG 75: Documents Relating to the Negotiation of
         Ratified and Unratified Treaties With Various Indian
         Tribes, 1801–1869
T967   RG 59: Copies of Presidential Pardons and Remissions,
         1794–1893
T1212   RG 59: Records of Special Agents for Securing the Florida
         Archives, 1819–1835
T1223   RG 59: Presidential Proclamations 1–2160, 1789–1936

PUBLICATION SHORT TITLES

The Autobiography John C. Fitzpatrick, ed., *The Autobiography of*
  of Martin Van   *Martin Van Buren*. Washington, 1920.
  Buren
Bassett   John Spencer Bassett, ed., *Correspondence of*
                     Andrew Jackson. 7 vols. Washington, D.C.,
                     1926–1935.

Burke	Pauline Wilcox Burke, *Emily Donelson of Tennessee*. 2 vols. Richmond, Va., 1941.
Calhoun Papers	W. Edwin Hemphill and Clyde N. Wilson, eds., *The Papers of John C. Calhoun*. 28 vols. Columbia, S.C., 1959–2003.
Clay Papers	James F. Hopkins et al., eds., *The Papers of Henry Clay*. 11 vols. Lexington, Ky., 1959–1992.
Correspondence of Jeremy Bentham	Timothy L. S. Sprigge et al., eds., *The Correspondence of Jeremy Bentham*. 12 vols. to date. London and New York, 1968–.
Hamilton *Reminiscences*	*Reminiscences of James A. Hamilton*. New York, 1869.
Hansard's Parliamentary Debates	Thomas Hansard, ed., *Hansard's Parliamentary Debates*. 3 ser. London, 1829–1891.
HRDoc	U.S. Congress, House of Representatives, *House Documents*.
HRRep	U.S. Congress, House of Representatives, *House Reports*.
House Journal	U.S. Congress, House of Representatives, *Journal of the House of Representatives of the United States*.
Jackson Papers	Harold D. Moser et al., eds., *The Papers of Andrew Jackson*. 8 vols. to date. Knoxville, Tenn., 1980–.
John Ross Papers	Gary E. Moulton, ed., *The Papers of Chief John Ross*. 2 vols. Norman, Okla., 1985.
Madison Papers	William T. Hutchinson et al., eds., *The Papers of James Madison*. 17 vols. Chicago, Ill. and Charlottesville, Va., 1962–1991.
Nat. Intelligencer	Washington, D.C., *Daily National Intelligencer*.
Niles	*Niles' Weekly Register*.
Parton	James Parton, *Life of Andrew Jackson*. 3 vols. New York, 1860.
Polk Correspondence	Herbert Weaver, Paul H. Bergeron, and Wayne Cutler, eds., *Correspondence of James K. Polk*. 11 vols. to date. Nashville and Knoxville, Tenn., 1969–.
Register of Debates	U.S. Congress, *Register of Debates in Congress*. 14 vols. Washington, D.C., 1825–1837.
Richardson	James D. Richardson, ed., *A Compilation of the Messages and Papers of the Presidents, 1789–1897*. 10 vols. Washington, D.C., 1896–1899.
SDoc	U.S. Congress, Senate, *Senate Documents*.
Senate Executive Proceedings	*Journal of the Executive Proceedings of the Senate of the United States of America*.

Senate Journal	U.S. Congress, Senate, *Journal of the Senate of the United States of America.*
Serial	*United States Congressional Serial Set.*
TPUS	Clarence E. Carter and John Porter Bloom, eds., *The Territorial Papers of the United States.* 28 vols. Washington, D.C., 1934–1975.
US Telegraph	Washington, D.C., *United States' Telegraph.*
Works of Jeremy Bentham	John Bowring, ed., *The Works of Jeremy Bentham.* 11 vols. Edinburgh, 1838–1843.
Writings of Sam Houston	Amelia W. Williams and Eugene C. Barker, eds., *The Writings of Sam Houston, 1813–1863.* 8 vols. Austin, Texas, 1934–1975.

ABBREVIATIONS

AJ	Andrew Jackson
BUS	Bank of the United States
GLO	General Land Office

Lists and Tables

1830 CHRONOLOGY

Jan 27 Daniel Webster concludes "Liberty and Union" speech, climaxing Senate debate with Robert Hayne

Jan 29–30 Jackson meets with secretaries Berrien, Branch, and Ingham to resolve Cabinet crisis over the Eaton affair

Mar 10 Senate unanimously rejects Henry Lee for consul general to Algiers

Mar 31 Pennsylvania legislative caucus proposes Jackson for a second term

Apr 12 Senate rejects Isaac Hill for Treasury second comptroller

Apr 13 Jackson toasts "Our *Federal* Union" at Jefferson birthday dinner

Apr 13 George McDuffie submits House Ways and Means report championing the Bank of the United States

May 6 Jackson sends two Choctaw removal treaty projects to the Senate

May 7 Charles Rhind concludes commercial treaty with Turkey at Constantinople

May 10 Senate confirms Amos Kendall as Treasury fourth auditor on Calhoun's tie-breaking vote

May 13 Jackson accuses Calhoun of treachery over his 1818 Seminole campaign; Calhoun responds May 29

May 27 Jackson vetoes Maysville Road bill. Navy secretary Branch sends Kendall's reports on Miles King's and John B. Timberlake's accounts to the House

May 28 Jackson signs Indian Removal Act

May 29 Jackson signs Preemption Act for public land settlers and law authorizing him to reopen the British West Indian colonial trade by proclamation

May 31	Congress adjourns. Jackson vetoes Washington Turnpike bill and pocket-vetoes Louisville and Portland Canal and lighthouse bills
Jun 1	Georgia law assuming state jurisdiction over Cherokees goes into effect
Jun 14	Jackson pardons mail robber George Wilson
Jun 17	Jackson departs Washington for Tennessee via Wheeling and the Ohio River
Jun 26	George IV of England dies; succeeded by William IV
Jul 1	"Great State Rights Celebration" held at Charleston, S.C.
Jul 2	Execution of mail robber James Porter at Philadelphia
Jul 6	Jackson arrives at the Hermitage
Jul 27–29	Three-day Paris uprising leads to overthrow of Charles X and installation of Louis Philippe as French constitutional monarch
Aug 8	General Land Office commissioner George Graham dies
Aug 10	U.S. minister to Russia John Randolph reaches St. Petersburg; departs for London Sep 19
Aug 31	Chickasaws and U.S. commissioners John Eaton and John Coffee conclude a removal treaty at Franklin, Tenn.
Sep 1	Jackson departs overland from the Hermitage, reaching Washington Sep 25
Sep 27	Choctaws conclude a removal treaty with Eaton and Coffee at Dancing Rabbit Creek
Oct 5	Jackson opens British West Indian colonial trade by proclamation
Oct 25–31	Jackson and Andrew J. Donelson correspond over the Eaton affair
Nov 8	War Department orders U.S. troops withdrawn from Cherokee country
Dec 6	Congress convenes; Jackson sends in his second annual message
Dec 7	Washington *Globe* begins publication
Dec 13	Alabama legislature elects Gabriel Moore senator over John McKinley
Dec 20	Jackson nominates Stockley D. Hays for surveyor of southern public lands

JACKSON'S PRESIDENTIAL PUBLIC PAPERS, 1830

DATE	DOCUMENT TYPE[1]	RECIPIENT	RICHARD-SON[2]	*JEPS*[3]	SERIAL SET[4]	*PAJ*[5]
Jan 2	Proclamation				196	
Jan 2	Proclamation				196	
Jan 2	Proclamation				196	
Jan 4	Message	Senate	464–65		192	
Jan 4	Nomination	Senate		35		
Jan 4	Nomination	Senate		41		
Jan 4	Nomination	Senate		35		
Jan 4	Indian Treaty	Senate	465	41		
Jan 5	Message	House	466			
Jan 5	Message	Senate	466		192	
Jan 5	Nomination	Senate		43		
[Jan 5]	Nomination	Senate		41–42		
Jan 6	Nomination	Senate		44		
Jan 13	Nomination	Senate		45–47		
Jan 13	Nomination	Senate		48		
Jan 13	Nomination	Senate		48		
Jan 14	Message	Congress	466		196	
Jan 18	Nomination	Senate		51		
Jan 19	Message	Congress	466–67		196	
Jan 19	Nomination	Senate		51		
Jan 19	Nomination	Senate		51		
Jan 20	Message	Congress	468		196	
Jan 20	Nomination	Senate		51		
Jan 20	Nomination	Senate		50		
Jan 20	Nomination	Senate		49–50		
Jan 22	Nomination	Senate		51–53		
Jan 25	Nomination	Senate		53		
Jan 25	Nomination	Senate		53–54		
Jan 25	Nomination	Senate		54		
Jan 26	Message	Congress	468		196	
Jan 26	Message	Congress	468–72		196	
Jan 26	Nomination	Senate		54		
Jan 30	Message	Congress	473		196	
Feb 3	Nomination	Senate		54		

DATE	DOCUMENT TYPE[1]	RECIPIENT	RICHARD-SON[2]	*JEPS*[3]	SERIAL SET[4]	*PAJ*[5]
May 1	Nomination	Senate	477	99		
May 4	Nomination	Senate		99		
May 5	Nomination	Senate		99		
May 6	Indian Treaty	Senate	478–79	97–99		228–30
May 6	Nomination	Senate		99		
May 6	Nomination	Senate		100		
May 6	Nomination	Senate		100		
May 7	Nomination	Senate		100		
May 7	Nomination	Senate		100		
May 12	Nomination	Senate		103		
May 13	Message	House	479–80		198	
May 13	Message	House	480		198	
May 13	Nomination	Senate		103		
May 13	Nomination	Senate		102–3		
May 14	Message	Congress	480		194	
May 15	Nomination	Senate		103		
May 20	Nomination	Senate		106		
May 21	Nomination	Senate	480	106		
May 22	Nomination	Senate		108		
May 24	Nomination	Senate		107		
May 25	Nomination	Senate		108		
May 25	Message	House	480		194	
May 25	Nomination	Senate		109		
May 26	Message	Congress	480–81		198	
May 26	Nomination	Senate		108		
May 27	Message	House				278–79
May 27	Veto	House	483–93		198	279–300
May 27	Treaty	Senate	481–82	112		
[May] 28	Nomination	Senate		114		
May 28	Nomination	Senate	482	113		
May 28	Nomination	Senate		113		
May 29	Message	House	482		194	
May 29	Nomination	Senate		115		
May 29	Message	Senate	482		193	
May 29	Nomination	Senate		115		
May 29	Nomination	Senate		115		

DATE	DOCUMENT TYPE[1]	RECIPIENT	RICHARD-SON[2]	JEPS[3]	SERIAL SET[4]	PAJ[5]
May 29	Nomination	Senate		115		
May 29	Nomination	Senate		117		
May 29	Nomination	Senate		119		
May 29	Nomination	Senate		117		
May 30	Nomination	Senate		121		
May 31	Message	Congress	483		198	
May 31	Veto	Senate	493–94		191	
[May 31]	Veto	Not Sent				323–31
Jun 5	Proclamation				206	
Sep 18	Proclamation		496–97			
Oct 5	Proclamation		497–99		203	
Dec 6	Annual Message	Congress	500–529		203	650–80
Dec 9	Indian Treaty	Senate	529	126	202	
Dec 9	Nomination	Senate		127		
Dec 10	Message	Congress	530		206	
Dec 10	Treaty	Senate	530	126		
Dec 11	Nomination	Senate		128		
[Dec 14]	Nomination	Senate		127–28		
Dec 14	Nomination	Senate		129		
Dec 15	Message	Congress	530		206	
Dec 15	Nomination	Senate		129		
Dec 15	Nomination	Senate		129		
Dec 15	Nomination	Senate		129–30		
Dec 17	Nomination	Senate		130		
Dec 17	Nomination	Senate		133–34		
Dec 18	Nomination	Senate		135		
Dec 18	Nomination	Senate		135		
Dec 20	Nomination	Senate		135		
Dec 20	Treaty	Senate	531	134		
Dec 20	Indian Treaty	Senate	530–31	134–35		
Dec 23	Nomination	Senate		136		
Dec 23	Nomination	Senate		136		

DATE	DOCUMENT TYPE[1]	RECIPIENT	RICHARD-SON[2]	JEPS[3]	SERIAL SET[4]	PAJ[5]
Dec 27	Nomination	Senate		137		
Dec 28	Nomination	Senate		138		
Dec 28	Nomination	Senate		138		
Dec 29	Indian Treaty	Senate	531	140		
Dec 29	Nomination	Senate		140		
Dec 30	Nomination	Senate	531	141		
Dec 30	Nomination	Senate		142		
Dec 31	Message	Congress	531–32		203	
Dec 31	Nomination	Senate		141		
Dec 31	Nomination	Senate		141		
Dec 31	Nomination	Senate		141		

1. Presidential communications to Congress are as follows. "Annual Message" is the general message reviewing the state of the Union, delivered to both houses of Congress at the opening of its regular annual session. "Nomination" is a message to the Senate, received in executive session, submitting or discussing nominations of civil or military officers whose appointments require Senate advice and consent. "Treaty" or "Indian Treaty" is a message to the Senate, received in executive session, submitting or discussing treaties whose ratification requires Senate advice and consent. "Veto" is a message rejecting a bill passed by Congress and returning it to the house where it originated. "Message" is any other message to either or both houses of Congress.

2. Page numbers in vol. 2 of James D. Richardson, ed., *A Compilation of the Messages and Papers of the Presidents, 1789–1897* (Washington: Government Printing Office, 1896), *House Miscellaneous Document* 210, 53d Cong., 2d sess., Serial 3265.

3. Page numbers in vol. 4 of *Journal of the Executive Proceedings of the Senate of the United States of America* (Washington: Government Printing Office, 1887).

4. Volume numbers within the *United States Congressional Serial Set*. For a document's number and location within the Serial Set volume, see the calendar listing for it herein.

5. Page numbers in this volume of *The Papers of Andrew Jackson*.

JACKSON'S DONELSON FAMILY CONNECTIONS, 1830

(ages on January 1, 1830)
(deceased persons in italics)
(Volume VIII correspondents in boldface)

First generation: sons and daughters of *John Donelson* and *Rachel Stockley*
      Second generation
            Third generation

Alexander Donelson, 78

Catherine Donelson, c77, m. *Thomas Hutchings*
      John Hutchings, their son
            Andrew Jackson Hutchings, 18, John's orphaned son

John Donelson, 74, m. Mary Purnell, 66
   their children:
      John Donelson, 42, m. Eliza Eleanor Butler, 38
      Lemuel Donelson, 40
      Rachel Donelson m. *William Eastin*
            Mary Ann Eastin, 19, their daughter
      Mary Donelson, 36, m. **John Coffee**, 57
            Mary Donelson Coffee, 17, their daughter
      William Donelson, 34, m. Elizabeth Anderson, 20
      Elizabeth Donelson, 33, m. **John Christmas McLemore**, 39
            Mary McLemore, 13, their daughter
            John Coffee McLemore, 11, their son
      Catherine Donelson, 30, m. James Glasgow Martin, 38
      Stockley Donelson, 24, m. Phila Ann Lawrence, 20
      Emily Tennessee Donelson, 22, m. Andrew Jackson Donelson[1]
            Andrew Jackson Donelson, 3, their son
            Mary Rachel Donelson, their infant daughter

Mary Donelson m. *John Caffery*
   their children:
      Donelson Caffery, 43
      Jane Caffery m. **Ralph Eleazar Whitesides Earl**, 41

William Donelson m. *Charity Dickinson*
   their children:
      Severn Donelson, 32

Jacob Donelson, 28
Martha H. Donelson, 20, m. **Robert Minns Burton**, 29
    Elizabeth Charity Burton, 2, their daughter
    William Donelson Burton, their infant son
Elizabeth Hays Donelson, 10

Jane Donelson, 63, m. *Robert Hays*
  their children:
    Rachel Hays, 43, m. **Robert Butler**, 43
    Stockley Donelson Hays, 41, m. Lydia Butler, 41
      Sarah Jane Hays, 15, their daughter
      Richard Jackson Hickory Hays, 7, their son
    Martha Thompson Hays, 39, m. William Edward Butler, 39
      William Ormonde Butler, 15, their son
    Narcissa Hays, 34
    Samuel Jackson Hays, 29, m. Frances Pinckney Middleton, 18
    Elizabeth Hays, 24, m. **Robert Johnstone Chester**, 36

Rachel Donelson m. **ANDREW JACKSON**
    Andrew Jackson Jr. (adopted), 21[2]

Samuel Donelson m. Mary Ann Smith, 48
  their children:
    Andrew Jackson Donelson, 30, m. Emily Tennessee Donelson[1]
    Daniel Smith Donelson, 28

Severn Donelson m. *Elizabeth Rucker*
  their children:
    James Rucker Donelson
    Andrew Jackson Jr.[2]
    Thomas Jefferson Donelson, 21
    Lucinda Rucker Donelson, 17

Leven Donelson, 53

    This listing is not complete. The marriages of Rachel Jackson's brothers and sisters produced more than fifty adult children and innumerable grandchildren. Only those named in Jackson's 1830 correspondence are shown here.

    1. Emily Tennessee Donelson married her first cousin Andrew Jackson Donelson.

    2. Andrew Jackson Jr., adopted in infancy by Andrew and Rachel Jackson, was the son of Severn Donelson and birth twin of Thomas Jefferson Donelson.

The Papers, 1830

PRINCIPAL CHARACTERS

The Cabinet

Secretary of State Martin Van Buren, of New York
Secretary of the Treasury Samuel Delucenna Ingham, of Pennsylvania
Secretary of War John Henry Eaton, of Tennessee
Secretary of the Navy John Branch, of North Carolina
Attorney General John Macpherson Berrien, of Georgia
Postmaster General William Taylor Barry, of Kentucky

In Washington

Vice President John Caldwell Calhoun, of South Carolina
Margaret O'Neale Timberlake Eaton, wife of the Secretary of War
Duff Green, editor and publisher of the *United States' Telegraph*
Isaac Hill, Second Comptroller of the Treasury
Amos Kendall, Fourth Auditor of the Treasury
William Berkeley Lewis, Second Auditor of the Treasury
Thomas Loraine McKenney, Superintendent of Indian Affairs
Philip Grymes Randolph, chief clerk of the War Department

Diplomats Abroad

Louis McLane, minister to Britain
William Cabell Rives, minister to France
John Randolph, minister to Russia
Anthony Butler, chargé d'affaires in Mexico
Charles Rhind, James Biddle, and David Offley, envoys to Turkey

Family

Andrew Jackson Jr., Jackson's adopted son
Andrew Jackson Donelson, Jackson's nephew and private secretary, and
    his wife and cousin—
Emily Tennessee Donelson, Jackson's niece and White House hostess
Mary Ann Eastin, Emily Donelson's niece and companion
Samuel Jackson Hays, Jackson's nephew
Andrew Jackson Hutchings, Jackson's grandnephew and ward

Companions and Confidants

John Coffee, of Alabama
Hardy Murfree Cryer, near the Hermitage
Ralph Eleazar Whitesides Earl, in Tennessee and Washington
James Alexander Hamilton, in New York City
Samuel Houston, with the Western Cherokees
Charles Jones Love, near the Hermitage
John Christmas McLemore, in Nashville
John Overton, in Nashville

January

To James Alexander Hamilton

[Although the twenty-year congressional charter of the second Bank of the United States (BUS) would not expire until 1836, the question of its renewal had already arisen during Jackson's first year in office. In November 1829, BUS president Nicholas Biddle (1786–1844) offered Jackson a plan by which the Bank would expedite retiring the national debt in return for an early recharter. In a private meeting, Jackson thanked Biddle but said he thought Congress had no power to charter banks outside the District of Columbia (Reginald C. McGrane, The Correspondence of Nicholas Biddle Dealing with National Affairs, *pp. 93–94). Then, in his December 8, 1829, first annual message to Congress, Jackson declared against recharter, saying that "both the constitutionality and the expediency of the law creating this bank are well questioned by a large portion of our fellow-citizens, and it must be admitted by all that it has failed in the great end of establishing a uniform and sound currency" (James D. Richardson, ed.,* A Compilation of the Messages and Papers of the Presidents, 1789–1897, *2:462).*

Jackson's attack on the Bank surprised many. James Alexander Hamilton (1788–1878), a son of Alexander Hamilton whom Jackson had appointed federal district attorney for New York, had helped Jackson craft the passage. Afterwards, a New York press report suggested that unnamed persons in the city had used their advance knowledge of Jackson's position to speculate in BUS stock. On December 16, Duff Green (1791–1875), editor of the administration's Washington organ, the United States' Telegraph, *wrote Hamilton to warn him of the charge. Green also accused Biddle himself of manipulating the Bank's stock by spreading false assurances before the message that Jackson would favor recharter. Hamilton wrote Jackson on December 22, enclosing Green's letter and denying any connection with BUS stock dealings (Jackson Papers, 7:645–46).]*

Washington Janry 1rst. 1829—

My Dr. Sir

your letter of the 22nd. ultimo was recd. in due course of mail, & in reply I have to observe that I regret that you should have thought it necessary to have declared to me that you had no agency in speculating in the

· 3 ·

bank stock, or making advantage of your knowledge of my opposition to a rechartering of the Bank of the U. States—you are surely aware of my exalted opinion of your virtue & honesty, & this must convince you, that I think you incapble of any thing dishonest, dishonorable, or unfair.

The last paragraph of Genl Greens letter surprised me, & I sought an interview with him to be informed on what he rested the assertion of Mr Biddles declarations, with regard to me & my cabinet being friendly to the rechartering of the Bank, he gave me the name of his informant, & reasons for his belief that it was true—for myself I cannot believe it, for Major Biddle acknowledged my frankness to him on this subject, to Major Lewis[1] & others, and I can scarcely believe that he for the sake of vile speculation, would state what he knew to be false—But the longer we live the more we will learn of mankind, & I fear its morale is not improving as fast as I could wish it.

Present to your amiable family the kind salutations of me & mine & believe me yr friend

Andrew Jackson

ALS, NN (14-1260). Hamilton *Reminiscences*, pp. 153–54.
1. William Berkeley Lewis (1784–1866) was AJ's political manager and the second auditor of the Treasury. Biddle had submitted his debt retirement plan through him.

To Susan Wheeler Decatur

[Jackson's appointment of Tennessee senator John Henry Eaton (1790–1856) to the Cabinet as secretary of war sparked a controversy at the administration's outset which deepened into 1830. On January 1, 1829, Eaton had married Margaret ("Peggy") O'Neale (1799–1879), daughter of Washington innkeeper William O'Neale (c1751–1837). Margaret's first husband, Navy purser John Bowie Timberlake (c1791–1828), had killed himself at sea in April 1828. His widow's quick remarriage to Eaton scandalized Washington. Philadelphia clergyman Ezra Stiles Ely and others charged Margaret with a history of promiscuous sexual relations, including a longstanding liaison with Eaton that presumably provoked Timberlake's suicide. Jackson repelled the charges and pressed for the names of the informants. In September 1829, Washington minister John Nicholson Campbell (1798–1864) revealed himself as the source for a story that Margaret had miscarried Eaton's child some years earlier while Timberlake was abroad. Jackson quit attending Campbell's Second Presbyterian Church, confronted him before the Cabinet, and nearly provoked a duel between Eaton and Campbell's friend, Army paymaster general Nathan Towson.

Susan Wheeler Decatur (c1776–1860) was the widow of naval hero Stephen Decatur. In his first annual message, Jackson had pressed her

claim for prize money for the frigate Philadelphia, *destroyed by Decatur in a daring raid in Tripoli harbor in 1804 after it was captured by Barbary pirates (Richardson, 2:462). On December 31, 1829, Susan Decatur wrote Jackson about her claim (Jackson Papers, 7:659). She also enclosed an anonymous note warning her not to associate with Mrs. Eaton.]*

Washington Janry. 2d. 1830—

My Dr Madam

I have the pleasure of acknowledgeing the receipt of your note of thursday last, together with its enclosure. You may rest asured, Madam, that my aid shall be most cheerfully accorded in support of your claim & getting it allowed by Congress. I believe it a just & righteous one, and should have long since been recognised by the Government, & paid. I have too much confidence in the disposition of Congress to do justice to those gallant men, and their Representatives, to believe for a moment they will refuse to mete to them the same measure of justice that has so often been extended to others in similar situations. It will however be necessary for you and your friends, to act with great caution and circumspection—studiously avoiding every thing that may by possibility be calculated to produce the least feeling on the part of the members of Congress.[1]

I perfectly agree with you that the anonymous letter you enclose me, is evidence not only of a *malicious* and vindictive community in this District, but also of *a corrupt* and *profligate* community. I believe no lady has been more basely slandered, or cruelly persecuted than Mrs. Eaton. I have heard much *said* to her prejudice, but no one has even yet had the hardihood to say to me, that he or she, of their own knowledge, knew any thing against her, as a moral virtuous, and correct woman

I have on all occasions, treated Mrs. Eaton with as much respect as any other lady in the District, because I have ever believed her entitled to it; and I shall continue to do so, unless I shall become convinced she is undeserving of it, in spite of the sneers and *tittle tattle* of a set of gossips who, in ~~every~~ many respect are greatly her inferiors, and in none, as I believe, her superiors. I hope, my dear madam, you know too well what is due to the sex, and your own character, to be intimidated by the threats of such *base, corrupt,* and *unprincipled villains* as your anonymous correspondents. I shall keep the letter you have inclosed me, with the hope of being able some day, of finding out the name of its *vile author*—I think I know *him & her*. I am with much respect your friend

Andrew Jackson

ALS, PP (14-1294). LS copy in William B. Lewis's hand, DLC (37).

1. A bill to compensate Susan Decatur and other claimants from Decatur's crew was reported by the House Committee on Naval Affairs on January 7, but did not pass.

From James Taylor

Columbus Ohio Jany 3d. 1830

Dear Sir

Our youngest daughter Jane has accompanied Mrs. Judge Mc.lean to your city. I presume she will spend part of her time with Mrs Barry.

She has just completed her education, & Mrs Taylor was desirous she should see something of the World having scarcely been as yet out of our immediate naybourhood. Mrs. T. expects & wishes some of our friends, Mrs Barry or Mrs. Mclean will make my daughter acquainted with your self & your household. We have endeavored to give her the best advantages our country affords, as to education, & I trust it has not be thrown away on her.

Mrs Taylor is still your devoted friend, and we both feel very anxious for your health, which we are pleased to learn is much improved latterly   Mrs Mclean is a very old & particular friend of Mrs. T. she spent considerable time with us, when single. our daughter will accompany Mrs Mc. to Phila. on a visit to her daughter & will, I understand return that way home.

The Message is generally approved, as far as my knowledge has enabled me to judge. It is not to be expected that the violent oppositionists will approve ~~much~~ any thing.

The greatest diversity of opinion on that able State paper, appear to be on the subject of the National Bank ~~question~~, it has its friends & a great many enemies in the Western Country. with great respect I have the honor to be Dr Sir your obed St

James Taylor

ALS, DLC (37). *Register of the Kentucky Historical Society*, 34 (1936): 334. James Taylor (1769–1848), of Newport, Ky., had been a militia general in the War of 1812. His wife was Keturah Moss Taylor (1773–1866) and his daughter was Jane Maria Taylor (1806–1872). Taylor's son James had married Susan, daughter of AJ's postmaster general William Taylor Barry (1784–1835) and his late first wife. Barry's present wife was Catherine Armistead Mason Barry (1793–1873). Rebecca Edwards McLean (1786–1841) was the wife of John McLean (1785–1861) of Ohio, appointed by AJ to the Supreme Court in 1829.

To Edward Livingston

Monday morning Janry. 4th. 1830—

Genl Andrew Jackson presents his respects to the Honble E. Livingston, will thank him to return by the bearer, the notes upon the U. States Bank, with the other manuscript.

AN, NjP (mAJs). Livingston (1764–1836), a U.S. senator from Louisiana, had been AJ's volunteer aide at New Orleans. In 1831 AJ appointed him secretary of state.

From Willie Blount

[Willie Blount (1768–1835) had been governor of Tennessee, 1809–15. He began this January 4 letter to Jackson by copying out a letter to himself from Parry Wayne Humphreys (1778–1839), a Tennessee congressman in 1813–15 and now a state judge.]

Clarksville Octr 22d. 1829

Dear Sir,

You request me to write you the substance of a conversation had with you, many years ago, relative to the first appointment of General Jackson in the service of the U. S—It will be difficult to recollect, at this time, the particulars—I then gave you a detail of the facts and circumstances: and as I now remember them, they are these—I think it was, in the winter of 1814, when I was a Repr. in Congress from this State, I recd. from you a letter, in which, you suggested the propriety of the General being employed in the U.S. Service—you spoke of his energy of character, talents, and qualification for command—In the Spring of that year, the republican party in Congress, favorable to the successful prosecution of the war, was much dejected and depressed, our military movements to the north having been unprosperous: the Treasury exhausted: the recruiting service, in some places, opposed: the credit of the Government reduced, and the administration censured and abused: Congress being about to adjourn, a general gloom was visable in the countenances of the republican members—a few days before the adjournment, I recd. from William G. Blount, a hand-bill giving an account of the battle of the Horse-Shoe, in which, the Creek Indians were entirely vanquished, and a termination, thereby, put to the Creek war—with the document in my hand I went, rather exultingly, to the House: as I approached the steps, which led to the Chamber of the House of Repts., I met Doctor Condict, of New Jersey, with other members: I observed to them, I had good news from the west, & gave the hand-bill to Doctor Condict:[1] he read it aloud, to the great delight of all present: when it was read through, I observed to the Company, that General Jackson ought to be in the regular army of the U.S:—Doctor Condict, after a few words of conversation on the subject said, if you will write a recommendation of him to the President, we will sign it—I observed, that General Jackson, being a Major General in the State service, would not accept the office of Brigadier; that we must recommend him for Major General, or we could not obtain his acceptance; this, was immediately agreed to—The Doctor and myself went to our Desks, in the Chamber, which were adjacent to each other: I there wrote two recommendations, one, to be signed by the Tennessee Delegation, the other, for the members generally. They were, severally, handed to Doctor Condict, who copied them, he, writing a fairer and more legible hand, than myself—They were then signed, to wit, that drawn for the Tennessee Delegation, by all the members from Tennessee, as they came to the House, except General Sevier,[2] to whom, it was not presented, he being absent: the other, was signed by about thirty of the members from other States: I inclosed them to the President—In a day, or two, afterwards, I was about starting home, when, I waited on General Armstrong, the then Secy War, to know the result of the recommendations: he told me, the subject was then under his consideration, seemed disposed to comply with the wish of the recommenders, but stated, there was some doubt, whether the Senate would sanction an elevation of a Major General, in the service of a State, over the heads of Brigadiers, in the regular service, that Body having, in one instance, refused to do so—I left him, and was satisfied that the appointment would be made, if practicable—some short time after I had returned home I learned, that General Jackson had been appointed Major General in the Army of the U.S.—This: all happened when Congress sat, in the Capitol, and before that edifice was burned by the enemy—Doctor Condict and myself were both very anxious, that the General should be appointed, fully believing, that the public service would be greatly promoted by having General Jackson at the head of the Army of the U. S—your respectful and sincere friend[3]

Signed, Parry W. Humphreys

Note on the above—I need not employ words to show my motive in writing to Judge Humphreys, at the time, & upon the occasion he alludes to when he says, he recd. a letter from me: nor to shew my gratification at your apptmt. to a place of usefulness in the army—[4]

Jany 4th 1830, near Turnersville
Robertson County, Tenn.

Dear Genl.

I well recollect, that shortly after Judge Humphreys returned home from Congress, about the period above stated, that he mentioned to me the above particulars: & also recollect, that when you recd. the apptmt. of Brigadier in the regular army & mentioned it to me, at Nashville, that I observed, accept it, that it would soon lead to your promotion to the rank of Major General: I dont know whether Humphreys ever knew, that you were first apptd. a Brigadier—after hearing you say when last at the Hermitage, that until lately before that, the manner in which you had been recommended for an apptmt. in the regular army, had been unknown to you, I, as soon as I saw Judge Humphreys, asked him to give me the particulars so far as related to the recommendation made by him and others;

and in justice to him, and to the other, then, members of Congress who signed those recommendations, respectively, as above stated, I transmit to you the foregoing copy of Humphreys's letter; presuming, that the information would be acceptable to you to have in your possession; and have done so, without the knowledge of Humphreys, or of any other of the signers: Humphreys, is a good & an amiable man, and as a sincere friend, I have known him, for twenty years, worthy of trust and confidence. Doctor Condict is, I believe, still a member.

Your very, very excellent message, on reading it, was as I expected it to be, and it occasioned my heart to leap for joy—Our mutual friend Major Baker died a few days ago, and has, no doubt, gone to Heaven[5]—He did not live to see your message, which, however, he expressed, repeatedly, his great desire to see: his exit was on the day of its coming to our vicinity— that your health is good, and that it may long continue so, is the earnest desire of your devoted friend

Willie Blount

I read the Richmond Enquirer—the Editor does justice to your administration—it affords me great pleasure to see his just applause, bestowed on the reports made by the heads of Depts.[6]—the political oppositionists don't know what to be at: they will however, worry themselves somehow, no doubt; but the foundation is knocked from under them, and away they will go, to Sea, without a rudder, where, they will founder & sink, & no matter as politicians of that order how soon—Branch, Eaton, & myself, are Carolinians, and you, Eaton & I, are Tenn-folks, our neighbourhood, hereabouts, has many Carolinians, acquainted with Eaton & Branch, and we sometimes get together and say, respecting them, well done, good and faithful men, and express thanks to the President, for appointing men to office who are both capable and honest, as well as ever engaged in usefulness like yourself, beloved by all—[7]

I have, by me, the rough draft of sundry letters, from me to you, none of which have yet been either copied or mailed: they relate to things gone bye, & so, no matter whether they are ever sent or not: they only speak of the pleasureable feelings I experience in the knowledge I possess of the motives & conduct in the various promotions of my friend, yourself, & the results of your efforts since the battle at Nickajack, commanded by Ore; where, as Sampson William says our friend the mountain Leader, the friend of man, was at that never to be forgotten good day's work in which, you lent an active useful hand, that gave peace to our frontier, never to be forgotten by me—[8]

In your letter you said you would like to see my digests in print—they were not intended for the press: their contents are already before the public: and to print mine, could be of no use to an intelligent & well informed public: but the perusal of those digests, by my grand children, & by the sons of a few friends, in manuscript, for whose perusal they are, in that dress, intended, may, possibly, be of use to them: & to me, for the present, they will enable me to say, amen, to your acts, founded on the principles contained in them: & if you had not have come into office, they might have assisted, to put your wrongheaded predecessor out of office—

Where is your Son Andrew, & how is he? hope he is studious & doing well—let Judge White know of Major Baker's death: he was the sincere friend of the Judge, & the Judge his—I see that Jonny Q. has arrived at his son's, at Washington: he will die hard—cunning & intrigue are engrafted in some men's system: their opus operandi et modus show it—I make latin to suit myself—[9]

Having all my life acted from my own counsel, and as life, owing to the variety of employment with me, has been eventful, and never having acted, except from what I thought good motive, free, as I have believed, from selfishness, have relied on my acts speaking for themselves, as far as they were known, and have but seldom indulged in giving, even best friends, any account of what it has fallen within my course to do: of late, have thought, that to you, & to Judge White, whom I have ever known and considered to be friends to each other, and to me, I would often write about matters and things long since gone by: at other times have thought, that both you & he had so much of more interest in charge, than any thing I could say about things past, that it would be an intrusion on your time, and his, to call off your attention to read my letters, commonly so long, as to be beyond the patience of men, of more leisure than either of you have, to read: but recollecting, when last I saw you, that you would expect to hear from me, occasionally, and my promise to do so, my long letters have been sent you—I have not, and of choice, do not wish or intend to have any thing to do more than to read and to write, and as writing letters is converse with a friend, fear my letters may be tedious to one who has much more to do than I have, & so thinking, do not mail the fourth part of my letters written and addressed to either you or the Judge, as they cannot be of any worth, beyond my own gratification, a thing I have no right to trouble another with or about. they generally relate only to what is past, & somewhat to the manner of acting in past scenes so familiar to others that I can raise no interest in what I touch on, and still my wish is, to have such manuscript by me: the only objection I ever had to any friends being in office, of his choice, is, that his necessary attention to the discharge of its duties, deprives me of the pleasure of social converse with him, & a great privation it is to one as fond of such converse, with a friend as I am, who am, your friend

Willie Blount

[Endorsed by AJ:] recd—2nd. Feb'y 1830—Govr W. Blount enclosing a letter from Judge Humphries to him, to be filed with my private papers

ALS, T (14-1311); ALS addendum and envelope with AJ endorsement, DLC (14-1315).

1. AJ effectively ended the Creek War with a decisive victory at Horseshoe Bend on March 27, 1814. His March 28 report of the battle was printed in the Washington *National Intelligencer* on April 18, the day Congress adjourned. William Grainger Blount (1784–1827), Willie's nephew, was Tennessee secretary of state, 1811–15, and later a congressman, 1815–19. Lewis Condict (1772–1862) was a New Jersey congressman, 1811–17 and 1821–33.

2. John Sevier (1745–1815) was governor of Tennessee in 1796–1801 and 1803–9 and a congressman in 1811–15. He and AJ had been bitter rivals.

3. AJ had been a major general of Tennessee militia since 1802. On May 22, 1814, Secretary of War John Armstrong (1758–1843) tendered him an appointment in the regular Army as brigadier and brevet major general. AJ accepted June 8, on the understanding that he would be nominated for a full major generalship once Congress reconvened. Meanwhile, however, the resignation of William Henry Harrison opened a vacancy at the rank of major general, to which AJ was immediately commissioned May 28.

4. This note is by Blount. He wrote it below his own dateline and then marked it for insertion at this point with the notation "I should have put the Note below, here, instead of under the date of my letter below."

5. John Baker (1753–1829) of Montgomery Co., Tenn., died on December 22, 1829. He was the father of Blount's first wife, Lucinda Baker Blount, who died in 1806.

6. Thomas Ritchie (1778–1854) edited the *Richmond Enquirer*. Its December 15 issue lauded the annual message and the departmental reports, especially Eaton's.

7. Blount, Eaton, and Secretary of the Navy John Branch (1782–1863) were all born in North Carolina. Branch was U.S. senator from the state, 1823–29, and then its first representative in the Cabinet.

8. In 1794 a militia force led by James Ore (1762–1812) that perhaps included AJ destroyed the Chickamauga Cherokee towns of Running Water and Nickajack. Sampson Williams (1762–1841), an early friend of AJ, participated. As a Tennessee congressman in 1797, AJ had worked to secure federal repayment of the expedition's expenses.

9. Hugh Lawson White (1773–1840), a former judge, was U.S. senator from Tennessee, 1825–40. AJ's son was Andrew Jackson Jr. (1808–1865), born to Rachel Jackson's brother Severn Donelson and his wife Elizabeth, and adopted by AJ and Rachel in infancy. In December 1829 former president John Quincy Adams (1767–1848) returned from Massachusetts to Washington, where he stayed with his son John Adams (1803–1834). An opus operandi is a "work of working," or operating principle; a modus operandi is a "way of working."

From Duff Green

Washington 4th Jany 1830

Dear Sir

It is impossible that you can be aware of the use that will be made of Mr. Baldwin's appointment to the Supreme Bench. You cannot know the course of your enemies in relation to it. Having been bitterly assailed and hearing from a source entitled to credit that you disapprove of what I have published in relation to him, and being induced to believe that that publication may have a tendency to ~~adv~~ promote his success, I ask as an act of justice to your own fame that you will give me permission to read to you a few papers & make a few explanations before his appointment is sent in—Permit me to say that I should not have troubled you on this subject if I did not believe Mr Baldwins appointment, under the circumstances of this case, will distract your friends, impair your fame, and inflict irreperable injury upon the republican party who have sustained you for the Presidency.

May I ask you say at what time I shall wait on you. Your sincere friend

D Green

LC, NcU (14-1318). Henry Baldwin (1780–1844) was a Pittsburgh lawyer and former congressman. He was considered for the Cabinet at the outset of AJ's administration, and had recently been rumored for the Supreme Court vacancy opened by the death of Associate Justice Bushrod Washington in November 1829. Green attacked Baldwin's candidacy in the *Telegraph*, on December 30 branding him as "among the most bitter personal revilers and political opponents of General Jackson" and a covert tool of Henry Clay. AJ nominated Baldwin to the Court on January 4, the day of this letter, and the Senate confirmed him on January 6 by 41 to 2. In a January 14 editorial, Green denied that the appointment marked "a declaration of hostilities" by AJ against the *Telegraph*.

From James Alexander Hamilton

[In his 1829 annual message, Jackson proposed, as an alternative to rechartering the Bank of the United States, a national bank "founded upon the credit of the Government and its revenues . . . which would avoid all constitutional difficulties and at the same time secure all the advantages to the Government and country that were expected to result from the present bank" (Richardson, 2:462). On December 19 Jackson wrote James A. Hamilton, who had helped draft the passage, for his ideas on such a bank—either a government bank of deposit, perhaps attached to the Treasury with the custom houses as branches, or a mixed institution like the BUS, but without infringing on state rights or the constitution (Jackson Papers, 7:642–43).

Printed here is Hamilton's response with its enclosed "Outline of a substitute for the United States Bank." Jackson later copied the entire outline into his memorandum book as possible text for a message to Congress (pp. 602–4 below). In his 1869 Reminiscences (pp. 154–59), Hamilton published a substantially different version of this letter, followed by a different paper entitled "A Project to Create Offices of Deposit in Aid of the Fiscal Operations of the Government, and to Establish a Uniform Currency." That longer document was perhaps the further "plan of a Bank of Discount as well as deposit" promised below. No manuscript version of the "Project" is known, and there is no evidence it was sent to Jackson.]

New York Jany 4 1830.

My dear Sir

I have the pleasure to enclose a few hints on the subjects of Banks or offices of Deposit to assist the fiscal operations of the treasury and to establish a uniform currency.

It is not expected that such an adjunct to the Treasury Department will perform all the functions of a Bank in its general acceptation: Indeed the principal end of such an institution, which is; to extend the circulating medium of the Country to the utmost limit which the laws of commerce assign to it by means of its credit, is expressly denied to the Managers of these Banks or offices of deposit. The issue of notes is confined to actual deposits of Gold or silver or bank notes convertable into coin of standard value; Whereas a Bank of discount limits, or ought to limit its issues, not by the amount of its specie Capital & deposits but by the amount of Circulation which the commercial operations of the Community can absorb: And this may be done without or with a very smal specie capital Provided the business of the Bank is confined as it ought invariably to be to discounting *business paper* or in other words *notes or Bills of Exchange created by commercial interchanges*—The Proposed Banks or offices of Deposit not having the power to make loans will not have the power of assisting the Government or individuals by loans or advances in any emergency; a defect which may be sensibly felt by both should the Country be exposed to war; but which is incident to their organization and cannot be avoided without incurring the risk of far greater evils: for it would be highly indiscreet to entrust the funds & the credit of the Government (private persons could not be induced to entrust theirs) for the purposes of loans or discounting to the management of individuals, unless; their industry, vigilence & caution should be called into action by the strong motives of personal and pecuniary interest; such an interest as the directors of a Bank who are stockholders are supposed always to have in the institution committed to their management: But as I do not mean to extend this letter to a dissertation upon Banking I must return to the matter in hand.

Preparatory to the formation of this project I have examined with care the different Banking systems that have been tried in different countries & ages and I have drawn from each such notions as seemed to be just and adapted to the end in view: The Bank of Amsterdam alone however is at all analagous to this (an account of it will be found in the 2d vol of Smiths Wealth of Nations p276) from it I have drawn the Idea of receiving a fee on deposits and but for the apprehension of exciting a clamour against *a novelty* I ~~might~~ would have introduced a further provision in regard to Bills of Exchange that might be made highly useful in regulating or assisting to regulate exchanges at home & abroad.[1]

This project is accompanied by notes explaining its different provisions and intended to meet those objections that have occurred to me: I could have wished for more time to mature the system but even with the advantage of more mature reflection I would not probably have thrown out any thing more worthy of you consideration; for I assure you I have no confidence in my ability as a projector of this kind—I have alone brought into the work the most ardent zeal for you service and If It shall be in the slightest degree useful to you I shall be amply compensated

I intend shortly to send you a plan of a Bank of Discount as well as deposit which will not be obnoxious to constitutional objections because like any other of its offices it will be under the exclusive direction & controul of the Government. With the truest attachment I remain your friend & obt Servt

James A Hamilton

P S I have been under the necessity of using my daughters pen in making copies and have not therefore made them as perfect as I could have wished

JAH

It ought to be recopied before it goes into other hands than yours

Outline of a substitute for the United States Bank.

The objections to the present Bank are—
    1. It is unconstitutional;
    2. It is dangerous to Liberty.
Yet, this Bank renders important services to the government and the Country.
    It cheapens and facilitates all the fiscal operations of the government.
    It tends to equalize domestic exchange and produce a sound and uniform currency.
    A substitute for the present Bank is desired, which shall yield all its benefits, and be obnoxious to none of its objections.
    Banks do two kinds of business:
    1. They discount notes and bills, for which they give their own paper.
    2. They deal in exchange.
    These two kinds of business have no necessary connection. There may be Banks of discount exclusively, and Banks of exchange exclusively. Both may be Banks of deposit.
    The United States may establish a Bank of Exchange exclusively based on government and individual deposites.
    This Bank may have branches wherever the government may think necessary.
    They may be clothed only with the power to sell exchange on each other; and required to transmit government funds without charge.
    They need only have such officers as their duties require, checked by frequent and rigid inspection.

The whole may be placed under the direction of the Secretary of the Treasury, through a separate bureau.

The present Bank is unconstitutional:

1. Because it is a corporation which Congress has no constitutional power to establish.

2. Because it withdraws the business of Bank discounts and the property of private citizens from the operation of State laws, and particularly from the taxing power of the States in which it is employed.

3. Because it purchases lands and other real estate within the States without their consent, under an authority purporting to be derived from Congress, when the General Government itself possesses no such constitutional power.

The proposed substitute would not be a corporation, but a branch of the Treasury Department; it would hold no property real or personal, and would withdraw none from the operation of the State laws.

The present Bank is dangerous to Liberty—

1. Because, in the number, wealth and standing of its officers and stockholders, in its power to make loans or withhold them; to call oppressively upon its debtors or indulge them, build houses, rent lands and houses, and make donations for political or other purposes, it embodies a fearful influence which may be wielded for the aggrandizement of a favorite individual, a particular interest, or a separate party.

2. Because it concentrates in the hands of a few men; a power over the money of the country, which may be perverted to the oppression of the people, and in times of public calamity, to the embarrassment of the government.

3. Because much of its stock is owned by foreigners, through the management of which an avenue is opened to a foreign influence in the most vital concerns of the Republic.

4. Because it is always governed by interest and will ever support *him* who supports *it*. An ambitious or dishonest President may thus always unite all its power and influence in his support, while an honest one who thwarts its views, will never fail to encounter the weight of its opposition.

5. It weakens the States and strengthens the General Government.

The proposed substitute would have few officers, and no Stockholders, make no loans, have no debtors, build no houses, rent no lands or houses, make no donations, and would be entirely destitute of the influence which arises from the hopes, fears and avarice of thousands. It would oppress no man, and being part of the government, would always aid its operations. It would have no stock and could not be reached by foreign influence. It would afford less aid to a dishonest President than the present Bank, and would never be opposed to an honest one. It would strengthen the States, by leaving to their Banks the whole business of discounts and the furnishing of the local currency. It would strengthen the General Government less than the Custom Houses, immeasurably less than the Post Office, and less than the present Bank when it acts in concert with the National authorities.

The proposed substitute would cheapen and facilitate all the fiscal operations of the government as completely as the present Bank.

It would in the same manner tend to equalize the exchange. Until since the last annual message of the President the present Bank charged a premium on all Exchanges, except for government, public officers and members of Congress. This practise will doubtless, be resumed should that Bank be rechartered. The profits of the exchange business heretofore done was sufficient, it is believed, to pay all the expences of the Bank. The proposed Substitute may charge such a premium on all Exchanges, excepting those for the government, as will suffice to pay its expences.

It might be made in the same manner, although not perhaps to the same degree, to operate upon the currency. By taking the paper of such local Banks in the vicinity as pay specie, it would restrain over-issues and tend to preserve the currency in a sound state.

The usual deposites of the government would be an ample capital for a Bank of Exchange. Independent of its capital, the Bank would always have cash on hand equal to its outstanding Bills of Exchange. But it might not be at the right points, and a small capital would be necessary to meet unequal calls at those points until the equilibrium could be restored. Exchange works in a circle. It is against the West in favor of the East, against the East in favor of the South, and against the South in favor of the West. By constant interchange of information and judicious management, little funds would be wanted at either point, other than those that would be raised by selling Exchange on another.

In time of war the capacities of this Bank might be increased by act of Congress.

Such a Bank would not be unconstitutional, nor dangerous to Liberty, and would yield to the government all the facilities afforded by the present Bank. Further than this, perhaps the General Government ought not to look. But its incidental advantages to the Country would scarcely be inferior to those afforded by the present Bank, while it would destroy a favored monopoly.

[Endorsed by AJ:] The within the only safe outline for a bank or government deposit. A. J.

ALS, DLC (37). Hamilton *Reminiscences*, pp. 154–55.
1. The Bank of Amsterdam was created in 1609 and dissolved in 1796. It accepted deposits of gold and silver, exacted a transaction fee, and furnished depositors with bank credit backed by the city of Amsterdam. Adam Smith's *Wealth of Nations*, first published in 1776, discussed it in Book 4, chapter 3, part 1. Hamilton's page reference matched the Glasgow edition of 1805.

From Amos Kendall

4th Auditor's Office
5th January 1830.

Sir,

I have read so much of Mr. Paulding's letter to you as speaks of my Report with surprize. I expected sensitiveness in some of those employed in the Naval Service; but not in Mr. Paulding. The part of my Report at which he takes exception is thus worded: "Who would doubt that the Navy Agents paid out for house rent, Clerk-hire &c. &c. the sums which have been allowed them under those names? Yet such is not the fact—at least in many instances?"

When I penned these sentences, Mr Paulding was in my mind's eye; for he was the only Agent, so far as I knew, who has been in the habit of rendering vouchers for these expenditures or a considerable portion of them and his was the only known case which would have prevented my making the assertion general. He does me great injustice, therefore, in supposing that I intended to cast any reflection upon him.

But I did not intend to reflect on any of the Navy Agents. These charges have been made by them in pursuance of regulations communicated to them from the Navy Department. It is the Department and not the Agents, which I hold to be responsible for systematizing falsehood in public accounts and demoralizing all around.

I deem Mr. Paulding to be one of the most honest, faithful and correct public men I have ever known and that it is fortunate for the government that a man of such strict integrity has held the agency at New-York during 'the worst of times.'[1]

But when I entered this office I determined to do justice to the country regardless of men. The truth must be told or what hope have we of reform? To make the administration pure is my only aim, if I know my own heart. I hope that I shall not, in the use of the means necessary to accomplish so great a good lose the friendship and respect of good men. It will give me pain if I do; but the truth must be told and justice must be done. I know I shall have *your* support in doing it, and if the time shall ever arrive when I cannot do it *in* office I shall endeavor to do it *out*.

Accept my thanks for submitting to me Mr. Paulding's note and be assured that my hopes for the perpetuity of our government in a very great degree rest on the success of your administration[.] With reverence & respect Your friend &c

Amos Kendall

ALS, CSt (14-1334). *Putnam's Magazine* (May 1868), pp. 541–42. Amos Kendall (1789–1869) was the fourth auditor of the Treasury, responsible for settling Navy Department accounts. Litterateur James Kirke Paulding (1778–1860) was navy agent at New York City and later secretary of the Navy under Martin Van Buren. AJ forwarded this letter to him on January 7.

Navy secretary Branch had asked Kendall in November 1829 to look into the causes of the "present confused and unsettled state of the fiscal accounts and concerns of the Navy Department." Kendall's response, forwarded to Congress with the Department's annual report in December, censured its "irregular and unlawful practice" of augmenting officers' admittedly inadequate salaries through improper allowances and reimbursements of fictitious expenses. The quoted passage charged that the navy agents' office allowance was really a covert income supplement. Kendall condemned Navy accounting as a system of "pretences and falsehoods" and called for strict financial accountability and transparency and an end to discretionary spending (*SDoc* 1, 21st Cong., 1st sess., pp. 262–74, Serial 192).

1. "The man who dares be honest in the worst of times" was a common accolade.

From Alfred Balch

Nash. 8th. Jany. 1830.

My Dear Sir,

Altho I am aware that you are incessantly engaged in the concerns of the public, still I offer no apology for engrossing a little of your attention—because I write under the influence of no motives of self aggrandizment but merely for the purpose of offering you my congratulations on the Message lately transmitted to Congress—I have read this document with profound attention—The style is pure—the tone moderate yet firm—the Doctrines sound and Constitutional.

I see so many evils in the exercise of the power by Congress to make internal improvments, that I am wholly averse to the whole scheme. When the day arrives that shall see our citizens paying tolls at Turnpike gates and on Canals for the benefit of the national Treasury—when the time arrives that our Members of Congress shall be scuffling for a division of the spoil to be gathered from the Treasury of the General Govt in order to sustain their own popularity and that of some corrupt administration, the *Sovereignty* of the States will be but a shadow—a mere name.[1]

If we must levy imports and thereby have money to dispose of, let all the workmen— undertaking jobbers—contractors &c in other words all the voters receive their reward from the state authorities, not from the overflowing means of a great splendid National Government—Of all the evils which may afflict us, let the evil of an overshadowing overwhelming *Central* power be the last—because it will prove the greatest & the most devouring.

The spirit of avarice and commerce is converting the Bank of the United States into a Mammoth Broker. The office here employs the smallest means to gather up a few nine pences—Such will always be the case when such institutions are conducted by men who only know how to sell tape, thread & needles. Mr Calhoun told us when he set up this Bank that it would give us a sound currency—would equalize exchange and be a blessing to the people. Let us have a little commentary on this text. Old Mr Crutcher told me a few days ago, that he had a check on the Bank of the U States last week, drawn by a public officer, payable at sight at Phila. He went to the office here and wished the cash for it—They charged him one per cent for advancing the money; Notes payable at the office at Boston are thrown in here—If you wish to receive silver for them you must pay two & half per cent.[2]

Instead of loaning money here at 6 per ct—they will buy a Bill on the office at New Orleans, charge you 1½ per cent premium & 6 per ct all payable in advance and the office at N Orleans will charge you 1½ per cent for accepting it there. So that the object of this immense institution is to make money—to secure a large dividend for the benefit of the great stockholders on the other side of the Atlantic.

As to the effects of the office here, they must in the end prove to the last degree calamitous. Those who borrow are encouraged in their extravagant modes of dressing & living—which are far greater than their solid means will justify   Many are building little palaces—furnishing them in very expensive style—and the children of many are dressed as tho they were the sons & daughters of Princes. What may remain of the wrecks produced by these splendid follies, will after a few years be seized on by this Mammoth Bank.

Our Legislature has not yet adjourned. We were engaged in the Trial of Williams for three weeks.[3]

Our town has been in a state of great excitement for the last week, in consequence of the statement made by Col Parrish that he had suffered certain individuals whom he would not name to the committee deputed by the Legislature, to over draw to the amount of between 60 & 70 thousand dollars. Conjecture was busy in naming the individuals. It was suggested that McLemore had overdrawn to the amt of 5 or 10 thousand dollars. Hearing this I went to McL. who stated that during his absence a note of his for 800 dolls had fallen due & a check had been accepted instead of the money for the note. But, that he had paid it up. I called on Parrish & had a confidential conversation with him in which he disclosed the names of those who had overdrawn—some of them by means the most dishonorable. In one instance, an individual had overdrawn 9000 dols. in this way—He handed Parrish checks on the Branch Bank here for this amt received his notes & made off—when the checks were presented there was no money there.[4]

I wish it may all turn out that Parrish had not himself over drawn largely. Many of the agents are found to be defaulters—and this cumbrous edifice, having in its first creation a vice fatal to its permanency, is about to tumble into ruins about our ears.[5]

I hope you will not be disappointed in your expectations of finding Mr V. Buren a safe and efficient *Statesman*—of politicians we have myriads   But, statesmen are as rare as Immortal & fine poets. My fervent hope is that V. Buren may realize the high estimation in which I have long held him—When that day shall arrive that he will be before the people of Ten. as a candidate, I shall draw the sword in his cause and throw away the scabbard. As I have never yet seen the day that I could compromise one single private or political opinion to get office from any man, & hope in God that I never will, I shall always be found either on one side the fence or the other. With my present feelings towards Mr V Buren, I shall support him if he does not get another vote in Tennessee. But the truth is, if your admn is successful of which I never had a doubt, Mr V. Bn will have overwhelming masses of friends in the four southwestern states.[6]

Already many are enquiring anxiously after him, and many are desirous to see his despatches to our Foreign Ministers—which of course will be made public in due season.

I flatter myself that Mr Bell will do justice to the interesting subject committed to his charge as Chairman of the committee of Indian Affairs— The removal of the Indians would be an act of *seeming* violence—But it will prove in the end an act of enlarged philanthropy. These untutored sons of the Forest, cannot exist in a state of Independence, in the vicinity of the white man. If they will persist in remaining where they are, they may begin to dig their graves and prepare to die.[7] With great respect I remain yr ob Sevt.

Alfred Balch

ALS, DLC (37). Alfred Balch (1785–1853) was a Nashville lawyer.

1. Congressional spending on transportation or "internal improvement" projects, long disputed on constitutional grounds, had grown under President Adams. A bill to place tollgates on the federally financed Cumberland or National Road was vetoed by President James Monroe in 1822. In his annual message AJ had proposed distributing federal surplus revenues to the states as a less contentious alternative to specific appropriations (Richardson, 2:451–52).

2. Headquartered in Philadelphia, the Bank of the United States at this time operated branches in twenty-two cities including Nashville. John C. Calhoun, now vice president, had championed the Bank's creation as a South Carolina congressman in 1816. Thomas Crutcher (1760–1844) was Tennessee state treasurer.

3. The Tennessee house had impeached circuit judge Nathaniel W. Williams (c1779–1833), a political foe of AJ, for misconduct. The senate acquitted him December 22.

4. Joel Parrish Jr. (d. 1834), a former military aide to AJ and a member of his 1828 Nashville campaign committee, was cashier of the Bank of the State of Tennessee. On January 3 he had secreted the Bank's books to prevent their inspection by a legislative investigating committee. Parrish admitted allowing overdrafts to his friends but declined to reveal their names. The investigation eventually uncovered losses of more than $150,000, largely due to overdrafts allowed by Parrish. John Christmas McLemore (1790–1864) was a Nashville businessman and husband of Rachel Jackson's niece Elizabeth Donelson McLemore (1796–1836).

5. The charter of the Bank of the State of Tennessee, enacted in 1820, mandated the establishment of an agency in every existing county of the state.

6. Martin Van Buren (1782–1862) of New York was AJ's secretary of state.

7. Tennessee congressman John Bell (1797–1869) chaired the House Committee on Indian Affairs, to which was referred the portion of AJ's annual message recommending Indian removal (Richardson, 2:456–59). Bell reported a removal bill on February 24 (*HRRep* 227, 21st Cong., 1st sess., Serial 200).

From James Gadsden

Wascissa
8 Jany 1830

My Dear General

Your very friendly letter of the 4th. ulto having been directed to Magnolia instead of Liponia P.O. Jefferson County was delayed more than a week in its reception. I am happy to find that through the assurance of Major Andrews you are disposed to believe Mr Slacum (untill otherwise proved) guiltless of the offences alledged against him.[1] I admit, you would have had good cause to be displeased with the friend, who knowing the charges against that Gentleman could notwithstanding have recommended him to you for office. No real friend could have been capable of it; I therefore felt the more anxious to hear from you direct on the subject, and would have received it still more kindly, if the first knowledge of the delicate attitude in which Mr Slacum had been thrown by his accusers, had been derived from you. For I should have been foremost in investigating his conduct, and the first to have withdrawn (if guilty) that confidence which you may very correctly suppose I had by my recommendation reposed in him. With you I am willing to believe Mr Slacum innocent untill he is convicted, and in this age of slander I will be exceedingly cautious in yielding credence to any but positive proof. It is singular My Dear General, if even suspicion could rest on Mr Slacum, that in an intimate intercourse with him for 2 years, and in the social circle of neighbours, most of whom are friends of Mr Adams, and between whom, Mr Slacum & myself repeated political discussions were held, that he Mr Slaccum never betrayed a disposition to indulge in disrespectful language to any of the parties or persons involved in the contest. On the contrary he was always curteous in his manners, arguing like a Gentleman & not as an inflamatory demagogue. His accusers may say he was prudent before me; & even before those of my neighbourhood, who thought politically with him. This is possible; and if true you will find me among the first to advise the withdrawal of the appointment which I was among the first to recommend him to. I favored his application for the qualities I knew he possessed & which I believed peculiarly fitted him for the office he subsequently received.

With regard to myself & the correspondence growing out of the Clerkship offered me; I have nothing more to add, other than an expression of a regret that you should have hazarded an offer which you seem to think I could not accept; and when my non acceptance was exposed to the misconstructions which others seem so very willing to put upon it. You do justice to my selection of a companion; in supposing she has added greatly to my domestic happiness; but these enjoyments are not associated exclusively with retired life, as you would seem to intimate; or do they disincline me for honorable public employment, when voluntarily conferred under a conviction of my ability of being useful.[2] There are many considerations strengthening the inducements to return to public life, and none more so than those connected with the relative situation I hold to a political community now in embryo.

I was much pleased to learn that the Seminoles are to share the fate of the Creeks. Their removal from our Territory would greatly advance its interests; & enlarge the sugar growing district to the enterprise of Emigrants. If I can in any degree be of assistance in forwarding your views I hope you will not fail to command me[.] I remain your friend

James Gadsden

[Endorsed by AJ:] Col Gadsden letter to be answered—A. J

ALS, The Gilder Lehrman Institute of American History (mAJs). Gadsden (1788–1858) had been AJ's military aide before settling in Florida. William Augustus Slacum (1799–1839) was serving as purser on the sloop *Peacock* under an interim commission issued by AJ in June 1829, for which Gadsden had recommended him. President Adams had previously nominated Slacum for purser to the Senate in February, but AJ withdrew this and other pending Adams nominations on taking office in March. In May 1830 AJ again nominated Slacum, and he was confirmed.

1. Timothy Patrick Andrews (1794–1868) was an Army paymaster.
2. In April 1829 Gadsden had declined an appointment as chief clerk of the War Department. He married Susanna Gibbes Hort (1786–c1858) in 1827.

From Samuel Delucenna Ingham

Try Dept.
8 Jay 30

The Secretary of the Treasury with his best respects to the President, has the honor to inform him that the ~~only appointment~~ nominations sent to the Senate only include, the appointments made to supply vacancies and reappointments of present incumbents—all the temporary appointments as well for custom houses as for Land offices remain yet to be sent. The formula will be prepared to day for all these and sent to the President—

[Endorsed by AJ:] Mr Ingham giving the officers sent to the Senate   only those whose terms are about expiring—Janry 9th. 1830—

AN, DLC (37). Samuel Delucenna Ingham (1779–1860) of Pennsylvania was secretary of the Treasury. Under the Tenure of Office Act of 1820, most civil officials requiring Senate confirmation were commissioned for terms of four years but were also "removable from office at pleasure." During the recess of the Senate between March and December 1829, AJ had removed a number of Treasury officers and replaced them with temporary appointees, none of whom had yet been nominated to the Senate for regular commissions. On January 13, 20, and 25, AJ nominated forty-seven customs officers and twenty-six land office registers and receivers to whom he had given temporary appointments, nearly all to positions made vacant by removal.

From Persis Brown Goodrich Lovely

Pope county A. T. January 9th 1830—

Sir

I intrude to solicit redress for what I feel as a wrong. You sir, was commissioner to negociate a treaty with the Cherokees held at Highwassee 1817 in which treaty the place where I then lived was secured to me for life. Majr Lovely my husband died a few months previous to that treaty: and there I have lived unmolested, untill 1828 when another treaty with the Cherokees took place, at Washington in which treaty a reservation of land was given to the Cherokees, that reservation included my home: which reservation has since been sold intire, and in consequince I am a houseless wanderer at sixty years of age. As soon as I saw the treaty I adrss'd a note to the Secretary of war, and an other to the Agent for the Cherokees, who was then at Washington: it was several months before the Agent returned to this countrey, when he told me he had been instructed to let me know that I might either select a place made vacant by the removal of the Cherokees; or have my place vallued; and recieve the amount in money: it was to late to select a place as all the places worth any thing were then taken up, my place was vallued by the Gentlemen appointed to value indian improvements, it was vallued to five-hundred dollars, which sum I have not recieved and am led to believe I never shall   I have prepared a petition to Congress which I hope is in the hands of The Honourable Member for Arkansas Territory: in which my claims are setforth: in which Sir I have to solicit your aid and influence if you consider the low voice of a distressd, & she thinks injured widow an intrusion sir for which you must blame your own exalted charecter for benevolence and Justice; for her attempt to interest you in her favour I have obtained permission to shelter my self in an house built by a Missionary: One mile from thier former establishment, call'd Dwight Mission[1]   If dear sir I might be permited to possess for life this place where the reverand A Finney lived with the little mill attached to it, which mill does not run more than four months in the year and recieve the valuation of the place I was obliged to relinquish I shall be content: but Sir five hundred dollars is a small remuneration for a home for life, especially to a woman who is a widow childless and lone in the world I confidently hope my Goverment will do me Justice: and pray your Excelency will interpose your aid that I may obtain relief. I am Sir with Respect & Esteem yours &c

Persis Lovely

[Endorsed by AJ:] Mrs. Lovely letter complaining of injury & requiring my aid to her petition to congress under the care of the Delegate from arkansa Territory   A. J.   The Delegate to be seen & conversed with on this subject   AJ

ALS, DNA-RG 233 (14-1360). *TPUS*, 21:148–49. Lovely (1770–1842) was the widow of William Lewis Lovely (1750–1817), who had been subagent to the Western Cherokees. The 1817 Cherokee treaty, negotiated by AJ as U.S. commissioner, vacated whites from the Western Cherokees' Arkansas domain but permitted the just-widowed Lovely to remain for life at her residence adjoining the agency near present Russellville. In the May 1828 Treaty of Washington, the Western Cherokees exchanged their Arkansas lands for territory in present Oklahoma. The Arkansas agency tract, including Lovely's square-mile farmstead, was to be sold to fund a saw and grist mill in the new Cherokee homeland. Lovely protested to the War Department, and in September 1828 Indian superintendent Thomas L. McKenney instructed Western Cherokee agent Edward W. Duval to appraise her property and offer payment for it (*TPUS*, 20:714–16, 750). Lovely considered the resulting $500 valuation inadequate and appealed to Congress for succor. Arkansas Territory delegate Ambrose Hundley Sevier (1801–1848) presented her petition on December 16, 1829 (*TPUS*, 21:133–35). A law of March 3, 1831, granted her lifetime possession of a half-section of land at her new residence and payment for her lost improvements.
    1. Dwight Mission, near present Russellville, was established in 1820 by the American Board of Commissioners for Foreign Missions. In 1829 its co-founder Alfred Finney died and the mission relocated with the Cherokees to Oklahoma.

To Hardy Murfree Cryer

Washington, Janry. 10th 1830

My Dr. Sir

I have recd. your letter of the 26th. ulto. and after duly noting its contents, hasten to answer it.

I certainly approve the course you have adopted with regard to my gray stud colt. Knowing the purity of his blood, I was anxious to have bred from him; Had I not have been compelled to leave home, I never should have consented that he should have been sold—and I am glad he is *again* my property—His name *is* & was *Bolivar*, and if he stands the ensuing season anywhere, I wish him advertised under that *name*—with such certificate as Colo. Elliot thinks he deserves—His blood you know—However it is as follows—His dam by *Pacolet*, grand dam by Truxton out of the noted *running mare opossum Filly* whose pedigree, Mr. James Jackson has, I think   She was *a Wildair & Medley*—she was a first rate four mile ~~animal~~ *runner* of her day—*his sire Oscar*, whose pedigree can be easily obtained.[1]

I would like to get Col Elliots opinion of the propriety of Training, and running him in the Spring; if he *thinks well of it*; I will give him fifty dollars for training him, and when he makes the experiment, if he chooses to enter him for his own benefit, he may do so; if not I will pay the entrance, & run him for the benefit of my son, if Col Elliot thinks his situation & wind will justify the experiment—I am of the belief, that by nature, if his breathing had not been injured, he was one of the first runners ever reared in america—Dunwody by neglect destroyed him as a runner & ruined my Oscar filly also as a runner.[2] *Consult Col Elliott in whom I have every confidence*, whether it is prudent to try him again upon the Turf—if he says he will train him, & thinks he can run him in credit, let him be placed wheresoever the Col may direct, say on my own farm, & treated as he may desire until the proper time for him to take him for training   If he advises him *not again to be trained*, then, Sir, you will either send him to my farm or place him at a stand that you may select, advertising him at fifteen dollars payable within the season, or twenty out, & in proportion the single leap, & insurance—Knowing the merit of his blood, you see I am determined to keep its credit up, until I can get it tested, by his offspring from a thorough bred mare—I shall direct the Virginian to be put to him, as the best blood I have except those that are too nigh a kin to him—as to a sale of him—I will not *now* take less than *one thousand dollars*, and that *on interest*, at one, two, & three years, if this sum can be got for him *well*, if not I will keep him, as I know he is of better stock than any that can be got in Virginia *now*—with these instructions you will please manage him for the best—& if he is my property in the spring, I wish the Virginian filley I got of you, *put to him*, her colt will test his merit as a foal getter & turf horse, ~~if her~~

with my kind salutations to your amiable family & best wishes for their & your happiness believe me your friend.

Andrew Jackson

P.S. If a good stand cannot be got for him else where, let him be advertised to stand at the Hermitage, & Dunwody to manage him, under the superintendence of my overseer. A. J.

ALS, THi (14-1366). Cryer (1792–1846) was a Methodist minister and horse breeder in Sumner Co., Tenn. He had written AJ on December 26, 1829, of his plan to reacquire Bolivar, whom Cryer called Tariff, from two Kentuckians who had bought him from AJ for $800, raced him, and lost when Bolivar had difficulty breathing (*Jackson Papers*, 7:647–49). AJ wrote Cryer again on February 28, and Cryer replied to this letter on March 4 (both below).

1. Truxton and Pacolet were renowned racers once owned by AJ. Oscar was undefeated before retiring to stud. George Elliott (1780–1861), a lieutenant colonel of Tennessee volunteers under AJ in the Seminole campaign, was a well-known Sumner County horseman. James Jackson (1782–1840), now of Florence, Ala., was an estranged former associate of AJ.

2. The slave Dunwoody (c1770–c1845), purchased to accompany Truxton in 1806, was the trainer of AJ's racing stock.

From Estwick Evans

Washington Jany 11th 1830

Sir—

Without making any apology to you, I hasten to do an act of justice to one of my fellow-citizens, which delicacy has, until now, prevented me from performing. I have, heretofore, taken [n]o part in the now existing contention amoung [the] Republicans of Portsmouth, New Hampsh[ire.] Both parties in this dispute have merits, & I am friendly to both. But in the *recent* proceedings of the Greenleaf party, so called, I perceive so much that is unfair & ungenerous—so much of the spirit of persecution, that I conceive it to be *my duty* to give you, very briefly, my views upon the subject. In doing this I assure you that Colonel Decatur has not the most distant idea of my interfering in the case, nor have I any reason to believe that he or his friends wish for such a step.

I have, sir, been acquainted with Col Decatur ever since his arrival in Portsmouth in 1824. His name gave him celebrity there; & this circumstance, connected with his address & his efforts to produce the present state of things, (made, not only there but in the interior & on the Maine side of the Piscataqua,) rendered him both efficient & conspicuous.

In such a place as Portsmouth every thing said & done is known; & yet, I can state that as far as I have seen or heard—as far as I have been able, by enquiry, to ascertain, Col Decatur's conduct has been unexceptionable.

The secret of the opposition to him is, that the Greenleaf party wished to monopolize to themselves all the patronage of the Government, &, of course, claimed all the credit of the revolution in public sentiment in New-Hampshire.

Colonel Decatur is very popular with a portion of the people of Portsmouth, among whom may be ranked many of the most influential republicans there. The federal party did, at first, speak much against his appointment, because they were offended at the removal of Mr Upham, &, of course, were grat[ifie]d to see the Greenleaf party denounce Col D., *[but]* here, sir, permit me to remark that the removal [of] Mr. Upham was loudly called for upon the salutary principle of rotation in office. He had filled a very lucrative situation for twelve or fourteen years; & to have continued him in it would have conveyed the idea that certain offices amoung us are for life. This would lead to corruption in the obtaining of them, & would be a bar to rising generations of men, who have a right to the *chance* of participating in the patronage of their country.

The appointment of Col Decatur was a very suitable one—the best that could have been made in Portsmouth. He is better qualified for the office than Mr. G in many particulars. Col D is a man of more standing—he is a man of a more ready mind; his commercial & nautical information gave him infinitely the advantage. His manners too & style of living are peculiarly well adapted to the paying of suitable attentions to strangers of distinction visiting the town. In these particulars Mr G is very deficient.

I observe again, sir, that Mr Greenleaf & his party have merits; but they are selfish—they are assuming—they lack that generosity of character without which many of the great virtues of the human heart can never flourish. These men, sir, highly respect you, but they do not love you as they ought.

The great difficulty is that Mr Greenleaf suffered himself to expect the office of Collector, & that his friends hoped for appointments under him. These persons continue their opposition to Col Decatur; &, by their flattery, lead Mr G on in the work. Mr G is, as it respects himself, well satisfied with the office of Post Master. I have heard him say that he prefers it to any other whatever.

I trust, sir, that Col Decatur will be sustained—fully sustained by the Government. This [c]an be done by a steady & quiet course—a course at once [dign]ified & politic. Here there will be no irritation; & the [e]xcitement of the Greenleaf party will be [. . .] out, &, finally, will die away. I do not think that this exc[ite]ment will at all affect the ascendency of the Republican party in New-Hampshire.

I pray you, sir, to excuse the freedom with which I have written upon this subject, & to believe that I am, with distinguished respect & sincere regard your humble servant

Estwick Evans

[Endorsed by AJ:] Mr. Evans in favor of Col Decatur—

ALS, THer (14-1378). Evans (1787–1866), formerly of Portsmouth and now a Washington resident, was a lawyer and the author of *A Pedestrious Tour of Four Thousand Miles, through the Western States and Territories* (1819). Timothy Upham (1783–1855) had been customs collector at Portsmouth since 1816. In April 1829 AJ removed him for John Pine Decatur (1786–1832), a brother of naval hero Stephen Decatur, who before this had been Portsmouth naval storekeeper since 1818. Decatur's appointment was strongly opposed by New Hampshire Jacksonians favoring Abner Greenleaf (1785–1868), who was appointed Portsmouth postmaster in April 1829 (*Jackson Papers*, 7:393–98). AJ nominated Decatur to the Senate on January 13. The Senate rejected him on March 29 by 43 to 1.

From John Thomson

Washington
Jan. 11th. 1830

Dear Sir

I had the honour this day of receveing your note inviting me to dine with you on Thursday next and requesting an answer

To which you will permit me to say that if health is continued I shall not deny myself the pleasure that it will afford me to mingle in your society at your own table   And I do most ardently hope that from henceforth you will number me among—not only your *warm*; but your most *sincere friends*—one with whome the people of the 12th congressional district of ohio thought proper to, out run, and, run out, the notorious John Sloane our common enimy

But sir I hope you will ponder this freedom in one with whom you as yet have little or no acquaintance and permit me to say to you that this is not flattery for the purchase of an office—no sir I have none to ask for, either for myself, or any of my immediat friends[.] I have the honour to Be most Respectfully Your Obt. Servt.

John Thomson

ALS, DLC (37). Thomson (1780–1852), a physician of New Lisbon, Ohio, had defeated incumbent John Sloane (1779–1856) for Congress in 1828. A Clay and Adams man, Sloane had helped lead the 1828 campaign attack on AJ for his execution of six militiamen in February 1815.

To Ezra Stiles Ely

(Copy)

Washington Jany 12th 1830

My D. Sir,

I expected this would have been handed to you by my son, but a slight indisposition and the inclemency of the weather have induced him to postpone his intended visit to Philadelphia for the present.

The object of this letter is to inform you that Major Eaton has lately received a letter from Mr Ogdon, Consul at Liverpool, covering one from Mr. Hyde, then in London, who is refered to in one of your communications to me last Spring, relative to the slanderous reports against Mrs. Eaton. I consider it my duty to apprise you of the receipt of this letter; and to inform you that Mr. Hyde denies in strong terms the correctness of the statement made to you. In the first paragraph of his letter he says, *in substance,* "Had you enclosed me charges of high Treason, prefered against me by my Government, you could not have astonished me more, or I more innocent of the charge than the one made which you enclose me." He goes on to state that he is unacquainted with Major Eaton and his lady—that he knows neither her, nor her relations, and has no recollection of ever having heard her name mentioned.

The scurrilous pieces published in the opposition papers against Mr. Eaton have, as I suppose, induced him to publish the card which, doubtless, you have seen.[1] I assure you, my dear sir, that he is fully prepared to expose the vile conspiracies against him—to unmask Mr. Campbell and his associates, and to vindicate his own character and reputation. The only evidence he wanted to enable him to do this fully and completely was a contradiction on the part of Mr. Hyde of the only unrefuted charge contained in your letter to me; and this he now has, ~~in his letter to Mr. Ogdon~~. The extraordinary conduct of Mr. Campbell must, at no distant ~~period~~ day, bring forth a full disclosure of all the facts and circumstances connected with this unpleasant subject. He and his friends are daily getting into new and greater difficulties. He attempted not long since to throw a fire brand into the Methodist Society, by relating a story which he said he had from an old lady—a pious matron of that church. When this reached the ears of Major Eaton's friends, the old lady refered to, was called on, who declared the story to be destitute of truth. She said Mr. Campbell applied to her under the garb of friendship and religion, to inform him concerning the character of Mrs. Eaton, and particularly with regard to a miscarriage she once had. The old lady informed him, as she has since stated, that she had long known Mrs. Eaton, and that she never in her life knew any thing, of her own knowledge, prejudical to her character as a lady; and that the abortion, about which this *pious* and *reverend* gentleman enquired, happened either a little before or after Mr. Timberlake left home; if after certainly not more than two or three months as she believes. She further stated to him that Mrs. Oneal, the mother of Mrs. Eaton, related the circumstance to her without making any secret of it—inded no one that she ever heard of believed for a moment that there was any thing wrong or improper in the affair.[2]

If we have faith in that portion of the scriptures which says—"by their ~~works~~ fruits ye shall know them"—surely we must believe that Mr. Campbell is any other than an Embassador of our blessed Saviour.[3] His conduct has done the Presbyterian Society much injury, as well as the cause of religion generally.[4] His conduct will be exposed either before the Presbytery, or before the nation, on a proper and fit occasion I have been *assured*. He cannot remain in credit here, and an inquiry any where will forever prostrate him as a preacher of the Gospel. I forwarned him of the *dilemma*—had he acted as a christian ought, and as our blessed saviour him, society would have rested in peace & harmony and his conscience would not nightly admonished him of his improper & unchristian course.

Present me affectionately to your lady & family to Mrs Carswell & hers, & to Mr. Lamb—and believe me yr Friend[5]

Signed—Andrew Jackson

LS draft mainly in William B. Lewis's hand, DLC (37). Presbyterian clergyman Ezra Stiles Ely (1786–1861) of Philadelphia was an old friend of AJ and Rachel. In his March 18, 1829, letter of accusation against Margaret Eaton, Ely related that at Gadsby's hotel in Washington "a man whom I shall not call a gentleman, said in the hearing of four persons, 'Mrs. E___ brushed by me last night and pretended not to know me. She has forgotten the time when I slept with her'" (*Jackson Papers*, 7:102). Ely cited New York merchant John Ellsworth Hyde (1781–1844) as his source. At Eaton's prompting, Francis Barber Ogden (1783–1857), newly appointed consul at Liverpool, wrote Hyde in London on November 22, 1829, demanding details of the story. Hyde disclaimed it on November 26 in the language AJ paraphrased here, and Ogden forwarded his reply to Eaton on November 30 (DLC-75).

1. Margaret Eaton's late husband John B. Timberlake had died an apparent defaulter to the government. In October 1829 an anonymous note to the Navy Department suggested that his records, then under review by fourth auditor Amos Kendall, would show that before his death he had suspiciously funneled funds to Eaton, who invested them in Washington real estate. Reports in the *New York Commercial Advertiser* on December 26 and Philadelphia *United States Gazette* on December 28 publicized the story and hinted that documents now in possession of Margaret's accuser Reverend John N. Campbell might implicate Eaton in fraud. In reply, Eaton published a card in the January 5, 1830, *United States' Telegraph* decrying the "anonymous imputations of the retailers of ribaldry and scandal" and challenging the "base calumniator" responsible to come forth. Kendall's report, transmitted to the House of Representatives in May, detailed Eaton's transactions with Timberlake but exculpated him of wrongdoing and surmised a conspiracy to defame him (*HRDoc* 116, 21st Cong., 1st sess., Serial 198).

2. Campbell had charged, first through Ely in March 1829 and then directly to AJ in September, that Margaret Eaton had suffered a miscarriage in or around 1821, when Timberlake's extended absence abroad precluded his being the father. AJ disputed the timing, and both he and Campbell sought corroborating witnesses. The "old lady" was a Mrs. Williams, likely Sarah Williams, a Washington milliner. AJ drew his account of her testimony from a report John W. Simonton wrote William B. Lewis on December 19, 1829, after interviewing her about her earlier conversation with Campbell (DLC-75).

3. Matthew, 7:20.

4. From this point on the handwriting is AJ's.

5. Ely's wife was Mary Ann Carswell Ely (c1792–1842) and his mother-in-law was Margaret Means Carswell. Philadelphia businessman Lemuel Lamb (c1786–1855) was married to Mary Ann Ely's sister.

To Martin Van Buren

Jan'ry. 12th. 1830

The President with his respects, reminds the Secretary of State of the Ratified Indian Treaties which require certain appropriations to carry them into effect—These must be laid before the House of representatives—& an appropriation asked for—does this action come from the Dept. of State, the War Deptt., or the President—The latter I would presume—The inquiry is made, that an appropriation may be promptly asked for—a copy of the Treaty must be laid before the House when the appropriation is asked for

AN, THi (14-1390). On December 30 and 31, 1829, the Senate had ratified three Indian treaties: a Chippewa, Ottawa, and Potawatomi treaty of July 29 and a Winnebago treaty of August 1, both signed at Prairie du Chien, and a Delaware treaty concluded at Little Sandusky on August 3. On January 14 Secretary of War Eaton submitted an estimate of appropriations to carry them into effect, which AJ transmitted to Congress with the treaties the same day (*HRDoc* 24, 21st Cong., 1st sess., Serial 196).

From Caleb Atwater

January 13, 1830.

Dear Sir,

The enclosed, is a letter from a son of mine, who was thirteen years of age, last March. The letter, is in his hand writing, and it is in, *his own words*. I send it, so that Gen. J. may judge of his qualifications for a midshipman's warrant, or a place, *at some future day*, in the Academy at West Point. I have shown the letter, to Maj. Eaton, but, not to the Secy of the Navy. The nation did expect, and do yet, that the President would not suffer an useless Branch, to grow on the tree of liberty, but, that he would select a Porter, to carry the burthens of the Navy; Or, they expected, that the President would select some man, who *Woodbury* all the errors of former administrations, in the great deep.[1] Until then, perhaps, it is the best, not to offer you my son, for that service. Gratefully your's forever

Caleb Atwater

[Endorsed by AJ:] Mr. Caleb Atwater enclosing a letter from his son applying for a cadets warrant or midshipman   To be retained on file in my office—A. J.

ALS, DLC (37). Caleb Atwater (1778–1867) was a lawyer and author of Circleville, Ohio. In 1829 AJ had appointed him commissioner to negotiate the Indian treaties at Prairie du Chien. He enclosed a December 28, 1829, letter from his son Richard Douglas Atwater (1816–1852), addressed to him at Washington and conveying news from home (DLC-37).

1. David Porter (1780–1843) had been a Navy captain and then commander of the Mexican navy. Levi Woodbury (1789–1851) was a U.S. senator from New Hampshire who succeeded John Branch as Navy secretary in 1831.

To John Henry Eaton

January 14th. 1830—

The case of E. W. Duval Indian agent & other public officers considered—

The act of Congress of the 31rst of January 1823, is positive that on failure to render his accounts quarterly, or within three months thereafter the officer, or agent, *shall be dismissed from the public service*, unless he shall account satisfactorily to the President for his default.[1]

It has been reported to the President that Mr E. W. Deval has not rendered his accounts for fourteen months past—and having rendered to the President no satisfactory reason for his disobedience of this positive injunction of law—It is therefore ordered that he be dismissed from the Public service[2]—and D. B. McComb disbursing on account of appelachecola River having rendered no vouchers to the Department for his Disbursments since the 30th. of September 1828, nor accounted to the President for this omission is likewise ordered to be dismissed from the Public service.[3]

Andrew Jackson

ADS, DLC (37).

1. AJ paraphrased the 1823 law, which applied to all officials entrusted with public funds. Domestic officers failing to render accounts within three months of the close of each quarter were to be reported to the president and dismissed unless they could make satisfactory explanation.

2. Edward Washington Duval (1789–1830) had been agent to the Western Cherokees since 1823. Eaton wrote to inform him of his dismissal on January 15 (DNA-RG 75, M21-6).

3. David Betton Macomb (1793–1837) of Tallahassee had been engaged by the Army's Engineer Department to remove obstructions from the Apalachicola River. The day after this order, Army chief engineer Charles Gratiot asked Eaton to suspend Macomb's dismissal, as his disbursements had been small and he had perhaps been unaware of the law. On January 16 AJ duly suspended Macomb's dismissal for a month. Failing still to render his accounts, Macomb was dismissed on February 26 and replaced by Gabriel J. Floyd (DNA-RG 77, M1113-2; *TPUS*, 24:367–68).

Memorandum regarding Miles King

[Jackson had removed Norfolk, Va., navy agent Miles King (1786–1849) in August 1829 after receiving complaints of his malfeasance and possible corruption. In settling King's accounts, Treasury Department second comptroller Isaac Hill (1789–1851) disputed certain payments to Norfolk baker Tildsley Graham (1773–1832), who had contracted to supply bread to the Navy in 1828. Jackson referred the matter for inquiry through Navy secretary John Branch to fourth auditor Amos Kendall. Kendall's report of January 6, 1830, submitted by Branch to Jackson on January 7 and recapitulated in this memorandum, charged that King, with the sanction of the Board of Navy Commissioners, had deliberately overpaid Graham for bread delivered in November and December 1828 to cover his losses on 52,500 pounds destroyed by fire at his bakery while awaiting delivery (HRDoc 115, 21st Cong., 1st sess., pp. 3–6, Serial 198). Jackson's review sustained Hill and Kendall. King complained to Virginia senator Littleton Waller Tazewell (1774–1860), who took up the matter with Jackson in mid-February (below).]

The case of Mr Miles King, on appeal from the decision of the 2nd. comptroller, considered

It appears from a contracted in writing bearing date 31rst. of Decbr. 1827 that Tildsley Graham of Norfolk Va. ~~entered~~ Baker stipulated with Miles King Navy agent Norfolk va. acting for and on behalf of the Navy commissioners to furnish all the bread required for the use of the Navy at Gosport for the year 1828 at two dollars and Eighty seven & half cents for every hundred pounds of bread made, delivered & inspected agreable to the intent & meaning of said written contract aforesaid, nothing to be allowed for the barrels or packages—on the 7th. of Novbr. 1828 it appears an indent or requisition was made upon Mr Graham for 52:500 lb of bread for the guerrier[1]—on the 14th. the bread was ready but not delivered at Gosport Navy yard on account of bad weather—on the 19 Mr Grahams Bake House were burned & the bread entirely consumed it is not even contended that payment was to be made for the bread until inspected & recd. by the Command.g officer of the Navy yard, but was at the sole risk of Mr Graham until it was delivered as pr contract—on the 2nd. of Decbr 1828 Mr Graham writes to the Navy Board & details his loss &c &c—on the 6th. of Decbr. 1828 the commissioner acknowledge having recd Mr Grahams letter & have determined to pay him for the bread so lost 52.500 lb. on the same terms as stated in the letter of the commissioners of the Navy Board to Mr King of the 14th. Novbr. 1828—[2]

Upon reference to the letter of the 14th. Novbr. it has no relation to the payment for the lost bread, but to the contract to be made for the year 1829—From the vouchers produced & suspended by the 2nd. comptroler of the Treasury that Mr Graham has recd. on the 31rst. of Decbr 1828 three thousand and 33 dollars & $^{62}/_{100}$ for 62,549 lb of Bread at $4/ $^{85}/_{100}$ pr hundred & on the 21, 24th. of November & Decbr 1st 1816 for bread at $^4/_{85}$ the sum of $466.61—in Novbr 6, & 27. & Decbr 22 the sum of $41.83—and it does not appear that all this bread ~~has been inspected~~ & was delivered—under the contract as the price paid was pr hundred $1.97½ more than was to be given under the contract—

The difficuty &c

AD, DLC (14-1253).

1. The *Guerriere* was a U.S. frigate. The Gosport (also called Norfolk) navy yard was at Portsmouth, Va.

2. Graham's contracted delivery price for bread in 1828 was $2.87 per hundred pounds. Following a sharp rise in flour, the Board of Navy Commissioners on November 14, 1828, authorized a new price of $4.85 per hundred pounds for 1829. Graham's bakery burned five days later. On December 6 Captain John Rodgers (1773–1838), head of the board, authorized King to allow Graham the new 1829 price for bread supplied in place of that lost by fire. Graham's deliveries to the end of the year were paid at the higher price (*HRDoc* 115, 21st Cong., 1st sess., pp. 28–29, Serial 198).

From Ezra Stiles Ely

Philadelphia Jan. 15th 1830.

Dear & Honoured Sir,

Your favour of the 12th instant. has just arrived. It would have given me pleasure with it to have received your son also: and I have only to regret that you were under the necessity of writing on a painful subject.

My letters to yourself I considered so entirely confidential that I did not take a copy of them; & therefore cannot recollect what were the words I used concerning Mr. John E. Hyde, merchant of New York. I think you will find, dear Sir, by a reference to my letters that I have given him as the person who told me that some man at Gadsby's public table on the morning after Mr. Vaughn's last public entertainment which preceded your inauguration, had said, as was reported, "that Mrs. E. brushed by him last night & pretended not to know him: that she had forgotten the time when he had slept with her."[1]

He did tell me that some one had thus spoken, in Gadsby's public eating room. He did not assert any thing more than this: & appeared to regret that such disgraceful things should be thus publicly spoken against the wife of one who was expected to be a member of the cabinet.

The Mr. Hyde to whom your last letter refers I should presume must be some other man, than the one of whom I wrote. It is true that Mr. John E. Hyde brought no charge of any kind against Maj. Eaton or his lady. A third person was present when Mr. John E. Hyde told me of this shameful speech of some fellow; & if he has not gone to France I shall endeavour get his statement. If Mr. Hyde is in N. York, I shall expect he will do me the justice to tell the truth. I shall write him.[2]

With the Rev. J. N. Campbell I have not had the least intercourse or communication since I left your truly republican palace. I have designed not to meddle with the character & conduct of Mrs. Eaton unless I should be compelled in my own defence. Every thing which I have done in relation to her, or said, will have my leave to be forgotten as soon as possible.

I know nothing of Mr. Campbell's designs at present. Of her I should be glad to hear that she makes Major Eaton a good wife, & gives you no trouble.

Since my letters may be important to refresh my own memory, I should be glad to copy them, or to obtain a copy were it not too great a tax upon your private Secretary.

I beg you to look at them again, dear Sir, & I think you will find that Mr. Hyde is charged with nothing but telling me what some one had said at table. He did not tell me that he heard the shameful speech; nor did he name, if he knew, the person who uttered it.

You will pardon me, I trust, Sir, for having sent you many papers of late on the Indian Question. They are intended for Mr. Donelson to hand to one of your friends, for the public good.

Be assured, Venerable Chief, of the sincere & ardent friendship of your much obliged fellow citizen.

E. S. Ely.

P.S. Mrs. Ely & myself present our kind regards to your Son Andrew, & desire him to come & lodge with us, at 144 South second Street. We should be well pleased to make him at home with us. He may visit & be visited just as much, & just as little as he may please. Our kind respects also we would present to Mr. & Mrs. Donelson, & Miss Eastin. We should give them all a right Tennessee welcome.[3]

[Endorsed by AJ:] Mr Elys letter 15th. Janry 1830 answered & enclosed to him a copy of his letter of the 18th. of March 1829 as requested—

ALS, DLC (37).
1. John Gadsby (c1766–1844) was proprietor of the National Hotel, Washington's leading hostelry. Charles Richard Vaughan (1774–1849) was the British minister to the U.S.
2. Ely wrote AJ again on February 10 (below).
3. AJ's nephew and private secretary Andrew Jackson Donelson (1799–1871), Donelson's wife and first cousin Emily Tennessee Donelson (1807–1836), and her niece and companion Mary Ann Eastin (1810–1847) made up AJ's Washington family. Andrew's father Samuel Donelson and Emily's father John Donelson were brothers of AJ's late wife Rachel.

From Charles Jones Love

Mansfield 15th January 1830

My Dear General,

You will find Inclosed an account of the Stock & Crop at the Hermitage, I found all well yesterday except one of the women and she was not much indisposed. Moses is sill with me he is getting much better & I hope will be well enough to go home next week   I am afraid he has not a good Constitution and a great deal of care must be taken of him, Joe is much as he was when I wrote you last, Joe has a brother that has had sore Eyes for several months the Doct has attended to him but they get no better he rimains about the Kitchen and is attended to &c[1]

Steel is takeing the large Timber out of the new ground, sending to the saw mill what will answer for Plank & Scantling the balance will be made into Coal they are diging Clay for Brick & &c[2]

Your stock looks will generally but the mares and young Colts are in very fine condition the stockholder Colt out of the brown mare that died will make an uncommon fine looking Horse he is now upwards of 15 hands high (your favourite) the sorrell one, has much Improved & grown considerably lately and will be a Horse of good size   The Colt from the Oscar mare had been weaned some time before I rec'd your letter on the subject of its sucking all the winter, It is in fine order and will do very well

On the subject of your mares going to a Horse next spring I would advise them being put to Sir William, If not all a part of them, I have seen Arab, although fine looking animal, I do not like him as well as William, at all events the sway back mare ought not to be put to him, as he is very much so him self; there is in an other reason with me, If he was this selebrated Horse, as he is said to be, he would not have left Virginia, Considerable offers have been made for Sir William, as I am informed, for the purpose of getting him back to Virginia; Sir William will be here the Hermitage, and the over seer can attend when the mares are put, last year one of the Colts, was very much Injured, by the travel up to Stockholder; you might enquire of some of your Virginia friends which of the two would be the most preferable and governable your self accordingly[3]

I wrote you in my last that Mr. Hill, advised me to purchase the Land of Mr. Mosely. I then gave you my reasons whi I did not, On Wednesday last he again advised me to make the purchase, and said it would suit him to take it out of your next crop of Cotton, I have seen Capt Mosely, he wishes you to get the Land, and will wait until I hear from you on the Subject, Mr Steel Informed me that Dr. Hoggat had offered 10$ for that part, I would have made the purchase, but I sent for the Capt. he said you should have the 150, but he wanted to sell more; the sooner you write me the better, William Donelson says you ought to perchase it, and advised me to close the bargain, but I could not go beyond my instructions, particularly as I have got the Capt to agree to wait you directions to me[4]

Steel said he wrote you as he could not please you, you had better look out for some other person, He in my opinion has not the least Intention of going away I am confident your last letter will still make him the more particular and attentive to your Orders at first he was some what offended with me, I told him I should do my duty and he must go agreeable to your Orders and that if he did you would not sensure him for aneything, even if it turned out badly[5]

I asked him to take Andrews Horse at the 125$ he says the Horse is much worse than when he agreed to give me that price, he now offers 75 my own Impression is that he never will get well, he is very badly spavined and will always be lame, you will say what Andrew will do on the Subject I said I would give him an answer in one month

In my next If you make the purchase of Mosely, I will give you my views of feeding Cattle with the surpluss Corn made on your Farms   I feel confident it will be more profitable in that way than aney other I am my Dear Sir Your friend

Ch J Love

Excuse this hastey scrall it is late at night

Memorandum of Stock crops &c &c at the Hermitage 15 January 1830

Corn cribbed—1276 Barrels
64   Stacks   fodder—
40— do—   Oats.
11   do   Rye.
51   Bales   Cotton 27.056 lbs—
11769 lbs pork killed
40 Hogs more to kill

Blooded Stock of horses &c

4 Brood mares
1—2 year old filley
1—3 do Constitution[6]
3—2 yr old Stockholders
3 young Sir Williams

common horses

11 work horses
4 work mules
1 mule colt
1 horse of Andrews
1 Bay mare bot by Andw with mule colt.
1—two year old filley

cattle &c

14 work steers.
7 fat steers.
65 cows & young cattle.
123 head sheep.
250 head Stock hogs.

Stock sold

1. Oscar horse[7] by Cryer—$800.00
44 Sheep
3 do given away one by you & other by Andrew.
4 cows to Lucius Polk.[8]
1 do given to Mrs Donaldson.

Deaths

5 work horses.
1 cow & calf.
1 Steer—.
6 Calves.
[2] yearlings.

Killed for use of farm.

4 Steers for beef.
4 smaller ones.
1 sold to Mitchell

3 Negroes died.
3 do increase[9]

Cash recd. for sheep butter & vegetables—	$126.24
Cash pd out for sundry purposes—	94.68
Balance	$31.56

ALS, DLC (37). Love (c1773–1837) was AJ's friend and Tennessee neighbor. Mansfield was his estate.

1. Moses was likely the 19-year-old son of AJ's slaves Tom and Molly. Joe, 14, and Elick, about 10, were sons of the slave Peter. Joe died in February and Elick also in 1830. They were attended by Nashville physician Samuel Hogg (1783–1842), a former congressman.

2. Graves W. Steele (d. 1838) was beginning his second year as Hermitage overseer.

3. AJ had previously put mares to stud horses Sir William and Stockholder at Hardy Cryer's stable. Arab, owned by Virginian William R. Johnson, stood at Cryer's in 1830.

4. On December 17, 1829, AJ had directed Love to close with Peter Guerrant Moseley (1776–1858) for the purchase of 150 acres adjoining the Hermitage holdings if AJ's cotton receipts for 1829 came within $500 of meeting the price (*Jackson Papers*, 7:639–40). Harry Rufus Willie Hill (1797–1853) was a partner in Nichol & Hill, AJ's marketing agent firm. William Donelson (1795–1864), son of Rachel Jackson's brother John Donelson, lived near the Hermitage and looked after AJ's affairs.

5. AJ had chastised Steele on November 7, 1829, for neglectful management (*Jackson Papers*, 7:539–41) and complained about him to Love and Donelson.

6. In 1826 AJ had put three mares to the stud Constitution, owned by John Shute of Nashville.

7. Bolivar.

8. Lucius Junius Polk (1802–1870) of Maury County, Tenn., was the son of William Polk. In 1832 he married Mary Ann Eastin.

9. Hermitage slaves who died in 1829 were Old Ned (b. c1770), Jack (b. c1809), and AJ's former military servant Jim or James (b. c1794). Children were born to Jim's wife Hannah (b. c1799), Creasy (b. c1799), wife of Argyle, and Candis (b. c1804), wife of Titus.

To *Samuel Delucenna Ingham*

January 18th. 1830—

The President with respects to The Secretary of the Treasury & returns him Mr Gordons letter.

The President sent the other day for Mr Inghams perusal, at the request of the artist Mr Wright, letters, warmly recommend.g him for the place of die sink[er] to the mint—amounghst which ought to have ben included Judge Spencers, of Congress which he now incloses, & will thank him to file with the other

AN, PU-Ingham Papers (14-1458). Charles Cushing Wright (1796–1854) was a renowned medallist and engraver. Ambrose Spencer (1765–1848) was a New York congressman and former chief justice of the state supreme court.

From *Young King et al.*

Seneca Reservation near Buffalo Jany 18th 1830—

Hond. Sir

We the chiefs and Warriors of the Six Nations of Indians take the liberty of addressing you at this time hopeing you will think well of it— you know probaly that for a long time there has been two parties of our tribes residing in the vacinity of this place, called christian and Pagans parties. We have been divided & on account of what you have told us all along back we have got so far as to think we have got light. We hope it has come from the Great Spirit, therefore we wish to inform you that we are again united. We have been a long time trying to settle our dificulties and have our children Educated. We are now once again united, therefore we again rejoice that the Pagan party that was, have with the christians agreed to have their children Educated by the *Friends Society*—We are all well pleased that such is the case and wish all our friends to have their children educated. it is expected that the *Friends Society* will send a school here and pay the expense of it them selves and we wish your consent that we may have such a school on our Reservation, this is all we have to say on this subject but wish you to write us on the subject of our school.[1] We have now agreed to do all we can at farming, and other work, and want to do all things that our Father the President may want of us. We further wish to speak of the treaty made with us by our former Great Father Washington We have thought much of our condition it make us think much of our Father the President as our Reservation is now so small that it is hardily large enough to turn round on it is our desire to Educate our children as soon as may be and do all other things that will please you, therefore we beg of you to have mercy on us. We beg of you to let our Lands what we have left remain for us and our children to live on, as we have but just enough for that, it makes us think of what was said to us by our Great friend Washington, you no doubt are aware of the fact that we together with others of the six nations, was with you and assisted in making peace with all other Indian nations in the United States, and did all in our power for the benefit of our Father the President of this we wish you to think, and further for the *Se[n]eca Nation* themselves in reference to the Treaty made at *Geneseo*. We was at that time (as was agreed by the authorised agent of the United States) to have the Sum of Six Thousand Dollars per year, for ever, and it has always been faithfully fulfilled until last year. Since the year 1828 we have not recd our money. We have seen our agent appointed by you and was astonished to see him bring in for us last fall only about one half the former sum of money. and we would not take that supposing there must be some mistake. and shall expect next spring to have the two payments in one Viz Twelve Thousand Dollars we hope you will send that amount as that will be justly our due.[2] We was very much pleased with our Goods and other presents last fall delivered us by our new agent and have only further to request that we may have an answer to this soon and will write you again if this is not answered—we wish further to add that it is our request that we may after this receive our money from the Govermnt on the 1st June of each year or near that time, as it will be much less trouble to have it at a stated period than to have to meet at diferent times to get our annuities, we generally meet in June and in the fall to receive our goods which we should like to have continued having at those seasons more time to spare for such business than at any other—with much Respect we are your children & ever faithful friends—

Young King	his	X	mark
Col. Pollard	his	X	mark
Capt. Billy	his	X	mark
Big Kettle	his	X	mark
James Robison	his	X	mark

[Fourteen additional signatures follow.]

DS, DNA-RG 75 (M234-832). Seneca chief Young King (c1760–1835) had fought on the American side in the War of 1812. He, Colonel (or Captain) Pollard, Little Billy (d. 1834), Big Kettle, and James Robison were of the so-called "Christian party" of Senecas, more receptive to missionaries and land cessions than the rival "Pagan party" headed by Red Jacket.

1. The Society of Friends, or Quakers, had been active among the Senecas.

2. Justus Ingersoll (1794–1842), a former Army officer, had been appointed Seneca subagent in July 1829. In a 1797 treaty signed at the Genesee River, the Senecas sold land for $100,000, to be held by the president for them in stock of the Bank of the United States. For years the fund, variously reinvested after the demise of the original BUS, had produced

a yearly annuity of $6,000. However, its present investment in three per cent government bonds returned much less. President Adams had made up the difference out of general funds, but AJ stopped the practice as unsanctioned by law. In 1829 the fund yielded only $3,385.60, which the Senecas refused. In December 1829 both AJ and Secretary of War Eaton brought the problem before Congress (*Jackson Papers*, 7:191, 193–94, 621–23). A bill to fix the annuity at $6,000 failed in 1830, but passed in 1831 after further protests from the Senecas.

To Stephen Pleasonton

Janry. 19th. 1829—

The President with his respects, requests Mr P. 5th. auditor to furnish him with the present state of the accounts of all our Foreign Agents who had accounts with the Govrt. on the 4th. of March last, & also, that of our Bankers, & other disbursing officers abroad.

The President draws the attention of the 5th. Auditor to the act of Congress of the 31rst. of January 1823, & the necessity of the due execution of that act, in all cases of disbursing officers.[1]

The President would suggest the necessity of the 5th. Auditors keeping a set of Books, so that the Debit & credit may appear in all cases at a glance & the real ballance due—so that whilst Justice may be done in all cases to our agents, disbursing officers may not be permitted to retain public monies to long in their hands.

AN, DLC-U.S. Finance Papers (14-1468). Pleasonton (c1775–1855) had been fifth auditor of the Treasury since 1817. He supplied the requested information on February 10, noting that accounts from bankers in London and Amsterdam for the last quarter of 1829 had not yet arrived.

1. The 1823 law gave officers and agents abroad who were entrusted with public funds six months to render their quarterly accounts or face dismissal.

To Sarah Bronaugh

Washington Janry 20th. 1830

My Dr Madam

I recd. your note by Dick—some few days ago, there was paid to Mr Skinner on 8th. of January, the Sum of two hundred—dollars—and two members of Congress is under promise to Doctor Hogg to advance a further sum, but as this business is entrusted to Major Lewis to whom I have handed your letters, I cannot state the amount, so soon as he can arrange, & receive the money promised, it will be remitted to you—I regr[et] that Mr Skinner had not communicated this circumstance to you, as it would have prevented you the trouble of sending Dick down before the money w[as] recd. from the members of Congress a[llud]ed to.

I have no wish to purchase any negroes; if Dick was not intemperate, Major Lewis having the mother & family of Dicks wife, might purchase, but as you have not named a price, I can give you no information as to the Majors determination on that subject—If I was disposed to purchase I have not the means—

I am Dr Madam very respectfully yr most obdt. servt.

Andrew Jackson

ALS, DLC-Donelson Papers (14-1479). Sarah Bronaugh (1784–1869) was the sister of the late Dr. James C. Bronaugh, an Army surgeon and AJ's friend and aide. When Bronaugh died in 1822, his slave Dick (b. c1781) was transferred to his mother, Rebecca Bronaugh of Loudon County, Va. She later deeded Dick to Sarah. Usher Skinner (b. c1791), the husband of Sarah's sister Rebecca, was collecting a debt owed to Dr. Bronaugh by Samuel Hogg. He wrote AJ about Dick on April 16 and 26 (below).

From John Caldwell Calhoun

Washington 20th Jany 1830

Dear Sir,

Majr. S. Clark is desireous of some appointment under the Government, and I cheerfully recommend him to your attention.

He is the son of Col Clark of Vermont a distinguished officer both in the late war and that of the Revolution. The Majr. served many years in the Army & he is possessed of good talents, and education, and is well qualified to discharge the duties, which usually attach to office. With sincere regard I am & &

J. C. Calhoun

[Endorsed by James Monroe:] To Major Saterlee Clark   In the view taken by Mr Calhoun, in regard to yr. conduct & character in the service according to my best recollection, I concur. Washington, Jany 20. 1830. James Monroe

Photocopy of ALS, ViFreM (mAJs). Calhoun (1782–1850), of South Carolina, was AJ's vice president. He had been secretary of war from 1817 to 1825 under President James Monroe (1758–1831). Satterlee Clark (c1784–1848), a West Point graduate, was dismissed as Army paymaster in 1824 for defaulting on his accounts. Clark had contested the charge and publicly savaged Calhoun. He was now sutler at Fort Howard in Wisconsin, where he remained until 1842. His father Isaac Clark (1749–1822) of Vermont had been a lieutenant colonel of militia in the Revolution and an Army infantry colonel in the War of 1812.

From Martin Van Buren

Jany 20th 1829

The Secretary of State presents his respects to the President and sends him, the papers in the case of Mr Breckenridge with an analysis made for his accommodation—

[Endorsed by AJ:] Case of atto. for District of western Pennsylvania—

AN, Thomas Coens (mAJs). In 1829 James Gray of Pittsburgh had brought charges of misconduct against Alexander Brackenridge (1792–1870), federal district attorney for western Pennsylvania (*Jackson Papers*, 7:428–29). State Department clerk Nicholas Trist had prepared a report on the case for AJ Donelson on January 12. Brackenridge vehemently denied all charges (DNA-RG 59, M639-3). In October AJ replaced him with George W. Buchanan.

From Eneah Micco et al.

Creek Agency. Creek Nation
Janry 21st. 1830—

We the head Chiefs of the Creek Nation avail ourselves of the opertunity of writing by our friend Genl. Brook to our farther the president to inform him that there are white people moving into our Country without our consent infringing on the rights guarenteed to us by U.S. Government and we do hope that our agent will be instructed to protect and relieve us from such oppressions our Negroes & Horses are taken from us by thiefs & we are not allowed our oaths to proove them.

Our friend Genl. Brook will tell you how we are situated more particularly.

Neha Micco his   X   mark
Tuscahenaha his   X   mark
Jim Chemoley   X
Mickey Barnard   X

Signed in presence of us.
Geo. M. Brooke Bt. Brigdr gen usa
Wm. Moore

DS, DNA-RG 75 (M234-222). Eneah Micco (d. 1836) and Tuskeneah, whose names were rendered variously, were leading chiefs of the Lower Towns, one of the two main population centers within the Creek nation. Brevet Brigadier General George Mercer Brooke (1785–1851) commanded at Fort Mitchell, Ala., on the Chattahoochee River, site of the Creek agency. He was preparing to visit Washington. William Moore was an agency blacksmith.

Confined entirely within Alabama since surrendering their last Georgia holdings in 1827, the Creeks had complained repeatedly of white incursions and pressures to remove westward. On January 21 the same four chiefs also signed two other documents, both witnessed by Brooke and sent on by him with this one the next day. One, addressed to AJ and Eaton, disavowed authorship or approval of reported complaints against Creek agent John Crowell. The other was directed to a Creek delegation that had been sent to Washington in December under authority of both Lower and Upper Town chiefs. It designated four delegation members as spokesmen, barred other members or Cherokees from speaking on its behalf, and urged it to press the Creeks' grievance against Alabama's extension of jurisdiction over them (DNA-RG 75, M234-222). On February 1 the Lower chiefs again wrote AJ about Crowell (below).

From Louis McLane

London Jan. 22. 1830

My dear Sir,

I have the pleasure to forward to you by the present Packet a book left with me for that purpose by Mr Watson: and in performing this service I beg to renew the assurances of my regard and the best wishes of myself and family for your continued health & happiness.[1]

I send no public dispatch by this Packet for I am yet without the answer of this government to our proposition. How long we may be kept so is somewhat uncertain. It is gratifying, however, to perceive that while the message has given a proud elevation to our national character with the British public, it has also inspired the most favorable disposition with the members of the Cabinet.

At a large dinner a day or two ago at Mr. Secretary Peel's, it was the subject of common gratulation by the members of the Cabinet, and the Foreign ministers, even the French Ambassador himself, did not ~~suppress~~ with hold the favorable expression of his sentiments tho' he thought "there was a little coquetry toward this government." I cherish the hope, therefore, that the feelings thus inspired will go far to counteract the constant exertions of the Shippers and Canadian interests to defeat my negotiation.[2]

The affairs of Greece are not yet finally arranged; tho I do not doubt that Prince Leopold will be ultimately placed at the head of the government, but under some other name than that of *King*—probably of *Protector*—the name of King being, as it is said, objectionable to the *King* of *England*![3]

I pray my regards with those of Mrs. ML. and my daughter to the Ladies, and have the honor to be dear Sir, with real respect and regard very faithfully your obedient Servant[4]

Louis M Lane.

ALS, DLC (37). McLane (1786–1857) of Delaware had been appointed minister to Britain in April 1829. On December 12, 1829, he made a formal proposal of reciprocal measures to reopen the West Indian colonial trade, which Britain had closed to American ships in 1826 after a diplomatic impasse with the Adams administration.

1. Ralph Watson's *A Brief Explanatory Statement of the Principle and Application of a Plan for Preventing Ships Foundering at Sea* (London, 1829) proposed lining ships with air-filled safety tubes to enhance buoyancy. AJ thanked McLane for it on March 17 (below).

2. AJ's first annual message spoke cordially of Britain (Richardson, 2:443). Robert Peel (1788–1850) was Home Secretary in the Tory government of Arthur Wellesley, Duke of Wellington (1769–1852). Peel's dinner party was January 16, at his house in Privy Gardens, Whitehall. The French ambassador to Britain was Anne Adrien Pierre de Montmorency-Laval (1768–1837).

3. Following the successful Greek War of Independence against Ottoman rule, the protecting powers Britain, France, and Russia sought a ruler for the nascent state. In February the Greek throne was offered to Prince Leopold of Saxe-Coburg (1790–1865), favored by France and Russia but not by Britain's George IV (1762–1830). Leopold declined in May, and the next year became King of the Belgians.

4. McLane's wife, Catherine Milligan McLane (1790–1849), and daughter Rebecca Wells McLane (1813–1893) had accompanied him to England.

To John Branch

Washington January 23d 1830

Sir,

The revolutionary spirit which has lately displayed itself in Mexico is so well calculated to favor the vicious employment of the captured Spaniards, who are lately returned to Cuba from that territory, that I consider we cannot place too soon in those seas the Frigate Brandywine, in order to guard our commercial interests, and keep down combinations for piratical objects. The calamity which has deprived us of the Hornet, makes this precaution absolutely necessary, at least during the absence of the sloops of War that belong to the West India Station[1]   You will therefore with as little delay as possible dispatch the Frigate Brandywine to the Gulf of Mexico, directing her captain to report from Cuba to the commandr of the Station; and having received his instructions, to proceed on to Tampico and Vera Cruz, where it is important that he should be seen by the authorities of these places—He should also proceed to Carthegena, and from Tampico to that place make inquiry for the Hornet; and throughout his cruize should be particularly charged to report to you from time to time, every capture made of pirates, and every exertion of force in behalf of our commerce.[2]

Such orders as you may deem proper to the commandr of the West India squadron so as to secure the return of the Brandywine within six months to the United States and of those seamen whose engagements are about to expire, in a national vessel should be transmitted with this dispatch. Very respectfully, I have the honor to be, yr. obt. servant.

Andrew Jackson

LS in AJ Donelson's hand, DNA-RG 45 (M124-122). The Navy's West India squadron, comprising four or five sloops and two schooners under Captain Jesse Duncan Elliott (1782–1845), was charged with suppressing piracy in the Caribbean and Gulf of Mexico. In September 1829, ships of the squadron were ordered to the Mexican coast to protect American citizens and property threatened by turmoil in Mexico and by an abortive Spanish attack on Tampico that was mounted from Cuba in July. After the Spanish invaders surrendered in September, Mexico allowed more than 1,200 of them to return to Cuba. To bolster the American presence in the Gulf, Congress in December 1829 passed a special appropriation to refit and man the frigate *Brandywine*, recently returned from the Pacific.

1. The sloop *Hornet* of the West India squadron vanished in a gale off Tampico on September 10, 1829, and was presumed lost. A letter from Elliott to Branch confirming its sinking appeared in the *Telegraph* this same day.

2. Branch embodied these instructions in orders to Captain Henry E. Ballard (1785–1855) of the *Brandywine* on February 15 and to Elliott on February 16 (DNA-RG 45, M149-18). The *Brandywine* sailed from New York on March 10, reached Havana April 1, and proceeded to Vera Cruz and Tampico before returning to Norfolk July 7. She brought home sailors from the squadron with expiring enlistments, exchanged for part of her own crew at Havana.

From John L. Allen

Washington City
January 23d 1830

Dear Genl:

On last evening while converseing with you, on the Subject of Major B F Smith Ageant for the Chickasaws, and the charges prefered against him by Major John B Duncain, and myself, I thought, that I could discover a disposition in you to doubt the truth of the Charges as I alledged in them, to exist—

I admire that trait in your character, that you are Slow to believe a bad report against an old frend, that you have once had a good opinion of— But sir, I was mortified to know that you did not give that credit to my statement that truth, and Justice demands.

I have not made up my opinion haistely about Major Smiths conduct, towards the Chickasaws, & I know well, the worth of character and I also know, full well, that if I was to make charges against Major Smith that I could not sustain, that it would *politically dam me*. But sittuated as I have been in the Chickasaw nation I could not but know the facts to exist in substance as I have alledged them against Major Smith to be true. More particularly, those charges connected with the interest of the Indians, and after they have come to my knowledg, I would think myself equeally gilty with him, were I to have concaled them from the officers of the Gen'l Gov't, untill he had Sliped from under their controle.

Had I taken a different course, and had said nothing on this subject untill after Major Smith had resigned; Then they mite have said to me, ? why did you not tell us all these things before, we accepted of his resignation, you have come too late we now have no controle over him—

Those are the causes that induses me to addopt the course that I have, for the good of our common country, with a view to support the purity of the republican party and fearless of consequences.

Genl Jackson, you have known me a long time, you know that I love to honor you, you know that I have offered my life as a Sacrafice on the field of Battle to support you and my countrys cause, and at a time when my Services were much needed and would again do so if circumstaces Should require it, and as I have never Misrepresented nor decived you, I think it extremely ha[r]d that I cant be believed at this advanced age—

Sir I have no ille will nor hatred, against Major Smith, except that natural dislike that every *honest man* Should feel aganst an individual, guilty of Such acts of official treachery. But I know full well that if Major Smith escapes a public Trial, that the Chickasaws will loose at least six thousand dollars, money they are Justly entitled to besides money to no inconsidderable amount due the Gen'l Gov't that he has procured false and fraudulent vouchers and rendered them in the settelment of his accounts with the Gov't thereby precureing a credidt for money that he never expended   Sir it is proclaimed in the Streets and in the public houses in the Town of Tuscumbia and other places, that Major Smith is a corrupt and dis honest man. the peuople call a loud for a public investigation, Justice & truth makes still a louder call, and Major Smith if innocent of the charges, would be much benefited by a public investigation, and if he is guilty it is due to the peuople that he should have a fair and impartial trial and receive the punishment due to his crime   I say nothing to you on this subject but what I know to be true, and that not with any intention to wound your feelings, for you well know that I would be the last man on earth that would give your Hart one pang—

I am fearful that if this investigation is refused, it will be handled with much Severity against you and Major Eaton, you because it is well known in Allabama and else where, that you, and Genl Coffee are Major Smith's securitys, and Major Eaton, because in a similer case (towitt) Tobias Watkins he was denyed the priviledge of resigning and compelled to stand a public trial—[1]

Twelve or fifteen days have now elapsed since we layed these charges before Major Eaton and have as yet recived no information as to the cours that he intends to persue and I am at considderable expense at the Tavern. I would like to heare as soon as possible the result of your deliberations on the foregoing subject—I have the honor to be sir your obt Servt

John L Allen

PS With regard to Major Duncain, I am now fully satified that indue prejudices exist with you, and others of you Cabinet against that individual, this I am sorry for & would be glad to eleveate and I will say to you without hesitation that in North Allebama his character stands fair with the exception of Major Smith   as a further proof of his respectable Standing in Society, I will respectfully refer you to the Hon John McKinley, Robert E B Barlor, John Kincaid, Robert Letcher, John Rowen & William T Barry   all of these Gentlemen are personally acquainted with Benjamin Duncain of Lincoln County Kentucky the father of John B Duncain and several of those Gentlemen are personally acquainted with this young man and his conduct through life since he has become a man to act for himself, further Genl Jackson I know you are not capable of an act of ingratitude, the father of this John B Duncain has been one of your Strong supporters and having Spent much time and money to support you in your Election to the Station you now hold, and for his son to be removed from office by a man who possessed wealth & influence; and for him to make an unsuccessful appeal to you for that which have never been denied any ma[n] under similar circumstaces, the injury becomes doubly afflicting[2]

J L A

ALS, DNA-RG 75 (M234-136). *Lexington Observer* (Ky.), June 25, 1831. Allen (d. 1865) was subagent to the Chickasaws. Benjamin Fort Smith (1796–1841) had been appointed Chickasaw agent in 1823, with AJ and John Coffee as his sureties. In 1828, then-subagent John B. Duncan and others accused Smith of swindling both the Indians and the government. In March 1829 the War Department cleared Smith and replaced Duncan with Allen (*Jackson Papers*, 7:536–38). Duncan and Allen came to Washington late in 1829 to press their complaint in person. Meanwhile, Smith resigned on December 16. On January 12, 1830, Duncan had written Eaton reiterating his allegations. At Eaton's behest, he and Allen subsequently submitted a sworn affidavit of charges before leaving town in March (DNA-RG 75, M234-135). No proceedings ensued against Smith. Duncan later published a card, dated April 25, 1831, accusing Eaton of covering up Smith's misdeeds to shield AJ from embarrassment, and then a documentary record of the controversy, including this letter, in the *Lexington Observer* of June 25. Smith published a defense and refutation in the *Nashville Republican* of October 4, 1831.

1. John Coffee (1772–1833), now resident in Alabama, was AJ's friend, relation, and former comrade-in-arms. AJ had removed Tobias Watkins (1780–1855) as fourth auditor of the Treasury in March 1829. He was subsequently convicted of embezzling public funds. Jacksonians had paraded the case as proof of the Adams administration's corruption.

2. The published version of the letter omitted this postscript. John McKinley (1780–1852) was a senator and Robert Emmet Bledsoe Baylor (1793–1874) a congressman from Alabama. John Rowan (1773–1843) was a Kentucky senator and John Kincaid (1791–1873) and Robert Perkins Letcher (1788–1861) were Kentucky congressmen.

To Martin Van Buren

[A series of Washington formal entertainments beginning in December 1829 tested Margaret Eaton's acceptance in polite society. The Russian minister to the U.S., Paul Baron de Krudener (1784–1858), hosted a ball attended by the Eatons but avoided by several Cabinet wives. Then, on January 6, 1830, Constantia Wilhelmina Vrijthoff Huygens (1772–1858), wife of Dutch minister Christiaan Diederik Emerens Johan Bangeman Huygens (1772–1857), threw a party to which Mrs. Eaton was not invited. In the next two weeks, Treasury secretary Ingham, Navy secretary Branch, and attorney general John Macpherson Berrien (1781–1856) followed with large parties that likewise excluded the Eatons.

Report reached Jackson that Madame Huygens had publicly declared her intent to ostracize Mrs. Eaton, an affront sufficient in his view to justify demanding her husband's recall. According to Van Buren's later account, Jackson asked him to investigate. He met with the Chevalier and Madame Huygens, who both denied the charge. Van Buren so reported to Jackson, and asked him to write this statement for the record.]

JAN'Y 24TH 1830.

MY DEAR SIR

Your note was rec'd, of this evening, when I had company, and so soon as they have left me I have hastened to reply—The story is this—Shortly after the party at Baron Krudener's it was stated that Madame H. was piqued at something that took place there and said she would give a party and would shew society that she did not recognize Mrs. E. as a fit associate and would not invite her to it.[1] The Heads of the Departments, say the gossips, would follow suit and Mrs. E. and the Major would be put out of society. This came to the ears of some members of Congress, and the attempt *thus*, by a Foreign Minister's family, to put out of society the family of a member of my Cabinet was thought to be such an attack upon me, who had invited this member to come into it, that it aroused their feelings and the communication was made to me. The three parties that followed, given by the three Heads of Departments, were well calculated to give credit to the story of a combination headed by Madame H. to put Major Eaton and his family out of society and thereby to assail my character for inviting him into it. These are the tales and I am happy Madame H. has stated they are not true as far as she is concerned. *This is the substance.* Yrs.

ANDREW JACKSON

Printed, *The Autobiography of Martin Van Buren*, pp. 354–55 (15-0014).

1. Reportedly Krudener took Margaret Eaton's arm to escort her in to dinner, while Madame Huygens reluctantly accepted John Eaton's. When she saw that her assigned seat was next to Margaret's, she and her husband left abruptly.

Memorandum Book

[Jackson wrote notes to himself on stray pieces of paper and also in a memorandum book, which he began keeping in April 1829. He made entries in the book irregularly and not in strict order. These passages appear on two facing pages, out of chronological sequence at the rear of the book.]

Note on Thursday night Jan'ry 21st. 1830—it was communicated to me by Major L.[1] as ~~two members~~ coming from a member of Congress Mr S that Madam H___s[2], had said that she ~~had made~~ would make a party for the purpose of shewing to the world that Major & Mrs. E. was not fit associates & would not be asked, so that they might be excluded from society—on the 22nd. had an interview with Mr. V ~~Buren~~ on night of the 23rd. had an interview with Mr. V___ who informed he had spoke to Ma. H___s on the subject who said it was not true—that Mrs. Th___p__n had come to her and after telling her a thousand things, asked her if Mrs. E. was invited to the party, when she said she had not—Mrs. T. is the niece of Mrs. S___ note[3] It is believed Mrs T was sent there by Mrs. S. and these gossips gave the signal, & the Parties given at Mr. Ing___s, Mr. B___s. & Mr Barriens was in concert—Whether this is true time will unfold, & action prompt will follow—

Mr. H. to be seen at one oclock on the 25th. instant—

on night of 24th. recd. a note from Mr. VB, & answered it—see note—

January 15th. 1830 It was communicated that a caucus was held—Genl. *[G.—H—]* Col. T. &c &c when the decision was that. T. would not challenge. E. But the Female gossips should be set to work, to Have parties, & not invite her to them—[4]

The information Recorded on the other page gives a strong presumption that the above is true—Time will unfold this base conspiracy—& it appears to be connected with the conspiracy of stealing the private papers from the Navy Department—[5]

AN, DLC (64).
1. William B. Lewis.

2. Madame Huygens.

3. This word is inserted, perhaps as a direction to the two paragraphs on the next page.

4. Colonel Nathan Towson (1784–1854) was paymaster general of the Army and friend of Eaton's accuser John N. Campbell.

5. These were the papers reported to be in John N. Campbell's possession implicating Eaton in fraud.

To Martin Van Buren

My Dr Sir

I have this moment recd. the enclosed (confidential) and without reading it through enclose it to you that you may forthwith direct the necessary process against all concerned against whom evidence can be had.

The District attos. at Newyork, Boston, Philadelphia, and Baltimore, if not already instructed, ought, forwith to be directed, to Execute the law against all concerned in this infraction of our nutrality.

Consider this confidential[.] yrs.

Andrew Jackson

ALS, DNA-RG 59 (15-0024). AJ enclosed a January 22 letter from David Porter, who had returned to the U.S. in 1829 after commanding the Mexican navy. Porter warned that a Mexican agent now in Baltimore, José Ignacio Basadre, was likely commissioning privateers against Spain on American soil in violation of law. Van Buren had already learned of Basadre's activities from British minister to the U.S. Charles Richard Vaughan on January 18 (DNA-RG 59, M50-15), and had alerted district attorneys in port cities on January 20 (DNA-RG 59, M40-21).

To John Branch

*[The public snubbing of the Eatons brought Jackson's Cabinet to a crisis. Later, after the Cabinet broke up in 1831, members Berrien, Ingham, and Branch each published his version of January's events. All three related that they had an interview with congressman Richard Mentor Johnson (1780–1850) of Kentucky on the evening of January 27, at which he delivered a demand from Jackson that their families socialize with Mrs. Eaton. All three claimed they had indignantly repelled this attempt at social dictation, and stayed on in the Cabinet only because Jackson himself soon retracted the demand (*Niles' Weekly Register, *July 30, September 3, 1831). Johnson published a contrary recollection that he had merely tried to play peacemaker by offering a suggestion, and had never presumed to give orders for Jackson or to speak by his authority (*Niles, *August 20, 1831).*

Meanwhile, in the note that follows, Jackson proposed a meeting between Branch and Eaton. In 1831 Eaton published a riposte to the *accounts of the three secretaries, in which he included Branch's response below agreeing to their meeting. Eaton dated the exchange of notes at January 28 and 29, just after the contentious Johnson interview, and he pointed to Branch's cordial tone to show that his indignation at Jackson had been feigned and his friendship for Eaton hypocritical (*Niles, *September 17, 1831). In rebuttal, Branch published the whole correspondence in the Raleigh* Star *with correct dates of January 26 and 27, before the Johnson interview. The Washington* Globe *then explained that Eaton's misdating had arisen from difficulty in deciphering the handwriting on Branch's note, which Jackson had passed on to him (*Globe, *October 10, 1831).]*

January 26th, 1830.

The President, with his respects to Gov. Branch, has the pleasure to inform him that he has seen Major Eaton, and he has authorized the President to say to him that he will with pleasure have a friendly interview with Gov. Branch in the presence of Major Barry, whenever it may suit Gov. Branch and his convenience. The P. communicates this with much pleasure, as he hopes all misunderstanding will be explained.

Printed, Raleigh *Star, and North Carolina State Gazette*, October 6, 1831 (mAJs). *Niles*, October 15 (15-0026).

From John Branch

[Printed here are three drafts of Branch's reply to Jackson's note above, the first by Andrew J. Donelson and the other two by Branch himself, and also the finished text as published by Branch in 1831. Eaton's version, published before Branch's, was identical in wording but dated January 29.]

Dr. Sir,

Disposed now as I have ever been to be well understood by you and those connected with the administration, I ~~cannot reject~~ cheerfully accept the proposition for an interview with Majr. Eaton which you have submitted in your note of this evening. Conscious however that the necessity for one, as introductive of that harmony and union which it seems to imply does not exist, has not originated in any conduct of mine; and being well satisfied that it has been the settled purpose of a party to misrepresent me in this respect, I deem it due to my own character to say that this proposition ~~is not the result~~ was not made ~~with my knowledge~~ at my instance. To you to Majr Eaton, and the world, I have observed the utmost frankness, both in regard to the circumstance which has prevented the intercourse of my family with Mrs. Eaton, and in all matters pertaining to our official connection—in which latter capacity I have been always desirous to cultivate the best feelings of friendship & respect. I have been induced to believe however, that a similar sentiment has not governed Majr Eaton & many others that are understood to be his particular & confidential friends. Rumours which I have heeded not, at various intervals during the last six months, and more than once traced to such individuals, have represented the failure of my family to visit Mrs. Eaton as the forfeit of my seat in this cabinet—These I allude to now as explaining the construction which I place upon the wish of Majr Eaton to meet me in the presence of *Majr Barry*, a Gentleman for whom I have always entertained the highest respect; but in as much as the Maj has deemed a witness necessary, I consider that a similar privilege will be allowed to me, without being understood to convey, as I do not, the slightest disrespect to that Gentleman; and for this purpose I beg leave to name Mr. Van Buren, at whose house at any time that the other Gentlemen may designate, I am willing the interview should be held—

Draft in AJ Donelson's hand, NcU (15-0058).

Washington City
Janry 27. 30

Dear Sir,

I have had the honor to receive and carefully to peruse your note of yesterdays date ~~with emotions which~~ with such emotions as a generous bosom ~~can~~ may imagine but which I will not attempt to describe. Unconscious as I am of ever having given *just* cause of offense to Maj. Eaton I cannot for a moment hesitate in accepting your friendly mediation ~~to preserve those friendly~~ *official* relations which it has ever been my anxious desire to cultivate. The Major thinking proper it seems ~~to have a witness and for that purpose~~ to desire the presence of Maj. Barry a gentleman for whom I entertain the highest respect to this I can have no objection.

AL Draft, NcU (mAJs).

Dear Sir,

I have received your note of yesterdays date and ~~will~~ do most cheerfully accept your friendly mediation, more however from a desire to give you an additional evidence of the friendly feelings which have ever actuated my bosom towards yourself than from a consciousness of having given to Major Eaton any just cause for the withdrawal of his friendship

As an additional evidence of the frankness which I trust ever will characterize my conduct, I agree to meet him in the presence of Maj Barry at ~~the Navy Department as being most convenient to all parties~~ Mr Van

Burens and his presence also ~~also if~~ at any time when it may be most convenient

AL Draft, NcU (mAJs).

Navy Department, Jan. 27, 1830.
Dear Sir:
 I have received your note of yesterday's date, and do most cheerfully accept your friendly mediation; more, however, from a desire to give you an additional evidence of the friendly feelings which have actuated my bosom towards yourself, than from a consciousness of having given to Major Eaton just cause for the withdrawal of his friendship. As a further manifestation of the frankness which I trust will ever characterize my conduct, I agree to meet him this day at two o'clock, in the presence of Major Barry, at Mr. Van Buren's, and in his presence also. Yours, truly,

JOHN BRANCH

Printed, Raleigh *Star, and North Carolina State Gazette*, October 6, 1831 (mAJs). *Niles*, October 15 (15-0060). After a further exchange about arrangements, Eaton and Branch met on January 28 at Berrien's office, with Berrien and Barry present. By both men's later accounts, they shook hands and parted amicably after agreeing that official cooperation in the Cabinet did not require familial intercourse outside it (*Niles*, Sep 3, 17, 1831).

From *Theodore Ingalls et al.*

Portland Jany. 27th. 1830
To the President of the United States.
 The undersigned members of the Senate and House of Representatives of the State of Maine and supporters of the measures of the administration of the General Government being assembled after an election seldom equalled in bitterness and asperity, most respectfully ask leave to represent what we believe to be the sentiments of the democratic party in this State upon the subject of *Reform*, so beneficially carried into effect in different parts of the United States.[1]
 It is probably well known to the Executive, that in this State, where pure republican principles, harmonising with the genius of our government and the measures of the present administration are entertained by a large and respectable portion of our citizens, almost every office under the last administration became, under the fiat "that there should be no neutrals" engines in the hands of an overbearing aristocracy, to break down the democratic party; and in many instances wholly to control the freedom of our elections. Having witnessed in the most obvious manner palpable instances of the perversion of the influence of office for the unjustifible purpose of supporting a corrupt administration and of stifling

the voice of the people, we have been led to believe that patriotism and justice were in those cases merged in the stronger feeling of self interest, and that long continuance in the enjoyment of lucrative offices has a direct tendency to lessen a proper respect for the will of the people. We here beg leave to name two gentlemen whom we consider as coming directly within the spirit of the principle above named. They are Benja. Green Marshall of Maine and Stephen Thather Collector of the port of Passamaquoddy. These Gentlemen have been distinguished by their early, constant, strong and decided opposition to the republican party. The former has heretofore sustained several offices under the State Government; and in all has been associated with the enemies of our free institutions. He presided at the first general State convention, called together immediately preceding the late presidential election; and must be considered as sanctioning and approving the violent measures & disgraceful proceedings of that convention, the design of which was to awe the Legislature and the people into submission to the last administration. We therefore have no hesitation in assuring the President that this Gentleman has not the confidence of the republican party; and we respectfully request his removal from the important and responsible office of Marshall of this District. We believe his removal would be perfectly in unison with public sentiment and in accordance with the principles and measures recommended by the Executive to secure a fair and free representation of the will of the people.

Mr. Thatcher, though less known, is by no means less obnoxious to the Republican party. And we have not a shadow of doubt that his reappointment to his present office would be highly detrimental to the public interest, as well as injurious to the spread of pure Democratic principles. We therefore pray that he may not be nominated for a reappointment thereto.

The undersigned refrain from an expression of their preference as to the successors who may be selected for the above named offices.

> Theodore Ingalls
> Charles Hutchings Jr.
> Robert P. Dunlap
> Thomas Davee
> John L. Megquier

[Seventy-three more signatures follow.]

DS, DNA-RG 59 (M639-9). Ingalls (c1790–1857) was a Bridgton physician and a Maine state senator. Benjamin Green (1764–1837) was appointed marshal by Monroe in 1824 and reappointed by Adams in 1828. Stephen Thatcher (1774–1859) was first appointed customs collector for the Passamaquoddy district by Monroe in 1818 and reappointed in 1822 and 1826. On March 29 AJ removed Green for Albert Smith and nominated Maine congressman Leonard Jarvis to replace Thatcher when his current term expired on April 1.

1. Maine's closely contested state elections in September 1829 produced an evenly divided senate and a disputed result for governor. In February the legislature declared anti-Jackson candidate Jonathan G. Hunton the victor.

To Martin Van Buren

Jan'ry. 28th. 1830—

The President with respects to the Sec. of State,—Having read Mr Deans letter now returns it—with this remark, that the charge of want of moral honesty would have prevented his first appointment—that he has been superceded on the charge by Govr Duval—if the Govr. will unite in a desire to suspend the nomination until further enquiry, there would be some grounds for a withdrawal for that purpose, but we cannot without this as both are here—If you should think proper you can give him this, or any other similar reply, if reply is proper

AN, DNA-RG 59 (M179-68). In June 1829, AJ had given John Dean of Alabama a recess appointment as marshal of Florida Territory's southern district. Territorial delegate Joseph M. White and others subsequently charged Dean with dishonesty (*TPUS*, 24: 311–12). Governor William Pope Duval (1784–1854), who was then in Washington, endorsed the charges in a letter to Van Buren of January 12 (DNA-RG 59, M639-23). Duval and White both recommended Lackland M. Stone to replace Dean. On January 19 AJ nominated Stone, superseding Dean. Dean, also in Washington, wrote Van Buren on January 27 voicing astonishment at the charges against him and asking a suspension of his replacement to give him time to repel them (*TPUS*, 24:338–39). Stone's nomination was not withdrawn, and the Senate confirmed him on March 4.

Memorandum of Interviews with John Branch, Samuel Delucenna Ingham, and John Macpherson Berrien

[At Jackson's request, secretaries Branch, Ingham, and Berrien met individually with him on January 29 and 30. Together with the previous meeting of Branch and Eaton, these interviews restored an appearance of harmony and averted an immediate Cabinet rupture.

Jackson apparently began this memorandum with the intention of conveying its substance through a friend (probably Richard M. Johnson), and then rewrote it as a record of his own conversation. Two subsequent versions in Jackson's hand survive. One is an elaboration and reworking of the entire text, the other a yet further polishing of its opening passage prefacing the account of the interviews. Both were evidently written out sometime later, most likely in the summer of 1831 during the burst of public recriminations that followed the Cabinet breakup. At that time,

Globe *editor Francis P. Blair addressed a public letter to Berrien, charg-*
ing that he, Branch, and Ingham had known all along that Jackson never
intended to dictate their social relations. To prove the point, Blair quoted
two extracts from a paper that he said Jackson had read to them at their
interviews (Niles, July 30, 1831). Blair's quoted language closely echoed
that of this memorandum and precisely matched that of Jackson's later,
reworked full version. In their expositions that followed Blair's letter, the
three secretaries vehemently denied that Jackson had shown or read them
any paper at all.]

The personal dificulties between some of the members of my cabinet
have assumed an aspect & *[received]* a bearing in regard to myself which
require an expression of my personal feelings—to prevent future misunderstanding I have deemed it expedient ~~that the same should be made~~
~~through a mutual friend~~ to have ~~an~~ this interview with Mr Ingham Mr
Branch & Berrien
    ~~I have therefore requested my friend _____ to say to~~ When we met I
said to them (Mr. Ingham, Mr Branch & Mr Berrien) ~~that~~ That the course
pursued by them towards Major Eaton & his family as reported to me ~~is~~
was in my opinion under the circumstances not only unjust in itself but
disrespectful to myself. The ground upon which this opinion is founded
are substantially these—[1]
    I do not claim the right to interfere in any manner in the domestic
relations or personal intercourse of any member of my Cabinet nor have
I ever in any manner attempted it. But from information, and my own
observation on the general course of events I am fully impressed with a
belief that ~~the gentlemen whom I have named, & portions of their~~ you
& your families have, in addition to the exercise of their own undoubted
rights in this respect taken measures to induce others to avoid intercourse
with Mrs Eaton and thereby sought to exclude her from society & degrade
him. It is impossible for me upon the fullest and most dispasionate view
~~of~~ & consideration of ~~the~~ this subject to regard this course in any other
light than a wanton disregard of my feelings & a reproach of my official
conduct. It is I, that have without solicitation or desire on his part called
Major Eaton into my cabinet, & it is I, that with the fullest conviction of
the injustice of the imputations which as I firmly believe malice & envy
have cast upon his wife continue him there If her character is such as
to justify active measures on the part of the members of my cabinet to
exclude her from virtuous society—it is I who am responsible to the community for this alledged indignity to public morals—I will not part with
Major Eaton from my cabinet & those of my cabinet who cannot harmonise with had better withdraw, for harmony I must & will have   It is
in vain to attempt to disguise the true aspect of the question, and it is not
in my nature to do so if I could; nor can I consent to harbour any feelings
toward those with whom I am in the habit of daily association without

distinctly expressing & apprising them of those opinions—my whole life has been at variance with such a course, and I am too old to practice it now—I must cease to respect myself when find myself capable of it.* ~~The relations between those Gentlemen you & myself are two fold—the one personal—the other official. This first communication will make known my feelings which my friend _____ is now requested to make will satisfy the claims of the former and place matters upon the footing upon which my own feelings imperiously require the should stand The other &the affect which this unhappy & I can truly say very painful state of things ought to have upon it is of a very different character, that will remain to be hereafter considered and upon which I shall when a proper time arrives express myself with the same sincerity & freedom.~~ interview I now have asked will place

~~Andrew Jackson~~

* Therefore have I sought this interview, to assure you if there are any truth in the report that you have entered into the combination charged, to drive Major Eaton from my cabinet that I feel it an indignity & insult offered to myself, and is of a character that will remain hereafter to be considered—

read to them

Andrew Jackson

[Endorsed by AJ:] private   to be put away with my *private papers*—this was ~~not sent~~ read to them & being informed by the gentlemen that as far as their influence went, it was exercised diferently, & their wish was to harmonise the cabinet—I determined not to dismiss them—

ADS, DLC (59; 15-0063).
1. The pointer is in the margin and may have been inserted when AJ composed his final revision of the opening passage, which concludes with "when we met I made the following statement ☞".

To William Donelson

Washington Jan'ry 30th. 1830—

Dr William

your letter of the 20th. ult. has been some time since received, and such has been the press of business ever since that really I had not time to answer it—I have sincerely to thank you for your attention to the subjects it embraced, for really I became so unhappy from information recd. of Mr. Steels inattention to my sick negroes & alledged inhumanity that I could not rest—I have recd. a very insolent letter from him lately, with a notice that he will only remain the present year & wishes to get away by July—I believe he has no intention of going but thinks I will coax him to remain—but I have wrote him a short answer, informing him I have noted that part of his letter & will be prepared to meet his wishes at the end of the year—our articles are that he is to House the crop—I am sure he can have no wish to go, for the crop of cotton will about pay his wages & the expence of the plantation & surely he could not expect to do better any where else—Genl Coffee writes me, that Hutchings farm will produce from 75 to 78 Bales Wt. 32000 lbs. this is 5000 lb. baled cotton more than I make with a third more hands—Mr Lemuel Donelson wrote me of a Mr Holt recommendg. him as a good overseer—If he is not engaged and can be had at a moderate price I would be glad if he could be engaged without letting Mr Steel know any thing about it, until the year is out unless Steels conduct is such that he ought to be removed—but I would not employ any man unless his honesty & humanity could be vouched for.[1]

I have recd. a letter to day from Col Love,[2] in which he stated that you gave it as your opinion that I ought to buy the one hundred & fifty acres of land from Capt Moseley adjoining Winstons place on the north running from my N. East corner north & then west to Wards line, so as to includge 150 acres—I have wrote him to day to buy it—and as you have been good anough to permit me to trouble you with my business I have to ask the favour of you to survay it for me. It may press me a little in my pecuniary matters, but it is a good peace of land, & serving a man in pecuniary distress.

I owe the heirs of our deceased friend James R. Donelson, which if needed & the note forwarded here, I will pay it—or send it home with part of my family here who will visit Tennessee in the spring, please send me the amount of the note.[3]

My young friend Thomas. J. Donelson wrote to my son that he wanted him to speak to me to loan him a bed, that he was about to go on his tract of land—poor fellow, when I read it, and reflect how often his poor aunt, spoke of him & his situation, the Tears trickled from my cheeks—my Dr William go over & give him the bed in the office, or if there is feathers anough direct Steel to have a new bed made for, ~~him~~ & give it to him—I believe the bed in the office is a new one—if he takes that, say to Steel & old Hanna & Betty that I want another bed made & put in the office—give Thomas the bed, & the bedcloaths, that is with it—If a new bed is made for him, let a *tick*, sheets, pair of blanketts, & coverlet be bought for it & Lucinda can make them up for him & present them to him—If his aunt had been living she would have done this, & it gives me pleasure to do it in remembrance of her—I well recollect when I was left an orphan, my situation was more desolate that his, but I have learned to feel for all in his situation, & I praise my god that I have the means to aid him in this little, but necessary boon, have this done for me[4]

How sincerely I regretted to hear of the sad accident that had befallen your dear mother, but I thank god she is, from the last accounts doing well, & is likely soon to be well. do william, have the steps of the House where she is in the habit of passing out & in, made so that she can pass them in safety—present me kindly to her & your father, with my prayers for both their happiness in this life & the world to come.[5]

I rejoice to hear that *Poor Poll* is still living say with my kindest salutations to your dear Elisabeth, how much I feel indebted to her for preserving it, should I live, I will reward her for her care of it—should I live to return, & find it alive it will be a great comfort to me—I value this bird more than any thing that my dear wife left—she thought so much of it— give my kind respects to Uncle Sandy, say to him I hope to see him once more, & wish him health & happiness in this life, & that which is to come—remember me kindly to Lucinda, & Thomas, & your uncle Levan, & Severn, & Jacob Donelsons & their families, & to all friends & neighbours, & believe me your affectionate uncle[6]

Andrew Jackson

P.S. Mr Steel writes me that Dr Butler sent a servant for my constitution stud colt, without on[ce] writing—Unless he has bought *[him]* from Parson Cryer I cannot u[nder]stand how this happened—I had di*[rected]* Mr Cryer if he could to sell him; a[nd] if the Doctor will give a fair pric[e] say $500 he can have him & two years to pay it in—The colts of the two cotton mares were long since to have divided, inform me if this is done— A. J.[7]

ALS, DLC-Donelson Papers (15-0075). William had written AJ on December 20, 1829, with news of the Hermitage and the neighborhood (*Jackson Papers*, 7:643–45).

1. AJ was the legal guardian of Andrew Jackson Hutchings (1811–1841), the orphaned son of Rachel's nephew and AJ's former business partner John Hutchings. The Hutchings estate, of which John Coffee was co-executor, included an Alabama plantation. Lemuel Donelson (1789–1832) was William's brother.

2. January 15, above. AJ had acquired the farm of his late neighbor Anthony Winston in 1828.

3. William's first cousin James Rucker Donelson (1805–1829), son of Rachel Jackson's brother Severn Donelson, had died August 18, 1829.

4. Thomas Jefferson Donelson (1808–1895) was another son of Rachel's brother Severn and the birth twin of AJ's adopted son Andrew Jackson Jr. Lucinda Rucker Donelson (1812–1837) was his sister. Old Hannah (b. c1770) and her daughter Betty (b. c1793) were Hermitage house slaves.

5. William's mother, Mary Purnell Donelson (1763–1848), had fallen from the steps and broken her arm. Her husband was Rachel Jackson's brother John Donelson (1755–1830).

6. AJ had purchased Poll the parrot in 1827. William's wife Elizabeth Anderson Donelson (1809–1841) was caring for it. Alexander "Sandy" Donelson (1751–1834) and Leven Donelson (1776–1833) were unmarried brothers of Rachel Jackson. Severn Donelson (b. 1797) and Jacob Donelson (b. 1801) were sons of her late brother William.

7. William Edward Butler (1790–1882) was the husband of another of Rachel's nieces, Martha Thompson Hays. Hardy M. Cryer had reported to AJ on December 26, 1829, that

he was looking for a horse to buy (*Jackson Papers*, 7:648). Horse breeder Henry Cotten or Cotton (d. 1828) had sent AJ two mares for breeding in 1826. AJ purchased one for AJ Donelson's son Andrew on August 30 (below).

From Black Hoof et al.

Wapaughkonnetta Janry 30th. 1830

Our Great Father the President of the U.S.

We the Chiefes of the Sawnoes Nation, wish you to lison to speach of your Children—we now deputise 2 of young Chiefes to hand our speach to you & we hope you will pay the same atention to it as if we ware speaking to you fase to fase

Father we have something that troubles our minds & when our minds troubled we cannot rest easy & we thought we would talk with our father and see if He could remove this rouble from our minds.

Father we still remember the Treaty held with G. Cass & Macarther others in the year 1817 at Ft Migs. were to receve $1,000 & give us reservations 1 on Hog Creek & the other at wapaughkonnetta and the treaty not ending we had Treaty with G. Cass at St Maries in the yeare 1818. at that time heard that our white brothers wished us to move west of the Mississippi & we metion the thing to Cass He said that he did not us to go, unless we wanted to move and that govourmet assist us to move, the Weyandots Senneca & we answered that we did not wish move west of the Mississippi—

Father we still remember the words of uor frend G. L. Cass he told us that govourment would bind themselves to pay 3,000 dollars yearly at wapaughkontta for ever as long as we ware a nation.

Father we consider that treaty still binding we cant see were we have broke it on our side, & after it become a law we thought our father would not brake it. we could see any way it could be broak—

Father we know that there ware a number of our People amaong us that ware continly runing after wiskey and brought trouble, & we often talked with them, not to do so. They would not listen us, And took a notion to move to Mississippi and often bring trouble yet to this place—

Father this all that we can see, and why sould the money be sent to Mississippi when all the Chiefes are all here that ware present at the Treaty

Father we have concluded to make a visit & see you as we are desireous to see our father President. And have a fare understanding on both sides we have often got our father McElwan to write to our grate Father, he told us that he had not yet receved sufficen answers as to be sure when the money would be recovered again or not.[1]

Father an another thing is lacking, that is our salt, we use to receved 5 Barrel of salt every year that we have not receeved none for 2 years past. All things we wish to have a fare understanding on both sides.

Father we must till you that we are all pleased with our Agent Mr John McElwane we have seen him twist the more we form acquintantance with the more we love him we think he wish to do nothing but what is wright and good towards us in evry thing[.] remains yours Effetionly

Black Hoof	his mark	X
John Perry	his mark	X
Thothweacaw	his mark	X
Pa H Tha	his mark	X
Leothaw	his mark	X
Little Fox	his mark	X

DS, DNA-RG 75 (M234-669). Black Hoof, or Catahecassa (c1734–1831), was the leading chief of the Ohio Shawnees. An 1817 treaty concluded at Fort Meigs on the Maumee River had pledged the Shawnees a perpetual annuity of $2,000 and reservations of land at Wapakoneta and Hog Creek, in return for their acceding to land cessions by several Ohio tribes. A supplementary treaty the next year at St. Mary's expanded the reservations and raised the annuity to $3,000. Black Hoof was the lead Shawnee signatory to both treaties; U.S. commissioners were Lewis Cass (1782–1866), governor of Michigan Territory, and Duncan McArthur (1772–1839) of Ohio. Starting before the treaties, parties of Shawnees had emigrated from Ohio first to Missouri and then, under an 1825 removal treaty, to present Kansas. On April 29, 1829, Thomas Loraine McKenney (1785–1859), head of the War Department's Bureau of Indian Affairs, had ordered $2,000 of the annuity paid to the western Shawnees. On February 23, 1830, McKenney endorsed this petition changing the ratio to give the Ohio Shawnees $2,000 and the western Shawnees $1,000. In 1831, John Perry (c1780–1845) and the remaining Ohio Shawnees signed a removal treaty surrendering their reservations and rejoining the previous emigrants in Kansas.

1. John McElvain (1789–1858) was Indian agent at Piqua, appointed by AJ in 1829. He had written McKenney about the annuity on January 12 (DNA-RG 75, M234-669).

February

From Eneah Micco et al.

Creek Nation
1 Feby 1830

Dear Father

From rumor we a few days since addressed you on the subject of a petition which appears to have made its appearance at Washington, with our names attached thereto, requesting the removal of our present Agent—Col. Crowell, and recommending a man by the name of Triplett as his successor.

Having now received correct information in relation to that petition, we as Head men of the Creek Nation and representing one half of said Nation, cannot in Justice to ourselves and Nation forbeare from again humbly solisiting your interferance in behalf of our Agent Col. Crowell; As we do assure you in the most posative terms, we have made no such request as above mentioned; It appears strange, and would be the hight of simplisity in us to recommend a man as our agent who is an entire stranger to us   We know nothing of this Triplett spoken of, We are however well acquainted with his brother, and if that is any criterian by which to judge him, Lord forbid us from wishing his acquaintance—[1]

From the interference of designd white men it is highly probable that some of the Upper Town chiefs have made such a request. Those men have used their influence to poison us against Col. Crowell   The have told us that all the talks which he had given us, as coming from you, were his own and made for his own purposes, and not yours;[2] they further told us if we would have him (Col. Crowell) removed, and a nother appointed in his stead, we could remain quietly on our present homes,

As the Talks were such as we but little expected, and such as we did not like, we were at first dispose to believe what was told us; but having now become convinced to the contrary, we cannot but express our entire confidence in Col. Crowell as our Agent; our people have but one objection to him, and that we presume would be attached to any other Agent who might be appointed, that is he wishes us to leave our present homes and move to a strange country—

Our condition as a free people is one which is to be lamented by all the Humane part of the community; We from our infancy have been taught to exercise our feelings as a *free* and *independant people*, subject only to the Laws and wishes of the United States, such a state of feelings have been our happy lott to experiance from time immemorial; but it now appears to us that, that happy fate of ours, so long exercised is about to be sealed; Our white Brothers on each side of us appear to have lost all the good feeling which formerly existed, all appear to have turned their hands to crush us; Justice on our part appear to have forever fled. We can but now rely on the ~~decision~~ good faith of the proud Americans, for our future destiny, If they withdraw their strong hands from beneath us, we will inevitably fall as a Nation to rise no more   We therefore as a dependant people look to you for protection, and sincerely hope that we as a Nation may prosper and that in a coming day we may be able proudly to say that the American people were our Friend

we rem yur humble & Loving children

signed
Nehoh Micar
Tuskenehaw
John Stoham
Efah Emorthle
Opefuske yohola

[Fifteen more names follow.]

in pres of *P Wager Bt Mjr 4. Inf[3]*

Copy, DNA-RG 75 (M234-222). The signers were chiefs of the historic Creek Lower Towns along the Chattahoochee River. The other main Creek population center, the Upper Towns, lay westward in central Alabama. Former Alabama congressman John Crowell (1780–1846) had been agent to the Creeks since 1821. A Creek petition to AJ of November 20, 1829, had begged Crowell's dismissal and the appointment of former Georgia state comptroller William M. Triplett in his place. A second appeal to AJ of December 10, written to accompany a Creek delegation to Washington, also complained of Crowell. Both documents purported to speak for the entire nation and bore the names of Lower and Upper chiefs including Eneah Micco (*Jackson Papers*, 7:563–65, 634–35). In Washington, Indian superintendent Thomas L. McKenney invoked this February 1 address and those sent previously on January 21 (above) to discredit the visiting Creek delegation. McKenney charged that the delegation's Cherokee secretary, John Ridge, had falsified its credentials and the complaints against Crowell to misrepresent the views of Eneah Micco and the Lower chiefs, who he claimed spoke for the preponderance of Creeks (DNA-RG 75, M21-6).

1. Thomas T. Triplett, William's brother, was a former Creek subagent, dismissed in February 1829 for abusive conduct.

2. As instructed, Crowell had delivered AJ's March 23, 1829, talk to the Creeks urging their removal west of the Mississippi (*Jackson Papers*, 7:112–13).

3. Brevet Major Philip Wager (d. 1835) was a career Army officer.

From Spencer Darwin Pettis

Wash.g. Feby. 2. 1830.

Sir,

Having had the honor of a personal interview with you the other day on the subject of the appointment of an Agent for the Shawnees, Delawares &c. in & near the State of Missouri I beg leave to submit my opinions in writing.

I think Mr. Rector should not be appointed because such an appointment would be very unpopular with both friends & foes. He is supposed in Missouri to be a very violent man and therefore has many enemies   He is unpopular because of the manner in which he left the State: having broken the custody of the Sheriff when he was on his trial on indictment for (I believe) *stabbing with intent to kill*. He made his escape—a verdict was found against him and he has not been back as far as I know or ever heard, to abide his trial. For these reasons I am opposed to his appointment. As a personal and political friend I have deemed it my duty to make this statement without feeling the least personal hostility to the gentleman in question. I have discharged my duty to you, to myself & to those I represent and now leave the matter to take its course.

I would however offer one other reason why Mr. R should not be appointed. There are many applicants from Missouri for places of that kind who are men of unexceptionable characters and who have at least as much capacity as Mr. R. His appointment over them would be very disagreeable to the great body of the people of that State. The pressing of Mr. Rs. appointment by gentlemen here is an evidence I think of *great indiscretion*. I have the honor to be Sir Your Obdt Servt

Spencer Pettis

[Endorsed by AJ:] Mr. S. Pettis on the Subject of appointment of Mr Rector Indian agent—refered to the Secretary of War—

ALS, DNA-RG 75 (M234-300). Pettis (1802–1831) was a Missouri congressman. Wharton Rector (c1800–1842) was a former Army lieutenant and recently elected Arkansas legislator. In 1826 a St. Louis grand jury had indicted Rector for "stabbing with an intent to kill" Augustus H. Evans, a clerk in the land surveyor's office with whom he had quarreled over a debt. At the trial in June 1827, Rector applied for a continuance on grounds of the absence of the only eyewitness, his brother Elias Rector, who could prove provocation and lack of intent to kill. The request was refused, and Rector broke custody and fled to Arkansas Territory. The jury convicted him two days later.

On February 5, three days after this letter, AJ nominated Rector as agent to the Shawnees and Delawares. Among his recommenders were Missouri senator Thomas H. Benton and Kentucky congressman Richard M. Johnson. On April 5, the Senate requested information from AJ respecting Rector's conviction and his fitness for office. AJ complied on April 6, submitting the court record and statements attesting to Rector's good character and claiming he had not received a fair trial. The Senate rejected Rector by 23 to 21 on May 20. AJ renominated him on May 28, citing the absence of two favorably disposed senators during the previous vote. On May 29 Rector was again rejected by 21 to 20.

To Mary Letitia Kirkman Call

Washington February 4th. 1830—

My Dear Mary

I was gratified indeed by the receipt of your kind letter of the 15th. ulto. handed by your friend Colo. Reed—He dined with me yesterday, from him I was gratified to learn that you & your amiable little family enjoyed health, that greatest blessing heaven can bestow, and great prosperity in life, as well as the rest of our friends in Florida.

It will always be a source of gratification to me to hear of your prosperity & happiness & that of your family, for which my ardent prayers as well as that of my Dr departed wife whilst living were continually offered up—she is gone, and alas, all my happiness here below—altho surrounded with company & labour, still I never shall cease to mourne her *loss.*

I beg you to receive my thanks for your kind wishes for the success of my administration, I shall endeavour, Mary, to do my duty, trusting to, & suplicating a kind providence to guide & direct me.

Mr. & Mrs. Donelson, with Mary Eastin, my son & ward A. J. Hutchings Joins in kind respects to you & family.

I fondly hope before this reaches you, your dear Husband will be restored to you in good health, to whom tender my respects, and accept the assurance of my sincere respects friendship & esteem

Andrew Jackson

P.S. Present me affectionately to Col. Butler & his family & to Mr. & Mrs. Eastin & theirs[1]

ALS, F (mAJs). Mary Call (c1801–1836) was the wife of AJ's friend and former military aide Richard Keith Call (1792–1862), now resident in Tallahassee. They had married at the Hermitage in 1824.

1. Robert Butler (1786–1860), AJ's former adjutant general and now surveyor of public lands in Florida, was married to Rachel Jackson's niece Rachel Hays. Florida newspaper editor Thomas Eastin (1790–1865) was an old acquaintance of AJ's and the brother of Mary Ann Eastin's late father William. He married Lucinda Gayle (b. 1789) in 1815.

From Louis McLane

London Feb. 6th. 1830

My dear Sir,

I have been asked by the author, to present to you the accompanying pamphlet in his name, and to offer to you at the same time, the assurances of his profound respect for your public character. I need scarcely repeat the pleasure it affords me to perform these services, and to add the assurance that such respect is rapidly infusing itself into all ranks in this country. The debates in the Commons upon the subject of the address, afford some evidence of this, and the speech of Mr. Secretary Peel may be considered the avowal from the highest authority of the sentiments now entertained towards the Chief Magistrate of the United States.[1] On this subject I have nothing farther to ask than that they will give us some practical proof of their disposition; and have ventured to say so to each gentleman who has complimented me upon the Message. I took the liberty of suggesting, that, some *practical proof* by this government, only could be equivalent to the independence (not easily to have been manifested by another) which enabled the Message with a firm hand to assail the remnant of prejudices which once prevailed to a great extent in the U.S.

My family desire me to present to you and the Ladies their affectionate remembrance; and with my best wishes that you may be long preserved in health & happiness to enjoy the love of your countrymen, and the respect of the world I remain dear Sir, with sentiments of real respect & regard very faithfully your Servant

Louis McLane.

[Endorsed by AJ:] (private) The Honble. Louis McLane of 6th. February & 22nd Janry   recd. & answered 17th. of March 1830—the copy of answer within—To be placed on file with my private papers   A. J.

ALS, DLC (37). McLane enclosed a pamphlet by English economist Nassau William Senior (1790–1864), perhaps *Three Lectures on the Cost of Obtaining Money; and on Some Effects of Private and Government Paper Money* (London, 1830), a compilation of talks given at Oxford in 1829. AJ replied on March 17 (below).

1. On February 4, in a House of Commons debate over a response to the King's speech to Parliament, Home Secretary Robert Peel had praised the tone of AJ's annual message and reciprocated its friendly expressions toward Britain.

From Samuel Delucenna Ingham

Try Dept.
9 Fby 1830

My dear Sir

The enclosed Letters from Mr White were recd this morning, in relation to the character of Livingston who was appointed not long keeper of a Light house at St. Johns—it is so difficult to know the truth as to the characters of men at such a distance, that I relied mainly on the Service of this man at N. Orleans when I recommended him to you—if however you think the enclosed letter affords sufficient ground to distrust his integrity, I will enter upon an enquiry as to his character and in the mean time suspend him from taking charge of the L. House—with great respect your obt svt

S D. Ingham

Photocopy of ALS, TU (mAJs). The letters were likely from Joseph M. White (1781–1839), Florida's territorial delegate to Congress. William Levingston, now of St. Augustine, had fought at New Orleans. AJ had recently appointed him keeper of the new lighthouse at the mouth of St. Johns River.

To Samuel Delucenna Ingham

Dr. Sir,

I have read Mr Whites letter & the one he refers to—I know nothing of Mr. Levingston more than he was an excellent soldier & fought as bravely as ever man fought, and was spoken of as an honest man. However there is gentleman just arrived, Col Piatt, at Gadsbeys, who knows him well, & who employed him in the quartermasters Deptt. at Neworleans on whom you can rely; and to whom I refer you for Mr Levingstons character[1]—I would only remark, that Levingston is a witness against Judge Smith, and it may be necessary to impeach his character to save smiths; and spaniards sometimes, can be induced to become instruments in the hands of bad men

Our duty is to have honest men, & if Col Piatt does not give him a good character, suspend his commission; forward to him a copy of those letters, & call upon him for a speedy answer. Mr. L. may be a bad man, but as I never have yet seen a *base* man, *brave*, I dout the charge[.] yrs.

Andrew Jackson

Photocopy of ALS, TU (mAJs). Levingston, with others, had charged Florida Territory district judge Joseph Lee Smith (1776–1846) with judicial oppression (*Jackson Papers*, 7:737; 13-0521). Smith had repelled the charges and censured Levingston's character (*TPUS*, 24:287–91, 326–27). AJ did not remove Smith, but replaced him when his four-year term expired in 1832.

  1. William Piatt (1773–1834) of Cincinnati, an Ohio Jackson presidential elector in 1828, had been a regular Army officer and AJ's quartermaster general at New Orleans. AJ appointed him an Army paymaster in May 1830. Levingston had been a master's mate and fought at New Orleans under Navy lieutenant Charles Crowley, who commanded one of AJ's batteries. Naval commander Daniel T. Patterson's January 27, 1815, report of the battle praised him by name. Ingham wrote Piatt inquiring about Levingston's character on February 15 (Ingham Papers, PU).

To Samuel Delucenna Ingham

Febr'y. 9th 1830

My Dr. Sir

  The enclosed was handed me by Dr. Thomas express from the Govr. & council, and Legislature of Maryland—can such an appeal be resisted—or I ought to have said, can we pass it over without action—It is called for to aid the republican party, our friends & ought I not to yield to it—I wish your opinion—

  I do not mean to send it in before the Senate unmasks its course—yrs

Andrew Jackson

ALS, Americashistory.org (mAJs).

From Ezra Stiles Ely

Philadelphia Feb. 10th 1830.

Dear & Honoured Sir,

  On my return from Washington, I received from Jeremiah Evarts, Esq. a letter of which the foregoing is a copy. I send it to you *solely* to confirm the truth of my assertion, that Mr. John E. Hyde told me a certain report. I do not wish you should rely upon my word, when I can confront Mr. Hyde's denial with such a letter as the one copied above. It is my desire that no other use may be made of the name of Mr. Evarts than to satisfy yourself that Mr. Hyde must have written very erroneously from England. Sorry, indeed, am I to trouble you with one line on this subject; but it is very natural, when I know myself to be a man of truth, that I should wish to be thought so, by one whom I so highly venerate & love as I do the President.

May the Lord bless you, & keep you, dear Sir, and continue to make you a lasting blessing to our country. Yours most respectfully,

E. S. Ely

ALS, DLC (37).

[Enclosure: Jeremiah Evarts to Ely]

Copy.

Boston Jan 26th 1830.

Dear Sir,

Your letter, inquiring whether I heard Mr. John E. Hyde, of New York, tell you of a certain report concerning Mrs. Eaton, was received a short time since. As your character for veracity has been impeached, I feel bound to state what I recollect on the subject; relying on your sense of propriety not to make any unnecessary exposure of what I write.

You inquire, whether I heard Mr. John E. Hyde "inform you that, at Gadsby's hotel on the morning after Mr. Vaughan's party, a fellow said, at the public breakfast table, that Mrs. Eaton brushed by him last night, and pretended not to know him; that she had forgotten the time when he had slept with her?"

In reply, I must say, that I cannot be positive as to the terms used, or the person using them. I was much in the company of a Mr. Hyde, of New York, a man of respectability; but I cannot speak as to his christian name. Both he and I were repeatedly in your company together. Some person, or persons, mentioned in my hearing more than once, that a declaration had been made on the morning after some large party, in substancially the words which you have used; in words at any rate, that implied that the person making the declaration had, at some previous time, had criminal intercourse with Mrs. Eaton.

My impression is that Mr. Hyde is the man, who reported the observation; but in this I would not be positive. Nor can I say, whether you were present, or not, though I think you were, when the observation was reported.

I owe it to Mr. Hyde to say that he was not forward to introduce the subject of Mrs. Eaton's character. I am Dear Sir yours sincerely

signed Jerh Evarts.

Copy, DLC (37). Jeremiah Evarts (1781–1831) of Massachusetts was a moral reformer and editor and a leader of the American Board of Commissioners for Foreign Missions. His celebrated "William Penn" essays in 1829 opposed Indian removal.

Decision concerning Moses M. Gove

Febry 10th. 1830

This is a case for violating the revenue laws by smuggling. The Executive clemency, in such cases, ought not to be extended on light ground. Where insolvant characters are employed in smuggling, imprisonment is the *only* punishment that can reach & deter them from a repetition of the offence— To liberate such persons would be to encourage smuggling unless where a strong case is made, supported by testimony under oath. The prayer of the Petitioner therefore is not granted

Andrew Jackson

ADS, DNA-RG 59 (17-0880). LC at August 13, 1830, DNA-RG 59 (M40-21). In December 1828, Moses M. Gove (1800–1847), a fisherman of Edgecomb, Maine, was apprehended for smuggling salt into the U.S. He was fined $1,000 and costs in federal district court in September 1829 and imprisoned for failure to pay. In January 1830 he petitioned AJ for pardon, pleading poverty and hardship, ill health, and ignorance of the law. Local officials and Maine congressman Joseph F. Wingate endorsed his plea. Appeals for clemency continued after AJ's decision, and AJ pardoned Gove on March 16, 1831.

To Daniel Todd Patterson

Washington Febry 11th. 1830

Sir

The 4th Auditor has made known to me that there are some dificulty in the settlement of the late Purser Timberlakes accounts; Mr. Timberlake having died on board the ship of which you had command, and you having appointed a purser to succeed him, as well as an individual to take an inventory of Purser: T. property on board said ship—The 4th: Auditor is desirous that you should be present whilst these witnesses are examined, that you may afford him all the information in your power to enable him to come to a just, & fair settlement of this account. you will please therefore to attend him this day at noon, and at such other time as he may appoint for the examination of witnesses and Purser. T. accounts[.] respectfully yrs

(signed) Andrew Jackson

Copy, DNA-RG 46 (15-0130). Kendall was investigating John B. Timberlake's apparent default. Patterson (1786–1839), a Navy captain and member of the Board of Navy Commissioners, had commanded the frigate *Constitution* on which Timberlake was purser at the time of his death in 1828. Patterson had then ordered Lieutenant Elie A. F. Vallette to conduct an inventory of Timberlake's property and had appointed Lieutenant Robert B. Randolph to serve as acting purser. On February 12 and 25, Kendall, Patterson, and second comptroller Isaac Hill examined Vallette, Randolph, and others in an effort to determine what became of the $11,750 in cash Timberlake had in possession at his death. Kendall's report, transmitted to the House of Representatives in May, pointed toward Randolph as the culprit in its disappearance (*HRDoc* 116, 21st Cong., 1st sess., Serial 198).

From William Piatt and Elijah Hayward

Washington City, Feb. 12. 1830

Sir,

The undersigned, citizens of the city of Cincinnati, and state of Ohio, have been informed, that Charles Hammond of Cincinnati, has procured, or caused to be procured, certain documents tending to prove that Moses Dawson Esqr. of the same place (whom it is said you have been pleased to nominate to the Senate, for the office of Receiver of Public moneys there) in procuring his certificate of Citizenship, had been guilty of some fraud, misrepresentation, or other dishonourable conduct; and that these documents have been communicated to the senate, without having been first submitted to your examination or that of the Secretary of the Treasury.

Without any personal knowledge of the facts to which these documents are supposed to relate, but as due to justice, we take the liberty of stating, that we have heard Mr. Dawson say, that Mr. Hammond had given him notice he should take depositions in relation to his citizenship, to be used before the Senate when his nomination as Receiver aforesaid should be considered; but that he (Mr. Dawson) had no fears on that subject—that he was willing Mr. Hammond should have the whole matter investigated, as he had done nothing but what was strictly correct in procuring his said certificate, or in the previous proceedings at Philadelphia—that the proceedings at Philadelphia were all conducted by a respectable Attorney at Law, who procured from the court there, and delivered to him, the documents or papers which Mr. Hammond had alleged were spurious.

We would further state, that we have been personally acquainted with Mr. Dawson, for the last ten years, and with his character and standing in Cincinnati, during that period; that he has uniformly sustained the reputation of an honest man, and we have never heard a reproach upon his character for honour, integrity, or probity (not even by his most violent political opponents) except in the matter connected with his citizenship, which Mr. Hammond has seen fit to agitate; and so firm is our opinion of his good moral character, and of his honesty and integrity, that we cannot but believe, that the attempts which have been and now are making, to prejudice his character, in the estimation of the Senate, are founded in some mistake as to facts, or in a wanton misrepresentation or gross perversion of them. We have the honour to be, sir, with the highest respect, Your obedient Servts.

W. Piatt
Elijah Hayward

LS in Hayward's hand, DNA-RG 46 (15-0138). Hayward (1786–1864) was a Cincinnati lawyer and Ohio Jackson leader. In September 1830 AJ appointed him commissioner of the General Land Office. Moses Dawson (1768–1844), a native of Ireland who came to the U.S. in 1817, was editor of the pro-Jackson *Cincinnati Advertiser*, and Charles Hammond (1779–1840) was the anti-Jackson editor of the *Cincinnati Gazette*. AJ had given Dawson a recess appointment as receiver of the Cincinnati land office in May 1829, and nominated him to the Senate on January 20, 1830. On February 3, Ohio senator Benjamin Ruggles introduced a remonstrance from Hammond charging that Dawson had committed fraud in seeking naturalization as a citizen (DNA-RG 46).

Under the laws in effect in 1817, an immigrant had to reside in the country five years and declare his intent to become a citizen in court three years before he could be naturalized. As Dawson explained to AJ through William B. Lewis on December 20, 1829 (DLC-37), he had landed in Philadelphia when court there was out of session. He was taken by a friend to what he thought was the clerk's office, declared his intention, and later obtained a certificate from his friend stating the circumstance. In 1822, he introduced this paper before a Cincinnati court to prove his five years' residency. The court refused it, and Dawson had to file a new declaration and wait another two years (Congress having reduced the time) before being naturalized.

Hammond charged that Dawson had attempted to pass off his friend's certificate (which had been partially burnt, obscuring its character) in Cincinnati as a legal document, a "false and fabricated" record of a declaration in fact never made before a Philadelphia court. To counter Hammond, Hayward penned this letter, which AJ passed on to the Senate. Both Hayward and Lewis told Dawson that AJ was prepared if necessary to nominate his son Washington Dawson in his stead (as Dawson had proposed) but believed Dawson would be confirmed (Feb 10–15, Moses Dawson Papers, OCX). The Senate rejected Dawson on May 10 by 42 to 5.

To Robert Johnstone Chester

Washington Febry 14th. 1831.

My Dr. Sir

I have just recceived your letter of the 26th. ulto. and hasten to reply to it.

Mrs. Hays has a right to dispose of the negroes as she may think proper—These negroes were purchased by me, paid for by me, and convayed by me to Severn Donelson now deceased in trust for Mrs. Hays, and subject to her disposition at her death—If I recollect correctly the Deed of trust recorded in Davidson Court, will shew, that they negroes were at her disposal at her death, and all she has to do is to make her will and by it leave such negroes as she thinks proper to a trustee for the use of Betsey during her life & then to her children—a Deed of trust to some one for Betseys use during life & then to her children would I suppose be legal & binding—Surely your uncle cannot be so foolish as to believe that he can make these negroes subject to his debt, nor do I believe the Negroes can be made subject to any debts during the life time of Mrs Hays—I think such is the Deed on record, which I refer you to—But still the Deed may be drawn to make them disposable by Mrs. Hays by sale or otherwise—but I think otherwise   I think they are secured to Mrs. Hays during life &

then disposable by her will—But sure I am, that no person can take them during her life.

I am happy to hear that the old Lady enjoys such good health; present me kindly to her & Narcissa, & to every branch of your & Doctor Butlers family Mrs. Hutchings & hers, & say to them all that A. J. Hutchings is in good health & learning *well*, & doing *well*[1]

Be pleased to say to Mrs. Hays, that her son Saml J. Hays with his charming little wife, is now with me, both in good health & will be with her in the spring—assure the old lady & every branch of the family, that she is a charming fine little woman, and I am sure she will be pleased with her—Saml. is well married.[2] I will see the postmaster Genl. on the subject of your letter—and should the Chekesaws & choctaws consent to remove X the Mississippi, I will endeavour to give you some profitable employment—so soon as the report on Indian affairs is acted upon I will write you again.[3]

I am labouring under a bad cold, & great pressure of business & must close this letter with my best wishes for your prosperity & happiness & that of Betsy & the sweet little children[.] yr frend

Andrew Jackson

Major Donelson & Emily with Mary Easton—Saml. J. Hays & his lady all join in kind salutation to you all, and particularly to the old lady   A. J.

ALS (misdated by AJ), James S. Corbitt (17-0513). Envelope, William R. Coleman (mAJs). Chester (1793–1892), the postmaster of Jackson, Tenn., was being sued by Robert Allen, his former business partner and widower of his mother's sister. Chester's wife, Elizabeth "Betsy" Hays (1805–1841), was Rachel Jackson's niece. Her mother, Jane Donelson Hays (1766–1834), was Rachel's sister and widow of the late Severn Donelson. The late Severn Donelson (1773–1818) was Jane and Rachel's brother. On May 11, 1807, AJ had deeded fifteen slaves to Severn in trust for Jane. In January 1831 Allen obtained a judgment against Chester for more than $10,000.

1. Narcissa Hays (b. 1795) and Martha Thompson ("Patsy") Hays Butler (1790–1857), wife of William E. Butler, were Betsy's sisters. Mrs. Hutchings was probably Catherine Donelson Hutchings (c1752–1834), another of Rachel Jackson's sisters and grandmother of Andrew J. Hutchings.

2. In November 1829, Betsy's brother Samuel Jackson Hays (1800–1866) had married Frances Pinckney Middleton (1811–1865) of South Carolina.

3. Chester had solicited an appointment as agent to the Chickasaws. AJ instead offered him a Florida Indian agency, which Chester had declined (*Jackson Papers*, 7:584–85, 635–36).

From James Lucas

Baltimore, Feb. 15, 1830.

Sir,

I am constrained at this time to address you on a subject of rather a serious nature respecting the wife and children of Mr. Sewell, who was keeper of the North Point Light in the river Patapsco—and who, about six weeks ago died, and during his sickness, which was some considerable time, she attended to the lights herself, and there was not the least shawdow of complaint; but since that she has been removed and one Riley appointed to attend to the lights, the consequence is that she, at that season of the year is thrown upon the charity of the public with her three children, one at the breast, and one cripple, without any thing for their support—I would not have thus annoyed you, but that I believe you are not aware of the distress it has occasioned, when it is known and generally believed she could have attended to those lights herself, and been enabled by the generosity of the government to have raised her small family in credit—but it is ordered otherwise, that poor old Mr. Sewell, who fought in the revolutionary war, should leave his wife and children at this time in want—I am convinced that you have a simpathy for those who shared in the dangers of the war of independence, and if you can consistently with propriety restore the old lady to the birth her husband once held, it is known, that she can attend to it as well as those that have been recently appointed, you will oblige one who has advocated your pretensions with an zeal to the Presidency and has seen no just reasons, as yet to forsake you although an humble individual[.] Yours

James Lucas printer
No. 19. South Calvert

P.S. I should, if not inconsistent wish an answer to the above

ALS, DLC (37). Lucas (c1795–1873) was a Baltimore printer. The North Point light at the mouth of the Patapsco aided ships approaching Baltimore from Chesapeake Bay. Thomas Sewell had served with Maryland's marine coastal defense in the Revolution. In 1828 he married Charlotte Coleman (c1791–1867). Sewell died on January 14, and the Treasury Department replaced him with David Riley (c1797–1834), who served until his death. Coleman remarried in 1830.

To *Thomas Hart Benton*

February 16th. 1830—

Dr Sir

I have just recd. the enclosed letter & submit it to you, f[or your] perusal   Should it contain your views, and you will so state to me in writing it will give me pleasure to bestow upon the offspring of the Patriot Genl Davidson who fell in our revolutionary struggle, an evidence of my reguard for his memory—If convenient I would ask you to give me Mr. Pettis views on this subject. *[Have]* the goodness to return to me Mr Ewings letter, accompan[ie]d with your views thereon—I am very respectfully yrs

Andrew Jackson

ALS, UPB (mAJs). Thomas Hart Benton (1782–1858) was U.S. senator from Missouri. William Lee Davidson (1746–1781), a Revolutionary officer from North Carolina, was killed at Cowan's Ford. His daughter Margaret (1774–1868) married Finis Ewing (1773–1841), a founding minister of the Cumberland Presbyterian Church. Pettis wrote AJ to recommend Ewing on March 15 (below).

From *John Henry Eaton*

16 Feby.

Sir

Public men must act, not merely not to deserve; but also not even to seem to deser[v]e censure. Accordingly I have sd to Genl S Houston, that we cannot make a *private contract* with him; but must advertise for proposals. He is quite satisfied with the course. I propose therefore if you approve it, to advertise say 30 days for proposals for supplying the Indians who may emigrate during this year, or may, for the next also— I submit it for yr consideration[.] Yrs

J. H Eaton

[Endorsed by AJ:] The President, with respects to the Sec of War, approves the within—February 16—1830—

[Later endorsement by Eaton:] Hou, called on me, he said by direction of the Pres. He wished to make a contract for the emigrating Indians at a price greatly below what the govt was paying on contracts made under the last admn. The President had refered him to me. He stated that the price of the ration was too great & besides that the Indians were defrauded

by the contractors. After conferring with genl Houston, I wrote to the President this letter—J. H Eaton   30 Apl. 1832

ALS, DNA-RG 233 (15-0143). *HRRep* 502, 22d Cong., 1st sess., pp. 66–67 (Serial 228). Samuel Houston (1793–1863) had resigned as governor of Tennessee and settled among the Western Cherokees in 1829. He arrived in Washington in January 1830. On February 18, two days after this letter, Indian superintendent Thomas L. McKenney advertised for proposals to supply rations to emigrating Indians, with a March 20 submission deadline. Bids were submitted, including one from Houston associate John Van Fossen, but no contract was awarded this year. Eaton and Houston were subsequently charged with colluding to steer the business to Houston, with the short thirty-day deadline purportedly intended to shut out competing bids from the West. In 1832 a House committee investigated, and this letter was introduced in evidence. Houston maintained that his aim was to protect the Indians from being cheated and short-rationed by a low bidder. The majority of the committee exculpated Eaton and Houston of attempted fraud, a minority dissenting.

From Josiah Goldsmith

auburn N Y february the 16—1830

Kind Sir

altho a stranger to you personly I shall Now apeal to you as a friend to Humanety and to the cause of the old soldier of seventy six the time that tryed mens Souls the Difecuilty with me is plainly this I want my pension as a soldier of the Revolusionary War as I inlisted and served one full year in a Ridgment Raised By Lord Sterling and William Windes Esqr of New Jersey the first men Raised in that state to Defend the fronteirs I inlisted as a Soldier at the House of said windes as he was as he was Liutenent Colonol of the sd Ridgment and He Being then an old man and wanted asistance in Raising men I at that time was a near Neighbor to him He called on me to Help him in the Buisnes of the Ridgment and was made an orderly sergent and waited on my old Colonol Dureing the year But continued to carry my gun and other acoutrements as a soldier tho seldom peraded in any Compeny as Colonol Windes Kept me other ways imployd Early in seventyfive He got His Comision and We Began to Raise men in the fall and so continud throu the winter and in the spring of 76 the Ridgment mustered in the Cyty of New york with Exspectasion to Be stasioned on Longisland But Lord sterling was made a Brigadier general and Windes Head of the Ridgment and ordered to Caneda and Did imbark and took the Ridgment to alboney By water in may—

Sir

the order to Caneda was so suden and unexpected to the old Colonol as he when he Enterrd the servis Expected to Be stasioned Near New york so as to Be near Home as he Had a Large farm and only Hired Hands to Depend on as he Had no Children He Concluded he Had a right to Lieve me Behind and Help the Recruiting servis that was then a Raising to gard New york and the fronteirs of New Jersey and Likewise to Hold a Corespondene with him untill he should send for me But he thought it was Best for me to Continu and Do Duty on the fronteer as it was Expected that the Enemy would atact New york soon as they Did in July come into york Bay a Large British fleet and Landed an army on straten Island and I continued to Duty on the Lines untill Novembar was at Elisabeth town point when general Washingtons army Retreated from the White plains to Deleware River and the Brigade I Belonged to was ordered Back to morris town and gard the fronteer and Wach the Enemys plundering partis—and I Did Duty on the Lines all Winter and was in several ingagements with the Enemy and served my Country faithfuly as a miletery man untill the End of the war

and Now Sir
Conserning my pension I Have proved my Enlistment and servises one full year By credable witnesses and have done all the Law Requirs of me yet the Excuse at the pension office is old general Bloomfeilds opinion was that my own Diclerasion and also the Evedence was not Correct and so over Ruled the Buisnes that I Never yet Received a pension and Now if old general Jackson will Be so kind as to Consider my situasion and Help me to a pension will Do me at the age of Eighty a great good as I am unable to Earn my Liveing and nothing to suport me But a few old Debts that is Hard to Be Colected—With mutch Respect I subscribe my self your Real friend and well Wisher

Josiah Goldsmith

[Endorsed by AJ:] Refered to the Secretary of War with this remark—If the Testimony brings him within *the pale* of Law, let it be granted—his days must be nearly numbered, & he ought, if really a soldier of the revolution, to be fed until *death*   A. J—

ALS, DNA-RG 15 (M804-1087). A law of 1832 eased the eligibility requirements for a Revolutionary pension retroactive to March 4, 1831. Under it Goldsmith (b. 1750) qualified to receive $60 per year. William Alexander, styled Lord Stirling (1726–1783), and William Winds (1727–1789) were Revolutionary generals from New Jersey. Joseph Bloomfield (1753–1823) was a Revolutionary major and was later congressman, governor of New Jersey, and a general in the War of 1812.

To John Henry Eaton

February 17th. 1830—

My Dear Sir,
I have received your note of the 16th. instant with Genl Gaines argument on the proceedings in the cases of Col Chambers & Woolly

Genl Gaines admits the commanding officer to be the proper judge of the number of officers who can be spared *without manifest injury to the serrvice*, to compose a Court Martial. In these cases the commanding officer exercised this discretion and conformed the details of the Court to the necessities of the service both as to number and grade. The fact that a majority of that number may be junior to the prisoner is not inadmissable according to his own construction of the law. There must be some defect then in the organisation or proceeding of the court to justify his conclusion. Does any appear? After being assembled, in the presence of the prisoner they are sworn and he is asked if any objections are entertained. He replies, none. The trial begins, the charges are read, and the prisoner pleads, not to the jurisdiction of the court, but generally to the charges. His own act of *record* thus admits the legality of the constitution of the court, and its competency to try him. But, notwithstanding, the Genl. argues, that the President ought *now* to enter upon an investigation to ascertain whether a larger number of officers of superior grade could not have been detailed for the trial without *manifest injury* to the service. And how is this investigation to be made? By referring to the monthly returns to falsify the report of the commanding General who ordered the court, and whose duty it is, at all times, to know precisely the situation of his command and what the interests of the service require. It would be strange indeed if more confidence should be placed in the monthly, than in the special report of a commanding officer where the conduct and character of a Brother officer are involved; and still greater where that officer by his own act testifies to the propriety and impartiality of the proceedings upon that report. Had the prisoner pled to the jurisdiction of the court, objecting to the number and grade of the officers composing the court, the President might have then considered this plea, and if sustained, set aside the proceedings, and awarded a new trial. It is otherwise now. Genl Gaines argument would carry us back to former administrations, and justify a reconsideration of decisions that have long since been executed. That in the case of Col King of the 4th Infantry is in point, and one of the severest known in our military history.[1]

I return the argument of Genl Gaines   yrs. Respectfully

Andrew Jackson

LS in AJ Donelson's hand, DNA-RG 107 (M222-27). In 1829 Lieutenant Colonel Abram Rall Woolley (1784–1858) was court-martialed and dismissed from the service for abusive conduct (*Jackson Papers*, 7:188–89). In 1826 Colonel Talbot Chambers was court-martialed and cashiered for drunkenness. Brevet Major General Edmund Pendleton Gaines (1777–1849), commanding the Army's Western Department, had argued to Eaton that both trials were invalid because the Articles of War adopted by Congress in April 1806 mandated a court of thirteen officers "where that number can be convened without manifest injury to the service" and stipulated that members not be junior in rank to the accused "if it can be avoided." Chambers was tried by five officers, all of them his juniors; Woolley by seven, four of them junior. Woolley subsequently appealed to Congress; a House committee looked into the matter but declined to intervene (*HRRep* 269, 22d Cong., 1st sess., Serial 225).

1. Colonel William King (d. 1826) served under AJ in the 1818 Seminole campaign. In 1819 he was court-martialed and suspended for five years for ordering to shoot deserters. King protested the proceedings as a malicious persecution. AJ admired King and believed him "much injured." In 1821 he appealed in King's behalf to President Monroe (*Jackson Papers*, 5:110–11).

To Samuel Delucenna Ingham

(private)

February 17th. 1830

The President with his respects, assures the Secretary of the Treasury that he has read the letter of Mr Johnston, with the endorsment thereon, with great satisfaction—It will put to rest all the false rumors of frauds practiced upon the Treasury, *in favour of the Foreigner* by our appraisers, to the injury of *our manufactoners*. He has little doubt but those *idle rumors*, has given rise to *some features* in Mr Mallarys Bill

AN, PU-Ingham Papers (15-0164). Vermont congressman Rollin Carolas Mallary (1784–1831) had introduced a bill on January 27 to tighten customs procedures for inspecting and appraising imported woolen goods. Its ostensible aim was to prevent evasion of duties through fraudulently low valuations. Critics considered it a scheme to protect domestic manufacturers by making importation onerous. A milder substitute by James Buchanan, applying not only to woolens, was signed into law on May 28.

To Samuel Delucenna Ingham

(private)

Febry 18th. 1830

My Dr. Sir,
    I have recd. & read with great care your two notes of the 17th. inst. with the enclosure—I had a conversation with Genl Smith on the subject of wines generally, & the propriety of equalising the duties thereon. Whether he has in his bill, provided for the wines of Portugal & Sicily, as I have not the bill before me, I cannot say, but it will be well for you to see & converse with him on this subject—that the views taken by Mr Jos. Ingham are correct there can be no doubt.[1] We are promised by the Portugal minister, an offer of a commercial Treaty on the broad basis of fair reciprocity, for which purpose he is waiting for instructions.[2] The increase of inspectors at Neworleans was much wanted, but I agree fully with you, that great care must be taken least we extend the increase too far—we must meet the real number whatever it may be, to secure the revenue & prevent smuggling, but we must endeavour to stop at that point

every where—I think an increase of appraisers at Newyork, the great emporium of our commerce, is much wanted, but even there, we must not let the great press for office carry us too far, but just so far, as will secure the revenue.[3]

I was informed last evening by an Eastern member that Collector Williams has been rejected by the Senate, if so, would it not be well to send them Mr. Freeman   I wish you to think of this & let me hear from you to day.[4]

I have read the report of Mr Goodsall with pleasure & would call your attention to that part of it that shews that at one point, one family occupy all the officers, this badge of aristocracy ought to be broke in upon, by removing at least some of them—I will return it to you to day—

I return Mr Ingham letter, & being surrounded close this hasty scrall[.] yrs

Andrew Jackson

ALS, MWiW-C (15-0194).
    1. Maryland senator Samuel Smith (1752–1839) had reported a bill on January 7 to continue an 1827 law permitting importation of brandy in casks and allowing a drawback of duties on re-exportation. AJ signed it into law on February 27. British merchant Joseph Ingham (d. 1833) was U.S. agent for a family trading firm that exported wine from Sicily.
    2. In presenting his credentials on October 2, 1829, Portuguese chargé d'affaires Jacob Frederico Torlade Pereira d'Azambuja had voiced his government's desire for a most-favored-nation trade relationship with the U.S. (DNA-RG 59, M57-2). A commercial treaty was concluded with Portugal in 1840.
    3. New Orleans customs collector Martin Gordon wanted more officers. Ingham had authorized hiring temporary inspectors for the six-month busy season, but Gordon rejoined that he could not get good men to work half the year. On February 12 Ingham authorized two new permanent inspectors and also four temporaries. Gordon refused the temporaries, and on March 19 Ingham, citing AJ's authority, ordered him to hire two (DNA-RG 56, M178-16). The May 28 customs law authorized an additional appraiser and four assistants at New York.
    4. In April 1829, AJ gave Lemuel Williams (1782–1869) a recess appointment as collector at New Bedford, Mass., removing Russel Freeman (c1780–1842). The Senate rejected Williams by 34 to 11 on February 17. On February 18, the day of this letter, the Senate voted to reconsider. Williams was confirmed, 26 to 20, on March 8.

To John Macpherson Berrien

February 19th. 1830—

The President with his respects to the attorney Genl U. States, requests to see him this evening for a few minutes at his office—The object of the President is to have his opinion whether the President can inforce the act of Congress of the 3rd. of March 1807—against the claimants under Zacariah Cox one of the yazoo purchasers who are now disturbing the settlers in alabama—If the P. can *legally, he is determined to enforce it,* as he *does know* that Zacariah Cox before he sold to John Smith T. had convayed all his right to M. Maher & Company—The P. will submit various points in this ~~question~~ case in due time for your opinion, but on the one proposed, he wishes to decide promptly   Therefore wishes the interview—

AN, DNA-RG 60 (15-0197). The law of March 3, 1807, authorized the president to evict trespassers on public lands. In 1795, as part of the infamous Yazoo fraud, the Georgia legislature sold much of north Alabama to Zachariah Cox, Matthias Maher, and others acting as the Tennessee Company. Entrepreneur and speculator John Smith T (1770–1836) had purchased from Cox and was now leasing out land under his title while seeking its confirmation in the courts. On February 23, Smith T's attorney William Kelly solicited Congress to buy him out for $100,000. AJ issued a proclamation ordering illegal settlers off north Alabama lands on March 6. Evidence disproving Smith T's title surfaced in April (AJ to Graham, Apr 16, below).

With this note, or perhaps at their interview, AJ gave Berrien a signed, dated formal memorandum requesting Berrien's opinion and stating AJ's personal knowledge of the case (DS, DNA-RG 60; DNA-0198). AJ related that Cox had sold out his interest to his Tennessee Company partners and then fraudulently resold the same land to buyers in Tennessee. In 1804 Smith T had paid a $5,000 debt to AJ with land scrip purchased from Cox. When AJ tried to sell the scrip in Philadelphia, the title it conveyed was shown to be worthless.

To William Ramsey and Thomas Hartley Crawford

WASHINGTON, February 19th, 1830.

GENTLEMEN:

I had the satisfaction yesterday to receive your polite note, offering for my acceptance two specimens of carpeting, manufactured by your constituent, Mr. Samuel Given, of Cumberland. Nothing can be more pleasing to me than the evidence which these products afford, that an American loom in Pennsylvania is already able to perform its part in the system of domestic economy, upon which this, and all other nations, must ultimately place the power to preserve their independence. I pray you to tender to Mr. Given my sincere thanks for thinking me worthy of such a present; and receive yourselves, Gentlemen, the assurances of my high regard,

Your obedient serv't.

ANDREW JACKSON.

Printed, Washington *Daily National Intelligencer*, February 24, 1830 (mAJs). *Niles*, March 27 (15-0205). Samuel Given (1804–1892) operated a carpet mill at Mount Holly Springs in Cumberland Co., Pa. On February 16, Pennsylvania congressmen Ramsey (1779–1831) and Crawford (1786–1863) had presented samples of his product to AJ and praised the tariff which enabled Given to compete with foreign imports. They addressed AJ again on April 5 (below).

To Littleton Waller Tazewell

Febr'y 19th. 1830—

My Dr. Sir.

Your letter of the 17th. instant with its enclosures was recd. on yesterday —finding from your letter that you were of opinion I had acted on the case of Mr Miles King without a full knowledge of *all the facts* of this case—that Justice might be done I forthwith refered it to the Sec. of the Navy, requiring him to cause to be made to me *a full & detailed report of all the facts*—which as soon as recd. you shall be furnished with.[1] In the mean time permit to say, my opinion is, that it is you, not I, from whom some of the facts have been witheld. I had before me the lucid, candid & impartial report of Mr Kendal with the letters & vouchers refered to, all which confirmed the justice of the conclusions formed, & to which you will be refered in the report preparing. I am very respectfully yr friend

Andrew Jackson

ALS, NjMoHP (15-0206). Tazewell had written AJ on February 17 asking him to re-examine Miles King's accounts. Tazewell said he was "most thoroughly" convinced that the accounting officers had erred, and that AJ's January 14 decision upholding theirs (above) was unsustainable because he had not seen "*all* the facts." Tazewell enclosed two opinions he had written for King. In the case of the alleged overpayment to baker Tildsley Graham at the end of 1828, Tazewell held that King was faultless, having simply followed orders from proper naval authority. Further, the payment was prudent. If not paid the higher 1829 price, Graham could simply have withheld delivery until the new year. He might also have pursued a fair claim for the entire value of the bread burnt on November 19, whose delivery had been held up by the government's unreadiness to receive it. Tazewell's other opinion concerned $500 for coping stone ordered for construction at the navy yard, for which the Treasury had also refused payment to King (*HRDoc* 115, 21st Cong., 1st sess., pp. 7–8, 10–13, appendix 1–7, Serial 198).

1. AJ sent Tazewell's letter and opinions to Branch this same day, asking for another full report and remarking Tazewell's charge that AJ had acted "without having before me *a full view of all the facts of the case*." Branch referred the request and papers to Kendall on February 26 (*HRDoc* 115, 21st Cong., 1st sess., p. 9, Serial 198).

From Littleton Waller Tazewell

Washington
Feby. 20. 1830.

Sir,

I have just received the enclosed from the Secretary of the Navy. The tone of this communication puts it out of my power to answer any such interrogatories when so propounded. But I owe it to myself to say *to you* sir, that in making the assertion which I now repeat, that "*all* the facts which the documents abundantly prove to constitute the case (referred to) are not disclosed in that upon which your judgment was given," I neither intended to prefer any such charge, as that the facts omitted to be stated had been "suppressed" "witheld" "suppressed" by the accounting officers of the Treasury, or by any of them; nor do I admit this to be a correct inference from my language quoted. The facts believed to be *omitted* in the case formerly before you, may readily be ascertained, by a comparison of your decision (in which the case is stated) with the facts represented in the cases upon which my opinion is given. These *omitted* facts were not communicated to me by any "person." They were infer'd by my own reason, from the evidence before me, by which evidence I still repeat, they are abundantly proved. The papers constituting this evidence, I received from Mr. King, as the papers which he had submitted to the accounting officers, or to some one of them, in support of the claims to which they refer'd. Of the correctness of his information I could not doubt, because many of these papers had the memoranda of some of these officers indorsed upon them; and some were official papers themselves, and refer'd to others by descriptions so precise and accurate, as not to permit of substitution or mistake. It would have been difficult moreover for me to have conceived a reason, why papers certainly intended to support a claim should not have been exhibited to those of whom the possessor of such papers was solicitous to obtain the allowance of the very demand which the exhibition of these papers was designed to establish. At what time these papers were laid before the accounting officers of the Treasury by Mr. King, I neither asked or was told as I believe: but if I was informed this fact is not now remember'd. Nor, in deciding the question *what are the facts which they establish*, does it occur to me, that the time when is of much more importance than the place where the papers were produced.

May I beg the favor of you sir, to return me the inclosed letter when you have perused it, as also to cause me to be furnished with copies of mine to you of the 17th: Instant, and of the two documents which it inclosed. I did not think it necessary to take any copies of these papers when I forwarded them to you, but the Secretary's letter, confirmed by a conversation I had with him this morning before the receipt of this letter, seems to be intended to warn me to prepare myself for defense against attack from a quarter where I little expected it. With great respect I am Sir, your mo: obdt. sevt.

L. W. Tazewell.

Feby. 21. 1830.
P.S. I have just received yours of yesterdays date, covering another written on the preceding day.[1] In reply permit me to say, that my sole object in addressing you as I did was to bring under your examination the case of one of my constituents who thought himself aggrieved. Concurring myself

in this opinion, and feeling the most perfect assurance that it would give you real pleasure to prevent injustice whenever you could be satisfied that error had been committed, I ventured to obtrude upon your attention some remarks. But if sir you entertain the opinion that the decisions to which I have refer'd are right, and that Mr. King has no just cause of complaint at being refused the two credits which he claims, altho my respect for you may cause me to regret any diversity of sentiment that may exist between us upon any subject yet I certainly do not wish to trouble you with the re examination of your decisions nor do I mean to continue my investigation into this matter further than I have done. I have no desire therefore, to be furnished with the reply of any one to the arguments I took the liberty of submitting to you. The case will of course be brought before the judicial tribunals of the Country. A Jury must hereafter decide what are the facts which constitute its merits; and a Court adjudge, what is the law arising upon those facts. It was principally with a view of preventing such a resort that I adopted the course I have done. I have failed of success, but I shall never regret that I have made the effort. Time will prove whether I was right or wrong in doing so. With great respect I am your mo: obdt. sevt.

L. W. Tazewell.

[Endorsed by Tazewell:] Copy of my letter to the President written Feby. 20. 1830 and then shewn to Judge White—P.S. written Feby. 21. but never shewn to any person

ALS copy, Vi (15-0213). AJ had referred Tazewell's February 17 letter asking a re-examination of Miles King's accounts to Branch. Branch wrote Tazewell on February 20. He construed Tazewell's statement about AJ not having all the facts as a charge against the accounting officers of "withholding" information, and demanded that Tazewell furnish a statement of the names of its suppliers, and the time of its submission to the Treasury. Tazewell did not reply (*HRDoc* 115, 21st Cong., 1st sess., p. 9, Serial 198).
    1. AJ had neglected to send Tazewell his letter of February 19 above, and enclosed it with an explanatory note on the evening of the 20th.

From David Henshaw et al.

Boston February 22d. 1830.

Sir
    The undersigned appointed by a convention of the Republican members of the Legislature of this State, assembled on the 11th inst to act as a Central Committee, in accordance with the wishes of the members of that Convention beg leave respectfully to solicit your consideration for a few moments to the subject of U.S. Marshal for the district of Massachusetts. We should not presume in common cases, after the executive had come to a decision, to press the subject again upon his attention. But believing that

the importance of the office at this time has not been duly estimated and that the conduct and political principles of the officer have been misrepresented we feel it a duty we owe alike to the government and its friends, to present this case for their consideration in its true light.

The office of U.S. Marshal, always a dignified and influential one is at this time unusually important. A Census of all the citizens is to be taken forthwith under the direction of the Marshal who will have to appoint numerous agents to assist him, and these agents will in the discharge of their duty be carried to the door of every housekeeper in the State. The political character of these agents cannot fail to affect the sentiments and feelings of those among whom they travel, in performing these duties. Though no effort be made by any of these agents to affect one way or the other the opinions of the citizens, yet their political character, whether friends or opponents to the administration will silently influence to a very great extent one way, or the other, the minds of the citizens. The moral influence thus produced is we conceive a legitimate power for the goverment to wield, and it would certainly seem more wise to have it in the hands of friends to be used for us, rather than in the hands of foes to be used against us.[1]

Then again the information local, statistical and other, which these numerous agents will gather in performing their duties is too valuable & important to be given into the hands of the opponents, or lost to the friends of the Administration. Our opponents in this State would not fail to make much use of this opportunity and this information. Such we apprehend was the view taken of this subject by the last Congress and consequently they referred the law for taking the Census to the present Congress, one year beyond the usual time, for the purpose of having suitable men appointed to perform this important service.

At this particular time the office of Marshal is one of the more importance than any other in the gift of the general goverment in this State, and it would be peculiarly unfortunate to have its power & influence in this State against the Administration.

Col. Harris, the present incumbent is no friend, and we presume he does not pretend to be, of this Administration, and consequently it is but reasonable to suppose that he will very naturally make the selection of agents to take the Census from his political friends, who are our political opponents. In fact many of these agencies are already promised to our opponents. We have no desire to disparage Col. Harris and have against him personally no feelings of unkindness, nor should we solicit his removal at this time but for the weighty considerations we have here suggested.

We have understood that Col. Harris' friends have represented that he has taken no active part in politics, and that he was not opposed to the election of the present executive. Col. Harris we presume would not himself make such a declaration. We by no means intend to censure any gentleman for an honest expression of his opinion of men or measures, however that opinion may differ from our own, but the facts in this case, whatever they may be, ought to be fairly understood, and as a convincing proof that the representations of Col. Harris' friends as above stated, are incorrect, we annex to this the proof-sheet of a circular address and letter in favour of Mr Adams signed by Mr Harris' own hand. What we consider particularly objectionable in this is, that in the post-script to the letter what you will perceive is erased in its place & directed to be inserted at the bottom of the circular, a request is made to those who correspond with them to direct all their communications to Aaron Hill the then Postmaster in this City, thus defrauding the revenue in furtherance of their political schemes.[2] This committee of correspondence, with a few others constituted what was called the "Adams Club," and that Club of which Mr Harris was a member was the soul of the Adams party. It planned all the measures for his support, and the attacks upon his opponents, and by means of the Post Office, (the Postmaster Dr. Hill, whose name signed by himself you will perceive next above that of Col. Harris, being one of the Committee) they circulated their gross scandals and libels, and communicated their intelligence at the charge of the public treasury. Col. Harris not only belonged to this Club, but up to nearly the close of the late election he was one of its most prominent and active members. These are facts notorious here.[3]

It will not be denied that Mr Harris has been a bitter, and in some cases an abusive partizan, and knowing as we do his political sentiments, and feeling as we do the immense importance of having friends rather than opponents appointed to take the Census, we venture again to express an earnest hope that Mr Harris may be speedily removed and a friend to the Administration appointed Marshal in his stead. With great respect we have the honor to be your Obedient Servants

David Henshaw
Charles Hood
John K Simpson
Sam. S. Lewis
Hall Jackson How
Nathl. Greene
John Wade
Ebenr Seaver
Wm Parmenter

LS, DNA-RG 59 (M639-21). On February 11, Jackson members of the Massachusetts legislature convening in caucus had nominated Marcus Morton for governor and named these nine men as a Central Committee to coordinate the campaign. AJ had given David Henshaw (1791–1852) a recess appointment as Boston customs collector in April 1829; his nomination, now before the Senate, was confirmed April 12. Nathaniel Greene (1797–1877) had edited the *Boston Statesman* before being appointed postmaster in 1829. Charles Hood (1787–1864), John K. Simpson (1787–1837), Samuel Shaw Lewis (1799–1869),

Hall Jackson How (1791–1849), John Wade, Ebenezer Seaver (1763–1844), and William Parmenter (1789–1866) were variously engaged in commerce and banking.

Samuel Devens Harris (1780–1855), an Army captain and brevet lieutenant colonel in the War of 1812, was appointed U.S. marshal for Massachusetts by President Monroe in 1821 and reappointed by Monroe and Adams in 1825 and 1829. The candidate to supplant him was Jonas L. Sibley, recommended to AJ in mid-February by Morton and others. On March 9 AJ Donelson intervened in Harris's defense (below).

1. Congress enacted regulations for taking the 1830 census on March 23. Marshals were authorized to hire assistants and were required to enumerate the population by personal inquiry at every household.

2. The senders enclosed a document from the 1824 campaign, a proof sheet of a circular sent by the Committee of Correspondence appointed by a meeting of Boston "Democratic Republicans" at Faneuil Hall on February 14, 1824. Harris chaired the meeting and both he and Aaron Hill (c1758–1830), then Boston postmaster, signed the circular. The circular touted Adams but mentioned no other name. It urged selecting a candidate by popular voice and condemned the congressional caucus nomination (of William H. Crawford) as unrepublican. The postscript invited responses to "Hon. Aaron Hill, Post-Master, Boston." Since postage on mail was paid by the recipient rather than the sender, making the postmaster the addressee might enable avoiding payment.

3. Boston's Adams "Club" formed in late 1823 and met weekly. It organized the Faneuil Hall meeting. Members included then customs collector Henry A. S. Dearborn and newspaper editors P. P. F. Degrand and Edmund Wright Jr.

From Littleton Waller Tazewell

[In a February 22 letter to Tazewell, of which only a brief abstract is available, Jackson upheld his decision disallowing Norfolk navy agent Miles King's payments to baker Tildsley Graham.]

Washington. February 24. 1830.

~~My dear~~ Sir;

I am under the painful necessity of again addressing you, in reply to your letter of yesterdays date, which I have this moment received. The dut~~y~~ies I owe to myself, to you, to Mr. King, and to ~~the publick~~ others, all combine, to cause me to do so; and ~~must be~~ constitute the only apology I have to offer for such repeated intrusions upon your precious time, in calling your attention to a small matter, from which I feel as much solicitude to withdraw my consideration, as I do to relieve you from the trouble its examination ~~will~~ may impose.

So far as I have had any ~~personal~~ concern with this subject, by reason of the agency I have taken in bringing it before you, I never entertained for a moment, the most remote suspicion, that *you* or any other person ever had, would, or could, charge, believe, or imagine, that "improper motives" had influenced my conduct. Nor could I conceive, that any occasion would ever arise, when I ought to prepare to defend myself, against any attack ~~from~~ to be made ~~by~~ upon me by *you*, or with *your* knowledge. A mere difference of opinion, as to the questions, what facts *ought to be* infer'd from ~~the same~~ certain evidence; what legal propositions the infer'd facts *fairly* present for decision; and ~~what is the law~~ how such legal propositions *ought to be* decided is a state of things of such ~~frequent~~ common occurrence, that ~~much less~~ but little intelligence ~~than even the worst of your enemies and calumniators are compelled to concede that you possess, cannot fail~~ is requisite to discern, that it did not involve either the purity of the heart or the soundness of the understanding of either of the differing parties. It is a difference of opinion ~~merely~~ only, which while it continues, equal independence ~~will~~ ~~must~~ will maintain; and which ~~is only to be removed by the~~ must continue until conviction ~~of error by their own reflexions~~ shall satisfy one of the parties of his error or mistake. Thus much is due both to you and to myself.

As to Mr. King, altho' I had formed the determination never again to ~~say~~ trouble you or any other of the Executive officers of this govt. with any suggestion of mine concerning his case, yet a part of your last letter seems to make it necessary that I should do so. I will therefore ~~merely~~ make a single observation. The perusal of the opinion given by you upon this case on the 14th. of January last, inclined me then to believe, and your last letter confirms this impression, that you suppose, Mr. King to claim credit, for a sum of money paid by him to Graham in satisfaction of a parcel of bread *never deliver'd to the U.S, but burnt while in Grahams possession and at his own risk.* ~~But~~ This is not the case as it exists most certainly. The money for which the credit is claimed, is money paid to Graham, in satisfaction of a parcel of bread made & *delivered by him to the U.S.*, regularly inspected & *received by their officers*, and actually *consumed* (not by fire) but *by those in the service of the U.S.* for whose use it was originally purchased. The only question is, not whether this bread so regularly delivered & received is to be paid for by the U.S. but at what price this payment is to be made. The accounting officers of the Treasury being perfectly satisfied of the delivery and receipt of the bread have allowed Mr. King credit for part of the money which he paid for it but they refuse to allow him credit for the residue of this sum upon the ground that the price at which it is charged in Grahams account exceeds the contract price. *He* contends, that he was order'd to pay this price, by the Commsrs of the Navy, and by the Commandant of the Yard at Gosport, the orders of ~~each~~ all of whom he was bound to obey; and therefore whether the charge be right or wrong he is entitled to the credit claimed for the payment made in pursuance of such orders.[1]

It seems to have been supposed by one ~~at least~~ of the accounting officers of the Treasury, that this *extra-price* directed by the Commsrs to be paid to Graham for the bread *actually delivered* by him, was a mere *device* to give him compensation for the bread *never delivered* by him but burnt; and as the Commsrs had no authority to ~~pay~~ direct the payment for the burnt bread directly, therefore they had no authority to direct such a payment to be made indirectly. ~~This is a serious charge~~ The defense of the ~~gallant officers of the Navy board~~ Navy Commissioners against ~~the~~

~~imputation of a fraud like this~~ this argument is not committed to me, I have not therefore touched it, further than to say, that I thought they had authority with the assent of the other contracting party, to alter all their contracts in any way ~~they thought~~ beneficial to the U.S. & That the alteration upon the present occasion was ~~probably~~ beneficial to the U.S. But even if this is not so, yet that all inferiors were bound by their orders, whether beneficial or not; and that these orders must sanction the acts done under them altho' the Navy Commsrs might be made to answer even with their lives and commissions for giving them.

~~As to the coping stone, which it is conceded admitted which is now no longer a misterious transaction, but perfectly understood, the only question seems to be to whom the~~ As to the coping stone, the price for which you say "is already ordered to be paid to the person entitled to receive it," I will only observe, that this order can never be productive of any effect. Mr. King can never receive any benefit from it because ~~it seems to be already deci~~ the order itself implies that he is not the proper person; and it ~~would be~~ seems difficult ~~indeed to decide~~ to conceive what other person could be so recognized while he retains the vouchers he has exhibited.[2]

In conclusion, I beg leave to repeat the request made in mine of the 20th. Instant, for copies of the two documents inclosed in mine of the 17th. Instant and which are not forwarded with yours of ~~the 22d. Instant~~ yesterday. These ~~opinions~~ papers are now wanted for Mr. King, for whose use they were originally intended, and as I have before stated to you no copies of them were retained by me. With great respect I am Sir, your mo: obdt. servt.

L. W. Tazewell

ALS draft, Vi (15-0245).

1. Composed of three senior officers, the Board of Navy Commissioners had charge of naval procurement. Captain James Barron (1768–1851) was commandant of the Gosport navy yard.

2. Tazewell's opinion accompanying his February 17 letter to AJ stated the facts as follows: King had ordered coping stone for navy yard construction from Ichabod L. Scranson of Connecticut for a price of $500 including delivery. King paid $61 freight when the stone arrived. Scranson himself soon followed and asked for payment of the balance. Lacking ready funds, King receipted Scranson's invoice, on which the Norfolk branch of the Bank of the United States advanced him the remaining $439 and separately charged it to King. Since Scranson's invoice showed the Bank, not King, as having paid him, the Treasury had refused King's repayment voucher. Tazewell remarked that Navy secretary Branch "calls this 'a mysterious transaction, which requires explanation;' but the greatest mystery about it seems to me to consist in discovering what there is in it that explanation can make it more clear than it now appears" (*HRDoc* 115, 21st Cong., 1st sess., pp. 10–13, Serial 198).

To *Littleton Waller Tazewell*

February 24th. 1830—

Dr. Sir,

Your note without date has just been received. I regret, I had not understood that you wished a copy of your opinions given Mr. King, as well as your letter, or they should have been transmitted, the originals are now returned to you, enclosed.

I find from your note before me, that a word of explanation by me is necessary. You mistake me when you suppose I am under the impression that the burnt bread was directly charged & paid for—but you have my meaning correctly when you understand that the sum of one dollar ninety seven & a half cents were added on every 100 lbs. of bread delivered over the stipulated contract price of 1828 for the supply of that year for the port of Gosport to cover Mr Grahams loss sustained by the bread being burnt; and Mr King, as agent, having made this contract, had thereby a full knowledge that the instructions to add this sum to the contract price were illegal, and if that had been positive, and the certificates & receipts in due form, with this knowledge before him, the duty he owed to his office, and the Government, ought to have induced him not to have paid for it; having *thus* paid it, with this knowledge it was in his own wrong, and the accounting officer, with all these facts before him, was bound, as I believe to disallow all the addition above the contract price; he did so; I therefore approved his decision, refering Mr. King to congress as the only power competant to give him relief, as there existed no legislative powers in the board of Navy commissioners.

This explanation I ~~deem~~ consider due to myself. I am my Dr. sir with great respect yours

Andrew Jackson

P.S. Surely, it cannot be thought by Mr King wrong, that he should produce from the mechanic a full receipt for the stone delivered without any condition endorsed on the back of the receipt—This done the credit will be admitted to him for the whole amount. A. J.

ALS, NjMoHP (15-0242). King was not credited for either the bread or coping stone payments. On May 15 the House of Representatives called for an explanation of his accounts. Kendall's report of May 26, transmitted by Branch to the House on May 27, included information newly obtained from navy yard commandant James Barron that the stone in fact had been refused as unfit for use and returned to King's custody. Kendall accused King of concealing this and using the Norfolk bank as an intermediary to obtain credit for a payment that he knew was illegitimate. Branch and Kendall charged King with years of careless or fraudulent accounting. Kendall calculated that he owed $3,835.20 to the U.S. and also $40,144.17 to the Bank of the United States for unauthorized advances to him on the government's behalf, besides the one to Scranson (*HRDoc* 115, 21st Cong., 1st sess.,

Serial 198). In February 1831 the government sued King for the $3,835.20. After prolonged adjudication, a judgment was rendered in King's favor in 1844.

From Simon Cameron

Harrisburg, Penna.
Feb. 24, 1830

Dr Sir

Mr Stambaugh, I am informed, is an applicant for the office of Marshal of this District; and understanding that some evidence of his claims, character and qualifications is necessary to warrant his appointment, I take the liberty of addressing you. I do so because, I have known Mr S. long and well. He was the editor of the "Penna. Reporter," the leading *Jackson paper* of this state in the publication of which I was concerned as joint owner. In the support of the party we were compelled to spend our money freely, for no one at the seat of government contributed a cent to our aid; and while I was engaged in other business, the health of Mr Stambaugh by a devotion to his editorial duties, was much injured. His character for morality and temperance I presume is not doubted, and his ~~qualific~~ capacity is equal to that, or any other situation which the government has to bestow. I speak thus freely, (and I trust, my dear sir, you will pardon my boldness) for I know Mr S. is in much need, being out of business, and for myself I have nothing to ask. Most respectfully Your friend,

Simon Cameron

ALS, DNA-RG 59 (M639-23). Cameron (1799–1889) was later a U.S. senator from Pennsylvania and Lincoln's first secretary of war. He and Samuel C. Stambaugh (1799–1864) began the Harrisburg *Pennsylvania Reporter and Democratic Herald* in 1827. AJ did not appoint Stambaugh marshal, but in June gave him an interim appointment as Indian agent at Green Bay. The Senate rejected his nomination in March 1831.

To Samuel Delucenna Ingham

Febr'y 25th. 1830—

The President with his respects to Mr Ingham brings to his recollection his note the other day on the subject of some certificates amonghst Mr Raguets papers, which you had furnished me with in the last summer, which on making search in my office, I could not find & suppose I had returned to you—they are the certificates of collectors of Baltimore Philadelphia & Newyork, & the date of the arival of all vessels &c &c—will Mr Ingham attend to this subject & have Mr R. furnished with them

[Endorsed by Ingham:] No papers in relation to Mr Raguet can be found in the Try Dept, is it not possible that in Mr Donelson's distribution he may have sent them to the Dept of State   will Mr V. Buren please to cause a search to be made   SDI

[Addressed by Ingham:] Secy of State

AN, DNA-RG 59 (M179-68). Condy Raguet (1784–1842) was appointed consul at Rio de Janeiro in 1822 and chargé d'affaires to Brazil in 1825. His harsh, threatening language in protesting Brazil's seizure of American ships and sailors in its war with Buenos Aires angered the Brazilian government and dismayed his own. In 1827 he abruptly demanded his passports and returned home. The Adams press severely censured his indiscretion.

In 1829 Raguet established the free-trade journal *Banner of the Constitution* in Washington. The settlement of American differences with Brazil in January 1830 prompted Raguet to commence, in the *Banner* of February 13, a self-defense which (he said) he had before withheld to avoid damaging current negotiations. Raguet accused the Adams administration of undermining his effectiveness in Brazil by first withholding his diplomatic credentials and then failing to furnish timely instructions. In his final installment in the *Banner* of February 27, two days after this note, Raguet printed certificates obtained in 1829 from the customs collectors of New York, Philadelphia, and Baltimore, stating the arrival dates of vessels carrying Raguet's 1825 and 1826 dispatches from Brazil. Raguet invoked these to show that Secretary of State Henry Clay must have been fully aware of his methods, including some provocative language that Clay later rebuked, when he wrote Raguet an approving message on October 22, 1826.

To Richard Riker

Washington
February 25th. 1830

Dear Sir,

In the numerous file of my private letters to which, I but seldom, have leisure to refer, I this morning observed your friendly one of the 16th. Decembr last. Unacceptable as the expression may now be I must thank you for the great pleasure its perusal afforded me.

The views of our policy, taken in my message, has been long entertained by me, as dictated by the best interests of the Union. Those to which you allude in relation to the distribution of the surplus revenue, and the evils of the U S Bank, I am aware will encounter the opposition of many able and virtuous men. But this was no reason why I should have suppressed them. Their discussion and thorough analysis cannot be the work of a day, or year. And whatever may be the judgment of the people upon them I owed it not less to myself than to them, to invite the investigation when partizan influences and those motives to political action which produce precipitancy and confusion, seemed likely to lose their usual sway.

It is too early yet for me to judge whether I can permit my name to be voted for again by the people. My own inclinations ever lead to retirement:

and unless they are overruled by the public will and interest, I shall obey them, with great respect yrs

signed A Jackson

[Endorsed by AJ Donelson:] Copy of a letter to Mr. Riker of New York

[Endorsed by AJ:] 25th. Febry 1830 This to be filed A. J.

LS Copy in AJ Donelson's hand, DLC (72). Riker (1772–1842) was a lawyer and the Recorder for New York City. In his first annual message AJ had advocated distributing the federal government's projected surplus revenue to the states (Richardson, 2:451–52).

From George Lowrey et al.

[With Jackson's election as president, the inherent tension between the sovereign claims of Indian nations and of state governments materialized into open conflict. Federal treaties guaranteed the Cherokee Nation's title to their eastern homeland, centered in northwest Georgia. In 1827 the Nation adopted a formal constitution asserting its authority over this domain. But Georgia, citing inherent state sovereignty and a formal pledge by the U.S. in 1802 to extinguish the Indian title as soon as possible, also claimed jurisdiction over Cherokee lands within the state. In 1828 and 1829 the legislature passed measures to extend state law over the Cherokee territory and to void all acts of the Cherokee government effective June 1, 1830. In an address that Jackson later called his own, Secretary of War Eaton told a Cherokee delegation in Washington on April 18, 1829, that the federal government would not sustain their claim to self-government within Georgia, and that their "single alternative" was to submit to Georgia's laws or remove west beyond the Mississippi, where some Cherokees had already gone.

A related controversy concerned the actual extent of the Cherokee domain within Georgia. The Creek Indians ceded their last Georgia holdings, lying south of the Cherokees', in 1827. State authorities claimed that in previously formalizing their boundary with the Cherokees in 1821, the Creeks had illegitimately conveyed to them about a million acres between the Etowah and Chattahoochee rivers, lands that were historically Creek and that therefore with the rest of the ceded Creek country now rightfully belonged to the state. In 1829 hundreds of whites entered the area, and the Cherokees complained to Washington. In October Jackson sent John Coffee to investigate and determine the historic Creek-Cherokee boundary. His report in December upheld the Cherokees' right to the bulk of the disputed region (SDoc 512, 23d Cong., 1st sess., vol. 2, pp. 226–29, Serial 245).

Meanwhile, in November 1829 the Cherokee General Council and Principal Chief John Ross (1790–1866) delegated the six signers of this address to visit Washington, meet with Jackson, and present grievances including intrusions into their territory and Georgia's infringements on their sovereignty (John Ross Papers, 1:177–79).]

Brown's Hotel, Washington City[1]
25. Feby. 1830.

Sir,

It is with the deepest regret, and most painful feelings, that we again address you on a subject that threatens our Nation with fatal consequences; and one which we had the honor of conversing upon at our late interview.

We, yesterday received a communication from the Pl. Chief of our Nation, detailing the melancholy circumstances which led to the murder of a cherokee by the intruders! Various other letters recd. confirm the intelligence communicated by the Pl. Chief, and which alone is sufficient, and convincing evidence of the facts. We are truly sorry that such an occurrence has taken place within the limits of our Nation; and has had a tendency to impress more deeply upon our minds that unless timely aid is afforded by the Govt. of the U.S. for the protection of the lives and property of our Citizens the most unhappy consequences must result.

The subject of intrusion was one of serious deliberation by the late Genl. Council of our Nation. For upwards of twelve months have their numbers been increasing, and with it the troubles and losses of our Citizens proportionably. Their removal has been urged upon the Govt. and implored as an act of justice; and we regret to say that the instructions issued & countermanded, has had the serious effect of adding to our distress. Many have taken advantage of the oppty. and settled upon our lands, under a sanguine hope that they would not be molested; nor has the Agent ever advised their removal as a matter of justice to themselves![2] The Nation, under the treaty of Holston, as will be seen by reference to the 8t. article (viz "If any Citizen of the U. States, or other person, not being an Indian, shall settle on any of the Cherokees' lands, such person shall forfeit the protection of the U. States, and the Cherokees may punish him or not as they please,") have an unquestionable right to adopt such regulations as are deemed proper, for the protection of the Citizens against all who may transgress as above.[3] This is a right however, to which our Nation has ever been averse to the exercise, fearful that some unpleasant circumstance might eventually be the cause, and relying upon the faith of the Genl. Govt. that a faithful execution of the intercourse laws and treaty stipulations would supercede any necessity, on our part, of such an exercise. Such, however, has been the nature of the many injuries sustained in this way, that the late Genl. Council, with great reluctance, passed an act vesting in the Principal Chiefs, 'by, & with the advice of the Executive Counsillors' to use such means as they deemed for the public good, to check the flow of intruders, and to some degree, at least, save the Citizens from total loss of property. Such has been the daring of these violators of the laws, that they have penetrated far into the interior of the Country; and against whom, more particularly, the provisions of this act was intended to operate. It was not intended, or anticipated, that a general removal of intruders, would be effected, by us, or that those who were nearer the borders of the Nation would be molested; nor was it adopted thro. any disrespect to the Genl. Govt., or to the countermand suspending the orders for their removal.

Application, it seems, was lately made to the Principl Chief, by our citizens, to exercise in some degree, the power vested in him; as their grievances were almost insupportable, and harmless individuals far in the interior of the Nation were suffering but too seriously the want of protection, many of whom, had been ejected, by violence, out of their houses. Yielding to this pressing application, a party of cherokees, among them some of our most respectable citizens, under a special injunction to treat the persons & property of the intruders with respect & humanity, and a forbearance of any harsh measures, repaired to a few places taken and occupied by white families, and there, after expostulation, carried their household goods out of the houses, and left them in flames. Not a cents worth of property belonging to the white families, was destroyed; and they forbore to act as the article above cited would have justified. The houses being the property of the Indians, themselves, they had a right to destroy them or 'not as they pleased.' On the returning of these men to their respective places of residence they seperated. In the mean time however, it seems, that a party of intruders upwards of 20 in number had assembled on Tarrapin Creek, fifteen or twenty miles west of the chartered line of Geo., and pursued the Indians, well armed, for some evil purpose, as is evident. At a certain place, they found four, one being drunk had been tied by his companions to quiet him, who were made prisoners & led off to Georgia. One, refusing to be tied, & led into the state, was so much beaten and mangled with their guns that he died in a few hours afterwards. The others sought an oppty. and effected their escape, one however, was severely wounded by several stabs with a large butchers knife. Returning they pursued different courses. Two reached home, but the third not heard of.[4]

The party of cherokees acted under the immediate eye of Majr. Ridge during the short time they were absent. He is a man of high repute in our Nation, and one in whom there is not a hostile feeling toward even those who have so grossly trampled upon our rights. The character of our Principal Chief Mr. Jno. Ross, is too well known by you, to require further proof of the kind and friendly feelings of the National authority towards the whites. That this unhappy occurrence will be reported as a *hostile* disposition, on our part, we doubt not, from facts heretofore demonstrated. But we can assure you Sir, and however much it is to be lamented, that *necessity alone on our part*, has brot. matters to the present crisis. It cannot be supposed, even tho. our people *are* Indians, (we mean no disrespect) that they can with calmness and submission, witness every act of injustice & plunder by the intruders, most of whom have fled from the justice of their own laws. It is a hard case for the father and mother to see the subsistence of their children wrested from their hands by cruelty and avarice; and one inconsiderate act, what might it not eventually prove to the whole nation? The Govt. of the U. States has now in its power the means of dispelling the dark clouds, that seem almost ready to burst upon our Citizens with destruction, by a speedy and efficient course of measures.

We humbly solicit that you will direct an order to be issued, forwith, to the Agent, that the intruders may be removed without any delay. We remember your promise on the subject; but hope that the truly unhappy situation, in which our Nation is thrown, will be a sufficient apology for again troubling you on the same subject.[5]

With sentiments of the highest regard and esteem we have the honor to be, respectfully your Obt. Servants.

> George Lowrey Asst. Pl. Chief Cher. Nation
> Lewis Ross
> William Hicks
> R Taylor
> Joseph Vann
> Wm. S. Coodey
> Cher. Delegation

[Endorsed by AJ:] The Sec of war will answer the within briefly noticing the orders issued on the recpt of the report of our agent—and admonishing them to instruct their people to be quiet & not attempt to *usurp* the powers of the Genl. Govt. that it has & will be exerted, to preserve all their possessory rights—assure them that the late order of their council was badly judged of, & might involve their nation in war—A. J.

LS, DNA-RG 75 (M234-74). Copy, DNA-RG 233 (15-0249). *HRDoc* 89, 21st Cong., 1st sess., pp. 33–35 (Serial 197). The delegates were assistant principal chief George Lowrey (c1770–1852); Lewis Ross (1792–1870), brother of John Ross; William Hicks (b. 1769); Richard Taylor (1788–1853); Joseph Vann (c1800–1844); and William Shorey Coodey (1806–1849). They had previously appealed to Eaton on February 11 (Serial 197, pp. 26–29), and addressed AJ again on March 26 (below).

1. Jesse Brown (c1768–1847) operated the Indian Queen Hotel in Washington.

2. Cherokee agent Hugh Lawson Montgomery (1767–1852) had standing orders from the War Department to remove intruders on Cherokee lands. Secretary Eaton instructed him in August 1829 to forbear for the present from forcibly evicting whites in the disputed region, then ordered their removal in October, then suspended the order on November 26 pending

Coffee's report on the boundary (DNA-RG 107, M6-12). Montgomery had reported to Washington on his efforts to stem intrusions but complained of their futility unless backed by military force (*HRDoc* 89, 21st Cong., 1st sess., Serial 197).

3. This was Article 8 of the Treaty of Holston, concluded in 1791 at present Knoxville, Tenn.

4. At the behest of the Cherokee Council, Principal Chief Ross on January 4 had authorized a foray against intruders along the Alabama–Georgia border. Major Ridge (c1770–1839), who had led Cherokee contingents with AJ in the Creek and Seminole campaigns and held numerous posts in the Cherokee government, commanded. Ridge and about thirty Cherokees expelled some eighteen white families and burned the houses they occupied, which had been recently vacated by Cherokees emigrating west. The four captured Cherokees from the raiding party were Cheewoyee, who died; Daniel Mills and the Waggon, who escaped; and Rattling Gourd, who was taken to Carrollton, Ga., jailed, and later released.

5. The previous day, February 24, Eaton had ordered troops from Fort Mitchell, Ala., into the Cherokee Nation to forestall further violence. On March 14 he instructed agent Montgomery to remove all Cherokees from south of the boundary determined by Coffee and all white trespassers north of it, excepting settlers on parcels that had been relinquished to the U.S. by individual emigrating Cherokees. Eaton dismissed the Cherokees' pretensions to autonomy, branded their action against intruders a "highly exceptionable" usurpation of federal authority, and reiterated that removal westward was the only solution to their distress (Serial 197, pp. 35–36, 39–40).

From Roley McIntosh and Benjamin Hawkins

[As defined by treaty in 1821, the domain of the Creek Nation comprised some ten million acres in Georgia and Alabama. In 1825 chief William McIntosh (1775–1825), who had commanded Creek allies in Jackson's Creek and Seminole campaigns of 1814 and 1818, signed the Treaty of Indian Springs, which exchanged most of the Creek country for new land in the west. The Creek National Council repudiated the treaty as a fraud and put McIntosh to death for violating its ban on unauthorized cessions. The Treaty of Washington, signed in 1826, voided and superseded that of Indian Springs. Under it and a followup agreement in 1827, the Creeks agreed to cede all their Georgia lands in return for various payments. The treaty also provided for the McIntosh faction's removal westward within twenty-four months at federal expense. In 1828 more than a thousand McIntosh Creeks emigrated to the Verdigris River near Fort Gibson in present Oklahoma.

In 1829 the emigrant Creeks complained to Jackson of the government's neglect and mistreatment (Jackson Papers, 7:83–85, 296–98). Later Roley McIntosh (c1790–1863), half-brother of William, and Benjamin Hawkins (d. 1836), a Princeton-educated lawyer and son of a U.S. senator and a Creek woman, came east to present their grievances in person.]

Gadsby's National Hotel
Washington City 25th. February 1830

Our Great Father Andrew Jackson President of the United States,

We have seen you and delivered to you the talk which your Red children the chiefs of the Arkansas Nation of Creek Indians in Council directed us to deliver. It is to our Great Father alone, that we can look for protection, and for the justice which is due to his Red Children beyond the Great River.

Father listen to us, and we will speak the words which our Brothers the chiefs of our Nation commanded us to speak—

Father when we assembled around the Council fire of our Fathers, we were a Great Nation. We had houses, and, land, stock, and Game and we were happy—But when our white Brothers were grown Great and spread like the yellow leaf when scattered by the whirlwilds blast, our Father the President advised us to seek a home beyond the great River. He told us we could not live in the land of our Fathers, and be prosperous, and happy, and that if we would leave the land of our Fathers and seek a new home we should have land enough for our people and their children while the grass grows and the water runs—We listened to the talk of our Father the President, and left the lands where the bones of our Fathers lie, and have moved to a distant and strange land—

Father listen to our talk—The land which our Father the President gave us is too little for our people—Many of our Brothers in the old nation wish to move to our Country—Our Father the President and our white Brothers want all to move: but if our Father the President does not give us more land, we cannot invite them to move. Part of the land on which our Brothers walked who first went into the woods over the great River to find our new home, has been since given by our Father the President to the Cherokee Indians   If our Brothers of the old Nation move to our Country all will perish unless our Father gives us more land—

Father, give us the land lying within the following boundaries, Begin at the head of the Verdigris river, if that river heads in the Rocky Mountains, and if it does not, then begin at the Rocky Mountains, due west of the head of the said River thence to the head of the said River thence down said river as the water runs to the arkansas river thence down the middle of said River to Fort Smith or to the western line of Arkansas Territory, thence South on that line to the Red River, thence up said River to the Rocky Mountains, thence along the range of said mountain to the begining.

Father this would be enough and not more than enough, for all our people and our Brothers of the old Nation who together make about Twenty three thousand; and this contains a less quantity of timbered land than our preportionable part of the country set apart for Indians.[1]

Father by various Treaties made between the United Sates and the Creek Indian Nation, the United States promised to pay the said Nation various annuities, some perpetual, some limited, and by the third and the supplemental article of the Treaty of Washington City made on the twenty fourth day of January Eighteen hundred & twenty Six, the United States promised to pay to the Chiefs of the Creek Nation to be divided among the Chiefs and Warriors of said Nation, the sum of Two hundred and forty seven thousand Six hundred dollars; and by the fourth article of the said Treaty the United States stipulated to pay to the said Nation an additional perpetual annuity of twenty thousand dollars—and by the Treaty made at the Creek Agency on the fifteenth day of November Eighteen hundred and twenty seven, the United States promised to pay to the said Nation the sum of Forty two Thousand four hundred and Ninety one dollars.

Father, we have received no part of the annuities thus promised by the United States since the murder of our Great Chief Genl. William McIntosh, nor of the two Sums one of two hundred & forty seven thousand six hundred dollars, and the other of Forty two thousand four hundred and Ninety one dollars promised by the United States to the Said Nation for the cession of their lands

Father, we are entitled to a full share of all the annuities to which the Creek Nation are entitled or have been entitled from the death of Genl. William McIntosh as well as a full share of the two last mentioned sums of money; in the proportion which our numbers bear to the whole number of the Creek Indians, including our people with the people of the old nation, because by the Fifth article of the Treaty made at Washington City in Eighteen hundred and twenty six it is provided that we "shall be admitted to all our privalages as members of the Creek Nation."[2]

Father, listen to us. By the ninth article of the Treaty of Washington City made in Eighteen hundred and twenty Six, the United States promised to present to us as the friends and followers of Genl William McIntosh the sum of one hundred thousand dollars in consideration of our exertions to procure a cession in 1825 at the Indian Springs &c, and of our past difficulties and our then contemplated removal, if our party should amount to three thousand persons, and in that proportion for a smaller number—We have received but Fifteen thousand of the last mentioned sum

Father, our people amount now to about twenty seven hundred, we are therefore entitled to such a proportion of the unpaid ballance of the one hundred thousand dollars as the present number of our people bear to three thousand.[3] By the seventh article of the Treaty of Washington made in 1826 it was stipulated that the emigrating party should remove in twenty four months from that time, during which time our agent was to have the power of going into the old Nation, among our Brothers there and point out to them the advantages which they would gain by going with us, but bad white men spoke to them with a crooked tongue so that but about one thousand of us emigrated within the two years—at the Expiration of that time our Father the President extended the time without limit, by ordering our agent to go into the old Nation for the purpose of inviting our Brothers to move, and by an act of Congress approved the ninth of may Eighteen hundred & twenty Eight the sum of Fifty thousand dollars was appropriated for aiding the Emigration of the Creek Indians and for the purpose of carrying into effect the provisions of the existing Treaty with the Creek Nation of Indians having relation to the aforesaid object.[4] We refer to this act to shew that Congress sanctioned the exertions Indefinately at the time for the removal of our people, and that therefore we are entitled to all the benefits provided by the Treaty of Washington as well as by an act of Congress passed in May 1826 to aid certain Indians of the Creek Nation in their removal to the west of the Mississippi, as if we had all Emigrated within the two years.

Father by the provisions of the last mentioned act our people were entitled to one Rifle Gun and ammunition, a Butcher Knife one Blanket one Brass Kettle and one Beaver Trap to each warrior, our people have not yet received all these things—The same act provides that the United States will pay to all such emigrants the actual value of all the improvements left by them and which were of a nature to add real value to the Land. Our people stand in need of what is due to them for their improvements left behind them, to enable them to live in the new country where they are now settled—Father the Third section of the same act provided, that there should be delivered to the agent appointed for our people in each and every year a fair and full proportion of all the annuities stipulated and promised to be paid by the United States to the Creek Indians according to the number of emigrants who should remove, and to enable the Government to divide the annuities fairly it was made the duty of the agents of the two parties of Creek Indians to make annual returns of the whole number of emigrants.[5]

Father, it is not the fault of our people that this act has not been complied with and we hope our Father the President will cause justice to be done to us—By the Eight article of the Treaty of Washington made in 1826 the United States promised to furnish our people with an Agent or Sub Agent and Interpreter to reside with them and also with a Blacksmith and a Wheelwright—Father Give to us an Agent to live with us who will speak to us and for us, with a straight Tongue; and to protect us against the evils of having the Brothers, Friends or Favourites of our Agent settled among us as traders contrary to our wishes. Make it necessary for the Agent to obtain the consent of a Council of our Chiefs before he can license any person to trade among us.[6]

Father we have no Wheelwright.

Father when our People Emigrated they left much property behind them, of various Kinds, which has been used by (and some of it now in) the possession of our Brothers of the Old Nation. We beg our Father the President to cause justice to be done between us and our Brothers of the Old Nation, who have used our Property or now have it in possession.[7]

Father, Before our People under their Great Chief Genl. William McIntosh fought with you against our Red Brothers in the late War between the United States and Great Britain they were prosperous and happy, but the recollections of the part which they took in that War rankled in the Breast of some of our Red Brothers, long after the termination of the War—It was therefore only necessary for the White man who was our Enemy to point at our Chief and he fell and we were swept away as by the blast of the Whirlwind of the Wilderness.

If our Father should now give to us an agent who had any connexion either by himself or his friends with the Quarrell between the Red People of the Creek Nation, our people who have fled from persecution will be again over taken and crushed by their Enemies

Father, listen to us. We are anxious to reconcile all our differences with all our Red Brothers of the old Nation and for them to settle with us in our New Country, and if our Father will let us choose an agent to live with us who has never had any thing to do with either party in the old Nation we will do every thing in our power to reconcile the two parties and to induce our Red Brothers of the old Nation to live with us, and we believe it can be done

But if our Father leaves it to a majority of all the Creek people to choose an agent then we will be again involved in all the evils which surrounded us in the old Nation

Father, our Red Brothers of the other party are stronger then we are, and if our Father will not give us our agent, let us live a lone and in peace.[8]

Father, the council of the chiefs of the Arkansas Nation of Creek Indians directed us to ask you

1st. For the country contained in the before described limits

2nd To say to you that the People of the Arkansas Creek Nation are entitled to a full share of all the annuities to which the Creek Indians are now entitled to, or have been paid from the death of Genl William McIntosh, or hereafter may be entitled to receive from the United States.

3d. That they are entitled to a full distributive share of the consideration money stipulated to be paid by the United States for a cession of Territory by the Creek Nation according to the provisions of the Treaty of Washington made in 1826 with its supplemental article, and the Treaty made at the Creek Agency in November 1827 the aggregate of which consideration money is $290.090

4th. That they are entitled to such proportion of $85.000 which is the unpaid balance of $100.000 stipulated in the 9th Article of the Treaty of Washington made in 1826 to be paid to the Emigrating McIntosh Indians as the whole number of persons in the Arkansas Creek Nation, bear to Three Thousand.

5th. That some of their People are entitled to the value of their improvements left in the Old Nation according to the provisions of an act of Congress passed in 1826

6th. To ask the President to give to the Arkansas Creek Indians an agent to be selected by them according to the provisions of the Treaty of Washington made in 1826.

7th. To say that they are entitled by the 8th Article of the last mentioned Treaty to a Wheelwright, 'do give us one.'

8th. To say that the Agent to be appointed ought not to have the power to license any person or persons to Trade in the arkansas Creek Nation without the consent of a council of the Chiefs of the Nation

9th. To ask the President to cause renumeration to be made by the Old Nation to our people for Property left by the Emigrating Creeks in the Old Nation.

10th. To say that the arkansas Creek Nation objects to the appointment of any person as their Agent who has been in any way connected with the Agency in the Old Nation or concerned in the Quarrell which took place between the two parties in that Nation

11th To object to a selection of an agent for the Arkansas Creek Indians to be made by a majority of the Creek Indians, the Indians of the Old Nation and of Arkansas Included

12th To say that the People of the Arkansas Creek Nation will be entitled to a fair and full Proportionable share of any and all sums of money which may be hereafter stipulated to be paid by the United States for any part or the whole of the land now in possession of the Creek Indians of the Old Nation

13 To beg the President of the United States to pay to the Arkansas Creek Indians the money which is now or may hereafter become due to them from the United States, through some other Agency or medium than the Agency of the Old Creek Nation, or the Persons connected with that Agency.

If our Father orders payment of the money which is now or may become due to us heareafter to be made through the Agency of the Old Nation, or any Persons connected with that Agency our People if they ever get it will be deprived of the use of it so long that in the end it will aid them very little in surmounting the difficulties by which they are surrounded in their New home

Father we want to go home, and we beg our Father to enable us to shew to our People on our return to them, that they have not looked in vain to their Great Father the President of the United States for justice

We beg our Father to give us an Agent, to live with us, and who will protect our rights, and Interests, and act for us in all things—We do not wish to leave our home, or ever come here again—

Roley McIntosh   his   X   mark
Benjamin Hawkins

DS, DNA-RG 75 (M234-236). McIntosh and Hawkins wrote AJ two days later, February 27, enclosing this petition and explaining their detour around usual War Department channels by their "extraordinary confidence in you." AJ referred it to Eaton who referred it to Indian superintendent Thomas L. McKenney. On March 2 McKenney reported back to Eaton emphatically rejecting the complaints. He charged that "some person in Washington," with intent to foment discord among the Creeks and thus thwart further emigration, had "injected" McIntosh and Hawkins with baseless grievances contrary to their instructions from the western Creeks (DNA-RG 75, M21-6). His response was shown to McIntosh and Hawkins, who remonstrated further on March 22 (below).

1. McKenney replied that the western Creeks' present land allocation was intended for the whole nation and was ample for its needs, that the Cherokee domain did not infringe on it, and that extending it west to the Rockies would frustrate the government's policy of civilizing the Indians.

2. The 1826 Treaty of Washington pledged to the Creek Nation $247,600 payable upon ratification and a perpetual annuity of $20,000. The 1827 agreement added a $27,491 payment for the remaining Creek lands in Georgia, plus $15,000 set aside for schooling, erection of mills, and purchase of equipment, blankets, and other goods. McKenney claimed that the first cash payment was made, as required, to the nation as a whole more than a year before the McIntosh party separated and emigrated. How the Creeks had then divided the money among themselves was their business and not the government's. Having already been amply and even specially compensated, said McKenney, the McIntosh Creeks had no right to any part of the additional payment of 1827. They had also received their fair share, if not more, of the annuities for 1828 and 1829.

3. The Treaty of Washington promised the McIntosh Creeks $100,000 if they numbered 3,000 and a proportionate sum if fewer, $15,000 of it payable at once and the rest on arrival in the west. McKenney claimed that further payments had in fact been made to them through their former agent David Brearley.

4. The Treaty of Washington promised payment of removal expenses and a year's subsistence upon arrival for Creeks who emigrated within twenty-four months. The government had continued to recruit emigrants after that time, and the annual Indian appropriation for 1828 included $50,000 to pay their way.

5. A law of May 20, 1826, implementing the Treaty of Washington included all these stipulations. McKenney claimed the items had actually been furnished and the improvements paid for.

6. The Treaty of Washington promised the emigrant Creeks their own agent or subagent, blacksmith, and wheelwright. The Creeks had accused their first agent, Adams appointee David Brearley (1786–1837), and his friends of cheating them in trade. AJ removed Brearley in 1829 and appointed John Campbell of Tennessee. Just five days before, on February 20, AJ had withdrawn Campbell's nomination from the Senate on learning that he was a defaulter to the government. Meanwhile subagent Luther Blake ran the agency.

7. McKenney dismissed this complaint as an internal matter for the Creeks to settle among themselves.

8. Although an advocate of removal, Creek agent John Crowell had joined the National Council in denouncing the Treaty of Indian Springs, and both the McIntosh Creeks and Georgia officials had blamed him for blocking the treaty and purportedly plotting William McIntosh's death. McKenney accused "intermeddling and designing white people" of poi-

soning the McIntosh party against Crowell to frustrate Creek reconciliation and thus foil further emigration.

From Littleton Waller Tazewell

Washington Feby. 25. 1830.

Mr. Tazewell's very respectful Compliments to the President ~~of the U.S.~~ and while acknowledging the receipt of his letter of the 24th. Instant announcing his definitive opinion in the case of Mr. King formerly submitted to him, Mr. Tazewell begs leave to repeat the expression of the regrets he feels, in having been the cause of so much trouble to the President.

ANS draft, Vi (15-0259).

To Hardy Murfree Cryer

Washington
February 28th. 1830—

My Dr Sir

I have been awaiting your answer to my last letter on the subject of my Gray stud colt *Bolivar*, to be informed what has been done with him, with a view to the instructions it may be proper to give to my overseer, if sent to the Hermitage, concerning him

I have but little doubt in meeting with a good markett for him in virginia if I can obtain Col Elliots certificate of his appearance figure & blood, including the circumstances under which he has laboured when started on the turf, as in truth he can give, which you will oblige me in procuring.

Any expence you have incurred since *Bolivar* has been taken back, you will please to have paid out of the first collections from the sum stipulated to be paid on his being taken back, & the ballance please have collected & apply to relieve your present pressure until it may be more convenient for you, or my wants may require it—my cotton crop, I learn has been a poor one, much short of what I was induced to believe from the report of my overseer—still you know I have learned to live within my means and oeconomise to keep clear of debt.

You will oblige me, by writing on the receipt of this, that I may know where the colt is, that I may give to my overseer instructions if sent to the Hermitage—I have a great wish to get some of his colts, you know I have a great partiality for his blood, and for this reason am I happy that I have got him again   I believe him one of the purest blooded horses in america—and I have no doubt from his strain that his colts will make valuable as a brood horse.

Present me affectionately to your amiable lady & family & believe me your friend.[1]

Andrew Jackson

ALS, THi (15-0262).
1. Cryer was married to Elizabeth L. Rice (1794–1833).

To *Charles Jones Love*

Washington
February 28th. 1830—

My Dr. Sir,

I have this moment received your two letters of the 13th instant, which advises me of your having closed the contract with Capt Mosely for the 150 acres of land, and the same has been survayed by William Donelson Esqr. That this is a choice peace of land I well know, & all important to make the Winston tract profitable, & valuable; and for these reasons, (added to the anxiety expressed by Capt Mosely to sell to me, under my cir[cum]stances in life) were the reasons that alone induced me to purchase—I am happy to find you have closed the contract, & will be prepared to meet the payment on your draft—I feel greatly indebted to Mr Hill for his kind & liberal proposition, but am determined not to be *indebted*, therefore, will expect you to inform me, whether I had better send on the amount there, or await your order here—I am in hopes that from the rise that has taken place in cotton in England, the demand for it in Europe, by the increased manufactories, added to the deficiency of the crops in america, that in all next month cotton will rise—if mine should not be sold before the middle of next month, I am well convinced it will bring me at Orleans, from eleven to twelve cents; should it, it will meet my debt to Mr Josiah Nichol, & I can meet the other here—but should my cotton prove deficient in meeting my debt there, the ballance I will remit, or meet here on a draft.[1]

So soon as I hear from you that the Deed is executed by Capt Mosely, I will write you fully on the plan of farming you propose—I have no doubt it will be profitable—and I will thank you to give directions to my overseer with regard to the quantity of corn & cotton to plant—about one hundred & fifty or 160 acres of cotton is as much as I think ought to be planted; and as much corn as the hands can, with moderate work, cultivate well—If the Deed is made by Capt Mosely, I wish you to say to my overseer, that I want him to see Mr Sanders, and get him to turn the Lebanon road from Mr Jones by Mr Sanders. and enclose the clear land bought of Capt Mosely by running my fence due north on the line to the

North East corner of the land bought, &c &c, and include it in the north field of Winstons, if his situation will permit him to do it this spring, but not to attempt it, if it will throw him back with his crop—The first moments leisure I shall write Mr Steel on this subject.[2] I had been advised by Mr Cryer that the Gray Stud coolt had been taken back—I directed that he should be sent home, as I intended to breed from him that is, I will have My Virginian, and the Cotton mare put to him, the others are too nigh *akin* to him. I have directed him to be called *Bolivar* & to be let to mares of fifteen in, & twenty dollars out of the season   Whether he will make a good stand in my neighbourhood I cannot say, and if a stand cannot be got for him, whether it would not be better not to advertise him at all, but just keep him for my own & Major Donelsons mares & such of my neighbours that I might choose to send to him

I believe he is a better horse than any in the west except Sir William & his blood is equal to his, but when leisure permits I will write you on this subject again

With my best respects to your amiable lady & family believe me yr friend[3]

Andrew Jackson

ALS draft, DLC (37). Love had purchased 151 acres from Moseley for AJ for $1812. The deed was drawn February 18 and registered May 20.

1. Josiah Nichol (1772–1833) was a Nashville banker and merchant. Payments to Josiah Nichol & Son of $1975.72½ in May, drawn from the sale of AJ's cotton crop, and of $324.52 in August settled AJ's account.

2. The road from Nashville to Lebanon, Tenn., ran past the Hermitage. William Saunders (c1776–1846) operated the nearby Fountain of Health mineral spa.

3. Love had married Frances Peyton Dixon (1785–1833).

Memoranda

report

John Grant collector & postmaster   this is improper must be seperated—The influence of this family & the various offices held by them—same[1]

The public works at Gennessee going on badly & with bad materials, such as an Engineer ought not to permit—let this be examined into & rectified—[2]

The mineral lands to be survayed   The commissioner of the land office to be called upon for an estimate—of the appropriation necessary for the survays of public lands, and particulary as to the late cession (*mineral*)[3]

Mr Colden, on the subject of Col Clinton the civil Engineers—law of 1824—says it cannot infringe the right of the corps proper to appoint Col Clinton in the place of Sulivan resigned—see Major Eaton—[4]

Mr Handy—The bill for establishing land office at St Josephs—if it passes Mr. Handy is recommended, by Judge Hayward & many of the members Judge   Mr Goodenow adds his name   Doctor Dickson recommended for the other office at St. Joseph[5]

Genl Reason Beall Mr Thompson recommends him—to visit the land offices in Wooster, Tiffen, Detroit & Munroe in Michigan T.[6]

Col Webber has called to know what conclusion the Govt. has come to on the subject of the osage that killed one of their people
2d. about the education of their children whether if they send them abroad, their education will be paid for out of the school funds—
3rd. as to the boundery of their lands, and what provision will be made for those who are emigrating from the East of the M. river—[7]

wrote a note to Commodore Patterson requesting him to attend the 4th auditor whilst examing purser T. accounts[8]

The militia of the District C.[9]

Judge Hayward—Genl McNeil—for Govr. Huron—and also Micaja T. Williams acting canal commissioner—[10]

George G. Kingman—Rochester in New york—recommended by Mr Hayward well educated—[11]

Col Chapin recommended for postmaster at Buffolow N.Y.—[12]

Sundry Recommended *Mr. Foreman*—Genl Ashly says he stands as low as any other individual—*Antony Carr & Major Strother*, ought not to be relied on—[13]

Gooddales Report—Doctor Sherwood collector is feeble constitution not able to attend well to his duty obtained the appointment by foul means &c &c[14]

AN, DLC (15-0083).
    1. John Grant Jr. (d. 1850) was postmaster and customs collector at Oswego, N.Y. In March AJ nominated him for a second four-year term as collector. He was replaced as postmaster by Samuel Hawley in January 1831.
    2. In 1829 the War Department began building harbor improvements at the mouth of the Genesee River near Rochester, N.Y. On April 8, 1830, Army chief engineer Charles Gratiot ordered an inspection of the work in response to allegations of faulty construction. He reported to Eaton on June 1 that the complaints were groundless (DNA-RG 77, M65-3).

3. The Indian treaty of July 29, 1829, at Prairie du Chien included cessions of mineral-rich lands in northwestern Illinois and southwestern Wisconsin. Surveyor general William Lytle appealed to General Land Office commissioner George Graham for authority to begin surveying them on January 30 (*TPUS*, 12:119–20). Lytle subsequently wrote AJ on May 8 (below).

4. AJ crossed this out and scrawled "Noted" over it. An April 1824 law authorized the president to employ civil and Army engineers to survey road and canal routes of national importance. President Monroe created a Board on Internal Improvements to conduct the surveys. John Langdon Sullivan (1777–1865) had resigned as chief civil engineer on the Board. De Witt Clinton Jr. (b. 1805), a former assistant engineer who had resigned in 1826, sought the post and was perhaps recommended by Cadwallader David Colden (1769–1834). On October 15, 1829, Eaton told Clinton he could not be inserted above others currently employed but that a place might be found for him (DNA-RG 77, M1113-2). By arrangement, Clinton withdrew his 1826 resignation as assistant engineer on February 23, 1830, and was retroactively reinstated by Eaton on February 26 (DNA-RG 107, M222-27). On June 9 he was appointed chief civil engineer (DNA-RG 77, M1113-3).

5. A bill to establish a new land office on the St. Joseph River at South Bend, Ind., was reported in the Senate on February 8 and passed on March 18, but did not pass the House. Henry S. Handy (c1804–1846) had edited a Jackson paper in Salem, Ind., and served on the state Jackson committee in 1828. John Milton Goodenow (1782–1838) was an Ohio congressman.

6. Reasin Beall (1769–1843) had been an Ohio congressman, brigadier general of state troops in the War of 1812, and land office register. Mr. Thompson was Ohio congressman John Thomson.

7. Western Cherokee delegates Walter Webber (c1790–1834) and John Brown had arrived in Washington with Sam Houston in January. The Western Cherokees had recently complained of the government's failure to punish the killing of a Cherokee by an Osage in 1822 and had asked for more land to accommodate new emigrants (*Jackson Papers*, 7:597–98). Eaton, speaking for AJ, wrote Webber and Brown on March 22 that the Cherokees had themselves already avenged the Osage murder and should now rest content and keep peace (DNA-RG 75, M21-6). In the 1828 Treaty of Washington, the U.S. had pledged $2,000 annually for ten years to educate Western Cherokee children "in their own country."

8. AJ crossed this out and wrote over it "This complied with." He wrote Patterson on February 11 (above).

9. On January 7, officers of the District of Columbia militia led by Henry Naylor solicited AJ to organize a new brigade to accommodate their growing numbers. On February 13 AJ referred the proposal favorably to Eaton, who ordered the change.

10. A bill to establish a new Huron Territory was reported in the House on January 6 but did not pass. Micajah Terrell Williams (1792–1844) of Cincinnati, a former Ohio house speaker, was one of two "acting" members of the state canal commission responsible for overseeing construction. In 1831 AJ appointed him surveyor general for Ohio, Indiana, and Michigan. Brevet Brigadier General John McNeil (1784–1850) resigned from the Army in 1830 to become customs surveyor at Boston.

11. George G. Kingman was a Rochester businessman.

12. Buffalo physician Cyrenius Chapin (1769–1838) had been a colonel of New York troops in the War of 1812. He was not appointed.

13. Stephen W. Foreman was a St. Louis editor. William Henry Ashley (1778–1838) was a leading St. Louis fur trader and later a congressman. Anthony V. Carr (d. 1830) of Missouri was appointed subagent to the Osage Indians in July. George French Strother (1783–1840) had been a Virginia congressman and St. Louis land office receiver.

14. In 1829 AJ had given physician Henry Hall Sherwood (d. 1848) a recess appointment as customs collector at Sackets Harbor, N.Y. On January 13 he nominated Thomas Loomis to replace him. Reuben Goodale (1783–1871) was a Watertown, N.Y., physician.

March

From John Coffee

Dear Genl.

I am under the necessity to ask your advice in the settlement of some of Andrew J Hutchings accounts—Andrew was a few weeks, say 2 or 3, at Columbia where he went to enter the College, but I understood he was not admited into College, before he learned some how or other, that you had permited him to go on to Washington City, which he determined on immediately, this was probably the cause of his short stay there—But as soon as I heard of his going to Columbia, I wrote Mr. Peter R. Booker, and enclosed him $100. and requested him to take charge of Andrew, and to enter him in College, and pay the fees usual or necessary, & to purchase for him any supplies necessary for his use from time to time, and pay the money for them, and have no running accounts in stores &c—But it so turned out that Andrew did not remain there, and I have not seen Mr. Booker since—about the beginning of this year a Mr. Moore & Co. sent me an account against Andrew for $129=49. and wrote me that Mr. Booker had approved of their sending me the account for payment—I could not of course be at any loss, for the proper course to be pursued by me—I wrote them back for answer, that I had engaged Mr. Booker to assume a guardianship over Andrew, and that I had placed money in his hands to meet all necessary demands, but if Mr. Booker said I aught to pay the account, I would certainly do it, But at the same time I protested against their policy in permiting boys at school to create accounts in stores without permission to do so, from their Parent or Guardian and pointed out some of the evils attending such course, and finally told them, if Mr. Booker disavowed the authority to them to raise the account, I could not, nor would I pay the account, untill directed to do so, from you—as I knew I was not authorised to pay such accounts, and if I did so, when at mature age, the allowing the payment might be rejected, and thrown on you and myself, besides the other evils attending such course—I wrote to Mr. Booker, and I send you his answer to shew you what he says about it—and I will be governed by your advice—the merchants wrote me back quite a starched letter, & finally said they would send the account to you for payment, who they had no doubt would pay it promptly—I informed them, if you ordered payment I would pay on the rect. of your orders to that effect. I really feel at a loss how to act on such occasions   I dont like to withhold payment altogether, and at the same time they aught to suffer awhile for their imprudence, but I will be governed by your letter of advice, if you will please to give it—Andrews account in Nashville with Josiah Nichol after you left there was $377=36¼ from January untill Novr. of 1829—and in the same time this account with Mr. Moore & Co. $129–49. and at Col. Jas. Walkers, as you will see in Mr. Bookers letter of $40. or upwards, and of Cash paid by Booker $51=50 and cash furnished him by myself at different times in the same time about $50—besides the sum of one hundred dollars put in his hands to travel on to Washington—making in the agregate $788=35. but this includes his traveling expences to Washington[1]—But there is to be added to this the money you paid for his board at the Nashville College, which was paid to him by the Steward when he left College there, as I was informed—thus in less than one year his accounts are $800. or upwards, I regret it, but really I dont know how to prevent it, if he comes back before he is of age, or that he learns more prudence and oeconomy, if you can retain him with you it will be greatly better for him, for no one here can have any influence or controul over him, and I dread his being within the reach, of some of his relations—will you let me hear from you as soon as convenient—my family are all well, and Polley joins me in our kind remembrance to you, and our relatives with you—Dr. Genl. your friend[2]

Jno. Coffee

[Endorsed by AJ:] (private) Genl J. Coffee 2d of March 1830 on the subject of A. J. Hutchings accounts—enclosing Mr Bookers letter to be preserved with care—recd. 17th. of March 1830 and acknowledged Same day   A. J.

ALS, DLC (37). In the summer of 1829, before AJ brought him to Washington, Andrew J. Hutchings had briefly planned to attend the academy of William L. Williford at Columbia, Tenn. Peter Richardson Booker (c1784–1839) was a Columbia lawyer and William S. Moore a merchant. Coffee enclosed to AJ a January 27 letter from Booker, explaining that Hutchings had run up extravagant charges with local merchants despite Booker's admonitions to them not to extend him credit (DLC-37). Booker denied sanctioning Moore's bill.

1. The sums listed by Coffee add to $748.35. James Walker (1792–1864) was a Columbia merchant and brother-in-law to James K. Polk. Booker estimated his bill at $40 and reported paying $51.50 himself for Hutchings's expenses.

2. Polly was Mary Donelson Coffee (1793–1871), Coffee's wife and Rachel Jackson's niece.

From John Coffee

(Private)

Near Florence 2nd. March 1830.

Dear Genl.

I have had the pleasure to receive yours of the first Ult. and for the information it contains and the explanation given me, I beg leave to tender you my thanks. In my report of the evidence obtained touching the boundary line between Georgia and the Cherokees I gave you a plain statement of all the evidence obtained—and in offering my opinion as to the true claim of both parties, I gave it frankly and according to the best lights of my Judgment. But in that part of my report concerning the Georgians setling on the vacated farms of emigrants and claiming it as Georgia soil (extinguished from the Indian title) I fear I may have indulged too far in expressing an opinion—for I was labouring under the impression that the U. States did not pretend that she had extinguished the claim of the Cherokee nation to the soil of the farms left by emigrants, and for which the U.S. had paid the individual Indian the simple value of his improvement. I well recollect the treaty which you made with the Cherokee nation, I think in 1817. and by which it was stipulated that when emigrants left their improvements and received pay therefor—the U. States took imediate possession of the improvements and rented them out to white men citizens of the U. States, who setled on and cultivated the farms amidst the Indian settlements—and had that treaty have remained inviolate, I have no doubt, but at this day every Cherokee in the nation would have been west of the Mississippi, and Georgia in quiet possession of her territory—but I was also under the impression that Mr. Calhoons treaty of 1819. revoked and made void the provisions of the treaty of 1817. and if so the provisions of the latter treaty, did not, as I understand them, extinguish the right of the soil left by the emigrants—This was my understanding and impressions at the time I sent you my report, but I may have been premature in forming that opinion, inasmuch as Georgia may in *this instance*, as in the case of the *treaty* with *Creek nation* at the *Indian Springs*, contend that the united states could not make void the treaty of 1817. without her consent—and I confess I do not see any material difference in the two cases, with the exception only, that she has remained silent in seting up her claim for more than ten years, which may be plead in bar against her, under the Statutes of limitations, and furthermore Georgia did, under the provisions of Mr. Calhoons treaty of 1819. remove her citizens (or the U. States removed them without any complaint on the part of Georgia) from the lands rented from the United States under the treaty of 1817. as I was informed while in the nation—and by that surrender of the soil, and so long of quiet possession by the Cherokees, may it not well raise doubts on the equity of her claim. I am aware of the importance of removing the Cherokees and giving to Georgia her entire chartered limits—there are a portion of the people of that state, who seem to thurst, and have their whole hearts fixed on that subject, and although I believe the interior, and better informed citizens of Georgia are not of the class spoken of, yet the pioneers and frontier setlers are so clamourous, that the authorities of the state feel bound to urge their claim even beyond the sober dictates of their better judgments, indeed it seems proverbial that a man in office in Georgia, must clamour on this subject, or be driven out of Office—for although some may and do differ in opinion, yet such must be silent, or be hunted down by the vociferous part of the community.

I am of opinion that the poor Indians would not be averse to emigrating under the liberal provisions offered by Govt. was it not for the influence of the Chiefs. Therefore deprive the chiefs of the power they now possess, take from them their own code of laws, and reduce them to plain citizenship, of *either* the *Indian* or the *whiteman citizen* of *Georgia*, and they will soon determine to move, and then there will be no difficulty in getting the poor Indians to give their consent. All this will be done by the state of Georgia if the U. States do not interfere with her laws—for if Georgia extends her laws over the nation, and take away the authority of the Chiefs, no matter how liberal otherwise the laws may be they will instantly withdraw when they find that neither Congress or the Executive will interfere—And I have no doubt but this is the true policy to pursue towards them to remove them, and make them thereby, trebly happy to what they now are, or will be, in a few years if they remain where they now are—If I am right in this position, would it not be well for the United States to be liberal with them in construing the treaties, in affording them protection, and in all her transactions as far as possible, maintain harmony, and above all, retain the confidence of the nation. This course will have a happy effect on the feelings of the civilized world—and it will put down and silence those in our own country who constantly seek for cause to complain. It may indeed turn them loose upon Georgia, but that matters not, it is Georgia who clamour for the Indian lands, and she alone is entitled to blame if any there be.

I have thought that you would not take it unkind, for me to give you this explanation of my views and motives, which governed me at the time of my report—with the greatest respect Dr. Genl. your friend & Leut.

Jno. Coffee

ALS, DLC (37). The Cherokee treaty of 1817, negotiated by AJ as U.S. commissioner, promised compensation to individual emigrating Cherokees for improvements on lands they left behind. Vacated improvements that lay within the Cherokee Nation's newly circumscribed boundaries were to be rented annually by the agent "to the Indians," with proceeds going to the relief of Cherokee poor. The treaty of 1819, negotiated by then secretary of war John C. Calhoun, voided the leases and required the U.S. to remove white intruders from the Cherokee country. Left unclear was the status of the vacated properties, for which the U.S. had paid individual consideration but which still lay within the Cherokees' acknowledged national domain. Coffee's official report on the historic Creek-Cherokee boundary in December 1829 did not touch the question, but in letters to Eaton of January 15 and 21, 1830, he severely censured Georgia's boundary pretensions and her encouragement of intruders in general (DNA-RG 75, M234-74).

On November 30, 1829, Eaton had sent to Georgia governor George Gilmer Indian superintendent McKenney's opinion that the U.S. payment for improvements did not purchase ownership of the soil, which still belonged to the Cherokees as a nation (DNA-RG 75, M21-6). Later in March, however, attorney general Berrien gave Eaton a legal opinion that the Cherokees held a mere right of occupancy, and that when this was quieted by purchase of their improvements full title to the land passed automatically to Georgia. Eaton exempted settlers on the vacated tracts from his March 14 and 17 orders to agent Montgomery to remove intruders (*HRDoc* 89, 21st Cong., 1st sess., pp. 39–41, 45–49, Serial 197). On June 1 he wrote Gilmer that the lands were "considered as not belonging any longer to the Cherokees" (M21-6).

To James Reeside

The pair of horses reached me on yesterday, safe and in good condition, and your driver has agreed to remain today to accompany my driver, a round or two in the city, so that he may become acquainted with the disposition of the horses [. . .] I have had but little time to look at the horses; as far as examined, I am pleased with them, and asure you, they fully meet my expectations. If they are of good disposition, true to the draft, & gentle, they will remain mine as long they live, and I *endure*—I hold myself ready to meet your draft for them should you think proper to draw, previous to your intended visit here in april next[.] I am very respectfully yr mo. obdt. servt.

Andrew Jackson

P.S. please give me the ages of the pair of horses—strange as it may seem, altho I have raised so many horses, I cannot tell by the mouth a four year old from that of ten years. A. Jackson—

Printed extract and ALS facsimile fragment, Charles Hamilton Galleries catalog, 1976 (15-0290); Envelope with ANS postscript, William C. Cook (mAJs). Reeside (c1790–1842) of Philadelphia was a leading mail contractor.

From William Ellis Tucker

Philada. Mar 3 1830

Permit me to present the accompanying small specimen of American Porcelain, manufactured from American materials, and made in part by

American workmen who have been taught the different branches of the art in my establishment since it was first founded in the City of Philad.

The materials constituting French China have long been known to exist in the United States, and for the last fifty years many attempts have been made to form a perfect porcelain from these materials without success— At Jersey City a few years since, under the direction of French & English artists, large sums were expended in repeated efforts to establish this manufacture. But the difficulty arising from the difference that appears to exist in the proportions of the component principles of the material of this country and that of France, requiring a process in the combination of those materials, at variance with all the known rules of these artists, baffled their utmost skill and ingenuity, so that a spurious article was produced, unsound in body and in glaze, and the establishment was finally abandoned.[1]

Having the advantage of being self taught and unrestricted by the preposessions of European practice, a wider range of experiments has been resorted to, and three years of unceasing personal devotion to the object has crowned my exertions with a happier result.

During this period I have encountered more than an ordinary share of the difficulties that are usually attendant on the introduction of a new manufacture. To which has been added the frequent shipment of porcelain to New York from France, in which the duties have been evaded, by the exhibition of invoices below the real cost, thus enabling the shipper to throw the article into the market at a very low price much to the injury of my American porcelain.[2]

But if after having expended seventeen thousand Dollars in the obtainment of this important national object, it is consistent with the policy of the government of my country to give such encouragement to the establishment as will enable me to erect a factory, and bring the article into more general use than my present limited finances will permit; it will not only secure a discovery to the country which will open a new source of useful and extensive employment; but will in time, from the genius of our american youth in the formation of the article, enable the United States to compete with France in every part of the world in the excellence and in the abundance of the manufacture

Impressed with these facts I am emboldened to present the following proposition for your consideration, and with profound respect submit to your superior wisdom & judgment to dispose of it as your sense of the interests of the country may justify. Viz In consideration of twenty thousand Dollars being secured to me by Congress, I will bend myself to impart to the Government of the United States after receiving the same a complete and perfect knowledge of every branch of my business in the formation of American Porcelain, so that the discovery shall for ever be secured to the country

This sum would enable me to build a factory and to bring the Article into general use, throughout the United States   I would just observe that the specimen of Porcelain now sent has not been specially prepared; but is a fair sample of what I am in the constant habit of manufacturing, and is taken of out sells already made for sale. I am with sentiments of high respect your friend & fellow Citizen

Signed Wm Ellis Tucker

LC, PPPM (mAJs). Tucker (1800–1832) pioneered American fine porcelain manufacturing at his Philadelphia factory, founded in 1826. AJ replied on April 3 (below).
    1. The Jersey Porcelain and Earthenware Company was incorporated in December 1825. The works failed and were purchased in 1828 by David Henderson, who reincorporated them in 1833 as the American Pottery Manufacturing Company.
    2. Imported porcelain paid a customs duty of 20% ad valorem.

To Martin Van Buren

March 4th. 1830—

Dr Sir
    I enclose for your examination a rough draft of a proclamation to be Issued, with certain instructions to accompany it as pointed out by the act of March 1807, for your examination & inspection—When it passes your inspection have the goodness to have it drew in a fair hand for signature as I want to place it in the hands of the Sec. of the Treasury as soon as possible
    yrs. respectfully

Andrew Jackson

P.S. The instructions is made out by the Sec. of the Treasury & commissioner   A. J

ALS, Memphis Pink Palace Museum (15-0296). The law of March 3, 1807, authorized forcible removal and prosecution of trespassers on public lands. On March 6 AJ issued his proclamation ordering illegal settlers in the Huntsville, Ala., land district to depart by September 1 (Richardson, 2:494–95). The accompanying instructions, issued on March 9 by General Land Office commissioner George Graham, allowed present occupants to remain as tenants at will by making application to the land office and forswearing any claim of ownership (*US Telegraph*, March 24, 1830). AJ's order stemmed from the dispute over land titles derived from John Smith T.

From Hardy Murfree Cryer

Gallatin Tennessee March 4th. 1830.

Dear friend

Your two last letters which have come to hand are of Decr. & Jany.[1]—
Pursuant to your request I have just returned from 'the *Hermitage*' a
name & place that combines an *association* of ideas & Sensations at
Once *brilliant* & *gloomy*—pleasingly mournful—I say it is so to me—
but I can only Speculate—it is for *You* dear Sir—to realize all that others
talk about! But we must not indulge a murmuring spirit—No—God our
heavenly is too Wise to err—and too good to chasten us but for our
profit—I will just say further—that the garden is in a state of forward
preparation—all is *neat* & *dry* around *the Tomb*—Your farm is in good
repair—your hogs & cattle look well for the Season—I examined all
your horses mares & colts—Bolivar will stand at the Hermitage—I have
no doubt it is the best place for him—as Mr. Clay has Sold Sir Wm. to
Some men abt. Franklin—in Williamson Cnty. price $4000. in one & two
years—I have written an advertisemt. for Bolivar which you will See in the
Republican—He will not do to train any more—Elliott says his Colt Jerry
is afflicted in the Same way but not so bad—and he has lost his reputation
as a Courser[2]—And as to his training any of your Younger Ones—He just
observed that he not room for his own—The secret is this—He & Mr.
Williams are so united with *James* Jackson—that there is no doing any
thing agt. his interest—& if Elliott & Williams were to train a Stockholder
& run him with *Success* why it would be *blocking* up the way of James
Jacksons *next* importation—if he Should *die* on the way! for you must
know that he is determined to *try* a third time—And on the other hand
if Elliott Should train & run a Stockholder *unsuccessfully* Shelby who is
a *censorious* little man would attribute it to design[3]—Your Constitution
Colt out of the Miller Mare is a Short heavy Colt—I suppose he is not
intended by natur for a *racehorse*—the brown Colt out the Same mare by
Stockholder is of better form for a Sprightly active horse—*his eyes* look
rather weak—time & moderate feeding may make all right—The Sway
back mare's filly of the Same age by Stockholder will make a large active
animal—& so will the Cotton mare's Sorrel filly—the *little* Sorrel *mother-
less* one from the brown mare; is improved very much—but the *large bay*
Colt from the Gray Pacolet—by Stockholder is *worth all the rest* of the
two year olds put to gether—he is very large and begins to Shew some
fine points—I know no man that would do a good part by him, but—Mr.
Cotten my Uncle—if he trains, perhaps he might consent to gentle him for
you—Your Oscar mare I think is in foal to the Cover Arab gave her, after I
got out with him—of which I gave you an account—her Colt by Wm. is a

good one—not so splendid as it is good—You have seen my advertisemt.[4] I expect to hear from you according to promise abt. the mares—&c.

Mrs. Cryer & children are all well & I hope to be in a *situation, say this year*—"to owe no man any thing but *good will.*" Little Rachel is very promising & her Mother thinks a great deal of her—Respectfully yours

H M Cryer

Present me to Gen. Desha & say to him that Madame Tonson has the best foal at her foot, She ever dropt—a filly[5]

[Endorsed by AJ:] The Revd. Mr Cryer answered 19th. of March 1830—

ALS, DLC (37).
1. December 8, 1829 (*Jackson Papers*, 7:630–31), and January 10, 1830, above.
2. Cryer's ad for Bolivar debuted in the *Nashville Republican* on March 5. It included his pedigree signed by AJ and a statement from trainer Jesse Haynie attesting his speed at short distances and quality as a sire. George Elliott's colt Jerry had "cramped and stopped" in the second mile of an October 1829 Nashville race it had been favored to win (*American Turf Register*, December 1829, p. 210). John W. Clay was a Davidson County horseman.
3. In 1828 James Jackson had imported an English brood mare named Stoughton Lass and a former racer named Abjer, who died before reaching Tennessee. In 1830 Jackson purchased the celebrated English stallion Leviathan, who stood at Elliott's stable. Williams and Shelby were likely Green Berry Williams (1778–1874) and Anthony Bledsoe Shelby (1789–1851), both Sumner County horsemen.
4. Cryer had been advertising Arab at stud in the *Nashville Republican* since January 1. John Brown Cotton (1778–1849) of Sumner County was the brother of Cryer's mother.
5. Cryer's daughter, Rachel Jackson Cryer (1829–1895), was just over a year old. Robert Desha (1791–1849) of Gallatin was a Tennessee congressman. Madam Tonson was a celebrated brood mare owned by Cryer.

From George Graham

5th March. 1830.

Sir,

I now submit in compliance with your request, those observations in relation to a Bill passed by the Senate, and now pending in the H of Reps "to grant pre emption rights to settlers on the public Lands," which were heretofore verbally communicated to you.

The 1st Sect. of this Act grants to every occupant of the public Lands now in possession and who cultivated any part of it in 1829, any number of acres not more than 320 to be taken by legal subdivisions. An amendment proposed in the H R reduces the quantity to 160 acres.

The 3d Sect. of the Bill declares that the act shall remain in force for one year from & after its passage. A substitute for this Section has been proposed in the H R which does away all limitations as to the continuance of the Act, and provides only for the mode in which the settlement & improvement shall be proved.[1] These provisions of the Act extend to all the public Lands, as well those which have not been proclaimed for sale, as those which have, and are now subject to entry at the minimum price. With respect to the first description of Lands the effect of the act will be to prevent the Executive from proclaiming for sale during the continuance of the act any of the public Lands; there being no limitation as to the time when the Lands to which the right of preemption may accrue shall be paid for, it is to be presumed that Congress intend that payment may be made at any time within the period for which the law may be in force—And again, as the Bill authorizes a selection of the Land to be made at the option of the occupant in four legal subdivisions as passed by the Senate, and in two of such subdivisions as proposed by the amendment in the House, it results that the occupant taking his improvement as a centre would have the privilege of making his Selections in the first instance from 49 of such legal subdivisions, equal to 3,920 acres, and in the second instance from nine of such legal subdivisions, equal to 720 acres.[2] The practical difficulty therefore of bringing those Lands into market until the preemption rights shall have been adjusted would be such as to deter the Executive from the attempt; independent of that respect which would be due to the presumed intentions of the Legislature. In fact the sale of the public Lands proclaimed previous to the introduction of this Bill has been postponed in consequence of its passage by the Senate.[3]

With respect to the second description of Lands, viz: those which have been offered at public sale and are now subject to entry at the minimum price, the settlers on which are very numerous, the effect of the provisions of the Bill, if it become a law, will necessarily be to produce embarrassment and prevent to a great extent the purchase of the public Lands at private entry, by those emigrants who are able and would be willing to buy, because as the right of selection in each occupant in 1829, would extend to a tract embracing 720, or perhaps 3,920 acres, lying in every direction around his improvement, it would be unsafe for a purchaser to enter any portion of this land until the occupant had entered and paid for his preemption. Agreeably to the 3'd Section of the Bill as proposed to be amended in the House, this period for payment is unlimited; by the Bill as passed in the Senate it is necessarily limited to 12 months after the passage of the act. It is however probable that but few of the present occupants of this description of lands will make payment under the act within the period last referred to. So far as these occupants have the means of purchasing they can now enter the Land occupied at the minimum price; to the wealthy occupant it is presumed Congress have no desire to extend gratuitous favors. If the poorer occupants have not the present means of paying for 80 Acres of Land, it is not to be expected that in twelve months they would generally have the means of paying for *160* or *320* Acres as the case may be; but encouraged by the provisions of the proposed

Act, they will aspire to the purchase ultimately of the maximum quantity allowed by the Law, and being unable to make payment within the time limited, will petition for a further indulgence as to time, and will consider themselves as debtors to the Govt. for the amount of the purchase money of the maximum quantity of Land to which the preemption right may extend—thus the Credit system which has been abolished with the general consent of the nation (and a debt incurred by individuals of sixteen or seventeen millions of dollars has been liquidated by allowances for discounts & the relinqt. of a portion of the Lands purchased) will again be revived and under more unfavorable circumstances than it originally existed.[4]

The real effects of the provisions of this Bill, if matured into a Law, will probably extend very much beyond its present limitations   The emigrant to the States & Territories in which the public Lands lie possessing the disposition and the means to purchase, but embarrassed in his selection by the privileges granted to those persons claiming preemptions by mere rights of occupancy in 1829, and perceiving no possible reason why the individual who took possessin of the public Lands in 1829, should have a better claim on the indulgence of the Govt. than he who should settle on the public Lands in 1830, will of course defer his purchase, settle down on the public Lands, and petition Congress for all those rights, privileges & indulgencies which had or might be extended to the settler on the public Lands in 1829. It does not require the spirit of prophecy to foretel that a system for the disposal of the public domain founded on the principles embraced in the Bill above referred to, would in a short period arrest the regular *Sales* of the public Lands, and throw those Lands into the hands of the occupants who would pay for them only when convenient, if at all. All which is respectfully submitted

George Graham

LC, DNA-RG 49 (M25-25). *HRDoc* 109, 21st Cong., 1st sess., pp. 2–4 (Serial 198). Graham (1770–1830) was Commissioner of the General Land Office.

Under the system in place since 1820, federal public lands were surveyed on a rectangular pattern and then proclaimed for cash sale at public auction in 80-acre parcels, with a minimum bid of $1.25 per acre. Tracts unsold at the auction remained open for subsequent "private entry," or purchase at the minimum price. Settlement prior to purchase was illegal trespass. Nonetheless, Congress had from time to time offered particular groups of settlers the privilege of pre-emption, or the right to purchase the tracts they occupied in advance of the auction and at the minimum price. In the 1820s agitation arose to make pre-emption general.

On January 13 the Senate passed a bill extending to every current occupant who had cultivated his holding in 1829 the right, good for one year from date of enactment, to pre-empt up to 320 acres in "legal subdivisions" of 80 acres each. The House Committee on Public Lands reported it on January 25 with an amendment reducing the pre-emption to 160 acres. On March 10 Graham sent an extract from this letter to Ohio congressman Samuel F. Vinton, who had asked his opinion of the bill (DNA-RG 49, M25-25). On May 25 the House asked Treasury secretary Ingham for copies of Graham's letter and any other pertinent documents. Graham, through Ingham, replied the same day with a copy of the letter and of reports from Alabama that squatters in the Cahaba district had organized to suppress competitive bidding at the upcoming auction by violence (*HRDoc* 109, 21st Cong.,

1st sess., Serial 198). On May 29 an amended House version of the bill passed both houses of Congress and was signed into law by AJ.

1. On February 22, Arkansas Territory delegate Ambrose H. Sevier offered an amendment waiving the Act's expiration date for settlers on lands that had not yet been surveyed, allowing them one year after completion of the survey to file their claims. The amendment failed in the House.

2. Under the Senate bill, a settler could pre-empt the subdivision containing his farmstead or "improvement" plus three more in any direction, making available to him a grid seven subdivisions high by seven wide. The House version limited the pre-emption to the improvement plus one contiguous subdivision, reducing the eligible grid to three by three. Until the pre-emptor made his selections, presumably nothing within the grid could be sold. The House later added a provision requiring that pre-emption claims be filed and paid for before the announced date of the public sale, which should not be delayed thereby. Despite this, the reduction to 160 acres, and the failure of Sevier's amendment, Graham informed Alabama congressman Clement C. Clay on May 28 that he remained "opposed in principle to the whole bill" (M25-25).

3. No new sales had been proclaimed since December 1829. On June 5 AJ signed proclamations for sales in eight states and territories. Transmitting them for publication in the *US Telegraph* on June 9, Graham explained that they had been held up "during the pendency of the pre Emption Bill" (M25-25).

4. Before 1820, the government had sold public lands on a credit of up to four years. Massive debts incurred by purchasers in the late 1810s led to the abolition of the credit system and its replacement by cash sales. Relief legislation to liquidate the lingering debt continued into the 1830s.

To Robert Young Hayne

[A minor proposal by Samuel A. Foot of Connecticut concerning the public lands provoked a celebrated Senate debate in January 1830 over the nature of the federal Union between Robert Young Hayne (1791–1839) of South Carolina and Daniel Webster (1782–1852) of Massachusetts. Hayne's second speech, on January 25, assailed the central government's usurpation of oppressive powers. Hayne defended South Carolina's threat to declare the protective tariff on imports unconstitutional and therefore null and void, claiming it as a remedy sanctioned by hallowed Jeffersonian precedent. Webster's second reply to Hayne reproved nullification and disunion and exalted American nationality, ending with the famous paean to "Liberty and Union, now and forever, one and inseparable!" The speeches attracted much attention and were widely circulated in newspapers and as pamphlets.]

March 6th. 1830—

My Dr. Sir

I have received your polite note of the 5th. instant accompanied with the present of your second speech in answer to Mr. Webster, which I accept with great pleasure. It shall occupy a place in my library next to the productions of the enlightened republican & sage of Monticello—"As you are contending for the republican principles of 98, the doctrines of the Virginia resolutions, & of Madisons report"—This is where it ought to be placed; for on Mr Jeffersons opinions these were all founded; and I have ever thought they were justly to be regarded as the great safeguards of our liberties, & our bond of union; and if practiced upon, our liberties will endure forever.[1]

The Indian affairs with other public duties hitherto have pressed upon me, that I have not had time to read, deliberately, your spech, I have barely glanced over it as it appeared in the newspapers—I intend shortly, to give it an attentive reading. I am Dr Sir with great respect yr friend

Andrew Jackson

ALS, NN (15-0309). Addressed by AJ to "Genl R. Y. Hayne in the senate." Whether AJ had once sanctioned Hayne's doctrines became an issue after his proclamation against nullification in December 1832. On February 28, 1833, Henry Daniel of Kentucky charged in the House that Hayne's ideas in 1830 had "met with the approbation of the President, as expressed in direct terms in a letter from him to Mr. Hayne. The terms employed were as strong as language can afford. They were to the effect that the speech contained an exposition of the true principles of republicanism, and that it should be bound up and placed in his library along with the works of Thomas Jefferson" (*Register of Debates*, 22d Cong., 2d sess., p. 1885).

1. Hayne had said that the "South Carolina doctrine . . . is the good old Republican doctrine of '98; the doctrine of the celebrated 'Virginia Resolutions' of that year, and of 'Madison's Report' of '99." In 1798 the Virginia legislature adopted resolutions drafted by James Madison which declared the Alien and Sedition Acts palpably unconstitutional and affirmed the right of states to "interpose" to enforce constitutional limits on federal power. The Kentucky legislature passed similar resolutions drafted by Jefferson. Madison's report of December 1799, adopted by the Virginia legislature in January 1800 to answer critical reaction from other states, defended and elucidated the principle of state interposition (*Madison Papers*, 17:307–50). The Virginia and Kentucky resolutions formed the core of subsequent state's-rights doctrine.

To Samuel Delucenna Ingham

March 6th. 1830—

Mr. Dr. Sir

I have this moment found on my table the enclosed recommendation of Mr Cornell for a warrant officer in the cutter service. It is impressed on my mind that I have made an appointment out for him & sent it to your office. If in This I am mistaken, I send herewith another, yrs respectfully

Andrew Jackson

I appoint Stephen Cornell a warrant officer in the cutter service of the U. States March 6th. 1830—

Andrew Jackson

ALS, DLC (75). Stephen Cornell (1797–1869) was from Newport, R.I. Ingham had recommended him to AJ the day before.

To Francis Preston

March 6th. 1830

The President with his respects to Genl F. Preston, sends, by his son, for his perusal, the manuscript spoken of yesterday—They originals are in his hands deposited for safe keeping.

The Genl will read and Judge for himself, whether ever he heard of as vile a conspiracy against character as it discloses. but truth being powerful, ever has, & ever will, prevail—When the Genl has perused, he will please return the paper.

AN, ViHi (15-0311). AJ addressed this note to Preston at Gadsby's hotel. Preston (1765–1835) of Abingdon, Va., was a former congressman and a longtime friend of AJ. The son was Andrew Jackson Jr. The manuscript AJ showed Preston was a version of his 93-page compilation of letters and affidavits containing the history of the Eaton affair from March to December of 1829 (DLC-75).

To Samuel Delucenna Ingham

March 8th. 1830—

My Dr. Sir,

yours of the 6th. with its enclosures was laid on my table on the night of that day, & remained unnoticed until this morning—having carefully examined its enclosures I hasten to reply.

I sincerely regret that there should exist any ground of complaint against any of our collectors, & particularly Mr. Gordon for too rigid a performance of duty, where the safety of the revenue does not require it—I think it will be proper for you to call upon Mr. Gordon for a statement of this case, and in the mean time to *admonish him*, whilst he strictly executes the *law & detects fraud*, he is to throw no unnecessary dificulties in the way of the honest & fair dealer, where there does not exist any suspicions of fraud.

I would barely add, that whilst we protect the honest and fair dealer from all unnecessary delays, we ought to exact from all, the faithful fulfilment of the laws, for at such a port as Neworleans where there are a great looseness of morals, the least relaxation of law will be used to defraud the govt., for the Spanish population have been educated to believe that it is no crime to cheat the Govt. It will not do to condemn an officer on the complaint *alone* of the interested merchant—Therefore, Justice to Mr Gordon would seem to require that he should be called on for a stateme[nt] of the case submitted, which when recd. we can better judge of the hardships of the case complained of—from the fair character of Mr Gordon, from his long experience as a public officer, and his high character as such, I would suppose that there is more in this case, than the mere defect of the tool of the P— enquiry before we condemn our officer is proper[.] very respectfully yrs

Andrew Jackson

ALS, The Gilder Lehrman Institute of American History (mAJs). Measures by New Orleans collector Martin Gordon (c1773–1852) to enforce the customs laws had prompted protests to the Treasury (*Jackson Papers*, 7:631–34). The New York merchant firm Meyer & Hupeden complained that Gordon had refused to allow a drawback of duties on imported goods shipped coastwise to New Orleans for re-export. On March 12 Ingham wrote Gordon for explanation. Gordon replied on April 4 that despite some discrepancy in the shipping labels on the goods he had not refused to issue the certificate permitting the drawback, but had merely been delayed by press of business (DNA-RG 56, M178-16).

To Francis Preston

March 9th. 1830—

The President with his respects to Genl F. Preston acknowledges the receipt of his note of the 6th. instant with return of the manuscript—assures him that there was not any injunction of secrecy imposed on its contents, except to the name of the writer of the first letter which lead to the correspondence & enquiry whose name, as far as connected with that letter, I would conceive confidential, but none other, and in no wise else, only as connected with writing the first letter—[1]

The President has just recd your note from Baltimore   he regrets he had not recd. it on yesterday—as his son would have considered himself much honored by waiting upon yr daughter & conducting her to our house—we had the pleasure of her company last evening, she was escorted by Col Morgan & Lady—The P. expects the pleasure of the Genls. his daughter & nieces company on wednesday next to dine with him and will be happy when the genl returns to the city to see, & converse with him freely, & fully, on the subject of the manuscript—

AN, ViHi (15-0317). Addressed by AJ to Preston at Gadsby's.
1. This was Ezra S. Ely's letter to AJ of March 18, 1829 (*Jackson Papers*, 7:101–4).

From Andrew Jackson Donelson

March 9th. 1830

Dear Sir

I have recd. from a friend in whom I place the highest confidence the enclosed papers in relation to Col. Harris the Marshal at Boston. They are submitted to you with an earnest hope that the application to remove him will not prevail unless he be brought fairly within the operation of the course prescribed in the inaugural address on the subject of removals.[1] My idea of his conduct and character, makes him an example worthy of the imitation, rather than the punishment, of our friends in office.

I may be mistaken however. He is a man I never saw and of whom I know nothing but from the statements of Genl Gaines and other respectable officers who served with him in the last war.[2]

yr. respectful srvt

Andrew J Donelson

ALS, DNA-RG 59 (M639-10).
1. In his inaugural address, AJ had pledged the "correction of those abuses that have brought the patronage of the Federal Government into conflict with the freedom of elections, and the counteraction of those causes which have disturbed the rightful course of appointment and have placed or continued power in unfaithful or incompetent hands" (Richardson, 2:438). A pre-inaugural memorandum targeted for removal those officers who were appointed against the public will, who electioneered in office, or who were of bad moral character (*Jackson Papers*, 7:60–61).
2. In 1814 Edmund P. Gaines had recommended Samuel D. Harris, then an Army captain, for promotion to lieutenant colonel for his "intelligence, honor, zeal, activity, discipline & courage" in service on the Niagara frontier (*Publications of the Buffalo Historical Society*, vol. 24, 1920, p. 342).

[Enclosure: Samuel Devens Harris to Nathan Towson]

Boston March 4 1830

Dear Colonel

When I had occasion some time since to trouble you on the subject of my office I think that I promised you, it should be the last & so I confidently hoped, it would be, but such is the passion with a few people here for office, who assume to themselves an exclusive right, to all the emoluments in the gift of the administration that they, by the way a very few, have again or will demand that my office be vacated. Not that its duties are not satisfactorily performed & to the perfect acceptation of the government & people. Not that the incumbent has not as good claims to it & as much merit as any other man here, both in war & in peace not that he is not one of the oldest Democrats or rather belonging to one of the oldest Democratic families in this section of the country.[1] Not that, he voted against Genl. Jackson nor that he voted for Mr Adams, not that he is supported by the almost entire population of this City of all ranks & parties & that he has always been the zealous personal friend of the General, but that *the few* must have all the offices.

It becomes me in duty to myself and to shield myself against the falsehoods & misrepresentations of any who are desirous for my place, to again call on you as the only friend I have at the seat of Govt, to state I am informed that J L Sibley of Sutton Cty of Worcester has left here for Washington to try for my office, he will be supported I presume by a small number of the Representatives of our Legislature, who assume to be the friends of the Administration, if it were necessary, I could send from the same body the support of ¹⁵/₁₆ths of it.² My present object is to guard against any misrepresentations to the President, and if you are not quite wearied out with your friends (for I understand that you are pressed on all sides by them) I *for once more* ask of you to see that the President is *not deceived*. It may be apropos to state that Mr Sibley has been recommended to me to be appointed as an assistant to take the Census, by the "Jackson County Committee for Worcester County," & that the Letter expresses a confidence that the President will not dismiss me.³ I enclose you a copy, it will shew you their feeling on the subject, that I voted for Mr Adams is a mistake, the fact is, having zealously supported Genl Jackson during his Military life & particularly when the arm of opposition was raised against him during his Campaigns in the South, I could not, with *my feelings*, oppose him when he was a Candidate for the Presidency. I therefor did not cast my vote, but observed a neutral ground. Believe me it has been quite an effort for me to make another requisition on your kindness at this time & nothing short of imperative duty to myself can be offered as an apology[.] your friend

Saml D Harris

[Endorsed by Donelson:] Please read Harris' letter

ALS, DNA-RG 59 (M639-10). Jonas Leonard Sibley (1791–1852) was a lawyer of Sutton, Mass. AJ did not remove Harris, but replaced him with Sibley when his term expired in 1833.

1. Harris's father Jonathan Harris and his grandfather Richard Devens, both of Charlestown, were active in the Revolution and later politically affiliated with the Jeffersonians.

2. Twenty-seven Massachusetts legislators had written AJ in mid-February recommending Sibley.

3. Jubal Harrington, chairman of the Worcester County Jackson Committee, wrote Harris on December 27, 1829, recommending Sibley for census taker. Harrington assured Harris that "though it is understood that he [AJ] was not your choice, still from your well known Republican principles and services in the second war of Independence, we have great confidence to believe the highly responsible office you now hold, will be continued in your hands by the Government—Genl Jackson is too much of a soldier to forget those who have fought for their Country and exposed their lives to the perils and dangers of war." However,

on February 16 Harrington and the Worcester County committee wrote AJ urging him to remove Harris for Sibley (DNA-RG 59, M639-21).

To Littleton Waller Tazewell

March 11th. 1830—

The President with his respects to the Honble. Mr Tazewell would thank him to have the nomination of Col A Butler acted upon at as early a period as possible—

The President is waiting the result to send out some necessary instructions to him

AN, Sotheby's (mAJs). In August 1829 AJ had dispatched Anthony Butler (1787–1849) to Mexico with instructions to U.S. minister Joel Poinsett. In October he recalled Poinsett and replaced him with Butler as chargé d'affaires. On January 22, 1830, AJ sent Butler's nomination as chargé to the Senate. It was referred to the Foreign Relations Committee on February 10 and reported out by Tazewell, its chair, on March 3. The Senate considered Butler on March 11 and confirmed him on March 12 by a vote of 35 to 12. AJ's special instructions to Butler (March 23, below) concerned the purchase of Texas.

To William Polk

Washington March 12th. 1830—

My Dr Sir

I have the pleasure of acknowledging the receipt of yours of the 7th. Instant, expressive of your wish that Mr Devreaux might not be removed from the office which he now holds. I am pleased to hear you speak so favorably of that gentleman as it is confirmatory of the good opinion expressed of him by others of his friends.

If any doubt had rested upon my mind as to the propriety, or policy if you please, of reappointing him, that doubt would have been removed upon the reading of your letter. However, it is with pleasure I inform you, that such was not the case; and his name had been sent to the senate before your favor came to hand.

Please present my kind regard to Mrs. Polk & your amiable family, and believe me to be very sincerely your friend

Andrew Jackson

ALS, DLC-William Polk Papers (15-0350). William Polk (1758–1834) of Raleigh, N.C., was a prominent soldier and politician and a relation of James K. Polk. His wife was Sarah Hawkins Polk (1784–1843). On March 11 AJ had nominated Thomas Pollock Devereux (1793–1869) for a third four-year term as district attorney for North Carolina. In May Polk's son Leonidas married Devereux's younger sister.

To *William Branch Giles*

[Giles had written Jackson soliciting a West Point cadetship for his son Thomas Peyton Giles. Printed here are Jackson's draft of his reply and the reply itself.]

Mr Giles letter to be answered, his letter recd. &c &c, that in that retirement that he has selected for the repose in of his declining days May that indulgent providence, who dispenses his blessings & his affections upon all for his own purposes, convert those afflictions visitted on him to his happiness here in the declining years & to his immortal happiness beyond the grave—our confidence in a heaven beyond the grave & our enjoyments there, gives peace to us here, and is a balm to our afflictions &c &c—

The little boon you have requested on the solicitations of your son will be granted with much pleasure—and in due time he will receive his warrant of which you can apprise him.

Altho our political horisons is at present a little clouded with protentous storms of consolidation &c &c still I do not despair of the republic   I have great confidence in the virtue of the people, and I trust ere long that our Legislation under the constitution will be restored[1] to the Republican Doctrine and practice of 98—and that a Just line will be again drew between the powers granted to the general Govt. and those reserved to the States & to the people

conclude with the assurance of my great Esteem & Respect, & best wishes for his happiness—retirement being the only where it can be enjoyed   A J

ALS draft, DLC-Donelson Papers (15-0357). Giles (1762–1830) had been a Virginia congressman and senator. His three-year term as governor had ended March 4. Eaton sent Thomas P. Giles (b.1812) a cadet's warrant on March 22.

1. AJ first wrote here simply "I trust ere long the constitution will be restored," then added words to alter the phrasing.

Washington March 13th. 1830—

Dr Sir

I avail myself of the earliest opportunity since the receipt of your favor of the 1rst. instant to thank you for it.

The little boon you have requested on the solicitation of your son will be granted with pleasure. He will shortly receive his warrant, of which you may apprise him.

Altho our political horison is at present a little clouded with the storms of consolidation, and other federal signs, I do not despair of the republic. I have great confidence in the virtue of the people by which our legislation will, I trust, be gradually brought back to the doctrine and practice of 98—we must look to the people for a more just discrimination of the powers granted to the General Government, and those reserved to the states.

You are now in the bosom of retirement. I congratulate you upon your enjoyment of it. altho the sufferer of much bodily affliction, you will derive from it a higher stimulus in the contemplation of the indulgence, wisdom, and mercy of Providence. It is the balm of declining years to know that they are silently approaching a Government in which there will be no need of the checks and restrictions by which we vainly strive to guard against the abuses, and corruptions, of our fellow men. That yours may be as sweet as human infirmity will admit, is the sincere prayer of one who has ever esteemed you, and will always take pleasure in hearing from you[.] your friend & fellow citizen

Andrew Jackson

ALS, PHi (15-0355).

From *Spencer Darwin Pettis*

March 15. 1830

Sir,

I take the liberty of recommending to you, Finis Ewing of Missouri to be Register of the Land Office at Lexington Missouri, in place of J S. Findlay. Mr Ewing is of a character entirely unexceptionable & in all respects qualified for the office. The present incumbent is rendered wholly unfit by reason of intemperance. Mr Ewing appointment will be approved by all discreet men—very Respectfully your obd Servt

Sp Pettis

[Endorsed by AJ:] nomination of Mr. Ewing 16th. March 1830   A. J.

ALS, DNA-RG 46 (15-0366). Jonathan Smith Findlay (1778–1832) had been register of the Lexington land office since 1823. AJ removed him and nominated Ewing on March 16.

To *Samuel Delucenna Ingham*

March 16th. 1830—

My Dr Sir

I have recd. your note of this day & sincerely regret to learn the Mr. Findly *removed*, is brother to Govr. & Genl Findly—when you read the recommendation of Mr Pettis you will find that he requests the removal of Mr Findley & the appointment of Mr Ewing because the incumbent Mr Findley *is incompetant from intemperance to discharge the duties of the office*—Col Benton has coincided with Mr. P. in this request—This charge therefore coming from such a high source could not be overlooked consistant with the rule that intemperate men cannot be permitted to remain in office, civil, naval, nor military, we must pursue principle, & deal out uniform justice to all, altho I regret when it falls upon the connection of our friends. yours respectfully

Andrew Jackson

ALS, PHi (15-0376). *Pennsylvania Magazine of History and Biography* 9 (1885): 239. Findlay's brothers were former Pennsylvania governor William Findlay (1768–1846) and Ohio congressman James Findlay (1770–1835).

From James Alexander Hamilton

New York March 16th 1830

My dear Sir,

We have news from London as late at the 10 ultimo embracing the Kings Speech and the debates thereon, a part of which together with the former I have the pleasure to enclose to you, as also to send you the following extract on the subject of your message from a private letter written by Messrs Daniel Crommelin & son the Bankers in amsterdam who made the late loan to the ohio canal addressed to Mr T W Ludlow of this City.[1] These Gentlemen deservedly rank first among their countrymen as to wealth and intelligence—"The Presidents Message"—"which seems generally to have made a good impression on the European Public—and which certainly is able, correct and manly & cannot but create good will with all that are well disposed in a Country and a government whose first magistrate comes forward with such sentiments   The Message is indicative also of the General prosperity of the Country we hope to see the messages during many years fraught on the whole in the spirit of the present one"—"The United States Bank"—"If that establishment be dissolved we suppose Government will have to make some arrangement to carry on its concerns"—"The Government evidently wants some such financial agent for manifold purposes"—

These are the opinions of men uninfluenced by political considerations and are therefore the more to be valued as evidence of the views of that mass of the honest and intelligent portion of Mankand who have the deepest interest in good government

It is a singular thing to see Mr Peel in the house of Commons quoting the opinions of an American President in order to sustain himself and his party with his own countrymen.[2]

You will observe that Wellington admits that their deep & general dis[t]ress in some measure results from "*foreign competition*" a most extraordinary admission of the effect our Tariff System and you will further

observe that the King invokes his Parliament not to forget what is due to
the inviolability of the Public credit—This latter and last paragraph of the
speech proves that there has been an extensive and growing disposition to
releve themselves from the public burthens either by reducing the Interest
upon the debt or otherwise to tamper with public faith—[3]

I have intended to write to you at large in relation to the state of things
across the water which I consider as uncommonly interresting to us in many
points of view and indeed so much so that the attention of an American
Statesman cannot be diverted from them for a moment; but my fear of
trespassing upon your time already so over burthened has detered me.

The excitement in France from plethora & a Spirit of Liberty and in
England from Starvation cannot fail to produce important results—

The Crown of Greece is the apple of discord between these powers and
the great Northern Bear.

With the truest attachment I remain your friend & svt

James A Hamilton

[Endorsed by AJ:] Col. Hamilton on subject of our relations with
England—

ALS, DLC (37). Hamilton *Reminiscences*, pp. 161–62.

1. Daniel Crommelin & Sons was a prominent Dutch banking firm that had brokered a
loan of $1,500,000 to finance construction of the Chesapeake and Ohio Canal. New York
financier Thomas William Ludlow (1795–1878) was their American representative.

2. Besides praising AJ's cordial expressions toward Britain, Home Secretary Robert Peel
in his February 4 speech had parried criticisms of his government by quoting AJ's annual
message to prove that Britain's recent commercial distress was shared in the U.S. and that
the two countries had pursued similar policies toward Dom Miguel of Portugal (*Hansard's
Parliamentary Debates*, 2d ser., 22:103–5).

3. George IV's speech from the throne to open Parliament on February 4 acknowledged "Distress . . . among the Agricultural and Manufacturing Classes in some Parts of
the United Kingdom," but concluded by cautioning against remedies that would "relax the
Determination which you have uniformly manifested to maintain inviolate the Public Credit,
and thus to uphold the high Character and the permanent Welfare of the Country." Prime
Minister Wellington in debate blamed depressed manufactures on "competition abroad"
rather than governmental neglect (*Hansard's Parliamentary Debates*, 2d ser., 22:3–4, 37).

From Francis Preston

Tuesday Morg. Mar. 16th. 1830

Dear Genl.

I have again read the Document with great care and attention, which
with the free and full conversation of yesterday has confirmed me in the
opinion that Mrs. Eaton is a persecuted woman and that for political
effect. Truth, time and correct deportment are all powerfull, and will
prevail

I intended yesterday to have congratulated you on your Birth day, but entirely forgot it—permit me now Sir to say that I hope you will enjoy many of them, even as you did on yesterday in good health, fine spirits and with a *Sincere friend*—[1]
I am off tomorrow. Adieu.

Frans Preston

[Endorsed by AJ:] Genl Prestons note March 16th. 1830—

ALS, DLC (37).
   1. AJ had turned 63 on March 15.

To Louis McLane

(copy)

March 17th. 1830—

Dear Sir,
   I had the satisfaction this morning to receive your notes of February 6th. & January 22d. last, the first offering to my acceptance the Lectures of Mr. Nassau William Senior, and the other Mr. Watson's plan of preventing ships foundering at sea
   These evidences of the estimation in which I am held by Gentlemen wholly unknown to me before deserve a return of my thanks which I beg you to convey to them. To an individual who has struggled the greater portion of his life against the adverse sentiments of his own countrymen, the assurance that the ultimate attainment of ~~different relations~~ their approbation ~~was attended abroad~~ obtains the sanction of those whose talents in the service of mankind are not confined to any country, cannot but be gratifying. If without the imputation of vanity I may be permitted thus to value the favorable expressions which you have communicated, it is not without a corresponding sense of the increased obligation which they impose ~~upon me~~ to persevere in ~~that the~~ a course of action which may terminate my public life without disappointing them. To do this is more than I can expect from my humble talents, but dependent as they are upon the cooperation of the other branches of the Government, and the aid of my friend I must not anticipate less for the character of my administration. The kind salutations of the Ladies &c &c[1]
Present & to Mrs. & Mr. Ml

Draft in AJ Donelson's hand, DLC (38). Ralph Watson had inscribed a copy of his *Plan for Preventing Ships Foundering at Sea* to AJ as "the Patron of Science, and Promoter of Your Nation's glory and general welfare" (THer).
   1. This last phrase is in AJ's hand.

From *Greenwood Leflore and David Folsom*

Council Ground Choctaw Nation March 18 1830—

To Our Father the President of the United States.

Your Red Children of the Choctaw Nation have heard the talk of their Father the President. We were told that the State of Mississippi would extend her laws over us, and, we are not permitted to look to our Father for protection. We are distressed. We see among us the aged warriors who fought for our white brothers many years ago; they tell us that our Great Father Washington promised them that our great father the President would always be the friend of the red people, and we see among us the widows and orphans of warriors who fought for our white brothers under our present father the President, and many of our warriours, yet feel the brotherly hand of our father, when he told them that our white brothers loved us: Our warriors were glad! Our white brothers have lived many years very near to your choctaw children, and when our white brothers told us that they were many in number, and wished land to make bread for their children our fathers heard the talk of their white brothers, and let them have land. Again our white brothers wanted land, and our fathers heard them and let them have land. Our white brothers told us that they were increasing and wanted land; we heard our fathers talk, but our land was small; most of our land we already had given up to our white brothers: where we now live is the place of our fathers homes. Here the bones of our fathers rest. We said we cannot sell our fathers homes, and leave the place of our birth. Our present Father the President told us that his white children would put their laws upon us. They have done so. Our Father tells us that we had better leave our land, and go to a land where he can protect us; and that he cannot protect us upon our present land. We love our land, but we cannot suffer our council fire to be extinguished by submiting to the laws of our white brothers, but to stain our hands with the blood of our white brothers we cannot consent. We never have done so. We know that our warriours are too few to defend ourselves; but our father knows that Choctaws are not affraid to die. Many of them have fought and bled by the side of our Father the President. We ardently wish to live in peace with our white brothers. Many among them love us. We could not think of injuring them were it in our power.

Most of our People have heard and are trying to obay the talk of the Great Spirit. This tells us to love even those who injure us; and that we may live in peace with our white brothers, we have determined to leave our homes, and the land of our fathers, and go to the land were our father promises to protect us. We have sent a talk to our Father the President by our brother David W. Haley; we hope our Father will not think we ask too much of him. It is not the hope of money that influences us to sell our country, but that we may live in peace, and under our own laws. We hope that our Father will send our brother Haley back in haste to tell us, that our Father still loves his Choctaw Children; and that he will do all that we ask of him; and also that he will appoint our brother Haley to go with us to our new home, and live among us as our Agent. We wish soon to hear, as we wish and assure our Father, that in two years we will all, or most of us, be in our new homes if he sanctions our talk sent by our brother Haley. Signed in behalf of the National Council

Greenwood Leflore
David Folsom

DS, DNA-RG 46 (15-0391). Greenwood Leflore (1800–1865) and David Folsom (1791–1847) were chiefs of the Choctaw Nation. Emulating Georgia, Mississippi had moved to assert jurisdiction over its Indian domains and disband tribal governments. In October 1829, AJ had deputed David W. Haley (1793–1857) of Mississippi to visit the Choctaws and Chickasaws and urge them to remove, using the arguments AJ and Eaton had already addressed to the Creeks and Cherokees (*Jackson Papers*, 7:494–95). On March 17, 1830, the day before this address, Leflore, Folsom, and other Choctaws meeting in national council signed a removal treaty which Haley carried to Washington. Mushulatubbe and other Choctaws sent a protest against the treaty to Eaton on March 25 (below). AJ submitted the treaty, accompanied by this address and the protest, to the Senate on May 6 (below).

To John Henry Eaton

March 19th. 1830—

My Dr Sir

I enclose a Resolution from the House of Representatives, which I beg leave to draw your early attention to. The military force now in that section of country being ~~now~~ competant for all the purpose of protection, will be still more so, as the number of emigrants increase—and the late reconciliation between the Mc.Intosh party, & those of the old nation, give proof of the friendly disposition and wishes of those now on the arkansa, that those of the old nation should unite *with them there*.[1]

I have given these hints, that they may be used in the report.

will you ride at 1/2 past noon today   yrs

Andrew Jackson

ALS, DNA-RG 107 (M221-110). A House resolution of March 18 requested information on Indian removal, including past and likely future expense, the condition of the Western country and the disposition of its present Indian occupants toward new arrivals, and the amount of military force necessary to protect emigrants against whites, other Indians, and each other. On April 13 AJ received Eaton's report, enclosing one from Thomas L. McKenney, and transmitted it to the House. Eaton opined that keeping peace would require no increase in frontier military force or expense and that the Creeks, Cherokees, Chickasaws, and Choctaws, having much in common, might "being contiguous, presently become one nation of people" (*HRDoc* 91, 21st Cong., 1st sess., p. 2, Serial 198).

1. McKenney's report predicted that "the Indians in the West would rejoice if their friends in the East would join them" (Serial 198, p. 9).

From Susan Wheeler Decatur

George Town, March 19th 1830—

My dear General,

I am overwhelm'd with despair at the rejection of my claim! and I do think it a most unjust and cruel persecution! From the first establishment of the Navy to the present day, this is the only case in which a vessel of war has been destroy'd whether in battle or from *ship wreck*, in which the Government has fail'd to make compensation; and yet all admit that it was an achievement which laid the foundation of all your Naval glory, and has sav'd millions of dollars to your Treasury! and yet make it the only case in which they have withheld the manifestation of their bounty and gratitude; I am the only individual of my unfortunate class (connected with the Navy) who has not receiv'd a pension; and yet they refuse me the compensation for my husband's services, which in every other instance they have granted without hesitation.

I am sorry to be so troublesome to you my dear General, but you will confer a very great favor upon me if you will have the goodness to call and see me for a few moments—I will be ready to see you on any day and at any hour you may have the goodness to name—My Servant will call at your door tomorrow about nine o Clock, to save you the trouble of sending so far—

I beg you once more, my dear General, to accept the assurance of my cordial gratitude for all the trouble and interest you have taken in my concerns, and to believe me always most sincerely & respectfully yours

S. Decatur

ALS, DLC (38). A bill to award $100,000 to Decatur's crew and their heirs, including $31,412.42 to Susan Decatur, was reported to the House on January 7 but was tabled on March 12 after extensive debate. A motion on May 1 by South Carolina congressman George McDuffie to take it up again was defeated.

From Edmund Pendleton Gaines

Hd qrs Nashville T. March 20, 1830

My Dear General—

The recent difficulties between the Cherokee Indians and Georgia Intruders, with the general threatening aspect of the habitual disturbers of the public peace in that quarter, added to a strong conviction upon my mind that some of our mutual *friends* entertain very erroneous views upon the subject, and that they have either misrepresented or misunderstood my opinions or principles—suggest to me the propriety of appealing direct to you; and of requesting your attention to the remarks which follow:

Although my views in regard to the friendly Indians residing within our limits (as to their natural rights and our duties towards them as enjoined by Treaties as well as by our superior degree of civilization and power, and their want of them) remain the same as expressed in my official Reports of 1825 and 1827;[1] yet, as I understand your views of the subject are in some respects different from mine; and as I constantly, upon every important point of duty call to mind the oath which I have taken; I can have no difficulty beyond that of making myself acquainted with my duties:—the most simple and impressive of which are summed up in one single word, and that word is *"obedience"*—But when acting under the orders of a constitutional commander in chief who I have long been in the habit of respecting, not merely as my most efficient commanding General, but of regarding as an affectionate friend, I cannot but be anxious that my judgment, and my heart, should always go along with my hands, in the discharge of every duty ordered by you; and if the time should ever come (which I should deeply regret) when I shall feel that I cannot cordially obey; then will I without loss of time desire you to supply my place with another.

I take leave now to submit for your consideration a few suggestions, which if approved by you, may tend to accomplish the removal of the Indians, south of us, without any sort of violence, either direct or indirect, being resorted to by the people of Georgia or any other state.

1—Texas was and is a part of Louisiana, as purchased by the United States. We had no constitutional right to divest ourselves of that part of our Territory. It must and will be restored to us. When the people of Texas, who have already much of the democratic *Leaven* amongst them, demand admission into the union, as one of our sovereign & Independent States, they cannot—will not be refused. We want no increase of states in any other way. In this way we shall probably in time have from 24 to 240![2]

2—The several tribes of Indians in the habit of wandering over the country between the head waters of the Sabine, Red and Arkansas Rivers and the Rocky mountain; and who have committed numerous acts of hostility along that border of our Territory, upon our citizens engaged in the trade of that quarter, must be punished before our intercourse with new mexico can be safe, and the coming summer and fall appears to me to be the proper time to punish them.

3—To effect this object, as those Indians consist of near 2000 warriors, all mounted, I would respectfully suggest the propriety of detaching a light Brigade, under that excellent officer General Atkinson—to consist of ten or twelve companies of Regular troops taken from the 1st. 3rd. 6th. and 7. Regiments of Infantry, with six or eight companies of the friendly southern Indians, cherokees, chickasaws choctaws and creeks, to be mounted and to have field and staff officers with captains of the army, and subalterns of their own people.[3]

The employment of the friendly Indians in this way it is believed will answer the twofold purpose of chastising the hostile bands, and at the same time of exploring the country, and acquiring an intimate knowledge of all its advantages & disadvantages. And if their reports are favourable, as I trust they will be, their respective tribes will not be likely long to hesitate in making the exchange, & move thither without delay. But if as some of them now imagine, they should not like the country upon the upper waters of the Red & Arkansas Rivers on our side of the present misplaced boundary; then they may ultimately in that event, decide in favour of a selection within the limits which the anticipated correct boundary will give us.

When the removal of the Indians was first urged by two of your predecessors, I then respectfully, but confidently, solicited them that it might not be attempted without first kindly assisting considerable number of their chiefs and warriors to explore and become well acquainted with the country offered them in return for theirs. I was convinced as I am still convinced that one of the principal obstacles in our way, was, and is an impression on the minds of the Indians that the lands which we offered them would not be such as they would like; and that this impression could only be removed by making them perfectly acquainted with the proffered lands; not by a trip of speculation and drunkenness, under the direction of a man remarkable for nothing but his known imbecility, in war & in peace,—but by a sober, careful, tour of Inspection under an officer whose qualifications and morals are above suspicion, and who can be held responsible for his conduct. Wishing you health & happiness, I am with perfect respect your unchanged & unchangeable friend.

Edmund P. Gaines
Major Genl by B.

ALS, DNA-RG 107 (M222-27).

1. Gaines appended a lengthy discussion of Indian policy to his report of an 1827 Army inspection tour. Deeming the present system "radically defective throughout," he extolled the Indian character and, on grounds of efficacy and humanity as well as military security, urged educating and civilizing the Southern Indians where they were rather than driving them westward (*SDoc* 101, 20th Cong., 2d sess., pp. 52–62, Serial 182).

2. The 1819 Adams-Onís treaty, by which the U.S. acquired Florida, also defined a southwestern boundary between the U.S. and Spanish Mexico, which included Texas. The Senate voted to ratify by 34 to 0. The idea that the U.S. had actually purchased Texas with Louisiana in 1803 and that the 1819 treaty unwarrantably surrendered it for Florida gained currency later and was endorsed by AJ in 1829 (*Jackson Papers*, 7:270–72).

3. Brevet Brigadier General Henry Atkinson (1782–1842) commanded at Jefferson Barracks, Mo.

From Daniel Sturgeon et al.

[Speculation about Jackson's willingness to stand for a second term in 1832 had begun almost with his election. To bring him out as a candidate, William B. Lewis composed a draft of this address for adoption by Jackson members of the Pennsylvania legislature and sent it to Samuel C. Stambaugh, who revised and circulated it for signature (Parton, 3:297–302). The sixty-eight signers were a majority of the legislature's 133 members.]

HARRISBURG, March 20, 1830.

To his Excellency, Andrew Jackson, President of the United States.

DEAR SIR:

The undersigned, members of the legislature of Pennsylvania, before closing the duties assigned them by their constituents, beg leave to tender to you their best wishes for your health and happiness, and to express to you the confidence reposed by them in the sound republican principles which mark the course of your administration. The second political revolution effected in 1829, is progressing in a way to attain those great results which were fondly anticipated, and which in the end, we ardently hope, will tend to cement in stronger bonds the republican feelings of the country. In a free government like ours, parties must and will exist—it should be so, inasmuch as it serves to make those who are dominant, vigilant and active in the discharge of the important duties which give life, health and activity to the great principles by which as a free people we should be governed. If the voice of Pennsylvania, which has recently been prominently and efficiently exerted in the election of our present distinguished chief magistrate can have influence, it will as heretofore be exerted in inducing you to permit your name and distinguished services again to be presented to the American people. We deem it of importance to the maintenance of correct republican principles, that the country should not thus early be again drawn into a warm and virulent contest as to who shall be your successor. If the people can indulge a hope that in acceding to their wishes as heretofore, the warmth of former contests may be spared, they will be able to repose in peace and quiet, and before the end of your second term, will expect with confidence that the great principles of governmental reform will be so harmonized and arranged, that the affairs of the nation, for the future, will move on certainly, peacefully and happily. Expressing what we feel and believe to be the language of our constituents, we claim to indulge the expectation that your avowed principle "neither to seek nor decline to serve your country in public office," will still be adhered to—that thereby the people may obtain repose, and toward the termination of your second term, be better prepared to look around and ascertain into whose hands can be best confided the care and guardianship of our dearest rights, our happiness and independence.[1]

This communication is not made with the intention of obtaining from you any declaration at this time upon the subject. We are aware that persons would be found to call such declaration premature before some general expression of satisfaction in relation to the course you have pursued had been exhibited, and time afforded for it to be evinced. Pennsylvania heretofore first to express her attachment upon this subject, seeks only to maintain the position she has assumed, and to express through her representatives her continued confidence in your stern political integrity, and the wise, judicious, republican measures of your administration; and to cherish the hope that the country may again be afforded the opportunity of having those services, the benefit of which she is now so happily enjoying. On this subject, sir, we speak not only our own sentiments and opinions, but feel that the people will accord to the suggestion, and every where respond to what we have declared.

Wishing you long life, health and happiness, we remain your friends and fellow- citizens.

Daniel Sturgeon,	Geo. Emlen,
Wm. G. Hawkins,	Jno. Blair,
Frederick Hambright,	N. P. Fetterman,
Samuel Houston,	Garrick Mallery,
Daniel A. Bertolet,	Henry Logan,

[Names of fifty-eight more legislators follow.]

Printed, Harrisburg *Pennsylvania Reporter and Democratic Herald*, April 23, 1830 (mAJs; 15-0423). Parton, 3:299–301. Sturgeon (1789–1878) was speaker of the Pennsylvania senate and later a U.S. senator.

1. Solicited in 1823 to stand for the presidency, AJ had famously replied that "My undeviating rule of conduct through life . . . has been neither to seek, or decline public invitations to office" (*Jackson Papers*, 5:253).

From Martin Van Buren

March 20 –30

Dear Sir

This will be handed to you by Dr Parker of Massachusetts who is the father in law of Mr Dimond Commercial Agent at Portau Prince & a gentleman of much worth & respectability. He wishes a salary to be allowed to Mr Dimond as was done to his predecessor. I have informed him that that question was last summer submitted to you & refused by you on the ground that Congress ought to make the appropriation if it was necessary & that you were indisposed to make such allowances out of the contingent fund. I have also informed him that an application has been made for the removal of his son in law & the appointment of Mr Irwin—the nephew of Genl Findlay but that that application had been denied.[1] Mr Parker however wishes an opportunity to pay his respects to you. He is a friend of much worth & consideration[.] Yours

MVB

ALS, THi (15-0425). Francis Moore Dimond (1796–1859) of Rhode Island was U.S. consular commercial agent in Port-au-Prince, Haiti, a post that paid fees but no salary. His wife's father was Benjamin Parker (1759–1845). In the absence of an American diplomat or consul in Haiti, Dimond's predecessor, Andrew Armstrong, had performed extra functions and received a $1,000 salary from the State Department contingent fund.

1. John Ramsey Irwin was a Baltimore merchant residing at Port-au-Prince. He had been recommended to replace Dimond, partly on grounds that Adams had earlier refused him the post for his politics (DNA-RG 59, M639-12). He was the son of Archibald Irwin, whose sister Jane had married Ohio congressman James Findlay.

Lewis Boudinot Hunter to Thomas S. Hamersley

Washington City,
March 20. 1830.

My dear Sir,

I have been requested by a friend to state what I know concerning you, your character, &c. I do so cheerfully; and conceiving that it may perhaps be of some service to you, I make my statement in the form of a communication to yourself.

I have had the pleasure of your acquaintance since July 1828, when I joined the Frigate Hudson, and during the time that has since elapsed, I have considered your conduct such as became an officer and a gentleman. I have always understood that you held a high place in the confidence of our Commander, until the unfortunate but unavoidable affair with several officers of the British Naval Service, at Rio de Janeiro. In that occurrence, I received from two eye-witnesses, who were not supposed to have been very friendly to Americans, the most favourable account of your behaviour. On the next day, myself being present, I can truly say your conduct was correct, dignified and manly, and such as raised your character in the estimation of all present.

On our return to the ship, I had reason to believe, and do still believe, that the affair was greatly misrepresented to the commander by an individual, in whose defence, when glaring insults were offered to himself and his country, you so gallantly, but unfortunately, as it afterwards appeared, stood forth. What were the views of this man in thus disgracing himself, I shall leave to others to determine.[1] Certain it is that the course pursued yourself was in my own, and I believe in the opinion of all who were privy to the circumstances, highly unjust and tyrannical. In the cruel and rigorous confinement afterwards endured by you, I know of very few officers in the Navy, who would have conducted themselves with more propriety than yourself did. Hated and persecuted for your political opinions and your defence of friends whose characters were wantonly aspersed by a faction, you were drawn into arguments, the warmth of which was represented to your disadvantage, as I firmly believe, by those in the confidence of, and of the same political party with, the Commander.[2] From these circumstances all your after difficulties may be said to have arisen.

In what I have said above, I have been actuated by a sincere desire that the true cause of your troubles should be known. In them, you have the sympathy of every just and honorable man who is acquainted with the details of your last cruize. Ardently hoping that you may continue to fill the station you have so much contributed to adorn, I am, With great esteem & respect, Your friend,

L. B. Hunter

[Endorsed on packet by AJ:] The case of Lt Hamersly   From the good character of this officer sustained as within—and the clear expression of propriety of his conduct on the last interview with the British officers, lays a good ground for the remission of the Sentence   referred to the Sec. of the Navy   A J

ALS, DNA-RG 125 (M273-25). Hunter (1804–1887) was a Navy assistant surgeon. Thomas S. Hamersley, a Navy lieutenant since 1816, was court-martialed in 1829 for drunkenness, disorderly conduct, insubordination, and brawling with British officers at Rio de Janeiro. He was found guilty and sentenced to be cashiered. AJ approved the proceedings on March 6. However, on March 4 Hamersley had protested to Branch that he was tried for resisting a "system of tyranny and oppression" by senior officers and for defending AJ against their "slanderous imputations" (DNA-RG 125, M273-25). Branch suspended the sentence on March 10, and over the next month he and AJ received appeals for leniency from naval officers and other notables vouchsafing Hamersley's good character and citing extenuating circumstances. AJ referred the matter to Branch for further consideration on April 9, but the sentence was allowed to stand and Hamersley was dismissed from the Navy in 1831.

1. The fight began when one of a party of British officers with whom Hamersley and acting sailing master John Colhoun had been drinking exclaimed "the damned Yankee Flag was furled" when the two Americans got up to leave. Hamersley, Hunter, and others returned and exchanged words, but no blows, with the British officers the next day. At trial, Colhoun testified that Hamersley had started the fight, while Hamersley claimed he had only joined it to extricate Colhoun.

2. Captain John O. Creighton commanded the frigate *Hudson* and preferred the charges against Hamersley. Officers serving under Creighton subsequently brought charges against him, including "excessive tyranny and oppression" in verbally abusing Hamersley and confining him for seven months before trying him (DNA-RG 125, M273-26). Creighton wrote AJ about the charges against him on March 30 (below).

To Martin Van Buren

March 22nd. 1830—

My Dr. Sir,

I have hastily run my eye over the enclosed report of Mr Wirt—and the order of the court—you will please apply thro' our minister at Madrid for copies of the original orders & instructions in those documents refered to, and also, instruct the atto for the District of Louisiana, to have careful inquiry, & search made for the orders refered to, which may be on file in the archives at N. Orleans. yr friend

Andrew Jackson

ALS, DNA-RG 59 (15-0432; T1212-3). Former attorney general William Wirt (1772–1834) had been engaged to defend the U.S. in suits to confirm private land titles based on purported Spanish colonial grants. On March 17, 1830, the Supreme Court held over two cases from Missouri, brought by claimants Julie Soulard and John Smith T, to allow time to obtain authentic copies of documents from the Spanish archives that would clarify the legitimacy of the claims. Wirt reported the decision to Ingham on March 20. On May 14 Van Buren instructed Cornelius P. Van Ness, the U.S. minister to Spain, to procure the needed documents as quickly as possible (*SDoc* 7, 24th Cong., 1st sess., pp.18–19, Serial 279). In 1836 the Court upheld Soulard's claim and rejected Smith T's. The district attorney at New Orleans was John Slidell (1793–1871).

From Samuel Houston

If the President deems it fit to appoint Colonel Arbuckle, Col. Chouteau, & myself (without fee or reward) to treat with the Pawanees; and to make peace between them, and the Osages, tranquility will reign in the Priara's.[1] The whole western Tribes will be at Peace. The lines of the Different Tribes on Arkansas can be laid of and harmony established between the Indian Tribes, and an acquiescense in the wishes of the Goverment, & the Executive insured. So long as Hamtramck is permitted to remain Agent for the Osages they can never prosper! They will only await the day to redress wrongs which they receive thro' him.[2] I will have no reward, nor do I wish to have any thing to do with money matters. If the Pawanees should receive of the Govt (and Kemanchees) from 5 to $10,000 Dollars per annum it would save the expense, of a guard to the Caravans[3]

And let the commissioners make quarterly reports to the War Department, of all their proceedings, and the reasons—Let them be authorised to employ Maj: Langham, or Colonel Arbuckle to select from his command a Surveyor for running off the Indian lands—and be instructed in all things to regard the objects of the Government, in the fair fulfillment of Treaties, and where the letter can not be pursued to follow the spirit of the Treaties.[4]

I will pledge my life upon the benificale result of the above suggestions, both to the Indians, & the Executive of the Union!

I am aware that it is not the most popular position for me to occupy in relation to the Indians, but justice and a regard to their real interests requires of me both risque, and sacrifice if necessary.

Sam Houston

[Endorsed by AJ:] Genl Houstons Letter—to be attended with its enclosure—[5]

ADS, DNA-RG 75 (M234-433). *Writings of Sam Houston*, 1:146–47. Sporadic violence had marked relations between the Osages and neighboring Indians for years. In February 1830 the *Arkansas Gazette* reported an Osage attack on a Pawnee village on the upper Arkansas in which nearly a hundred Pawnees were slain.

1. Colonel Mathew Arbuckle (1776–1851) commanded at Cantonment Gibson in Arkansas Territory (now Oklahoma). Auguste Pierre Chouteau (1786–1838) was a well-known fur trader.

2. The Osages had accused their agent John Francis Hamtramck (1798–1858), a former Army officer, of cheating them. Eaton dismissed Hamtramck on March 31, citing his failure to reside with the Indians and keep them at peace (DNA-RG 75, M21-6). In April AJ appointed subagent Paul L. Chouteau, brother of Auguste, to replace him.

3. Trading caravans on the thousand-mile Santa Fe road from Missouri to New Mexico had been subject to frequent Indian attacks. In 1829 the Army began providing armed escorts as far as the Mexican border.

4. Angus Lewis Langham (c1788–1834), an Army major in the War of 1812, had surveyed western Indian boundaries for the War Department.

5. Houston enclosed letters from Marcus Palmer and William F. Vail seeking support for their Indian mission schools (DNA-RG 75, M234-774).

From John Stevens

Hoboken Mar: 22 1830

His [Excl]y. [A]ndrew Jackson Esqr. [Pre]st. U.S.

It is now more than a dozen years ago since I ventured to suggest to Government the necessity of reform in respect to the Navy Department, both as to economy and efficiency by the introduction of an entire new species of naval tactics, viz, by the use of steam vessels propelled by steam.[1] Whilst the present Navy Board are continued in active employ nothing to any this purpose *[can be effec]*ted. Let these Nautical Gentlemen then be promoted to the rank of Admirals, and if a should an annuity for life be given to each of them to the amount of $10,000 a piece; nay, we may safely raise it to $100,000 each, and still the country would be immense gainers. No man whose prejudices are so violent and inveterate, as the your nautical man—as an old seafaring Man and the reform now contemplated never can, in such hands be carried into effect. But the absolute necessity, at the [pr]esent juncture of *[this]* vital reform cannot admit of a particle of doubt. ~~It will~~ The struggle must *[. . .]* the commencement of the next naval conflict, and wo be to that naval power who shall then remain unprepared to meet it.

*[It is as]*serted in the Southern Review that "one of the most experienced and scientific of our officers not long since visited Europe, for the purpose of looking into the condition of the naval establishments on that continent." "It is," says this ~~Gentleman~~ "experienced & scientific officer," "believed ~~also~~, that both France & England have made provision of steam-engines, preparitory to the [introdu]ction of steam-vessels into future naval warfare."[2]

I shall say no more, but merely that as I so long ago had the honor of suggesting this gigantic improvement to Government, for which, however, I have been most scandalously vilified I would now *[ask]* the indulgence of a hearing to the proposal I am *[. . .]* to take the liberty of bring forward

After the present Navy Board have been descently laid on the shelf, pardon the liberty I take of suggesting to your Excellency the propriety and expediency of appointing my Son R. L. S. as an independant and special engi[neer] for superintending the construction and fitting ~~all Vessels~~ up of steam-engines, and other machinery &c [in]tended to be employed on board of "steam vessels in future naval warfare." But further, should the General Government ~~be inclined~~ finally determine to establi[sh] rail-ways along the Post Roads, that the superintend[ing] thereof be also ~~bestowed upon~~ committed to him, as notoriously the mo[st] capable.[3]

This you may consider as a mighty modest sort of a request on my part in behalf of my son—But all I ha[ve] to say, in justification of this my modest assurance, is tha[t] In the first place I consider him as by far the fittest man in every respect to be found any where for ~~such a business~~ an employment requiring such uncommon science *[. . .]* and such preeminent dexterity and tact in the execution & science. And, in the next place, I can assure you that of the proposal I now ma[ke] he is entirely ignorant. Nay! I have reason to doubt h[is] acceptance, were the offer made him—

But I will not detain Your Excellency longer than will be barely necessary to express my profound respect and to assure you how much I am your Obedt Servt.

Until I had finished the above letter, it did not occur to me that Robt L Stevens as the ingenious inventor of the elongated exploding shells, ~~my son Robt~~ was, in every point of view, best entitled to such an office[. In] deed, to preserve secretcy, it becomes absolutely necessary that, as far as regards the manufacturing of these shell, the business be executed under his immediate superintendance & control.[4] And as [for] the r[ail]-ways— You may rest assured that under his active guidance in less than 3 years they [. . .] to pervade the whole of these U.S. and thus we shall [. . .] knit together as one people

AL draft, NjHi (mAJs). Stevens (1749–1838) was a renowned inventor and engineer who pioneered the development of steam navigation and railroads in the United States. He wrote AJ again on April 7 (below).
    1. Stevens had written President Monroe on June 13, 1817, proposing to defend the U.S. with oceangoing steam frigates that would mount fewer and more powerful guns than sailing warships at a fraction of their cost. He warned that this "entire revolution in Naval Tactics" would be resisted by professional officers (DNA-RG 59, M179-37).
    2. Stevens quoted from pages 191 and 194 of an article on the Navy in the February-May 1830 issue of the Charleston, S.C., quarterly *The Southern Review*.
    3. Engineer and inventor Robert Livingston Stevens (1787–1856) had followed his father as a leading innovator of improvements in steam transportation. In April 1830 he was made president of the new Camden and Amboy Rail Road and Transportation Company.
    4. In 1818 the War Department had contracted with Robert L. Stevens to produce elongated percussion shells of his own invention.

Roley McIntosh and Benjamin Hawkins to John Henry Eaton

Washington City
22nd March 1830

Our Father,
    When we came to the City, it was on the business of our people who are far from you and therefore they sent us to speak to you in their behalf and that you might remove their troubles from them.
    We spoke to the Great Father, and to you also, and we were heard, and you spoke kind words to us. We were glad and rejoiced, because the cloud of many sorrows seemed as if it would pass by, and with it our troubles would also pass away. It was but a dream. Troubles yet darken our hopes, and our sorrows rest upon us like the foot of an enemy.
    Colonel McKenney wrote to us some days since and told us that we had told untruths, and that we had no claims for the money which we asked out of the annuities of the old nation, and the promises which were made to us under Treaties. We need not write about our troubles when this man has to act upon our claims. He has always hated us and he yet hates us. We must be still in our distress until our Father can look upon his Red Children, for he will do them justice. General Jackson has never told his Red Children a lie, nor has scolded them but in war, and when they had struck his white children. Colonel McKenney hates us in peace. He is angry with us because we do not love Colonel Crowell. We have no cause to love him. He has slain our friend,[1] and we will not praise him.
    The claims which we made, we will still insist upon, and we will tell our people what we have done when we meet them. Our Great Father says our lands shall be good and plenty for our people.

Colonel McKenney says some white men "injected" bad notions into us but we don't believe that he thinks so. This was told him by our Enemy and he has sent us his words, and tries to persuade us that we don't know what we want. He scolds us very much because we ask for what we think just but he praises his friend as much as he abuses the Indians. He says money has been paid out to us by the Government, but we have not received it, and surely if the agents of Government keep the money and do not pay it to the Indians, the promises of the Treaties were of no use to the Indians an[d] it were better they should have *none*.

Colonel McKenney says that we are trying to *thwart* the wishes of the President. Now this he does not believe. He tries to make our Great Father angry with us, by saying that white men have made us say all that we have said to you our Father. It is not so, for the Treaties we claim under are many, and white men do not trouble themselves to see when the Indian has been wronged. But the Indian does not forget a promise when it is once made to him, nor can the Mc'Intosh party forget that Mr McKenneys hand has laid heavy upon them.

He says we were not told to speak against Colonel Crowell when we left our homes, and that Mr Blake told him so.[2] We do not know whether Mr McKenney wrote that part of his talk, and therefore we will not blame him for it; and if he did, it was done to praise his friend and to make us ashamed and unhappy. We say again that we do not wish Colonel Crowell ever to have any thing to do with us, or for us, and if you and our Great Father will send us a Good Agent and keep Colonel Crowell where he can never reach us we will pay him a salary of $1500. every year out of our annuity as long as he lives and be made happy by the swap.

To shew our Father that we have told no lie about Colonel Crowell, we will lay matters before his eyes, and let him look upon them and be satisfied that we speak the truth.

Last June we heard that Colonel Crowell was to be sent to us, as our agent and we were miserable and had no peace in us   We sent a Memorial to our Great Father. It was signed by twenty five of our Chiefs, and we came to Cantonment Gibson to get Colonel Arbuckle and the officers to witness it. They did so, and it is now in the office. The words which we put in the Memorial were these. "Another subject of deep sorrow to us is the information that Colonel Crowell is to be sent to us as our Agent. This we hope is not true. Nor can we believe that General Jackson would make us so unhappy. He well knows the sorrows that we suffered in the old nation. He has not forgotten the murder of Mc'Intosh. He knows that his blood yet lies on the ground unburied.

Mc'Intosh was a warrior of General Jackson. The General told him he would protect him, but Jackson was far off, and Colonel Crowell near at hand. He whispered to the enemies of Mc'Intosh. He pointed at him and he perished. McIntosh has friends and children yet living. They cannot be happy when they think of his death, nor can they ever receive the man who caused (it)   If he were amongst us the same men are yet living that killed Mc'Intosh and the Agent might point at another Mc'Intosh. Whenever we think of Colonel Crowell our hearts are sorrowful. We hope General Jackson will not make us miserable and that he will keep this man from among us. Our miseries in the old nation drove us from the land of our Fathers, and we hope General Jackson will make our new homes happy. Division amongst us at this time would prevent the old nation from coming and if a good Agent is given to us and we are happy the people of the old nation will flock to us, to share our happiness."[3]

You then wrote in answer to our talk above stated and told us that Colonel Crowell should not come amongst us.[4] This made our people happy until we heard in Council from Hillabee Tustennuggee who came to us last summer that when himself and the Chiefs of the Euphawlees went to see Colonel Brearley, and to remove to Arkansas, that Colonel Crowell told them that their Father had turned against the Tribe on Arkansas, and had removed their Agent and that he, (Colonel Crowell) was appointed in his place, and if they would return to their homes and stay for one year that a party by that time strong enough would move over and be able to put down the McIntosh party, and rule the Nation. But the Chiefs told Colonel Crowell that they had sold all their provision and stock, and must move over to Arkansas   This was told to the McIntosh party, and we will ask our Father if we can love Colonel Crowell or wish him to be our Agent. But we have more cause than this to dislike him. The Delegation of Creeks which we met at this place assured us that Colonel Crowell and Captain Walker did know that McIntosh was to be killed, and that they did both wish it done.[5] It was done and the man who commanded the party was at one time prepared to tell all about it, but that a man persuaded him not to do so. We believe these things to be true and if they were not so we cannot know it. We know that the Indians of themselves never killed a Chief like McIntosh. But bad men are in all countries and there were white men who would have killed General Jackson, if they had dared to have done so, and why not kill a Red Chief when it is their inter-est to do so?

Now, can our Father think that we have no ca[use] of complaint, when we hear and believe these things, and when Colonel Crowell told us that our Father had told him that he should be Agent on Arkansas if he wished to be so. We have told our Great Father since we came to the City that Colonel Crowell was our enemy, and that we did not wish him to send Colonel Crowell to us, but some man that would be our friend and do us justice.

Mr McKenny has told our Father and us that we are trying to defeat the Executive by what we are doing, and to prevent the Creeks from moving to Arkansas. There would be no use in saying to our Father this is not true, for our Father can see that Colonel McKenny is trying to set him mad at us, and make him think that the Agent and himself are good men and friends to General Jackson. We never said they were not friends to General Jackson, but we say they are both enemies to the McIntosh party.

If our Father would believe what Colonel McKenney says to us, and do what he wants done, we would be worse than Negroes. He says if we or any other Indians should send any thing to our Father, that it should be "sent back to them, and if the Agents prove incompetent or negligent, or in any manner unfaithful, the remedy is with the Executive." Now we will ask our Father to think of this business, and see how the poor Indians would be situated, if this rule were pursued as Colonel McKenny wishes it to be. Say for instance that the Agent chooses to injure an Indian either in person or property, or to withhold the annuities, and monies of the nation and send on forged receipts. Would the Agent tell these acts to the Government? No, he *would* not, yet he is the "official channel," and the Indians dare "seek" none other, or if they do, the "communication *is* to be sent back to them" as Colonel McKenney would have it. Would not this course destroy even the hope of the Indian? But even this according to Col. McKenney would not have "so deleterious a tendency as to allow these people to communicate by and through whomsoever they may incline persons wholly irresponsible, When the Government keeps Agents to serve them at its cost, who are bound by bond and the oath of office to act correctly."[6] Now if an officer thus bound should violate all bonds official and moral no report but his own of that violation is to be regarded if the opinion of Colonel McKenney is adopted by our Father. And how then is his corruption to be known? Father, this is the man who tells you and us that we wish to trouble the Great Father and make divisions among our people   The party of McIntosh and their youngest children love General Jackson, and the Creeks are all tired of troubles and quarrels, and if they dare speak what they think they would be glad to have the man who caused them taken away from them, that they might be united and happy. We hope our Great Father will take him away from us, and we will pay him out of our own money his salary as long as he may live.

We will not trouble our Father any more at this time, but assure him and our Great Father that we will always listen to his words, and that his counsel shall light our path, and we will hold our White Brothers by the hand, and if they fall we will fall with them.

Roley McIntosh   his X   mark
Benjamin Hawkins

[Endorsed by AJ:] The complaints of the Arkansa Creeks are heard their request will be granted to them A. J.   refered to the secretary of war— A J.

DS, DNA-RG 75 (M234-236). This appeal responded to, and quoted from, Thomas L. McKenney's March 2 letter to Eaton (DNA-RG 75, M21-6) rebutting McIntosh and Hawkins's previous approach to AJ on February 25 (above).

1. William McIntosh.

2. McKenney had charged that the complaints against Crowell were hatched in Washington by ill-designing whites. He claimed that the Western Creeks' instructions to McIntosh and Hawkins said nothing against Crowell, and that subagent Luther Blake (c1799–1861), who was present when they were drawn up, had assured him the Indians' real feelings were "directly the reverse." The Western Creeks' November 28 written authorization to McIntosh and Hawkins, witnessed by Blake, did not mention Crowell (DNA-RG 75, M234-236).

3. Roley McIntosh et al. to AJ, June 22, 1829 (*Jackson Papers*, 7:296–99).

4. Eaton's reply of August 3, 1829, to the Western Creeks' June 22 appeal did not mention Crowell, but promised a replacement for David Brearley who "will alike regard the interest of the Indians and the business of the Government" (DNA-RG 75, M21-6). AJ had since appointed and then withdrawn John Campbell.

5. William Walker (c1774–1836), a son-in-law of the late Creek chief Big Warrior, was employed as a subagent for the removal of Eastern Creeks.

6. McKenney had used this language in protesting the reception of Indian complaints made through unofficial channels, which he said fatally undermined the agents' authority.

To Anthony Butler

[In October 1829 Jackson recalled U.S. minister to Mexico Joel R. Poinsett, whom the Mexican government had accused of meddling in the country's internal affairs, and replaced him with Anthony Butler as chargé d'affaires. State Department instructions to Poinsett and then Butler stressed the importance of acquiring Texas and proposed possible terms of purchase. In private letters to Butler, Jackson suggested strategies for winning Mexican confidence and managing the negotiation (Jackson Papers, 7:364–68, 487–90, 498–99).

On January 5 Butler wrote Van Buren "a private unofficial letter" reporting that the new Mexican government of President Anastasio Bustamante was partial to Britain and hostile to the U.S., either out of antipathy to Poinsett or aversion to republicanism (Butler Papers, TxU). Butler vowed to "feel my way" with "vigilance and caution" and make friends as best he could, but offered little hope of a successful negotiation until the government stabilized and feelings subsided.

Below are Jackson's undated draft of a reply and the finished letter of March 23. An intermediate draft by Andrew J. Donelson, dated March 17 (DLC-72), approached the final version.]

Col Butler

your letter of the 5th. of Janry has been recd. & read with attention. I regret the revolutionary Spirit that disturbs the repose of Mexico, & is likely to jeopardise if not change its republican government.

The hostile temper of its present rulers towards us, I sincerely regret, as it may interrupt that friendly intercourse, & prevent those commercial regulations from being concluded so necessary to the prosperity of both and all important to the peace, prosperity & tranquity of Mexico. Still, Sir I do not despair that your prudence ~~by~~ in not interfering with ~~the party feelings~~ either party, or the internal concerns of that republic, but you will ~~acquire~~ regain that confidence ~~in~~ with its rulers that the ~~imprudence~~ incautious conduct of your predecessor ~~by rousing~~ which roused their jelousy involved him ~~in~~.

As you are well acquainted with the Spanish character, I have no fears but your ~~upright & pruden~~ prudent and cautious conduct will regain you the confidence of that Government, *be they whom the may*, and whenever that is obtained, by pursuing the course pointed out to you in my former *private letter* you will be able to place our commerce with them on the broad basis of ~~mutual~~ reciprocity ~~and friendship mutual benefit which will secure to true & lasting friendship,~~—It will be then in your power advantageously to open a nagotiation with them with regard to our boundery and to convince them of the real propriety and necessity for the peace of both of extending our limits to include those Tribes of Indians so hostile to them and mischievous to our borders the chastisement of whom ~~has roused them~~ may arrouse their Jelousy by ~~sometimes~~ being compelled to enter their Territory in pursuit of those marauders to protect their citizens & property, as well as our own—I repeat, by attending to the *reasoning pointed to, in my former private letter* you cannot *fail of success.*[1]

Their interest & security, as well as ours, both combine to induce them to enter into this territorial arrangement which will form the basis of a lasting peace, friendship & good will between the two republics—This is an object I have greatly at heart, and I am sure the moment their present jelousy subsides you can make such an *appeal to their understanding & feelings* that must convince them ~~of it being their~~ that it is the real *interest* of the republic to come into the measures proposed in your instructions— *From the* ~~instructions & the~~ *hints in my private letter*, you possess the means of making a *strong appeal to their* ~~understanding~~ *feelings* that ~~will~~ must succeed.

I have to repeat that if you obtain a cession, all private grants except those that the conditions are fulfilled must be set aside & there can be none except Austins that the conditions are fulfilled, if that—~~To do this, part of the amount that you are autho~~

The frauds in Florida has admonished me that this must be *a sine qua non*—If a cession is obtained it must be free from incumbrance, and the consideration to be given must, in part, be employed to that object— When you find the minds of the rulers prepared you will open cautiously the subjects upon which you are instructed to negotiate—[2]

AL draft, DLC (72).

1. AJ's private letter of October 10, 1829, had suggested ways Butler might play on Mexican fears of American invasion or Texas rebellion, as well as ministerial greed: "I scarcely ever knew a spaniard who was not the slave of averice, and it *is not improbable* that this *weakness* may be *worth a great deal to us, in this case*" (*Jackson Papers*, 7:487–90).

2. In the Florida treaty of 1819, the U.S. had pledged to honor earlier Spanish land grants, even with unperfected titles. Large land claims, many presumed to be fraudulent, subsequently plagued the government and engendered much litigation. Stephen Fuller Austin (1793–1836) and his late father Moses (1761–1821) had received an empresario grant in Texas in 1821.

Washington City March 23d. 1830

Dear Sir,

Your letter of the 5th. of January has been received and read with great attention. That the revolutionary spirit should be still disturbing the repose of Mexico and is likely to paralyse for a considerable period, if not change altogether, her Republican Government, is a source of the most painful regret. This spirit must of necessity be hostile to us—opposed to the conclusion of those commercial regulations which the interest of both countries calls for and particularly that of Mexico. These are as necessary to her prosperity, as peace and internal repose are to her integrity. But if she will be blind to their importance it does not become you to give her *eyes*. No contingency can authorise your interference with her concerns. Let them take what form they may in setting up and pulling down rulers, friendly or unfriendly to the principles of free Government, yours is the part of neutrality which should dictate at all times a respect for the existing powers and a discret avoidance of whatever can commit your character, either in your public or private relations, to the exclusive interests of a party. This is the course of duty as well as prudence. With your knowledge of the Spaniards it will enable you to make the most out of their present condition—which should it become permanent, or sufficiently so to allow of a negotiation, will then admit the application of the views which I expressed in my former private letter, as the best for your guide in establishing a Treaty of commerce.

It may also place it in your power to discuss advantageously the many important questions connected with the establishment of the boundary line—not the least of which is the condition of the Indians on either side of it, as it is now supposed to exist. The United States should include within their limits all the Indians who have intercourse with their citizens. The power to regulate their trade and to punish their aggression ought to be complete. It cannot be so whilst its assertion may compel us to cross over into ~~Spanish~~ Mexican Territory.[1]

Another great inducement for a new territorial arrangement, as the basis of a lasting peace between the two republics, arises from the influence which the population of Texas is fast acquiring, and which there is some reason to fear on account of the law liberating their slaves is in a state of considerable disaffection. Deriving their ideas of Govenment from the United States, their collisions may from this cause weaken the confidence of that [repub]lic in this. At all events prejudices arising from this source in order to be corrected may *be touched in connection with the other motives for a new boundary*, without justly exposing us to the charge of ambition or unfriendliness in the eyes of that republic. In my *estimation* they afford *an argument for the cession* almost *irresistable.*[2]

I have to repeat if you obtain the cession, that all private grants except those in which the conditions are fulfilled must be set aside. I have no knowledge of but one of this character and that is Austins. The frauds in Florida are and will continue for a long time to come, the source of the most vexatious and expensive litigation. All liability to such must be removed in this instance, by making *the consideration itself effective in this respect.*

I refer you to the State Department (the papers transmitted herewith) for the news of the day; and remain as usual yr. friend

[Andrew Jackson]

[In margin:] Should you enter upon a negotiation of boundary it will be proper for you to pursue the course, *with regard to yourself*, mentioned in your private letter.

LS in AJ Donelson's hand (signature removed), TxU (15-0434). Draft of March 17 in AJ Donelson's hand, DLC (72). Facsimile of envelope, Robert G. Kaufmann catalog, 1985 (15-0438).
1. The correction is in AJ's hand.
2. Mexico had abolished slavery in 1829.

From Samuel Delucenna Ingham

Try Dept 23 March
My dear Sir
Will you have the goodness to state what may be the value of Gen Brahan Plantation near Florence—he proposes to convey it as security for the balance of his debt and has refered me to yourself for its value—I have the honor to be with great respect

S D Ingham

[Endorsed by AJ:] Mr Ingham on the value of Genl Brayan farm, near—Florence—

ALS, DLC (38). AJ had known John Brahan (1774–1834) as an Army captain stationed in Tennessee, a supply contractor during the Creek War, and a fellow investor in north Alabama. He had given Brahan a letter of introduction to Ingham on March 2. As receiver of the Huntsville land office in 1819, Brahan had purchased largely at the public auction (allegedly to defeat a speculators' cabal to suppress competitive bidding) and became indebted to the government for more than $80,000. Brahan settled the principal in 1830 but at his death still owed more than $30,000 in accumulated interest. In 1839 Congress passed a law to relieve his heirs of the outstanding debt.

To Samuel Delucenna Ingham

(copy)

March 23rd. 1830—

Dr. Sir,

In answer to your enquiry—I am acquainted with the tract of Genl Brahan near Florence—it is a tract formerly owned by Col E. Ward and costs him on an average about $20 per acre, some fifty, & some one hundred dollars pr acre—has a good mill & ginn on it contains about 1000 acres, & I would suppose at its present depressed value, would be worth ten thousand dollars in cash—

The Genl has also a tract on Town Creek containing about 800 acres with a mill on it[1]—this is very valuable   I should suppose it worth in cash nine thousand dollars—This is a property the Genl intends to reserve for himself & children & I suppose would not take $25,000 for, it will be good security I am sure for the ballance of his debt if not over fifteen thousand dollars[.] yrs respectfully

Andrew Jackson

ALS draft, DLC (38).
  1. Town Creek is in Lawrence County in northern Alabama.

Mushulatubbe et al. to John Henry Eaton

[On May 6 (below), Jackson submitted this protest to the Senate along with the March 17 removal treaty sent him by Greenwood Leflore and David Folsom to which it objected.]

Choctaw Nation March 25. 1830

Friend and Brother,

The subject on which we would wish to address you, is one of the utmost importance to the welfare, and happiness of the Choctaw Nation. At no period with the Choctaws has there been so much distress and disatisfaction existing among the people as there are evidently felt at this time with at least more than two thirds of the community and we know not to whom we could better pour forth our greviances than to our Great Father the president, the fountain head of power, where all his red children can if they speak be heard and listened to. Friend and Brother, we would wish you to open to us your ears, and attentively listen to what we shall say in behalf of our afflicted and distressed Country. We are sorry, we are distressed. And this is owing to the late proceedings of some of our head men in the nation at a Council held in the uper Towns. The result of this Council was made known to us but three sleeps ago, and which is, that a proposition has been made to the Goverment for the soil of all of our Country East of the Mississippi river. We have no objection to sell our Country, and go west of the Mississippi river, for there we know we can live umolested as long as we are a nation, and where we shall be out of the jurisdiction of all the States in the Union, and where we know our Great Father the President can, and will protect us. This you have told us, and we believe it to be true, but we have a serious objection to any Treaty being made where it does not meet the full approbation of at least one half of the nation, and most particularly when it is done entirely unknown to the people, and understood only by a few individuals and when it will be made to give to those same individuals ten Sections of land to each, who have done more injury to the Nation than good. The persons to whom we allude is Folsom and Leflore and other designing half breeds who have got themselves into office by management and intrigue.[1] Why should Folsom and Leflore receive ten Sections of land each, and our beloved Mingo Musholatubby who served his nation more than Sixteen years, and who at all times was the true friend of the Americans, in time of peace as well as in war, should not receive no more than a Common warrior of the land which he alone can say as his Father the Beloved Mingo said, this land is mine, all this country is mine, and why is it that the halfbreeds alone are to be benifitted more by a Treaty than the real pure Choctaws. Is it because we are ignorant, and because we are poor that we should be neglected. If any people in the world that can call any portion of the land of this world their own we the real Choctaws can truely say that this is our own land, This is our own Country. Therefore if this Country is to be treated away, who but the real Choctaws should have the honour of selling it. Our right to the soil we live on is paramount to all others. Let then the Goverment treat with us your Children, who are the true inheritors of all this Country, and who alone have the right of selling or disposing with it as they may think propper. We say we are your Children. You have acknowledged us as such. It was a full blooded Choctaw that first gave his hand to the Great and Good Washington and called him Father. It was no proud and conceited half breed. As Children we have been dutifull towards you, we have not been unrully & fractious at no time as many of our other red Children have been and done you injury, no; we have at no time ever done you any injury, but we have done you good whenever we had it in our power so to do. We ask of our Great Father the War Chief Jackson who was it that fought by his side in the late war. was not it our Pushmataha and Musholatubby and their brave warriors? Let him remember the good deeds we have rendered for the United States and for our great Father. Let him remember our unchangable friendship and above all remember us as a poor helpless and distressed people. If there is a treaty made between the Goverment and the Choctaws let all, the full blooded, as well as the half breeds, be equals in the proffits arising from the Treaty. This will be the only way to give satisfaction to all   We say we are willing to sell our Country, but never under any conditions where in it will make a few very rich; 5 sections seems has been allowed Garland, two for Joel R Nail and the same to J L McDonald Israel Folsom and George Harkins.[2] Here you see in this propposition which has no doubt been presented to you by David W. Haley as being from the whole nation and which if it is agreed to will make only the half breeds rich. Israel Folsom and Nail have never done anything for the nation in no way whatever, but there are many others who have spent the whole of their time in the service of their Country, and men the means of doing a great deal of good and yet they are no more benefitted by this treaty than a common warrior and the reason is they are no relations to the Chiefs who have made this proposition, and they are not halfbreeds is another cause of this. You have no doubt been also informed that Greenwood Leflore ~~is now~~ has been made the principle Chief of the whole nation in consequence of the resignation of Folsom of this District (North East) and Garland of the Southern District.[3] But we will inform you that Folsom had no Office to resign, he had lost it some time since at an ellection, and it was through disapointed ambition that made him act as he has in this respect. Musholatubby is the only Chief in this District as he was reinstated by a large majority of the people and is now considered as in full Office. The reason why Garland of the six towns resigned as he said himself in Council (as Folsom did also) that his warriors were all forsaking him. Folsom and Garland in this situation gave themselves up to Leflore with a few of their warriors and relations and acknowledged him as the principle Chief of the whole nation, but Leflore can not be the principle Chief unless he is ellected by a Majority of the people in the whole nation. The people in this District and also in the other Districts has ever had the privellege of selecting and making who they please as their Chief, and removing them from office whenever it suited them, but never have there been as yet a single instance where the Chief had the power of transfering his warriors into the hands of any other Chief or mingo at their own option, but however Folsom and Garland have assumed a privellege and a power that never was placed in the hands of any Chief in the Choctaw Nation. And we therefore warn you in time not to agree to the propposition which was made at the late Council by Leflore and his party, for we assure you it is not a general understanding among us. and we are fully determined to never agree to it let the Consequence be as it may. Some of us were at the Council when the propposition for the sail of our Country was made   It was formed by Folsom and Leflore in a secret apartment without the consideration of any other individual, except two or three missionaries, and when they had finished it, the people were called togather at a late hour of the night, when it was read to them. We were displeased with it, and we found others to be also even those who signed their names to the talk to be sent to our Great Father, but what was more displeasing to us, and truely disgusting, was when we saw those Individuals (Folsom and Lefore) so uncommonly anxious for the people to sign this talk. Every thing was urged and done in a hurry, and not even a minutes time was allowed for deliberation. If you have a mind to do justice by us I know you will not agree to any treaty made with our nation unless it is with the whole nation and where it will give satisfaction at least to all the full blooded Choctaws, Therefore in order that this may be the case we would be glad if it is the wish of your Goverment to treat for our lands that you would send Commissioners to the nation and we will show them that we have the power and will sell our Country, but we will make a fair and an honest treaty with them, and not under such considerations as that which is proposed by Leflore and Folsom. When we make a treaty we do not want the missionaries to be present. Let them attend to their propper vocations, and meddle not with the concerns of the Nation. The missionaries we are sorry to inform you that they are a meddlesome set and have not done much good among us, no, but they have been the cause of a great deal of injury to the nation and also to the Goverment. For they are the very set that has ever opperated against the policy of your Goverment towards the Choctaws and thereby deprived us of those advantages and those blessings which it has been the wish of your Goverment to bestow on us. We have always been confident that your Government would not wrong our people, nor recommend us to nothing but what would tend to our happiness and prosperity, but nevertheless your views as respects for the removal of our nation to the west, have heretofore disapointed by Missionary Counsel and intrigue. I wish our father the President but knew these people as well as we do. We would not wish you to think because we do not the missionaries that we do not wish to encourage among our people the habits of civilized life—that we do not wish our youths to be educated and brought up as white people. As a people, that we are disposed to the reverse of this, we will present to you as an instance of it our Cherished institution in Kentucky The Choctaw Academy. Musholatubby was the founder of that Academy, and sent his sons there to be educated.[4]

Friend and Brother

In consequence of the iniquitous proceedings of the Halfbreed Chiefs and their party a great many of the people from most every Section of the Country have met together and joined in making you this communication. They have at the same time appointed a General Council, to take place on the 16th of April, where every man is to attend with Guns and deadly weapons, we are determined to die, or have justice done us and never to consent or agree to any treaty that is made in the dark by designing and avaricious men. Such as Leflore and Folsom.[5]

We have the honour of subscribing ourselves your friends and brothers.

Mingo Mushulatubby	his	X	mark
Mingo Nittukaichee		X	
Mingo Eyarhokatubby		X	
General Talking Warrior		X	
Captain J. Kincaid	his	X	mark

[Thirty additional signatures follow.]

We Do Certify that the above is a true Interpretaion

John Pitchlynn
M. Mackey, US Intrs.

DS, DNA-RG 46 (mAJs). The Choctaw Nation was organized in three districts, each headed by an elected "medal chief." Mushulatubbe (d. 1838) had been chief of the northeastern district before being replaced by David Folsom in 1826. Nitakechi or Nittakaichee (1772–1845) was a nephew of the late Choctaw chief Pushmataha (c.1764–1824). John Pitchlynn (d. 1835) was a white man who married a Choctaw woman and had long served as an interpreter for the Choctaw Nation. Middleton Mackey was also an interpreter.

1. Greenwood Leflore and David Folsom had white fathers and Choctaw mothers.

2. Southern district chief John Garland, Joel R. Nail, James L. McDonald, David Folsom's brother Israel Folsom (1802–1870), and Leflore's nephew George Washington Harkins were prominent Choctaws. The reservations of land for them and for Greenwood Leflore and David Folsom were in Article XXVII of the treaty.

3. At the national council on March 16, the day before the removal treaty was signed, Folsom and Garland resigned their offices in favor of Greenwood Leflore as sole national chief.

4. Mushulatubbe was the lead Choctaw negotiator of the 1825 Treaty of Washington, pursuant to which a Choctaw Academy funded through the War Department was established near Georgetown, Ky., under the supervision of then-senator Richard M. Johnson.

5. On April 16 Choctaws from the northeastern and southern districts met in council and elected Mushulatubbe and Nitakechi to replace Folsom and Garland. The next day they wrote Choctaw agent William Ward (c1769–1836) seeking protection from Leflore, who had written Mushulatubbe on April 7 asserting his authority as sole chief, inviting Mushulatubbe's cooperation with the treaty, and threatening "strong measures" if he resisted (DNA-RG 75, M234-169).

From George Lowrey et al.

Brown's Hotel, Washington City
26th. March 1830.

Sir,

It becomes our painful duty, to again address you on the unpleasant subject of intrusions upon our lands, by white citizens of the U. States.

For several weeks past we have been receiving the complaints of our citizens, respecting a new species of intrusion which is now practising to an alarming extent. The Principl. Chief of our Nation, has also urged us to lay before you the subject as early as possible, as our agent, probably, has not yet reported the facts, tho. complaints have been made to him by the Executive of our Nation. It appears that there are hundreds of whitemen searching and digging for gold within the limits of the Nation, and at some distance from the portion of disputed lands, to the no small annoyance of the natives.[1] The number of these intruders had been variously stated from one to two thousand, and from the most authentic information there is evidently upwards of a thousand persons engaged in this business, which we cannot but consider as depriving us of property for which the faith of the Govt. is pledged for our protection. Whatever minerals, and however valuable, that may be found upon our lands must surely be considered the undisputable and indefeasible property of the Cherokees; and thus to be deprived of their value and advantages is a subject of too much importance to be neglected by us, or that will escape your early attention, as we humbly hope. The losses already sustained by the illegal conduct of these persons are great, & daily increasing; besides the injury and perplexity our Citizens have to undergo, in consequence of their pernicious behaviour—we therefore, respectfully solicit that orders for their removal may be issued, as early as practicable, and that measures be taken to guard against a future recurrence of this evil—we take the liberty of enclosing an extract from a letter recd. some days since, from the Pl. Chief of our Nation on the subject—

We beg leave, again, to call your attention to the subject of the complaints laid before you by our late Delegation, against our Agent and requesting the appointment of another in his place. This may be a subject of some delicacy, yet a just regard for our rights, and preservation of that good understanding with the Govt. which has heretofore existed, and which it is our sincere desire ever to maintain, as well as good faith through the medium of its proper agent, has made it necessary, on our part to solicit a change. The facts stated by our late Delegation are strictly correct; and from the encouragement received by them at your parting interview, we had flattered ourselves that another would have been appointed. We hope you will pardon in us the liberty of mentioning a remark of yours at that time—viz—That there were some reasons necessary, to be submitted before the Senate for his removal, & that a copy of a certain document, relative to some reservation Lands, which the agent had neglected, would be sufficient. This document was obtained & transmitted by Mr. Ross soon after his return, & which we hope you have recd.—It is, we assure you, with unpleasant feelings, that we press this matter, and that personally, we respect our agent, but in the discharge of his official duties, the Cherokees are greatly dissatisfied.[2]

We humbly request that you will consider the subject, as soon as the pressure of business will admit, and if possible grant the wishes of our people. Between the Agent and the Indians over whom he is appointed you well know the most perfect good understanding should exist, & a mutual interchange of good feelings; were this the case in regard to ours, we should be silent.

With sentiments of the highest regard and esteem, we have the honor to be respectfully, Yr. Obt. Servts.

George Lowrey
Lewis Ross
William Hicks
R Taylore
Joseph Vann
Wm S Coodey
Cher. Delegation

Extract of a letter from Mr. Jno. Ross, Principl. Chief of the Cher. Nation to the Cher. Delegation now in Washington, dated, Head of Coosa C. N. March 3d. 1830—

"Mr. Moses Daniel arrived here last evening, by whom I am informed that the report respecting the gold mines on the branches of Etowah River, in Hickory log district is fully confirmed. He says that Judge Martin has lately been at the mines, and it is supposed that there are not less than One thousand whitemen, Citizens of the U. States, engaged in this public robbery. I have written two or three letters to the Agent on the subject, but you well know his apathy & reluctance to do his duty when justice is demanded in behalf of the Nation"—"It is estimated that these transgressors, procure from 1500 to 2000 dollars worth of gold pr day. Ought not the U. States to make good this robbery of our public property by their Citizens? are they not in justice bound to do it? The act is committed in the face of day, and in violation of their own laws, and to the Contempt of their public Agent who stands here with folded arms as it were, merely to witness the rights of the Cherokees invaded & trampled under foot with impunity."[3]

The Gentlemen named above are persons of unquestionable veracity. Judge Martin is at present National Treasurer, & for many years a Judge of the Superior Court.

Cherokee Delegation

[Endorsed by AJ:] refered to the secretary of war, if those people are at work within the Indian Limits, instruct the agent that they come under his order for removing intruders—& inform the delegation that orders have been issued to remove all such intruders & the agent *will obay* we cannot take ex party evidence against our agent he must have time to explain— enclose the agent a copy of the charge & ask him for explanation—

[Endorsed by Eaton:] make out a Copy of the charges against Montgomery which are on file   J H E

LS, DNA-RG 75 (M234-74). Copy (extract), DNA-RG 233 (15-0463). Extract, *HRDoc* 89, 21st Cong., 1st sess., pp. 43–44 (Serial 197). The extracts communicated to and printed by the House omitted the two paragraphs complaining of agent Hugh Montgomery. Eaton replied to the delegation the next day, March 27: "Your letter of yesterday, to the President, complaining of intrusions upon your lands, has by him been referred to this Department, where it should have been addressed by you, instead of the President. Heretofore you were informed, verbally, that orders had issued from the Department, to remove present intrusions, and to prevent them for the future. Upon this subject the agent has been fully instructed." Besides instructing Montgomery, Eaton on March 16 and 17 had ordered troops from Fort Mitchell to warn off intruders and, if necessary, remove them by force and destroy their property (*HRDoc* 89, 21st Cong., 1st sess., pp. 41–43, 45, Serial 197).

1. Gold was discovered in northeast Georgia in 1828. John Ross had complained to Montgomery of gold-seeking intruders in the Nation on February 19. On February 22 Montgomery wrote Eaton asking how best to proceed against them (*HRDoc* 89, 21st Cong., 1st sess., pp. 31–32, Serial 197).

2. In March and April 1829, a Cherokee delegation in Washington headed by John Ross had complained to AJ of agent Montgomery's neglect of duty and misuse of his office for private enrichment. On June 24, at AJ's suggestion, Ross had sent him court transcripts showing that lawsuits to defend Cherokee land titles had been dismissed because Montgomery failed to appear (*Jackson Papers*, 7:82–83, 144–46; *John Ross Papers*, 1:165–66).

3. Moses Daniel (c1782–1848) was a Cherokee and John Martin (1781–1840) was a prominent Cherokee official. Hickory Log on the Etowah River was in the eastern part of the Nation southwest of Dahlonega, which became the center of the gold region.

To John Nicholson Moulder

WASHINGTON CITY, March 27, 1830.

Respected Sir:

I regret that the duties of my office will not allow me to avail myself of the polite invitation conveyed in your note of yesterday. It would afford me the highest pleasure to unite with my Masonic Brethren of this District in laying the *Corner Stone* of a Religious Edifice proposed to be built in Alexandria, and in marching afterwards *in form* to the Tomb of Washington. The memory of that illustrious Grand Master cannot receive a more appropriate honor than that which Religion and Masonry pay it, when they send their votaries to his Tomb fresh from the performance of acts which they consecrate.

I am, very respectfully, Your obedient servant,

ANDREW JACKSON.

Printed, Washington *Daily National Intelligencer*, April 7, 1830 (mAJs). *Niles*, April 24 (15-0470). Moulder (1792–1839), a Treasury clerk in the second comptroller's office, was Grand Master of the District of Columbia Masonic Grand Lodge. On March 29, about 500 Masons laid the cornerstone of the Associated Methodist Church in Alexandria, Va., then went by steamboat to Mount Vernon to pay homage at Washington's tomb. AJ and Washington were both prominent Masons. Washington was the founding Master of the Alexandria Lodge, and AJ had been Grand Master of the Tennessee Grand Lodge in 1822–24.

From Spencer Darwin Pettis

March 27. 1830

Sir,

I beg leave to call your attention to the recommendation of William Wright of Missouri to be Register of the Land office at Palmyra Missouri in place of Mr. Carson

The reasons for the removal are set forth in the recommendation of Col Benton & myself. Your very Obdt Servt

Sp Pettis

[Endorsed by AJ:] Wm Wright—appointed—A. J.

ALS, THer (15-0471). AJ removed William Carson (1798–1873) and nominated William Wright for register of the Palmyra, Mo., land office this same day. On April 1, Senator David Barton of Missouri offered a motion to inquire of AJ "for what cause or causes of unfitness, or for what act of official misconduct, William Carson has been removed." The Senate tabled Barton's motion, 22 to 15, on April 26 and confirmed Wright on May 29.

From Spencer Darwin Pettis

March 27. 1830

I take leave also to call your attention to the recommendation of Col. Benton & myself in favor of Richard W Cummins to be Receiver of Public monies at Lexington Mo. in place of A. S. McGirk.

Our reasons for the removal are set forth in our letter to the Secretary. In this case as well as the case at Palmyra I am decidedly of opinion that the incumbents should be removed. Respectfully

Sp Pettis

[Endorsed by AJ:] Mr Pettis on the subject of appointing Mr. Wright Register at Palmyra—and Col Cummins receiver at Lexington M—Wright ordered to be nominated & Cummins posponed until the 30th of Decbr next When the incumbents time expires—to be filed A. J.

ALS, THer (15-0473). AJ nominated Richard W. Cummins for agent to the Shawnees and Delawares on May 29, after the Senate had twice rejected Wharton Rector. On December 23 he nominated Edwin M. Ryland for receiver at the Lexington land office in place of Andrew Stephen McGirk (1792–1842), whose term expired December 21. Cummins and Ryland were quickly confirmed.

From Samuel Swartwout

New York 27 March 1830

Dear Sir,

I am overwhelmed with grief that you should have had so much trouble with me. I will barely trouble you farther with regard to my unfortunate nomination and matters connected with it, to assure your Excellency, upon *my honor*, that any representations which have been made to you, or others at Washington, or elsewhere, with regard to the objects of a certain supper got up on the 4th of March, in honor of your inauguration, with an intent to make it be believed that I took an interest in it, further than to unite with my fellow Citizens, in the expression of that single sentiment, is utterly untrue—[1]

The miserable subterfuges which are hourly & secretly resorted to to injure me in your good opinion, have induced me to trouble you with this explanation of a very trifling matter & I hope it will be credited. What will next be attributed to me, I am unable to conjecture, but of one thing I beg you to be assured, that after the evidences you have given me of your personal regard & confidence, I would sooner die than deceive you or do any thing that should occasion you pain or regret.

I am, Dr Sir, with every sentiment of veneration & regard, most sincerely & affectionately Your Obt. Servt.

Saml. Swartwout

P.S. I beg you to further assured, *all reports* to the contrary notwithstanding, that I have not expressed any opinion but one on the subject of the next Presidency & that is for your reelection—I confine myself wholely & solely to the duties of my office.

[Endorsed by AJ:] Mr Swartwout private to be filed private—A. J.

ALS, DLC (38). AJ gave Samuel Swartwout (1783–1856) a recess appointment as New York City customs collector in April 1829 and nominated him to the Senate on January 13, 1830. In March the Senate collected evidence on Swartwout that included a remonstrance from customs inspectors whom he had dismissed, a complaint of chaos in the customs office by Gerret Forbes, several testimonials in Swartwout's favor including one from Ingham, and letters from Swartwout explaining his association with Aaron Burr and disclaiming any connection with his defaulting brother Robert Swartwout (DNA-RG 46). The Senate confirmed Swartwout on March 29 by 25 to 21.

1. A banquet to honor the first anniversary of AJ's inauguration was held at Tammany Hall on March 4.

To Samuel Delucenna Ingham

March 29th. 1830—

The President with his respects to the Sec of the Treasury, and informs him that he wishes to send up this morning to the Senate all nominations that may be ready—The Collector for Passamaquoddy, aught to go up this morning

AN, PU-Ingham Papers (15-0528). Later this day AJ nominated three customs officers, including Maine congressman Leonard Jarvis (1781–1854) for collector of the Passamaquoddy district to replace Stephen Thatcher. The Senate confirmed Jarvis on April 5. He elected to stay in Congress, and AJ instead appointed James W. Ripley.

To Samuel Delucenna Ingham

March 30th. 1830—

The President with his respects to Mr Ingham informs, ~~him~~ that Mr Swan, as atto. for this District, applied to him for permission to call to his aid as counsel Mr Key in the case, U. States vs Orr & his securities—which he represents importan[t]   the P. has yielded his assent to his application & has requested Mr Key to wait upon, & agree with you on the amount of compensation to be recd—

AN, PU-Ingham Papers (15-0534). Thomas Swann (1765–1840) was the federal district attorney for the District of Columbia, and Francis Scott Key (1779–1843), author of "The Star Spangled Banner," was a Georgetown lawyer. Benjamin Grayson Orr (c1763–1822) had been a Washington resident and mayor. The U.S. was pursuing claims against Orr's estate and sureties for his failures as an Army supply contractor to AJ's Southern Division troops in 1817–18. Four suits, which had been pending since 1821, were prepared for trial in the spring of 1830 and finally decided in Orr's favor in the circuit court for the District in 1831. The Supreme Court affirmed the judgments in 1834.

From John Branch

Navy Department
March 30th. 1830.

Sir,

It has been proved to my satisfaction, that Lieutenants Edmund Byrne, and Hampton Westcott, Passed Midshipman Charles H. Duryee, and Midshipman Charles G. Hunter, of the Navy of the U. States, were recently concerned in a duel, which took place between the last named Officer, and William Miller Jr. of Philadelphia, which resulted fatally to the latter.

I respectfully recommend to you, that the names of the said Officers, Edmund Byrne, Hampton Westcott, Charles H. Duryee, and Charles G. Hunter, be erased from the List of Officers of the Navy of the United States. I am, very respectfully, &c.

Jn Branch

[Endorsed by AJ:] Let the above named officers of the Navy, be striken from the Roll of the Navy, March 31rst. 1830—Andrew Jackson

LS, DNA-RG 45 (mAJs). LC, DNA-RG 45 (M472-1). *Niles*, April 10, 1830. An assault by R. Dillon Drake upon Henry Wharton Griffith in a Philadelphia billiard room on February 19 triggered an escalating public quarrel that drew in friends of both men, including Navy officers Hampton Westcott (c1804–1837), Edmund Byrne (d. 1850), Charles G. Hunter (1812–1856), and Charles H. Duryee (c1811–1861). On March 17 Hunter challenged Drake's friend, Philadelphia lawyer William Miller Jr. (c1809–1830). They fought in Delaware on March 21, with Byrne present as Miller's second and Westcott and Duryee as Hunter's. Miller was killed. The Pennsylvania legislature formally commended AJ's action on April 2. All four officers were later reinstated: Byrne in 1831, Westcott in 1832, and Hunter and Duryee in 1833.

From John Orde Creighton

Sir

After serving my Country for thirty years If not with equal ability at least with a zeal and Fidelity not surpassed by any of my contemporaries, I have been recall'd from my command and arrested upon charges emanating as I am officially informed from Lieut: Homans and others lately serving in the Squadron under my Orders.

That complaints had been exhibited against me from any source whatever I was not officially informed of until my arrival in this City when I was deprived of my sword and a Court Martial immediately convened for my Trial. Ignorant at the time of my removal of having committed any offence, as well as the Nature of the complaints alleged against me, no reasons whatevr having been assigned by the Secretary of the Navy for so stron the adoption of so strong a measure, I was of course deprived of the opportunity of bringing Home such witnesses as are essential to my defence, and consequently my trial has been postponed. Removed from my command like a culprit, in the midst of foreign Squadrons and Representatives of foreign Governments—Vituperation and abuse poured upon me by a licentious press—my Enemies Triumphing even at this moment in my mortification and distress, I would ask *you* Sir as the Guardian of us all if this be not a case of extreme hardship and one calling for alleviation. Under a supposition therefore that you cannot be apprised of all that I have suffered on this occasion and am still struggling with, I have come to the determination of soliciting the favour of a personal interview, or if most agreeable to yourself that you will allow me to explain in a written communication the charges prefered against me, satisfied that if either mode be granted I shall be able ~~not only~~ to remove every unfavorable impression ~~but~~ and prove that I am not only an innocent but a deeply injured individual

In addressing my self directly to You Sir, I beg that I may not be understood as intending to convey the slightest disrespect to the Head of the Navy Department, my sole object is to bring the subject immediately before You, and if possible to disperse the cloud which at present ~~hangs~~ throws a shade over my character, and professional reputation. With perfect Respect I have the Honor to be sir Your Obedt and Humble St.

J. Orde. Creighton.

ALS draft, PPRF (mAJs). AJ replied on April 3 (below). Creighton (c1785–1838), a Navy captain, had commanded the frigate *Hudson*, flagship of the Brazilian squadron. He was ordered home in June 1829 and put under arrest in February 1830. In January 1831 he was court-martialed in Philadelphia on charges instigated by Lieutenant James T. Homans (1805–1849) and Lieutenant Thomas W. Freelon (c1799–1847) of conduct unbecoming an officer, tyranny and oppression toward subordinates, neglect of duty, and drawing double pay. On February 17 the court acquitted Creighton on all charges except claiming salary twice for one month, which it deemed an inadvertent error. The court sentenced Creighton to be admonished by the secretary of the Navy to be more careful in his accounts. It appended to its verdict a rebuke of Homans and Freelon for their "unworthy manner" of circulating and forwarding their complaint against Creighton, "opposed to every principle of Naval discipline and to the express orders of the Navy Department," for usurping a right to judge Creighton's governance of his ship in "matters of mere usage," and for having "wantonly imputed to him base and unworthy motives which imputations have been supported by no proof whatever" (DNA-RG 125, M273-26).

To Martin Van Buren

March 31st. 1830

The President presents his respects to the Secretary of State, having carefully considered the case of Mr. Witherell secretary of the Territory of Michigan and the letter of Mr. Biddle which is herewith returned. It seems clear, from old age and other causes, that he is not competent to the proper discharge of his duties, and a fit subject therefore for removal. The Secretary of State will please send a nomination of Mr. Mason of Kentucky in his place.

N in AJ Donelson's hand, DNA-RG 59 (M639-27). *TPUS*, 12:147. James Witherell (1759–1838), a former Vermont congressman, was appointed a Michigan Territory judge in 1808 and territorial secretary in 1828. AJ and Van Buren had received complaints that Witherell was, in the words of Michigan Territory congressional delegate John Biddle (1792–1859), "perfectly imbecile from age and infirmity." On March 31 Biddle repeated to Van Buren that Witherell's "faculties were quite impaired and that he was under the influence of very unsafe consellors" and "no longer capable of doing justice to his station" (*TPUS*, 12:138, 146). Appeals in Witherell's defense included one from his son (April 24, below). John Thomson Mason (1787–1850) was the son of late Virginia senator Stevens Thomson Mason. AJ nominated him to replace Witherell on May 6.

Memorandum Book

[These undated entries in Jackson's memorandum book, probably from March and April 1830, directly follow those from circa November 1829 in Jackson Papers, 7:592–93.]

Stephen Thatcher Collector of Pasamaquode, Judge Preble, says, ought to retained, & pledges himself for the rectitude of his conduct—his time expires 1rst. of April 1830—requests him to be renominated.[1]

Judge Emmerson & Govr Vaness says the Navy agent Harris must be removed and Mr Broadhead appointed in his stead—all parties in Boston expect it—Judge E. is to furnish documents to shew the wish of the great body of both parties in Boston that he must be removed.[2]

Mr Wadels report on the subject of Messengers to be considered & if approved to be brought to the view of Congress in a Message—[3]

The letters of recommendation to the President & heads of Departments for office belong to the Executive, and aught not to be sent to committees of the senate &c. The senate have no right to call for them—The President has the constitutional power to appoint; he does this on the best information he has obtained, and it is anough for them, informally, to know, that the officer was deemed both honest, fit, & capable—The letters will therefore be safely kept in the Depts. and the Head thereof, will if applied to answer the enquiry as above.[4]

change suggested.

1st. The first comptroller to be relieved from the superintendence of the customs, and that duty to be assigned by some officer created by law for that purpose—This appears to have been attempted by a bill to "establish a commissioner of customs" some years ago, by the committee of ways & means—*Examine the necessity*.

2nd. It is believed that the commissioner of the General Land office should be relieved from the examination of the accounts of the receivers of public mony & this duty assigned to the Fifth Auditor.

3rd. That the duties of the 2 & 3rd auditors be assigned to one of those officers; and that the other be charged with the examination of the Post office accounts. This P.O. accounts is now assigned to 5th. auditor—
Note—This requires legislation—[5]

Northern & Northwestern boundery—The Grand Portage on Lake Superior, our boundery by treaty stipulation—The British claim to the bottom of the lake being the south west point of said Lake—The treaty when refered to will settle this matter—Mitchels map being refered to by the treaty, will be the guide, & must settle this dispute—The falls of St Marys, is another disputed point—who owns the Island, the map & treaty here also the guide.[6]

Claims on France—
3 kinds—first the antwerp claims about three millions $
2 Those burnt at sea without condemnation   These are so just that France has, nor cannot make an argument against them
3rd. class disputed—The best mode to obtain the consent of claimants to designate a gross amount, & urge the question with energy—& payment cannot be refused, by a magnanimous & just nation who has admitted the justice of the claims.[7]

AN, DLC (64).
1. AJ replaced Thatcher on March 29 (above). William Pitt Preble (1783–1857) of Maine, appointed minister to the Netherlands by AJ in 1829, was Thatcher's brother-in-law.
2. The navy agent at Boston was Richard Devens Harris (1782–1847), brother of U.S. marshal Samuel D. Harris. His term expired April 19. On April 24 AJ nominated Daniel Dodge Brodhead (1802–1885), son of New Hampshire congressman John Brodhead, to succeed him. Brodhead had been extensively recommended to AJ in 1829. The Senate confirmed him on May 29 by 18 to 17 after an inquiry into a contract Brodhead held to supply the Navy with slop clothing. Thomas Emerson (1781–1853), postmaster at Windsor, Vt., was a former state legislator and local judge. Cornelius Peter Van Ness (1782–1852), former governor of Vermont, was appointed minister to Spain by AJ in 1829. The two "parties" in Boston were rival Jackson factions.
3. William Coventry Henry Waddell (1802–1884) was the Agent of the State Department, responsible for its financial administration.
4. Beginning January 6 and continuing through the session, the Senate entertained various resolutions asking AJ to furnish credentials for certain nominees and explanations for his removals. A March 18 resolution by Samuel A. Foot of Connecticut, which did not pass, asserted in general terms "the unquestionable right of the Senate to call in respectful terms upon the President of the United States for such information as may be in his possession, and which the Senate deem necessary to the faithful discharge of the duties imposed upon it by the Constitution" (*Senate Executive Proceedings*, 4:72). AJ complied with two resolutions that did pass on April 5 and 12, requesting information on Wharton Rector and John Hamm respectively. He and his Cabinet also informally supplied credentials for some nominees to Senate committees.
5. A law of March 3, 1817, prescribed the duties of the Treasury's five auditors and two comptrollers. The first auditor prepared the accounts of the Treasury Department, and the fifth auditor those of the State Department, General Post Office, and Indian bureau, for review and certification by the first comptroller. The second and third auditors prepared War

Department accounts, and the fourth auditor those of the Navy Department, for submission to the second comptroller. The first comptroller also supervised customs collections. In 1826 the House Ways and Means Committee reported a bill creating a commissioner of the customs to assume this duty. Proposals to reorganize the accounting offices continued through AJ's administration. Congress created a customs commissioner in 1849.

6. The Treaty of Paris of 1783 ending the Revolutionary War drew a border between the U.S. and British Canada based on John Mitchell's 1755 map of North America. In the northwest the treaty prescribed a water boundary through the middle of Lake Huron to Lake Superior and thence via "Long Lake" to Lake of the Woods. Later negotiations between Britain and the U.S. failed to resolve the meaning of this and other unclear locations described in the treaty, especially on the Maine border, and in 1827 the two countries agreed to neutral arbitration on the basis of Mitchell's map. One disputed point in the west concerned ownership of Sugar Island in the St. Marys River below Sault Ste. Marie; another concerned the identity of Long Lake and the point where the boundary exited Lake Superior toward Lake of the Woods. The U.S. and Britain agreed to submit their positions to the arbiter, William I, King of the Netherlands, by April 1, 1830. His award in January 1831 was not accepted, and the Webster-Ashburton Treaty of 1842 finally settled the boundary. It gave the U.S. Sugar Island and designated a route west from Lake Superior starting up the Pigeon River at Grand Portage.

7. The U.S. had long sought recompense from France for spoliations on American shipping committed during the Napoleonic Wars. The "Antwerp claims" were for American ships and cargoes which French officials at Antwerp and elsewhere had sequestered and later sold without condemnation by a prize court. The disputed claims, AJ's third class, were mainly for ships and cargoes formally condemned under authority of Napoleon's Berlin and Milan decrees of 1806 and 1807. The U.S. maintained that these edicts themselves violated treaty obligations and the law of nations and that all condemnations under them, regardless of circumstances, were therefore illegal. In dispatches of February 16 and 25, 1830, U.S. minister to France William Cabell Rives (1793–1868) reported that the French ministry seemed disposed to recognize all claims for property either seized without formal condemnation or destroyed at sea, corresponding to AJ's first two classes. He suggested proposing to France a joint commission to adjudicate the third class based on the particulars of each claim (*HRDoc* 147, 22d Cong., 2d sess., pp. 80–92, Serial 235). Rives's February 25 dispatch arrived April 10, and AJ wrote Van Buren the same day preferring a lump settlement by France to a joint commission (below).

April

From Henry Petrikin

Harrisburg April 2nd 1830

Dear Sir

I wish you to read this letter: I am to you personally unknown, but I have been, and continue to be, your warm friend and admirer. For the services which you performed; for the sacrifices which you made, for your country; I, with thousands of others, most sincerely *advocated* your election to the distinguished station which you now hold. To say that you, in the discharge of the arduous duties necessarily devolving upon you, have verified the predictions of your friends, would not be saying enough—even your enemies award to you praise without qualification! I am to be understood as confining myself in these observations to Pennsylvania. The *people* are heart and soul with you. You have more *real friends* in this State than you had at the late election. Those who occupy themselves only with the domestic cares of life, anxiously wish you to be a candidate for re-election, and you will receive the undivided vote of those who love their country for their country's sake! Those who supported you for the sake, and in the hope of Office; will be governed in their choice by the *gratification* or *disappointment* of their selfish purposes. I am an obscure individual, scarcely known beyond, (if known at all) the limits of the State. To you I am totally a stranger. But I have presumed to address you on a subject which is of more interest to the people than to yourself. You are "public property," and I claim the right to be heard on the part of those who are their country's friends, and whose patriotism is not measured by a thirst for office. I will (and hope not to incur the charge of vanity in stating it) say to you, in evidence of standing in my native State, that I have represented the County I come from (Centre) in the Senate, and am now a member of the House of Representatives, and have been for sometime past. A few evenings since a meeting of the Democratic members of the Legislature, friendly to the National Administration, was called. I attended, and was appointed one of the Secretaries of the meeting. A committee was appointed to draft resolutions for the consideration of the meeting. The 2nd resolution reported was in these words:

Resolved, *That,* "*should it* (The Administration) *continue to be characterised by the same wholesome measures and sound republican principles with which it has commenced,*" the best interests of the country will be maintained and promoted by the re-election of the present distinguished Chief Magistrate.

On motion of Mr Cunningham, of Mercer, that part which is underscored underwent debate whether it should be struck out. The striking out was warmly opposed by Dr. Burden and all the friends of Samuel D. Ingham. I supported the motion to "strike out"—as did Wise, of Westmoreland, Wilkins, of Allegheny, Cunningham of Mercer & some others.[1] The question was, whether a resolution so doubtful in its phraseology; so luke warm in its expression of adherence to the "People's Choice"; so evidently open to doubt whether it was a sincere expression of our sentiments, should be adopted; or whether one more bold, more decided, without *if* or *ands*, should be substituted. It was evident that the friends of Ingham wished to hold themselves in reserve, and unpledged, to be governed by circumstances. If by their intrigue, for which in this State they are famous, and in which consists all their power, for they are few in number, they could manage to get you out of the way, then their whole energies would be put in requisition in support of John C. Calhoun. They dare not openly declare themselves against you. They are aware the people would frown them down. But they are at work to destroy you in the affections of the people in a covert way. I assure you on the word of one who never asked you for an Office and never will, that their task is a vain one. The people demand it at your hands to be again a candidate, and the result of the meeting of the *members,* called by the few adherents of Ingham and Sutherland in the Legislature, to answer their own selfish views and base purposes, should operate powerfully with you to suffer yourself to be again a candidate.[2] The resolution above quoted was voted down, & you will see by the public papers the opinion of the meeting in the preamble and resolutions adopted. The honest yeomanry of the country are well represented in the sentiments therein contained.

But your sincere friends—those who never asked you for an Office—are surprized that you retain in your Cabinet a man who is plotting, (not only your destruction, but) against the peace and welfare and best interests of the Country. You are loudly called upon, and justice to your friends in this State, requires it at your hands, to dismiss from your confidence & patronage, Samuel D Ingham and the creatures attached to his fortunes, who through his exertions were appointed to Office in this State. He and they came into your support at a late hour, and only when they found that a vast majority of the people were against their favorite, Calhoun. They never were your sincere friends; and although for the little service they performed, they were well rewarded with Office, they are uneasy and will never be satisfied until their ends are accomplished in the promotion of their favorite. They have attempted to make you believe that they were the *pillars* upon which your popularity in Pennsylvania rested, and to ingratiate themselves more readily, Baldwin and Barnard must be destroyed and weakened in your estimation.[3] That was a part of their plans. These two men were your zealous, efficient and sincere supporters from the first, and remain as much attached and as sincerely devoted to you as ever. I am intimate with them both, and assure you I speak to you the truth and nothing but the truth in pledging to you their sincerity and devotedness at all times and now.

I have considered it a duty, before retiring from this place, to address you this letter. I could not have my own consent to remain silent, or suffer you to remain in ignorance of the intrigues of Ingham. It is the first and last time I have or shall appear before you. I intend giving you a cordial support for re-election, not only for your own virtues, but for the sake of our beloved country, whose happiness I consider involved in your continuance at the Head of our Affairs. I conclude by asking you to pardon me for obtruding myself on your notice. I speak to you from my obscurity, but it is the voice of one who admires you as a Warrior and Statesman; who loves you for his country's sake, and whose most ardent prayer is for your temporal & eternal happiness.

May Heaven bless & preserve you

H Petrikin

ALS, DLC (38). Petrikin (1798–1849), editor of the *Bellefonte Patriot*, represented Centre and Clearfield counties in Pennsylvania's house of representatives. Jackson members of the legislature had caucused on March 30 and 31. The first day they appointed a committee which framed resolutions that conditionally endorsed AJ's renomination. The next day's full meeting rejected the committee's draft and instead unanimously resolved that AJ's administration "meets the cordial and decided approbation of the democratic party, and of the people of Pennsylvania" and that "the unanimity and harmony of the great Democratic party of the Union, will be greatly promoted by again placing the name of Andrew Jackson before the people as a candidate for re-election."

1. State senators Jesse R. Burden (1798–1875), Jacob M. Wise (b. 1795), and Thomas Scott Cunningham (1790–1855) and representative Ross Wilkins (1799–1872) had all been on the drafting committee.

2. Joel Barlow Sutherland (1792–1861) was a Pennsylvania congressman who, like Ingham, had supported John C. Calhoun for president in 1824 before switching to AJ.

3. Supreme Court justice Henry Baldwin and Isaac Dutton Barnard (1791–1834), U.S. senator from Pennsylvania. On April 1 Ross Wilkins had written Barnard a letter very similar to this one, which also came into AJ's hands. Wilkins charged that the equivocal resolutions put forth by the meeting's organizers exposed a plot "concerted in Washington" to "destroy Jackson covertly: and advance Calhoun upon his ruins" (DLC-38).

To John Orde Creighton

April 3rd. 1830—

The President with his respects to Capt. J. Ord. Creighton acknowledges his note of the 30th. ultimo, informs him, that he will receive any explanation of his case that he may think proper to make to him in writing, or in a personal interview, should the latter be prefered by the Capt; at any time he may think proper to present himself for that purpose.

The President assure the Capt that his note would have received an earlier answer, had it not have been for the press of business with which he was surrounded when it was recd.

AN, PPRF (mAJs).

To William Ellis Tucker

[This letter survives only in later printed versions.]

WASHINGTON, April 3, 1830.

SIR,—

I have had the honor to receive your letter of the 3d of March, and, since, the porcelain which it offered to my acceptance. I was not apprised before of the perfection to which your skill and perseverance had brought this branch of American manufacture. It seems to be not inferior to the finest specimens of French porcelain. But whether the facilities for its manufacture bring its cost so nearly to an equality with that of the French as to enable the moderate protection of which you speak to place it beyond the reach of competition in the markets of the world, is a question which I am not prepared to answer. If Congress could be made acquainted with the experiments on the subject, and they should confirm your favorable anticipation, there would be scarcely a doubt of its willingness to secure the important results of the manufacture. I do not see, however, any mode by which this can be effected on any other principle than that of protection. You would probably have a right to a patent for the discovery, but this right would have to be determined in the usual way. Congress have refused to make a donation to the heirs of Robert Fulton for the national benefits resulting from his discovery, upon the principle that the Constitution does not provide any other reward for the authors of useful discoveries than that which is contained in the article in relation to patents. The same objection would of course defeat your application for twenty thousand dollars as a remuneration for this discovery, or as a reward for its free communication to the world.[1]

It will give me much pleasure to promote the objects you have in view, so far as they are within my constitutional sphere. There is no subject more interesting to me than that which concerns the domestic economy of our country, and I tender you my sincere thanks for an example of its success so creditable to yourself.

With great respect, believe me Yr. Obt. Svt.,

ANDREW JACKSON.

Printed, *Lippincott's Monthly Magazine* (December 1892), p. 768 (mAJs).
1. A Senate bill to grant a township of public lands to the heirs of steamboat inventor Robert Fulton was defeated by 33 to 9 on March 11 after unrecorded debate.

To William Ramsey and Thomas Hartley Crawford

WASHINGTON, APRIL 5th, 1830.

GENTLEMEN:

I have the honor to acknowledge the receipt of your note of this morning, presenting me with an axe and hatchet, from the Manufactory of Messrs. Dunlop & Madeira, in the borough of Chambersburgh, which I accept with great pleasure. These samples of the skill employed in that establishment, fully illustrate the capacity of our citizens to contend successfully with the ingenuity and enterprise of other nations. They, in fact, refute the idea, too prevalent in several portions of the Union, that the policy of protection is, in every view of its effects, unequal to the anticipations of its friends.

I pray you to present to those gentlemen my warmest wishes for their prosperity, and to accept for yourselves the renewal of the obligations which I owe you, for the many instances of your friendship and regard.

Your obedient servant,

ANDREW JACKSON.

Printed, Washington *Daily National Intelligencer*, April 8, 1830 (mAJs). *Niles*, April 24 (15-0583). James Dunlop (1795–1856) and George A. Madeira (c1788–1856) manufactured edge and other iron tools at their Lemnos Factory in Chambersburg, Pa.

From Ralph Eleazar Whitesides Earl

Fairfield 5th April 1830.

Dr. Sir,

I have the honor to address to you the letter from the residence of my friend Major Lewis' in answer to your kind favor of the 7th. last month, and should have answered it before but had previously written to the Major giving him nearly every information required in your letter to me.[1]

I regret it was not in my power to have accompanied Judge Overton at this time on to Washington—If the Judge could have waited two weeks longer would have done so, but he was fearful if he delayed that long the waters would be too low on his return to bring him back again, and business also which required him to be at home at a certain time.[2]

I shall this month have completed all my engagements here, and ~~shall~~ will be ready to leave this by the first steam boat that offers after the 25th.—You express'd a desire of getting a Miniature likeness of Mrs Jackson from one of my late portraits of her. The only one which I would wish to send forth to the world as a correct ~~likeness~~ representation of that good and pious woman is in the possession of Genl. Call. Upwards of twelve months ago I wrote to him by Col. Robert Armstrong who delivered the letter himself to Call at the City, in which I informed him ~~I wished with~~ it was my desire to have an engraving taken from the Portrait of Mrs Jackson then in his possession; and also to have a Miniature taken from it for you. On this subject I had written to Mr Longacre and received a letter from him informing me that Genl. Call had called on him and promised immediately on his arrival in Tallahassa he would forward the portrait to him. The Genl. also sent me the same message by Col. Armstrong. On the receipt of your letter I wrote to Call, and also sent him an extract from that part of your letter in which you express'd a desire to have a Miniature of Mrs Jackson taken from one of my late portraits of her, and requested him (if he had not already done so) soon as convenient to have it sent to Longacre of Philadelphia—where Major Bradford has my full approbation to have any engraving taken from it he may think proper.[3]

I have been so much engaged of late that I have not had time to visit the Hermitage, but intend doing so shortly, and will then write you from there very particularly.

Mr. McLemore and family are all well, except his son John who was supposed to have been bitten by a mad-dog a day or to ago and which to prevent any ~~apprehensions~~ thing of a serious ~~consequences~~ nature had an opperation performed on him by cutting out the flesh at the spot which was bitten—the dog has since been proven not to be mad.[4] I presume in the hurry of Mr. Mc.Lemore business who is very much perplexed at this time had forgotten to deliver your friendly offer as regarded funds—my friend Major Lewis previous to your favor of the 7th had offered me ~~any~~ assistance in that way, and fearful I might be in want, not being able to collect my dues accepted of his friendship, and also return you my sincere thanks for your kind offer to the same

Your friends here are all well—the Judge will give you the particulars of all local information—~~Poor Parrish's misfortune you have long before this heard of—God grant he may come out well, he has always been my~~

~~friend and I shall always respect him as such—With great respect~~ I remain
your friend and very humle. Ser.

R. E. W. Earl

ALS, DLC (38). ALS copy, MiDbEI (15-0578). Earl (1788–1838), a well-known portrait
artist, was AJ's close friend and the widower of Rachel Jackson's niece Jane Caffery.
1. William B. Lewis's estate, Fairfield, was near Nashville.
2. Tennessee lawyer and jurist John Overton (1766–1833) was AJ's longtime friend and
political backer.
3. Earl had painted Rachel Jackson for Richard K. Call around 1827. James Barton
Longacre (1794–1869) was a renowned Philadelphia engraver who had collaborated
with Earl to publish a likeness of AJ in 1828. Samuel Fisher Bradford (1776–1837) was
a Philadelphia publisher, and Robert Armstrong (1792–1854) was Nashville postmaster
and a friend of AJ. John Eaton had asked AJ to get Earl's consent for Longacre to engrave
and Bradford to publish a likeness of Rachel based on Earl's portrait (Earl to Longacre,
Jun 21, 1830, TU). Longacre received the portrait from Call in June 1830. It is now at The
Hermitage and in *Jackson Papers*, 1:93.
4. McLemore's son was John Coffee McLemore (1818–1882).

Order of Pardon for David H. Dyer

April 5th. 1830

David H Dyer some time since was convicted of robbing the mail. The
Judge of the District of Alabama who presided at his trial, and numerous
citizens have petitioned for his pardon. His youth being only 19 years old
at the time of committing the offence, and induced by older offenders to
commit the crime, & his subsequent good conduct & repentance of error,
are urged as considerations why Executive clemency should be extended.

While the President is indisposed to interfere with the laws, & to
restrain their operation, where crime is fairly and fully disclosed, he cannot be insensible to the high regard which should be paid to the application of respectable citizens where they give evidence of repentance and
reformation; and more especially to the recommendation of the Judge
who sat upon his trial, and has recommended the prisoner to mercy.

In consideration therefore of his age and that he has already suffered a
long confinement, which it is hoped, may for the future direct him to the
path of correct and moral conduct—Let him be pardoned on payment of
costs.

Andrew Jackson

[Endorsed by AJ:] order for the pardon of David H. Dyer—The pardon to
be sent to Mr. Clay representative in congress from Alabama—

DS, DNA-RG 59 (15-0615). In October 1828 David H. Dyer was convicted in federal court
at Huntsville, Ala., and sentenced to ten years' imprisonment for stealing banknotes from
letters at the Florence post office, which adjoined the printing office where he worked. On

January 14 and February 26, 1830, Alabama congressman Clement Comer Clay (1789–1866) forwarded AJ appeals for clemency from federal district judge William Crawford, who had presided at Dyer's trial, and from other leading citizens (15-0590). AJ pardoned Dyer April 6.

To John Pitchlynn

copy

Washington Apl 6th. 1830

Friend & Brother—

Such are the various and important dutes which engross my time and attention, that it is not in my power to reply to your letter fully as I otherwise would desire to do. Already I have told you my sentiments as regards your removal beyond the Mississippi. In that, I have spoken to you candidly as a friend, one—who if he could, would not deceve you. When was it, that I attempted to take advantage of my Indian friends. Brother—In all the intercourse had with them, in peace and amidst the ravages of war, my constant object has been, to speak to them as friends and brothers. I never have deceived them, and never shall. Let me say to you then—with that candour which always has been practiced, that it is vain and idle for you to expect to live happily where you are. Have you not tried it long enough and do you not perceive that your nation is daily sinking, growing fewer in numbers and becoming less powerful, Look to all the tribes which have dwelt in our country surrounded by their white brethren, and you will perceive that their character and consequence as a people, have wholly disappeared. From this fate I desire to save you— and believe it is only to be effected by a consent on your part, to remove west of the Mississippi   There you can be happy—there you will have a home, you and your children for ever, free from the interposition, or interruption which now assails you—and which must continue to assail you, whilst you reside among your white brothers. Go then to the west, where happiness and peace await you. There the state laws cannot molest or disturb you. The lands granted will be yours and will belong to your children, when you are no more, fertile & rich, they will yield an ample sustenance. To those who shall chose to indulge in agriculture, while such of your people as shall insist on the chase, will find a region opening to and stretching back on the mountains, where game is abundant and fine   If under all circumstances the choctaws sensible of their true interest, shall be disposed to remove and leave their trouble behind them. Terms the most liberal will be granted. The people of the united states want no advantage of their red brothers. they will meet in council & act with them on the most liberal and enlarged terms. Their great purpose is to make them a happy people, and indulge a hope that they may be perpetuated as a great & lasting people. If then your people shall consent to go, I shall not hesitate, to send a confidential messenger to make conditions with you, or if prefered to receive a delegation here, to arrange and settle all differences. If they be agreed to by the nation, and a delegation be sent, clothed with full powers to make a treaty on these points, all their expences in coming & returning will be paid. Make all this known to your nation[.] Your friend—

Andrew Jackson

Copy in John Dabney Terrell's hand, A-Ar (15-0623). Terrell (1775–1850), of Alabama, had been a special agent to the Chickasaws. Pitchlynn sent him a copy of this letter on May 3.

To John Branch

april 7th. 1830—

My Dr. Sir,

I have received the within from Mr. Eckford, and refer it to you that enquiry may be made of the Navy Board, as to the quality of the Timber, & value. If it is as represented by Mr Eckford, suitable for a Frigate of the first class, & repairs of our Frigates, it ought to be contracted for at the reduced price proposed. If the real price for such timbers are from $133 to 137 the cubic foot, with chance cut timber amonghst it—This choice Lot of *picked timber ought to be secured* by the U. States at $106 cents the cubic foot. The letter is therefore refered to your consideration[.] yrs

Andrew Jackson

ALS, DNA-RG 45 (M124-123). Henry Eckford (1775–1832) was a renowned naval architect and shipbuilder. He had written AJ this day offering a complete ship frame and additional cut pieces of select timber, ready at New York, for 106 cents per cubic foot.

From John Stevens

Hoboken April 7 1830

[Sir,]

In rev[iewin]g the copy of the letter which I lately took the liberty of addressing to your Exy, I now find I have taken liberties therein which, on more deliberate investigation I consider unwarrantable on my part—and am therefore induced to intreat you to pardon whatever you may find exceptionable—more especially as I now promise to be more guarded in my expressions in future on the present occasion.

I view both the objects brought forward for your consideration as involving Interests of the utmost magnitude to the general welfare &

prosperity of these ~~happily~~ U.S. If, as Your Exy. has recommended, we should discontinue building any [more] ships of war, in case [of ru]pture with a naval power we [shall be] taken unprepared—and before a naval force could be got in rea[diness,] we ~~shall~~ should be liable to sustain great injury along our coast[1]

[The plan I have] suggested would [put us into immediate] possession of [the] means of [de]fending ourselves—[Ve]ssels of all sizes and [descrip] tion [from a pil]ot boat to a ship [of large] size, are at all times procurable in our numerous seaports. And should the machinery for the steam engines and propellers be always in readiness—a very short time will [be r]equired to bring these vessels into actual service—and—unless met with a force equiped [in t]he same way—These steam Vessels would very soon clear the coast of ships of war of any size. Here then we have a plan of defence decidedly *efficient*, and, at the same time *economical* beyond calculation when compared with the present mode of ~~attack~~ naval defence. But, on this momentuous subject, I shall dwell no longer.

I shall now take the liberty of saying a few words on the subject of rail-ways and steam carriages—A very small appropriation would be [su]fficient [to put my] plan to the test of actual experiment. Now when we [take into considera]tion the enormous expenditure of money incurred in the con[struction and oper]aration of the [Natio]nal Road ~~from~~ to Weeling ~~road~~, we surely [. . . in bestowing a few] thousand dollars in the formation of rail-wa[ys.]

These rail-ways can be constructed at one thir[d of the expense of the Road] mentioned—And, as to repairs from their mode of construction scar[cely] any will be re[quired.]

How magnificent!—how beautiful! a theatre will be exhibited [to travel] with the celerity of lightning velocity of a bird in all directions, and to the uttermost extremities of these ~~well~~ highly favored States. As I have in my former letter observed—time and space will ~~be~~ thus be nearly annihilated. But there is one circumstance which will give to this improvement an unappreciable value. It will be capable of being brought to a completion in a most wonderfully short space of time. Under such superintendence and arrangements as I have taken the liberty of suggesting and recommending Rail-~~Roads~~ ways may be made to pervade every section of these States in ~~the~~ two, three or four years at farthest. Our external commerse, [from] various circumstances, [is] at the present moment [in a] somewhat [lan]guishing state. But Rail-Ways ~~will~~ would ~~thus~~ soon revive our [wonted vigorous] exertions. Commerce furnishes us with the means of ma[king beneficial ex]changes of the [products of our] own soil with [those of other climes, but th]e effect of the [improvement] now proposed will, [in] a great me[asure], remedy the ~~loss~~ diminution, or even total loss, of foreign intercourse. The v[ast] extent of our territories embraces sites of every ~~temperature and~~ variety of soil & climate. All that is wanting is to render the intercourse [easy, cheap, and] expeditious. Of every variety of what is usually called the rough materials of fabrics and manufactu[res] we possess an abundance. ~~It is the~~ We want then only a facility of transportation to make our internal communications supply very soon to a great extent and ultimately, completely any interruption of foreign intercourse. By this [mode] of [communication] I shou[ld] not be surprised should we be able soon to procure abundant supplies of oranges, limes, [lemons,] pine-apples &c in one third of the time it now takes in obtaining our supplies of these ar[ticles in the] usual way, by water—And this too at one half the expense. H[ow transcendently] meritorious will that administration prove by whose efforts these [improvements in this] mode of transportation are introduced and accomplished[. Improvements that will] bestow blessings on future generations to the end of time.

AL draft, NjHi (mAJs). Typed copy, InU (15-0640). The manuscript is badly deteriorated. Missing text has been supplied from the typescript.
   1. AJ's first annual message had recommended stockpiling materials for rapid naval construction if necessary, rather than incur the heavy expense of building and maintaining unneeded warships in peacetime (Richardson, 2:459).

From Martin Van Buren

Will the President have the goodness to inform Mr Van Buren whether his decision in regard to Mr Witherels case has undergone any change

[In AJ's hand:] The President informs the Secretary of State that he has not come to any other decision in the case of Judge Wetheral than the one endorsed on the papers, towit, that whenever the Sec of State was ready to make out the nomination of Mr Mason he would send it up—nor has he ever told any person otherwise—That he might have said that this nomination would not go up before May nex[t] may be true but has no recollection even

AN, DNA-RG 59 (15-0559). On April 7 Michigan territorial delegate John Biddle asked Van Buren if it was true, as he had heard, that AJ intended putting off a decision to replace James Witherell until May (DNA-RG 59, M179-72).

Clement Comer Clay and John McKinley to Martin Van Buren

Washington—April 8th. 1830.

Hon. M. Van Buren:

Sir,

Enclosed you will receive a letter addressed to us by G. W. Higgins, Henderson Lewis and Samuel B. Moore Esquires, acting as a corresponding committee, appointed at a meeting of sundry citizens of Jackson County, Alabama, held at Bellefonte, on the 8th. ult.—The object in view seems to be the procurement of a grant, or grants of land, within the limits of the Mexican Government—the motives, and purpose of the committee, & of those whom they represent, are however fully explained in the paper referred to. Our reflections upon the subject have resulted in the conclusion, that the propriety of any direct communication, on our part, with the Representative of the Mexican Government, would be at least questionable. We have, therefore, thought proper to submit the address of the committee to your consideration; and to request, if consistent with your views of propriety, that you will communicate with the Minister of the Mexican Government upon the subject; or that you will please to inform us of the course most proper to be pursued. We have the honor to be, very respectfully, your obt. svts.

J. McKinley
C. C. Clay

[Endorsed by State Department chief clerk Daniel Brent:] McKinley J & Clay C C   Washington, 8 April 1830 Recd 12th.   Grants of land in Mexico NB The memorial did not come into my Hands, with this letter   D B

[Endorsed by AJ:] The President cannot have any thing to do in the project—The Mexicans would at once think we were engaged in plots against them   A. J—

LS, DNA-RG 59 (M179-68). Samuel B. Moore (1789–1846) was an Alabama legislator.

To John Coffee

(private)

Washington April 10th. 1830—

Dr. Genl.

I wrote you on the 8th instant by Mr Saml J. Hays to be mailed at Nashville enclosing you the receipts of the expenditure of the $500. dollars transmitted to me, for the use of Master Hutchings education, cloothing &c &c, which when recd. you will please place on file with the other papers & give me credit for the $500– on the Books.[1]

I now write you by A. J. Hutchings who goes on in the stage with Mr Bedford of Nashville, to be mailed at Nashville, on the receipt of which I will thank you to write him. I have directed him to go to Mr Williford at Columbia & finish his mathematical studies—Here, is a bad place for a youth, who has not a constant eye over him, & my situation is such, that every moment is employed on my public business, and I have no time to attend to any one, my life is one of incessant labour, I may really say it is a dignified station of abject slavery, and if I can only realise the hopes of my country, by bringing back the Legislature of this union, to the real principles of the Constitution as understood when it was first adopted, & practiced upon in 1798 & 1800, I shall not complain of the sacrafice I have made, by being placed where I am—but altho I never despair, still from the extraordinary course pursued by the present Congress, I cannot say I am sanguine of success—The most unacountable state of electioneering, *secretely*, commenced at the commencement of this session of Congress—The first object was to lessen my popularity, by a determination that nothing should be adopted that I had recommended, by which the nation might be induced to require a change in the Presidency—This will account to you, for the amendment recommended by me to the Constitution, *sleeping*, Mr McDuffie being the *chairman* &c &c[2]—I need not point to you, further the great actor in this secrete drama—It is plain Mr VanBuren whose situation has identified him with the success of the administration, could not be using his influence against it—no, he is firm to the core, but it is his *rival*—The late proceedings at Harrisburgh, has proved a damper on those ambitious views, & will give peace in the republican ranks & we will, I trust, progress smoothly on with the public business, and these restless spirits will have to yield to the determination & will of the people—could I see you, I have evidence to unfold to you, the base hypocracy of the great secrete agent, as it respects myself, as early as 1818—under the most positive assurance of his friendship but of this hereafter.[3]

I wrote you about the account against Hutchings in Columbia some time since—When that merchant is punished a little and it is convenient for you to spare the amount, let it be paid—and let it be understood that no account will be paid hereafter of Hutchings contracting unless by your authority—Mr Booker will be a proper agent to place Hutchings under— From the documents forwarded by Mr Hays, you will find Hutchings has behaved well at college here, but he has such a great dislike to this place, & his health not good that I have consented to let him return under a promise that he will abandon his extravagance—he has asked me permission to visit his grandmother Hutchings before he joins college, I have granted this request.

I have just recd. a letter from Mr Hume, informing me of his visit to the Hermitage & Capt John Donelsons and of the weak & debilitated state of the Captain—I fear my old friend is not to be long with us, I despair of seeing him again—If I can, I will return, even for a few days, to the Hermitage this summer, & if he should be spared, once more take & shake him by the hand—What a life of toil & trouble has been mine, & now, even in my decline, forced into public life, in constant labour & bustle, without one hope of care or comfort to myself; be it so, it is the will of providence & I submit—[4]

Present us all affectionately to your amiable family, & with a hope of seeing you here next fall, believe me yr friend

Andrew Jackson

ALS, THi (15-0656).
1. In 1829 Coffee had furnished AJ with $500 from Andrew J. Hutchings's estate to cover his expenses and schooling in Washington for a year.
2. AJ's annual message in December 1829 had recommended amending the constitution to make the president electable by direct popular vote for a single term of four or six years or, failing that, at least to bar congressmen from receiving executive office from a president chosen by the House. On December 10 the House referred these proposals to a special committee chaired by George McDuffie (1790–1851) of South Carolina. On February 1, 1830, McDuffie reported a complicated constitutional amendment to elect a president by popular vote within districts, each district casting one electoral vote. A second election between the two top candidates would follow if neither obtained a majority of districts in the first. No further action ensued.
3. The secret agent was John C. Calhoun, whom AJ would soon accuse of treachery over his 1818 Seminole campaign (May 13, below).
4. John Donelson, Rachel Jackson's brother and father of Coffee's wife Mary and of Emily Tennessee Donelson, died April 21. William Hume (1770–1833) of Nashville was a Presbyterian minister and friend of AJ.

To Martin Van Buren

private & for Mr Van Burens own eye—

April 10th. 1830—

I have examined Mr Rives dispatch, hastily. I am clearly of opinion that all kind of mixed commissions ought to be avoided if possible by agreeing to a gross sum to be paid for all spoliations committed by France & our commerce, from a certain date to the present, say for instance six millions of dollars, if that sum will be sufficient to cover all the *just* claims of our citizens, and let commissioners be appointed by the United States to adjudicate, and apportion all the claims of our own citizens against France; and when adjudicated aportioned agreable to the amount thus stipulated to be paid—This mixed commission will be both tedious & expensive & ought to be avoided if possible—But if Mr Rives should find that the French minister would prefer leaving it to this mixed commission, it appears to me, that one commissioner & arbatrator, on each side, would be sufficient, and in the event of disagreement, the arbatrator selected by lot to determine; three men will dispatch business more expeditiously than five, & with as much justice—Still I am in favor of a gross sum which will cover all our just claims for time is every thing for merchants & if a gross sum is agreed upon, our merchants will receive their mony in half the time that a mixed commission will pass upon & settle the claims.[1]

On the subject of our negotiation with great Britain—we ought to be prepared to act promptly in case of a failure—we have held out terms of reconciling our difference with that nation of the most Frank liberal & fair terms—Terms, if England really had a wish to harmonise, and act justly towards us, ought to have been meet in that spirit of frankness & candor & friendship with which we proposed them—These terms being rejected our national character & honor requires, that we should now act with that promptness & energy due to our national character—Therefore let a communication be prepared for congress recommending a non intercourse law between the United States & Canady, and a sufficient number of Cutters commanded by our naval officers & our midshipmen made revenue officers, and a double set on every vessel &c &c—This adopted and carried into effect forthwith and in six months both Canady and the westindia Islands will feel, and sorely feel, the effects of their folly in urging their Government to adhere to our exclusion from the west India trade[2]

will Mr. Van Buren—Think of these sugestions and see me early on monday to confer upon this subject

Andrew Jackson

[Endorsed by AJ:] Mr Van Buren will please bring this with him on Monday morning A. J

ALS, DLC (38).
1. Rives's dispatch of February 25, received on April 10, proposed that the U.S. and France each designate two commissioners and one arbitrator to settle disputed American spoliation claims. The four commissioners would adjudicate claims, with one arbitrator drawn by lot joining them when necessary to break ties. AJ noted his preference for a lump settlement by France in his memorandum book (above, p. 168). On April 20 Van Buren instructed Rives to try for a gross payment or at least for a smaller commission, but to

accede to French insistence on either point if France would agree to settle the claims (*HRDoc* 147, 22d Cong., 2d sess., pp. 35–38, Serial 235).

2. A series of retaliatory trade restrictions between the U.S. and Great Britain had culminated with the latter closing its West Indian colonial ports to American shipping in 1826, effectively ending their direct trade to the U.S. In July 1829, Van Buren instructed U.S. minister to Britain Louis McLane to offer a recision of American discriminatory measures if Britain would reciprocate by opening the colonial trade to the U.S. on the same terms permitted to other nations. McLane proposed the arrangement to the British ministry in October 1829 and pressed it thereafter but could get no definite response. His dispatch of February 26, 1830, received in Washington April 9, reported no progress in the discussions and remarked that further British delay would injure American dignity. Van Buren had already advised McLane that British obstinance might prompt U.S. retaliation against Canadian shippers, who carried an indirect American commerce with the West Indies in lieu of the direct trade (*SDoc* 20, 21st Cong., 2d sess., Serial 203; DNA-RG 59, M30-33).

From Hestor Lockhart Stevens

Rochester 10 April 1830

The Petition which I have the honor of forwarding you I sincerely hope may meet with your favourable consideration. The father of Thomas Sloan is a very worthy man, and by the enlistment of his son is very unfortunately situated

Being a foreigner by birth & having come late in life to this country he does not so readily become familiarized to the manners & customs of our country, and his son also having had charge of his business heretofore and it still being necessary that some one should continue to assist & indeed to support the old gentleman makes the situation of the father peculiarly unfortunate.

No blame whatever attaches to Lieutenant Harris in relation to the subject, as I have been informed and do not doubt that he took the necessary precaution previous to his enlistment, to ascertain whether he really wished to be enlisted. The friends of Sloan who saw him about the time he enlisted, say that one not well acquainted with him, might not have observed anything peculiar in his appearance or conduct. With sentiments of the highest esteem and consideration I have the Honor to be your Obt Servt

H. Stevens

ALS, DNA-RG 107 (M222-28).

[Enclosure: Hestor Lockhart Stevens et al. to AJ]

Rochester NY. 7" April 1830.

Your petitioners would humbly represent That Mr Thomas Sloan an Irishman by birth, but now a resident of the county of monroe and state

of New York was enlisted in the U States army at the recruiting establishment in this village on the 18' day of March last as a private soldier—Mr
Sloan is a very respectable young man and until his enlistment resided
with his father (an aged man) and who looks to his son for support and
protection of his old age. Your petitioners feel assured that at the time this,
to him unfortunate circumstance occurred Mr Sloan was not sensible of
the act he was doing, and we know that he now deeply and bitterly regrets
the course he has pursued. On the 17' of March the natives and friends of
Ireland celebrated in this village the Festival of St Patrick, and Mr Sloan
with many others came in from the country to join in the festivities of the
occasion, and we regret to say that indiscretely he became intoxicated,
and as will appear from the certificates and affidavits accompanying this
petition continued so until after his enlistment.

Your petitioners are assured that intemperance is not a vice to which
Mr. Sloan is habitually addicted and also that nothing could be further
from his intention, than this enlistment had he been in a rational and
sound state of mind.

Considering the advanced aged of Mr Sloan the father, and that his son
is his only stay & support and also that the son has done in a moment
of excitement, and we might say of alienation of mind what in his sober
moments he would not have done Your Petitioners would most humbly
solicit that he might be discharged from the Army. And your Petitioners
as in duty bound will ever pray—

> Hestor Stevens
> Mortimer Strong
> Luther Tucker.
> James Seymour
> Henry O'Reilly
> Jacob Gould
> Seth Saxton

[Endorsed by AJ:] refered to the Sec. of War—application for the discharge of Sloan—irregularly enlisted—

[Endorsed by AJ:] The President with his respects refers the enclosed
Statement to the Secretary of war, for his examination & decision—The
enlisting of men whilst intoxicated must be pud be put down—it is disgraceful to our national character   april 20th—1830

[Endorsed by John H. Eaton:] Majr. Genl Macomb, will examine this
case, & report to me, who the officer is who attends the recruiting service;
also whether the order of last summer forbidding the enlistment of intoxicated persons, has not been issued to the army—J. H. E 21. April 30

DS, DNA-RG 107 (M222-28). Stevens (1803–1864) was a Rochester lawyer and later a Michigan congressman. On April 22 Major General Alexander Macomb (1782–1841), commanding general of the Army, reported to Eaton. He submitted proofs that Lieutenant William L. Harris (1800–1837), who recruited Sloan, had correctly followed a series of required procedures designed to guarantee against the enlistment of intoxicated persons (DNA-RG 108, M857-1).

Daniel W. Wright to Powhatan Ellis

Hamilton, Aprill 11th. 1830

Dear Judge

This morning I received a communication from Majr. Pitchlynn of the Choctaw Nation, requesting me in behalf of himself Mushulatubbe Hihagotoba, the Talking Warrier, and the head men and Captains of the Northern and South Eastern districts of the Natition, to address the President on the subject of what they call their distressed situation

As my acquaintance with the President was at a period of my life when my years were few in Number it is possible that he may not now recollect me, and as I have heretofore written to you the subject of Indian affairs in our State I deem it most prudent to address you, and make their communication to you, and if you in your discretion may think it worth presenting to the President you can do so

you will recollect that Majr. Pitchlynn has been Interpreter for the United States in the Choctaw Nation of Indians for forty years, and that although he is a white man resident among them with an Indian family he has ever both in and out of the Nation, sustained a fair & reputable Caracter

I will give you their communication *verbatim*, with the exception, of ading a word or two to make it read intelligable

They request me to say to the President, that they are a distressed People and want the help of their Great Father the President who has never told them a lye

That a few half Breed Chiefs, and the Missionaries have robed them of their rights and happiness. That they are all (Except the Majr.) full Blooded Indians

That they understand, Greenwood Lalflour, David Folsome and John Garland thre half Breed Chiefs, has sent on by Majr. Hailey, propositions to the President to treat away their Country without their Consent or knowledge, and without hardly any of the Indians knowing any thing about it, and as they have heard upon such terms as will not benefit the Common Indians and give them Justice

That they have always had Chiefs of their own until now and have never been compelled to serve a Chief without their own consent, and that they are now determined not to do it, for they understand Fulsome & Garland the former Chiefs of their Districts have resigned in favor of

Laflour who is to be the only Chief for life This they say they can not bear

They say they the persons before named are the head men of the Northern & South Eastern Districts and their Captains & warriers speak as they do. That they are ready if the President will send Commissioners on to treat with them for their two districts   That they will, give the Government a better treaty than the half Breeds and Missionaries have offered them and that they will go west of the Mississippi river or any where the President may think best for them to go &c.

I set out by stating that I wold give the Communication *verbatim* but when I came to transcribe it I found that I had best give it in substance as it is made in the true Indian Stile of communicating Ideas

Thus you see the Condition of the Choctaws and it is now in the power of the United States to make a favorable treaty with them, one which will enable the Govt. to display its Magnanimity, towards those persons, for they are at this time entirely at the Mercy of the Govt. their own internal dissentions producing the effect

I have no doubt those two districts *en mass* will conform to the policy of the Govt. and the other will be compelled to come into the measure

you will pardon me when I give it to you as my opinion that the earliest action on the part of the Govt. in this respect will be most sure to effect the object of the Govt. & the interest of the Indians, as also it may prevent the effusion of Blood by those poor deluded and missguided people, for from what I can learn there is every probability that the 16th. Inst. will date the Commencement of a civil war among them

This fact I believe I mentioned to you in my last letter

I shall set out on wednesday next for Madison Court and shall stay on the Night of the Sixteenth in the Neighbourhood of the Council so soon as I hear the result of their meeting I will inform you

I am with sentiments of great respect your Friend

D. W. Wright

PS. Col. Pruett[1] who passed through the Nation the other day, says he understood The Talking Warrier had beat his War Drum, and was performing the Indian Ceremonies usual preceeding *war* &c.

[Endorsed by AJ:] Colo. Wright to Judge Ellis—

ALS, DNA-RG 46 (15-0673). Wright (1795–1844) was a Mississippi lawyer and former legislator, and Powhatan Ellis (1790–1863) was U.S. senator from Mississippi. Wright's summary of objections to the Leflore and Folsom treaty closely matched the remonstrance sent by Mushulatubbe and others to Eaton on March 25 (above). AJ enclosed this letter to the Senate with the treaty on May 6 (below).
    1. Likely Abner Prewett (1789–1871), later a Mississippi state legislator.

From Nicholas Philip Trist

Washington, Apr. 12. 1830.
Dr Sir,

~~I have~~ Having just now heard of the rejection of Mr Hill, I will lose no time in saying to you, as I did some ~~time~~ weeks since to Mr Donelson, that shd. a vacancy occur in, & shd. it suit yr. views to appoint me to, any of these high offices in the Treasury, I wd. thankfully avail myself of ~~the~~ such a disposition. Lest ~~it~~ this comment ~~shd. appear~~ shd. strike you as evincive of greediness on my part, I will state that it is as much with a view to the comfort of Mrs Randolph & her family as my own, that this letter is written. I shall not trouble you with any recommendations. Shd. these be wanting, a suggestion to that effect will be attended to, by yr. obt. servt.

N. P. T.

ALS draft, DLC-Trist Papers (15-0682). Trist (1800–1874) was a State Department clerk. His wife's mother was Thomas Jefferson's daughter Martha Jefferson Randolph (1772–1836), now a widow in financial straits. On this day the Senate rejected AJ's nomination of Isaac Hill for second comptroller. Action on Amos Kendall's nomination as fourth auditor, sent to the Senate February 4, was still pending. Trist remained in the State Department. He was later consul to Havana under AJ and negotiated the Treaty of Guadalupe Hidalgo ending the Mexican War under Polk.

Toast at Jefferson Birthday Dinner

[On April 13, Jackson attended, by invitation, a public dinner at the Indian Queen Hotel in honor of Thomas Jefferson's birthday. A committee consisting of Thomas Hart Benton of Missouri, George M. Troup of Georgia, and Warren R. Davis of South Carolina had prepared twenty-four regular toasts, many of which applauded principles of state's rights and warned of federal oppression. Jackson's was the first volunteer toast to follow.]

Our *Federal* Union—*It must be preserved.*

[Endorsed by William B. Lewis:] The above toast was given by President Jackson, at the Jefferson Birth Day dinner on the 13th. Apl 1830, and published in the Washington Telegraph the 17th. from the original manuscript. W B L

[Endorsed by AJ Donelson:] Genl. Jackson's Toast at the Jefferson Dinner in 1830.

Copy in William B. Lewis's hand, DLC (72). *US Telegraph*, April 17, 1830. Calhoun imme-diately followed AJ's toast with "The Union: Next to our liberty, the most dear; may we all remember that it can only be preserved by respecting the rights of the States and distributing equally the benefit and burden of the Union." Van Buren then toasted "Mutual forbearance and reciprocal concession." AJ's toast was widely interpreted as a rebuke to Calhoun and the nullifiers.

To Martin Van Buren

April 15th. 1830—

Dr Sir

I have perused the report of Genl Call with the accompanying papers and now return them—His account rendered compared with the reported service rendered is reasonable—

In the instructions sent out to our minister in spain by the agent con-templated to be sent out to obtain the documents in the judicial order, might be added, the archives which of right belong to Florida, were to be delivered with the country by positive stipulations in the treaty, & which have not—If such an order can be obtained from the King of Spain by our minister, then our agent could return by Havanna, and Bring them here—I submit this for your consideration before you make out the instructions to be sent by our special agent[1]

I have directed the original draft of the communication to be made to the Senate with the Choctaw Nation to be handed to you—I wish your criticism upon it, with any addition you may please to suggest[2]—yrs.

Andrew Jackson

ALS, DNA-RG 59 (15-0727; T1212-3). *TPUS*, 24:395–96. Richard K. Call had returned in March from his mission to Cuba to retrieve records of Spanish land grants in Florida, which the cession treaty of 1819 said were to be turned over to the U.S. Call reported that he had obtained some documents but was refused others. He suggested asking the Spanish government to instruct Cuban authorities to deliver them (*TPUS*, 24:384–88). Call submit-ted expenses of $1,231.50, of which the Treasury disallowed $51.00.

1. On May 25, Van Buren instructed U.S. minister Cornelius P. Van Ness to seek an order from Spain to Cuban officials to surrender the documents. Atkinson H. Rowan, sent as special agent to retrieve Spanish documents for the pending Supreme Court Soulard and Smith T cases, carried the instructions to Van Ness. On February 15, 1832, the Spanish government ordered immediate surrender of the documents and informed Van Ness.

2. AJ addressed the Senate regarding the Choctaws on May 6 (below).

From Anthony Butler

City of Mexico 15. April 1830.

My dear Sir,

In my dispatch of the 10th. forwarded by the way of Vera Cruz, I apprised the Government of the present state of affairs in Mexico, and of the prospect before us. Since the departure of Mr. Poinsett the aspect of things is materially changed for the better as I think; and all the public functionaries so far as professions go, indicate the strongest desire to unite the two Governments in bonds of the strictest intimacy. There seems now to be a probability of my effecting all the objects with which this Legation is charged not only in relation to the Treaty of Commerce, but also the Treaty of limits including the Cession of part or the whole of Texas.[1]

This latter will no doubt be attended with some difficulties but I am not without hopes of being able to reconcile this Government to an acquiescence in our views upon that most important subject. As yet nothing more than conversations have passed between the Secretary of State and myself, but they have been so frequent, so full and explicit—and his observations so pregnant of good will towards the United States, with professions of the strongest desire to advance the interests, and accommodate the wishes of our Government, and to strengthen by all proper means the relations of amity between Mexico and the United States; that every thing favours the opinion of our settling amicably and to mutual advantage all the questions now open between the two Governments, provided the Executive power remains in the hands of the Men who at this time administer the Government.

When first accredited by this Government, the political state of the Country was so disordered and unsettled, and the men in power held their Offices by a tenure so precarious, and apparently so short lived, that it seemed to me useless to attempt any thing of important character, as the proceeding was liable to be interrupted from day to day by the threatened ejection from office of those who held the Executive power. Besides, after the repeated suspensions of the most important Negotiations between the two Nations caused by the acts of the Mexican Government itself, we having performed every thing it was necessary on our part to do, for perfecting the arrangements entered into between Mexico and the United States; it seemed to me due to the dignity of our Government no less than in conformity with the Tenor of my General instructions that I should wait for the manifestation of a desire on the part of the Mexican Government to renew the Negotiation. This manifestation has several weeks since been made, and Mr. Alaman the Secretary of State then assured me that so soon as the Government could dispose of the questions connected with the continuance of the present Administration in power—So soon as the prevailing insurrectionary spirit was quelled, and the factions in arms at different points in the Republic were subdued, he would immediately commence with me the discussion and adjustment of a Commercial Treaty; as well as a Treaty of limits; and that the earliest moment would be seized on for doing so.

In a very recent conversation the Secretary stated his hopes of being able in a very short time to commence on the Commercial Treaty—that communications had been received very lately from the different points where disaffection had most threat'ned the Administration to induce the belief that opposition would be entirely suppressed, and tranquillity restored throughout the Republic.

Amongst other reasons for strengthening my belief in an amicable and successful termination of all our differences with the Mexican Government is the apprehended invasion from Spain. In this event it is obvious that Mexico would desire to stand well with the United States, for notwithstanding the well known policy pursued at all times by our Government of preserving a neutral attitude between Belligerents, I can perceive that Mexico is not without hopes that in her extremity we might lend her aid in preference to seeing the Country once again subjugated to the dominion of Spain.[2] This has been clearly indicated to me in a Conversation held not long since with Mr. Alaman, who directly proposed to me the question "What do you suppose would be the course of your Government in the event of a second invasion by Spain and of Mexico being seriously pressed? Did I believe that any aid could be counted on from the United States to relieve Mexico in her difficulties?" To these questions I replied of course, that it was not in my power to return any satisfactory answer—that I had no instructions on that subject—That he (the Secretary) knew the Character of our policy but that certainly events might occur to induce a relaxation of that policy, and a contingency happen when the Government might feel itself not only justified, but called on to depart from the course hitherto uniformly pursued, and deemed as part of a system adopted upon the fullest deliberation, and tested by long experience, as the one best calculated to secure peace and promote the happiness and interests of our Community. That whenever such a Contingency should arise, Government would take the part which a just regard to our character and interests might indicate. In this way I promised nothing, but by mistifying a little left him not without hopes. I have besides other ground on which I found a hope that the Mexican Governmt. may be induced to yield Texas, whenever we come to a discussion of that question. Yet I confess there are great difficulties to be overcome, and perhaps the Negotiation with all my hopes may utterly fail. You have heard already from Mr. Poinsett his opinions: they are no doubt such as he conveyed to me *viz*: "that Texas never would be ceded to *us*:" He may be correct, and my opinions erroneous, for I freely admit that during a five years intercourse of the most free unlimited character, he had more ample means for forming a true estimate of this people, than I can possibly acquire in the same number of months, and with the additional advantage of speaking the Language like a Native. Yet with all this I repeat, my hopes are strong that success will attend me—The result may convict me of error, but at present my impressions are clear that I shall manage this people better than Mr Poinsett was able to do.

Before I close this letter already a very long one, you will permit me to suggest for your consideration one fact. I am here comparatively a stranger to the Spanish Language: it is true that for ordinary purposes I can read, understand and translate with sufficient accuracy to obtain their meaning—Yet with regard to Official communications, and more especially on subjects of moment, where misunderstanding the true import of one word, might make an essential difference in the character and meaning of a sentence, I have felt it necessary to have perfect translations made—This costs me, and will hereafter cost me a great deal when in discussing the articles of a Treaty, long communications will be frequently received that must be replied to. In this event what shall I do? Shall I employ a Secretary to be paid by the Month, or must the translations be made as the contingency shall occur? Hitherto I have made no charge in my Contingent account for disbursements of that sort, because in all my Correspondence with the Departments of the Government, relative to the detention of Vessels in port and other questions that have arisen under their Revenue Laws, I have been able with but two exceptions to understand with sufficient clearness the different Notes addressed to me so as to return replies or make explanations. I am aware that heretofore clerks have been allowed to chargé d'affaires and their hire paid out of the Contingent fund, but previous to my entering on that account an item for such services (although its performance will be indispensable to me) I beg you will advise Mr. Van Buren on the subject, so that he may communicate to me his instructions. My salary will at present scarcely support me in the style of a gentleman in Mexico, and such a drawback on it, I presume the Government neither desire or intend. Let me hear from you on this matter at your earliest convenience.[3]

With best Wishes for your Health and happiness, and my fervent prayers that your fame may increase with your years I remain as ever your obliged and sincere friend

A. Butler

ALS, DNA-RG 59 (M97-6). Copy, CU-BANC (15-0712). Extract, HRDoc 351, 25th Cong., 2d sess., pp. 323–24 (Serial 332).
1. Butler's dispatch to the State Department of April 10, 1830, described Mexican fears of an imminent Spanish invasion and his conversations with Lucas Alamán (1792–1853), Mexico's Minister of Interior and Exterior Relations, about the prospect of American aid in that event. He reported that Alamán also suggested that the U.S. annex or extend a protectorate over Cuba in the likely event of its separation from Spain—a separation which Butler believed Mexican agents were working to effect by fomenting a Cuban revolution or slave revolt. Two commercial treaties between the U.S. and Mexico, signed in 1826 and 1828,

had failed of ratification in the Mexican Congress, and a boundary treaty of 1828 (which left Texas with Mexico) was ratified only after the deadline to do so had expired. Both matters therefore remained unresolved. In his first instructions to Butler in October 1829, Van Buren had charged the ratification failures to "the political perverseness and inattention of the Mexican government" (*HRDoc* 351, 25th Cong., 2d sess., p. 44, Serial 332).

2. A Spanish force from Cuba had attacked Tampico in July 1829.

3. AJ wrote Van Buren on June 26, enclosing this letter and approving a translator for Butler (below).

To John Henry Eaton

April 16th. 1830

The President refers to the secretary of war, the subject of a claim upon Genl John Brown, on a bond that will be produced by Major Taylor of the cherokee delegation to him—question; ought not the agent to be instructed to enforce a compliance with this obligation by Genl John Brown

I shall see you shortly before I ride out—

AN, DNA-RG 107 (M222-26). John Brown (1779–1846) of Roane County, Tenn., had commanded Tennessee volunteers under AJ in the War of 1812. The claim was on behalf of George Fields, who fought with AJ's Cherokee auxiliaries in the Creek campaign. Fields held Brown's bond for two of his slaves that Brown had taken from a Cherokee named The Broom in 1813. On April 28 Thomas L. McKenney instructed Cherokee agent Hugh Montgomery, who had forwarded the bond to Richard Taylor in Washington, to recover its amount "by suit or otherwise" (DNA-RG 75, M21-6). In 1833 Congress paid Fields $700 compensation.

To George Graham

April 16th. 1830—

Dr. Sir,

I have just recd. Judge Kelly' letter, read, & now return it to you.

I am uninformed, what the costs of the suits against the U. States would amount to; therefore, cannot determine whether it would be to the interest of the U. States, to meet Judge Kellys proposition "that he will dismiss the suits on the United States paying the costs"—I would refer you to the secretary of the Treasury, & attorney General, for consultation, & advice upon this subject, & if they recommend it, I will approve, as it may quiet the minds of the citizens in possession of the land, and increase the amount of sales. yours respectfully

Andrew Jackson

ALS, DNA-RG 60 (15-0737). William Kelly (1786–1834), a former U.S. senator from Alabama, represented John Smith T in the pending Supreme Court suits to establish his title to north Alabama lands purchased from Zachariah Cox. On April 15 Kelly had written

Graham that a deed from Cox, now in possession of the Senate Committee on Public Lands, proved that he had fully relinquished his interest in Tennessee Company lands before selling it to Smith T, thus exploding the latter's claim. Kelly offered to dismiss the suits if the government would pay costs, on grounds that if he had been shown the deed earlier he would have abandoned Smith T's case at once (DNA-RG 60, 15-0721). On April 27 Berrien wrote Kelly that AJ agreed (DNA-RG 60, M699-1). Kelly dropped the suits and abjured Smith T's claim, and Graham forwarded his account to Ingham for payment on May 1 (DNA-RG 49, M25-25). Meanwhile, on April 22 the Senate Public Lands Committee rejected Kelly's alternative proposal to buy Smith T out (SDoc 129, 21st Cong., 1st sess., Serial 193).

From John Macpherson Berrien

Office of the Attorney General U.S.
16th. April 1830.

Sir,

I have the honor to acknowledge the receipt of your communication of yesterday asking my opinion,

Whether the rejection by the Senate of the nomination of Mr. Isaac Hill to the office of second Comptroller of the Treasury, has vacated the Commission granted on the Executive appointment of that officer, made during the late recess of the Senate?

Or whether a Commission issued under an Executive appointment, continues until the end of the succeeding session of Congress, or until another commission shall be issued on a nomination approved by the Senate?

Mr. Hill was appointed during the last recess of the Senate, to fill a vacancy occurring during the recess—That appointment was made in pursuance of the third clause of the second section of the constitution which declares that "The President shall have power to fill all vacancies, that may happen during the recess of the Senate, by granting commissions, which shall expire at the end of their next session"—The commission issued to Mr. Hill, was I presume in conformity to these provisions—It was then a grant of the office, to the end of the next session of Congress succeeding its date, subject intermediately, as all such offices are, to the pleasure of the President.

Under the preceding clause of the same section of the Constitution, the President is authorised to nominate, and by and with the advice and consent of the Senate to appoint, all officers of the United States, whose appointments are not otherwise provided for in the Constitution, and which shall be established by law—with a provision which is inapplicable to the present enquiry, that Congress may vest the appointment of such inferior officers as they may think proper, in the President, alone, in the Courts of law, or in the heads of departments—

In the exercise of the power thus conferred upon the President, Mr. Isaac Hill was during the present session of Congress nominated by him to the Senate, and the nomination has been rejected by that body—I apprehend that the commission granted to Mr. Hill in the recess, remains untouched by this nomination and the rejection of it—

The limitation which is affixed to it by the Constitution is *the end of the present session of Congress*, unless it be sooner determined by the pleasure of the President—To this, the decision of the Supreme Court, in the case of the *United States vs. Kirkpatrick* has superadded another limitation—That Court has in that case decided that the acceptance of a commission issued after the confirmation by the Senate of an Executive appointment made during the recess on a nomination to that body of the same individual is a virtual superseding and surrender of the commission granted on the original appointment[1]—So that by force of that decision if Mr. Hill's nomination had been confirmed, and a new commission had issued under an appointment made in conformity to the advice and consent of the Senate, after the acceptance by him of such new commission, that which he originally held, would have been virtually superseded and would not have continued until the end of the present session of Congress—but this would be the result of the concurring acts of the President and the officer, of the former in the new appointment, consequent to the advice and consent of the Senate—of the latter in the acceptance of the Commission issued under such new appointment—

In the case under consideration whether the commission of Mr. Hill shall continue until the end of the present session of Congress, or be sooner determined, seems to me to depend on the pleasure of the President—He certainly has the power by and with the advice and consent of the Senate, to determine it by a new appointment to take effect immediately—but this power is derived from his right of removal—If he abstains from the exercise of that power—if he delays the nomination until the last day of the session—or nominates immediately, specifying that the appointment is to take effect at the end of the present session, in either case, Mr. Hill's commission, undetermined by any act of the Executive will, is left to expire by its own constitutional limitation, at the end of the present session of Congress—

The following precedents which have been adverted to, among others, seem to conform to this view of the subject—

On the 5th. of March 1799, Mr. Adams then President, appointed *Eugene Brenan* an Inspector of the Revenue—On the 4th. of the following December, he nominated that individual to the Senate for the same office—On the 10th. of that month, the nomination was rejected by that body—and on the 12th. of the same month, he made a new nomination in the following terms—"I nominate Julius Nicolls Jun of South Carolina to be Inspector of Survey number three in that State, in the place of Eugene Brenan, *whose commission will expire at the end of the present session of the Senate*"—and on the 13th. the Senate advised and consented to that nomination—[2]

On the 17th. January 1814 Mr Madison nominated to the Senate as principal assessor for the 28th. collection district of New York, *Homer R. Phelps* who had been appointed to that office, during the recess—On the 24th. of that month, the nomination was rejected by the Senate, and on the 31st. the President nominated sundry assessors, and among the rest, "Asahel E. Paine for the 28th. collection district of New York, *in room of Homer R. Phelps*" which nomination was confirmed on the second of February—[3]

In the first of these cases, Mr. Adams left the officer to enjoy the benefit of the commission granted during the recess, until the end of the then current session of Congress, altho' his nomination was rejected in the early part of that session—In the second Mr. Madison conforming to the opinion of the Senate as expressed in their vote of rejection, determined this Executive appointment, by appointing a new officer *in the room* of the person so appointed—

In the first, the President forbore to exercise the power of removal, but left the Executive commission granted during the recess, to expire by its own limitation—The Executive commission granted in the second case, was determined by the exercise of that power—

Upon the whole, I am of opinion that the commission granted during the recess to Mr. Hill, will continue until the end of the present session of Congress, unless it be sooner determined by his resignation, or by the pleasure of the President—I have the honor to be Very Respectfully Sir Yr. obt st

Jn: Macpherson Berrien

LC, DNA-RG 60 (T412-3). Copy, DNA-RG 46 (15-0729). *HRDoc* 123, 26th Cong., 2d sess., pp. 759–61 (Serial 387). AJ had issued Hill a temporary commission as second comptroller on March 21, 1829, during the congressional recess, and nominated him to the Senate on February 4, 1830 . The Senate rejected him by 33 to 15 on April 12. On May 25 AJ nominated James B. Thornton to replace him.

1. The Kirkpatrick case, decided in 1824, concerned whether the liability of Pennsylvania revenue collector Samuel M. Reed's sureties under his recess commission of 1813 continued after he was nominated to the Senate, confirmed, and recommissioned in 1814.

2. Eugene Brenan was actually issued a recess commission as an inspector of revenue in South Carolina on June 27, 1799, and nominated to the Senate on December 5.

3. Asahel Ellsworth Paine was actually confirmed on February 7, 1814.

From John Branch

Navy Department
April 16th. 1830

The Secretary of the Navy has the honor to return to the President of the United States, the original memorandum forwarded to The Secretary of State relative to certain expressions used by Comde. Biddle in the

Mediterranean; and to send a copy of the letter addressed to him by the Navy Department upon this subject.

(Copy)

Navy Department April 9th. 1830

Sir,

In a communication lately received from the Mediterranean by the Government the following statement is made

"I heard him" Mr. Biddle "say, in my presence, and of several officers, in his Cabin That no language could express his detestation of our present administration"

It cannot be necessary to remind you that declarations of this kind, made by the commander of a squadron under the circumstances mentioned in the above extract, are subversive of the proper discipline of the Navy, and a violation of the laws enacted for its government: and that a charge of this nature having been brought against you, on respectable authority, it becomes the duty of the Department to notice it. It would be very satisfactory to the Department to find upon investigation, that your expressions on this occasion have been misconceived.

This communication is made with a view to give you an opportunity of offering such explanation as you may think proper, and this it is requested you will do as soon after the reception of this letter as may be convenient to you. I am Respectfully Sir, Your obt. servt.

(signed) Jno. Branch

[Endorsed by AJ:] To be placed on file in State Dept.   A. J.

D, DNA-RG 59 (M179-68). LC, DNA-RG 45 (M472-1). LC of enclosure, DNA-RG 45 (M149-18). Captain James Biddle (1783–1848) was commander of the Navy's Mediterranean squadron and brother of BUS president Nicholas Biddle. The memorandum accusing him was by Charles Davenport Coxe (c1769–1830), U.S. consul at Tripoli, who sent it to Van Buren on December 6, 1829 (DNA-RG 59, M179-68). Biddle received Branch's letter on August 16 and answered the next day, branding the charge "utterly false" and remarking "that self respect and the respect due from me to the Chief Magistrate of my Country equally forbid my using such language anywhere, but especially in the presence of the Officers under my command" (DNA-RG 45, M125-151). Branch replied on November 27 that he had never believed the charge and that Biddle's "unqualified denial" was "entirely satisfactory" (DNA-RG 45, M149-19).

From Usher Skinner

April 16th 1830
Roseville Loudoun County Va

Dear Sir

Mrs Bronaughs Sirvants Dick & Sally informed their mistres (on their Return from Washington) that you would Perchase them if she would write to you immedeately and let you kno her Price. Mrs Bronaugh on hearing this Requested me to say to you that she would take it as a favour if you would Perchase Dick and his family as thay ware very ansus to Return to Tennessee. I inclose you a cirtificate of valluation of them by Mr Johnston Cleaveland and John Fitshugh. She authorises me to say if you think the vallue Prices set on them too hie you can have them for what you think them worth when you see them   Mrs Bronaugh will be compeled to dispose of some Propurty in order to Pay the Debt of her husband which is a greate hardship on her considering how much of her property he had wasted Previous to his deth.[1]

Mrs Bronaugh would not Part with Dick and his family to any one that they ware not willing to go to it being her mothers Request. If you should think Proper to Perchase them you or Mr Donaldson will have the goodniss to write to me or Mrs Bronaugh assoon as convenient at Roseville Loudoun County Va and oblige Sir your Obdt servant

Usher Skinner

[Endorsed by AJ:] Mr. Skinners letter on the subject of the sale of Mrs Bronaugh wishing to sell Dick & his family to be answered—answered 20th April 1830—note within

[Endorsed by AJ:] answered 20th April 1830—that if Mrs Bronaugh will take $900 for Dick, Sally & their family I will purchase them

ALS, DLC (38). Skinner wrote AJ again on April 26 (below).
    1. Sarah Bronaugh had married Martin Bronaugh, perhaps a cousin, in 1819. Johnston Cleaveland or Cleveland (c1764–1834) was a Loudoun County planter.

From Arthur Peronneau Hayne

Private

Charleston 17 April 1830.

Dear General:

It is my wish, if the hard times will permit me to do so, to visit you for a few days this Summer. With this object in view, it would be gratifying to my feelings as an old Soldier to repair to West Point as one of the visiting Committee.[1]

Be pleased to present Mrs. Hayne & myself respectfully to all under your roof, & accept for yourself our best wishes for health & happiness. Our little Frances sends you a kiss. She owes her Grandmother a visit, & Mrs. H. & herself will accompany me. I am dear General, your faithful friend

A. P. Hayne

[Endorsed by AJ:] If the visitors to the military accademy have not been filled it would be grateful to me to have Col Hayne the writer of the within appointed—Andrew Jackson

ALS, DNA-RG 94 (15-0747). Hayne (c1788–1867), brother of South Carolina senator Robert Hayne, had served as an Army colonel with AJ at New Orleans. His wife was Elizabeth Laura Alston (1799–1867) and his daughter from a previous marriage was Frances Duncan Hayne (b. c1819). Her grandmother was Martha Callender Duncan (c1766–1852).
    1. The War Department appointed a board of visitors to monitor and report on the instruction of cadets at West Point.

To Samuel Jackson Hays

(private)

April 19th. 1830—

Dr Saml
    I have just returned from paying the last respect to ~~Genl~~ the mains of Genl Smyth of va. who was buried to day[1]—When I wrote you this morning enclosing a letter to your dear wife, I had not time to say any thing to you on the subject of my farm which you have been kind anough to say that you & Frances would visit.
    I have a three year old colt (my sons) that I had directed Mr Steel if he could to sell at $500; if he is not in figure & size calculated for a brood horse, it would be well to have him changed—I wish you to examine him, and instruct the overseer what to do with him, if he cannot be sold at the price of *$500* at one or two years, it is better to have him changed as my son will want a horse if he goes on this summer, & he must make a good saddle horse—you will oblige me by giving me a full description of all my mares & colts & their looks & vallue—and my Dr Saml. give a faithful description of the Garden, the tomb of my dear wife, & whether the roses & flowers, which I directed to be planted around it, has been so planted, & whether the row of flowers between the House & front gate is attended to—say to old Hanna & Betty that all those that were planted by the directions of your dear aunt, I wish carefully cultivated & preserved, until I return   That garden is now to me a consecrated spot, & I wish it carefully attended to, particularly the square around the sacred Tomb.
    With my best wishes to you & Frances believe me yous affectionately

Andrew Jackson

ALS, ArU (15-0753). Hays replied on May 5 (below).
    1. Virginia congressman Alexander Smyth (1765–1830) died April 17.

From Eneah Micco et al.

Creek Nation
20th April 1830

Our Father

We the Chiefs & head men of the Creek Nation in Council Convened inform you that they sent a delegation to Washington City and they have returned. Our Agent was there & heard their talk to you—On the return of the delegation the Chiefs of the Nation was assembled and a deputation appointed to address you another letter begging to be protected on the land they now inhabit—Our Great father has known for some time that we did not wish to emigrate west of the Mississippi—some of our people have gone but we do not wish to go but wish to be protected by our Great Father on our land. While the delegation was at Washington they were informed that some confusion had arisen among the Chiefs of the Nation & when the delegation returned they found it was the case. The Agent has long since known that the Upper Towns wanted Neothlocco Hopoy (or Little Doctor) to be thier head man and they have broken Tuskina and appointed him in his place—This is all the talk we have at present but when our Agent returns we will get him to write you again on some of our business.[1]

The Secretary at War sent us a letter by Benj. Hawkins and Rolly McIntosh while we were in Council advising us to emigrate but we say to him as we said before that we do not wish to leave our Country[2]—Neo Micco & Neothlocco Hopoy were present at the Council where the above talk was given & the deputations appointed to represent the Nation to address you

Little Doctor	X	Tuckebachu
Neo Micco	X	Capitan
Tuskeenehaw	X	" "
Octiache Emartla	X	Oswychee
~~John Steadham~~	~~X~~	Sowagalow

[Eight more signatures follow.]

Signed in the presence of
N F Collins
B. Marshall
Joseph Marshall

[Endorsed by AJ:] Creek chiefs and Captains, wish to be protected where they are—and their present agent continued. refered to the Sec of war— who will prepare a reply—That they will be protected in their posses-

sions free from intruders but will have to be subordinate to the laws of Alabama   A. J.[3]

DS, DNA-RG 75 (M234-222). *Augusta Chronicle* (Ga.), April 28. Little Doctor of Tuckabatchee was head chief of the Creek Upper Towns. Nathaniel F. Collins was a lawyer, and the brothers Joseph and Benjamin Marshall were prominent Creeks of mixed parentage. Newspaper printings of the address listed Daniel B. Asbury, clerk of the Creek nation, as witness instead of the Marshalls.

In the manuscript, Little Doctor's name appears to have been inserted at the head of the signers. On May 1, Roley McIntosh charged to Eaton that the address was a fraud concocted by agent John Crowell's brother Thomas and his friend Collins. McIntosh claimed that the meeting lacked Upper Town representation and was not a formal council, that Little Doctor was not present, and that some of the signers were known to favor emigration and had signed the address without knowing what it said (DNA-RG 75, M234-222). Another message witnessed by Collins and the Marshalls was sent to AJ this same day. Its thirty-seven signatories, headed by Eneah Micco and Tuskeneah, included ten of the thirteen names affixed here, though not Little Doctor's. Speaking as "a deputation representing the whole Nation," the signers again avowed their faith in Crowell and branded calls for his removal as fabrications.

1. Tuskeneah was the son of Big Warrior, late head chief of the Upper Towns. Tuskeneah himself was deposed as head chief in 1827, later restored, and demoted again after he accosted a mail stage in February 1830.

2. Roley McIntosh and Benjamin Hawkins had come from Washington bearing a March 20 letter from Eaton, which they read to the Creeks in council on April 7. In AJ's name, Eaton urged the Creeks to reconcile among themselves, abandon idle hope of federal intervention against Alabama, and agree to remove west for their own happiness and safety (DNA-RG 75, M21-6). McIntosh and Hawkins sent a report of their reception to Georgia senator George M. Troup, who gave it to AJ on April 27 (below).

3. Eaton replied for AJ in mid-May, telling the Creeks that they would be protected in their property but that neither he nor anyone could stop Alabama from extending its laws over them. Eaton repeated that "there is now no hope or prospect for your contentment and happiness and prosperity as a Nation, but in a voluntary and free consent" to remove westward (DNA-RG 75, M21-6).

From Edward Everett

House of Representatives
22 April 1830

Sir,

I beg leave to enclose to you a letter from Dr S. G. Howe on the subject of affairs in Greece. This gentlm. originally went to G. as a volunteer surgeon & conducted himself with great credit. This led to his being employed as an agent to distribute the cargoes of clothes & provisions w'h were sent to Greece. In this way he has been with short intervals about six years in Greece during which time he has acquired the language of the Country; made the acquaintance of its leading men and gained their respect; and at the same time rendered himself well known to the people as a public benefactor. I have presented the Secretary of State copies of two letters recently received from him which with this which I have the honor now to enclose besides considerable information as to the State of things in Greece afford a fair specimen of Dr. Howe's talent & mode of thinking.

It is Dr Howe's wish to be employed by the Gv't of the U. States in Greece. In addition to the evidence of his qualifications furnished in these letters, I may add that he possesses very estimable personal qualities and great physical energy. I render this attestation at the request of his friends with the greater pleasure, as I believe as far as he has taken any part in politics, he has been (I know his father has been) on an opposite side from myself.[1] I have the honor to be with high respect, Sir, Your obedient servant

LC, MHi (maJs). Everett (1794–1865), at this time a Massachusetts congressman, had been a Unitarian minister and Harvard professor and would later be governor, senator, and briefly secretary of state. He had supported Adams in 1828. Trained as a physician at Harvard, Samuel Gridley Howe (1801–1876) aided the cause of Greek independence as a soldier, physician, and organizer of relief. He later gained fame for his pioneering work in educating the blind as director of the Perkins Institution in Boston.

1. Howe's father, Joseph Neals Howe (1772–1847), was a Boston shipowner and rope manufacturer.

From Charles Rhind

Constantinople 23d. April 1830

I have the honor of announcing to Your Excellency, that on the 13th. Instant I finally closed a Treaty with the Sublime Porte by which Americans are to be received on the footing of the most favored Nations and that the Navigation to and from the Black Sea, shall be free and open to American Vessels.

It is most gratifying to my feelings to inform Your Excellency, that this great acquisition has been effected entirely by ourselves without the *assistance*, or *even knowledge* of any *Powers or Persons* whatever and that the Sublime Porte has on every occasion expressed the highest opinion of our Country, and repeatedly assured me that they considered the United States among the first Powers.

I had concluded the Basis of the Treaty on the 17th. of March and considered the affair finished, but the moment the circumstance became known to the English they arrested the business and their disgraceful intrigues have cost me nearly a month to defeat them, but we have proudly accomplished our object in defiance of all their efforts. I shall take an early opportunity of forwarding to Your Excellency, a detailed account of the Negotiation. With the highest respect I have the honor to be Your obt. hu. St.

Chas Rhind

ALS, DNA-RG 59 (M46-3). Rhind (1779–1857) was a merchant and U.S. consul at Odessa. In September 1829 he, Navy captain James Biddle, and diplomat David Offley (1779–1838) had been commissioned to conclude a commercial treaty with Turkey. To minimize visibility and the risk of foreign interference, Rhind was instructed to conduct the negotiation alone, with Biddle and Offley not to join him in Constantinople until the finished treaty was ready to sign. On May 10 Rhind sent AJ an account of his negotiation. He accused the English of encouraging Turkey to insist on a discriminatory 5% duty on American trade, unacceptable to the U.S. The Porte dropped the demand on April 13, and a treaty placing commercial relations on a most-favored-nation basis was concluded and signed by Rhind on May 7 (*HRDoc* 250, 22d Cong., 1st sess., pp. 77–94, Serial 221). Biddle and Offley arrived from Smyrna on May 24, and wrote AJ with their objections to the treaty on June 8 (below).

To John Henry Eaton

April 24th. 1830—

The President with his respects, informs the Secr'ty, that he sees accpts of military officers, of the army, & Navy, presented for payment

The President requests that orders be Issued to the surgeon Genl. & his assistant to attend all officers who may be here at any time under orders, & may be sick—similar orders are directed from the Navy Department— These are acpts that hereafter are inadmisable—

AN, DNA-RG 107 (M222-27). Eaton issued a directive this same day, requiring the surgeon general to provide medical care to Army officers on duty in Washington and refusing their future claims for medical expenses unless they first sought treatment from him (DNA-RG 107, M6-12).

From Benjamin Franklin Hawkins Witherell

Detroit April 24th AD 1830

To His Excy the President of the United States—

It has been for some time past understood here that accusations had been made by Petitions & otherwise, against the Secretary of the Territory—Judge Witherell—the substance of the Petition & affidavits were, not till *this day* made known to Judge Witherell or his Friends   a Copy of them is, for the first time, procured; and knowing what the accusations, set out in the affidavits are & the statements made in the Petition, they can be easily, Explained & refuted and such an Explanation will be transmitted immediately; in the meantime, if consistent, & as a matter Justice to Judge Witherell, I would respectfully request that the Charges may not be acted on till such explanations shall be reviewed by you[.] I Remain Very Respectfully Your Obt Hbl Servt

B. F. H. Witherell

[Endorsed by AJ:] The President with his respects sends the enclosed for the perusal of the Secretary of State—
It occurs to the President that any further delay in the removal would be useless & embarrassing—Therefore as soon as you think proper to send me the nomination in favour of Mr Mason I will send it to the Senate

May 6th. 1830—

ALS, DNA-RG 59 (M639-27). *TPUS*, 12:159–60. Witherell (1797–1867) was an attorney and son of Michigan Territory secretary James Witherell. Besides incapacity due to age, charges against his father included abuse of the patronage and obstructing the return of fugitive slaves. Witherell's defenders attributed the charges to personal spite. AJ nominated John T. Mason to replace Witherell on May 6. He was confirmed May 20.

From Tuskeneah et al.

Creek Nation
April 25th 1830

To the President of the United States
having understood that some of Colo Crowells enemies were trying to induce some of our people to apply to you for his removal—We thought it our duty in justice to ourselves as well as Colo Crowell to write you a few lines on the subject—They have told our chiefs that they could no doubt have whom they pleased for Agent if they would make a Treaty—Now sir all of us that sign this letter have already agreed to emigrate with Colo Crowell—and we have hundreds ready to go with us & It was with Colo Crowell that we agreed to go—Colo Crowell read to us a letter from the President stating that he was to be our Agent & go with us if we would emigrate[1]   We therefore hope that the President will not after we have agreed to move break his promise to us—to gratify a few designing Chiefs & White men—who wish to get Colo Crowell removed in hopes of getting his place.
There is but a small part of the whole nation that is opposed to Colo Crowell—and they have nothing against him only he has advised them to move—We did not believe that the President would remove Colo Crowell without some good ground—but as there was some complaints against him we thought it our duty to say what we have & to let our Father the President know our feelings & the feelings of a Large majority of our nation towards Colo Crowell—It is impossible to get an Agent to please all in the present state of affairs—We have no hesitation in saying that Colo Crowell can do more with those people than any other that could be sent here—he can carry more of them to Arkansas than any stranger—For many of those that have already agreed to go would not like to go with a stranger & all that has been done by Colo Crowell would be lost—Those

are the sentiments & feelings of your children that have taken your talk—
we therefore hope that Colo Crowell will be permitted to take charge of
us conduct us to our new home & remain with us untill we are comfortably settled

Tuskenahar   X
Caracchu Yarlolar   X
Pasenfar hargo   X
Tustuneggu Emartha   X
Hase Eamarther   X

[Forty more signatures follow.]

Witness
Benjamin Marshall

[Endorsed by AJ:] Refered to the Sec. of war—A. J.

DS, DNA-RG 75 (M234-222).
   1. AJ's address of March 23, 1829, read by Crowell to the Creeks, urged them to move
west and called Crowell "my agent, and your friend" (*Jackson Papers*, 7:112–13).

To Robert Young Hayne

(confidential)

april 26th. 1830—

My Dr Sir
   The Navy agency at Giberalter is now vacant, would Col Arthur P.
Hayne accept of this—It is worth, say, about *$7000* a year, and if he
is acquainted with the mercantile world, & would embark a commission business, four years would ensure him an ample fortune—will you
give me, confidentially, yr opinion on this subject   I wish to write your
brother tomorrow—
   When I recd. his letter on Saturday I immediately sent it to the Sec
of War and I regretted to learn that we had not the means to require
his services as a visitor to West point being only $30 of this fund left—
I really think the Col could spend two or three years profitable up the
Mediterranean until something better might offer—please answer this
note, & give me your opinion
   yrs very respectfully

Andrew Jackson

ALS, DLC (38).

From John Pope

Pittsburg april 26th 1830

Dr Sir

I reached here yesterday after a most unpleasant trip in a crowded stage & will leave here at three oclock for Louisville—In renting out the lands on arkansas river acquired from the Cherokee Indians I acted in compliance with orders of the government and I shall perform my duty to the government whether popular or unpopular[1]—It is just that those who enjoy the improvements paid for by the government should pay something & that they should pay some reasonable additional price for the land so improved at the expence of the government and I thought it my duty as an officer of the general government to tell you so but I am aware that there is an aversion to the payment of rent in that quarter or for the improvements & if it is demanded there will be some clamour about it—The relation I hold to the government forbids me to advise any course to advance my popularity at a sacrifice of the public interest but I assure you that I shall as an individual be gratified if the government can waive all claim to rents or compensation for Improvements—You ought at least to make them pay enough to satisfy the agent for his services—The government made a bad bargain for the improvements three times as much has been paid for them as they are worth and it merits your consideration whether the small amount the government will gain by demanding rent & compensation for them, will be an adequate equivalent for the clamour & discontent which will be the consequence—If the rent & payment for improvements should be waved I wish it done at the instance of Colo Sevier because he is a good fellow a friend & it will help him in that quarter[2]—The lands for a mile or two round Little Rock should be sold in Lotts & small tracts to raise a fund for useful purposes & ought not to be subject to the floating claims of the Country—The attention of the secretary of the treasury should be drawn to this subject

I wish this letter to be shewn to Genl Eaton & when you & the secretary at war have Leisure I wish you would take into serious consideration the propriety of making the Governor of the arkansas Teritory superintendant of Indian affairs over all the Country west & south of Little Rock—There is a fitness in this growing out the geograpical situation & connection of the indian tribes on Red River & the arkansas with the arkansas Teritory & the white people in the vicinity of the Indians—I would occasionale visit the indians & agents & see how they managed the business confided to them & make them settle their accounts at Little Rock subject to revision at washington—I would be able to check frauds on the government & if the Indians & agents were taught to look upon the Governor as the Lord paramount & head of the Territorial department he could interpose with more effect in settling disputes between the Whites & Indian tribes & preserving peace in that quarter—I should not visit the agences or Indians with a view to charge the government eight dollars a day—I only ask or expect a conpensation adequate to sustain the dignity of the office I hold—my conpensation as superintendant I would cheerfully submit to the discretion of the government—I dont want something for nothing—The plan I suggest would add to the dignity & importance of the office—I accepted it with much hesitation & I really am unwilling to be humiliated by a trifling salary & an abridgment of the power & authority heretofore assigned to the governor of that Territory[3]—Instead of putting the little inoffensive tribe of Quapaws under the care of a distant agent it would be better & more satisfactory to them to assign them to the secretary Fulton who would attend to them for one or 200 dollars & he would attend to them with kindness & justice—Should accident the pressure of my business in Kentucky or other considerations remove me from the Territory I beseech you to make Fulton my successor—He is you know an honest & vigilant man & will have become acquainted the people & business & no appointment could be more satisfactory[4]—Permit me to remind you & the Genl of my friends smith & wife—Genl Eaton by his conduct to them has made a strong impression on me in his favour as a gentleman of liberality & good feelings & if you can without embarrassment or incovenience add a little to their comfort I shall be particularly gratified—I ask this not on the ground of political relation but as matter of personal favour to me—accept assurances of my high respect & personal regard

John Pope

[Endorsed by AJ Donelson:] Gov. Pope on the concerns of his Territory—to be shewn to Mr. Eaton Secy. of War—

ALS, DNA-RG 107 (M222-28). *TPUS*, 21:219–20. Pope (1770–1845), a former senator from Kentucky, was appointed governor of Arkansas Territory in March 1829. He was now returning there from Washington.

1. In the 1828 Treaty of Washington by which the Western Cherokees agreed to remove from Arkansas Territory, the U.S. pledged to pay emigrating Indians for improvements they left behind. The War Department later ordered these vacated lands to be leased out to settlers at rates based on their assessed value. In November 1829 Pope and the Arkansas legislature protested the leasing policy (*Jackson Papers*, 7:530–32). Pope wrote Eaton further in August and September 1830 about the difficulty in collecting rents, and in November Eaton ordered the efforts stopped (*TPUS*, 21:248–50, 268–71, 288–89).

2. In a letter of December 17, 1830, published in the *Arkansas Gazette* on January 19, 1831, Arkansas Territory congressional delegate Ambrose H. Sevier took credit for procuring Eaton's recision of the leasing policy.

3. The 1819 law creating Arkansas Territory made its governor *ex officio* superintendent of Indian affairs. In June 1829 Pope claimed a $750 stipend for this duty. Eaton replied that as there were no Indians left in Arkansas, Pope had no duties and would receive no stipend (*TPUS*, 21:46, 61). In November, Pope and the Arkansas legislature petitioned to give the governor superintendency over Indians neighboring the territory (*Jackson Papers*, 7:529–30). On March 15, 1830, Pope, then in Washington, renewed his claim to Eaton, saying the money had been paid to his predecessors and promised to him and that he had in

fact dealt officially with emigrating Cherokees and returning Quapaws (*TPUS*, 21:194–96). Eaton referred the matter to Thomas L. McKenney, who on March 16 recommended paying Pope a half-year's stipend to compensate his dealings with the Cherokees and their former lands (DNA-RG 75, M21-6). Pope was accordingly paid $375 on March 17.

4. The Quapaws had ceded their Arkansas lands in 1824 and removed to the Caddo country on Red River, but many had recently returned in distress. Pope favored allowing them to stay and providing them with land and aid. The Quapaw agency was at Natchitoches, La. William Savin Fulton (1795–1844) was appointed secretary of Arkansas Territory in April 1829. He succeeded Pope as governor in 1835.

From Usher Skinner

Loudoun cunty Va April 26

Dear Sir

your Letter of 20th came to hand and I have this day made its contents known to Mrs Bronaugh She Requests me to say to you that she will Take the $900 for Dick his wife & children and if you and major Lewis should conclude to take them when it will sute you—I will come to wahsington and Deliver the Negroes and Reced the money for them, Mrs Bronaugh will perhaps go with me to W___ city when and whare she will be able to make a good and sufficnt Title to you for the negroes, in the Event of her not going to washington she will give me full Powers to sel and conveigh them. the negroes ware Left to Mrs Bronaugh by her Mother by will to whome they ware Left By the Late Dr JC Bronagh who Perchased Dick of the Distributes of his father and Sally of Major Wm. B. Lewis, with sentiments of Respect I remain your Obt Sirvant

Usher Skinner

[Endorsed by AJ Donelson:] Mr. Skinner son in law of Doct Bronough—says that she will take $900 for the negroes—

[Endorsed by AJ:] recd the 4th. of May 1830 answered the same day that the negroes will be recd. at $900—& Cash paid on the receipt of them, & title made   A. J.

ALS, DLC (38). AJ paid Sarah's half-brother Jeremiah W. Bronaugh $900 for Dick, Sally, and their four children on June 3. Skinner was brother-in-law, not son-in-law, to the late James Craine Bronaugh (1788–1822) and his sister Sarah.

To Arthur Peronneau Hayne

Washington April 27th. 1830—

My Dr Colo.

Upon the receipt of your letter I forthwith by the hand of our mutual friend Col. Gibson made known to the Secretary of war my desire that you should be appointed one of the visitors to the military academy, and regret to find from his letter, which I herewith enclose, that the appointments had been made previous to the receipt of your letter, & the fund so limited & exausted, that he could not comply with my wishes on this subject.[1]

It will afford me much pleasure to see you your amiable Lady & daughter in Washington, when I will expect you & family to take a room in my House during your stay in the city, & where it will afford me pleasure to make you & them comfortable.

I have it in contemplation if possible after the adjournment of congress to take a journey to the north & west, & visit the tomb of my dear departed wife, before I return to this city, and hope to see you & your family here before I set out; if I can leave this city this summer I must set out shorty after congress rises—of this tho, I cannot as yet determine—but Mrs. Donelson & our niece Miss Easton will travel as far as Newyork, & I am sure will be pleased to have the company of your amiable family

I had a thought of tendering to you the naval agency at Giberalter which is worth $7000 pr annum which is now vacant, & on last evening wrote a confidential note to your brother Genl Hayne, who, in answer, gave it as his opinion that you would not leave this country & would not accept it—you may be here before I am *obliged to fill this office* it is sought for by many.

I pray you to tender my affectionate regard to your amiable lady & daughter & believe me yr friend

Andrew Jackson

ALS, DLC (38). Hayne accepted the navy agency on May 22.

1. Brevet Brigadier General George Gibson (1775–1861), the Army's commissary general of subsistence, had served as quartermaster general under AJ.

From Richard Templeman Brown

[On March 10, the Senate rejected Jackson's nomination of Henry Lee to be consul general to Algiers by a vote of 46 to 0. Lee (1787–1837) was the son of Virginia Revolutionary hero Henry "Light-Horse Harry" Lee and the elder half-brother of Robert E. Lee. An Army major in the War

of 1812, Lee had served Jackson as a publicist and political operative in the 1828 campaign. Jackson appointed him consul general during the Senate recess in April 1829 and he sailed for Algiers in August. Jackson nominated Lee to the Senate on January 22, 1830. The United States' Telegraph *claimed on March 13, after Lee's defeat, that he had been nominated on recommendation from public men who knew him well, including Supreme Court justices John Marshall and John McLean, Senator Edward Livingston, and House speaker Andrew Stevenson. Widely known but rarely discussed openly was the scandal in Lee's past: in 1820 he had seduced and perhaps impregnated Elizabeth McCarty, his ailing wife's nineteen-year-old sister and his own legal ward.]*

Sir,

In behalf of many respectable Citizens of Westmoreland County (Va) I send herewith the expression of their sentiments in relation to Major Henry Lee our country man and his late rejection by the Senate of the United States.

This much has been thought due to their respect for your appointment of the Consul General to Algiers—and to a gifted individual who though not exempt from human infirmity is yet in common with erring mortals;—and especially for the high & honorable qualities which his ordinary life has exhibited;—entitled to hope for charity from fallible man, and to expect that an implacable and remorseless spirit of persecution should not incessantly pursue him through every Lane of life down to the last step of his existence.

The signers of the accompanying Address tender through me, their respects to yr. Excellency; and I ask permission to subscribe myself Yr fellow citizen & ob. st.

L, Lee-Kendall House, Arlington, Va. (15-0275). Brown (1777–1840) was a Westmoreland County merchant and a friend of Lee's.

[Enclosure]

To his Excellency Andrew Jackson President of the U[nited States]

We have viewed with feelings of concern the rejec[tion,] by the Senate, of the nomination of our countryman Ma[jor Lee] as consul general to Algiers. What circumstances unknow[n to the] public have influenced the decision of that honourable b[ody we] are unable to say, but we cannot help believing that th[eir vir]tuous indignation has been grossly abused by the most [exag]gerated statements and malicious invectives. Educated [in as] strict a moral code as his most vindictive persecutors, [we] equally condemn *one* circumstance of his life, but we d[o not] consider it a generous policy or a christian virtue to p[ursue] forever with unrelenting ferocity the unfortunate vic[tim] of *a single* act of human passion. We were grat[ified]

at your nomination of Major Lee to foreign station, [as a means] of bringing into public servi[ce and con]sideration his ackno[wledged] talents
& noble qualit[ies] which tho' sullied [with a stain,] would have been
an ornament to his coun[try, and we] deeply regret that your generous
intention[s towards an] unfortunate man have been unhappil[y frustrated]
and converted to his ruin.

With s[incere wishes for your personal wellfare and the successful operations of your administration we are &c &c—]

Copy (fragment), ViW; Typescript, DLC-Lee Family Papers (mAJs). Ethel Armes, *Stratford
Hall: The Great House of the Lees* (1936), p. 396. Bracketed text is supplied from the
typescript.
    Writing from Paris to William B. Lewis on July 26, 1833 (ViHi) and to AJ on December 27,
1833 (DLC-43), Lee quoted from a letter he said AJ had sent him on June 4, 1830: "I need
not say to you the mortification I experienced on your rejection by the Senate. When you
return to your country, you will be advised by whom, aided by all the opposition this has
been brought about. Your fellow citizens in the County of Westmoreland have addressed
me upon this subject, which from their number and respectability is honourable to you and
consoling to me. *This is preserved.*"

From Lewis Clephane and John Gardiner

Washington 27th April 1830
Sir,
    The Petition for leave to copy the Portraits (of Indians) in the War
Department which we presented to you, and you referred to the Secretary
of War, was by him referred to Colo McKenney: he has refused to grant
our Petition because "the Portraits are the property of the nation, because
he has refused numerous other applicants who were desirous of copying
the Portraits, because he *thinks* they should not be copied for exhibition
unless they were accompanied by a national work containing the History
of the Aborigenes, &c &c."

    We trust *you* will grant our Petition, & thus gratify the curiosity of
those who wish to see the Portraits & pay us for the sight at their own
homes, instead of coming to this City to see them. Other Governments
& those monarchical, permit their subjects not only to view the national
paintings, but their Artists to copy them, and it is strange that a subordinate clerk should dare to refuse to permit the Artists of the Republic
to copy the Public paintings for the gratification of all the Citizens who
may be willing to pay the Artists for their labour in copying them, and
who cannot conveniently come to the Seat of Government[.] We are most
respectfully Sir, Your Obt Servts.

Lewis Clephane
John Gardiner

[Endorsed by AJ:] The President with his respects to the Secretary of war, sends for his perusal the above letter, and adds, that it might be well to permit them to copy the pictures if they will do so, in the Portrait room— they ought not to be taken from the room. A. J. April 28th 1830—

LS, DNA-RG 75 (M234-433). Lewis Clephane (1752–1833) and John Gardiner (c1770– 1839) were artists residing in Washington. On April 22 they had written AJ for permission to borrow the Indian portraits displayed in the War Department for copying. McKenney refused on April 26 in language paraphrased here (DNA-RG 75, M21-6). On May 7 Clephane and Gardiner again asked Eaton if AJ would "trust us with two or three portraits at a time for a few days" for copying (DNA-RG 75, M234-433).

McKenney had been acquiring Indian portraits for the War Department since 1822. His letter refusing Clephane and Gardiner envisioned incorporating the portraits in a national scientific study of the Indians, a comprehensive work to show "a connecting link in the great chain of the history of man." One hundred twenty of the portraits were reproduced in *History of the Indian Tribes of North America* (Philadelphia, 1836–44), which McKenney co-authored with James Hall. An 1865 fire in the Smithsonian Institution destroyed the originals.

From George Michael Troup

Senate Chamber
27th April 1830

GM Troups Complts to the President—encloses for his reading communications just receivd from McIntosh & Hawkins

[Endorsed by AJ:] I have read the enclosed will converse with you this evening on the subject   yrs   A. J.

[Endorsed by AJ:] The Secretary [of War]

AN, DNA-RG 107 (M222-28). Troup (1780–1856) was a former governor of Georgia and now U.S. senator.

[Enclosure: Roley McIntosh and Benjamin Hawkins to Troup]

Creek Nation April 15th. 1830.

To the Honble. George M. Troup.

Friend & Brother—Enclosed is a copy of a Letter which we have addressed to the Secretary of War. The mail is about closing and we have but few minutes to devote to this letter. Our prospects at present are not very flattering, for we believe a strong effort is making in the nation to reconcile the Indians to the present Agent, and if they succeed, we fear all hopes of his removal will be lost. We desire his dismissal above all things. He will continue to be an obstacle to a reconciliation among our people.

We think that during this summer a majority of the Indians here will be disposed to emigrate, and would it not be well for Congress to make some arrangement to hold a treaty with them so soon as the consent of the majority is obtained. Let them before their adjournment make the appropriation in anticipation of the event. If the Agent was removed, a treaty could be held with them very shortly. On the 7th. inst. at the Council, a partizan of Col. Crowell, by the name of Doyle made the following remarks to the chiefs. He said that he did not belong to the white people that he had lived a long time with the Indians, was their friend. Genl. Jackson he said was a bad man, and was now verry old, and would very shortly die and then, the Indians would not have to leave their country—some good man would be elected President who would protect them. He advised them not to give up "their country—"[1]   It is by such like men in the nation, that the views of Government are defeated, and the Indians are kept blind to their interests.

We wish you to get the Secretary of War to write the letter to us which he promised on the subject of our stipend.

Perhaps we may write to you again before you leave Washington

Rolly McIntosh   his   X   mark
for himself & Benj. Hawkins

DS, DNA-RG 107 (M222-28).
  1. Nimrod Doyle or Doyell was a white trader among the Creeks.

[Enclosure: Roley McIntosh and Benjamin Hawkins to Eaton]

Creek Nation April 12. 1830

Friend & Brother

In complying with our promise to write, it grieves us that we have no glad tidings to communicate. We have partially failed in the objects of our friendly mission—The talk which you placed in our hands to deliver to the chiefs has been presented to them & rejected by them.[1] It was our intention to have had it interpreted to them at their homes by their firesides, believing that they might there be more disposed to listen to the voice of reason and reciprocate the friendly feelings that we desire to cultivate; but shortly after our arrival here, we were informed that a council was to be holden in a few days, and concluding that the occasion would be a favourable one to deliver the talk, we determined to embrace it. The council convened and on the 7th inst. the Talk was accordingly tendered to them. At first they refused to receive it. We addressed the chiefs. We urged upon them the great importance of a reconciliation among our people—they had become divided by the designs of bad men—their divisions had already brought calamities enough upon them, and if persevered in, would soon operate their total distruction. Once we were a united and contented people; happy as individuals and prosperous as a nation; but what was our condition now? a distracted and miserable race hating one another, withe no prospect before us but that of leading degraded lives and leaving wretchedness as an inheritance to our children. And what was the cause of this unfortunate condition? We told them that it was owing to the animosities that prevailed among us—it was time to drop them. When we were united in the bonds of love and peace, we were a flourishing and powerful people; and to become so again, it was only necessary to unite in affection and assemble once more as a common nation. It was for this purpose that we had visited them; we came to bury the Tomahawk and restore tranquility; our arms are open to receive our enimies—let offences and resentments be remembered no longer. We informed the Council, that we were instructed by our brethren in Arkansaw to make this overture of peace and friendship, and to invite them to a participation of the blessings that are enjoyed in the west. There the atmosphere is salubrious, the soil fertile and the land abounds in game. Those who are there are satisfied; and desiring peace and harmony with their brethren here, they entreat them to come and share the advantages of the country and form once more a united, happy and powerful people—your situation (we said) requires your removal and circumstances will very shortly compel you to remove. You are needy and defenceless and who is to aid you? Your great Father the president has told you that it is out of his power to protect you—that you will have either to remove to the Arkansaw or come under the laws of Alabama. Are you prepared for the latter alternative? By adopting the former you go to a country superior to the one you now occupy—will be received with pleasure by your brethren—protected by the President and free from the annoyance of the White man; but if you remain where you are, living among people of uncongenial habits & tempers, and subjected to laws which you cannot participate in making, you will be an easy prey to the repacity of bad men, and soon dwindle away under a system of Government which you are incapable of comprehending—We then earnestly entreated them to accept our overtures of peace and friendship, and to receive the Talk which by order of the President had been sent them for their own welfare—

Friend & Brother, we grieve even now at the recollection of the coldness with which we were received; and at the reluctance with which they finally consented to hear the Talk. It was interpreted to them—they listened to it with indifference. After the reading was finished, some of them remarked on that part of your Talk where you recommend the immediate repeal of their law against emigration, that the Government of the United States had no right to dictate to them about their laws—that it was their privilege to make and enforce whatever law they thought proper—that the white people were very jealous of this right themselves—that they spent much time in making laws and would not allow other nations to control them in their Legislative powers.[2] Without any dispassionate consideration of the Talk they returned it to us, saying that they had no regard for it, and had no reply to make.

Brother, as discouraging as this circumstance may appear, we are not dispirited from making farther efforts in a cause upon the good or ill success of which depends the prosperity or extinction of so many of our brethren. Another Council is to be held in a few days, at which we design renewing our endeavours to awaken our people to a sense of their real situation, and prevail on them to consider more seriously the advise of their Father the President, who had never deceived them or spoken falsely to them. We attribute in part the ill success of our efforts at the first council, to the absence of some of the most influential members of the Delegation, who were with us at Washington City. We were persuaded from conversations held with them, that they would give us their active co-operation but when we attended the Council on the 7th inst. they were not present. We expect however to meet them at the ensuing Council and hope to receive their aid.[3] We should certainly not have the heart to say any thing further to our brethren here, if we were not fully sattisfied that the ill success which we have met with, is attributable to other causes than an unwillingness on the part of a majority of the nation to emigrate. We are convinced that a large portion of them are ready to move cheerfully to the west, but are restrained from an avowal of their feelings through fear of the Head Men, who exercise over them unlimited power, and find no difficulty in controling their opinions (or restraining their expressions) upon almost all matters. Those who in conversation with us signify their willingness to remove, impose secrecy and beg us not to tell upon them; and now if the word Arkansaw be named to the common Indians, they immediately anticipate our business and answer "Ask the Chiefs." Their law against emigration has great effect in retarding its progress—it ought to be repealed and the Indians emancipated from the fear of their Chiefs.

Friend & Brother, we still retain the opinion expressed to you on other occasions that the present is a very unsuitable agent for the nation under existing circumstances. He is too unpopular to have much influence in promoting emigration. Very few of the Indians have any affection for him or place any confidence in his word. We cannot help thinking that if some good man was appointed in whom all would have confidence; to whose consels they would listen and whose motives they would not distrust, they would soon consent to remove and go cheerfully. The present agent may remove them by opperating on their fears, he may be able to drive them off by threats, but we do not wish them to go in that way, we wish them to go friendly and voluntarily. You must forgive us the expression of these sentiments—we feel the force of their truth. Brother we are the injured party—our dear relations have been sacrifised, and their characters blackened; yet we come not in the habiliments of war—with the ensigns of peace we approach our brethren, and with open arms invite to our bosoms those who have aggrieved us most. We do this because of our attachment to our people, and from an anxious desire to see them once more united as a nation in interest and in affection. The great concern of our mission is to effect a reconciliation with our brethren before they remove to Arkansaw. If they go there with all their unkind feelings about them—if their animosities be not extinguished—if the feuds which have divided us here be revived and cherished there, then will their emigration be a curse rather than a blessing to our people. Enemies cannot dwell in harmony together—war will ensue—blood will be shed. Hence our great anxiety to bury the Tomahawk here and smoke the calumet of peace. All that we ask is the appointment of some good man who will enter heart and hand in accomplishing this desirable & all important end; one who has no partialities to extend to one party or resentments to gratify on the other. If we thought that our voice could have weight with our great Father the President, we would plead with our latest breath, for the dismissal of him who stands in the way of the best interest of our deluded people.

Brother In conversation with you at Washington you promised to write us a letter giving us information in regard to the mony coming to the emigrated party in Arkansaw—The letter has not yet been received. Our departure to the West will be delayed for some weeks to come and in the mean time we should be glad to hear from you. Previous to our leaving Washington, you promised to let each of us have One hundred & fifty dollars to defray our expenses home—we did not receive that amt. We recd. only Sixty a piece, & are unable to account for the circumstance, we have been in consequence brought in debt—Direct you letters to us at Columbus Muscogee Co. Geo where we can most readily obtain them—[4]

Rolly McIntosh his X mark
for himself & Benjamin Hawkins

Copy, DNA-RG 107 (M222-28). DS, DNA-RG 75 (M234-236). The original sent to Eaton contained a postscript explaining that Hawkins had approved the letter but was called away before it was copied out, giving McIntosh authority to sign for him.

1. McIntosh and Hawkins bore a March 20 letter from Eaton to the Alabama Creeks, urging them to reconcile their differences and agree to remove (DNA-RG 75, M21-6).

2. Eaton's letter admonished the Creek council to "repeal a law, you never should have made—the law, which punishes any who shall offer to dispose of the lands of the Creeks." He chided them for thus attempting to suppress free speech among themselves.

3. This was the meeting that produced the remonstrance of April 20 against removal (above), and which McIntosh complained on May 1 was not a proper council.

4. On March 20 the War Department had paid McIntosh and Hawkins $120 to visit the Alabama Creeks. Their complaints of February 25 and March 22 (above) about payments due the Western Creeks were yet unanswered. On May 15, Eaton wrote Georgia congressman Wiley Thompson, who had inquired for Hawkins, that the Western Creeks would receive everything promised to them but that Hawkins had dealt falsely by deterring instead of encouraging removal, and that Eaton would therefore "hold no further intercourse, or communication with him" (DNA-RG 75, M21-6).

To Samuel Smith

April 28th. 1830

The President with his compliments to Genl Smith, thanks him for his communication thro Doctor Sims, & receives it as the evidence of his sincere friendship, and assures him it will be adopted.[1]

The President rejoices to hear of the Genl.s. improving health, & hopes soon to have the pleasure of hearing of him in the Senate chamber.

The President returns to the Genl. enclosed the letter he had the goodness to present for his perusal, with his thanks, and requests him to accept of his best wishes, for his heath & happiness

AN, DLC-Samuel Smith Papers (15-0830).
1. Thomas Sim (1770–1832) was AJ's Washington physician.

To John Christmas McLemore

April 30th. 1830—Washington

My Dr. Sir

yours of the 15th. instant is just to hand, and I will see Major Eaton in an hour & through him inform Genl Dibble of your wishes—The money will be reserved for you.

Judge Overton left us yesterday, but before he did, I got him to make a statement of the vallue of your Memphis & Nashville property whereon you live, which was quite satisfactory, and which I have placed in Major Eatons hands—Thus you see it is only necessary for you to have the Deeds executed and brought on with you, to ensure you the loan—or to send them on here executed in due form—but your comming on here will be better, as you can arrange your matters to your own satisfaction and have your cash in U. States notes of the mother Bank which will be, one percent, in your country better than the Branch Bank bills   I shall expect to see you in all the month of May next—as I have some hopes of being able to leave here for a while in the summer, travel to the north, then to niagara falls, & then to the Hermitage, & would delight to have you along, as I will travel constant & soon reach the Hermitage where my heart constantly yearns once more to behold.

I had seen a postscrip of our friends Mr Thos Crutchers letter to major Lewis in which he stated that our old friend Capt Jno. Donelson was fast going & could not remain long—the day I read this I had wrote him by Genl D. S. Donelson who had just left us for Tennessee before I had seen the P.S.[1] I am fearful he will not survive to read it—If so I shall regret it—

but I hope he is prepared, and his change is to a happier & better world than this—
with my respects to your dear wife, & sweet little family, and all friends,
May heaven prosper & guard you, & give you prosperity   farewell

Andrew Jackson

P.S. our friend overton will be able to give you the news of this place to whom I refer you.

ALS, James F. Ruddy (15-0862). McLemore was selling land to clear off debts, including his liability as a security for defaulting state bank cashier Joel Parrish Jr. McLemore wrote AJ Donelson on April 3 that he had ample property but needed to raise about $10,000 to meet pressing demands. He declined the tender of the navy agency at Gibraltar, saying the appearance of personal favoritism would embarrass AJ (Donelson Papers, DLC).

1. Daniel Smith Donelson (1801–1863) of Sumner County was AJ Donelson's brother and a brigadier general of Tennessee militia.

To George Graham

The commissioner of the lands office will, if Mr Kelly has signed the agreement prepared by the atto. Genl, & dismissed they suits, instituted by John Smith T. and those claiming under him, you will prepare a proclamation or orders for Publication, that all permits required by the proclamation shall be suspended, until further directions from the President of the U States

AN, DLC (15-0552). On May 15, Graham ordered the suspension of proceedings under AJ's March 6 proclamation and its attendant instructions of March 9, which had required north Alabama land claimants under John Smith T's title to vacate their holdings or obtain permits from the Huntsville land office to remain as tenants at will. The *US Telegraph* first published his announcement May 22.

May

To James Alexander Hamilton

WASHINGTON, May 3, 1830.

MY DEAR SIR:

Your letter of the 29th ultimo, marked private, reached me this morning; I hasten to answer it. Mr. Forsyth has made no communication to me as yet; should he, you shall at an early day be apprised thereof and with its contents.[1]

I find from your letter that you have not seen Mr. McDuffie's Report upon the U.S. Bank. I herewith send it to you; I presume it to be, a joint effort, and the best that can be made in its support, and *it is feeble.* This is intended, no doubt, as the first shot; it will pass without moving me.[2]

I will thank you for your ideas on this report when leisure will permit.[3] Although intended to wound me, it will not injure me, but it will not go unanswered when a proper time arrives. Let me hear from you soon, and Believe me your friend,

ANDREW JACKSON.

Printed, *Reminiscences of James A. Hamilton*, p. 164 (15-0876).

1. John Forsyth (1780–1841) was a U.S. senator and former governor of Georgia. On May 12 he gave AJ a letter from William H. Crawford concerning Calhoun's role in Cabinet deliberations in 1818 over AJ's Seminole campaign. AJ acknowledged the letter to Hamilton and confronted Calhoun with it on May 13 (below).

2. On December 10, 1829, the House of Representatives referred the portion of AJ's annual message concerning the Bank of the United States to the Committee of Ways and Means, chaired by George McDuffie of South Carolina. On April 13 McDuffie submitted a detailed report upholding the Bank's constitutionality and defending its operations and management. Against AJ's charge that the Bank "has failed in the great end of establishing a uniform and sound currency," the committee held that "*it has actually furnished a circulating medium more uniform than specie.*" The report excoriated AJ's proposed government bank as a giant fount of executive patronage and corruption, and warned that failure to recharter the BUS would do the country "great injury" (*HRRep* 358, 21st Cong., 1st sess., pp. 14, 23, Serial 201).

3. AJ repeated this request on May 18 and 29 (below).

From Martin Van Buren

With Mr Van Burens respects. Will it be possible to send him out in a public ship. It would be well if it could be so—

AN, DLC-Van Buren Papers (15-0915).

[Enclosure: John Randolph to Van Buren]

Richmond May 2d. 1830.

Mr Dear Sir,

Your letter of the last of April was recd. yesterday. A long notice is sometimes not better than a short one. However, nunquam non paratus[1] is my maxim; & although not quite so well prepared as I was two months ago, I am ready.

I shall set out immediately for my own residence, where I shall await further advice from you. I have repressed the inclination that I had to write to the President in consideration of the heavy demands upon his time. I would prefer sailing this month, or the first of June, to the risk of the calms of July. How do you propose to deport me? In a publick vessell, I hope; if I am to go up the Baltick. I dread a land journey over the sands of the North of Germany. I expect to find a letter from Hamilton,* when I reach home, containing news of Mr Cruger.[2] Is it the President's pleasure that I should wait upon him in person?

The mail for Charlotte C. H. leaves Washington every Tuesday & Friday, by the Southern route. I shall remain at Roanoke until I hear from you.[3] When does Congress propose to adjourn? faithfully yours

J. R of Roanoke

*I write to him to day.

ALS, DLC-Van Buren Papers (15-0917). John Randolph (1773–1833) had been a Virginia congressman and senator. In September 1829 AJ had offered and Randolph had accepted appointment as minister to Russia.

1. Latin for "never unprepared."

2. AJ had promised Randolph his choice of secretary of legation, and South Carolina politician James Hamilton Jr. (1786–1857) had proposed his brother-in-law, Henry Nicholas Cruger (1800–1867), who was then abroad. Unable to contact Cruger to confirm his interest, Hamilton withdrew his candidacy later in May, and Randolph chose John Randolph Clay instead. AJ commissioned him June 4.

3. Randolph's "Roanoke" estate was in Charlotte County, Va.

To Martin Van Buren

May 4th. 1830—

My Dr. Sir

your note enclosing Mr Randolphs to you, of the 2nd. instant, has been recd. & duly considered—I have been urging the Sec. of the Navy to have one of our Sloops ready as early as *possible*, to convay our friend to the Baltick; & another to convay Porter; both these Sloops are destined for the Medeterranean to relieve our vessels there. I hope they will be ready for sea in a few weeks—I have sent for the sec. of the Navy, & will give you the time he may report the one will be ready—I am always perplexed with the tardiness of the public *vessels* on repair—I *will alter it*.[1]

you may, with my respects, assure Mr Randolph it would afford me at all times pleasure to see him; but I leave it entirely to his own pleasure & convenience, which rout he may take—we can send his instructions to him, & I have full confidence in his wisdom & prudence that our concerns with Russia will be well maintained by him[.][2] yr friend

Andrew Jackson

P.S. Send me his nomination, that I may send it up on *Thursday next*. A. J[3]

ALS, DLC-Van Buren Papers (15-0919). Addressed "(Private)."

1. On May 5, Branch wrote the navy yard commanders at Portsmouth, N.H., and New York for readiness reports on the sloops *Concord* and *Boston* respectively (DNA-RG 45, M149-18). Randolph sailed from Norfolk on the *Concord* on June 28. David Porter, Henry Lee's replacement as consul general to Algiers, sailed from New York on the *Boston* on June 29. The two sloops relieved the *Warren* and *Lexington* in the Mediterranean.

2. Van Buren answered Randolph on May 6 that a sloop would be ready to take him in mid-June from either New York or Norfolk as he preferred, that while AJ would be glad to see him there was no need to visit Washington, and that Congress's adjournment was uncertain (Van Buren Papers, DLC).

3. AJ nominated Randolph as minister to Russia on May 24. The Senate confirmed him May 26.

To Martin Van Buren

[Federal power to fund transportation works, known as "internal improvements," had long been contested. Under Presidents Monroe and Quincy Adams, Congress had underwritten several projects by subscribing for stock in canal companies incorporated by state legislatures. On April 29, 1830, the House of Representatives passed and sent to the Senate a similar bill to subscribe for 1,500 shares in the Maysville, Washington,

Paris, and Lexington Turnpike Road Company, incorporated by the state of Kentucky.

Van Buren presented the exchange of notes below in his Autobiography, published posthumously. The manuscript he gave Jackson was a brief he had prepared some time before on the internal improvements question. With the Maysville Road bill now pending in the Senate, Jackson had asked to see it.]

(Private.)

MAY 4TH, 1830.

MY DEAR SIR,

I have been engaged to day as long as my head and eyes would permit, poring over the manuscript you handed me; as far as I have been able to decipher it I think it one of the most lucid expositions of the Constitution and historical accounts of the departure by Congress from its true principles that I have ever met with.

It furnishes clear views upon the constitutional powers of Congress. The inability of Congress under the Constitution to apply the funds of the Government to private, not national purposes I never had a doubt of. The Kentucky road bill involves this very power and I think it right boldly to meet it at the threshold. With this object in view I wish to have an interview with you and consult upon this subject that the constitutional points may be arranged to bear upon it with clearness so that the people may fully understand it.

Can I see you this evening or Thursday morning? Your friend

ANDREW JACKSON

Printed, *The Autobiography of Martin Van Buren*, p. 321 (15-0921).

From Martin Van Buren

PRIVATE.

W. *May 4th 1830.*

MY DEAR SIR.

I thank you for your favorable opinion of the notes. This matter has for a few days past borne heavily on my mind, and brought it to the precise conclusion stated in your note. Under this impression I had actually commenced throwing my ideas on paper to be submitted to you when I should get through, to see whether it is not possible to defeat the aim of our adversaries in either respect, viz; whether it be to draw you into the approval of a Bill most emphatically *local*, and thus endeavor to saddle you with the latitudinarian notions upon which the late administration acted, or to compel you to take a stand against internal improvements generally, and thus draw to their aid all those who are interested in the ten thousand schemes which events and the course of the Government for a few past years have engendered. I think I see land, and that it will be in our power to serve the Country and at the same time counteract the machinations of those who mingle their selfish and ambitious views in the matter. We shall have time enough; the Bill has not yet passed the Senate and you have, you know, ten days after that.[1]

I want to see Mr. McDuffie this evening upon the subject of the outfits and may not, therefore, call. I should prefer too to complete first the arrangement of my ideas, and then we can take up the subject more satisfactorily. Yours truly

M. VAN BUREN

Printed, *The Autobiography of Martin Van Buren*, pp. 321–22 (15-0922).
1. The writing Van Buren had commenced may have been his draft of AJ's Maysville Road veto of May 27 (below). The bill passed the Senate on May 15 and was signed and presented to AJ on May 19.

To John Branch

May 5th. 1830—
verbal as well as written

Reported that Thos. W. Barry was appointed gunner 2nd. July 1813 Navy yard at Washington—that charges was prefered against him & thro' Commodore Tingy he was permitted to resign[1]—that B. left the country & went to Mexico, returned and in 1827 was appointed Gunner—and now holds the appointment of Gunner and store keeper—

That he should hold these two appointments to the exclusion of other meritorious officers are made ground of reiterated complaints—

¿What is the duty of store keeper and how far does it comport with the responsibility of Gunner—

The claims of Major Broom are presented for the office of store keeper alledging that the two offices in one man is improper—

This subject is refered to the Secretary of the Navy—& if there is no saving to the Govrt. by uniting them in one person—let them be seperated & Major Broom appointed store keeper—But if there are saving to the Govt. by keeping them united let them so remain[.] respectfully

Andrew Jackson

ANS, CtHi (mAJs). On the other side of AJ's note is a memorandum concerning Barry, perhaps composed by a Navy Department clerk. Thomas Barry (c1779–1842) had been a gunner in the Navy, serving prominently in the War of 1812. He resigned in 1826 and was reappointed in 1827. The memorandum stated that although Barry drew pay as a gunner, his only duty at the Washington navy yard was keeping the powder magazine, a job performed elsewhere for less pay. The Navy Department subsequently sought a post for Barry that would justify keeping his gunner's status and salary, and in July reassigned him to the New York navy yard as ordnance chief (DNA-RG 45, M149-19). Marine captain Charles R. Broom (c1795–1840) was appointed magazine keeper at Washington in June.

   1. Captain Thomas Tingey (1750–1829) had commanded the Washington navy yard in 1826. According to the memorandum, Navy lieutenant Thomas Crabb had preferred charges against Barry. He withdrew them at Tingey's instigation and Barry resigned.

From Samuel Jackson Hays

Nashville May 5th. 1830

Dr. Uncle

   I have great pleasure being just in receipt of two letters from you—They have relieved me of all unpleasant feeling on the subject of the horse

   I wrote you on the day of my arrival here in which I endeavoured to give a general & correct view of every thing at the Hermitage I did not descend to particulars on the subject of the Tomb &c for fear of irritating unnecessarily old wounds & of exciting unpleasant & melancholy feeling. Mr. Steel seems to have paid great attention to every thing about the Tomb & I think it presents such appearance as you would be pleased with. The garden was found in fine order the sides of the walks handsomely paved with brick & every thing looking very luxuriantt & fine—The prospect of an abundant crop of straw-berries which were just begining to turn red—Frances was very much pleased with the neighbourhood & would have liked to remain a few days longer & partake of the straw-berries but for our anxiety to visit Mother[1] & our relations in the District, who have urged us to visit them as soon as we can

   You ask for information relative to the horse which you gave Andrew   I spoke of horses generally in my letter to you & now have no hesitancy in saying that he is decidedly too fine a horse to think of changing —Mr. Steel informs me that Dr. Butler[2] is pleased with him—I will see the Dr. in a few days & will know whether he would like to purchase—I should say he is likely worth $450 or 500 I don't profess to be a great judge of a horse but according to my opinion he is a very fine colt

   The brown colt is said to be the very image of his father & I have no doubt will become one of the fleetest horses in the country—we found all our friends well here & many kind enquiries after you—we staid last night at Mr McLemores who speaks of visiting you Washington—he is a sterling fellow & will I hope get thro' with all his difficulties. We leave here in the morning for Jackson   I will drop Mr. Steel a line before I go—I have taken Felix. Mr Steel having assured me he could spare him without injury to the crop & have left the grey horse with him, which he will plough after resting a short time   we can exchange it some other time, indeed Hutchings may ride Felix in if I can get a horse to do me in the interim. I will sell the horse I purchased if I can well, for after his purchase I barely have funds enough to take me home after which however I will not have need for any.

I am now writing in Mr. Crutchers office, who is well &c.

Mr. Earl has been with me a good deal speaks of leaving here in the course of 8 or 10 days for the City.

Poor Houston is here & not well recd. I understand there are resolutions by the people of Sumner Cty. coming out agst. him in to morrows paper! He has informed me he will leave in the morning.[3]

Present our respects to all the inhabitants of the "White House" say to Andrew I will write him from Jackson & accept for yourself our love

S. J. Hays

I have seen Dr. Stith & others from Franklin who say the good people of Williamson Cty. will give Major Eaton & family a cordial reception should they visit there this summer—I can speak for at least one here McLemore

Nashville is crowded at this time with doctors from all parts of the state *[who]* have assembled at the instance of *[the]* Legislature for the purpose of suppressing *quackery* by establishing a medical board & censors & by not permitting any one to practice who has not been licensed It has produced considerable excitement. Hogg & Dr. Roane were the opposing candidates for President   the latter succeeded[4]

[Endorsed by AJ:] To be answered   A. J.

ALS, DLC (38). AN postscript and envelope postmarked May 7, DLC (15-0949). AJ replied about May 31 (below).

1. Jane Donelson Hays.

2. William E. Butler, Hays's brother-in-law.

3. In April 1829, Samuel Houston's bride of three months, Eliza H. Allen of Sumner County, separated from Houston and returned to her parents. Houston abruptly resigned as governor of Tennessee and quit the state. On April 26, 1830, while Houston was in Nashville on his way from Washington to Arkansas, a public meeting convened at Gallatin, the Sumner County seat, and appointed a committee to vindicate Eliza's character. The committee's report, adopted unanimously by the reconvened meeting two days later and published (after Houston left) in the *Nashville Whig* of May 7, praised her virtue and blamed the separation on Houston's "unfounded jealousies" and groundless suspicions. Calling Houston a "deluded man" and Eliza "an innocent and injured woman," it accused him of trying to excuse his desertion and arouse public sympathy by spreading insinuations that she was unchaste.

4. In January 1830 the Tennessee legislature incorporated the Medical Society of Tennessee, with 151 physicians as charter members. The Society was directed to establish boards of censors to examine and license medical practitioners. As stipulated by the charter, the Society first met at Nashville on May 3. James Roane (c1790–1833) of Nashville was elected president, and Ferdinand Stith (d. 1855) of Franklin and Samuel Hogg were elected to the board of censors for the Middle Tennessee district.

To the United States Senate

[On March 17, Choctaws headed by Greenwood Leflore and David Folsom signed a proposed removal treaty and sent it via David W. Haley to Washington, where it arrived in April. On May 6 Jackson submitted it to the Senate along with an alternative treaty of his own, drawn up in the War Department. Printed here is Jackson's draft of his May 6 message to the Senate, followed by the two treaty proposals that accompanied the message. (The final sent version of the message, without the treaties, appears in Senate Executive Proceedings, *4:97–99, and in Richardson, 2:478–79). With this message Jackson also enclosed communications from Leflore and Folsom of March 18, from Mushulatubbe of March 25, from Daniel W. Wright to Powhatan Ellis of April 11 (all above), and from Eaton of April 27. Eaton's letter, enclosing a statement from Thomas L. McKenney, itemized the existing Choctaw annuities that Jackson's proposed treaty would supersede.*

*The Senate ordered Jackson's message and its attachments to be printed in confidence and referred them to the Committee on Indian Affairs. On May 27, chairman Hugh Lawson White reported that the Leflore and Folsom treaty did not clearly have the assent of the Choctaw Nation and that in any case its provisions, notably Articles 3, 12, 16, 18, and 20, were so unreasonable as to require rejection. The committee opined that the payments offered in Jackson's treaty were perhaps too generous, but concluded that for the Senate to try to stipulate precise terms in advance would impede rather than aid a successful negotiation. On May 29 the Senate adopted the committee's resolution formally advising Jackson not to ratify the Leflore and Folsom treaty (*Senate Executive Proceedings, *4:111–12, 119).]*

To the Senate of the United States

Propositions in the form of a Treaty have been recently sent to me, by a special messenger from the choctaw nation of Indians, proposing to cede their entire country to the United States east of the Mississippi river. This has been an act exclusively of the Indians themselves   The Goverment was not informed of it, and was unrepresented at the council that formed it—The Indians convened of their own accord, drafted & executed the propositions which are now presented, consenting to be bound by them if within three months, the president & senate should approve. It will be perceived that they declare, in the last article, that if those which are now offered, shall be rejected, none others will be assented to, or submitted by them.

It is certainly desirable, & of great importance on various accounts, that some agreement should be concluded, that would effect an object so important as removing the Indians beyond the Territorial limits of the States. In such arrangement I should be disposed to extend to them terms as liberal, as it might be inferred the senate would sanction. I could not however, on constitutional grounds, consent to adopt the provisions contained in the present proposed treaty, nor ~~yet~~ do I consider it advisable or proper to withold it from the consideration of the senate

first, such is the request of the Indians

2nd. That the opinion of the Senate in relation to the terms proposed by the Indians, would have a salutary effect in further negotiations if this should be deemed advisable

3 That the propositions altho' objectionable in certain particulars, are believed to be susceptible of modification which might render them conformable to the humane and liberal policy, which it is desirable on the part of the Goverment to our red Brethern and be made at the same acceptable to the Indians—To these modifications, and to any suggestions of the Senate, The President in the exercise of Peculiar functions would give the most respectful consideration

4th. Such a course is abundantly justified by precedent in the earlier administration of ~~our~~ the Goverment and though not used for some years past, may it seems to me be now properly resorted to under the peculiar circumstances of our present relations with the Indian tribes from a consideration of the magnitude of the results which are contemplated, and from a conviction that the measures, thus framed from their origin, by the united councils of the two branches of the treaty making power will be more satisfactory to the american people, who have taken a deep interest in this question, as well as the Indian tribes[1]

5— This mode of communicating with the senate in relation to compacts which it is proposed to enter into with the Indian tribes, is believed not to be liable to the objection, which might, perhaps, be properly made to its application to our negotiations with civilized nations—The secrecy which it is indispensable to preserve in the latter case, is comparatively unimportant in the former—

With ~~these views of the subject~~ this view the President submits to the Senate, the ~~suggestions~~ alterations which have occurd to him as proper in relation to the propositions made by the choctaw nation, ~~and his view of the~~ They are such modifications ~~which might~~ as may render those proposals acceptable to the parties respectively—Such are the views which occur to the President ~~by his reflection on the proposal of the choctaw nation—willing to~~ He will cheerfully however yield ~~mine~~ his to the correction which may result from ~~the~~ a frank interchange of opinion with ~~his~~ constitutional advisers. He submits ~~for~~ therefore to the Senate the following ~~questions~~

~~Will the Senate advise and consent to the ratification of the Treaty with the Choctaws herewith presented—~~

☞ Will the Senate advise & consent to its ratification, with any and with what amendments—

AD draft with corrections by Eaton, DLC (76). DS, DNA-RG 46 (15-0927). *Senate Executive Proceedings*, 4:97–99; Richardson, 2:478–79. This may have been the draft AJ showed Van Buren on April 15 (above). In its final sent form, the message named both the Leflore and Folsom treaty and the protests against it as "voluntary acts of the Indians themselves." It also more directly identified the alternative treaty as one "I have drawn up." The order of text in the message was rearranged somewhat, and the phrase "civilized nations" replaced with "foreign nations." A new concluding paragraph acknowledged that the payments AJ proposed were large, but deemed the money of minor importance: "The great desideratum is the removal of the Indians, and the settlement of the perplexing question involved in their present location, a question in which several of the States of this Union have the deepest interest, and which if left undecided much longer may eventuate in serious injury to the Indians."

1. The Constitution gives the president "Power, by and with the Advice and Consent of the Senate, to make Treaties." Presidents Washington and John Adams had sought Senate counsel on pending negotiations as well as concluded treaties, but the practice had since fallen into disuse.

[Treaty project from Greenwood Leflore, David Folsom, et al.]

Articles of a treaty between the United States of Amearica and the Choctaw Nation of red people.

Whereas the Choctaw Nation of red people have always lived under such laws as were judged and admitted in their national councils to be just and equitable, and suited to free men, and whereas the General Assembly of the State of Mississippi has extended all the laws of said State to all the persons and property within the chartered limits of said State, and the President of the United States has expressly told us that he cannot protect the Choctaw people from the exercise of Mississippi law, but that he will be under the necessity of sustaining said State in the exercise of her laws—Now therefore, We the Choctaw Nation of Red People in National Council assembled have determined that we never will submit to or be governened by laws in the anactment of which we are not permited to participate, and as the Constitution of the State of Mississippi does not secure the representation of Red people in the Legislative Councils of said State, and that we may continue under our own laws in peace with the United States, and the State of Mississippi, we have further determined to propose to sell all our claim to lands East of the Mississippi River, and emigrate to the Choctaw lands West of said river on the following conditions.

Article I. The United States shall secure the said Choctaw Nation of red People the perpetual, peaceful possession of all that tract of country known and described in a treaty as the Choctaw lands West of the Mississippi River embraced in the following lines and limits, viz. beginning on the Arkansas River one hundred paces East of Fort Smith, and running up said River to the mouth of the Canadian ~~River~~ Fork ~~of~~ thence up said fork to its source, thence a due South course to Red River, then down said Red River to the point or place where a due South line from the beginning would strike said Red River, thence along said South line to the beginning on the Arkansas river which last line it is expressly stipulated shall be the perpetual, and perminent boundry line beween the Teritory or State of Arkansas and the Choctaw Nation, and immediately on the ratification of this treaty, a patent shall be issued by the President of the United States, Granting, and transfering to the said Choctaw Nation of red people a full and perfect title in fee simple to all the land within the before described limits, and forever warranting and defending the peacable possession of the same to the Choctaw Nation, their decendants and citizens.[1]

Article II. The Government and people of the United States are hereby bound and obligated, to secure to the said Choctaw Nation of red people the jurisdiction and government of all the persons and property that may be within the limits pointed out in the first article so that no teritory or State, or the United States shall ever have a right to pass laws for the Government of the Choctaw Nation of red people, their desendants or citizens, and that no part of the above described land shall ever be embraced in any teritory or state, but that the United States shall forever defend said Choctaw Nation from and against all laws, but such as from time to time may be enacted in their own National Council of said Choctaw Nation. Provided always that nothing in this article shall be so construed as to subject the Agent of the United States, his family or property, or any other person, particularly employed by the United States, and recognised by the Chief, to the laws of said Choctaw Nation as citizens, but being in the immediate employment of the United States for the benefit of the Choctaw Nation, their persons and property shall be under the protection of the Nation, and under the protection of the United States, but in all cases where the Legislative Council of said Choctaw Nation shall complain to the President of the United States that the Agent is guilty of transgressions of the laws of the Nation, to the injury of said Nation the President shall remove him; And in all cases where other persons in the employment of the United States, shall transgress the Laws of the Nation, they shall be removed by the Agent, on the application of the Cheif and legislative Council; But as above stated, all other persons shall be subject to the laws of said Nation, and neither the United States, nor any other power, or government shall ever have a right to protect them from the laws of said Choctaw Nation if they reside within the limits pointed out in the first article

Article III. Greenwood Leflore is hereby acknowledged as the Chief of the Choctaw Nation West of the Mississippi, and shall be so recognized and respected during life, or the faithful discharge of his duties, and David Folsom is hereby acknowledged as the Supreme judge of the Choctaw Nation West of the Mississippi River, and shall be so recognized, and respected during life, or the faithful discharge of his duties. And it is moreover ~~agree~~ understood and agreed upon that but one Cheif of the Choctaw Nation shall be recognized at any one time by the United States

Article IV The United States are hereby obligated and bound to protect the Choctaw ~~Nation~~ Citizens from foreign enemies, on the same principles that the Citizens of the United States are protected, that whatever would be a legal charge upon the United States for self defence, or for spoilations committed by an enemy, shall be equally binding in favour of the Choctaws, and their citizens; And in all cases where the Choctaws shall be called upon by ~~the~~ a legally authorized officer of the United States to fight an enemy; such Choctaws shall receive such pay and other emoluments, as the citizens of the United States receive in such cases.

Article V. Should a Choctaw or Choctaw Citizen commit any act of violence upon the person or property of a citizen of the United States, or join any war party against a neighbouring tribe of Indians without the command of his Captain, or with the authority of his Captain, except to oppose an actual or threatened invasion, such person so offending shall be delivered up to an officer of the United States, if in the power of the Choctaw Nation, that such offender may be punished as may be provided in such cases by the said United States; but if such offender is not within the controul of said Choctaw Nation, then said Choctaw Nation shall not be held responsible for the injury done by said offender.

Article VI. All acts of violence committed upon the persons and property of the Citizens of the Choctaw Nation, either by citizens of the United States, or neighbouring tribes of red people shall be refered to the Agent of the United States, who shall examine into such cases, and see that every possible degree of justice is done to said injured citizen of the Choctaw Nation.

Article VII. Offenders against the Laws of the United States, or any individual State, shall be apprehended and delivered to the Agent, or any duly athorized officer, where such offender may be found in the Choctaw country, having fled from some part of the United States: but in all such cases, application must be made to the Agent, or Chief, and the expense of his apprehension and delivery provided for.

Article VIII. Any citizen of the United States who may be ordered from the Nation by the Chief, or supreme judge, and refusing to obay, or returning to the Nation without the consent of the Chief, shall be subject to such pains, and penalties, as may be provided by the Choctaw Council in such cases.

Article IX. Citizens of the United States traveling peacably shall be under the protection of the Nation

Article X. The United States shall aid the Chief when called upon, to suppress any insurrection of any part of the Choctaw Citizens against the laws of the National Council (which council shall be composed of the Chief and the Captains of the Nation, and the laws enacted by said council shall govern and protect equally all the Choctaws and citizens of the Nation) and the United States shall be particularly obliged to assist the Chief in excluding ardent spirits from said Nation, unless for purposes of real necessity

Article XI No person shall expose goods, or other articles for sale as a trader without a written permit from the Chief, under the penalty of forfeiting all such articles to the Nation; and the Cheif shall not license any person to trade in the Nation, unless he resides in the Nation, and is subject to all the laws of the Nation.

Article XII. The United States shall immediately have Red River made navigable forty miles into, or along the Choctaw line, or at least to the mouth of Riamisha, and to the mouth of the four blues when necessary, and shall continue said stream in a navigable state; and shall improve the navigation of the Arkansas, if necessary, as high as the mouth of the canadian fork, and said rivers shall forever continue free for the navigation of the Choctaw citizens, without subjecting said citizens to pay any toll for navigating said rivers or the Mississippi. The United States are further obliged to open, and keep in repair a good road from Natchitoches to such two points in the Southren, and Northern portions of the Choctaw Nation West of the Mississippi river as the Chief shall direct, and from such point in the Northren District as the Chief may have selected to intersect some other main road leading to the City of Washington. And the United States shall establish a regular weekly Northren, and Southren mail along such road through the Choctaw Country, and shall establish at least two Post Offices, & as many others as may be necessary for the accommodation of the citizens of the Choctaw Nation.

Article XIII All persons other than Choctaws shall be removed, by the United States from the Choctaw lands West of the Mississippi, at any time when so requested to do by the Chief, after the ratification of the Treaty.

Article XIV No United States Soldiers shall be stationed in, or marched through the Choctaw lands without the consent of the Chief, and in all cases private property shall be respected, and not taken for the use of the United States soldiers, in their service, without fully compensating the rightful owner for the same.

Article XV As it is necessary that the Choctaws should have confidence in the United States Agent residing among them, and attending to the complaints of Choctaws against citizens of the United States, therefore the United States Agent shall only hold his office for four years, but may be reappointed by the recommendation of the National council, but in all cases the President of the United States shall remove the Agent and appoint some other person on the petition of the Cheif and two thirds of the legislative Council of said Nation. It is further stipulated that the wish of the Cheif shall be particularly attended too in the appointment of an Agent immediately on the ratification of this treaty, who shall be the only United States Agent for the Choctaw Nation for the time being, and said Agent shall fix his residence in the Southren Section of the Nation, and all future Agents shall reside in said Southren Section, unless the contrary shall be agreed upon by the Cheif and Legislative Council. It is further stipulated that whenever a Choctaw or Choctaw citizen shall be delivered to the United States as an offender, that the United States agent shall employ counsel to defend said offender, and in the absence of the Agent the Judge before whom said accused person shall be tried, shall appoint counsel, for the accused person which counsel shall be paid by the United States

Article XVI Any and all Choctaws wishing to continue on the land where they now reside shall be secured a full section, or six hundred and forty acres of land to each family in fee simple

Article XVII All Choctaws requesting it may have the value of their improvements paid by the United States, or like improvements made for them on their future places of residence West of the Mississippi.

Article XVIII. All Choctaws wishing to make their own improvements West of the Mississippi shall be allowed six hundred and forty acres of land in fee simple to each family, and three hundred and twenty acres and to each man capable of serving in the defence of his country. Said land to embrace the present improvements of such families, or being subject to be located upon any unocupied land within the limits of the present residence, or lands of the Choctaws East of the Mississippi. A family shall be considered to consist of a man and his wife, or child, or children or a woman with a husband or a child or children and the men provided for as being capaple of defending their Country, are understood to be men without families, and each family of children without a parent living shall be viewed as a family. Such persons as wish it shall have a certificate or certificates issued in his, her, or their names, and shall dispose of said certificate as they may think proper, and the legal holder of said certificate shall locate, on any Choctaw lands now known as Choctaw land East of Mississippi, and the President of the United States shall issue patents to the legal holders of said certificates, for such quarter sections as shall cover the largest part of the improvements or claim of such legal holder of such certificate, provided that no certificate shall call for more than six hundred and forty acres, and every certificate shall be laid on land adjoining, so that a certificate calling for six hundred and forty acres although laid on quarter sections of different sections (when survayed) such quarter sections shall be adjoining but it is not to be understood that the location of different certificates shall be connected. But nothing in this Treaty shall secure a certificate of claim for a sale made of such claim untill the certificate has actually issued. It is further stipulated that the National Council shall appoint commissioners for the Choctaw Nation in the West who shall receive the certificates of claims as above, for persons who wish such claims, but are not capable of affecting their sale, or are not accustomed to attend to such business, the said commissioners shall be approved of by the Agent of the United States, who shall certify that said commissioners are authorized to sell said claims, and that the legal holders of them will receive a patent from the President, then said commissioners shall sell such claims on the most advantagous terms in their power, and appropriate the proceeds, according to the medium price of the same to the improvement of the new homes of the original claimants, and should any surplus remain it shall be paid to such claimants in such property as they shall be least likely to spend. The National Council shall determine on the compensation to be allowed said commissioners. The accounts of said commissioners shall be at all times open to the inspection of the Chief, and the United States Agent, and said commissioners may be removed at any time by the national Council.

Article XIX. The United ~~Council~~ States shall pay to the National Council, through the United States Agent, at such times as may be called for by said council, the sum of fifty thousand dollars to be appropriated by said council in building school houses, purchasing books &c, and also twenty five thousand dollars to be appropriated in erecting council houses, and also twenty five thousand dollars to be appropriated in erecting places of Divine Worship.

Article XX The United States shall immediately appoint a person to issue the above certificates of claim or claims, so soon as the Agent of the United States shall assertain who wish such certificates, and this shall be ascertained by the attendance of the agent at such places and times as may be appointed by the Cheif of the Choctaw Nation. The Agent shall take down the name of each man having a wife or child, and shall assertain whether he wishes a claim to land for to be sold, or whether he wishes his improvements assessed and like improvement put on the place of his new home, or whether he wishes his improvements paid for. The women having children, or men without families, shall likewise specify their wishes as above, but in all cases of a child, or children without parents, a certificate shall issue to the commissioners as above in favour of said orphan or orphans.

Article XXI The United States shall appoint a person or persons whose duty it shall be to assess the value of the improvements of those who wish such assessment in preference to a claim of land for sale, and the aforesaid person shall also assess the value of all furniture to be left by Choctaws or present citizens of the Nation, and shall take charge of such tools as may be delivered to him or them at suitable places, by Choctaws or citizens (Citizens being in this place understood to be white persons married to red persons or having been so married and now residing in the Nation, and being particularly permitted to remove with the Nation by the Cheif) which said furniture, and tools shall be paid for or replaced at their new residence West of the Mississippi by the United States. The above appointed persons, or others duly appointed shall take charge of all hogs and cattle that may be pened and delivered at places appointed by the Chief, or such other places as the Chief may direct and all hogs shall be paid for by the United States at the rate of two dollars ahead, or a like number furnished at their new residence in the West, at the option of individuals; and all horned cattle thus delivered shall be paid for by the United States, or a like number furnished, west of the Mississippi to the persons delivering them here, and six dollars ahead shall be the price of all those horned Cattle paid for as above. White men with red families, and permitted to remove with them as above shall be equally entitled to the above provisions as tho. they were native Choctaws, provided that all persons wishing to remove their stock shall be aided by having a supply of corn for their hogs upon an average of one bushel to every hundred head daily to be delivered.

Article XXII. The United States shall open a road from the present Choctaw Agency to the big sand Landing on the Yazoo, and from Col Leflores to the best crossing on the Mississippi, to be selected by the Agent and Chief and shall provide a suitable number of waggons to accompany such part as may remove by land, and shall furnish a sufficient supply of provisions for them from the time they shall form encampments by the direction of the Agent of the United States, untill they shall disperse to their homes, or be directed to do so by said Agent when they have arrived in the neighbourhood of said homes, in their country West of the Mississippi river. And the United States shall furnish an ample and ful supply of provision for twelve months to each Choctaw and his family, or persons known as citizens of the Choctaw Nation as pointed out in the twenty first article. The United States are further obligated to furnish Steam boats to carry all those who may wish to go by water, and all such as are aged and infirm together with such females and children as would be unfit for a journey by land; said steam-boats shall carry them from the landing near Greenwood Leflores to some point on the Arkansas, and from thence shall furnish waggons to carry the sick and infirm to the vicinity of their future homes, and shall have them supplied with provisions on their passage & for one year after their reaching their new residence, as in the case of those who move by land and in all respects those who move by water shall share equal advantages with those who remove by land and in both cases the United States Agent shall accomodate and provide for the Choctaws in their emigration with such tents as he may judge necessary for their comfort, even although not especially provided for in this article. The provisions provided for in this Article for the supply of the Choctaws and their familes &c ~~and~~ shall be furnished at such places as the Agent & Cheif may agree upon, and shall consist of a daily ration as allowed to a United States soldier with the exception of at least one bushel of corn per month in place of whisky and as large a supply of bacon as may be requested by the Cheif in the room of beef to each individual to be delivered daily, weekly, or monthly as the Cheif may request.

Article XXIII According to a former Treaty the United States are obligated to furnish every man emigrating to the West with a good rifle gun and ammunition together with a blanket and brass or copper Kettle; These articles shall be furnished to every man, and each man shall be furnished with an ax, hoe and plow, and each woman shall be furnished with a spining wheel and cards, and each five families with a loom, so soon as their future places of residence shall be prepared for them; the United States shall also furnish two black smith shops at the expense of the United States on the principles of the shop now furnished the Nation.[2]

Article XXIV All white men with their effects now connected with the Nation as having red families or having had such shall be removed to the future home of the Choctaws ~~as thou~~ on the same principles as though the were Choctaws, by the particular permit of the Chief, and shall be entitled to one years support as a choctaw; And all Ministers of the Gospel, and teachers of schools now labouring in the Nation, together with their families shall likewise be entitled to the removal of themselves, and their effects and a years provision as above by the request of the Cheif in writing.

Article XXV To enable the Choctaws to defend themselves in their new home, each warriour shall annually be furnished for five years by the United States with a full supply of good rifle powder and lead; but while the new homes of the Choctaws are preparing and the people emigrating, or preparing to emigrate the United States shall station such troops as may be necessary in such position on or near the Choctaw line, or other situation as may be requested by the Chief so that the Choctaws may safely settle untill they feel themselves sufficiently strong to protect themselves; but at all times the United States shall assist the Choctaws if invaded or threatened with an invasion. Further it is stipulated that the Cheif of the Choctaw nation shall be ~~annually~~ furnished with a good six pound brass piece of Artilary well mounted, together with a supply of powder and balls

Article XXVI As the Captains will have much trouble for the first four years of keeping their people in order and settling them, the United States shall furnish each Captain, the number of whom shall not exceed one hundred, with a good suit of Clothes, and a substantial broad sword as an outfit, and shall pay each Captain fifty dollars annually for the first four years; also the Cheif of the Nation shall appoint fifty men as rangers, who shall occupy and hold the grade of Captains, and each of them shall receive the outfit and salary of a Captain for the first four years. These rangers shall execute the orders of the Cheif and travel as messangers.

Article XXVII. Whereas the Cheif of the Choctaw Nation must be at great expense and trouble in traveling and attending to the business of the Nation for the first four or five years, therefore the Cheif shall be allowed the pay and emoluments of a Col. in the United States Army for the first four years, and whenever called into the service of the United States shall hold the grade of a Col. and receive a Col's pay and emoluments. The pay above secured to the Cheif of the Choctaw Nation shall be paid by the United States, and in consequence of the expense of a chief in the West in entertaining the large number of foreign visitors who would frequent his house, together with the number of his people who would visit on business that the Cheif of the Choctaw Nation may prove the advantages of settled homes and civilized habits to the wandering tribes of the West, it is desireable that his situation should be very comfortable, therefore the Cheif Greewood Leflore shall make selections of ten sections of land to be located so as to embrace his pesent improvements or any other unocupied land in the Nation on the East of the Mississippi such location to be made in such body as may suit the purchasers of his claims, and to embrace in each seperate quarter section, if sold seperate the largest part of the improvement, or claim of the holder of the certificate of the claim of said quarter section; and the United States shall cause patents in fee simple to issue to the legal holders of said claim. Whereas David Folsom has made heavy sacrifices for the good of the Nation in his late responsible office of Cheif and in his new station of Supreme judge must of necessity continue to devote his time assiduously in behalf of the Choctaw Nation it is stipulated that said David Folsom shall select and sell ten sections of land on the same principles as specified in the case of the Cheif. And said David Folsom shall receive from the United States one ~~hundred~~ thousand dollars annually for the first four years. Also John Garland a late Cheif shall have five sections of Land, and Joel R. Nail, Isreal Folsom George W. Harkins & James L McDonald shall each be allowed two sections of Land, to be selected and sold as in the case of the Cheif, for their own benefit.

Article XXVIII Whereas the United States now pay annuel amounts to the Choctaw Nation for lands heretofore sold to said United States to the Amount of about twenty four thousand dollars for the support of said Choctaw National government, and for schools, and for other purposes, a large part of which annuel sum is paid as an interest on a capital in the hands of the United States, now therefore, we the Choctaw Nation in National Council assembled do hereby relinquish all our claims for said annuities, and all claims heretofore provided for, for individuals, and sell relinquish and transfr to the United States all our claim for lands on the East side of the Mississippi except such as are provided for by liberal construction of this Treaty; and we do hereby revoke all Treaties inconsistant with the provisions of this Treaty, in consideration of which the United States are held and firmly bound to pay the Choctaw Nation, as an interest on one million of dollars the sum of fifty thousand dollars annually for twenty years, and if said Choctaw Nation shall call for the said principal of one million of dollars at the expiration of said twenty years, the said United States shall pay said Million of Dollars to said Choctaw Nation but if the said Choctaw Nation fail to call for the principal at that time, the said United States shall continue to pay the sum of fifty thousand dollars annually untill paid, and said sum of one million of dollars shall be paid at the expiration of any ten years after the first stipulated term of twenty years. Two thousand dollars shall be annually appropriated by the

National Council for the support of the poor, the afflicted and aged. One thousand shall be annually appropriated by the National Council to the Comfort of the aged Choctaws who fought under General Wayne in the United States army, and for such aged warriours as fought for the United States, at any period pevious to the year eighteen hundred and ten. Two thousand shall be annually appropriated by the National Council for the comfort and support of such persons as fought in the United States armies in the last war, provided that such persons are poor and need the aid of the proposed assistance, or their Widows or orphans need such support, provided also that no warriour his widow or orphan shall receive more than twenty five dollars annually. Any surplus of said last appropriations shall be at the disposal of the National Council, and at the death of persons thus provided for the said appropriations shall constitute a part of the National founds. One thousand dollars each shall be annually paid after the first four years to the Cheif and supreme judge out of said annuity. And one thousand dols shall be annually appropriated for a secretary for the Cheif, and clerk for the supreme Court, at five hundred dollars each, who shall keep correct accounts of all moneis received, and paid out by the Cheif, and shall annually lay a correct account of the same before the National Council; the affore said Cleark shall register all laws, and do other such other business as the supreme judge shall direct. Also twelve thousand dollars shall be annually appropriated by the National Council for schools in the Nation under the care of said National Council, The remaining sum of thirty thousand dollars annually shall be appropriated by the National Council for the support of machancial institutions for Blacksmiths iron and other articles of husbandry, and for the support of the National Government and other purposes[3]

Article XXIX A liberal construction shall be given to all the articles of this Treaty in favour of the Choctaws, and in all cases of doubt the desision shall be in favour of the Choctaws. No advantage shall be taken for the want of form in any part but what shall appear to be the meaning and design of the parties shall be the governing principal in fulfiling the provisions of this Treaty of the Choctaw Nation. The United States Agent shall have the power of appointing his sub-Agent, and removing him at pleasure. The Agent of the United States shall appoint two interpreters for the Choctaw Nation, by the recommendation of the Cheif, and Supreme judge and upon complaint of said Cheif and Supreme judge shall remove either of them. The United States are obligated to appoint such an agent as the Nation has confidence in, and it is felt to be an object of the first importance that the removal of the Nation should be conducted by men who will use every possible means to conduct them with as little suffering as possible. Therefore the Agent to be appointed immediately after the ratification of this Treaty shall be the principal conducter of said Nation, and shall appoint such persons as assistants as may be recommended by the Cheif or supreme judge if approved of by himself and on the complaint of the Cheif or Supreme judge, the said principal conductor shall remove any assistant complained of

Article XXX This Treaty is the only proposition of that the Choctaw Nation will ever make to the United States and proposes the only terms on which the said Nation will emigrate to the West, and it would not propose to emigrate on any terms were there hopes of living in peace and friendship with the Whites and continuing to occupy their country East of the Mississippi; but as they cannot consent to be governed by laws in the enactment of which they are forbiden to participate and as they ardently wish to live in peace the foregoing Treaty shall be binding on said Choctaw Nation if ratified by the President and Senate of the United States within three months from this date; and shall take effect from and immediately on its ratification in such cases as will prudently admit of so taking effect but the Choctaws shall not be obligated to surrender their present country to the United States sooner than two years after the ratification of this Treaty; but any person purchasing claims herein provided for in this Treaty may remove to the lands upon which such claims may be located by the writen permission of the Cheif and S or Supreme judge.

It is expressly understood that nothing in this Treaty shall bind the United States to improve the navigation of Red River within the State Louisiana, or open roads within the said State, should said state object to the fulfilment of such stipulations as are contained in the Treaty, on these subjects

For the fulfillment of all the Articles of this Treaty, we the undersigned Chief, Supreme judge, and Captains bind ourselves and the Choctaw Nation if ratified as above, in witness whereof we have hereunto set our hands this seventeenth day of March eighteen hundred and twenty thirty

Capt.	Chilita	X	his mark
"	Thomas Lflore	✓	his mark
"	John Garland	✓	his mark
"	Samuel Cobb	✓	his mark
"	Is tunok hacho	✓	his mark

[Two hundred eighty-seven more signatures follow.]

We Greenwood Leflore Cheif of the Choctaw Nation and David Folsom late Cheif of said Nation do hereby approve of and sanction the within Treaty and do also hereby certify that the within Treaty has been duly sanctioned by the within named Captains, Headmen, and Warriours in a regularly appointed National Council, which Council was composed of all the Leading men and most of the Captains in the Nation

Greenwood Leflore
David Folsom

We the undersigned witnesses were present at the National Council, to whom the within Treaty was proposed, and we do hereby certify that the said Treaty was sanctioned by said Council, and that we saw the within Treaty signed by the within named persons

Alexander Talley
David W. Haley
Martin Sims
Robt. D. Smith[4]

DS, DNA-RG 46 (mAJs).

1. These were essentially the boundaries of the western Choctaw domain as defined by the 1820 Treaty of Doak's Stand and 1825 Treaty of Washington.

2. The Treaty of Doak's Stand stipulated the blacksmith shop and a rifle and ammunition, blanket, and kettle for each emigrating warrior.

3. Thomas L. McKenney's tabulation, submitted by Eaton to AJ on April 27 and transmitted herewith to the Senate, showed that the U.S. was presently paying the Choctaws $24,300 annually under four treaties: $6,000 to support a school, $11,400 in perpetual tribal annuities, a $6,000 twenty-year annuity, $600 to support a troop of light horse, and $150 each to two chiefs. General Anthony Wayne (1745–1796) conducted frontier Indian campaigns in the southwest during the Revolution and in the northwest in 1793–95. The Treaty of Dancing Rabbit Creek, signed in September 1830, pensioned surviving Choctaws who had fought with him.

4. Signer Thomas Leflore (c1795–1857) was Greenwood Leflore's cousin. Witness Alexander Talley (1789–1835) was a Methodist missionary.

[Jackson's treaty project]

Proposed.

Articles of a Treaty between the United States of America, and the Choctaw Nation of Red People.

Whereas the Choctaw Nation of Red People have always lived under such laws as were judged and admitted in their National Councils to be just and equitable, and suited to freemen, and Whereas the General Assembly of the State of Mississippi, has extended all the laws of said State to all the persons and property within the chartered limits of said State, and the President of the United States has expressly told us that he cannot protect the Choctaw people from the exercise of Mississippi law, but that he will be under the necessity of sustaining said State in the exercise of her laws. Now therefore we the Choctaw Nation of Red People in National Council assembled have determined that we never will submit to, or be governed by laws in the enactment of which we are not permitted to participate, and as the Constitution of the State of Mississippi does not secure the representation of Red People in the Legislative Councils of said State, and that we may continue under our own laws in peace with the United States, and the State of Mississippi: We have further determined to propose to sell all our claim to lands East of the Mississippi River, and emigrate to the Choctaw lands West of said River, on the following conditions:

Article 1. The United States shall secure the said Choctaw Nation of Red People the perpetual peaceful possession of all that tract of country known, and described in a Treaty, as the Choctaw lands west of the Mississippi River embraced in the following lines and limits, viz: beginning on the Arkansa River one hundred paces East of Fort Smith, and running up said River to the mouth of the Canadian Fork, thence up said fork to its source, thence a due south course to Red River, then down said Red River until it reaches the Western boundary of Arkansa Territory, and thence North with said line to the beginning on the Arkansa River, which last line it is expressly stipulated shall be the perpetual and permanent boundary line between the Territory or State of Arkansa, and the Choctaw Nation. And so soon after the ratification of this Treaty, as Congress shall authorize it, a Patent shall be issued by the President of the United States, granting, and transferring to the said Choctaw Nation of Red People a full and perfect title in fee simple to all the land within the before described limits, and forever warranting and defending the peaceable possession of the same to the Choctaw Nation and their descendants.

Article 2. And in consideration of the provisions contained in the several articles of this treaty, the Choctaw Nation of Indians consent and hereby cede to the United States, the entire Country which they own and possess within the State of Mississippi, as is defined within their recognized limits and boundaries; and agree within two years from the date of this instrument, to remove beyond the Mississippi River; and will so arrange their removal, that as many as possible of their people, not exceeding one half of the whole number, shall depart during the Spring of 1831, while the waters and rivers are in order for their transportation—the residue to follow during the succeeding Spring, whereby a better opportunity will be afforded the Government to extend to them the aid and care which it is so desirable should be extended, in conveying them to their new homes.

Article 3. The Government and people of the United States, are hereby bound and obligated, to secure to the said Choctaw Nation of Red People the jurisdiction and government of all the persons and property that may be within the limits pointed out in the first article, so that no territory or State, shall ever have a right to pass laws for the government of the Choctaw Nation of Red People, and their descendants; and that no part of the above described land shall ever be embraced in any territory or State; but that the United States shall forever defend said Choctaw Nation from and against all laws, except such as from time to time may be enacted in their own National Council, not inconsistent with the Constitution, Treaties, and laws of the United States; and except such as may be, and which have been enacted, by Congress, to the extent that Congress under the Constitution, are required to exercise a legislation over Indian Affairs.

Article 4. The United States are hereby obligated, and bound to protect the Choctaws from foreign enemies, on the same principles that the Citizens of the United States are protected, that whatever would be a legal

demand upon the United States for self defence, or for spoliations committed by an enemy on a Citizen of the United States, shall be equally binding
in favor of the Choctaws; and in all cases when the Choctaws shall be
called upon by a legally authorized officer of the United States to fight an
enemy, such Choctaws shall receive such pay and other emoluments, as the
Citizens of the United States receive in such cases: Provided no war shall
be undertaken, or prosecuted by said Choctaw Nation, but by declaration
made in full Council, and to be approved by the United States; unless it
be in self defence against an enemy marching into their Country, in which
case, they shall defend themselves until the United States are advised
thereof. It is furthermore agreed that the United States will acknowledge,
such persons as Principal and Subordinate Chiefs of the Nation, as by the
constituted authorities of the Nation may be appointed.

Article 5. Should a Choctaw commit any act of violence upon the person or property of a Citizen of the United States, or join any war party
against a neighboring tribe of Indians without the authority in the preceding article, and except to oppose an actual or threatened invasion, such
person so offending shall be delivered up to an officer of the United States,
if in the power of the Choctaw Nation, that such offender may be punished, as may be provided in such cases by the laws of the United States;
but if such offender is not within the control of said Choctaw Nation,
then said Choctaw Nation shall not be held responsible for the injury
done by said offender.

Article 6. All acts of violence committed upon persons and property of
the people of the Choctaw Nation, either by Citizens of the United States,
or neighboring tribes of Red People shall be referr'd to the agent, by him
to be referr'd to the President of the United States, who shall examine into
such cases, and see that every possible degree of justice is done to said
injured party of the Choctaw Nation.

Article 7. Offenders against the Laws of the United States, or any individual State, shall be apprehended and delivered to the agent or any duly
authorized officer, where such offender may be found in the Choctaw
Country, having fled from some part of the United States: but in all such
cases, application must be made to the agent, or Chief, and the expense of
his apprehension and delivery provided for.

Article 8. Any Citizen of the United States, who may be ordered from
the Nation by the agent and constituted authorities of the Nation, and
refusing to obey, or returning to the Nation without the consent of the
aforesaid persons, shall be subject to such pains, and penalties, as may
be provided by the Laws of the United States, in such cases. All Citizens
of the United States travelling peaceably and under the authority of the
laws of the United States, shall be under the care and protection of the
Nation.

Article 9. The United States will aid the Choctaw Nation, when called
upon, to suppress any insurrection of any part of the Choctaws against

the constituted authorities of said Nation, so that peace and harmony may be preserved amongst them; and the United States shall be particularly obliged to assist in excluding ardent Spirits from said Nation unless for purposes of real necessity.

Article 10. No person shall expose goods, or other articles for sale as a trader without a written permit from the Constituted authorities of the Nation, or authority derived from the United States, under the penalty of forfeiting all such articles; and the said constituted authorities shall not license any person to trade in the Nation, unless he resides in, and is subject to all the laws of the Nation.

Article 11. It is understood and agreed that the Navigation of Red River and Arkansa shall remain free to the Choctaws, and that they shall be subject to no higher toll or rate of duty than Citizens of the United States may be at any time subject. The United States agree further, that they will establish one or more post offices within the territory of the Choctaws; and may establish such military and post roads as shall be considered necessary.

Article 12. All intruders shall be removed, by the United States, from the Choctaw lands, West of the Mississippi, at any time when so requested to be done by the constituted authorities of said Nation, after the ratification of this Treaty. Private property shall be always respected, and not taken for the use of the United States, without fully compensating the rightful owner for the same.

Article 13. As it is necessary that the Choctaws should have confidence in the United States agent among them, and attending to the complaints of Choctaws against Citizens of the United States, therefore, the United States agent shall only hold his office for four years if not sooner removed; but may be reappointed. In all cases the President of the United States, shall remove the agent, and appoint some other person on the petition of the constituted authorities of the Nation, he being satisfied that there is sufficient cause therefor. It is further consented that the wish of the constituted authorities shall be respected in the appointment of an agent, immediately on the ratification of this Treaty, who shall be the only United States agent for the Choctaw Nation, for the time being, and said agent shall fix his residence in the Nation; and all future agents shall reside at the agency, so long as the United States shall conceive it advisable to keep one. It is further stipulated that whenever a Choctaw shall be delivered to the United States, as an offender, that the United States agent shall employ Counsel to defend said offender, and in the absence of the agent, the Judge, before whom said accused person shall be tried, shall appoint Counsel for the accused person, which Counsel shall be paid by the United States.

Article 14. Any and all Choctaws wishing to continue on the land where they now reside, shall be secured in a full section, or Six hundred and forty acres of land, to each family in fee simple. But this provision shall not attach except to such as shall continue to reside on the same for five years from the ratification of this treaty; and who shall have signified a determination to become Citizens of the State of Mississippi.[1]

Article 15. The United States, to afford to the Choctaw Nation of Indians an earnest of their good feelings, and at the same time to enable them the better to settle themselves to the West, agree, that as full compensation for such improvements abandoned as may add increased value to the land, which shall be assessed, by one or more Commissioners, to be appointed by the President, they will pay, for the term of three years, by which time it is hoped they will be enabled to render their farms productive, 75,000$, annually, to commence from the date of removal, which said annuity shall be apportioned amongst those who shall leave improvements, and agreeably and in proportion to the respective value of the same. The United States agree further to pay them the sum of 10,000$ for the purpose of erecting one or more houses of public worship—also 10,000$ for erecting School houses, 5,000$, for a Council House—2,000$ for a house for the Principal Chiefs, of the Nation: and 10,000$, annually, for ten years to be applied under the direction of the President for the purpose of educating the Children of the Choctaws. And as it is hoped that the Chickasaw Nation will be disposed to unite to the West with their Choctaw neighbors; in which event it will be desirable to place them near to the homes of their ancient friends and neighbors, the Choctaws; it is hereby agreed, that on their consenting to remove, the United States shall have authority to assign to them a home within the limits of the Choctaw Country, West of the Mississippi, not exceeding the quantity of acres owned by them in the State of Mississippi; and as consideration for this, the United States will pay the Choctaw Nation the sum of 15,000 dollars, for twenty years; and will extend the Choctaw West boundary, directly west, over any land they now own, and may have a right to convey, to the extreme western limits of the lands of the United States—Or if preferr'd by both Nations, the Chickasaws to be adopted into the Choctaw Nation, with all the rights and privileges which belong to the people of the Choctaws.

Article 16. It is agreed, that the United States shall support the Indians with sound and wholesome food while they shall be encamped, by the agent of the United States, previous to their departure for their new homes; also during the time they may be engaged in removing; and for twelve months after their arrival—and to enable the Government the better to comply with this article, they stipulate, to purchase at valuation price, the hogs, and cattle, of the Indians which they may be able to supply, for this purpose. Such as may not be wanted, may be travelled to their new homes, to be supported on their way, far as it may be practicable to obtain supplies, at the expense of the United States. The tools, and personal property of Indians left behind, if deposited at one or two designated points, by the agent, shall be sold by the agent, or some authorized persons, and the proceeds thereof, be hereafter paid over, for the benefit of the Indians who may have left them. The United States consent to furnish at proper points such wagons and Steam boats as the President may conceive necessary for the removal.

Article 17. According to a former Treaty the United States, are obligated to furnish every man emigrating to the West, with a good Rifle Gun, and ammunitition, together with a blanket, and brass or copper Kettle. These articles shall be furnished to every warrior; and each farmer shall be furnished with an axe, hoe, and plough; and each family shall be furnished with a Spinning wheel, and Cards, and each five families with a loom, so soon as their future places of residence shall be prepared for them; The United States, will also furnish One Blacksmith Shop, at the expense of the United States, on the principle of the Shop now furnished the Nation, for a period of 20 years.

Article 18. To enable the Choctaws to defend themselves in their new home, each warrior shall, annually, be furnished for four years, by the United States, with a reasonable supply of good Rifle powder, and lead; but while the new homes of the Choctaws are preparing and the people emigrating, or preparing to emigrate the United States shall station troops on, or near the Choctaw line, or other situation as the President may designate, so that the Choctaws may safely settle until they feel themselves sufficiently strong to protect themselves; but at all times, the United States, shall assist the Choctaws if invaded or threatened with an invasion— Further it is stipulated that the Choctaw Nation shall be furnished with a good four or six pound piece of Artillery, well mounted, together with a supply of powder and ball.

Article 19. As the Captains will have much trouble for the first four years of keeping their people in order and settling them, the United States shall furnish each Captain, the number of whom shall not exceed one hundred, with a good suit of Clothes, and a substantial broad sword, as an outfit, and shall pay each Captain fifty dollars, annually, for the first four years; also the constituted authorities of the Nation shall appoint fifty men, as rangers, who shall occupy and hold the grade of Captains, and each of them shall receive the outfit as aforesaid, and also the salary of a Captain, as aforesaid, for the first four years. These rangers shall execute the orders of the Chiefs, and travel as messengers. They shall also be liable to be called into the Service of the United States by the President, and when thus employed shall receive at the rate of one hundred dollars additional, per annum. The principal Chief when in the Military service of the United States, by authority of the President shall have the rank and pay of a Colonel.

Article 20. All annuities heretofore secured to the Choctaw Nation, and which have not already become due, and payable, shall cease from the date of the ratification of this Treaty, with the exception of 6000 Dollars, secured under the 2nd. Article of the Treaty of the 20th. of January, 1825, concluded at Washington, which shall continue for ten years, from the date of the ratification of this Treaty, and no longer.[2] It is also covenanted and agreed, that for the purposes and objects secured by the provisions of this Treaty, and with a view fully to satisfy the Choctaw Nation, of the kind feelings entertained towards them, in addition to other sums herein stipulated for, the United States, agree to pay to the Choctaw Nation 50,000 Dollars, annually, for 40 years, of which 7,000$, a year shall be applied to the use, and purposes of a Common School, or Schools, to be established west of the Mississippi—under the direction of the Secretary of War—1,500 Dollars, annually, under the same direction, for two or more Teachers of the Christian Religion of different denominations, and the residue to be apportioned by the agent amongst the different families of the Indians, for their particular use and benefit except 1,250 Dollars, which shall be paid, annually, to the principal Chiefs. It is agreed, further, that in all matters of doubtful construction under this Treaty, it shall be construed most favorably towards the Choctaws. It is further agreed, that no one shall be disturbed or interrupted on account of his religious opinions.

Article 21. Of the land ceded, East of the Mississippi River, the United States will cause 50 Sections to be laid off, & surveyed, of which _____ of said sections shall be sold and the proceeds paid to Greenwood Leflore, and David Folsom. also to be surveyed and disposed of as aforesaid _____ Sections of the same for the benefit of Mushulatubbee, and John Pytchlynn. Also _____ Sections, in manner as aforesaid to be disposed of for the benefit of each of the following persons, John Garland, Joel R. Neil, Middleton Mackey, Israel Folsom, George Harkins, James L. McDonald. The residue to be disposed of, and the proceeds given to Such other persons of the Choctaw Nation, as may be agreed upon in National Council at the ratification of this treaty. Said surveys shall in all cases include the improvements of the persons entitled; and where no improvement is had, the United States shall designate where the survey shall be made. The proceeds whereof shall be paid so soon as sales of the land so reserved are made. or the United States shall take them by paying, within three months from the ratification, $1.25/100, if the parties entitled shall consent to it. Said surveys shall be made to conform to sectional lines, and shall not interfere with other previous rights under this treaty.

Article 22. So soon as this Treaty shall be ratified by the parties making it, the United States shall have authority to survey and prepare the Choctaw Country for sale, free of interruption, and said lands thus ceded shall remain as a fund pledged for the payment and satisfaction of the different sums stipulated herein to be paid. But the Indians shall not be interrupted in the possession of their Country, until the expiration of two years from the 15th. of May, ensuing; tho' it is agreed that they will remove earlier if practicable. But, by that period, to wit: the 15th. May, 1832, it is stipulated they shall remove. It is also understood and agreed, that all white persons who at the date of this Treaty, are identified with, and who are members of the Choctaw Nation, by virtue of existing laws, or Indian regulation shall be considered as included under the general term "Choctaws" used and employed in this Treaty.

D, DNA-RG 46 (mAJs).
1. The phrase "from the ratification of this treaty" in this sentence is an insertion by Eaton.
2. Article 2 of the 1825 Treaty of Washington provided $6,000 annually for Choctaw schooling. Eaton's April 27 letter to AJ, sent herewith to the Senate, proposed retaining this annuity for ten years to ensure continued funding for the Choctaw Academy in Kentucky.

To John Coffee

I enclose you an account which my ward A. J. Hutchings left unpaid to my great mortification—you will see from Mr Mulledys letter which accompanies the account that I had wrote him by Hutchings to be informed if all his college dues had been paid, that by H. he had wrote & enclosed me the account which Hutchings never delivered—The President supposing I was unadvised addressed me the enclosed letter with the account which I now forward that you may place on file with the other receipts for money expended for his use.[1]

By Mr Saml. J. Hays I forwarded you vouchers for the five hundred you had remitted me for A. J. Hutchings in which I requested you to notify every one that no accounts would be paid only those authorised by you—This will be necessary to ~~preserve~~ save him from bankruptcy & ruin—Hutchings has promised me he will create no accounts but by your authority & that he wil[l] ocomise. I hope he will reform—I wrote you by him, which I hope you have recceived.

We all here enjoy tolerable health & unite in our kind & affectionate regards to you, Polly, & the children   we are in a Gloom expecting when we hear from Capt J. Donelson that he is no more, our last information was that he could not last long—we hope he may yet a little be spared, but the Lords will be done.

Major Lewis has recd. your letter & trying to get Genl Hinds to close the Indian Treaty account—strange that he has been here for five months & until urged by Major Lewis has taken no step to have it closed   Major Lewis will urge him until it is closed[2]   it is now eleven oclock P.M. I am in hopes by the first arrival to hear that we have accommodated with England our constest about the West India trade *satisfactory*. This will wind up our congress at least satisfactory to the nation, and the executive, & much to the disappointment of congress—for it is not expected by them

Let me hear from you, how you all are, how my son progresses with his education, & how business progresses on Hutchings farm & How Capt

Jack & his family are, & how he gets on with his Irish neighbours[.] In haste your friend

Andrew Jackson

P.S. I open this letter May 9th. to state we have just heard that Capt Donelson died on the 21rst. ult. we are without advice from any but my overseer—

ALS, THi (15-0959).
1. Thomas F. Mulledy (1795–1861) was president of Georgetown College. AJ enclosed a copy of his bill, which he had paid, for $40.12 in miscellaneous expenses by Hutchings from December 1, 1829 through March 24, 1830 (14-0793).
2. In 1826, Coffee and Thomas Hinds (1780–1840), now a Mississippi congressman, had served with William Clark as U.S. commissioners in a failed effort to negotiate removal treaties with the Choctaws and Chickasaws. Their account for expenses was still unsettled. AJ wrote Ingham about it on June 9 (below).

From *Charles Jones Love*

Nashville 8th May 1830

My Dear Sir

I recved yesterday your favr of the 20th Ultimo. I have just seen Mr Hill he says you may send him a Check on the branch Bank at this place the amount will be by the small paper enclosed 1848$—Mr H. says he will go up with me next week and divide the Cotton stock. I will then give Mr Steele my opinion about the stud Colts my present opinion is they ought to be altered as they will sell for much more as they are, you I hope will be out this summer and can then decide your self and if you wish it they can be altered in the Fall. I am requested by one of your friends to ask of you what you would take for the Sir Williams colt out of your Oscar filley. I think a good price may be got if you feel disposed to sell. If you are, name the price and I will show him that part [of] the letter. I am for the present to keep the horse to my self, but you will not hesitate to trust the Gentleman   He is a very fine Colt and you will soon be over stocked If you would get *a good* price I think I would sell

Your Cotton was not sold on the 27 of April I hope you will get the full benefit of all the rise in England[1]

Mr Earl is very much engaged at this time but say he will soon be with you I will write you again soon after the Cotton stock is divided[.] In the mean time I subscribe myself your friend

Ch J Love

[Endorsed by AJ:] answered 24th. of May 1830—and enclosed a check to Mr Hill for $1848—agreable to the within instructions & requested Mr

Love to close finally all this business finally for the purchase of the land from Capt P. Mosely—

ALS, DLC (38).
1. Recent press accounts reported rising demand for cotton in England.

From William Lytle

Surveyor Generals Office.
Cincinnati, 8th. May 1830.

Sir,

I beg leave, respectfully, to call your attention to the subject of the public lands in the southern part of the *North-West Territory*, which have been purchased of the Indians, by the late Treaty at Prairie du Chien; particulary that part of cession which embraces the *Mineral region*, on Fever River, and bordering upon the Mississippi.

Presuming it to be the intention of the government to cause these lands to be immediately surveyed and prepared for sale; and yet apprehensive that the press of business before Congress, as the session draws to a close, *may cause* the Act which may be necessary to authorize the survey, to be laid over; I would respectfully suggest to you, sir, the importance of an early survey of these lands, and that there ought to be no delay in adopting such measures as may be necessary for that purpose. I have the honor to be, very respectfully Sir, Your Obt. St.

Wm. Lytle

[Endorsed by AJ:] The Commissioner of the Genl. Land office will attend to this subject—he knows the wishes of the P. to bring all public land into markett at the shortest day possible—A. J.

[Endorsed by AJ:] Refered to the Commissioner of the Genl Land office—A. J.

ALS, DNA-RG 49 (M478-8). LC, DNA-RG 49 (M477-4). Lytle (1770–1831), of Cincinnati, was appointed surveyor general of public lands in Ohio, Indiana, and Michigan Territory in 1829. By treaties concluded at Prairie du Chien in July and August, 1829, the Chippewa, Ottawa, Potawatomi, and Winnebago Indians ceded lands in southwestern Wisconsin and northwestern Illinois that included the mineral-rich Galena (or Fever) River district. No appropriation for surveying public lands passed Congress in 1830.

To Isaac Dutton Barnard et al.

May 10th. 1830—

The President of the United States, with his respects, informs the Honble I. D. Barnard, Wm Marks, J. B. Steriger, D. M. Miller and J. B. Sutherland that he has recd. their note by Mrs. Craig, with the papers praying a pardon for her husband.[1] Finding no recommendation from the attorney who prosecuted, or the judge before whom he was tried recommend'g Craig to the clemency of the Executive, which he has laid down in most cases for his guide. The President requests the Gentlemen above named that they give to him their opinion, whether in this case Executive clemency aught to be extended—The respect the President has for the opinion of they Gentlemen, if in the affirmative, will induce him to act in the absence of the opinion of the attorney who prosecuted & the judge before whom the prisoner was tried

[Endorsed by Barnard:] I have read this note of the President, & have resealed it, to be shewn to the other gentlemen named   I. D. B.   I would name Genl. Marks's quarters to meet at 6. this Evening.

AN, The Gilder Lehrman Institute of American History (mAJs). Barnard and William Marks (1778–1858) were Pennsylvania's U.S. senators, and John Benton Sterigere (1793–1852), Daniel H. Miller (d. 1846), and Joel B. Sutherland were Philadelphia-area congressmen. In 1827 the U.S. circuit court in Philadelphia convicted John W. Craig of forging Bank of the United States notes and sentenced him to 16 years in prison. The two judges at his trial, Richard Peters and Bushrod Washington, had both since died, and the prosecutor, district attorney Charles J. Ingersoll, was replaced in 1829. Craig was not pardoned. He escaped from prison in November 1830 and continued his career as a counterfeiter.
    1. Craig's wife Martha was the sister of Ebenezer Gleason, the head of Craig's counterfeiting ring, who was likewise convicted in 1827.

To Amos Kendall

MAY 10, 3 P.M.

The President with his respects to Mr. Kendall informs him his nomination is confirmed by the casting vote of the Vice President. The President will be glad to see him for a few minutes.

Printed, *Cincinnati Commercial*, February 4, 1879, DLC (38). AJ had given Kendall a recess appointment as fourth auditor of the Treasury on March 21, 1829, and nominated him to the Senate on February 4, 1830. The nomination had been sent to a select committee and twice postponed. On May 10 the Senate confirmed Kendall on a vote of 24 to 24, with Vice President Calhoun breaking the tie in favor.

From Thomas Lilly Smith

T. L. Smith's respects to the President and takes the liberty of enclosing for his perusal the remarks of Mr. C. J. Ingersoll of Philadelphia at the Dinner recently given to Mr. Poinset. It is upon a subject of much interest and more particularly at this time.

[Endorsed by AJ:] Mr. Ingersols Speech upon the Jeffersonian doctrine of the constitution at Mr P. din[ner] to be kept o[n] file—A J

AN, DLC (38). Smith (1787–1871), of New York, was register of the Treasury, appointed by AJ in 1829. At a dinner held in Philadelphia on May 3 to honor returning minister to Mexico Joel Poinsett, Charles Jared Ingersoll (1782–1862) gave a speech acclaiming AJ's toast at the Jefferson Birthday dinner. Denying that Jefferson had ever sanctioned South Carolina state's-rights doctrine, Ingersoll said of AJ that "by the master stroke of a mere toast, he *nullified* the *nullification* he was invited to magnify. While thus he defends the country and the constitution, he is worthy and welcome to govern the one and administer the other." Ingersoll had been U.S. district attorney from 1815 until his removal by AJ in 1829. His speech was published in Philadelphia on May 6 and by the Washington *National Journal* on May 10.

To Cephas Grier Childs

May 12th. 1830

Dear Sir,

I received through Mr. Atwater the series of views which you were good enough to *present* to me, and acknowledged their receipt, soon after his arrival in this city; but finding from your note of the 21st ulto that my note did not reach you; I take pleasure in repeating an expression of my thanks.[1] Please consider me a subscriber to their publication and believe me, very Respectfully, yr. obt. Servant

Andrew Jackson

LS in AJ Donelson's hand, Bloomsbury Auctions sale, November 19, 2008 (mAJs). Abstract of cover, Robert F. Batchelder catalog, 1997 (mAJs). Childs (1793–1871) was a Philadelphia engraver and publisher. From 1827 through 1830 he issued six numbers of a work entitled *Views in Philadelphia, and its Vicinity; Engraved from Original Drawings.*

1. Caleb Atwater had arrived in Washington from Philadelphia in November 1829.

From "Renodau"
(William Sylvan Phiquepal D'Arusmont)

[The writer of this pseudonymous letter was a French-born educator named William S. Phiquepal D'Arusmont (1779–1855). Phiquepal was trained in the methods of Swiss pedagogical reformer Johann Pestalozzi and came to the U.S. in 1824 under the patronage of philanthropist and geologist William Maclure. He accompanied Maclure in 1826 to Robert Owen's community at New Harmony, Ind., where he taught school and met the Scotch-born social reformer Frances ("Fanny") Wright. In January 1830 Phiquepal accompanied Wright to Haiti to resettle thirty-one slaves from her failed emancipationist community, Nashoba, near Memphis, Tenn. The two returned to the U.S. separately, Phiquepal sailing via New Orleans, and reunited in Philadelphia in April. In 1831 they married in France. Printed here is a translation of Phiquepal's letter, all of which but the postscript was written in French.]

Philadelphia, May 12, 1830

Mr. President,

Permit me, as a friend of the United States and of your administration, to reveal to you the necessity of sending to New Orleans one or two ships of war, to be there in a state of readiness this coming summer, for the purpose of disrupting the execution of a plan formed by the Haitian government to foment an insurrection of Louisiana's blacks, kill the whites, pillage, destroy the city, and seize the most suitable ships with good crews to carry their booty back to Haiti, along with fifteen or eighteen hundred men and women of color who may wish to return with them.[1] These people, by succeeding, believe that they will strengthen the power of their government, which is held in high esteem by blacks, but they will not in fact bring back any of that color, not even those who contributed the most to their success. They have chosen the end of summer over any other season, because they know that then the town is practically deserted by those whites who are best able to resist them; and that September is the most favorable time for them, because of the heat and the maladies which whites have reason to fear because of the accompanying fatigue—not to mention the many other inconveniences that create difficulties so great as to be insurmountable.

It is not as an informer that I do myself the honor of writing you, but, rather, as a friend to the preservation of order and tranquility, and I assure you that no motive of self-interest guides me on this occasion. I pray you forgive the loan I've made of another name as well as believe what I have said. With feelings of the most profound respect for your Excellency, your most humble and most devoted servant,

By Renodau

[In English:] It is but few days since I have arrived From there.

[Endorsed by AJ:] ~~for the young Ladies to translate AJ~~

[Endorsed by Nicholas P. Trist:] Pseudonymous letter addressed to the President by some fool

Translated from ALS, NjP-Livingston Papers (mAJs). The French text is as follows:
Monsieur le Président
    Permettez-moi comme ami des Etats unis et de vôtre Gouvernement de vous exposer la nécéssité denvoyer à la Nouvelle Orléan, un, ou deux batiments de Guerre, pour y être en Estation pendant l'été prochain, afin d'empêcher l'éxécution d'un Plan Formé par le Gouvernement Haïtien, d'insurger les négres de la Louisiane, d'y assassiner les blancs, Piller, et bruler la ville, aprez prendre les batiments les plus convenables avec de bons Equipages pour emporter en Haïty le pillage avec quinze ou dix-huit cents hommes, et femmes de couleur qui veulent y aller. Ses gens en reussissant considérent qu'ils rafermiront la Puissance de leurs Gouvernement fort Jalousé par les noirs, et de cette couleur ils ne veulent-pas en porter un seul, pas-meme ceux qui auront contribuez le plus à les faire reussir, ils ont choisi la Fin de l'été à tout autre saison, parce qu'ils savent qu'alors la ville est déserte presque de tous les blancs, qui sont les plus capable de les resister, et qu'en Septembre c'est le temps le plus Favorable pour eux, à cause de la chaleur, et des maladies que les blancs ont tant à redoutter à cause des fatigues que nécéssiterait un pareil événement, sans parler de plusieurs autres inconveniens qui rendrait les difficultés si grandes que peut être on ne pourait y rémédier.
    Ce n'est-pas comme délateur que je me fais l'honneur de vous écrire, mais bien comme ami de la Conservation de L'ordre et de la tranquillité, et afin de vous assurer que nul motif d'intéret, ne me guide dans cette occasion. Je vous prie de me pardonner l'emprunt que je fais d'un autre nom comme de me croire, avec les Sentiments du plus profond respect de vôtre Excellence Le plus humble & le plus dévoué serviteur,
    1. People of color, or *gens de couleur*, were free people of mixed African and European ancestry.

From George Michael Troup

Washington May 12 1830

Sir
    Pardon me for asking your attention to the case of Capt Woolsey who has been aggreived by a recent & very unexpected order of the Navy Dept. His high Character as an Officer so universally acknowledged & his amiable & gentlemany Deportment have acquired for him a numerous circle of Friends who take a deep interest in his welfare & in that of his interesting & growing family—they are of course sensibly alive to whatever may affect his feelings or reputation—as an old schoolmate & Friend I cannot withhold my own sympathies which are indeed warmly enlisted & the more so as this grievance would seem to have been the result of mis-

take or misapprehension[1]—I have good authority for beleiving that Capt
Woolsey has left Pensacola with the universal regret of the Community in
which he had uniformly lived in the highest estimation & that no Officer
can be appointed to succeed him who would conciliate in greater degree
its confidence & affections & yet it is for the supposed want of these that
the recal complained of has been made—I am persuaded that the President
will not suffer an act of the Government which must be regarded at least
as a diminution of its confidence to affect injuriously a deserving Officer
unless it can be justified by some reasons stronger than those assigned for
the removal of Capt Woolsey. With high respect & considr

G M Troup

[Endorsed by AJ:] refered to the secretary of the Navy—for his
consideration   A. J.   May 13th. 1830—

ALS, DNA-RG 45 (M124-124). Navy captain Melancthon Taylor Woolsey (1780–1838)
had been relieved in March from command of the Pensacola navy yard. Troup enclosed
a clipping from the April 17 *Pensacola Gazette* lamenting his departure. Navy secretary
Branch reported to AJ on Woolsey's removal on May 14 (below).
    1. Troup and Woolsey had both attended Erasmus Hall academy on Long Island, N.Y.

To John Caldwell Calhoun

*[On December 26, 1817, Calhoun, then secretary of war under
President James Monroe, ordered Jackson, then U.S. major general in
command of the Southern Division, to take direct command of troops
on the southern frontier and suppress Seminoles raiding from Spanish
Florida into Georgia and Alabama. Explicitly authorized to pursue the
Indians across the border, Jackson from March through May 1818 conducted a lightning conquest of Florida itself, capturing Spanish bastions
at St. Marks and Pensacola, arresting and executing two British nation-
als, and installing a provisional government. Jackson's campaign brought
foreign protest and domestic criticism, including a congressional inquiry
and debate. While restoring Florida to Spain (which shortly ceded it to the
U.S. in the Adams-Onís treaty of February 1819), the Monroe administration publicly backed Jackson; and he claimed, then and later, that all his
operations had had its full sanction. With this letter he reopened a long-
smoldering private controversy about Calhoun's role in secret Cabinet
discussions over whether to repudiate him.]*

(copy)

May 13th. 1830—

Sir

That frankness which I trust has always characterised me thro' life, toward those with whom I have been in habits of friendship induces me to lay before you the enclosed copy of a letter from Wm. H. Crawford Esqr, which was handed me on yesterday. The submission you will perceive is authorised by the writer. The statements and facts it presents, being so different from what I had heretofore understood to be correct, requires that it should be brought to your consideration. They are different from your letter to Governor Bibb, of Alabama of the 13th. of May 1818, where you state "Genl. Jackson is vested with full power to conduct the war in the manner he may judge best."[1] And different too, from your letters to me at that time which breaths throughout a spirit of approbation & friendship; and particularly, the one in which you say, "I have the honor to acknowledge the receipt of yours of the 20th. ult. and to acquaint you with the entire approbation of the President of *all* the measures you have adopted to terminate the rupture with the Indians."[2] My object in making this communication is to announce to you the great ~~sacrafice~~ surprise which is felt, and to learn of you whether it be possible that the information given is correct—whether it can be, under all the circumstances of which you & I are both informed, that any attempt seriously to effect me, was moved and sustained by you in cabinet council when, as is known to you, I was but executing the *wishes* of the Government, and cloathed with the authority "to conduct the war in the manner I might judge best."

you can, if you please, take a copy, the one enclosed, you will please return to me. I am, Sir, very respectfully yr Humble servant

Andrew Jackson

[Endorsed by AJ:] sent to Mr Calhoun by Major Donelson on the 13th. of May 1830—A. J.

[Endorsed by AJ:] copy of a letter sent to Mr Calhoune on the 13th. 1830 of May by A. J Donelson, enclosing a copy of one from Wm. H. Crawford to Mr Forsyth, detailing an account of a movement made to have me punished in a cabinet council by Mr. C.—These papers to be carefully preserved—A. J.

ALS draft, DLC (72). *US Telegraph*, February 17, 1831; *Calhoun Papers*, 11:159–60.
1. Calhoun wrote Alabama Territory governor William Wyatt Bibb (1781–1820) on May 13, 1818, that "Genl. Jackson is vested with full powers to conduct the war, in the manner which he may judge best" (DNA-RG 75, M15-4; *Calhoun Papers*, 2:291).

2. In response to Calhoun's orders of December 1817, AJ reported from Nashville on January 20, 1818, on his measures to mobilize and concentrate troops at Fort Scott in southwest Georgia "to inflict speedy and merited chastisement on the deluded Seminoles." Calhoun wrote back on February 6 to acknowledge AJ's letter "and to acquaint you with the entire approbation of the President of all the measures which you have adopted to terminate the rupture with the Indians" (*HRDoc* 14, 15th Cong., 2d sess., pp. 42–43, 38–39, Serial 17). AJ arrived at Fort Scott on March 9 and began the campaign the next day.

[Enclosure: William Harris Crawford to John Forsyth]

Copy.

Wood Lawn, 30th April 1830.

My dear Sir

Your letter of the 16th. inst. was received by Sunday's mail, together with its enclosure. I recollect having conversed with you at the time and place, and upon the subject in that enclosure stated, but I have not a distinct recollection of what I said to you, but I am certain there is one error in your statement of that conversation to Mr. ____ I recollect distinctly what passed in the Cabinet meeting, referred to in your letter to Mr. ____[1]

Mr. Calhoun's proposition in the Cabinet was that Genl. Jackson should be punished in some form, or reprehended in some form, I am not positively certain which. As Mr. Calhoun did not propose to arrest Genl. Jackson, I feel confident that I could not have made use of that word in my relation to you of the circumstances which transpired in the Cabinet as I have no recollection of ever having designedly mis-stated any transaction in my life, and most sincerely believe I never did. My apology for having disclosed what passed in a Cabinet meeting is this. In the summer after that meeting, an extract of a letter from Washington was published in a Nashville paper in which it was stated that I had proposed to arrest Genl. Jackson, but that he was triumphantly defended by Mr. Calhoun and Mr. Adams. This letter I always believed was written by Mr. Calhoun or by his directions. It had the desired effect. Genl. Jackson became extremely inimical to me and friendly to Mr. Calhoun. In stating the arguments of Mr. Adams to induce Mr. Monroe to support Genl. Jackson's conduct throughout, adverting to Mr. Monroe's apparent admission that if a young Officer had acted so, he might be safely punished, Mr. Adams said that if Genl. had acted so, that if he was a subaltern Officer, *shooting was too good for him*. This however was said with a view of driving Mr. Monroe to an unlimited support of what Genl. Jackson had done and not with an unfriendly view to the General. Indeed my own views on the subject had undergone a material change after the cabinet had been convened. Mr. Calhoun made some allusion to a letter the General had written to the President, who had forgotten that he had received such a letter, but said if he had received such an one he could find it and went directly to his cabinet and brought the letter out. In it Genl. Jackson approved of the determination of the Government to break up Amelia Island and Galveztown and gave it also as his opinion that the Floridas ought to be taken by the U.S. He added it might be a delicate matter for the Executive to decide; but if the President approved of it he had only to give a hint to some confidential member of Congress, say Johnny Ray, and he would do it, and take the responsibility of it upon himself.[2] I asked the President if the letter had been answered. He replied no; for that he had no recollection of having received it. I then said that I had no doubt that Genl. Jackson in taking Pensacola believed he was doing what the Executive wished. After that letter was produced unanswered I should have opposed the infliction of punishment upon the Genl. who had considered the silence of the President as a tacit consent; yet it was after this letter was produced and read that Mr. Calhoun made his proposition to the Cabinet for punishing the Genl. You may shew this letter to Mr. Calhoun if you please. With the foregoing corrections of what passed in the Cabinet, your account of it to Mr. ____ is correct. Indeed there is but one inaccuracy in it, and one omission. What I have written beyond them is a mere amplification of what passed in the Cabinet. I do not know that I ever hinted at the letter of the General to the President yet that letter had a most important bearing upon the deliberations of the Cabinet at least in my mind, and ~~probably~~ possibly in the minds of Mr. Adams and the President, but neither expressed any opinion upon the subject. It seems it had none upon the mind of Mr. Calhoun for it made no change in his conduct.

I am dear Sir Your Friend and most Obedt Servt

(Signed) Wm H. Crawford.

[Endorsed by Forsyth:] A true copy from the original in my possession. John Forsyth   May 12 1830

[Endorsed by AJ Donelson:] Copy of a letter from Wm. H Crawford to Honble John Forsyth put into the hands of the President on the 12th. of May 1830 detailing the views of the cabinet in relation to the arrest of Genl Jackson for his measures in Florida *[in AJ's hand:]* —with a copy of a letter to Mr Calhoun within—These to be carefully preserved A. J.

Copy, DLC (72). *US Telegraph*, February 17, 1831; *Calhoun Papers*, 11:160–61. William Harris Crawford (1772–1834) of Georgia had been secretary of the Treasury in Monroe's Cabinet. John Quincy Adams was secretary of state.

1. On January 29, 1828, James A. Hamilton, whose name was omitted here, wrote Forsyth asking him to query Crawford "whether the propriety or necessity for arresting and trying General Jackson was ever presented as a question for the deliberation of Mr. Monroe's Cabinet." Forsyth replied on February 8 that Crawford told him that Calhoun had indeed "submitted to and urged upon the President the propriety and necessity of arresting and trying General Jackson. Mr. Monroe was very much annoyed by it; expressed a belief that such a step would not meet the public approbation; that General J. had performed too much public service to be treated as a younger or subaltern officer might, without shocking public opinion. Mr. Adams spoke with great violence against the proposed arrest, and

justified the General throughout, vehemently urging the President to make the cause of the General that of the administration." On April 16, 1830, Forsyth enclosed a copy of this letter to Crawford and asked him to verify its accuracy and authorize him to show it to AJ (*US Telegraph*, Feb 22 and Mar 29, 1831; *Calhoun Papers*, 10:341–42, 11:149–50).

2. AJ wrote Monroe from Nashville on January 6, 1818, before receiving Calhoun's December 26, 1817, directive to assume field command. He praised the administration's intent, announced in Monroe's first annual message to Congress on December 2, 1817, to suppress the smuggling haven at Amelia Island off Florida's Atlantic coast (and also, though not mentioned by AJ, at Galveston). But he criticized as ineffectual Calhoun's recent order of December 16 to General Edmund P. Gaines, then commanding at Fort Scott, which authorized him to cross into Florida and attack the Seminoles "unless they should shelter themselves under a Spanish post." Instead, AJ urged that "the whole of East Florida [be] seized & held as an indemnity for the outrages of Spain upon the property of our citizens: this done, it puts all opposition down, secures to our Citizens a compleat indemnity, & saves us from a War with Great Britain, or some of the Continental Powers combined with Spain; this can be done without implicating the Government; let it be signifyed to me through any channel, (say Mr. J. Rhea) that the possession of the Floridas would be desirable to the United States, & in sixty days it will be accomplished" (*Jackson Papers*, 4:166–68). John Rhea (1753–1832) was at that time a Tennessee congressman. Monroe later noted on AJ's letter that he was ill when it arrived and did not read it until some time after.

To James Alexander Hamilton

(Private)

Washington May 13th. 1830

My Dr. Sir

I on yesterday received from Mr Forsyth the communication which you aluded to in your letter.[1] My son is not yet returned, and I have not time to make you a copy—as I am much pressed, & have been engaged making a copy for Mr Calhoun, who I have written to this morning & enclosed him a copy—in due time you shall have ~~a copy~~ one & as Mr Crawfords letter alludes, to another communication, if you have any information to whom it was made I would like to see it in connection with the one handed me yesterday[2]

with my kind salutations to you & family believe me yr friend

Andrew Jackson

P.S. If my son is in Newyork, please to say to him that I wish him forthwith to return, *I want him very much*   A. J.

ALS, NN (15-0989).
1. May 3, above.
2. Forsyth's February 8, 1828, letter to Hamilton, enclosed by Forsyth to Crawford on April 16, 1830.

From John Caldwell Calhoun

Washington
13th May 1830

Sir,

Agreeably to your request, I herewith return the copy of a letter signed Wm. H. Crawford, which I received under cover of your note, handed to me this morning, by Mr Donelson, and of which I have retained a copy, in conformity with your permission

As soon as my leisure may permit, you shall receive a communication from me on the subject to which your note refers.

In the mean time, I cannot repress the expression of my indignation at the affair, while I must express my gratification, that the secret and mysterious attempts, which have been making by false insinuations for political purpose for years to injure my character, are at length brought to light. I am very respectfully Yours &c &c

J C. Calhoun

ALS, DLC (38). *US Telegraph*, February 17, 1831; *Calhoun Papers*, 11:162–63. Calhoun answered fully on May 29 (below).

To John Overton

Washington May 13th. 1830—

My Dr. friend

I had the pleasure to receive your letter from Wheeling of the 5th. instant advising me of your safe arrival at that point & in good health—I gave this pleasing intelligence to the Gentleman requested, with the tender of your kind salutations which was gratefully received, & a request that I should reciprocate them.

The Packett from England, expected shortly after your departure, has not yet arrived; her detention is ascribed to continued adverse winds—we are expecting her daily, and as congress has to be in session on the 25th. instant we must receive intelligence from England before that time—When received I will loose no time in communicating the result to you   I have no doubt but it will be pleasing[1]

On yesterday was placed in my hands the copy of a letter, a copy of which I enclose you—My usual course of frankness I thought in this case was best to be pursued, and I hastened this morning to address him, enclosing him a copy of Mr Crawfords letter—I enclose you a copy of mine to Mr Calhoun & his reply—from which you will see, that I am promised an answer in due time—I think you will discover in this a confirmation of what you first conceived in 1818 before I got home from the Seminole ampaign, and took the stand to arrest it, *fully verifyed*, but you, and I, both believed that the dagger was in other hands than Mr. Calhoun—I might well exclaim, if the narative by Mr Crawford be true, "et tu Brutus."

The papers will shew you the extraordinary course pursued by the Senate—Hill, Noah, & Dawson and Gardiner rejected—Gardiner was recommended by all the republican of the Legislature of ohio, and if the injunction of secrecy can be removed the two Senators will have to account with their constituents for their stewartship; be it so. Our friend judge Tazewell remained to vote against all the Printers, but could not have Kendal rejected—I do suppose he does not mean to continue in Public life—The people of Virginia have denounced the course of Tazewell & Tyler in the Senate, *some most bitterly*—Richie condemns them in a private letter ~~most bitterly~~—The people will correct those evils.[2] Strange as it may seem, the appropriations for the year 1830, up to the first of this month has exceeded, by nearly half a million, the whole expenditures of 1829—The opposition endeavour to make appropriations as great as possible, and the friends, or rather, pretended friends, of the administration, go with them—their objects plainly are, to make this, a more extravagant administration, than the last—Theer may be another object, it is this, Clay in his american System, lays it down, that congress has the constitutional power to make *roads & canals, without limitation*, as well local, as national; the internal improvement mania prevades congress, the log rolling principles has fully displayed itself, and large appropriations are proposed for private & local roads, such as from Maysville Kentuckey, to Lexington with the view to compell me to approve them, & thereby acknowledge Mr. Clays doctrine, or disapprove them upon constitution grounds[3]—I am prepared to meet the crisis if it comes—from Mr Jeffersons, Mr Madisons & Mr Monroes precedents set, it is a perplexing question, & requires great consideration, more than I have now time to bestow upon it—still my friend, as I take public good for my aim, & the constitution for my guide, & trust in a kind providence to direct me, I will do right, by following the conviction of a pure intention, & exercising my best judgt.

It is getting late & I have no time for friendship but what I take from my hours that I ought to sleep, I therefore must close with asking you for your opinion, Whether [I] have not adopted a proper course with Mr Calhoun by promptly & frankly addressing him and laying the copy of Mr. Cs. letter before him

With my prayers for your & your families happiness in this life & that which is to come I am your friend

Andrew Jackson

ALS, THi (15-0994).

1. AJ was hoping for news from Louis McLane on the West Indian negotiation before Congress adjourned. No date was yet set, but Congress would be in session at least until May 25, when the Senate was scheduled to resume a judicial impeachment trial.

2. On May 10, the day Kendall was confirmed for fourth auditor by Calhoun's casting vote, the Senate rejected three other AJ nominees: Mordecai Manuel Noah (1785–1851) for New York City customs surveyor, by 25 to 23; James Booker Gardiner (1789–1837) for register of the Tiffin, Ohio, land office, by 46 to 0; and Moses Dawson for receiver of the Cincinnati land office, by 42 to 5. These four and Isaac Hill, rejected for second comptroller on April 12, had all edited Jackson papers in the 1828 campaign. Virginia senators Tazewell and John Tyler (1790–1862), later the tenth President, voted against all five. Senate proceedings in executive session were ostensibly secret, but congressman Henry R. Storrs of New York remarked in his diary that Tazewell spoke zealously against all the printers and especially Kendall, accusing him of gross official misconduct (NBuHi). Thomas Ritchie of the *Richmond Enquirer* had complained of AJ's appointment of editors in 1829 (*Jackson Papers*, 7:129–32).

3. In 1824 Henry Clay (1777–1852) had given the name "American System" to his program of national economic development through a protective tariff and federal sponsorship of internal improvements.

From John Branch

Navy Department
14th. May 1830

Sir

In relation to the case of Commo. Woolsey, I have the honor to state that he was ordered to take command of the Pensacola Station on the 27th. Octr. 1826. Being in command for upwards of three years, a change was deemed advisable; and accordingly on the 19th. of March last, he was detached from the Navy Yard, and Captn. Alexr. J. Dallas appointed to succeed him in the command.[1]

In addition to the above, Charges and Specifications have been preferred by Master Commandant John H. Clack against Como. Woolsey. These are still under consideration; but they will probably lead to an investigation, so soon as the trial of Master Commandant Clack shall have been completed[.][2] I am Respy.

J B

LC, DNA-RG 45 (M472-1).

1. Navy captain Alexander James Dallas (1791–1844) was the son and namesake of Madison's secretary of the Treasury and the brother of George M. Dallas, presently U.S. district attorney in Pennsylvania.

2. Master Commandant John Henry Clack (1791–1844) had served under Woolsey at Pensacola. The two men clashed and Woolsey brought charges against Clack. Clack was transferred from Woolsey's command in November 1829 and court-martialed in September 1830. In May 1830 he in turn filed countercharges against Woolsey. AJ approved Clack's court-martial on November 23 (below).

From Maunsel White

New Orleans May 14th. 1830

Dear Sir

Annexed you will find the account Sales of Fifty one Bales Cotton which I recd. the 10th. Feby last at which time the article was extremely dull, & would not as a lot have brot. over 8½ cents. the quality too is not so good generally as you have been in the habit of raising but this may be easily accounted for by your absence from Home the Nt. proceeds $2246 ³⁹⁄₁₀₀ I have paid over to Messrs. Nichols & Hill your agents. you will see from the sales that there was three qualities, choice prime & Inferior—I have had the pleasure of addressing you one or two Letters since your residence at Washington, but have not had any answer to either.

There is a Rail Road about to be made on Marigny Canal, which has allready enhanced the value of Lots 100 pCent. Miss Eastins is now worth $600. & when the Road is Completed may be worth $1000.[1]

with best wishes for your Health & happiness I remain very Sincerely your Friend & obt. st.

Maunsel White

ALS, DLC (38). White (1783–1863) was AJ's cotton factor at New Orleans. His account showed sales for AJ on April 28 of 12,802 pounds at 10½ cents for $1,344.21, 5091 pounds at 9¾ cents for $496.37, and 8218 pounds at 8⅝ cents for $708.80, totaling $2549.38 minus $302.99 in freight, insurance, and 2.5% commission.

1. Completed in 1831, the five-mile Pontchartrain Railroad connected the New Orleans Mississippi riverfront with Lake Pontchartrain.

From Samuel Delucenna Ingham

The Secretary Try with his best respects has the honor to submit for perusal of the President, the Letters recd from Mr Strother in relation to the transactions in Missouri—from which it will be seen that we shall have some trouble with him—It is much to be regretted that Col. McCrea declines, especially as OFallon is represented to have an adverse interest as to a part of the property—Strother will probably not deliver the property until his compensation is fixed, but it occurs to the Secy of the Treasury that it will be best to associate the District Attorney in place of McCrea, order Strother to deliver up the property papers &c account for which he has recd, and if he refuses, direct the District Atty to file a bill in Chancery to enjoin him, and get Receivers appointed to take charge &c   The property on which OFallon has a claim, may be placed exclusively into the care of the District Atty—

AN, PU-Ingham Papers (15-1030). The Bank of Missouri failed in 1821, owing the U.S. $159,163.87. To cover the debt it transferred $189,237.19 in mortgages and other assets and claims. The government entrusted these to George F. Strother, then receiver of the St. Louis land office, as its agent for liquidation. On April 6, 1830, the House had called for information on the collections. Ingham reported on May 18 that Strother had thus far paid in less than $20,000 in cash and scrip and rendered no account for the rest. To speed the work, the Treasury had selected William McRee (1787–1833), the surveyor of public lands in Missouri, Illinois, and Arkansas, and Benjamin O'Fallon (1793–1842) to assist Strother; but McRee declined and Strother resigned. George F. Shannon (1787–1836), U.S. district attorney for Missouri, would instead be instructed to work with O'Fallon (*HRDoc* 111, 21st Cong., 1st sess., Serial 198).

To Samuel Delucenna Ingham

May 15th 1830—

I fully approve the measures proposed by the Secretary of the Treasury within—The attorney for the District Mr Shannon is a proper & fit person to be appointed; and ought to be instructed to act promptly in this business—The usual compensation ought to be allowed Mr. Strother upon his fully & faithfully accounting for his stewartship, and no more

AN, PU-Ingham Papers (15-1032).

To Samuel Delucenna Ingham

May 15th. 1830—

The President with his respects, request the Secretary of the Treasury to inform him what proportion of the estimated balance in the Treasury on the 1rst of January 1831 are unavailable—The balance as estimated is, 4,494,545.02   This is requested to see how the appropriations by Congress for the year 1830, corresponds with the real available funds in the Treasury—and if they exceed, how much, the available funds in the Treasury

AN, PU-Ingham Papers (15-1028). AJ attached to his May 27 Maysville Road veto an earlier Treasury estimate showing receipts and cash on hand for 1830 of $28,250,071 minus $23,755,526 in expected expenditures, leaving a projected balance on January 1, 1831, of $4,494,545. An updated statement below showed unavailable funds of $3,883,719 in bad debts and holdover expenses from 1829, and $25,072,215 in appropriations passed or likely to pass the current Congress. These together, subtracted from the $28,250,071, left a projected shortfall in the Treasury of $705,863 (*HRDoc* 113, 21st Cong., 1st sess., p. 11, Serial 198).

To Martin Van Buren

PRIVATE.

May 15th, 1830

DEAR SIR,

Your note is received. I am happy that you have been looking at the proceedings of Congress. The appropriations now exceed the available funds in the Treasury, and the estimates always exceed the real amount available. I have just called upon the Secretary of the Treasury for the amount of the estimated available balance on the 1st January 1831.

The people expected reform retrenchment and economy in the administration of this Government. This was the cry from Maine to Louisiana, and instead of these the great object of Congress, *it would seem*, is to make mine one of the most extravagant administrations since the commencement of the Government. This must not be; The Federal Constitution must be obeyed, State-rights preserved, our national debt *must be paid*, *direct taxes and loans avoided* and the Federal union preserved. These are the objects I have in view, and regardless of all consequences, will carry into effect. Yr. friend

A. J.

Mr. V. B. *Sec. of State.*
Let me see you this evening or in the morning.

Printed, *The Autobiography of Martin Van Buren*, p. 322 (15-1036).

From John Forsyth

May 18. 1830.
Senate Chamber.

John Forsyth has the honor to hand to the President ~~the~~ a copy of the letter referred to in the letter of Mr Crawford delivered to him last week

[Endorsed by AJ:] Major Forsythe of U.S. Senate enclosing a copy of a letter to Major J. A. Hamilton on the subject of an Executive or Cabinett council where it was proposed to punish me by Mr. Calhoun for my conduct on the Seminole Campaign—Let this be carefully filed with Mr. C. letter to Mr. F. My letter to Mr. Calhoun & his reply—A. J. May 18th. 1830

AN, DLC (72). The enclosed letter was Forsyth's to James A. Hamilton, February 8, 1828.

To James Alexander Hamilton

(Private)

Washington May 18th 1830

My Dr Sir

In my last I promised to forward you a copy of Mr. C. letter just placed into my hands; but being informed that a copy had been sent you, I declined it—On the receipt of Mr. C.s letter I addressed a note to Mr Calhoune enclosing him a copy, with such remarks as the facts stated, with other references to his *professed confidence*, & approbation ~~expressed~~ of my conduct, in his various correspondences with me, on the subject of the Seminole war, sugested—he acknowledged the receipt of my note, and has promised, so soon as leisure will allow, to answer it. Thus you see, he will either have to deny the truth of the statement, in Mr Crawfords letter, or be in a delicate situation, if he admits the fact—Major Forsyth has this moment placed in my hands a copy of his letter, I suppose to you, which is refered to by Mr Crawford—you will hear from me soon—in the mean time I have to ask you for the criticism on Mr Mc.Duffie' report—In haste yr friend

Andrew Jackson

ALS, NN (15-1043).

To Samuel Delucenna Ingham

May 18th. 1830—

The President with his respects, requests the Secretary of the Treasury to furnish him with the amount of money appropriated under different laws for the construction, & repairs, of the cumberland road from its commencement to this date.

AN, PU-Ingham Papers (15-1045). The Cumberland or National Road ran west from Cumberland, Md., to Columbus, Ohio, and Indianapolis, with a planned extension to the capitals of Illinois and Missouri. Its construction at federal expense was sanctioned by the laws admitting Ohio, Indiana, Illinois, and Missouri to the Union, which allocated 2% of net federal land sale proceeds in those states for roads leading to them. AJ attached to his May 27 Maysville Road veto a Treasury statement showing total appropriations for the road from 1806 through 1829 of $2,620,243.60, far outdistancing the 2% fund (*HRDoc* 113, 21st Cong., 1st sess., p. 22, Serial 198).

From Samuel Houston

Steam Boat Nashville
18th May 1830.

Dear Sir,

You will by the time this reaches you have seen a useless publication against me by sundry respectable citizens of Sumner County. The object must have been to injure me, because it could not benefit others to review this subject at this time. They were axious to publish my letter and they have done it. They state untruly when they say it was after the seperation, it was before it. The letter was written under a state of vast excitement and with a view to quiet matters, until the election for Governor was over, and a friend of the country elected Speaker of the Senate, when I would have resigned and left the world without the slightest noise, and left it in darkness, as to the causes and all things connected with the whole matter.

Therefore I said I was "satisfied," I was, as to the course I would, and ought to pursue. It is stated that my treatment induced her to return to her Fathers house for protection. This is utterly false, and without any foundation. By the publication of my letter they adopt a contrary state of facts, for in that I aver that I never was unkind to her, and I refer to her to bear witness. If I had been, would she not have said so, and would they not have published the facts to the world? Yes they surely would have done so. They alledge as an excuse that public sympathy was excited in my behalf. Who did this? I did not. I would not claim nor even wish sympathy to be extended to my case by mortal being. To me the thought of it is, as cold as the breezes of Norway. I never sought to injure her with any one. To you, even *you* sir, in whose estimation I have been most proud to stand honorable & fair, I appeal to know of your heart, if I cast the slightest reflection upon her, or her immediate family. But I have drank the cup, and the *dregs* only remain, for me to consume. I feel well satisfied, nor will I ever permit myself to abandon the ground which I have assumed. I have sacrificed every thing that was Glorious to my peculiar necessities & conscious Honor, and rectitude only remain as my companions. They are old friends, and will not desert me in time to come.

This recent attack would not have been made upon me, if it had not been supposed that I was down in society. I am not down. The effections of the people of Tennessee are with me and if I would present myself to them again, they would shew the world that they have confidence in me, and care nothing about my private matters, which they cannot understand. So soon as I can reach home I will let you know the condition of the Indians, and whether the Mexican Troops have reached the Borders of the U. States. I pray you to accept my best wishes for your health and happiness, with assurances of my perfect respect.

Sam Houston.

Typed copy, DLC (72). *Writings of Sam Houston*, 1:149–50. The April 1830 Summer County meeting that issued a public condemnation of Houston published a letter he had written to his wife's father, John Allen, on April 9, 1829, a week before he resigned the governorship (and, said the meeting, just after the couple separated). In it Houston reported that a "most unpleasant and unhappy circumstance has just taken place in the family." He complained of coldness from Eliza but acquitted her of unchastity: "That I was *satisfied* and *believed her virtuous*, I had assured her on last night and this morning. . . . That I have and do love Eliza, none can doubt—that I have ever treated her with affection, she will admit—that she is the only earthly object dear to me, God will bear witness" (*Nashville Whig*, May 7, 1830).

To Francis Smith

(copy)

Washington May 19th. 1830

Dr. Sir,

This will be handed to you by my son, by whom I take occasion to tender to you my thanks for your kind attention to him on his late tour to the North.

I am fearful he has committed an error. If he has, I trust, you will ascribe it to his youth, diffidence and inexperience, and allow him to make atonement for it—for which purpose I send him to you. He has made known to me, since his return, the attachment he has formed for your amiable daughter, which he informs me has been expressed to her and if not reciprocated, has at least won her favorable opinion. He has erred in attempting to address your daughter without first making known to you and your lady his honorable intentions, and obtaining your approbation; but he has been admonished of this impropreity, and he now waits upon you to confess it. I find his affections are fixed upon her, and if they are reciprocated with your approbation, that he looks upon the step which would follow their sanction as the greatest assurance of his happiness. Mine, since the bereavement which the loss of my dear wife has inflicted upon me, has almost vanished except that which flows from his prosperity.

He has been reared in the paths of virtue and morality by his pious and amiable Mother, and I believe has walked steadily in them; is the only hope by which I look to the continuation of my name; and has a fortune ample enough with prudence and econemy, and more than enough without them. With these prospects he presents himself again to your daughter. If you have any objections I am sure you will with frankness communicate them to him, when he will withdraw from any further suit and desire only to be ranked with your and her friends. I mistake your character if in thus approaching you either he or myself run the least hazard in being misunderstood. It has been a rule with me thro' life not to permit the forms of ceremony to prevent a free expression of my feelings on a subject which touches those of others.

I will soon be left alone as Major A. J. Donelson and family are preparing to go to Tennessee upon a visit to their disconsalate Mother. In their absence I cannot bear to be seperated long from my son. should his anticipations not be disappointed any arrangements for their completion will be at your pleasure, and on his return to me he will be prepared to meet them

With a tender of my kind salutations to your amiable lady and daughter Believe me most respectfully yr. sert

signed Andrew Jackson

[Endorsed by AJ:] (copy) letter to Major Francis Smith May 19th. 1830—

LS Draft in AJ Donelson's hand, Heritage Auctions sale 675, October 2007 (mAJs). Francis Smith (d. 1840) operated a salt works at Abingdon, Va. His wife was Mary Trigg Smith (1781–1839) and their daughter was Mary Frances Trigg Smith (1812–1890). In August 1831 she married Wyndham Robertson, later governor of Virginia in 1836–37.

From G. G. & S. Howland et al.

New York, 19th May, 1830.

To his Excellency the President of the United States.

We, whose names are hereunto subscribed, having had business to transact at the Custom House in this City, during the past year, beg leave respectfully to represent to your Excellency, that we have always found the Surveyor, Mr. Noah, at his post, attentive to his duty, obliging in his disposition, and accommodating in all his arrangements for the protection of the interests of Government and the convenience of the citizens.

Mr. Noah has, heretofore, filled the state office of High Sheriff of the City and County of New York, and his discharge of the arduous duties of that delicate and important station was such as to elicit the most unqualified and general approbation of his fellow citizens.[1]

We cannot but regret, therefore, that the nomination of this tried citizen was not confirmed by the Honorable the Senate of the United States, and we sincerely hope that, on a more mature consideration of the subject, that Honorable body may see fit to reconsider their vote and confirm the nomination.

G. G. & S. Howland
Will & Sam Craig

Garcia, Arcos & Co
Fish Grinnell & Co
John Hone & Sons
Stephen Whitney
John Flack

[Thirty more signatures follow.]

[Endorsed by AJ:] memorial in behalf of Major Noah, to renominate him—

DS, DNA-RG 46 (15-1050). G. G. & S. Howland, headed by brothers Gardiner Greene Howland (1787–1851) and Samuel Shaw Howland (1790–1853), was a leading New York City merchant firm. AJ had given Mordecai Noah a recess appointment as New York customs surveyor in April 1829 and nominated him to the Senate in January 1830. The Senate rejected him on May 10 by 25 to 23. On May 21 AJ renominated him, claiming he had been rejected "through misapprehension." To prove his fitness AJ submitted this memorial and a May 20 letter of praise to Noah from New York merchant Peter Remsen (15-1056). The Senate confirmed Noah on May 28 on a vote of 22 to 22, with Vice President Calhoun breaking the tie in favor (*Senate Executive Proceedings*, 4:101, 106, 114).
   1. Noah had been sheriff of New York in 1821–22.

To John Henry Eaton

May 20th. 1830—

Sir
   I have examined the papers & order of the commander in chief countermanding & recinding the orders of Genl Gains which appears very improvident.
   The transfer of the Troops as proposed by Genl Gains could have no beneficial tendency, and would increase the expense five thousand dollars.
   a proper economy in every department of the Government in the disbursement of public money must be observed—You will therefore return to Genl Gains his letter which must have been written under some improper feelings & without his usual reflection; inclose him likewise, the report of the quartermaster Genl shewing what this unnecessary & useless movement would cost the united States; and notify him that hereafter no expense by any unnecessary change of the position of the troops in his Department be ~~made~~ incured[.] very respectfully

Andrew Jackson

ALS, DNA-RG 108 (15-1053). On March 7 Gaines had ordered a rotation of infantry companies among four western posts. On April 3 Army commander General Alexander Macomb countermanded the order, instructing Gaines that troop dispositions were not to be changed without his authority (DNA-RG 108, M857-1). Gaines wrote Macomb an apparently inde-

corous protest on April 24, which Macomb passed on to Eaton. Eaton wrote Macomb of
AJ's decision on May 21. Macomb enclosed it to Gaines on May 24 (DNA-RG 108, M857-
1), and Gaines composed a remonstrance to AJ on July 12 (below).

From Balaam Duke Fields

Pikeville
State of Alabama Marion County
May the 20—1830

Mr Andrew Jackson as an Individual I take liberty of adressing you
although not personaly aquainted wee see sir a proclamation advertised
in the Huntsville Democrate with your own signature asignd siad to have
Bin done by your own hand at the Citty of Washington that [per]sons
whoo ar in posesion of or Residing on aney of the public Lands of the
united States within the district of Alabama subject to sail at Hunstville
to Remove ther from by the 1st day of September I have thought proper
thearfore to comunicate a few Lins to you opon that subject as ther is
a large majority of the poor people and citisans of marion county oco-
pian the Lands belonging to the united States and subject to sail at the
Land offises of Huntsville and all Intertaing of diferant opinons as to the
sbstance of the artical avertis Some beleave it to be the Lands which ar
Relinquished of forferted[1] others beleave it to be that large and valuable
Boddy of Land liing in the tennessee valy which is claimed by Col. John
T. Smith and some entertain an Idea that the artical has been advertised
by some person whoo will be In opposition to you at the next presidential
term all Intertaing of Diferant oppinons and ascribeing them to intier
diferant causes became each a critic to the uninformd I thearfore hope
you will comuncate to me a few Lins opon the subject as my frends and
self ar all anxiously waiting on you for an ansur which will dispell doubt
and Bring forth facts to stand substinatualy as thay ar with sentamints of
sincear esteem I am sir you moust obdent frend and servant

Balaam. D. Fields

[Endorsed by AJ Donelson:] B. D. Fields of Alabama in relation to the
proclamation (Smiths case)

ALS, DLC (38). Fields (1807–1862) later moved to Mississippi. A debate had erupted in the
Huntsville *Democrat* following its publication of AJ's March 6 proclamation ordering off
trespassers in the Huntsville land district. Attacking the proclamation, "Civis" on April 30
and May 14 charged AJ with abusing his authority and violating the government's historic
tolerance of settlement on unsold public lands. The *Democrat*'s editors answered that the
proclamation was clearly aimed only at holders under John Smith T's title, not occupants at
large, and accused "Civis" of distorting facts to injure AJ.

1. Relinquished and forfeited lands were those purchased under the old pre-1820 credit system on which payment had not been completed. A law of March 31, 1830, offered purchasers several options to commute the unmade payments and obtain title.

From James Taylor

Bellevue (Newport Ky)
May 22d 1830

I had the pleasure to see a few days ago Col John S. Smith U.S. atty for this district, who informed me that he should previous to our annual elections (1st. Monday of Augt) resign his appointment, & become a candidate for the Legislature.

Colo John W. Tibbatts my son in law, would gladly accept the office. He is a young man of fine education, a graduate of Transylvania University, & a man of fine acquerments, sober, industrious, discreet & popular, and a good speaker.

He was, and still is, a warm supporter of the cause which brought you to the executive chair.

He is a member of the bars of the Fed Courts of this State & Ohio, and is considered inferior to no atty at the bar of our court & the adjoining Counties. He was a member of the two last Legislatures & acquired much reputation as a man of business.

In consequence of some embarassments by security ships, I have not been able to give my children much productive property. Our slaves leave us in considerable numbers, & he as well as my self, has been unfortunate in this way. He has therefore but little productive property & a growing family.

I refer you to the Hon. W. T. Barry for information of his qualifications to fill the office with honor to himself & credit to our Country.

If he should be so fortunate as to meet your approbation, you would confer a lasting obligation on Mrs. Taylor, myself & whole family

I hope this may find you in improving health, & your household in the enjoyment of that most estimable of blessings.

I have the honor to be with great respect & esteem Dr sir you obed. St.

James Taylor

[Endorsed by AJ:] refered to the Secretary of State to await the Resignation of Major Smith   A. J.

ALS, DNA-RG 59 (M639-24). John Wooleston Tibbatts (1801–1852), later a congressman, had married Taylor's daughter Anne Wilkinson Taylor. John Speed Smith (1792–1854) was U.S. district attorney for Kentucky. AJ Donelson endorsed Tibbatts's candidacy to Van Buren on June 4. William T. Barry wrote AJ about the vacancy on July 10 (below).

To Sylvanus Thayer

Washington May 24th 1830

Dear Sir,
I take the liberty of sending a line to bespeak your kind attention for the bearer Cadet Wm. S. Reid who is the son of my old Aid de Camp in the southern campaigns of the last war. His Father was a most intelligent, brave and useful officer, and as is too often the fate of such men left a very dependent family to his country. This young Gentleman I hope will see the importance of the education which is placed within his reach at west Point, and turn to the best account the advice which he may occasionally need under your superintendence and care.
I am with great respect yr. obt. servant.

Andrew Jackson

LS in AJ Donelson's hand, NWM (15-1079). Thayer (1785–1872) was superintendent of the United States Military Academy at West Point. William Steptoe Reid (1813–1899) was the son of AJ's late military aide and biographer John Reid. AJ wrote similar letters to Thayer on June 1 for cadet John W. Smyth, the son of recently deceased Virginia congressman Alexander Smyth, and on June 16 for William B. Giles's son Thomas P. Giles. AJ wrote Reid's grandfather, Nathan Reid, about him on November 16 (below).

From Mary Wilson

[On April 13, 1830, a federal grand jury in Philadelphia indicted James Porter (c1804–1830) and George Wilson (b. c1801) for robbing a mail carrier on December 6, 1829, by use of deadly force, a capital crime under an Act of 1825. The two were tried separately and convicted, Wilson on May 1 and Porter on May 6. On May 27, presiding judge Henry Baldwin sentenced them to hang. Mary Wilson was George's mother. Porter appealed to Jackson for clemency on May 28 (below), as did Wilson's sister Mary Wilson on May 29.]

Philadelphia May   1830

Sir,
The mother of an unfortunate youth, condemned by his own crime and the Laws of his country, respectfully addresses you—In the hope of exciting your sympathy, and awakening your mercy—Surely in a country whose boast is the lenity of its Laws, the mother may plead before the Executive of that country, for a stay of the sentence of death, in favour of her only son!! Decrepid from age, and entirely impoverished by misfortune, I have no opportunity of adding by *personal* intreaty to the force of my

application—Enclosed within the precinct of a poor house, and verging on to the *last* residence of humanity, I pause, to invoke your clemency, to save me from that dreadful and heart rending calamity, the public execution of my only child! Oh! Sir, think upon the schock which my poor, weak, and debilitated system would undergo from such an occurrence—Consider Sir, that he is my only child, my last tie upon the bosom of the world, and think Sir, upon his being thus awfully taken from me, by the hand of the common hangman! Precipitated at once, in crime, and ignominy, into the presence of his God! Oh Sir! Nature calls out from my heart, she bids me raise my feeble voice to your ear, she calls on me to stir up your own feelings, and humbly ask you, can I contemplate his exit from this, and his too probable fate in the world to come, and not send forth my prayer to you who have the power, to hold back the dreadful sentence. Can it be Sir, That there is no power in my woe, nor any weight in my misfortune; and that you must let fall the sword? Oh! cruel must be the heart, that can respond thus to my supplication. You Sir, I am sure, have felt the stroke of some cruel misfortune, and yet I feel persuaded that however it may have passed down the tide of life, that some secret traces of it, in your heart still remain, to aid my hope and excite your sympathy. Must I refer to his offence for a gleam of mercy? Oh Sir, then remember that he shed no blood—Yes, if consolation remain to a heart torn by the enormity of my child, it springs from this—no being will stand before the bar of his Creator in the day of his judgement and charge him with having steeped his hand in blood at the moment that he broke the Laws of his country! And Sir, when you consider the temptation for such an addition to his already great crime, when you find him preferring the solemn risk of dis- covery ending in his own death, rather than take away the life of his fellow men, I sincerely hope you may discover traces of good feeling, that under other auspices, might form the ground work of complete reformation —And Sir, When you couple this with the fact, that in our state, where blood has not been shed or life destroyed, That the offence no matter how enormous is never punished by the death of the criminal, and that the state of public feeling does not require that any such forfeit should follow, I hope you will find something to mitigate the terrible execution of the law—I well know Sir, that you are not responsible for aught but its faith- ful execution.[1] But mercy is as much your prerogative as the other your duty—And who will question your decision on the side of mercy? How then can I a poor distracted creature derive any thing but despair from my son's destruction? For nature cannot but abhor the fatality of the Law that policy may demand and parent-like I only question its expediency— Ah, Sir! You well know that youth is too often the victim of passion; and here a double woe is mine. The influence of a wretched father, nurtured the poison that so fatally destroyed my son, and *poverty* accelerated, what vice designed—As his mother, many, many circumstances of pallia- tion present themselves to my gloomy mind, and I solemnly intreat you to pause, ere you condemn him to death! The sterness that so well befits a Judge, might seem too severe in the executive: his office bearing the alternative of life and death.—And whilst the Law incapable of distinction equally condemns the old and hardened offender, with the young and imprudent one. Yet the voice of religion, nature and mercy jointly plead in favour of youth. I beseech you Sir, by the sacred feelings of an agonized parent, to have pity on my age and infirmities and believe me that your future life will be sweetened by the reflection that you gave this youth an opportunity to amend his life, and at the same time plucked from an aged mother's pillow—the sharp thorn of his untimely death. And while life lingers shall my prayer hourly rise to the throne of God for your happiness both here and to come—Your distressed humble servant

Mary Wilson

[Endorsed by AJ:] Mary Wilsons Pathetic appeal for the pardon of her son—

D, DNA-RG 59 (15-1414), postmarked May 24. Thomas Porter, *The Mail Robbers, or Evils Attendant on a Sinful Life* (Philadelphia, 1830), pp. 14–16. Mary Wilson (b. c1770) lived in the Philadelphia almshouse. Thomas Porter (c1798–1846), a Baptist clergyman, befriended the prisoners and their families and may have helped craft this appeal. The trial transcript was published as *The Mail Robbers: Report of the Trials of Michael Mellon, the Lancaster Mail Robber; and George Wilson and James Porter alias May, the Reading Mail Robbers* (Philadelphia, 1830).

1. The postal law of 1825 prescribed death as the only penalty for mail robbers who wounded a carrier "or put his life in jeopardy, by the use of dangerous weapons." Wilson and Porter held up the mail stage with pistols but did not shoot. The driver testified against them at trial.

To Martin Van Buren

May 25th. 1830

The President with his respects, informs the Sec. of State that he awaits the nomination of Genl Lytle as Survayor Genl. to send it to the senate—The P. supposed this nomination had long since been sent to the senate but he supposes he is mistaken—The P. requests to be informed whether there is any persons recommended as commissioner & survayor to run the line between Louisiana & Arkansa, if so, please send them that the appointment may be made & given to Mr Sevier

AN, DNA-RG 59 (M179-68). AJ had given William Lytle a recess appointment as surveyor general for public lands in Ohio, Indiana, and Michigan Territory in May 1829. His nomination, dated this day, May 25, was received and confirmed in the Senate May 26. A law of May 1828 authorized appointment of a U.S. commissioner and surveyor to join with Louisiana officers in running the line between Louisiana and Arkansas Territory. AJ queried Van Buren for a candidate again on June 1. On June 8, AJ commissioned James Sevier

Conway (1796–1855), first cousin of Arkansas congressional delegate Ambrose H. Sevier, as boundary commissioner and William Pelham as surveyor.

From Anastasio Bustamante

PALACE OF THE FEDERAL GOVERNMENT,
Mexico, May 26, 1830.

MR. PRESIDENT:

I avail myself of the occasion the return to the United States of Don Antonio Mexia, of the Mexican legation, affords, to address your excellency particularly.[1] I would have had this pleasure earlier, if my attention to current business had not wholly occupied my time. The liberty I now take may possibly be deemed strange by your excellency, having never had the good fortune to have had any previous communication with you; but I hope that your excellency will excuse the frankness of a soldier, who is not arrested by forms, when he sees any promised advantage to his country. After the frequent changes to which unfortunately this people have seen themselves subjected in preceding years, public opinion, loudly pronounced, has produced a state of things more tranquil, and which promises to be confirmed. The attempts to subvert it, although encouraged and fomented by appearances, and names heretofore respectable, have been various; and with great reluctance I have found myself obliged, in some few cases, to use the force of arms. The conviction of my mind is, that they have been employed constantly with beneficial effects.

The attention of the Government will now be directed to the reparation of the evils caused by a storm of such duration; to open the fountains of inexhaustible prosperity with which Providence has endowed this country, and to extinguish discord which has been so prejudicial. The means by which I propose to effect this are very simple. Having been employed many years in the profession of arms, I cannot accustom myself to the subtleties of the politician; and always inclining to the simplicity of my military habits, I prefer frankness and uniformity of procedure. The march of the administration shall be open and undisguised; past offences and resentments forgotten: the most strict impartiality with respect to men who, in less happy times, have belonged to different parties. Such is my system. Uniting to this a rigid economy and strict accountability in the treasury, and an exact discipline in the army, I promise myself that Mexico will re-establish herself, and prove that we can be happy. The same principles applied to our foreign relations will prove to your excellency that I shall personally devote myself to extinguish every trace of disgust or ill feeling which, from causes to which it is not necessary to refer, are believed to exist between our respective countries. I behold in your republic the oldest friend to the independence of this. I believe the bond of friendship which unites us should be strengthened, and I consider it a primary obligation to promote the most intimate relations between the two people. It has so happened that internal cares have scarcely left me a moment to direct my attention towards pending treaties with the United States; and if I have not already taken up that with the first nation which recognised our independence, and the first to which we are bound by the faith of treaties, I will take care at least for the future that every cause of delay shall be removed. This will produce a thousand benefits, and especially at a time when a new invasion is announced by our eternal enemies the Spaniards, Mexico ought to count upon the good will of her no less constant friends; and in this respect I can do no less than to avail myself of the occasion to manifest to your excellency my gratitude for the good offices which your Government has interposed, in order that the independence of this and the other new republics of America may be recognised by Spain. If Spain knew her true interests she would accord it. The continuation of the war can only bring upon her injury and disgrace; for on this point there is not a single Mexican, whatever his opinion may be on other political subjects, who is not resolved to sacrifice himself if necessary to sustain independence. I fear that you may find this letter too long for a first communication. I have here exposed my motives; and in concluding I make bold to ask of your excellency that you will treat me with equal frankness, and permit me to consider myself among the number of your friends; and accept the assurance that I am, with every consideration, your most attentive and obedient servant,

ANASTACIO BUSTAMENTE.

A true copy: Mexico, May 26, 1830.

ORTIZ MONASTERIO.[2]

Printed translation, HRDoc 351, 25th Cong., 2d sess., pp. 642–43, Serial 332 (mAJs). Copy (in Spanish), DNA-RG 59 (M54-1). AJ received this letter on October 6 and replied October 7 (below). Anastasio (or Anastacio) Bustamante (1780–1853) became vice president of Mexico in 1829 and assumed the presidency in January 1830 after overthrowing Vicente Guerrero.

    1. José Antonio Mexía (1790–1839) was secretary of the Mexican legation in Washington.

    2. José María Ortiz Monasterio was clerk of the Mexican foreign office.

From Martin Van Buren

[Not having received the expected word from Louis McLane in London on a resolution of the West Indian colonial trade controversy, Jackson addressed Congress on May 26, asking for authority to reopen the trade by proclamation should an agreement be reached during the pending six-month congressional recess. Jackson closed by offering to furnish "any information in the possession of the Executive which you may deem *necessary to guide your deliberations" (Richardson, 2:480–81). The next day, May 27, the House adopted a resolution by New York congressman Churchill Cambreleng asking the president for "such information relating to our negotiations with Great Britain, concerning the colonial trade, as he may deem compatible with the public interest" (House Journal, 21st Cong., 1st sess., p. 743, Serial 194).]*

Department of State
Washington 27th. May 1830

To the President,
The Secretary of State to whom has been referred a Resolution of the House of Representatives of this date, requesting the President to communicate to that House "such information relating to our negotiations with Great Britain, concerning the Colonial Trade, as he may deem compatible with the Public Interest,"—has the honor herewith to submit the accompanying copies and extracts from the correspondence between this Department and the Minister of the United States at London, and between that Minister and His Britannic Majesty's Government.

M Van Buren

DS, DNA-RG 233. LC, DNA-RG 59 (15-1175). Van Buren enclosed correspondence from July 1829 through April 1830 between himself, Louis McLane, and British foreign secretary the Earl of Aberdeen, detailing the progress of the negotiation.

To the United States House of Representatives

(Confidential)
Washington 27th. May 1830.

To the House of Representatives of the United States
In compliance with the Resolution of House of Representatives of this date, requesting the President to communicate to that House "such information, relating to our negotiations with Great Britain, concerning the Colonial Trade, as he may deem compatible with the Public Interest," I herewith communicate a Report from the Secretary of State, which, with the documents accompanying it, affords the desired information.

Anxious that you should be fully informed of every step which has been taken by the Executive Department of the Government for the restoration of the Colonial Trade, as also of my views upon the subject, I have deemed it proper to cause the entire instructions which have been given thereon to our Minister at London, to be laid before you—

It will be seen by the documents now submitted, that if an arrangement is made upon the terms which have been authorized by this Government; the vessels of the United States will be allowed to enter the British Colonial ports with the same kind of American produce as may be imported in British vessels, the vessels of both Countries paying the same charges; and that the produce of the United States will not be charged, in said ports with any other or higher duties than similar produce is charged with when imported from any other foreign country.

Although these papers contain nothing which, in ordinary circumstances, would be considered as of a secret or strictly confidential nature, yet, inasmuch as the matter of which they treat is still the subject of pending negotiation, I am induced, by considerations of public interest, to ask that this communication may be regarded as confidential[1]

Andrew Jackson

DS, DNA-RG 233; LC, DNA-RG 59 (15-1166). Before adjourning, Congress on May 29 passed an Act authorizing the president to open American ports to British colonial shipping by proclamation on his receiving word that Britain would drop its discriminatory restrictions on American ships and cargoes entering colonial ports. AJ issued a proclamation reopening the trade on October 5 (Richardson, 2:497–99).

    1. The House considered AJ's message behind closed doors and did not have it printed. Most of the attached diplomatic correspondence was communicated to the Senate in 1831 and printed in *SDoc* 20, 21st Cong., 2d sess., pp. 3–39 (Serial 203).

Maysville Road Veto Message

[A bill "Authorizing a subscription of stock in the Maysville, Washington, Paris, and Lexington Turnpike Road Company" passed the House of Representatives by 102 to 85 on April 29 and the Senate, after a test vote of 24 to 18, on May 15. It directed the Secretary of the Treasury to subscribe for 1500 shares ($150,000) of stock in the company, which was chartered by the state of Kentucky. The bill was enrolled, signed, and presented to Jackson on May 19. On May 27 he returned it to the House with his veto, the first of his presidency. A bid to override the veto, requiring a two-thirds majority, failed in the House on May 28 by a vote of 96 in favor to 92 against.

Jackson accompanied his veto message with two Treasury statements, which he had solicited from secretary Ingham on May 15 and 18 (above). The first showed that appropriations already made or likely to pass in the current Congress would exceed available funds by $705,863, and that other bills introduced in House and Senate would appropriate $8,273,918 more. The second statement tabulated cumulative Cumberland Road expenditures of $2,620,243 since 1806. The veto with the attachments was printed in HRDoc 113, 21st Cong., 1st sess. (Serial 198), and appears without the attachments in Richardson, 2:483–93. In the Library of Congress are original drafts of the message by Jackson, James K. Polk, and Martin Van Buren, and revised drafts by Andrew Jackson Donelson

(DLC-76), who also wrote out the finished text (DS, DNA-RG 233 [15-1108]). Presented here are all the drafts except Donelson's.]

Draft by Andrew Jackson

notes—
The Maysvill road bill—considered
1rst. its constitutionality.

The objects intended by the confederation of States in framing the constitution & the people who ratified it, were to give to Congress the power of Legislation over all exterior & interior national matters ~~confin~~ reserving to the States exclusively the sovereign power of regulating on all their local ~~matters~~ concerns

~~There are no grant within the constitution, giving to Congress the power to make roads other than national~~ The grants are specific: To regulate our foreign relation for defence, for the regulation of commerce, and to establish, not make, post roads—can this Bill be ~~applied~~ considered to come within any of these grants—no. The sages who formed the constitution viewed it as a government of experiment and granted all powers thought necessary for ~~all~~ national purposes, never expecting that congress would attempt to Legislate and appropriate money only where the powers granted gave them jurisdiction ~~of~~ over the subject—and certainly it will not be contended where congress have no juris over the subject that it can appropriate money to that object—The framers of the constitution viewing it a Government of experiment in which it might be discovered that powers not granted, might be necessary for the prosperity & safety of the country provided for its amendment—and therefore it was presumed that Congress would never exercise doubtfull powers, but where doubts existed a call would be made on the people to grant the power necessary—~~is there any~~ There are no powers granted by the ~~States & people, for~~ the constitution to authorise the United States to become a ~~members~~ of corporations created by the states,* this power is no where to be found in the constitution—adopt this system & where would you stop, where draw the distinction, would not every incorporated body by they states have equal claims upon your membership & on your bounty, & I repeat—where could you stop—would the people suffer themselves to be taxed for such purposes—would not such a power be too dangerous to your liberties   what would it result in, in this, that the United States by ~~their banks, by their being~~ becoming stockholders in every petty state corporation, to the amount of half the stock, ~~it~~ would weild its power in your elections & all ~~your domestic~~ the interior concerns of the state, this would lead to consolidation & that would destroy the liberty of your country—

I can no where find, ~~under the first~~ in our early Legislation under the Federal constitution, where the power by congress was assumed to appropriate money to objects where the constitution had not given jurisdiction over the subject, or where the object was not clearly national, ~~not local~~ whereever the general Government have jurisdiction over the subject, & can appropriate money for its improvement, the power follows & is incidental, to pass all laws to protect & preserve it, & punish all persons ~~to~~ who violates its regulations, nay to exercise exclusive jurisdiction over it—with this view of the subject & the powers exercised by congress to tax the people for local objects of improvements of a state, what power cannot congress exercise over & within a state & what jealousy will not arise from the partial legislation, by combinations in congress will not follow—we have seen this spirit prevail, & there can be no doubt it will increase in future. Believing as I do that the constitutional powers of Congress in Legislation under the granted powers of the constitution are entirely national—all local matters being reserved as appropriate objects of the States, I recommended in my message, the speedy payment of the public debt, and then an appropriation of the surplus revenue amonghst the States for internal improvement &c &c This I then & still do believe is the only just fair & Federal mode in which our surpluss revenue could by applied—leaving to the States their constitutional rights to regulate all their interior concerns & the General Government all its national—

The expediency—The voice of the people from Main to Louisiana during the last canvass for the presidency has answered this in the negative—they have cried aloud for reform, retrenchment in public expenditures, & oconomy in the expenditures of the Government—they expect the public debt to be speedily paid, not increased by appropriations for local not national concerns, by subscribing to & becoming partners to brokers, corporations & insolvant Banks   What is the fact. during the present congress, up to the 1rst. of May the appropriations have exceeded the whole expenditures of the year 1829 by ____ and the bills reported to the House if acted upon & passed will far exceed by many millions the amount available in the Treasury for the year 1830—is it not then inexpedient & unjust at this time if the constitutional power existed to exaust your Treasury on local improvements & create the necessity of resorting to a System of direct taxes, to cover the arreages, or to loans, to redeem the national pledge in these subscriptions & appropriations—

*where is the grant in constitution, for the united States, to become a member of corporations created by the States, it is ~~inconsistent~~ corrupting & must destroy the purity of our govt. it must lead to the consolidation & the destruction of State rights; ~~and~~ The Govt. of the United States owning half the capital in each State corporation will weild ~~your~~ the State elections by corrupting & destroying the morales of your people. This will be more injurious & destructive to the morals & Liberty of the people than the U. States Bank so much & so justly complained of—~~This is a direct~~ This is not a power granted to congress, & of course is an infringement upon the reserved powers of States, & at once destroys that harmony that by the framers of the constitution was intended to exist between the two govts. and which has for years destroyed the harmony of the union, and might have been avoided by ~~at first~~ submitting an amendment of the constitution, for this purpose, to the people—These considerations ~~lead~~ induced me to recommend the speedy payment of the public debt, & as soon as that was paid, to distribute the surplus revenue amongst the States, as the most, just fair & Federal distribution of it, & by which ~~the~~ flagitious Legislation arising from combinations if you vote with me I will vote with you so dangerous to our country, would be prevented—

[Endorsed by AJ:] Maesvill road bill—veto—A. J

AD, DLC (38).

Drafts by James Knox Polk

[Polk (1795–1849), later the eleventh president, was at this time a third-term congressman from Tennessee.]

Having carefully examined the Act ____ presented to me for my signature on the ____ Instant, I find myself constrained to return it to the House of Representatives in which it originated with my objections—

Aware of the prevailing sentiment on the subject of Internal Improvements generally, and apprized of the variety and conflict of opinion concerning it I ought not to be indifferent to public ~~opinion~~ sentiment, but cannot hope to avoid giving disatisfaction to many whether I approve or disapprove of this act.

Feeling the high responsibility of my situation, I have looked to the Constitution, to experience and to reason for lights to direct me in the best course to promote the permanent prosperity of our country.

The advocates of the power of the Federal Government to make Internal Improvements, within the limits of the respective states, deduce it by construction from the Constitution, and not ~~from~~ in any express grant, except the clause concerning "Post Roads"—the meaning of which is earnestly contested. What this Government may or may not do in particular circumstances or in cases of emergency, is very difficult to define; but I think it may well be questioned, if not safely denied, that the power claimed was ever intended to be conferred on this Government as part of its ordinary functions.

Our statesmen of most distinguished talents have differed as to the existence of this power, and among those who recognize it, there is an indefinite variety of opinion as to its extent. These diversities of sentiment must necessarily produce gross inequality and injustice in its exercise; but it has progressed far enough already to satisfy us, from actual experience, that it is attended with other evils, prejudicial to general harmony, and dangerous to the purity of our institutions.

There is no absolute, nor urgent necessity for exercising such a power; partial convenience alone calls for it; and that may well resort to other means or await public opinion expressed in a *safer mode.*

The National debt is not yet paid. It is an object to which, all agree, we have the right of applying money; and its discharge is of the first importance, claiming all our resources beyond the ordinary demands of the Government. By pursuing this policy we may expect the debt will have been entirely discharged in a few years; and if our resources should yield a surplus of revenue, beyond the necessities of ~~the~~ Government, it may then be disposed of as the people may direct. In the meantime it may be well for Congress to submit to them such propositions for amending the Constitution, as may seem best calculated to obviate any existing difficulties.

This ~~Bill~~ act proposes to take stock in a company, and while it avoids some, it creates other objections against making or aiding such works by this Government. I have therefore though it safest, without indulging in distinctions among the various modes which have been proposed, respectfully to recommend a reference of the whole subject, to the people, for suitable amendments of the Constitution, and to withhold my signature from this ~~Bill~~ act for the following reasons.—

1st. The Constitutional power of this Government over the subject generally, is at least questionable.

2nd. The diversity of opinion, and uncertainty as to the existence of the power, and its extent, render it impossible to exercise it with tolerable equality and justice.

3rd. There is no indispensible use for the contemplated work; and the manner of disposing of any surplus revenue, with a view to this, or to other objects, may be satisfactorily adjusted before the final payment of the Public Debt.

4th. The annual receipts into the Treasury, which may remain after defraying the ordinary expenses of the Government, and such extraordinary expenses, as may be necessarily incurred, for the accomplishment of objects, unquestionably within the reach of Federal power, should be applied in my opinion, exclusively to the payment of the Public Debt.

[Endorsed by AJ:] view of internal improvements

The power to *construct* roads within the jurisdictional limits of the states, is not in my opinion conferred upon Congress by the Constitution. ~~Most~~ Some of my predecessors in this high trust have denied the existence of such a power, whilst others ~~have been di~~ under particular limitations have been disposed to concede the power to *appropriate* money for the construction of such works. Having anxiously sought in the Constitution the grounds on which this power rests, I am brought to the conclusion, upon a full review of the whole grounds, I am brought to the conclusion, that the existence of the power is too questionable to justify its exercise, and presents just such a question as should be refered to the people, in the mode prescribed by the constitution. Its exercise is not indispensible to the progress or prosperity of the Government, and if it present a question of real doubt such a reference is preferable, to the assumption of such a power, which all admit is derived from no express grant in the constitution but from construction. Considering therefore the weight of authority, and the conflict of opinion which exists on either side of this important question, and the dangers to be encountered whenever when ever the Federal Government, shall pass beyond the boundaries prescribed by the Constitution, limiting its powers, it is in my opinion safest not to exercise it, but refer its decision in the constitutional mode to the people.

But waiving the constitutional question presented by this Bill, and conceding it to be matter of great doubt, I withhold my signature from it for the following reasons. First the annual receipts into the Treasury, which may remain after paying the necessary expenses of the Government, should in my opinion be applied exclusively to the payment of the Public Debt.

Second—Because the appropriations made by Congress for the expenses of the current year, already exceed those of the preceeding year, and if large additional appropriations are now made, for objects of Internal Improvement, there is danger that there will not be money in the Treasury to meet the annual sinking fund applicable to the debt, and in that event, it may become necessary, to increase the revenue by a direct tax, or in some other mode which may be provided by Congress.

Third—That the road contemplated to be made by the Bill is not in my opinion necessary to effect any *National* end.

Fourth—If after the Public Debt shall have been discharged, it shall be impossible to devise any system of revenue, which shall make the annual receipts and expenditures precisely equal, and if of necessity, for the safety of the Government, there must be an annual surplus in the Treasury, it is submitted whether it would not be expedient, to provide in anticipation of that state of things, for its distribution in some equitable proportion among the different members of the Union.

Impelled by a deep sense of my duty, under the constitution, and fully aware of the high responsibility which I assume, in withholding my approbation from a measure which has received the sanction of a majority of Congress, I return the Bill with the consolation that if in the opinion of a Constitutional majority, I have erred, that my opinion will be overruled; or if not, that it may lead to some amendment of the Constitution which will restore harmony of opinion in the National Legislature, upon this interesting question of policy and Constitutional power.

[Endorsed by AJ:] a view of the Constitutional power of ~~the~~ Congress to appropriate money for internal improvements

AD, DLC (76).

Draft by Martin Van Buren

[This full draft by Van Buren provided the basis for the message in final form. Subsequent copies in Andrew J. Donelson's hand adjusted the phrasing and added detail while retaining this version's core structure, argument, and vocabulary. Jackson then supplied several insertions and amendments to Donelson's text, all given below.]

To the House of Representatives
Gentlemen

I have maturely considered the Bill entitled ____ and now return the same to the House of Representatives whence it originated with my objections thereto.

Sincerely friendly to the improvement of the Country by means of roads and canals I regret that any difference of opinion should exist between us to the mode of contributing to so desirable a result. If in stating my objections to the immediate measure under consideration I go beyond what the occasion may be deemed to call for I hope to find my apology, if any be necessary, in the grave importance of the general subject—an unfeigned respect for the high source from which the measure under consideration has emanated, and an anxious desire to be fully understood by my constituents in the discharge of every duty that devolves upon me. Diversities of opinion in regard to particular measures among public functionaries actuated by the same general motives are incident to all governments and are the more to be expected in one which like ours owes its existence and depends for its continuance upon the freedom of opinion. All that our constituents have a right to ask is that the views of their agents should be formed with an exclusive reference to the public good—that they should be honestly maintained and frankly expressed. That done—our respective duties are discharged and the result may be safely left to those for whom we act; relying with confidence, as we well may, that under all circumstances our respective opinions will be canvassed by the people with the indulgence which is due to the imperfections of our nature & that whatever is wrong will in due time find its correction in their deliberation and unbiassed judgment.[1]

The question as to the constitutional power and proper agency of the Federal Government in the construction or promotion of Internal Improvements presents itself in two points of view viz

First—The right to construct roads & canals within the respective states and to exercise over them & the territory they occupy jurisdiction sufficient for their enjoyment & preservation—

Secondly—The right to appropriate money from the national treasury in aid of works of that character when made by virtue of state authority.

The first is an open question & can be decided without embarrassments arising from the usage of the Government. Although frequently & strenuously attempted that power has not yet been in a single instance exercised by this Government. It does not in my opinion possess it. No bill therefore which asserts it can receive my official sanction.

The remaining question is differently situated. The ground taken upon this point at an early period of the Government was—"that whenever money has been raised by the general authority, and is to be applied to a particular measure, a question arises, whether the particular measure be within the enumerated authorities vested in Congress. If it be the money requisite for it, may be applied to it, if not no such application can be made."[2]

The document in which this principle was first advanced is of deservedly high authority & should be held in permanent & grateful remembrance, as well on account of its immediate agency in rescuing the Country from existing abuses & the constitution from the dangers which menaced it, as for its conservative effect upon many of the most valuable principles of the Government. The symmetry of the system & the sobriety of its operation would doubtless have been better preserved by the proposed restriction of the right of appropriation, if that restriction had been found compatible with its sufficiency for the attainment of the ~~great~~ avowed objects of its institution. But the fact is undeniable, that this construction, though doubtless at all times respected for its abstract fitness has been departed from by every subsequent administration of the Government; embracing a period of thirty out of the forty two years of its existence. It is not my purpose to detain you by a minute consideration of the particular acts by which this assertion is sustained. anxious however that the subject should be viewed in its true light by those whom it so deeply concerns and hoping much from the ultimate action of the people upon it, I cannot refrain from noticing such of them as are most prominent.

The administration of Mr Jefferson is distinguished by two acts ~~which~~ the bearings of which upon the question under consideration have not been surpassed, if they have been equalled, by any subsequent events. I allude to the payment of ____ millions for the purchase of Louisiana, and the original appropriation for the Cumberland Road; the latter act deriving increased weight from the recorded acquiescence and approbation of three of the most powerful and patriotic of the original members of the Confederacy expressed through their respective Legislatures.[3] Although the circumstances of ~~that~~ the latter case may ~~not have been such as to give to such~~ be such as to deprive so much of it as relates to the actual construction of the road, of the character of an obligatory exposition of the constitution; it must nevertheless be admitted that so far as it concerns the appropriation of money it is of a very imposing character. No less than ____ different laws have been passed through all the forms of the constitution appropriating ____ millions of dollars out of the national treasury in support of that object with the approbation of every President of the U S. from the period of its first adoption to & including my immediate predecessor.[4]

Independent of his sanction given to appropriations for the Cumberland & other roads & objects the administration of Mr Madison was characterized by an act ~~by~~ which furnishes the strongest evidence of his opinion upon the subject at that period. A Bill was passed through both Houses of Congress and presented for his approval "setting apart & pledging certain funds for constructing roads & canals, and improving the navigation of water courses, in order to facilitate promote & give security to internal commerce among the several states & to render more easy & less expensive the means & provisions for the common defence."

Regarding the Bill as asserting a power in the Federal Government to construct roads & canals within the limits of the states with ~~their~~ assent of the particular states ~~through~~ in which they were made he objected to its passage on the ground of its unconstitutionality:—declaring that the assent of the respective states in the mode provided by the Bill could not confer the power in question;—that the only cases in which the consent and cession of particular states can extend the power of Congress are those specified & provided for in the Constitution: superadding to those avowals his opinion that "a restriction of the power 'to provide for the common defence & general welfare,' to cases which are to be provided for by the expenditure of money, would still leave within the Legislative power of Congress, all the great and most important measures of Government, money being the ordinary & necessary means of carrying them into ~~effect~~ execution."[5] I have not been able to place any other construction upon this declaration than as a concession that the right to appropriate money is not limited by the power to carry into effect the measure for which the money is asked as was formerly contended.

The views of Mr Monroe upon the point were not left to inference. During his administration a bill passed the two houses conferring & prescribing the mode of exercising jurisdiction by the Federal Government over the Cumberland road. He returned with objections to its constitutionality; & in assigning his objections he took occasion to say—that in the early stage of the government he had inclined to the construction, that the Federal Government had no right to expend moneys except in the performance of acts authorized by the other specific grants of power, according to a strict construction of them; but that on further reflection and observation his mind had undergone a change—that his opinion then was "that Congress have an unlimited power to raise money, & that in its appropriation they have a discretionary power, restricted only by the duty, to appropriate it only to purposes of common defence, and of general not local, national not state benefit;["] and this principle was avowed to be the governing one in this respect through the residue of his administration.[6] The development of the principles of the last administration in this regard were so ample & are of such recent date as to render a particular reference to them unnecessary. It is well known that the money power to the utmost extent which had been claimed for it in relation to Internal Improvement was fully exercised.

This brief reference to known facts will be sufficient to shew the difficulty not to say impracticability of bringing back the operations of the Government in this regard to the construction of the Constitution set up in 1798; admitting that to be true reading of the original text. I am f

I am fully aware of the dangerous tendency of interpretations which derive their authority from the Statute Book instead of the Constitution. No man can be is more so, or more earnestly disposed to guard the Constitution with sleepless vigilance from all interpolations which derive their chief sanction from acts of successful encroachment upon the definition & partition of the powers of Government contemplated & established by the framers of that sacred instrument. But and But although I shall be among the last to give an my official sanction to the obligatory character of occasional usurpations, effected through the conjunction of peculiar & facilitating circumstances, I am nevertheless free to admit; that the public good & the nature of our political institutions require, that plain palpable & long enduring acquiescence by the people and confederated authorities, in particular constructions of the constitution, upon doubtful points ought not to be disturbed on ordinary grounds.

The case before me does not require the expression of a more definite opinion as to the particular circumstances which will warrant the appropriation of money by Congress in aid of works of Internal Improvement; for although an extension of the power to apply money beyond that of carrying into effect the work object for which it is appropriated has for a long time been claimed & largely exercised by the Federal Government, such grants have always been, professedly at least, under the controul of one general principle viz—that the works which might be thus aided should be "of a general not local, state national not state character."

A disregard of this distinction would of necessity involve the subversion of the Federal system. That the qualification is an unsafe one, subject to arbitrary distinctions and consequently liable to great abuses is are positions at least obvious if they have not been already confirmed by experience. It is however sufficiently certain & imperative to constrain require forbid my approbation of the Bill entitled ____. I have given to its provisions all the consideration which is was demanded as well by the a due regard to the interests of those of our fellow Citizens who have requested its passage and to the respect which is at all times due to the house & source from whence it has originated, but I have not been able to view it in any other light than as a matter of purely local concern. If it can indeed be truly ~~regarded~~ considered as a national object, it does appear to me that no further distinction between the appropriate duties of the General & State Governments in this regard need be attempted; for I find it difficult to conceive of any public improvement which may not with equal or nearly equal propriety be so called. I am therefore constrained by an imperious sense of duty to object to the passage of the bill herewith returned to you.[7]

But although I might not feel it to be my official duty, to interpose the Executive veto to ~~one~~ the passage of a bill appropriating money towards the construction, of such works as are ~~undertaken~~ authorized by the States & as are national in their character, I do not wish to be understood as expressing an opinion that it is expedient for this Government now to embark in a system of that character ~~or to do more than~~ Anxious that my constituents should be possessed of my views upon this as well as upon all other subjects which they have been pleased to commit, in part, to my discretion, I shall state them ~~briefly~~ frankly ~~but~~ and briefly. Independent of many minor considerations there are two prominent views of the subject which have made a deep impression upon my own mind—which I think are well entitled to your serious consideration, and will I hope be ~~deep~~ earnestly and maturely weighed by the people. From the official communication submitted to you it appears that if no adverse & unforeseen contingency happens in our foreign relations & no unusual diversion be made of the funds set apart for the payment of the national debt we may look with ~~entire~~ confidence to its entire extinction in the short period of fi____ years.[8]

The extent to which the realization of this pleasing anticipation is dependant upon the course to be pursued upon the particular matter now under consideration must be obvious to all & the events of the present Session are already well calculated to awaken public solicitude upon the point.[9]

The improvement of the Country by means of roads & canals is deservedly an object of much interest. Although many of the States are with a laudable zeal and under the influence of an enlightened policy successfully applying their separate efforts to objects of that character; yet the desire to enlist the aid of the General Government in the construction of such works as from their nature ought to devolve upon that Government and to which the means of the individual states are inadequate—is at once rational & patriotic. There are however time & circumstance for all things. If those wishes cannot be realized now it does not follow that ~~therefore~~ they never will be. The general intelligence and ~~known~~ public spirit of this people furnishes a sure guarantee that in good time that policy will be made to prevail, under circumstances more auspicious to its successful prosecution than those which now exist. Great however as that object undoubtedly is, it is not the only one which demands the fostering care of the Government. The preservation & success of the Republican principle ~~is in~~ rests with us~~, & to~~. To elevate its character and extend its influence deservedly ranks among our ~~first &~~ highest duties. The appropriate means to effect those desirable ends are to rivet the attachments of our Citizens to the Government of their choice by the comparative lightness of their public burthens; and to entitle it to the admiration and respect of the world by the ~~comparative~~ superior success of its operations. Although through the favour of an overruling & indulgent providence our Country is blessed with general prosperity and our Citizens are exempted from the pressure of taxation which other & less favoured portions of the human family are obliged to bear; it is nevertheless true that the taxes collected from our Citizens through the medium of imposts have for a long time been of a very onerous character. In many particulars those taxes have borne severely upon the laborious and less prosperous classes of the community by their being imposed upon the necessaries of life; and that too in cases where the pressure of their imposition was not relieved by the consciousness that their present burthens would in their ultimate effects contribute to make us independent of foreign nations for articles of prime necessity by the encouragement of their growth and manufacture at home. These taxes have been cheerfully paid because they were necessary to the support of Government and the payment of debts unavoidably incurred in the acquisition and maintainance of our national rights & liberties. But have we a right to calculate on the same cheerful acquiescence, when it is known that the necessity for their continuance would cease, were it not kept up by irregular, improvident and unequal appropriations of the public funds. By the extinction of the national debt the people would be relieved from a great portion of the taxes they now pay. Those which it would be necessary to continue for the support of Government might be so arranged as to contribute to the support and encouragement of our manufactures; still ~~in any event leaving~~ leaving I trust without oppression to any particular section of the Country a constantly accumulating surpluss ~~placed~~ fund subject to the disposition of Congress.

Should such results be ~~reali~~ effected the question as to the manner in which the Federal Government can or ought to ~~const~~ embark in the construction of roads & canals & the extent to which they will continue or impose burthens upon the people for that ~~avowed~~ purpose may be presented to them upon its own merits, free from all disguises and relieved from all embarrassments except such as spring from the Constitution. Assuming that those objects may be obtained and it appears to me neither extravagant or unreasonable to do so—will not our constituents require that the course by which alone they can be effected shall be pursued. Ought they not to require it. I have no hesitation in saying that with the ~~very~~ best disposition to aid as far as I can conscientiously do so, whatever is proposed by Congress with the sanction of their constituents, in further-

ance of works of Internal Improvement; my ~~decided~~ opinion nevertheless is, that the best and soundest views of national policy point in that
direction.[10]

But ~~if~~ its ~~inf~~ bearing upon the individual interests of our constits. is not
the only nor the most interesting view of this ~~subject~~ course. How much
deeper is the interest it would acquire from its influence upon the character of our government. What a sublime spectacle would this Republic
present to an admiring world; if, superadded to a comfortable & happy
population of ____ millions who are surpassed by none that the sun shines
upon in any great & good quality—to resources almost unlimited—to
political institutions which secure the greatest degree of liberty that society can endure & which require only to be honestly used to hand down
to posterity the blessings they confer on the present generation She could
also exhibit the unprecedented example of a nation in the 54th. year of
existence as a free people, after having passed through two protracted &
onerous wars with a great & powerful people   The one for the acquisition of its liberties & the other for the maintenance of its rights—without
a national debt & with all its immense resources ~~of the in the hands of its~~
~~citizens subject to~~ at free & unfettered disposal of its government. What a
salutary influence would not such a ~~spectacle~~ exhibition exercise ~~in~~ on the
course of liberal principles & free Governments throughout the world—
what encouragement would it not give to our sister Republics of this
Hemisphere ~~who are now~~ engaged ~~in~~ as they are in an apparently hopeless
struggle to acquire the proud eminence which we occupy. ~~What a contrast~~
~~between results like these~~ What Is it probable that our constituents, will,
when the question is fairly honestly & plainly put to them, hesitate in
their choice—between the realization of results like these and the possibility of its failure by ~~the~~ a continuance ~~in the~~ of a mortifying not to
say disreputable scramble for detached appropriations ~~which are~~ without
reference to any general system—the good effects of which must of necessity be very limited—~~& which~~ which are too often resorted to as successful expedients to shift from individuals upon the Government the losses
of unsuccessful private speculations & ~~which are~~ not unfrequently ~~made~~
urged for no other purpose than to minister to personal ambition—~~& in~~
~~every case thus having a direct~~ thus tending to sap the foundations of our
government and to taint its administration with a demoralizing & corrupting influence.

~~Next~~ An other interesting view of the subject and the only remaining
one which it is ~~at this~~ my intention to present to you at this time is that
which involves the expediency of ~~the Government~~ embarking in a entering
upon a system of Internal improvements without a previous amendment of
the Constitution explaining and defining the precise powers of the Federal
Government over the subject. Assuming ~~that~~ the right to appropriate
money to objects of national concern to be either warranted by the original text or to ~~have~~ result from cotemporaneous and continued exposition

& acquiescence, its ~~uncertain~~ insufficiency for a successful prosecution of the object in view must be admitted by all candid men. If it be sustained on the ground of usage that will be found so variant—embracing so much which has been successfully overruled & would not now be sustained, as to involve the whole subject in the most painful uncertainty & to render the execution of our ~~offic~~ respective duties replete with ~~much~~ difficulties and embarrassments. The general principle that the right to appropriate ~~has~~ is not restricted by the right to carry into complete effect has as we have seen been extensively acquiesced in. It is in regard to ~~Internal~~ public improvements & the acquisition of additional Territory that this practice has obtained its first footing. ~~The~~ In most if not all other disputed questions as to appropriation the construction of the Constitution may be regarded as an open if the right to apply money in the enumerated cases is placed on the ground of usage.

This subject has been one of much and I may add to me painful reflection. It ~~possesses an interest~~ has bearings which cannot fail to exert a most powerful influence upon our hitherto prosperous system of Government. It is one of the [only] matters which can ever on public account excite despondency in the breast of an American Citizen. I will not detain you with professions of zeal in the cause of Internal Improvements. If to be their friend~~ly to them~~ is a virtue which deserves particular commendation, our country is ~~rich in such~~ blessed by an abundance of that sentiment for I do not believe that there is ~~not~~ a sane man in the nation who does not wish to see them flourish. But although all are in favor of Internal Improvements—all, are not I trust regardless of the means by which they are promoted. ~~On~~ There are on the contrary I trust but few so degenerate as to desire even ~~that~~ so great a good if it is to be obtained by a violation of that sacred instrument upon the preservation of which rests our countries hopes. If the ~~hopes of the~~ expectations ~~of any rest on~~ are ~~found~~ entertained in any quarters upon a different result—if it is believed that the people of this country reckless of their constitutional obligations & prefering their interest to principle will go for the former regardless of the latter—such expectations will in the end be wofully disappointed. If it be not so—then indeed has the world but little to hope from the cause of free Governments. If an honest observance of a constitutional compact cannot be obtained from communities like ours, it cannot be expected any where; and the cause in which there has been so much martyrdom & from which so much has been expected must be abandoned. The degrading truth that man is unfit for ~~free g~~ self government admitted, & the management of public affairs surrendered to those who claim authority beyond the ~~popular~~ will of the people. But I entertain no such apprehensions. If it is the wish of the people the construction of roads & canals within the States should be ~~undertaken~~ conducted by ~~this Govern~~ the Federal Government it is not only ~~necessa~~ highly expedient but indispensably necessary that a previous amendment of the constitution confering upon it the necessary power, & restricting & defining its exercise with reference to ~~security~~ the sovereignty of the States should be previously made. ~~That without~~ Supposing an occasional disregard of the Constitution nothing extensively useful can be effected without it. The right to exercise as much jurisdiction, ~~at least~~ as much as is necessary to preserve ~~it~~ the works & to raise funds by the collection of tolls for keeping ~~it~~ them in repair cannot be dispensed with. The Cumberland road is a perpetual and should be an instructive ~~lesson~~ admonition of the consequences of acting without it. ~~No general system~~ Whilst one Congress may claim and exercise the power their successor may deny it & the ~~unavoidable~~ consequence of such a fluctuation of opinion must ~~be~~ unavoidably be fatal to any scheme which ~~could be~~ from its extent & ~~character~~ nature would promote the interests & elevate the character of the Country. The experience of the past has shewn that the opinions of respective Congresses are subject to such fluctuations.

If it be the ~~opin~~ desire of the people that the agency of the Federal Government should be confined to the appropriation of money in aid of works undertaken in virtue of state authorities then the occasion—the manner & the extent of such appropriations should be made the subject of constitutional regulation. It is necessary that this should be so to make them equal & therefore equitable among the States[11]—to preserve other parts of the Constitution from being undermined by the exercise of doubtful powers or the too great extension of those which are not so & to protect the whole subject against the debauchery & deleterious influence of combinations to carry, through concert, measures which ~~regarded~~ considered by themselves would meet with but little countenance.

That a constitutional adjustment of this ~~subject~~ whole matter upon equitable principles is in the highest degree desirable must be admitted & it cannot fail to be promoted by every sincere friend to the success & permanency of our political institutions. In no government in the world are appeals to the source of power in cases of real doubt more suitable than ours. What good motive can be assigned for the exercise ~~of a pol~~ of power by the constituted authorities while those for whose benefit it is to be exercised have not given & are not now willing to give. It would seem to me that an honest & successful application of the conceded powers of the Government to the ~~Internal~~ advancement of the general weal ~~affords~~ presents a sufficient scope to satisfy ~~the~~ a reasonable ambition ~~of any reasonable~~. The difficulty and ~~by some~~ supposed impracticability of obtaining an amendment in this respect is I firmly believe in a great degree unfounded in fact. I do not so understand the character of the american people. The time has never yet been when their intelligence & patriotism were not fully equal to the exigencies of the case & it never will whenever the subject matter calling for their interposition ~~shall~~ is plainly & honestly presented to them. To do so in this regard & to urge them to an early zealous & full consideration of its deep importance ran[ks] in my estimating among the ~~most acceptable~~ highest of ~~the~~ our public duties ~~the duties which can rest upon any good Citizen~~.

The strong desire of those more immediately interested in the success of local appropriations has given rise to suggestions which I have heard with regret. I allude to ~~the~~ a supposed connection between appropriations for Internal Improvements and the system of ~~protecting~~ duties for national defence, and the arrangement of our domestic labor. My opinions upon the latter subject have been at all times freely communicated to those who had a right to know them. That ~~my views of public duty~~ they have ~~in this respect brought me in collision of sentiment with~~ frequently placed me in opposition not only to individuals, but ~~with~~ to whole communities, in whose patriotism I have unlimited confidence, and ~~whose~~ have the strongest claims upon my esteem and gratitude has been to me a source of deep regret; but I trust that there has not been any thing in my public course which has exposed me to the ~~degrading~~ suspicion of being thought capable of sacraficing my views of public duty to personal considerations.

~~The encouragement of domestic~~ manufactures by means of protecting duties has received, and, as long as it is directed to national ends & supported on public grounds, it shall receive from me a temperate but steady support. I do not however ~~see any necessary~~ see ~~such~~ the connexion between ~~them as~~ the two systems which is suggested. It appears to me on the contrary that the supposition of their mutual dependence ~~and the~~ is ~~well~~ calculated to bring the protecting system into ~~disre~~ public disfavour. The grounds on which it has hitherto been sustained by its advocates ~~has~~ are—that it is not inconsistent with the letter or spirit of the Constitution— that its origin is to be traced to the assent of all the parties to the original compact, and that having the support and approbation of a majority of the people it is at least entitled to a fair and full experiment. The suggestions of which I speak refer to a forced continuance of the national debt by means of large & exhausting appropriates of the funds of the nation as a substitution for the security which the system derives from the principles upon which it has hitherto been sustained. ~~Could~~ Would not such a course be justly construed to indicate either an unreasonable distrust of the people or a consciousness that the system does not possess sufficient soundness for its own support? ~~Is there not reason to suppose~~ must not its claim upon public confidence ~~would of nece~~ be ~~greatly~~ unavoidably diminished by thus descending from the high ground of principle ~~to for~~ to an expedient which would speaks as plainly as language could speak, the belief of its friends, that the system is not safe when it rests upon the voluntary choice of the people. Those who believe that any policy can be long sustained in this country which is not so founded have been unprofitable observers of events. If the majority of the people should think it wise and just to ~~sustain the~~ foster their own labour, by protecting ~~system~~ duties after the national debt is paid they will not be at a loss for the means—if they should think differently no devices however spurious will induce them to do so.

AD, DLC (76).

1. In the final text, AJ's first insertion below, quoting his annual message, precedes the next paragraph.

2. Quoted, not quite exactly, from James Madison's December 1799 report to the Virginia legislature on state and federal powers (*Madison Papers*, 17:315).

3. The Cumberland Road passed through parts of Maryland, Pennsylvania, and Virginia. The three legislatures had given formal consent to its construction.

4. The final text fills these blanks with "twenty-three" and "upward of $2,500,000." The accompanying Treasury table showed twenty-one Cumberland Road appropriations from 1806 through 1829, totaling $2,620,243.60.

5. Quoted from Madison's veto of the "Bonus Bill" to fund internal improvements, March 3, 1817 (Richardson, 1:584–85).

6. Quoted from Monroe's May 4, 1822, message on internal improvements, supplementing his veto of a bill to erect tollgates on the Cumberland Road (Richardson, 2:173).

7. In the final text, AJ's second insertion below, concerning national and local improvements, precedes the next paragraph.

8. The final text fills this blank with "four."

9. In the final text, a section protesting excessive appropriations and referring to the Treasury statements, derived from AJ's draft below, is inserted here.

10. The final text replaces this paragraph with wording based on AJ's fourth insertion below.

11. In Donelson's version of this sentence, which closely followed Van Buren's, AJ at this point inserted "that harmony & kind feeling may be preserved between members representing different sections of the country." In final form the sentence reads: "This is the more necessary in order that they may be equitable among the several States, promote harmony between different sections of the Union and their representatives, preserve other parts of the Constitution from being undermined by the exercise of doubtful powers or the too great extension of those which are not so, and protect the whole subject against the deleterious influence of combinations to carry by concert measures which, considered by themselves, might meet but little countenance" (Richardson, 2:492).

Draft insertions by Andrew Jackson

[The second version of this passage was inserted nearly verbatim into the final text of the message, between the second and third paragraphs of the Van Buren draft (Richardson, 2:483–84).]

In the message which was presented to the consideration of Congress at the opening of its present Session, I endeavoured to present the views which I entertained upon this important and highly interesting subject; that the Representatives of the people might consider, after what mode, a system could be resorted to, calculated to reconcile the diversity of opinion which prevailed. In that message the following sentiments will be found "After the extinction of the public debt &c &c" insert that, & its following paragraph—

I again repeat, that a Subject so full of embarrassment, should not be confided to accident and chance. If an appropriation is obtained one year, for purposes of improvement; a succeeding congress may determine the purpose to be local, not general & national, & refuse to carry it on. uniting with corporations cannot vary or ~~improve~~ render the subject matter under consideration national: it will still be open to the enquiry whether it be so or not. If to be associated with a corporation can create a difference & authorise an appropriation, then there is nothing to prevent the Govt. from connecting itself with every local incorporated institution in every state of the union to be made liable and answerable for the acts, thereby extending the patronage ~~of~~ & influence of the General govt., to the ultimate destruction of the independence & sovereignty of the states—

√ first sheet 2nd page

In the message, which was presented to congress at the opening of its present session, I endeavoured to exhibit briefly my views, upon the important and highly interesting subject, to which our attention is now to be directed. I was desirous of presenting to the Representatives of the several states in congress assembled, the enquiry whether some mode could not be devised, which would reconcile the diversity of opinion concerning the powers of this government over the subject of internal improvement, and the manner in which those powers, if conferred by the constitution, ought to be exercised—the act which I am called upon to consider, has therefore been passed with a knowledge of my views on this question, as these are expressed in the message referred to—In that document, the following suggestions will be found

"After the extinction of the public debt, it is not probable that any adjustment of the tariff, upon principles satisfactory to the people of the union, will, until a remote period, if ever, leave the Government without a considerable surplus in the Treasury, beyond what may be required for its current service. As then the period approaches when the application of the revenue to the payment of debt will cease, the disposition of the surplus will present a subject for the serious deliberation of Congress; and it may be fortunate for the country that it is yet to be decided. Considered in connection with the dificulties which have heretofore attended appropriations for purposes of internal improvement; and with those which this experience tells us will certainly arise, whenever power over such subjects may be exercised by the General government; it is hoped that it may lead to the adoption of some plan which will reconcile the diversified interests of the states, and strengthen the bonds which unite them. Every member of the union, in peace & in war, will be benefitted by the improvement of inland navigation, and the construction of highways in the several states. Let us then endeavour to attain this benefit in a mode which will be satisfactory to all. That hitherto adopted has by many of our fellow citizens, been deprecated as an infraction of the constitution, while by others it has been viewed as inexpedient. All feel that it has been employed at the expense of harmony in the legislative councils." And adverting for the constitutional power of Congress, to make what I considered a safe, just and federal disposition of the surplus revenue, I subjoined the following remarks. "To avoid these evils, it appears to me that the most safe, just, and federal disposition which could be made of the surplus revenue, would be its apportionment among the several states according to their rates of representation; and should this measure not be found warranted by the constitution that it would be expedient to propose to the states an amendment authorising it"

[page torn] "watchful and auxiliary operations of the state authorities. This is not, the re-

AD, DLC (76). The quotations were from AJ's first annual message to Congress of December 8, 1829 (Richardson, 2:451–52). The last page of the manuscript is torn off near the top, just below "authorising it"; the final fragment of text, which comes from further down in the annual message, survives on the reverse. This passage as inserted into the veto message ends at the point of the page tear, suggesting that AJ wrote out a longer excerpt from his annual message, then tore off the part he decided not to use.

[This paragraph was inserted nearly verbatim in the final text (Richardson, 2:487–88).]

5th. Sheet, 2 page

¶Considering the magnitude & importance of the power, and dificulties, and embarrassments to which, from the very nature of the thing, its exercise must necessarily be subjected, the real friends of internal improvement ought not to be willing to confide it to accident and chance—What is properly *national* in its character or otherwise, is an enquiry, which is often extremely dificult of solution—The appropriations of one year for an object which is considered national may be rendered nugatory by the refusal of a succeeding congress to continue the work, on the ground that it is local. No aid can be derived from the intervention of Corporations. The question regards the character of the work to be done, not that of those by whom it is to be accomplished—notwithstanding the union of the Government with the corporation by whose immediate agency any work of internal improvement is carried on, the enquiry will still remain, is it national and condusive to the benefit of the whole—or *local* and operating only to the advantage of a portion of the union.

AD, DLC (76).

[These drafts remarked upon the Treasury statements that accompanied the message. Some of Jackson's figures here adjust the Treasury numbers to reckon in the effect of an Act reducing import duties on coffee, tea, and cocoa, which Jackson had signed into law on May 20. A passage of this general tenor, referring to the Treasury statements but without citing specific numbers, was inserted into the final text about midway through (Richardson, 2:488–89).]

From the statement derived from the secretary of the senate

From the statement of the Secretary of the Senate corrected by the Secretary of the Treasury hereto appended and marked A. it appears, that from acts published to the 21rst. of May 1830—and the report of bills pending on amendments between the two houses & bills pending which will probably pass there are an estimated deficiency in the Treasury of $73,378—which added to the reduction of the revenue on coffee & cocoa estimated at $708,240.98 will make an agregate deficiency of $781,588— and when we take into view the appropriations contained in bills that have passed the Senate & are now pending in the House of Representatives of $1,275,201 and the appropriation in bills that have passed the House of Representatives and are now pending in the Senate of $376,685 and of appropriations in bills in the Senate which have not as yet passed that body of $5,734,127——and of the appropriations in Bills of the House of Representatives still pending in that House of $2,085,271 we have an agregate of $9,471.284, to add to the other deficiency in the Treasury which if they bill do not pass this session, if we are to judge from the present appearances of the sentiments entertained by a majority in congress will pass next Session and which must be provided for by a system of direct taxes, or suspend the payment of the national debt—It is therefore proper that these things should be placed before the people and let them be the judge whether a system of internal improvement should not first be well organised and adopted before it is entered and the national debt be first paid The national debts should be first paid before and a System of internal improvement be first well organised and adopted before they shall be burthened with such onerous taxes as the present plans if presisted in must load them with—

From the Statement of the Register of the Treasury, together with those from the clerk of the House & Secretary of the Senate hereto annexed, & marked A. B. C &c shews that the bills which have passed into laws, & those which in all probability will pass after the 20th instant, added to the reduction of decrease of the revenue which will accrue from the decrease reduction of duties on coffee & cocoa, will overrun the available amount in the Treasury for the year 1830 the sum of $781,588.79.

From the foregoing it appears whilst we are reducing the revenue on the one hand, by appropr on the other by appropriations for internal improvements, we have exausted the Treasury, overrun its available funds the above sum of $781.588.79 whilst the bills pending before the two houses if passed, & become laws will augment that sum to upwards of ten millions of dollars which will have to be provided for by direct taxes, or leave the national debt unpaid. *The national Debt must be paid.*

[*Endorsed by AJ:*] memorandum on the appropriations exceeding the available amount in the Treasury $73,328 amt over the sum available & $708,240.98—The sum reduced by reduction on coffee & cocoa—

781,568.98	1 633,910
9,471,228.84	1 560,532
10,252,797.72	73,378

AD, DLC (76).

[This text replaced earlier wording in the Van Buren and Donelson drafts. The final version closely followed Jackson's (Richardson, 2:490).]

Strike, page 15 out, & insert—
Under this view, the question as to the Manner in which the Fed. Govt. can or ought to embark in the construction of roads & canals, & the extent to which demands upon the people shall be made for these purposes may be presented upon its own merits, free of all disguise and of every embarrassment except such as may arise from the constitution itself. assuming these suggestions to be correct, will not our constituents require the observance of a course by which they can be effected¿ ought they not to require it. with the best disposition as far as I can conscientiously, to aid in furtherance of works of internal improvement, my opinion is, that the soundest views of national policy at this time point to such a course. In it much benefit is diserned. Besides &c—see page 16

AD, DLC (76).

[Van Buren's draft lacked a closing. The final text of the message reduces this draft conclusion by Jackson to a one-sentence paragraph: "In presenting these opinions I have spoken with the freedom and candor which I thought the occasion for their expression called for, and now respectfully return the bill which has been under consideration for your further deliberation and judgment" (Richardson, 2:493).]

In presenting these opinions I have spoken freely & frankly, it is due to myself that I should do so. of what avail is it, to pursue any other course, and by a sacrafice or concealment to obtain the approbation of those who may entertain a belief, that the constitution is broad anough to cover any & every expenditure of public money. While the approbation of my fellow citizens will be always ~~pleasing~~ gratifying to me, it can only be so, when obtained without the sacrafice of principle, or the best interest of my country.
My earnest desire is that the country in which I have lived & in which I shall die, which secures to every man freedom in its broadest sense of right, may avoid every thing that may lead to consolidation and proceed on prosperous & flourishing, that posterity may come to the glorious inheritance which our forefathers procured by their blood & privations, and bequeathed to us. These results, are only to be obtained, by adhering

strickly to the land marks & principles of the constitution, as by *the states*, they have been established. The sages who formed ~~our constitution~~ it viewed it, as one of experiment & provided for its amendment; if therefore at any time it is conceived that the powers granted are too limited, apply to the people, and they will if they so think, enlarge, them, if too enlarged they will limit them; These alterations ~~being~~ if believed by them to be for their prosperity they will not refuse to grant ~~the application~~ where they believe the object is proper. But to preserve in safety the benefits now enjoyed, every thing of forced construction, and usurpation must be avoided, for when once commenced, it will be dificult to say, or even conjecture, where they may end, or what evil consequences may not arise from them, to disturb the future repose of our happy country. Encroachments and power, always move onward, they never voluntarily retreat; and once advanced position being gained, will be relied on as a mean of succeeding to the possession of another, & stronger one, until the definite partition of powers between the landmarks of the general & state governments, would be entirely destroyed by the extension of the constructive powers of congress—Therefore ~~I~~ have I witheld my signature from the bill, not doubting, but the beneficial objects will be obtained by a resort for the necessary powers, to the states and to the people, who never will withold powers, when to be exercised, for their prosperity & happiness.

Andrew Jackson

ADS, DLC (76).

To John Overton

Washington
May 27th. 1830—

My Dr Sir

I enclose you my objections to the Maysville &c & bill, which I this day returned to the House without my approval—read it with attention and give me your Frank opinion on this important subject—all important, as my judgment told me to the perpepuation of our happy Government. ~~This~~ Such system must destroy it.

This morning we received advises from England, but our negotiation on the West India trade not finally closed, but all concerned admitted that it would be, on the principles held out to us in 1825—by which we are to be placed on the same footing as all other foreign nations &c &c—we have also this morning recd a Treaty concluded with Denmark, in which is stipulated *at last, payment*, for the spoliations for our commerce by which $ we have obtained $150,000, more than our merchants had agreed to accept as full indemnity—the sum to be paid being *$650,000* $500,000 haveing been offered by our merchants to have been recd. in full[1]—Kendal has sent up his report today in Kings case, and in the Navy agent Randolph who succeeded Mr Timberlake—These will disclose the villany of these two men, attempted to be screened by Tazwell & Tyler—the will be published tomorrow—[2]

I have had the pleasure to receive your letter of the 10th from Louisville Ky. and trust in a kind providence that you have reached yr family in safety & health[.] in haste yr friend

Andrew Jackson

ALS, THi (15-1162).

1. By a convention signed at Copenhagen on March 28, Denmark agreed to pay the U.S. $650,000 to satisfy damage claims for Danish spoliations on American commerce during the Napoleonic Wars. AJ submitted the convention to the Senate this day (Richardson, 2:481–82). The Senate approved it unanimously on May 29, and AJ ratified it on June 2 and proclaimed it June 5.

2. On this day, Navy secretary Branch sent to the House fourth auditor Kendall's reports on the accounts of Miles King (HRDoc 115, 21st Cong., 1st sess., Serial 198) and on those of John B. Timberlake and Robert Beverley Randolph (1790–1869), suggesting fraud by King and Randolph (HRDoc 116, 21st Cong., 1st sess., Serial 198).

From John Rowan

Sir

The rejection of Colo. Rector by the Senate took place in the absence of Mr McClane and myself—we were both confind to our rooms by illness— Had we been present his nomination woud have been confirmd—I believe that if he were again placd before the Senate—his nomination woud be confirmd—and shoud therefore be ~~gratified~~ pleasd. if he coud. be again nominated[.] I have the honor to be yr obt

J Rowan

ALS, DNA-RG 46 (15-1165). Senate Executive Proceedings, 4:113; Richardson, 2:482. On May 20, the Senate had rejected AJ's nomination of Wharton Rector for agent to the Shawnees and Delawares by 23 to 21. Rowan of Kentucky and John McLean (1791–1830) of Illinois were absent. AJ renominated Rector on May 28, appending this note. He was again rejected on May 29 by 21 to 20, Rowan and McLean voting to confirm.

From Robert Young Hayne

(Confidential)
Friday Morning.

My Dear Sir,

Well grounded apprehensions of exposing the health of my Wife & children to great danger, by longer delaying my departure for the South, compel me leave Washington today and I regret that I am unable to do myself the pleasure of waiting upon you to take my leave. I have delayed my departure more than a week, and to the very latest moment, & even now, I would not have left the City, if it had not been in my power *to take one of our political opponents off with me.* I am gratified to be able to add that by taking the Steam Boat *today,* I shall be in Norfolk tomorrow, & will be able along the whole route to give the public mind a favorable direction with regard to the *Maysville road* which I assure you I shall do with *the utmost pleasure.* With my best wishes for the triumphant success of your administration, & your personal welfare believe me to be very truly yours

Rob. Y. Hayne

P.S. My brother will be here, as you will hear from him *in a few days.*

ALS, DLC (38). Hayne's wife was Rebecca Brewton Alston Hayne (1792–1853).

From James Porter

Philadelphia Prison
May 28th. 1830.

To his Excellency The President of the United States of America

The Petition of James Porter respectfully shows
That he has been convicted in the Circuit Court of the United States for the Eastern District of Pennsylvania of the offence of robbing the mail by the use of deadly weapons, and he has received the awful sentence of death. Under the deepest impressions of his unhappy and almost hopeless situation, he turns to your Excellency with a prayer that he may yet be saved from the extreme vengeance of the law. Your Petitioner will not arraign the justice of his sentence. He has been found guilty by an impartial tribunal, and he yields to the decree. But he ventures to hope that he is not without claims to mercy. The offence charged, though heinous in the Eye of God and Man, was still free from blood shed. Your Petitioner is young, and anxiously prays for a continuance of life, that he may amend it, and expiate by future good conduct, his past irregularities. He has a wife who throws herself at the feet of your Excellency, and an infant that will one day bless you. He is under conviction for another offence, which will afford ample opportunity to inflict a proportioned punishment without depriving him of life. He trusts that the laws will be considered as sufficiently vindicated by his present suffering and future imprisonment,

and he prays that a pardon may be granted to him of that portion of the charge which is punishable with death.

James Porter

[Endorsed by AJ:] Petition for the pardon of Porter—Mail Rober—P.a.

DS, DNA-RG 59 (15-1189). Notes appended to Porter's petition showed that if pardoned the capital offense, he was still liable to serve 90 years on lesser federal and state charges of robbing the mail and the passengers on the stage. On June 3 AJ declined to act until a warrant for execution had been issued (below).

To Robert Minns Burton

(Private)

Washington May 29th. 1830

My Dr. Sir

An apology is due to you for my neglect to answer your letter of Novbr. received in last Decbr. It is due to myself to state, that I thought I had answered it when recd. and so I thought, until yesterday when my son in looking over my letters, informed me your letter remained unanswered. This I sincerely regret, but the truth is, that at the time I received it, I was surrounded with business, & circumstances, that absorbed all my attention, & time and the subject in part which it embraced, occasioned tears to flow, which will never cease to flow, for departed worth, which threw my mind at the time into such a state, that I could not answer, and the croud of business, & other circumstances, I forgot it until brought to my view yesterday. The circumstances I alude to are, the secrete & wicked combination to destroy Eaton for political effect, by which, it was expected to injure me for having taken Major Eaton into my Cabinet, than whom, a more correct, & faithful agent, & honest man, does not exist; in him I have a faithful friend & the Government a talented honest & faithful agent—

Congress will rise on Monday next, the report of the Secretary of the Navy and my return of the Maysville bill with my objections have given rise to some animated debates in congress—The report will give you some idea of the wicked & secrete course adopted to injure Major Eaton—My objections to the Maysville &c &c Turnpike company bill you will see in The Tellegraph of yesterday, when you read, give me you opinion of it[1]

Surrounded as I am, I must defer, until Congress rises, a full answer to your letter—your views are correct, but before your friends application reached me, there was such a *scuffle* for the office, from others that I decided to give it to him, who was the most needy, who was capable, and who, had the least patronage, and required something to aid him into life. These motives have always governed me thro life—I think them correct.

I will rejoice to see you here. I am told Genl Desha intends retiring from public life—Present me to your Dr. Martha & two sweet little ones and to Elizabeth, & present them with my blessing   say to My Dr Martha, when she passes the Hermitage to call & see the garden, and you & her to pertake of its altered, but still, friendly hospitality—[2]

How my mind is pained on hearing of the course of Severn—I fear he is past recovery, gone to destruction by drink how melancholy the reflection—when you, present me to him & Jacob and their families—I have a hope to reach the Hermitage this Summer but is but a hope—should I I will endeavour to see you & your family—in haste yr friend

Andrew Jackson

P.S. present us respectfully to Mr Curothers his lady & family, & Major Donelson Emily, Mary Easton & son desires to be presented to you & yours & to them affectionately[3]

A J.

ALS, CtY (15-1201). Burton (1800–1843) was a Lebanon, Tenn., lawyer.

1. Kendall's report on John B. Timberlake's accounts, sent by Branch to the House on May 27, suggested the existence of a plot to smear Eaton (*HRDoc* 116, 21st Cong., 1st sess., Serial 198).

2. Tennessee congressman Robert Desha did not stand for reelection. Burton had married Martha H. Donelson (1809–1873), daughter of Rachel Jackson's brother William Donelson (1758–1820). Their children were Elizabeth Charity Burton (b. 1827) and William Donelson Burton (b. 1829). "Elizabeth" may have been Martha's sister Elizabeth Hays Donelson (1819–1850). Severn and Jacob Donelson were Martha's brothers.

3. Robert Looney Caruthers (1800–1882) was a lawyer residing in Lebanon. He married Sarah Saunders (b. 1806) in 1827.

To James Alexander Hamilton

(private)

May 29th. 1830—

My Dr Sir

I have just recd. your letter of the 26th. and have duly noted its contents —Mr Forsythe has handed to me the letter without address. Why this is so, I cannot say, time will unravel all things—

I advised you in my last, that the moment I recd. from Mr. Forsythe Mr Crawfords letter, I addressed a note enclosing a copy to Mr Calhoun of that letter, & asking, after extracting from several letters from him to me approving *all* my proceedings, on the Seminole campaighn, *if this could be so*—Mr Calhoun has acknowledged the receipt of this note & has promised a reply, *so soon as his leisure will permit*—when his answer is recd. I will have it in my power to form a just opinion upon this case—

I have had the fullest confidence in Mr Calhoun's frankness, honor, & integrity—but should he not be able to clear up satisfactorously the conduct charged against him you can easily judge without my expressing, the feelings & opinions, I am forced, from his conduct, to form of him. I have never abandoned a friend, without being forced to do so, from his own course to me—and I never break with one, without giving him a fair opportunity, first, to explain. In pursuing this course, the moment I had any thing tangible, with my usual frankness, I addressed him—you shall in due time see the correspondence—but it is due to him, & to justice, to give him time to explain—*he shall have it*—but I am afraid, he is in a dilemma, how he will get out, I wait for him to shew.

you will see by the papers of yesterday, my reasons assigned for withholding my approbation from the Maysville &c &c & *bill for the subscription of stock*—I am told, it raised some excitement—They reports of Kendall & the sec. of the Treasury, created a great deal; and much; philippic, & heat, in debate—for *all*, I refer you to the papers

I will thank you for your criticism on Mr McDuffies report on the Bank—

Present me affectionately to your amiable lady & family & believe yr friend, *in great haste*

Andrew Jackson

ALS, NN (15-1205).

From John Caldwell Calhoun

Washington
29th. May 1830

Sir,

In answering your letter of the 13th Inst. I wish to be distinctly understood that however high my respect is, for your personal character, and the ~~high~~ exalted station, which you occupy, I cannot recognize the right on your part to call in question my conduct on the interesting occasion, to which your letter refers. I acted on that occasion in the discharge of a high official duty, and under responsibility to my conscience and my country only. In replying, then, to your letter, I do not place myself in the attitude of apologyzing for the part, I may have acted, or of palliating my conduct on the accusations of Mr Crawford. My course, I trust, requires no apology, and, if it did, I have too much self respect, to make it to any one, in a case touching the discharge of my official conduct. I stand on very different ground. I embrace the opportunity, which your letter offers, not for the purpose of making excuses, but as a suitable occasion, to place my conduct, in relation to an interesting publick transaction, in its proper light; and I am gratified, that Mr Crawford, tho far from intending me a kindness, has afforded me such an opportunity.

In undertaking to place my conduct in its proper light, I deem it proper to premise, that it is very far from my intention to defend mine, by impeaching yours. Where we have differed, I have no doubt, but that we differed honestly, and, in claimg to act on honorable and patriotick motives myself, I cheerfully accord the same to you.

I know not, that I correctly understand your meaning, but after a careful perusal, I would infer from your letter, that you have learned for the first time, from Mr Crawfords letter, that you and I placed different constructions on the orders, under which you acted in the Seminole War; and that you had been lead to believe previously, by my letters to yourself and Governor Bibb, that I concurred with you in thinking, that your orders were intended to authorise your attacks on the Spanish posts in Florida. Under these impressions, you would seem to impute to me, some degree of duplicity, or at least concealment, which required, on my part, explanation. I hope, that my conception of your meaning is erroneous, but, if it be not, and your meaning be such, as I suppose, I must be permitted to express my surprize, at the misapprehension, which I feel confident, that it will be in my power to correct, by the most dicisive proof drawn from the publick documents, and the correspondence between Mr Monroe and yourself, growing out of the dicision of the Cabinet on the Seminole affair, and which passed through my hands at the time, and which I now have his permission to use, as explanatory of my opinion, as well as his, and the other members of his administration. To save you the trouble of turning to the file of your correspondence, I have enclosed extracts from the letters, which clearly prove that the dicision of the Cabinet on the point, that your orders did not authorise the occupation of St. Marks and Pansacola, was early and fully made known to you, and that I, in particular concurred in the dicision.

Mr. Monroe's letter of the 19th July 1818, the first of the series, and written immediately after the dicision of the Cabinet, and from which, I have given a copious extract, enters fully into the views taken by the Executive of the whole subject. In your reply of the 19th August 1818, you object to the construction of which the administration had placed on your orders, and you assign your reasons at large, why you conceived, that the orders under which you acted authorised your operations in Florida. Mr Monroe replied on the 20th Octr. 1818, and after expressing his regret, that you had placed a construction on your orders different, from what was intended, he invited you to open a correspondence with me, in order, that your conception of the meaning of your orders, and that of the administration, might be placed, with the reasons on both sides, on the files of the War Department. Your letter of the 15th. Novr. in answer, agrees to a the correspondence, as proposed, but declines commencing it, to which Mr Monroe replied, by a letter of the 21st December, stating his reasons, for suggesting the correspondence, and why, he thought, that it ought to commence with you. To these I have added an extract from your letter of the 7th December; approving of Mr. Monroe's message, at the opening of Congress, which, tho' not constituting a part of the correspondence, from which I have extracted so copiously, is intimately connected with the subject under consideration.[1]

But it was not by private correspondence only, that the view, which the Executive took of your orders, was made known. In his Message to the House of Representatives of the 25th March 1818, long before information of the result of your operation in Florida was received, Mr. Monroe states, that "orders had been given to the General in command not to enter Florida, unless it be in pursuit of the enemy, and, in that case, to respect the Spanish Authority, wherever it may be maintained; and he will be instructed to withdraw his forces from the Province, as soon, as he has reduced that tribe (the Seminoles) to order, and secured our fellow citizens, in that quarter, by satisfactory arrangements against its unprovoked and savage hostilities in future."[2]

In his annual Message, at the opening of the session of Congress in Novr. of the same year, the President speaking of your entering Florida says, "In authorising Majr. Genl. Jackson to enter Florida, in pursuit of the Seminoles, care was taken not to encroach on the rights of Spain;" Again "in entering Florida, to suppress this combination, no idea was entertained of hostility to Spain, and, however justifiable the commanding General was, in consequence of the misconduct of the Spanish officers, in entering St. Marks and Pansacola to terminate it, by proving to the Savages and their associates, that they could not be protected even there, yet the amicable relations between the U. States and Spain could not be altered by that act alone. By ordering the restitution of those posts, those relations were preserved. To a change of them the power of the executive is deemed incompetent. It is vested in Congress alone."[3] The view taken of this subject met your entire approbation, as appears from the extract of your letter of 7th December 1818, above referred to.

After such full and decisive proof, as it seems to me, of the view of the executive, I had a right, as I supposed, to conclude, that you long since knew, that the administration, and myself in particular, were of the opinion, that the orders under which you acted, did not authorise you to occupy the Spanish posts, but I now infer from your letter, to which this is an answer, that such conclusion was erroneous, and that you were of the impression, till you received Mr Crawford's letter, that I concurred in the opposite construction, which you gave to your orders, that they were intended to authorise you to occupy the posts. You rely for this impression, as I understand you, on certain general expressions in my letter to Govr. Bibb of Alabama of the 13th May 1818, in which I state, that "General Jackson is vested with full powers to conduct the war in the manner, he shall judge best;" and also in my letter of the 6th Feb.

1818 in answer to yours of the 20th January of the same year, in which I acquainted you "with the entire approbation of the President of all of the measures you had adopted to terminate the rupture with the Seminole Indians."

I will not reason the point, that a letter to Govr. Bibb, which was not communicated to you, which bears date long after you had occupied St Marks, and subsequent to the time you had determined to occupy Pansacola, (see your letter of the 2d June 1818 to me, published with the Seminole documents) could give you authority to occupy those posts.[4] I know, that in quoting the letters, you could not intend such an absurdity, and I must therefore conclude, ~~that~~ it was your intention, by the extract, to show, that at the time of writing the letter, it was my opinion, that the orders under, which you did act, were intended to authorise the occupation of the Spanish posts. Nothing could have been more remote from my intention in writing the letter. It would have been in opposition ~~of~~ to the view, which I have always taken of your orders, and in direct contradiction to the President's message of the 25th of March 1818, communicated but a few weeks before to the House of Representatives, (already referred to), and which gives a directly opposite construction to your orders. In fact, the letter on its face proves, that it was not the intention of the Government to occupy the Spanish posts. By refering to it, you will see, that I enclosed to the Governor a copy of my ~~other~~ order to Genl. Gains of the 16th Decr. 1817, authorising him to cross the Spanish line and to attack the Indians within the limits of Florida, unless they should take shelter under a Spanish post, in which event, he was directed to report immediately to the Department, which order Governor Bibb was directed to consider, as his authority, for carring the war into Florida, thus clearly establishing the fact, that the order was considered still in force, and not superceded by that to you, directing you to assume the command in the Seminole war.[5]

Nor can my letter of the 6th Feb, be, by any sound rule of construction, interpreted into an authority to occupy the Spanish Posts, or as countenancing, on my part, such an interpretation of the orders previously given to you. Your letter of the 20th January, to which mine is an answer, ~~bearing~~ bears date at Nashville, before you ~~sat~~ set out on the expedition, and consists of a narative of the measures adopted by you in order to bring your forces into the field, where they were directed to rendesvous, the time intended for marching, the orders for supplies given to the contractors, with other details of the same kind, without the slightest indication of your intention to act against the Spanish posts; and the approbation of the President of the measures you had adopted, could be intended to ~~extend~~ apply only to those, detailed in your letter.

I do not think, that your letter of the 13th Inst. presents the question, whether the executive, or yourself placed the true construction, considered as a military question, on the orders under which you acted. But I must be permitted to say, that the construction of the former is in strict conformity with my intention in drawing up the orders, and that, if they be susceptible of a different construction, it was far from being my intention they should be. I did not then suppose, nor have I ever, that it was in the ~~competency~~ power of the President, under the constitution, to order the occupation of the posts of a ~~power~~ nation, with whom, we were not at War, (whatever might be the right of the General, under the laws of nations, to attack an enemy sheltered under the posts of a neutral power), and had I been directed by the President to issue such orders, I should have been restrained from complying, by the higher authority of the Constitution, which I had sworn to support. Nor will I discuss the question, whether the order to Genl Gains, inhibiting him from attacking the Spanish posts, (a copy of which was sent to you) was in fact, & according to military usage, an order to you, and of course obligatory, till rescinded. Such certainly was my opinion. I know that yours was different. You acted on your construction, believing it to be right, and in pursuing the course which I have done, I claim equal right to act on the construction, which I conceive to be correct, knowing it to conform to my intention, in issuing the orders. But in waiving now the question of the true construction of the orders, I wish it, however, to be understood, it is only because, I do not think it presented by your letter, and not because, I have now, or ever had, the least doubt of the correctness of the opinion, which I entertain. I have always been prepared to discuss it on friendly terms with you, as appears by the extracts from Mr. Monroe's correspondence, and more recently, by my letter to you of the 30th April 1828, covering a copy of a letter to Majr. H. Lee, in which I decline a correspondence, ~~which~~ that he had requested on the subject of the construction of your orders. In my letter to Majr. Lee, I state, that "as you refer to the publick documents only for the construction, which the executive gave to the orders, I infer that on this subject, you have not had access to the General's (Jacksons) private papers; but, if I be in an error, and if the construction, which the administration gave to the orders be not stated with sufficient distinctness, in the then President's correspondence with him, I will cheerfully give, as one of the members of the administration, my own views fully in relation to the orders, if it be desired by General Jackson; but it is only with him, and at his desire, that under existing circumstances, I should feel myself justified, in corresponding on this, or any other subject, connected with his publick conduct;" to which I added, in my letter to you, covering a copy of the letter, from which the above is an extract, "With you I cannot have the slightest objection to correspond on this subject, if additional information be desirable." You expressed no desire for further information and I took it for granted, that Mr Monroe's correspondence with you, and the publick documents, furnished you a full and clear conception of the construction, which the executive gave to your orders, under which impression I remained, till I received your letter of the 13th instant.[6]

Connected with the subject of your orders, there are certain expressions in your letter, which, tho' I am at a loss to understand, I cannot pass over in silence. After announcing your surprise at the contents of Mr Crawford's letter, you ask, whether the information can be correct, "under all of the circumstances of which you and I are both informed, that any attempt seriously to effect me was moved and sustained by you in Cabinet council, when, as is known to you, I was executing the *wishes* of the Government." If by *wishes*, which you have underscored, it be meant, that there was any intimation given by myself, or any other individual directly or indirectly, of the desire of the Government, that you should occupy the Spanish posts, so far from being "informed," I have not the slightest knowledge of any such intimation; nor did I ever hear ~~of~~ a whisper of any shuch before. But, I cannot imagine, that it is your intention to make a distinction, between the wishes and the publick orders of the Government, as I find no such distinction, in your correspondence with the President nor in any of the publick documents; but, on the contrary, it is strongly rebutted by your relying for your justification constantly and exclusively, on your publick orders. Taking then the "wishes of the Government" to be, but another expression for its orders, I must refer to the proof already offered to show that the wishes of the Government, in relation to the Spanish Posts, were not such, as you assume them to be.

Having, I trust, satisfactorily established, that there has not been the least disguise, as to the construction of your orders, I will now proceed to state the part, which I took in the deliberations of the Cabinet. My statement will be confined strictly to myself; as I do not feel myself justified to speak of the course of the other members of the administration, and, in fact, only of my own, in self defence, under the extraordiny circumstances connected with this correspondence.

And here, I must premise, that the object of a Cabinet council is not to bring together opinions already formed, but to form opinions on the course, which the Government ought to pursue, after full and mature deliberation. Meeting in this spirit, the first object is a free exchange of sentiment, in which doubts and objections are freely presented and discussed. It is, I conceive, the duty of the members thus to present their doubts and objections, and to support them by offering fully all of the arguments in their favor, but, at the same time, to take care not to form an opinion, till all of the facts and views are fully brought out and every doubt and objection carefully weighed. In this sperit, I came into the meeting ~~in question~~. The questions involved were numerous and important; whether you had ~~violated~~ transcended your orders, if so, what course ought to be adopted; what was the conduct of Spain and her officers in Florida; what was the state of our relations ~~to~~ with Spain, and, through her, with the other European powers, a question at that time of uncommon complication and difficulty. These questions had all to be carefully examined and weighed, both separately and in connection, before a final opinion could be wisely formed; and never did I see a deliberation in which every point was more carefully examined, or a greater solicitude displayed to arrive at a correct dicision. I was the junior member of the Cabinet, and had been, but a few months in the administration.[7] As Secretary of War, I was more immediately connected with the questions, whether you had transcended your orders, and if so what course ought to be pursued. I was of the impression, that you had ~~violated~~ exceeded your orders and had acted on your own responsibility, but I neither questioned your patrotism, nor your motives. Belv'g that when orders were transcended, investigation, as a matter of course, ought to follow, as due in justice to the government and the officer, unless there be strong reasons to the contrary, I came to the meeting under the impression; that the usual course ought to be pursued in this case, which I supported by presenting fully and freely all of the arguments, that occurred to me. They were met by other arguments, growing out of a more enlarged view of the subject, as connected with the conduct of Spain and her officers, and the course of policy, which honor and interest dictated ~~should~~ to be pursued towards her; with which some of the members of the Cabinet were more familiar than myself, and whose duty it was to present that aspect of the subject, as it was mine to present that, more immediately connected with the military operations. After deliberately weighing every question, when the members of the cabinet came to form their final opinion, on a view of the whole ground, it was unanimously determined, as I understood, in favour of the course adopted, and which was fully made known to you, by Mr Monroe's letter of the 19th July 1818. I gave it my assent and support, as being that, which, under all of the circumstances, ~~which~~ the publick interest required ~~should~~ to be adopted.

I shall now turn to the examination of the version, which Mr Crawford has given of my course in this important deliberation, begining with his "apology for having disclosed, what took place in a Cabinet meeting." He says "in the summer after the meeting, an extract of a letter from Washington was published in a Nashville paper, in which it was stated, that I (Mr Crawford) had proposed to arrest General Jackson, but that he was triumphantly defended by Mr Calhoun and Mr Adams. This letter I always believed was written by Mr Calhoun, or by his direction. It had the desired effect. General Jackson became inimical to me, and friendly to Mr Calhoun."

I am not at all surprised that Mr Crawford should feel, that he stands in need of an apology for betraying the deliberations of the Cabinet. It is I believe, not only the first instance in our country, but one of a very few instances to be found in any country, or any age, that an individual has felt absolved from the high obligation, which honor and duty impose on one, situated as he was. It is not however my intention to comment on the morality of his disclosure. That more immediately concerns himself, and I leave him undisturbed to establish his own rules of honor and ~~morals~~

fidelity, in order to proceed to the examination of a question, in which I am more immediately concerned, the *truth* of his apology.

I desire not to speak harshly of Mr Crawford. I sincerely commiserate his misfortune.[8] I may be warm in political contests, but it is not in me to retain enmity, particularly towards the unsuccessful. In the political contest which ended in 1825 Mr. Crawford and myself took opposite sides, but whatever feelings of unkindness it gave rise to, have long since passed away on my part. The contest ended in an entire change of the political elements of the country; and in the new state of things, which followed, I found myself acting with many of the friends of Mr Crawford to whom I had been recently opposed and opposed to many of my old friends, with whom, I had, till then, been associated. In this new state of things my inclination, my regard for his friends who were acting with me, and the success of ~~a~~ the cause, for which we were ~~mutually~~ jointly contending all contributed to remove from my bosom any feeling towards him, save that of pity for his misfortune. I would not speak a harsh word if I could avoid it, and it is a cause of pain to me, that the extraordinary position, in which he has placed me, compels me in self defence to say any thing, which must in its consequence, bear on his character.

I speak in this sperit, when I assert, as I do, that his apology has no foundation in truth. He offers no reason for charging me with so dishonorable an act, as that of betraying the proceedings of the Cabinet, & that for the purpose of injuring one of my associates, in the administration. The charge rests wholly on his suspicion, to which I oppose my positive assertion, that it is ~~false~~ wholly unfounded. I had no knowledge of the letter, or connection with it, nor do I recollect, that I ever saw the extract. But why charge me and not Mr Adams also? I had then been, but a few months in the administration, and Mr Crawford and myself were on the best terms, without a feeling, certainly on my part, of rivalry, or jealousy. In assigning the motive, that he does, for the letter, he forgets, the relation which existed then between you and himself. He says it had the desired effect; that you became friendly to me and extremely innimical to him. He does not remember, that your hostility to him, long preceded this period and had a very different origin. He certainly could not have anticipated, that a copy of his letter would be placed in your hand.

These are not the only difficulties accompanying his apology. There are others still more formidable, and which must compel him to assign some other reason for disclosing the proceedings of the Cabinet.

Mr. McDuffie's letter to me of the 14th Inst (of which I enclose a copy) proves, that Mr Crawford spoke freely of the proceedings of the Cabinet on his way to Georgia in the Summer of 1818; and dates will show, that he could not, at that time, have seen the extract from the Nashville paper, on which he now rests his apology.[9] The deliberation of the Cabinet took place between the 14th and 25th July 1818, on the former day Mr Monroe returned to Washington from Loudon, and on the latter a general exposition of the views of the government, in relation to the operations in Florida, appeared in the Intelligencer. The letter of Mr. Monroe to you of the 19th July 1818, fixes probably the day of the final decision of the Cabinet. Mr Crawford passed through Augusta on the 11th August, as announced in the papers of that city, on which day, or the preceding, his conversation, to which Mr McDuffie's letter relates, must have taken place. On a comparison of these dates, you will see, that it was impossible, that Mr Crawford could have seen the extract from the Nashville papers, when he was in Edgefield, and he must consequently find some other apology, for his disclosures. This was not the only instance of his making the disclosures before he saw the extract. He was at Milledgeville on the 16th August 1818, a few days after he passed through Augusta, and, a little after, there appeared a statement in the Georgia Journal, some what varied from that made in Edgefield, but agreeing with it in most of the particulars. I cannot lay my hand on the article, but have a distinct recollection of it. You no doubt remember it. Circumstances fixed it on Mr Crawford, and it has not, to my knowledge, been denied.[10]

With such evidence of inaccuracy, either from want of memory, or some other cause, in what relates to his own motives and action, it would be unreasonable to suppose, that Mr Crawford's statements will prove more correct, in what relates to me. I will now proceed to examine them. He first states, that I proposed, that you should "be punished in some form or reprimanded in some form;" and to make my course more odious, as I suppose, he adds, that Mr Calhoun did not propose to arrest General Jackson. I will not dwell on a statement, which on its ~~statement~~ face is so absurd. How could an officer under our laws be punished without arrest and trial, and to suppose, that I proposed such a course, would be ~~to~~ indeed to rate my understanding very low. His next ~~charge~~ allegation requires much more attention. He says "Indeed my own views on the subject had undergone a material change after the Cabinet had been convened. Mr. Calhoun made some allusion to a letter, that General Jackson had written to the President, who had forgotten, that he had received such a letter, but said, if he had received such a one, he would find it, and went directly to his Cabinet and brought it out. In it General Jackson approves of the determination of the Government to break up Amelia Island and Galveztown, and gave it also as his opinion, that Florida ought to be taken by the U. States   He added, it might be a delicate matter for the Executive to decide, but if the President approved of it, he had only to give a hint to some confidential member of Congress, say Johnny Ray, and he would do it, and take the responsibility on himself. I asked the President, if the letter had been answered. He replied no, for that he had no recollection of having received it. I then said, that I had no doubt, that General Jackson in taking ~~Florida~~ Pansacola believed, he was doing what the executive wished. After that letter was produced unanswered, I should have opposed, the infliction of punishment on General Jackson, who had considered the silence of the President as ~~silent~~ a tacit consent, yet it was after the letter was produced and read, that Mr Calhoun made the proposition to the Cabinet for punishing the General." Again "I do not know, that I ever hinted at the letter to the President, yet that letter had a most important bearing on the deliberations of the Cabinet, at least in my mind and possibly on the minds of Mr Adams and the President, but neither expressed any opinion on the subject. It seems it had none on the mind of Mr Calhoun, for it made no change in his conduct."

It will be no easy matter for Mr. Crawford to reconcile the statement, which he has thus circumstantially made, with his conduct in relation to the Seminole affair, from the time of the decision of the Cabinet till the subject ceased to be agitated.

How will he, in the first instance, reconcile it with his Edgefield Statement, of which Mr McDuffie's letter gives an account. The contrast between that, and the present, is most stricking, to illustrate which I will ~~quote~~ give an extract from Mr McDuffie's letter. Mr McDuffie says that "he (Mr Crawford) stated, that you (Mr Calhoun) had been in favour of an enquiry into the conduct of General Jackson, and that, he was the only member of the Cabinet, that concurred with you. He spoke in strong terms of disapprobation of the course pursued by Genl. Jackson, not only in his military proceedings, but in prematurely bringing the grounds of his defence before the country, and forestalling publick opinion; thus anticipating the administration. On this point he remarked, that, if the administration could not give direction to publick opinion, but permitted a military officer, who had violated his orders to anticipate them; they had no business to be at Washington and had better return home." Such was the language then held and such his tone of feeling, at that time. We hear not one word of the letter, which makes so conspicuous a figure in his present statement, not one word of the change it effected in his mind in relation to your conduct, not a word of his taking a course different from me, but, on the contrary, he then stated directly, that he concurred with me in favoring an enquiry, and indicated no difference on any other point, and so far from exempting you from the charge of breach of orders, as he now attempts to do, he asserted positively, that you had violated your orders. Shall we find the explanation of the ~~difference~~ contrast in the two statements, in the difference of his motives then and now? Is his motive now to injure me, and was it then to attack another member of the administration? Or must it be attributed, as the more charitable interpretation, to the decay of memory? Whatever may be the true explination, all will agree, that a statement, when the events were fresh in the memory, is to be trusted in preference to one made twelve years after the transaction, particularly, if the former accords with after events, and the latter does not, as is the case in this instance. At the next session of Congress your conduct in the Seminole war was severely attacked in both branches of the Legislature. Let us see, if the course persued by Mr

Crawford and his personal and confidential friends can be reconciled to the statement, which he now gives of his course in the Cabinet. Mr Cobb of Georgia, ~~who lately died~~ now no more, was then a prominent member of the House of Representatives. He was the particular personal and confidential friend of Mr Crawford, his near neighbour, and formerly a law student under him. What part did he take? He led the attack, he moved the resolutions against you, he accused you expressly ~~with~~ of the violation of your orders, and sustained the accusation with all his powers.[11] All this ~~can be reconciled~~ accords with Mr Crawford's statement of his sentiment and his course at the time, but how can it be reconciled to his present statement? How could he, on any principle of justice, stand by and hear you thus falsely accused in the face of the world, when he, according to his showing now, knew that it was all false? And how can he reconcile his silence then, when you stood so much in need of his assistance, with his disclosures now, when the agitation has long since passed away, and his aid no longer required? But let us turn to the other branch of the Legislature, and see whether any occurrence there can explain this apparent mystery. Genl Lacock of Pennsylvania, the particular friend of Mr Crawford, and in the habit of constant intercourse with him, was the Chairman of the ~~military~~ Committee in that body, To ~~this Committee~~ whom the part of the Message, which related to the Seminole war, was referred. Mr Forsyth, then and now, a Senator from Georgia, and who now acts a prominent part in the transaction which has given rise to the present correspondence, was also a member, and was then, as he is now, an intimate personal and political friend of Mr Crawford. With two such able and influential friends on the Committee, he had the most favourable opportunity, that could be offered to do you justice. According to his own statement, he felt no obligation to observe silence, in relation to the proceedings of the Cabinet. Why then did he not interfere with his friends on the Committee to do you justice? That he did not, I need not offer you arguments to prove ~~that~~. The report of the Committee is sufficient testimoney. Should he say, that he was restrained by feelings of delicacy from interfering with his friends and the Committee, how will he reconcile, on the principles of justice and honor, his silence after the report, so severely assailling your motives and conduct, was made, when, admitting his present statement, it was completely in his power to shield you from censure.[12]

But why should I waste time and words to prove, that Mr Crawford's whole course is in direct conflict with his present statement of the proceedings of the Cabinet, when there remains an objection, that cannot be surmounted. The statement is entirely destitute of foundation. It is not true. Strange as it my appear, after an account so minute and circumstantial, no such letter, as he refers to, was ever before the Cabinet, or alluded to in its deliberations. My memory is distinct and clear, and is confirmed by the ~~less~~ no less distinct recollection of Mr Monroe and Mr.

Wirt, as will fully appear by copies of their statements, herewith enclosed. Feelings of delicacy, growing out of the political relation of Mr Adams and Mr Crowninshield, the other members of the then administration, both towards you and myself, has restrained me from applying for their statements, but I have not the least apprehension, that they would vary from Mr Monroe's or Mr. Wirt's.[13]

Comment is useless. I will not attempt to explain so gross a mistatement of the proceedings of the Cabinet, but will leave it to those friends of Mr Crawford, who have placed him in this dilemma, to determine, whether his ~~false~~ erroneous statement is to be attributed to an entire decay of memory, or to some other cause; and if the former, to exempt themselves from the responsibility of thus cruelly exposing a weakness, which it was their duty to conceal.

It now becomes necessary to say something of your letter of the 6th January, to which Mr Crawford has given, in his statement, so much prominence. My recollection in relation to it accords with Mr Monroe's statement. I came into his room, when he had appearantly just received the letter. He was indisposed at the time. I think he opened the letter ~~while~~ in my presence, and finding, that it was from you, he gave me the letter to read. I cast my eyes over it, and remarked, that it related to the Seminole affair, and would require his attention, or something to that effect. I thought no more of it. Long after, I think it was at the commencement of the next session of Congress, I heard some allusion, which brought the letter to my recollection. It was from a quarter, which induced me to believe, that it came from Mr Crawford. I called and mentioned it to ~~you~~ Mr. Monroe, and found that ~~you~~ he had entirely forgotten the letter. After searching some time, he found it among some other papers, and read it, as he told me, for the first time.

Having stated these facts, I should be wanting in candour, were I not also to state, that, if the facts had been otherwise, had Mr. Monroe read your letter and intentionally omitted to answer it, and had it been brought before the Cabinet, in my opinion it ~~ought~~ would not ~~to~~ have had the least influence on its deliberation. The letter was not received till several weeks after the orders to you were issued, and could not, therefore, as you know, have had any influence in drawing them up; and such I conceive was your opinion, as I do not find any allusion to the letter in your publick, or private correspondence, at the time, which would not have been the case, had it, in your opinion, formed a part of your justification. You rested your defence, on what I conceive to be much more elevated grounds, on the true construction, as you supposed, of your orders, and the necessity of the measures, which you adopted, to terminate the war; and not on any supposed secret wish of the executive in opposition to the publick orders, under which you acted. Mr. Crawford in placing your justification *now* on such grounds, not only exposes your motives to be questioned, but as far as his act can greatly weakens your defence.

On a review of this subject, it is impossible not to be struck, with the time and mode of bringing on this correspondence. It is now twelve years since the termination of the Seminole war. Few events, in our history, have caused so much excitement, or been so fully discussed, both in and out of Congress. During ~~this~~ a greater part of this long period, Mr Crawford was a prominent actor on the publick stage, seeing and hearing all that occurred, and without restraint, according to his own statement, to disclose freely all he knew, yet not a word is uttered by him in your behalf, but now, when you have triumphed over all difficulties, when you no longer require defence, he, for the first time, breaks silence, not to defend you, but to accuse me, who gave you ~~my~~ all the support, in your hour of trial, in his power, when you were fiercely attacked, if not by Mr Crawford himself, at least by some of his most confidential and influential friends. Nor is the manner, less remarkable than the time. Mr Forsyth, a Senator from Georgia, here in his place, writes to Mr Crawford, his letter covering certain enclosures, and referring to certain correspondence and conversations in relation to my conduct in the Cabinet deliberation on the Seminole question; Mr Crawford answers, correcting the statements alluded to in some instances, and confirming and amplifying in others, which answer he authorises Mr Forsyth to shew me, if he pleased. Of all this Mr Forsyth gives me not the slightest intimation, tho' in the habit of almost daily intercourse in the Senate, and instead of shewing me Mr Crawford's letter, as he was authorised to do, I hear of it, for the first time, by having a copy put into my hand ~~by your~~ under cover of your letter of the 13th Instant, a copy with *important blanks* and unaccompanied by Mr Forsyth's letter with its enclosures, to which ~~it~~ Mr Crawford's is an answer.

Why is this so? Why did not Mr Forsyth himself show me the letter, the original letter? By what authority did he place a copy in your hands: None is given by the writer. Why is your name interposed? Was it to bring me into conflict with the President of the United States? If the object of the correspondence between Mr Crawford and Mr Forsyth be to impeach my conduct, as it would seem to be, by what rule of justice am I deprived of evidence material to my defence, and which is in the hands of my accusers; of a copy of Mr Forsyth letter, with the enclosures, of a statement of the conversation and correspondence of the two individuals, whose names are in blank in the copy of Mr Crawford's letter furnished me? Why not inform me who they are? Their testimony might be highly important, and even their *names alone* might throw much light on this mysterious affair.

I must be frank. I feel, that I am deprived of important rights by the interposition of your name, of which I have just cause to complain. It deprives me of important advantages, which would otherwise belong to my position. By the interposition of your name, the communication, which would exist between ~~him~~ Mr Forsyth and myself, had he placed Mr Crawford's letter in my hands, as he was authorised to do, is prevented, and I am thus deprived of the right, which would have belonged to me, in that case, and, which he could not in justice withold, of being placed in possession of all of the material facts and circumstances connected with this affair. In thus complaining, it is not my intention to attribute to you any design to deprive me of so important an advantage. I know, the extent of your publick duties, and how completely they engross your time and attention They have not allowed you sufficient time for reflection in this case, of which evidence is afforded by the ground, that you assume in placing the copy of Mr Crawford's letter in my hand, which you state was submitted by his authority. I do not so understand him; the authority was as I conceive to Mr Forsyth and not to yourself, and applied to the original letter, and not to the copy, both of which, as I have shown, are very important in this case, and not mere matters of form. I have asked the question, why is this affair brought up at this late period, and in this remarkable manner. It merits consideration, at least from myself. I am in the habit of speaking my sentiments and opinions freely, and, I see no cause, which ought to restrain me on the present occasion. I should be blind not to see, that this whole affair is a political manoeuvre, in which the design is, that you should be the instrument and myself the victim, but in which the real actors, are carefully concealed, by an artful movement. A naked copy, with the names referred to in blank, affords slender means of detection, while, on the contrary, had I been placed, as I ought to have been, in possession of all of the facts, to which I was entitled to be, but little penetration would probably had been required, to see through the whole affair. The names, which are in blank, might of themselves, through their political associations, ~~have~~ point directly to the contrivers of this scheme. I wish not to be misunderstood. I have too much respect for your character to suppose you capable of participating, in the slightest degree, in a political intrigue. Your character is of too high and generous a cast to ~~be capable of~~ resorting to such means, either for your own advantage, or that of others. This, the contrivers of this plot, well knew, but they hoped through your generous attributes, through your lofty and jealous regard ~~of~~ for your character, to excite feelings, through which they ~~hoped~~ expected to consummate their designs. Several indications, forewarned me long since, that a blow was meditated against me, I will not say from the quarter, from which this comes, but in relation to this subject. More than two years since, I had a correspondence with the District Attorney for the Southern District of New York on the subject of the proceedings of the Cabinet on the Seminole war, which tho' it did not then excite particular attention, has since, in connection with other circumstances, served to direct my eye, to what was going on.[14]

Of Mr Crawford I speak with pain and only in self defence; but that you may more fully realize, the sperit, which actuates him, and how little scrupulous he is of the means, that he uses, where I am concerned, I would refer you for illustration to facts in the possession of one, who stands to you in the relation of a constitutional adviser, and who, from his character, is entitled to your entire confidence, I mean the Post Master General. No one knows better than yourself how sacred the electoral college, for the choice of President and Vice President, should be considered, in our system of Government. The electors are the trustees of the high sovereign power of the people of the States as it relates to the choice of those ~~high~~ magistrates, and on the degree of fidelity with which the trust may be discharged, depends in a great degree the successful ~~of~~ operation of our system. In order to prevent, as far as practicable, political intrigue, or the operation of extraneous influence on the choice of the electoral College, it is provided, that they shall meet in their respective states, that they shall vote throughout the Union on the same day and be elected within thirty-four days of the time designated for the election, thus excluding with the greatest care all other influence on the choice of the electors, except the will of their constituents; but where the object was to injure me; the sacred character of the College was an insufficient restraint. Mr Crawford wrote to Majr. Barry in October 1828 (a copy of whose letter he has furnished me at my request) requesting him earnestly to use his influence with the electors not to vote for me as Vice President, tho he could not be ignorant, that I had been ~~named~~ nominated for that office on the preceding 8th January, when your friends nominated you in a state convention for the high station, which you now hold, and that the electors were pledged to vote for you as President, and myself as Vice President. This is not the only instance of his interference. He pursued the same course in Tennessee, and Louisiana, as I am informed, on the highest authority.[15]

At an earlier period, he resorted to means not much less objectionable to injure my standing, and to influence, as far as I was concerned, the election. I am not ignorant of his correspondence with that view, and which, I feel confident, has not escaped your observation. But I will not dwell on this disagreeable subject. I have no resentment towards Mr Crawford. I have looked on in silence, without resorting to any means to counter act the injury, which he intended me; and I now depart from the rule, which I have carefully observed ever since the termination of the Presidential election in 1825, because his present attack comes through a channel, my high respect for which, would not permit me to be silent. I have, however, in noticing, what I could not pass over, situated as I now am, endeavored to limit myself by the line of self defence, and if I have apparently gone beyond in making any remarks on his conduct, which his letter did not naturally suggest, my apology will be found in the necessity of showing the state of his feelings towards me, so that the motive which influenced him in the ~~transaction~~ course, which has caused this correspondence may be fully understood. I am Sir, very respectfully your obt. servant,

J. C. Calhoun

ALS, DLC (38). *Calhoun Papers*, 11:173–91. Calhoun published the entire Seminole correspondence, including this letter and its enclosures with added notes and commentary, in the *United States' Telegraph* on February 17, 1831.

1. Monroe wrote AJ on July 19, 1818, that "in transcending the limit prescribed by those orders [the previous orders to Gaines to stop short of attacking the Spanish posts in Florida], you acted on your own responsibility." The executive could not authorize an attack on a foreign power without a declaration of war, but "cases may occur, where the commanding general, acting on his own responsibility, may with safety pass this limit, & with essential advantage to his country." Un-neutral conduct by Spanish officers in Florida in arming, aiding, abetting, and sheltering the Seminoles would present such a case. AJ should gather and forward evidence of such provoking misconduct, and the administration, while returning the posts to Spain, would justify him against Spanish protests and domestic criticism on that ground. Monroe invited AJ to revise past communications of his that might have suggested any other motive or implied a precalculated intent to seize the Spanish posts (*Jackson Papers*, 4:224–28; Calhoun's extract, DLC-25).

AJ replied on August 19, 1818, that Monroe's distinction between the administration's responsibility and his was misconceived and that he had not transcended orders. An executive order to accomplish an object without specifying means or limits "leaves an *entire discretion* with the officer as to the choice and application of means, but preserves the responsibility, for his acts in the authority from which the order emanated. under such an order *all the acts* of the inferior are the acts of the superior." Calhoun's orders of December 26, 1817, gave AJ full power to conduct the campaign as he saw fit and superseded the previous orders to Gaines (*Jackson Papers*, 4:236–39; Calhoun's extract, DLC-25).

Monroe wrote back on October 20, 1818, complimenting AJ's motives and regretting "that you understood your instructions, relative to operations in Florida, differently, from what we intended." For the record, and for use in fielding inquiries from Congress, he suggested that AJ write Calhoun stating his view of the powers under which he acted; this would be answered "in a friendly manner by Mr. Calhoun, who has very just and liberal sentiments on the subject" (Bassett, 2:398; Calhoun's extract, DLC-25). AJ replied on November 15, agreeing to an explanatory correspondence if Calhoun would initiate it, but insisting that he had always claimed to be acting fully under orders, as the War Department should have known. He had so informed it in a dispatch of May 5, 1818—a dispatch which, AJ surmised, the "base unprincipled" Crawford might have waylaid to cause trouble between himself and the administration (*Jackson Papers*, 4:246–48; Calhoun's extract [dated Nov 15, 1830], DLC-38). Monroe replied on December 21 that he had only proposed the correspondence so that AJ could state his position "on the strongest ground possible, so as to do complete justice to yourself." Monroe agreed that nothing in the official record revealed a difference of opinion over AJ's orders, since to mention such would have implied "a censure on your conduct, than which nothing could be more remote from our disposition or intention" (*Jackson Papers*, 4:257–59; Calhoun's extract, DLC-26). Meanwhile, AJ wrote Monroe on December 7 that he had read Monroe's November 16 annual message to Congress, which justified the Florida campaign as an imperative response to Spanish officers' misconduct, "with great attention and satisfaction" (Bassett, 2:402; Calhoun's extract, DLC-26).

2. Richardson, 2:31–32.

3. Richardson, 2:42–43.

4. On June 2, 1818, AJ reported to Calhoun on the conclusion of the Seminole campaign, including his seizure of Pensacola on May 24 (*HRDoc* 14, 15th Cong., 2d sess., pp. 86–89, Serial 17; Bassett, 2:379–81).

5. Calhoun's May 13, 1818, letter to Bibb enclosed a copy of his December 16, 1817, order to Gaines, and said, "you will consider it as furnishing authority to the troops of the territory to pass the Florida line, should it be necessary" (*Calhoun Papers*, 2:291).

6. In March 1828 Henry Lee, who was researching a biography of AJ, wrote Monroe and Calhoun querying their construction of AJ's orders in the Seminole campaign. Suspecting Lee's motives, Calhoun replied to Lee declining an answer and advised Monroe to do the

same, while writing AJ on April 30 that he would gladly discuss the matter with him (*Calhoun Papers*, 10:376–81; *Jackson Papers*, 6:450–51).

7. Calhoun joined the Cabinet early in December 1817, nine months into Monroe's first term.

8. A paralytic stroke in 1823 and subsequent defeat in the 1824 presidential election had ended Crawford's public career.

9. George McDuffie's May 14, 1830, letter to Calhoun related that Crawford, in conversation at Eldred Simkins's home in Edgefield, S.C., around the summer of 1818, had strongly criticized both AJ's actions in Florida and the Cabinet's failure to discipline him (DLC-38; *Calhoun Papers*, 11:163–64).

10. Branding AJ a "*military despot*," the Milledgeville *Georgia Journal* on August 25, 1818, reported rumors of an equal division in the Cabinet over whether to arrest him.

11. Georgia congressman Thomas Willis Cobb (1784–1830) led the drive to censure AJ in the 1818–19 winter session of Congress, introducing and speaking for resolutions that declared the Seminole campaign a violation of orders and of the constitution.

12. Abner Lacock (1770–1837) of Pennsylvania had chaired a Senate select committee, appointed on his motion, to investigate AJ's Seminole campaign. Lacock's report, delivered February 24, 1819, condemned the entire campaign as an act of military usurpation and severely censured AJ (*SDoc* 100, 15th Cong., 2d sess., Serial 15).

13. William Wirt had been Monroe's attorney general and Benjamin Williams Crowninshield (1772–1851) his secretary of the Navy. Calhoun enclosed to AJ copies of his letters of May 17, 1830, to Monroe and of May 28, 1830, to Wirt, asking their memory whether AJ's January 6, 1818, letter to Monroe, inviting a private authorization to conquer Florida through John Rhea, had been before the Cabinet during its deliberations. Monroe's reply of May 19 and Wirt's of May 28, copies of which Calhoun also enclosed, both denied it. Monroe's recollection, coinciding with Calhoun's, was that when the letter arrived he had shown it privately to Calhoun and also to Crawford, but, being ill, he had then laid it aside, forgot it, and did not read it himself until months later. Wirt said the letter was to him "a thing perfectly new, and of which I never heard before" (DLC-38; *Calhoun Papers*, 11:164–65, 171–72).

14. On February 25, 1828, James A. Hamilton, whose name was omitted in the correspondence AJ showed to Calhoun, had written Calhoun asking him to confirm that arresting AJ was never proposed in the Cabinet. Calhoun declined on March 2, citing Cabinet confidentiality. Calhoun, unaware of Hamilton's simultaneous correspondence with Forsyth that elicited Crawford's disclosures against himself, understood from Hamilton that his answer was wanted only to help repel an anticipated campaign attack on AJ. He asked Hamilton for the information that had prompted his query, which Hamilton declined to reveal (*Calhoun Papers*, 10:354–56, 359, 361, 365–66).

15. Crawford wrote Van Buren on October 21, 1828, proposing that New York's electors vote for Nathaniel Macon instead of Calhoun for vice president. Crawford said he was urging the same course on "distinguished individuals" in every state outside New England (Van Buren Papers, DLC).

To John Caldwell Calhoun

May 30th. 1830—

Sir

Your communication of the 29th. Instant was handed me this morning just as I was going to church, and, of course, was not read until I returned.

I regret to find that you have intirely mistaken my note of the 13th instant. There is no part of it which calls in question either your conduct, or your motives, in the case alluded to. Motives are to be infered from actions, & judged of by our god. It had been intimated to me many years ago, that it was you and not Mr Crawford, as I had supposed, who had been secretly endeavouring to destroy my reputation. These insinuations I indignantly repelled, upon the ground that you, in all your letters to me, professed to be my personal friend, and approved *entirely*, my conduct in relation to the Seminole campaign. I had too exalted an opinion of your honor and frankness to believe, for a moment, that you could be capable of such deception. Under the influence of these friendly feelings (which I have always entertained for you) when I was furnished with a copy of Mr Crawfords letter, with that Frankness which ever has, and I hope ever will characterise my conduct, I considered it due to you and the friendly relations which had always existed between us, to lay it forthwith before you, and ask, if the statements contained in that letter could be true. I repeat I had a right to believe that you were my sincere friend, and until now, never expected to have occasion to say of you, in the languague of Cesar—*et tu Brute.* The evidence which has brought me to this conclusion is abundantly Contained in your letter now before me. In your and Mr. Crawfords dispute I have no interest whatever, but it may become necessary for me, hereafter, when I shall have more leisure, and the documents at hand to place the subject in its proper light, to notice the historical facts & references in your communication, which will give a very different view of this subject.

It is due to myself, however, to state that the knowledge of the Executive, ~~the~~ documents and orders, in my possession, will shew conclusively, that I had authority for all I did, and that your explanation of my ~~orders~~ powers as detailed to Govr. Bibb shews your own understanding of them. Your letter to me of the 29th., handed to day, and now before me is the first intimation to me that *you* ever entertained any other opinion or view of them. Your conduct, words, actions & letters, I have ever thought shew this

Understanding you now, no further communication with you on this subject is necessary[.] I have the honor to be very respectfully yr mo. obt servt.

Andrew Jackson

[Endorsed by William B. Lewis:] Copy of a letter from Genl. Jackson to Mr. Calhoun—dated 30. May 1830

ALS draft, DLC (73). *US Telegraph*, February 17, 1831; *Calhoun Papers*, 11:192–93. Calhoun replied on June 1 (below).

Louisville and Portland Canal
and Lighthouse Bill Veto Message (not sent)

[Congress adjourned on Monday, May 31. On that day Jackson sent to the Senate his veto of a bill to subscribe for 4,500 shares in the Washington Turnpike Company, chartered by the state of Maryland to build a road from the District of Columbia line to Frederick. For his reasons Jackson's brief message referred the Senate to his May 27 Maysville Road veto, a copy of which he enclosed. A motion to pass the bill over his veto, requiring two-thirds, failed in the Senate by 21 in favor, 17 opposed.

Jackson drafted vetoes for two other improvement measures before Congress adjourned. The first, a bill to subscribe for 1,000 shares of stock in the Louisville and Portland Canal Company (S. 74), passed the Senate on March 15 and the House on May 29. The state of Kentucky had chartered the company in 1825 to build a canal around the falls of the Ohio at Louisville. Under President Adams, Congress had already subscribed for 1,000 shares of its stock in May 1826 and for up to 1,350 additional shares on March 2, 1829.

The second bill made sundry appropriations for lighthouses and lightboats, other navigation aids, and harbor and channel improvements in twenty-two states and three territories (H.R. 304). It passed the House on April 7. The Senate passed an amended version on May 13 and the House concurred on May 29. Both bills were presented to Jackson on May 31, the day of adjournment.

Printed here are sequential drafts, in Jackson's hand, of a veto message covering both bills. Jackson did not send this message in. Instead he pocket-vetoed the two bills by withholding his signature. He returned them both to the reconvened Congress with his second annual message of December 6, 1830, explaining his reasons therein.]

The Portland & Light House Bill

 The President in his objections to the Maysville Bill, has passed definitively upon two points

 1st That the Federal Government possesses no authority to construct roads & canals, exclusively within the limits of a state & to exercise jurisdiction over the same with, or without the assent of a state.

 2d That congress has no right to appropriate money for internal improvements which are not of general ~~not~~ but local character.

 He has intimated an opinion, that the right to make appropriations for national objects, has been acquired by the general federal Government thro' usage, & the long acquiescence of the states. He has likewise, intimated that such appropriations, on the ground of expediency, ought to be deferred untill the national debt be paid; and that the public interest imperiously demands an amendment of the constitution before any general system shall be adopted. In reference to all appropriations for internal improvements, which can be considered general, & national, some certain and definite ground should be taken. There should be established some rule, which shall give the greatest practicable precision to the power to appropriate money for objects of general concern, that is, to lay down some test by which to determine their nationality, & to establish some rule for the regulation & erection of light Houses, and for the regulation or improvement of commerce so far as our rivers are concerned

The propriety & expediency of omitting all appropriations for these objects except for those which shall be considered of fixed national character until the public debt shall be paid is matter for reflection, as well on account of the importance of that consideration as to afford time for the adoption of some general constitutional arrangement, whereby the whole subject may be placed on better grounds—an arrangement which never can be seriously attempted, so long as scattering appropriations are made, and a scramble for them thereby encouraged.

Besides those ~~sanctioned~~ improvements in the country ~~which rest upon usage~~ sanctioned by usage, and the acquiescence of the states in that usage, ~~a second~~ another power is derived, under the grant to congress to regulate commerce amongst the several states. under this ~~grant~~ power, charts of our sea coasts have been made; obstructions to navigation removed, inlets improved, Light Houses & buoys erected, and a Break water begun. But all these benefits are derived without any expence or exaction or tolls from the commerce of the country. They are paid for out of the funds of the people, and they, free of expence receive the advantages conferred. A river constituting a great high way thro' which general commerce passes, must have been considered a matter of constitutional concern, under the authority given to regulate commerce, ~~equally as tho~~ as much so as if it were an arm or inlet of the sea. It is not the salt, or fresh quality of the water, but the beneficial purposes to which it may be applied and the difusive advantages it presents which gives a determined ~~idea, as~~ character to the powers ~~which are ex~~ to be exercised over it, under this grant of authority. ~~By virtue~~ In Consequence of practiced usage and acquiescence, a right exists to ~~assist in~~ improveing the Ohio River; but in the expenditure to be incurred for this purpose, like other improvements which congress have begun & finished in aid of commerce, it should be free; exempt from all demands; or otherwise it is ~~not~~ the exercise of a power, not to regulate commerce, but for the purposes of taxation & revenue; a description of ~~bills~~ cases which by the extreme caution of the constitution is required to originate in the House of Representatives   The ohio River, like the inlets & bays along the sea coast, is constitutionally placed by practice & usage of the Gvt. under the care & consideration of congress. By the provisions of the Portland Bill, the navigation of the stream is intended to be aided, but under the proposed arrangement, it is to be done at an expence to the citizens; while other similar improvements, to wit, Light Houses, buoys and break waters, which also assist commerce, are made at the expense of the Goverment, ~~the privileges of which are~~ and its benefits enjoyed without exactions of any ~~sort~~ kind. As the ~~priviledges of which are enjoyed without exactions of any sort~~ improvement of our bays, Rivers and harbours, rests then, upon the authority to regulate commerce, certainly no variation can arise whether the improvement to be made, be on the stream itself, or by canal around an ~~impending~~ impeding obstruction, & which, without such resort would be without remedy.[1]

The falls of ohio consists of ledges of Rocks which crossing the bed of the stream, at low water interupt the navigation. The opinion entertained is, that to remove them would create a strong current, and perhaps, by reducing the quantity of water above, ~~would~~ produce shoals & rapids. The most approved plan therefore was a resort to the shore ~~that by~~ by opening a canal thereby preserving the level of the river. The obstruction might be overcome without encountering the inconveniences anticipated, by attempting ~~an~~ unsuccessfull, and expensive experiments on the bed of the stream. Had this been done by the general Govt. with its own resources under the sanction of Kentuckey, unconnected with any private association & company, nothing could be perceived in the undertaking, at variance with that uniform practice & acquiescence, which has obtained in relation to the improvement of our bays & inlets, under the grant, to regulate commerce, ~~but~~. This course was not pursued: a subscription was made, & an association formed with a view to impose a tax upon all who should receive the benefit of the improvement, thereby depriving the citizens who may navigate the stream of those ~~priviledges~~ benefits which are enjoyed from works of similar character along our sea coast.

There are strong objections to connecting the government with private companies. If in making canals &c, the united states may associate with one incorporated company within a state, they may connect themselves with another, & another, untill excessive, & unlimited partnerships for these objects are created in all the states. In every local Bank ~~they~~ it may become a partner & thus the entire original character of our confederacy be changed & ~~mangled~~ lost, & a new one created. When this shall be the case, consolidation, and, as a consequence, the destruction of our libertyies will follow. ought we not to guard against these? The high privileges our country enjoys, have been purchased surely at too dear a price to be staked at such a hazard. To encourage improvements by canals & roads is desirable, but they should not be undertaken at the expense of any principle of the constitution. ☞ connect chesepeak & ohio canal here

Why ~~therefore~~ on the score of policy should not the states project works of local character in their individual, rather than in their federative capacity. The funds necessary to their completion are to be obtained by the general government no where else than from the people; and surely it will prove as salutary, from time to time, to diminish the amount of taxes from imports upon articles which do not enter into competition with our own home industry, thus leaving the amount which would be drawn from the people in their own pocketts that thereby strengthening their resources, a capacity may be afforded to the states respectively to project & execute such works themselves. Better feelings will be the consequence of such a course—jealousies will be prevented; & that prodigality will be avoided which might induce the representatives of one state, to seek after appropriations, because they have been granted to another. Then will be witnessed no scramble; no electioneering after the public funds. Improvements clearly determined to be national being such only as will then come under the supervision of congress, every cause for unpleasant feeling will be ~~taken away~~ removed and the action of the Representatives of the people made to depend entirely, on what reason & their best judgments may clearly decide to be works of this description. But on the other hand, continue the practice which has obtained, of extending appropriations to objects merely local, and the funds of the people will be drained, & lavished upon every little by way thro' the country! The efforts then to be witnessed, will be, who by the most adroit management, & forward supplication shall obtain most from the public Treasury to be expended within his District that his popularity may be assisted and retained.

These considerations constitute my objections to they Bills. whether the improvement contemplated & desired by the Portland &c bill can most advantageously be reached thro' the bed of the river, or by a resort to the shore by ~~the~~ a canal is still matter of uncertainty. Congress, it appears, was not fully informed upon this subject, inasmuch as the Portland & Louisville Canal Bill makes an appropriation in aid of the canal, while the Light House Bill which passed at the same time contains an appropriation for a survay of the channel of the River to ascertain if the obstructions might not be removed, and the navigation consequently left free from toll. Both resorts cannot be necessary, both cannot be national—one or the other may be dispensed with; and since the improvement of the river is preferable as imposing no exactions upon the people the bill is not approved, that measures may be taken, if congress deem it expedient, to ascertain if the latter proposed method be not acceptable & preferable.[2] As it regard the other, usually denominated the Light house bill, there is so much exceptionable matter, & such a variety of interests & appropriation contained in it, that any examination of its provision more minute & particular than what has already been offered in the consideration of this, & the Maysville Road ~~Bill~~, appears unnecessary. Under all the circumstances which rest in connection with these Bills, & under the exercise of my best judgment, I have concluded ~~to reject~~ disapprove them. They are accordingly returned for the further consideration of congress, renewing to them the desire I have already heretofore expressed that they may pursue such a course of economical expenditure of the public money, that the public debt may be speedily paid. This being the case, and the duties reduced on all articles which do not enter into competition with the industry of our citizens, happiness & good feelings throughout the various sections of our extended & rapidly advancing country will be found. Then will the direction & appropriation of our surplus revenue become a subject of interest, worthy the representatives of ~~the~~ a great free & powerful people; and with proper deliberations & care may be placed upon a footing to conduce permanantly & steadfastly to the general benefit of the whole; and above all, to procure harmony & friendly feelings amonghst the States, considerations which never can be two highly regarded.

☞—Hence the Delaware & chesapeak, & the chesapeak & ohio canals considered as national objects should be seperated from the state corporations by purchase of their interests, and freed from all exaction & tolls, as all other national objects are by the constitution where improvements have been made for the benefit of commerce—These are of recent occurrence, & cannot be supported as constitutional growing out of long usage & acquiescence of the States—[3]

☞ hence all improvements considered as national objects, that have been made, or are now in progress in which the general Govt. has become a partner, under the authority to regulate commerce should be seperated from State corporations, ~~by a pur[chase] of the individual interest or sale by Govt~~ exonerated from all exactions & tolls, as all other national objects have been where the improvements were made for the benefit of commerce, under the constitutional usage of the country.

The Delaware & chesapeak—The chesapeak & ohio, with the Portland & Louisville canal may be considered as falling under this head; These are of recent occurrence, and cannot be supported as constitutional, growing out of long usage & acquiescence of the States—

[Endorsed by AJ:] Portland & Louisville canal bill & the Light House bill so called

AD draft, DLC (72).

1. The Louisville and Portland bill, like other canal subscriptions, provided for the government to receive its share of toll revenues paid to owners of company stock.

2. The lighthouse bill appropriated $300 to survey the Ohio rapids on the Indiana side opposite Louisville, to determine the feasibility of clearing obstructions from the channel.

3. In 1825, under President Monroe, Congress had subscribed for 1,500 shares of stock in the Chesapeake and Delaware Canal Company. In 1828, under Quincy Adams, it subscribed for 10,000 shares in the Chesapeake and Ohio Canal Company. These, the two previous Louisville and Portland Canal subscriptions, the vetoed Maysville Road bill, and the present Louisville and Portland bill all provided for the government to vote its shares in the election of company officers and to receive its due portion of toll revenues.

To the Senate of the United States
Gentlemen

I have maturely considered they bills—one proposing to authorise "a subscription of Stock in the Portland & Louisville canal company—the other the Light House bill so called, and now return them to Congress, with my objections to their passage

The President in his objections to the Maysville bill, has passed definitively upon points

1rst. That the Federal Govt possesses no authority to construct roads & Canals, exclusively within the limits of a state; and to exercise jurisdiction over the same with, or without the assent of a state.

2nd. That congress has no right to appropriate money for internal improvements which are not of general but local character.

He has intimated an opinion, that the right to make appropriations for national objects, has been acquired by the general federal Government thro' usage, and the long acquescence of the states—He has likewise, intimated that such appropriations, on the ground of expediency, ought to be deferred until the national debt be paid; and that the public interest imperiously demands an amendment of the constitution before any general System shall be adopted.

In reference to all appropriations for internal improvements, which can be considered general & national, some certain and definite ground should be taken. There should be established some rule, which shall give the greatest practicable precision to the power to appropriate money for objects of general concern, that is, to lay down some test, by which to determine their nationality—and to establish some rule for the regulation and erection of Light Houses, and for the regulation or improvement of commerce so far as our rivers are concerned.

The propriety and expediency of omitting all appropriations for these objects, except for those which shall be considered of fixed national character until the public debt shall be paid is matter for serious reflection, as well on account of the importance of that consideration, as to afford time for the adoption of some general constitutional arrangement, whereby the whole subject may be placed on better grounds—an arrangement—which never can be seriously attempted so long as scattering appropriations are made, and a scramble for them thereby encouraged.

Besides those improvements sanctioned by usage in the country, and the acquiescence of the states in that usage, another power is derived under the grant to congress to regulate commerce ~~amonghst~~ amongst the several States. Under this power, charts of our sea coasts have made, obstructions to navigation removed, inlets improved, Light Houses and buoys erected, and a Break water began. But all these benefits are derived without any expence or exaction on tolls from the commerce of the country—They are paid for out of the funds of the people, and they, free of expense receive the advantages conferred. A river constituting a great high way thro' which general commerce passes, must have been considered a matter of constitutional concern under the authority to regulate commerce, as much so, as if it were an arm or inlet of the sea. It is not the salt, or fresh quality of the water, but the beneficial purposes to which it may be applied and the difusive advantages it presents, which gives a determined character to the power to be exercised over it, under this grant of authority. In consequence of practised usage and acquiescence, a right exists to ~~assist in~~ improve the ohio river; but in the expenditure to be incurred for this purpose, like other improvements which congress has began & finished in aid of commerce, it should be free; exempt from all demands, or otherwise it is the exercise of a power, not to regulate commerce, but for the purpose of taxation & revenue—a description of cases which by the extreme caution of the constitution is required to originate in the House of Representatives.

The ohio river like the inlets and bays along the sea coast, is constitutionally placed by practice and usage of the government under the care & consideration of Congress. By the provisions of the Portland & Louisvill canal bill, the navigation of the stream is intended to be aided, but under the proposed arrangement it is to be done at an expence to the citizens, while other similar improvements, to wit, Light Houses, buoys, and breakwaters, which also assist commerce, are made at the expense of the government, and its benefits enjoyed without exactions of any kind. As the improvements of our bays, rivers, and harbours rest then upon the authority to regulate commerce, certainly no variation can arise whether the improvements to be made, be on the stream itself, or by a canal around an ~~impending~~ impeding obstruction, and which without such resort would be without remedy.

The falls of ohio consist of ledges of Rocks which in the bed of the stream, at low water interupt the navigation   The opinion entertained is, that to remove them would create a strong current, & perhaps, by reducing the quantity of water above would produce shoals & rapids. The most approved plan therefore was a resort to the shore by opening a canal, thereby preserving the level of the river; that the obstruction might be overcome without encountering the inconveniences anticipated, by attempting an unsuccessfull & expensive experiment on the bed of the river—Had this been done by the general government with its own resources, with the sanction of Kentuckey, unconnected with any private association or company, nothing could be perceived in the undertaking at variance with that uniform practice, and acquiescence, which has obtained in relation to the improvements of our bays & inlets, under the grant to regulate commerce. This course was not pursued: a subscription was made, & an association formed with a view to impose a tax upon all who should receive the benefit of the improvement, thereby depriving the citizen who may navigate the stream of those benefits which are enjoyed from works of similar character along our sea coast. These are strong objections against connecting the government with private companies. If in making canals &c &c, the united States may associate with one incorporated company within a state, they may connect themselves with another and another, until excessive & unlimited partnerships for these objects are created in all the states—In every local Bank it may become a partner and thus the entire orriginal character of our confederacy be changed & lost, and a new one created. When this shall be the case, consolidation, and, as a consequence, the destruction of our liberties will follow. Ought we not to guard against these? The high priviledges our Country enjoys, have been purchased, surely, at too dear a price, to be staked at such hazard. To encourage improvements by roads & canals is desirable, but they should not be undertaken at the expence of any principle of the constitution. Hence all improvements considered as national objects, that have been made, or are now in progress in which the general government has become a partner under the authority to regulate commerce should be seperated from state corporations ~~by a purchase of the individual interest or sale by the Govt.~~ & exonerated from all exactions & tolls, as all other national objects have been where the improvements were made for the benefit of commerce under the constitutional usage of the country—They Delaware & chesapeak, the chesapeak & ohio, and the Portland & Louisville canals may be considered as falling under this head. These are of recent occurrence, and cannot be supported as constitutional, growing out of long usage and acquiescence of the states.

Why on the score of policy should not the states project works of local character in their individual, rather than in their federative capacity. The funds necessary to their completion are to be obtained by the general government no where else, than from the people; and surely it will prove as beneficial & salutary, from time to time, ~~to leave~~ to diminish the taxes from imports upon articles which do not enter into competition with our own home industry, thus leaving the amount which would be drawn from the people in their own pocketts, thereby strengthening their resources, a capacity may be afforded to the states respectively, to project and execute such works themselves—Better feelings will be the consequence of such a course—jealousies will be prevented, and that prodigality will be avoided which might induce the representatives of one state to seek after appropriations, because they have been granted to another. Then will be witnessed no scramble, no electionering after the public funds. Improvements clearly determined to be national being such only as will, then, come under the supervision of Congress, every cause for unpleasant feeling will be removed, and the action of the Representatives of the people made to depend entirely on what reason and their best judgments may clearly decide to be works of this description. But on the other hand, continue the practice which has obtained of extending appropriations to objects merely local, and the funds of the people will be drained and lavished upon every little by way thro' the country. The efforts then to be witnessed will be, who by the most adroit management & forward supplication shall obtain most from the public Treasury to be expended within his own district that his popularity may be assisted and retained.

These considerations constitute my objections to they Bills. Whether the improvement contemplated & desired by they ~~Portland canal~~ bills can most advantageously be reached thro the bed of the river, or by resort to the shore by a canal is still matter of uncertainty. Congress, it appears, was not fully informed upon this subject, inasmuch as the Portland & Louisville canal bill makes an appropriation in aid of the canal, while the Light House bill which passed at the same time contains an appropriation for a survey of the channel of the river to ascertain if the obstruction might not be removed, and the navigation consequently left free from toll. Both resorts cannot be necessary, both cannot be national—one or the other may be dispensed with; and since the improvement of the river is preferable, if practicable, as imposing no exations or tolls upon the people, the bill is not approved, that measures may be taken, if congress deems it expedient, to ascertain if the latter proposed method, if practicable, be not acceptable & preferable. As it regards the other usually denominated the Light House bill, there is so much exceptionable matter, and such a variety of interests and appropriations contained in it, that any examination of its provisions more minute and particular than what has already been offered in the considerations here presented, and in the objections to the Maysville road &c, &c, appears unnecessary. Under all the circumstances which rest in connection with these bills ~~adding thereto, their having been finally passed on Sunday, and~~ under the exercise of my best judgment, I have concluded to disapprove them—They are accordingly returned for the further consideration of congress, renewing to them the desire I have already heretofore expressed that they may pursue such a course of oconomical expenditure of the public money, that the public debt may be spedily paid. This being the case, and the duties reduced in all articles which do not enter into competition with the industry of our ~~country~~ citizens, happiness, harmony, and good feelings throughout the various sections of our extended and rapidly advancing country will be found. Then will the direction and appropriations of our surplus revenue become a subject of interest worthy the representatives of a great free & powerful people; and with proper deliberations & care, may be placed on a footing to conduce permanantly, & steadfastly, to the general benefit of the whole; and above all to procure harmony and friendly feelings amongst the states; considerations which never can be too highly regarded.

[Endorsed by AJ:] The Portland & Louisville canal & Light House bills, considered & reasons for disapproval—

AD draft, DLC (72).

To John Coffee

May 31rst. 1830—
My Dr. Genl,
Congress has this day adjourned, after a very stormy session, and on Saturday night and Sunday morning, after they knew the Treasury was exhausted by former appropriations, passed many laws appropriating nearly one million of dollars—two of which, containing upwards of half a million, I have retained under consideration until next session of congress, having before put my veto upon one & today upon another; the reason assigned by me I herewith enclose you, with my best wishes for your happiness & that of your family—we are all well here & all join in kind salutations to you & family—we hope to be able to visit Tennessee this summer, but it is as yet a mere hope with me—your friend

Andrew Jackson

ALS, THi (15-1232).

To Samuel Jackson Hays

you and your Dr Frances [. . .] far progressed in safety & in health, but was mortified to hear that Frances had such alarm by the falling of the Horse.

I am happy that the overseer was able to accommodate you in a horse to take you out, & I hope you will make Hutchings return & go to Columbia to school as early as possible—I hope to be in Tennessee this summer for a few days, but what rout as yet I have not determined— Congress has just adjourned, after appropriating for internal improvements at least a million and a half more than is in the Treasury—Col Crockett joined the opposition in all its profligacy, & voted against the Indian bill throughout—Mr Webster was seen walking hand & arm with him, and it is proper that his constituents should [. . .][1] Stockly has either betrayed your confidence or communicated what you said to him to his mother as she has communicated to Daniel, that you should have said to Stockly that Major Eaton was so enraged at the treatment of Emily to his wife that it was with some dificulty that I prevented Major Eaton from making it a serious matter with Andrew—My Dr Saml. you ought to have had more prudence than to communicate any thing that would have given any pain to that amiable old lady—all matters having here gone to rest any thing that has taken place here, or that you might casually hear ought not to have been communicated   I do not know what precisely you have been said to have communicated—one thing is certain that a story always grows as it *[. . .]* If friends *[cannot . . . har]*mony we cannot complain of our enemies—[2]

If the gray horse you took out should suit you better than the one I gave you—you can take him—and if Doctor Butler will take the constitution colt he can have him at *$500*—

Present me kindly to your mother your Dr frances, Narcissa and all friends—say to Mr Chester I have recd *[his letter &]* will, if time permits, answer it before I leave this for Nashville[3]

May health & happiness be yours[.] yr friend

Andrew Jackson

ALS fragment, William C. Cook (15-1239). This letter replied to Hays's of May 5 above.

1. Tennessee congressman David Crockett (1786–1836), later of the Alamo, spoke and voted against the Indian removal bill, which passed the House on May 26 by 102 to 97.

2. "Stockly" was Emily T. Donelson's brother Stockley Donelson (1805–1888). Their mother was John Donelson's widow Mary Purnell Donelson. Daniel Smith Donelson was AJ Donelson's brother and first cousin to Emily and Stockley and to Samuel J. Hays.

3. William E. Butler and Robert J. Chester were Hays's brothers-in-law. Narcissa Hays was his sister.

From Robert Butler

Private

Tallahassee May 31st. 1830

My Dear Sir,

Your interesting letter of the 9th. inst. came to hand by last mail and I was much pleased to learn that you & family were all enjoying good health. The Death of our old friend Capt. Donelson had been communicated to us a few days before your letter reached. He had lived a round age, not generally allotted to men, and his life had been a useful one; his departure leaves a void in that neighborhood not easily supplied—[1]

You will have received my letter and inclosure on the subject of your correspondence with Doctor Bronaugh in the hands of Colo. Walton. How far that gentleman can reconcile the statement to Colo: Tutt with the one given in his letter to me is not for me to determine; and the whole matter seems mysterious that he should withhold the letters for a moment unless he thinks of being an applicant for office, and holds them as a bribe for success. Such a course might do under an administration where "Patronage" was power and corruption the watch word; *but times are changed* and the line of honesty begirts the nation.[2]

I do most sincerely hope & trust that some effectual course will be adopted to stop such a blood sucking system from draining the Treasury of its last dollar, as seems to pervade the Congress of the Union under the plea of General Welfare. The Press throughout the Union favorable to the existence & welfare of the nation, ought to take this matter in hand & I think the Telegraph & Courier & Enquirer would be doing much better than throwing slang at each other, which is sickening their readers very fast in this quarter. To be candid; I think Duff Green was about to trip when the Enquirer attacked him, and your surmises in a previous letter on the subject of secret canvassing between certain great men, induces me to believe they had Duff by the collar and would soon have led him without much difficulty; but good old Pensylvania & New York has blown their golden dreams "sky high"—[3]

I long to hear and know, that you have succeeded in your negotiations with England—to have a perfect understanding with that power, and France on the subject of our claims will be a *killing frost* to the *National Republicans* of *Hartford Convention* and *War pestilence & famine* memory.[4] That you may be enabled to bring light from darkness; make crooked things strait, establish the Jeffersonian doctrine of the constitution, thereby rendering perpetual our union; pay the national debt, complete our fortifications, remove the Indians, establish reciprocal commerce with all the world, and retire to the Hermitage to close the evening of your days in happiness & tranquility, is wishing no more than you can accomplish if properly seconded by the other arms of the Goverment & provided it pleaseth Providence to give you health—

My family are all in health, desire to be rememrd. to your family, and for yourself accept our warmest Affections—Truly yours

Robert Butler

[Endorsed by AJ:] Col R. Butler on the subject of Bronaughs letters in the hands of Walton—

ALS, DLC (38).
1. John Donelson had died April 21 at age 75.
2. George Walton (c1790–1863) of Pensacola, former secretary of Florida Territory, was a friend of AJ's late aide Dr. James C. Bronaugh and the administrator of Bronaugh's estate. Either with this letter or earlier, Butler sent AJ copies of correspondence detailing his recent efforts, made at AJ's behest, to retrieve AJ's confidential letters to Bronaugh, now presumably in Walton's hands. On April 19, Butler had written Walton conveying AJ's request for the letters. Walton replied on April 27 that he had "already been applied to on this subject by Charles P. Tutt Navy Agent here, who read to me a long homily on the sacred character of that correspondence, said to have been written by Mr. Donelson at the instance of the President." Walton told Butler that he would have answered a direct query from AJ, but that "this circuitous method" used instead "to *extract* correspondence from me," accompanied by insinuations that AJ feared his making "improper use" of the letters if not surrendered, was "very mortifying and insulting" and would be answered by silence. Butler replied on May 16 that neither he nor AJ had intended any insult, nor did he now see "any thing objectionable in the mode of application" for the letters, which by right belonged to AJ (DLC-38). Charles Pendleton Tutt (1780–1832) was navy agent at Pensacola, appointed by AJ in 1829.
3. Duff Green's *United States' Telegraph* and James Watson Webb's *Morning Courier & New York Enquirer* had been dueling over the presidential succession, Green touting

Calhoun and Webb favoring Van Buren. The dispute turned personal when the *Telegraph* charged on March 31 that Webb, a former Army lieutenant, was "driven from the army in disgrace" when he resigned in 1827. On May 6 Webb accosted Green outside the Capitol in Washington, intending to thrash him. Green drew a pistol in defense. Both editors published accounts of the affair, Green calling it a "ridiculous farce" and Webb posting Green as a coward as well as a slanderer.

4. The Hartford Convention, attended by delegates of the New England states, met in December 1814 to concert measures of opposition to the War of 1812 and the Madison administration. Its name came to symbolize seditious ultra-Federalism and was habitually linked by Jacksonians to the National Republicans of John Quincy Adams and Henry Clay. In an 1828 campaign address, Clay had famously said that he would rather see his country visited "with war, with pestilence, with famine, with any scourge other than military rule or a blind and heedless enthusiasm for mere military renown" (*Clay Papers*, 7:273).

From Thomas Kennedy

Hagers Town May 31—1830

Dear Sir,

I have just read your Message to Congress on the rejection of the Maysville and Lexington Turnpike Road, and it does you great credit.

You have come out openly and honestly in expressing your sentiments on a great National question, and although your enemies may secretly rejoice at your rejection of this bill, your enemies in Kentucky particularly, yet when the truth, the whole truth comes to be made known to the People, they will approve your conduct and sustain you in your views.

If the Maysville and Lexington Road is to be regarded as a National Work, then there are few Roads or Canals in the U. States which may not come under the same description, and here your enemies will find, that they have over-reached themselves.

I am and always have been a friend of Internal Improvements, and have always considered that Congress had power to appropriate money for great "National Purposes"—and introduced a Resolution into the Legislature of Maryland avowing this principle at the session of 1825 and which passed.[1] Yet it would be well to have this question settled finally, so that we should not at every session of Congress have the subject and the principle agitated.

The Government of the U.S. was certainly intended to protect us from Foreign Nations, and to take especial care of our external concerns—each State like a family must take care of its own interests, and as we are all of one family, I trust we shall seldom differ on questions which have for their main object, the public good.

There is another Road Bill—which if it passes, I have no doubt you will approve—I mean the Road from Washington to Frederick; That certainly is a National object; more so, much more so, than any other Road, or Canal, in the United States.[2]

Go on as I said in my last letter, do your duty fearlessly and you will be sustained by the People—You have thousands and tens of thousands of friends who will never leave you, never forsake you—and among them you may count on one until death is

Thos. Kennedy

ALS, DLC (38). Kennedy (1776–1832), at this time a state senator, had served in both houses of the Maryland legislature since 1817. He wrote again on June 5 (below).

1. Kennedy's resolution, introduced in the House of Delegates on January 9, 1826, declared "That the Congress of the United States does possess the power, under the constitution, to adopt a general system of internal improvement, as a national measure."

2. AJ vetoed the Washington Turnpike bill this same day.

June

To John Branch

1st. June 1830

Dear Sir,

Desirous of placing the solicitor of the Treasury in one of the four buildings occupied by the several Departments, the least crowded with clerks, I request a report from you giving me an account of the rooms and the manner in which they are used (stating the number of clerks in each) in your Department, in order that I may see in which a suitable selection may be made for the solicitor[.] yr. Respectfully

Andrew Jackson

[Endorsed by Branch:] Mr Boyle will furnish the information askd.[1]

LS, DNA-RG 45 (M124-124). A law of May 29, 1830, created the office of solicitor of the Treasury to oversee the Department's legal business. Virgil Maxcy of Maryland was nominated and confirmed the same day. Four buildings flanking the White House housed the State, Treasury, War, and Navy Departments. Branch replied to AJ on June 3, detailing the use of space in the Navy Department building. On June 5 Van Buren reported no room to spare in the State Department. On June 16 AJ ordered a shift of offices in the War Department to make room there for the solicitor general.

1. John Boyle (c1777–1849) was a Navy Department clerk.

From John Caldwell Calhoun

Steam boat Potomac
1st June 1830

Sir,

Tho' you intimate to me in your letter of yesterday, that no further communication is necessary with me on the subject to which it refers, I feel my self impelled to notice some of your remarks, lest my silence should be construed, into an acquiescence in their justness. I shall be as brief as possible.

You say, that I have entirely mistaken your letter of the 13th May, in supposing, that it questioned my motives, or conduct. I am not aware, that I charged you with an impeachment of my motives, but I certainly did understand, that you had questioned the sincerity and frankness of my conduct, and, I must add, that your present letter, notwithstanding the most demonstrative proof to the contrary, shows clearly, that I understood you correctly, and of course was not, as you suppose, mistaken.

I have no doubt, but that there are those, who actuated by enmity to me, and not friendship to you, have in the most artful manner for years, intimated, that I have been secretly endeavoring to injure you, however, absurd the idea, but I must be permitted to express my surprise, that you have permitted insinuations, as base as they are false, to operate on you, when every word and act of mine gave to them, the lie direct. I feel conscious, that I have honorably and fully performed towards you every duty, which friendship imposed, and that any imputation, to the contrary, is wholly unmeritted.

You mistake in supposing, that I have a dispute with Mr Crawford. That he bears me ill will is certain, but whatever feelings of unkindness, I ever had towards him, have long since passed away; so much so, that instead of returning his attacks on me, the line of conduct, which I had prescribed to myself, was to bear patiently and quietly all that he might say, or do, leaving it to time and truth to vindicate my conduct. If I have apparently departed from the rule, that I had prescribed, in this case, it was not because there was any disposition on my part to alter the line of my conduct, but when you interposed your name, by placing in my hand a copy of his letter addressed to Mr. Forsyth, I was compelled by an act of yours, in order that my silence might not be imputed to an acknowledgement of the truth of Mr. Crawford's statement, to correct his errors, and to expose the motives of enmity, which actuated him, and which sought to use you, as an instrument of its gratification.

You intimate that at some future time, when you may have more leisure, you will place the subject of this correspondence in a different light. I wish you to be assured, that I feel every confidence, that whenever you may be disposed to controvert the correctness of my statement or conduct in this affair, I shall be prepared, on my part, to maintain the truth of the one, and the frankness, honor, and patriotism of the other, throughout this whole transaction.

That you honestly thought that your orders authorised you to do, what you did, I have never questioned, but that you can show by any document, publick or private, that they were intended to give you the authority, which you assumed, or that any such construction was put on them at any time by the administration, or, myself in particular, I believe to be impossible. You remark, that my letter of the 29th Inst was the first intimation you had, that I had taken a different view from yourself of your orders. That you should conceive, that you had no intimation before, is to me unacountable. I had supposed, that the invitation of Mr Monroe in his letter to you of the 20th Octr 1818 to a correspondence with me with the intention, that the different views, taken by you and myself of the orders, should be placed in the files of the Department, and my letter to you of the 30th April 1828, covering a copy my letter to Majr. Lee in which I referred to the publick documents and private correspondence between you and Mr Monroe, as containing the views taken of your orders, and the offer, which I made to present my views more fully, if not given sufficiently explicitly in the documents refered to, were, at least, an intimation, that we differed in the construc of the orders, and I feel assured, that neither "my conduct, words actions or letters," afford the slightest proof to the contrary.

The grave charge, which you have made against me, of secret hostility and opposition, which, if true would so vitally effect my character for sincerity and honor, and which has caused a rupture in our long continued friendship, has no other foundation, but that of a difference between us in the construction of your orders—orders issued by myself, the intention of which I of course could not mistake, whatever may be their true construction in a military point of view, and the right and duty of interpreting which belonged especially to me, as the head of the War Department. The mere statement of these facts must give rise to a train of reflection, the expression of which, I cannot repress. Your course, as I understand it, assumed for its basis, that I, who, as Secretary of War, issued the orders, had some motive to conceal my construction of them, as if I had no right to form an opinion, whether the officer to whom they were given had transcended them or not, while the officer was at perfect liberty to express and maintain his construction. My right, as secretary of war, was at least as perfect as yours, as commanding officer, to judge of the true intent and limits of your orders, and I had no more motives to conceal my construction of than you had ~~yours~~ to conceal yours. The idea of concealment never entered my conception, and to suppose it, is to suppose, I was utterly unworthy of the office, which I occupied. Why should I conceal? I owed no responsibility to you! and if you were not affraid to place your construction on your orders, why should I be affraid to place mine? It was an affair of mere official duty involving no question of private enmity, or friendship, and I so treated it. I conclusion, I must remark, that I had supposed, that the want of sincerity and frankness would be the last charge brought against me. Coming from a quarter, from which I had reason to expect far different treatment, and destitute, as I know it to be of the slightest foundation, it could not fail to excite feelings too warm to be expressed with a due regard to the official relation, I bear to you. I have the honor to be Very Respectfully

J. C. Calhoun

[Endorsed by AJ:] Mr. Calhouns—letter, june 1rst. 1830—not to be answered—but placed on file

ALS, DLC (38). *US Telegraph*, February 17, 1831; *Calhoun Papers*, 11:196–99.

To John Macpherson Berrien

June 2nd. 1830—

The President with his respects to the atto. Genl—will thank him to look into the case of Joseph Shaw a Revolutionary pensioner, in whose behalf an act has been passed, without making any appropriation ¿is there any fund, appropriated, out of which this claim can be paid.

AN, DNA-RG 60 (15-1257). Joseph Shaw (c1761–1844), late of Massachusetts and now of St. Lawrence County, New York, had served in the Continental Army in 1778–80, entitling him to a life pension of $8 per month under an Act of March 1818. He applied for a pension in 1818, mis-stated the command in which he served, and was refused because his name was not on the muster rolls. In 1827 he reapplied with a corrected statement of service and was granted a pension. On May 28, 1830, AJ signed an Act directing the secretary of war to pay Shaw his back pension from 1818 to 1827. Apparently by accident, the Act omitted the usual clause designating from which appropriation the money should be drawn. On May 31, Ingham wrote a note that Shaw could only be paid from the general appropriation for Revolutionary pensions, but Eaton replied that this was improper (DNA-RG 60, 15-1260). Pursuant to AJ's direction, Berrien wrote Eaton this same day opining that Shaw could lawfully be paid from that fund (*HRDoc* 123, 26th Cong., 2d sess., p. 765, Serial 387).

From John Forsyth

[Jackson showed Calhoun's May 29 letter to John Forsyth, who wrote Calhoun on May 31 explaining his part in the affair. Forsyth said that he had not, as Calhoun charged, "interposed" Jackson into the controversy by furnishing him Crawford's April 30 letter, but had done so at Jackson's own request. Forsyth denied withholding information from Calhoun and offered to show him any of the correspondence he had not seen. He demanded to know if Calhoun's charge of conspiracy was meant to include him, and asked Calhoun's leave to show Crawford his May 29 letter (DLC-38; Calhoun Papers, 11:194–95). Calhoun's response of June 1 appears below. Forsyth enclosed copies of both letters with this letter to Jackson.]

Norfolk, June 2, 1830

Sir

The letter of Mr. Calhoun to you of the 29th. of May is of such a character, that I think, in justice to Mr. Crawford, he should know the contents of it. For Mr. Crawford's use I, therefore, respectfully request a copy of that letter, and of the documents sent with it. The enclosed copy of a correspondence, I have just had with Mr. Calhoun, is communicated to shew, that he is apprised of my design to make this application to you, and his opinion, that the propriety of granting it, rests wholly with you.

With great respect I have the honor to be Your friend and Obedient Servant.

John Forsyth

LS, DLC (38). AJ replied on June 7 (below).

[Enclosure: John C. Calhoun to Forsyth]

Copy.

Steam Boat Potomac
1st. June 1830.

Sir

I have just received your letter of the 31st, May, which was handed to me by Mr. Archer, since I came on board of the Boat.[1]

It gives me the first intimation, that I have had, that the President applied to you to obtain information of what took place in the Cabinet of Mr. Monroe, on the subject of the Seminole Campaign, and of course, as I suppose, that you were acting for the President, and not for yourself in your correspondence with Mr. Crawford. Neither the copy of his letter to you placed in my hands by the President, nor his Note covering that copy, gave me the slightest intimation of this fact; but on the contrary, I had a right to presume, from Mr. Crawford's giving you authority to shew me his letter, if you pleased, that the correspondence originated with yourself, and was under your control, and not, as I now infer, at the request of the President, and for his use. The view, in which I regarded the correspondence, and which I was justified to do, by the facts before me, fully explain my remarks in my letter to the President, as far as you are connected with them.

In the direction, which this affair has taken, it is not for me to determine, whether you ought to furnish me with any information, or what it should be. Had I supposed, that, under the circumstances in which I am placed, such a right belonged to me, I would have claimed it previously to my answer to the President's letter, so as to have had the advantage, before making my reply, of whatever light might be furnished from the sources, I therein indicated.

That there are those, who intend, that this affair shall operate against me politically by causing a rupture between the President and myself, and thereby affect, if possible, my standing with the nation, I cannot doubt, for reasons which I have stated in my answer to the President; but, I must be permitted to express my surprise, that you should suppose my remarks comprehended you, when they expressly referred to those, whose names did not appear in the transaction, and, consequently, excluded you.

My letter to the President is his property, and not mine, and consequently it belongs to him, and not me, to determine to whom he shall, or shall not furnish copies. I am respectfully Yours &c. &c.

(signed) J. C. Calhoun

Copy, DLC (38). ALS copy, DLC (38). *US Telegraph*, February 17, 1831; *Calhoun Papers*, 11:195–96.

1. William Segar Archer (1789–1855) was a Virginia congressman.

To John Macpherson Berrien

June 3rd. 1830—

Dr Sir,

I have after mature deliberation determined, in all cases, to leave the Execution of the sentence of the law to the direction of the Court without Executive interference, resting confident that in all cases the court will give a reasonable time for the interposition of executive clemency, where it ought to be interposed. you will please communicate this, to The Honble. Henry Baldwin & Jos. Hopkinson—respectfully yrs

Andrew Jackson

ALS, DNA-RG 60 (15-1273). Supreme Court justice Henry Baldwin and federal district judge Joseph Hopkinson (1770–1842) had presided at the Philadelphia trials of mail robbers James Porter and George Wilson. Baldwin pronounced the death sentence—the only penalty allowable by law—on May 27. On June 1, Baldwin and Hopkinson queried the administration if it wished to intercede before they issued a warrant and set a date for execution. Pursuant to AJ's direction, Berrien wrote them declining on June 4 (DNA-RG 60, M699-1). On June 8, Baldwin and Hopkinson issued a warrant for Porter and Wilson's execution on July 2. They wrote AJ to tell him so on June 10. AJ pardoned Wilson on June 14 (below).

To James Alexander Hamilton

(Private)

Washington June 3rd. 1830—

My Dr Sir

Your letters of the 28th. & 30th. ult. with the *remarks* accompanying them, have been recd.—but the hurry & bustle incident to the close of, & adjournment of Congress, has prevented me from answering until now—

I have had no conversation with Mr. McDuffie on the subject of Banks, nor never did I contemplate such, as in his immagination he has assumed, & commented on his report—I have often spoken of a national Bank, chartered upon the principles of the checks & ballances of our Federal government, with a Branch in each State, the capital apportioned agreable to representation and to be attached to, & be made, ~~part~~ subject to the supervision of the secretary of the Treasury, and an expose of its condition be made annually in his report to Congress as part of the Revenue—Which might be a bank of Deposit only, which I have always thought more consistant with our Government, than that it should become a broker, or Banking establishment for discount & deposits—But if the Federal Government should have any thing to do in Banking establishments beyond that of a safe deposit for our revenue, which might give aid to our fiscal concerns in a state of war—that it should belong to the nation exclusively, all its emoluments to accrue to the nation, to the whole people, and not to a few monied capitalists, to the exclusion ~~to~~ of the many, and I have no doubt but it could be so guarded in the charter, that it would be less dangerous to the liberties of our country, than the present Hydra of corruption, so dangerous to our liberties, by its corrupting influence every where, & not the least, in the congress of the union.[1]

I shew you when here my ideas on a Bank project, both of Deposit, (which I think the only National Bank that the Government ought to be connected with) and one of discount & deposit, which from the success of the State Bank of So. Carolina I have no doubt could be wielded profitably to our Govt. & less demoralising affects upon our citizens than the Bank that now exists[2]—But *a national*, entirely *national* Bank of Deposit is all we ought to have; But I repeat—a national Bank of discount & deposit, may be established upon our Revenue & national faith Pledged, & carried on by salary officers, as our Revenue is now collected with less injury to the morals of our citizens & to the destrution of our liberty than the present Hydra of corruption, and all the emoluments accrue to the nation as part of the Revenue—and I wish your ideas of a plan of each when leisure presents itself—

I have examined your remarks enclosed—I return them that Mr Calhouns name may be striken out—from a correspondence lately between him & myself in which I was obliged to use the language of Cesar—*et tu Brute*—it might be thought to arise from personal feeling, and arrouse the sympathy of the people in his favor—you know an experienced Genl always keeps a *strong reserve*; and hereafter it may become necessary to pass in review the rise & progress of this Hydra of corruption, when it will be proper to expose its founders & supporters by name—then, & then only, can his name be brought with advantage & propriety before the nation—I return it for this correction, which, when made, and two following numbers forwarded with it, I will have them published in the Tellegraph—This is the paper for *more reasons than one*.[3]

I have attempted five times to write you this scrall, & have been a dozzen of times interrupted since I commenced it—you must receive it as it is, I have no time to correct it[.] yr friend

Andrew Jackson

P.S. I am pleased with your commencement, & wish you to proceed—you cannot be too severe upon the report—A. J—it deserves it—

ALS, NN (15-1276). Hamilton *Reminiscences*, pp. 167–68.
1. McDuffie's April 13 House Ways and Means Committee report took AJ's proposal in his first annual message of a "national" bank "founded upon the credit of the Government and its revenues" to mean a full bank of discount and deposit, with branches throughout the states, acting wholly under executive control. The report warned of "this tremendous engine of pecuniary influence," which by wielding a vast patronage and dispensing tens of millions of dollars upon political motives would sink the country in corruption and despotism (*HRRep* 358, 21st Cong., 1st sess., pp. 25–28, Serial 201). Hamilton's first essay on the report, published in the *US Telegraph* on June 30, branded McDuffie's interpretation a "palpable absurdity," a "project of a bank, which his imagination had bodied forth," not resembling anything proposed or intended by AJ.
2. The Bank of the State of South Carolina was chartered in 1812 and run by a president and twelve directors, elected annually by the legislature. The bank was state-owned, and state funds made up its capital. It was empowered to issue notes, make loans on real and personal property, and receive deposits, including deposits of all public monies.
3. Hamilton's four essays criticizing McDuffie's report appeared, unsigned, in the *US Telegraph* on June 30, August 14, August 21, and September 21.

To John Randolph

(Copy)

Washington June 3rd. 1830

D. Sir,

I have appointed Mr. Clay Secretary of the Legation of the U. States in Rusia & will be happy to contribute whatever else may be in my power to give facilities to your mission.[1] I regret however to inform you, that in the hurry & confusion of the closing scenes of Congress the Bill making appropriations for your & other outfits remained unacted upon. as the necessity for this expenditure accrued during the Session of Congress, & was distinctly brought to their notice by a letter from the Secretary of State, I do not feel that I would be justified in considering it as contingent expense which ought to be properly paid out of the fund set apart for such purposes. I am however very anxious that you should arrive at your ~~place of destination~~ post sufficiently early to enable you to carry into effect the object of your mission in season for my annual message to Congress; in the practicability of which, I have strong confidence. I should therefore regard it as a public misfortune if the omission of Congress to act upon the subject of outfit were allowed to delay your departure. That the appropriation will be made at the commencement of the next Congress there can be no doubt; indeed, if it will be any accommodation to you, I will cheerfully accept a draft drawn upon me, individually, through one of the virginia Banks, payable about the 1rst. of January next, & trust to the appropriation being made for this object, before that time.[2] Please to let me hear from you upon this subject.

It would have given me sincere pleasure to have taken you by the hand before you leave the united States, but as that will not be the case, I have only to wish you an happy and successful mission. I hope to leave Washington for Nashville in a few days. I have the honor to be with sincere regard yr mo obdt. servt.

Andrew Jackson

[Endorsed by AJ:] copy to be filed   A. J.

ALS copy, DLC (38). Copies, NcD, PHi (15-1282); Copy, DLC-Randolph Papers (mAJs). Randolph replied June 8 (below).
1. The next day, June 4, AJ commissioned Randolph's namesake and protégé John Randolph Clay (1808–1885) as secretary of legation at St. Petersburg.
2. Congress had included a salary but no outfit for the minister to Russia in the general appropriation for 1830, signed into law on March 18. The next year's appropriation, passed March 2, 1831, allocated $9,000 for Randolph's outfit.

From James Alexander Hamilton

Private

New York June 3d
1830 midnight

My dear Sir,
I have just completed the whole subject except that which will treat of the first point made in the Report and upon that I shall be very brief combating merely some of the arguments put forth in the report and referring to ~~others which~~ those in opposition to the power which have heretofore been urged—and then I have done—I fear I have been already too difusive and too ~~smart~~ caustic ~~with Mr McD~~. The subject grew upon me as I advanced and my feelings of disapprobation of the author of this flimsy & unfair report became more excited as those characteristics became more apparent. You will, having the whole before you temper & expunge such parts as may require ~~it~~ either—[1]

Mr Van Buren informs me by a letter I received ~~yeste~~ today that you would set out for the Hermitage in the Course of this month—I trust you intend to take New York in your way   If you should not so intend I should like to know when you leave Washington in order that If I can find the time I may run away to Washington to pass a single day & night with you: So many events of ~~int~~ deep intent have occured since I left you that I feel the strongest desire to commune with you in the unreserved manner I have been heretofore permitted to do.[2]

with my most earnest prayers for your continued health & happiness I remain your sincere friend

James A. Hamilton

[Endorsed by AJ:] Recd. 6th. June 1830—to be answered

[Endorsed by AJ:] Mr J. A. Hamilton answered 7th of June 1830—

ALS, DLC (38). Hamilton *Reminiscences*, pp. 166–67.
1. The first point McDuffie's Ways and Means Committee report addressed was the constitutionality of the BUS. It maintained that Congress's power to charter such an institution was "a postulate no longer open to controversy" (*HRRep* 358, 21st Cong., 1st sess., p. 1, Serial 201). None of Hamilton's four published *Telegraph* essays argued the question.
2. Van Buren had written Hamilton on May 31 of AJ's plans to leave for the Hermitage in mid-June (Hamilton *Reminiscences*, p. 166). Hamilton came to Washington and met with AJ on June 14 and 15. On June 17 AJ left for Tennessee.

To John Branch

June 4th. 1830

Dr Sir

To prevent any dificulty hereafter in a Foreign Port between our Commanders of Ships of War and Consuls residing in ~~Foreign~~ said Ports

The following regulations is submitted to the secretary of the Navy for his consideration, and when adopted to be promulgated by his order—

In all Foreign Ports where consuls reside, the commander of our ships of war upon entering the port shall send a boat with an officer on board, who shall wait upon the consul and tender him a passage on board said Boat to visit said vessel.

This is the rule of all Foreign government, and such the instructions to all commanders of their vessels, so far as I am informed—This appears to be proper, as it may not be in the power of the consul to procure a boat to visit the armed vessel when she arrives, and I am informed some ~~incon~~ bad feeling has arisen because our consuls has not visited our armed vessels when they have come to anchor in a foreign Port, when it was out of their power to do so, for the want of a boat—

Think of this, & if such rule, does not exist, it will be proper to adopt it. yrs.

Andrew Jackson

P.S. it may be well to converse with the Navy Board on this subject— A. J.

ALS, DNA-RG 45 (M124-124). AJ wrote Van Buren on the same subject June 5 (below).

To Martin Van Buren

June 5th. 1830—

Dr Sir,

I have read, & now return the enclosed, as you have requested—

On yesterday I wrote a note to the Sec. of the Navy, on the subject matter of the enclosed note—conforming his order to the British mode—you will please converse with him on the subject—The distinction taken between squadrons and single ships, I think proper, and on your suggestion I have no doubt but the Sec. will have his order to conform to the idea[.] yrs—

Andrew Jackson

ALS, DNA-RG 45 (M124-124). AJ enclosed an undated memorandum by David Porter saying that a protocol for establishing relations between U.S. consuls abroad and visiting naval commanders was "absolutely necessary to preserve good feeling." Porter described British procedure, in which the consul came to the ship at the captain's invitation on a boat supplied by him, and French, by which the captain himself came ashore and paid the first call (DNA-RG 45, M124-124). On June 22 Branch drafted a circular order to all naval commanders. Following Porter's recommendation, it prescribed the British method—a first meeting on board ship—for all encounters involving squadron commanders and/or regular consuls. But in the case of a single ship commander and a consul general, the former should make the first call (DNA-RG 80, M977-1). Branch furnished the order to Van Buren on June 23. He approved, and on June 25 the State Department circularized consuls to conform to it (DNA-RG 59, M179-68).

From James Alexander Hamilton

Private

N.Y. June 5 1830

My dear Sir:

I enclose herewith the last portion of the criticism and must confess it is that part with which I am least satisfied—I had hoped to have put my hands upon the arguments of Mr Jefferson & the Atty Genl Mr E Randolph when this question first arose & from them I intended to have stated their views at large but I have been unable to find those papers and have therefore omitted that part of my plan of an argument rather than delay the paper any longer.

I can only add that I wish this offering of my industry & zeal to serve you was more acceptable than it is

Perhaps further reflection and more leisure may enable me to add something further on this subject & particularly the last Branch of it.

The hour for Closing the Mail having arrived before my transcriber has completed his task I send this letter without its companion to say that the latter will be forwarded tomorrow. I remain in haste with the truest attachment your friend & servt

James A. Hamilton

ALS, DLC (38). In February 1791 President Washington had consulted his Cabinet on the pending bill to incorporate the first Bank of the United States. Secretary of State Thomas Jefferson and Attorney General Edmund Randolph submitted opinions arguing that it was unconstitutional.

From Thomas Kennedy

Hagers Town Md June 5 1830

Dr. Sir,

I wrote to you about a week ago after seeing your Message in regard to the Lexington and Maysville Road, and expressing a hope that the Rockville and Frederick Road Bill would meet with your approbation, as its character was much more National than the other but it seems you have also refused to approve it—I regret this for many reasons, particularly as I believed the Road of great importance to the government, to the Post office Department particularly, and to the whole Western Country, and at this particular crisis in the affairs of our State, it will give in some Counties the vantage ground to the opponents of your administration, and this I do no wish to see them obtain.

Your true friends however duly appreciate your motives, and when the whole ground is fairly viewed by the people, the excitement will pass away. And although we have wily and desperate foes to contend with, who take all advantage by rousing prejudices, and making misrepresentations, we shall I think again defeat them in Maryland—at least we shall try. I was much pleased to find that Mr Noah's appointment was at last confirmed—He is a Hebrew, but has more liberality in his disposition than one half of our Christians.

I have seen many of your friends passing through Hagers Town since the adjournment of Congress. Let me suggest to you a short visit to Annapolis this summer. The Court of appeals sit in June, and during the term the Governor and Council will also very probably meet. It is well worth a visit if you have never been there, and if I knew when, it would give me pleasure to meet you there. Mrs. Bland and the Chancellor would be much gratified and so would many of your other friends.[1]

Wishing you every happiness now and hereafter, I am your friend

Thos. Kennedy

ALS, DLC (38). Kennedy wrote again on June 26 (below).
    1. Theodorick Bland (1776–1846) had been Chancellor of Maryland since 1824. His wife was Sarah Glen Davis Bland (c1768–1854).

From Ann Maria Gage

Shalersville   Portage county Ohio   June 6th. 1830

Dear and Highly Honored President Of the United States

May his goodness excuse my humble and limited capacity and at the same time the liberty which I am necesiated to take in asking his highness to grant me the privilege of obtainining his honored Signiture on a deed for Six hundred and forty Acres of Land lying near the mouth of St. Josephs river in Michagan Tereto[ry] and wishing him to mention the same on the deed as it must be in such manner as the President may direct   I am a poor *widow* and haveing three orphen sons who *[have]* not arived at maturer years sufficient to advi*[se]* with me I have paid five hundred dollars in specia land all that I possessed and without the permission of the President of the United states I can hold no legal claim I therefore lean upon his hiness as a friend to the widow and the orphen and beg he will Sanction my deed and direct the same *[to be given]* as soon as convienant which will *[reflect]* lasting favor on my and my helpless Chillren[.] respectfully your Obedient and Humble Servant

Ann Maria Gage

[Endorsed by AJ:] refered to the commissioner of the General Land office

ALS, DNA-RG 49 (15-1305). Gage had purchased title to a square-mile section of land from Rebecca Burnett, a Potawatomi Indian, to whom it was reserved by an 1821 treaty. By terms of the treaty, the reserve could not be sold without the president's consent. On July 21, General Land Office chief clerk John M. Moore wrote Gage that AJ could not approve the sale because Burnett's tract had not yet been located and surveyed (DNA-RG 49, M25-25).

To John Branch

June 7th. 1830

My Dr. Sir—

Finding that no Legislative act has been passed relative to the Navy, it is now ncessary that some System should be adopted, by which all pay & emoluments of the Navy may be tested, and uniformity preserved, in every respect.

These reflections make it proper that I should call your *particular attention*, to the act of 1806. This law appears imperative. It declares that no officer in the Navy shall receive more than half pay, during the time *they shall not be under orders for actual service*

your attention is drew to this law that we may conform to it, and that a report may be made of the officers in servie & under orders, entitled to full pay, & those not, who are only under half pay, & paid accordingly— you will please note in this report, if any, what, deviation has been made by former administrations, from this law. The law must be strictly adhered to, unless where ~~the law~~ it authorises the department to make rules, then the rule must be in writing, & approved by the President—where this is not the law must, in *all cases* be our guide, yours respectfully

Andrew Jackson

ALS draft, DLC (73; 15-1308). A law of April 21, 1806, limiting the size of the peacetime Navy, decreed that shipboard officers should receive no more than half pay "during the time when they shall not be under orders for actual service." On February 4, 1830, the House of Representatives called on Branch for a comprehensive accounting and justification of pay and allowances to all naval officers and agents in 1828 and 1829. Branch responded on May 29 with a report by fourth auditor Amos Kendall. It showed that in 1819 Navy secretary Smith Thompson had ordered full pay for all officers except those on furlough, and that in 1824 Navy secretary Samuel Southard had ordered such officers "to hold themselves in readiness for active service." Construing this to mean they were "under orders" entitled them all to full pay, evading the 1806 law (*HRDoc* 121, 21st Cong., 1st sess., p. 3, Serial 198).

Branch answered AJ on June 9 with a copy of the naval register, marked to show officers on active duty at sea or on shore. Officers on furlough, on leave of absence, or waiting orders were unmarked, although, Branch noted, many of those on leave "have recently returned from long cruises." Branch enclosed Smith Thompson's 1819 regulation authorizing full pay for all officers not on furlough (DNA-RG 45, M472-1). In March 1835 Congress passed a comprehensive law regulating naval salaries. It prescribed specific lower rates of pay for officers on leave, on shore duty, or awaiting orders.

To John Forsyth

Washington june 7th. 1830

Sir

I have received your letter of the 2nd. instant inclosing a copy of ~~your letter~~ one from you to Mr. Calhoun of the 31rst. ultimo, and his reply thereto—all which I have duly noted.

you have requested a copy of Mr. Calhoun' letter to ~~you~~ me of the 29th. of May last, for the purpose of shewing it to Mr Crawford. Mr Calhoun in his reply to you, does not consent, nor yet object to your being furnished with a copy, but refers the matter to my discretion.

A copy of the original letter of Mr Crawford to you, having been submitted to me, it occurred to me as being proper & correct, that you should be apprised of Mr Calhouns answer, and therefore it was shewn to you. I cannot on reflection perceive any impropriety in now according to you the request you have made, particularly as on your refering this matter to Mr Calhoun, he does not object. I accordingly send it with this injunction, that it be used for no other purpose but the one you have stated, "to be shewn to Mr Crawford."

In the letter which you addressed to Mr Calhoun, you state as follows, "Having at the request of the President to be informed what took place in the Cabinet of Mr Monroe on the subject of the Seminole campaign, laid before him a copy (except the omission of a name) of a letter from Mr. Crawford &c &c";[1] This is construed by Mr Calhoun into a declaration, that I requested you to furnish me with the information. I am satisfied it was not by you so understood, and I would be glad you would so explain to him. I never conversed with you upon this subject previous to the time when you sent me Mr Crawford's letter. The facts are these. I had been informed, Mr Crawford had made a statement concerning this business which had come to the knowledge of Col James A. Hamilton of N.Y. on meeting with Col Hamilton I enquired of him and received for answer that he had; but remarked, that he did not think it proper too to be communicated without the consent of the writer—I answered, that being informed that the marshal of this District had, to a friend of mine, made a similar statement to that, which was alledged to have been made by Mr Crawford that I would be glad to see Mr Crawford's statement, and desired he would write and obtain his consent—my reasons for this request, were, that I had, from the friendly professions of Mr Calhoun always believed him my friend throut all this seminole business, and had therefore a desire to know if in this I had been mistaken, & whether it was possible for Mr Calhoun to have acted with such insincerity and duplicity towards me.[2] I have inclosed a copy of this letter to Mr Calhoun, and I am Sir, with respectful regard yr mo obdt. servt.

Andrew Jackson

[Endorsed by AJ:] (Copy) To the Honble. John Forsythe Agusta Georgia June 7th. 1830   To be copied & inclosed to Mr Calhoun—

ALS draft, DLC (38). *US Telegraph*, February 17, 1831; *Calhoun Papers*, 11:199–201. Forsyth replied June 17 (below).

1. Forsyth's May 31 letter to Calhoun began with these words (DLC-38; *Calhoun Papers*, 11:194–95).

2. Tench Ringgold (1776–1844) was marshal of the District of Columbia. The friend who conveyed his statement was William B. Lewis.

To John Caldwell Calhoun

Washington june 7th. 1830

Sir

On the 5th. instant, I received a letter from Mr Forsythe, of the Senate, requesting a copy of your letter to me of the 29th. of May last. I have not been able to perceive any objections, to comply with his request. A copy of my letter to him on this subject, I have thought it proper, should be sent to you, it is therefore inclosed.

I am sir, very respectfully yr mo, obdt. servt.

Andrew Jackson

[Endorsed by AJ:] (Copy) to Mr. J. C. Calhoun 7th. June 1830—inclosing him a copy of mine to Mr J. Forsythe same date—To be copied—& inclosed to Mr C—ne

ALS draft, DLC (38). *US Telegraph,* February 17, 1831; *Calhoun Papers,* 11:199.

From James Alexander Hamilton

New York, June 7, 1830.

My Dear Sir:

Your kind letter of the 3d instant was received to-day, together with Number 1, which I have altered in the manner you suggested, and in such other respects as were suggested to my mind on its perusal; and I have the honor to enclose it herewith. The last part was forwarded on Sunday. You cannot do any act that will be more gratifying to me than to return any of the other portions as you have done this, with your intimations for the purpose of revision and amendment, for you will thus evince your confidence in my desire to serve you. I hope at my earliest leisure to be enabled to put in the form of heads for a Bill, such a scheme of a Bank of *Discount* and *Deposit* as you have suggested. At the same time I must differ from you in the opinion you have expressed that it ought to be exclusively in the hands of the Government and its paid officers. A bank of deposit may be safely so arranged, but it will want the ability in certain exigencies to aid the fiscal operations of the Government which a bank of discount and deposit would possess, while the latter could hardly be safely left to the direction of persons who were not interested in the faithful and cautious administration of its affairs. I have thought of a plan in which the credit and revenues of the Government would be the foundation, and with which individual interest could be united in such a way as to preserve a preponderance to the Government, and in which the direction would be so managed as that the Government would appoint the whole—one half of its own mere volition, uninfluenced by the interference of the individuals interested, and the other half to be appointed from a list of nominees chosen by the individuals interested; which should be submitted to the President for his selection; the President of the Institution to be appointed by Government, the Cashier by the President and Directors. The difficulties to be avoided on the one hand and the other are these: a bank, the capital of which should be furnished by the Government under the direction of paid officers, would be exposed, 1st, to the danger of having its funds loaned to irresponsible persons who might be of the family or friends of the directors, and thus wasted and destroyed; and next, that these directors, influenced by the power which created them, might use this money with reference to political influence, and thus endanger the purity of our institutions, as well as waste the capital. The only way I now see in which these evils can be avoided, is to secure the untiring watchfulness of individual interest, always better managers of pecuniary concerns simply, than Governments are; and so are private individuals better than corporations; to permit them to purchase a part of the capital thus furnished, for which the Government will be paid at par (and thus raise the means to discharge its debt, if that should not have already been done), and for which and no more it will ultimately be responsible. But it is quite clear that individuals will not so invest their funds unless they can participate in the management of the bank; for they will naturally say, a bank exclusively under the direction of persons appointed by Government may go on very well in time of peace, but in war, when the Government wants means, these directors will lend the whole capital and credit and all to it. I would, therefore, to secure the confidence of the Government and individuals, form a direction in the manner I have stated, and I would superadd that no individual loan should be made without a concurrence of two out of three of the public directors; or to the Government, without the sanction of two out of three of the private directors. I throw out these suggestions for your consideration just as they occur to me. With all this I would connect so much of that part of the plan of a bank of deposit, which I sent to you, as would secure the faithful disbursement and safekeeping of the public revenues. I had intended to have thrown out some hints of a plan of a bank, but my time is so little my own, as to compel me to defer them to a future day. With the truest attachment, your friend, &c.

Printed, *Reminiscences of James A. Hamilton*, pp. 168–69 (15-1312).

From James Biddle and David Offley

Constantinople June 8th. 1830—

Sir

We have the honor to transmit herewith a copy of a treaty signed by us in French on the part of the United States, with the Sublime Ottoman Porte, together with a separate secret article

As there exists a difference of opinion between us respecting the secret article, we shall make, as to it, separate communications to the Honorable the Secretary of State. We also transmit the original in Turkish signed by the Reis Effendi on the part of the Porte.[1]

The presents made by us will be covered by the sum authorized to be expended upon effecting a treaty. The whole expence incurred will exceed the sum authorized. The excess however will be of trivial amount.[2]

We have the honor to be, with great consideration and respect your most Obedient humble servants.

James Biddle
David Offley

Mr Rhind declines signing the above. He disagrees with us as to the propriety of forwarding these documents by a public Vessel of the United States and informs Mr. Offley that he intends to protest in the British Chancellery against our doing so. We therefore forward this communication without his signature.[3]

LS, DNA-RG 59 (M46-3). Copy, DNA-RG 233; Copy (extract), DNA-RG 46 (15-1318). *HRDoc* 250, 22d Cong., 1st sess., p. 95 (Serial 221). The nine public articles of the treaty concluded by Charles Rhind on May 7 covered commercial matters, including reciprocal most-favored-nation status, consular privileges, and American navigation of the Black Sea. A separate and secret article, which Biddle and Offley accused Rhind of concealing from them until four days after their arrival on May 24, authorized the Turkish government to arrange through official channels for the procurement of American-built warships of the same quality and price as those built for the U.S. Navy. Rhind explained to Van Buren on June 1 that the article, though crucial in concluding the treaty, was not a *sine qua non* for its ratification and did not bind the U.S. to do anything (*HRDoc* 250, 22d Cong., 1st sess., pp. 94–95, Serial 221). Biddle and Offley believed the article violated Van Buren's instructions that the treaty "should extend only to objects of commerce and navigation, and should, in no event, interfere in the neutral obligations of the United States" (Serial 221, p. 72). But rather than scuttle the treaty and risk Turkish retaliation, they signed it with the secret article on May 30. Beginning the next day, Biddle and Offley sent Van Buren a series of complaints against Rhind, which he reciprocated against them (DNA-RG 59, M46-3).

1. Mohammed Hamid was the Turkish Reis Effendi, the minister responsible for foreign affairs.

2. A sum of $20,000 had been put at Biddle's disposal for treaty expenses, mainly presents or bribes to Turkish officials (*Jackson Papers*, 7:427–28). On June 15 Biddle sent AJ an account showing actual chargeable expenses of $21,136.

3. Rhind considered the treaty his accomplishment and claimed the right to bring it home to present to AJ in person. He also objected to Biddle and Offley's participation in awarding presents and refused to join them in an official audience. Rhind did not, as threatened, lodge a formal protest in the English Chancellery against Biddle and Offley's proceedings, but sent one to Van Buren this same day. He wrote AJ on June 21 (below).

From Charles Jones Love

Mansfield 8th June 1830

My Dear Sir,

I recd. on yesterday only your favor of the 24th ultimo covering the Check for Nichol & Hill you will find Inclosed a receipt for the amount.[1] I wrote you last week & stated that your Cotton had been sold & &

I am really afraid your friends in the Senate or rather your pretended friends are disposed to place you in an unpleasant situation before the people, by acting so contrary to your wishes, and the good of the Nation   I cannot account for it unless it grows out of the next Presidential question

your not sanctioning the law for the apropriation of the Maysville Turnpike Road will give general satisfaction in this part of the state. I cannot for a moment doubt that it will be very popular generally, let that question be settled and at the next Congress you would have applications for millions for the same perposes   We have a law to make a Turnpike Road to Murfreesobro & Franklin which will take 180 thousand easily and I assure you we should have made a similar application and Indeed all the States would (save one or two), how can the nationl debt be paid off if the money is otherwise appropriated & you then would be sensoured for it by your enemys[2]   your friends know you will act from the purest motives and leave party feelings out of the question.

I regretted very much the rejection of our friend Majr Lee what is to become of him or what can be done for him he must not be lost   I hope providence will yet smile on him

The weather is very cold for the season we are now sitting by afrid it will make the cotton dwindle and turn yellow

Mrs Love desires to be affectionatley remember to you   I am deare your friend

Ch J Love

ALS, DLC (38).
1. AJ had presumably sent Love a check he wrote to William B. Lewis for $1,848 on May 24. Love paid that sum to Nichol & Hill for AJ on June 7.
2. In its 1829–30 winter session the Tennessee legislature incorporated a turnpike company from Nashville to Murfreesboro, with Love as a charter member, and another from Nashville to Franklin, each with an authorized capital stock of $75,000.

From John Randolph

Roanoke June 8th. 1830

My dear Sir,

Your most esteemed letter of the 3d. Instant was received yesterday by Mr Clay. Whilst I tender you my warmest acknowledgments for the very liberal & disinterested offer which you hold out to me, I cannot prevail upon myself to accept it. I have about half the amount of an outfit in Bank; & last year's crop of Tobo. to pay the charges of the current year upon my estate—For by God's blessing, I have kept clear of Debt & thus have been enabled to preserve my independence. The chief inconvenience that I shall sustain will be the obligation to forego a most eligible & advantageous purchase by using my private funds in the publick service. others have risked purse & person for their country, & poured out their blood like water in her cause.

I purpose being in Norfolk on the 16th provided the ship shall have reached Hampton Roads, which I shall know at Richmond, by the Steam Boat of the preceding day. She shall not be delayed by me.

In case that I shall be so fortunate as "to carry into effect the object of my mission, in season for your annual message"—shall I be deemed too encroaching if I ask leave to spend the winter in the South of Europe; provided I see no prospect that the publick interest may suffer thereby?

In the hurry of departure, I trust that some excuse may be found for the brevity of this Letter. I have no command of language that will do justice to the sense of profound respect & regard with which I am, Dear Sir, your obliged & most faithful Servant

John Randolph of Roanoke

[Endorsed by AJ:] Let the request be granted well aware that he will be always at his post when duty calls   A J

ALS, DLC (38). Randolph's official instructions of June 18 included permission to leave Russia for the winter if his mission did not suffer thereby.

To Samuel Delucenna Ingham

June 9th. 1830—

The President with his respects to the Secretary of the Treasury & encloses him the opinion of the attorney general in the case of Genls. Hinds & Coffee; which appears to me him to be conclusive, that they are entitled to a credit for the amount deposited by them, & not subject to the loss by depreciation

AN, PU-Ingham Papers (15-1333). In 1826 John Coffee and Thomas Hinds had served as commissioners to treat with the Choctaws and Chickasaws. They drew $15,000 for the expenses of their mission and at its end returned $3,646.03 in unspent funds. Of this, the Treasury rejected $2,375 in notes which were "uncurrent," that is, not presently accepted for specie or for other notes at par. On June 8, attorney general Berrien submitted an opinion to AJ that Coffee and Hinds, having drawn their funds in the only paper available and returned that same paper to the government, were not liable for any deterioration in its value.

From Margaret O'Neale Timberlake Eaton

Washington City June 9th. 1830
4 oclock

My Dear Genl
My dear husband since his return from the office has expressed to me the desire you had for me to dine at your house to day. You know the cheerfulness with which at all times I should be willing to do any thing which could contribute to your idea of propriety, but in cases where my feelings are concerned I know you would not require me to do what they would not sanction. Circumstances are my dear Genl are such as that under your kind and hospitable roof I cannot be happy. You are not the cause, for you have felt and manifested a desire that things should be different. I could not expect to be happy at your house for this would be to expect a different course of treatment from part of your family, different ever yet it has been my good fortune to meet. You meet on such occasions to enjoy ourselves, but there would be none to me. I agree to the suggestion my husband has made that it may be a triumph to some if it may be said I were not invited, but what of that it will only be another feast to those whose pleasure it is to make me the object of their censures and reproaches. I ask to say to you that whatever may be the cause of the unkind treatment I have recd from those under your roof, whose course could not but be a serious injury in the opinion of others one consolation is had, that I have done all in my power to avoid it. I do not know what *tales* may have been *borne* of *things* said by me to their prejudice, but I know very well that whatever they may have been they are untrue. I have spoken of your family in no other manner than a respectful one. Much injustice as I think they have done me, I claim to say in the language which we are commanded to regard, that I have ever endeavored to return good for evil. But if in moments of cruel suffering I have permitted any harsh or unkind expression to escape me is not an apology found in those persecutions which heaven grant no member of your family may ever feel. But I have never done so. I challenge any one to say they ever heard me. Enough

pardon me for this interruption, but I could not say less in justice to you and myself, and hope I have said nothing that is improper[.] y

signed Margaret Eaton

Copy taken 9th. June 1830

[Addendum by AJ Donelson:] The only *unkind treatment* which my family can have pacticed towards Mrs. Eaton is their refusal to acknowledge her right to interfere with their social relations. all else is imaginary or worse. This letter is abundant evidence of the indelicacy which distinguishes her character, and is disgraceful to her husband. Instead of coming to me as the head of my family for explanations where objections to my conduct were entertained, they have invariably approached the President with childish importunities, first aiming to excite his sympathies, and then to pour upon them the poison which they had concocted for all who did not bow to her commands. pursuasion, personal threats, and finally banishment from the presence of the President to whom I have stood from my infancy in the relation of son to Father, have served their turn as the wretched expedients in their hands to gratify the vain desire of being understood to possess the controul of his confidence and favor.

A. J D
10th. June 1830

Copy in AJ Donelson's hand, DLC-Donelson Papers (15-1328).

From James Ronaldson

Louisville Ky June 9 1830

Sir

It is now a week since I arrived here, the time has been almost exclusively devoted to understand the present state of the Louisville & Portland canal (which by the bye should have gone by some other name) its natural state and relation with other parts of the union, and the prospects of its completion: And considering the interesting connection your situation forms with this National work, independent of the interest as a private individual you feel for the industry and prosperity of this Union, I deem it a duty I owe you to communicate what has occured to me; should the views I have taken be wrong, or my ideas not be properly expressed, the errors will be in my capacity not my intention.

You are personaly acquainted with the location of the canal, and the fall of some thing over twenty feet, that has most fortunately been by nature formed at this place, from a ledge of rocks crossing this fine river, and every thinking man must be aware that to overcome the inconveniency, a canal is the only rational way; inconsiderate men have spoken of cuting the rocks that form the fall: If this was done the water above would be run of, and the river ruined; where a three hundred ton vessel can now sail, a man on horseback might forde the river. The canal admits of being formed on both sides, Kentucky, or Indiana, and is simply a task of labor, which when reduced to a money estimate might on the Indian side cost a million of Dollars, or one third less on the Kenucky side, this excess of cost would be more than remunerated by the increased value land in the neighbourhood of the canal would experience, at present it is comparatively low. I mention this natural state of things only to notice as a fortunate circumstance as respects the nation, because the time may come when the trade will require both, and it affoards opportunity to unmask the apethey of those interested in the prosperity of Louisburgville, for the million that would be added by the Canal to Indiana land; would be lost to Louisville; and whenever the makeing a second canal commences the property of Louisville will fall in value; yet in the face of this, the Louisville and Portland canal has very few friends here; in proof of this, the citizens own only about $7000 of the stock, they prise the carting of goods from the vessels above and below the falls, the gains of Hack coaches, storeage, and commission, more than the canal; I assure you it is no favourite with Lousiville or Potaland; and should have been called by some other name—"The nine States canal" "the United States Canal" would have been more apropriate and something like truth the present name is wrong.[1]

As matters now stand this place gains by the carting &c &c aluded to, but the increased business that will result from the canal, will many times compensate all that is lost by hacks & drays; but if this was not to happen, the business relations of nine or more states, should not be intercepted, or the vast exchange of produce and merchantdize of all discriptions exposed to delay, or injury, carting or any other tax or expence that can be avoided: The profit of the Louisiana cotton grower, and the Pittsburg joiner for example, are small enough already, and can ill affoard a transit tax to Louisville which is now the case, and they must remain payers of this tax untill the canal is opened, and how or when this will be is now the question.[2]

Accounts of the Bill authorising the United States to subscribe another hundred thousand dollars to the stock of this canal has been received here, and also the reasons from the Executive for not concuring in the Maysville Road appropriation: There is with the Officers of the canal great anxiety on this subject; this anxiety grows out of the present empty state of their treasury, and a fear that the principles and reasoning on the Maysville road bill may be extended to this Canal: The practice of Congress delaying to the last hours of the session the passing of laws and at once sending to the President for his concurance great numbers of them, dos not affoard that Officer reasonable time for the human mind to examin the principl, the detail, or even the gramatical, and correct wording of the law, a defect in which might be the source of great error or trouble: It has been said that an edition of the Bible came from the press in London and some copies were sold, before it was discovered a very essential—NOT was left out of one of the Ten Commandments, thus directing, in place of forbiding a sin:[3] Now in this mass of Laws it is possible the fate of the Louisville and Portland canal bill may be decided by takeing it in with the Maysville road which is a local not even a state affair, and the other a National one so far as the interests of Nine or more States can make it so, This canal has all that can characterise a National work and one in which the Nation has already invested a considerable amount of money, which will for a considerable time be rendered unproductive stock to the Treasury, and what is equally to be regretted unserviceable to the western states: If the work for want of funds is stoped for only one month, a great loss must be the consequence the season will be lost and the canal being so exposed in its unfinished state to the effects of the Ohio floods it is certain to suffer great injury.

The present state of the working is good, I presume much better organised and going on better then at any former period, and if no interuption takes place I think there is a fair prospect of finishing this year and it is exposed to interuption from two causes only viz the river riseing, or want of funds, the former can be to some degree guarded against and if unfortunately water should get in by a rise the Steam engine now erected would in no great span of time remove it; and let the work go on. The treasury is empty, and no provision has been made for the contingency of the United States not takeing this other $100000 worth of the stock: The Contractors, their labourers must have their pay weekly, they cannot do without the means of subsistance, no one here is able or *willing* to lend the money, and five, six, or eight weeks will be required to negociate a loan or procure subscriptions in the Atlantic States, or where people take an interest in the Ohio being uninterupted in its navigation.

What is to be done in this interm I am not able to say, be assured I am at present under the influence of no very enviable feelings   I fear the work will be suspended and there may, [or we] may say, will result from this a loss perhaps forty or fifty ℔ Cent on the whole cost, which will finaly become a tax to that proportion on the industry of Nine or more States in proportion to their industry is connected with the navigation of the Ohio, the toll of the canal will be just so much higher—

I regret its not haveing been my fortune to have seen all these things sooner, or that some one has not made the Government and those interested in the Canal acquainted, with them, that due provision might have been made to prevent the ills that threaten the work, and I should be delighted to see it brought to a creditable conclusion under your auspices, it will prove on of the most useful works the Nation has yet engaged in

To me, it appears this Nine State Canal will pass a greater mass of property than the celebrated Canal that joins Clyde & Forth devideing

Scotland by uniteing those two arms of the sea and the effects of the Ohio Canal on American industry will be greater than the effects of the Clyde and Forth Canal has been on British[.][4] With sentiments of undiminished Respect I am your most obt. ser

James Ronaldson

PS—I expect to remain here not more than one week longer

ALS, DLC (38). Ronaldson (1770–1841) was a leading Philadelphia typefounder, capitalist, and philanthropist, the president of Philadelphia's Franklin Institute, and a large investor in the Louisville and Portland Canal Company.
1. Much of the canal company's stock was owned in Philadelphia.
2. The canal passed its first steamboat in December 1830 and began limited regular operations in 1831.
3. The so-called Wicked Bible, printed in London in 1631, omitted a "not" from Exodus 20:14, making the seventh commandment read "Thou shalt commit adultery."
4. The 35-mile Forth and Clyde Canal, completed in 1790, bisected Scotland to connect the North Sea with the Atlantic.

From John Randolph

Richmond June 11. 1830
half past 10 A. M.

Dear Sir

By making an exertion as great as my strength would allow, I arrived here within a quarter of an hour past. no tidings of the Concord. Should the boat tomorrow night bring tidings of her I shall ~~return~~ go down on Sunday morning (the 13th) so as to reach Hampton Roads two days sooner than the time as directed by your letter (15th). It gives me the greatest pleasure to anticipate your commands. I hope that Mr Van Buren will give me a meeting on board the Concord. It is very desirable that I should have an interview with him.[1]

I renew the assurances of my most profound respect & devotion

J R of Roanoke

Mr Clay arrived here last night

ALS, DLC (38).
1. Van Buren went to Norfolk and on June 20 gave Randolph private instructions for a commercial negotiation with Russia.

To John Henry Eaton

June 12th. 1830—

Sir

I have recd your note enclosing the paymaster Generals letter. Congress not having passed a law upon the subject, the opinion of the committee, can only be regarded with that respect due to the opinion of the Gentlemen who gave it. But as the Surgeon Genl is receiving fuel & quarters, it will be just to allow it to the paymaster Genl. The allowance must be paid out of the appropriations founded upon the estimate of the present year. The arreages if paid, must be out of the appropriations made for arreages, upon estimates for this purpose; or in other words, each appropriation must be confined & applied to the specific object for which it was appropriated, and where there has been no estimatione and appropriation for a particular object it must remain unpaid, until an appropriation is made. Therefore if no estimate & appropriation for these arreages, they cannot be paid out of any other fund. The committee ought to have reported a bill appropriating for this object   yours

Andrew Jackson

ALS, THi (15-1358). Pursuant to Army regulations, both the surgeon general and paymaster general had drawn a fuel and quarters allowance until 1827, when the paymaster general's was stopped on the ground that it was unsanctioned by law. Paymaster General Nathan Towson protested the inequity, and in his December 1829 annual message AJ asked Congress to clarify the matter (*Jackson Papers*, 7:513–14). On January 4, 1830, the House Committee on Military Affairs reported a bill (H.R. 58) declaring both officers' right to the allowance, but it did not come to a vote. On June 11 Towson complained to Eaton that the government's accounting officers were still denying him the allowance despite the opinion of AJ, Eaton, Berrien, and the entire House committee that he was fairly entitled to it (DNA-RG 107, M222-28). Towson's allowance was subsequently restored as of January 1, 1830, and in March 1832 Congress authorized payment of his lost arrears.

From the Western Creeks

Council ground Western Creek Nation 12th June 1830.

Genl Jackson.

Great Father.

You have spoken to our Fathers, and to us; and told us; that your ears should be open unto us; and that your arm should protect us. We have spoken to you from a distance; but you have not answered our words; nor have you taken away from us, the cause of our sorrows. We spoke to you, of Colonel Brearley, and he was removed from us as our agent, and we were told by the Secy of war, that "the object of the President, *would* be to place with *us*, one, who he *hoped would* alike regard the interest of the Indians, and the business of the Government," ~~of the~~ and moreover he said to us, that our Father wished his red children to remove from the Old Nation to this country; and that "they would be able to find repose, and happiness" and said "He believes so, or would not say it." These things were said to us after we had sent to our Father two memorials, asking for the fulfillment of promises, made to us by the Government, and justice from it. We are then asked by the Secy of War, "When did ever he (your Great Father) deceive you? and he answers "never!" We can not think he ever will deceive us unless bad men deceive him, and we hope he is too great to be blinded by wicked men, but we fear that he has not read our talks, and that others read them, and talk to us for, him, with crooked tongues, and say to us words to suit them, and their friends; whose hands are stained with the blood of men, and whose pockets are filled with the money of the poor Indians.[1]

When we came to this land where corn had never grown, we were promised money, and many things else—We were promised an agent to take care of us. We have had none. Col Brearly did not take care of us—he was removed and a subagent was sent to us, by Col Crowell, but not by the President. ~~He came as we believe to make money, and to treat us as Colonel Crowell had done in the old nation, but not to pay us the money sent to us, as promised.~~ But he has given us no money, that was promised to us, if we would come here! The Secy of war sent us another man, and told us to love him. It was Genl Campbell. We met him, and he talked to us, as Colonel Hawkins, had before talked to us. We loved him as we were told to do. And hope became bright in us. We talked to our wives, and our young men, and our children, and told them that we were happy—Our fires were kindled, early in the morning, because our joy was lively, and we could not sleep, ~~because~~ when there was sunshine on our path! This joy lasted but a few moons! Mr Blake went to the city, saw some people there, and came to us again; and told us, that he was to be our Agent until Col Crowell should come to us; and that our Father had said that he was to be our Agent. That General Campbell was taken from us: We then had a council and Genl Campbell, told us that he was recalled, but advised us if he had made us good talks, to walk by them; and told us that our Great Father, was Great, and good, and would do us justice, and make us happy! Our old men & warriors shed tears, but those tears have not washed away our sorrows. They are fresh within us, and when we rise up in the morning from our sleep ~~and~~ we part with it, as our best friend; because it takes away our sorrows from our memory.[2]

Why can not our Father give us General Campbell for our Agent? We ~~are told~~ have heard, that he was a warrior, among the white people, and that he is honest! The white people, some times allow their slaves to choose their masters; and surely our Father will allow his red children to choose their agents. We have walked in a stright path, to the house of our Father; nor has our Mockasen tracks; been seen, leading to the blood of his white children—When he sends us his talks we want them brought in a straight path, and if we have to shake hands with his agents, we do not want their hands to be bloody! Our agents for years back have talked to us, as Masters, but Genl Campbell has spoken to us as a Father talks to his children. We loved him because he brought with him, his wife & family—He brought no store with him, to cheat us, and make us poor, & unhappy. But he told us, that he would let traders come among us, if they would not bring whiskey, to destroy us.[3]

Last summer we worked hard—raised corn and sold it many thousand bushels to Mr Blake for the Goverment; but we have not been paid for it. He gave us his paper for it and promised us money but we can get none; And we would sell our paper, where it says that it is worth $500 for $450. We don't think our Father knows, of these things; or he would send us the money! If we had money, we could buy ploughs, & hoes, and such things as we may need—raise more corn; & be like white people   Our women were happy, when they looked upon the wife of Genl Campbell, because she told them to spin, and weave, and make clothes for them, and us, and our children, and that she would learn them—Words which had not been told to them, since Colonel Hawkins went to the Great Spirit!

If our Father will send us a good Agent (and we would rather have Genl Campbell than other man) our fires shall burn bright in our new homes; and we will be happy to see all our Brothers here from the Old Nation; and live with them as one family, and all smoke in peace!

When we left the Old Nation, we buried Tomahawks, because our Father told us, to do so; and that they would be of no use to us, in our new homes, where we were to be happy—War parties have passed by us, and offered to us the Tomahawk but we have refused it; because of our Great Fathers wishes, and his promises—The sorrows of three years now rest upon us—our load is too heavy to bear! If our Great Father, intends to keep Mr Blake here until he sends Colonel Crowell to us, we hope he will let us know it, (for he cannot fear those who love him) that the his Muscogee children may seek a new home, very far to setting sun; and so soon as they find a fair land, their warriors, shall dig up the Tomahawk; and they will march before their women, and children, and their aged people, until they find rest & peace! Our hunters step shall be no more seen on the Arkansas—the bark of our dogs shall no more be heard Our fires, shall no longer burn upon the Arkansas—the barking of our dogs shall cease be heard no more; and the footstep of our hunters shall be seen no more no more be seen! But in sorrow we will think of the promises of our Great Father—

Draft, Tx (15-1348).

1. The Western Creeks had petitioned to AJ to remove agent David Brearley on March 7 and June 22, 1829 (*Jackson Papers*, 7:83–85, 296–99). The quotations are paraphrased from Eaton's reply of August 3, 1829, giving news of Brearley's removal (DNA-RG 75, M21-6).

2. AJ had appointed John Campbell (1777–1858) as Western Creek agent in September 1829, then withdrew his nomination from the Senate on February 20, 1830, on report that he was a public defaulter. Subagent Luther Blake ran the agency before Campbell's appointment and after its withdrawal. AJ reappointed Campbell on March 2, 1831. Former North Carolina senator Benjamin Hawkins Sr. (1754–1816) had served as Creek agent from 1796 until his death.

3. Campbell had been an Army colonel and Tennessee militia general. His wife was Mary E. Cowan Campbell (1798–1880).

From John Randolph

Richmond June 12. 1830.

Dear Sir,

I wrote you a few hurried lines yesterday as well as a gouty right hand would permit. and I take the liberty to intrude upon your time again to day with a request to know whether the Concord has orders to touch any where in her passage to the Baltick.[1] It would have been a sensible accomodation to me to have been apprized a short time ago of the name &c of the vessel in which I was to sail. I have had but a very short time (since your letter by Mr Clay) to make my arrangements.

The Bank of Virginia offers to take my draft on government for my outfit, so that I shall only lose the discount; but I know not whether to draw on the Secretary of the Treasury, the Treasurer, or the Secretary of State.

I shall go down tomorrow, provided we have news of the Concord by tonight's boat; otherwise on wednesday (16). Hoping to have the pleasure to hear from you either by Autograph or through Mr Van Buren, I remain Dear Sir you most faithful Servant

J. R of Roanoke

P.S. am to draw on our Bankers in Europe for my Salary as it falls due—or how am I to receive it

ALS, DLC (38).
1. On June 14, Navy secretary Branch ordered Matthew C. Perry, commanding the *Concord*, to follow Randolph's wishes regarding route and ports of call (DNA-RG 45, M149-19).

To David Campbell

Washington 14th. June 1830

Dr. Sir,

I beg leave to introduce to you my son who will hand you this, and avail himself of the polite invitation which you were pleased to address to me in your letter of the 31st. ult., to take shelter under your hospitable roof on his way to Nashville. The facility which I am assured I can obtain at Wheeling, of a water transportation to Louisville, will induce me to take that course, and lose the pleasure of seeing you & Mrs. Campbell in company with my son.

I pray you to accept for yourself and family a renewal of my best wishes for your prosperity and happiness; and believe me very sincerely yr. obt. svt

Andrew Jackson

LS in AJ Donelson's hand, NcD (15-1383). David Campbell (1779–1859) of Abingdon, Va., the brother of U.S. Treasurer John Campbell, was a former Army colonel and later governor of Virginia, 1837–40. His wife was Mary Hamilton Campbell (1783–1859).

To John Coffee

Washington June 14th. 1830—

Dr Genl

We intend setting out for Tennessee on the 17th. instant. My stay in Tennessee cannot be long, but will be happy to see you if your own convenience will permit you to come to Nashville whilst I am in its neighbourhood & visit me at the Hermitage. The choctaw chiefs, thro their agent sent on here, have requested that I should meet them near Nashville, to which I have answered, that upon their principle chiefs of the whole nation uniting in that request, I would comply with their wishes—This my principle business, still my desire is once more to visit the Hermitage & if possible once more see you—

Altho congress has acted very strangely & contrary in most things to what was expected, still my administration is going on pretty well—but still there has been, & are things that have coroded my peace, & my mind, & must cease, or my administration will be a Distracted one—which I cannot permit. I wish to see you, will be at the Hermitage early in july—with my love to your family & the salutations of all here, I am sincerly your friend

Andrew Jackson

ALS, THi (15-1385).

To *Samuel Smith*

My Dear Sir,

In the great mass of business which the knowledge of my intention to depart in a few days on a visit to my farm in Tennessee, has thrown upon me, I can scarsely find a moment to acknowlege the receipt of your favor of the 10th. instant; But I must thank you for its contents.

It is gratifying to me to know that the considerations which produced the veto on the Maysville road bill, are likely to be satisfactory to the great body of my friends, tho' there may be many, like the citizens interested in the Rockville bill, whose local situations, rather than their judgment, will force them for a while to withold their acquiescence. In relation to this class of my friends, this step must take its chance, appealing to their reason and patriotism alone. If the evils which it anticipates are worth avoiding, as dangerous to the purity of the Government, and the durability of our union, I have the fullest confidence that their zeal in the cause of internal improvements will be so far moderated as, at least, to give me the credit of good intentions.

I pray you to accept my best wishes for your happiness and believe me sincerely yr. obt. svt

Andrew Jackson

[Endorsed by Smith:] Gen. A. Jackson President. U. States 14 June 1830

LS in AJ Donelson's hand, The Gilder Lehrman Institute of American History (mAJs).

From *Jeremy Bentham*

Jeremy Bentham, London, to Andrew Jackson
President of the Anglo-American United States

Sir,

When your last predecessor in your high office was in this country in the character of Minister Plenipotentiary, towards the close of his residence here it happened to me to commence with him an acquaintance which ripened into an intimacy ~~from~~ which in my capacity of legislative draughtsman for any political community which should feel inclined to accept my services, was of very essential service to me. Besides some concerns of a private nature he condescended to take charge & become the bearer of a packet of circular letters to the several Governors of the United States as then constituted, from several of whom I had the honour of receiving favorable answers. By candid and authentic information on several topics of high importance he was of use to me in various more ways than you have time to read of or I to write. Days more than one in a week he used to call on me at my Hermitage as above, and to accompany me to the Royal Gardens at Kensington, in my neighbourhood, where after a walk of two or three hours he used to return to a tête à tête dinner with me. What gave occasion to our first meeting was a letter to me of which he was the bearer from the President Madison. A letter of introduction which I took the liberty of addressing to him (Mr Adams) in favor of an intellectual character, a relation of my friend Joseph Hume M.P. (of which last-mentioned friend of mine the reputation cannot be altogether unknown to you) experienced that reception which I could not but anticipate.[1]

These things considered, you will not be at a loss, Sir, to conceive what must have been my disappointment upon my learning of his failing to receive the customary addition to his term of service. Judge, Sir, of the consolation—the more than consolation—which I experienced when, upon reading your Inaugural Message, I found that upon the whole your sentiments were not only as fully in accordance with mine as his had been (and in politics and legislation I do not think there was a single topic on which we appeared to differ) but that they were so, and I trust remain so, in a still more extensive degree—embracing several topics which between him & me had never been touched upon. With Mr Rush I was also upon such a footing that in a letter of his which I still have, written some months before his departure, he had the kindness to offer himself to me as my *"Agent and Fac Totum"* (those are his words) upon his return to the United States: notwithstanding which, several months before his departure, from some cause which I never heard nor can form so much as the slightest guess at, he dropt my acquaintance & took his departure without so much as a farewell message. Since his retreat from office, I have however been favored by him with the copy of a pamphlet of his without further explanation.[2]

I might mention in like manner my friendship with Mr Lawrence, late Chargé d'Affaires from your country to this; and Mr Wheaton Minister to Denmark to whom I have been obliged for various important and, to me, honorable services. But of this more (you will say) than enough.[3]

I now look back to a letter I had been dictating between 3 & 4 months ago—Cause of the long interval, how deservedly regretted by me, not worth troubling you with. What now follows had been completely forgotten when what you have seen above was commenced—this oblivion years of age more than 82 render but too natural

[4]I have this moment finished the hearing of your Message: I say the hearing; for at my age (as above mentioned) I am reduced to ~~hear~~ read mostly by my ears. Intense is the admiration it has excited in me: Correspondent the sentiments of all around me.

'Tis not without a mixture of surprise and pleasure that I observe the coincidence between your ideas and my own on the field of legislation. The coincidence of mine with those of Dr. Livingston, the Louisiana Senator, are perhaps not unknown to you.

The flattering manner in which he is pleased to speak of my labors in that field is in the highest degree encouraging to me. The herewith-transmitted publication entitled "Codification Proposal" may serve to bring it to view.[5]

These circumstances combined concur in flattering me with the hope that the present communication will not be altogether unacceptable to you. Annexed is a list of some of my works which solicit the honour of your acceptance.

Here follow a few observations which I take the liberty of submitting to you, on some of the topics touched upon in your above-mentioned Message

1st. Navy Board—In this subdepartment of the Defensive Force Departmt you find I perceive many-seatedness established: by you I see single-seatedness is preferred—so is it by me: for this preference your reason is, responsibility—so is it for mine. But in my account, though the principal reason, it is but one among several. This may be seen in my the accompanying copy of the first part of my Constitutional Code Ch IX §3[6]

2nd After that you come to the Judiciary. If I do not misrecollect, in your superior Judicatories the bench is singleseated. In my leading Chapter on the Judiciary, to all the reasons which apply to the Administrative department in all its subdepartments (twelve or thirteen in number) several which are peculiar to the Judiciary are added.

3rd. Utter inaptitude of Common Law for its professed purpose—guidance of human action. Places of in which you may find this topic worked—1. Papers on Codification &c. 2. Codification Proposal—3. Petition for Codificatn. Justice in the Vol. of "Petitions"[7]

4th. Superfluous functionaries. In this number my researches have led me to reckon the whole of your Senate. Not merely is the whole expense thrown away, but the whole authority much worse than useless. Responsibility in greatest part destroyed by a single functionary, what must it be by a multitude so numerous. Functions legislative and administrative thus united in the same body: thus the same men are judges over themselves. In my view of the matter the administrative and the judiciary are two authorities employed to give execution & effect to the will of the Legislative, in which accordingly ought to be in the instance of every Member of each at all times distinct—the legislative being by means of the power of location & dislocation, though not by that of imperation, subordinate to the people at large—the constitutive.

Knowing nothing of the facts, my theory leads me to expect to find that the sort of relation that has place between the Presidt. & the Senate is—that each of these functionaries—the Prest. included—locates within his field of patronage a protégé of his own without any check from the authority of the rest.

This is nothing more than a faint, imperfect, and inaccurate outline drawn momentarily by a broken memory from the recollection of a short paper written several years ago: should it afford any prospect of being of any use, and you will favour me with a line to let me know as much, I will get it copied & transmitted to you: possibly I may not even wait for such your commands.

It occurs to me that should our opinions agree on this subject there might be a use in the idea's being delivered as coming from me or anybody rather than yourself: seeing ~~from~~ the wound from the opposition it would be sure to meet with from those who are satisfied with things as they are, the wound such an opposition might give to your popularity, which is as much as to say the interests of the State.

5th. Defensive Force—by sea & land—its organization. Tactics (of course) neither in land nor water service am I, who know nothing of the matter, absurd enough to have comprised in it; but the part that I have undertaken has undergone the minute examination & received the considerate approbation of leading minds of the first order distinguished ~~by~~ not only by talent, but by experience & splendid success: and who, indeed, though without having published on the subject had in great part anticipated me.[8]

An intelligent man, who is in the confidence of the Duke of Orleans, ~~who~~ and bears the whimsical name of *Le Dieu* has been here in London for some time publishing a periodical in French under the name of "*Le Représentant des Peuples*"—He is thought to be the author of an address to the French army that after having been written here and either printed or lithographized has been transmitted to & circulated in France—it has for its object the engaging the army, should matters come to a crisis, to act not against but for the people. The above-mentioned periodical I have not had time to look into—I am told it advocates monarchy; whh. considering the connectn. of the author with the family so near ~~th~~ to the ~~crown~~ throne as the D. of Orleans is, he could not choose but do. Thinking you might possibly have the curiosity to look into it I send you a copy of such of the numbers of it as have appeared. La Fayette is a dear friend & occasional correspondent of mine: but unless it be for some special purpose we have neither of us any time to write.[9]

Forgive the liberty I take of suggesting the idea of your putting in for a copy of our House of Commons Votes & Proceedings—the annual sum I pay for them is between 16 and 17 £, included in which is a copy of our Acts of Parliament—Infinite is the variety of the political information which they afford: for scarcely any document that is asked for is ever refused. As to the price scarcely wd six or eight or ten times (I believe I might go further) the money procure the same quantity of letterpress from the booksellers. Trash relatively speaking, of course, is by far the greatest part; but if in the bushell of chaff a grain of wheat were to be found, the above-mentioned price you will perhaps think not ill bestowed in the purchase of it—Dr Livingston, if either of the packets I have endeavored to transmit to him through the same official channel have reached their destination, will be able to show you a few articles of the above-mentioned stock.

If I do not misconceive you, you are embarked or about to embark on a civil enterprize in which Cromwell notwithstanding all his military power failed ~~in~~—I mean the delivery of the people from the thraldom in which every where from the earliest recorded days of Rome they have been held by the harpies of the law.[10] Having yourself ~~been~~ officiated in the character of a Judge you are in possession of an appropriate experience, which in his instance had no place. But will you be able to resist their influence over the people? In opposition to you, so long as you are engaged or believed to be engaged in any such design, it were blindness not to look to see their utmost influence employed. The interest of the lawyers and that of their fellow ~~creatures~~ citizens in the character of clients (need it be said?) is utterly irreconcileable. You cannot ~~be~~ assuage the torments of the client, but you diminish in proportion the comforts of the lawyers. If this be really of the number of your generous designs, I cannot but flatter myself with the prospect of being for that purpose an instrument in your hands: the contents of the accompanying packet will insofar as you have time to look at them show you on what grounds.

With the most heartfelt esteem and respect I subscribe myself, Sir, Yours

Jeremy Bentham

Eyes will not permitt my looking over what is above   It is in great part written from dictation.

List of Books &c herewith sent   June 1830

1. Rationale of Judicial Evidence—5 vols
2. Constitutional Code—1st Vol
3. Rationale of Reward—1 vol.
4. Justice and Codification Petitions—1 Vol.
5. Papers on Codification—1 Vol.
6. Codification Proposal—1 Vol.
7. Leading Principles of a Constitutional Code—A pamphlet
8. Westminster Review, No XXII containing "*Bentham, & Brougham, & Law Reform.*"
9. Article on Real Property—from *Westm. Revw.*
10. Equity Dispatch Court Proposal—Pamphlet
11. Letters to Toreno on Penal Code
12. Truth versus Ashhurst—Pamphlet
13. Radical Reform Bill
14. King against Edmonds &c—and—Rex v Wolseley, &c Pamphlet
15. Emancipate your Colonies

16. Draught of a Plan of a Judicial Establishment in France—1 Vol.
17. Scotch Reform
18. Representant des Peuples—No 1 to 11
19. Hauman's Prospectus of Brussel's Edition of J. B's Works
20. Official Aptitude Maximized Expense Minimized—1 Vol
21. "Financial Reform" Scrutinized—By General Sir Samuel Bentham[11]
22. J. B's Challenge to Brougham—
23. Political Tactics—4 to
24. Panopticon—&c—2 vols.
25. Article "Militia" from *Morning Herald*—in slips—3 copies
26. Constitutional Code—2nd Vol. *Ch X—Defensive Force*—Not yet published—the remainder of the Volume not being yet printed.
27. Naval Essays, by Sir S. Bentham.
28. Naval Papers, Nos 1, 2, 3, 5, 6, 7, 8—No. 4. not as yet published.

LS, DLC-Nicholas P. Trist Papers (15-1371). *The Works of Jeremy Bentham* (Edinburgh, 1843), 11:39–42. Bentham (1748–1832) was an English utilitarian philosopher and prolific writer on law, government, political economy, and reform. He evidently composed this epistle over a span of months. The version published in his *Works*, taken presumably from a retained draft, is in two parts dated April 26 and January 10, 1830. But neither date is on the letter itself, while the publications list that accompanied it is dated June. Probably both were sent together with the June 14 letter that follows.

1. John Quincy Adams, U.S. minister to Britain in 1815–17, helped distribute Bentham's writings to American public officials, including his June 1817 twin circulars to state governors proffering his plans for legal codification and for a system of public education. Bentham published the circulars, along with his letter of October 30, 1811 to President Madison offering to codify the laws of the U.S. and Madison's belated May 8, 1816 reply, in *Papers Relative to Codification and Public Instruction* (1817). Bentham's "Hermitage" was Queen Square Place, his family estate in Westminster. Dr. Joseph Hume (1777–1855) of Scotland was a longtime Member of Parliament. Bentham had recommended Hume's brother-in-law, William Hardin Burnley (1780–1850). Adams and Burnley dined in Washington in October 1826.

2. Richard Rush (1780–1859), Adams's vice-presidential running mate in 1828, had succeeded him as minister to Britain in 1817 and served until 1825. On February 3, 1824, he wrote Bentham offering to be his agent and factotum in the U.S. (*Correspondence of Jeremy Bentham*, 11:344).

3. William Beach Lawrence (1800–1881) was appointed secretary of legation at London in 1826 and served as acting chargé d'affaires in 1827–28. Henry Wheaton (1785–1848) had been U.S. chargé d'affaires in Denmark since 1827.

4. A new page begins here. The *Works* version headed the preceding text with a date of April 26, 1830, and the remainder beginning here with date of January 10, 1830.

5. Edward Livingston was a leading American proponent of reforming and codifying the criminal law. His publications credited Bentham's seminal influence, and in a letter to Bentham of August 10, 1829, he praised his inspiration and "superior sagacity" (*Works of Jeremy Bentham*, 11:23). The enclosed pamphlet was Bentham's *Codification Proposal, Addressed by Jeremy Bentham to all Nations Professing Liberal Opinions*, first published in London in 1822.

6. In his December 1829 annual message, AJ had proposed replacing the Board of Navy Commissioners with separate bureaus like those in the War Department, each under a single head, thus instilling a "wholesome responsibility" productive of efficiency and economy (Richardson, 2:460). Bentham published the first volume of his *Constitutional Code; for the*

Use of all Nations and all Governments Professing Liberal Opinions in 1830. Chapter 9, §3 argued the advantages of unitary executives over administrative boards.

7. In the *Codification Proposal* (1822), *Papers Relative to Codification and Public Instruction* (1817), and *Justice and Codification Petitions* (1829), Bentham criticized the inherent confusion and injustice of the common law.

8. Bentham enclosed his "Defensive Force," later published as Chapter 10 in the second volume of *Constitutional Code*.

9. *Le Représentant des Peuples* was a short-lived weekly edited by the French liberal writer Louis François Joseph Le Dieu (b. 1791). Louis Philippe (1773–1850), the Duke of Orléans, became King of the French in August 1830.

10. Oliver Cromwell (1599–1658), Lord Protector of the Commonwealth from 1653 until his death, had advocated reform of the administration of justice.

11. Samuel Bentham (1757–1831), Jeremy's brother, was a noted inventor and engineer, at one time general in the Russian army and Inspector General of Naval Works in Britain.

From Jeremy Bentham

Private and Confidential

14 June 1830.

Anti-*Senatica* Papers.

Of the paper in its present state—in this worse than rough state—a state, in which it never was destined to make its appearance—not having undergone the author's revision—the only use is the enabling you to form a conjecture, whether, as to the purpose in question it would be of any use that, from this same author it should receive the amendments necessary to its being regarded by him as completed: in case of the affirmative, you have but to give me an intimation to that effect, and I will do what depends upon me towards the rendering it fit to be sent to the press.

Had my own reputation been my principal object, never could I have trusted it these papers out of my own hands in such a state: but, being, (as I told Mr M'Lane,) at heart more of a United-States-man than an Englishman, it cost me little or nothing to subject myself to this exposure.

The whole mass, taken in the aggregate, was written at different times: each time without looking back for what had been written before: which, for one reason or other, has been the case with no small portion of my scrawl. Hence, no small quantity of repetition and perhaps of some incongruities —this however will not prevent its answering the purpose—the only purpose, which, as above, I had in view in sending it.

I suspect that there will not be time for my hearing read, for the purpose of rendering it intelligible more than half of the copy I have got taken of it, time enough to go by the present conveyance.

Jeremy Bentham

[In Bentham's hand:] Information of the receipt of this letter and the accompanying packet which might by a line or a leter to Mr MacLane *[without]* waiting to write to me would much oblige me.

LS, DLC-Nicholas P. Trist Papers (15-1368). Bentham's enclosed Anti-Senatica papers, composed in 1822–24, were a series of essay fragments attacking the U.S. Senate as aristocratic (*Smith College Studies in History* 11 [July 1926]: 221–67).

Order of Pardon for George Wilson

[On June 10, judges Henry Baldwin and Joseph Hopkinson wrote Jackson that they had issued a warrant for the execution of mail robbers James Porter and George Wilson on July 2. The next day, prominent Philadelphians Samuel F. Bradford, attorney John Kintzing Kane, and clergyman Thomas Harvey Skinner wrote Jackson urging clemency for Wilson. More than four hundred citizens headed by printer Joseph Rakestraw signed a printed petition to spare Wilson's life; a few signers added Porter's name as well. The appeals stressed Wilson's youth, his full confession and evident contrition, his certain punishment by many years in prison, and the severity of the death sentence.]

June 14th. 1830—

Let a pardon Issue remitting the punishment of death awarded by the District court of the United States for East Pennsylvania against George Wilson for mail robery for which a warrent of Execution has been Issued by said court to the marshal of said District to carry the judgment of said court ~~in said~~ into execution on the second day of July next. But this pardon is to have no other effect but to remit the punishment of death in the case of Georg Wilson leaving him subject to any ~~decree~~ judgment that may be made against him by said court in all and any other case or cases pending before said court

Andrew Jackson

[Endorsed by AJ:] Fiat for pardon to be made out for the signature of the President but to be kept from the knowledge of the world, the bearer of this Mr Bradford will be entrusted with it A. J.[1]

ADS, DNA-RG 59 (15-1446). Wilson's formal pardon for his capital offense was issued this same day. It cited appeals by "a numerous and respectable body of petitioners" and Wilson's liability for long imprisonment on other federal and state charges as reasons for clemency. James Porter was not pardoned, and was executed July 2.

    1. Vincent Loockerman Bradford (1808–1871), nephew of Samuel F. Bradford and one of Wilson's defense lawyers, had come to Washington to plead for his life.

To Philip Grymes Randolph

june 15th. 1830

The President with his respects request the acting Secretary of War to send him any charges on file made against Mr Rowland Marshall of Michigan acting as pension agent for said Territory & the testimony on which the charge is sustained

AN, DNA-RG 107 (M222-27). Randolph (1801–1836) was chief clerk in the War Department and acting secretary in Eaton's absence. Thomas Rowland (c1784–1849) was both marshal of Michigan Territory and a pension agent under the War Department. In a series of letters to Van Buren and Eaton beginning January 13, 1830, John P. Sheldon of Michigan accused Rowland of peculation and fraud in both his official capacities. Rowland repelled the charges, and Sheldon countered his denials. A report from Van Buren to AJ on June 14 cleared Rowland of misconduct as marshal (DNA-RG 59, M639-20; *TPUS*, 12:142, 144–45, 157–58, 160). Randolph replied to AJ on June 16 (below).

To John Macpherson Berrien

Washington june 16th. 1830

Dear Sir

As I am about to be absent from the Seat of Government, and circumstances may render it proper for you to proceed to Georgia, or to the Creek or cherokee nation during the interval, I have thought it proper to put you in possession of the authority under which you will act—

Having conversed with you fully on the subjects connected with the relations of the Government of the united States with the state of Georgia and those tribes, you will be able to express my views to the constituted authorities of that State, and to the chiefs ~~and~~ warriors of the tribes—~~and~~ ~~can and~~ can communicate with me from time to time, as circumstances may require—In the mean time, this letter will serve to evince to those with whom you may have occasion to transact any business connected with these subjects, that you are acting with my approbation, and under my authority

Keep me advised of the information received, from your correspondents in the south, and of the time you leave here. I am very respectfully yr mo obdt. servt.

Andrew Jackson

ALS, GHi (15-1468).

To James Biddle

Washington 16th. June 1830

Sir

Allow me to acquaint you with the bearer Col. A P Hayne of So. Carolina who has been recently appointed Navy Agent for Gibralter. Having served with me in the Southern campaigns which I had the honor to conduct during the last war, and being a considerable period one of my staff in the capacity of Inspector Genl of the Army, I have had every opportunity to understand his character, of which I cannot speak in terms too favorable. And in entrusting to his care the interests of the Navy at that station, so far as they are connected with that office, I feel therefore every confidence that they will be well attended to; and if any improvements, economical or otherwise, should be suggested by the experience of the commander of the squadron, or by future observation that they will find in the zeal and intelligence of Col. Hayne the most cordial and useful support. I have the honor to be with great respect yr. obt. servant

Andrew Jackson

LS in AJ Donelson's hand, Uk (mAJs). Hayne had served intermittently as AJ's inspector general from 1814 to 1820.

To Francis Preston

(Private)

Washington june 16th. 1830—

My Dr. Sir,

Some time since, I had the pleasure to receive your letter on the subject of the 2nd. Comptroller, under the existing circumstances, New Hampshire being unrepresented in the Executive Dept. of our Government, claimed this office—Virginia being represented fully, your brother could not receive it[1]

I am on the eve of setting out to the Hermitage; hearing that the Ohio is still in good boating condition, I take the rout by Wheeling to save labour—it is a warm season, but the choctaw chiefs have intimated a wish to see me personally, & to gratify them, & to get them peaceably & voluntarily to their permanent home, I undertake it—should I return the virginia rout, I shall do myself the pleasure to pay my respects to you & your amiable family, to whom be pleased to present me respectfully.

My son will hand you this, and I beg leave to recommend him to your attention during his short stay in Abington—I expect him to meet me at the Hermitage.

Accept the assurance of my esteem & regard & believe me yr friend

Andrew Jackson

ALS, ViU (15-1473).

1. AJ had appointed James B. Thornton of New Hampshire second comptroller after the Senate rejected Isaac Hill. Preston had likely recommended his brother James Patton Preston (1774–1843), former governor of Virginia and present Richmond postmaster.

From James Gowen

PHILADELPHIA, 16th June, 1830.

Dear Sir:

It appears that women and children are engaged in this city, soliciting signatures to a petition praying a pardon for Wilson, one of the mail robbers. The same spirit and morbid sensibility that obtained signatures against the removal of the Indians, characterize the proceedings in this case.

Far be it from me to throw any obstacle in the way of clemency, but I conceive it my duty to apprise your Excellency, that if Wilson be pardoned and Porter executed, it will produce a *strong sensation among the Irish*, who ascribe the sympathy in favor of Wilson to *sectarian* and *sectional feelings*. They say Porter is an Irishman. I pay but little attention to those things myself, but it is not an easy matter to combat the prejudices of others, and prevent them from drawing their own inferences. Of one thing, however, I am certain, that neither the motives nor the principles of those who would have you *avert the hand of justice* in the case of a FELON, who was a CONVICT IN BOYHOOD and RIPENED IN VILLANY WITH YEARS, are worthy of your consideration.

Most respectfully yours, &c.

JAMES GOWEN.

Printed, *United States' Telegraph*, August 23, 1832 (mAJs). Irish-born James Gowen (1790–1873) was a Philadelphia merchant. Gowen read this letter in his opening address, as chair, to a mass "Irish Anti-Jackson Meeting" in Philadelphia on August 6, 1832, in which he denounced AJ for bigotry against the Irish in pardoning George Wilson "for no other *apparent* reason than that Wilson was a native, and Porter a foreigner." Gowen wrote AJ again on July 3 (below).

From John Overton

Travellers Rest 16th June 1830

My Dear Genl

In your last you did me the honor to ask my opinion. Business in which, I then was engaged in court, put it out of my power to offer any reasons for the result of my reflections on the subject, but promised that I would do so, at as early a day as practicable. Weakness with a slight inflamation in my eyes, occasioned by dust and smoke in my tour to the east, makes it painful to write or read, even, at this moment.

Considering the situation in which Mr Calhoun is placed, with the tenor of his answer to your note, his object is very apparent. He is aspiring we all know, and his eye has never been averted for a moment, from the presidency, since he became a member of Mr. Monroes Cabinet. This is not unnatural for talented men. Hence, no man saw with more pain (Mr Clay not excepted) the rise and elevation of your character, during the last War. And rest assured my friend, that both Monroe and Adams, had the same feeling, and Crawford far from being exempt from them, because though he did not see the consequences so clearly   This was all the difference. Knowing the character of Mr Monroe, and the members of his cabinet, as I thought when it was formed, as well as your character, I came to a conclusion, respecting the disposition of that cabinet towards you, immediately on sight of the *order* to take command of the army, and conduct the War against the Seminole Indians

All those men, I knew, were jealous of the rising strength of the west; all averse to the president, coming from that quarter

In this Mr Jefferson, and all the eastern folks perfectly agreed, at that time   In the fame you had already acquired they, (I mean the cabinet, for three of them were aspirants) saw a most appalling, distressing obstacle. Hence, this *general order*, in the conduct of the War   It was an object to terminate the War to be sure; they knew your talents and character, of which there was no longer a doubt, and well knew how you must do it, by following the Indians into Florida, and dislodging the British their allies, if found there, as well as remove all impediments thrown in the way, by the Spaniards. All this they were obliged to foresee, unless they had suddenly lost their senses

These were my views, upon your shewing me the order, and if proof were wanting, Mr Crawfords letter a copy of which you have enclosed greatly strengthens the impressions then made on my mind Viz before you left home on the Seminole campaign. My firm belief is, and was, that the object which that Cabinet had most at heart, was, by an alleged infraction of orders, or the law of Nations, to get you out of the way

There can be no mistake in this General—nor should you have the least unpleasant feeling or ill will, about the matter. It was so. It was quite an ordinary business, with such men as Adams and Monroe, who had received the principle part of their education as politicians, in Europe, where the sacrifice of a meritorious officer to state policy is by no means uncommon

Neither Crawford nor Calhoun, interested, as they thought they were, would make awkward hands at such work

Crawford, in his letter, virtually admits his disposition was hostile, or rather to let you down, *until Mr. Monroe found the letter, you had written him referring to John Rhea* &c. Calhoun, he says, stood out even after that: that may be true, though it acquires no manner of credit from *his statement*

Why, it may be asked? My answer is, because Mr Crawford has shewn himself to be unworthy of credit, by violating his sacred duty, as a Cabinet Minister. He was opposed to you until he saw the letter, *which Mr Monroe had forgot, went and found it*! A poor tale this, scarcely fit to deceive a sensible school boy of a dozen years of age   As a minister of the government, Mr Crawford, is forced to admit a knowledge of the *general order*, or *carte blanche* to conduct this war. *Was this nothing!* Or of so little account, as not to be noticed, when Monroe and his cabinet, had you on trial, or under deliberation, whether to be court martialled, shot, or otherwise dealt with!!

None of these statesmen and lawyers, for they were all, such; in the course of this deliberation on your case, seemed to have thought for one moment, that you had conducted this war, agreeably to orders; in other words, according to the *law of nations*, which, under the general and discretionary order ~~had~~ received, was your guide, as an honest man!!! But the truth is, which Mr Crawford has suppressed; the president and his minister did think of that. The people had taught them through the writings of Aristides (republished in the Natl. Intr and other prominent papers in the U. S which see) Cato, first published in the Nashville Impl Rview and other writers on the same subject, this lesson, or what was the law of nations— and beside taught them all to know, that if there was any blame (of which there was not the semblance, but the strongest grounds of approbation) Mr Monroe, himself, was responsible; and not his commanding officer, who had acted honestly in the transaction.[1] I could safely tell Mr Crawford, sir, it was not the finding of the letter by the president, that changed your opinion—or the opinion of Monroe or Adams; for all of you, aye, every mothers son, as well as Calhoun would have given all the good things you had in this world, to have had it in your power to have got Jackson out of the way, at that time. But alas! You had heard the voice of the people, from one end of the Continent to the other, in a tone too strong and distinct to be misunderstood. The least move against Jackson, would have produced a burst of indignation, not to be resisted. Jackson was directly in the way of three of you, Adams Crawford & Calhoun; and Monroe was alarmed at the idea of a Western president. Three of you shrunk back. Calhoun, more bold, and inexperienced, than Adams & Crawford, and seeing then was his best chance, held on. Now, as to all this matter, I view the whole of them as precisely on the same footing, not an iota of difference, as to intention   If any thing, Calhoun has it, as discovering the greatest determination, though the most folly—Clay also saw, or believed, that then was his time to push, and if the secrets of all hearts could be laid bare, I would risque my all on the fact, that, as to anxiety and feeling there was not much difference at that time between Adams, Crawford Calhoun & Clay—Monroe, of the same opinion that you should be kept down, though not with the same feelings—All this, is, and always has been but too common to be repined at by you, who have met, and stilled, and quieted the storm   It is an affair of by gone days—of a Cabinet, which in honor ought never to be divulged, for I am of opinion, as in war, right or wrong, every man ought to fight for his country; so in moral intercourse, no man ought to violate the principles of duty and honor in any event. But you will say, that I must be wrong, as Mr ~~Calh~~ Monroe, told you, in answer to an enquiry, that there never was any thing like such a deliberation in his cabinet, as Mr. Crawford speaks of

This is nearly the account of what you told me Mr Monroe, said to you, when in this Country on his tour.[2] In this respect I believe Mr Crawford & not Mr Monroe. The circumstantial evidence, on my mind is conclusive with me. I was then all alive, watching movements such as I am now incapable of.

Thus far, I have thought it necessary to give you a sketch of past events, in order to understand the present state of things. Your ascension to the presidency thwarted the views of these aspirants, but rest assured, that neither Calhoun nor Clay, have let go their hold; they are still aspiring and using every exertion. The course of events will bring them into the same ranks, Calhoun as the leader for the presidency and Clay for the Vice presidency. A community of feeling will bring them and their friends together, in this way; for with Clay, half a loaf is better than no bread— especially when it will gratify his hostile personal feelings toward you. In this he is weak, and much the inferior of Mr Calhoun, as well as in many other respects.

No doubt, Mr Calhoun was highly pleased on the receipt of your note, as affording an opportunity of coming before the public; probably, in the first instance, by a short answer, but certainly, in a pamphlet, by some friend or himself. It is precisely, what suits his case, as an aspiring politician, in these our days; as we do know, from actual experience; and probably what would happen in all past times, in a government of the people

The probability is, that he will endeavour to draw from you, a further written correspondence, as your note does not contain quite enough of hostility to him—This he wants for Van Burens use as he is your Secretary

&c. If he should fail in a further correspondence, with you, which I hope he will, still you may expect to see a lengthy expose on his side, laid before the Nation, probably justifying the correctness of the opinion entertained by him in Cabinet Council, abusing Crawford, handling you roughly, on that and other points   It will please Clay & his friends (whom your friends should attend to)—to the life. They will all chime in. I shrewdly suspect, that the plan has been laid by Calhoun himself. His letter shews too much pleasure, not to have understood it before. I beg you my friend, trust nobody—How common is it, especially among politicians, to keep up appearances of open hostility—when underneath, there is the most perfect understanding. This, has ever been the case, since governments existed, conferring honor and riches. This, is an old game, that will be played, as long as man exists

Both Calhoun & Clay, are writing under the severest agonies of impatience   Hopes deferred, maketh the mind sick, thinks Mr Calhn   Every effort must be now made, or I sink into perpetual obscurity. It is true, thinks Clay, I see plainly now, that I never can be president, tho necessary to keep up the expectation of my friends for the present, from whence I will ease myself down, but a small distance into the Vice Presidency, in conjunction with Mr Calhouns friends. But both will necessarily conclude that this man, Jackson, will be in our way, as he was before. Hence, the severe blight which fell on their hopes, by the Pensylva & N.Y. resolutions[3]   Oh God! they would exclaim, this course is next to death itself! Jackson must be broken down before the end of four years for if elected for the next four years, we are irretrievably lost. True, gent. that is so, and must be so, in the nature of things but do not blame Genl. Jackson with your failures—It was the great body of the people, who are the true owners of the govt. who called upon him to serve them, in the office he now holds, and which you want. It was his duty to serve them, when asked, without fraud, trick or contrivance. How can you think hard of Jackson; blame, his, and your superiors, the peeople, and not him. You, Mr C & Mr C have no more cause of complaint in truth & fact, than I have, or any other man in the nation. You are only Citizens, & so am I, or any other man. The people have a right to chuse whom they please, without cause of complaint with any one. "But Jackson, is lending his official influence to his Secretary V. B"   How does that appear Gent.; he has never concerned with your, or Mr V. B.s pretensions; he has left you all, or the friends of each to maintain your respective pretensions as they may think proper. He does not concern by word, act, or deed. It is true, you have assailed and slandered Jackson; it is the bounden duty of Genl Jacksons friends, to support him and repel these slanders & misrepresentations. It is a duty they owe to society & the Nation

If, in doing so, your pretensions are spoiled, be it so, as you brought it on yourselves, and thrown the pretensions of Mr V. B, who, too, like Jackson has been silent performing his official duties—ahead of yours.

This, in part is my view of things. Mr. V. B.s destiny is necessarily interwoven, with Genl J— whose administration must be good and popular, else V. B, has no chance. It has ever been your character to be honest & faithful, and consequently, never for your own promotion, to deceive the people—It is now equally the interest of Mr V. B, whose duties are identified with yours. It is not necessary that either of you, should ever say one word directly in favor of each other. That wd be an injury to you both. Let each do his duty honestly and satisfactorily, the people prospering and Mr V Bn is president of course, when you retire; in spite of all Mr C or Mr C can do; it must be so, so long as the government hangs on the hinges it now does

Well, who, is to blame for this? Not Genl J. for he was obliged to have a Secretary of State. Not Mr V. Bn because it was his duty to serve his country, if able, when called on, either as Secretary, or president.

I repeat, let but the president & Secy of State, act their parts prudently, and for the good of the people, the Secy must be the next president; in ordinary times of peace and quiet: Such is my reading of the law of natures not to be changed by Mr Calhoun or Mr Clay.

From principle, you know it is not my wish that it should—not that I have any objection to Mr V. B. or Mr Calhoun. Either wd. make a good president I have no doubt

To Mr Clay I have sold objections. I repeat I should be satisfied with either Mr Calhoun or Mr V. B. the latter I should hower prefer much, provided the two great states of N. Y and Pensyla, by their deligation in Congress, should, before the expiration of your four years, greatly alter the Tariff, which, in wisdom & justice they ought to do; and which Mr Cambrelings commercial report, gives a fair promise, they will do. By the by, this is an able state paper, founded generally, in the immutable principles of truth.[4] This Tariff excitement, is the very thing for Calhoun & Clay, bating a little, for the nullifying doctrine. But they are heading off from that, as fast as they can. Still, there is no earthly doubt, but that there is great and just grounds agt. the tariff of 1828, alias one branch of Mr Clays American System. It is for the middle states to put an end to this uneasiness, when the anti-tariffites shall behave a little better. Sooner, would not do. This, not being done, may make a great difference in Mr. V. Bs. prospects—But, let N.Y. and Pensylva which always should have gone together as to the presidency or ought now to do so—reasonably modify the Tariff, and the prospects of Mess. Calhoun & Clay, instantly vanish and none will soon be seen but Mr V: B.s

I think Genl: you will agree with me, that there would be impropriety in permitting yourself to be drawn into any further written correspondence with Mr Calhoun, or his friends. It is not the interest of you or your friends to fight the battle of argument, respecting your Conduct in the Seminole Campaign over again. You, and they, have once obtained a decisive and triumphant, victory before the people & in Congress. It is the wish of C and C to go to war again—to fight the battle over again, hoping to deceive the people. It is not the interest of you or yr friends to do so, or put to hazard the ground they occupy. We want rest, and to repose among our justly earned laurels

My eyes have given out, and I have no doubt your patience. Accept my best wishes. Present my kindest wishes to the members of yr. Cabinet including Mr Calhoun, providig he may not chuse to fall out openly with you, feeling a hope you will not with him[.] As usual

Jno Overton

ALS, DLC (38).

1. On September 19 and 26, 1818, the *Nashville Whig* printed articles by Overton, under the pen name Aristides, vindicating AJ's conduct in Florida under the law of nations and rules of war. The *National Intelligencer* reprinted them on October 10 and 20, 1818.

2. President Monroe took an extended southern tour in 1819. AJ was with him for four weeks in June and July, including two stays at the Hermitage.

3. A meeting of New York legislators on April 13 had seconded the Pennsylvania legislative caucus resolutions of March 31 calling on AJ to stand for a second term.

4. On February 8, 1830, New York congressman Churchill Caldom Cambreleng (1786–1862) submitted a report from the House Committee on Commerce blasting the protective tariff as wrong in principle and calamitous in practice, "injurious to every interest and to every section of the country" (*HRRep* 165, 21st Cong., 1st sess., Serial 199).

From Philip Grymes Randolph

War Office
June 16th 1830

Sir

I have the honor to enclose Mr Rowland's defense against charges preferred for maladministration whilst U S Pension Agent. Mr Ellis Doty has been appointed to supercede Mr Rowland who will be apprised of the fact as soon as Mr Doty's bond is received—with great Respect

P G Randolph
Actg Secty of War

[Endorsed by AJ:] Mr Rowland has been removed as Pension agent—will it not appear strange that he should be retained as Marshal—under this circumstance consistancy, says remove him   send me a proper name to appoint.—A. J.

ALS, DNA-RG 59 (M639-20). LC, DNA-RG 107 (M127-2). On May 5 and 8, Thomas Rowland had sent Van Buren evidence and affidavits repelling John P. Sheldon's "false and malicious" accusations, including the charge of exacting improper fees from pensioners. Copies of his defense were furnished to the War Department and also to Sheldon, then in Washington, who reiterated the charges (DNA-RG 59, M639-20). Ellis Doty (c1783–1843), Rowland's replacement as pension agent, was a Wayne County justice of the peace. Before leaving town on June 17, AJ removed Rowland as marshal and appointed John L. Leib. On August 14 Rowland wrote Van Buren demanding to know the cause of his removal (*TPUS*, 12:180, 195–97). AJ nominated Leib to the Senate on December 14, and on February 18, 1831, nominated Sheldon for receiver of the Monroe, Mich., land office. On March 2 the Senate rejected Leib by 35 to 5 and Sheldon by 19 to 18.

From John Forsyth

Augusta June 17. 1830

Sir

I have had the honor to receive your letter of the 7th. inst & the copy papers enclosed with it. The papers will be shewn to Mr Crawford & no other use of them made by me.

I did not intend to convey to Mr Calhoun the idea that any personal communications ever took place between us prior to the date of Mr Crawfords letter relative to the occurrences in Mr Monroes cabinet on the question of the Seminole War. What I intended he should know & I suppose he will now understand, if I have inadvertently misled him is that I did not volunteer to procure the information contained in Mr Crawfords letter; but that it was obtained for your use, in compliance with your request. Major Hamilton requested me in your name to give you what I had previously given to him—Mr Crawfords account of the transaction. With this request I complied after having first obtained Mr Crawfords consent & received his correction of a mistake I had made in repeating his verbal sentiment. I have the honor to be with great respect yr friend & ob. Serv.

John Forsyth

a copy of this will be sent to Mr Calhoun

[Endorsed by AJ:] Mr Forsythes letter acknowledging the recpt of mine enclosing a copy of Mr Calhouns for Mr Crawford—recd. July 8th 1830   To be copied—to be copied & enclosed to Mr Calhoun—

ALS, DLC (38). *US Telegraph*, February 17, 1831; *Calhoun Papers*, 11:205.

From George Rockingham Gilmer

Executive Department
Milledgeville 17th June 1830

I transmit to the President for his information two proclamations, one of which is designed to notify the Indians within the State of the extension of its jurisdiction over them, the other white persons as well as Indians to desist from trespassing upon the property of the State by taking gold or other valuable minerals from its ungranted land. Before these proclamations had reached the part of the State occupied by the Cherokees, the U States troops had driven from it all persons except Indian occupants.

The President is aware that such an exercise of power is believed not to be authorized by the Constitution of the U States, and more especially since the passage of the law by Georgia extending the jurisdiction of the State over all its Indian territory. It is however so important an object with the State to obtain from the U States the execution of its contract of 1802 to remove the Indians from within its limits that it has been unwilling to create the least embarrassment by any assertion of its rights in opposition to the policy of the General Government.[1] This disposition has been increased by the special confidence reposed in the present administration.

From information just received there is much reason to apprehend considerable disturbences and perhaps bloodshed from the manner in which the orders of the President to remove intruders has been executed by the officers commanding the regular troops. The persons who have been removed by them were those engaged in mining for gold. Their number amounted to several thousand most of whom had found their employment exceedingly profitable. The Indians in their immediate vicinity so far from objecting to the occupation of their country by the gold miners it is said favored their prescence, They were not interrupted in the accustomed enjoyment of their country by the taking of gold from its soil.

The gold region is situated very near the thickly inhabited part of the frontier of the State.

When the gold diggers were removed by the troops altho much discontent was felt they retired to their homes without any actual resistance   It however soon became known that the mines from which they had been driven were immediately taken possession of by the Indians, and the whites connected with them, and that they were permitted to take the gold therefrom without any resistance from the troops who had dispossessed the citizens of the State. Very great excitement is said to be the result of this state of things.

There is much reason to apprehend that the Indians will be forcibly driven from the whole of the gold region unless they are immediately prohibited from appropriating its mineral wealth to themselves ~~immediately~~.[2]

Since the discovery of gold in the Cherokee Country, the opinion has very generally prevailed, that those who were engaged in digging for it violated no right except that of the State, & that after the passage of the law extending the jurisdiction of the State over that Country, the Government of the U States would have no authority to enforce the nonintercourse laws.[3] What effect the proclamation prohibiting all persons both Indians & whites from digging for gold may have in allaying the excitement among the persons who have been removed as intruders is very uncertain. It is probable that it may prevent an immediate attack upon the Indians who are so employed from the expectation that they will be restrained by the authority of the State.

I shall be compelled to resort to the tedious process of the courts for this purpose, the laws of the State not having invested the Governor with the power to protect the public property by military force. In the mean time it is very desirable that the President would direct the officers commanding the U States troops to prevent intrusion upon the property of the State by the Indians, at the same time that they are defending the occupant rights of the Indians from intrusion by the whites.

The President will perceive that in the proclamation forbidding all persons both whites & Indians from taking gold from the territory of the State in the occupation of the Indians that the right of the state to all the gold and silver in its ungranted land is directly asserted. It is believed that the President requires no argument in support of that right thus claimed for Georgia. All the European nations who made discoveries, conquests, or took possession of any portion of this continent claimed the exclusive right to all the gold and silver found within their possessions. This was in fact the first and strongest inducement to the enterprize of the early adventurers to this country. In addition to this right assumed by all European nations the King of Great Britain claimed by virtue of the common law of England to be the sovereign owner of all the lands within his kingdom and especially in the American Colonies   Upon the Independence of the States their Governments became entitled to all the rights of sovereignty over the territory within their limits which had before belonged to the crown of G Britain. The State of Georgia is therefore entitled to the gold & silver in its territory occupied by the Indians as well by the customary law established by the nations by whom this country was settled, as the fee simple or paramount title which it derives from the crown of G Britain. The courts of this State have uniformly determined that the Government of the State is the universal proprietor of all the ungranted lands within it including those in the occupancy of the Indians. Such is believed to be the legal doctrine of all the other States it is certainly that of the supreme court of the U States as to the lands of Georgia.[4] It is believed that if the Indians are permitted to take possession of the gold mines thro the assistance of the U States Government that instead of being removed they will become fixed upon the soil of Georgia. It is said that preparations are making by a large number of the wealthy Cherokees to remove into the gold region, for the purpose of participating in its mineral riches. If they can be protected in so doing by the U States We shall thus not only retain the Cherokees who have hitherto occupied the lands of the State but many of those who reside in Tennessee, Alabama and North Carolina. The U States are bound by contract to prevent this state of things and no doubt is entertained of the disposition of the President to perform the obligations of the Government in good faith. The State of Georgia cannot permit her rights to be violated by persons subject to her jurisdiction as the Indians are acknowledged to be without applying a remedy adequate to the removal of the evil. In exercising this power however if it should unfortunately become necessary it will be the object of the State to do it in such a manner as to aid rather than thwart the policy of the present administration, & carefully to guard from violation the rights intended to be secured to the Indians[.] Very Respectfully Yours &c

George R Gilmer

P.S. I have this moment received information which may be certainly relied upon that when the Executive Proclamation was received at the gold mines, all the native Indians desisted from work and expressed their determination to obey the orders of the Government of the State, but that most of the whites and wealthy half breeds continued digging for gold. I have not yet understood what effect the proclamation has had upon the intruders who have been driven off & who have evinced a disposition to act with violence. An Agent of great discretion and firmness will be immediately sent to the gold regions with directions to enjoin by process from the Courts, all persons who may be found digging for gold. In this way strong hope is entertained confirmed by the late intelligence that peace & order may be restored to our frontier.[5]

George R Gilmer

LS, DNA-RG 75 (M234-74). LC, G-Ar; Copy, DNA-RG 46 (15-1483). *SDoc* 512, 23d Cong., 1st sess., vol. 2, pp. 229–31 (Serial 245). Gilmer (1790–1859) was governor of Georgia. He enclosed two official proclamations, both issued June 3. The first declared in effect Georgia's law of December 19, 1829, which annexed the Cherokee domain to five Georgia counties, extended state jurisdiction over it as of June 1, disbanded the Cherokee government and voided its laws, and prescribed criminal penalties for resisting state authority or attempting to deter Indians from emigrating. The second proclamation ordered all unauthorized occupants, Indian and white, to vacate the gold country (*SDoc* 512, 23d Cong., 1st sess., vol. 2, pp. 231–36, Serial 245).

With AJ and Eaton absent, acting Secretary of War Philip G. Randolph received this letter. As instructed by AJ, he conferred with Berrien, who wrote AJ on June 25 (below).

1. On April 24, 1802, U.S. and Georgia commissioners concluded a formal agreement by which Georgia ceded its western domain (later Alabama and Mississippi) to the U.S., on condition "that the United States, shall, at their own expense, extinguish, for the use of Georgia, as early as the same can be peaceably obtained, on reasonable terms, the Indian title" remaining within the state.

2. Gilmer appended letters warning that evicted intruders might resort to mob violence against those who had taken their place at the mines (*SDoc* 512, 23d Cong., 1st sess., vol. 2, pp. 236–37, Serial 245).

3. An Act of March 30, 1802, "to regulate trade and intercourse with the Indian tribes" barred unauthorized entry onto lands "belonging, or secured by treaty" to the Indians and empowered the president to remove intruders by military force.

4. In *Fletcher v. Peck* (1810), Chief Justice John Marshall declared the opinion of the Court majority "that the nature of the Indian title, which is certainly to be respected by all courts, until it be legitimately extinguished, is not such as to be absolutely repugnant to seisin in fee on the part of the state."

5. On June 21, Gilmer appointed Yelverton P. King as superintendent of public lands in the Cherokee country and instructed him to obtain writs against trespassers.

To William Berkeley Lewis

(Private)

Cumberland
June 21rst. 1830

Dr Major

We arrived here this evening all in good health—you may say to our friends in the city, that the veto is working well—widely different to what our enemies anticipated—we leave here at 5 in the morning, & will write you from Wheeling—I will be happy to hear from you at Nashville when I reach there.

Present me to all friends, & in your letter, advise me whether Mary Ann got her pairysol we happened to bring on when we separated & sent back from clarksburgh—say to Mr Van Buren I will be glad to hear from him often—In haste yr friend

Andrew Jackson

ALS, NNPM; Copy, NN (15-1519). Mary Ann Lewis (c1814–66) was Lewis's daughter.

From Charles Rhind

Constantinople 21st. June 1830.

I crave permission to refer Your Excellency to the Despatch I had the honor of addressing you under date of 10th. Ulto. in which I mentioned that after having successfully combated the Intrigues of the English, and obtained finally the sanction of the Sultan, I nevertheless considered that I would be hazarding the interests of the United States if I left the business unfinished, and accordingly exercised plenipotentiary power, and signed and exchanged the Treaty on the 7th. Ulto. but in compliance with the wishes of Your Excellency immediately dispatched a special Messenger with passports for my Colleagues to repair here and sign it also.

They arrived at Pera on the 24th Ulto. they both declined signing the Treaty, and declared they *never* would do so, and that they would pay no money on account of it. On reasoning with them and requiring their objections in writing, (which were entirely futile) they at last had the baseness to say that if I would expunge the paragraph which recites that the

Treaty was negotiated by me, *they* would sign it!! I spurned the degrading proposal, as became an American.[1]

They then gave me to understand that they would pay no money, to this I replied that I trusted I could raise it on the credit of our Government among the Merchants, Mr. Offley thought I could not, I told them in such case I would apply to the Minister of some Friendly Power to extricate me from the degrading dilemma in which they had placed me, but finding eventually that I could raise the money, they thought it prudent to add their Names to the Treaty *already finished*. On the 9th. instant they left this for Smyrna.[2]

Those Gentlemen evidently came here to mar the Negotiation if they could, and the Documents I have already forwarded to the Honb. Mr. Van Buren will prove this fact. The Funds that were appropriated for the purpose of making this Treaty with the exception of 143,000 piastres (about Nine thousand Dollars) which I drew for the customary presents on *making* a Treaty, they have used as they pleased, all that I have received of that Fund is *Five hundred Dollars*!! which will hardly cover my expenses before I reached this! and they had the baseness to refuse payment of a Draft I made for 10,000 piastres (about Six hundred & fifty dollars)— there is nothing left undone by them, which could disgrace and degrade our Country or heap indignity upon me, I have documents to prove the facts I assert, and shall have the honor of presenting them personally to you; shortly (I hope) after you receive this for nothing is left me now but to return to Washington and meet face to face before Your Excellency this Commodore Biddle whose recall I have respectfully requested in my protests.[3] I venture to assert and pledge myself to prove, that since the formation of our Republic, nor even in the annals of Diplomacy, is there to be found an instance of such disgraceful conduct as those two men have shewn on this occasion, but most fortunately it was not in their power to mar the business.

When all the facts are laid before Your Excellency I repose entire confidence that the expression of your censure will be *marked*, to those who deserve it, if I have acted amiss I will bow with deference to your fiat, and I hope if You find that it is my Colleagues who have disgraced their Country, You will not spare the censure they merit

I proceed immediately to Odessa for the purpose of naming a Vice Consul *ad interim* & Agents at such ports as may be deemed most necessary, until my return to Russia   I shall remain there but a very few days and return to Washington with all possible dispatch.[4]

With profound respect I have the honor to be Your obt St.

Chas Rhind

ALS, DNA-RG 59 (M46-3). This letter repeated the substance, and some of the language, of the sworn protest Rhind had sent Van Buren on June 8 (DNA-RG 59, M46-3).

1. Pera was a Constantinople suburb. The secret article identified Rhind as "Commissioner and Plenipotentiary" "with full powers to treat of and conclude, separately,

or jointly" with Biddle and Offley, a broader statement of his authority than in the treaty's preamble. Biddle and Offley reported to Van Buren that they had considered not signing the secret article or appending a disclaimer to their signatures, but dropped the idea on learning the Turks would reject the treaty unless signed unconditionally by all the commissioners.

2. Biddle wrote Van Buren on June 9 that he had never withheld funds from Rhind. On May 26, he had approved payment of 143,500 piastres (about $10,000) for nine jeweled snuff boxes that Rhind had already distributed as presents to Turkish officials. He later told Rhind he would not have done so had he then known of the secret article—a remark, he said, that Rhind misconstrued as a refusal of funds (DNA-RG 59, M46-3).

3. Rhind's June 8 protest concluded by asking AJ "to order James Biddle home, that he may personally appear with myself before His Excellency and answer for his conduct."

4. After designating vice consuls at Odessa and Taganrog on the Black Sea, Rhind sailed from Smyrna in September and reached New York on November 14.

From John Caldwell Calhoun

Pendleton 22d June 1830

Sir,

I embrace the first leisure moment, since my return home to enclose to you a copy of a letter from Mr Forsyth, the original of which was handed to me on my passage from Washington to Norfolk on board of the Steam boat, and also a copy of my answer.

You will learn by a perusal of Mr Forsyth's letter, that it refers to the correspondence between us, and that it places the subject of that correspondence in a light, in some respects, different from what I had previously regarded it. I had supposed, from the complexion of your letters to me, that the copy of Mr Crawford's letter to Mr Forsyth had been placed by the latter in your hand, without any previous act, or agency on your part, but by Mr Forsyth's letter to me, I am informed, that such is not the fact. It seems, that he acted as your agent in the affair. He states, that you applied to him to be informed of what took place in the Cabinet of Mr Monroe on the subject of the Seminole ~~affair~~ campaign; and I infer, as the information could be obtained only from some one of the members of the Cabinet, and as Mr Forsyth was not one, and, as far as I am informed, not particularly intimate with any of the members, except Mr Crawford, that the object of your request was obtain information through Mr Forsyth from Mr Crawford; and that consequently in writing to him and in placing the copy of his letter in your hand, he can be regarded in no other light, but as your agent.

Under this new aspect of this affair, I conceive, that I have the right to claim of you to be put in possession of all of the additional information, which I might fairly have demanded of Mr Forsyth, had the correspondence been originally between him & myself, on the supposition, on which I acted previously to the receipt of his letter. He avows himself ready, if desired by me, to furnish me with the additional information, but a sense of propriety ~~will~~ would not permit me to make the request of him.

Considered *as your agent* in this affair, it is not *for me* to make the request of information *of him*.

What additional information, I conceive myself to be entitled to, my letter to you of the 29th May will sufficiently indicate. A part of that information, it seems from Mr Forsyth's letter, is already in your possession, and there can be no doubt, but that the whole would be furnished, at your request.

I make this application solely from the desire of obtaining the means of enabling me of to unravel this mysterious affair. Facts and circumstances light of themselves may, when viewed in connection, afford important light, as to the origin and object, of what I firmly believe to be a base political intrigue, got up by those, who regard your reputation and the publick interest much less, than their own personal advancement.

I must remark in conclusion, that the letter of Mr Forsyth affords to my mind conclusive proof, that the intimations to my prejudice, to which you refer in your letter of the 30th Ultimo, and which you seem to think made no impression on your mind, have not been without their intended effect. On no other supposition can I explain the fact, that, without giving me any intimation of the step, you should apply for information, as to my course in the Cabinet to one, whom you know to be so hostile to me, as Mr Crawford is, and who could not, as you know, make the disclosure consistently with the principles of honor and fidelity, when my previous correspondence with you ought to have satisfied you, that I was prepared to give you frankly and fully any information, which you might desire in relation to my conduct on the occasion. I am very respectfully your &&

J. C. Calhoun

ALS, DLC (38). *US Telegraph*, February 17, 1831; *Calhoun Papers*, 11:206–7. Calhoun enclosed copies in his hand of John Forsyth's letter of May 31 and his reply of June 1 (DLC-38), both of which Forsyth had already sent to AJ on June 2 (above). AJ replied on July 19 (below).

From John Macpherson Berrien

[Converging events in mid-1830 pushed the question of Indian nations' status within the United States further towards resolution—or confrontation. On May 28, Jackson signed the controversial Indian Removal Act, which empowered the president to arrange with Indian tribes or nations to exchange their lands within existing states and territories for others west of the Mississippi. It appropriated $500,000 for costs of negotiation and emigration. On June 1, Georgia's law of December 1829 extending jurisdiction over its Cherokee domain took effect. On June 17, the day Jackson left Washington for Tennessee, the War Department ordered

*that tribal annuities henceforth be distributed to individuals and families
rather than leaders or governments. For the Cherokees, the change was
to "be attended to immediately" (DNA-RG 107, M6-12). Meanwhile, on
June 4 former U.S. attorney general William Wirt wrote Governor Gilmer
of Georgia that he had agreed to represent the Cherokees in challenging
the state's authority over them before the Supreme Court.]*

Washington 25th. June 1830—

Dear Sir,

Doctor Randolph called this morning to converse with me on the subject of the accompanying communication and documents, transmitted by
the Governor of Georgia.[1] After a careful examination of them, I have
advised him to have

1. an order to the officer commanding the US troops in the Cherokee
nation, instructing him, until further orders, to prevent all persons from
working the mines or searching for or carrying out of the nation, any
gold, silver or other metal—

2. To advise the Governor of Georgia, that such order had been issued
ad interim—and that his communication & the accompanying documents
would be forwarded to you, that you might take such other or further
steps, as you might deem necessary—

3. To write to the agent of the Cherokees, announcing to him this order
& instructing him to recommend to the Cherokees and other persons in
the nation to conform to it—

4. To forward the papers to you with a statement of what had been
done—[2]

Having mentioned to Doct Randolph my intention to write to you
by this mail, he has requested me to forward to you the accompanying
papers, with these explanations—

As I do not doubt the right of the State as the owner of the fee, to the
gold and silver found in the soil, I thought it due to the conciliatory course
which has been pursued by Gov: Gilmer, that any proper efforts should
be made on the part of this Government to prevent the disturbances,
which he apprehends. I had the less difficulty in recommending the order,
because the papers will be with you so soon, that if you should desire
to make any change of arrangement, you can promptly effect it—Genl
Macomb will accordingly issue the order tomorrow—

The remaining memoranda require no particular explanation. I beg
leave however to suggest to you some reflections which have occurred to
me on the subject of carrying into effect, the act of the last Congress, so
far as it concerns this tribe. With the existing Government (as it is called),
there is I think no hope. The Chiefs who now rule in the Cherokee nation,
have secured for themselves, too many privileges, to consent to change
their position, while the possession of the treasury, furnishes them with
pecuniary means to defend it. An exchange of lands is moreover forbidden

by their Constitution.³ While therefore we recognize that Constitution by acknowledging its functionaries as legitimate, it is in vain for us to hope for success. My plan then is, without stopping to negociate with them (the chiefs) to go directly to the nation, and the present circumstances are favorable to such an operation—

The Constitution divides the nation into eight districts from which Representatives are elected. I propose the appointment of a competent agent, who should go under the protection of the military now in the nation, to ascertain successively the will of the *native* Indians in each district—I say native, because I would not allow any american citizen, by assuming the Indian character, to thwart the wishes of his own Government—and I provide that the agent shall go under the protection of the military, in order that the common Indians may see that they will be supported in the free expression of their opinions, if they should differ with their chiefs—If you could select an intelligent agent near you, whom you could at once dispatch on this errand—who would frankly represent to these people the views of the Government, and assure them from you, that the soldiers of the United States would protect them, against their chiefs, if they attempted to interfere with them, for agreeing to remove, I think he would succeed—and having done this in any one district they should be immediately called upon to select a person to represent them in negociating with you the terms—

The two great difficulties with which we have to contend, are the possession of the treasury and of the press acquired by the Chiefs—The first you have perhaps done all in your power to control—but the order is prospective and the present year's annuity has I fear already gone into the Treasury—Is it too late however for the agent under instructions from the Secretary, to insist upon its distribution among the Indians at large? If this could be done, it would incline them to receive the proposals of the person you should send to them more favorably—The remaining consideration relates to the *press.* If that could be transferred with the school fund to the *West of the mississippi,* our work would be half accomplished—You can judge better than I can, of the practicability of this measure, but I cannot too strongly urge its importance—⁴

I have written to Gov: Gilmer and have sketched an answer to Mr. Wirt's letter—It is a delicate operation, but I trust he will view it properly —and at any rate, from your view of its importance, I did not feel myself at liberty to abstain from it—I shall write to him again by the present mail—⁵

I send you a letter received this morning from Genl Coffee of Georgia. I think the projected visit to Alabama, may probably be advantageous at this crisis—At any rate it will give him an opportunity of knowing personally, what reliance is to be placed on the assistance of Lucas & Fitzpatrick.⁶

I have written to you freely on the several subjects of this letter, and though I would not tax you in your retirement, I should be very much gratified to hear from you—my feelings and my judgment concur so entirely on the propriety of these measures, that I need not repeat my readiness to give any aid in my power—

We have been gratified here, that you have had such fine cool weather for your journey, which has I hope been a pleasant one—Supposing that you may have arrived at Nashville, by the time this letter can be transported there, I direct to that place—I beg to present my respectful compliments to your family, and to assure you of the respectful regard, with which I am Dear Sir your friend & obt st

Jn: Macpherson Berrien

[Endorsed by AJ:] Judge Berrien—to be acknowledged   recd. 8th of july 1830

ALS, DNA-RG 75 (M234-74).

1. Above, June 17.

2. All these things were done. On June 26, acting Secretary of War Randolph issued orders through General Macomb for troops to prevent all persons from working the mines or carrying off metal, by force if necessary. Randolph sent copies the same day to Governor Gilmer, to Cherokee agent Hugh Montgomery, and to AJ (*SDoc* 512, 23d Cong., 1st sess., vol. 2, pp. 237–39, Serial 245).

3. The Cherokee constitution of 1827 declared that the Nation's boundaries "shall forever hereafter remain unalterably the same" and that all lands within them "are, and shall remain, the common property of the nation." It further forbade the sale or disposal of individual improvements to the U.S. or state governments or to their citizens (*HRDoc* 91, 23d Cong., 2d sess., p. 11, Serial 273).

4. Citing AJ's orders, and following on his own directive of the day before, Randolph on June 18 had instructed agent Montgomery to pay annuities henceforth to individual "Chiefs, Warriors and common Indians, and their families" rather than to the Treasurer of the Cherokee Nation, adding that "this mode of distribution is not under any circumstances to be departed from" (DNA-RG 75, M234-74, M21-6; DNA-RG 107, M6-12). Since February 1828 the Nation had published a newspaper, the *Cherokee Phoenix*, in both English and Cherokee.

5. Berrien had evidently seen a copy of Wirt's June 4 letter to Gilmer. Gilmer had already on June 19 sent Wirt an indignant reply (*Niles*, Sep 18, 1830).

6. John Coffee (1782–1836) of Georgia, a cousin of AJ's friend John Coffee, had been a state militia general and was later a congressman. Walter Ballard Lucas (1795–1862) was a trader and innkeeper in Montgomery County, Ala.; Benjamin Fitzpatrick (1802–1869), later governor and U.S. senator, was a lawyer and planter. Berrien and Coffee had been attempting to enlist their aid in inducing the Creeks to remove. On May 3 Berrien wrote Coffee proposing to meet Lucas and Fitzpatrick in Milledgeville. He enclosed with this letter to AJ Coffee's June 15 response from Milledgeville, saying that Lucas and Fitzpatrick had not come and that he would now go to Alabama and confer with them. If they would not help, he would sound out the Creek chiefs himself (DNA-RG 75, M234-74). Coffee wrote AJ on July 10 (below).

From Martin Van Buren

W. June 25 1830

My dear Sir

I returned from Norfolk on Tuesday being absent only three entire days. The vessel had not yet arrived but is doubtless there if not off before this time. I found Mr Randolph in reasonable health and excellent spirits. He entered very fully & intelligibly into all your views—will leave the U.S. with the very best intentions & as I hope & believe do credit to himself & his employer. He desired his respects & regards to you. Nothing has occurred since you left us worth noting except the news from Columbia which you will see in the papers. Moore has as usual laboured with discretion but grieves much that Bolivar leaves the country, which I do not; viewing the preservation of his fame as if not the only certainly the most important tangible point of value in that Country at the present moment. He had halted several days twelve miles from Carthagena were it is understood means were using to induce him to remain which I hope he will not do. Mr Moore has no doubt they will re-elect him in Feby. & insist upon his return. The men now in power at Bogota & Carthagena are his friends.[1] I have read more newspapers since you have been gone than in the ~~wh~~ a year before. The message continues to cleave its way nobly. Your friends exhult & your enemies cower. Gales has made some civil but weak observations & is evidently glad to be rid of it.[2] The papers (Ritchie leading the way) are taking strong ground in regard to the removal of Miles King.[3] I shall leave here on the 5th. July & wish you would direct your letters to me at Albany from whence they will be sent to me wherever I may be. I shall be extremely happy to hear from you frequently & will write you as often as I have any thing to say. If any favorable changes are produced in a matter which has given us all so much uneasiness—which I most ardently hope may be the case, I would take great pleasure in being informed of it.

Remember me affectionately to Mr & Mrs Donelson & to my good friend Miss Eastin & believe me to be Truly your friend

M Van Buren

[Endorsed by AJ:] The Sec. of State recd. 11th. 1830 answd—12th. july Do—directed to Albany N.

ALS, DLC-Van Buren Papers (15-1527).

1. Thomas Patrick Moore (1797–1853), a former Kentucky congressman, was U.S. minister to Colombia. Simón Bolívar (1783–1830), famed liberator of South America, had relinquished the Colombian presidency in April 1830. In dispatches received in Washington on June 24, Moore reported on political upheaval that portended the imminent breakup of the country. Bolívar, he said, had left Bogotá on May 8 for Cartagena on his way to the U.S.

Moore lamented his departure but expected that his friends, presently in power, would elect him president and compel his return in February 1831 (DNA-RG 59, T33-6).

2. Joseph Gales Jr. (1786–1860) and his brother-in-law William W. Seaton published the anti-Jackson *National Intelligencer*. A long editorial on June 24 criticized the Maysville Road veto on various grounds.

3. On June 22 Thomas Ritchie's *Richmond Enquirer* defended AJ's removal of Norfolk navy agent Miles King. Repelling charges of "political persecution," the editorial said AJ "was actuated by no spirit of political hostility" and that King's loose and possibly fraudulent accounting "required and justified his removal" as a "public duty."

To *William Berkeley Lewis*

(Private)

Board Steam Boat
Wheeling june 26th. 1830—

Dr Major

We arrived at Mr Steenrodes last evening, where we were met by Mr McClure, Postmaster,[1] who delivered me the package forwarded by you & your letter of the 19th. instant marked private—its contents duly noted, I have barely time to remark, that the conduct of Genl. D. Green, is such as I suspected—from me he never had a hint of the writer of those strctures upon Mr McDuffies report, and the only thing that ever passed between us on the subject of that report was after the adjournment of Congress when I asked him for a copy, & observed, that it was necessary, *as he had been silent*, that some notice should be taken of that, & Genl Smiths, of the Senates, report—here our conversation ended, and since, I have never changed one word with him on that subject—his remarks, therefore, that he knew the author, must have been gratuitous, for from me he never had any other hint, but the one I have detailed—should he write me, which I cannot believe he will, he will receive a proper reply   The truth is, he has professed to me to be heart & soul, against the Bank, but his idol controles him as much as the shewman does his puppits, and we must get another organ to announce the policy, & defend the administration,—in his hands, it is more injured than by all the opposition. I have not time at present to say more on this subject, I shall expect to hear from you at Nashville[2]

I have recd. inclosed from Major Barry a long communication from Col. A. Butler, which I herewith inclose to Mr Van Buren—it promises well & holds out fair prospects of success, in that quarter—[3]

The veto I find will work well, altho' it is to be reviewed by Mr Gales— The opposition has made some noise but like the anti-masonic, bubble is wasting in the common sense of the people—little sectional interests feel a disappointment, whilst the great body of the people hail the act, as a preservative of the constitution & the union.[4]

I am greatly disappointed in not meeting with, or hearing from Major Eaton at this place; I leave him my compliments and hope to meet him at Louisville or Cincinnati—at those places, if I should not meet him I will write him—

We are all well, and all unite in our love to you & my Dr Mary Ann, to whom present me kindly—

Present me to Major Barry & his family & all the heads of Departments respectfully & believe me yr friend

Andrew Jackson

ALS, NNPM; Copy, NN (15-1532).

1. Daniel Steenrod (1784–1864) kept a tavern at Wheeling, and Richard McClure was the postmaster.

2. The unnamed author was James A. Hamilton, prompted by AJ to write a critique of McDuffie's Ways and Means Committee report on the Bank, the first installment of which ran in the *Telegraph* on June 30. On March 29, Samuel Smith had reported from the Senate Committee on Finance that the BUS, contrary to AJ's charge in his annual message, already provided the country with a perfectly safe and uniform national currency (*SDoc* 104, 21st Cong., 1st sess., Serial 193). Green's "idol" was John C. Calhoun.

3. Anthony Butler to AJ, April 15 (above).

4. The disappearance and presumed murder in 1826 of William Morgan of Batavia, N.Y., who was planning to expose secret rituals of the Order of Freemasonry, triggered a popular furor against Masonry that assumed political form as the Anti-Masonic Party. The Anti-Masons elected governors in Vermont in 1831 and Pennsylvania in 1835, and ran William Wirt for president in 1832.

To Martin Van Buren

(Private)

Board Steam Gondola
Wheeling june 26th. 1830—

My Dr. Sir

I have this moment arrived here, and on board the Boat received the enclosed from Col A. Butler, which I send for your perusal & answer.

you will find he is in good spirits & under present circumstances, if it can be done agreable to usage, and with propriety, let him be authorised to employ a translator whilst engaged in his negotiations on those two important subjects, a commercial treaty, and of limits. I do not see how he can do without one, and I suppose it will be an expence that may be, with propriety, paid out of the contingent fund—with these remarks I leave you to give him the answer.[1]

I am, as I have been all the rout, surrounded with a croud—I write for your own eye—when I get to the Hermitage I will write you more in detail—say to Col Butler my situation, & why I have not wrote him at present. The *veto, works well*, we have nothing to fear from it   it will lead to stability in our government, & a system of internal improvement that will be durable & beneficial to our country, keeping the agency & powers of the Federal Govt. within its proper sphere, & the States to manage their own concerns in their own way.

I shall expect to hear from you at Nashville where I expect to arrive in nine days, at farthest—accept assurance of my sincere regard & esteem, present me to all the heads of Departments & believe me in great haste yr friend

Andrew Jackson

ALS, DLC-Van Buren Papers (15-1539).
    1. AJ enclosed Anthony Butler's letter of April 15 (above), requesting authority to hire a translator. Van Buren wrote Butler on July 1 that federal law prohibited chargés from hiring secretaries or clerks at public expense. However, Butler could charge the cost of translating individual official papers to his contingent account (*HRDoc* 351, 25th Cong., 2d sess., pp. 64–65, Serial 332).

From Thomas Kennedy

Hagers Toun June 26th. 1830

My dear Sir,

I hope you have had a pleasant journey since you left Hagers Toun which is just about a week ago. I send you by this Mail the Hagers Toun Mail of the 18th. & 25th. the Annapolis Gazette of the 24th. The Baltimore Republican of Tuesday and Wednesday last, and the Rock Ville Free Press of Wednesday. The pieces signed Maryland as well as the others marked /—/ were written by a friend of yours here to whom you presented a book on the Eye.[1]

Your rejection of our Frederick Road caused some *excitement* at first, but it is subsiding fast, and I now believe it will ultimately make you stronger with the People, although every means will be used to misrepresent your views; and it will keep us busy here for a few months in order to counteract the attempts of your enemies. The grand object at present is to gain the State of Maryland and for this every nerve will be strained, but I still have hopes that "All's Well."[2]

I thought when you were elected by so large a majority, that the opposition would have submitted with a good grace, and I thought last fall after we had gained Maryland, that the State would have been suffered to rest in peace for a season, but your enemies are desperate and reckless, with them it cannot be worse—yet they have those to encounter who although they did not seek the battle will not shun it. A U. States Senator is to be elected by our Legislature, as Mr. Chambers term expires next March, and next year the Senate have to be elected for five years—I still hope for the best.[3]

I received a letter from Colo. Geo. E. Mitchell M. C. from the Eastern Shore he has lately been in several Counties, and thinks your *Veto* on the Road Bills has made you stronger on the Eastern Shore.[4]

I am now glad that I am still out of Office, as I can speak my mind more freely, but I hope we shall settle all matters to our satisfaction this fall in Maryland, and all that is necessary to gain the Victory is to Keep the People well informed, and so far as regards Washington County particularly and Maryland generally I shall try to do my part. Yr friend

Thos. Kennedy

Present me to Mrs. Donnelson—Miss Eastin and Maj. Donnelson—I take the ladies first you see—even at Boonsborogh I had to speak first to the ladies—for although I like the President well, the ladies are always prefferrd by me to man. To Mrs. Hayes and Mr. Hayes please to remember me—I often think of her and Annapolis. I may send you papers occasionally, but do not expect answers.

[Endorsed by AJ:] Mr Kennedy Hagers Town Maryland recd. July 8th 1830—to be acknowledged

ALS, DLC (38).
　　1. The Annapolis *Maryland Gazette* in mid-1830 ran a series of political essays signed "Maryland." Number 6, on June 24, and numbers 4 and 5, reprinted in the *Hagerstown Mail* of June 18 and 25, defended AJ's internal improvement vetoes.
　　2. Columns signed "ALL'S WELL" in the June 18 and 25 *Hagerstown Mail* justified AJ's vetoes and predicted they would not impair his popularity.
　　3. Jacksonians lost the annual legislative elections in October, and anti-Jackson senator Ezekiel Forman Chambers (1788–1867) was elected by the Maryland legislature to a new term in 1831.
　　4. George Edward Mitchell (1781–1832), an Army brevet colonel in the War of 1812, was a Maryland congressman, 1823–27 and 1829–32.

From William Lytle et al.

[Cincinnati Jackson men met on June 23 to plan his welcome to the city. A committee of seventeen, accompanied by a band of music, took a chartered steamboat on June 26 to meet Jackson coming down the Ohio. They rendezvoused with him late the next night, about 135 miles above town. The two steamboats were lashed together and the following addresses were exchanged.]

Sir—

It becomes my duty, as Chairman of the committee appointed at a public meeting of the friends of the administration of the general government, in the City of Cincinnati and county of Hamilton, Ohio, for welcoming the arrival of the President of the United States, to congratulate you on this interesting occasion, and in their name to assure you that their confidence in your integrity and patriotism is undiminished; that the measures of your administration generally, are cordially approved, and especially your reasons for disapproving the bill appropriating the public funds for local roads;—and although a few may have made your veto on the Maysville turnpike bill a pretence for leaving our ranks, we are convinced that our real strength has been increased rather than diminished by that document. The Committee are instructed to bid you heartily welcome, and to request the favor of your company, at Cincinnati, for as long a period as your engagement will admit.

Printed, *Cincinnati Advertiser*, June 30 (mAJs). *US Telegraph*, July 7 (15-1543).

To William Lytle et al.

SIR—
I should be insensible to the pleasure flowing from the conscientious discharge of duty, did I not find in the sentiments expressed by you on this occasion, a tribute to my good intentions, which I may accept without weakening the restraints imposed by a just sense of my present accountability as a public servant.

Of part of my administration, and particularly that relating to the bills to which you have alluded, it is a source of the deepest regret to me that my views were such as not to admit the modification necessary to place me on grounds of unanimity with all my friends. Acting for the whole, and not a part of our union, which was formed for general purposes, I could not shrink from the exercise of my constitutional right to oppose the adoption of a policy calculated to extend the action of the general government to the local concerns of the states, and to confound all distinction between the powers of Congress and those reserved to the people. Such I conceive, would be the effect of a precedent for the appropriation of the money of the United States to aid the execution of works purely of a local nature; and I was therefore called upon by every consideration that could demonstrate my attachment to my country and my confidence in the virtue and intelligence of its citizens, to refuse my assent to it. Whether those considerations are supported by a fair construction of the constitution, and a just conception of the practical effect of the principle involved in this question of power, it remains for the people to decide: and I feel gratified that those you represent on this occasion, not only allow me the credit of honestly entertaining them, but the happiness of recurring to them hereafter, as affording a new proof of their respect and esteem for my character.

I pray, you, Sir, to be assured of the high value I set upon the approbation you bestow upon the general course of the administration, and of the great pleasure it will afford me to take by the hand my fellow citizens of

Cincinnati and Hamilton county, with whom my engagements will not permit me to stay longer than 12 o'clock on Tuesday.

Printed, *Cincinnati Advertiser*, June 30 (mAJs). *US Telegraph*, July 7 (15-1544).

From James Alexander Hamilton

New York June 27th. 1830.

My dear Sir.

In compliance with my promise to Mr Malibran who is the writer of the enclosed letter I have to say that I verily believe he is wholly unable to pay the amount of the Judgment—Prior, & larger debts to the U.S. & others having swept away all his property—Should he be released He might aid his Trustees to obtain payment of debts assigned to them to pay the U.S.—at all events I can not believe that expediency or Justice requires that he should be longer detained in confinement—Should you agree with me in this opinion two courses are presented one: To order him to be discharged on payment of Costs. the other—To order a reference of the Petition to the Dist attorney of this District to inquire into the truth of the facts stated in the Petition & upon his report you may decide what ought to be done[1]

We have nothing new here of particular Interest—as far as I have had an opportunity to Judge your *veto* is approved in this State & Pennsilvania.

I had the pleasure to see one of the examiners at West Point who met Genl Eaton there. He speaks of his mode of doing business his demeanour & of him in all respects in terms of very great approbation & expresses this as the opinion of the board of visitors. This Gentleman is a Clergyman of this City distinguished for his learning & Piety[2]

We have news from England to the 18th of May. The King was much better & nothing else of importance   I believe these changes are merely the flickerings of the expering light and that he will not live long[3]

Do me the favor to remember me to all my friends[.] with the truest attachment your friend & Srt

James A Hamilton

ALS, DLC (38).

1. In December 1828, French-born New York City merchant François Eugène Malibran (1781–1836) was imprisoned on order from the federal district court for nonpayment of a penalty of $2,000 plus $359.09 in damages and court costs for violating the law against the importation of slaves. Malibran had already assigned all his assets to cover an outstanding debt to the U.S. of more than $20,000 on custom house bonds from a previous business failure in 1826. On June 26 he petitioned for release, explaining that as a foreigner he had been ignorant of the slave-trading law and that he had already been tried and acquitted for his incidental role in the offense, which consisted only of outfitting the ship. Further, he could better repay his past judgments if he was free to pursue in person the collection of debts owed him outside the U.S. (DNA-RG 59, 16-0402). On July 12 (below), AJ referred the

petition back to Hamilton. On September 4 Hamilton, in his official capacity as U.S. district attorney, reported that Malibran's statements were true and recommended his release. On October 16 AJ ordered Malibran's release on payment of court costs.

2. Eaton had briefly been at West Point during the board of visitors' inspection in June. The clerical gentleman was Jonathan Mayhew Wainwright (1792–1854), rector of Grace Church in New York City and later Episcopal bishop of New York.

3. George IV died on June 26.

To William Berkeley Lewis

(Private)

Cincinnati June 28th 1830—

Dr Major

From wheeling was my last—on our passage, on the morning of the 27th. we broke our shaft—and were left to float with the current *always fortunate*, at nine at night we were met by a committee from cincinnati who with Genl Lytle at their head were charged to conduct me to that hospitable city; their boat took us in tow, and with the aid of the clinton who met us above the city, lashed to us, delivered us at the city where we were greeted by at least six thousand people assembled on the shore to receive us. The numerous assemblage on such short notice require some explanation—some few days ago, Mr Barton was given a public dinner, where many speeches were made, & toasts drunk, of the most violent party kind.[1] The line, it is said, has been fairly drew, my veto upon the Maysville bill the theme of the opposition, & as informed by all, where it has lost me one, it has gained me five friends, and in Kentuckey has done no harm. I am told by judge Burke & Mr Dawson & judge Brown that this was the cause of this numerous collection, as the opposition had drew the line, my friends were determined to display their increased strength— and surely it was a more numerous crowd, than I ever before witnessed here, some say eight, but I do suppose *at least* six thousand people.[2] You will see the canvass has began, the campaign will be a hot one, my friends sanguine of success, and pleased with my course. Judge Burk who has just returned from a tour through the interior of ohio states that Stansbury is prostrate. This is as it should be, and evinces virtue in the people, & a determination to punish hypocracy and double dealing.[3] I spend this night with Genl Lytle & will leave here tomorrow, as early as I can get away.

I have heard nothing of Eaton, will leave a note for him with Mr Dawson in hopes he will overtake me at Louisville. I have taken a little cold, & am not so well as I could wish. Say to Major Barry & Van Buren & the other heads of Depts that I think all is well in this quarter, all we have to do is to continue stedfast in our course, keeping constantly in view the constitution, and the prosperity of our country founded upon its provisions—should we, on these principles not obtain the full approbation of our country, we will have the pleasing consolation of our own, which is above all others.

I write for your own eye, present me kindly to Mr Kendal, say to him amonghst his other arduous duties, he must attend to Mr McDuffies report—the feeling of the people are in a good time to receive a criticism on this subject, and it would have a good effect pending the electioneering campaign to bring this subject before the people

with my respects to Mary Ann, and best wishes for yourself in great haste adieu.

Andrew Jackson

P.S. I find it is expected that I should have a survay of the falls made—This I will order as soon as I see the sec of war—I find the suspension of the Light House & Louisville canal Bills, are approved on the ground that the canal & clearing the falls cannot both be national

ALS and Copy, NN (15-1546).

1. Anti-Jackson senator David Barton (1783–1837) of Missouri was guest of honor at a large public dinner at Cincinnati on June 18. Henry Clay was enthusiastically cheered, and Barton gave a speech denouncing AJ's removals from office and internal improvement vetoes.

2. William Burke (1770–1855) was the Cincinnati postmaster. Ethan Allen Brown (1776–1852), former Ohio supreme court judge, governor, and U.S. senator, had been appointed chargé d'affaires at Brazil by AJ in May. Burke, Brown, and Moses Dawson were among the steamboat delegation that greeted AJ.

3. William Stanbery (1788–1873) was an Ohio congressman. Elected on a Jackson ticket in 1828, he broke with the administration and won reelection in October 1830 as an anti-Jacksonian.

From John Randolph

Concord at Sea Monday
June 28. 1830. Six A. M.

Sir

The Concord arrived in Hampton Roads on Tuesday last about sunset. She was found to require caulking; a leak having found it's way to her Magazine, which rendered it necessary to take out her powder. There were other causes of unavoidable delay. Too much praise cannot be given to Capt. Perry & the officers under his command for the activity with which they have prepared the ship for sailing—We should have put to sea last eveng, but that we had to wait for Surgeon Heerman, who delayed coming on board until too late. I myself repaired on board in the morning —& have made good my pledge "that the ship should not wait one hour for me." Many persons, conversant in these matters, pronounced that we could not possibly get ready to sail before the end of this week or the beginning of the next—but all difficulties vanished before the energy of Capt Perry.[1]

The Concord is a fine ship & I have but one fault to find with my situation—it is, that Capt. Perry's politeness has induced him to give up his own state Room & dressing Room to me, & I fear to straiten his own quarters. I have every accomodation that the most fastidious person could possibly desire. Nothing can surpass Captain Perry's polite & kind attentions to myself & Mr. Clay.

In consequence of the defect of appropriation I have had to buy bills at 7 perCent advance. Shall I be deemed unreasonable in asking, that, when the appropriation shall have been made, credit shall be given me for it upon our Bankers in Europe? Thus placing the outfit & Salary on the same foot. This will perhaps be not more than a fair equivalent for seven months delay, & the inconvenience to which I am exposed in drawing upon my own funds. If however you shall deem that there is the slightest impropriety in this request I shall be cheerfully consent to lose the interest & the advance also upon the exchange. For I would not have my pecuniary transactions with the Govt tarnished with the slightest indelicacy for any imaginable consideration. No person can comprehend or appreciate this feeling more readily than yourself. With the highest respect I have the honor to be Sir your most faithful Servant.

John Randolph of Roanoke

P.S. I left my residence to take upon me the duties of my Mission on Wednesday the 9th. of June 1830   Mr. Clay departed the day before.

ALS, DLC (38).
1. Master Commandant Matthew Calbraith Perry (1794–1858) was captain of the *Concord*. Naval surgeon Lewis Heermann (1779–1833) had just been ordered aboard to join the Mediterranean squadron as fleet surgeon. Randolph's quotation paraphrased his promise to Van Buren on June 7 that he would not delay the ship (Van Buren Papers, DLC).

John Crowell to John Henry Eaton

Creek Agency
June 30th 1830

Sir

I have received your letter of the 14th. Inst.

I am not prepared at this time to give you any satisfactory information in regard to the disposition of the nation to send a delegation to Tenassee to meet the President. A National Council is ordered on the 15th of July, which was the earliest day the Chiefs were willing to have it, at this Council I will learn their views on that subject and give you the earliest information.

Most of the Indians who expected to be removed this spring & summer are greatly disappointed at the delay, many of them have not planted, any Crop, and seem to be quite uneasy about their situation and think they are not well treated—those opposed to emigration cease upon that circumstance, & use it to considerable effect against the cause—I learn since my return to the Agency that the stock of those who had openly declared their intention to emigrate have been destroyed to a considerable extent.

Hawkins & McIntosh are in this nation, & I regret to say doing much injury to the cause of emigration. I have the Honor to be your Obt. Srvt

Jno. Crowell
Agt for I a

[Endorsed by AJ:] Crowel to the Secretary of War.

ALS, DNA-RG 75 (M234-222). On June 4, Eaton had instructed Crowell to address the Creeks and give them a choice between submitting to the laws of Alabama or treating for their removal as a body (DNA-RG 75, M21-6). On June 17, acting secretary Randolph wrote Crowell with AJ's instruction to keep him and Eaton informed of the Creeks' disposition to emigrate (DNA-RG 107, M6-12). Crowell met the Creek chiefs in council on August 4, and the next day they gave him a declaration declining to treat with AJ for removal and invoking his protection under treaties and federal laws against Alabama's assumption of jurisdiction. Crowell wrote Eaton on August 8 that further efforts at negotiation at present would be useless (DNA-RG 75, M234-222). Saying that several thousand Creeks were ready to remove, he instead recommended resuming enrolling them individually for emigration, which Eaton had told him on June 4 to discontinue.

To Julia Maria Dickinson Tayloe

June, 1830.

Let wisdom all my actions guide,
And let my God with me reside.
No wicked thing shall dwell with me,
Which may provoke thy jealousy.

ANDREW JACKSON.

Printed, *In Memoriam Benjamin Ogle Tayloe* (Washington, 1872), p. 36 (mAJs). Julia Tayloe (1799–1846) and her husband Benjamin Ogle Tayloe entertained at their home on Lafayette Square in Washington. Julia collected autographs from distinguished visitors in her album. AJ's entry is from Isaac Watts's rendition of Psalm 101.

July

From James Gowen

[On July 2, mail robber James Porter was hanged in Philadelphia before a crowd reported at 40,000.]

Philada. 3rd July 1830—

My dear Sir,

I had this pleasure on the 16th. ultimo—I then took occasion to apprise your Excellency of my apprehensions, should Wilson, one of the Mail Robbers, become the recipient of Executive Clemency. It is with mortified feelings and deep concern, that I inform you, that all I then foresaw and apprehended, have been but too faithfully realised.

Your ancient and bitter enemies, have insiduously operated upon, an over sensative and too ardent part of the community, who reproach you with ingratitude and injustice, in drawing a distinction betwixt a native and an Irishman, by pardoning the one, when, as is contended, there were not one mitigating circumstance that could be plead in extenuation, and executing the other, who morally & physically was the better man— merely, *because he was an Irishman.*

It is impossible to tell you all that I have felt and suffered for the last three or four days—The reproaches and threatnings of as generous and as brave a Class of Men as breathe the free air of heaven, & as disinterested too—Men who with a solitary exception would have spilt the last drop of their blood for you.

I threw myself as became me betwixt you & them—I pledged myself for the purity of your motives and the absence of all partiality—That had you a bias twas *Irish*—I have told them of the courtesy and hospitality I have experienced under your roof, and at your table, and that I always placed it to the a/c of being an Irishman, somewhat distinguished and respected among my countrymen—conjured up their former friendships and shewed the danger of deciding too hastily. Thank God no rescue was made, and whatever others may think I am free to say, that no other class of men in this community, feeling as much as the Irish *did feel* on the day of the Execution, would have so respected the Laws—This your

Excellency may think but a negative compliment, yet if you knew as I did know, the extent of their feelings on that occasion, and how easy it would have been for them, to have rescued Porter—the compliment would apply with some force.

The Marshall was much to blame in too so early exposing the Pardon—his circulars were ill judged, and done incalculable mischief—Reeside the Mail Contracter and the Post Master Genl. are greatly to blame.[1]

This unfortunate business originated with Wood the Keeper of the Penetentiary, who found in Wilson an old convict, and a Protogee. He spur'd on Reeside, who values himself much upon influence, and who talked of disclosures to Barry—then came the Bradfords, as *contemptible* and *hypocritical* set a set as you can well immagine, a rotten root of aristocracy, who naturally hates Irishmen & Democracy—with other unprincipled enemies, and hollow hearted friends, who falsified the case, and induced you to an act, that has caused such excitement, as is hardly proper for me to mention in detail. At one time was talked of, with the rescue of Porter—The hanging Barry & the Marshall—Reeside to be the Gallows—The Bradfords the Confessers, and Wood the Executioner—This was one of the projects.[2]

I have now, one most urgent request to make, and which I hope for your own sake, and for the character of the country you will be pleased to grant—that is, that you will have the goodness to state—the motives, causes and considerations that induced you to draw a distinction betwixt Porter & Wilson, and to disavow, that which I know you can disavow—that *you were not actuated by any national prejudice*—Do this for me. I stand in the very vortex of this most unnatural excitement, and I want something, other than my own assertions and protestations, to rescue you from so base and ill founded accusations—alike dishonorable to the accused, and the accusers. Most Respectfully & Devotedly Your Friend

James Gowen

ALS, DLC (38). AJ replied on July 22 (below).

1. Former congressman John Conard (1773–1857) was the U.S. marshal for eastern Pennsylvania. On July 1 he summoned a posse of citizens to attend Porter's hanging to quell resistance and a possible rescue attempt "by ignorant and infatuated men." Conard's call, quickly published, revealed that Wilson but not Porter had obtained a pardon. On July 3 Conard issued a public thanks to Philadelphia's mayor and police for helping to keep order.

2. Samuel R. Wood (d. 1858) was superintendent of the new Eastern Penitentiary where Porter and Wilson were held. He had previously befriended Wilson when Wilson was jailed for a youthful larceny, found him a job upon release, and succeeded for a time in reforming his character. Mail contractor and postal agent James Reeside testified at Wilson's trial that Wilson had voluntarily confessed to him after his arrest. Reeside's testimony painted Porter as the instigator and Wilson as a reluctant accomplice. Thomas Bradford Jr. (1781–1851), brother of Samuel F. Bradford and father of Wilson's attorney Vincent L. Bradford, was a lawyer and an inspector of the Eastern Penitentiary, who showed Wilson kindnesses during his confinement. Postmaster General Barry had carried Wilson's pardon to Philadelphia. He wrote AJ on July 10 (below).

From Moses Dawson

Cincinnati 5th July 1830

Dear General

In accordance with your desire I now take the liberty of reminding you of the vacancy caused by the resignation of General Herrick as United States' attorney for the district of Ohio—In recommending to your notice Robt. T. Lytle for that office I believe I am placing before a young man fully qualified for the office—He once held the office of prosecuting attorney for this City and performed the duty with ability and integrity and would have still held it had his politicks agreed with the City Council elected in the spring of 1828 by a trick of which you may have heard—before the election it was held out that no party principle should be involved but no sooner were they elected than it was trumpeted abroad as an administration triumph and one of their first acts was to dismiss every municipal officer who was known to be favorable to your election—and among others Mr. Lytle was a victim—although the Mayor himself an administration man acknowledged the duty had never been more ably or faithfully done[1]

As I mentioned to you before Mr. Lytle is a popular young man—he has lately been elected Captain of one of our Uniform Companies has been in the state legislature by a majority of 1690 votes and nothing but his youth prevents him being sent to Congress next Election in the room of the present incumbent—his appointment therefore will I believe meet the approbation of the district and also of Judge Campbell who I have reason to believe is sincerely his friend and would greatly desire his appointment[2]

As to my good and much esteemed friend Mr. Robert Punshon I can say that the government never had in its employ a man of better principles as a Republican nor of more integrity as a man—He was during both the Canvases for the Presidency a fearless advocate of true republican principles and an adent supporter of your cause—and although surrounded by your opponents and attacked at all quarters he fought the battle and continues to do so with equal talent and fidelity to the cause—He has been an assistant to Mr. Burke in the Post office and also in the ministry for several years—his pay is but small and his family large—If therefore Major Barry could place him in a situation in the post office department—if he had occasion for a secret travelling agent or if a vacancy should occur in any post office sufficiently productive to support his family—he would not only be securing a faithful and talented officer but provide for an honest and persevering adherent to the Republican Cause—[3]

I would here take the liberty of suggesting the great utility to this part of the western Country of having an active and faithful postmaster at

Wheeling—who would take the trouble of forwarding the mail by steam boat when the stage of water would admit it—great complaints I have heard against the unaccommodating spirit of the present Post master and of his hostility to your cause not only before but after the election— provided there were to be a change in that office the appointment of Mr. Punshon would be hailed as a valuable one to the people of the whole Miami Country—as he would be alive to their interests and convenience in forwarding the mail by every possible opportunity—In this office or that of secret agent I do think he is eminently qualified—[4]

I regret much that opportunity did not serve to enable me better to understand what kind of Bank you ~~would~~ think would best answer as a substitute for the present Bank of the U.S.

If consistent with your views you would take the trouble of communicating to me a few hints through Major Donnelson or any other friend it might be useful—I have both publicly and privately contended that the Bugbear conjured up by Mr Mc.Duffie, on your plan of a Bank, never entered into your conception; but not knowing your views on the subject exactly I could only say, that it was not your desire to have a Bank created that would be productive of the evils pointed out by that gentleman and which evils I had reason to believe you attributed to the present institution and therefore desired a change—

It has always appeared to me that you deprecated a Bank that would either give undue influence to the General Government or that could be carried on independent of state sovergnty or of state taxation—that foreign capital should be employed within the U.S. and not contribute toward the national burthens or that foreigners beyond the jurisdiction of the United States should enjoy not only the profits of American industry but have a degree of influence always consequent to wealth that might some day be prejudicial to the public interest—Such a Bank it is generally admitted is the present—not to touch upon the question of Constitutionality—its expediency becomes questionable—

That a Bank or exchecquer is necessary for the management of the national funds both as to collection and disbursement I do not doubt— nor do I doubt the practicability of creating an institution adequate to these purposes without any of the inconveniences above hinted at—

So far as I can form a judgment on the subject a Bank or national exchequer should not be a Bank of discount the lending or dealing in money should be left to private individuals—For the purpose of having a convenient circulating medium paper might be issued in the payment of the officers of the Government, contracts &c &c—this paper should not be in notes for less than $20—and should be confined to the amount of the annual expenditure of the Government so that no more should be affloat than could be redeemed in one year—and if received in payment of taxes imports and for public lands there would be perhaps no necessity for providing for its redemption in specie or that at most one third being provided for would enough—

If it would be found necessary to establish branches throughout the Union for the purpose of collecting and disbursing—perhaps an arrangement might be made for the convenience of traders that drafts or treasury notes might be given for specie—the former at a premium not to exceed the mere expense of transit

These are confess but very crude ideas on the subject but as the discussion is now all important to the nation I am anxious to have light thrown on it at the same time I feel timorous to embark in it without having some idea of what has occurred to you on the subject—and I feel lest my notions might conflict with those who better understand or who better digested it—

I have since my arrival at home attentively perused the document sent me by Major Lewis—There most assuredly has been a deep laid plot to destroy the character of a virtuous and deserving individual—it really shocking to humanity—but it cannot have the desired effect—the slander defeats itself—no man of common sense can believe the tale as it is related—it carries falsehood on its face—none but the most abandoned of wretches could attribute such conduct to any human being born and educated in a civilized or christian country—It would be only necessary to have it known as related to have it stamped with ignominy and falsehood —I am determined however to let it rest till the slanderers here come out with their hints and innuendoes—and then I shall challenge them to produce their authority if silent I will brand as calumniators and if they should go into detail I am then fortified with such evidence as will confute and consign them to the infamy of slanderers and destroyers of character—[5]

The Major is not yet arrived and if the Calumniator means to make an attack it will either be in announcing his arrival or remarking on his departure—I shall therefore be on the watch and act accordingly—[6]

You may observe by the papers that the Ebonites here are endeavouring to detract from the public expression of approbation of your Executive conduct and to have it believed at a distance that you have lost the confidence of the people of the west—But my dear Sir you may rest assured that they fail in every attempt—and that so far from losing old friends you have formed many new ones.[7]

With my best respects to the ladies and Major Donnelson I have the honour to be Sir your obedt servt

Moses Dawson

Before sending this letter I have heard from Mr. Burke that a letter from the P. M. of Columbus states that your veto has made from 30 to 50 Converts there and that the same spirit pervades the northern part of the state[8]

[Endorsed by AJ:] Mr Moses Dawson recommendg. Mr Lytle to fill the vacancy occasioned by the resignation of Mr Herrick as atto. for the District of ohio—& on the Bank—answered 17th. July 1830—

ALS, DLC (38). AJ replied on July 17 (below).
    1. Samuel Herrick (1779–1852), a former congressman, was appointed district attorney by AJ in 1829 and resigned on June 30, 1830. Robert Todd Lytle (1804–1839), son of William Lytle, had served in Ohio's lower house in 1828–29. Isaac Gouverneur Burnet (1784–1856) was mayor of Cincinnati.
    2. Cincinnati congressman James Findlay, a Jacksonian, was reelected in October. John Wilson Campbell (1782–1833), a former congressman, was appointed Ohio federal district judge by AJ in 1829.
    3. Robert Punshon (1777–1848) was a leading Cincinnati Jacksonian. He and postmaster William Burke were both Methodist ministers.
    4. Richard McClure remained as Wheeling postmaster through AJ's two terms.
    5. William B. Lewis had written Dawson on February 10, 1830, of AJ's intention to send him his documentary compilation on the Eaton affair (OCX-Moses Dawson Papers).
    6. The major was Eaton. The calumniator was Cincinnati editor Charles Hammond, who had attacked AJ's marriage in the 1828 campaign.
    7. "Ebonite" was a derisive term for Adams men, taken from his widely ridiculed cryptic toast to "Ebony and Topaz" at an October 1827 celebration of Baltimore's defense in the War of 1812.
    8. Bela Latham (1794–1848) was the Columbus postmaster.

From William Carroll

Philadephia July 7. 1830.

Dear Sir:
    When I parted with you at Washington, I calculated on reaching Nashville before you; but in consequence of a severe attack of fever, which has confined me for the last three weeks, I am still here. I am now fast recovering, and hope in a few days to be able to set out for home, though I shall not start until my physicians say that I can travel in safety.
    I understand that the chiefs of the four tribes of Indians are to meet you some time in August at Nashville—I hope that they may do so, and that you may be able to persuade them to remove west of the Mississippi. I have heard much said on the subject, and as *you* know a diversity of opinion prevails. Should you be able to have the law executed on any thing like reasonable terms all will be well; but should it require a large expenditure of money, it will be a subject upon which opposition will never cease to harp. If I can render you any aid in this business when I return it shall be most cheerfully given.
    You have doubtless heard of the excitement among the Irish in this city in consequence of the execution of Porter, and the pardon of Wilson. The fever is gradually abating, and the circumstances, except among a few of the Irish will shortly be forgotten. Mr. Van Buren left here this morning for New York in good health.

Hoping to see you shortly, I am dear sir, Most Respectfully Your Obt. Servt.

Wm. Carroll

ALS, DLC (38). Carroll (1788–1844) was governor of Tennessee.

From Thomas Claiborne et al.

[Jackson arrived home at the Hermitage on July 6.]

Nashville 8th. July 1830

Sir

The Citizens of the town of Nashville, having heard of your arrival at the Hermitage, have deputed the undersigned to wait on you, and in their name, to offer to you their congratulations.

Your long residence among them, has furnished the best means of an intimate acquaintance with you, as well in private as publick life.

They have often greeted you heretofore, as the victorious champion of our country on the crimsoned field. They now hail you, as the head of the civil institutions of that country which you so well and ably defended in peril and battle.

None could have regarded the measures of your administration, with more interest than the people of Nashville; they had aided by every honorable means in their power, your elevation to the chief magistracy, under the most solemn conviction that they would thus render an important service to their common country; and at this day it affords them sincere pleasure in declaring their satisfaction with the measures pursued in your administration of the government.

Anxious to see you among them that they may individually offer to you the homage of their esteem, the undersigned have been directed to request you to attend a publick dinner to be given to you in the town of Nashville on such day as may be most convenient and agreeable to you.

The undersigned avail themselves of this occasion to renew to you the assurances of their undiminished regard and individual attachment

Tho. Claiborne
H. R. W. Hill
D. Craighead
Alexr. Porter
David Barrow

DS, TNJ (16-0003). *National Banner and Nashville Whig*, July 12, 1830. *Niles*, July 31. Thomas Claiborne (1780–1856) was a lawyer and former congressman. David Craighead (1790–1849) was a lawyer and later state legislator. Alexander Porter (d. 1833) was a Nashville merchant, and David Nicholas Barrow (1800–1831) was a lawyer.

To Thomas Claiborne et al.

JULY 8th, 1830.

Gentlemen:—

I receive the congratulations so politely presented in your note of the 8th instant, in the name of the citizens of Nashville, with a sensibility peculiar to the relation which I have so long sustained as their neighbor and friend. Within this relation is included the greater part of my life, and it would be vain for me to attempt an enumeration of the many causes which combine to make my whole public and private career, an inadequate measure for the honors it has bestowed upon me, and the happiness it now confers. I can only say that all my heart can feel, or reason suggest, as the subject of gratitude, unite in giving sincerity to thanks which are due to this renewal of your confidence and regard.

Your approbation, Gentlemen, of the course of my administration thus far, is peculiarly gratifying; although its responsibility is to the people of the whole Union, there is yet a pleasure in the assurance that it meets the anticipation of its earliest friends, which I trust, I may enjoy as a useful stimulus in the future prosecution of my duties.

Having since my departure from Washington declined various invitations to partake of public dinners, I hope, gentlemen, that my fellow citizens of Nashville will pardon the same course on this occasion. It will afford me much pleasure to meet them at the Nashville Inn on Tuesday next, and give them a cordial shake of the hand as an earnest of my friendship for them. I have the honor to be, very respectfully, your obedient servant,

ANDREW JACKSON

Printed, *National Banner and Nashville Whig*, July 12, 1830 (16-0006). *Niles*, July 31.

To John Coffee

Hermitage July 9th. 1830—

My Dr. Genl.

I reached this on Tuesday last, & on last evening recd. yours of the 5th. instant & hasten to reply to it.

I sincerely regret your sudden indisposition which has prevented your journey hither, but rejoice to hear of your fair prospects of returning health, & still hope to have the pleasure of seeing you, and your family, before I leave this section of country for the city, and will, with judge Overton, meet you at Franklin if advised of your coming.

I cannot precisely say how long I may remain, as it will depend on the movements of the Indians with whom I will communicate, so soon as Major Eaton arrives, who I expect every hour—he was to have met me at Cincinnati, but I suppose has been retarded in his movements, by the indisposition Judge Rowan of Ky. and also that of Mrs. Eaton who I learn was not in good health when she left Philadelphia

The Major had to pass the military academy, & Mrs. Eaton was under engagements to spend some days with her friends Mrs. Dudley, Mrs. Sanford & Mrs Swartwout &c &c &c of Newyork, wives of the two Senators & of the collector of Newyork—They first two Ladies having spent the winter in washington—I am tho, expecting to hear of their arrival every hour, at Tyres Springs where I am to send a carriage for them.[1]

I am well advised of the difference that exists between the chiefs of the choctaws, their remonstrance was forwarded to me, & laid before the Senate; we will recognise the chiefs chosen in each Department of the nation, & have invited them thro' their confidential agent to meet us in the neighbourhood of Franklin T. but as yet have not heard from them—I will write Peachlin & Hailey so soon as Major Eaton arrives.[2]

My Dr friend I am anxious to see & converse with you—I have on my mind something, that has filled me with grief, and really what I was not prepared to expect—and since I have reached home, have heard whispers that has filled me, ~~with~~ not only with regret, but amasement—when I see you, I will fully unfold to you all, & council with you as a friend—

Please present me kindly to Polly & all the children—say to her that it will afford me sincere pleasure to have the opportunity, ~~to~~ once more, to shake her by the hand & present her with my most friendly greetings—I would rejoice to see Andrew J. Coffee.[3]

Judge Overton is now with me & joins me in kind salutations to you Polly & all the family—Major Donelson Emily & children together with Mary Easton are in good health & at the old Ladies—in haste

[Andrew Jackson]

P.S. give my respects to Capt Jack & Elisa—& say to them I would be happy to see them[4]   A. J.

ALS (signature removed), THi (16-0007).

1. Charles Edward Dudley (1780–1841) and Nathan Sanford (1777–1838) were New York's two U.S. senators. Their wives were Blandina Bleecker Dudley (1783–1863) and Mary Buchanan Sanford (1800–1879). Samuel Swartwout's wife was Alice Ann Cooper Swartwout (1789–1874). Tyree Springs was a watering place in Sumner County, north of Nashville.

2. John Pitchlynn and David W. Haley.

3. Coffee's son, Andrew Jackson Coffee (1819–1891).

4. Coffee's brother-in-law John Donelson (1787–1840) and his wife Eliza Eleanor Butler Donelson (1791–1850).

From William Taylor Barry

Washington 10. July 1830

My Dear Sir

Since your departure from Washington I visited Philadelphia and remained there a few days with my family, and had the happiness to find my Son Armistead much improved in his health and recovering slowly though in the opinion of the Doctors certainly.[1] As you requested I delivered the pardon for the Mail robber Wilson to the District Attorney Mr. Dallas and made it known to informed the Marshall.[2] Upon consultation it was thought best to let it be known a short time before the day fixed for the execution. It appears that Clergymen of different sects had visited the two prisoners since sentence was pronounced upon them, the Presbeterians attended Wilson, the Episcopalians Porter. As soon as it was known that the executive clemency was extended to one and not to the other, it produced an affect upon the minds of the clergymen who had attended Porter, and it was insinuated artfully with a view to create excitement, that Wilson was saved by the influence of the Presbeterians & Dr. Ely was censured, and as Colo. Armstrong informs me since I left that City, has found it necessary to disclaim from the pulpit any participation in the efforts that led to the pardon.[3] It was also industriously intimated that the pardon was in blank with power to myself to insert the name of one or both culprits, and that I had been operated upon to discriminate after my arrival at Pha. This utterly ridiculous notion was so far accredited as to cause several intelligent gentlemen to call and make enquiry of me. Mr. Reeside was assailed violently for the part he had taken. The Irish portion of the population were particularly excited and their indignation greatly aroused because a distinction had been made in favor of a native born citizen in preference to an Irishman. To these causes of excitement were added many falshoods in relation to the characters and conduct of the criminals, representing Porter as an innocent young foreigner taken in by Wilson an old & practiced offender. Your political enemies as was to be expected used those weapons, but the excitement would have been checked in the commencement if friends had been firm & faithful. Political men who ought to have acted promptly in informing the public, and removing prejudices, stood aloof, thinking more of their popularity than duty as citizens. There were several who were prompt and active in disabuseing the public mind, and allaying the ferment, amongst others were Messrs. Dallas, Toland, the Marshall & Mr. Reeside.[4] Some timid friends who had just passed through the Market House & heard the threats against of the Irish Butchers against Reeside, informed him of it and urged him to leave the City until the ferment subsided. Instead of listening to their counsels, he immediately went in amongst the Butchers, talked to the leading men of them, and succeeded in satisfying the most intelligent & reflecting that the discrimination ~~between~~ made in favor of Wilson was just, and that under existing circumstances, to have declined pardoning him would not only have been unjust but cruel. In addition to the circumstances made known to you here, I ascertained to my satisfaction that not only did Wilsons confession lead to the detection of Porter and to the ultimate conviction of both, but that these confessions had been elicited by assurances to Wilson that they should not be used against him, which promises were denied at the trial. The Irish catholics were much aroused at first, but they are becomeing indifferent about it, since it is ascertained that Porter was a Protestant and an Orange-Man.[5] After you left this many more Petitions came in for Wilson, and amongst others as Mr. Reeside informs me, are seven of the Jury who sit upon the trial of Wilson. Mr. Reeside will be here in a day or two, and I have thought it will be proper, to give to the public a concise statement of facts, that distinguish the case of Wilson & operated to mitigate his punishment.[6] I have been thus tedious supposeing it would be agreeable to you to know the circumstances connected with the excitement in Philadelphia, which although considerable, has been much magnified, both by pretended friends & foes. I have observed the tone of the public prints of that City, and am reluctantly led to the conclusion, that although there are several papers friendly to the Administration ~~in that City~~ yet not one of them did their duty with becomeing candour & firmness. All things as far as I am informed go on well here. I see Dr. Randolph very frequently, he appears very attentive to his public duties, prudent and discreet in the discharge of them.[7] Majr. Lewis & Miss Maryann have gone to the North, they were both in very good health when they left Washington. I had like to have forgotten to mention that I have recd. a letter from Genl. John Adair, recommending his Son in law Colo. T. B. Monroe as the Successor of Colo. J. Speed Smith in case of a vacancy in the office of Attorney for the District of Kentucky, I know Colo. Monroe to be well qualified for the station. In his letter general Adair remarks, that your course upon the subject of internal improvements is the correct one, that it is the only one that will preserve the Union, that a perceverance in it will be successful and entitle you to the gratitude of the nation. Genl. Mc.Afee writes to me, that Genl. Adair upon all suitable occasions, vindicates your course, and sustains the grounds assumed in your Veto.[8]

I beg to be presented to Majr. Donelson & the ladies of your family[.] I am with very high regard very truly your friend & ob. St.

W. T. Barry

ALS, DLC (38).
1. Armistead Barry (d. 1845), suffering from a hip problem, was under care of noted physicians Philip S. Physick and Thomas Harris in Philadelphia.

2. George Mifflin Dallas (1792–1864), later vice president under Polk, was the U.S. district attorney for eastern Pennsylvania.

3. Episcopal ministers Jackson Kemper and Francis L. Hawks attended Porter in prison and at his execution. Other clergy, Presbyterian, Methodist, and Baptist, visited both prisoners. In his newspaper, the *Philadelphian*, Ezra S. Ely denied influencing AJ to save Wilson but not Porter.

4. Henry Toland (c1785–1863) was a Philadelphia merchant.

5. Orangemen were Irish Protestants, mainly from Ulster, originally followers of William of Orange who deposed the Catholic James II of England, succeeded him as William III, and defeated him at the Boyne in 1690.

6. In an early August letter, Barry named anti-Jackson congressional candidate John G. Watmough as the only Wilson juror who had signed his pardon petition. The statement was published August 12. Watmough angrily denied it, charging a possible forgery of his name, and Barry recanted. In a letter published by Watmough in the Philadelphia *United States Gazette* of August 19, Barry explained that he, Reeside, and Attorney General Berrien, examining the petition together, had mistaken another signature for Watmough's.

7. Philip G. Randolph.

8. AJ had already the day before directed the appointment of Thomas Bell Monroe (1791–1865) to succeed John Speed Smith as U.S. district attorney for Kentucky. John Adair (1757–1840), Monroe's father-in-law and a leading Kentucky politician, had commanded Kentucky troops under AJ at New Orleans and later publicly quarreled with him over their performance. A *Biographical Sketch of General John Adair*, published in Washington in 1830, praised Adair's conduct at New Orleans but also commended AJ's. Robert Breckinridge McAfee (1784–1849) was a Jackson supporter and former Kentucky lieutenant governor.

From John Coffee (of Georgia)

Fort Mitchell
July 10 1830.

Dear Sir,

Persuant to the letter of Judge Berrien, I have had an interview with Mr. Lucas of lime creek Allabama, on the subject of the removal of the Creek Indians. And now have the honour of submitting for your consideration his views of the subject. After satisfying myself that his influence could accomplish this desireable object, if properly aided by the agents of the Government; I deemed it proper to see Captain Walker who lives near Tuckabachee, and whose aid he particularly required, and learn from him, how far he would cooperate with Mr. Lucas in this matter.[1] he verry promptly declared that every private feeling (if any existed) should yield to the public good, and that Mr Lucas might calculate on his aid to the full extent of his influence. I have had two or three meetings with these gentlemen, and we have conversed freely on this subject. They both perfectly agree as to the course necessary to be persued to insure success. It is known that any effort made in public council without a previous understanding will fail, these people have been so long in the practice of violently opposing every thing like emigration, and abusing those of their people who expressed a wish to remove, and so jealous are they of each other, that no influence could induce any one of them to advocate any measure in council that had for its object an exchange of country, without he knew that he would be sustained by other influential Chiefs, hence the necessity of a previous understanding.

It is therefore proposed to see five or six of the principle chiefs seperately at first, and have a perfect understanding with each of them; These men are then to be assembled and propositions for a treaty submitted to them, and explained untill they understand each article and give their assent to it, and their pledge to each other to sustain it in council. They are then to assemble the principle town chiefs, and explain to them the necessaty of the measure, and sign the instrument. Mr. Lucas, and Cap Walker are both of opinion that no other course can succeed and that this, if prudently conducted cannot fail.

Relying much upon the opinions of these two gentlemen I have declined pressing the subject on the chiefs myself, but as far as I have thought it prudent to go, I have had flattering assurances of success.

They are evidently preparing the minds of their people for the result some of them are making selections for the purpose of taking reserves, and some have come up from Allabama under the impression that they will be permitted again to take reserves. Opoith le yoholo (the pivot on which all the important affairs of this nation turns) in a late talk to his people told them that "he would hold on to the country as long as possible, but when he found it impossible to contend longer, he would rise up and tell them so, and then they must with one voice say, let us go." Notwithstanding I am opinion that Opoith le yoholo has determined on his course. I have thought it proper to strengthen him in his resolution, by bringing to bare on him, every influence in my power for this purpose I have made arrangements (unknown to him) for William McGilvery and others, who he knows have always been his friends, to call upon him at various times and use every argument in their power to convince him of the necessity of giving up the country, and removing.[2]

Mr. Lucas is of opinion that it will require from fifty to an hundred thousand dollars, to effect this object, Capt Walker is of opinion that the first named sum will be amply sufficient, by giving fifty or perhaps more of the town chiefs reserves. To avoid much trouble, it is desirable to conduct this matter, in a way that it will be impossible for the Cherrokees to know any thing about it, untill it is over, this is an addition reason for persuing the plan suggested. Should you approve the plan purposed, and determine on opening a negotiation with them, I have promised to mention the name of Benjamin Fitzpatrick Esq of Allabama as a fit person for a commissioner, he has managed some important law suits for Opoithleyoholo and is believed to possess considerable influence over him; from what inquiries I have been able to make, I find that Mr. Fitzptricks character unexceptionable, and beleave his appointment would give general satisfaction to the citizens of Allabama. permit me to hope however that the services of Judge Berrien will not be dispensed with in this business, I deem it of high importance that the Judge, or some gentleman possessing your entire confidence, and well acquainted with all your views on this subject should be on the mission. I have thus sir given you a plain statement of all the important facts of this business. If the course persued meets your approbation I shall deem myself happy. I have the honour to be with the highest respect your obedt servt.

Jno Coffee

ALS, DNA-RG 75 (M234-237).
    1. William Walker.
    2. Opothle Yoholo (c1798–1862) was a leading Creek spokesman. William McGilvery was a Creek chief.

From Philip Grymes Randolph

Department of War
July 10th. 1830.

Sir,

I have the honour to enclose to you a copy of a talk of the Choctaw Chiefs to the Secretary of War dated the 2d. June 1830. very respectfully your obedt. Servant

P G Randolph
Acting Sect'y of War

LS, DNA-RG 107 (M222-27). LC, DNA-RG 107 (M127-2).

[Enclosure: Mushulatubbe et al. to Eaton]

Choctaw Nation, June 2d. 1830.

Friend & Brother,

Your communication of the 1st. ultimo to our friends Mingo Mushulatubbee and Major John Pitchlynn, has been fully made known to us in general council of the North East and Southern districts.[1] We have also heard the talk of our great father the President to our old Interpreter Major Pitchlynn.[2] We are truly happy that the proposals, which was prepared by a few designing men in the nation, and sent to our great father by D. W. Haley, has been considered inadmissible, and that Commissioners will be appointed to come and treat with us for our lands. We are now fully confident that ere long all things will terminate in giving general satisfaction to all parties in the nation—that the poor as well as the rich will receive their just rights, and that those who would wish to usurp the rights of the poor Indians may not be able to carry on their odious projects. As it would be useless at this time to make any more remarks respecting Folsom and Leflore, we shall decline saying anything about them; but however it would be well for you and our great father to know that Folsom, the former chief of the North East district has lost entirely the confidence of all the Captains and warriors of the Southern as well as the district he lives in, with the exception of a few, and they are such as those who joined the Missionary church and are related to him, but even these are fast leaving him. Leflore has no influence beyond the limits of the districts in which he rules as chief. Mingos Mushulatubbee and Nittukaichee has been unanimously acknowledged by all the Captains and warriors of the aforesaid districts as principal chiefs, and accordingly invested with full power to act in that office—but of this you doubtless have been informed by your agent, Colo. Wm. Ward, whose report will confirm what we wrote you from the Council at Yarmibbie Old towns.[3] We are termed the Republican party, and Leflore the Despotic. Our party has now double the power or number of warriors over Leflores'; and we are daily increasing in number. We are truly proud to inform you that our most intelligent white brethren who have any knowledge of our cause, have commended our proceedings and have enlisted their feelings in our behalf. We are advised not to desist, but to persevere in our cause, and finally to establish whenever we may be so situated as to allow it, a government similar to that of the United States under which our people may flourish and be perpetuated as a nation. As we have no knowledge of our Country west of the great river Mississippi, we have concluded in Council that we would send a delegation of 16 men to explore it, but unfortunately we have not funds to defray their expenses. We therefore entreat our great father to furnish us funds sufficient to defray the expenses of said delegation; and so soon as we are informed of the nature of said Country we shall then feel perfectly willing to meet Commissioners and treat with them; but in the present case to dispose of our country here and to emigrate to one of which we have no knowledge, would be acting, as we think, unwisely. In this we hope our great father will not consider us unreasonable, and that he will extend to us his beneficence. If our great father agrees to the above proposition, and think it necessary to appoint an agent to conduct the exploring delegation, we would be glad for him not to give that appointment to D. W. Haley, for we know he is not qualified to fill the appointment, and besides we have no friendship for him. We the headmen and Mingoes of the North East and Southern districts wish that all communications made to us from our great father the President hereafter be directed to Mingoes Mushulatubbee, Nittukaichee, and Major John Pitchlynn. We are your friends and brothers.

Mushulatubbee ⎱ Nittukaichee ⎰	Principal Chiefs
Eyahokartubbee ⎱ Eyahchah Hopia ⎰	Speakers of the Council

Unnahubbee	Chief of the six towns—
	but under Nittukaichee
Holubbee	Major
Chah tah ma ta haw	
Pistarmby	

[Forty-seven additional names follow.]

We certify that the above is the talk of the principal Chiefs and head men of the North East and Southern Districts of the Choctaw Nation.

(signed) John Pitchlynn, U.S. Interpreter
M. Mackey, U.S. Interpreter
(signed) P. P. Pitchlynn, Secretary of the Council[4]

[Endorsed by AJ:] acting Secretary of War enclosing a talk from part of the choctaw chiefs—wishes to explore the country before—
The country laid out has been explored by many of the chiefs & I suppose, the request only made to procrastinate—

Copy, DNA-RG 107 (M222-27). DS, DNA-RG 75 (M234-169). The June 2 date on this address is likely incorrect. It appears a plausible response to a communication sent by Eaton on June 1. Neither that, nor news of the Senate's rejecting the Leflore and Folsom treaty in late May, could have reached the Choctaws by June 2. Eaton replied on July 24 (below).
1. Eaton wrote all the Choctaw chiefs on June 1, informing them of the Senate's refusal to approve the Leflore and Folsom treaty and of the passage of the Indian Removal Act. He urged them to accept removal and to confide in Haley. Eaton invited the chiefs to meet himself and AJ in Tennessee, but only if they were ready to conclude a treaty (DNA-RG 75, M21-6).
2. Perhaps April 6, above.
3. William Ward was the Choctaw agent.
4. Peter Perkins Pitchlynn (1806–1881), later principal chief of the Choctaws, was the son of John Pitchlynn.

To *James Alexander Hamilton*

Hermitage July 12th. 1830—

My Dr Col

I have just recd. yours of the 27th. of june last accompanying Mr Malibran Petition, which I have herewith inclosed & refered to you for your report of the truth of the facts stated in his petition.

I reached this place on the 6th. instant found my farm in good order, & my family in good health, my crop suffering for the want of rain—I have been constantly in a croud since I left the city, altho I have declined all public dinners, & really I wish I could return to ~~the city~~ it, in an air balloon to avoid the great fatigue I have encountered on my way hither. I have every reason to believe that my veto, will be sustained by a large majority of the people of the u. states, be this as it may, one thing I do know, that the faithful discharge of my constitutional duties pointed to the course I adopted, & I pursued it without enquiry who would or might condemn, or approve the measure

I am alway happy to hear of Major Eatons increasing popularity, & prosperity—I have long known him, & a more virtuous honest man, does not exist—he is worthy of confidence, & will never violate it—

I have agreed to meet my fellow citizens on tomorrow in Nashville to give them a shake by the hand & friendly greeting—

Major Eaton & his lady has not reached me, what delayses him, I have not heard, until he arrives, I cannot commence my arrangement with the Indians, a subject I have much at heart, & as soon as it is acted upon I will hasten back to the city to attend to my duty there. with my respects to your Lady & family believe me yr friend.

Andrew Jackson

ALS, NN (16-0015). Hamilton *Reminiscences*, p. 171.

To Martin Van Buren

Hermitage July 12th. 1830—

My Dr Sir

We reached this place on the 6th. instant all in good health, found my family well, my farm in exellent order, but suffering for the want of rain— The bustle of the journey has fatigued me, & I want rest, I fear that will not be mine, in this life; for I am engaged to meet, & greet, my friends with a hearty shake by the hand on tomorrow, & on thursdays to meet my farmers in the neighbourhood—I have declined all public dinners since I left the city, & I hope during life.

I had the pleasure last evening to receive your letter of the 25th. and am happy to hear that Mr. R. enjoys fine health. I have full confidence of his good intentions to promote our views & in his talents to carry them into execution—I have strong hopes that he will succeed.

I have not heard yet from the Indians, all communications from the agents being addressed to the Sec. of War, and he, not as yet having united with me, I have not recd the information expected from them. I expect Major Eaton in a few days, when we will enter upon the Indian business with zeal, close it & return to the city. Of the other matter to which you allude I cannot speak with certainty, but do suppose during next winter will live quite a batchellors life, would to god I had commenced it with my administration, it would have prevented me from much humiliation & pain that I have experienced, and have prevented much injury to the innocent, by the secrete slanders circulated here & fed from the city—time will unfold the authors—

I expect Major Eaton & family here in a few days where he will be met by judge Overton & conducted to his house

The, veto, has become what my enemies neither wished, or expected, very popular, I have no doubt but it will be sustained by a large majority of the people.

I will be happy to hear from you often—I have presented your respects to Major Donelson Lady & Miss Mary Easton, who requests me to say that they reciprocate them, my s*[on has]* just joined me [. . .] yr friend

Andrew Jackson

ALS, DLC-Van Buren Papers (16-0017).

From Edmund Pendleton Gaines

Nashville Tennessee
July 12th. 1830

Sir—

I have received from Major General Macomb a paper from the Secretary of War, purporting to give the contents of a letter from the President of the United States, dated the 20th of May last, of which I have the honor to enclose herewith a copy submit to you a copy enclosed herewith.[1]

My conviction of the propriety and utility of the movement in question (and the necessity of that movement being made before the approach of hot weather) as well as of the soundness of the military principle which governed me in issuing my orders requiring that movement; added to a vivid recollection of your views and opinions having been for many years past in accordance with those which I have taken for my model and my guide, upon every cardinal principle of military law, suggest to me the possibility of some mistake in the letter, and the consequent propriety of my requesting the favour of you to inform me whether the enclosed contains a true representation of your views regarding my conduct; and whether you directed my letter, vindicating my conduct against the animadversions, errors and censures of Major General Macomb, to be returned to me.

The movement in question was ordered by me in obedience to the instruction given me in the year when in command of the western department in the years 1821, 22 and 23—instructions from the department of war and General in chief instructions that had never been to my knowledge revoked or abrogated, and were therefore deemed to be as much in force, as any of the printed orders or contained in the Book of Regulations, emanating from the same source,—namely—the Department of war

That the Major General, as well as qr. M. Genl. Jesup, should each, in turn endeavour attempt *extrajudicially*, to prove that I have neither capacity to give that I have neither military mind to give proper orders,

~~nor capable of being sufficient~~ nor honesty to take ~~due~~ care of the public treasure, were but to continue the invidious labours in ~~the system of intrigue~~ which they have ~~ignorantly or wickedly~~ employed their pens and pamphlets against me, for some time past, since they volunteered ~~against me~~ in the Brevet controversy—into which I was forced in self defence ~~which they figured so ingloriously as to render and in which they figured so unfortunately as to render~~ my triumph of 1828 was the hapless cause of their unmitigated enmity and ~~insidious~~ secret opposition ~~to me~~: they would each, I have no doubt gladly prove ~~to you~~ that ~~I have always been~~ I am worse than useless to the public service.[2] Nor should I be at all surprised if Mr. Secretary Eaton should have imbibed similar sentiments towards me—for he also has calumniated me; and it is yet to be seen whether he may not, like the two Washington City Generals, be found incapable of doing an act of justice towards one who he has under the fair exterior of respect wantonly injured. But I cannot permit myself to believe that the President of the United States—~~chosen by a majority of his countrymen, mainly upon the supposition that he had the wisdom and moral courage to do right, and to abstain from doing wrong~~—would knowingly give countenance to such an opposition; or that he can be so changed as to sit in judgment against me upon the ex parte statements of my known vindictive enemies, and condemn me without ~~such a hearing, such as the rules and articles of war prescribe~~ a hearing such as the law prescribes.

AL draft, DNA-RG 393 (16-0012).
1. AJ to Eaton, May 20, above.
2. Thomas Sidney Jesup (1788–1860) was quartermaster general of the Army. In the 1820s Gaines had engaged in a protracted public quarrel over seniority with Winfield Scott. A law of 1821 reduced the peacetime Army to a single major general and two brigadier generals. Gaines and Scott were the two brigadiers, both commissioned on March 9, 1814. As a brigadier Gaines outranked Scott because of his earlier past promotions, but Scott had received a major general's brevet in the summer of 1814 three weeks before Gaines, giving him a claim to precedence. In 1823 Jesup published a pamphlet favoring Scott. In 1828 Macomb, previously junior to both Gaines and Scott, was commissioned as major general and appointed commander-in-chief over the protests of Scott, who claimed that his brevet made him the Army's ranking officer. War Department orders in 1829 confirmed the precedence of commissioned over brevet rank, and therefore of both Macomb and Gaines over Scott.

From David W. Haley

Doaks Stand Mi
July 13th. 1830

Sir
I have not visited the choctaws in their own country as yet, owing to the health of my family   I have ~~seen~~ [*writen*] several influential men from the nation, and received several letters from citizens of the nation on

the subject of a Treaty and I cannot hear of a man that is willing to *[send]* a delegation to Tennessee. it would be imposible for a part of the nation to conclude a Treaty that would be satisfactory to all. if the Treaty is concluded in the nation every man, woman, & child can be present, that has a wish to be.

I have been invited to a large Council that is to meet at or near the Factory, on the Tombigbee in a few days and had not sickness in my family prevented me I should have been present. it is to be hoped they will settle their form of government shortly and adopt a constitution, by which they will be governed when they arrive at their new home on the Arkansaw & Red River. should they continue under several chiefs of equal power so *[long]* they will continue divided and in a few years would become separated into different bands. the government should act on this point with precaution. they may be forced to submission while east of the Miss, but when in the mountains and barrens of the west, it would in all probility cost money and the lives of valuable soldiers to keepe them at peace now is the proper time to get things settled in a friendly manner. There will be a form of a constitution submited to them shortly, perhaps on the 27th inst. as there is to be a Council at that time in the centre of the nation, which Council I will be at.

There is a wish that you should send your commissioners as soon as posible. a supply of provisions may be furnished in a few days at the centre of the nation say at Wilsons stand on the Robinson Road, and if you cannot finde a more proper hand to under take to furnish supplies I will do it.

dont give your self any uneasiness about the disputes between the parties in the nation, as they will come to a good understanding I hope in a short time, if let alone and not be incouraged by persons who are not their real friends[.] I have the honor to be your obt. svt.

D. W. Haley

[Endorsed by AJ:] Major Haley of 13th. July 1830—

ALS, DNA-RG 75 (M234-185).

From James Alexander Hamilton

N.Y. July 13th 1830

My dear Sir,

I enclose to you a Slip from The Even Post containing *Leopolds* letter abdicating the Crown of Greece with Lord Aberdeens remarks upon the subject in the House of Lords. I believe this is an event in which the Peace of Europe is involved Russia has probably induced The Greek senate to take the Course refered to by Leopold in order by acting upon his *feeble* character to deter him from taking the place   other motives are attributed to him connected with the demise of the King but I think those remote and ~~indistinct~~ unwarranted—[1]

Two questions now arise 1° will Greece submit to have a King chosen for her 2d. will the 3 powers agree upon any other man   War, war, war, will follow. To have established a new Kingdom & to have selected a Prince for that Kingdom Peaceably would have been more wise & tranquil Than the Kings of the Earth are wont to be

We live in a remarkable age   This would be too great a wonder to be anticipated—

I have a letter from McLane of the 27° May He is desponding The Act of Congress may do for him what nothing else can do.[2]

Rhind writes under date of the 26° April & says he has concluded a Treaty

Lewis & his daughter are with me The Latter will go to the Springs with my family. Van Buren is here & in health. Miss Adelaide Huygens is to be married tomorrow[3]

Do me the favor to remember me Kindly to Mr. & Mrs Donaldson & Miss Eastin & to believe me to remain with the truest attachment your friend & Servt

James A Hamilton

ALS, DLC (38).

1. The July 12 *New York Evening Post* carried Leopold's May 21 letter declining the Greek throne and speculation on its motive. Leopold himself cited the opposition of the Greek Senate and people to the arrangements made by the Allied powers, which included a surrender of territory to Turkey, and his unwillingness to govern a resistant people by force of foreign arms. Addressing the House of Lords on May 24, Aberdeen blamed Leopold for posing unreasonable terms of acceptance and then hastily withdrawing.

2. McLane wrote Hamilton on May 27, despairing of a favorable British response on the West Indian trade and wishing he were home, where he could be of more use (Hamilton *Reminiscences*, pp. 164–66).

3. Adelaide Charlotte Woldemarine Huygens, daughter of the Dutch minister, married Dominique D'Arbel of France on July 14 in New York City.

From *William Ellis Tucker*

Philada. July 13—1830

Dear sir

About six weeks ago, I received an order from you, for the manufacture of some Porcelain, which I immediately commenced, and had it finished, excepting in the last burning.

The kiln in which it was placed for the purpose of completing this process, was unfortunately lost, owing to a long continuance of wet weather. The moisture penetrated through my oven and prevented the fire from having its usual good effect—Inasmuch as I understood that the Porcelain in question was designed for use during your stay at your country seat I declined recommencing the order (as it would require six or eight weeks to finish it) until I should learn from you, your pleasure respecting it—Your obliging answer to my last letter came to hand, and I am disposed to believe that your view respecting the impracticability of Congress doing any thing for me, excepting in the way of an additional duty is correct—If a fair duty was placed on the article, and imposition & fraud on the part of European manufacturers, guarded against, the country might be supplied without difficulty with a quantity of Porcelain sufficient for the demand. But as it now is, I have so many difficulties, as greatly to impede my progress—There is only twenty per Cent of duty laid, and the French manufacturer gets over the payment of at least one half of that small amount, in the following manner: he becomes the vender of his own china by sending an agent to New York with an Invoice, not at the price the article is selling for in France, as was the design of congress, but at the price which he supposes the article costs him to manufacture it, which he is careful to place at a very low rate. This is the Invoice shewn at the Custom House, and in this way the object of Congress is defeated by the duplicity of the French manufacturer—[1]

I have exhausted my finances, and spent a large portion of my time in perfecting the manufacture of Porcelain; and, unless something is done, I am fearful that I shall be swept away before the torrent of opposition & difficulty to which I am subjected; and in that case, the àrt will be for a time lost to the country, as mine is the only successful establishment in the United States[.] With sentiments of much respect I am yours &c

signed Wm E Tucker

LC, PPPM (mAJs).
1. The 1828 tariff law required customs appraisal of imported goods at their "true and actual value, any invoice or affidavit thereto, to the contrary notwithstanding."

From Benjamin Tucker

Philada. 7—14—1830

Much Respected Friend

In common with my son William Ellis Tucker, I deeply regret the accident which has occasioned a failure in the completion of thy order for American Porcelain so as to have had it at the time requird   And I feel under sensible obligations for thy obliging reply of April 3rd last, to his application on the subject of his discovery in the manufacture of this Article.

It is to be regretted, if Congress are prohibited by the Constitution from patronising an establishment, which it will be admitted is amongst the most important that has ever been introduced into our Country; because in addition to its intrinsic value, it is perhaps one of the most difficult of attainment.

Besides the sacrafice of private fortune in the attempt, the Government of France devoted large and liberal contributions in bringing this interesting national object to no higher degree of perfection than what a self taught american citizen, by his talent, and by the dint of unceasing application, with the fearless devotion of the whole of his pecuniary resources has exhibited to his Country.

The ordinary mode of securing a benefit to a discover, by patent, (alluded to in thy letter) is, in this case impracticable—The deposit of a specification in a public office would qualify the unprincipled, immediately to form the compound; and yet by the addition of some neutral substance that would not injure the china, they would be enabled to boldly assert its dissimilarity to the patented article; and from the impossibility of analyzing burnt ware, would very readily shield themselves from penalty. Besides, secrecy, if it were attainable is not the object of my son. Were he remunerated for the expence he has been at (and $20,000 would do it) in bringing to perfection an art, of immense advantage to any country, so as to furnish him with the means for carrying it on with spirit, and with advantage to himself; it would give him the highest pleasure to see the manufacture of American Porcelain in the various states of the Union, so as to secure to the United States a revenue from its extensive exportation—

From thy generous and public spirited offer to promote the object of my son, so far as within thy constitutional sphere, I feel happy in believing he will not be forgotten and that if any thing can be done in favour of his establishment it will receive thy friendly aid—With sentiments of the most respectful regard I am thy friend

B T
No 44 no 5 St

LC, PPPM (mAJs). Benjamin Tucker (c1768–1833), William Ellis's father, was a Philadelphia china-shop owner and educator.

To Moses Dawson

[Printed here is Jackson's retained draft, followed by the letter itself.]

(Private)

Hermitage July 17th. 1830

My Dr Sir

yours of the 5th. instant reached me some days since, but such was my situation, that I could not answer it until now.

On my arrival here I was met by a letter from the Secretary of State, informing me of the resignation of Mr Herrick, enclosing me strong, numerous, & respectable recommendations for Mr. Noah H. Swayne, with a blank commission to be filled ~~up for him~~. I have given the subject a full consideration & notwithstanding the respectable recommendations of Mr Swayne with two members of Congress at its head, I should have selected Mr Lytle, but in doing so, it would have violated the republican rule we have adopted to take but one of a family into office at a time. Having appointed Genl Lytle survayor Genl we could not consistant with this ~~republican~~ rule, fill this vacancy by his son Mr Lytle who you have presented, & who, I have no doubt would have discharged the duties with credit to himself & benefit to the Govt. Noah H Swayne was appointed[1]

I have not time to go into the Bank question at present, can only observe, that my own opinion is, that it should be purely a *national Bank of deposit*, with power in time of war to Issue its bills bearing a moderate interest & payable at the close of the war, which being guranteed by the national faith Pledged, & based upon our revenue, would be sought after by the monied capitalist, & do away, in time of war, the necessity *of loans*. This is all the kind of a bank that a republic, should have. But if to be made a bank of discount as well as deposit, I would frame its charter upon the checks of our Govt. attach it to, & make a part of the revenue, & expose its situation as part ~~of the revenue~~ thereof annually to the nation, the profits of which would then anure to the whole people, instead, ~~as in the present case, to~~ of a *few monied capitalists*, who are trading upon ~~the credit of~~ our revenue, & enjoy the benefit of it, to the exclusion of the many. The Bank of deposit, & even of discount would steer clear of the constitutional objections to the present Bank, & all the profits arising would accrue, & be disposable as ~~the~~ other revenue for the benefit of the nation ~~as part of its revenue~~ company crouds me & I must close. with great respect your friend

A. J.

ALS draft, DLC (38).
1. Noah Haynes Swayne (1804–1884) had been an Ohio legislator. He served as district attorney through AJ's two terms, and was appointed by Lincoln to the Supreme Court in 1862.

(Private)

Hermitage July 17th. 1830
My Dr Sir
Yours of the 5th. instant reached me some days since, & such was my situation, that I could not find time to answer it until now.

On my arrival here I was met by a letter from Mr Van Buren, informing me of the resignation of Genl Herrick & enclosing numerous, respectable recommendations for Noah H. Swayne Esqr, with a blank commission to be filled.

I have given the subject a full consideration, and my private feelings at once would have decided in favor of Mr Lytle, notwithstanding the respectable & numerous recommendations of Mr Swayne—but in doing so, it would have violated the republican rule we have adopted to take but one of a family in office at a time. Having appointed the father survayor Genl, we could not consistant with this rule fill this vacancy by the son, who you have presented, & who I have no doubt, would have discharged the duties with credit to himself and benefit to the Govt. Noah H Swayne was therefore selected.

I have not time to go into the bank question at present—have only time to observe, that a republic should only have a *national Bank of deposit*, with powers in time of war, if the emergency required it, to issue its paper bearing a moderate interest payable at the end of the war; The payment of these notes being guranteed by the public faith pledged, & based upon our revenue, would do away the necessity of loans in time of war, and be sought after by the monied Capitalists. But even if made a bank of discount, as well as deposit, its charter might be so framed as to steer clear of most of the constitutional objections against the present Bank, by attaching it to, & making it a part of your revenue, do away all secrecy, & expose it annually as a branch of your revenue, making the whole profits anure to the nation, & not to a few monied capitalists to the exclusion of the many as is at present, but by adopting in its charter the principles of checks & ballances, I have no doubt but a national bank of discount & deposit, could be carried on with as much facility, & security, as your present system of revenue is collected. But I have always thought republics ought never to become brokers, therefore never ought to have any other bank but one intirely national, & that of deposit only—I am in great haste respectfully yr friend

Andrew Jackson

ALS, OCX (16-0022).

From Samuel Delucenna Ingham

Washington 17 July 1830

My dear Sir,

It appears from various Letters recd from the members of Congress from Maine that Leonard Jarvis has resigned the office of Collector of Passamaquoddy—Mr Anderson says he has seen a Letter from Jarvis addressed to the Editor of the Eastern Argus, Gen Ripley says he has recd a letter from Jarvis to the same effect informing him that he had sent on his resignation to Washington, Mr McIntire M. C. from Maine repeats the same   I am persuaded therefore that there can be no doubt of his resignation having been sent altho I have not received it—The office is one of considerable importance and it is desirable to have it filled as soon as may be practicable   I therefore forward a Commission in blank—I think you expressed the opinion that James W. Ripley was now your choice his having been a member of Congress could no longer be an objection to him seeing that Mr Jarvis was appointed since he resigned—I am persuaded that you cannot select a more worthy or fit man—[1]

I enclose a copy of a Letter from Mr Henshaw on the subject of L. Houses and shoals which will give a slight glimpse of the character of part of the Light house bill   it is no doubt redundant with such cases—the letter he encloses is full of interesting facts, the old Captain says "I was almost discouraged and reconciled to expect thousands on thousands of dollars again voted away for this ill fated purpose but I do not know when I was more agreeably surprized than when I first read the paper that the President had detained the L House Bill my only fears were that ~~the President~~ he might afterwards be persuaded to sign it"—there is nothing to fear from the effect of this measure on the Atlantic—[2]

I hope this will find you in health and in the more substantial enjoyment of the comfort of domestic Life than is permitted to those in public stations when on the theater of action—my children have been quite sick   our public affairs go on so far as I know very well, Mr Barry has informed you of the scenes in Philada.—but for the great good sense and prudence of Mr Gowan, aided by the advice of Mr Dallas there would have been a town meeting the result of which under the excitement which existed and the Diabolical advice that kept it in motion, none could have foreseen—

The new Law in relation to the customs gives some trouble, but the N. York customs House gives much more   each one has his whims and interests & every man who apprehends the slightest disturbance of his convenience or interest can conjure up objections to the most obvious improvements, the consequence is that the work goes on slowly and I am sorry to add rather reluctantly—but it will get in order in time[3]—accept my best respects Your obt sert

S D Ingham

ALS, DLC (38). LC, PU-Ingham Papers (mAJs). AJ replied on July 31 (below).

1. Maine congressman Leonard Jarvis, already confirmed by the Senate as customs collector at Passamaquoddy, had declined the office. James Wheelock Ripley (1786–1835) had resigned his seat as a Maine congressman in March. John Anderson (1792–1853) and Rufus McIntire (1784–1866) were also Maine congressmen. Thomas Todd (c1798–1854) edited the Portland *Eastern Argus.*

2. Ingham enclosed a copy of a July 9 letter from Boston customs collector David Henshaw (DLC-38). Henshaw had sent Ingham a letter from John Prince (1762–1848) of Marblehead, a former sea captain and Massachusetts legislator, and an 1826 state senate report co-authored by Prince opposing new lighthouses. Henshaw derided several specific Massachusetts lighthouses and harbor improvement projects as utterly useless, saying of one that "it would be about as feasible to attempt to bail the Ocean dry." A June 10 letter from Prince to Henshaw, matching the sense but not the language quoted here by Ingham, appeared in the *US Telegraph* of August 13.

3. "An Act for the more effectual collection of the impost duties," signed into law on May 28, aimed to tighten customs operations. Through June and July Ingham fielded complaints from New York collector Samuel Swartwout that the new procedures it mandated were either unclear or unworkable (DNA-RG 56, M178-17).

To William Berkeley Lewis

Hermitage July 1830

My Dr Major

I have just recd. your letter of the 5th instant enclosing one from Mr. Calhoun—This displays the knawings, of a guilty conscience, and with what delight he would seize upon any thing that could shew I had been making enquiry into his deceiptful course as it regards myself. I shall, on tomorrow, bring to his view in my reply the gross & wanton error he has fell into, and there leave him, Mr Crawford, & Major Forsythe, to settle their matters in their own way, which he may publish as soon as he pleases—

The other confidential matter fills me with regret, but I trust Major Barry will, agreable to his promise to me, attend to the war Department— Major Eaton has not yet arrived, so soon as he does, without naming the source of information, I will cause him to write the Doctor[1]—your note is the very first intimation I have had of his intemperance, or I assure you, displease whom it might, I should not have appointed him—The evil shall be remedied quickly—

I pray you to keep your eyes wide awake, & advise me of every occurrence—Mr Earle is with me & will write you tomorrow, & joins me in affectionate regard to you & your amiable daughter & believe me yr friend

Andrew Jackson

ALS and Copy, NN (16-0026).
   1. Philip G. Randolph.

To John Caldwell Calhoun

Hermitage 19th of July 1830—

Sir

Your letter of the 22nd of june last, has just been recd. via Washington City. I regret that mine to you of the 7th. of May[1] covering a copy of one to Mr Forsyth from me of the same date, had not reached you as it would have prevented you from falling into the gross errours, you have, from the unfounded inferences you have drawn from Mr Forsyths letter to me, and would have informed you that I had no conversation or communication with Mr Forsyth on the subject alluded to, before the receipt of the copy of Mr Crawfords letter which I so promptly laid before you—To correct the errours into which the inferences you have drawn from Mr Forsyths letter have led you, I herewith again enclose you a copy of my letter to Mr Forsyth of the 7th. of May, and his answer thereto of the 17th. of june last, which I recd. on the 8th instant—and I have to regret that any interruption of the mail prevented your receipt of mine of the 7th of May, which was mailed at the same time mine to Mr Forsythe was—

Mr Forsyth having promised in his letter to me of 17th. of june that he would explain, and by letter, to you correct you in the unjust & unfounded inferrences which you had drawn from his letter, and I must add here, for your information, that if I understand your other allusions, they are as equally unfounded, I have never heard it even intimated except in your letter, that the man individual, to whom, I suppose you allude, had the slightest knowledge on the subject, or the most remote agency in the matter. In conclusion I have repeat that I have always met the intimations that you had of your having originated made before the cabinet in secrete session council against me, injurious movements with flat, & positive denials, & brought into view by way of rebutter, your uniform & full approval of my whole conduct on the Seminole campaign, so far as I, or any of my friends had heard you on the Subject, and the high character you sustained, for fair, open, and honorable conduct in all things, was entirely opposed to the secrete uncandid & unmanly couse ascribed to you by these intimations, of conduct in the secrete council, and I banished from my mind what I conceived to be unjust imputations upon your honor by ascribing duplicity to you, and never until after the intimations were communicated to me of the suggestions of the Marshal as stated in my letter to Mr Forsythe (a copy of which was enclosed to you) it was then that I had a desire to see the statement said to have been made by Mr Crawford, & when informed by Col Hamilton that such statement had been seen in writing that I made the request to see it, with the object of laying before you, which I then supposed would meet your prompt & positive negative—but I regret that instead of a negative which I had a right to expect I had the poignant mortification to see in your letter an admission of its truth—understanding the matter, now, I feel no interest in this altercation, and leave you Mr Crawford & all concerned to settle the affair in your own way, and now close this correspondence for ever. I am very respectfully yr mo. obdt. servt.

Andrew Jackson

ALS draft, DLC (73). *US Telegraph*, February 17, 1831; *Calhoun Papers*, 11:208–10. Calhoun replied on August 25 (below).
    1. Actually June 7 (above).

To John Coffee

(private & confidential)

Hermitage July 20th. 1830—

Mr Dr. Genl

From circumstances that have arisen, but which ought not to have arose, but which, my early & friendly admonitions endeavoured, but could not as it appears prevent, it would afford me great pleasure to see you—firm to my public course where duty guides and stedfast to friendship, so far as it can be continued consistant with my public duties and official station, and even then, tho, duty may compel a seperation, my friendship cannot cease—But from the most surprising combination & situation of society here formed by the intrigue of well disciplined politicians, a combination of the most heterogeneous mass of base enemies, & boosom & dear friends, I am filled with sincere regret—The ground of that regret I will fully disclose to you when I have the pleasure to see you—My course is a plain one, and open one, from which I cannot depart—folly & pride may have induced others to believe, that it would be dishonorable, *now,* for them to recede—and I would sacrafice my life before I would advise, or consent that my friend or connection, should submit to a dishonorable or degrading act—as to myself, I never have, nor never will; I have never asked it, nor never will from others. I therefore have a great desire to see you—and judge Overton who has just left me, has requested me to say to you, should you come in he wants to see you on your way, & requests that you would call at his house. I would be also glad you would.

Present me affectionately to Polly & your amiable family and believe me yr friend

Andrew Jackson

P.S. I have said my course is a plain one, I have nothing to dread, pursuing the principle I have adopted for my guide, no harm can befal me; whatever may happen to others. My duty is, that my household should bestow equal comity to all, and the nation expects me to controle my household to this rule—would to god my endeavours by council & persuasion had obtained this—happiness would have been mine & peace in the administration. The latter, cost what it may, must be maintained

A. J.

ALS, THi (16-0031).

To William Berkeley Lewis

(confidential)

Hermitage July 21rst. 1830—

My Dr Major

Lt Smith being on his way to the city I cannot forego the pleasure of droping you a line by him—Major Eaton has reached Frankling, him, & his lady, in good health

The great magicians have been at work & by their agents here have been endeavouring to prevent that attention due to Mrs. & Major Eaton—I am at no loss, *now*, to determine, why the Genl chose his head quarters at Nashville—but all the combination will fail at last, or I calculate badly[1]—but strange as it may appear, some of our friends have acted *most strangely*—you know I am immoveable—It may so happen that I shall return to the city in company with my son alone—on this event I shall want a Secretary, who can write & compose *well*—one who can from a brief do justice to any subject—will you make enquiry where such a young Gentleman can be had, without making it positively know that he is wanted for my Secretary.

My connections have acted very strangely here, but I know I can live as well without them, as they can without me, and I will govern my Houshold, or I will have *none*   I expect to go to judge Overtons in a few days when I shall see Major Eaton & his family—The judge is to give them a dinning shortly—Present me to the heads of Departments—To Kendal, Smith & Jones, P.M. & Genl Green[2]—My health is not so good as when I reached here but I hope it will be quite good in a few days; it has proceeded from a cold, which produced a cough which is wearing away.

My son joins me in kind respects to you & Maryann[.] yr friend

Andrew Jackson

ALS and Copy, NN (16-0035).

1. The general was Edmund P. Gaines, who on assuming command of the Army's Western Department in January 1830 relocated its headquarters from Jefferson Barracks near St. Louis to Nashville.

2. Amos Kendall, Thomas L. Smith, Washington postmaster William Jones (1790–1867), and Duff Green.

From William Clark

St. Louis July 21st. 1830.

Dear Sir,

Having been informed you were at the Hermitage, I do myself the honor to enclose to you herewith, a copy of a letter from the Commissioners to the Hon: Secretary of War, by which you will learn the result of our negotiations with the Tribes between whom we were authorized to effect a peace, and of whom a purchase has been made of a portion of their country, intended as a common hunting ground for the Tribes ceding the same, and with a view also of locating thereon such other Tribes as the President may deem proper.[1]

A slip of Land of forty miles in width, and about two hundred & fifty in depth has also been purchased of the Sacs & Foxes, and the Four Bands of Sioux of the Mississippi. This Land extends from the Mississippi, and runs south westwardly to the purchase made as above on the Missouri; and is to be considered as neutral ground, on which no Trader shall be permitted to settle.

Although the Yanckton and Santie Bands of Sioux were prevented by unavoidable circumstances from sending Deputations to this convention, I have no doubt but they will give their assent to the Treaty. For this purpose I shall in a day or two despatch Major Bean, an active, zealous & efficient Agent, who will be supplied with the means of rendering those two Bands as well satisfied with this Treaty as their neighbors, and of making them parties thereto. This officer will also be instructed to bring a small Deputation from each of those Bands to meet a Deputation of the Sacs & Foxes at this place in order to communicate in person, to the last named Tribes, the assent of their Bands to the provisions of both the Treaties, and to smoke the pipe of peace in my presence. This arrangement is in compliance with a request of the Sacs & Foxes in Council, and agreed to by the commissioners.[2]

I should also have mentioned that my arrangements for this Treaty had nearly been frustrated by a most determined opposition of the Sacs & Foxes, growing out of their reluctance to make a peace after the recent loss they had sustained by the murder of some of their chiefs and principal men below Prairie du chien. Two parties of those Tribes had made preparations and were on the eve of their departure on a war excurtion: they were stopped on hearing that I was on the way up, and also of the decisive measures about to be taken with them.[3]

The Presidents message however, had all the effect which could have been wished by those who were inclined to peace, and was finally well received by the whole of them. The appearance also of the Troops, shortly after my arrival at Prairie du chien, had a good effect, as I am now very much inclined to the belief that their presence prevented very serious difficulties among them, and which from their excited feelings during the first two or three days after their arrival, appeared inevitable; this however was previous to their assembling in council, and of hearing the message.

The prompt measures which have been taken by Genl. Atkinson on my application, has effected the removal of the intruders, and will prevent any further intrusion of the whites on the mineral Lands of the Sacs & Foxes west of the Mississippi, (which are found to be much superior to those on the East side) particularly as a detachment of the Troops will be left at Dubuques mines to prevent the miners from returning, which they had openly declared they would do, after the Troops had descended.[4]

Finding that the Deputations of Sacs & Foxes were not prepared to cede their mineral country above Rock Island for the compensation, I was willing to make them, I declined entering on the subject with them, untill I should be further instructed thereon by the Government. They appear willing to sell their mineral country above Rock Island, but expect something like the annuity given to the Winnebagoes & Puttowattamies, and for a much greater term of years, and also the payment of debts due to their Traders, of about $60,000. They expressed a wish to consult with their Nation on this subject, and said they would inform me of their decision, & state their terms at the time they come to meet the Deputations at this place, from the Yanckton & Santie Bands of Sioux, in October next.[5] I have the honor to be, with sentiments of the highest consideration & respect your most obt. serv.

Wm Clark

[Endorsed by AJ:] Genl Clark Indian Treaty—to be handed over to the Sec of War

ALS, DNA-RG 107 (M222-27). LC, KHi (mAJs). William Clark (1770–1838), co-leader of the famed Lewis and Clark expedition, was Superintendent of Indian Affairs at St. Louis. On July 15, 1830, he and fellow commissioner Willoughby Morgan, an Army colonel, concluded a treaty at Prairie du Chien with the Sacs and Foxes, four bands of Sioux, and other Indians. The Indians jointly ceded roughly the western third of present Iowa, to be allocated by the president as a tribal residence and hunting preserve. The Sacs and Foxes and Sioux also separately ceded two parallel strips, each twenty miles wide, running diagonally westward across northern Iowa from the Mississippi to the larger cession's eastern edge on the Des Moines River.

1. Clark and Morgan wrote Eaton explaining the treaty on July 16 (DNA-RG 75, T494-2).

2. Jonathan L. Bean (1800–1853) was subagent to the Sioux. Yankton and Santee delegates signed the treaty at St. Louis on October 13.

3. In April 1830 the War Department had ordered the positioning of troops to try to prevent an imminent general war between the Sacs and Foxes and the Sioux. On May 5, Sioux and Menominee warriors attacked a party of Foxes who were on their way to Prairie du Chien, killing ten. At a council in St. Louis on June 14, Sac and Fox chiefs complained to Clark of the murders and protested his instruction to meet the Sioux at Prairie du Chien (DNA-RG 75, M234-749 & M234-728).

4. At Clark's behest, Henry Atkinson at Jefferson Barracks had sent troops to evict white intruders who crossed the Mississippi from Galena to occupy recently vacated Fox villages around Dubuque.

5. The Sacs and Foxes ceded their lands in eastern Iowa along the Mississippi, including the Dubuque mineral district, in September 1832 after the Black Hawk War.

To John Henry Eaton

P.S.

Instruct Mr Donelly to appoint a day that the chiefs will be at Franklin—or if they will not come, but give assurances that they will treat, to appoint a day & place in the nation   I want the chiefs to come here—Laflour can influence the cherokees, & as soon as we make arrangements with the choctaws by sending Laflour to the cherokees, he can bring a delegation to meet us on our way to Washington in East Tennessee.

I have just recd. a letter from Major Barry, all is well in the Department of War—Having just recd. a letter from Genl Coffee who says he will be at Franklin on the evening of the 28th. I will be there with judge Overton to see him—present me respectfully to your lady, mother & Doctor Brethit & Lady, & excuse the haste in which this is written[1]

A. J.

[Endorsed by AJ:] The Sec of War

ALS fragment, DNA-RG 75 (16-0047). On June 28, the War Department had sent instructions from Eaton to Choctaw agent William Ward and Chickasaw agent Benjamin F. Reynolds to ascertain the Indians' willingness to remove. If they were ready, each agent was to bring a delegation, not larger than twenty or twenty-five, to treat with Eaton and AJ at Franklin between August 1 and 15 (DNA-RG 75, M21-6). John Donly was an Alabama mail contractor with Choctaw relations. Eaton wrote him on August 4 (below).

1. Franklin, about twenty miles south of Nashville, had been Eaton's home. His mother Elizabeth Eaton (c1753–1843) still lived there, as did his sister Mary Pauline (1790–1847) and her husband, physician Edward Breathitt (1790–1837).

To James Gowen

Hermitage July 22nd 1830—

My Dr Sir

I have just received yours of the 3rd instant and hasten to answer it. I regret to learn the great excitement that has been produced on the pardon of Wilson. The absurdity that I should have pardoned Wilson because he was an american, and permitted Porter to be hung, because he was an Irishman is too palbable to deserve one single comment from me, when it is known my parents were Irish.

The facts as *presented* in favour of Wilson were these, upon which he received the pardon

Wilsons confession led to the apprehension of Porter & associates in the mail robery, and to their ultimate conviction—that this confession had been elicited from Wilson by assurances ~~to Wilson~~ that it should not be used against him, which promises were denied ~~him~~ upon the trial, and instead of Wilson being made the witness he was convicted upon his own confession thus elicited—that it appeared upon the trial that Wilson was a young man & coerced into this daring robery by Porter & associates & that seven of the jury who tried him united with ~~thousands~~ hundreds of respectable citizens for the pardon of his life—[1]

Under these circumstances to have permitted Wilson to have been hung would have left an indeliable stain upon the character of our Government—Wilsons life was spared, and he left subject to 60 years imprisonment, a poor, but necessary boon—What was Porters situation as represented—not only a mail rober, but one of the most hardened villains & cold blooded murderers, who had confessed to the murder of two men for their mony—one man near the city of washington on whom he had found but three nine penny peaces which so much enraged him that he cut off his head; could such a monster in human shape, let him originate from what country he might, be pardoned, when robery and crime, had become so frequent, that an example for public safety, had become necessary—I do not recollect whether in any of the petitions for pardon, the country of their birth was named—be this as it may, I never shall regret my action in this case. I am very respectfully yr mo obdt. servt.

Andrew Jackson

ALS, NcD (16-0041). Philadelphia *American Daily Advertiser*, November 5, 1832. Gowen replied on August 13 (below).

1. William T. Barry had supplied some of this information on July 10 (above).

From James Alexander Hamilton

New York, July 23, 1830.

My Dear Sir:

I congratulate you upon your arrival at your peaceful abode, where I hope you will enjoy that tranquillity which is denied to you elsewhere. I intend to send to you, with this letter, a debate which occurred in the House of Commons of a character deeply interesting to us. The impudent assumption of a right asserted on the floor of that House to extend their right to interfere to preserve a balance of power in this quarter of the globe, is unequalled.[1] That nation has extended its hands to every quarter of the world for the purpose of creating a colonial dependence upon her power. She now contains more than eighty millions of souls, distributed throughout every continent and sea, she herself not amounting to more than twelve millions; and yet presumes to create alarm at a disposition in our Government to extend its control over a contiguous territory which is almost without population. And to what end? in order that this territory may be cultivated by a hardy race of freemen, who will enjoy all the blessings of a free and liberal government; in the direction of which they will participate in common with every other member of the nation. From all I learn, I very much fear that our negotiation will not be successful, unless the late Act of Congress should, by depriving the Duke[2] of all pretence for refusal, obtain that from their sense of shame which their sense of justice could not induce.

Yours truly, &c.

Printed, *Reminiscences of James A. Hamilton*, pp. 171–72 (16-0045).
1. This debate was also remarked by Ingham, immediately below.
2. Prime minister Wellington.

From Samuel Delucenna Ingham

My Dear Sir

I have recd your esteemed favor of the 9th and am happy to learn that you have arrived safely among your old friends   I have written to Mr Neville on the subject of the accidents which happen to steam boats and have also opened a correspondence with persons in England & France—There is now a great effort making among the practical & scientific men of the old & new world to discover the immediate causes of and the best means of preventing these calamitous accidents and I have much confidence that something will be elicitted which may lead to an efficient remedy. I shall spare no exertion to accomplish it.[1] I do not despair of restoring the customs House of N. York to the confidence of the country altho it is very difficult to conquer lazy habits.

you will have seen Mr Peels speech in the Brittsh Parliament declaring on the authority of Mr McClane whom he eulogises "as a very honorable man" that the U S. Govt. had no view to an extension of her territory into Mexico—This may all be a finesse of Mr Peels; but it is of course worthy of notice here[2]—The prospect of the revenue is not quite so flattering as at the corresponding period of last year, but the returns of the first quarter of the year are now all in, and we shall soon be able to ascertain the prospect with more certainty when I will advise you of the result—I am sorry to hear that our new Register & Receiver have issued between 70 and 80 of the certificates for the spurious Brittish grants—Mr Graham is reported some what better to day & we have hope of being able to get him home again[3]—Gov. Branch return'd to day with his daughters, his family have been quite sick in his absence both Mrs B. and the children, they are now better. I have heard nothing lately from the Philada. excitement it is of course subsiding   The veto will I am sure be sustained in all the Atlantic States—The opposition do not even make a point of it out of Maryland, if they had no other ground for hope in Massachusetts & Connecticut, this wd fail them even there.

The movements in Charlestown have evaporated. Mr Cheves speech is certainly the most mischievous that I have seen. Hamilton's has not yet come to hand—tis said to be fiery, but there is nothing in all this to disturb the Govt. and it is most to be regretted as affording the example of good men for future mischief to be deceived by wicked ones[4]   accept my best respects and earnest wishes for your health & happiness and believe me very sincerely your obt Sert

S D Ingham

Letters to day say that Gen Boyd is not dead tho very ill of an apoplexy[5]

ALS, DLC (38). AJ replied August 7 (below).

1. On May 4, the House of Representatives had directed the Treasury secretary to report on means of preventing steamboat boiler explosions. On August 1 Ingham distributed a questionnaire for engine manufacturers and steamboat operators about the cause of explosions. He reported to the House on March 3, 1831, that his inquiries had so far yielded little information (*HRDoc* 131, 21st Cong., 2d sess., Serial 209). Morgan Neville (1783–1839) was a prominent Cincinnati businessman, editor, and author.

2. In a May 20 speech in the Commons, William Huskisson called on his government to safeguard British commercial and maritime interests in the Gulf by enforcing peace between Mexico and Spanish Cuba and by foiling American designs on both places. Peel replied that he "relied with confidence on the statements of the American minister to this country, than whom a more honourable man did not exist," that the U.S. harbored no expansionist designs on either Mexico or Cuba (*Hansard's Parliamentary Debates*, 2d ser., 24:875–94).

3. On April 27, General Land Office commissioner George Graham had instructed Thomas G. Davidson and Alexander G. Penn, register and receiver of the Saint Helena, La., land office, to stop issuing certificates for land claims based on old British grants. On July 20 Graham's chief clerk John M. Moore wrote Davidson and Penn revoking the certificates already issued. Too ill to return home, Graham died near Washington on August 8.

4. On July 1 a large public dinner was held at Charleston, S.C., to honor Senator Robert Hayne and congressman William Drayton. Billed as a "Great State Rights Celebration," it featured militant speeches against the tariff and in defense of nullification. Lead organizer and gubernatorial aspirant James Hamilton Jr. championed bold resistance to federal oppression. Langdon Cheves (1776–1857), a former congressman and BUS president, decried the South's "colonial suffering, dependence, and disgrace" under the tariff, but counseled a cooperative response and deprecated separate state action "as premature and impolitic."

5. John Parker Boyd (1764–1830), a onetime Army brigadier, was appointed naval officer for the Boston and Charlestown customs district by AJ in 1829. He died October 3.

From David W. Haley

Jackson Mi
July 24th. 1830

Sir

I have just returned from a short visit to the nation, and it is with much satisfaction I can informe you the Choctaws have settled all their disputes, and are now prepared for business. I often stated to you while at the city that Leflore would and should rule the nation   he is the only man they have that can keepe them united and promote them to a state of civilization. when your commissioners meets them and sees Leflores men by the side of the other districts they will at once acknowledge the fact. I leave home to morrow to visit Leflore and the Choctaws on the Yazoo and on my return I will write you again and at what time will suit the nation best to meet in council. though about the first of September will be the most proper time, as new corn can be used by that time. your commissioners must come out liberal in the out set of the negotiation in a manner that all parties will be satisfyed for should they conclude a Treaty and apart of the nation should take it in their head to object to it you well know two thirds of the Senate would not approve it and any Treaty that is made in the bounds of Equity and agreed to by the unanimous body of the nation will be approved of by the senate and the appropiations made by the house without difficulty. I have the honor to be your obt sevt

D. W. Haley

ALS, DNA-RG 75 (M234-185).

John Henry Eaton to Mushulatubbe et al.

Copy.

Franklin 24th. July, 1830.

Friends & Brothers,

Your talk of the 2nd. June, directed to me at Washington, has been forwarded, and has just reached me at this place.[1] It is matter of surprise and some regret, to find, that you are desirous to make a visit to the country west of the Mississippi, before you are prepared to decide, as to the propriety of a removal. The experience of the past has abundantly shewn, that you cannot reside peaceably where you are. The laws of Mississippi, subjecting you to a different government, than you have been accustomed to, and which will restrict you to the usages and customs, and rule, to which your white brothers conform, are already extended over you. This your Great Father cannot prevent; and repeatedly, he has told you so. Are you prepared to submit to this state of things, and to become citizens, for such must be the case? If you are so prepared, then is it unnecessary to say more, or to speak to you further on the subject. These matters have been discussed already long enough; and it is high time, there should be an end of the argument, and a decision had, whether you will remain where you are, surrounded by the whites, and made subject to their laws, or peaceably remove to the west, there to live on your own soil, under your own ancient usages and customs, and free from those interruptions which now on every side beset you. One or the other you must resolve upon. Further delay, is not only unnecessary, but is attended with hazard to your best interest.

Why should you solicit time to visit the Country which has been assigned you to the west. Already you are well advised, that it is situated in a pleasant, agreeable Climate, even more so, than that you are about to leave; and in all respects equally fertile. Bounded by the Arkansa to the North, and by Red River, to the South, and embracing nearly twenty millions of acres, it is a Country infinitely more desirable, and larger in extent, than the one you occupy. All the information possessed shews this to be the fact.

Of your own accord during last winter, you forwarded to your Great Father, a treaty, ceding your entire Country. He laid it before his great Council, the Senate; but in doing so, he told them of your differences, and discontents; and that while a portion of the Nation desired the treaty to be agreed to, another, was of a contrary opinion. The Senate, did not approve what you did. One reason was, that the terms proposed were too extravagant; but another and a strong one was, they did not desire any arrangement to which the Nation was not with general approbation assenting. The same language is now declared to you. We want no dissatisfaction, no heartburnings to abide after a treaty shall be made. Your Great Father is satisfied, that your peace, prosperity and happiness, depend upon your removal; but he will take no course which shall not be entirely satisfactory to his red children. He does not merely desire their removal, but he desires it to take place under such circumstances, as shall conclusively satisfy them, that justice, and liberality, are the terms upon which their departure is asked. Beyond the Mississippi, he is solicitous for them to remove, tho' still under such circumstances as shall retain them as his children, and friends; a result which he is persuaded is to be obtained only, by suffering them to depart, with a full conviction that their interest has been regarded, and their happiness as a people, consulted.

But these things cannot be so fully explained at a distance. Major Haley, your friend and agent, was so informed, and he was instructed to tell you, that with a view to a perfect understanding of every thing, the President and the Secretary of War, would be in Tennessee this summer, near to you, and face to face, would confer with you. Now that they have come, instead of meeting, to enter into an arrangement for a removal as your previous acts and conduct had indicated a disposition on your part to do, you propose an examination of the Country; information already sufficiently possessed, whereby, to defer longer, doing that, which every sensible man in the Nation perceives must happen, if you would preserve yourselves.

Friends and Brothers—Your Great Father will not attempt disguise—he will in nothing deceive you. He will not now do, what in all his former intercourse with you, he never attempted. Truth and justice, are his object, and they are the great land marks, which in his intercourse with you, he would carefully preserve and maintain. In a spirit of frankness then, he assures you of what shortly you cannot but discover, that it is vain and idle for you to expect to dwell in peace where you are. Difficulties, and severe trials, must and will be yours. Surrounded by the whites on all sides—made subject to their laws and customs, so variant from your own, it is not to be expected that you can dwell under them with any thing of security, or quiet to yourselves. Your own reflection and reason cannot fail to teach you the certainty of these suggestions. How you shall conclude to act, is for yourselves to decide. We shall do no more than to persuade, not coerce you, to what your interest requires.

A just regard to your happiness demands of you to pursue the course that has been suggested. Why then defer it? why not at once arrive at the conclusion which reason and experience prove, is the only sure one to which you can arrive. It cannot be accounted for on any other principle, than that you are deceived and imposed upon by designing men, who would persuade you to error, and to a course which cannot fail ultimately to involve your Nation in ruin. I warn you to be upon your guard against these intruding and obtrusive advisers who disregarding your true interest would advise you to a course, of which in the end, you may have cause for deep and lasting repentance. I urge you to beware of such evil Counsellors, for they have any other object before them, than your welfare; On the other hand, what motive adverse to you, can have influence with the President. In past times, you have known him to be your friend, and he will not now be different from what he has been: While, as Chief Magistrate of this Country he will on all occasions consult the happiness and prosperity of the whites, I take occasion to assure you that he will never do so at the expense of his red children—no such course will be demanded of him by the people of this Country.

Friends and Brothers—Your Great Father is here, not distant from you, where it was understood you would gladly meet him, to treat for a final removal to a home, which promises to you greater happiness than you can possess where you are. A country will be yours, not on the principles of mere occupancy, but one which your Great Father will give you to hold forever, as his white children possess their lands—a Country where being to yourselves and at a distance from the whites, there will be none to disturb or make you afraid—where he can and will protect you from all interruptions. Such an opportunity of furthering your interest may no more occur. Your Great Father and his Secretary of War are here, to hold council with you, to extend to you terms liberal as can be admitted. Hereafter this may not be the case! He may be constrained to send his Commissioners to see you, and then the advantages now presented may be impaired. It is in his power at present to pay all the expenses of your removal, and to take care of you at your new homes for twelve months until your crops can be made. He may not have it in his power hereafter to do this, inasmuch as Congress may change that policy which they have adopted, and thereby place it out of his reach to do, what at present it is in his power to affect. The whole scheme of emigration, if it be now deferred, may require hereafter to be carried into effect thro' your own means and at your own expense. Then you may call for help, when the power to extend it, may not be possessed.

Under these considerations your Great Father has instructed me to send his friend, and your friend, Mr. Jno. Donnelly, to converse freely with you, and to tell you, in detail more than I have time to write. Listen to his counsel, for he comes from your Great Father and will not deceive you. He comes to tell you the truth—to point you to your true condition, and to warn you, of what experience in a short time will convince you, that to remain where you are, happy, and preserved as a Nation, is what no sensible and reflecting man can look to, or hope for. Where now are the tribes of former years—the Tuscaroraws—Six Nations, and others which once, were numerous and powerful. Easy to learn the vices, but slow to acquire a knowledge of the virtues and morals of their white brothers, they have gradually disappeared, until now scarcely are they known as a people. The same fate must be yours; and reflection and observation should convince you of the correctness of the assertion. To escape, is in your power; but defer your removal for a time, and the just expectations which are now within reach may fail you, no more to return.

These things have repeatedly been brought to your consideration. A long time ago, your Great Father, who at this time presides over the affairs of the Country, told you truly what your condition would be—what, the certain result that awaited you. Then, as now, you heeded not his opinions, but listened to the advice of bad men, who had no regard for you; and whose object was to deceive. At present you may not, but by and by, when probably it may be too late for you to be benefited, the truth of what he has asserted may be perceived. To discuss the matter longer is unnecessary: it is a waste of time and words to repeat, what so often has been told. Decide then fully in reference to the merits of your case and let that decision be final. Either you must make up your minds to become citizens of Mississippi, subject to her laws and her government, or conclude to remove to the Country which has been assigned you beyond the Territory of Arkansa: Already you have had ample time to deliberate upon this subject; and if further consideration and deliberation shall be necessary, your Great Father cannot undertake to promise, that any provision will be made by the Government for your removal and support, as is now the case. The people of this Country already complain of the ample and liberal provision which has been made for their Indian brothers, and may induce Congress to forbear further assistance, and hence when circumstances and your own necessities shall compel you to remove, it may be at your own expense, and upon your own resources. The Government then may not supply the means of assisting you to your homes. How important is it, then, that you should seriously reflect upon these things, and at once decide and act: it may presently be too late for you to do so. Your friend & Brother

John H. Eaton.

Copy, DNA-RG 46 (mAJs). AJ sent this copy to the Senate with the Treaty of Dancing Rabbit Creek on December 9, 1830. The Senate had it printed in confidence.
    1. Enclosed by Philip G. Randolph to AJ, July 10 (above).

From Samuel Delucenna Ingham

Washington 25 July 1830

My dear Sir,
    I omitted to mention when I last wrote that the Marshal of Tennessee has not been able to account for the money advanced to him, and according to the rule adopted last year of which notice was given by a circular, no further advance could be made untill the amounts of the previous term were settled and the money accounted for—the balance in the hands of Mr Purdy at the last settlement as reported by the accounting officers was $1979 to which may be added a further remittance of $500 asked for to pay rent for the court House and some jail fees—the balance in his hands is estimated to be ample for the expenses of the longest terms of the Court—I mention this that you may be fully apprized of the facts, should it happen, which I hope may not be the case, that Mr Purdy is not able to meet the expenses of the approaching term, and that you may not be annoyed without knowing the cause by the complaints of Jurors & witnesses &c, which are to be expected whenever they are not punctually paid. Mr Purdy is fully aware, if he has recd my letters, of the reason why no more money was sent to him—[1]
    we have had extremely warm weather for the last 2 weeks, you very fortunately escaped it on your journey: it has proved fatal to very many of the poor fellows on the Canal, there have died in the neighborhood of Georgetown as many as 6 of a day besides several others in other pursuits[2]—The new minister of France has been here several days[3]—the public business goes on very quietly, I am not aware of any thing that

has rquired your presence since you left us, altho we shall be very glad of your rturn. I trust you will not think of it untill there is some assurance of cooler weather. The opposition are certainly preparing for a more violent contest than even the last. Their pens are all dipped in gall, and no effort will be left untried to carry the war as Mr Clay says into "every hamlet"   The Toasts have indicated Mr Southard as the Candidate for the vice Presidency on Mr Clays ticket.[4]

my family is still in the country on account of the health of our youngest which is still very precarious—

accept the assurance of my very best respects & believe me sincrly your obt Svt.

S D Ingham

ALS, DLC (38).

1. Robert Purdy (1757–1831) was U.S. marshal for the west Tennessee district.

2. On July 27, the *National Intelligencer* reported that temperatures had exceeded 90° the last twelve days, causing "a number of sudden deaths" among immigrant workers on the Chesapeake and Ohio Canal.

3. Jean Baptiste Gaspard Roux de Rochelle (1762–1849), the new minister from France, arrived in Washington July 20.

4. In his 'war, pestilence, and famine' address in 1828, Henry Clay had also said that if he could he "would visit every state, go to every town and hamlet, address every man in the Union, and entreat them" to oppose AJ's election (*Clay Papers*, 7:273). At an Independence Day celebration held by Clay men in Washington on Monday, July 5, Samuel Lewis Southard (1787–1842) of New Jersey, former Navy secretary under Monroe and Adams, was toasted for vice president.

From Martin Van Buren

Saratoga Springs July 25th 1830

My dear Sir

I am here taking the waters in peace, seeing many of our friends, thinking on public affairs as much as is consistent with recreation, & attention to some agreeable ladies, & improving my health. I shall remain two weeks & then go slowly south (unless hurried by events) and reach W. some time in April. You will not I hope think of getting there before the first of October. September is a bad month in W. & you should not run any hazard without adequate cause.

I have been disappointed in not hearing from you but am in daily expectation of that pleasure. There has been no political act in many years which has given such universal satisfaction in this State as the Veto. The Republicans are vociferous in their approbation and the Opposition silent in regard to it—many even approving it in terms. The same may be said of Pennsylvania & New Jersey. But I am really sorry to say to you, that the moment of suspense as to its effect served to shew the cloven foot on the part of our friend Baldwin.[1] He has been tampered with by the friends of Mr Clay, & believing at the moment that the Veto would ruin us in Pennsylvania & the West, he was ready to go with the current. Of this there is no manner of doubt. You know I am not suspicious, or credulous, & I feel therefore that I may claim your confidence when I assure you that I have such evidence of the fact, as makes it absolutely certain. I should not trouble you with the circumstance but for prudential reasons. As matters have taken a different turn we shall probably hear no farther about it, unless we should again be considered in danger, when he will again be deceived by the belief that by clubbing his interests with Mr Clay they can attach Pennsylvania & the West, & carry the whole on their joint account. The South looks better than it has done for years. The last exhibition at Charleston will be the valedictory upon the subject of nullification, & the honest & good men who have figured in the scene, will gradually return to better feelings, & sounder principles. New Hampshire & Maine will certainly be with us—this state though sorely distracted by anti-masonry & Working-men's faction will I trust sustain herself nobly in regard to her local politics, & in regard to national politics she is not in question.[2]

If you had not seen too much of politicians not to be surprised at any somersets, on the part of those who have once placed themselves in the current, you would experience that feeling, on learning that our quondam friend Judge Spencer, after all his bitter denunciation of Mr Clay, is out openly for him.[3] The fact is nevertheless so, & although I have no positive evidence of it, I have sufficient to satisfy my own mind, that he had a secret agency in deluding M̶r̶ Judge Baldwin—they are old cronies—t̶h̶e̶ Judge Spencer spent some time on his way up with his brother of the Bench. In no sense can the course of Judge Spencer be injurious to us, & in some it will be a positive advantage. So much for domestic concerns. I have several letters from McLane without adding much to our stock of information. I send you Hughes letter to amuse you. If there is any confidence to be placed in the creature there is some importance in what he says about the Duke of Clarence.[4] Cambreling tells me that a Mr W. who has written a Pamphlet (sent to us by McLane) agst. the opening of her colonial Ports by G. Britain to our commerce, has written a letter to New Brunswick, stating, that the Ministry had determined to open the ports, as soon as they were satisfied that the measure would be properly appreciated by Congress. My belief is that as soon as they get our proceeding— the King is dead, and the old ministry relieved from apprehension, they will conclude a satisfactory arrangement. The French Ministry have taken the ground intimated some time ago—viz pretending that they understood Mr Rives as admitting the construction they put on the Louisiana Treaty, and insisting that the negotiation must be broken off unless we do so. Mr. Rives was informed before the note, taking this position, was written, that that course was necessary, even if they should find an arrangement on different grounds practicable. It is resorted to, to, regain the ground occupied by preceeding administration, & which the Prince Polignac had lost by opening the negotiation, & by admitting portions of our claims, before theirs, arising from that source, were brought under discussion. Mr Rives has sustained himself admirably, & I see nothing discouraging in the general aspect of affairs in that quarter.[5] Mr Rhind has succeeded in negotiating a general Treaty of Commerce & Navigation with the Sublime Porte upon the terms of the most favoured nation. The Treaty has not yet been recd. but is doubtless on its way. My last direct accounts from Mr. Rhind were after all the terms had been agreed upon, & when the Treaty was waiting the arrival of Biddle & Offley for its signature. The Mexican Minister is here, & informs me this morning, that from his last Dispatches he has no doubt that he will receive the Commercial Treaty between the U.S. & Mexico before the next session of Congress.[6] So that the pace of affairs touching our foreign relations may be said to wear a very favorable aspect. Remember me kindly to Major Donelson & all the members of your family & to Major & Mrs Eaton if they are with you. Tell Miss Eastin if she does not write me I will give her up as a bad girl, & ask Mrs Donelson to kiss my daughter for me, if little Jackson will allow it by that name.[7] Yours truly

M Van Buren

ALS, DLC-Van Buren Papers (16-0050; mAJs).

1. Supreme Court justice Henry Baldwin.

2. A Working Men's Party was organized in New York City in 1829 and fielded candidates in that fall's legislative elections. It dissolved in 1830.

3. Congressman Ambrose Spencer.

4. Christopher Hughes (1786–1849) was the U.S. chargé d'affaires in Sweden. Writing Van Buren from London on June 1, he related his recent visit to the country seat of William, Duke of Clarence, who became king on June 26 at the death of George IV. Hughes reported that "I never saw a man, of 63, in a better condition of health, physical & moral, to enter upon the discharge of any duties, political or *Kingly*." He found William well informed about the U.S. and well disposed toward AJ (Van Buren Papers, DLC).

5. In earlier exchanges, France had met American spoliation claims with a counterclaim based on alleged American failure to honor the eighth article of the 1803 Louisiana Purchase treaty, which granted France most-favored-nation trading status in Louisiana ports. In March, Rives reported that the French foreign minister, the Prince de Polignac (1780–1847), had again suddenly interjected the Louisiana pretension as an "indispensable preliminary" to settling American claims. After seeming to relent, Polignac repeated the demand on May 20. While refusing both the linkage and the legitimacy of the Louisiana claim, Rives explored informally offering a compensatory benefit in a reduction of U.S. duties on French wines (*HRDoc* 147, 22d Cong., 2d sess., pp. 92–118, Serial 235).

6. The new Mexican minister was José María Tornel y Mendívil (1789–1853).

7. These were Emily and AJ Donelson's children, Mary Rachel (later Mary Emily) Donelson (1829–1905) and Andrew Jackson Donelson (1826–1859).

From Daniel W. Wright, John H. Hand and De La F. Roysdon

Columbus (Miss) July 26th. 1830.

Dear Sir

By the accompanying preamble and Resolutions setting forth the proceedings of a meeting of a large and respectable collection of the Citizens
of this County; you will discover that the undersigned compose a committee, which they respectfully ask you to receive as the only appology for the
present address.

Your Excellency will discover that the object and result of the meeting
was to solicit the exercise of your personal popularity, and just influence; which your high character and personal acquaintance has given
you among the Chiefs, and head-men of the two tribes of Indians; (the
Choctaws & Chickasaws) occupying a large portion of the Territory
embraced within our chartered limits.

The numerous feuds and turmoils which have latterly arisen in the
Choctaw Nation, have assumed an aspect, foreboding of evil, and deliteri-
ous consequences. Between three and seven hundred armed Indians have
within the last ten days been marched by one of their Chiefs, (Greenwood
Leflour) in warlike array from the South Western to the South Eastern
part of their Territory; spreading terror and alarm to their more peaceful
and defenceless brethren, who did not join in the array. The consequences
arising from a procedure of this kind cannot be foretold.

The State of Mississippi has recently made the Indians residing within
her limits Citizens; and divested their Chiefs and headmen of power forever, and yet in defiance of her laws; we find one of their Chiefs daring
enough to arm a force and march in all the terror and parade of war: The
consequence is that the State of Mississippi must succumb and submit to
the outrage of an Indian Chief or assert the supremacy of her laws. This
from present appearances must eventuate in collission and disturbance;
an event greatly to be deprecated, and one which should by all means be
avoided. The only means of obtaining this desired object is to prevail on
them to sell their Country and remove West of the Mississippi.

That you have had many hours of painful reflection on the best means
to be adopted for the peaceful, equitable, and speedy removal of the
Indians within the limits of the States; the Committee have no doubt. If a
person in whom the Indians had implicit confidence; one to whom they
could look as a father and friend were to make propositions of treaty: we
have no doubt but that they would acceed. From our knowledge of the
Indian character, and from their great faith and confidence (in common
with their white brethren) in your wisdom and justice we believe there is

no person whatever who could make with them a treaty so advantageous to the Government, and at the same time so satisfactory to them, as yourself in person. The Indians look upon you as a father and a friend; as a kind of mediator betwen them and the States; your presence would quiet all disturbance and allay all rancorous animosities: and we do not hesitate to say, that should you visit them in person, you could effect a treaty and induce them to remove.

The effectuation of this object by you, would be another great achievement in the cause of humanity, and would add another laurel to your brow—

We therefore in the name of our fellow Citizens; and by all the ties of humanity for those unfortunate beings the Indians, call upon and invite you to come in person and use your endeavors to effect a treaty with them. It is true that a request of this kind is, so far as the committee are informed, unprecedented in the history of our Government; so also is the crisis of Indian political affairs: and from our knowledge of the alacrity with which you discharge every duty for the good of your Country, whether in the Cabinet or in the field; in the Temple of Justice, or in the Indian wigwam, asking for a peaceable cession of his Country: we are not deterred by the novelty of the thing, from making the invitation; but on the contrary, we and our fellow Citizens rely with the utmost confidence on your compliance with the request, should you not be prevented by paramount official duties.

The wise and just policy prescribed by your excellency for the action of the Government towards the Indians, for their removal West of the Mississippi River; is, in the opinion of the Committee, the only course that can be pursued, which will redound to the honour of the American people as a Nation; and in its operation save those unfortunate remnants of a once numerous people from extinction. Think not that we would laud and eulogise any man whose measures were not in strict accordance with our views of a wise and just policy.

The Committee must close this address, which has from the importance of the subject been spun out to too great a length. In conclusion we have to request a speedy answer from your Excellency, informing us of the result of our application—

We have the honor to be with sentiments of great respect and consideration, your Excellency's most Obedient and humble servants—

> D. W. Wright
> J. H. Hand
> De La F Roysdon

P.S. We have no doubt but that the County of Monroe will cooperate with us; so would the State generally; in the foregoing solicitations; but for fear that official duties might call you back to Washington, we have from the exigency of the case thought it best to forward on this communication immediately. We would also here mention, that should your Excellency think proper to come on; if you will inform us of the time, we will do ourselves the honour of waiting on you at the Hermitage, or any other designated point: and escort you to our State—

D. W. W.
J. H. H.
D. F. R.

LS, DNA-RG 107 (M222-28).

[Enclosure]

At a numerous and respectable meeting of the citizens of Lowndes County, (Mississippi), on the 24th. of July Inst, Silas Mc.Bee Esqr. having been called to the chair, and De La F. Roysdon appointed Secretary; Colo. Daniel W. Wright offered the following preamble and resolutions, which were unanimously adopted, viz

Whereas it is understood, that our beloved and highly esteemed fellow-citizen, the Chief Magistrate of the U. States, is at this time, on a visit to the Hermitage, his former place of residence in Tennessee, and knowing that the brightest ornament in his truly illustrious character is his prompt and unwearied attention to any and every service, for the advancement of the interest of our common Country, which may be within his power to effect; And whereas we are aware that the all absorbing subject to the citizens of this State, and the union in general, that of the removal of the Indians, occupying a portion of the Territory within the chartered limits of our State, and sister States, forms a subject of the wisest policy of the present Administration, founded in the truest principles of humanity & philanthropy, towards the Indians, on the part of our beloved President; and whereas, from our intimate knowledge of the Indian character and their present politics, no person will so certainly, we believe, be able to effect the wisely devised policy of the present administration, that of the removal of the Indians by treaty, as the President himself in person;

Therefore, it is resolved, by the unanimous vote of this meeting, that a committee of three citizens be appointed, to visit the President, at the Hermitage, or elsewhere, to confer with him by letter, or in person, and to entreat him by all arguments in their power, to attend the Indians in person, by calling upon the United States' Agents, to cause the reputed Chiefs, head men and warriors, to assemble at some designated point, for the purposes above expressed—

Resolved, that the citizens of our sister County (Monroe) be solicited to assemble, and co-operate, by adopting Similar resolutions.

Whereupon the meeting unanimously appointed Colo. Danl. W. Wright, of Monroe County, Doctor John H. Hand and De La F. Roysdon of Lowndes County, the committee, for the purposes expressed in the above resolutions—When it was resolved that a copy of the foregoing proceedings be forwarded on to the President of the United States, at the Hermitage—

And then the meeting adjourned—

Silas Mc.Bee chm.
De La F. Roysdon secy

DS, DNA-RG 107 (M222-28). Silas McBee (1765–1845) resided in Lowndes County.

Benjamin Lewis Goodman
to Hugh Lawson Montgomery

Head of Pigeon Roost 27th. July 1830

Sir

We the citizens of Georgia who are engaged in the gold digging business in the Cheeorkee nation beg leave to make the following communication (to wit) We are well awar that it is wrong for us to intrude upon the rights of Georgia by digging for gold upon her unappropriated & unsurveyed lands, as we have been doing for some time past & that we of right ought to be stoped   Therefore at the time you visited us, in June last (at your request) we abandoned our searches for gold in the nation and returned to our homes   But finding that your reasonable request and the exertions of Capt Brady had not induced the citizens of other States to abandon their searches we again returned to the nation[1]   And our excuse for thus acting may be found in this   That we believe the soil of the nation and the minerals therein contained properly belong to Georgia and that we have a prospective interest in the same, and that we are more excusable than the citizens from other states or the people of the nation   Therefore we thought while others were grasping after the wealth of our State that we would strive for a part   But Sir notwithstanding all this; we are now willing to abandon our searches for gold again, provided all other persons are compeled to do so—But let it be distinctly understood that if affective means are not adopted to restrain & prohibit all other persons from digging that we will again return with the full determination of being the last to quit the mines upon any subsequent occasion.

~~Therefore~~ It is unanimously Resolved that the foregoing Communication be signed by the Chairman in behalf of the citizens of Georgia present and countersigned by the secretary and forwarded to Col. Hugh Montgomery.

B. L. Goodman
Chairman—
M. H. Gathright Secy.

DS, DLC (38). Benjamin Lewis Goodman (1798–1865) was later an Alabama state legislator. Milton H. Gathright was later a Lumpkin County, Ga., editor and judge.

1. As commander of U.S. troops in the Cherokee Nation, Captain Francis W. Brady was charged with carrying out the War Department's June 26 order to expel gold-seeking intruders.

To William Berkeley Lewis

(Private)

·Franklin July 28th. 1830—

My Dr Major

I reached here on yesterday, and found without the least intimation of it before I set out a large assembledge of people collected to give Major Eaton a barbecue   a committee waited upon me & invited me to the barbecue, which I declined, but agreed after dinner to ride out & shake hands with my old acquaintances neighbours & soldiers—at half past 3 oclock, I rode out, where I met between three & 500 of Major Eatons old neighbours & friends, who greeted me in the most friendly manner—The ladies of the place had received Mrs. Eaton in the most friendly manner, and has extended to her that polite attention due to her.

This is as it should be, and is a severe comment on the combination at Nashville, & will lead to its prostration. Until I got to Tyres Springs I had no conception of the combination & conspiracy to injure & prostrate Major Eaton—and injure me—I see the great Magicians hand in all this—and what mortifies me most is to find that this combination is holding up & making my family the tools to injure me, disturb my administration, & if possible to destroy my friend Major Eaton. This will recoil upon their own heads—but such a combination I am sure never was formed before, and that my Nephew & nece should permit themselves to be held up as the instruments, & *tools*, of such wickedness, is truly mortifying to me—I was pleased to see the marked attention bestowed upon the Major & his family on their journey hither and the secrete plans engendered at the city & concluded here, & practised upon by some of my connections have been frustrated by the independant, & virtuous portion, of this community—but I shall write you on my return to the Hermitage—I have come here to meet Genl. Coffee, who writes me, he will be here to night—after I have an interview with him I shall be able to form some opinion of the course of my connections—mine you know is fixed—with my kind salutations to Major Barry & his family, Kendall & his, & all my friends, with the request that you write to Mr Van Buren, that I am in ordinary health, will write him soon

I bid you for the present adieu[.] yr friend

Andrew Jackson

ALS and Copy, NN (16-0061).

From James Alexander Hamilton

New York July 29th 1830

My dear Sir,

I learned with very great pleasure from your letter of the 12t received on the 27t Inst, that you was in good health at home where all things were found by you in good order—I could well conceive from what I had before observed on a former & some what different occasion that you would be harrassed by the Crowds of persons who would interrupt your passage home—

I have for some days past contemplated writing to you in relation to our affairs as connected with events and opinions abroad but I have been prevented from doing so by ~~the~~ my continued engagements in Court which have only ceased to day

An English Newspaper If I can obtain it (containing a discussion of our ~~intention~~ Policy in intending to obtain The Texas) will accompany this letter and as soon as I have leasure I will do myself the pleasure to communicate to you the views which this discussion has presented to my mind—

I forwarded to Mr Van Buren yesterday a letter from Constantinople in which Mr Rhind informed him that he had signed a Treaty with The Porte thus puting the last hand to this business

From a letter I have received from McLean I have reason to fear unless The Late act of Congress in relation to our navigation with the Colonies shall work a Change with the English Ministry that he will not be successful —much is to be hoped from that *act*—

Duff Green has published The first Branch of the Criticism on Mc Duffies Bank Puff & since that has filled his paper with The Report itself[1]

Among other Changes required at washington It is indispensably necessary that The administration should change its *official organ*—The announcement of this Treaty with The Turk ought to be made in a manner which would give your administration the credit it deserves by contrasting your success & the means you have employed with the meanes & unsuccessful efforts of your Predecessor & yet I venture to say The General will merely announce the fact—

In the hope of writing to you again in a few days I close this hasty letter by wishing you all health & happiness[.] Your sincere friend

James A Hamilton

ALS, DLC (38).

1. The *Telegraph* ran the first installment of Hamilton's critique of McDuffie's Bank report on June 30 and the second on August 14.

To Samuel Delucenna Ingham

Hermitage july 31rst. 1830

My Dr. Sir

yours of the 17th. instant with its enclosures ~~are~~ is just recd. Being advised by yours of the resignation of Leonard jarvis of the office of Collector of Passamoquoddy, I hasten to enclose you a commission for James W Ripley to fill the vacancy occasioned by the Resignation of Mr L Jarvis, which you will please forward as early as possible to Mr Ripley.

I have read Mr Henshaws letter on the subject of the Light Houses, & shoals, with attention. it affords a good comment on the loose Legislation of Congress, and confirms me in the propriety of withholding my approval from the Light House bill as presented to me.

I regret to hear that the new law in relation to the customs gave trouble, and that N.Y. should give more, I hope the customs House officers are not aiding in creating dificulties, should this be; there are remedies.

Before the receipt of yours I was fully advised by letters from Mr Gowen & others of the excitement attempted to be created on the pardon of Wilson—I am well advised that Mr Gowen and Mr Dallas acted well their part to keep & put it down whilst others, from whom, every aid was expected to maintain order & aid in the execution of the law ~~and order~~ and keeping down improper excitement, was silent, if not secretely exciting the tumult. These excitements produced for political effect, without any just ground to sustain ~~it~~ them, will always recoil upon the heads of their ~~originators~~ authors. a review of this case.[1] I feel justified on every principle of justice & good faith in yielding to the various petitions in favour of the pardon of Wilson, & was it now to do, with a knowledge of all the excitement that has been created, I would ~~now~~ pardon him, regardless of the consequences—This excitement, because two was not hung instead of one cannot be based on philanthopry & justice. The one to whom executive clemency was extended was young & his confession ellicited on a promise that it should not be used against him—contrary to this, ~~being~~ he was convicted upon ~~it~~ his own confession The justice, & dignity & good faith of the Government required that he should not be ~~punished~~ put to death on his own confession thus ~~acquired~~ ellicited—his life was spared—The other an old offender—who had confessed the commission of two of the most cruel & cold blooded murders ever committed & this for base lucre—the frequency of crime required an example, & Porter presented a fit subject, & the law was permitted to take its course— was there any cause here for excitement—still much has been made out of it, but it will soon die with its political exciters & be buried with them in oblivion

I sincerely regret to read of the bad health of your children but hope they are recovered & that you & your family enjoy health²—mine has been a little checkered from bad colds—but still I am in travelling condition & my colds better. I am waiting in daily expectation of hearing from the Indians—should the agents of the opposition prevail in preventing them from coming in we have prepared ~~& sent them~~ an address assuring them, that the Executive will now leave them to themselfs ~~& to chance;~~ ~~& congress to give them~~ that the Executive has made his last offer &c &c & I will set out forthwith for the city—Major Donelson his lady & Miss Eastin are well & join in kind respects to you your Lady & family, to whom present me respectfully and believe me yr most obt. Servt

A. J.

ALS draft, DLC (38).
1. This phrase is inserted above the line.
2. Ingham and his wife Deborah Kay Hall Ingham (1796–1862) had three young daughters.

From Felix Grundy

Nashville, July 31st 1830—

Dear General,

During this week, I have been anxious to hear of your return from Franklin, that I might go to the Hermitage and see you—On yesterday I heard of your return and prepared to set out, but am disappointed, it is out of my power to do so—

I wished among other things to communicate to you all the intelligence I have received respecting the effects of the Veto to the Maysville road Bill—I find, that in New Hampshire & Maine, the strenth of the Administration is increased by it—In Pensylvania it has done no harm   In Newyork it has given strength—In Ohio & Kentuckey, no satisfactory opinion can be formed—In Maryland, it has operated both ways—On the Eastern shore, the effects are beneficial, not so in the Western parts—Taking the whole South, there is scarcely any opposition to it—The result of the matter in my mind is, that altho your friends ~~are~~ may not be numerically increased, their attattchment is now of a stronger texture—formerly it consisted in a degree in an affection for the man and an admiration of his character & public services and confidence in his virtues—Now is added, an adherence to political republican principles; the former are very good recommendations to get a man into office, the latter the safest reliance for him when in—If your friends can only be kept from differing among themselves, so as not to give fresh hopes to the opposition, I am persuaded, nothing is to be feared, and no opponent will present himself at the next election—*To my certain knowledge*, the calculation of your enemies is in a scism among your friends, and the least appearance of that will give them courage; at present they are perfectly at fault, and cannot tell what to do—Since I had my conversation with you—I have reflected very much upon the political condition and prospects of our Country and I verily believe that the present contest for principle is to decide for many years to come the fate of our Institutions; If the Government can be brought back to its true principles all is well—If not we are on the high way to ruin—your reelection, I do not consider a matter of any consequence to your personally—but it is of deep concern to the Country, and the principles you advocate—

I am anxious to learn what is doing in the way of negociation with the Indians, but shall see Majr Eaton on Monday at the Franklin Circuit Court—and shall then learn what may be proper to be known—I shall be to see you so soon as I can return from Franklin and If I can be of any service to you, will return at any time—

I have looked closely into the proceedings at the public dinners &c. and can discover no signs of an opposing Candidate from among your late supporters—& in Charlestown (S C) all seem to wish your reelection—

I am told Genrl. Coffee is with you, give him my best respects, and shew him this letter—yr friend

Felix Grundy

P S—I have seen Isacks and conversed with him on the subject of Internal improvements—and what should be his course in future—I think he will do right, that is, he will not surrender his old opinions, but will not agree to harrass the Executive of his choice, with Bills which cannot be signed—this is all that need be asked of him—and I hope he will do so—he became very sick while I was at Winchester, which prevented me from another conversation—[1]

Gr

ALS, DLC (38). Grundy (1777–1840) was a Nashville lawyer and U.S. senator from Tennessee, elected in 1829 to fill John Eaton's vacated seat.

1. Jacob C. Isacks (1767–1835), of Winchester, was a Tennessee congressman. An advocate of federal internal improvements, he had voted to override the Maysville Road veto.

August

From Cornplanter

Kenzua Warren County Pennsva. th 2 Augst 1830

Father for by that name I always address the President

It is now many years since I sold most of my lands to my white Brothers and by sundry regulations we have annually received Six Thousand Dollars and in 1828 not receiving our Money in due time we prevailed on our Agent to go to Washington and the then Secretary of War informed us that it was the intention of the President that we should receive Six thousand Dollars annually & we felt satisfied that we should have justice done us,[1] but in 1829 we received none at all but we were told that we could have 2,500 Dollars but if we received that we should get no more for that year and now in 1830 we are told by the Indian agent that we can have but 3,000 Dollars & if we take that we can get no more for this year and it fills our minds with concern that we cannot get our Money nor be informed why we should not receive as in former years

Father I am anxious to know from you for to ease my own mind and that of my Nation the reason that our Money has become almost nothing

Father I am Old and my time here cannot be long and I have a great desire to see my People in peace & to cultivate their land in quietness when we received all our Money it was but a little but it enabled us to purchase Salt & some Blankets and that would be a great help to those who are active & till their land

Father I am very Old having seen the frost and Snow of almost a hundred Winters and cannot expect to act as a head Man but a little while and I hope you will be pleased to let me know from your own hand what we are to expect hereafter in regard to our Money so that our minds may be at rest and to know how much we are to receive and the probable time we are to receive it

Father I have almost done and I hope you will not neglect to attend to and answer a poor Old Indian who has been once a Warrior and now feels that he is a poor dependant being

Father I have done all but hoping the Great Spirit will be pleased to Smile on you and that you may smoke the Pipe of Peace the remainder of your days.

John his X mark Obail
known by the Name of Cornplanter
head chief of the Seneca Nation

Father I almost forgot to mention that I think that I ought to have some compensation for all the trouble I have for the Nation the sum to be taken out of the annuity

DS, DNA-RG 75 (M234-808). The celebrated Seneca chief Cornplanter, or John O'Bail (c1750–1836), lived near Kinzua Creek on a tract deeded him by the state of Pennsylvania in 1791. With AJ and Eaton absent, acting Secretary of War Philip G. Randolph replied to Cornplanter on September 2. Randolph recounted the history of the Seneca annuity (above, pp. 40–41), offered payments for 1829 and 1830 of $3,385.60, representing the fund's current yield, and remarked the president's inability, despite his good will, to make up the deficiency in the accustomed $6,000 without the consent of Congress (DNA-RG 75, M21-7).

1. On June 5, 1828, Indian superintendent McKenney had notified Seneca subagent Jasper Parrish (1767–1836) that the annuity would likely be reduced to match the fund's dwindling return. Parrish protested for the Senecas on July 26, and on September 25, after consulting then-Secretary of War Peter Buell Porter (1773–1844), McKenney pledged the full $6,000 for 1828 and future years—a decision that AJ later reversed as unsanctioned by law (DNA-RG 75, M21-4, M234-808, M21-5).

To John Henry Eaton

Private & for your own eye.

Hermitage August 3rd. 1830—

My Dear Major

I send my son to meet you at Judge Overtons, and to conduct you and your lady with our other friends to the Hermitage where you will receive that heartfelt welcome that you were ever wont to do, when my Dr departed wife was living—her absence makes every thing here wear to me a gloomy & malancholy aspect, but the presence of her old & sincere friend will cheer me amidst the malancholy gloom with which I am surrounded.

My neighbours & connections will receive you & your Lady with that good feeling that is due to you; and I request you & your Lady will meet them with your usual courtesy, which is so well calculated to gain universal applause even from enemies, & the united approbation of all friends— Our enemies calculate much upon injuring me, by raising the cry, that I had forced A. J. Donelson from me, & compelled him to retire, because he would not yield to my views, which they call improper; I mean to be able to shew that I only claimed to rule my Houshold, that it should extend justice & common politeness to all & no more, & thus put my enemies in the wrong, and if my friends desert me that it is theirs, not my fault.

Genl Coffee has, since here, produced a visable, & sensible change in my connections, & they will all be here to receive you and your Lady, who I trust will meet them with her usual courtesy & if a perfect reconciliation cannot take place, that harmony may prevail, and a link broken in the Nashville conspiracy—

I trust you are aware that I will never abandon you or seperate from you, so long as you continue to practise those virtues that have always accompanied you, nor would I ask you, or any friend to pursue a course to compromit, or be degrading to themselves, or feelings—but I am anxious that we pursue such a course as will break down the Nashville combination, which I view as the sprouts of the Washington conspiracy—This effected, and we have a peaceful administration, and when we have waded thro' our official Labours, a calm retirement. I wish us also to heap coals upon the heads of our enemies, by returning good for evil. When I see, I have much to say to you—I have recd. letters from Major Haley & Peachlynn & a string of resolutions from the citizens of Mississippi all of which will be presented to you when here   with my compliments to your Lady [Dr.] B.[1] & his, I am in haste yr friend

Andrew Jackson

ALS, DLC (38).
    1. Eaton's brother-in-law, Edward Breathitt.

From Friedrich List

Philadelphia August 4. 1830.

Sir

Desirous to serve this my adopted country I had composed the annexed article with the intention of communicating a french translation of it to the editor of the revue encyclopedique when it occurred to me that it might promote the public interest in a more effectual manner if I would communicate it at first privately to your Excellency.

I hope my good intentions will excuse the liberty I have thus taken in case it should be found deficient of merit.

The printed sheets containing the first chapter of a criticism of the different systems of political economy which I have at present under press I take the liberty to enclose because the matter contained in it has in many respects reference to the subjects treated in the essay.

I am with sincere veneration Your Excellencys most obedient and humble servant

Frederick List

[Endorsed by AJ:] Frederick List—on the commerce between France & U.S. sends a communication on the subject of a commercial Treaty with France—

ALS, DLC (38). List (1789–1846) was a German-born political economist. In March 1831 the *Revue Encyclopedique* published his "Idées sur des Réformes Économiques, Commerciales et Politiques, Applicables à la France," promoting railroad development and Franco-American trade. List sought a consular appointment from AJ on October 20 (below).

John Henry Eaton to John Donly

Hermitage Davidson 4th. augst. 1830
Wednesday

Sir

Last evening I recd. your letter from Columbus   In answer I have to request that you will remain & attend the council on the 10th., and exert yourself to induce the Chactaws to meet the President; and arrange upon some plan for their departure west of the Mississippi. Their *interest, happiness, peace* and prospects depends upon their ~~choice~~ course. A great deal has been said and explained to them on this subject, and I forbear to say more.

To enable them to remove, & comfortably to arrange themselves at their new homes, Congress has done much in the liberal appropriations they have made. It was a measure the President sought to effect, because he was satisfied that the Indians could not possibly dwell under the laws of the state. If now they shall refuse to accept the liberal terms which are offered, they only, must be liable for whatever troubles and difficulties may arise. The President will feel a consciousness that he has done, all he could for his red children; and if any failure of his good intention arises, it will be attributable to their want of duty to themselves, not to him. The President requests that you will remain & attend the council & explain fully every thing as you have been instructed. He wishes nothing of concealment to be practiced, but a full and fair explanation of every thing to be made. Those people sent a treaty to Washington: the senate refused it, & rightfully; for they asked too much. The President is now near them agreably to their wishes as expressed through their agent Mgr. Haley, having previously sent word by the bearer of that treaty (Mgr Haley) that he would be here, & confer with his Chactaw children, if they would come. But it seems, they are not willing; what then is he to believe, but that their whole design in sending Mgr. Haley on to Washington, was but mere pretence; and a disposition on their part to impose on their great father? It can be nothing else; and he can consider it in no other light—If they were sincere, they would not hesitate to meet him and asuage all difficulties—

Their great father is resolved, that if they now refuse, he will trouble them no more, but leave them to remove or not as they please, & when they please and at their own expense. If they believe they can live under the laws of Mississippi, he is perfectly willing they should do so; but should they find they cannot, & become desirous to seek a new home, let them understand, that they must seek it as they can, & in their own way; for no other application will be made to them for a treaty—If they will not listen and be advised, be all the consequences which may follow on themselves.

Soon as you shall ascertain that they are resolved to refuse the offers sent them; and to live under the laws of Mississippi; write me; for we are anxious to prepare for a return to Washington; & to have this buisness ended in some way

To the Chactaws tell these things candidly and freely, for we have no desire but to tell them the naked truth—very respectfully

J. H. Eaton

P.S. We must leave here by the 10th. of Sept.

Copy, DLC (38). Donly replied to Eaton on August 14 that Choctaws of the Southern District had not attended his August 10 meeting, and that confusion and division reigned generally among them. Still all the Choctaws seemed ready to treat for removal, but they were afraid to venture off their own ground. Donly recommended that Eaton and John Coffee come to them as commissioners (DNA-RG 75, M234-169).

To John Pitchlynn

[Words in italic brackets are insertions by Eaton.]

Hermitage August 5th. 1830—

Dr Sir

your letter of the 24th. of july has just been received. I would have been happy to have seen you at Nashville and ~~have~~ received your views as it regards the permanent settlement of the choctaws west of the Mississippi. I am aware of your friendship for them & the great anxiety you have for their future welfare; but great as I know it *[to be]*, it cannot be more so than mine. At the request of their confidential agent, Major Haley, who communicated to me the great desire the choctaw chiefs had to see me, & enter into arrangements ~~with them~~ to surrender their possessessions ~~where they now are~~, & remove across the Missisipi to the country provided for them, *[& at his suggestion that the desired to see me,]* that they had great confidence ~~in me~~ that I would do them liberal Justice, ~~that~~ I am now here to meet *[& to confer with them]* their chiefs, agreably to the promise made

· 465 ·

to Major Haley, ~~that at the requests of the chiefs, made thro him~~   The Secretary of War & myself ~~would~~ *[are here ready to]* meet them in the neighbourhood of Franklin. ~~We have been here since the 6th. of July, and have as yet~~ *[Of this they have for some time past been informed, & as yet we have]* heard nothing from them of a positive character. Whether they chiefs are comming to meet us or not *[we are not certainly advised.]* our official business urges a return to the city of Washington & we cannot stay much longer here to meet them. We therefore request that you will make known to them that we are now ~~here~~ *[present]* awaiting there arrival agreeably to my promise to their confidential agent Major Haley   I beg of you to say to them, that their *interest happiness* peace & prosperity depends upon their removal beyond the jurisdiction of the laws of the State of Mississippi. These things have been *[often times]* explained to them fully and I forbear to repeat ~~them~~; but request that you make known to them that Congress to enable them to remove & comfortably to arrange themselves at their new homes has made liberal appropriations. It was a measure I had much at heart & sought to effect because I was satisfied that the Indians could not possibly live under the laws of the States. If now they shall refuse to accept the liberal terms offered, they only must be liable for whatever evils & dificulties may arise. I feel conscious of having done my duty to my red children and if any failure of my good intention arises, it will be attributable to their want of duty to themselves, not to me.

~~I enclose you a letter which~~ I have directed the Secretary of war to write *[you fully & finally on this subject so important to the interest of the Choct]* make it known to my red children—and tell them to listen well to it—it comes from a friend and the last time I shall adress them on the subject should the chiefs fail to meet us now. I am your friend

A. J

ALS draft, DLC (38).

John Henry Eaton to John Pitchlynn

Nashville 5th. Aug. 1830

Friend and brother

The President has sent Magr. Donnelly to see you, and this day has instructed me again to write to him, and direct him soon as possible to see the Chactaws and explain fully every thing to them. It is time this buisness was in some way concluded   The President having the great and numerous affairs of the country to attend to cannot give his consideration time after time to the affairs of his red children, especially when they shew no disposition to receive and reguard his advice. Before he left Washington the friend and agent of your people, Magr. Halley suggested that the chiefs of the Chactaw would gladly avail themselves of the opportunity afforded them by his visit to Tennessee to meet him and arrange all things as to a removal; but now that he has come, it appears they are indisposed to do so.

Have your people looked to all the consequences of a refusal? The laws of Mississipi are to constitute the rule of Indian action for the future, & your great father will not interfere to prevent this, because he has no right no authority to do so. What then? Can you live under these laws, and be governed by them? You all know that you cannot. In this situation, with the sanction of Congress, your great father approaches and tells you, to go, for your peace and happiness depends upon it, That he will treat with you upon liberal terms, and giving you absolute title to a country, larger than the one you have, & of better soil, place you in a situation where being out of a state; and where no state will ever be formed, you will find happiness and be able to live under your own laws. The means are within his reach too of paying the expences of the removal, & supporting your people for a year until their crops can be grown. And will you pass all these advantages by? Reccollect that a little longer delay on your part may place it out of the power of the President to extend this kindness to you, and should this be the case, do not omit to bear in mind that the fault is all the Chactaws.

Justice and truth demands him to say and let it be explained to the nation, that he will no more trouble himself to render his Chactaw children happy on this subject. He has earnestly besought them to be so, & to remove, because, he foresaw that surrounded by the whites, & made subject to their laws a miserable state of ~~things~~ being was before them. If now they respect his offers, & refuse to act, he will interfere no more, but leave them to remain where they are; & when they shall find they cannot do so in peace, they must go, as they can, & at their own expense to their new homes. He will feel it to be his duty at the next Congress to say, that he has pursuded his Indian friends to remove and be happy; but they will not;[1] & to recommend accordingly that all appropriation be withdrawn, & they left to find their new homes as they can. Say these things to them, that they may understand, truly what their situation is—respectfully

J. H Eaton

LS draft, DLC (38).
1. From here on the writing is in Eaton's hand.

To *Samuel Delucenna Ingham*

Hermitage August 7th 1830

My Dr. Sir

I have received yours without date acknowledging The receipt of mine of the 9th ult; I am happy to learn that the Scentific men of our day, have turned their attention and skill, to the invention of something, that will prevent the calamities of Steam boat explosions. I sincerely hope that it may be rimedied, and Mr. Neville will be able to afford you important information on this subject, and that you may be able to lay before Congress such information as will lead to an efficient remedy.

I am happy to learn that you will have it in your power to restore the Custom House to the confidence of the Country.—but regret that our revenue is falling off a little, we must pay the National Debt and remedy this defect by economy, and apply the whole ammount applicable to its payment, I wish you to have an eye constantly to this subject.

I am awaiting the movements of the Indians. Their grand and last Council are to be held on the 10 inst, when we will be informed whether The Cheifs will *meet us* or *not*, The moment That I am informed *They will not.* we will set out on our return to the City, and reach there as early as possible. If the Cheifs agree to come in, we will have to wait their arrival, & conclude a Treaty with them, after which with all haste we will repair to Washington. I regret to hear of the illness of Majr Graham, & pray for his speedy recovery.

I inclosed sometime since the Commission for Ripley as Collector for Passamaquaddy—with my respects to your family & all other friends believe me, yours Respectfully &c

Andrew Jackson

LS, NIC (16-0075). ALS draft (at August 1), DLC (38).

To *William Berkeley Lewis*

Hermitage August 7th. 1830

My Dr Sir

your letters of the 23rd. & 25th. ult. has just been recd with their inclosures—having *duly noted their contents*, I have it only in my power to say that I hope all things will be well—I shall have no female family in the city ~~this~~ the ensuing winter, Mrs. D. remains with her widowed mother—and it is probable Mrs. Eaton may remain with her mother, if not until next Spring, *at least*, to January or February next.[1] Whether Mr Donelson will or will not accompany me to the city has not as yet been determined on by him, whether he will leave his wife & little ones to whom he is greatly attached, he will determine today or tomorrow.

As you observe they dificulty has been created by those from whom I had a right to expect better things—but we cannot get back, we must now look forward, and all friends will unite in admonishing all concerned from imprudent acts, of every kind   My feelings have been much coroded here; I found the combination of Washington, to have extended itself here, & in *Nashville*, a full combination that none of the Ladies were to visit Mrs. E.—Mrs. Stuart, Mrs. Hall & a few others waited upon her as she passed, the Major having reached Nashville late, & set out for Franklin in a hack early next morning, where Mrs. E was met by all the ladies in the place with open arms, *but one—*

Mrs. & Major Eaton with judge Overton & his Lady, Mrs Stuart & Mrs. Judge Barker of N York, & the Miss Bradfords, has just left me. The dined with me on wednesday, with all the ladies in this neighbourhood, Mrs. Genl Overton of the number.[2] I have a hope that the Ladies will remain here this winter, & surely the vindictive persecution will cease, and the contempt of the pious & good, will frown it down. Genl Coffee is now here, is himself, has perfectly accorded with me in my course—

I have to assure you that there has been thro some channel the most foul & extraordinary combination formed here—The, *Idoll*, as Mr Hill would say, is the great magician that has worked the wires, and some of the military & others the machines—I will purge the military in due time, of all its unworthy members.

I have had a great deal of company & must close—will write you from Franklin where I will be next week at *large*

We are awaiting the final result of the choctaws, there last, & *general* council on the 10th instant—Donelly is awaiting the result, & will communicate it without delay, & if they decline coming in, we will set out without delay to the city—present my respects to judge Barrien, & say to him I have recd. his several communications & am awaiting further advices from Georgia before I write him—I would by to days mail have wrote him, but have not time, the correspondence with the chiefs occupy every moment I have from company—present me affectionately to the heads of Departments & of Bureaus, and write Mr Van Buren the prospects I have given you & say why I have not written him oftener was, that I had nothing either positive, or pleasant to communicate, but that I have much to say to him, & information to give, that will astonish him as much as it has me—but I think I have arrested the sting from the adder—

With my best regard to Mary Ann believe me your friend

Andrew Jackson

ALS and Copy, NN (16-0081).

1. Mrs. D. and her mother were Emily Tennessee Donelson and Mary Purnell Donelson. Margaret Eaton's parents lived in Washington. AJ meant her mother-in-law, Elizabeth Eaton, who lived in Franklin.

2. John Overton's wife was Mary McConnell White May Overton (1782–1862). Annache Livingston Barker (1792–1865) was the wife of Pierre Augustus Barker (1790–1870) of Buffalo.

To *William Berkeley Lewis*

Nashville August 10th 1830—

Dr. Major

Genl Daniel S. Donelson goes on to Washington in company with Mr. Mc.Lamore. I have requested whilst in the city that they make our House their home—you will therefore cause the servants, & stewart, to attend & provide for them. I request that you will kindly attend to them

I refer you to the Genl & Mr. McLamore for the news of this country. I am on my way to Franklin to arrange matters for a meeting with the choctaw chiefs who I expect in shortly, if *they come to meet me*—This day their general council in the nation is to be held, & our agent is there awaiting their final answer. Should they conclude not to come in & meet me, I shall set out in a few days on my return to the city. so soon as I am advised of the result of the council I will write you.

Present me to all the heads of Departments, & Bureaus with their families—say to Kendal that his reply to King has given satisfaction to all, that he was rightfully removed, respectfully yr. friend

Andrew Jackson

ALS, NNPM; Copy, NN (16-0091). On June 23 the *US Telegraph* published a response by removed Norfolk navy agent Miles King to the May 27 Navy Department report on his accounts. King denied any wrongdoing and charged the administration with incompetence and malicious persecution. Amos Kendall replied in the *Telegraph* of July 15 with a review of King's accounts to show that his charges to the Treasury were so irregular, extravagant, and disregardful of law as to "imperiously require" his removal.

From *John Macpherson Berrien*

Washington 10th August 1830—

Dear Sir,

Having received no answer to the several letters, which I have addressed to you, I am fearful I may be intruding upon your time, perhaps already too much occupied with more important matters. Yet it seems to me to be my duty to submit the enclosed letter to your perusal, as I believe the writer to be both zealous and discreet. It is accordingly transmitted.

I have concluded also to send to you a letter received from Gov: Gilmer, as it may be desirable to you, to know his views at this moment—[1]

After consultation with Major Barry and an examination of documents, a statement in relation to the pardon of Wilson was inserted in the Telegraph—[2]

I hope your health continues good—with my compliments to your family, I am respectfully Dear Sir your friend & st

Jno. Macpherson Berrien

ALS, NjP (16-0090).

1. Gilmer wrote Berrien on July 5, 1830. He condemned William Wirt's "most wicked and selfish attempt to embarrass the Administration" and warned of "disastrous consequences necessarily flowing" should the Supreme Court intrude into Georgia's dispute with the Cherokees. Gilmer applauded the measures taken by federal troops, and also detailed his own, to interdict intrusions and head off confrontations between whites and Indians in the gold country while avoiding any action that could give ground for judicial intervention (DNA-RG 107, M222-27).

2. The item, entitled "Wilson the Mail Robber," ran in the *US Telegraph* on August 4. It explained that AJ had pardoned George Wilson on account of his youth and inexperience in crime, his full confession and Christian penitence, and the "earnest supplications" of his mother, sister, distinguished clergymen, officers of justice, and hundreds of disinterested citizens. James Porter's case, by contrast, lacked a "single alleviating circumstance." He was the ringleader and a hardened violent criminal; he showed no penitence or remorse, but spurned and mocked Christian counsel; and his appeal was backed by few. The article cited the June 14 date on Wilson's pardon to disprove the story that AJ had given Barry a blank pardon, to have the name decided once he reached Philadelphia.

[Enclosure: Andrew Dunlap to Berrien]

Boston August 4th 1830.

Dear Sir,

I have just been informed that, the District Judge of New-Hampshire is dead. It is of consequence to the friends of the Administration in New England; who are increasing in strength constantly, that a firm, and faithful friend of the Administration, possessing the confidence of the firm, and faithful friends of the Administration in this part of the Country should be appointed, it also of consequence that he should be a man of honourable principles; and respectable talents and attainments, and it is also of great consequence, that there be no more rejections of nominations for the "Granite State." Now to produce a good result, all which is necessary, is that proper time should be taken, and my object in addressing this letter to you, is, to ask you to exert your influence to secure, the taking of ample time for examination and deliberation, so that no mistake may be made. The friends of the Administration, here in New England, particularly the lawyers, have much to contend with, for it is a regular system of our opponents to underrate our abilities and qualifications and as we have all the Senators from New England, except Mr Woodbury opposed to us, there is great necessity for caution and deliberation. There is no need of any haste in this business, for during something like three years, the late judge has been so entirely incompetent, that he has not held a Court, and the little business in his Court, has been according to the Statute, certified into the Circuit Court, and it has produced no inconvenience in that State.

As this question is interesting to *all* the friends of the Administration in *New England*, and it is of great importance to our cause throughout the *whole of this part of the Country*, that we have no more rejections of New-England appointments, nearly all of which, have been, and will be furiously opposed, by those who think it doing God service to calumniate and injure all, who are not their partizans and tools. I have taken the liberty, without having any wishes of my own, in relation to any particular individual, respectfully to suggest a hope, that the appointment may be delayed, till there can be the most full examination had, and the best selection made[.] I am Sir with the highest respect your obt servt

Andrew Dunlap

[Endorsed by AJ:] Mr. Barien—answered by Major Eaton—

ALS, DLC (38). Andrew Dunlap (1794–1835) was the U.S. district attorney for Massachusetts. John Samuel Sherburne (1757–1830), U.S. district judge for New Hampshire since 1804, died August 2. On November 2 AJ appointed New Hampshire governor Matthew Harvey to replace him. The Senate confirmed Harvey in December.

Mushulatubbe and Nitakechi to John Henry Eaton

August the 10th. 1830 C Nation

Friend and Brother.

Sir your letter of the 24th. of July has been Recd. we have had it Read and Interpreted to us we have appointed a General Council for the Chiefs and head men of the Chocktaw Nation to meet on the 15th. Inst. to have your ~~by~~ Communication sent by Mr. Donnolley Read and Interpreted when we will prepare ourselves to go on to meet our Father the president we Intend to go on with all powers from our Nation to act and Transact business for the Nation but whither Clothed with full powers or not we are Determined to go on to see our Father the president agreable to his wishes we shall set out Immediately after our Council is over we are your friends and Brothers

Mushuletubbee Chief N East Destrict
Netuckeche Chief South Destrict Choctaw Nation

P S Our Council Could have been on the Ninth but through some mistake or bad management of the Agent it was posponed till the fifteenth the particulars of which we can tell you when we see you—

DS, DLC (38).

To Hardy Murfree Cryer

Judge Overtons
August 11th. 1830—

My Dr. Sir

When last at my House I did intend to pay you the ballance on account of mares, say $21 or thereabouts, but my mind being drew to some other object, you left me without my recollecting it—expecting to have seen you, & your Lady at my House, I did not send it by the boy that carried the note to you—I am anxious to see you before I leave the country when the ballance on above account shall be paid you, or I will remit it agreable to any directions you may please to give.

I am on my way to Franklin where the necessary arrangements will be made for the reception of the choctaw chiefs if they come in—yesterday was their final council in the nation on this subject, & our agent is there awaiting their determination, who, will in a few days communicate to us the result; should they decline coming to see me, I will forthwith set out for the city, I shall return to the Hermitage next sunday, & if you could meet me there on sunday night, it would afford me great pleasure, or on monday—where I may be after that, I cannot now say, as I have all my private concerns to attend to, & arrange before I leave the country—

With my best wishes for yr health & happiness & that of your amiable family I am yr friend

Andrew Jackson

ALS, THi (16-0096).

From John Pitchlynn

Chocktaw Nation.
Augst 11th. 1830.

Dear Friend

The communications bearing date of the 24th. of July last which was sent by the Secretary of War, to the chiefs Mashulatubbee and Nitokgachee; and the seperate one to myself, was in due time handed to me by Maj. Donelly—I immediately forwarded the letter which was directed to the chiefs, which was interpreted to them by Mr. Mackey the other interpreter for the U.S. This was the first news they had received on the subject. The Agent had, to be sure, told them at the Annuity ground on the fifteenth of the last month (July) that he held a communication to the chiefs from their father the President; the reading of which was defered until the hurry of the annuity should subside. as soon as the Annuity was distributed the chiefs called on the Agent for the communication, informing him that they were then ready to attend to it. The Agent informed them that he had handed it to Laflour. The chiefs were somewhat displeased at this— and observed that they would not go to Laflour to get news from the President. There were some other careless remarks made about it and the matter dropped without further investigation.

To the careless treatment of your first communication must in part be attributed the delay of the delegation; for immediately on receiving the communication which was directed to the chiefs of the republican party by the Secretary of War, they proceeded to call a council, which from the scattered situation of our people could not be effected to hold the appearance of a national council sooner than the ninth of the present month. The chiefs of the republican party are determined to see their father the President they are desirous of being clothed with proper authority to treat should a reasonable offer be made them; And these powers cannot be vested in any other way but in national council

We could easily have had the council on the 9th. but unfortunately the Agent was somewhere in the neighborhood of columbus on business of his own when he received the communication from the secretary of war, and could not, or did not attend to it till six days after the chiefs and myself had received letter of the same date. To these facts must be attributed the delay. For I am certain, that, had the first letter which was sent to our Agent have been interpreted at the time of our meeting at the factory, which was on the 14th. of last month; the delegation would now have been on their way to Tennessee—

We have now, however, got matters in a proper train and as soon as it can possibly be effected we will be at the place appointed by our father the President.

It would not be amiss here to inform you that the Agent appointed a meeting at Wilson's on the 10th (yesterday) But that place is in Laflour's district, and as he keeps an armed fource of seven or eight hundred men continually about him, the chiefs of the republican party would not meet at that place.

The chiefs of the republican party, from the communication addressed to them by the Secretary of War; had appointed a meeting to be held on the 9th, at the house of the old chief Mashulatubbee. But when the Agent returned and made an appointment for a meeting at another place, to be on the day after the appointment at Mashulatubbee's, for the purpose of giving the people an oppertunity of attending both councils, it was thought proper to withdraw the order for the meeting at Mashulatubbee's and set it on the fifteenth at another place more centrical to the popelation of the two districts. Unfortunately for our nation there are two distinct parties amongst us, one, tho' it is a disgrace to the name is called the christian party—the Other the republicans—Laflour is the chief of the former party, and as the Agent has gone amongst them with the Secretary's commucation it is very likely that there will be a delegation from them, which I hope may be the case; as by that means the nation will be fully represented when the delegation from the republican party comes on, which at farthest will not be more than five days behind them.

All these things I thou't it my duty to communicate to you, that you might be fully apprised of what is going on in our devoted country; and that you may not be deceived by misrepresentation; for it is more than likely that Laflour, ~~and his party~~ will represent his party as a national delegation, which I sincerely hope will not be regarded as such by your excellency.

I could not attend the council at Wilson's on account of bad health—I shall endeavour to attend the council on the fifteenth—and shall accompany the delegation to Franklin if Possible—Mr. Mackey is doing all he can to bring the thing about, and will also accompany the delegation—I am dear sir, as ever Your friend and Brother

John Pitchlynn

LS, DLC (38).

Benjamin Franklin Reynolds to John Henry Eaton

Chickasaw Agency
11th. August 1830

Dear Sir

I arived at the council house on the 9th Inst and found that the chiefs had dispersed and could only learn that Col. Foster had been with them and that they had concluded to meet the President and yourself at franklin Ten. but not meeting with any of the Chiefs I have not been able to learn particulars as respects there feelings in regard to an exchange of countrys. Pitman Colbert informed me on my way to this place that four from each district was appointed to meet the President and would be at this place on tomorrow evening on their way and expected to get their horses shod

I am prepareing for them and will use every exertion to expedite them on their way   Colbert also informed me that the Chiefs expected me to conduct them to Franklin which servis I am ready to perform. Indians are slow in their movements but so soon as I can get them off I will advise you of the day they will be at Franklin

I have depossited the Anuity at Col. George Colberts in the care of the Sub Agent who will keep it in charge untill my return beleaveing it to be the best disposition I could make of it as it could not be paid out untill the return of the Chiefs[.][1] With greate respect your Obt Srvt

Benjn. Reynolds

ALS, DLC (38). Reynolds (1788–1843) was agent to the Chickasaws.
1. The Colberts were a leading Chickasaw family. George Colbert (c1764–1839) was a trader and Pitman (c1797–1853) was his adopted son. John L. Allen was the subagent.

To Martin Van Buren

Franklin Tennessee
august 12th. 1830—

My Dr. Sir

Being here on a visit to Major Eaton & to make arrangements for the meeting with the chiefs of the choctaw & chikisaw nations, which we are advised (not officially), will be here on the 20th. instant I have recd yours of the 25th ult and hasten to apprise you of it—

I have wrote you but seldom since I have been here, the reason was I had nothing worthy to communicate, nothing very interesting in any way. I have a sanguine hope that we will be able to get the choctaw & chikisaw chiefs here, & if they come, we will make the necessary arrangements for their removal—so soon as this is done, or we are advised they will not meet us, I will set out for the city. Major Eaton & Major Donelson will leaving the Ladies with their aged mothers to console them under afliction and bereavements, for a while.

I have noted your opinion of our judges—I hope as to Baldwin your information is incorrect—his pledges have been of such a nature, that he must be a man of deep duplicity if you are well informed. From the late contest in Kentucky it is evident Clay has lost & not gained strength in Ky. With all the aid that they *judges could give him*, my opinion is, Clay will never be sustained in ohio Ky. again—he never can be, unless Pennsylvania or Newyork could be brought to take him up, then he might hope for success in ohio & Ky. & unite other states in his favour—

When I receive official information from the Indian chiefs I will again write you. I have much to say to you, which I shall pospone until we meet. I hope to be in the city about 20th. or 25th. Septbr. will expect to meet you there.

Major Eaton & his lady are in good health & joins in kind salutations to you   Major Donelson & the ladies are at home   with my prayers for your health & happiness for the present adieu—

Andrew Jackson

Govr Carrol has got home in good health & speaks in high praise of you

ALS, DLC-Van Buren Papers (16-0099).

From David W. Haley

Doaks Stand Mi
Augt. 12th 1830

Sir

You will learn all the perticulars respecting the choctaws by Major Donly. should you sende commissioners to hold a Treaty with them, they will stand in nead of some articles from Vicksburge. I would also recommend to you to have three or four thousand pounds of bacon and about one of coffee and three of sugar hauled up and delivered out to the indians at the Treaty. they want the bacon to cook with their beef. if you conclude to give them the above mentioned articles I will have them on the Treaty ground by having a few days notis will furnis the beef at three cents pr pound. You must order the Treaty to be held at or near Mr Wilsons, on the Robinson road.

It will be all important that Major Eaton should attend the Treaty. I hope you will prove by your acts that your are the true friend of the choctaws   Majr. Donly can informe you what is neaded to satisfy them on this point. Your friend & obd. servt. in hast

D. W. Haley

PS. there will have to be 10 or 12 sacks of salt furnished. the whole amount I have proposed can be delivered for four thousand dollars or there abouts—

D. W. H

ALS, DNA-RG 75 (M234-169).

To Ralph Eleazar Whitesides Earl

Franklin August 13th. 1830—

Dr Sir

I leave here this morning for judge overtons where I will be to night and where I would like to meet my son if in Nashville, by whom send the papers & letters that may have reached Nashville yesterday & to day—I dine with the Judge tomorrow, where I would be glad to see you & in the evening will go with you to Fairfield, & early on Sunday to the Hermitage—

If my son is not in Nashville can you come to the judges to night—please call upon Messhrs Nichol & Hill for my account & Mr Josiah Nichol   I want to close my old account with them before I go, & my individual account, so that I may leave nothing unsettled[1]—yr friend

Andrew Jackson

ALS photocopy, Anonymous (16-0104).

1. On August 20 AJ wrote a check to Nichol & Hill for $948, noting it as full payment on all his accounts with Nichol & Hill and with Josiah Nichol & Son.

From James Gowen

PHILADELPHIA, August 13th, 1830.

MY DEAR SIR—

I have the honor of acknowledging receipt of your letter of the 22d inst. in answer to mine of the 3rd ultimo. Neither this letter, nor that of the 16th June, was indicative of any feeling or doubt entertained by me, that in the exercise of a constitutional prerogative, you would manifest any partiality, much less, a prejudice against my *poor country*. Both letters were induced, solely, by the warmth of my attachment for you. The letter of the 16th June, especially, to save you from acting on representations, whether from friends or foes, that were likely to lead to disastrous consequences. Having premised so far, permit me to advert to the prominent points in your letter, which I am sorry to say, are confirmatory, that gross misrepresentations have been adduced in favor of Wilson, by the managers in that farce. If the grounds were tenable, I should have taken leave to publish your letter, and claimed a triumphant approval.

The worst possible defence would be that which extenuates the crimes of Wilson, and reflects on the character of Porter; this community being in possession of facts which enable them to judge of the relative demerits of each. That the information furnished by Wilson, was used as testimony against him and ultimately led to his conviction, is rather sublimated, and is susceptible of denial.

That seven of the jury recommended him for pardon, is utterly denied. It is asserted that but *one* of the jury recommended, and even this is matter of doubt. The Juryman alluded to is John G. Watmough, the adjunct of Jonathan Roberts in his itinerant revilings of you through the neighboring counties—the brother-in-law of John Sergeant, and *now* the opposing candidate of your friend Dan'l H. Miller, in the 3rd Congressional District. But you will not be troubled with Watmough at Washington as a member of Congress, until Henry Clay be President, and that will be—never![1]

As relates to my warm hearted countrymen, they are fully convinced, *how unjust were their suspicions*. I have read to many of them the extract from your letter, very properly showing, how unnatural it would be for *you*, not to be the friend of Irishmen.

It were proper, perhaps, that I should apologise for the freedom with which I have addressed your Excellency, as well as the little caution there seems about me, in passing on men and things—yet these neither emanate on the one hand, from a want of due respect, nor on the other can it be ascribed to indiscretion. There lives no man, more *devoted to your person and administration than I am.* So much do I prize both, that I dare be at issue with friends and foes, and am, thank Heaven, in every sense, too independent to fear the consequences.

I am, most respectfully, Your devoted friend and hum.b sv't.

JAMES GOWEN.

Printed, Washington *Globe*, November 1, 1832 (16-0105).

1. On August 12, the name of John Goddard Watmough (1793–1861) was published in Philadelphia, on information from William T. Barry, as the sole Wilson juror who had petitioned for his pardon. Watmough denied it, and Barry at his demand recanted the claim. Jonathan Roberts (1771–1854) was a former U.S. senator from Pennsylvania. John Sergeant (1779–1852) of Philadelphia, husband of Watmough's sister, was a former congressman and Henry Clay's vice-presidential running mate in 1832. In October Watmough defeated Jacksonian incumbent Daniel H. Miller for Congress.

From John Branch

Washington City
Augt. 14th 1830

My Dear Sir

I have several matters of some little importance, which I was about to transmit to you by mail but upon reflection I have determined to permit them to remain untill your return, as the public interest can sustain no detriment thereby and as I presume your mind is occupied with other business of more pressing importance.

One subject I will barely mention. On a partial inspection of the Navy Yard at Norfolk as I was returning from North Carolina I was surprised to find a new Sloop of war almost ready for launching   On enquiry I ascertained that she was put on the stocks in March last, and that she was intended to bear the name and supply the place of the John Adams *reported to the last Session of Congress for repairs.* I am further informed ~~that~~ by the Navy Comrs. that they have felt authorised to build this vessel in consequence of instructions, (verbal I presume) which were given by Mr Southard   I must acknowledge that I have been somewhat embarrassed by this unauthorised expenditure. First because we have not one cent appropriated for *building* new Sloops. And secondly by a reference to legislative enactment it will appear that not even a barge has been built in time of war even without the express direction & sanction of Congress, with the exception of two or three cases under the last Dynasty   I dislike very much to practice such a deception, to do by indirection what we cannot do directly and above board   Again the policy of building new vessels when we already have afloat more than we can *employ, repair* or *preserve from premature decay* may well be questioned *as in truth it was in your last Message to Congress.*[1] I have therefore directed that she should be preserved on the stocks untill your opinion can be obtained   If it is the wish of the government to supply the place of those vessels which may be either lost at sea or may be condemnd as the John Adams was as being unfit for repair, let them say so & appropriate accordingly. The Nation expects economy in the disbursement of the public monies and they have a right to expect, nay *to require* their executive officers to execute the law as they find it written and not as they believe it ought to be written. I have however done in this as I trust I shall in every other case what I believed to be my duty, and solicit most earnestly your counsel   We look forward to your return with unaffected pleasure

Pray present us in kind terms to Maj & Mrs Donelson and Miss Mary and accept for yourself our united good wishes and esteem

Jn Branch

What will become of Clay after his recent signal discomfiture in Kentucky? No alternative but to be laid on the shelf with his prototype Burr. May such be the fate of all traitors to their country[2]

[Endorsed by AJ:] Govr Branch—to be replied to—that the *[. . .]*

ALS, DLC (38). Branch submitted an official report on the *John Adams* on October 2, to which AJ replied on October 28 (below).

1. In his first annual message, AJ remarked that the Navy had more ships than it needed for its peacetime duty of protecting commerce, and that those idled in harbor quickly decayed and became useless. He recommended discontinuing construction of the larger classes of ships and instead stockpiling finished materials ready for rapid assembly, reckoning expansionist capability rather than ships afloat "as the index of our naval power" (Richardson, 2:459).

2. Aaron Burr (1756–1836), once vice president under Jefferson, retreated into obscurity after his acquittal on treason charges in 1807 for purportedly conspiring to separate the trans-Appalachian west from the U.S.

From James Knox Polk

Columbia August 14th. 1830

Dear Sir

Many of your old friends in this quarter of the country, who have not had it in their power to visit you, have expressed a warm desire to see you before you returned to Washington, and if it would comport with your convenience to visit Columbia, nothing would gratify them more. Knowing that the rule of conduct which you have prescribed for yourself, on your present visit to your residence, would prevent you from accepting any public demonstration of that respect which they sincerely ~~feel~~ entertain for you, they have tendered none. I hope however that you may have it in your power at some time most convenient to yourself, to dine with me, and thus afford an opportunity in an informal manner, to your very numerous personal & political friends here, personally to greet you. ~~If it will not impose upon you too much fatigue, I must insist on you If you can visit us as~~ I hope you can, be pleased to inform me on what day. ~~If you come,~~ If it will not impose on you to much fatigue, I must insist on you to come, & if you do I hope you will accept of my House as your quarters, during your stay with us.

Very Respectfully, yr obt & very Hul svt

James K. Polk

ALS draft, DLC-Polk Papers (16-0106). *Polk Correspondence*, 1:325. AJ replied on August 18 (below).

To William Berkeley Lewis

(In haste & private)

Fairfield August 15th. 1830—

Dr. Major

On my return from judge Overtons to the Hermitage, I determined to spend a night at this your hospitable mansion, & enquire, & see how all your family were, Mr Earle accompanied me. I found every thing as it ought to be—your family enjoying health, your premises in good order, your crop fine, and your overseer doing his duty faithfully. I have spent a pleasant night here & leave it this morning by the way of Col Loves, to the Hermitage to make my arrangements to return to the city at as early a period as the engagements with the Indians, who are to meet me at Franklin on the 20th instant will permit me.

I have examined the Paintings of you & your deseacd relatives by Mr Earle—they are excellent, and do much credit to the artist. There never was a more striking likness than yours & they Mrs Lewises.

Judge Overton gave a dinning on yesterday to Major Eaton and his lady, which was numerously attended by the neighbourhood and a few from Nashville. There were upwards of forty Ladies, & as Mr Wood observed, here said he, is the bone & sinew of the country. The unaccountable combination in Nashville, has, & will be met by the citizens of Franklin & the neighbourhood as it ought, and the combination, which has extended itself from the city of Washington to Nashville, put down.

No Ladies will return with me. Major A. J. Donelson, my son & Mr Earle will consitute my family, & I hope Major Eaton will accompany me, & leave his Lady until the rise of the waters, when old Mrs. Eaton will accompany her with Doctor Breathit as their protector. To this the Major is willing, whether Mrs. E. will finally consent to this arrangement (she says she will) I cannot say—I have much to say to you when I we meet which would not do to be committed to paper.

Kentuckey has done her duty—as far as heard from, there are ten of a majority against Clay in the State Legislature.

I expect the Indians on the 20th instant at Franklin. I shall set out for Washington so soon as I meet & talk to them, & form a treaty. I am anxious to be there—with my compliments to the Heads of Departments & Bureaus I am yr friend

Andrew Jackson

ALS and Copy, NN (16-0110).

From John Henry Eaton

Sunday. 15. Aug. 30—12. Oclock

Dr Genl.

I send you all I recd by the mail to day—The Choctaws will come—but as the Council does not meet till the 10th. no information is had when they will be here—No doubt the Choctaws & Chickasaws will arange to come together, and will perhaps not be in earlier than the 25—of this I may be able to advise you by the mail on Tuesday—

our Choctaw agent seems to be behaving badly—if so, we should get clear of him—I will keep you advised of all I get—The mail waits[.] yours

Eaton

[Endorsed by AJ:] Major Eaton inclosing Peachlynn & Mushulatubees letters to be returned to the Sec of War—A. J—

ALS, DLC (38). This same day, AJ formally commissioned Eaton and John Coffee to treat with the Chickasaws and such other Indians as might attend at Franklin for their removal west of the Mississippi.

From *Mushulatubbe et al.*

Council ground Chocktaw Nation
August 16th. 1830—

We the Chiefs, Captains, and Warriors of the northeastern and southern districts of the chocktaw nation, having met in open council, this day, for the purpose of listening to a talk which we understood had been received by the Agent from our Father the President—The Agent had made an appointment at Wilson's Stand in the Western district of our Nation (on the 10th of august) but on account of an unfriendly misunderstanding between that district and the districts to which we belong the people would not assemble at that place   To remedy this evil we appointed a council in our districts on the 15th. of August five days later, so that the Agent might have the oppertunity of attending to both Councils, of this arrangement we gave the Agent timely notice—and we met on the ground with the hope of meeting him and Maj. Donelly, who we understood had been sent on as special Agent with a great talk from our father the President, explanatary of the vews of the Government on this important subject. But when we came there to our great mortification, neither Agent, Maj. Donelly, or the Presidents talk were to be seen, but instead thereof a Mesenger from the Western district with a letter directed to our Chief declaring that they would not send a delegation to meet our father the President. This news put the prospect of our sending a national delegation out of the question; for it could not be called a national delegation unless all three of the districts were represented, and we were instructed to come clothed with full powers &c.

The two letters which were sent to Maj John Pitchlynn one from our father the President, and the other from the secretary of War and bearing the date of 5th. August, were duly interpreted in open council, the contents of which we clearly understand   But as we could not come clothed with full powers to do national business, we were compelled, though much against our will, to neglect the invitation of our father the President.

That our Father the President may not think that our nonattendance has originated from an unfriendly disposition in us, we have made out this report and sent it to him by our confidential friends, Maj John Pitchlynn, U.S. Interpreter, Peter P. Pitchlynn Pierre Juzan, Thomas Wall, and Mr. John Bond, who are instructed to wait on our father the President, and explain to him our views more fully than we can do by writing.

We wish our father the President would send us a talk by some good men, who will give us time to call a full council, and who will explain to us the views of the Government on the subject of the removal of our people west of the Mississippi. We will all gather and meet them, listen to their talk and give them a positive answer, what we will do either to remove west or remain where we are receive the law, and abide by the consequences.

Respecting what Mr. Haley told our Father the President as to our meeting him in Franklin or any other place; we can say we do not know the man have never seen him, and therefore can assure our Father the President, that he was wholly unauthorized to make any propositions coming from us—

And further, We understand that the report which was sent on to our father the President from the Western district of our nation, contained an accusation against our Interpreters, Messrs. Pitchlynn and Mackey— Stating that they are dishonest men and at the head of all the disturbances in the Nation, and that except they are removed from office there cannot be any thing done with the people of this Nation &c. In justice to the Interpreters we feel it our duty to state, that we have always found them honest and true men, that they are much in favour of sending a full delegation to meet our Father the President, and that they have in all cases given impartial interpretations, so far as has come to our Knowledge—as such we wish them to remain in office so long as they live.[1]

We sincearly hope that our father the President may not fault us for not attending to his invitation; for did he but know the difficulties which we have to encounter, we are sure he would pitty sooner than blame us—

Done in open Council at Coon chitto, and subscribed to, the day and date above written—

Mu,shoo,la,tub,bee	his	X	mark
Ne,tuk,ai,che		X	
J,ah,ho,ka,tub,bee		X	
E,ah,ho,pi,e		X	
Ah,ho,lub,bee		X	

[Eighty-seven additional signatures follow.]

[Endorsed by AJ:] The Eastern & Southern chiefs of the choctaws talk to the President to be safely kept by the Sec of War—A. J

DS, DNA-RG 75 (M234-169).

1. Writing to Eaton on August 14 with news of the failed August 10 general council, John Donly recommended removing interpreter Middleton Mackey, saying the Choctaws lacked confidence in him. Donly charged Mackey with fomenting dissension and refusing to perform his duties. He proposed replacing him with David Folsom while retaining "the old & faithful Interpreter" Pitchlynn (DNA-RG 75, M234-169).

To William Berkeley Lewis

(Private)

Hermitage August 17th. 1830—

My Dr Major

I have just received yours of the 27th. ulto. and hasten to acknow-ledge it.

Before the receipt of yours, I had recd. from Mr Ingham information that Mr Jarvis had resigned, and I sent to him the appointment for Mr Ripley.

I have duly noted the information you have recd. from Mr Biddle, and when I reach the city I shall act upon those cases as propriety may dictate —and the justice due Mr Gardiner may render necessary & proper.[1]

The news from Kentuckey of the late election is quite grateful—Clay has lost a majority in the State Legislature, as our friends believe, of about ten, or fourteen—even five, will give him a quietus there—Ohio will prove true to her republican principles so long as New york & Pennsylvania remain firm Ohio will never seperate from them.

you ask what has become of Major Eaton¿ he is at Franklin enjoying all that happiness that the hospitality & good feelings of that place, & its vicinity can afford him & his lady—They have been treated with marked respect there, & every where else, but in Nashville, and they have not put it in the power of the coalition there, to treat them well or ill—for he reached Nashville in the stage late in the evening, & went on in a hack the next morning, visiting no one, but Mr Stuart whose lady waited upon, & took them to his house with Mrs. Judge Barker who travelled with Mr & Mrs. Eaton from Buffaloe—I left Major & Mrs. Eaton on the 14th. at Judge overtons where they had been invited to dine, and where about thirty ladies & as many gentlemen were assembled of the most respect-able character. Mr R. Wood was there with his family—and as Mr Earle informs me, when he saw the company observed "here is the bone & sinew of our country"—so you see the coalition in Nashville headed by Mrs. Kirkman & Doctor McNairy, Genl Gains & Co. Major Claibourne &c &c, are surrounded & in rather a bad way—The thing is now clear to me, that the Washington coalition has been extended *here*, by the vilest secrete concert   They are unmasked, and in time will be made to feel very sensibly—[2]

you must excuse the want of information in my letters I have not one moment any where without interuption—There has two Gentlemen arrived since I began this hasty scrall and I have to close.

The Indians will meet us—The chikisaws on the 20th. & the choctaws on the 25th—I am only awaiting their arrival to set out for washington

I will be accompanied with Major A. J. Donelson, my son, Col Earle & I hope Major Eaton; Mrs. Donelson *will remain, with her widowed mother*, and I suppose Mrs Eaton will remain & await the rise of the waters, that her aged mother Mrs. Eaton can accompany her, when Doctor Breathit will accompany them—with my respects to all friends. I remain yours

Andrew Jackson

ALS and Copy, NN (16-0119).
   1. Lewis wrote James B. Gardiner on August 5 that he had written to AJ urging Gardiner's claim to office (DLC-Lewis Papers).
   2. The persons AJ named were Richard K. Call's mother-in-law Ellen Jackson Kirkman (1774–1850), Nashville physician Boyd McNairy (1785–1856), Edmund Gaines, and Thomas Claiborne.

From Francis Preston Blair

Frankfort. Aug. 17. 1830

Dear Sir

I have taken the liberty to transmit to you by this days mail, a paper containing a list of the members elect to the general Assembly of Kentucky, with a designation of the political cast under which they received the suffrages of the people. The information upon which this statement is founded, is of the most unquestionable character. I have no fears that any defection will take place, that can change the complexion of the Legislature, from that given to it in the Argus.[1]

The Election in this county was a most extraordinary one. It was distinguished on the part of Mr. Clay's friends by the foulest bribery & fraud. Votes were notoriously purchased with large sums of money; and the Officers at the polls conducted every thing with marked partiality & injustice to favor the election of Mr. Crittenden—notice has been served that the election will be contested, & unless the most iniquitous influence shall prevail, & controul the result, Mr. Sanders must obtain the seat by a considerable majority. It is not improbable that the funds applied to carry the election here, as well as in other counties of the state, was furnished by the Branch of the Bank of the U.S. at Lexington. Genl. McCalla is in possession of evidence that will go far to establish this fact.[2]

The friends of your administration in this section of the state, & those, who from the deep interest they feel in your fame & continued success & prosperity, boast a nearer feeling for you individually, are extremely anxious that on your return to Washington you would take this place in your route. Many have desired that I should express this wish to you—& should the gratification of this general feeling, comport with the course which higher considerations will doubtless direct, permit me to ask the favor that I may be informed of it.

You will I trust pardon the trouble I give in calling your attention to a matter with regard to which I feel some solicitude. Colo Monroe, (the son in law of Genl Adair) is I understand, an applicant for the Office of U.S. Attorney made vacant by the election of J. S. Smith Esq. His appointment would give general satisfaction to the Republican party in Kentucky. He is eminently qualified, & merits on many accounts the favor he solicits at your hands. I am Sir, with the greatest respect yr. mo. ob. st

F. P. Blair

[Endorsed by AJ:] Mr F P. Blairs 17th. august 1830. recd 24th. & answered A J.

ALS, DLC (38). Blair (1791–1876) had been Amos Kendall's collaborator at the Frankfort *Argus of Western America* and succeeded him as editor in 1829. AJ replied to him on August 24 (below).

1. The list, published in the *Argus* on August 18, claimed 56 of 98 persons elected to the state house of representatives as "decided friends of the administration," reducing Clay from a majority of 22 to a minority of 11 on joint ballot in the legislature.

2. In Franklin County, once and future U.S. senator John Jordan Crittenden (1786–1863) defeated Jacksonian candidate Lewis Sanders Jr. (1796–1864). John Moore McCalla (1793–1873) was the U.S. marshal for Kentucky, appointed by AJ in 1829.

To James Knox Polk

(Private)

Hermitage August 18th. 1830—

My Dear Sir

I have recd. your favor of the 14th. instant, & hasten to reply—that my public engagements will prevent me the pleasure of visiting you in Columbia. The chikisaw Indians are to be at Franklin on the 20th. and, I suppose, the choctaws on the 25th instant. I set out tomorrow to meet them, will be at Franklin on Saturday, from whence I mean, if business will permit, to visit & stay one night with my friend Genl Wm Polk, of which you will be advised, & where it will afford me pleasure to meet you. I will be happy to see you at Franklin, & will, if I can spare the time, ride with you to Genl Wm. Polks—I am much pressed with business, must return to the city the moment I have had an interview with the Indians and arranged business with them, I am much wanted there.

Mr Van Buren writes, that our Agent Mr Rhind, has concluded a treaty with the Port placing us on the footing of the most favored nations.

The King of England still lingers, and our minister there awaiting, with anxious solicitude, a final answer on the arrangement of our west India Trade—Guerrero in Mexico, having defeated Genl Bravo, last accounts place him within three Leagues of Mexico—It is fair to conclude, if this be true, that by this time Gustamenta is deposed, & Guerrero the Executive

of Mexico[1]—we had just commenced negotiations with them, under sanguine prospects of general success, which a change must greatly delay, if
not defeat. With my kind respects to your Lady, mother, & family—yr
friend[2]

Andrew Jackson

ALS, DLC-Polk Papers (16-0132). *Polk Correspondence*, 1:325–26.
    1. AJ's news was incorrect. Deposed Mexican President Vicente Ramón Guerrero
(1782–1831) failed to regain power. In January 1831 his followers were defeated in battle
by pro-Bustamante forces led by Nicolás Bravo Rueda (1786–1854). Guerrero was later
captured and executed.
    2. Polk's wife was Sarah Childress Polk (1803–1891). His mother was Jane Knox Polk
(1776–1852).

From *"annonymous"*

D. Sir
    I suppose from one so obscure as myself, you would not deign to take
advice—but be that as it may, I think it my duty as a citizen to warn even
the President of danger when I know it, altho' he may not believe it til
he feels the dagger in his side, or tasts the poison in his bowl—You must
know then I have been in Washington—and last winter a most tragical
plot was made, and *you are the victim*—Your worse enemies are those of
your own house—You have real friends and false ones—you have friends
who did not, nor would not support you, or this warning would never
have came from me—I heard the plot, but the conspirators have not the
least idea that any but themselves ever heard a whisper—You are to live
til by holding you up as a candidate excitement gets to its highest pitch,
than suddenly you some of your now pretended warm friends are to put
a *veto* on your existence, and after a false show of great mourning come
out in your place—You may think this weak logic, but be assured there
are those who look upon it as a sure steping stone to the seat you now
fill—You have been a meritorious General, and as such I love you, and
for that, I give you this warning—you are now advised of your danger
take warning and live. Dont do like Ceasar when Spurina warned him of
his danger.[1] If you wish to live dont suffer your flatterers to influence you
to be a candidate any more and then you will pass your time calmly & I
assure you then you will have nothing to fear, for you will not be viewed
as in the way   Once more *take warning*—If you should be a Candidate
again be cautious how you go alone, or with whom you trust your life—
The bane of your life is near you—Mind how you drink in the fall of
1832—Farewell thou faithful General, and may God cause you to take
this adice from your friend

annonymous

[Endorsed by William B. Lewis:] This letter was recd. and opened by me this morning—it came thro' the City Post Office. Wednesday Augt. 18th. 1830. W B Lewis

AL, LNT (16-0128). The handwriting and tone strongly resemble that of "Citizen," who wrote President Adams on August 14, 1827, urging him and AJ both to withdraw from the presidential race to avoid impending bloodshed (Adams Family Papers, MHi).

1. On the Ides of March, Julius Caesar's wife Calpurnia tried to dissuade him from going to the Senate, having had a premonition of his murder.

From John Henry Eaton

18 augst 30

Dr Sir

I have time only for a line or two before the mail starts

The enclosed letters shew that LeFlores party will not come—The Missionaries no doubt prevent. Pitchlens party met on the 15th. & I have full confidence that party will come; & if so LaFlores, & Fulsoms will come in self defence—Fridays mail will more fully explain—without the Choctaws I do not expect we can do any thing with the Chickasaws, understanding from Mr Foster who has just returned that they wish to be located within the Choctaw Country to the west

A letter from Col Reynols dated at Lawrenceburg yesterday (17) says the Chickasaws are that far on their way 20 Chiefs. They will arrive here Friday morning—In haste yours—

J. H. Eaton

[Endorsed by AJ:] Indian letter enclosed by Major E. Secy of War to be carefully kept—

ALS, DNA-RG 75 (M234-169).

From Samuel Delucenna Ingham

Washington 21 Aug 30

My dear Sir

Mr Francis Dickins will hand you this, he goes to Nashville on business of the Dept for the prosecution of Hugh Moore who has committed some very gross frauds upon the Try but which have been prevented by the vigilance of Mr Dickins   We are all well and I am not aware that any public business has suffered by your absence, but we shall be very happy to see you return in health for the arduous duties that await you, accept my best respects for yourself and family—Mrs I is still in the County—very respectfully yours

S D Ingham

ALS, NcU-Asbury Dickins Papers (mAJs). Francis Asbury Dickins (1804–1901) was a Treasury agent and the son of Treasury Department chief clerk Asbury Dickins (1780–1861). He went to give evidence against Hugh Moore of South Carolina, who had been arrested in Nashville on a deposition from Ingham that he was fraudulently collecting pension payments in the name of a long-dead Revolutionary officer named John Nelson (DNA-RG 15, M804-1806). Moore pled guilty to two charges of forging pension applications and was sentenced to five years' hard labor.

From Henry Lee

Port Mahon 22nd. August 1830

My dear Sir

I am greatly obliged to you for your letter of the 4th of June, which was handed me by my successor Comre. Porter. I regret that you should have experienced concern on ~~acept.~~ account of my rejection by the Senate. The proof however which this gives me of your confidence, and other kind expressions in your letter, place me far above the reach of oppression or injustice. The partial estimate you put upon my ability to promote the cause of wisdom and justice in a great branch of our government, is highly pleasing to me; as it shews that if my merit is below your estimation, the place I hold in your favour depends exclusively on the kindness of your feelings toward me. When I do return I shall be glad to employ myself in a task so honourable

But I am still more gratified with the prospect you hold out of entrusting to me the important subject of national history which grows out of your management of the Seminole War. I never doubted the truth of my apprehensions respecting the prime mover of all the persecution, by which, for that great service to your Country, you were so cruelly and so constantly assailed; and I shall devote myself to the labour of bringing before the publick a fair and full account of that campaign, with the utmost alacrity and the sincerest zeal. But my dear Sir, there is one obstacle in the state of my private affairs that makes it impossible for me to return to the U. States at this moment. You will remember that I mentioned to you my being involved in a securityship for Peter R. Beverley of Alexa. a friend of mine, in a case which threatened a judgment against me for about 5.000 dollars—& that the apprehension of some annoyance from that entanglement rendered me anxious to leave the U.S. last summer without delay. My brother writes me from Newyork that a judgment for the amt. mentioned had actually been obtained against me, & was hanging up in Washington in wait for my return—but he adds that Beverley has instituted proceeding in the Chancery Court of Fredericksburg Va. which in all reasonable probability will exonerate me, in the course of april next from this liability. The case was originated in that Court. Now if I return at once to the U. States I shall have to keep out of the District until either by selling Beverleys house over the heads of his wife (a most amiable and delightful woman) & children, or raising by some other means an adequate sum, I shall ~~have~~ be able to pay the judgment ~~or submit~~. otherwise I must, in order to get in the district, surrender myself to the Marshall. My object therefore is as my brother advises me, to remain in Europe so as not to return, if I can help it, until next spring. I have saved 1000 dollars of my salary, & the govt. allows me 1000 more to pay my passage home. With this sum I propose passing through the principal cities of Italy—surveying all the great battle fields of that interesting country—and intending to reach Paris on or before the 1st. Day of December. There, if I can get no help from home, I shall be compelled by want of means, to embark at Havre for the U. States—and I must keep away from the District until april or May.[1]

One mode of prolonging my stay usefully to myself and to you, until the proper period, has occurred to me—and it is this. I have reason to apprehend that the treaty which has lately been negotiated by Mr. Rhind Mr. Offley & Comre. Biddle with the Ottoman Porte, will not be ~~nego~~ ratified in all its articles—and I infer therefore that it will be found necessary to reopen a negotiation touching the offensive stipulation at Constantinople. As Mr. Rhind was the author of the exceptionable article and from intemperance of habits is unfit for business (all the officers of the squadron who saw him here & at Smyrna unite in this allegation), I hardly think with a ~~gov~~ potentate so *[punitive]* and obstinate as the Turk, it will be thought prudent, to attempt a rectification of the instrument by means of the same agent whose work is objected to. And it does appear reasonable to suppose that on principles of common prudence & justice, a fresh agent for this operation would be preferable. In this case I feel authorised to propose for your consideration, myself for this service. My zeal, I flatter myself you can rely on, and I suppose the little acquaintance I have made ~~of~~ with the Turkish character & habits will be no disadvantage. But of this you & your advisers will judge. I shall be in paris by the 1st. of December certainly if I live, & you propose being at Washington by the 1st. of November. If then you should not deem it proper to ratify the treaty, or to submit it to the Senate in its present shape, as from what I have gathered I think probably will be the case, and if you should incline to honour me with this agency, either alone or in conjunction (as I should like) with Comre. Biddle & Mr. Offley, by enclosing the necessary instructions to me under cover to Mr. Rives, our envoy at Paris, I should be on the spot to receive them, & in five or 6 days afterwards could join Comre. Biddle at this place. This employment, I think I should have as good a chance as any other person, of conducting in a manner that would be advantageous to the country and satisfactory to yourself. It would completely relieve me from the effects of the Senates injustice, by showing that you had not withdrawn your confidence from me, & would enable me to take a position on my return home agreeable to myself & useful to my friends. I send this letter under cover to the Secy. of State, & as I shall write to you again in a few days by the sloop of war Lexington, will defer until then some remarks I propose making on your arguments in explanation of your veto. I wrote to you some time ago mentioning that I had a wild boar of Africa which I intended to send you. I had also a gazelle for little Jackson, but the French soldiers stole the gazelle & let the wild boar loose—so that I lost them both. I hope you will approve of my conduct at in staying at Algiers during the invasion and taking command of the Consular garrison that we erected there and that was placed under my flag. I presume it is the first and only garrison you ever had under your govt. or authority, in Northern Africa.[2] I am afraid your patience will be exhausted by this long letter—and therefore begging you to Consider all that part which relates to the obnoxious article of Mr. Rhinds treaty, as strictly confidential, I hasten to conclude by assuring you of my own and of Mrs. Lees gratitude for your constant and generous kindness to us, and of my unalterable respect & faithful friendship[.] Yr. ob st.

H. Lee

P.S. I shall probably write & publish a journal of my travels in Italy, & should I go there, in the sulans dominions—which if they should be worth publishing, I should like to be allowed to dedicate to you.

ALS, DLC (38). Lee's wife was Ann Robinson McCarty Lee (1797–1840).
1. At its December 1829 term, the U.S. district court in Washington found Lee liable as surety for a debt of Peter Randolph Beverley (b. 1780). Lee's half-brother Charles Carter Lee (1798–1871) represented him at trial. Beverley's wife was Lovely St. Martin Beverley (1790–1867). On December 24 Lee wrote AJ a long letter describing his travels in Italy.
2. French troops captured Algiers in July 1830.

From John Randolph

particularly private & confidential
St. Petersburgh Augt. 10/22 1830[1]
My dear Sir
For reasons which I am now reducing to writing, but cannot detain the Concord to finish, I desire to return home in time to take my seat in the next Congress (provided that my old constituents see fit to elect me) where I may fight under your banner; & I acknowledge no other leader; against Mammoth, Leviathan, Legion, or _____ " whatever title pleases his ear, your adversary & mine—"the adversary of God & Man"—whose friends are the foes of us & of the people, whose friends foes, wheresoever found, are our friends & their friends.

There I may sustain you. Here I can do you no good (altho I might have done you some but for this strange dilatoriness)

[In margin:] meanwhile, should Mr R. or Mr. Mc.L. wish to return also; I would be glad to be at P. or London in my present Station. I would give 20,000 now to be at either. I am in the Bastile, cut off by Despotism from the surrounding world

Let me beg you to refer to our correspondence once more. Decr. 30. Mr. Secry. V. B. writes.

"The letters to Mr M. were sent off immediately ~~on~~ after my return" (from Richmd) "& the moment we hear from him, the other matter" (my appointmt.) "will be announced. I shall be anxious to see you off as early in the spring as may be found practicable, having reference to all circumstances."

Mr M. it seems, has played back upon the S. of S. his own game. Be that as it may, we have lost *time* & *tide which wait for no man.* Cincinnatus, the Warrior-Ploughman, knows & none so well, that if seed time be neglected there can be no Harvest.[2]

Sir, there is something wrong. My mind misgives me. My best regards to Mr Branch whom I greatly respect. He is an honest man & your friend—personally attached to you, with no ulterior views. We get it on both sides of the House it seems. Mr Chairman of the Ways & Means the Patroclus of Mr Achilles C. was no doubt too much occupied with his much-bepraised Defence of Leviathan, to think of an appropriation bill for outfits.[3] Thus, nurse engrossed with dandling & kissing her own sweet Baby, forgets the nursling in the cradle, sits upon it & over lays the poor thing.

Sir, such a circumstance would have cast ridicule & reproach upon the Admns. of Jefferson or Madison—& has done more to lessen yours to say nothing of injury to the Publick service than any *act* could do. It never could have happened when J. R. was in that chair. No former Secry. or Chairman of W. & M. could have made such a blunder. But was it an oversight? Willis Alston would have done better[4]

Perhaps you'll say what is R. at now? Is he Ratting with the Chiltons & Stansberrys & *John Holmes*! no this last name settles the question, if the Bank did not do it. No true coalitionist is anti-Bank.[5] "Is he then for t'other candidate?" (the V. P.) That question too is answered: & if it were not, all our strong doses; Tariff, Bank & all, are from that quarter. I thought once the penitent had confessed & been reconciled to the Catholick Church of State-Rights, with Hayne & my gallant friend Hamilton. But on Webster's touching the sore place, He winced. All that he had recanted in private to Father Macon & brother Roanoke went for nothing—& he has made a reservation, which (as Mr. Secry. V. B. would say) will enable him to act hereafter "according to all circumstances," or events to come[6]

"Is R. then mad? as they say. Is he an Ishmaelite or a John Holmesite? Does he love to be in a minority? Has he taken opium & does he mean like a Malay to "run a muck"? None of these except that he *will* "run a muck" not drunk with opium or wine against the aforesaid Leviathan, Mammoth Legion, who is now doing what the Bank of England & the E. India Company are doing, buying votes & seats.

For three days except a broiled rasher of Virginia bacon for br'kfast with my coffee & Virginian bread I have taken only a crust of bread & glass of wine, in lieu of dinner   It has enabled me to support myself; under unparallelled exertion. I mean such as I never before made. Poor Clay is quite low & indisposed: Since 3 this morning—it is now ten & these are the last lines I write by the Concord I have been driving the pen. There is an impalpable dust here which with the heat & glare from the streets & white Houses is fatal to the eyes. Farewell! most faithfully your steadfast friend

J. R of Roanoke

Sunday Augt. 22. 1830

It is Sunday. Last half sheet of letter paper but the envelope left

Just heard but know not what to believe that the Duke of Orleans is proclaimed King.

Yesterday La Fayette was at the head of affairs—a bad augury of success. He might make a capital chairman of the W. & M. or Chancellor of Exchequer for he is a first rate financier in one respect   No one better knows how to raise the supplies, than M. de La. F.[7]

He would never forget to take money out of the Treasury—The appropriation bills at least would not

[Endorsed by AJ:] private & confidential

ALS, DLC (38).
    1. Randolph gave dates in both Old Style, still used in Russia, and New.
    2. Henry Middleton (1770–1846) of South Carolina was Randolph's predecessor as minister to Russia. Van Buren wrote him a letter of recall on June 16 (DNA-RG 59, M77-8).
    3. In Homer's *Iliad*, when Achilles sulks and refuses to fight the Trojans, his friend Patroclus dons his armor and is slain by Hector. Randolph's Patroclus was House Ways and Means Committee chairman George McDuffie and his Achilles was Calhoun. The defense of Leviathan was McDuffie's April 13 report sustaining the Bank of the United States.
    4. Randolph had chaired the Ways and Means Committee from 1801 to 1807. Willis Alston (1769–1837) was a long-serving North Carolina congressman.
    5. Like William Stanbery of Ohio, congressman Thomas Chilton (1798–1854) of Kentucky had switched sides, announcing his support for Clay in March 1830. Senator John Holmes (1773–1843) of Maine, a onetime Federalist and later Jeffersonian, had also come out against AJ's administration during the congressional session. The "coalition" was

a derisive Jacksonian term for Adams and Clay men, harking back to the supposed corrupt bargain of 1825 which made John Quincy Adams president.

6. Calhoun and his South Carolina confederates had once championed nationalizing economic measures. Daniel Webster highlighted their inconstancy in his Senate exchange with Hayne. Longtime North Carolina congressman Nathaniel Macon (1758–1837) was, like Randolph, an apostle of "Old Republican" strict construction and state's-rights doctrine.

7. American revolutionary hero the Marquis de Lafayette (1757–1834) helped install Louis Philippe as the new king of France. AJ wrote him on October 1 (below).

To the Chickasaw Indians

[On Monday, August 23, negotiations for a removal treaty began at Franklin between U.S. commissioners John Eaton and John Coffee and twenty delegates of the Chickasaw Nation. Eaton and Coffee opened the proceedings by reading an address from Jackson. Printed here is Jackson's retained draft of the address, mainly in the handwriting of Ralph E. W. Earl with changes by Earl, Jackson, and Eaton. Jackson's insertions are in brackets. The version in the official treaty journal (DNA-RG 75, T494-2) and later copies closely followed this text as amended.]

Franklin Tennessee
Monday 2~~2~~3nd. Aug: 1830

Friends and Brothers

Your Great Father is rejoiced once again to meet and shake you by the hand; and to have it in his power to assure you of his continued friendship and good will. He can cherish ~~nothing~~ none but the best feelings for his red Children, many of whom during our late war fought with him in defence of our Country.

By a communication from your elder brothers and neighbours the Chactaws during last winter your great Father learned, that in consequence of the laws of Mississippi being extended over them they were under great alarm; & of their own free will and without any application from him, they asked to leave their Country and retire across the Missi. The treaty sent [by them to him] was laid before the Senate [of the United States] and they refused to approve it.

The rejection of this treaty was communicated to the Chactaws by their confidential agent [Major Haley]. He was instructed [by me] to do so, and I was ~~informed~~ [assured] by him [this should be made known to them]. It was ~~also communicated~~ also [made known to me by Major Haley,] that the Chactaws were desirous to see and converse with me on this important subject; and in obedience to that desire I assented to meet them at this place. with regret I now learn they have declined their engagement.[1]

Solicitous to avoid every act the tendency of which might be to deceive or impose upon ~~my~~ his Red children he laid the treaty which was [presented] ~~to me,~~ to him ~~was laid~~ before the Senate with the protest which had been forwarded by the opposite party [against it], that all the circumstances might be fully known. It was rejected. Of these things their confidential agent [Major Haley] was advised, and he was requested to make them known to the Chactaws. Understanding from him that they were desirous to see and converse with ~~me~~ their Great Father on this important subject in accordance with that desire ~~I~~ he agreed to meet them at this place. With regret ~~I~~ he now learns they have declined their engagement

~~Congress b~~By an act [of Congress] ~~passed; placed it~~ [it was placed] in ~~my~~ his power to extend justice to the Indians, to pay the expences of their removal, to support them for twelve months, and to give them a grant for lands which should endure "as long as the grass grows or water runs," ~~I~~ A ~~determine~~dation ~~to advise my~~ was taken immediately to advise his red children of the means which were thus placed at ~~my~~ his disposal to render them happy and preserve them as ~~a~~ nations. It was for this, that ~~I~~ he asked ~~my~~ his ~~chactaw~~ [chikisaw & other] friends to meet ~~me~~ him here. You have come, and ~~I~~ your Great father rejoices to see you and ~~be able~~ face to face, to tell you the truth, and point you to a course which cannot fail to make you a happy & prosperous people. [Hear &] ~~D~~deliberate [well] on what ~~I~~ he shall say; and under the excersise of your ~~best~~ [own reason, & matured] judgement, determine what may appear ~~to~~ you ~~advisable~~ [best] to be done, for the benefit of yourselves and your children.

Brothers—You have long dwelt upon the soil you occupy: and in early times before the white man kindled his fires too near to yours, and by settling around, narrowed down the limits of the [chase], you were then ~~an~~ uninstructed, yet a happy people. Now, your white brothers are around you; they compass you about every where. States have been ~~erected~~ created within your limits which claim a right to govern and control your people as their own citizens; and to make them answerable to their civil and criminal laws. Your great Father has not the authority to prevent this state of things; and he now asks if you are prepared and ready to submit yourselves to the laws of ~~Alabama~~ [Mississippi]—make a surrender of your ancient laws, and customs, and peacably, and quietly live, under those of the white man?

Brothers Listen: The laws to which you must be subjected are not oppressive, for they are those to which your white brothers conform and are happy. Under them you ~~would~~ [will] not be permited to seek private revenge—but in all cases ~~of agrievement to submit thro' them to their laws~~ & where wrongs may be done you thro' them, to demand redress. No taxes upon your property or yourselves, except such as may be imposed upon a white brother, will be assessed against you. The Courts will be open for the redress of wrongs, and bad men, will be made answerable ~~there~~ for whatever crimes or misdemeanor may be committed by any of your people or our own.

Brothers—To these laws [where you now are,] you must submit: there is no preventive—no alternative. Your Great Father can not, nor can his

Congress prevent it: The states only can. What then? I pray you brothers to listen. Do you believe that you can live under those laws—that you can surrender all your ancient practices [habits], and [the] forms by which you have been [so long] controlled so long? If so, your great Father has nothing to say, or to advise. He has only to express a hope that you may find happiness in the determination you shall make, whatever it may be. His earnest desire is that you may be perpetuated and preserved as a Nation; and this [he believes] can only be secured by a your consent on your part to remove [to a country] beyond the Mississippi to a Country, where [which] for the happiness of our Red friends was laid out by the government a long time since; and to which it was expected ere this, they would have gone. Where you are, it is scarcely [not] possible you can be [live] contented and happy. Besides the laws of Missi, which must operate upon you, and which your great Father cannot prevent, white men, continually intruding are with difficulty kept off your lands; and every day inconvenience and difficulty continue to increase around you.

Brothers—The laws of Congress usually called the intercourse act, has been resorted to, to afford relief; but in many instances it has failed of success. Our white population has so extended around in every direction, that difficulties and troubles are to be expected. Can [not] this state of things not be prevented? Your firm determination alone [only] can do it.

Brothers—The only plan by which this can be done and tranquility for your people obtained, is that you pass across the Missi, to a Country in all respects equal if not superior to the one you have. Your great Father will give it to you forever, that, free from future interruption it may belong to you and to your Children so long as while you shall exist as a Nation.

Brothers There is no unkindness in the offers made to you. I seek not No intention or wish is had to force you for [from] your lands; My object is but rather to advice you on the score of to your own interest. I know tThe attachment you feel for the soil which incompasses the lands [bones] of your ancestors is well known, our forefathers had the same feeling, when a long time ago, to obtain happiness they left their lands beyond the Great waters and sought a new and quiet home in those distant and unexplored regions. If they [had] not done so, where would have been their children; and where the prosperity they now enjoy. The old [world] would scarcely have afforded support for a people, who by the change of Country, their Fathers made, have become prosperous and happy. So iIn future time so will it be with your posterity [children]. Old men arouse to energy and lead your children to a land of promise and of peace, before the great spirit shall call you to die. Young chiefs forget the prejudices you feel for the soil of your birth, and go to a land where you can preserve your people as a Nation! Peace invites you there! Annoyance will be left behind. Within your limits no state or Territorial Authority whereby to disturb you will be permitted. Intruders, traders, and above all ardent spirits so distructive to health and morals, will be kept from among you, only as the laws and ordinances of your nation may sanction their admission. And that the weak may not be assailed by ~~any of~~ their stronger and more powerful neighbours care ~~will~~ shall be taken, and stipulations made that the United States by arms, if necessary, ~~shall~~ will preserve and maintain peace amongst the tribes, and guard them from the assaults of enemies of ~~any~~ every kind, whether white or red.

Brothers Listen ~~to me~~ These things are for your serious consideration and it behoves you well to think of them. The present is ~~all~~ the time in which you ~~have~~ [are asked] to do so. Reject the opportunity which is now offered to obtain comfortable homes, and the time may soon pass away when such advantages ~~can & will~~ [as are now within your reach may not] again be presented. If from the course you now pursue this shall be the case, then call not upon your great Father hereafter to relieve you, of your troubles; but make up your minds conclusively to remain upon the lands you occupy and be subject to the laws of the state where ~~may~~ you [now] reside, to the extent that her own citizens are ~~required to submit~~. This you must do, & complain no more hereafter—for ~~complaining~~ it will be useless and unnecessary. In a few years, by becoming amalgamated with the whites, your national ~~chactaws~~ character will be lost; and then like other tribes who have gone before, you ~~will~~ [must] disappear and be forgotten.

Brothers! If you are disposed to remove say so, and state the terms you may consider just and equitable. Your great father is ready and ~~disposed~~ [has instructed his commissioner] to admit such as shall be considered liberal, to the extent that he can calculate the Senate will sanction; and terms of any other character it would be ~~idle~~ useless ~~for him to offer, or~~ for you[2] to ~~require~~ insist upon; as without their consent & approval no arrangement to be made could prove effectual. ~~But~~ Should you ~~decline the offers made, &~~ determine to remain where you are candidly say so, & let us be done with this subject no more to be talked of again—[~~But should you on the other~~] But if disposed to consult yr. true interest, & to remove, present the terms on which you are willing to do so, to my friends & your friends the Secretary of war & Genl Coffee, who are authorised to ~~act~~ confer with you; & who in the arrgemts to be made will act candidly—fairly & liberally towards you

[Signed][3]

[Endorsed by AJ at bottom:] copy of an address directed to be delivered to the chickisaw chiefs by the commissioners, The Sec of War & Gen John Coffee, before entering upon the subject of negotiation

[Endorsed by AJ at top:] ~~a copy~~ The original of The ~~above~~ within was handed to the commissioners, Sec of War & Genl Coffee, to be read to the chiefs in council & to be explained to them—after a short talk delivered to them by President on this day _____

Draft in Ralph E. W. Earl's hand with corrections by AJ and Eaton, DLC (38). Copy, DNA-RG 75 (T494-2); Copy, DNA-RG 46 (16-0137). *HRRep* 488, 22d Cong., 1st sess., pp. 16–19 (Serial 228). *SDoc* 512, 23d Cong., 1st sess., vol. 2, pp. 240–42 (Serial 245). *US Telegraph*, September 15, 1830.
    1. This whole paragraph is crossed out, and does not appear in later versions.
    2. From here on the text is in Eaton's hand.
    3. All later versions were signed "Andrew Jackson."

To *Francis Preston Blair*

Franklin. T. August 24th. 1830—

Dear Sir

I have this moment received your letter of the 17th. instant with the paper enclosed. It would appear that Kentuckey is herself again. She has aroused from her lethergy and again struggles for the true principles for which she, and the other republican states, contended in the years 1798, & 1800   I think the republic is safe.

I have been detained too long here with the Indians to comply with your polite invitation to take Frankfort in my way to the city. My duties require my presence there; and where duty urges, I must obay, & repair to Washington by the most expeditious rout.

I thank you for the intelligence you have communicated, and am Sir with great respect yr mo, obdt. Servt.

Andrew Jackson

ALS, DLC (38).

From *William Hume*

Nashville Aug. 24th 1830

Dear Genl

I have returned to Mr Earl the "Private Correspondence" between yourself and Dr. Ely of Philadelphia, and the other Documents appended thereto, in relation to Mrs. Secretary Eaton's character, and by your request I commit to writing the opinion which a cool, impartial, and diligent examination of them has compelled me to adopt, viz, that they prove abundantly and satisfactorily, that the numerous and almost numberless allegations, against that lady's chastity, are utterly false, malicious and unfounded, and that they fully substantiate her innocence. I am with great respect yours

Wm. Hume

To *William Berkeley Lewis*

Franklin August 25th. 1830—

My Dr. Major—

I have just recd. your several letters with their enclosures. The one advising me of the death of Major George Graham, and the various applicants have been duly noted—no appointment will be made until I reach the city to which place I will set out the moment after I know whether the a delegation from the choctaws will come in; By the mail of this morning we expect to receive the result of their council, which was to have been held on the 16th instant.

The chikisaws are now here, & on this day we expect their answer on the subject of their election to cross the M. river, or to remain where they now are. If they agree to remove, we will make a treaty with them—the choctaws not being here in whose boundery we wish to settle them will produce some dificulty, as the chikisaws, are not acquainted with the land adjoining the choctaws on their north boundery, which is the only point where we can place them without interfering with other tribes. I have a sanguine hope the choctaws will be in to day—I will keep this open until the southern mail arrives & by a P.S. give you the news.

I have recd & noted the letter inclosed from the *Gentleman* in So.C. I was aware of the hostility of the influential character aluded to—I sincerely regret the course taken by Hamilton & Hayne. The people of South Carolina will not, *nay* cannot sustain such nulifying Doctrines   They Carolinians are a patriotic & highminded people, and they prize their liberty too high to jeopardise it, at the shrine of an ambitious demagogue, whether a native of Carolina or of any other country. This influential character in this heat, has led Hamilton and Hayne a stray, and it will, I fear, lead to the injury of Hamilton & loose him his election. But the ambitious Demagogue aluded to, would sacrafice friends & country, & move heaven & earth, if he had the power, to gratify his unholy ambition. His course will prostrate him here as well as every where else. Our friend Mr Grundy says he will abandon him unless he can satisfy him that he has used his influence to put down this nulifying doctrine, which threatens to desolve our happy union.

The creeks have officially informed us, that they will not meet us—we have answered, that we leave them to themselves, & to the protection of their friend Mr Wirt, to whose protection they look, and to whom they have given a large fee to protect them in their rights as an independent nation; and when they find that they cannot live under the laws of Alabama, they must find, at their own expence, & by their own means, a country, & a home. The course of *Wirt* has been truly wicked—it has been wielded as an engine to prevent the Indians from moving X the Mississippi & will lead to the distruction of the poor ignorant Indians   It must be so, I have used all the persuasive means in my power; I have exonerated the national character from all imputation, and now leave the poor deluded creeks & cherokees to their fate, and their anihilation, which their wicked advisers has induced. I am sure the stand the Executive has taken was not anticipated by their wicked advisers. It was expected that the more the Indians would hold out, and oppose the views of the Government, the greater would be the offers made by the Executive, and all they missionary, and speculating tribe would make fortunes out of the United States. The answer sent, has blasted these hopes and if I mistake not, the Indians will now think for themselves, and send to the city a delegation prepared to cede their country & move X the M.

I have just discovered that Major Haley has been acting the double part with the view to obtain large reserves for the Indians, and to participate in them—he is the tool of Laflour, & has advised him not to meet us here, expecting that we would send commissioners into the nation, when he would become the contractor for their supplies, and when we would be so anxious to treat that we would yield to any terms demanded of us. If the eastern & Southern section of the Choctaw nation send in a full delegation; being two thirds of the whole nation, we will treat with them & leave the halfbreeds & wicked whitemen disappointed & at leisure to comment upon their own folly.

The current in Nashville begins to change its course, and the prime movers in this wicked persecution will ere long be left in a ridiculous situation. If Mrs. E. would consent to remain untill midwinter here, she would obtain a complete triumph every where, & the enemies, *here*, of Major Eaton compleatly put down—but I fear that the admonition of her friends will not be able to prevail. Major Eaton must forthwith repair to the city. I will be with you as early as possible, I travel thro' Virginia, write & say so to Mr Van Buren, I will notify you of the time I leave here—say to Mr Ingham I have recd his letter & am delighted to find that ~~we can~~ the revenue will permit us to apply so much to the discharge of the national debt—present my respects to all the Heads of Departments & Heads of Bureaus, & to Major Barrys family—say to him I have recd. a letter from Mr Blair Frankfort Ky and that she has done her duty. Ky is herself again, *& will sustain the republican Doctrine of 98 & 1800*—I am respectfully yr friend

Andrew Jackson

ALS and Copy, NN (16-0145).

To *William Polk*

Franklin August 25th. 1830—

Genl A. Jackson with his kind respects to Genl William Polk and lady, regrets to inform them, that it will be out of his power to pay his personal respects to them as he expected and intended. He is here, awaiting the movements of the Indians, and to hear from the Choctaws; and his duty urges him to the city of Washington to which, he must set out the moment he can leave the all absorbing subject which now engrosses his attention. He refers you for other reason to Colo. Polk who will hand you this. The Genl begs you to present his blessing to his name sake to whom he will send a momento of his friends, so soon as he can have it prepared—

AN, NcU (16-0159). AJ's namesake was William Polk's son, Andrew Jackson Polk (1824–1867).

From *John Caldwell Calhoun*

Fort Hill
25th. August 1830

Sir,

I received on the 6th Inst your letter dated 19th June, but which, I suppose, was intended for the 19th July, with its enclosures. On the 24th of June, I received the note of Mr Forsyth, covering a copy of his letter to you of the 17th of the same month, but owing to some delay in the conveyance, for which I am unable to account, I did not receive your letter of the 7th June, covering a copy of your letter to Mr Forsyth, till the 14th July

You regret, that I did not receive your letter of the 7th June, before I wrote mine of the 28th of the same month, on the ground, to use your own language, that it would have prevented me from falling into the gross errors I have from the unfounded inferences, I have drawn from Mr Forsyth's letter to me. You cannot more sincerely regret, than I do, that any delay in the mail deprived me of the advantage of your statement in your letter to Mr Forsyth, seeing that you deem it material to a correct understanding of the facts; but I must say, after a careful perusal of your letter to him, as well yours to myself, I am utterly at a loss to perceive the "gross errors" of which you accuse me. As far as I can understand you, they seem to consist in the supposition, that I infered from Mr Forsyth's letter, that you applied to him personally to obtain the information from Mr Crawford of what took place in the Cabinet on the Seminole question, whereas, in fact, you applied, not to him, but to Mr James Hamilton of New York, and that it was he, and not you, who applied to Mr Forsyth to obtain the information. If there be a difference in principle between the two statements, I can only say, that I am not responsible for it. The charge of error ought to be made against Mr Forsyth, and not me. His words are, "Having at the request of the President to be informed what took place in the Cabinet of Mr Monroe, on the subject of the Seminole Campaign, laid before him a copy (except the omission of a name) of a letter from Mr Crawford, which has been since communicated to you & &." Now, Sir, if I had infered from these words, as you suppose I did, that you had personally applied to Mr Forsyth to obtain the information for you, I would have done no more, than what I fairly might, without the imputation of "gross errors." But I made no such inference; on the contrary, I have used almost the very words of Mr Forsyth. My language is, "I have supposed from the complexion of your letters to me, that the copy of Mr Crawford's letter to Mr Forsyth had been placed by the latter in your hand, without any previous act, or agency on your part, but by Mr. Forsyth's letter to me, I am informed, that such is not the fact. It seems, that he acted as your agent in the affair. He states, that you applied to him to be informed of what took place in the Cabinet of Mr Monroe, on the subject of the Seminole Campaign." In my letter to Mr Forsyth I use almost verbatim the same language. As far as I am capable of understanding the force of words, my language does not vary, in the smallest degree, in its sense, from that used by Mr Forsyth in his letter to me, and most certainly does not more strongly imply, than his does, that you applied to him personally for the information. But suppose, I had fallen into the "gross errors" of infering from Mr Forsyth's letter, that you had personally applied to him, when, in fact, it was not you, but your agent James Hamilton, who applied for you, in your name, as Mr Forsyth informs you in his letter of the 17th June, it requires more penetration, than I possess, to discover how the difference can in the slightest degree effect the only material question, whether he acted, as a mere volunteer, or as your agent. Mr Forsyth himself decides this question. He tells you expressly, that he did not act, as a volunteer, and it is on the ground, that he acted for you, and not for himself, that I claimed of you to be put in possession of certain facts connected with the subject of our correspondence, which were in the possession of Mr Forsyth, and which I deem important to a full developement of this affair; but, instead of complying with so reasonable a request, you reply, not by denying the justice of the request nor that he acted for you and not for himself, but by accusing me with "gross errors," on an assumption, on your part, at once gratuitous and immaterial, that I had infered, that you had applied to Mr Forsyth personally, when in fact the application had been made for you in your name by Mr Hamilton. I must say, that I cannot see in your statement the least excuse for witholding from me the information requested, and I am constrained to add, that I have looked in vain in the course, which you have pursued, for the evidence of that frankness, which you assured me in submitting the copy of Mr Crawford's letter to me, has ever characterized your conduct towards those, with whom you had been in habits of friendship.

As connected with this point, let me call your attention to a fact, which has not been explained, tho in my opinion it ought to be. It now appears, that when Mr Forsyth placed the copy of Mr Crawford's letter in your hand, he also placed with it a copy of his letter refered to by Mr Crawford. Why was it, that a copy of this letter of Mr Forsyth did not accompany Mr Crawford's, when you placed a copy of the latter in my hand? Calling on me in the sperit of frankness and friendship, as you informed me you did, I had a right to infer, that every document connected with the charge, and in your possession, calculated to afford light, would be placed in my possession, and such in fact was my impression, but which I now find to be erroneous. It is with regret, that I feel myself const bound to state, that Mr Forsyth's letter, with the subsequent correspondence, has given an aspect to this affair very different from what, I received from your first letter.

You have stated some suggestions of the Marshall of the District, which were communicated to you, as the reason, why you have agitated this old affair at this time. You have not stated what they were, to whom made, or by whom communicated, which of course leaves me in the dark, as to their nature, or character, but whatever they may be, the course you adopted, considering the friendly relation, which I had reason to suppose existed between us, is well calculated to excite surprise. Instead of applying to the Marshall, in order to ascertain, what he did say and from whom he derived his information, and then submitting his statement to me, which course friendship and the high opinion, which you say you entertained for my character, "for fair, open and honorable conduct in all things" manifestly dictated, you applied for information, as to my conduct, to the man, who you know felt towards me the strongest enmity. I wish not to be understood, that you had mere general information of his ill will towards me. Your information was of the most specifick character, and was of such a nature, as ought to have made you distrust any statement of his calculated to effect my reputation.[1]

Knowing the political machination, that was carring on against me, and wishing to place me on my guard, a friend of mine placed in my hand, some time since, a copy of a letter written by Mr Crawford to a Nashville correspondent of his in 1827. It constitutes one of the many means resorted to, in order to excite your suspicion against me. In it, Mr Crawford makes an abusive attack on me, but not content with thus assailing me in the dark, he offers to bring into the market the influence, which Georgia might have on the Presidential election, as a mean whereby to depress my political prospects. To avoid the possibility of mistake, I will give extracts from the letter itself, in full confirmation of what I have stated. Speaking of the Presidential election, Mr Crawford says, that "the only difficulty that this state" (Georgia) "has on the subject" (your election) "that if Jackson should be elected Calhoun will come into power." Again, "If you can ascertain that Calhoun will not be benefitted by Jackson's election, you will do him a benefit by communicating the information to me. Make what use you please of this letter and show it to whom you please." That the letter was intended for your inspection cannot be doubted. The authority to his correspondent to make what use he pleased and to show it to whom he pleased, with the nature of the information sought, whether I was to be benefitted by your election, which could only be derived from yourself, leaves no doubt on that point; and I am accordingly informed that you saw the letter. A proposition of the kind, at that particular period, when the Presidential election was the most doubtful, and most warmly contested needs no comment, as to its object. To say nothing of its moral and political character, stronger proof could not be offered of the deepest enmity towards me, on the part of the writer, which ought, at least, have placed you on your guard, against all attacks on me, from that quarter. The letter will not be denied, but, if contrary to expectation, it should, I stand ready by highly respectable authority to prove its authenticity[2]

You well know the disinterested, open and fearless course, which myself and friends were pursuing at this very period, and the weight of enmity, that it drew down on us from your opponents. Little did I then suspect, that such secret machinations were carring on against me at Nashville, or that such propositions could be ventured to be made to you, or, if ventured, without being instantly disclosed to me. Of this, however, I complain not; nor do I intend to recriminate, but I must repeat the expression of my surprise, that you should apply to an individual, who you knew from such decisive proof to be actuated by the most inveterate hostility towards me, for information of my course in Mr Monroes Cabinet. It affords, to my mind, conclusive proof, that you had permitted your feelings towards me to be alienated, by the artful movements of those, who have made you the victim of their intrigue, long before the commencement of this correspondence.

Instead of furnishing me with the information, which I claimed, in order to a full understanding of this extraordinary affair, and which you could not justly withold, you kindly undertake to excuse the individual, to whom, you suppose, some allusion of mine to be made. I know not to whom you refer. I made no allusion to any one particular individual; but be that as it may, you must excuse me, if on subjects, which personally concern me, I should prefer my own judgement to yours, and, of course, if I should not be satisfied with your opinion, as a substitute for the facts, by which I might be able to form my own.

After I had so fully demonstrated the candour and sincerity, with which I have acted through out this whole affair, I did not suppose that you would reiterate your former charges; but having done so, it only remains for me to ~~contradict~~ repeat, in the most positive manner, the contradiction. I never for a moment disguised my sentiment on this, or any other political subject. Why should I in this instance? I had done nothing, which I ought to desire to conceal. I had violated no duty, no rule of honor, nor obligation of friendship. I did your motives full justice in every stage of the Cabinet deliberation, and, after full investigation, I entirely approved and heartily supported the final decision. In this course, I was guided, it is true, not by feelings of friendship, but a sense of duty. Where our country is concerned, there ought to be room neither for friendship, nor enmity.

You conclude your letter by saying, that you understand the matter now, that you feel no interest in this altercation and that you would leave me and Mr Crawford and all concerned to settle this affair in our own way, and that you would close the correspondence for ever.

It is not for me to object to the manner you may choose to close the correspondence on your part. On my part, I have no desire to prolong it. The spectacle of the first and second officer of this great Republick engaged in a correspondence of this nature, has no attraction for me, at any time, and is far from being agreeable at this critical juncture of our affairs. My consolation is, that it was not of my seeking; and, as I am not responsible for its commencement, I feel no disposition to incur any responsibility for its continuance. Forced into to it to repel unjust and baseless imputations on my character, I could not retire in honor, while they continued to be reiterated. Having now fully vindicated my conduct, I will conclude the correspondence also, with a single remark, that I too well know, what is due to my rights and to self respect, in this unpleasant affair, to permit myself to be diverted into an altercation with Mr Crawford, or any other individual, who you may choose to consider, as concerned in this affair. I am very Respectfully

J. C. Calhoun

[Endorsed by AJ:] to be carefully put on file with the other papers— A—J—   This is full evidence of the duplicity & insincerity of the man & displays a littleness & entire want of those high dignified & honorable feelings which I once thought he possessed—

ALS, DLC (38). *US Telegraph*, February 17, 1831. *Calhoun Papers*, 11:220–25.

1. AJ inserted a pointer here and wrote in the margin: "☞The reason I did directly apply to Mr Calhoun"

2. Calhoun quoted a Crawford letter of December 14, 1827, to AJ's friend Alfred Balch. Georgia congressman Wilson Lumpkin (1783–1870) forwarded it to Calhoun on January 27, 1829, with an assurance that AJ had seen it (*Calhoun Papers*, 10:554–56).

To the Chickasaw Indians

*[After deliberating over Jackson's August 23 address, the Chickasaw
delegates at Franklin composed a response on August 25 and presented
it to Eaton and Coffee on the 26th. While branding the assumption of
state jurisdiction over them "an act of usurpation . . . unparalleled in
history" and intended only "to drive us from our homes," they credited
Jackson with a sincere concern for their welfare and pledged to "talk in
earnest about an exchange" after they had seen their proposed new country and satisfied themselves of its quality. Eaton and Coffee responded on
August 26. Promising an equal exchange, they stressed the Chickasaws'
dire circumstances and urged them to "act, and act at once" lest the best
western lands be claimed by other emigrating Indians (HRRep 488, 22d
Cong., 1st sess., pp. 19–23, Serial 228).*

*This address by Jackson is not mentioned in the official treaty journal
(DNA-RG 75, T494-2). It may, according to its date, have been delivered
on August 26 in tandem with the reply of Eaton and Coffee. Alternatively,
it may be the text of the unrecorded remarks with which, according to the
treaty journal, Jackson took leave of the Chickasaws after their address to
him of August 27 below.]*

Friends & Brothers

I have received your talk—being an answer to my address to you of
the 23rd. instant. It has been laid before me by the commissioners I ~~had~~
directed to treat with you. It is such, as I had calculated to receive from
my chikisaw children. It shews that they have deliberated well, and are
mindfull of their true interests, and willing to do what in all future time
shall prove a lasting benefit to their children.

Brothers

your great father does not desire to place you in a country, where you
will not find soil and climate equal to the one you have. He will never
consent to place you where you would be in a worse ~~condition~~ situation:
his great desire is to make your condition better; not worse.

Brothers—Bad men have said; and they have told his red children, that
it was the intention of their great Father to drive them from their lands—
to compel them to seek a new home; and in the wilderness, to leave them
to suffer. Believe not these idle tales—your father has the frost of many
winters upon his head. From early youth he has lived near to ~~the~~ his red
children. He has slept with them—Hunted with them—and fought with
them; towards them, he has always entertained feelings of strong regard;
and will not fail to be their friend, if they shall permit it, and repose
confidence in him; He will ~~seek~~ have sought for them a good home, & one

large anough for all their purposes. He wants no land west of the Arkansa Territory for his white children, they will have enough without it—all that region of country west of it, he desires his red children to live upon, & be happy—each tribe to have anough for all reasonable purposes, to be defined by certain, & fixed bounderies; no more to be interupted or disturb. No laws, of a state or Territorys, will be permitted to operate over them, but they will be left subject to their own—no wars will there rage. The Red man, in peace & friendship with their great Father, will have his favor, & protection, from all enemies & bad men.

Brothers. Go on then, & conclude a treaty with the commissioners, I have appointed, on the principles you have stated. Have confidence in what they tell you—and hear what I now repeat to you, that a country every way desirable, and as good at least as the one you leave, shall be survayed and laid off for you, & your children forever; and if on examination you find it not such, then will your great father make ample amends to you for any inferiority and deficiency it may be found to contain

Brothers. Business calls your great Father to the City of Washington. He leaves his commissioners with you, to conclude this important Treaty as relates to your welfare, happiness, & perpetuation as a nation—and prays that the great spirit above may take you in his holy keeping, & guide, & direct you always

Andrew Jackson

[Endorsed by AJ:] reply of 26th. august

ADS, DNA-RG 75 (16-0162).

To the Choctaw Indians

Franklin 26. Aug. 1830

Friends & Brothers of the Choctaw Nation

The talk of the Chiefs, Captains, and warriors of the North Eastern, & Southern Districts, of the Choctaw nation of Indians in full council assembled, has been presented to me by your trusty friend Major Pytchlyn. I have listened to your complaints; feel for your distress, & will immediately appoint trusty and faithful friends to you & me, to see, & to confer with you. If possible the Secretary of War, will come, to explain fully every thing for me, as if I myself was present. Your old & tried friends Genl. Jno. Coffee, & his Excellency genl. Wm. Carroll, in whom I have every confidence, will be present with you as Commissioners to speak my sentiments, & advise you to your true interests. Confide in them. They are charged to act justly towards you, & see, that no wrong is practised. They will be instructed to meet in the nation and make a treaty with you in Council, that those of the Choctaws who have a desire to remove, may have the means afforded to them of doing so. They may then settle upon lands, given to them by Grant, which shall be theirs, & their childrens forever

Friends & Brothers

I have directed my commissioners to receive & acknowledge as medal chiefs, those who have been elected & acknowledged such, by the warriors within their respective Districts. It is the right of a majority to rule; and those who are so appointed, ~~are~~ in reference to the rights of the people are to be respected

Friends & brothers

Hear well, & listen! The time appointed for my commissioners to meet you is the 15th. of September, at Dancing Rabbit Creek, near to where the trace crosses it, leading from the agency, to the Counsha Towns, where from the talk sent ~~him~~, your Father expects you all, both medal, & the other chiefs to meet ~~him~~. There he hopes a treaty may be made, which shall make you happy, & settle you finally on land west of the Mississippi, that shall belong to you by Grant always, & make you happy forever

Brothers Listen

You must now make a voluntary choice: remove—seek a home beyond the Mississippi, or else remain, where you are, under the laws of the State, & as good people endeavour to conform to them. No other alternative is presented!

Andrew Jackson

[Endorsed by AJ:] Talk of the President U.S. to the chiefs of the Choctaw Nation—to be forwarded to them by Major Pitchlynn

DS in Eaton's hand, DNA-RG 75; ADS draft, PHi; Copy, DNA-RG 46 (16-0166). Eaton's finished text presented here closely followed AJ's draft.

From John Pope

Little Rock august 26th 1830

Dr sir

Before the receipt of your letter from Genl Eaton's I had been apprised of the result of the suit between Colo Combs & my nephew Mr Trotter[1]—I shall not visit Kentucky before the first of november—my business there will require an absence of six or eight weeks—There are frequent complaints made here by the Indians & whites living near our western boundary line about hunting stock which passes the line from each party— Colo arbucle has written me from Cantonment Gibson proposing a plan for regulating this matter, a copy of which I have transmitted to the war department & have declined acting on the subject without special instructions from you or Genl Eaton—I presume that this business properly belongs to the agents or some superintendant of indian affairs but whether within the pale of my duty as Governor of this Territory or not you may be assured of my prompt attention to whatever you or the secretary may deem most adviseable on this subject—If you could be certain of having at all times *a good Governor* here I would press on your consideration the expediency of making him superintendant & head of Indian & Territorial matters in this quarter—but the imputation of pecuniary motives to which I should expose myself constains me to forbear presenting my views again on this subject—I have sent you a copy of this letter of Colo Arbuckle & made this communication to you at the Hermitage with a hope that you & Genl Eaton may find it convenient to advise me on the subject before your return to the City—I have issued a proclamation notifiing the Indians not to hunt in this Territory & warned the militia officers to avoid as far as practicable the use of force or harsh measures to prevent them—I have spoken to the prosecuting attorney to Indict & use the proper means to punish if guilty the white man who killed the Indian in Pope County in this Territory—I feel much solicitude for your success in effecting an amicable arrangement with the southern Indians for their removal to the west of this Territory—I have no doubt that the measure will conduce to their good & the good of the nation—It is very desirable to have their consent upon any tolerable terms—Colo arbuckle is very desirous to have some arrangement made without delay between the whites & Cherokee Indians for the recovery of their stock & if compatible with the convenience of yourself & Genl Eaton I should be gratified to be advised immediately on the subject—The plan proposed may be attended with some expence— With high respect & consideration &c I am yours &c

John Pope

ALS, DLC (38). *TPUS*, 21:262-63. Pope enclosed a copy of a July 18 letter from Mathew Arbuckle, which he had also forwarded to the War Department. Arbuckle reported Western Cherokee complaints of an unpunished murder of a Cherokee by a white man and of interference and threats of violence against Cherokees who tried to retrieve cattle and horses that strayed into white settlements. Arbuckle proposed either sending a troop detachment or designating leading citizens to keep the peace and protect the Cherokees (DLC-38; *TPUS*, 21:245–46). Acting war secretary Philip G. Randolph replied to Pope on September 7 that disputes between whites and Indians over property or goods should be handled by Indian agents (*TPUS*, 21:267). In 1829 the War Department had rejected a proposal by Pope to assume superintendency of the Indians adjoining Arkansas, and to receive a stipend therefor (*Jackson Papers*, 7:529–30).

1. Presbyterian minister John Pope Trotter (d. 1839) was the son of Pope's younger sister. Leslie Combs (1793–1881) of Kentucky was a political foe of AJ. In 1828 he had enraged AJ by impugning his conduct as negotiator of an 1818 Chickasaw treaty.

To John Coffee and John Henry Eaton

Franklin 27. Aug: 1830

Being about to leave the State of Tennessee for Washington City, &
not knowing what business may arise with the Choctaws & Chickasaw
Indians in my absence, I do hereby appoint & authorise you to arrange
not only what has been confided to you by; but any other business which
said tribes may desire to transact, you are authorised to arrange & settle
fully, & make report of the same
  Given under my hand at Franklin

Andrew Jackson

DS in Eaton's hand, DNA-RG 75; Copy, DNA-RG 46 (16-0182).

From George Colbert et al.

Franklin Ten. Augst. 27th. 1830.

To our Great Father, the President.
  Your red children, the chiefs and head men of the Chickasaws, have
had under consideration the talk of our father and also, the talk delivered
to us by the commissioners, Majr. Eaton and Genl. Coffee.
  The subject submitted for our consideration, is, to us, of great importance to us. The decision we this day make and declare to you, and to the
world, depends our fate as a nation, and as a people.
  Father; You say that you have travelled a long ways, to talk to your
red children. We have listened, and your words have sunk deep into our
hearts. And as you are about to set out for Washington City; before we
shake our father's hand, perhaps, with many of us, the last time, we have
requesting this meeting to tell you, that after sleeping upon the talk you
sent us, and talks delivered to us by our brothers, Major Eaton and Genl.
Coffee, we are now ready to enter into a treaty, based upon the principles,
as communicated to us by Major Eaton and Genl. Coffee. Your friends
and brothers.

G. Colbert.
L. Colbert.
Jas. Colbert.
Wm. McGilvery
Jas Brown.

[Fourteen additional signatures follow.]

J. McLish
Secretary for the nation.

Copy, DNA-RG 75 (T494-2). Copy, DNA-RG 46 (16-0180). *HRRep* 488, 22d Cong., 1st sess., p. 23 (Serial 228). *SDoc* 512, 23d Cong., 1st sess., vol. 2, pp. 246–47 (Serial 245). *US Telegraph*, September 13, 1830. Levi Colbert (c1759–1834) and James Colbert (1768–1842) were George Colbert's brothers. James Brown and William McGillivray (c1754–1844) were Chickasaw chiefs, and John McLish (1780–1838) was secretary. The official treaty journal reported that AJ replied that he had indeed traveled far to see them, that important business now called him to Washington, and that he left the negotiation to his commissioners with instructions to act liberally. He then took his leave.

From Henry Lee

Port Mahon 29th. August 1830

dear Genl.

It is some days since in a letter which I enclosed for forwarding to our consul at Marseilles, I acknowled the recpt. of your kind and gratifying favour of the 4th. of June last—which was delivered to me here by Comre. Porter. As it will be satisfactory for you to learn that our intercourse was not disturbed by any pitiful jealousy or jarring, I take the liberty of enclosing ~~the copy of~~ a letter from him, shewing the spirit in which I rendered & he recd. such services as it was in my power to afford him, conducive to the discharge of his public duties. I need not add that his gallant services public spirit, and the unworthy treatment which they recd. at the hands of Messrs. Adams & Southard, made it a pleasure to me in vacating my office, to assist him in filling it with honour & success.[1]

In my former letter I mentioned that I should take the first opportunity of reading your argument in support of your veto on the Maysville Road Bill. This I have done & find it perfectly satisfactory not only as being irrefutable, but as taking away from the opposition every point of reasonable controversy. I shall have no longer the least confidence in the influence of reason and honesty over the public mind, if the motives and conclusions expressed and demonstrated in that paper ~~does not~~ do not satisfy the great mass of our fellow citizens, that in the conscientious discharge of your public duty, it was a matter of moral necessity that you should reject the bill. I trust they will be grateful ~~to you~~ for your firmness & not less so for the fearless manner in which you have exposed and arrested the vicious schemes invented by their unreflecting or profligate represenatives of pouring out the public treasure ~~for~~ in these unconstitutional channels instead of paying off the public debt—& of making this debt a pretext for a heavy tariff of duties in order that funds to be directed to these illicit and corrupting ~~channels~~ objects may be ~~provi~~ unadvisedly supplied by the deluded people. In this scheme the grand object of internal improvement is prostituted into an instrument for the selfish benefit of a few northern speculators—instead of being carried on by constitutional means, & for the advantage of those communities by ~~means of~~ whose labour and health, its several branches are to be executed. The first stalking horse behind which these sharpers operated was our sense of national independence. That being now seen through by a majority of the people, they have determined to substitute the strong and laudable anxiety that animates ~~the~~ various quarters of the Union, to bring our national resources into full & active development—as an instrument of similar delusion. Your clear and forcible argument will I trust render this attempt as frustrate as it its predecessor—

In my former letter I took the liberty of mentioning that I have been induced to believe that owing to the treachery or infidelity of Mr. Rhind—an old drunken Scotch merchant captain, as I am informed—a secret article had been attached to the Treaty lately negotiated with the ottoman porte, so much at variance with the ~~views~~ instructions of Mr. Van Buren, and the spirit of our international policy, that a reasonable certainty existed of your refusal to accept the treaty in its present shape. As I have never seen the treaty—the secret article or the instructions by which you wished our commissioners to be guided, I must not be understood as giving any opinion in presumptively forestalling of yours—but merely as stating, a hearsay conjecture, in order to introduce the application that follows. If the treaty should be rejected by you—it would seem to follow that a fresh negotiation and a new agency must be resorted ~~into~~ in order to correct the errour into which Mr. Rhind, it would appear, has fallen. If he has blundered in the manner he has been reputed to have blundered, & has led his colleagues into an errour by the false and entrapping measures he is said to have pursued—or if he is guilty of the gross intemperance which he is reported ~~to indu~~ on the best authority to indulge in, without looking to his foreign origins, his previous [. . .] pursuits & misfortunes, & his numerous other existing disqualifications, I should suppose you would not wish again to confide to him this delicate & important agency. If as I believe my small acquaintance with the Turkish character, be a small advantage, & you can place a full reliance on my zeal, as I trust you can, I hope to be excused for saying that I should be proud & happy to be employed in this business—and that I shall be in Paris about the 1st. Decbr. next ready to receive and to act on the earliest instructions that after your return from Tennessee can be sent out to me—and in a situation to repair to the scene of operations, by uniting with Comre. Biddle at this place much sooner than I could do—by coming out from the U.S. by the way of Gibraltar direct to this place. The letter above alluded to contained a full statement of the reasons which incline me to remain some months longer on this side of the Atlantic & as I have detailed them again to Donelson & Lewis I refer you to them, instead of fatiguing you with a second recital of them.

Before I conclude justice to myself renders it proper to say that I do not think my rejection by the senate for one office should necessarily be disqualify for appointment to another, neither under the provisions of the constitution, nor in the eyes of common sense. Noah was rejected & confirmed by the same senate, for the same office and during the same session. I am dear Genl. truly & gratefully yr. frd. & sert.

H. Lee

ALS, DLC (38).
1. Lee enclosed a copy of an August 22 letter from David Porter to Van Buren, thanking Lee effusively for his assistance and advice (DLC-38). Court-martialed in 1825 for his over-zealous actions in suppressing Caribbean piracy and for subsequent insubordination, Porter had resigned his commission and accepted command of the Mexican navy. Daniel Carroll Croxall (c1793–1877) was the U.S. consul at Marseilles.

Deed of Gift to Andrew Jackson Donelson (1826–1859)

I have this day presented to Andrew Jackson Donelson, son of Andrew, J. and Emily Donelson, the full blooded mare Bellasena, formerly the property of Henry cotton, with a stockholder filly at her foot—which I bind myself to warrent the title of said mare and mare colt to him & his heirs forever—His father has agreed to take charge of them for his son, & to him they are hereby delivered for the above purpose, & use—witness my hand this 30th. day of August 1830

Andrew Jackson

[Endorsed by AJ:] A Jackson To Jackson Donelson son of Andrew bill of sale of Belasena & her colt

ADS, DLC (73). On this day AJ purchased from Henry Cotten's estate one of the two mares he had been keeping at the Hermitage and her filly. In 1837 the *American Turf Register and Sporting Magazine* gave the mare's name as Bellissima. The filly was Lady Nashville.

To Gerard Chittocque Brandon

[On August 31, commissioners Coffee and Eaton concluded a treaty with the Chickasaw delegation at Franklin. Supplementary articles, mainly concerning private claims and reservations, were added September 1. By the treaty, the Chickasaws ceded all their lands east of the Mississippi in return for a fee simple title to a domain of equal size and quality west of Arkansas Territory, to be selected by a Chickasaw scouting party. Failure to find a suitable country would void the entire treaty. Half the

Chickasaws were to remove in the fall of 1831 and the rest a year later. The U.S. would bear all expenses, pay an annuity of $15,000 for twenty years after removal, and in the new country furnish supplies, tools, buildings, a blacksmith and millwright, and funds to pay teachers. Emigrating Chickasaws would be paid for their land and stock, and families choosing to remain were each to receive title to a half-section (320 acres) of land (DNA-RG 75, T494-2; Kappler, Indian Affairs: Laws and Treaties, (Washington, 1904), 2:1035–40).]

Hermitage near Nashville
August 31st. 1830

Sir

I have the pleasure to inform you that on this day the Chickasaws concluded and signed a Treaty with our Commissioners stipulating for the exchange of their whole country East of the Mississippi for lands West of that river.

In the 18th. clause of the Treaty it is stipulated that "the President will use his good offices and kind mediation and make a request of the Governor and Legislature of the State of Mississippi to prevent the laws being extended over the chickasaw people, or to suspend their operation until the fall of 1832, that time may be afforded them to remove."[1] Agreeably to this request, which is both reasonable and just, I take pleasure in addressing you, and thro' you the Legislature of your state, confident that the suspension of the laws until the fall of the year 1832, to give these people time to remove, will be promptly and cheerfully granted to them. This step under all the circumstances, will be regarded by the Indians as an act of kindness worthy of the justice and magnanimity of your State. It will enable them to leave us with feelings of friendship which it certainly is the duty of the General Government, and the common interest of both the Indians and our own citizens, to foster and cherish

I will be greatly indebted to you excellency to address a letter to Major John H. Eaton, Secretary of War, at the Choctaw agency, giving him your opinion, whether the Legislature of your State, will gratify this request of the Indians. The information that they will, or the expression of such an opinion from you, would no doubt have a good effect upon the Treaty pending with the Choctaws, who in all probability will imitate the example of the Chickasaws. You may judge therefore of my anxiety, that your Excellency and the Legislature of Mississippi, seeing the good effects which are likely to result from the suspension of the laws which the Indians look upon as unfavorable to their interests, will take the most timely means to secure it. I am Sir with great respect your most obt. servant

Andrew Jackson

LS in AJ Donelson's hand and Copy, Ms-Ar (16-0185). Brandon (1788–1850) was governor of Mississippi. He wrote Eaton on September 15 that "I have no hesitation in pledging myself that it will be done so soon as our Legislature convenes in November, so far as the Indians are concerned, but not as to the white men living in the nation" (Ms-Ar).

1. AJ closely paraphrased the treaty's final clause, following its seventeenth and last numbered article.

To *William Berkeley Lewis*

Hermitage August 31rst. 1830.

Dear Major

On last Saturday I returned from Franklin where I had been detained for Eight days, awaiting the conclusion of the chikisaws on the subject of a negotiation proposed to them—on Saturday they gave a written address & reply, that they would Treat upon the Terms I had proposed to them thro' my commissioner. I have this moment recd. from Major Eaton & Genl Coffee a letter informing me that on this morning They ~~have~~ signed a Treaty & in all the year 1832 they will cross the Missippi. Thus far we have succeeded against the most corrupt & secrete combination that ever did exist—and we have preserved my chikisaw friends & red brethern. Two thirds of the choctaws have requested me to send commissioners and they are prepared to treat & cross the Mississippi. I have directed The Sec. of War Genl Coffee, & have added Govr. Carroll, for certain reasons—to meet them on the 15th. proximo in the choctaw nation—where, notwithstanding, all the opposition, we will make a treaty with the choctaws. From their Chiefs & messengers sent to me; & the talk received & returned; I have no doubt of it myself. I therefore set out on thursday morning via virginia, & will reach the city at as early a day as I can—of this, advise Mr Van Buren, for really I am too much engaged with matters with the Indians, to write to Heads of Departments. I expect to reach the city *just as the official account from England gets there to open the West India trade by proclamation.* Should an express be sent to me on this subject, let it pass thro charlottsville va—and the main rout to abington. It is now eleven oclock P. M. and I must wish you good night—yr friend

Andrew Jackson

[Endorsed by AJ:] This not for publication—That the Treaty is signed may be given in the Tellegraph that it is a fair & just one

ALS, NNPM; Copy, NN (16-0191).

To James Knox Polk

August 31st. 1830
Hermitage
My Dear Sir,

After the conclusion of my talk with the Indians, the result of which you have no doubt heard before this, I felt too much oppressed by the ~~fatigue~~ heat of the weather, and the necessity of hastening the tedious journey which I am to undertake tomorrow, to comply with the polite request expressed in your note of the 14th inst. It would have afforded me the greatest pleasure to have seen you & Mrs. Polk and our common friends at Columbia, but I trust our old acquaintance with each other can readily pardon the postponement of it to another time. Present me kindly to Mrs. Polk and believe me sincerely yr. friend

Andrew Jackson

[In AJ's hand:]
(Private)
P.S. The Treaty with the chikisaws, satisfactory to all, has this day been signed & duly executed, & I have no doubt but the choctaws will follow the example, leaving the cherokees, & creeks, under the guardianship of *Mr. Wirt.* If I mistake not, the creeks will have a delegation at Washington before congress meets. They did not expect such an answer—as I directed to be made to them.

When you see my friends—Genl Polk & Lady, make my kind salutations to them, & Lucius, & particularly to my son.[1] I am off tomorrow morning. I have in the chikisaw treaty destroyed the serpent, & I hope so soon as I arrive at the city, to have the satisfaction of opening the West india trade to our country. This, if it be, will enable me to make, *a short, but pleasing communication to congress*—A. J.

LS in AJ Donelson's hand, DLC-Polk Papers (16-0197). *Polk Correspondence*, 1:330.
1. Lucius and AJ's "son" were Lucius Junius and Andrew Jackson Polk, sons of William Polk.

Memorandum on the Creek Indians

The Sec of War to the President on the subject of the creeks—answer directed to be returned that we leave them to their own will & guidance of Mr Wirt & *[the]* other evil councillors—directed the agent to be ready to settle as we might withdraw the agent entirely as it was doubtful of the propriety of keeping one since the Indians have been made citizens

AN, DLC (38). AJ wrote this on an undated envelope from Eaton, addressed to him at Nashville for hand delivery.

September

From John Henry Eaton

Franklin 1 Sept 30

Dear Genl.

The enclosed letter from J. Stewart at his request I send to you. He certainly will not answer for the 1st. place he proposes for—Commissioner in Grahams place—His next is for the Indian Department in McKenneys place   If he would answer there I should surely have no objection to ~~the man~~ him; if you have none you would prefer. As regards that, the Indians being removed there can be no great labor, or high mental powers wanted. The principal & most important duty would be, to arrange the amount of appropriations for that service, & by cautious attention see that they were properly drawn upon & at no time exceded[1]

The Chickasaw treaty may rouse the Cherokees & Creeks. I will write to Crowell, & this morning will dispatch Col. Lowry to the Creeks. I shall limit his service to some short period, and allow him only 3 dollars a day, which will about meet his expences   What he may do, will not exceed $150.[2] It will be *wonderful* if we get through with all the tribes before Congress meets; & now I should not be surprised if we did so. We shall now be run after by the Indians. Our treaty with the Chickasaws is I think liberal & excellent[.] Yrs truly

J. H Eaton

ALS, DLC (73). Eaton enclosed an August 26 letter from Nashville merchant James Stewart to AJ, asking to be named commissioner of the General Land Office, superintendent of Indian affairs, or to some other post. Stewart said Eaton had given him "every possible encouragement" to apply.

1. Thomas L. McKenney's post as Indian superintendent was technically a War Department clerkship. With Eaton away, acting secretary Philip G. Randolph notified McKenney on August 16 that he would be terminated September 1 (DNA-RG 107, M6-13).

2. This same day, Eaton instructed John Lowrey of Tennessee to visit the Cherokees (not Creeks) as special agent "and employ all fair arguments you can" to persuade them to remove. Lowrey reported back in late October that he had offered the Cherokees a proposition patterned after the Chickasaw treaty. The Cherokee Council refused to consider removal on any terms, though Lowrey reported a rising disposition among many Cherokees to submit and accept individual reservations, especially if their appeal to the Supreme Court should fail (*SDoc* 512, 23d Cong., 1st sess., vol. 2, pp. 98–99, 178–79, Serial 245).

From Felix Grundy

Nashville, Sept 1st 1830—

Dear Sir,

I now comply with the suggestion made, when I last saw you. Mr A Dunlap of Boston writes me, that the District Judge of New Hampshire is dead. I am strongly impressed with the propriety of your appointing Mr Woodbury to that place—he is certainly highly qualified, no man more so—that is the great point of recommendation to any office, and I apprehend all minor considerations concur in pointing to him. I think myself the office is too small for ~~that~~ the man, of that, however, he is the Judge—

I was anxious to see you before you left Tennessee and called at the Hermitage, on saturday, before you got home. I will endeavor to be at Washington a few days before Congress meets. At present the signs are, that Mr Clay will oppose you—& be beaten. I still think he & his friends will think better of it before the time arrives—yr friend

Felix Grundy

ALS, DNA-RG 59 (M639-27). Grundy wrote Levi Woodbury on August 24 that AJ had requested him to propose Woodbury for the judgeship in writing after Grundy had given assurance, based on a letter he had received from Woodbury, that Woodbury would accept (Woodbury Papers, DLC).

Andrew Jackson Donelson
to Emily Tennessee Donelson

Septr. 7th. Knoxville

Dear Emily:

Tho' very late at night I cannot defer the duty of apprising you of our safe arrival at this place this evening. Having been refreshed by several showers since we reached the mountains our journey on the whole may be said to have been much favored. We travel at the rate of about 30 miles a day, take a cup of coffee in the morning by candlelight, our breakfast at 10 or 11 after about 12 miles ride, our dinner at night; and then to sleep, but I, not without many thoughts about you and our dear little Jackson and Mary Ratchel. I hope indeed at some point between this and the city to hear that Jackson is restored, and that you and the babe are strong enough for excursions among your friends in the neighbourhood, and even to Washington should state affairs require your presence there.

Uncle is quite well—as much caressed on this route as he was on the other, and cheered by the most flattering accounts of the success of Mr.

McLean. There is but one thing to regret in all his administration, and that perhaps will soon be consigned to oblivion: at least I hope so, in all but that part of it which I may remember, as exalting you still higher in my Love and honor. You have too true a sense of what is due to virtue ever to pine at your own conduct, too just a respect for the honest opinion of others, ever to quarrel with it. In relation to this subject you have only to remember that whatever others do, you cannot change your position—you cannot visit the madam.

I shall write you occasionally on the route. In the mean time be happier than I can without you, kissing Jackson & Mary, and enjoying the kindness of your best of mothers, and the society of your affectionate brothers and sisters.

Remember me to them all, and especially to mother, Stockly & sister Philia[.][1] yrs. affectionately

Andrew J Donelson

I send this scrawl knowing it will be more acceptable than none.

[Envelope franked by AJ:] Free Andrew Jackson

ALS, DLC-Donelson Papers (16-0211).
1. Phila Ann Lawrence Donelson (1809–1851) was the wife of Emily's brother Stockley Donelson.

From Samuel Jackson Hays

Woodlawn
Sep. 12th. 1830

Dr. Uncle

I have the happiness to inform you, on last evening Frances presented me with a fine son.

She proposes calling him after you, & I should be the *last* to prefer an objection; all of her attendants have concurred in pronouncing him an extraordinary fine child—Unusually large

I hope before this reaches Washington you will have arrived there & have recovered from the fatigue of the journey.

I have no further news worth communicating. Many parts of the District have been characterised this season with an unusual degree of sickness. Our immediate family have escaped with the exception of the Dr. & his son William who have had slight attacks of the fever.[1]

The drought has been so inveterate & prevalent, that we won't realise half a crop of cotton—early corn excellent. We have neither seen nor received the scrape of a pen from brother since he went to see you at Nashville—begin to fear he must be sick, tho' I suspect he must be detained by the Federal court where he was summonsed as a witness—he might have written however.[2]

I had liked to have forgot to tell you that Frances & son are doing as well as could be expected. She unites with me in affectionate love to yourself—present us to such of our friends as may be with you[.] yours ever affectionately

S. J. Hays

N. B. The baby has very black hair & is said to be pretty much of an Hays in appearance. S. J. H.

[Endorsed by AJ:] S. J Hays & A. J. H. letters answd. 2nd. octbr. 1830—

ALS, DLC (38). Woodlawn was Hays's Jackson, Tenn., estate. The new baby was Andrew Jackson Hays (1830–1878). AJ replied on October 2 (below).

1. Probably Hays's brother-in-law Dr. William E. Butler and his son William Ormonde Butler (1814–1881).

2. Samuel's brother was Stockley Donelson Hays (1788–1831).

From George Vashon

Cant. Gibson 12th Septbr. 1830

Sir,

Under the impression that it is the duty of Ind Agents to apprize you of every procedure which may have a tendency to counteract the views of the Governt. as exhibited by treaties, laws, or regulations on the subject of Ind Affs. I beg leave to present to your notice the following communication.

I am informed from a source entitled to confidence, that Col: Augst. P. Chouteau a trader, & brother to the present Agent for the Osages, has purchased up the Reserves on the Neosho, granted by treaty 2 June 1825, to half breed Osage Children & others, and that two of said reserves containing a valuable Saline, has just been sold by said Chouteau to Genl S. Houston & a Mr. Drenen a mercht. of Nashville, who appears to be connected in trade with Genl H. in the Cherokee country & within 3 miles of this post, and I have good reason to believe they have purchased these reserves from Col. Chouteau, with the view & expectation of prevailing on the Governt. to purchase them out, at an exorbitant price, by availing themselves of an undue influence over the Cherokees to induce them to demand of the Governt. the removal of persons unacceptable to them, under the 3 Article of the treaty of 6 May 1828; the application would be, I presume, for removing the Osage grantees.[1]

The case of Genl. S. Houston, which has been reported by Col Arbuckle to the Secrety of War for his decision, was accompanied by a certificate of the adoption of Genl H. into the nation, with the right to exercise all the privileges of a native, and under which he claims the right to trade without License, deeming the laws, regulating trade & intercourse inapplicable to his case. The 9th. Art of treaty of Hopewell & 6th Art of treaty of Holston, gives to Congress the sole & exclusive right of regulating trade carried on by natives & others, but I have not seen any law restraining the exercise of the right of the natives or of the adopted whites among them, to trade in any way—the Whiskey trade carried on by Indians is a growing evil, and greatly to be deplored through out every Indian Tribe, and therefore deem it my duty, as it appears the existing laws on the subject does not embrace such cases, to solicit your attention thereto, and to suggest the necessity of instructing Agents how they are to consider white persons who are permitted by the Indians to reside amongst them.[2]

Permit me also to suggest what appears to be requisite to effect a speedy & satisfactory adjustment of the conflicting claims of the Cherokees & Creeks to the territory ceded to them by treaty, and to solicit your approbation of the course I am pursuing in furtherance of that object. The map of this country furnished the War dept. by Col: Arbucle, being considered too imperfect for the requiste purpose, I have deemed it my duty to request Col Arbuckle to employ without delay the most efficient means in his power to obtain a correct survey of the Canadian & Arkansas from their junction to such point as he may deem necessary to enable the Governt. to make such a partition of the country, as the just claims of the parties under their respective treaties may require: and with a view to ascertain what partition of the country would be most satisfactory & acceptable to the parties, I have requested the co-operation of Genl Campbell, and if accorded will report progress to the Dept. so soon as essential facts can be ascertained—and should it be proven as is expected, that the country west of the old territorial line between Arkansas & Canadian, together with that section of country now occupied by the Creeks in the fork of the Verdigris & Arkansas, will be found sufficiently large for the settlement & accommodation of the whole Creek nation, I have no doubt that the country north & west thereof to the Osage line, would be accepted by the Cherokees for the deficit of their seven million acres & perpetual outlet.[3]

By the statement of Genl Campbell, since his return to the Creek Agency, it appears to be the intention to cede to the Creeks the whole of the country in the fork of the Canadian & Arkansas, including the land east of the old territorial line in said fork (which is considered as having been heretofore ceded to the Cherokees) together with the whole of the country in the fork of the Verdigris & Arkansas to the Osage line—Hence it is my duty to apprize you without delay of the probable effect which such partition of the country is likely to produce—about 60 or 70 families of Cherokees have settled on their lands in the fork of Canadian & Arkansas east of the old territorial line, and the nation justly considers that portion of their country more valuable than any other—the uneasiness produced by this rumer has induced many of the most intelligent to request me to inform them if it is possible that such rumer can be true;

adding that the Creek treaty did not authorize them to make any selection east of the old territorial line, and therefore it ought not now to be contemplated by the Governt. to violate the vested right to that portion of their country which they think must be admitted to be solemnly guaranteed to them by their late treaty; and that no fair construction of the proviso to the ratification could infringe their legal claim to said land. I deemed it my duty to assure them that their rights would not be violated, and that the Governt. would certainly fulfil their treaty stipulations in good faith—that I considered their view of the subject perfectly correct, and that I had no doubt the Governt. would sustain their claim.

Permit me to say that I think it important to the interest of all parties that every doubt upon the subject should be promptly removed.

And it is deemed a duty also to apprize you of the state of feeling which this question, and the long continued delay of payment under treaty stipulations has produced among these people—they appear to feel as if they had good reason to believe that the Governt was disposed to pay but a very limitted observance of a faithful compliance with treaty provisions, after effecting the removal of the Indians, and feelingly point to the distressed condition of their emigrant families.[4]

I am induced to believe if that portion of their country should be disposed of to others, they will assert their rights, and maintain possession to the last—they say their right to it shall never be surrendered.

Please indulge the privilege of expressing my solicitude for the early receipt of such information & instructions together with the requisite means which may be deemed necessary to enable me to fulfil & accomplish the views of the Governt. relative to the duties of my agency. I have the honor to be Your most obt & hum servt.[5]

Geo: Vashon
Ind Agent C. W. M.

P.S. I have been under the necessity of providing an office & quarters for myself ever since the commenct of my duties in the Ind dept.[6]

[Endorsed by AJ:] recd. Octbr. 24th. 1830—Capt Vashon Indian agent—To be answered—That justice will be done the cherokees—Their lines will be spedily run and marked, at least as soon as, Congress will appropriate for this object, and the Treaty in good faith carried into effect—This to be retained a few days for the arrival of the Sec. of War—

ALS, DNA-RG 75 (M234-77). Copy, DNA-RG 46 (16-0239). *SDoc* 512, 23d Cong., 1st sess., vol. 2, pp. 113–14 (Serial 245). Vashon (1786–1836) had been appointed agent to the Cherokees west of the Mississippi in February 1830.

1. An Osage treaty signed at St. Louis in 1825, ceding lands in present Kansas and Oklahoma, reserved individual square-mile tracts for a number of "half-breeds," including relatives of fur trader Auguste P. Chouteau and his brother Paul Liguest Chouteau (1792–1851), now Osage agent. The 1828 Treaty of Washington, by which the Western Cherokees exchanged their lands in Arkansas for a domain in Oklahoma, placed these res-

ervations within Cherokee territory. It also obligated the U.S. to remove from that territory all whites and any others "unacceptable to the Cherokees." On September 1 Chouteau sold to Houston, in partnership with traders John Drennen and David Thompson, two Osage reservations containing salt springs on the Neosho River near present Salina, Oklahoma. They were later acquired by Cherokee chief John Rogers.

2. The Cherokee treaties of Hopewell (1785) and Holston (1791) recognized Congress's exclusive right to regulate Indian trade. On July 23 Mathew Arbuckle, commanding at Cantonment Gibson, had written Eaton challenging Houston's claim to exemption from regulation on the basis of his adoption by the Cherokees on October 21, 1829. Acting Secretary of War Philip G. Randolph replied on September 11, concurring with Arbuckle that the Cherokees could permit U.S. citizens to live among them but could not confer on them privileges incompatible with federal law. Houston, like other traders, would have to provide bond and obtain a license from the agent (DNA-RG 75, M234-77). Attorney General Berrien upheld this decision in a formal opinion on December 21 (*HRDoc* 123, 26th Cong., 2d sess., pp. 800–802, Serial 387).

3. The 1828 Western Cherokee treaty moved Arkansas Territory's western boundary more than forty miles eastward, to the present state line, and guaranteed the Cherokees seven million acres within a prescribed area immediately west of it, plus an open outlet to the western limit of American terrain. In potential conflict was the previous Creek Treaty of Washington of 1826, which authorized the emigrating McIntosh Creeks to occupy a reasonably sized domain of otherwise unallocated lands "wherever they may select" in the same region. Flowing eastward through Oklahoma, the Arkansas River is joined by the Verdigris from the north and the Canadian from the south. Vashon wrote AJ again on November 21. He recommended confining the Creeks north of the Arkansas where most were already settled, moving the Osage further north if necessary to accommodate the whole Creek nation there, and leaving the Cherokees in sole possession, as promised in the 1828 treaty, between the Arkansas and Canadian.

4. Vashon complained to Eaton on December 2 that the Western Cherokees were still owed more than $68,000 in unpaid annuities, spoliation claims, and emigration stipends promised them by treaty (DNA-RG 75, M234-77).

5. Vashon had written Eaton for instructions on August 28 (DNA-RG 75, M234-77). Randolph sent him general instructions for operating the agency on October 15 (DNA-RG 75, M21-7).

6. Randolph's October 15 instructions directed Vashon to locate a permanent site for the agency and submit a cost estimate for construction of buildings, quartering himself meantime at Cantonment Gibson.

To William Berkeley Lewis

Botetourt Springs
Septbr 18th. 1830—

Dr Major
We reached here this evening all well, my horses a good deal jaded— proceed on tomorrow a Sabath days journey; and hope, if my horses hold out, to reach the city in 6 or 7 days
with my kind salutations to heads of Depts. & of Bureaus & all friends believe me yrs.

Andrew Jackson

ALS, NNPM (16-0250). Botetourt Springs is near present Roanoke, Virginia.

From James Duane Doty

[Treaties, or compacts, concluded under federal auspices in 1821 and 1822 between Menominee and Winnebago delegates and prospective emigrant "New York Indians"—largely Oneida, Stockbridge, and Brothertown—undertook to provide the latter a home in the Fox River region of present Wisconsin. The Menominees and Winnebagoes subsequently repudiated the agreements, saying they were unauthorized and gave up too much land. In the 1827 Treaty of Butte Des Morts with the U.S., they agreed to refer the dispute for final decision by the president. Jackson to that end on June 7, 1830, appointed a commission composed of New Yorkers Erastus Root (chairman) and James McCall and Michigan Territory secretary John T. Mason. Eaton instructed them on June 9 to fix a definite domain within the contested area for the New York Indians. The commissioners convened in Detroit in July and met at Green Bay in August with representatives of the Indian nations. They submitted their report on September 20 (SDoc 512, 23d Cong., 1st sess., vol. 2, pp. 8–13, 99–103, 123–68, Serial 245). Doty (1799–1865), later Wisconsin territorial governor and congressman, was at this time a federal judge for Michigan Territory and served as counsel for the Menominees before the commission.]

Green Bay
Septr. 18. 1830.
Sir,

The leading commissioner of the Indian Embassy which has just left this place, attempted to intimidate the white people whilst here to prevent them from doing what they had never done to wit, ejecting the N.Y. Inds., & he threatens that so soon as he can reach Washington he will utterly destroy them by insinuation & sarcasm. Nevertheless, I will venture to presume so far, as to solicit of you a perusal of the enclosed paper which will best inform the govt. whether there was or is any disposition manifested here to oppose or thwart its views. The original was filed with the Commissioners.[1]

It would not be difficult, I am informed, to induce the most of the N.Y. Indians who propose to establish themselves here, to remove at once to some suitable portion of the country west of the Mississippi. I have stated the question to them, and the only opposition which it has received is from one or two individuals who expect to receive a large part of the tract claimed here. They will forever prevent an amicable and just settlement of the claims of the N.Y. Indians to this country. You will perceive that they are not even satisfied with what two of the Commissioners—and those two from New York—say is sufficient for their use.[2]

The Fox and Wiskonsin Rivers are the natural Indian boundaries at the present day, between the Great Lakes and the Mississippi. And I would ~~take the liberty to~~ respectfully suggest, that if no *new* Tribes are introduced into the country *south* of these streams the day is not distant when the whole of those Indians now residing in this portion of the country will cheerfully emigrate. A residence of twelve years in what has been considered the Indian country has satisfied me that the course which you have adopted respecting the Indians is the only practicable method left to preserve them. And I have no doubt that an act of Congress extending the Laws of the Territory over those of the New York Tribes who have settled here, as well as over other civilized Indians, ought to be passed. The Committee of Elections in Congress in 1826 in ~~their~~ Report declared the votes of such persons legal.[3] I am Sir, ever respectfully Your obedient servant—

J D Doty—

ALS draft, CSmH (16-0248).

1. The disputed compact of 1822 had granted the New York Indians shared tenancy of the whole Menominee domain of more than five million acres, far larger than their presumed needs, in return for a payment of $3,000. At the commission hearings in Green Bay, the New York Indians claimed that the Menominees had deliberately given them co-ownership of all their lands so they could help "keep off the white man." On September 10, Doty protested to the commissioners that the compact frustrated government policy by interdicting white acquisition and settlement of Menominee lands and making the New York Indians "guardians and trustees" of "an Indian country, subject to their own exclusive and independent control." In December, Root charged that Doty's interest in white land claims underlay his counsel to the Menominees to repudiate the compact (*SDoc* 512, 23d Cong., 1st sess., vol. 2, pp. 156, 131, 211–12, Serial 245).

2. Commissioners Root and McCall proposed assigning the New York Indians about 300,000 acres. (Mason declined his assent, saying they were exceeding their authority.) As they reported on September 20, all parties at Green Bay opposed this settlement: the Menominees and Winnebagoes for yielding too much land, the New York Indians for giving them too little (*SDoc* 512, 23d Cong., 1st sess., vol. 2, pp. 123–27, Serial 245). On September 8, Green Bay Indian agent Samuel C. Stambaugh wrote AJ asking permission to lead a Menominee delegation to Washington to present their case in person. The delegates arrived in December, and in February 1831 they concluded a treaty ceding about 500,000 acres to the U.S. for the New York Indians in return for a payment of $20,000.

3. The Act authorizing election of a congressional delegate from Michigan Territory entitled every qualified "free white male citizen" to vote. In investigating charges of illegal balloting in a contested 1825 election, the House Committee on Elections opined that Indians, not tribal members, who were "assimilated to, and associated with, the great body of the civilized community" could be permitted to vote (*HRRep* 69, 19th Cong., 1st sess., pp. 6–7, Serial 141).

From Stockley Donelson Hays

Jackson
Sepr 21st. 1830.

Dr Genl.

I learn from several quarters on the Border, that many of our good orderly, but enterprising citizens intend forthwith, to move over on to the Chickisaw lands to procure occupant claims—

There is a treaty stipulation to prevent this procedure—[1]

Untill the U States troops can arrive, Would it not be well to issue your proclamation on the subject—to prevent the great mischief which may otherwise ensue.

I write this at the suggestion of several of our friends here.

all friends here are in good health. With a tender of my ardent wishes for your health & happiness, I remain your unchanged friend & obt Srvt.

S. D. Hays.

[Endorsed by AJ:] The acting Sec. of war will instruct the chikisaw agent to forwarn all person from moving to, or intruding on the chikisaw lands assuring them that ~~they~~ all trespassers will be removed from it and their houses burnt & every thing destroyed   A. J.

ALS, DNA-RG 75 (M234-136). Copy, DNA-RG 46 (16-0254). *SDoc* 512, 23d Cong., 1st sess., vol. 2, p. 174 (Serial 245). AJ forwarded this note to acting secretary Randolph on October 7 (below).

1. The Chickasaw treaty forbade U.S. sale of ceded lands until after the Indians had removed. It did not add, as did the Choctaw removal treaty in September, an explicit prohibition on settlement within the ceded country previous to removal and sale.

From Comstick et al.

In council Seneca Village
September 22d. 1830—

To Andrew Jackson Our Great Father
President of the United States.

Our Great father is again requested to give his red children his ear. They sent to him a year ago their application, informing him of their desire to dispose of their reservation on the Sandusky river in Ohio, and their wish to go away beyond the Mississippi   They have received no answer to their request   They are fearful that their Great Father has not been made acquainted with their wishes. His red children are now more anxious than ever to emigrate—They wish to exchange their Lands here for other on the west side of the Mississippi. The game is destroyed around their Lands in Ohio, and their young people are daily learning bad habits from the white people. They therefore wish to leave this country as soon as their Great Father will allow them to exchange their Lands, and give them the means of departing for their new home. They will then have some hope of reclaiming such of their children as have fallen into bad habits, and be more likely to prevent their young children from contracting similar ones.

Father, your red children request that some person may be sent to them, to council concerning the exchange of their Lands for other Lands in the west. Or should our Father think proper to permit his red children to come on and see their Great Father, and send them word, they will come on and see their fathers face and treat with him for their new country, which he will give them beyond the Mississippi.

Father your red children know that you are a great warrior. They know that you are just and wise in Council, and they believe that you love your red children, and will give them a kind answer—your red children will wait patiently until their Father shall send them word.

Father we thank you for appointing our good brother John McElvain our Agent—he is very kind to his red friends and gives them good advice.

Father your red children sincerely wish that you may live very long and be always well and may the Great spirit now and hereafter bless you.

Comstick	Chief	his	X	mark
Small cloud	"	his	X	mark
Seneca Steel	"	his	X	mark
Tall Chief	"	his	X	mark
Curley Eye's	"	his	X	mark

[Fourteen more signatures follow.]

Henry C. Brish	Assistant Agent[1]
Martin Lane	Interpreter

DS, DNA-RG 75 (M234-669). Copy, DNA-RG 46 (16-0256). *SDoc* 512, 23d Cong., 1st sess., vol. 2, pp. 169–70 (Serial 245). Comstick (also rendered as Cornstick or Coonstick) was principal chief of the Sandusky Senecas, numbering about four hundred. The Seneca chiefs had previously solicited AJ for a removal treaty in October 1829 (*Jackson Papers*, 7:496–97). A delegation led by Comstick, Small Cloud Spicer, and Seneca Steel went to Washington and signed a removal treaty there in February 1831.

1. Henry Colgate Brish (1799–1866) had recently been named subagent for the Ohio Senecas.

To James Henry Handy

SIR—

I take pleasure in acknowledging the receipt of your letter of yesterday, as it affords me an opportunity of expressing my concurrence with the result of the election in the Second Presbyterian Church, to supply the place of Mr. Campbell. I have great confidence in the piety and zeal of Mr. Baker; and had I been present when he was put in nomination, would have voted for him.

I am, very respectfully, your obedient servant,

ANDREW JACKSON.

Printed, *The Life and Labours of the Rev. Daniel Baker, D. D.* (Philadelphia, 1858), p. 154 (mAJs). John N. Campbell, AJ's adversary in the Eaton controversy, had resigned his pulpit at the Second Presbyterian Church in Washington for one in Albany, N.Y. Daniel Baker (1791–1857) had preceded Campbell at Second Presbyterian before accepting a Savannah, Ga., pastorate in 1828. Handy (1789–1832) was a church elder and a clerk in the fourth auditor's office. On September 27 he also wrote John Q. Adams, who attended Second Presbyterian when in Washington, asking his approval of the call to Baker to help quell opposition in the congregation. Adams responded similarly to AJ. Baker declined returning to Washington.

To Charles Richard Vaughan

I have received with deep regret the dolefull intelligence of the decease of your august Sovereign George the 4th. and offer you my sincere condolence at an event so well calculated to remind nations of their dependence upon the author of all good. But whilst I thus mingle my sorrows with yours, permit me to congratulate you and your Majestys subjects generally, that this dispensation of providence has been so mercifully ordered as not to be without a solace which may well excite their gratitude. In the Succession of his brother William the 4th. I feel confident that the people of England will find all the blessings of the succeeding reign; & that Foreign powers will see in it the same gurantees for a just & liberal intercourse preserved & strengthened. The long experience of his Majestys first minister confirms this pleasing anticipation, & would authorise us to look for a policy calculated to avert forever if it were possible, the horrors & miseries of war.

Permit me to assure you that the intercourse ~~that~~ which it may be my lot to have with your majestys Government will be dictated by an earnest desire to cultivate the same feelings of good will and friendship which were maintained with his predecessor—

AD, DLC (73). At an audience on September 28, Vaughan presented letters of June 29 and 30 from William IV, announcing George IV's death and his succession and renewing Vaughan's credentials as minister. This was AJ's reply.

From John Coffee

[On September 27, after a ten-day negotiation, John Coffee and John Eaton acting as U.S. commissioners concluded a removal treaty with the Choctaws at Dancing Rabbit Creek in the Choctaw Nation. Greenwood Leflore, Mushulatubbe, and Nitakechi headed the 151 Choctaw signatories, who also included David Folsom and John Garland. By the treaty the Choctaws ceded all their lands (individual reservations excepted) east of the Mississippi in return for a deed in fee simple to the country west of Arkansas Territory between the Canadian River to the north and the Red to the south, where the western Choctaws already resided. The Choctaws were to remove in three groups in the fall of 1831, 1832, and 1833. They were guaranteed permanent exemption from state or territorial authority, and all previous annuities to them were reaffirmed with an additional annual payment of $20,000 for twenty years after removal. White settlement within the present Choctaw country previous to removal was banned. Supplemental articles, signed September 28, authorized a party to scout the new country promptly at U.S. expense and also provided numerous private reservations for individual Choctaws and connected whites.]

Chocktaw Agency
29th. Sept. 1830.

My dear Genl,

I have the satisfaction to inform you, that on yesterday we closed a treaty with the Choctaws for all their country on the east side of the Missipi. River—Between five and six thousand of the Indians attended the treaty, and I think they are generally satisfied—when we first met them, great discontent prevailed; the first thing was to reconcile them among themselves, which we succeeded in pretty generally—then we went into the subject of the treaty, and with much difficulty their situation was made plain to their view by the Secty. of War (who was of himself a host on that occasion) when well understood by them, there was not much difficulty afterwards to frame a treaty—the terms allowed them are liberal, as you instructed us to make for their comforts, yet I think it a good treaty for the U. States.[1] I shall not enter into detail now, (as we are pressing on homewards) Major Eaton will write you as soon as he reaches Franklin and give you the details—Genl. Carroll did not come out with us, I understand he said, his health was not very good, so it is he declined coming, and fortunately we have been able to succeed without him—I hope you will approve the treaty when you see it.

I should be gratified to hear from you, how your health is, and how you got along with your fatigueing Journey—Major Eaton & myself are in good health—he joins me in friendly salutations to you—Dr. Genl. yours—

Jno. Coffee

ALS, DLC (38). AJ replied on October 16 (below).

1. When the Choctaws during the negotiation suddenly balked at removing, Eaton delivered an address charging them with deceit and threatening to break off the talks and leave them forever to their fate under Mississippi's laws (DNA-RG 75, T494-2; *SDoc* 512, 23d Cong., 1st sess., vol. 2, pp. 260–61, Serial 245).

From John Randolph

London September 17th/29th 1830. Wednesday

My dear Sir

The first law of man's nature, Self Preservation, has compelled me to anticipate your kind indulgence & to leave St. Petersburgh much sooner & more abruptly than I had intended. I left that Capital on Sunday the 7/19 Instant & landed at the Custom House wharf this morning at 8, via Hamburgh.

Nothing could have surpassed the affability & cordiality of my reception by their Imperial Majesties of all the Russias, & by the minister Prince Lieven. His Highness has won upon my esteem & his kindness has excited my regard.[1]

This is the last day that I can write by the Packet, which leaves Liverpool on the 1st. of next month. (the day after tomorrow.) I shall therefore reserve my further communication for the packet of the ~~forthcoming~~ next week (the 8th.)   The following extract from a Memo: of Mr Clay will suffice to show that (health out of the question) I have not compromitted any interest of our Country, or acted contrary to your instructions or wishes, in leaving that deleterious & deadly climate (for such it is in the summer & autumnal months) so soon.

Extract from Mr Clay's Memor: of his interview with His Highness Prince Lieven; by Mr Randolph's command.

"He (Prince Lieven) took the paper & read a few lines: suddenly stopping, he enquired after Mr. Randolph's health.

I told him that "Mr Randolph desired me to say to His Highness, that he thought his dissolution was approaching, & that the only way in his opinion to arrest it was to leave St Petersburgh immediately. That such being the case, Mr R. desired that His Highness would cause Passports to be made out for himself & his two black servants; that he would have written to His Highness, but that he was past writing, having made his last effort, yesterday, (Sept 7th) in the note which he had then the Honour to address to His Highness & which he *wrote lying on his back*." I then proceeded to state that on the day that Mr R. had the Honour to be presented to His Imperial Majesty & His August Consort, he (Mr. R) was in the hot stage of an ague.

Prince Lieven. "Was he indeed?," expressing great concern) Mr Clay— "& on the day of his last ~~audience~~ interview with ~~His~~ Your Highness Mr R. was obliged to be borne from his carriage, by his servants, to the ante chamber of the audience Room; & that he had been sinking ever since.

His Highness expressed the utmost concern & gave orders that "the Passports should be immediately made out."

"He then enquired whether or not I was to be left Chargé d'Affaires?" I told him "I thought not—but simply Secretary of Legation." I then told His Highness that "Mr. Randolph desired me to ask for the" (papers left for the consideration of the Imperial Ministry) which were accordingly sent for.

His Highness told me that "he had referred the Papers to the ~~Committee~~ Ministers of Finance & of Commerce; that Russia was in every way amicably disposed towards the U.S. *but that the subject of Navigation & Commerce was one of great importance & that he thought it would be impossible to give an answer in time to meet the wishes of the President."*

The papers being brought His Highness put them into my hands, & desired me "to tell Mr Randolph that he (Prince Lieven) was much concerned to hear of Mr Randolph's illness, & that he would call upon him that day (Septr. 8) and asked me where Mr R. was at present" (I had given up my House & removed to an English widow Lady's to be nursed) "I told him that Mr R. was at present at the Chancery of the Legation no 192* English Back Line. I then made my obeisance & retired."

*"This was a great blunder for the number is 197 & not 192." This note is written by Mr Clay.

and to this "*blunder*" it was owing that I did not see His Highness, who was obliged that Evening to attend the Emperour at Czarsko Selo where he was engaged long after the time fixed for my departure; which was prolonged by the detention of the Steam Boats from Lubec by bad weather.[2]

I trust my dear, Sir, that you will excuse this hurried letter written in pain & sickness. By the next packet ship you shall hear more fully. I purpose going to the continent to try & renovate my shattered system. If the season were a fortnight earlier I would embark at once for the U.S. as it is I shall if it pleases God return to St. Petersburgh (with your approbation) in the Spring & to the U.S. in September next, if not sooner. I am my dear Sir with the highest esteem & regard, your most faithful servant

John Randolph of Roanoke

ALS, DLC (38). AJ replied on December 3 (below).
    1. Nicholas I (1796–1855) was Emperor of Russia. His wife was Alexandra Feodorovna (1798–1860), the former Princess Charlotte of Prussia. Christopher Andreievitch Lieven (1774–1839), Russia's ambassador to Britain, was serving as interim foreign minister.
    2. Tsarskoe Selo (now Pushkin) was the royal family's country estate outside St. Petersburg.

To John Overton

Washington Septbr. 30th 1830

My Dr friend

I reached this place on the night of the 25th. instant all in good health but much fatigued with the rough roads—on the first part of our journey suffocated with dust, and experiencing much inconvenience from the scarcity of water for our horses—on the latter part deludged with constant & heavy falls of rain—on the 27th. I received your very friendly letter of the 14th. and after perusal & noting its contents disposed of it as requested.

I rejoice at your increasing good health, but sincerely regret that my good friend, your amiable Lady, is checkered, but I trust in the goodness of an all wise providence that with care her health will be perfectly restored, and she will be permitted long to live, as a blessing to you, and your dear children.

The drougth has been severes generaly; the corn & cotton in North & South Carolina on their uplands are very short, & the late storm has done much injury to their low lands, as far as my information extends, there will not be half usual crops and the price will rise; for myself I do not calculate on more than 200 lbs of seed cotton to the acre, if it should, as you state, produce five hundred, I shall be content, and when it is tested will thank you for the information of its product.

We are waiting daily to receive from England the final result of the negotiation about the West India trade, have every right to expect a favorable one—by the first arrival we must have it, which is daily expected—Indeed I travelled hard expecting it to be here awaiting my arrival; but the rejoicing & feasting on Williams Succession to the throne, has delayed all business, but from the Kings expressions to, and kind attention to Mr McLean, I have no doubt but the result will be as we expect it—a few days will decide.

Business has greatly accumulated in my absence—I found every thing well and have just ordered two millions more of the national debt to be paid—This will make in all this year about 12 millions   This will leave about 16 millions of the 5 & 4-½ prcent unpaid—13 millions of the 3 per-cent & 7 millions of the Bank stock which we can sell for 120—advance—and if I live on the 4th. of March 1833 I will, I hope, by the sale of land pay the last dollar—[1]

It is late, I must close—do write me often, and give me all the news—I wish Major Eaton was here, his Department wants his presence very much, and untill he does arrive, will throw much labour upon me—I hope before this reaches you he will be here, as I expect he will take the stage leaving his family to come on with Doctor Breathit.

Present me kindly to Mrs O. and all your family. Major Lewis & Colo Earle, with my son, and Major Donelson, desire to be presented respect-fully to you & Mrs. O. & family, *Genl Daniel Donelson is to marry Miss Branch this day fortnight.*[2] May god take you in his holy keeping, & preserve your health & permit you to visit me this winter, and believe yr friend

Andrew Jackson

ALS, THi (16-0277).

1. As reported by the Treasury, the total national debt stood on January 1, 1831, at $39,123,191.68, mainly in securities paying three, four and a half, and five per cent. Payments of $11,354,630.09 in 1830 included $9,442,214.82 in reduction of principal. The government owned $7,000,000 in stock of the Bank of the United States, priced in market above par. Western land sales were the government's second largest revenue source, behind the tariff.

2. On October 19, John Branch's daughter Margaret (b. 1811) married Daniel Smith Donelson, brother of AJ Donelson.

October

To the Marquis de Lafayette

Washington October 1rst. 1830—

My Dr Sir,

In reply to your letter of the 8th. of August, which I had the happiness to receive a few days ago, I am at a loss for words to convay the sentiments which the recent events in France have awakened in my bosom. More sudden in their developement than any which the world had witnessed before, they are yet signalised by a wisdom and moderation worthy of the principles which produced them, and shed a glory upon France which other nations will delight to acknowledge.

you will see, my Dr Sir, from the public journals some evidence of the spirit in which these tidings have been received in this country; and that the effective part which you have acted is only the more distinguished by the unpretending manner and the modest self devotion under which it lays. no doubt you were right in calling the Duc of orleans to the throne— he will be the instrument of a free people, subordinate to those principles of civil and religious liberty, whose greatest champion you have been, and whose success now is a sufficient compensation for the toils and hardships of your long and eventful life.

Suffer me also to congratulate you, sir, upon the station you now fill in the new Government. Tho not the highest it is one which your character makes the most enviable. May all the other functionaries second your efforts in it, to give tranquility, liberty and peace, to France and the world, is the sincere prayer of your friend

Andrew Jackson

ALS, NIC (16-0290). Draft in AJ Donelson's hand, DLC (38). A three-day Parisian uprising in July 1830 led to the ouster of King Charles X of France and the installation of Louis Philippe, Duke of Orléans, as King in a new constitutional monarchy. Lafayette helped manage the transition. Under Louis Philippe he resumed command of the National Guard, a post he had first held in 1789 during the Revolution.

To Samuel Jackson Hays

Washington Octbr. 2nd. 1830—

Dr Samuel,

I reached the city on the evening of the 25th. ult. much fatigued but my health good, and on yesterday received your letter convaying the pleasing intelligence of Frances having presented you with a fine son, and that she was doing well; and further, that you designed honoring me with his name—for this token of your joint respects, I make to you both, my sincere acknowledgements—Kiss the babe for me, and accept of my sincere prayers that he may long live become an ornament to the society in which he may ~~live~~ be placed, and an honor and comfort to his parents in their declining years.

The late revolution in France has filled all hearts with rejoicing here, and I hope, may settle down in peace & tranquility throughout France, and that the Holy Alience may not attempt any more to combine against the rational liberty of man. should they attempt to restore charles torrents of blood must flow, and rational liberty ultimately prevail.[1] The lot of Lafayette has been a happy one, it appears that providence has preserved him as an instrument in his hand for the happiness of the human race & thro whom to give liberty to man—when he first was called to the command of the national guards, it was to protect the person of the King, second, to protect the people from the tyrany & usurpation of the King—You may look for a revolution in Spain & Portugal—for the present I would rejoice that there it might stop for a season, but the Piedmonters, &c &c may rise, and bring austria & prusia both into the field, when France will succor, for her own safety, the former, which may lead to a general European war.

I have not as yet got over the soreness occasioned by my late journey—and our house has a loansome appearance to me.

Colo Stockely travelled a few miles with me the morning I set out, I intend to [do] something for him as soon as it can be with propriety, but you know, under such a pressure for office, how hard it is to get a connection in, without great censure—I am astonished that he had not returned before the date of your letter, as he told me he would go directly home—he was in fine health.

I have been much oppressed with business since my return, & will be for some time—will be happy to hear from you often & when I have more leisure will again write you

Present my kind wishes to Frances & the dear boy—& to your dear mother & Narcissa, and every branch of the connection my kind salutations, & accept for yourself the assurance of my continued friendship and esteem

Andrew Jackson

P.S. My son is with me, reached here the next morning after I did—*still single* I fear his dulcinea is coquetting him

ALS, Dennis S. Hays (16-0299).
1. Established in 1815 after the defeat of Napoleon and restoration of the Bourbon monarchy in France, the Holy Alliance led by Russia, Austria, and Prussia sought to maintain the European status quo against democratic and revolutionary impulses.

To Martin Van Buren

Your note enclosing Mr. McLean's dispatch is recd. I send you the act of congress wanted. I have no idea that anything in the act of Congress will stand in our way. The sooner the proclamation can be issued the better. I will expect to see you in this evening. Your friend, Andrew Jackson.

Extract, Robert F. Batchelder catalog, 1976 (16-0307). Louis McLane's dispatch of August 20, received in the State Department October 3, announced a successful end to his negotiation. He enclosed a note from foreign secretary Aberdeen pledging to lift Britain's restrictions and reopen the West Indian colonial trade once the American government did so. Congress on May 29 had authorized AJ to reopen the trade during its recess by proclamation, upon his receiving assurance that Britain would reciprocate. However, Aberdeen pointed out to McLane that ambiguous phrasing in the May 29 Act could be read as requiring concessions to the U.S. that were allowed to no other nation. In particular, the Act predicated reopening the West Indian trade upon Britain's providing "that the vessels of the United States may import into the said colonial possessions from the United States any article or articles which could be imported in a British vessel into the said possessions from the United States." Parliamentary legislation of July 1825 restricted entry into British colonial ports to those foreign ships bringing only their own country's goods, not others produced elsewhere. Aberdeen conditioned Britain's pledge to reopen the trade on McLane's verbal assurances that the May 29 Act of Congress was not meant to be construed as challenging this restriction (*SDoc* 20, 21st Cong., 2d sess., pp. 43–53, Serial 203).

To John Coffee

Washington Octbr. 3rd. 1830

Dr. Genl

I have this moment received the dispatch from our minister at London which contains the arrangement for opening the trade with the British West Indias—Should you & Major Eaton have succeeded with the Choctaws, then will my success be compleat, and the prosperity of our country be promoted as far as executive exertions can promote it, and all cause removed from my enemies to found just complaint, & much cause for my friends to exult. I have only time to add that I hope you have succeeded in your mission & have returned in good health to the bosoom of yr amiable family, *where alone there are any earthly happiness*—I reached here on the night of the 25th. travelling 90 miles the two last days, expecting this day week ago, to have met Mr McLeans dispatch—I was just in time and my proclamation will be out tomorrow opening the West India trade; When promulgated I hope the opposition papers will no longer pronounce it a hoax for electioneering purposes.

Present me affectionately to Polly & every branch of your family & believe me yr friend

Andrew Jackson

P.S. Andrew J. Hutchings has wrote requesting I would write you on the subject of purchasing Col Wards place for him, I have not time to say more than name it to you.[1] A. J.

ALS, DLC-Coffee Family Papers (16-0304).
1. Coffee wrote AJ about Edward Ward's plantation on December 12 (below).

To Martin Van Buren

My Dr Sir

I have examined the private letter of Mr McLean. I have turned to the different laws refered to & can see nothing to prevent us from adopting & sanctioning the measure by proclamation—

The instructions being before congress when the act was passed, the intention must have been to authorise the P. to issue his proclamation &c &c &c whenever we were placed on the same footing with regard to this trade as all other nations were, and all the acts refered to, speaks of american products—it would follow as a consequent where the act speaks of articles which British vessels were entitled to import that it refers to american products—I for myself only wait to see the regulations adopted, to act upon them[.] yrs

Andrew Jackson

ALS, DLC-Van Buren Papers (16-0314). On October 5 AJ issued a proclamation reopening the trade in conformity with the May 29 Act of Congress.

To James Alexander Hamilton

WASHINGTON, October 5, 1830.

MY DEAR SIR:

Your letter, with the slippers presented, was received two days ago, but we have been so busied with the despatches opening the West India trade, some little difficulty having arisen in the mind of the Secretary of the Treasury on the subject of the instructions to be issued to the Collectors, that no leisure was presented to me until now. We arranged this last evening, and I hope our return despatch will reach New York in time for the packet of the 8th.[1]

I sincerely thank you for the solicitude you take with regard to my health, and have the pleasure to inform you that it has improved, although a little checked by a bad cold taken since my return to this city. It would afford us great pleasure to see you here. I have much to say to you, and some letters to show you that might afford you some amusement, which would not be proper to submit in a letter. Major Donelson, Lewis, and my son all join in their respects to you, And believe me, Sincerely your friend, &c.

Printed, *Reminiscences of James A. Hamilton*, p. 187 (16-0319).

1. Ingham circularized customs collectors on October 6 with instructions to open their ports to British colonial shipping in accord with AJ's October 5 proclamation. Van Buren wrote McLane on October 5 enclosing the proclamation, urging prompt British reciprocation, approving McLane's construction of the Act of May 29, and praising his handling of the negotiation (*SDoc* 20, 21st Cong., 2d sess., pp. 53–54, 56–57, Serial 203).

To Martin Van Buren

My Dr Sir

I enclose for your perusal and free remark my answer to the President of Mexico, which when read & made, you will please return, that I may enclose it with a private letter I am preparing to Col A. Butler, in which I charge him to deliver, with such remarks as may be suitable on the occasion.[1] This may expedite the conclusion of a Treaty so much desired, on our boundary and commerce.

I return you Mr Livingstons letter—it breaths the feelings of a large majority of the nation, which will increase in the ratio of one hundred percent pr annum, if we continue our course with prudence & with care looking solely to the good and prosperity of our country.

When will you be able to send me your corrections & additions to my view of the points on the Light House, & Portland & Louisville canal bills—I am beginning to look now to the Message, still hoping to hear from Rives and Butler favorably in due time for the Message[.] yr friend—

Andrew Jackson

ALS, DLC-Van Buren Papers (16-0320).
1. Anastasio Bustamante's May 26 letter to AJ (above) was received October 6. AJ replied on October 7 (below).

To Anthony Butler

Washington City
Octbr 6th. 1830

Dear Sir,

I had the pleasure to receive a letter from you at Nashville where I have spent July and August of this summer in the neighbourhood of my old associates and friends. Before my acknowledgement of that letter I had hoped to have heard again from you, but am as yet disappointed.

We have at length gained the long sought for privilege of the direct trade between the ports of the United States and those of the British colonial ports, upon the ~~same~~ terms of the ~~trade to the British European ports which is regulated by our commercial convention~~ act of parliament of 1825. Mr. McLane, within a few days past, has transmitted to us the note of Lord Aberdeen, putting within our reach this valuable commerce, of which you will see the proper notice in the proclamation which will accompany the dispatch from the Department of State. This event is hailed with great and deserved joy by our citizens, not only on account of the direct benefit which they will derive from it, but as indicating a disposition on the part of Great B to meet us half way in establishing the relations between the two countries upon that fair and reciprocal basis which is the only sure guarantee for their future peace and the steady advancement of their prosperity and fame. How gratifying would it be to me to include within the list of our good works in the foreign relations of the Union, a Treaty with Mexico adjusting the points in dispute in regard to *our boundary*, and establishing a proper commercial intercourse! Will you not be able to communicate to us something for the message to Congress which will justify a more flattering view of this subject that we could now present?

The agents or pretended agents of Mexico are stirring up strife by appearing in the Arkansas Territory, opening offices for the sale of lands within our settlements, and giving Mexican protection within the limits of our jurisdiction. The evils of such proceedings I need not point out to you. Every forbearance on our part will be practised in order that Mexico may have time to see their character, and not suspect the sincerity of our disposition to avoid whatever can militate against her peace and integrity: a disposition which we have always professed in our intercourse with her, and which we shall not cease to feel even if we are forced to drive within her limits those of her citizens who are trespassing upon our rights.[1]

The views with which you were before charged touching the policy of establishing a boundary as far westward as the *Desert or grand Praire*, remain unaltered. But if Mexico should resist them as incompatible with her ultimate safety and happiness, do not allow them to postpone a negotiation *for such a boundary* as will prevent the *collisions that must grow out of the one now contended for by her agents, who pretend to hold grants under her*. In this way alone can we prevent the difficulties with which we are daily threatened for the causes mentioned. Be guarded in any event *whatever territory may be affected by the line*, recognise no grants but those that are perfected in all their terms or conditions, or so much so that it would be a want of good faith not to comply with them. Leaving Mexico to settle with the patentees out of the consideration received.[2]

I send you a copy of a letter which I have recd. from Bastamante, to which I have replied in a corresponding spirit of frankness and friendship. From this spirit I hope much. Write to me by every conveyance, so that I may be advised of your progress. with sincere respects yr. friend & obt. sevt

Andrew Jackson

LS in AJ Donelson's hand, TxU (16-0322). Draft by AJ Donelson, DLC (73).

1. Beginning in August, Arkansas Territory governor John Pope sent warnings to Van Buren and AJ that persons claiming Mexican title were colonizing settlers on lands just south and west of Red River, in an area the U.S. claimed lay on the American side of the still unsurveyed border. On September 28 Van Buren, speaking for AJ, instructed Pope to uphold American jurisdiction in the disputed region while avoiding violent collision (*TPUS*, 21:253–54, 263–66, 274–75). AJ further instructed Van Buren regarding the boundary on October 15 (below).

2. This sentence is inserted in AJ's hand.

To Anastasio Bustamante

Washington City
Oct. 7. 1830.

Dear Sir,

I had the happiness to receive upon my return from an excursion, which I had taken in the past summer to my residence in Tennessee the letter which your Excellency did me the honor to address to me by Mr. Mejia of date May 20th. 1830.[1] Nothing can be more gratifying than the opportunity which this letter affords me of acknowledging myself a debtor to the sentiments which the frankness of a soldier employs in the cause of his Country, disregarding forms and the many obstructions which the routine of diplomatic correspondence may interpose to the prompt attainment of what is really honorable and right. Like yourself unfitted by taste and habit for the subtleties of the politician, my rules of action lead directly to the objects to be attained, disdaining the circuities which too generally display more of the dexterity of vice than the enduring force of Justice and virtue: and the satisfaction which I derive from the reflection that the Executive power of the two Countries is in the hands of men who can thus meet each other in the congenial simplicity of their military char-acter is much increased by the concurrence which I am enabled to express of our views upon the general policy of their administration. Economy in the public expence, fidelity in the application of the Revenues to the purposes of the Union, a careful abstinence from all power not delegated, and a sincere reliance upon the principle of Responsibility in the exercise of every public function are the Cardinal points in our Republican System; and recognised as they are by you, will not fail I trust to procure for Mexico the reestablishment of her peace and prosperity.

The determination which your Excellency has formed of hastening the consideration of the subjects that form concern the intercourse of the two Countries, has been read with peculiar gratification—I trust that Col. Butler our Representative near the Government of Mexico has been so fortunate as to present the views of the United States in a proper light. The character of *earliest friend* which you so much honor by mentioning can be benefitted by no arrangement that does not act reciprocally upon the two Countries and promote their mutual safety and prosperity.

Col. Butler in addition to his many merits has that of honesty and frankness which are so well taught in the school of War: on which account I cannot close this letter without commending their character to your Excellency as being the medium through which I would be truly happy to see the best and most harmonious relations between the two Countries restored and perpetuated.

That every blessing public and private may attend the exertions of your Excellency in the service of the Mexican Republic is the sincere prayer of your Most obedt. & Humble Servant

Andrew Jackson

Copy in Anthony Butler's hand, TxU (16-0326).
1. Actually May 26 (above).

To Anthony Butler

[This letter is available only in typescript.]

(Private)

Washington City October 7th 1830

My dr Sir,

Just as I was closing my letter of the 6th inst, yours of the 8th of July last was handed me, thro Mr Bankhead Secretary of the British Legation here, to whom Mr Buchan had forwarded it from Baltimore, and of course I have not had the pleasure of seeing him personally, but when I do, I shall extend to him that kindness and hospitality due to him as a gentleman, and your friend[1]—I rejoice that you are progressing with a commercial Treaty, and I trust with a Treaty of boundary, and if President Bustamente, practices that frankness which he has professed to me in his letter, a copy of which I enclose, you cannot have much difficulty in the negotiation. In my reply you will find I have met him with the frankness of a soldier and hinted to him as a reason why you were selected, that you were a soldier and appreciated the character and would in all your acts with that Republic, use that frankness necessary and proper to produce and foster the prosperity and happiness of both, and a lasting harmony, peace and good will between our respective Republics:—And you may with all the frankness of a *soldier* urge the policy of adopting the Grand Prararie, as a permanent boundary between us, as a source of lasting peace & harmony, for I say to you confidentially, whenever the present boundary is run and our western Citizens find the imposition that has been practiced upon them, no power can restrain them, and they will be sufficiently numerous to declare themselves independent & maintain it.—There will be one county of Arkansas thickly populated, cut off by the line, as is now contended for.[2]—Our future peace with Mexico depends upon extending our boundary farther west. And if you cannot get it to the grand prararie, obtain to the *Brasos* or another point giving for it in proportion to the extent, in equal ration to the amount, authorized by your instructions.

But candour dictates that the fact should be disclosed that the Government possessing the Mississippi must at some day possess all its *tributary streams*.

Therefore the grand prararie including this would be a boundary that would give permanent peace to the two Republics:—Our right by the Louisiana Treaty, being once complete to all this boundary and more.— The citizens of the U States will never be contented until this boundary is acquired, when they become informed it was wantonly given away to keep down the prosperity and growing political influence of the west.—These hints will bring to your view the importance of obtaining this boundary as the future peace and harmony of the two Republics mainly depend upon it.—Therefore your best exertions are expected, and I have no doubt will be used in this negotiation to obtain both the important objects entrusted to you, at as early a day as possible.—Should you succeed you lay a sure bases for the peace & prosperity of the two Republics, and sweep from Texas the means of revolution that must disturb Mexico at some future day, the strength of our government being able to govern that, when added to our boundary, will keep Mexico free from harm in that quarter.—The late Treaty with the Sublime port, our arrangement with Great Britain about the Colonial Trade, has placed us upon high ground, it only requires a speedy and happy result in your negotiations to put it in my power to say, I have placed the nation on grounds of lasting prosperity and peace, if a proper harmony are continued and cultivated on principals of reciprosity with foreign nations.

The late and glorious revolution in France which must be followed by Spain and portugal, will give lasting security to the Southern Republics— from all foreign invasion, and is a sure guarantee to the whole world of rational freedom & representative governments.—I have only to add that the people of the U States are in good spirits, my political friends gaining ground, the veto on the Maysville bill notwithstanding.—I leave the enclosed letter to President Bustamente open for your perusal with a request that you seal and deliver it, on which occasion you can say many things, that the occasion will suggest to you, with the assurance that I will meet him on all matters that relate to the peace, harmony, & prosperity of our two Governments, in the spirit of that frankness that is the constant companion of the real soldier. Very respectfully your friend

Andrew Jackson

Typed copy, TxU (16-0330).
 1. Charles Bankhead (c1797–1870) was secretary of the British legation in Washington.
 2. The disputed region beyond Red River embraced all of Arkansas's Miller County and part of Lafayette.

To Samuel Delucenna Ingham

Washington Oct 7. 31.

The President with his respects to Mr Ingham acknowledges the receipt of his note of to day enclosing Mr Gowens letter of complaint against Mr Guier Inspector and guager for the port of Phila with the interrogations of Mr Gowen to and answered by Mr Thompson subgager appointed by Mr Guier, all of which he has read with attention & now returns with this remark. Having no direct power to remove an inspector &c &c can only suggest a proper course on this occasion and that is that Guier should be forthwith furnished with a copy of the letters containing the charges against him thro the collector of the Port & by him called upon for explanation & defence of the charges made.[1] Should the facts charged be substantiated he ought to be dismissed on both grounds, first for want of capacity, and farming out his office & second on the principles of using his official influence to controle state elections which is believed to be inconsistent with the true principles of our govt its officers should not interfere with state elections more than as a citizen to vote and decorously give his opinion if they choose for their preference beyond this if tolerated in the officers of the U S, may lead to consolidation, by the executive patronage being wielded to controle state elections which is a species of corruption that ought not to be permitted in a republic. State elections ought to be free and unbiassed by any action of the Genl Govt, by or thro its officers. To dismiss under existing circumstances without any notice to the accused or defence by him would be wielded against us by our *political opponents* with great force. with these suggestions I return the papers for your and the collectors action, excuse the haste in which this is written.

Copy (misdated), PU-Ingham Papers (mAJs). George Guier was a gauger in the Philadelphia custom house and an active supporter of John G. Watmough for Congress. James Gowen had charged Guier with incompetence, farming out his office for a portion of the fees, and "intermeddling" with politics to the neglect of his duties. John Thompson was the deputy gauger to whom Guier had allegedly delegated his work. Guier denied the charges. AJ wrote Ingham again about him on October 16 (below).

1. A gauger was a subordinate officer appointed by the port collector. James N. Barker had appointed Guier after AJ appointed Barker collector at Philadelphia in March 1829.

To Philip Grymes Randolph

Octbr. 7th. 1830—

The President with his respects, to the acting secretary of war, draws his immediate attention to the enclosed. Request the agent to notify the department if military force may be necessary & part of the Detachment, if not the whole from the cherokee country will be ordered to his aid to remove the intruders.

AN, DNA-RG 75 (M234-136). Copy, DNA-RG 46 (16-0334). *SDoc* 512, 23d Cong., 1st sess., vol. 2, p. 174 (Serial 245). AJ enclosed Stockley D. Hays's September 21 letter above. Randolph wrote Chickasaw agent Benjamin Reynolds this same day, instructing him in AJ's name to immediately circulate a notice that all intruders on Chickasaw lands would be ejected and their improvements destroyed (*SDoc* 512, 23d Cong., 1st sess., vol. 2, p. 38, Serial 245). With Reynolds gone to accompany the Chickasaw scouting party in the west, subagent John L. Allen replied to Eaton on October 23 that the notice had been circulated and some "Obstinate Intruders" removed. Allen declined Randolph's offer of troops, suggesting that the best way to keep intruders out of the Chickasaw country would be to engage secret operatives to arrest them before they entered it (DNA-RG 75, M234-136).

From Samuel Delucenna Ingham

Mr Brodhead who has just arrived from Boston desires to have a conversation on the subject of the appointment of Naval officer in Boston—Several additional Letters have been recd by the last mail and others expected by the next recommending another gentleman a Mr Lewis very strongly—the bond for Parker is not yet signed and if the President desires a further examination of all their claims there will be a full opportunity

S D I

ANS, PU-Ingham Papers (16-0345). John P. Boyd, naval officer for Boston and Charlestown, had died October 3. Leonard Moody Parker (1789–1854) of Charlestown was a lawyer and Massachusetts legislator.

To Samuel Delucenna Ingham

Octbr. 8th 1830—

The President with his respects to the Secretary of the Treasury acknowledges the receipt of his note & replies, as the appoint of Naval officer has been made upon good recommendations, to open it again would be a bad precedent, ~~& would~~ & lay a ground on which we would be much annoyed—From the recommendations of the atto. Dunlap, & others, the gentleman appointed must be worthy and capable, therefore I am not disposed to open it—

AN, PU-Ingham Papers (16-0346). The *US Telegraph* announced Parker's appointment on October 11.

From William Barnard and Lee Compere

Great Father

We are in trouble—our friend Col McKenney is going away—we want to go with him we dont want to stay Here without him He is our friend we love him he is good to us—Do not Father let us be taken away from him —We ask you to Let us go with him He is like a Father to us we come from our nation With him when we leave him we want to go back—But we Do not want to go back if we can go with him We come to see our Father with this talk—we hope he will not deny what we come for

William Barnard
Lee Compere

DS, DNA-RG 75 (M234-774). Thomas L. McKenney, *Memoirs, Official and Personal* (New York, 1846), p. 190. Barnard (b. c1814), a Creek, and Compere (b. c1817), a Yuchi, were Indian youths brought to Washington from Georgia by Thomas L. McKenney in 1827. They had lived with him while attending school in Georgetown, and McKenney planned to take them north with him and continue their education after his dismissal as Indian superintendent. However, on October 5 acting secretary of war Philip G. Randolph instructed him to leave them in Washington (DNA-RG 75, M21-7). McKenney protested, and the boys were given an audience with AJ on October 9, where they delivered this note.

To Philip Grymes Randolph

Octbr. 9th. 1830—

The President with his respects to the acting Sec. of war, encloses him a request of William Barnard and Lee Compere, that they should be permitted to go with Colo. McKenny who is about to remove to N. York

The President has advised them to remain with their present Teacher in George Town, Mr McVain and under ~~my~~ his care; The Secretary of War will make arrangements with Mr McVain for their schooling & Through the Indian Bureau for their board with some good moral, & religious family, where they will be well Treated and attended to

AD, DNA-RG 75 (M234-774). The War Department notified McKenney this same day (DNA-RG 75, M21-7). Barnard and Compere boarded with Presbyterian minister James McVean (1796–1847) and attended his academy at government expense until April 1832, when they returned home at their parents' request.

From James Gwin

Nashville October 10th. 1830

Dear general
    according to promise I send you these few lines which leaves me and my Family in good helth and I pray God that they may find you in the enjoyment of the like blessing
    I had the pleasure to see many of your friends a few evenings ago being Called on to perform the rites of Mattramony between Col G. W. Martin and Loucinda A R Dallasan.[1] all your friends are well I spent the evening at the Hurmitage and returned there agane after supper and

stayed all night It is quite Lonesum to be there now I conversed with your Overseear. He says his cotton turns out much better then he expected, so it seems generly through the cuntry. It has been and is now an excelent time to get out cotton. It is clean and white there being no rain to dusty it,

We have had no news from the Treaty with the chocktaws Generall Carroll did not go on being taken sick about the time the other commissioners went on. The dockument is read with considerable interest Mr. Grundy is now reading it. So far as it hath gone it has proved to be suffishent to produce a reaction in feelings and Centiments. Some of those who first told me they did not wish to read it, are making application to me for it. George Mc.clain came & spent an evening with me. We had a long conversation on the Subject by Ourselves. He was of the Opinion that Mrs. E character was in such a state of rueian that she could not be restored to Society in Washington. He regrated very much that you had meddled with the matter that it had done you much injury—and that he was fearful it would do you more yet. That your best friends thought you should not pay any attention to it. I remarked to him that the attack was made on you by Dr *Ely* that it became your duty to reply to Dr Ely's letter—and to call upon him for prouf to support the charge he had against Mrs. E. as it was about to destry the piece of your Family He spoke much in favour of Dr Ely & Mr. Cambell as being pious men & your real friends. I told him that Dr Ely had failed entirely in supporting his charges and that the whole of them were proved to be false (As I conceived) I named some of the gentlemen who had given testimony in the case. Among the rest I named old Mr Rayland who he says is a man of unblemished character.[2] He appeared to be greatly asstonished that Ely had failed to support the charges and remarked that he neaver knew any thing Criminal aganst Mrs. E of his own knowledge but—thought she was an imprudent woman I had a Conversation with Grundy on the subject He thinks the woman innocent & wishes his wife to be sattisfied of her innocency as she will go on with him to Washington this fall.[3] Since I commenced this letter Maj. Ettan has returned with the good news that they have affected a teaty with the chocktaws information of which you will get before this reaches you I think every honest man must say that Ettan is one of the most useful men in your Cabbinate I rejoice it is so for he is pursecouted shamfully but he will live in the affections of all sober thinking honest men when his persecuters are dead and gone, it is thought by some that you will *dismiss* Maj Ettan when congress meets on account of his beloved wife this cannot be Ettan has done his duty. *He will do his duty.* He is our man, you have confided in him, you will not dismiss him or any other faithful offices while true to their trust I remain as ever your sincear friend Mrs. Gwin & the children sends their love to you[4]

James Gwin

Dear Sir I have read the corspndine between you and Dr Ely My opinion is that the Dr has totally failed to support his charges aganst Mrs. Ettan—and should have returned and done all in his power to have healed her *feelings* and *character*

As to Mr. Cambell I think his conduct towards Mr. & Mrs. Ettan has been unchristian ungentlemanly and dishonest and of corse he will never try to make any redress for injury he has done them as to Mrs Ettan my opionion is that she has been most *Basely* slandered and that the object was to injure you through her together with your administration But truth will pervail and rightousness will triumph

James Gwin

[Endorsed by AJ:] The Revd. Mr. James Gwin to be carefully filed with the papers relative to Mrs. E.

ALS, DLC (38). Gwin (1775–1841) was a Methodist minister and a Sumner County neighbor of AJ.
    1. Lucinda Rucker Donelson married George Washington Martin (1792–1854) on September 30.
    2. The document was AJ's compilation of letters and affidavits on the Eaton affair (DLC-75). It included AJ's correspondence with Ezra S. Ely and John N. Campbell and also a September 28, 1829, testimonial to Mrs. Eaton's good character from William Ryland (1770–1846), a Methodist minister in Washington who had presided at her marriage to Eaton.
    3. Felix Grundy's wife was Ann Phillips Rodgers Grundy (1779–1847).
    4. Gwin's wife was Mary Adair McAdams Gwin (1773–1858).

To Samuel Delucenna Ingham

(Confidential)

Octbr. 11th. 1830—

The President with his respects to the Secretary of the Treasury, encloses him the four queries shewn him the other day on the subject of the Indians and the sovereign power of Georgia to extend their civil jurisdiction over them, & to protect the mines for its own use &c &c, with the remarks of the attorney genl on each point. They are laid before the Secretary for his consideration how far he coincides with the attorney General in the view he has taken, & if he differs with him, in what.

The Sec. will be pleased to take a copy & return the originals, that they may be laid before the Sec. of War, & Navy & Postmaster general   the Secretary of State has taken a copy

AN, PU-Ingham Papers (16-0360).

To Samuel Delucenna Ingham

Octbr 11th. 1830—

The President with his respects to Mr Ingham encloses a letter this moment recd. from the marshal of Kentuckey, Genl McCalla, for his perusal & consideration. The President will thank Mr. Ingham for the reasons why the remittances have not been made, that I may answer Mr McCalla understandingly

So far as is usual & customary in like cases, let remittances be made to Mr McCalla, for to meet the expence of the approaching Federal court in Kentucky

AN, PU-Ingham Papers (16-0362). The duties of marshals included paying the expenses of holding federal courts.

To John Moore McCalla

(Private)

Washington Octbr 11th. 1830—

Dr Sir

your letter was received by this days mail, and I forthwith laid it before the Secretary of the Treasury for explanation, & the enclosed note is his reply which I hasten to forward to you. so soon as I receive a full report it will be sent to you for your information & satisfaction. I hope the amount sent will relieve you from your late embarrassment.

With a tender of my sincere regard I am very respectfully yr mo. obdt. servt.

Andrew Jackson

ALS, THi (16-0369).

From Thomas ap Catesby Jones

near Prospect Hill
Fairfax County Va.
October 11th. 1830—

Sir,

Understanding that the Reverend Mr. Colton of Washington, is an applicant for the office of Chaplain in the navy, I beg leave to recommend him to your *particular* consideration.

Fully persuaded that whatever tends to improve the moral condition of the navy, must of necessity, not only add to its physical strength, but must greatly increase its reputation and means of general usefulness: and here may I be permitted to say, that I hope the day is not very distant when no *ship* in our navy will be permitted to sail from the United States, without a *chaplain* in every respect well qualified, to Instruct, and watch over, and to point out to the younger officers & youths of the ship the many obstructions which lay in their path to honor, and future usefulness to their Country. I have the honor to be, Sir, most respectfully, Your Obdt Srt.

Thos. ap Catesby Jones
Capt. U.S. Navy

ALS, DNA-RG 46 (16-0367). Jones (1790–1858), who had commanded a squadron at AJ's New Orleans campaign, was at this time the Navy's inspector of ordnance and ammunition. Walter Colton (1797–1851) was a Congregational clergyman, author, and editor. He wrote AJ on October 26 (below).

From William Ward

Choctaw Agency Octbr. 11th 1830

Sir

I deem it my duty to inform you as Prehaps the Secy. of war may not be in his place that since the late Treaty with the Choctaws One of the Missionaries by the name of Louring S. William has been as it is said trying to get the Indians to meet in a Council and oppose the Treaty as lately Concluded on by the Hon. Secy. of War and Genl. Coffee; It is said that he has gone on to the southern part of the nation and has said many things against the Treaty or those Indians that signed the Treaty.[1]

Mingo Mushulatubbee has Just this moment sent a man to apprise me of the conduct of Williams and states that some fears are entertained for the safety of himself and friends, I have not time to write much in detail as I have detained the mail untill I give you this *Hint*. Would it not be Expedient for you to advise the Executive of Mississippi to furnish such a Number of Militia as will remove out of the Indian Country all persons who may be known to oppose the views of Government.

You know that an Agent can only order of such people, but he has no force to carry his orders into effect. I give you this hasty scrawl as you may be apprised of what is going on (rather secretly.) It is said that if the Inds. did not like there bargain that the Secy of war said It should be revoked; I heared him say If they disapproved the treaty before he left the ground he would tare it up. But that was only talk and every thing is said to put the whole business as wind which was not the fact. If funds were placed into the hands of Mr. G. S. Gains or some other sufficent to take two or three Thousand off It would have been much better then to send him with Ten or Twelve Indians to Explore their Own Land.[2] Many applications are dayly made to me to get the means to go of entirely to the west—Eighty or One Hundred has started to see the Arkansas Country and select the best places to remove too. I have thought the sooner the people without much to subsist on were got of the better for Government and the poor Indians, as they might be induced to raise corn to support those who emigrate afterwards

I have the Honor to be very Respectfully your Mo Obdt. Survt.

W Ward Agt. C N.

[Endorsed by AJ:] Choctaw agent   the Agent to be instructed to apprehend Williams & hand him over to the civil authority   give an order to authorise the agent to call on Capt Wager for military aid, if he finds it necessary

[Endorsed by AJ:] refered to the secretary of war that he may address a letter to the agent instructing, to have arrested & sent out of the choctaw nation all whitemen who are disturbing the peace of the nation, with orders not to return and if force is required instructions to call upon Major Wager for a company of regulars, and to prevent all Whitemen from intruding or settling on their land—A J[3]

ALS, DNA-RG 75 (M234-169).

1. Loring S. Williams (1796–1879) was a Presbyterian missionary to the Choctaws under the auspices of the American Board of Commissioners for Foreign Missions. He and three other Board missionaries had been banned from the treaty ground at Dancing Rabbit Creek by Eaton and Coffee, despite their pledge to conduct only religious ministrations and "studiously avoid" any interference with the negotiations (DNA-RG 75, T494-2; *SDoc 512*, 23d Cong., 1st sess., vol. 2, pp. 252–55, Serial 245).

2. Choctaw trader George Strother Gaines (1784–1873), younger brother of Edmund P. Gaines, had been designated to lead a party of nine to twelve Choctaws to examine the western country, as authorized by the supplementary articles to the Treaty of Dancing Rabbit Creek.

3. Acting war secretary Philip G. Randolph wrote Ward on October 29, instructing him in AJ's name to remove from the Choctaw country all whites who were disturbing the peace or counteracting the government's aims. If Williams was doing so, Ward was to immediately apprehend him and turn him over to civil authorities. Randolph authorized Ward if necessary to call on Major Philip Wager for troops from the Cherokee country. Four days later the War Department withdrew this authority and instead ordered troops sent in from Jefferson Barracks (DNA-RG 75, M21-7). Ward reported on November 14 and December 2 that he had broken up plans to oppose the treaty by confronting Williams and the other schemers and threatening them with expulsion, and that all was now quiet (DNA-RG 75, M234-169).

To Samuel Delucenna Ingham

Octbr. 13th. 1830—

The President with his respects to the Secretary of the Treasury, will thank him to return by the bearer, the Queries, with the attorney Genls remarks, on the powers of Georgia over the Indians, which he sent him on yesterday, if he has taken a copy, as he wishes to lay them before the Sec. of the Navy & Postmaster General—

AN, PU-Ingham Papers (16-0374).

From Peter Carl Frederik von Scholten

Mr President!

When His Majesty the King of Denmark, my Master, directed me to proceed to the United States in the capacity of His Majesty's Minister Plenipotentiary, on a special Mission, having for its object to propose and enter upon a negociation with the United States Government, if so disposed, for the purpose of regulating the commercial intercourse between the United States and His Majesty's Westindia Possessions in a manner, consistent with just and equitable principles, and thus far satisfactory to both countries, His Majesty imposed upon me as a sacred duty, to assure the President of the United States, General Jackson, not only of the high esteem and regard His Majesty bore to the President as the head of a great and liberal nation, but also of the personal regard and attachment he entertained for him as a Man and a Soldier.

Mr President! Allow me to express on my own account, and with the utmost sincerity of my heart, the very great satisfaction I feel in performing this duty, and how gratifying it would be to me, if by the confidence, with which His Majesty has honored me upon this occasion, I might be the means of confirming and extending an intercourse, the continuance of which may be considered of high importance, as well to the United States as to Denmark, but more particularly to the Inhabitants of His Majesty's Westindia Possessions, the administration of which for several years has been confided to my care.

The liberal principles, which more particularly under Your Administration have characterised the commercial intercourse of the United States with other Nations, and the entirely friendly relations, which at all times have existed between the two Countries, with a single exception of a temporary character only, and for which the United States have been fully and as I trust satisfactorily indemnified by His Majesty, make me indulge in the hope, that the Negociations, which You as President of the United States may authorize, will be conducive to a satisfactory result.[1]

P v. Scholten

DS, DNA-RG 59 (M52-1). Von Scholten (1784–1854), governor general of the Danish West Indies, had been accredited by King Frederick VI of Denmark (1768–1839) to negotiate with the U.S. concerning the colonial trade. He delivered this address at his official presentation to AJ on October 13, furnishing an advance text to Van Buren the previous day.
   1. The single exception concerned spoliations in the Napoleonic Wars, for which Denmark had paid indemnity in the claims convention of March 28.

To Peter Carl Frederik von Scholten

Sir,

I hear with great satisfaction the expression of friendly sentiments entertained by his Danish Majesty toward myself individually and this Government, which as his special representative you have just delivered. Let me assure you that I sincerely reciprocate them both in their general and personal application, in which last respect particularly, your own high character & friendly feelings so often manifested in your intercourse with this country are esteemed as a pledge which it will be my pride not to disappoint.

Please communicate to his Majesty that altho', in the late arrangement respecting the claims of our merchants, the indemnification falls short of what was considered due to them, it is nevertheless what the govt., of the United States haves agreed to take and is therefore satisfactory; that upon the future relations of the two Governments This arrangement will have no unfavorable influence; and[1] that upon all occasions I shall be found ready to meet the proposals for a commercial Treaty upon the principles of a just reciprocity, and to draw closer in other respects the bonds of friendship and good intercourse which it is the interest of both countries to preserve.

The Secretary of State will be charged to open a free discussion with you upon these subjects

AL draft, DLC (16-0795). Complaining of injury from American duties on rum and sugar, von Scholten on October 27 proposed an arrangement for exclusive trading privileges between the U.S. and St. Croix. Van Buren declined the proposal on November 29 as conflicting with other treaty obligations and with congressional authority over the tariff. Von Scholten then asked that the correspondence be submitted to Congress, which AJ did on December 31 (SDoc 21, 21st Cong., 2d sess., Serial 203).
   1. A revised closing in Van Buren's hand is marked for insertion here: "that I shall upon all occasions receive every proposition made to this government by that of his Danish Majesty for a commercial arrangement with a sincere desire to do all that it will be proper for me to do to advance the interests of both countries & to draw closer the bonds of friendship & good intercourse which it is their interest to preserve."

From James Reeside et al.

WASHINGTON CITY, 13*th* Oct. 1830.

To the PRESIDENT *of the United States*:

SIR:

In compliance with the instruction of a number of citizens, concerned in the transportation of the United States' mail, assembled, at this time, in Washington, at Brown's Hotel, desirous to testify our respect for the Chief Magistrate of this Nation, we ask leave to hand to you the following resolutions, unanimously adopted:

1. *Resolved*, That we present to the President of the United States our heartfelt acknowledgements and cheerful thanks, for his wise, prudent, and patriotic conduct in the Executive chair; never, in our opinion, more ably and uprightly filled since the days of his illustrious and venerated predecessor, Gen. GEORGE WASHINGTON.

2. *Resolved*, That we cordially approve and applaud his interpretation of the letter and the spirit of the Federal Constitution, in placing his constitutional *veto* on the Maysville road bill.

3. *Resolved*, That we deem his act on the aforesaid occasion, as emanating from the most exalted, moral, and political courage; and as eminently worthy of the patriot and statesman, who has "filled the measure of his country's glory;"[1] as well as an earnest of the perpetuation of sound political principles, and a just exposition of the text of that sacred instrument which binds together our happy and prosperous Union.

4. *Resolved*, That we are on the whole, so highly gratified with his wise administration; with the choice of his Cabinet Counsellors, and the selection of his public officers, generally, that we are anxious and solicitous to see him continue in the administration of our national concerns, and are ready, again, to support him with our exertions and interest, for that exalted station, for the next constitutional term; for we may truly exclaim, "*Well done thou good and faithful servant!*"

5. *Resolved*, That a copy of these resolutions be handed to General Duff Green, with a request to give them a place in his paper.

6. *Resolved*, That the foregoing resolutions be signed by the Chairman and Secretary.

JAMES REESIDE, Chairman.

GEORGE BOWEN, Secretary.[2]

Printed, *United States' Telegraph*, October 15, 1830 (16-0375). The *Telegraph* reported that a committee of eight, representing some two hundred mail contractors then gathered in Washington, delivered this address in person to AJ at an audience on October 14.

1. A paraphrase of Thomas Jefferson's oft-quoted toast at a dinner for AJ at Lynchburg, Va., on November 7, 1815: "Honor and gratitude to those who have filled the measure of their country's honor."
2. George Bowen was a mail contractor with routes in South Carolina.

To James Reeside et al.

GENTLEMEN:

I receive the testimonial so kindly accorded to my official conduct by the resolutions which you have just presented to me, with a full sense of my responsibility to the people, and a gratification proportioned to the desire to deserve their approbation by a faithful and conscientious discharge of my duties. It is the duty of our citizens to look with vigilance to the conduct of those to whom they have delegated power; and its performance on your part cannot be the less salutary or proper on account of the relations you sustain to the Government, by which you are rather invited to a severe scrutiny of its actions, than tempted to relax a just one.

I am thankful, gentlemen, for the kind feelings you express for me personally, and salute you in return with a cordial shake of the hand, and a sincere reciprocation of your good wishes.

Printed, *United States' Telegraph*, October 15, 1830 (16-0375). Draft in AJ Donelson's hand, DLC (73).

To Martin Van Buren

Octbr. 15th. 1830—

The President with his respects to Mr. Martin Van Buren Secretary of States acknowledges the receipt of his note with the enclosure from Mr Conway, and now return it with these remarks. It is inexpedient for any agent of the Govt. to run an experimental line between the Mexicans & us—let him extend the Louisiana line as far west as the State runs, or is supposed to run, taking in the 30 miles west of the line now claimed by the Mexican Colo—if necessary, Informing Mr Conway, that we have instructed Govr. Pope to continue to exercise jurisdiction over all citizens, heretofore ~~supposed~~ believed to be within the Territory of arkansa, and to coerce obedience from them as citizens until the boundery is run by the authority of the two Govts.

P.S. I had a very bad night, but am better—A. J.

AN, DNA-RG 59 (M179-69); *TPUS*, 21:279–80. AN draft, DLC (38); Bassett, 4:185. James S. Conway, appointed U.S. commissioner to run the Arkansas–Louisiana boundary in June, had written Van Buren on September 17 querying how far west his line should extend. The intersecting longitudinal line north from the Sabine River to the Red River that was to form the international border between the U.S. and Mexico had not yet been located, leaving a zone of undetermined nationality some thirty miles wide between Arkansas and Louisiana on the east and Texas on the west. Conway recommended fixing the international line as soon as possible and meanwhile carrying his survey westward to the far end of the disputed zone to counteract the measures of Benjamin Rush Milam (1788–1835), an American emigré and Mexican colonel who was colonizing settlers in the disputed area and offering Mexican title (*TPUS*, 21:272–74). Van Buren enclosed Conway's letter to AJ, who returned it with this note. Van Buren accordingly instructed Conway on October 18 not to try to run a provisional international north-south line, but to extend his own survey to the western limit of the disputed zone. Van Buren also told Conway, as he already informed Governor Pope on October 11, that he had asked the Mexican government on September 28 to stop Milam's surveys and sales (*TPUS*, 21:279–80; *HRDoc* 351, 25th Cong., 2d sess., pp. 650–51, Serial 332).

To John Coffee

Washington October 16th. 1830

My Dr Genl

I have the pleasure to acknowledge your letter of the 29th. ultimo, dated at the choctaw agency, just received, communicating the agreable intelligence that you & Major Eaton had on the day preceeding concluded a treaty with the choctaws for a surrender of *all their land East of the Mississippi river*. This to me is grateful news, and it is the more so, as it is done without the aid of Governor Carroll, as if you had failed, many of our enemies would have aledged, that if he had been there success would have attended the Mission

The Treaty I have no doubt is a good one, and if you have secured a country for the chekisaws, all is right. Providence appears to Smile upon our endeavours, to preserve these people from *anihilation as tribes*, and athwart the machinations of ours and their worst enemies; not having heard from you from the date of Major Eatons letter of the 7th. ult. I was fearful that something unfavorable had arisen that might prevent a successful termination of your mission; you can judge therefore the gratification I felt on the recpt of your letter this morning.

you will have seen before this reaches you that we have succeeded in restoring the West india trade—our enemies now says it is worth nothing that the circuitous trade thro Canady was more advantageous than the direct trade—These men think the people fools, & that they can be gulled with any thing—

The late glorious revolution in France, has delayed the final arrangement with that nation on our claims for spoliations—but I am sanguine that with France & Spain we will succeed shortly—and I am daily in expectation of receiving from Col. A. Butler information that he has succeeded in concluding a treaty with Mexico. The Treaty with the Port, our arrangement with great Britain by which the Colonial trade is restored, our Treaties with the Indians, will afford, if we get nothing more, a good ground for a communication to Congress.

My health is a little checkered since my arrival here, I took cold & have a cough, am better, & my general health has somewhat improved.

I will be happy to hear from you often. I have not had a letter from any of my friends since I left Tennessee except my old friend judge Overton and Col Love. With my prayers for your and your families welfare both in this & the world to come believe me yr friend, present me kindly to your whole family—

Andrew Jackson

ALS, DLC-Coffee Family Papers (16-0394).

To Samuel Delucenna Ingham

Washington Oct 16th 1830.

The President returns his respects to the Sec of Treasy and acknowledges the receipt of his note of the 15th this day handed to him, with Mr Guiers letter inclosed, which he now returns with this remark—that he anticipates from the protest, that considerable political excite is to grow out of this matter, whilst the govt disclaims having anything to do with individual quarrels, yet it is responsible for the faithful performance of the duties assigned to its officers. Gentleman holding offices under the Federal Govt should not improperly interfere in state elections if this were tolerated, it must tend to consolidation of the union and in the end destroy the purity of elections within the states, whether Mr Guier has acted imprudently in this case is not for the Prest to say—It is a subject which belongs exclusively to the head of the Treasy Dept. in whom the Prest has every confidence that he will do what is right in the ____ The Prest will conclude therefore by observing that if Mr Guier has rendered himself obnoxious to the principles laid down for the govt of this administration after a full investigation into all the circumstances attending the charges prefered against him, then the only power the govt has to correct such abuses must be applied, *removal from office.*

Copy, PU-Ingham Papers (mAJs). Ingham ordered an investigation by U.S. district attorney George M. Dallas, before whom Guier refused to testify. On December 14, Ingham forwarded Dallas's evidence against Guier to Philadelphia collector James N. Barker with instructions to pursue an internal inquiry. Barker reported back on January 3, 1831, that Guier's performance was exemplary and that Gowen's charges were groundless and prompted by a private quarrel. Louis McLane, Ingham's successor as Treasury secretary, formally exonerated Guier on June 5, 1832 (DNA-RG 56, M178-21 & M178-23).

To *Samuel Delucenna Ingham*

Octbr. 16th. 1830—

The President with his respects to the Sec of the Treasury in explanation of the note he wrote him the other day, would from some sugestions made to him, request his opinion whether the good of the public service, requires the removal of the first auditor—if so, that it will be promptly done—it has been communicated to the P. that he is incompetant to the performance of the duties required in that office, and the first comptroller reports in favor of retaining him

The P. has just red the grateful intelligence of a treaty with the choctaws for all their land east &

AN, PU-Ingham Papers (16-0400). Ingham replied on October 19 (below). The first auditor prepared accounts of the Treasury Department for review and certification by the first comptroller. Richard Harrison (1750–1841), appointed by George Washington in 1791, was first auditor and Joseph Inslee Anderson (1757–1837), once a senator from Tennessee, was first comptroller.

From *Robert Minns Burton*

(Private and confidential)

Lebanon
October 16th AD 1830

Dear General

I was pleased to learne through the medium of the news papers that you arrived at the City on the 26th ultimo in good health: where you found—as I trust that the business in the several departments had been conducted in your absence with that harmony, energy, and unceasing diligence that should ever characterise public officers engaged in the service of such a country as ours.

In conformity with my promise—I avail myself of this opportunity of guiving you a brief account of the late movements of *Bragadier Genl Desha* as connected with myself—shortly after I parted with you I determined to become a candidate for Congress and thought it as good a plan as any to beard the *Lyon* in his *den*—so while at the Gallatin Court about three weeks since I announced myself as a candidate—*Desha* happened not to be in town—he came blustering in next day he seemed to think I had set his high pretentions greatly at defiance and that it was necessary for him to make a speech to put things aright he collected the people at the Court house and in his speech stated to the people that you were now

opposed to him and did not want him reelected and that the grounds of
your opposition to him were that he had waited on you and advised you
not to take Maj Eaton into the Cabinet—that he had stated to you that
Mrs Eaton was an abandoned woman and that she had not been recieved
into genteel society for five years before Maj Eaton had married her—and
as another ground—of your opposition to him that he had voted against
the bill making an appropriation to Mrs Decatur and that I was friendly
to Maj Eaton and had taking my family to see Mrs Eaton—and a grat deel
such like stuff   when I come to reply to him and present him in his true
character as drawing from domestic retirement a persecuted and injured
female before the public to assist him as an electionering hobby—(that in
this he had guiven full evidence of a want of that magnanimity and tender
sensibility that should ever be attached to the character of the *Soldier* if
not the Statesman) the indignation of the croud seemed to be arroused to
an unusual height—but when I come to enquire who was the man that
waited on the Chief Magistrate of the US. States—to advise him who were
suatable persons to compose his Cabinet was he some Statesman that
had distinguished himself on the floor of Congress? Some man high in
the nations Confidence? Oh no such a man would not presume unasked
to intrude his counsel—but that individual was no less a personage than
our Bragadier Genl. *Bob Desha "that every body Knows"* the house was
in an uproar of laughter to his great discomfiture   many other things
were said and done by Desha which satisfied all disinterested witnesses
of the meane and detestable Character of the man—he said to the people
that they might look on him as a candidate and my opperations were
directed accordingly—but when he found that the Sparks I had struck
out were Kindling into a flame—he suddenly declined and Genl Hall was
announced as a candidate—the people are already crying out *combination
coalition* & the like—and I think Genl Hall will find great difficulty in
satisfying the people that this comfortable arrangement was not expressly
agreed on between him and *Desha*[1]   I have been thus particular as to
the interview betwn Desha and myself for feare of misrepresentation by
some one to you more especially as I received a letter on yesterday from
Stokely Hays—who informed me that Stokely Donelson was guiving in
Nashville to everyone that would listen and untrue version of my reply to
Desha toching the character of Mr. & Mrs Eaton[2]—Since I have been a
candidate I have rode over most of Sumner & Smith the matter seems thus
far to stand favourable enough—yet it cannot be told at this distant day
how the matter will terminate   I have presented to the consideration of
the people the subject of our Western lands—the plan I have suggested for
thier disposition is to guive the actual or intended settler the preferrance
of entering a guiven quantity of acres—the price to be Graduated by the
quality of the land—the quantity of acres that the Government owns as yet
unsold—after allowing for the probable expenseis of surveying—schools
&c. according to the best estimate I can make is 250 millions of acres—

this quantity of land at the proposed pricies of—50 cents—25 &12½ cents would at the highest price bring into the Treasury 125 millions of dollars—at the sencond—62 millions 500 thousand—at the third rate 31.250 thousand at which lowest rate would be more than sufficient to pay the national debt—would it not be the wiseest policy in a Government like ours—to place this land at a reduced rate—so that a *home* will be within the reach of the man in humble life (in whom is often found the most zealious advocate of his Country's cause and the boldest defender of her invaded rights) than for the Government to become a land jobber as it were holding out to her citizens every incentive calculated to whet the appetite of avarice and speculation in consiquence of which policy hundreds of her citizens heretofore and many in time to come will be swallowed up in eternal bankruptcy? by the settlement of these lands trod only now by the wild beast of the forrest—agriculture will be progressing—the several States or Territories will derive benifit from the population—and millions will rise up and call themselves blessed in the possession of homes to end their earthly time upon while our Country may be still said to be truly going on "growing in her growth and strenthning in her strenth."

Should you think with me on this subject I should like to have your views in extenso guiven in a way to enable me to support my opinion by the aid of yours without being known in any other way than as a correspondent in which attitude you could not be considered as attempting to guive any direction either way in the contest betwen my opponent and myself—upon this subject as well as the rechartering of the US. Bank I would be glade you would write me fully and guive me all the information in your power   I was much pleased to learne the successfull negotiation of our minister at London and that the west India ports were now open: added to this the making of treaties with the Chocktaw and Chickasaw Indians constitute within themselves subjects of great gratulation to you and to the American people—the surveying of this newly acquired Teritory will I suppose be commenced soon after the ratification of the Treaty   a number of our young men intend going as adventurers to this newly obtained Country and are all anxiously waiting to know who will be the favorite that will get the appointment of Surveyor Genl. an office considered more valuable than any at this time within the guift of the President and which is desired by so many in our part of the Country

passing from one topic to another I apprehend I have drawn out my letter to a tiresome lenth   you will remember me respecfully to your family and to Majors Eaton Lewis and Earle   my family joine with me in the warmest salutations—for your health and happiness—I have the honour to be very Respectfully your friend & obt sert

Robert M Burton

ALS, DLC (38). AJ replied on November 6 (below).

1. William Hall (1775–1856), Burton's opponent to succeed Robert Desha in Congress, had been a Tennessee brigadier general in the War of 1812, a state legislator and senate speaker, and briefly governor in 1829 after Samuel Houston's resignation.

2. Stockley Donelson and Stockley Donelson Hays were first cousins, both sons of Rachel Jackson's siblings.

From James Alexander Hamilton

NEW YORK, October 16, 1830.

MY DEAR SIR:

I had the pleasure to receive your letters of the 5th and 8th instant, informing me of your safe arrival and improved health.

Your success in adjusting that difficult matter, the West India Trade, is very properly appreciated here by all ranks and parties, except the factious cavilers, who deceive themselves in their efforts to delude the people. We daily see in the *Post* the evidence, and receive information from those further East, which assure us that it will give greatly increased activity to our commerce.

Among the measures of congratulation to you, the increase of our impost revenues is not to be overlooked. This will not only afford the means, more rapidly than was anticipated, of absorbing the public debt, but it tends to show that the protective system has not been productive of the evils to our commerce which were so confidently anticipated by its opponents.

The recent events in Europe are full of interest here, as well as on the other side of the water. Ought we not to look to a general war as an event at least so probable, as to prepare the outlines of a system suited to such a state of things? But more of this when we meet, which pleasure, I regret to say, appears likely to be deferred until after the 5th or 6th of the next month, owing to the continued sessions of the U.S. Courts in this district. With my best wishes I remain, dear sir, your friend, &c.

Printed, *Reminiscences of James A. Hamilton*, pp. 189–90 (16-0398).

To Hardy Murfree Cryer

Washington Octbr. 18th. 1830—

My Dr Sir

I arrived here from the Hermitage on the 25th. ultimo all in good health & just in time to meet & act on the official communications from our minister at London, making arrangements with England, for the opening to us the direct trade with the British Westindia colonies—you will see from my proclamation, that this important trade to the Western &

Southern states are again open to us. This with the favorable treaty concluded with the Port, by which the commerce of the black sea are opened to us, must add to the prosperity of our cotton growing states as well as the commercial, as it will open a mart for more of our course cotton fabrics, & spun cotton, than any other country. These arrangements—added to the Treaties lately negotiated with the chikisaws & choctaws, by Major Eaton and Genl. Coffee, will I trust, lead to happy results, and silence our political enemies; at least it will be gratifying to our friends, and beneficial to our beloved country, which I am sure will be gratifying to you hear.

You will have seen an account of the Glorious revolution in France which gives a sure guarantee of rational liberty, & representative Government, to the world, it appears that Genl Lafayette is an instrument in the hand of providence, to bring about & give rational liberty to all Europe.

I have not heard from you and your amiable family since I left the Hermitage—it will always be a pleasure to me to hear of your welfare, & particularly how your dear little Rachael grows, that child from its name is very dear to me, knowing as I do, how much, her, for whom it was called, if she had lived, would have loved it, I hope to live to see it.[1]

I have recd. a letter from my overseer who gives a flatering account of the performance of my colts. The bay stud colt out of my Pacolet filly that died, which I have named, Citizen, with the sway back mares filly by Stockholder, will be, if his accounts true, first rate. The Brown stud colt out of the Miller mare got splinted, & lame, was turned out without a trial, he bids fair to be a good runner, if the splint does not injure him. I must have them next year with Mr Cotton if possible.

My overseer says he will want two or three mules able to plow next year if such you can get in your arrangements with those that are indebted, will be a convenience to me.

I have casually seen a letter giving an account of a meeting between Mr Burton & Genl. Desha, at Gallatine, and of their addressing the people, that I would like to have a full account of from you in whom I can confide. I am the more anxious on this head because, I am sure Mr Burton must have been misrepresented, as it states that he declared to the people that he was solicited to come out & oppose Desha by me—now this being utterly without foundation, I cannot credit it—will you on the receipt of this, write me a full account of this matter.

My Dr friend, should you be passing to Nashville will you call at the Hermitage, take a look into the Garden where lies all that made this world desirable to me, and inform me, whether it is attended to—altho the House is closed, its doors will always be open to you & yours, and it will give me pleasure to hear that you partake of its hospitality—with my best wishes for your & that of your amiable families happiness, I am yr friend

Andrew Jackson

ALS, The Gilder Lehrman Institute of American History (mAJs).
1. Rachel Jackson Cryer (1829–1895) was born in February 1829, two months after Rachel Jackson died.

To *Samuel Delucenna Ingham*

Octbr. 18th. 1830—

The President on Saturday last sugested to the Sec. of the Treasury a desire to obtain

1rst. The amount of appropriations which have hitherto been made for internal improvements, and the manner in which it has been distributed among the several states

2nd. The estimated amount of improvements of which survays only have been made & the manner in which they are distributed among the several states as near as it can be ascertained—with the survays in progress with their estimated amount—(for this, I the President haves applied to the Engineer Dept, but as there was a ~~report~~ publication on this subject, founded on a report, I would be glad to get it.

3rd. a particular description of the most objectionable objects, of which survays are authorised by the Ligh House bill—for this purpose, I would ask your ideas, & thank you for the prominent objections, of your correspondant on the subject of Light Houses, that the Sec. of the Treasury spoke of on saturday last—so soon as it will meet the convenience of the Sec. of the T. the President would be happy to be in possession of all the information on these several subjects, he can afford him

A. J

[Endorsed by Ingham:] The President in relation to subjects for the message

ANS, PU-Ingham Papers (16-0434).

To *Martin Van Buren*

octbr. 18th.

My Dr Sir

I sent you the information I obtained from the Engineer Department, so soon as I receive a reply from Mr Ingham will send it to you. The most objectionable objects of survays, in the bill, are those for ascertaining the expediency & expence of improving the navigation of rivers running from navigable streams into a county or neighbourhood, or even state; These cannot be considered national; nothing can be so considered, but those great leading and navigable streams from the ocean, and passing through two or more states, and an obstruction that prevents commerce from passing thro' other states, which when removed will give an uninterrupted passage to those other states, can be viewed as comming within the constitutional powers of congress—If this boundery is once passed, then every creek, or small river, emtying into a navigable stream, they not being navigable, & extending into a county may claim to be survayed ~~under this implied~~ and improved at the national expence

Such for instance in the State of Main The survay of Cathanse river to ascertain the expediency & expense of improving the navigation of the same—New Hampshire—the survay of Lamprey river to ascertain the expediency of improving the navigation of the same, the same might be said to the survay for improving the Cocheco branch of the piscataqua &c &c &c &c &c—[1]

I would wish you to come over & we will run our eyes over the whole bill. I informed you by note that there were in the bill an appropriation for a survay of the falls of ohio, with a view to clearing the obstructions in the channel; I have recd. a letter from Mr Ronaldson today now there, complaining that the river is now lower than ever known & the people are quarrying the stone from the bar that will destroy the upper navigation & ruin the canal.

I have been so busy today that I have had no time to examine the Light House bill & I now submit these crude ideas to you. yrs

Andrew Jackson

P.S. after I had sealed this Mr Ingham sent me the enclosed—preserve all & return them when you have done with them

ALS, DLC-Van Buren Papers (16-0439).
1. The vetoed lighthouse bill appropriated $200 each for navigational surveys of the Cathance and Lamprey rivers and $2,400 to improve the Cocheco branch of the Piscataqua.

To Samuel Delucenna Ingham

Octbr. 19th. 1830—

The President with his respects to the Secretary of the Treasury requests to be informed, whether Mr. Allen is still receiver of public monies at St Augustine—from the Register it appears, he was appointed on 22nd. of May 1826, of course his four years has expired, unless he has been appointed lately.

AN, PU-Ingham Papers (16-0453). William Henry Allen (1794–1836) was appointed receiver at the St. Augustine land office by President Adams in 1826. AJ had nominated him in March for a new four-year term beginning May 22, 1830, and the Senate confirmed him in May. By oversight, his new commission had not yet been sent nor his appointment listing updated.

From Samuel Delucenna Ingham

Oct 19th 1830

My Dear Sir

Owing to an unremitting pressure of business I have delayed until now replying to your note of friday last requesting to know whether in my opinion the good of the public service requires any change in the appointment of the 1st Auditor

My personal respect for that officer and the persuasion that he performs his duties according to the best of his ability and the absence of any specific matter to allege against him all disincline me strongly to suggest any thing that might lead to his removal and I regret therefore to find myself obliged to say that what with the natural tendency to relaxation in all public institutions the force of habit and the great reluctance and incapacity of men far advanced in life to adopt any material change of practice or system or to exert the energies of earlier life I have been led to conclude that it is not practicable for the head of that office to carry into effect the improvement which in my judgment the public service requires. It is the first office for the examination of the accounts of revenue officers and is the most proper to have charge not only of the chief scrutiny into their accounts as they are from time to time forwarded for settlement but of all the correspondence in relation to such accounts and more especially with ascertaining and detecting defaults peculations and frauds of every kind. under the present organization of the revenue system there is no check upon many custom house officers except what may be exerted from the Treasury Department   That this check has been wholy insufficient as heretofore constituted, to prevent or detect defaults and frauds is proved by experience. many of those discovered within the last year might never have been known but for the removal of the officer, and I believe none of those discovered before removal were detected by means of any information derived from the accounting officer. The office of the 1st Comptroller is already too heavily burdened with business which must be done by the head to bear an additional load that of the 1st auditor is not so burdened. besides there seems to be a peculiar fitness in charging the office which first examines the accounts with all the responsibility of preventing and detecting defaults and peculations so far as it may be practicable among all the officers whose accounts he settles. There can be no doubt but that an efficient and capable officer entering willingly and zealously upon the discharge of this duty and being considered responsible for its performance would insure to the Govt. lasting advantage. Defaults &c will not merely be detected and punished what is much better they will be prevented. Such an action would operate as a preservative principle throughout the whole machine of Govt. in promoting the morals of public functionaries and inspiring the people with confidence and veneration for these institutions.

The intellectual power of the officer at the seat of Govt. can only be employed to the best advantage where the intellectual labour is properly distributed and some competent person made specially responsible for the proper management of every transaction that may occur. It is not possible for the heads of Department to examine all the details of the vast machine committed to their charge much less search for and discover malversations in the various branches of service. This can only be done by their auxiliaries the heads of Bureaus immediately superintending and their various clerks[.] all which is respectfully submitted by your humble servant

(Signed) S D Ingham

LC, PU-Ingham Papers (mAJs). First auditor Richard Harrison was not removed. He resigned in 1836.

From Friedrich List

Washington Oct. 20 1830

Mr. President

I take the liberty of applying to you for the appointment of Consul General of the United States for Saxony, Bavaria; Hesse Cassel and Alsace. I would serve in the said capacity without remuneration but consider it as an additional favour if at present or on some future day, as your Excellency think proper, a particular Consulship or some other agency would be attached to it, yielding emoluments adequate to the services I propose to render or may have rendered. Having done my best hitherto to serve the American people, I am animated by the same sentiment in presenting to you this respectful application.

With sincere veneration I am Mr. President Your most obedient and humble servant

Frederick List

ALS, DNA-RG 59 (M639-14). List enclosed this application in a letter to Van Buren of the same day, proposing if he was appointed to pursue in Europe a ten-point program of promoting internal economic development and commerce with the U.S. (DNA-RG 59, M639-14). Van Buren forwarded List's application to AJ, who wrote back on October 23 (below).

From Addison Powell and William Rosser Hinton

Respected Sir,

The undersigned Addison Powell of the state of Virginia and Wm. R. Hinton of the state of North Carolina, the Agents and representatives of a meeting of gentlemen assembled at Washington City in the afternoon of the 19. instant to take into consideration the case of the acceptance on the part of the Postmaster General of a bid made by Messrs. Reeside Porter & Co. to run a line of stages from Washington City to Fort Mitchell in the line between the states of Georgia and Alabama, for the sum of $67,950, whereby the public has been greatly injured, and many of the individuals thus met together, as well as others taken by surprise, and their rights compromitted & sacrificed to the cupidity of this wealthy, rich and powerfully influential company of gentlemen, have found it necessary in the discharge of the trust committed to them to present themselves with the cause of these gentlemen whom they represent before your Excellency, and to ask at your hands a redress of grivences by them felt & complained of which redress has been denied them by the Post Master General to whom application has been made in the full hope and confidence of success.[1]

It is a matter of great felitation to your appellants that they are making petition to one who is both able & willing, to do that which is right if it can be ascertained by him, as well as to correct that which is wrong when the same shall be made appear; nor will he require any set form of address, or of sycophantic supplication; but the erect posture of an independant freeman, feeling as he should the injustice done him, & frankly, manfully & boldly demanding of him as the Stervart of their mutual master the redress of grievance complained of. We then, Sir, proceed to lay before you a statement of our case.

In a publication of the Postmaster General of the United States he advertised that he will receive proposals untill the 12 of octr. instant for carrying the mail on the multifarious routes therein stated comprehending most if not all within the states of Virginia, North Carolina, South Carolina, Georgia & Alabama & the Territory of Florida. That the decisions on such proposals as he shall *thus* receive, will be announced on the 19. also instant. In conformity to the frank & fair terms of this invitation, your petitioners and those whom they represent, together with very many others came forward & handed in their proposals for carrying the mail on the routes specified. But as the object of our solicitations is limited to one or two routes, we of course shall confine our selves to the routes from Washington City to Fort Mitchell on the line of Georgia & Alabama, a distance of more than 800 miles, and comprising about 15 numbers or Sections as partitioned in the said proposals; and, of the route branching off from that just named at Fayetteville, via Georgetown to Charleston,

S. Carolina, a distance of 199 miles & comprehending three Nos. or Sections as aforsaid.

We will direct your attention in the beginning to the route first named, and which is one of more interest and importance, than any other in the southern States. It would of course call forth more bidders, & excite more attention than any others. The persons whose case is now before you were principally bidders on this route, had come forward & with their proposals in the full assurance, that all proper regard & consideration would be extended to the bid of each worthy & responsible person that its relative merit should justly deserve & that in every thing in relation to receiving the proposals & making the final decission on them, the plainness, simplicity & frankness of the advertisement would have been kept up, and carried through. But to our utter confusion & astonishment the first route that was announced was proclaimed to have been given to Reeside, Porter & Co. for $67,950—the length & partitions of which have been before stated. Now, Sir, we do not object to the contract being given to the gentlemen who may compose this company, sooner than to a like number of active, spirited & efficient citizens composing any other company who by their energy, competency & faithfullness in such laborious service had secured their private interest while they subserve that of the public. our objections to this procedure is of a much graver & more elavated character. We protest against this act of the Department as not in accordance with the tenor & spirit of the Laws of Congress, which directs the duty, in establishing post offices & post roads; in dividing, apportioning & letting the same out as therein prescribed to contractors. As fostering a system of favouritersm, by bestowing its favors & emoluments on such of its friends & favorites as may, by a course of fawning & subserviency to the Department or any of its officers, render themselves acceptable. By enabling the subtle peculator who has & ever will, inveigle himself into office, to prosecute his Schemes of rapine & fraud of the public treasure. Because it is calculated to encourage & cherish the domineering spirit of the capitalist, already too triumphant over men of moderate means & fortune. Because in the present case, it is bestowed upon an association of many persons in exclusion of many associations of fewer persons; at a much higher price, than the latter propose to take the different Sections at—involving a clear loss to the government of a very large amount of the public money. Because in the present case it bestows on persons who already, in the North & in the South, in the East & in the West, the individuals composing the same company designated by a name some little, and but little, different from that under which this is awarded to them are enjoying very large and extensive contracts under the government, producing to them very great emolument & profit. Because one and perhaps two of the members of this firm, in one or more of the large southern contracts as it is known, & it is believed in many, if not all, in which this company is concerned was *lately*, a most favoured & efficient officer or officers of the General Post office, and since their inductions into office have amassed large, nay splendid fortunes—that under the tutelage & protection of those two individuals, or of one of them, most if not all, of the members making up this company, have been from time to time introduced into the public Service, and by the direct gift or bestowment of them, or one of them, do now enjoy many of the most valuable contracts under their direction. In short that your petitioners protest against the procedure as repugnant to the plain & homely garb, of our system of Government which excludes every thing like trick, artifice, or management, in obtaining such favors, & will countenance nothing but an erect & strait forward course.[2]

If the privilege had not been denied to your memorialist at the Department to compare the Several bids made on this route they would have had been able to have shewn in a manner quite satisfactory that they were the lowest bidders for the different Sections & therefore entitled as they conceive to the contract—not content with this refusal, and feeling a firm & confidential assurance in the justice of our cause, we addressed a letter to the Post Master General, his reply together with our rejoinder, & the final letter of that officer putting an end to further correspondence with him, accompany this memorial & we beg may be received as apart of it. Sundry certificates and affidavits of individual persons also accompany it, and exhibit some facts in relation to the transaction in the General Post Office which we think justify us in the suspicions we have expressed that "there is something rotten in the state of Denmark." Your fiat to that branch of the Government & its officers can cause the blazing light to shine before you, in which you may behold the whole case & we have full confidence that if our case shall not exhibit claims to your remedial power, that you will say so—and that if it does you will bestow the contracts where of right & justice they belong.[3]

We also protest against another decission of the General P. Office lately announced in favor of Charles P. Mallett, giving to him the contract of the route from Fayetteville N.C. via Georgetown S.C. to charleston 199 miles at $20,000 pr. annum when Allen, Evans & Teling tendered proposals for the same service for $19,100 pr annum. Thus exhibiting a loss to the Government in four years of $3,600. We claim the contract for the latter and submit their case.[4]

When we first entered upon the investigation of this business our only object was to ascertain who was really the lowest bidder, & to satisfy the gentlemen who had been *thus* repudiated. Every step in its progress has inforced upon us the imperative duty we owed to our fellow citizens to persevere in it, & expose such, as we think it a wanton breach of private right and justice. We will further add that we were not willing a measure, like this, so discouraging to the citizen, & in itself so reprehensible in all its features, should be covered over by the mantle of the perpetrators, to be hereafter spread before the people in all its deformity to the injury

of your standing as their public functionary. We, all, both principals &
agents were unwilling that our attachments to your self & your administration should be confined to a mere less service. But choose rather "that
our faith should be judged of by our works."

To your final adjudication we commit our case, fully believing that
you will cause right & justice to be done. We are Honored Sir, your Obt.
Sevts

(Signed) A. Powell
W. R. Hinton

Copy, DNA-RG 46 (16-0487). Powell (c1795–1840) and Hinton (1796–1839) were southern mail contractors.

1. Mail contractors Edwin Porter & John H. Avery were associates of Reeside.

2. The two former postal officers were assistant postmaster general Abraham Bradley
(1767–1838) and his brother, second assistant Phineas Bradley (1769–1845), both dismissed
by Barry in 1829.

3. Powell and Hinton attached a sheaf of affidavits charging collusion in awarding mail
contracts. One accused an unnamed Post Office clerk of tipping off Reeside and his associates that they had been outbid and that "great management" would be required to retain
their contract. AJ wrote Powell this same day asking for the clerk's name. Powell replied that
North Carolina bidder Caleb Leonard, who had witnessed the conversation, did not know
the clerk's name but could identify him. However, Leonard had since left town. AJ also wrote
twice to Postmaster General Barry this same day about the other charges (below).

4. Thomas Evans, Matthew Allen, and E. Sterling had bid on mail contracts.

To William Taylor Barry

(Copy)

Washington City Oct. 23. 1830

Sir,

Addison Powell & William R. Hinton on behalf of themselves & others,
having appealed to me (by their memorial) from your decisions upon the
bids for the contracts on the mail routes from Washington City to Fort
Mitchell & from Fayetteville, N.C. via Georgetown, S.C. to Charleston, I
request you to inform me—

1. Upon what considerations the first named of said routes were
assigned to Reesides, Porter & Co., & the last named to Charles P. Mallett,
in preference to the memorialists and those whom they represent?

2. If the suggestion of improvements by these bidders effected your
determination in the premises, whether you gave public notice that the
suggestion of improvements would be considered by you in deciding on
the bids?

3. Whether the suggestion of improvements by bidders and their consideration by the Postmaster General in determining the bids are of recent origin or have been heretofore and uniformly practised in the Department.

4. Whether the comprizing of several routes in one bid has been practised by other proposers for mail contracts than Reesides Porter & Co. and in reference to other routes than those assigned to them in the contract complained of—and whether the Postmaster General's regarding such as proper and valid proposals is in accordance with the law and the usage of the Department.

These enquiries are made in order to ascertain if there has been in the matters complained of a departure from the established & salutary principles & the sound discretion that should govern in such cases. I am respectfully your obdient servant

(Signed) Andrew Jackson

Copy, DNA-RG 46 (16-0469). In Barry's absence, Assistant Postmaster General Charles Kitchel Gardner (1787–1869) replied to AJ on October 26 (DNA-RG 28, M601-47). Gardner explained that the successful bid of $67,950 from Edwin Porter & Co., James Reeside, and John H. Avery for the twelve routes comprising the line from Washington to Fort Mitchell included a number of improvements over the contract specifications, among them faster and more frequent service, an armed guard at company expense whenever needed, free carriage of government expresses, and use of four-horse coaches instead of two-horse stages. These enhancements would save the Department several times the $4,869 by which the bid exceeded the combined low bids of $63,081 from eight separate contractors for the individual routes. Further, one low bidder had performed poorly on a previous contract, another was insolvent, and a third was an unknown party with no record or recommendations, while Porter, Reeside, and Avery's "energy and ability to perform are well tried." Similarly, Charles P. Mallett was awarded the Carolina contract, comprising four routes, for $22,800 because the faster service and armed guard in his proposal would save more than the $700 by which it exceeded the aggregate low bids of $22,100.

Gardner also said that by "long established usage" contract advertisements contained standard language inviting bidders to propose enhancements in service and promising them "due consideration." Consolidating several routes into one bid was likewise "an old established custom," in fact rather the rule than the exception. Powell and Hinton themselves had submitted such proposals.

To William Taylor Barry

(Copy)

Washington City Oct. 23. 1830.

Sir,

I desire you to investigate the following charges filed with me against your chief Clerk, Obadiah B. Brown Esqr. and report thereon to me. Said charges are contained in affidavits of which the following are abstracts.

That Obadiah B. Brown Esqr. told a Servant or porter on the 13th. October instant between the hours of 9 & 12 oclock A.M. in the presence of affiant to go to his (Browns) house and bring the bids or proposals that were left there on the night before. (Sworn to by John A. Byrd)

That Mr Reesides on the 19 instant before the decissions on the proposals were announced went into a room in the West end of the building of the Post office Dept., and in a short time O. B. Brown left the said room with him & walked to the opposite side of the building, & there had an earnest conversation with Mr. Reeside & this was repeated several times—the deponent believes it was on the subject of mail contracts & heard the Hon. Wm. T. Barry say that he did not hear of such intercourse. (Wm. R. Hinton is the affiant)

That Mr. Brown & Mr. Reesides had frequent intercourse & conversation with each other before the doors were opened to announce the decissions on the bids—that shortly before that event Brown & Reeside left the room together, adjoining the Postmaster Generals room, & went out into an aisle or passage & had a long & interesting conversation—And affiant believes that "information reciprocal" was given respecting mail contracts (Wm Gholson affiant—A. Powel makes affidavit to same occurrence)

That on the 19th instant, O. B. Brown came out of his office with Reesides & had a spirited conversation with him—& then returned to his office. That the affiant Powell & Hinton went into the Postmaster Generals room after the decissions had been declared, that they found the book opened Powell commenced reading & Hinton taking notes that shortly after Mr. Brown came in & told Mr. Powel that he must have the book & notwithstanding Mr. Powel declared that he only wanted a copy of the bids & Mr. Reeside said in a "flourishing manner" let them see; Mr. Brown persisted & took away the book. (Luke Fox affiant)

I am respectfully Your obdt Servant

(Signed) Andrew Jackson

Copy, DNA-RG 46 (16-0472). Affidavits from mail contract bidders John A. Byrd, William Gholson (1775–1831), and Lark Fox (1782–1833) were submitted with Addison Powell and William R. Hinton's memorial. Obadiah Bruen Brown (1779–1852) was chief clerk of the General Post Office. On October 26, Assistant Postmaster General Charles K. Gardner sent AJ Brown's "explanation and reply" to the charges (DNA-RG 28, M601-47). On October 29, AJ wrote Barry asking for sworn affidavits from Brown and Reeside about their conversation. Barry wrote AJ on November 12, denying collusion between Brown and Reeside and other charges made by Powell and Hinton. AJ wrote Powell on November 13 (below).

To Martin Van Buren

Octbr. 23rd. 1830—

The President with his respects to Mr V. B. encloses Genl S. Smiths letter which he has read with attention—his remarks are such as would flow from a source of good common sense, & great experience & I have no doubt are sound—[1]

My health is better—will you ride to day at 12—the day bids fair to be fine—P. wishes to converse with you on the subject of our national concerns—encloses you Major Eatons letter giving an outline of the treaty with the choctaws—it is liberal, our enemies cannot complain on this score, and our friends will not. Mr. V. B. will return it when Perused.

AN, DLC-Van Buren Papers (16-0506).
   1. On October 3 Samuel Smith wrote Van Buren a letter which he asked him to show to AJ. He applauded Louis McLane's conduct of the West Indian negotiation and urged AJ, in keeping with his forthright character, to immediately issue a proclamation reopening the trade, rather than repeat the error of previous presidents and lose a satisfactory settlement by hesitating or caviling over details (Van Buren Papers, DLC).

To Martin Van Buren

Octbr. 23rd. 1830—

The President with his respects to the secretary of State, acknowledges the recpt. of his note this morning inclosing Mr. Lists to him. The President believes much useful information may be derived thro' Mr List. Therefore, if there are a consulate vacant where he solicits the appointment it would meet my wishes to bestow it upon him, as he is willing to accept one not for emolument of office, but to place himself in a Situation to be usefull.
   The P will ride at 11 oclock if that hour will suit the sec. of State—
   The note of Mr List is returned.

A. J

AN, DLC-Van Buren Papers (16-0504). On October 28 List wrote Van Buren from Philadelphia, asking to be appointed consul at Hamburg and enclosing a recommendation to AJ from eight prominent citizens including Henry Baldwin, Charles J. Ingersoll, Henry Horn, George M. Dallas, and William J. Duane (DNA-RG 59, M639-14). AJ gave List a recess appointment to replace John Cuthbert as consul at Hamburg on November 8 and nominated him to the Senate on December 14; but the Senate rejected him on February 8, 1831, by 37 to 6. In 1832 List was nominated and confirmed as consul at Baden, and in 1834 as consul at Leipzig.

From Joel Roberts Poinsett

Charleston
23 Octr. 1830

Dear Sir
   When we parted at Washington in May last, I mentioned to you, that I was returning to Carolina in order to oppose, by any influence I might possess there, the strange and pernicious doctrines advanced by some of the leading men of our state and which, if not counteracted might lead to the most serious and fatal consequences   On that occasion I understood you to say, that you regarded them as "utter madness"; and I left

Washington in the firm conviction, that I was acting in conformity with your wishes and for the good of our common country in controverting doctrines, which I regard as subversive of the best interests of that country, and in declaring myself opposed to principles which if they could be detected in the letter or spirit of our constitution by any subtlety of the human intellect would render that instrument a ~~useless~~ worthless document, would entirely destroy the practical utility of our confederation and convert our bond of union into a rope of sand.

On my arrival in Columbia, where I went in order to ascertain the extent of the evil, and that my sentiments might be more generally known throughout the state, I found the public mind poisoned by the opinions uttered at Washington by our leading politicians there, and by the pernicious doctrines of the President of that College Dr. Cooper, whose talents and great acquirements give weight to his perverse principles, and make him doubly dangerous.[1] On conversing confidentially with ~~some~~ several old and valued friends in that place I found that they too, deprecated the measures proposed to be adopted as a remedy against the operation of the tariff law ~~by our leading men in the state~~; but regarded opposition as hopeless against such an array as had declared in favor of ~~calling a convention of the people to nullify the law~~ nullification. I found the same sentiments prevailing and the same fears entertained ~~by~~ among the moderate men in Charleston: but after frequent conferences with my friends Judge Huger, Mr. Pettigru, Mr. Pringle, Dr. Johnson and others it was resolved at all hazards to organise an opposition to schemes which we considered likely to ~~be~~ prove so ruinous in their consequences. In this determination we were confirmed and very much aided ~~in the execution of~~ by Col. Drayton's honorable and public declaration of his sentiments in favor of the union.[2]

The Nullifiers try to make us believe, that the union party ~~were~~ are acting against your wishes—This has been already & on several occasions broadly asserted by the advocates of the rights of the states to nullify the laws of the general government and besides the respectable names of the Vice Prest. of McDuffie, Genl. Hayne and Major Hamilton we have had to contend against these assertions of your views on this question, which the censure or dismissal of Mr. Pringle would tend to confirm for he is I believe the only officer of the general gov. in Charleston in favor of the Union party[3]—The opposition which was commenced in Charleston has been extended throughout the rest of the state and the favorable result of the elections lead us to hope, that we shall prevent the call of a convention, which might have ended in an act of insurrection, for I can regard in no other light the consequences of this state nullifying an act of congress.[4] It has been asserted of us that we have been induced to oppose ourselves to these doctrines because we are in favor of Mr. Clay and of the American System. This Mr. President is not so—Mr. Clay and his system have no partizan in this state & so entirely do we rely upon your wisdom and sense of justice & do we hope that you will finally obtain for us a modification of the system wh. really is injurious and oppressive in its operation upon us, that we severally and universally desire, that you should consent to serve another term

AL draft, PHi (16-0481). Poinsett (1779–1851), a Charleston native, had been a South Carolina congressman and minister to Mexico.

1. Thomas Cooper (1759–1839) was president of South Carolina College and a leading nullifier. In an 1827 speech against the tariff he had famously declared that "we shall 'ere long be compelled to calculate the value of our union; and to enquire of what use to us is this most unequal alliance? By which the south has always been the loser, and the north always the gainer?"

2. Judge and legislator Daniel Elliott Huger (1779–1854), former state attorney general James Louis Petigru (1789–1863), Charleston customs collector James Reid Pringle (1782–1840), and physician Joseph Johnson (1776–1862) were prominent South Carolina Unionists. In his speech at the Charleston "Great State Rights Celebration" on July 1, congressman William Drayton (1776–1846) pledged opposition to the protective tariff but reprobated nullification as an unconstitutional recourse leading to disunion and civil war.

3. Poinsett sent this letter to AJ through Robert Oliver of Baltimore. His covering letter to Oliver of October 23 urged him to impress upon AJ that Pringle's removal at the instigation of the nullifiers would devastate South Carolina Unionism (MdHi). AJ replied to Oliver on October 26 (below). Pringle was not removed.

4. Unionists had narrowly won Charleston's city election in September. In October state elections, nullifiers fell short of winning the two-thirds legislative majority necessary to call a constitutional convention.

To Mary Ann Eastin

Washington Octbr. 24th. 1830

My Dr Mary

At length a leisure moment this good sabath night has offered, & I take up my pen to drop you a hasty line.

We have been here since the night of the 25th. ulto. & accept from my old friend judge Overton & Col Love I have not recd. a single line from any of my other friends. Major Donelson has recd. several from Emily, & informs me you all enjoy health. As usual I am crouded with business & office Hunters. Many friends call to see me, and the ladies have been very kind, altho, Mrs. Watson has never been to see me nor one of the family. We are getting on prosperously with our national concerns, & Genl Donelson was joined in holy wedlock to Miss Margaret on the 19th. it having been posponed by the Sickness & death of her unkle Mr Southall—They left here the next morning for Newyork will return in a few days. My son went with them to Philadelphia.[1]

Major Donelson has informed you that the House appears lonesome, and on his account it would give me great pleasure that you & Emily with the sweet little ones were here   I have often experienced in life the privation of leaving my Dr wife, when contending against poverty, seeking for a competency, therefore can feel for him. But I fear if you were here the disagreable scenes heretofore experienced might be acted over again ~~here~~; of which I hear, & see, great Symtoms, which nothing when you come here, can prevent, but a determined resolution & energy in Emily & you ~~can prevent~~, and a duty to myself & my friend Major Eaton will require me to have observed, & which Emily has promised me that ~~if~~ when she comes she will observe.

I shall forever much regret that Emily & you did not at first pursue my advice, it was then in your power I knew to have kept from my doors & put down, that wicked political combination of Slanderers, & to have prevented those disagreable consequences that have ensued, and by the easy mode of extending equal civilities to all & particularly to the heads of departments & their families—you both knew Eaton was my steadfast friend and the able defender of your dear aunt when assailed by these wicked political monsters—& I further told you that the stroke was only ostensibly against Eaton, when levelled thro' him at me—I then knew it, and after finding the combination began & engendered here extending to Nashville with Doctor McNairy & Mrs K. in the van, it confirmed me in this well founded opinion, and the late letter published in the Lexington Reporter is proof as strong as holy writ—and what was the most cruel thing of all, my own connections included in this unholy wicked & unjust conspiracy against female character, by which I was to be reached, and the memory of my Dr wife, who ought to have been dear to all her connections, indirectly, ~~as well as~~ if not directly assailed.[2]

I have long knew the hypocrite who was at the bottom of this secretely wielding his pupets afraid to act in open day—his hand is seen in the letters from Washington, as well as those from Nashville, but he will fail in this, as he has before when he attempted to stab me in the dark, when to my face & to the public, crying out he was my friend & would support me. These acts will recoil upon his and his wicked agents head & fall harmless at the feet of those whose injury he has been seeking. I now think it proper to bring this to Emily and your view, for I hope you will come together when you do come, that you may well consider whether you can when you come here assume that energetic, dignified & independent course, that will shake from you, the ~~constant~~ particular association and attention of those, to the exclusion of friends, that have been the cause, of inducing you to spurn my advice, which has been the cause of so much disquietude to me, and has lead to a division of my House, where ~~alone~~ the advice of the head ought, & must govern, with the wicked purpose in view, of leading to my distruction. This tho, was under the hypocritical garb of friendship, that imposed upon Emily & you unacquainted with the arts of the experienced in calumny, and of political intrigue, altho well understood by me, and who, I now find where I expected them, associating with my worst enemies.

I have therefore only to add, that it would give me much pleasure to see you both here, provided you will persue my advice, and assume that dignified course that ought to have been at first adopted, of treating every one with attention, & extending the same comity and attention to all the heads of Departments, & their families which is the only course that my situation can permit. This will be a task that will require great firmness and energy, for you may rest assured that these satanic combination having once got your ears, ~~will~~ when you arrive will surround you with redoubled vigor & earnestness, knowing as they do, that it is the only hope for success, to create a seperation between my houshold, by which, they may hope to turn it to my injury, and so soon as they can accomplish their object, would wheel upon ~~you~~ & if possible destroy you—for those wicked ones who live & thrive upon slander, & are base enough to assail female character for political views, will stop at nothing—with these remarks I conclude, it will afford me pleasure to see you here, under a determination to adopt & pursue the course here pointed out, without such determination your own good sense will dictate to you both, the propriety of not coming until such arrangements are made here, to secure harmony for the future, better to put up with the seperation for a short time than to come on & introduce again those scenes here that has cost me so much pain, which first & last has almost destroyed me, & this too produced by my dearest friends, uniting with & pursuing the advice of my worst enemies. This is what I cannot again endure. I have never asked any sacrafice of either of you, I never will, but I have a right to expect my advice in my own House & to my own family will be obayed, and that is only that the same comity will be extended to all the families of the Heads of Departments & to all others & that my enemies will not be my families associates in exclusion of my long tried & sincere friends. Those who have been couselling you to your ruin, and inducing you to believe it is meritorious to disobay my admonitions & follow theirs and thereby destroying the Harmony of my family. Keep clear of the Slanderers, they are always dangerous—with a resolution to conform to the rule laid down here, which was the only one ever required by me and I will be more than happy to see you here—

one word more, has judge overton Randal McGavock, Lemuel Donelson, General Coffee, & thousand more injured their standing & character by associating with Major Eaton & his family, I think not. But the persecutor & Slanderers will always meet their reward sooner or later & all who associates with them[3]

Present my kind compliments to Emily, kiss Jackson & Mary Rachel for me & shew her this letter altho written in haste it is intended for her due consideration, and accept for yourself my best wishes & believe me your friend

Andrew Jackson

P.S. You will receive by Genl Donelson a small present, as a remembrance, it is sent as you have no parents to provide for you, it has been selected by our mutual friend Major Lewis who sends his compliments to you & Mrs. Donelson   A. J.[4]

ALS, NHi (16-0509). Burke, 1:246–47.

1. Methodist minister Daniel Southall (1768–1830), husband of John Branch's sister Patience, died October 15. Elizabeth Courts Love Watson (c1778–1853), sister of Charles J. Love, had been a close friend of Rachel Jackson.

2. On September 29 the Lexington *Kentucky Reporter* printed an unsigned letter, dated September 15 at Nashville. The author censured AJ for trying to browbeat the Indians into removing, and also for trying to force an unnamed infamous female into society and "into his own domestic circle (to the great dissatisfaction of the young, amiable and excellent female who presides there)." The letter commended the ladies of Nashville for repelling AJ's effort "to remove the barrier between purity and pollution" by foisting the tarnished woman upon them. On December 6 AJ wrote John Coffee naming Boyd McNairy as the author (below).

3. Randal McGavock (1768–1843) had been mayor of Nashville.

4. The present was a dress, to be delivered by Daniel Smith Donelson.

To George Gibson

Washington Octbr. 24th. 1830—

Dr. Sir,

Complaints appear to be the order of the day. The enclosed I have just received, and hasten to lay it before you, that you may lay before me a report of this case, and an answer to the charge made; of giving the contract to another when Craig, was (as stated by him) the lowest bidder.

you will please, with your answer, return Mr Craigs letter herewith enclosed, & believe me to be as usual yours respectfully

Andrew Jackson

ALS, DNA-RG 192 (16-0515). AJ enclosed a complaint of October 16 from Silas Craig (1794–1854) of Georgetown, Ky., that he was not awarded the contract to supply provisions to the Army posts at New Orleans and Baton Rouge despite submitting the low bid. On October 25 Gibson wrote Craig, with a copy to AJ, stating that Cleon Hawkins, who won the contract, had in fact underbid Craig by $110.80 (DNA-RG 192).

From Andrew Jackson Donelson

Octr. 25th. 1830

Dear Uncle

Reflecting upon the delicate subject of our mornings conversation, and the ground upon which you thought it right to place the social intercourse of Mrs. Donelson, before she is invited to return to the city, I have thought it best to give you my views in writing as the least painful mode of communicating them.

I have never had an agency in an issue of facts touching the general character of Mrs. Eaton, and shall not be forced to make one except in defence of my own conduct or that of my family.

It is impossible that a delicate female, introduced to a new social circle as was Mrs Donelson in the winter of 1829, should not be governed in some degree by the views of character which she found prevailing in it. An insensibility to such an influence would imply the absence of a moral sentiment which I should be unwilling to ascribe to any virtuous woman, much more to one that possesses my love and is the mother of my children. How, let me ask, was this safeguard of character treated in her case? Altho' from motives of friendship and duty to you, which it is my greatest happiness to know have never ceased to animate both Mrs. D and myself, we commenced an intercourse with the family of Majr Eaton, which as far as civilities of an ordinary kind from us could have any effect placed them upon the same footing that other respectable members of society occupied & yet a short time after your inauguration a letter is addressed to Mrs. D by Mr. Eaton in which he descends to the insinuation that she has placed herself under the guardianship of slanderers. This denunciation is applied to a very respectable family in this place, one member of which was an old and long esteemed friend and correspondent of our lamented Aunt, whose worthy example in "not deciding upon people's character" it also professes to respect. I refer to this letter not for the purpose of assailing the motives of Mr. Eaton, but of marking how well it corresponded with intimations which preceded it and have since followed it, that my power to hold my place here depended upon my subserviency to the wishes of Mrs. Eaton.[1]

Whilst however I permitted no circumstance to alter my conduct and am not sensible of but one trivial exception on the part of Mrs. Donelson which no sooner occurred than it was reported to you and satisfactorily explained, what is the fact in regard to Mrs. Eaton? A visit which I paid to her in your company was misrepresented to a member of the family, and was made the burden of a message which was not only insulting, but indicative of the artifice by which it was designed to make your feelings the minister of her threats. I mention this as another fact not depending upon rumour.

The next step in the history of this affair was the trip to Norfolk.[2] Altho' I was not an eye witness to the circumstances which gave Mrs. Eaton so much offence on this occasion, I am constrained to believe that they grew out of her habitual proneness to mistake the proprieties of her sex. Understanding that something had occurred which excited the astonishment of the passengers, and seeing Mrs. Eaton betray and extraordinary discomposure of temper, I proffered my arm to her in descending the hill to the steamboat for the purpose of ascertaining the cause. She informed me I think that Mrs. Donelson had not accepted her fan nor used her cologne bottle when offered to her, and shew a disposition not to be intimate with her: She also added that the emotions which then agitated her bosom were the result of pity for my family, for that you had agreed, if we did not behave differently from what Mrs. Donelson had then done, to send us back To Tennessee: and that she did not consent to take the excursion to Norfolk until you made that promise.

It is painful to me to refer to these incidents, and this last I should not name did it disclose any thing which rested on my memory alone. But the truth is I had the means of establishing the existence of similar impressions in the society in which I every day moved before that trip, and since after it from another unquestionable source. Whatever hopes I may have entertained previous to that disclosure of regulating my intercourse with the family of Majr Eaton so as not to allow my example to take the course of others who on different grounds had held none with it, they were now completely banished. It was impossible that I could submit to the degradation of having a tribune of this character constituted for the purpose of determining within what limits my good behaviour might secure the station which I held. Honorable as I deem that station I scorn to hold it at the will of any one but yourself, or at the expense of those principles with which have grown up my love and gratitude for you.

With the discretion of Mrs. Donelson on this subject I have never interfered until the occurrences of the Norfolk trip and those which followed it the day or two after our return to this city. They have satisfied me that no partial intercourse which I could hereafter prescribe for myself could save me from exposure to fresh insults, or what is worse representations calculated to withdraw your confidence from me. I feel it therefore to be my duty whatever may be the advice of Mrs. D.s other friends not to permit her further intercourse with Mrs. Eaton, except in your house, if you think proper to invite her return.

I do believe, Uncle, that the time will arrive when the difficulty which you now experience in reconciling my conduct to that tenderness of feeling which your unbounded goodness ought to create in the heart of filial love and gratitude will be removed. If however it never should, altho' the consequence is hazardous and full of danger to my future prospects, I hope to be able to bear up under it, and demonstrate to those who may still take an interest in my welfare, if I have erred, that I was not tempted by those considerations which usually assail integrity of motive and uprightness of heart. Affection can have no purer link than that which binds me to your interests, to your private happiness, to the honor and glory of your public services. To the ardour of this sentiment I may possibly owe the misfortune of its being misconceived: for I have with difficulty restrained its indignation when I have seen this petticoat affair employed in prejudicing old friends and in creating new ones. But I do not mean to find fault with the conduct of others here. All that I desired to do was to express in as delicate way as I can, my unwillingness for Mrs. Donelson to take her place in this house again, unless she can do so without being required to visit Mrs. Eaton or to hold an intercourse with her out of it. Yr. affectionate nephew

Andrew J. Donelson

[Endorsed by Donelson:] Duplicate letter to Genl Jackson dated Oct. 25. 1830. produced by his declaration that Mrs. D had been invited thro' Mary Eastin to return under a pledge to visit Mrs. Eaton and to practise the same comity to her out of his house, that she did to the families of the other heads of Department—

ALS copy, DLC-Donelson Papers (16-0518). AL draft, DLC (73). AJ had shown Donelson his October 24 letter to Mary Ann Eastin.
    1. On April 8, 1829, Eaton had written Emily Donelson admonishing her to shun the confidence of Washington slanderers and busybodies. He singled out Harriet Love Sim, wife of physician Thomas Sim, and Jane Love Watson Graham, wife of George Graham, respectively the sister and daughter of Rachel Jackson's friend Elizabeth Watson. Eaton recalled Rachel telling Washington tattlers that "I did not come here, to listen to little slanderous tales, & to decide upon peoples character." He warned Emily that she herself, like Rachel and his own wife, might "presently become a victim to those meddling gossips" (Donelson Papers, DLC; Bassett, 4:29–30).
    2. The Eatons and Donelsons had accompanied AJ on a steamboat excursion to Norfolk in July 1829, on which at one point Emily visibly spurned Margaret Eaton's offer of a fan and cologne bottle to help revive her when she felt faint.

To Andrew Jackson Donelson

Genl A. J. with his respects informs Major Donelson that he has recd his note & will to night make in writing a reply to it with candeur & in friendship, & has only to regret that he sees in his note, all that prejudice derived from the slanderers of Mrs. E. & the major, which he thought did exist, when neither he, nor any of his family would read the Testimony in her defence—I perceive this deep rooted prejudice & regret it. & I hope riper years will shew the danger of acting on rumor, or secrete retailers of slander, I hope in god not experimentally—but god only knows, for it has visited the fairest character & I will only remark, that as good, virtuous & respectable characters, has visited, does visit Mrs. E. as any others, & I hazard nothing in saying more virtue that many of her slanderers. all people have a right to select their society, every head of a family have the right to govern their House hold

AN, DLC (73).

To Robert Oliver

Washington Octbr. 26th. 1830—

Dear Sir

I had the honour this evening to receive your letter of the 25th. instant with its enclosure, and agreable to your request herewith return it, with a tender of My thanks for this token of your friendship & regard.

I had supposed that every one acquainted with me knew, that I was opposed to the nulifying doctrine, and my toast at the Jefferson dinner was sufficient evidence of the fact. I am convinced there is not one member of Congress who are not convinced of this fact, for on all occasions I have been open & free upon this subject. The South Carolinians, as a whole, are too patriotic to adopt such *mad projects* as the nulifyers of that state propose.

That Mr Van Buren should be suspected of such opinions are equally strange. I am Sir with great respect & regard your mo, obdt. servt.

Andrew Jackson

ALS, PHi; Copy, MdHi (16-0553). Oliver (c1759–1834), a Baltimore merchant, had transmitted Joel Poinsett's October 23 letter above to AJ. This reply was forwarded to Poinsett on October 28.

From Walter Colton

Washington City
Oct 26 1830

Most Excellent Sir

Allow me to trouble you with the enclosed Letters.

Please accept the accompanying Pamphlet as a token of my respect for that *decision*, which struck from the Naval list the rash and guilty youth engaged in the *duel* at Philidelphia.[1]

Will you permit me to solicit your attention to the *moral* condition of the Navey Yard at Pensacola. There is now no Chaplain ther, and no Protestant Clergyman in the *Place*. With profound respect I am Your obedient humble servant

W Colton

ALS, DNA-RG 46 (16-0543). AJ appointed Colton chaplain of the Pensacola navy yard on November 6.

1. On March 31 AJ had stricken junior officers Edmund Byrne, Hampton Westcott, Charles G. Hunter, and Charles H. Duryee from the Navy list for involvement in a Philadelphia duel. The enclosure was likely Colton's 1828 *Remarks on Duelling*.

To Andrew Jackson Donelson

Octbr. 27th. 1830—

Dr Andrew

When you read the hasty & I may say unintelligable scrall, handed you this morning I wish to have a free, friendly, & full conversation with you on the subject of your letter to which mine was intended as an answer[.] yours

A. Jackson

ALS, DLC-Donelson Papers (16-0563).

From Andrew Jackson Donelson

October 27th. 1830

Dear Uncle,

I have read with great care the contents of your letter in answer to mine of the 25th. It was not my intention in that letter to extract from you any thing for the justification of my conduct if I should ever be called upon to make one. You had thought it proper if Mrs Donelson returned to have it first understood that she should be on terms of social intercourse with Mrs Eaton. This was a concession which I believed I ought not to make considering the relations which now exist. You have decided the question as you have a right to do. The only remaining one for me to consider is also depending in some degree upon your decision, how long shall I remain seperated from my family?

If you desire my services any longer there is no ~~personal~~ reasonable sacrifice which I am not ready to make, provided the arrangements that are now made for my family do not become burdensome to ~~her friends~~ my mother in law.

I will when I have more leisure correct some inacurracies of fact contained in your letter; and also allow myself a wider latitude in noticing the views you have taken of my duty & of the whole subject, than I did in my first note to you.

As the condition ~~has no qualification~~ of Mrs. D.s return has no qualification in her favor, ~~it may be most proper~~ and as the ~~ballance of~~ remainder your term of office is a longer period than I ~~can would~~ ought consent to charge any friend or relation with the care of my family, it may be ~~well~~ best for you to look to some one to take my place at once, and in the mean to allow me to be employed in putting in more intelligible files the papers of the office, preparatory to my retirement from it[.] Believe me with the greatest affectionate yr. grateful nephew

Andrew J Donelson

[Endorsed by Donelson:] copy to Genl. Jackson dated 27 Oct.

ALS draft, DLC (73).

To Andrew Jackson Donelson

Dr Andrew

on the subject of your note of this morning I will this evening have with you a conversation, & full understanding—

I would wish before your further reply to my answer to your note to have & correct it as it was written in haste with a bad head ache & in the late hours of the night from memory without refering to memorandum for dates—and really not expecting that with you a long written correspondence would be the result—yours respectfully—

A. Jackson

[Endorsed by Donelson:] The President answers my note of the 27th—the letter referred to returned according to his desire—oct. 28th. 1830, in the morning—

ALS, DLC (73).

To Samuel Delucenna Ingham

Octbr. 27th. 1830—

The President returns his respects to Mr. Ingham, acknowledges the receipt of Genl Haynes confidential letter, is well acquainted with Major Lavall to whom he refers, and would freely provide for him as he has claims upon his Government should a proper occasion present, where, with propriety, he can be provided for.

If there can be established against the Collector such conduct as brings him in within the rule laid down, then he ought, & will be removed—but this is *another* delicate case, that must be investigated with great care. I am charged with being a nullifier, & embracing & countenancing the So. Carolina nullifying doctrine, nothing than which is farther from the truth, & the removal of the inspector under these circumstances, & appointing Major Laval, would be introduced as proof positive of this fact. I The

President will be happy to see, & converse with ~~you~~ Mr Ingham on this subject.

AN, PU-Ingham Papers (16-0566). William Jacint Laval (1788–1865), an Army captain in the War of 1812 who was breveted major for his part in AJ's assault on Pensacola in 1814, had been recommended to replace James R. Pringle as customs collector at Charleston.

From Ann Mason Chichester Tutt

Locust Hill Octr. 27th 1830

My Dear Sir

You were so kind last winter as to grant us permission to go out to Pensacola in a Public Vessel—in a late letter from Mr. Tutt he informs me the Ship Vincennes will shortly sail from New York to that port—will it be presuming too far to beg the favor of you to order her to touch at Norfolk and take us on board? I have a large and helpless family of Daughters and I am confident your goodness of heart will pardon the liberty I have taken—we were making arrangments to commence our journey on the first day of next month by land as far as Wheeling which would be a most fatigueing and expensive rout and it would be a great relief to us if you can with convenience grant our request—

With sincere wishes for your health and happiness both spiritual and temporal believe me Dear Sir with great respect and affection yours

Ann M. Tutt

PS. Will you be so good as to let me hear from you as early as convenient, and if we should be so fortunate as to get a passage on the Vincennes we will be in Norfolk on any day you will be pleased to name

A M T

[Endorsed by AJ:] refered to the Secretary of the Navy who will afford the necessary information on this subject—If the indulgence can be offerd I will be gratified, if consistant with the convenience of the officers & the good of the service   A. J.

[Endorsed by John Branch:] Inform Ms. Tutt that no vessel will be sent to the West Indies for some months and that the Vincennes is not destined for that squadron

ALS, DNA-RG 45 (M124-125). Ann M. C. Tutt (1789–1882) was the wife of Pensacola navy agent Charles P. Tutt. The *Vincennes* was a Navy sloop. Branch wrote Ann Tutt on October 30 regretfully declining her request (DNA-RG 45, M209-6).

To John Branch

October 28th. 1830—

Sir,

I have carefully examined the Correspondence between yourself and the Commissioners of the Navy Board relative to the repairs of the Ship John Adams, accompanying your letter to me of the 2d. inst. and return them with the following remarks.[1]

It appears from the correspondence laid before me, that the Ship John Adams was rebuilt instead of repaired, under the act of Congress making appropriations for repairs, without your knowledge, and without any act of Congress directing her to be rebuilt—And upon this fact coming to your knowledge, you ordered a suspension of the work until the case should be refered to me.

In the reply of the commissioners of the Navy Board to your call upon them for a report of the circumstances of this case, they state, "the rebuilding of the John Adams originated under your predecessor, with whose concurrence it was commenced. It was his decision, and it was the duty of the Commissioners to carry it into effect; The state of the Ship was reported to him, and it was also reported to you in 1829 time enough to have arrested her repairs or her rebuilding; if your disposition to reverse the decision had been made known to the Commissioners, *and insist*, that under the word repairs, used in act of appropriation, connected with former precedents in like cases, and the acts of Congress are Synonimous to repair, and therefore argue that the application of the funds for repairs was legally applied to the rebuilding of this Ship.[2]

From a full view of this case, and examination of the acts of Congress refered to, I have no hesitation to say, that the late Secretary of the Navy, and Navy Board have mistaken the law in this particular. The appropriation for repairs means, that it be applied to repairing the rotten, or decayed part of vessels or to rebuild a decayed part; these must be a foundation on which the repairs are to be made, or to be rebuilt upon.

The act of Congress of the 30th of March 1812 clearly points out this distinction; the first section of the act of the 30th of March 1812 provides for the repairs of vessels by name. The third section provides for the rebuilding of vessels by name, one of which has been burnt & entirely destroyed, & the others rotten & useless; it is therefore clear, that if Congress had thought to repair and to rebuild, were synonimous it would have included all the vessels in the first section of this act under the word *repairs*, not having done so, clearly shews their view was, that all vessels to be built or rebuilt, must be so directed, by special act of congress.[3]

The derictions of the late Secretary of the Navy to the Board of Commissioners, which they were bound to obey, with precedents in like cases is a sufficient justification for them to have commenced to rebuild, but it being our duty to execute the law, having no power to Legislate, no precedents of short duration, can justify a departure from it; Therefore hereafter no vessel is to be rebuilt until reported to congress, and by it, authorised by an appropriation for the same or annual estimates for *rebuilding vessels.*

The changes that have recently taken place in Europe may possibly make it necessary that we should have a larger force of this class of vessels afloat: you will therefore order that the Sloop of war John Adams be finished, launched, & made ready for active service, and the expence of the finish, be paid out of the funds arising from the sales of the vessels under act of the 3d of March 1825, and the case of the John Adams reported to the next Congress at its session.[4] yours very Respectfully

Andrew Jackson

LS, DNA-RG 45 (M124-125). ALS draft, DLC (38). Except for one excised paragraph, the sent letter closely followed AJ's draft.

1. On October 2 Branch had reported to AJ on circumstances leading to his order on August 6 to suspend construction on the sloop *John Adams.* He accused the Board of Navy Commissioners of usurping authority and practicing deliberate deception in building a new sloop under guise of repairing the old (DNA-RG 45, M472-1).

2. Branch's October 2 report quoted language similar to this from the Board's answer of August 11 to his demand for an explanation when and under what authority the new *John Adams* was begun.

3. Branch's October 2 report had made this point. In AJ's draft another paragraph follows here: "The act of 3rd. of March directs the vessels on the lakes to be sold & makes the proceeds of sales applicable to the *repairs,* & *rebuilding* of sloops of war—here again is an explicit congress has shewn that repairs are not intended to be considered synonimous with repairs rebuilding, or it would not have used the term *rebuild.* Therefore the construction you have placed upon the law is approved." The Act of March 3, 1825, authorized the sale of warships on the Great Lakes and directed the proceeds "to the repairs and building of sloops of war," including up to ten new ones.

4. The *John Adams* was completed and launched in November. Branch's annual Navy Department report, sent with AJ's annual message to Congress in December, briefly summarized the controversy and stated that, as ordered by AJ, in future "no vessels shall be built or rebuilt, unless authorized by a specific appropriation."

From George Rockingham Gilmer

Executive Department
Milledgeville 29th October 1830

Sir

By an Act of the Legislature of Georgia passed at its last session, all the Cherokee territory, and the persons occupying it, were subjected to the ordinary Jurisdiction of the State after the first of June then next ensuing. This Act has gone into operation. The acknowledgement by the President of the right of the State to pass such an Act renders it unnecessary to say any thing in its justification. The object of this letter is to request the President that the U States troops may be withdrawn, from the Indian territory within Georgia. The enforcement of the non-intercourse law within the limits of the State is considered inconsistent with the right of Jurisdiction which is now exercised by its authorities and must if continued lead to difficulties between the officers of the U States and State Governments, which it is very desirable should be avoided. No doubt is entertained that the object of the President in ordering the U States troops into the Cherokee territory, was the preservation of the peace of the Union. The motive is duly appreciated. The Legislature of this State is now in session. The special object of its meeting is the enforcement of the laws of the State within the Cherokee Country, and the punishment of intrusion into it by persons searching for gold. Its powers are amply sufficient for that purpose. As it is expected that the law for the punishment of trespassers upon the public lands will go into operation within a few days, the President is therefore requested to withdraw the troops as soon as it can be conveniently done.[1]

The conduct of Major Wager has been very severe to the gold diggers. In some instances unoffending citizens have been made the subjects of punishment in violation of their rights and the authority of the State. Complaints have been made to this Department and redress asked for. The removal of the troops is believed to be the most effectual means of preventing the repetition of such injuries—Information has been also received at this Department that the digging for gold is still carried on, in various parts of the Cherokee territory, and that the extent of country containing mines is so great that it is wholly impossible to prevent it by the use of military force alone. It is said that the Indians are even more extensively employed in taking gold than before the arrival of the troops—This proceeds from their residence within the country, intimate acquaintance with it, and other means of avoiding the operation of the troops. The fear of the whites had restrained them previously.

The President is assured that whatever measures may be adopted by the State of Georgia in relation to the Cherokees, the strongest desire will be felt to make them accord with the policy which has been adopted by the present Administration of the General Government, upon the same subject. Very Respectfully Yours &c.

George R Gilmer

LS, DNA-RG 107 (M222-27). LC, G-Ar (mAJs). Copy, DNA-RG 46 (16-0576). *SDoc* 65, 21st Cong., 2d sess., pp. 9–10 (Serial 204). Anticipating action by Georgia, the War Department issued an order to Major Philip Wager to withdraw his troops from the Cherokee country on November 8, before this letter arrived (*SDoc* 65, 21st Cong., 2d sess., pp. 8–9, Serial 204). AJ received Gilmer's letter and asked Eaton to reply on November 9. Eaton wrote Gilmer on November 10, informing him of the troop withdrawal and adding a regret that in executing his orders Wager "should have found himself constrained to resort to measures, which may have operated hardly upon some individuals" (DNA-RG 107, M6-13).

1. Gilmer had called the Georgia legislature into early session on October 18 to address the problem of trespassers. A law of December 2 put the governor in possession of all mines in the Cherokee country and made unauthorized digging punishable by four years at hard labor.

To Andrew Jackson Donelson

Octbr. 30th. 1830—

My Dr Andrew

In looking over your note of the 27th. instant to me, I find it requires an answer, this should have been attended to sooner but from the pressure of business & the state of my health.

From the first of this disagreable business to this time, the course adopted by my family I have & must ever, sincerely regret—all I ever required has been that the same comity should be by them extended to Major Eaton & family on all necessary occasions as to the rest of the heads of Departments and theirs, leaving you & your family as part of mine, to govern yourselves as to your social intercourse as you might think proper. This I have ever thought was due to me from you & your family knowing as you did the relations between Major Eaton & me, & believing as I have ever done, exacting nothing that ought not to have been yielded, to prevent my family from being pointed to by others, as was the case, so giving countenance to the slanderous & groundless reports, circulated, as I believe by one of the most wicked combinations that ever existed to destroy my friend, with the view of injuring me, this I always declared to you & refered you to the proof.

The course I requested of my family I thought due to the station I hold, & to Major Eaton & to justice, having invited him into my Cabinett, all which has been fully explained to you & your family, part mine—that I could not, nay would not seperate from Major Eaton under circumstances that would destroy him, disgrace me, and be doing precisely what the combination expected to compell me to do. The letter to Miss Mary Easton to be shewn to Emily, was written & thought necessary from information received, that if a change of conduct to Major Eaton & family could not take place, then & in such case, that it would be improper for them to come on, until some arrangements could be made, and harmony in this respect be restored, as I could not again be exposed to experience the disagreable scenes I had heretofore done. This letter I thought proper to shew to you, which has drew from you the dclaration that such a concession you could not make, and makes it necessary that you should withdraw from me & return to your family   However painful this decision is to me, and for which I cannot now nor never could see any real cause for, the course you have thought proper thus to adopt, upon a full review of the whole ground from the beginning, as I am sure, I have asked or required nothing that from my situation, ought not, and from yours could have been yielded without any sacrafice on your part, and from which perfect Harmony as to myself & family, could have been fairly maintained. But you have surely a right to judge for yourself & family, and have judged, & come to the determination that the *"condesension"* required cannot be yield to. Therefore my Dr Andrew as you have made your election, and view the requirements requested by me, as a sacrafice, & which, as a sacrafice I cannot receive but only as an act of justice, I have determined, like Mr Jefferson, to live without any female in my family, that cannot yield the same comity to all the heads of Departments & their families; This is a duty I owe to myself & the situation in which I am placed, for the sake of my own quiet, & justice due to others.

If you should not think it too great a sacrafice, for that I ask of none, I will be glad that you remain until after the meeting of Congress, or even to the rise of it, in the mean time arrangements may be made that may restore harmony & peace. But you are to be the judge, when you will withdraw; whenever it may be your pleasure to notify me, the means for your return are ready, but I shall expect a short times notice that I may look out for another, which I will not do, until that notice is given.

I have found for upwards of a year, that you appeared to be estranged from me, & entirely taken up with strangers, but what I most regretted was your constant malancholy, & abstraction from me which under my bereavements made my tears to flow often. I pray you cheer up my tears are dried. When you leave, whatever cause I have to regret or complain, you will carry my friendship with you, and my prayers for your happiness, and that of your amiable family. They two little cherubs Jackson & M. Rachel who I can never cease to love.

I found on my return to Tennessee the combination of my own connections, were interwoven with those of my enemies, that when I expected you & Emily to go to my House & remain with me as part of my family it was declined—and from information since derived from Tennessee some of the connection, still engaged in measures not very pleasant to me, all of which I have & will continue to regret, altho I was unable to controle.

I have not time to take a copy, when leisure permits make me one. I am very affectionately your uncle & sincere friend

Andrew Jackson

ALS, DLC-Donelson Papers (16-0583).

From Andrew Jackson Donelson

Oct. 30th. 1830

Dear Uncle:

I have taken according to your request a copy of your letter to me of this date which is enclosed. The letter to which it replies was the answer to that of yours which you requested to be returned and was accordingly returned.[1]

I have no wish to have that letter sooner than your leisure and convenience will enable you to give it; as the views I intend to take of it and the whole subject will, I trust, be a termination of the unpleasant correspondence, and besides I do not desire to present those views until the limitation which you have imposed upon my residence here expires.

In your house, my dear Uncle, as your guest I acknowledge that the same comity and politeness are due to Mrs. Eaton that are to the ladies of the other cabinet officers or those of other gentlemen. A pledge to secure this for the future, altho' it implies that without it a distinction would be drawn, I have never refused to make. Whether there be justice in requiring this pledge considering what has passed, I did not undertake to enquire; but I certainly did consider it as given both in my conversations and in the expressions of my letter.

Out of your house I claim only the same general discretion in behalf of my family that is possessed by all others. To require them to pay a visit to Mrs. Eaton or any one else, where it is obvious that there is no reciprocal respect is at once to degrade them. The same principle would oblige me to submit to all the insults which private intercourse is subject to in every sphere of life. You did not when a prisoner in the revolutionary war obey the order of the enemy who had you in his power to clean his boots. Yet you find fault with my determination merely to keep out of the way of insult[2]

I had as well here as elsewhere notice the allusion you have made to Mrs. Donelsons making her Mother's house her home instead of the Hermitage during your recent visit there, because it seems to be interpreted in an unfriendly manner. You have not forgotten the note of Mrs. Eaton in which she refused to dine with you because my family was in your house just before you started for Tennessee.[3] I have not forgotten the language which you employed on that occasion, and the determination you then expressed of carrying us home and leaving us there. Where was our home? Were we not bound from respect even to your feelings not to put ourselves in the way of the honors you intended to pay to Mr. & Mrs Eaton at the Hermitage? Was there nothing in Mrs. Donelsons long absence from her Mother to excuse the desire to stay with her without incurring your disapprobation? yr. affectionate nephew

Andrew J Donelson

[Endorsed by Donelson:] answer to Genl Jacksons letter of date 30th. oct. 1830

ALS copy and ALS draft, DLC (73).

1. In Donelson's draft a crossed-out paragraph followed here: "I do not desire that letter for the purpose of defence. Whenever that becomes necessary I have material enough without ~~involving you~~ connecting you with the responsibilities of other men. But I desire it as an of justice to you and the views ~~I think are due to the confidential household family relations that~~ which it made incumbent upon me to take of it, lest my silence might hereafter be taken for my condemnation."

2. Before correction, this sentence in Donelson's draft read: "Yet you find fault with my determination not to expose myself to the insults of a woman."

3. Margaret Eaton to AJ, June 9 (above).

To Andrew Jackson Donelson

Octbr. 30th. 11. oclock P.M.

My Dr Andrew, for so I must still call you

your note with the copy of my letter requested is recd. & read with haste but attention.

There is one paragraph that requires a few remarks from me, and gives me pain to see.

You are pleased to say in your letter "In your House my Dr Unkle as your *guest* I acknowledge that the same comity and politeness are due to Mrs. Eaton that is due to other ladies of your cabinett" &c

When my Dr Andrew were you my guest or how & when treated only as such. The term applied to me is surely unjust—you & Emily with Mary was considered by me as my family—you were so considered by the world, so introduced, and so treated, and in that situation as the representative of my dear & ever to be lamented wife was Mrs. Donelson here considered by me, and as such received & treated by all, and as such did she receive the ladies & Gentlemen at public dinners and Levees, being alway conducted to table by the secretary of State, and as such did I require only the same comity on all necessary occasions to Mrs. Eaton as to the rest. Review this expression it is unjust to me, nay, it is Humiliating to us all, and all the world must condemn it.

You were my family, my chosen family, and was placed where I was delighted to see you, and where, had it not been for bad advisers, by which my advice at first was disreguarded we would have been living in peace with all, and in my Bosom forever

This remark I could not in justice to myself refrain making, but I have done, every time the subject is named it makes my heart bleed afresh, for since the remark in S. D.[1] letter my tears are dried. I am yr affectionate uncle

Andrew Jackson

ALS, DLC-Donelson Papers (16-0588).
1. Stockley Donelson.

From Andrew Jackson Donelson

30th. Oct. 1830[1]

Mr Dear Uncle:

Allow me to correct the reading of the remark made by me in my note of yesterday and which you have quoted in your answer to it.

"In your house, my dear Uncle, I acknowledge that the same comity and politeness are due to Mrs. Eaton as your guest, from my family, that are due to the ladies of your other cabinet officers or those of other gentlemen." I hope you will allow the foregoing to be substituted in the place of your quotation. Nothing was farther from my mind than to express such an idea as that we considered ourselves, or were considered by others, as guests in your house. The whole difficulty of the case turns in my mind upon our duty as a part of your family to your guests.

What I wrote yesterday evening was done by twilight and I did not take a copy. yr. affectionate nephew

Andrew J Donelson

[Endorsed by Donelson:] copy to Genl Jackson 31st. Octr. 1830

ALS copy, DLC-Donelson Papers (16-0613).
1. Actually October 31.

To Martin Van Buren

I send for the perusal of Mr. V. B. Capt Princes letters that will fully prove, the inutility, and falacy, of our Light House System, that the are dangerous except on our capes, & leads to the destruction of our ships & lives of our seamen, by deceiving & bewildering them—you will please bring these, when you come over this morning—

A. J.

ANS, DLC (59; 14-1244). John Prince of Marblehead, Mass., campaigned against the lighthouse system as not only wasteful but dangerous. Ingham wrote AJ about him on July 17 (above). One of Prince's letters, published in the *US Telegraph* on August 13, hailed AJ's veto for warding off "mischief and disaster." AJ's second annual message on December 6 remarked that "from representations upon the subject which are understood to be entitled to respect" it appeared that multiplying lighthouses induced accidents by causing confusion among mariners (Richardson, 2: 508–9).

From Willie Blount

Turnersville P. O. Octr. 1830

Dear Sir,

You assure me, in your last, that you will do your best to preserve the Union: without such an assurance I know you would do so; and I know full well, that he who has thrice saved it before this, will save it a fourth time, & again, & again, when efforts to do it may be necessary: I fear no dissolution of our beloved Union as long as we have a beloved chief at the helm—about all such matters I feel as easy as the most perfect confidence in you can inspire me—he who takes his stand on the ramparts of the Constitution will ever preserve the Union, the sheet anchor of the Constitution—he who administers justice, in an evenhanded manner, will ever be supported by the People, who, own the Country, the Constitution, the Govt. and all belonging to either—the people are the sheet-anchors of the Union—

I see that the French are again in the field, in support of liberty: their doings startle the Crown'd head of Europe: one Crowns, not obtained from the people, fear of the people cometh; and Crowns, conferred by the people, will give way to republicanism, sooner, or later—I never did put any value on any mode of Govt., unless it was republican; & it, is little better than none, unless purely, ably, & usefully administered, for the benefit of community—such a Govt. is valuable.

I see that a treaty has been concluded with the Choctaws: thanks to all concerned—in a little time, the army of the U.S. could hardly keep the Creeks and Cherokees from going west of Missi. also—opponents are disappointed—Wirt & his man Ross will fail in their objects.

The opposition folks, every where, are singing out, Oh dear what can the matter be? Oh—the best song for them—I wonder the two Adams's, and their gangs, never saw that Washington, Jefferson, Madison, Monroe & Jackson administered the Govt. just as it should be done!!! Strange they could not, & will not see the right way to usefulness & true renown—your friend

Willie Blount

The papers inform us that the Jackson men in Maine are uppermost & have thrown Johnny Holmes into the ditch, and as Grundy assigned him to the Devil, there, let him remain[1]—If Johnny Q., Clay & Southard should run into Congress they will soon be glad to gallop out again—it is said that Governor Barbour's county people will excuse him from a seat in the Virginia Assembly, & it is thought that the Electors of President

& Vice P. will have no use for his services as V. P. to Clay at the next Presidential election—[2]

[Endorsed by AJ:] Gov. Willie Blount recd Novbr. 4th. 1830

ALS, DLC (73).
1. In his second Senate speech on Samuel A. Foot's resolution on January 25, Robert Hayne had assailed New England obstructionism in the War of 1812, recalling that Federalists had branded those who aided the war effort as allies of "James Madison, Felix Grundy, and the Devil." Excepting the mass of patriotic New Englanders from Hayne's strictures, John Holmes of Maine recalled that his own support of the war could have earned him a place at the end of the list. Grundy answered on March 1 that it was time to replace the old firm of "James Madison, Felix Grundy, His Satannic Majesty, and John Holmes" with two new ones: "Andrew Jackson and company," to include himself, and "the Devil and John Holmes" (*Register of Debates*, 21st Cong., 1st sess., pp. 53, 167, 219).
2. James Barbour (1775–1842) had been governor of Virginia, U.S. senator, and then secretary of war and minister to Britain under John Q. Adams. In 1830 he won a close election to the Virginia House of Delegates from Orange County. The results were contested and a new election held in December. Barbour again won narrowly in the official count but resigned the seat, conceding that he was not the true choice of the majority.

Drafts by Andrew Jackson Donelson

[In his October correspondence with Jackson over the Eaton affair, Donelson promised a fuller statement of his position when time permitted. These two undated fragments may have been intended for that exposition, or they may be discarded drafts of his actual letters to Jackson between October 25 and 30.]

It is due perhaps to the vindication which the blind advice of those to whose agency I ascribe my separation from you, may render necessary hereafter, to state briefly the view ~~which has decided my conduct in the intercourse with~~ of my social rights which I ~~feel have been outraged~~ have endeavored to maintain in this city. No man ~~has had~~ could ever have been placed in a more delicate situation. None I trust could have felt more sensibly the obligations which your goodness, your greatness, and my paternal duties, ~~imposed have created~~ have interwoven with all the affections of my heart and all the ~~emotions reflections~~ sensibilities of my mind. These can never be weakened, however they may be agitated, by being torn loose from the ~~relation~~ shelter under which they have been cultivated, ~~and are now to~~. They inspire a sense of virtue and the fortitude to practice it, far beyond the influence of those who think they are to be benefitted by their degradation. They inculcate a security in ~~the consciousness of self approbation~~ a self approving conscience which can defy their acts and pity their misfortunes.

I was acquainted with the character of Mrs. Timberlake, before she married Majr. Eaton. ~~Majr Eaton knows, as all do~~ Majr. Eaton must be sensible, ~~with~~[1]

In what estimation did I find the character of Mrs. Eaton upon my arrival in this city? and how did it become me as a member of your family to regulate my conduct in relation to it; are thé questions which I hope I will be pardoned for answering ~~satisfactorily~~, in order that the incidents which to which I shall refer in the course of this letter, may be fairly understood.

No intelligent and ingenuous citizen of this place can deny that from some cause or other, we found upon our arrival here the public mind so far as it can be collected from the evidence which its social intercourse speak, ~~was in a higher~~ in a high degree reluctant to accord to Mrs. Eaton ~~that respect which is usually paid to virtue~~ those civilities which usually ~~mark the~~ indicate the good name of one of its members. Whether this was just or not was not a question for me to decide. I did not attempt it, altho' aware myself of some of ~~the~~ many rumours which no doubt had ~~their~~ an effect in strengthening prejudices which might have been deservedly founded on other considerations, ~~than the~~ not affecting her character as a virtuous lady, ~~it was obvious to my mind that it was my duty to notice neither~~ I saw in the prominent relation which her husband had borne to you, and was about to occupy as a member of your cabinet, every inducement to restrain

AL draft, DLC (73).
  1. This paragraph is X-ed out.

as early as the 8th. of April 1829, Majr Eaton undertook to select Mrs. Donelson's society for her, denouncing the family which had always possessed the friendship and regard of our lamented Aunt, and ungraciously reminding her that ~~the tales of slander~~ her associates were slanderers and gossips. an allusion was made in a written communication to her to the attempt to misrepresent the character of our dear Aunt, for the purpose of operating upon our feelings, and inducing us to regard the case of Mrs. Timberlake as analogous to that. I disregarded at the time so unmanly an appeal, but could not but see in it ~~a hidden determination~~ a readiness on the part of Majr Eaton & his friends, to claim at your hands and those of our family their selfish cooperation in procuring for him & his a ~~verdict in favor of his wife~~ favorable verdict before the American people. His language is "I should presume that some recent events which gave pain on your own bosom would lead you to forbear attaching any importance to tales of slander. If fire side whispers shall have influence on intelligent minds, it is questionable whether character be worth any thing. Under such an order of things, you yourself may presently become a victim to those meddling gossips."

"When your excellent Aunt arrived here in 1825 (I have heard her tell the story) some of those busy folks, always and every where to be found, undertook to tell her of the people here, and amongst other things that a certain lady was not a proper character for her to associate with. Her answer alike creditable to her head as to heart was, I did not come here to listen to little slanderous tales, and to decide upon peoples character." "Mrs. Sim like her husband is wholly undeserving your confidence and you will after a while find it so. As for Mrs. Graham I have uniformly contemned her, and ever shall."[1]

Now at this time but little more than a month had elapsed since your inauguration, Mrs. Donelson had visited Mrs. Eaton, I had visited her and was frequently at Eaton's house. I had been at special pains to inform Col. Towson, Dr. Lovell & others respectable Gentlemen of the city, that my family had nothing to do with the question of Mrs. Eatons character, that we felt it our duty to leave the matter with the society which had originated it, and that ~~in~~ our associations ~~we~~ should ~~disregard~~ be independent of it.[2] But this does not satisfy Majr Eaton, he takes the ground that he has the right to express his contempt of a part of the respectable population, and ~~by calling up the~~ with a hypocritical veneration for the memory of our departed Aunt abuses the principle which governed

AL draft, DLC-Donelson Papers (16-0286).
1. Donelson quoted Eaton's April 8, 1829, letter to Emily Donelson (Donelson Papers, DLC; Bassett, 4:29–30).
2. Joseph Lovell (1788–1836) was surgeon general of the Army.

November

Memorandum Book on the
Bank of the United States

*[These three consecutive entries in Jackson's memorandum book directly
follow those above from circa March and April 1830. The first passage
was composed not later than November 1, when Jackson sent a copy
to Van Buren (below). It appeared, slightly revised, in Jackson's second
annual message to Congress on December 6 (Richardson, 2:528–29). The
second passage was copied directly from the outline James A. Hamilton
had sent Jackson on January 4 (above). The third passage is crossed out
in the book with vertical lines. These two latter passages were apparently
written after the first but before the entries that came next, which were
copies of correspondence in April and June 1831 between Jackson, John
Rhea, James Monroe, and John Overton, followed by early notes for
Jackson's third annual message to Congress in December 1831.]*

Message for 1830—

Bank—
    The importance of this subject requires that I should again call the
attention of Congress to the approaching expiration of the charter of the
United States Bank. Nothing has occurred to lessen, in any degree, the
dangers which many of our safest statesmen apprehend from that institution as at present organised, nor is the opinion of its unconstitutionality
less extensive or less deeply impressed. In the spirit of improvement and
compromise which distinguishes our country and institutions it becomes
us to enquire, whether it be not possible to secure the advantages afforded
by the present Bank, through the agency of a Bank of the United States
so modified in its principles and structure as to obviate constitutional and
other objections
    It is thought practicable to organise such a Bank with the necessary
offices as a Branch of the Treasury Department, based on the public
deposits, without power to make loans or purchase property, which shall
remit the funds of the Govt. without charge, and find a moderate premium ~~on~~ upon exchange furnished private citizens, the means of paying

its expences. Not being a corporate body, having no stockholders, debtors or property, and but few officers, it would not be obnoxious to the constitutional objections which are urged against the present Bank; and having no means to operate on the hopes, fears or interests of large masses of the community, it would be shorn of the influence which makes that Bank formidable. The states would be strengthened by having in their hands the means of furnishing the local paper currency through their own Banks, while the Bank of the United States, though issuing no paper, would check the Issues of the State Banks by taking their notes in deposit and for exchange only so long as they continue to be redeemed with specie. In times of public emergency, the capacities of such an institution might be enlarged by act of congress.

These suggestions are made, not so much as a recommendation, as with a view of calling the attention of Congress to the possible modification of a system which cannot continue to exist in its present form, without occasional collisions with the local authorities and perpetual apprehensions and discontents on the part of the states and the people.[1]

Therefore the following—

Outlines of a substitute of the United States Bank is presented for your consideration

The objections to the present Bank are

1. It is unconstitutional;
2. It is dangerous to Liberty.

Yet this Bank renders important services to the Government and the country.

It cheapens and facilitates all the fiscal operations of the government.

It tends in some degree to equalise domestic exchange, and produce a sound and uniform currency.

A substitute for the present Bank is desired, which shall yield all its benefits, and be obnoxious to none of its objections.

Banks do two kinds of business:

1 They discount notes and bills for which they give their own paper.
2" They deal in exchange.

These two kind of business have no necessary connection. There may be Banks of discount exclusively, and Banks of exchange exclusively. Both may be Banks of deposit.

The United States may establish a Bank of Exchange exclusively based on Government and individual deposites.

This Bank may have branches wherever the government may think necessary.

They may be cloathed only with the power to sell exchange on each other; and required to transmit government funds without charge.

They need only have such offices as their duty require, checked by frequent and rigid inspection.

The whole may be placed under the direction of the secretary of the Treasury, through a seperate bureau.

The present bank is unconstitutional:

1. Because it is a corporation which Congress has no constitutional power to establish.

2. Because it withdraws the business of Bank discounts and the property of private citizens from the operation of state laws, and particularly from the taxing power of the states in which it is employed.

3 Because it purchases lands and other real estate within the states without their consent, under an authority purporting to be derived from congress, when the General Government itself possesses no such constitutional power.

The proposed substitute would not be a corporation, but a branch of the Treasury Department; it would hold no property real or personal, and would withdraw none from the operation of the State laws.

The present Bank is dangerous to Liberty—

1. Because, in the number, wealth and standing of its officers and stockholders, in its power to make loans or withold them, to call oppressively upon its debtors or indulge them, build houses, rent lands & houses, and make donations for political or other purposes, it embodies a fearful influence which may be wielded for the agrandisement of a favorite individual, a particular interest, or a seperate party.

2. Because it concentrates in the hands of a few men, a power over the money of the country, which may be perverted to the oppression of the people, and in times of public calamity, to the embarrassment of the government.

3. Because much of its stock is owned by foreigners, through the management of which an avenue is opened to a foreign influence in the most vital concerns of the Republic.

4. Because it is always governed by interest and will ever support *him* who supports *it*. An ambitious or dishonest President may thus always unite all its power and influence in his support, while an honest one who thwarts its views, will never fail to encounter the weight of its opposition.

5. Because it is always

5. It weakens the states and strengthens the General Government.

The proposed substitute would have few officers, and no stockholders, make no loans, have no debtors, build no houses, rent no lands or houses make no donations, and would be entirely destitute of the influence which arises from the hopes, and fears and averice of thousands. It would oppress no man, and being part of the government, would always aid its operations.

It would oppress no man

It would have no stock and could not be reached by foreign influence. It would afford less aid to a dishonest Presidents than the present Bank, and would never be opposed to an honest one. It would strengthen the states, by leaving to their Banks the whole business of discounts and the furnishing the local currency. It would strengthen the general Government less than the Custom Houses, immeasurably less than the Post offices, and less than the present Bank when it acts in concert with the national authorities.

The proposed substitute would cheapen and facilitate all the fiscal operations of the government as compleatly as the present Bank.

It would ~~give~~ in the same manner tend to equalize exchange. Until since the last annual message of the President, the present Bank charged a premium on all exchanges, except for government, public offices, and members of Congress. This practice will, doubtless, be resumed should that Bank be rechartered. The profits of the exchange business heretofore done; was sufficient, it is believed, to pay all the expences of the Bank. The proposed substitute may charge such a premium on exchanges, excepting those for the Government, as will suffice to pay its expences.

It might be made in the same manner, although not in the same degree, to operate upon the currency. By taking the paper of such local Banks in the vicinity as pay specie, it would restrain overissues and tend to preserve the currency in a sound state

The usual deposites of the government would be an ample capital for a Bank of exchange. Independent of its capital, the Bank would always have cash on hand equal to its outstanding Bills of exchange. But it might not be at the right points, and a small capital would be necessary to meet unequal calls at these points untill the equilibrium could be restored. Exchange works in a circle. It is against the west in favour of the East, against the East in favour of the south, and against the south in favour of the west. By constant interchange of information and judicious management, little funds would be wanted at either point, other than those that would be raised by selling exchange on another. In time of war the capacities of this Bank might be increased by act of Congress.

Such a Bank would not be unconstitutional, nor dangerous to liberty, and would yield to the goverment all the facilities afforded by the present Bank. Further than this perhaps the general Government ought not to look. But its incidental advantages to the country would scarcely be inferior to those afforded by the present Bank while it would destroy a favored monoply—

This continued in Page marked �96.[2]

Again the Bank is unconstitutional and impolitic
Unconstitutional. Because
1rst. Congress has no power to legislate upon any subject, unless such power is *expressly* given in some part of the constitution, or is *necessary* and proper for the attainment of some object for the attainment of which there is an express grant.

Before the formation of the Federal constitution each state was sovereign, and independent, within *its own limits*, and no state is deprived by the Constitution of any power it once possessed, unless in the exercise of its own sovereign powers it has made an express surrender to the Federal Government.

Who can point his finger to the paragraph in the constitution which this power is conferred? I answer no person—Had it intended to confer so important a power by the framers of that instrument, the grant would have been clear and explicit—now all ought to admit, if such power exists, it is doubtful from what paragraph it is to be infered. Some of its advocates deduce it from one passage—some from another, and the very circumstance of this disagreement, is a strong argument that it cannot be legitimately, deduced from any of the grants of power which have been made. It has been very appropriately termed "a vagrant power crawling over the constitution for a *soft place* in the instrument, where it can make a settlement."[3] It cannot as, I think, be fairly contended that a Bank owned by *individuals* in whole, or in part, is necessary to enable congress to exercise[4]

AD drafts, DLC (64).

1. The copy sent to Van Buren on November 1 ended here.

2. This note was evidently added later. The page marked (96) follows in the memorandum book after the notes for AJ's December 1831 third annual message. Headed "Again the U.S. Bank is unconstitutional and impolitic," it is a draft of AJ's Bank veto message of 1832.

3. In a February 1811 speech opposing the recharter of the original Bank of the United States, Henry Clay complained that "this vagrant power to erect a bank" had "wandered throughout the whole constitution in quest of some congenial spot whereupon to fasten" (*Clay Papers*, 1:530). His phrase was often repeated with variants in wording.

4. The page ends here. The next pages in the memorandum book are missing. A note inserted by James A. McLaughlin says that they contained copies of letters written in 1831 concerning AJ's 1818 Seminole campaign which McLaughlin, at AJ's request, cut out on December 21, 1842, and sent to Amos Kendall for use in his biography.

To Martin Van Buren

Novbr 1rst. 1830—

My Dr. Sir

I have read Mr. Camberlngs letter with attention, it augurs well for the republican success—you know I never despair, I have confidence in the virtue & good sense of the people—god is just, & while we act faithfully to the constitution, he will smile upon, and prosper our exertions.[1]

I have read the consul, for the Kingdom Saxonys letter with some interest, his remarks embrace good common sense, and are worthy of consideration. In my message, while a judicious revision of the Tariff & a reduction of duties may be recommended, still we must also recommend, a just adherence to the rule that will give us the means of national defence in time of war, by placing our own labour on grounds of fair competition with that of Europe, by raising the necessary revenue from articles that come in competition with our own Labour; & so soon as the national debt be paid a reduction on all articles that do not come in competition with our own labour. In your sugestions the other day I think you fully embraced this idea, & when you digest them please send them, that I may prepare & arrange them for my message—[2]

I will send you today, what I propose to say on the Bank for your remarks

so soon as you get through the Foreign relations, I would like to have it—room can be left for any news from Mexico or France &c &c—

I have read Mr Pringles letter   I shall not touch him for the present. I return the letters—yr Friend

Andrew Jackson

P.S. Please send me the names of the Rusian charge de affairs, & srvt—[3]

ALS, DLC-Van Buren Papers (16-0633).

1. Elections were held in New York this same day, November 1. Cambreleng wrote Van Buren on October 23 predicting that Jacksonian acting governor Enos Throop would win election to a full term and that "we shall carry our tickets all round" (Van Buren Papers, DLC). Throop was elected governor and Jacksonians won fifteen of twenty-eight congressional seats and legislative majorities in both houses.

2. Christian Friedrich Goehring (d. 1834) was the U.S. consul in Saxony. On July 12 he wrote Van Buren from Leipzig to suggest that reducing prohibitive tariff duties to a competitive level would both increase revenue and spur domestic manufacturers to improve their product, ultimately to their benefit (DNA-RG 59, T215-1).

3. The Russian chargé d'affaires at Washington in the absence of minister Baron von Krudener was Baron de Sacken.

To Martin Van Buren

Novbr. 1rst. 1830—

The President with his respects to sec of State, sends the enclosed for his inspection, & critisism, which he please to make & return it with such as he deems proper to make.

AN, DLC-Van Buren Papers (16-0637). The enclosure, headed "Bank," was a copy, in AJ Jr.'s hand, of the passage in his memorandum book proposing a substitute for the Bank of the United States (above).

Memorandum on the Boundary with Mexico

note—

The Mexican Minister complains, that he has been informed officially, that the uncivilised tribes of Indians from the United States are approching the frontiers of Mexico in the direction of red river and Arkansas, and that several of these tribes, the Shawnees, Kikapoos, Delawares and cherokees have already passed wholly or in part, into the Mexican Territory. Eight hundred famelies of cherokees & seven hundred of creeks have lately been introduced.[1]

To this complaint it may be replied that the Shawnees Kiccopoos Delawares, have resided west of the Mississippi time out of mind, & that the Cherokees, have been settled where they now are north of the Red river ever since 1803, immediately after the U.S. acquired a title to Louisiana & have occupied their present position ever since, that the choctaws have occupied the country where they now are north of the Red river under a treaty with the United States since 1820, and the creeks have settled north of them, by treaty also, none of which tribes are within the ~~compass~~ limits of Mexico, as ever claimed by Spain agreable to her late Treaty or can be claimed by conquest from Spain by Mexico—

A Col Bean & some other officers of Mexico, lately come into our known & exercised jurisdiction, and attempted to allure our citizens, & did prevail upon some to buy lands, and take the oath of Elegience to Mexico—Col Bean attempted to erect a Mexican Garrison in the county of Miller within our dense settlements, this the Governor of Arkansa promptly forbade and the Mexican Col. has desisted for the present— Colo. Bean had been in Miller county and selected a site for a Fort on Red river at a place called the Spanish Bluffs.[2] Lafayette & Miller counties have for many years been populated by our citizens and our civil jurisdiction have been always exercised over that country. I will add that Possession of this country was taken ~~possession of~~ by the orders of our govt. by the military under command of Genl Wilkison in the year 1806, & spring 1807—as part of Louisiana, and we have had undisturbed possession of this country as part of Louisiana ever since, by the ~~consent~~ acquiescence of Spain.[3] The boundery in the Treaty with Spain could not have intended to dismember our country & citizens, and we being in peaceable possession for Twenty six years of that section of Country, it cannot now be claimed by Mexico, as a conquered country from Spain. Mexico, never having possession of any territory east of the Sabine—But the truth is, there are no part of the country ocupied by the Cherokees, Choctaws, or Creeks by the authority of the U.S. are within the limits of

Mexico, ~~or near it,~~ and the other tribes have resided where they now are time out of mind.

A. J.

ADS, DLC (73). On November 1, Mexican minister José María Tornel had written Van Buren protesting what he termed an "invasion" of Mexican territory by Indians from the United States. He asked Van Buren for copies of all U.S. treaties with the Indians, to prove that the tribes had transgressed their limits and to justify Mexico in repelling them by force. Van Buren replied on November 20 that Tornel's "information is calculated to excite great surprise, and to inspire much doubt as to its correctness." Closely paraphrasing AJ's memo, Van Buren said it was "notorious" that the western tribes had long resided where they now were, in areas never claimed by Spain or Mexico. Government agents among them had reported no incursions across the border. Van Buren enclosed a volume of U.S. Indian treaties and voiced a hope that Tornel would realize "that he had no good ground for the protest which he has thought proper to make to this Government upon these subjects" (*HRDoc* 351, 25th Cong., 2d sess., pp. 654–56, Serial 332).

1. This paragraph repeats nearly verbatim the opening passage of Tornel's letter to Van Buren.

2. American-born Peter Ellis Bean (1783–1846) was a colonel in the Mexican army and superintendent of Indian affairs for the Mexican province of Texas. In correspondence with Arkansas governor John Pope he had upheld Mexico's claim to the disputed area south and west of Red River, and like Benjamin R. Milam he had encouraged settlement under Mexican title. Pope reported Bean's scout for a fort site to Van Buren on November 2 (*TPUS*, 21:264–65, 283).

3. Brigadier General James Wilkinson (1757–1825), then the Army's senior officer, was ordered to command in Louisiana upon its acquisition in 1803.

To Robert Minns Burton

Washington Novbr. 6th. 1830—

Dr Sir

I have the pleasure of acknowledging the receipt of your letter of the 16th ultimo, and am greatly surprised at the declarations of Genl Desha with regard to my hostility to him, in his address to the people at the time of which you speak, and so soon after he had paid me a friendly visit at the Hermitage staid with me all night, & parted with all his former expressions of good feelings.

I am not disposed to interfere in political controversies in Tennessee or in any other state, but I feel bound to correct his wilful mistatements, so far at least as I am concerned.

In the first place you say, Genl Desha stated to the people that I was opposed to him because he waited on me and advised me not to appoint Major Eaton one of my Cabinett. That Mrs. Eaton was an abandoned woman and had not been received into ~~good~~ genteel company for five years before she was married to Major Eaton &c. Now this is wholly gratuitous, and entirely destitute of truth. I was not opposed to Genl Desha for that or any other reason. It is true he came to me unsolicited on my part and undertook to advise me against the appointment of Major Eaton;

I was not disposed to fall out with him on that account, altho, a proper delicacy should have forbidden, after I had given him my opinion fully on this whole matter, the frequent obtrusions of his advice upon this subject unasked for, and displayed an improper spirit of vindictiveness against Major Eaton, unworthy of a man of truth or justice. I had known Major Eaton much longer, and much more intimately than Genl Desha had, and felt myself fully competant to select my own Cabinett. I knew Major Eaton to be a pure upright & honest man, a sincere friend on whom in all things I could rely, (*a rare thing to be found in these days among demagogues & politicians*)—endowed by nature with a strong and comprehensive mind; surpassed by few in the country, and vastly superior to many who stand high in public estimation for talents. But these high qualifications pass for nothing in Genl Deshas estimation, because, as he says, he married "*an abandoned woman*," who for five years previously had not been recd into *Genteel* company. Is this true? Genl Desha has acknowledged to me he knows not aught against her of his own knowledge, and I deny the correctness of either assertions as it regards Mrs. Eaton. I believe her to be as virtuous as the best of those who refuse to associate with her, has as good testimonials as they can produce of good & virtuous character, & from as high sources of respectability, of which Genl Desha was informed, but *would not look at*, but who has solely listened to the *tales* of a combination formed for political, and other purposes, to destroy her. I do not know by what rule, or standard, Genl Desha judges of "*Genteel* society." but I do know in 1823 & 24 when I lived at her fathers, in the same House with Mrs. Eaton, that she enjoyed the company, & associated with as *genteel* company as Genl Deshas family, or of any of his connections. This I can testify to, because I saw it with my eyes, when I was in the Senate and a boarder with her father, where she lived, for the space of six months. Since her marriage, I am sure there is not a day, scarcely, she is not visited by Gentlemen & ladies, as respectable and *genteel* as any in the city, and I have never understood that any of them have suffered in either reputation or standing.

In the next place you say, the Genl represented me as being unfriendly with and opposed to him, because he voted against the Bill making an appropriation for the benefit of Mrs. Decature & others. This is untrue, and Genl Desha knew it to be such when he uttered it. I oppose no ~~man~~ member of congress on account of his opinions, or his votes he has a constitutional right to both. I thought it a claim which the government long since should have satisfied. The heroic deed which gave rise to it, was the foundation on which has been raised the super structure of our Naval glory. It is one of the most brilliant actions recorded on the page of history and will transmit to the latest posterity the names of those gallant spirits who achieved it. And shall we Genl Desha's opposition notwithstanding not *meet to them*, the same justice which has been awarded to others in like cases? I thought justice required it, and so I recommended in my last message. Genl Desha however entertained a different opinion, and as he had a right to do, voted against the claim   Far be it from me, to impugne his motives, or censure his course in this particular—*I never have done so.*

you will shew this letter to Genl Desha and to all others who heard his unjust imputations as far as I am concerned, & do any thing with it but one that is you are not to permit it to get into the news papers. Present me kindly Patsey & the children, to Mr Caruthers and his lady, & to all enquiring friends & believe me very respectfully yours

Andrew Jackson

ALS, MNS (16-0649). Copy dated November 8, DLC (38).

To Samuel Delucenna Ingham

Novbr. 6th. 1830—

The President with his respects, informs the Secretary of the Treasury, that he has not been able to lay his hands upon the printed report, containing all the appropriations for internal improvements since the commencement of the Government—if sent, it is mislaid so that he cannot now lay his hands on it—has therefore to request that he will send him one if to be got—if not, that he will direct the proper officer to have one made out for him.

The President hopes the Secretary has had leisure to day to notify the respective Mayors of the three corporations of this district that the interest, or first instalment on the loan has not been made agreable to the contract, and that we will execute the duties imposed upon us by the act of Congress to a *tittle*, agreable to the specific terms of the loan, and that no indulgence will be given by us, having no discretion on the subject. This is our imperious duty to prevent blame being thrown on us, and to keep the Government free from any responsibility hereafter. It will be necessary, as early as possible, to appoint collectors as specified by the act of Congress[1]

AN, PU-Ingham Papers (16-0653).
1. An Act of May 24, 1828, authorized the three District of Columbia corporations of Washington, Georgetown, and Alexandria to borrow money to subscribe for stock in the Chesapeake and Ohio Canal Company. The Act levied a property tax within each jurisdiction and provided that if the corporations did not collect it in time to make the required loan payments, the president was to appoint collectors to do so. AJ wrote Ingham again about this on November 14 (below).

To Robert Johnstone Chester

Washington Novbr. 7th. 1830—

My Dr Sir

your letter of the 25th. ultimo has just been recd. and I hasten to reply to it.

There are no complaints here against Genl Purdy, nor have we recd, any intimation of his intention to resign—but should the office become vacant you may rest assured your enemy shall not be appointed.

I recd. a letter from Mr Steel my overseer informing me that Charlotte had applied to you to purchase her, being disconted where she now is. I bought her being the wife of Charles at his request, he appears now desirous that she with her children be sold. I have therefore come to the resolution to part with her. But from the great reduction of hands on my plantation by recent deaths since the first of the year 1829—having lost six of my best hands, I was glad to hear that you had said to my overseer, that you would pay me here, so that I can get Andrew to reinstate, Charlotte by purchase here in due time to aid in the next years crop. I have therefore concluded to let you have them, that is to say charlotte with her three children for Eight hundred dollars, paid here in all the month of February next, and on your application for them, and ~~sending~~ handing to Mr Steel on a note payable in this Bank to me with Doctor Butler endorser, I have directed him to deliver them to you—or if it will suit you better, to plaice a note in Bank at Nashville, due & payable, by the 10th. of Feb'ry next, which will enable the cashier to remit a check for the amount to me here by the last of February, it will answer as I wish to send my son out early in March, by whom I would send the purchase in lieu of charlotte & her children[1]

I give my overseer $500 pr annum & my hands have decreased so much, that really this year with the bad season I will not clear from my farm what its culture has cost me—

I think I have placed charlotte & her children as low as they could be bought now here, & sent to my farm, but I do it that she may be contented. let me hear from you on the receipt of this letter.

I wish you to say to Colo. S. D. Hays, that he must get, & send on here, as early as he can, testimonials of his sobriety & capacity as a survayor; This will be necessary, for so sure as an opportunity offers if one should, to give him a survayers District, that in order to mortify me ~~that~~ his appointment will be opposed in the Senate & Crockett & Desha, will represent him as intemperate. Let the recommendations be strong and go to his capacity, and ability to give the necessary *security, if required.* This must be attended to early to be here by the middle or 20th. of Decbr next if practicable[2]

Present me to Betsy & the children & all friends—to my good old friend Mrs. Hays, Narcissa, to Saml J Hays & his sweet little wife, & kiss my namesake for me: To the Doctor & Patsey & son, to Stockly & Lydia jane & little hickory and believe me yr friend[3]

Andrew Jackson

ALS, THi (16-0669).
1. A January 1829 inventory of Hermitage slaves listed Charlotte, age about 30, and her children Aggy, age 5, Jane, 3, and Maria, 1. Her husband Charles, age then about 35, was AJ's carriage driver (*Jackson Papers*, 7:8). AJ wrote Chester again about the sale on November 25 (below).
2. Stockley Donelson Hays was Chester's brother-in-law. Recommendations for him were soon sent from Tennessee, including one on November 27, below.
3. Stockley D. Hays's wife was Lydia Butler Hays (1788–1852). Their children were Sarah Jane Hays (1814–1860) and Richard Jackson Hickory Hays (1822–1899).

From Robert Butler

Lake Jackson November 8th. 1830.

My Dear Sir.

It is now more than four months since I had the pleasure of a line from you although in your last written on the day of your departure from the City you stated that we should hear from you while in Tennessee, but I suppose the multiplicity of your cares prevented.

I learn from the prints that you returned to Washington in fine health for which we are thankful and happy. The opening of the West Indies ports, the Veto, the removal of the Indians (which I find you are effecting without much difficulty) and I expect you will soon, and certainly, obtain from the "Republican King of the French" remuneration for depredations committed on our commerce; when, (with what you have done & will do in the way of reform and liqudating the national debt) I think the measure of your "*iniquitous*" Administration will be full; and that you will have to carry without aleviation the Anathemas of the opposition as long as you live. You never can be forgiven. The present state of Europe may in the future, give you some trouble and anxiety in your foreign diplomacy, but I hope and trust that our relations with foreign powers may be kept by your foresight and prudence, within the strict letter of neutrality, and our Commerce will march on to a state of improvement that will again enable the Agriculturalist to stand upon the ground of bold relief—and the means for paying the national debt, will flow to you as a charm. When you shall accomplish that ever to be desired end, I shall then say, you have seen the summit of your greatness.

My family are all in good health, our youngest, came very near leaving us this summer by a disorganization of the stomach but, she is now fat and hearty.[1] My cotton crop will be short of my expectations but enough to square the yards and I hope my sugar business will succeed, and if so will realize $1000 from it. I am so weak handed that I labour to a disadvantage and could I borrow at fair Interest 5 or 6000$ ~~this~~ next fall for 4 or 5 years I could realize a handsome fortune from my state of preparation. Could such an accommodation be had in any of the banks in Washington. If so I would pay a visit the coming summer to the White House and gladden my heart once more with a shake of your hand. I feel satisfied that I could realize $4000 pr year with the addition to my force of about 12 or 14 hands, *clear of expences*, & I believe my present crop including sugar will realize 3000 Dollars—under any circumstances I shall be clear of the world as soon as it is sold. Under such a state of things with 4000$ added to my salary yearly, and my young negroes coming in yearly to my assistance (which have heretofore been an expence to me) and my expences met without touching this fund you may readily imagine what my prospects would be, having as valuable a tract of Land as Florida affords to act upon.

Will you have the goodness to reflect on this subject and give me your thoughts thereon, resting satisfied that I can effect what I have stated, *and under favorable seasons much more*—My Buildings &c. since I came to Florida has cost me $10.000 all paid including House, Gin house sugar house &c—& have never hired a negro—*260 acres open land*.

We all unite in love to you. Remember us affectionately to Capt. D. Mr. E. & your son Andrew iff with you—(is he married). Affectionately yours

Robert Butler

[Endorsed by AJ:] answered when recd 1rst. Decbr. 1830—

ALS, DLC (38).
    1. Born January 10, 1830, Mary Lucinda Butler died in September 1831.

From Preserved Fish et al.

New-York November 8th. 1830

To the President of the United States of America, the Memorial of the undersigned Citizens of the United States residents of New-York.

Respectfully Sheweth

That the late happy Revolution in France while it secures the liberties of that gallant nation and gives to public sentiment a controling influence in the measures of the Government also in the opinion of your memorialists affords a most favorable opportunity to urge the long neglected Claims of our Citizens upon the consideration of that Government—that the prevalence of more liberal and equitable principles in the French Cabinet and the influence of La Fayette in her Councils are circumstances which warrant a strong belief that the just claims of the citizens of this republic for spoliations on their property will not be treated with neglect—how long this favorable conjuncture may continue it is impossible to foresee and prudence dictates that the fortunate situation of affairs should be improved—With the view therefore of availing ourselves of the present favorable disposition of the French Government and of the sympathetic feeling of the French nation your memorialists pray that if it be not incompatible with the present state of the negotiation a special mission be appointed to convey the congratulations of the American people to that Government upon its glorious revolution and to urge the adjustment of the only subject of difficulty and disagreement between the two countries.

Your memorialists further pray that in the adjustment of these losses—the Claims of American Citizens upon the French Government for property seized in Holland and at St Sebastians by its authority be always considered as inseperably connected with the other claims upon that government.

Your memorialists would also beg leave to suggest that the claims of American citizens upon the Neapolitan Government for similar spoliations would long since have been settled had not the influence of that branch of the Bourbon family which has been deprived of power by the French nation been exerted in the Cabinet of Naples against the admission of Claims growing out of similar outrages and sustained upon the same principles as those upon the Government of France—That influence now no longer exists and your Memorialists would also respectfully submit the propriety of Clothing the same Minister with authority to urge upon the Neapolitan Government the necessity of liquidating claims founded in justice and which cannot be denied without a continued violation of those principles which establish and preserve harmony and good feeling between Independant powers—[1]

All which Your Memorialists do ever Pray

Preserved Fish	}	Chairman
John G. Coster	}	
Geo Griswold	}	
Philip Kearney	}	Committee
Davd. Clarkson	}	
J Blunt	}	

[Sixty-eight additional signatures follow.]

DS, DNA-RG 76 (16-0689). Fish (1766–1846) and the other signers were prominent New York City businessmen. They had previously solicited a special mission to settle spoliation claims against France in 1829 (*Jackson Papers*, 7:219–22). AJ wrote Van Buren about this memorial on November 18 (below). Identical memorials were sent from Portsmouth, N.H., on November 27 and from Newburyport, Mass., on November 29.

1. The Kingdom of the Two Sicilies, with its capital at Naples, was ruled by a branch of the Bourbon family. Negotiations to settle American spoliation claims arising from seizures made by its Bonapartist government during the Napoleonic Wars resumed in 1831.

From Andrew Jackson Donelson

Novr. 9th. 1830

My Dear Uncle

Understanding you in that part of our conversation last evening relating to the return of Mrs. Donelson to this city, to say, that I must not anticipate this happiness, until I could consent to her visiting Mrs. Eaton, or in other words would coerce an intercourse between Mrs. Eaton and Mrs. Donelson out of your house as well as in it, as far as ~~Mrs. Donelson~~ the latter was concerned; it becomes my painful duty to apprise you again that ~~these~~ such terms ~~will never~~ cannot receive my approbation.

If I have misconceived your meaning, pray, let me know what are the difficulties which I have to remove before my family can be allowed to occupy the same house that I do? Your grateful and affectionate nephew.

Andrew J Donelson

P.S. I do not wish another correspondence on the subject—all that I desire is the knowledge of your wishes in relation to the ~~visits~~ extent of the intercourse in question, in order that I may be able to be governed by them or occupy no longer than may be necessary a position which you think unfriendly to them. yr. &c

A J D

ALS, DLC (73).

From James Alexander Hamilton

New York Novr. 9th 1830

My dear Sir,

I have the pleasure to enclose to you herewith a Memoir on the subject of our Foreign intercourse & commerce with certain parts of Europe; embracing also some reflections upon the present condition of the same portion of the world; written by me on the suggestion of our friend Mr Edward Livingston.

This work was begun and finished during those engagements in the courts of the U.S. which have so much occupied my time during the last month; and is therefore more imperfect than it would have been under other circumstances—Permit me to ask you to consider it as intended for your indulgent Eye alone.

any correct views as to what will be the course of events in Europe ~~must~~ might be referred rather to a Spirit of Prophecy; than be deemed to result from a just course of deduction from any previous example in the History of the world—There is none like it. I therefore do not pretend to speak with confidence in any respect except that it is a dictate of wisdom on our part to be prepared for the worst—a General war. Heretofore in such a state of things; we proclaimed a strict neutrality & endeavoured honestly to maintain it; but being unable to place the country in a situation to enforce our Neutral rights; we were driven to submit to the aggressions of all nations; From England & France to those of Denmark & Naples. And ultimately, our resources being considerably diminished by these very aggressions, drawn unprepared into the war. Let such recent experience teach us as soon as it is ascertained that a ~~state of~~ general war must ensue to declare to the Beligerents what our course will be, and to prove to them by the energy and extent of our preparations that we mean to sustain our rights as Neutrals; if it be necessary; even by force

It is not at all improbable that England may for a length of time keep out of the contest; and thus by her situation be called to cooperate with us in sustaining the same views. It would be well if this should be so; *to endeavour* while she is so circumstanced to have some understanding with her as to what the rights of Neutrals are—Altho it is hardly probable that she will suffer herself to be committed on the subject inasmuch as she has heretofore treated Neutral rights as depending wholly upon Beligerent will.

If hostilities should be rendered more certain before the meeting of Congress might you not hint as the probable necessity for such preparation as affording an additional and a very strong reason for your refusal to concur in ~~the~~ expenditures for internal improvements.

Pardon me for imposing upon you the necessity for reading this long letter and believe me to remain with the truest attachment your friend & sert.

James A Hamilton

ALS, DLC (38). Hamilton *Reminiscences*, p. 175. Hamilton's enclosed memoir, dated October 1830, surveyed American political and commercial relations with Europe. Hamilton predicted that the Holy Alliance would move to suppress "the pure and holy spirit of liberty" now set loose in France, and that a general war between princes and their subjects must follow. Americans, while remaining neutral, "have no right to hold back in the great struggle for the political regeneration of the world." Rather, the U.S. should expand its diplomatic presence to further the spread of republican political principles which form "the foundation of our system, and the only true basis of all governments." To advance its own interests and publicize "our benign and beautiful system," the U.S. should send diplomats to more countries and redirect their efforts from seeking indemnities for past wrongs to opening new commercial opportunities (DLC-38; Hamilton *Reminiscences*, pp. 175–87).

To Andrew Stevenson

Private

Washington Novbr. 10th. 1830

My D. Sir,

The Secretary of State has submitted to me (confidentially) yours, to him of the 8th. instant. your own reflections cannot fail to satisfy you of the impropriety of his entering into unofficial explanations upon the points refered to. In addition to the communications received by the Department of State from Mr Randolph at St. Petersburgh, one addressed to myself from him at London (the only one from that place) has been recd.; From which the following is an extract "I trust my dear, Sir, that you will excuse this hurried letter written in pain and sickness. By the next Packet Ship you shall hear more fully. I purpose going to the continent to try and renovate my shattered System. If the season were a fortnight earlier I would embark at once for the United States; as it is, I shall if it please god return to St Petersburgh (with your approbation) in the spring, and to the U.S. in september next, if not sooner."[1]

Mr Randolphs communication is altogether affectionate & in an suitable spirit. Every step that has been taken by the Executive branch of the government in relation to his mission has passed under my own observation, and by them he has received as he shall unto the end receive, perfect & strict Justice. His friends, accustomed to the misrepresentations which his political opponents have always been in the habit to indulge in, respecting him, should wait with patience the result, trusting as I do, that it will never appear that he has been wanting in duty.

By Mr Randolphs original instructions the state of his constitution and the delapidations to which his long career of public service had exposed it, was taken into consideration, and he had a discretion given to him to leave St Petersburgh and spend the winter in a milder climate if he should be satisfied that, that indulgence would work no prejudice to the business of his mission.[2]

The reservation of privacy imposed upon this letter is only to be considered as imperative in regard to newspapers & indiscreet publications of its contents. Whenever it is clear and, in the exercise of a sound discretion, necessary to communicate its contents in relation to facts, you are at liberty to make it—trusting to your discretion not to do so on slight grounds, and much less to repel mere newspaper slander which is not of a character to injure any one. I am Sir with great respect yr mo. obdt. servt.

Andrew Jackson

[Endorsed by AJ:] a copy to the Honble A. Stevenson Novbr. 10th. 1830

ALS copy, DLC (38). Stevenson (1784–1857) was a Virginia congressman and, since 1827, Speaker of the House of Representatives. Recent press reports, including one appearing in both the Washington *National Intelligencer* and *National Journal* on October 30, had related incidents of bizarre behavior by John Randolph in Russia and censured his hasty exodus. A *National Journal* editorial on November 8 charged him with being drunk every day in Russia and then "running away" to vacation in London and the South of France.

    1. Randolph to AJ, September 29, above.

    2. Van Buren's official instructions to Randolph on June 18 gave him AJ's consent to winter in the south of Europe if he concluded a treaty with Russia in time to be reported in AJ's annual message. Also, if "any accident or unforeseen contingency" prolonged the negotiation, and if nothing were to be lost by his absence over the winter—a judgment Van Buren left "entirely to your own discretion"—Randolph was authorized to "repair to a milder climate, under a conviction that your patriotism and your own sense of duty will call you to your station whenever the exigencies of the public service will require it" (DNA-RG 59, M77-8).

Memorandum by Andrew Jackson Donelson

The 10th. Novr. 1830—

On this day about 12 oclock the President remarked to me that he had received my note of yesterday in relation to the difficulties which opposed the return of Mrs. Donelson to the city of Washington. The views which he took of that subject were so extraordinary and indicate so firm a determination to hold the members of his cabinet as well as myself who had not coerced their families into an intercourse with Mrs. Eaton, officially responsible to him, that I have felt it due to mself hereafter to reduce to writing what passes as leading to this object. Tho well aware from the moment of the organization of the cabinet that the repugnance of society to recognize Mrs. Eaton as a proper associate would deeply affect the feelings of the President and expose his excitements to the arts of office seekers and to the many biasses which must naturally attend the incorporation of private feelings with the action of the Government, yet I relied upon the checks, which, an overruling sense of justice, the tendency of time and good counsels, and the inherent weakness of such combinations contained, to dispel the delusion, and ultimately redeem the administration from the odium of such a feature. This anticipation has been banished by the conversation which the President held with me to day. An infatuation kept alive by the timidity of weak friends and the interests of the political party which have used Majr Eaton as an instrument first to obtain the confidence of the President and afterwards to controul him, has long since classed those who associated with Mrs. Eaton or who countenanced her pretensions to virtue and innocence, as the confidential friends of the President, and those who did not as secretly favoring the views of an opposition to his fame and character. The circumstances which ought to have removed this infatuation have confirmed it. It has now become a principle of the administration, and as such consigns to destruction those who do not subscribe to the means which are necessary to secure it power.

Independently of the importance of the subject in this point of view, it is more so to me individually, in another. My relation to the President as his private Secretary, the object of his early favor and care, and but for this ~~interruption of it probably~~ impediment the sharer with his adopted son of his estate; this and all the influences which it sets in motion calculated on the one hand to enjoin obedience, forbearance, conciliation, love & gratitude, as my duty; and on the other, opposite and corresponding vices or faults as the just measure of my character, if my agency in this event seperates me from his person; are considerations of the deepest import to my future happiness. That the world may know that they have been justly appreciated—that if I am borne down as others are by this evil tide, neither my honor, my character, nor my duties are sunk beneath it, by whatever standard they may be estimated—I have ~~resorted~~ yielded to the necessity of ~~some evidences~~ preserving up to this period some evidences of my conduct in relation to the attempts of Mrs. Eaton to subdue the moral sentiment of society, which will be found in another part of this book. The same necessity has also induced me to reduce to writing the conversations which I hold with the President, and I commence with that of this day.

The following letter was before him dated 9th. Novr. 1830

My Dear Uncle

Understanding you in that part of our conversation last evening relating to the return of Mrs. Donelson to this city, to say, that I must not anticipate this happiness until I could ~~anticipate~~ consent to her visiting Mrs. Eaton, or in other words would coerce an intercourse between Mrs. Eaton and Mrs. Donelson, out of your house as well as in it, as far as the latter was concerned, it becomes my painful duty to apprise you again that such terms cannot receive my approbation.

If I have misconceived your meaning, pray, let me know what are the difficulties which I have to remove before my family can be allowed to occupy the same house that I do. yr. grateful & affectionate nephew.

Andrew J Donelson

P.S. I do not wish another correspondence on the subject—all that I desire is the knowledge of your wishes in relation to the extent of the intercourse in question, that I may be able to be governed by them, or occupy no longer than may be necessary a position which you think unfriendly to them[.] yr. &c

A J D

The President said he had read with much pain this letter—that I knew very well he would not part with his friend Majr Eaton, and that this was the object of those who did not allow their families to associate with Mrs. Eaton.

I replied to him that whatever might be the views of others in regard to Majr Eaton that mine only looked to his fame and the protection of my own honor and character. That I had never seen any authority for his inference that a non intercourse with Mrs. Eaton was evidence of Political hostility to Majr. Eaton or himself—

The President continued. It is evidence of hostility to me. The refusal of my cabinet to associate with Mrs. E has already produced a coldness between several of them, which was daily exhibited. That he would not look to the cause of that coldness, but would at a proper time remove it by appointing officers that would harmonise in all their relations. I am, Sir, advised of the combinations which were formed in this city to keep Mrs. Eaton out of society, and the existence of similar ones at Nashville and elsewhere. They will fail. I shall never seperate from Majr. Eaton—no influence can ever force me to do it. The time is not far off when I will give the Gentlemen of my cabinet who cannot harmonise with Majr Eaton some honorable proofs of my confidence in new stations—vacancies will shortly take place in the corps of foreign ministers. They must take those or retire. I can do without them.

I replied to him. This will be a fatal step. It is that which your enemies are looking for. You have not a right to interfere with the private family relations of the cabinet, and the attempt to do it must be seriously injurious. It was to avoid such an imputation that I chiefly desired the return of Mrs. Donelson, whose absence had been already ascribed to his determination to coerce her into an intercourse with Mrs. Eaton.

He said. It was not true that he wished to coerce the intercourse, but that Mrs. D should not return until such intercourse could be maintained, or until she could be on the same terms with the families of all the Heads of Departments. That forty members of Congress during the past winter, understanding that the female part of his family and the ladies of the cabinet officers did not associate with Mrs. Eaton, had asked him if Genl Jackson was at the head of the Government—that this was the language of his friend every where. It was the language of truth and he would shew the world that Genl Jackson was at the head of Government—that he would not put up with what Mr. Monroe did—he knew his duty and would produce harmony.[1] He also spoke in bitter terms of Govr. Branch as having treated Majr Eaton cruelly (I was struck with this remark as corresponding with one of Mr. Triste's in which he mentioned that westcott said every body knew that Eaton appointed the cabinet, and that Govr. Branch among other things was reproached with ingratittude to Majr Eaton—Mr. Triste so informed me to day. It may be proper also to state that Westcott has recently been foiled in an attempt to get his Brother a midshipman reinstated—is one of Mr. Van Buren's officers, and has been quite indecorous in his official intercourse with the Secretary of the Navy)[2]

I was stating my opinion of the error into which the President had fallen by not discriminating between the rights of society as it regarded the character of Mrs. Eaton, and his own, when we were interrupted by the appearance of Leut Smith.

Novr. 13th—

On this day the Pensylvania enquirer containing the proceedings of the dinner given to Col Watmough was in the hands of the President when I entered his office. He had the day before authorised me to apprise Mr. Simpson of his determination to appoint him commissioner to distribute the indemnity which Denmark had agreed to pay to our claimants, if he would resign his clerkship under Mr. Girard who was a claimant.[3] Simpson attended this dinner, has long been known to the President as a violent enemy of Mr. Ingham, and as a mortified candidate for office had in various ways exhibited his hostility to the Administration. The toasts will shew that the sentiments of Mr Simpson were the prevailing ones at the dinner. The President read many of them in my presence. He did not seem to feel the slightest regret at the open assault which they made upon the character and services of Mr. Ingham but rather to acquiesce in it. In relation to the inquiry which had been instituted at the Treasury Department into the charges which had been exhibited by Mr Gowan against Mr. Guyer, and which was the subject of the most unfeeling remark at the dinner in question, the President expressed much discontent, and disclaimed any agency in it. I told him that he had certainly authorised it, and had given an order to Mr. Ingham to dismiss Mr. Guyer if upon investigation he should find the charges substantiated. He answered that the subject ought not to have been presented by the Department—that Gowan had acted incorrectly, and should have fought it out without troubling the Government. These expressions were evidently much excited, and I could not account for them, until I reflected that Majr Lewis had left the room soon after I entered it. His known agency in the election which had resulted in the defeat of Mr. Miller by representing him as having lost the confidence of the executive, which was the foundation of Mr. Gowans difficulty, readily explained the cause of the Presidents excitement, which did not stop here.[4] He expressed his doubts of the sincerity of the counsels of Mr. Ingham, and a determination hereafter to be more guarded in his intercourse with him.

It will be found that the President not only authorised the inquiry in question but on being informed that Mr. Guyer had refused to answer the interrogatories touching one of the charges (alleging the want of power in the Government to question his exercise of the right he possessed to govern himself as he pleased as a voter), he the President directed Mr. Ingham specially to prosecute the investigation in relation to this.

Novr. 17th.

after the receipt of the letter of this date to me in which I am informed that I am at liberty to retire from the office of Private Secretary, I called upon the President to let him know the injustice he had done by the assertion that I represented myself and family as his guests. In my letter to him of the 30th. of Oct speaking of the duty which I owed his guests, I unfortunately then expressed myself. "In your house, my dear Uncle, as your guest, I acknowledge that the same comity and politeness are due to Mrs. Eaton that is to the ladies of your other cabinet officers." He ~~made~~ considered the term *guest* as applied to myself and family in his house, altho the whole subject forbid such an idea. The context shews clearly my meaning. But that there might be no misapprehension about it; I begd leave to correct the sentence so as to make it read as follows—"In your house, my dear Uncle, I acknowledge that the same comity and politeness are due from my family to Mrs Eaton as your guest, that are due to the ladies of your other cabinet officers or those of other Gentlemen." after this no one can deny that the allegation that I had made an unfounded and ungenerous statement going to shew that Mrs. D and myself had been considered and treated by the President as his guests, is altogether erroneous. The President however admitted it verbally, but in writing will not acknowledge it. In conversation he will not reject the force of truth and honor. But in writing Mr. V & Mr. Lewis are his counsellors, and he will express no ideas that are not capable of perversion or material to the game which they have made the President play from the commencement of his disagreement with me; and which aims at my destruction.

He flew from the criminations of my conduct which are contained in his letter of ~~this date~~ the 16th; and indulged in observations upon the conduct of Mr. Ingham shewing that he is completely estranged from him. He also alluded to the Post office Department as obnoxious to the same influence which did not harmonise with his friend Majr. Eaton. said that he had written to Col. Powell and explained the conduct of Majr. Barry[5]

Novr. 21st

The President handed me a letter from Col. Hamilton to him as well as one from the same Gentleman to myself[6]   They both related to the removal of Majr. Laval by the city authorities of charleston, which had very highly excited the feeling of the States right party in which no doubt the friends of Genl Jackson were nearly all ranged. The object of the removal and the circumstance of its being effected thro' the agency of Mr. Pringle the collector whose influence was stated to have been used in such a manner as to make him obnoxious to the principles which the President had avowed in his Inaugural speech, formed the leading features in the letters of Col. Hamilton who had recommended the removal of Pringle and the appointment of Laval in his place. It became necessary for me to write such a letter in reply as the President would approve. This I did. After he read it, he said that Hamilton's indiscretion in this case was as great as that of Gowan's in guyer's: that both cases were directed by the influence of Mr. Calhoun whose hypocrisy and selfish ambition knew no limits, and would destroy his best friends to accomplish his purposes. He connected these incidents with the Watmaugh celebration, which he considered as a development of public sentiment which ~~was~~ had been cherished by Calhoun and was designed to destroy Mr. Ingham for the purpose of reaching ultimately the President himself.

I told him that the influence which had gotten up the Watmough dinner was composed of disaffected men—men who had from the organization of his administration had taken bold ground against it, and particularly against Mr. Ingham: and instanced Simpson and Jack as the leading spirits at the dinner. He said that Simpson was his friend—that the voice of his old friends called for his appointment, and he would obey it—that Mr. Ingham was becoming unpopular in Pennsa, and would fall a sacrifice to the intrigues of Calhoun—that Ganes was one of the puppets of the latter as was evinced by his letter to Watmough, and by his general deportment.[7]

He added other general remarks all pointing to a change in the cabinet, and such a change as would ensure harmony. A cabinet he said ought to be a unit; otherwise like the interests of a divided house it must fall. These views were followed by others denouncing Calhoun as having attempted to stab him in the dark. He mentioned a declaration of Mr. Ringgolds, the present marshal of the district, to Lewis, that Mr. Monroe resisted the inclination of Mr. Calhoun to arrest Genl Jackson for having transcended his orders in passing the Florida line—that Genl Jackson owed a great deal to Mr. Monroe &c. It ought to be stated here that Ringgold was interceding for Lewis favor and influence in behalf of Mr. Monroe's accounts against the Govrmnt, which are yet pending before Congress: and that it is probable he saw no better plan than that of access to the Presidents prejudices against Calhoun. Lewis was a fit and is always a ready instrument in such an operation.[8]

AD, DLC (73).

1. Monroe's Cabinet had been notorious for disharmony among its members, three of whom—Crawford, Adams, and Calhoun—were rival presidential aspirants in 1824.

2. James Diament Westcott Jr. (1802–1880) had been briefly a clerk in the State Department with Nicholas Trist before being appointed secretary of Florida Territory in June 1829. His brother Hampton Westcott was one of the four naval officers AJ had dismissed for dueling on March 31.

3. On November 11 the Philadelphia *Pennsylvania Inquirer* reported a "Democratic Festival" on November 8 to celebrate John G. Watmough's election to Congress over incumbent Daniel H. Miller. Toasts at the dinner chided AJ for "his neglect of early and tried friends" and branded Ingham an "obnoxious Minister" whose unpopularity would bring down the administration (*US Telegraph*, Nov 23). Stephen Simpson (1789–1854) was a Philadelphia author and editor. An early supporter of Jackson, he had quarreled with him in 1829 over appointments and had strenuously opposed Ingham for the Cabinet. Simpson was a clerk in the private bank of Stephen Girard (1750–1831) of Philadelphia, America's

leading financier. At AJ's direction, Donelson wrote Simpson on November 13, proposing to appoint him a claims commissioner under the treaty with Denmark if he would resign his position with Girard. Simpson wrote back on November 17 (below). AJ nominated Simpson on December 9. The Senate rejected him by 25 to 18 on March 2, 1831.

4. Campaigning for Watmough, George Guier in Gowen's presence had invoked Lewis as his authority for saying that Miller's votes in Congress against Indian removal and for the Maysville Road had cost him AJ's confidence. Gowen denied it and the two quarreled.

5. AJ wrote Addison Powell on November 13 (below).

6. James Hamilton Jr. wrote AJ on November 14 (below).

7. Charles J. Jack of Philadelphia had unsuccessfully sought appointment as marshal in 1829. Edmund P. Gaines had written Guier a letter for publication on September 12, praising Watmough's valor as an artillery lieutenant at the battle of Fort Erie in 1814, where he was severely wounded (*Louisville Public Advertiser*, Oct 21, 1830).

8. By Lewis's later account, Ringgold told him that Monroe alone in his Cabinet had defended AJ's Seminole campaign (Parton, 3:322–23). Monroe was a claimant before Congress for reimbursement of various expenses and losses incurred on government service.

To Duff Green

Novbr. 11th. 1830—

The President with his respects to Genl D. Green will be happy to see him as early as possible this morning, & before his paper of today goes to press. He finds a great error in his paper of yesterday wherein Mr Randolph is concerned, which is proper to have corrected to day

We find that we were mistaken in supposing as we did yesterday that the Presidents permission to Mr Randolph to visit the south of France had been sent to him recently. He was authorised ~~by original~~ by his original instructions to do so if the state of his health should make it necessary & the affairs of the mission would admit of his temporary absence without injury to the public service

AN, THer (16-0709; mAJs). Remarking John Randolph's "strange conduct," the *National Intelligencer* on November 10 said that if he indeed had AJ's permission to winter in France, as the *US Telegraph* had said, then he must have obtained it before leaving the U.S. for Russia. The *Telegraph* retorted that evening, assailing the *Intelligencer*'s credibility and surmising that AJ's consent was instead "communicated in reply to a request of Mr. R. transmitted in consequence of the present state of his health." The *Telegraph* ran AJ's correcting paragraph verbatim on November 11, the next day.

To Samuel Delucenna Ingham

Novbr. 13th. 1830

The President with his respects to Mr Ingham, draws his attention to the enclosed petitions & proceedings thereon, and then to the Act of the 3rd of March 1797—chaptr. 361 (LXVII) Section first, which vests the power in the Secretary of the Treasury to *remit* or *mitigate* such fine forfeiture or *penalty* &c &c. The judgt. not being final the power he conceives are in the Sec. of the Treasury & not in him. The P from the facts disclosed has no hesitation in saying the prosecution ought to be discontinued.

AN, PU-Ingham Papers (16-0719). The 1797 law (Chapter 67 in the 1828 Boston edition of *Public and General Statutes*) laid out a procedure for mitigating or remitting fines, penalties, or forfeitures for violations of customs and shipping laws where the offense committed did not involve willful negligence or fraud. Petitions for relief were to be submitted to the federal district judge, who was to collect facts and report to the Secretary of the Treasury. The Secretary had power to remit or mitigate the penalty, or to halt a prosecution for its recovery "upon such terms as he may deem reasonable and just."

To Addison Powell

(Copy)

Washington November 13th. 1830

Dr. Sir,

The absence of the Post Master General has occasioned a short delay in bringing the investigation of the matters complained of in your memorial to a close. I have now the honor of enclosing to you, the reply of the Post Master General to your memorial, and to your rejoinder to his reply with the affidavits of the Revd. Mr. Brown & Mr. Reeside with the statement in the declaration of the Clerks in the Post Office Department. These documents clearly shew, that no unfairness was practised in the transactions complained of.

When it is taken into view that the Post Master General is bound to look to the public good alone, and render impartial justice to all, I trust you will conclude with me, that he has, in this case, as in all others, faithfully performed his duty—

(Signed) Andrew Jackson

Copy, DNA-RG 46 (16-0721). Barry's letter of November 12 denied that the Bradley brothers held any interest in mail contracts or that a postal clerk had divulged information about competing bids to James Reeside.

To Samuel Delucenna Ingham

14 Nov. 1830

The President with his respects, acknowledges the receipt of the note of the Secretary of the Treasury of the 13th. with one from the Mayor of Washington enclosed, and is happy to find that partial payments have been made and others pledged so that the unpleasant duty of executing the law may be avoided; but as the President has no discretion in this case, he has to observe that such a guarantee of payment must be given as will satisfy the Secretary that the money will be in the Treasury on the first day of January next, before proceedings can be delayed.

N in William B. Lewis's hand, PU-Ingham Papers (16-0731). John Peter Van Ness (1770–1846) was mayor of Washington. Ingham had replied to AJ's note of November 6 (above).

From James Hamilton Jr.

Charleston Nov 14th 1830

My Dear Sir.

I beg leave to enclose you two Letters—one for Mr Donaldson and the other for Mr Hays. The latter contains a remittance which I am particularly anxious he should receive safely I will therefore thank you to place it under an evelope & give it a proper direction.

I feel much interest & concern in Hay's prosperity and shall at all times be exceedingly gratified to learn of his success in life. I regret that the embarrassments of Mr. John Middleton's Est. continue so as to prevent his immediately realizing any very considerable resources from So. Cna. but I trust the day is not far distant when he will derive important assistance from this quarter in the mean time I trust he is pushing his fortunes in Tennessee with energy & the best auspices.[1]

I find on my arrival here that Major Laval did not strike for the Collectors office but was content to make application for the humble & subordinate Post of Measurer of Salt & Coals. As he selected his own object neither he nor his friends have any right to find fault with you for giving him this birth instead of the more responsible office in which I desired to see him placed. In fact I have been so much mortified at Lavals not striking for Mr Pringle's place by which if it had been necessary we should have sustained both you and him by the political power of the State, that I beg leave to withdraw the Letter I wrote you from Columbia, in his favor, as the selection he made I deeply regret. Mr Pringle's removal would have been an act of justice, the removal of Old Mr Cardozo The

Measurer of Salt & Coals Major Laval ought not to have sought. It is true from bodily infirmities the poor old man had to discharge his duties by his son, but they were well performed. He was poor was appointed in Mr Jefferson's administration and I believe was wounded at the seige of Savannah.[2] If I had been in the City when Laval started for Washington this thing would not have occurred. Under the circumstances in which you were placed you could not have done otherwise altho' I regret, I could not have communicated with you in time.

As I leave town in the course of an hour I have not a moment to spare to write you on the subject of our State Politicks but I hope to find leisure in Country to do so. You may rest assured that my account shall be given with all possible frankness as I feel satisfied that the State right Party (who were your original and are now your zealous supporters) have quite as little to conceal as they have to be ashamed of.

I beg leave My Dear Sir to assure you of the great esteem with which I am very respectfully & faithfully your friend & obt. Sert.

J. Hamilton Jun

ALS, DLC (38).

1. The late John Middleton (1784–1826) of South Carolina was a cousin of Hamilton and the father of Samuel J. Hays's wife Frances. He had left property in South Carolina to her and her siblings. AJ wrote Hays on November 21 (below).

2. David Nunez Cardozo (1751–1834) was wounded at Savannah in 1779 and captured by the British at Charleston in 1780. AJ had just directed his replacement by William J. Laval as measurer of salt and coal at the Charleston custom house. Cardozo was soon appointed weigher, a lesser post, at which his son Isaac N. Cardozo later succeeded him.

To Martin Van Buren

Novbr. 15th. 1830

The President with his respects returns the letter, of Master Smith, & presents his thanks for its perusal—

What a gem! cherish it, never let a bloom of it be withered by oppression —change his position, unless the superintendant *atones* for the punishment of innocence; for who can *doubt the candor*, when he "swears to the Bible." I would not take a *million* for such *a son*, and I protest against permitting his *high sense* of honor & *propriety* from being subdued into abject servility, by newengland despotism—take him away, & send him to Nashville, or Educate him here—

This is in haste—

AN, DLC-Van Buren Papers (16-0733). Van Buren's son was Smith Thompson Van Buren (1817–1876).

To Andrew Jackson Donelson

Novbr. 16th. 1830—

Dr Andrew

After the last full & free conversation I had, & held with you upon the painful subject, to which yours of the 15th. instant alludes, & which was this evening handed by yourself, I had a hope my feelings would no more be harrowed up by your written communications when you were daily with me, and could orally have communicated your views upon this, or any other subject. I had supposed that my views were well understood by you. I had often repeated them to you, & Emily.

Were you and Emily ever constrained by me to become part of my family, I thought it was of your free choice; have I ever attempted to retain you against your will; I believe not; tho, would always be happy to have you both part of it, so long as you would conform to such rules as I deemed proper all my family should, & no longer. That whenever the rules of my House became irksome to you & her, you were at liberty to withdraw.

When Emily was placed in my house as the representative of my dear departed wife I did not suppose that she would have thought it discreditable to fulfil those duties to my friends, that if my Dr Mrs. J. had been living she would with pleasure have fulfilled. Emily was never required to do more than to extend equal comity to every one of the heads of the Departments & their families. This from me, & my household was due to them—the moment that this could not be submitted to, by such an important member of my family as Emily; it became her duty to withdraw. If an idea has been taken up that I wished to constrain you & Emily to remain part of my family when you would not conform to the rule before stated for the Government of my family when you wished to withdraw, you have laboured under a great mistake, for I have often said & at all times repeated, that I could not have any one a member of my family that would not conform to this rule; and particularly one as Mrs Donelson who, was placed as the representative of my Dr departed wife, from whom if living, or her representative when dead, justice required that the same comity should be extended to all.

One remark & I am done writting to you upon this subject—you must hereafter speak, not write to me upon it. ¿Why ~~have~~ do you ask me for a copy of a letter that I burnt before your eyes? You cannot have forgotten the reason why they were committed to the flames. You must recollect the ungenerous & unfounded statement you had mad to me in one of yours that "you and Emily had only been my *Guests* &c—When I brought this to your view, your calm reflection had brought conviction to your mind of the great injury in *this*, you had done me, and you asked to correct it. To think that you who your father had called for & bequeathed to me, that I had raised & loved as a child, should under the same roof be carrying on a written correspondence filled me—I burnt the correspondence, & hoped I was done with the subject—I *keep no black books for my friends*, I have no copy.

I have said before my Dr Andrew, whenever your own inclination leads, & you determine, you are welcome to withdraw. and when my friends & companions, are in your opinion, not fit companions for you, & yours, surely I would be the last man on earth that would desire to restrain you—all I wish is, that your *newly* acquired friends may act as faithfully to you, & protect your honor & your morals, as well as I have done. Therefore whenever you desire to withdraw, you have only to name the day, and means & those shall be ample are ready for you. To conclude, I hope no one may ever attempt to controle you from the management of your own houshold, and your own family—should they, it is a duty you owe yourself to resist it.

When you retire from me, you will *still* carry with you, my prayers for your welfare & that of your family—yours affectionately

Andrew Jackson

[Endorsed by AJ Donelson:] This letter recd. the morning of the 17th. Novr. 1830

ALS, DLC-Donelson Papers (16-0735).

To Nathan Reid

Washington Novbr. 16th. 1830

My Dr Sir

On the receipt of your letter of the 14th. of October last, on the subject of your Grandson Wm. J. Reid, I lost no time in laying before the proper department, your letter that it might be forwarded to the superintendant of the military academy, that the situation of your grandson might be fully known, and such preparatory steps taken as would prevent mortification to the youth, or unpleasant feelings to you. I have now the pleasure to inclose for your satisfaction, the reply of Lt Col. S. Thayer on this subject, which I trust will be fully satisfactory to you.

Permit me to recommend it to you, to write your grandson to lay out of view every idea of leaving the institution until he graduates. This will stimulate him to diligence and put out of his view all idea of leaving the institution, & when this is the case, he has genius, that will surmount all dificuly, & place him in a respectable standing in his class. Tell him, that

his future prospects in life mainly depend upon his continuing the & procuring when it is within his grasp, a thorough education.

I assure you my affection for the father has decended to the son, and
as far as I can with propriety, he will be protected in all his rights, and
encouraged to do right.

Accept I pray you my best wishes & believe me your friend

Andrew Jackson

Photocopy of ALS, T (16-0740). Nathan Reid (1753–1830), a captain in the Revolution,
was the father of AJ's late aide John Reid and grandfather of cadet William S. Reid. Young
Reid withdrew from West Point in 1831.

From William Craig

Philada. Nov 16 1830

Respected Sir

The recent removal of Mr John Cuthbert, from the Consulate of
Hamburg, having excited feelings of regret among the friends of that
Gentleman, I beg leave to lay before your Excellency, the enclosed evidence of the good will of the Citizens of Philada. towards him. I am with
with great respect Your friend & Svt

William Craig

[Endorsed by AJ:] recd. 17th. Novbr. 1830—refered to the Sec. of State—
That if he thinks the subject requires an aswer, that he may, say to Mr
Craigg—by whom Mr List was recommended, the public interest required
a change & the present incumbent had been a long time in office &c &c

ALS, DNA-RG 59 (M639-5). William Craig (c1784–1869) was a Philadelphia merchant.
He enclosed petitions of November 13 from Philadelphians headed by William Phillips and
Henry Toland, asking AJ to reconsider his removal of John Cuthbert (c1776–1848) as con-
sul at Hamburg. On November 9 AJ had replaced Cuthbert, a Philadelphian appointed by
Adams in 1826, with Friedrich List.

To John Henry Eaton

Novbr. 17th. 1830—

The bearer, Mr Jones, whose recommendations are on file in your office,
for the appointment of Sutler at Ft Trumbull; has applied to me for a decision on his application as he is desirous to return home—I have refered
him to you, and wish you to make a decision on his case.

Speaking of Suttlers brings to my mind, Genl Nicks—he was with me last evening says, he has presented to you from the officers of the army a full expression of their desire that he should be retained. If so, it will be well to try him longer, by a renewal of his appointment.

I shall expect you & Major Barry at six this evening

AN, DNA-RG 94 (M567-54). Joel W. Jones, a recently discharged artillery sergeant, was appointed sutler at Fort Sullivan in Maine. John Nicks (d. 1832), a former Arkansas Territory militia brigadier, was the sutler at Cantonment Gibson.

From Stephen Simpson

Philadelphia November 17. 1830.

Sir,

Our mutual friend A. J. Donelson Esq. has by Letter dated the 13th. current, notified me that by making known to you my determination to resign the Situation I now hold in the Banking House of M. Girard, the appointment of Commissioner under the Treaty with Denmark, will forthwith be forwarded to me.

In accordance with this intimation, I have now the honor to acquaint you, that upon the receipt of the Commission I shall instantly resign the place I hold in the Banking House.

It is hardly necessary to remark that the two would be utterly incompatible. I have the honor to be, With much consideration & regard, Your obt. humbl St.

Stephen Simpson

Major Donelson's Letter is only *this moment* received—

ALS, DNA-RG 59 (M639-21). Simpson wrote again on November 24 (below).

To John Henry Eaton

Novbr. 18th. 1830—

Dr Sir

In reply to your note of this morning enclosing the letter from the Govr. of Georgia I have to observe, that I can see no good to be derived to the State of Georgia, or the United States, by the enrolling plan, but an accumulation of expense to the Goverment, & a constant draw to our Treasury—suppose 1000 enrolled for emigration, this does not lessen the claim of the cherokees, as a tribe, to the territory now claimed by them within Georgia, and from the temper that has lately appeared amongst them to emigrate, it is evident to my mind, that they chiefs must shortly will propose a treaty under which the whole will emigrate, that do not intend to remain as citizens; but if the enrolling System is commenced, it will have the effect to lessen the ardor that now begins to show itself for emigrating to the west. This ardor ought to be increased, & delay in the business will have this effect, until the rising spirit of the Indians will compel their chiefs to send Deputies duly authorised to treat for the whole country. Therefore you will answer the Govr. of Georgia that this enrolling scheme ought to be posponed for the present until the course the Legislature of Georgia may take on this subject is fairly developed, and until it is seen what effect the late spirit for emigration, by many of them, may produce upon the whole nation.

I have no doubt but the common Indian seeing that their chiefs have become wealthy by the course pursued by them, whilst the common Indians have been reduced to beggary, will soon burst their bonds of Slavery, & compel their chiefs to propose terms for their removal. for the present the enrolling scheme ought to be posponed[.] yrs

Andrew Jackson

ALS, DNA-RG 75 (M234-113). Copy, DNA-RG 46 (16-0799). *SDoc* 512, 23d Cong., 1st sess., vol. 2, pp. 186–87 (Serial 245). On November 4, Governor Gilmer had forwarded to Eaton, for AJ's consideration, a letter from three citizens of Milledgeville saying that hundreds of Cherokee families would now enroll for emigration if given an opportunity (DNA-RG 75, M234-74).

To Martin Van Buren

Novbr. 18th. 1830.

The President with his respects, returns the memorial; remarks, that he will await the arrival of further intelligence from Mr. Rives, before he can take into consideration the subject of a special mission, The other point is embraced in Message

AN, DNA-RG 76 (16-0802). AJ returned the November 8 memorial from Preserved Fish and others (above), which had been sent to him from New York through Van Buren.

To Louis Philippe, King of the French

Washington 20th. November 1830.

Great and Good Friend,
I have received the letter which your Majesty was pleased to address to the United States, on the 22d. of August last, announcing to us your acces-

sion to the Throne of France, to which you had been called by the voice of the two Chambers, and the general assent of the Nation, and which you had ascended with the title of King of the French. Impressed with a deep sense of the importance of the change which this event has wrought in the destinies of a friendly and powerful People, while we deplore with your Majesty the calamitous occurrences which have attended it, and the misfortunes of the elder branch of your family, the people of these United States can but rejoice at the triumph, in regenerated France, of the great principles of Freedom and self Government secured by that glorious revolution, and which we hail as the harbinger of happy days to her. We sincerely congratulate your Majesty upon an event which has placed you at the head of liberal institutions in France; and with equal sincerety, we congratulate the French People on the selection they have made of a Monarch whose known integrity and constant attachment to the cause of Freedom will surround his throne with the power of public opinion; and, who faithful interpreter of the National will, will establish the empire of the laws, and spread over his Kingdom justice, order, happiness and glory. I avail myself of this opportunity to renew to your Majesty the assurance of the high esteem and regard with which I am, Your Majesty's good friend,

> Andrew Jackson,
> M. Van Buren, Secretary of State.

LC, DNA-RG 59; Copy, FrPMAE; Draft, DLC-Van Buren Papers (16-0811).

To Samuel Jackson Hays

> Washington Novbr. 21rst 1830—

My Dr Saml,

I have this moment recd. a letter from Col James Hamilton jnr. inclosing to me the within, saying it contains a remittance to you & requesting I should forward it to your address which I now do with pleasure, with a hope, that it will reach you in safety

I am & have been much engaged preparing for congress. I have been surrounded with circumstances & things last summer, that has made my life very unpleasant—some of my connections have pursued a course both unpleasant & injurious to me—I forgive them—still I cannot forget it. I still love them, but their course I can never appove—hereafter I will explain to you all matters. Now I cannot. I shall be happy to hear from you often, and when you visit Carolina will be happy to see you here where I shall expect you & your dear Frances to spend with me some time

My son is not in good health   Except him, we are all well—my health is checkered, but still I think my general health improved.

Present me kindly to your dear Frances & kiss the son for me, present me kindly to your dear mother & Narcissa, and to every branch of your family & to all inquiring friends & believe me truly yours

Andrew Jackson

P.S. All join in love to you & Frances, Mr Van Buren in good health and spirits   the Newyork Elections have put him in high spirits, and our Foreign relations we have a right to believe will all terminate well. If my family had stuck by me, I could have been happy—the administration is progressing well—altho the course taken by some of its heads, has been foolish & weak and cannot end in harmony, *but division*, and the course of my connections in uniting with them has displayed more weakness and folly than any thing I have ever witnessed thro' life—*but it is done*—let me hear from you—A. J.

ALS, J. Walker Hays III (16-0825).

To John Branch

Novbr. 23rd 1830—

The Honble Secretary of the Navy

You will please order the first of our armed vessels, that may be return-ing from the Mediteraen Squadron, to Touch at Cape de Verd Island, for the purpose of bringing home from thence, British sailors, deserters from their service, charged with mutiny on board the Brig Florenzo, of Philadelphia and that said vessel take charge of them, bring them to the U. States, that they may be handed over to the civil authority, and brought to a speedy trial for said offence[.] respectfully yours

Andrew Jackson

ALS, DNA-RG 45 (M124-125). In May 1829 several sailors, deserters from the British navy, were arrested and imprisoned at Santiago in the Cape Verde Islands at the instigation of the U.S. consul for making a mutiny as crewmen on the American merchant brig *Florenza*. Two died in prison, and on November 16, 1830, British minister Charles R. Vaughan wrote Van Buren asking on humanitarian grounds that the others be brought to the U.S. for an imme-diate trial. On November 23, the date of this note, Van Buren explained to Vaughan that merchant captains' reluctance to take on the prisoners had caused previous delay, but that AJ had now ordered a warship to the task (DNA-RG 45, M124-125). Following AJ's note and a seconding message from Van Buren on November 27, Branch on December 1 gave orders for the frigate *Java* to collect the prisoners on its way home (DNA-RG 45, M149-19). The *Java* picked up five prisoners at Santiago in February 1831 and delivered them to the U.S. marshal at Norfolk in June.

Approval of John Henry Clack's Court-Martial

Novbr. 23rd. 1830—
The proceedings of the general (Naval) court martial whereof Capt
A. J. Dallas, of the Navy, was President, and before which John H. Clack
master commandant in the U States Navy was tried and convicted are
approved. The secretary of the Navy will therefore Issue the necessary
orders for carrying the same into effect

Andrew Jackson

[Endorsed by AJ in March 1831:] The above sentence & confirmation
reviewed, on the application made by judge Thompson & judge Baldwin
after being submitted to the atto. Genl. and for the errors assigned set
aside, & Capt Clack nominated to the Senate & confirmed—Capt Clack
is restored to his command with his former rank—[1]

Andrew Jackson

ADS, DNA-RG 125 (M273-24). Clack was court-martialed at Pensacola in September 1830
on an array of charges brought by Captain Melancthon T. Woolsey, including official oppression, ungentlemanly and unofficerlike conduct, cowardice, disobedience of orders, misap-
propriation of public property, and disrespect and contempt toward a superior officer. The
charges stemmed from incidents occurring while Clack was stationed at the Pensacola navy
yard under Woolsey in 1828–29. Clack denied the charges and accused Woolsey of persecution. The court found Clack guilty and sentenced him to dismissal from the service. AJ made
detailed notes while reading the lengthy trial record (DLC-72; 16-0841). The proceedings
were subsequently challenged and on March 2, 1831, Attorney General Berrien submitted
an opinion that the absence of one of the court's five officers during much of the trial made
its verdict "illegal and void." AJ nominated Clack the same day for restoration to the Navy
without interruption in rank. The Senate confirmed him March 3.
    1. Smith Thompson (1768–1843) was a Supreme Court justice and former secretary of
the Navy.

From Stephen Simpson

PHILADELPHIA, Nov. 24, 1830.
Sir,—
Major Lewis did me the honor to call yesterday, at your request, to
desire that I would resign my present situation, in order to remove all
obstacles to the appointment with which you said you intended to honor
me, on the 2d day of the Session of Congress. I stated in reply, that I had
made every arrangement to resign, and should do so forthwith.
    Will you do me the favor to intimate whether I understand Major
Lewis correctly, as the measures I have taken to surrender my present
occupation, will very naturally cause me to experience some anxiety, lest

any misapprehension should arise, which to me, and my numerous family would be fraught with the most painful consequences.

With great respect, &c.

STEPHEN SIMPSON.

Printed, *Liberty Hall and Cincinnati Gazette*, November 3, 1831 (mAJs). The *Gazette* reprinted this letter from a series, "Illustrations of Jacksonism," in Simpson's own newspaper, the *Pennsylvania Whig*. According to Simpson, he received an answer "requiring an immediate resignation" of his clerkship with Girard. He resigned and was then left without sustenance when the Senate rejected him for claims commissioner under the treaty with Denmark.

To Robert Johnstone Chester

Washington Novbr. 25th. 1830—

My Dr Sir

Yours of the 5th instant has been some days since received. My last to you in reply to yours from Nashville on the subject which interests you, will have, ere this, satisfied you that you have nothing to fear from that source.

My overseer had communicated to me the wish expressed by charlotte to be sold to you. She had before I left the Hermitage expressed the same desire to me, I then told her I would sell her if you wished to buy her, but not her children—the fact was I did not wish to seperate her & her children, from charles, particularly his children, and I had promised to let him return as soon as I reached this city; but upon the receipt of Mr Steels letter I enquired of charles whether he was contented to part with her & the children; he replied in the affirmative, and I wrote you immediately and placed the lowest price at which such a family would cost me here, including the expence of taking them there. From the loss of so many of my hands, by death, on my farm in the two last years, I have not sufficient force to justify the employment of an overseer on the terms I have to pay, and I can save no funds from my salary here, to replace the reduced hands there—hence it is, ~~that~~ why, I am willing to gratify charlotte by selling her to you, if I can from her sale, replace her and family on my farm. If you think they are too high I am sure I it was not my intention to place them beyond what they would command in cash, and you shall have them at a fair price—for I assure you I have often wished her from my plantation, altho', one of the best servants I ever saw, if it was not for her ungovernable temper, and tongue—she has three of the finest children on my plantation, and I do think worth the sum proposed, & much more to a rising family—but of this you are to be the judge.

On the subject of the judgment & other claims against Col Stockly Donelson deceased, I think I handed them over to Colo. & Doctor Butler some years ago, when they had some intention of bringing suit vs Colo. McClung. The judgt. was recovered by Athelred Williams vs Colo. Donelson & Colo. Hays became his security to prevent him from being taken by a ca. sa. I think the judgt. was recovered in Nashville, but of this I am not now certain. The transfer I think I made to Mrs. Hays, and at the same time transfered three bonds I held on Col S. Donelson—if this was not done, I do not know where the bonds are—if not handed over as I have stated, they bonds must be still in my papers at the Hermitage, but I am almost certain they were—however if the judgt. has not been transfered, it shall be at any time, and the bonds, when found, as I never mean to do any thing with them myself—

Mr William Lytle was the agent of Mr Williams, and can tell you at once, where the judgt was recovered, and on the record, it may have been transfered by me, to Mr Hays, as I think upon the judgt. being paid, it was transfered to me—but really the whole circumstances has almost escaped my memory, and without being at home where I could turn to memorandoms, I cannot say any thing positive upon the subject.[1]

With my kind salutations to Betsy, Mrs. Hays, & every one of the connection, believe me sincerely your friend

Andrew Jackson

P.S. I am so surrounded with business preparing for congress, I have no time to write to a friend, unless in the late hours of night, & have no time to correct this. I will be happy to hear from you

A. J.

ALS, ICHi (16-0869).
   1. Rachel Jackson's brother Stockley Donelson (c1759–1805) had speculated largely in land. Robert Hays (1758–1819), Robert Chester's father-in-law and Stockley Donelson's brother-in-law, had stood personal security for the latter's debts to Etheldred Williams (d. 1847) of Grainger County, Tenn. Williams obtained a judgment against Hays for $3600 in 1804. AJ, brother-in-law to both Donelson and Hays, settled the debt in 1807. Charles McClung (1761–1835) of Knoxville had been involved in Donelson's land dealings. William Lytle (c1779–1839) was a Nashville businessman and state legislator.

From Thomas Claiborne et al.

Nashville 27th. Nov. 1830

Sir

Having understood that the Office of Surveyor General of the Publick Lands in the State of Mississippi is about to become vacant, and understanding that our friend Colo Stokely D Hays is desirous of receiving that appointment, we beg leave to recommend him to your notice for the Office. We think him qualified, and that his services and patriotism during the late war entitles him to the favorable consideration of the Government[.] Very respectfully Yr. Obt. Svts

Th. Claiborne
Will. Williams
Jo. Philips
R Armstrong
Jn. Overton

[Eighteen additional signatures follow.]

[Endorsed by AJ:] The Governor of Tennessee judges Born of Tennessee with many of the most respectable citizens of Nashville & its vicinity recommendg. S. D. Hays for survayor Genl. South of Tennessee—

LS, DNA-RG 46 (16-0891). Other signers included Tennessee governor William Carroll, state supreme court judge Robert Whyte and circuit judge Parry W. Humphreys, Tennessee house speaker Ephraim H. Foster, U.S. marshal Robert Purdy and district attorney James Collinsworth, former U.S. attorney Thomas H. Fletcher, and AJ's friends Samuel Hogg and John C. McLemore. Recommendations for Hays sent from his Jackson, Tenn., neighborhood about this time included one signed by Adam Huntsman and thirty-three others, stressing his scientific qualifications and self-sacrificing Army service in and after the War of 1812 (DNA-RG 46, 16-0872). On December 20 AJ nominated Hays to be surveyor of public lands south of Tennessee in place of Joseph Dunbar, who had resigned effective January 1, 1831. AJ wrote George Poindexter about the nomination the same day (below).

To Emily Tennessee Donelson

Washington Novbr. 28th. 1830—

Dear Emily

your kind letter of the 8th. ult. has been some days received, & has, owing to the press of business, been laid over for answer until now. I thank you sincerely for this letter, it is the only one I have recd. except one from Mary Easton, from any of my connections since I left the Hermitage, one from Mr. Mc.Lamore accompanied yours.

I intended my Dr Emily when I sat down to have given you a long friendly answer to your kind favor, but was interrupted in this intention by the receipt of a letters from Mr Caruthers, & others, giving me a detailed account of the disgraceful & unwarrantable course of Genl Desha at Gallatine. The last I saw of him was at my own House where he visited me as a friend, and parted with me as such, I know I had never said or thought harm of him, & any objection to his course, I had freely named to him on his enquiries made of me, and to him alone, and never suspected his friendship, until a few days after he left my house, I was informed by a friend, that he had declared in gallatine on his return home that he intended to come out against Major Eaton & myself, and what astonished me still more, was the positive falshood he stated as the ground of his hostility to me. I must confess this sommersett of the Genls. did not much surprise me, for I had cause from my first appointment of Major Eaton to believe, that he was united with the combination, & wielded by the great political magician who has worked all the political wires in this drama, to coerce me to abandon Eaton, & thereby bring on me disgrace for having appointed him, & thereby weaken me ~~thereby~~ in the affections of the nation, & open the way to his perferment on my ruin. I now clearly see, (as I thought I did from the beginning) in this movement of Deshas, the first public movement under the conspiracy here on the great political chess board. The Nashville letter, the secrete slander whispered as it is said by a certain judge, refered to by the Genl who was an invited gest at the marriage, & whose attendance give the lye direct to the assertion, or is proof of the abominable hypocracy, & baseness of the judge; the anti-masonic meetings & the late movements in Philadelphia, begin to unmask themselves & will be fully developed before long, when I must have my Cabinett a unit, when harmony will prevail; when it will give me pleasure to bring you & your sweet little ones here. I have suffered much & may suffer much more in feeling, but never can I seperate from my friend without cause—what a wretch he must be who can—"a friend in need is a friend indeed," & he who can forsake his friend in distress—against whom one of the most base & wicked conspiracies have been formed here, under the sanctity of religion to destroy him followed up in Tennessee with a malignity of persecution, against an innocent & unoffending man, that none but demons can possess—and in none has this demoniac spirit been more conspicuous than in Genl Desha. His late conduct at Gallatine has set a mark of disgrace upon him that he must feel to his grave, and the pit of disgrace that his immagination had prepared for Major Eaton & myself, he has tumbled into ~~himself~~. These remarks are founded upon the relation I have before me from Mr. Caruthers & others that I know to be men of truth, and name it to you that your brother Stockly may be more guarded, or he will get into dificulties, from which danger of disgrace may arise. A House divided cannot stand."

I thank you my Dr. Emily for the privation you are willing to forego in the seperation from your Dr husband—no one can appreciate more than me such a privation, & none will remove it with more pleasure that I will, when it can with propriety be done. I at first my Dr child saw, & with heartfelt sorrow regretted that my counsel could not prevent it. I knew the depth of intrigue with which we were surrounded, & the hypocritical cant of friendship & piety, with which it approached innocence, & inexperience, when they would have destroyed any, & every one, who stood in the way of their vengeance, and ambition—but it is done, and ought to be left behind us, & only remembered as a buoy to guard us from quicksands a head. My Dr Emily, I never *desert a friend without cause; I never will, a friend in distress*, and particularly ~~when that friend~~ one who has displayed his acts in so many ways as Eaton has to me, & mine. If I thought there could be an earthly influence that could induce me to do such a base act, I would despise myself, and be certain that I never could obtain the smiles of a just my god, whose atributes is, love, charity, & justice; I will write you again as soon as leisure will permit. in the mean time, accept of my prayers for your health and that of your sweet little ones, who I beg you to kiss for me. Your Dr Husband is well, but like myself busy. Daniel & Margaret is still here, may leave here next week. My son is here & well, who with yr Andrew, my son, Major Lewis Mr Earle, all request me, with Mary Ann Lewis, to be presented affectionately to you. Please present me to your mother & all enquiring friends, say to Mary Eastin, with my kind salutations, that she some time promised to write me, when she visited the garden at the Hermitage to let me know, whether there were sufficient care taken of the shrubery planted by her Dr Aunt in the garden, that I had directed to be planted around her tomb. I am affectionately yrs

Andrew Jackson

ALS, DLC (73).

To Martin Van Buren

Novbr. 29th. 1830—

The President returns Govr. Popes letter and at present has no remark to make upon it—its receipt might be acknowledged & his attention again drew to the instructions forwarded him in your last. The suggestions about more additional boundery, has been noted, but our negotiation with Mexico, m[ust] settle that matter—

AN, DNA-RG 59 (M179-69). John Pope had written Van Buren on November 2 describing his measures, including a threat of force, to uphold American authority in the disputed border region against the Mexican colonizing efforts of Benjamin R. Milam and Peter E. Bean (*TPUS*, 21:283–84). He also suggested procuring additional territory from Mexico on which to settle emigrating Indians. Van Buren had instructed Pope not to use force against Mexican claimants without explicit permission from Washington.

To Samuel Delucenna Ingham

The President with his respects to the Secretary of the Treasury, will thank him at as early a day as his convenience will permit to furnish him with a statement of the recipts into the Treasury for the fiscal year of 1830, & with the expenditures. The amount of Principle & interest of the Public debt paid in 1830—and whether any & if any what further provisions may be necessary for the better security of the revenue against smuggling.

Whether any, & if any what changes would be beneficial in the credit system of duties. Whether any additional ware Houses are necessary for Deposits of Foreign merchandise, to give greater security to the collection of our revenue, with any other information he may conceive it would be proper to be communicated to Congress at their next session—

AL, Christie's (mAJs).

December

From Robert Mayo

[This letter survives only in published form.]

Washington City, D. C. Dec. 2, 1830.

To General Andrew Jackson, *President of the United States*:

The enclosed is the scheme of a Secret Alphabet in the hand-writing of a Mr. Hunter, which came into my possession in the manner hereinafter mentioned, and which I confide to your excellency, together with the following statement of facts, to be used in any way your excellency may deem proper. Written out, the Alphabet stands thus:[1]

In making the following statement, it seems to me desirable, with a view to brevity, without impairing or obscuring the facts, to avoid that circumlocution which a minute detail of contingent and immaterial circumstances would involve.

Some time in the month of February last, as nearly as I can recollect, certainly very shortly after General Samuel Houston arrived in this city, I was introduced to him at Brown's hotel, where both of us had taken lodgings. Our rooms were on the same floor and convenient for social intercourse; which, from the General's courteous manners, and my own desire to be enabled to do him justice in my own estimation, relative to his abandoning his family and abdicating the government of Tennessee, readily became frequent and intimate. Upon what he perhaps deemed a suitable maturity of acquaintance, he spoke freely and minutely of his past history. He spoke of his separation from Mrs. H. with great sensibility, and deprecated the injurious impression it had made upon a considerable portion of the public mind, disparaging the *sanity* of his intellect, or rectitude of his moral character. Judging favourably, no doubt, of the progress of our acquaintance, and the prepossessing impression it had made on me in relation to the salubrity and general competency of his intelligence, with rectitude of impulses, he complained of the inadequate defence volunteered in his behalf by the editor of the Richmond Enquirer, and solicited me to write communications for the columns of that paper, and use my friendly interest with the editor for their publication.[2] I promised to make a sketch of something anonymous respecting my favourable impressions, and show it to him. But before I had time or full pliancy of mind to digest any thoughts upon the subject, our frequent interviews, and his confidence in my serving his ends, doubtless, induced him to avow to me more particularly, the ground of his solicitude to have his character and mental competency elevated before the public. He descanted on the immense fields for enterprise in the Indian settlement beyond the Mississippi, and through that as a stepping stone, in Texas; and recommended me to direct my destinies that way. Without making any promises or commitments, I did not discourage, at this stage, his inflated schemes for my advancement, as I had a curiosity now on tip-toe, to hear his romantic projections, for his manner and his enthusiasm were at least entertaining. Accordingly, he went on to develope much of a systematic enterprise, but not half what I have since learnt from another source; perhaps because he discovered that my interest in the subject did not keep pace with the anticipations he had formed for the progress of his disclosures. I learnt from him these facts and speculations, viz:

That he was organizing an expedition against Texas; to afford a cloak to which, he had assumed the Indian costume, habits, and associations, by settling among them, in the neighbourhood of Texas. That nothing was more easy to accomplish, than the conquest and possession of that extensive and fertile country, by the co-operation of the Indians in the Arkansas Territory, and recruits among the citizens of the United States. That in his view it would hardly be necessary to strike a blow to wrest Texas from Mexico. That it was ample for the establishment and maintenance of a separate and independent government from the United States. That the expedition would be got ready with all possible despatch—that the demonstration would and *must* be made in about twelve months from *that time*. That the event of success opened the most unbounded prospects of wealth to those who would embark in it, and that it was with a view to facilitate his recruits, he wished to elevate himself in the public confidence by the aid of my communications to the Richmond Enquirer. That I should have a surgeoncy in the expedition, and recommended me in the meantime, to remove along with him and practise physic among the Indians in the Territory.

As the matter began to assume the shape of a close and substantial proposition, I felt myself under the necessity to be decisive, which put an end to the further detail of his plans. I declined the overtures for my participation; and farther told him, by way of *exonerating* myself from the promise to make communications to the Enquirer, without exciting his apprehensions of my *active* hostility to his views, that it would be very *impolitic* to attract the public attention toward himself in that general and indiscriminate manner, that it would surely invite inquiry from some quarter, about the motives of such communications; which would probably issue in ferreting out his whole scheme. After this, our interviews fell into neglect—our intercourse consisted only of salutations of civility—he sought not my company, and as a matter of prudence I rather avoided his.

In the early part of our intercourse, Gen'l Houston informed me that he had volunteered to assure the president, that he had no desire for an appointment of any sort under his administration—that he believed the president would give him almost any thing he would request—but that he took into consideration, the prejudice with which an appointment conferred on him might be regarded by the public subsisting the circumstances and causes of his exile. Yet I have understood from indisputable authority, that Gen'l Houston did apply for and solicit the appointment to furnish provisions, &c. for the Indians, &c. at the charge of the United States in that quarter, which was denied him—but whether that wish has not been, as to his views, sufficiently substituted by the successful application of a most intimate friend of his, Gen'l Van Forsen, lately of New York, is a problem perhaps not unworthy of inquiry.[3] In the month of March, Gen'l Houston visited Baltimore, Philadelphia and New York, and did intend to have gone as far as Boston, as he informed me, under such circumstances as made the inference of his business a matter hardly to be doubted.

Some time in the month of June, shortly after the adjournment of Congress (or possibly in May, a short time before adjournment) having returned to Richmond, I met with a young gentleman in that place by the name of Murray, from Tennessee, on his return home through the southern states.[4] I had become acquainted with him, in this city, early in the winter. He had also told me that he wanted no employment from the government, but was travelling rather for his personal gratification. A considerable portion of the winter he had passed in a town to the north. When I called on him in Richmond, I made an oblique turn of conversation, upon the mysterious conduct of General Houston; and expressed a surmise, that he must have some very deep views in exiling himself from the civilized world, to settle among the Indians. This, Mr. Murray readily confirmed, apparently, as if he thought it a perfectly innocent and legitimate matter, or, as a thing of common rumour, and of no concern to him—by remarking, that the general was organizing an expedition to take possession of Texas. Upon my asking him how he knew *that*, he replied, 'that it was a good deal spoken of at Washington.' I did not press the subject sufficiently to satisfy my mind whether it was by common rumour, or among recruits only, that Mr. Murray meant it was spoken of, as Mr. M's movements indicated to me, some agency in the business; and too much curiosity on my part, after having declined co-operation, with which he might already be, or might become acquainted, would possibly excite alarm, and induce the parties to re-model their plan with greater secrecy and security.

Shortly after my return to this city, a few weeks ago, a Mr. Hunter, lately dismissed from West Point, came to take lodgings in the house where I boarded. He presently discovered himself to be very indiscreet, and boastful of himself, whether in relation to advantages real or imaginary. On a visit to my apartment, being in pecuniary embarrassments and unable to redeem his baggage from the house he last boarded at, he fell to boasting of the funds he was daily expecting by the mail, of his father's present riches, and still greater wealth before his misfortunes, and of his own possessions, independent of his father, whereof he had already spent five thousand dollars in enjoying life. But, says he, all that is nothing to the unbounded prospects I have of wealth in the future. Indeed! said I, how is it that you can engender wealth to repair your extravagance, with such facility? Ah, says he, that is a secret. I will lay my life said I, it is a scheme upon Texas. He, hesitatingly, said yes, something like it. And said I, General Houston is the projector and conductor of the enterprise? At this, he was so impressed with the conviction that I knew all about the plan, and was one of the recruits, that he declared it to be his belief, and asked me some questions to that effect. I declined answering, remarking that I did not believe he knew any thing about it, and should tell him nothing. Upon this issue, to vindicate his knowledge and alleged fraternity, he set in to tell me every thing.

Says he, there is your name, writing my name on the table in cipher, where it yet stands unobliterated. I was still incredulous. He asked for pen, ink, and paper, and wrote the scheme here enclosed, and then wrote my name at the bottom.

That he was a *bona fide* agent for the recruiting service for this district; and that there were agencies established in all the principal towns, and various parts of the United States; and that this conventional alphabet was the channel of correspondence. That several thousands had already enlisted, along the sea-board, from New England to Georgia, inclusive. That each man paid thirty dollars to the common fund, and took an oath of secrecy and good faith to the cause, on joining the party. That they were to repair, in their individual capacities, as travellers, to different points on the banks of the Mississippi, where they had already chartered steamboats, on which to embark, and thence ply to their rendezvous, somewhere in the territory of Arkansas, or Texas, convenient for action, (the plan not specified to me). That it was contemplated to supersede General Houston in the civil government, when the military operations were over, and that they meant to establish an independent government, and resist any attempt of the United States to wrest so valuable a prize from them.

He finally appealed to me again, with some concern, to say if I were not one of the party. I observed, that I should tell him nothing about it, and changed the subject to some levity, and afterwards avoided his further importunities, &c. I am, very respectfully, your obedient servant,

R. Mayo.

[Endorsed by AJ:] Dr. Mayo—on the contemplated invasion of Texas Private & confidential—a letter to be written (confidential) to the Secretary of the ~~Terittory of~~ the T. of Arrkansa with copy of confidential letter to Wm Fulton Esq sec to the T. of Florida[5]

Printed, Robert Mayo, *Political Sketches of Eight Years in Washington* (Baltimore, 1839), pp. 119–22 (16-0974). Mayo (1784–1864) was a physician and journalist of Richmond, Va. His *Political Sketches* was an exposé of Jacksonian perfidy. This letter appeared in a chapter titled "Of the conspiracy of General Houston to dismember the Mexican dominions, and the connivance of President Jackson to give it effect."

1. Here follows a cipher code with lines and dots representing letters of the alphabet.
2. A brief piece in the *Richmond Enquirer* on May 15, 1829, defended Houston as a "gallant & generous man" who "became the victim of a vague, most unfounded and unjust suspicion." It denied stories that Houston had used violence toward his wife.
3. Houston's associate John Van Fossen (c1789–1858) was later a Michigan politician.
4. Probably Maury.
5. A facsimile of this endorsement in AJ's hand follows the printed letter in *Political Sketches*. AJ wrote Fulton on December 10 (below).

To John Randolph

(Confidential)

Washington Decemb 3d 1830,

My Dear Sir,

My views in regard to the more immediate subject of your letters are so fully detailed in the official communication from the Department of State, which accompanies this, as to leave me but little to say in a private letter.[1] My principle object, therefore, in writing is to assure you of my sympathy in your personal sufferings from bad health, and my continued confidence in your disposition and capacity to serve your country. I beg you to speak your feelings and wishes in regard to the future without reserve, and to count with confidence in the steadiness of my friendship for you. Thoroughly convinced that the interests committed to us by the people, will never be intentionally prejudiced in your hands, you shall not as far as I can avoid it, suffer by the implacable malice of your enemies; And allow me as an act of justice to add that in this ~~particular~~ sentiment and desire, no one more sincerely participates than our mutual friend Mr. Van Buren. From the first inception of your mission to the present moment he has evinced a solicitude for your success and personal credit which could not have been exceeded by your nearest relations. It is unnecessary to enlarge upon the reasons for the preference I have directed to be expressed in the letter addressed to you from the State Depmt. that you should return to St. Petersburg in the Spring, if your health will admit of it, and you should have reason to believe that you will be able to accomplish the whole or a part of what is desired. The motives for that desire will be obvious to you. If however either circumstance should be wanting and you should prefer to return to the U States, in the Spring, let me know your wishes freely; and as early as practicable, and I will see that the necessary directions are sent to you without delay. Altho. I should in common with your friends regret the necessity which compels you to come home, I will nevertheless cherish the hope, that the Country will not in that event, if your life is spared, be wholly deprived of the benefit of your talents and experience. You will probably, by the same conveyance which brings you this, receive my Message to Congress. That every part of it will meet your approbation, is perhaps not to be expected. The condition of the Confederacy will scarcely admit of one which will be entirely acceptable to every part of the union. If you find in it, more to approve than to question, it is perhaps, as much as I have a right to expect.

We are on the eve of a short but I fear a stormy and intemperate session. It is too plain to be disguised that the opposition are determined not to be pleased with any thing that advances the public interest, and mean to throw every obstacle in our way which their malice can invent, and their ingenuity suggest.

I have however no apprehensions for the general result. The people are honest and firm, and if we do not receive their ultimate approbation, it will be because we do not deserve it.

Write me occasionally, and believe me to be your sincere friend

Signed—
Andrew Jackson

Copy, DLC (38). Randolph replied on January 5, 1831.

1. Van Buren instructed Randolph on December 2, approving his temporary absence from Russia while regretting the ill health that compelled it. He gave AJ's consent to Randolph's September 29 proposal (above) to return to Russia in the spring, and then to the U.S. in September or sooner if his health required it (DNA-RG 59, M77-8).

From Mary Ann Eastin

Florence Dec 5th 1830

You see my Dear Uncle that I am again on the wing—Mary McLemore & myself accompanied Mary Coffee out about three weeks since to visit our friends in Alabam[a.] I was delighted again to see my Dear Aunt & Uncle Coffee to whom I am greatly attached, & whom I have a right to include amongst my Dearest & kindest friends but the pleasure of seeing them was greatly embittered by the loss of one whom I had been accustomed to see with them, that was nearer & dearer than any I had on earth. We have paid Uncle Jack & Aunt Eliza a visit, & found her in much better health than usual, & very happy in her fine son.[1]

Before I left home I had the pleasure of receiving your kind affectionate letters, to the first you have before this received Aunt Emilys answer,
making known her intentions with respect to the subject presented to
her view in your letter which seemed more directly to call for an answer
from her, & which I hope if not entirely satisfactory has convinced you of
her affection for you. I am grieved My Dear Uncle to find your mind still
harrassed by this subject & likely to continue so, much agravated by the
idea that your connections have deserted you; but I hope you have or will
discard this idea as unworthy them, & impute their opposition to your
wishes to any thing else than disaffection to you. It is a subject that I have
ever deplored & I hope my Dr Uncle is sensible that I have ever wished &
endeavoured as far as lay in my power to conform to his wishes. It is the
first wish of my heart to see all things reconciled & harmony restored, so
that you may again be happy in the enjoyment of your *friends* around you
& in the affection of those from whom you should naturally expect it, to
solace, & comfort your declining years.

I feel highly gratified My Dr Uncle at the affectionate manner in which
you are pleased to express yourself towards me, & for your kindness in
offering me a place in your family I feel particularly grateful, for which &
innumerable other kindnesses, my heart shall ever be filled with gratitude
& Love

Mary & myself will return home in the course of this or the next weeks,
when I hope to hear some news from you & when I shall again write you.
Tomorrow your busy season commences, & you have to undergo another
winter's siege, it will be shorter than the last however, & I hope not so
toilsome. My best respects to Mr Van Buren & say to him that I condole
with him on the marriage of his belle Miss Calvert which I saw announced
in the last paper[2]

Remember me to Andrew and say to him that I should be very happy
to hear from him, & that in return he shall have all the news that can be
interesting to him—Uncle & Aunt send their love to you—& the Mary's
desire to be affectionately remembered. Mary McLemore is making you
a beautiful map of the world which will be sent on as soon as finished. I
have not heard from home since I left and cannot tell you any news from
there. I have not heard whether cousin Daniel has returned or not.

Give my love to Uncle Andrew—My best respects to Meg Lewis &
all enquiring friends. With many wishes for your health & happiness I
remain your sincerely attached niece

M A Eastin

PS. I have not received your present yet, but suppose it is with Cousin
Daniel, & I assure My Dear Uncle it will be kindly & gratefully
received   I have one request to make of you, which I have alway felt a
delicacy in asking, that is some small token or remembrance of my Dear
Aunt & I hope I need not assure my Dear Uncle that it will be held sacred

by me, as a remembrance of one whose memory I so highly venerate &
who when living I so loved & esteemed[.] Believe me yours truly

M Eastin

[Endorsed by AJ:] Mary Eastin to be answered—

ALS (at December 5, 1836), DLC (49).
    1. Mary McLemore, Mary Coffee, and Mary Ann Eastin were all first cousins and nieces
of Emily Tennessee Donelson. Mary McLemore (b. 1816) was the daughter of John C.
McLemore and Emily's sister Elizabeth; Mary Donelson Coffee (1812–1839) was the daughter of John Coffee and Emily's sister Mary; and Mary Ann Eastin was the daughter of
William Eastin and Emily's sister Rachel. Emily's brother John ("Captain Jack") Donelson
and his wife Eliza had a son, Edward Butler Donelson (1830–1851), born January 18.
    2. On November 11, Rosalie Eugenia Calvert (1806–1845) of Prince George's County,
Md., married Charles Henry Carter of Virginia.

Second Annual Message to Congress

*[On December 6 the Twenty-first Congress convened for its second reg-
ular session and Jackson sent in his second annual message. Signed manuscript copies, accompanied by annual reports of the executive departments
and their subsidiary bureaus, were delivered to both houses and printed
by their order (DSs, DNA-RG 46 and DNA-RG 233 [16-0988]; SDoc 1,
21st Cong., 2d sess. [Serial 203]). The message was widely published and
appears in Richardson, 2:500–529.*

*The Jackson Papers in the Library of Congress contain multiple drafts,
many of them fragmentary, of the message and its component parts (DLC-
76). Principal draftsmen besides Jackson included Martin Van Buren,
Andrew J. Donelson, Amos Kendall, and Nicholas P. Trist. Printed here
are all the drafts by Jackson and the most significant versions by others.]*

Outline by Andrew Jackson

The Message—
    1rst Introduction
    2nd. Our Foreign relations & concerns—
    3rd. the amendment of the constitution &c &c—
    4th. The state of our country, agriculture commerce & manufactures—
and operation of the Tariff, graduation of duties &c so as to place our
own on a fair competition of other countries
    5th. The Treasury—& our public debt—long credits injurious to our
revenue—ware houses for deposits—Smuggling—The Supervisor of the
Treasury—bring again to the view of C. the necessity of power to discharge persons debtors to the Govt.—

6. war Department—military accademy—Indians—The course pursued since last cession under The act of Congress—The result—

7th. The Navy Department—it improvement &c—The case of the John Adams—marine corps—recommend the pay of the Navy officers placed on the same footing as the army

8th. The Post office Department—

9th. Call their attention to the Judiciary & refer to message of last year

10th. The Census being taken, a law apportioning the representation &c &c—

11th. The Bank of the U.S. again brought to view & my former message refered to &c

Introduction—

Foreign affairs—*west India Trade*—Black Sea Treaty with *Turkey*— . . . Russia

The Light House &c & Portland bills . . . noted, sentence constitution will soon afford an opportunity of choosing another & &c—alteration suggested by Mr Barrien—to be looked over

Constitution—

Indians—

Tariff—

public debt—& revenue—Treasury—

war Dept.

Navy Dept

Postmaster Genl

atto. Genl & solicitor &—

District of Columbia

Bank of the United States

The conclusion, in the form of the last Message—

AD, DLC (76). AJ began this outline on the back side of a draft of the conclusion of his first annual message (*Jackson Papers*, 7:629–30).

Draft by Martin Van Buren on foreign relations

[This initial draft, subsequently polished by Andrew J. Donelson, closely prefigured the text in final form (Richardson, 2:500–508).]

I congratulate you Fellow Citizens on your return to the seat of the national Government to resume the important duties committed to you by the People.

It is cause for general satisfaction & for thanks to almighty God, that the return of this period finds our beloved Country in the enjoyment of unequalled prosperity & happiness.

In the midst of these blessings, we are called upon to witness changes in the affairs of other nations which impart the deepest interest to their condition; and may in their consequences, require the exercise of all our patriotism, together with the best exertions of our public functionaries to conduct our concerns in safety through the hostile struggles & convulsions of a disturbed world.

The recent acts of the French People have elicited in this Country a spontaneous and universal burst of applause. This vivid effusion of public sentiment, so creditable to the intelligence and spirit of the American people, was no less consistent with that principle in our foreign policy which, consecrated by the dying admonitions of the Father of his Country enjoins a total abstinence from intervention in the private concerns of other nations. From a people who feel themselves Sovereign—who know that from this proud characteristic is derived much of the unequalled happiness they enjoy—who can point in triumph to their free institutions and challenge comparison with the fruits which they bear, and the intelligence moderation & discretion with which they are administered—from such a people the deepest sympathy was to be expected in such a struggle as that to which I have adverted. The more especially was this to be expected when that struggle was, like the present, of a character to disarm Revolution of its terrors—when it so emphatically announced itself as the noble fruit of great moral developements, dissimilar in every thing from those displays of brute force provoked by grinding oppression which extorted tears of blood by their excesses. Among the considerations which give interest to this undissembled homage of a free people to the great cause of human rights, its perfect exemption from aught like personal feelings or individual preferences, is not the least gratifying. Notwithstanding the high character given of the present King of the French, by him whom we all so warmly love & so highly admire—a character which if sustained to the end, will secure to him the proud appellation of Patriot King—it is nevertheless not in his success, but in that of the great principle which has borne him to the Throne—the paramount authority of the public will—that the American people rejoice.

In turning our attention to affairs more immediately affecting ourselves, we find cause for gratification in what has been, & for hope in what remains to be done.

I am happy to inform you that the anticipations which were indulged at the date of my last communication on the subject of our foreign affairs have been in several important particulars fully realized.

An arrangement has been effected with the Government of Great Britain in relation to the trade between the U.S. and her West Indian & North American colonies. By it, a ~~topic~~ question which has for nearly forty years afforded matter of contention and almost uninterrupted discussion, and been the subject of no less than ~~five~~ six negotiations, has been finally settled in a manner which is thought to promise results highly favourable to the parties.

The abstract right of Great Britain to monopolize the trade ~~of~~ with her colonies, or to exclude us from a participation therein has never been denied by the U.S. But we have contended, & with reason, that if G. B. deems the productions and resources of this Country to be at any time necessary to her colonies, we cannot permit them to be supplied except upon principles of fair reciprocity: and, further, that when she conceives it to be for her interest to open her colonial ports to the vessels of other nations, it is making an invidious and unfriendly distinction to keep them closed agt. those of the U.S.

Antecedently to 1794, a portion of our productions were admitted into the colonial Islands of Great Britain by ~~proclamation of her Executive~~, concessions limited always to the term of one year, but generally renewed from year to year. In the carriage of these productions however, our vessels were not allowed to engage: this being a privilege reserved to British shipping; by which alone our produce could be taken from us, & that of the Islands brought back in exchange. From Newfoundland and her continental possessions all our productions, as well as our vessels, were excluded: with occasional relaxations in regard to the former, by which, in times of distress, they were admitted in British bottoms.

By the Treaty of 1794 she offered to concede to us for a limited time, the right of carrying to her West Indian possessions, in our own vessels not exceeding seventy tons burden, and upon the same terms as British vessels, any productions of the U.S. which British Vessels might import therefrom. But this privilege was coupled with conditions which are supposed to have led to its rejection by the Senate, viz, that American vessels should land their cargoes in the U. States only; and moreover, that they should, during the continuance of the privilege, be precluded from carrying molasses, sugar, coffee, cocoa or cotton either from the said Islands or from the U. States to any other part of the world. G. Britain readily consented to expunge the article from the treaty: and subsequent attempts to arrange the terms of the trade, either by treaty stipulations or concerted legislation, having failed; it has been successively suspended & allowed, according to the separate and varying legislation of the parties.

The following are the prominent points which have in later years separated the two Governments: Besides a restriction whereby all importations into her colonies in American Vessels are confined to our own products carried ~~directly~~ hence—a restriction to which it does not appear that we have ever objected—a leading object on the part of G. Britain has been to prevent us from becoming the carriers of British West India commodities to any other Country than our own. On the part of the U. States it has been contended; 1st. That the subject should be regulated by Treaty Stipulations in preference to separate legislation; 2d. That our productions when imported into the colonies in question, should not be subject to higher duties than the productions of the mother Country or of her other colonial possessions; and 3d. That our vessels should be allowed to participate in the circuitous trade between the U.S. and ~~G. B. through her colonies~~ the British ~~possessions~~ dominions.

The former point, after having[1]

~~a different aspect, they constitute a nearer approach to it than has ever yet been allowed.~~ That the prosperity of the Country, so far as it depends on this trade, will be greatly promoted by the new arrangement, there can be no doubt. Independently of the more obvious advantages of an open and direct intercourse, its establishment will be attended with other consequences of a high value. That which has been carried on since the mutual interdict, under all the expense & inconvenience unavoidably incident to ~~the landing & reshipment of cargoes at what are termed the neutral ports~~ it, would have been insupportably onerous, had it not been in a great degree lightened by concerted evasions in the mode of ~~doing the business~~ making the transhipments at what are called the neutral ports. These indirections are inconsistent with the dignity of nations who have so many motives, not only to cherish feelings of mutual friendship, but to maintain such relations as will stimulate their respective Citizens & subjects to efforts of direct, open & honorable competition only; and preserve them from the influence of seductive & vitiating circumstances.

When your preliminary interposition, was asked at the close of the last session, a copy of the instructions under which Mr McLane has acted, together with the communications which had at that time passed between him & the British Government was laid before you. Although there has not been any thing in the acts of the two Governments upon the subject which requires secrecy, it was thought most proper, in the then state of the negotiation to make that communication a confidential one. So soon however as the evidence of execution on the part of G. Britain is received, the whole matter shall be laid before you. It will then be seen that the apprehension which appears to have found its way into the act passed at your last session, that the restoration of the trade in question might be connected with other subjects, & was sought to be obtained at the sacrafice of the public interest in other particulars was wholly unfounded: and that the change which has taken place in the views of the British Government has been induced by considerations as honorable to both parties as I trust the result will prove beneficial.

☞ This desirable result was, it will be seen, greatly promoted by the liberal and confiding provisions of the act of Congress of the last session; by which our ports were upon the reception and annunciation by the President of the required assurance on the part of Great Britain forthwith opened to her vessels before the arrangement could be carried into effect on her part; pursuing in this act of prospective Legislation a similar course with that adopted by great Britain in abolishing by her act of Parliament in 1825 a restriction before that time existing and permitting our vessels to clear from the colonies on their return voyages for any Foreign Country whatever, before British vessels had been relieved from the restriction imposed by our law, ~~but which she trusted would in due time be done,~~ of returning directly from the U. States to the Colonies—a restriction which she required & expected that we should also abolish. Upon each occasion a limited and temporary advantage was given to the opposite party, but an advantage of no importance in comparison with the restoration of mutual confidence and good feelings, & the ultimate establishment of the Trade in question upon fair principles.[2]

It gives me unfeigned pleasure to assure you that this negotiation has been throughout characterized by the most frank & friendly spirit on the part of Great Britain; and concluded in a manner strongly indicative of a sincere desire to cultivate the best relations with the U. States. To reciprocate this disposition to the fullest extent of my ability is a duty which I shall deem it a privilege to discharge.

Although the result is itself the best commentary on the services rendered to his Country by our minister at the Court of St. James it would be doing violence to my feelings, were I to quit the subject without expressing the very high sense I entertain of the talent & exertion which have been displayed by him on the occasion.

The injury to the commerce of the U. States resulting from the exclusion of our vessels from the Black Sea, and the previous footing of mere sufferance, upon which even the limited trade enjoyed by us with Turkey has hitherto stood, have for a long time been a source of much solicitude to this Government & Several endeavors have ~~consequently~~ been made to obtain a better state of things. Sensible of the importance of the object, I felt it my duty to leave no proper means unemployed to acquire for our flag the same privileges that are enjoyed by the principal powers of Europe. Commissioners were consequently appointed to open a negotiation with the Sublime Porte. Not long after the member of the commission who went directly from the U. States had sailed, the account of the Treaty of Adrianople, by which one of the objects in view was supposed to be secured, reached this Country. The Black Sea was understood to be opened to us. Under the supposition that this was the case, the additional facilities to be derived from the establishment of commercial regulations with the Porte were deemed of sufficient importance to require a prosecution of the negotiation as originally ~~concluded~~ contemplated. It was therefore persevered in and resulted in a Treaty, which will be, forthwith, laid before the Senate. By its provisions, a free passage is secured, without limitation of time, to the vessels of the U. States to & from the Black Sea, including the navigation thereof; and our trade with Turkey is placed on the footing of the most favoured nation. The latter is an arrangement wholly independent of the Treaty of Adrianople: and the former derives much value, not only from the encreased security which under any circumstances, it would give to the right in question; but from the fact ascertained in the course of the negotiation, that, by the construction put upon that Treaty by Turkey, the article relating to the passage of the ~~Black Sea~~ Bosphorus is confined to nations having Treaties with the Porte. The most friendly feelings appear to be entertained by the Sultan, and an enlightened disposition is evinced by him to foster the intercourse between the two Countries by the most liberal arrangements. This disposition it will be our duty & interest to cherish.

(leave a blank of a quarter of a page for Russia).

You are apprised, although the fact has not yet been officially announced to the House of Representatives, that a Treaty was in the month of March last, concluded between the U.S. & Denmark; by which $650,000 are secured to our Citizens as an indemnity for spoiliations upon their commerce in the years _____.[3] This Treaty was ratified by the Senate at the close of its last session; and it now becomes your duty to pass the necessary laws for the organization of the board of Commissioners to distribute the indemnity amongst the claimants. It is an agreeable circumstance in this adjustment, that its terms are in conformity with the previously ascertained approbation of the claimants themselves; thus removeing all pretence for a future agitation of the subject in any form.

(leave a blank of half a sheet for the negotiation now going on with Denmark)

The negotiations in regard to such points in our foreign relations as remain to be adjusted, have been actively prosecuted during the recess. Material advances have been made which are of a character to promise favourable results. Our country is, by the blessing of God, not in a situation to invite aggression; & it will be our fault if she ever becomes so. Sincerely desirous to cultivate the most liberal & friendly relations with all; ever ready to fulfil our engagements with scrupulous fidelity—limiting our demands upon others to mere justice, ~~and~~ holding ourselves ready to do unto them as we would wish to be done by—and avoiding even the appearance of undue partiality to any nation; it appears to me impossible that a simple and sincere application of our principles to our foreign relations can fail to place them ultimately upon the footing on which it is our wish that they should rest.

Of the points referred to the most prominent are—our claims upon France for spoilations upon our commerce—Similar claims upon Spain, together with embarrassments in the commercial intercourse between the two countries which ought to be removed—the conclusion of the treaty of commerce and navigation with Mexico, which has been so long in suspense; as well as the final settlement of limits between ourselves and that Republic, and finally, the arbitrament between the U.S. and Great Britain in regard to the North Eastern Boundary.

The negotiation with France has been conducted by our minister with zeal and ability; and in all respects to my entire satisfaction. Although the prospect of a favourable termination was occasionally dimmed by counter-pretensions to which the U.S. could not assent, he yet had strong confidence of being able to arrive at a satisfactory settlement with the !ate Government. The negotiation has been renewed with the present authorities; and sensible of the universal & lively confidence of our Citizens in the justice and magnanimity of regenerated France, I regret the more not to have it yet in my power to announce the result so confidently anticipated. No ground inconsistent with this expectation has however been taken; and I do not allow myself to doubt that justice will soon to be done us. The magnitude of the claims; the length of time they have remained unsatisfied, & their incontrovertible justice make an earnest prosecution of them by this Government an urgent duty. The illegality of the great mass of seizures & ~~condemnations~~ confiscations out of which they have arisen has never been disputed; and whatever distinctions may have heretofore been set up in regard to the liability of the existing Government, it is quite clear that such considerations cannot now be interposed. It would therefore[4]

The subjects of difference with Spain have been brought to the view of that Government by our minister there with much force & propriety; and the strongest assurances have been received of their early & favourable consideration.

The steps which remained to be taken to place the matter in controversy between G. Britain & the U States fairly before the arbitrator have all been taken in the same liberal & friendly spirit which characterized those before announced. Recent events have doubtless served to delay the decision, but our minister at the court of the distinguished arbitrator has been assured that it will be made within the time limited by the Treaty.

I am particularly gratified in being able to state that a decidedly favourable, &, as I hope, lasting change has been effected in our relations with the neighboring Republic of Mexico. The unfortunate & unfounded ~~disposition~~ suspicion in regard to our disposition, which it became my painful duty on a former occasion to advert to, have been I believe entirely removed; and[5]

command in the adjoining Mexican State; by which it is hoped the quiet of that frontier will be preserved, until a final settlement of the division line removes all ground ~~for future~~ of controversy in future.

The exchange of ratifications of the Treaty concluded last year with Austria has not yet taken place. The delay has been occasioned by the non arrival of the ratification of that Government within the time prescribed by the Treaty. Fresh authority has been asked for by the ~~agent of~~

Representative of Austria; & in the mean time the trade & navigation of the two countries has been placed upon the most liberal footing of our navigation acts.

Several alleged depredations have been recently committed on our commerce ~~under the authority of the King of~~ by the ~~public~~ national vessels of Portugal. They have been made the subject of immediate remonstrance & reclamation. I am not yet possessessed of sufficient information to express a definitive opinion of their character; but expect soon to receive it, no proper means shall be omitted to obtain for our Citizens all the redress to which they may appear to be entitled.

AD, DLC (76).

    1. A page is missing here.

    2. This paragraph is inserted on a separate sheet.

    3. In the margin here Van Buren wrote "get dates." The sent message filled the blank with "1808, 1809, 1810, and 1811" (Richardson, 2:505).

    4. A page is missing here.

    5. A page is missing here.

Drafts by Martin Van Buren on internal improvements and surplus revenue

[A long, very rough draft by Van Buren (DLC-Van Buren Papers [16-1241]) provided the initial basis for the section of the annual message that addressed federal expenditures for internal improvements (Richardson, 2:508–17). These fragments of a subsequent Van Buren draft brought two passages in that section, explaining the pocket vetoes of the Louisville and Portland Canal and lighthouse bills and proposing the distribution of surplus federal revenues among the states, into an approximation of their final form (Richardson, 2:508–10, 514–15). Donelson executed a final stylistic revision.]

    at your last session and almost at the moment of its adjournment two Bills viz the one entitled "an act making appropriations, for building Light Houses, Light boats, beacons & monuments, placing buoys, and for improving harbours & directing surveys—& the other "an act to authorize a subscription for Stock in the Louisville & Portland company were submitted for my approval. It not being in my power to give them the consideration due to their character and importance I was under the necessity of holding them over the session for deliberation. Not having been able to reconcile an approval of all their enactments with my views of duty, they did not receive my signature within the constitutional period, & have of course failed to become laws.[1] They are now returned to the houses in which they respectively originated with the reasons for withholding my approval.

    The practice of defraying out of the Treasury of the U. States the expenses incurred by the establishment & support of Light Houses beacons buoys, & public piers within the bays inlets, harbours & ports of the U. States to render the navigation thereof safe & easy has been co-~~equal~~eval with the adoption of the constitution, & of uninterrupted and undisputed continuance.

as our foreign commerce encreased & was extended into the interior of the Country, by the establishment of ports of entry and delivery upon our navigable rivers, the ~~seats~~ sphere of those expenditures received a correspondent enlargement. Light Houses ~~& other~~ beacons & buoys & public piers, ~~were authorized~~ and the removal of sand bars sawyers & other partial and temporary impediments in the navigable rivers & in the harbours which were embraced in the revenue districts from time to time established by law, were authorized & directed by Congress, upon the same principle, and the expenses incurred thereby defrayed in the same way.

That those expenses have at times been extravagant & disproportionate is very probable. The circumstances under which they ~~were~~ are incurred are well calculated to lead to such results; unless applications of that character are subjected to a close scrutiny. The local advantages arising from the disbursement of the public money, the liberal prices usually paid for the ground on which the light houses are placed, & the creation of a new office in each case, too frequently, it is to be feared stimulate to applications for appropriations for objects of that description which are neither necessary nor useful. The number of light House keepers is already very large and the Bill before me proposes to add _____ more.[2] From some representations upon the subject which have fallen under my observation & which are understood to be entitled to respect there would seem to be the best reason to believe that there has not only been great improvidence in the past expenditures of the Government upon these objects but that the security of navigation has in some instances been injuriously diminished by the multiplication & consequent change of the lights upon the coast. It is in this as well as in other respects our duty to avoid all unnecessary expenses as well as every encrease of patronage not called for by the public service. But in the discharge of that duty in this particular it must not be forgotten that in relation to our foreign commerce the burden & benefit of accommodating and protecting it necessarily go together, and must do so as long as the public revenue is drawn through the custom House. Whatever gives facility and security to navigation cheapens imports, & all who consume them, wherever residing, are alike interested in whatever has that effect. If they consume they ought as they now do pay. If they do not consume they do not pay. The consumer in the most inland State derives the same advantage from the necessary and prudent expenditure for the facility and security of our foreign commerce and navigation as the consumer in a maritime State. Other local expenditures have not of themselves a correspondent operation.

To a bill making *direct* appropriations for such objects I should not have with-held my assent. The one now returned does so in several particulars but it also contains appropriations for surveys of a local character which I could not approve. I have therefore allowed it to fail and it gives me satisfaction to find that no serious public inconvenience has resulted from the act, nor will it I trust be cause of regret that an opportunity will be thereby afforded for Congress to review its provisions under circumstances better calculated for full investigation than those under which it was passed.[3]

In speaking of *direct* appropriations I mean to exclude the practice which has obtained to some extent, & to which I have in one instance, & in a different capacity, given my own assent—that of subscribing to the stock of private associations.

Positive experience and a more thorough consideration of the subject have convinced me of the impropriety as well as inexpediency of such investments. All improvements effected by the funds of the nation for general use should be open to the enjoyment of our own Citizens exempted from the payment of tolls or ~~other~~ any impositions of that character. The practice of thus mingling the concerns of the Government with those of the States or of individuals is inconsistent with the objects of its institution and highly impolitic. The successful operation of the Federal system can only be preserved by confining it to the pure and simple but yet important objects for which it was designed. The practice referred to if allowed to progress as it has recently done must in a short time change the entire character of this Government. Nor can I perceive how bills authorizing such subscriptions can be otherwise regarded than as bills for revenue and consequently subject to the rule in that respect provided by the constitution. If the interest of the Government in private companies is subordinate to those of individuals, the management & controul of a portion of the public funds is delegated to an authority unknown to the constitution & beyond the supervision of our constituents. If superior its officers & agents will be constantly exposed to imputations of oppression and favouritism. Direct prejudice to the public interest or an alienation of the affections & respect of portions of the people, may therefore, in addition to the general discredit resulting to the Government from embarking with its constituents in pecuniary speculations, be looked for as the probable fruits of such associations. It is no answer to this objection to say that the extent of consequences like these cannot be great from a limited & small number of investments because our experience in other matters teaches us & we are not at liberty to disregard its admonitions, that unless an entire stop is put to it, it will soon be impossible to prevent their accumulation until they are spread over the whole country & be made to embrace many of the private & appropriate concerns of individuals.

This mode of aiding such works is also in its nature deceptive & in many cases conducive to improvidence in the ~~app~~ administration of the ~~public~~ national funds. Appropriations will be obtained with much great facility & granted with less security to the public interest when the measure is thus disguised, than when definitive & direct applications of ~~the~~

~~public~~ money ~~is~~ are asked for. The interests of the nation would doubtless be better served by avoiding all such indirect modes of aiding particular objects, & in a government like ours more especially, should all ~~its~~ public acts be as far as practicable simple undisguised & intelligible, that they may become fit subjects for the approbation, or correction of the people. The Bill authorizing a subscription to the L & P. canal affords a striking illustration of the difficulty of withholding additional appropriation for the same object when the first ~~wrong~~ erroneous step is taken by the instituting a partnership between the Government & private companies. It proposes a third subscription on the part of the U.S. when each preceding one was at the time regarded as the extent of the aid which Government was to render to that work; and the accompanying bill for Light Houses &c contains an appropriation for a survey of the bed of the river, with a view to its improvement by removing the obstruction which the canal is designed to remedy, & which improvement if successful would afford a free passage of the river, & thus render the canal ~~comparatively~~ entirely useless. To such improvidence is the course of legislation in regard to internal improvements which has hitherto obtained subject, even with the best intentions on the part of Congress.

although the motives which have influenced me in

AD, DLC (76).
1. AJ circled the wording after "views of duty" in this sentence for replacement by "I cannot approve them. They are now returned &c &c." The final text omitted the sentence altogether.
2. The final text filled the blank with "fifty-one."
3. AJ circled "allowed it to fail" for replacement by "disapproved it." The final text omitted the phrase.

appropriations should insist on being redressed in those hereafter to be made, at the expense of those States who have already so largely, & disproportionately participated, we have as matters now stand, but little security that the attempt will ~~not merely~~ do more than to change the inequality complained of from one quarter to another.

Thus viewing the subject, I have heretofore felt it to be my duty to recommend the adoption of some rule for the distribution of the surplus funds, which may at any time ~~come into~~ remain in the Treasury after the national debt ~~is~~ shall have been paid, among the States, in proportion to their respective representations, in Congress, to be applied, by them, to objects of internal improvement.

although this plan has met with favour in some portions of the Union, it has also elicited objections which merit ~~deli~~ the most deliberate consideration. A brief notice of those objections here, will not therefore, I trust be regarded as either out of place or irrelevant.

They rest, as far as they have come to my knowledge on the following grounds, viz 1st an objection to the ratio of distribution 2ly. an apprehension that the existence of such a regulation would ~~lead to~~ produce improvident and oppressive taxation, to raise the funds for distribution, & ~~lastly~~ 3dly. that the mode proposed would lead to the construction of works of a local nature, to the exclusion of such as are of a general & as would consequently be of a more useful character, & lastly that it would create a discreditable & injurious dependence on the part of the State Governments upon the Federal power ~~derogatory to their character~~. ~~Those Some~~ Of those who object to the ratio of representation as the basis of distribution some insist that the exportations of the respective States would constitute one ~~that is preferable~~ that would be more equitable, & others again, that, the extent of their respective territories would furnish a standard, which would be more expedient, & sufficiently equitable. The ratio of representation presented itself to my mind, as it still does, as one of obvious equity, because of its being the ratio of contribution, whether the funds to be distributed be derived from the customs or from direct taxation. It does not however follow that its adoption is indispensable to the establishment of the system proposed. There may be considerations appertaining to the subject, which would render a departure from the rule of contribution to some extent, out of respect to claims of a different character, expedient, & as it respects the interests of the whole equitable; ~~It is not~~ nor is it absolutely necessary, that, the basis of distribution be ~~necessarily~~ exclusively confined to either ground. It may, if in the judgment of those whose right it will be to fix it, it is deemed politic & just to do so, have regard to all.

In my first annual Message I stated it to be my opinion "that it was not probable that any adjustment of the Tariff upon principles satisfactory to the people of the Union, will, until a remote period, if ever, leave the Government without a considerable surplus in the Treasury beyond, what may be required for its current service."[1] I have had no cause to change that opinion, but much to confirm it. Should these expectations be realized, a suitable fund would thus be produced for the plan under consideration to operate upon & if ~~not~~ there be no such fund its adoption will in my opinion work no injury to any interest. For I cannot subscribe to the apprehension that the establishment of the proposed system would tend to the encouragement of improvident & excessive legislation of the character supposed. Whatever the proper authority, in the exercise of constitutional power, shall at any time hereafter decide to be for the general good will, in that, as in other respects deserve, & ~~doubtless~~ receive the acquiescence, & support of the whole country; & we have ample security, that every abuse of power in that regard, by the agents of the people, will receive a speedy & effectual corrective at their hands. The views which I take of the future, founded on the obvious & encreasing improvement of all classes of our Fellow Citizens, in intelligence, & public, & private virtue, leave me without much apprehension on that head.

I do not doubt, that those who come after us, will be as much alive as we are, to the duty obligatory upon all the trustees of political power, to ~~save~~ exempt those for whom they act, from all unnecessary burthens and as sensible of the great truth, that, the resources of the nation, beyond those which are required for the immediate & necessary purposes of Government, can no where so well be deposited, as the pockets of the people who supply them.

It may sometimes happen that the interests of particular States, would not be deemed to co-incide with the general interest in relation to improvements within such states; But if the danger to be apprehended from this source is sufficient to require it, a discretion might be reserved in Congress, to effect improvements of a more general character, affecting several states, and which such states might not be disposed to provide for, by directing the application to such objects of the quotas of such state, or in some other manner. It may however be assumed as a safe general rule, that such improvements as serve to increase the prosperity of the respective States in which they are made, by giving new faclities to trade, and thereby encreasing the wealth, & comfort of their inhabitants, constitute the surest mode of confering permanent and substantial advantages upon the whole. The strength, as well as the true glory of the confederacy, is ~~primarily~~ mainly founded on the prosperity & power of the several independent sovereignties of which it is composed, and the ~~facility~~ certainty with which they can be brought into successful active co-operation through the agency of the Federal Government.

It is moreover within the knowledge of such as are at all conversant with public affairs that schemes of Internal Improvement have from time to time been

AD, DLC (76).
   1. Richardson, 2:451.

Draft fragment by Andrew Jackson Donelson on federal relations

[This fragment by Donelson begins with a revision of the closing sentence in Van Buren's original long draft on internal improvements and surplus revenue, making it nearly identical to the final text (Richardson, 2:517). The paragraph that follows resembles nothing in Van Buren's draft or in the message itself.]

within the sphere ~~of operations~~ intended ~~for it~~ by those who modelled and those who adapted it—which shall lead to the extinguishment of the national debt in the shortest period, and impose the lightest burthens on our constituents, shall receive from me, ~~by whomsoever it may be suggested,~~ a firm and cordial support.

In conclusion I beg leave to say that something is due even to the prejudices and passions of our political brethren, because we are all subject to like infirmities. Who would sacrifice our union to the pride of opinion or the point of honor? It is better to yield much that it is right than to sacrifice the inestimable blessings of our present Government. How will that man stand before God and posterity who in struggling to obtain some local or temporary good though of much importance, shall break asunder the bonds of our union and convert millions of brethren into aliens and enemies. Least of all will he stand excused, who, wielding the powers of the General Government, shall abandon the safe course of leaving to the States the management of their internal concerns, and, in attempting to subject them intirely to a central power, force them to seek in seperation the preservation of their useful existence and of the liberties of the people. The world is governed too much. We partake of the common error. We do not reflect that it is more the true end of Government to protect than to direct or control. Men need Government to enable them to pursue their several occupations unmolested. Our states established the general Government to enable them to exercise their sovereign powers unmolested. Men do not choose a Government to oppress them, nor did our states create the General Government to destroy them. They expected to be left independent in the exercise of every reserved power. The cords of union may be drawn too tight. There are interests, opinions, habits and prejudices which must not be brought into conflict. Why has the fairest portion of Europe been recently drenched in blood? Not because Holland and Belgium had not a common interest in Union, but the union was too close. Had each been left to the unrestrained indulgence of its own peculiar opinions and prejudices and the management of its

AD, DLC (76).

Draft by Nicholas Philip Trist on changing the mode of presidential elections

[This is the earliest extant draft of a passage in the annual message recommending amendment of the constitution to provide for a direct popular vote for president (Richardson, 2:518–19). Subsequent versions by Trist and Donelson revised and expanded the text into final form.]

Among the objects of domestic concern, I cannot forbear to bring to your consideration, as first in importance, that part of the constitution which relates to the election of chief Magistrate. The necessity for an alteration of the present mode, has been made so clear by experience of its evils, &c as well as the many able discussions which these have elicited on the floor of Congress & elsewhere, that I feel I should be wanting in a proper solicitude ~~for~~ in the value of our institutions, if I omitted to recommend the adoption of some new provision, for the exercise by the People, of this important attribute of their Sovereignty. Our system fortunately contemplates this reccurrence to first principles, without endangering its harmony, or interrupting the operation of the Government: differing, in this particular, from all that have preceded it; and thus secured, it is to be hoped, against that decay which has marked the progress of every former republic. Our fellow citizens too, who have kept steadily in view, the principles on which our system is founded; when they perceive ~~in~~ the incompetent action ~~of~~ in any part ~~of it~~, do not require to be reminded of the duty which they owe to themselves to correct it. While they are sensible that every ~~abuse~~ evil arising in the exercise of power, is not necessarily indicative of defective organization; and that temporary causes may sometimes, without calling for interference, give to one or more of the political elements an undue preponderance over others: yet, when the habitual recurrence of ~~those~~ such evils, or a single instance traced to its source, manifests an organic defect; this ~~will should~~ will not, surely, ~~be suffered to remain~~, through too scrupulous a veneration for the work of our ancestors, be suffered to remain. The framers of the Constitution considered it an experiment, committed to the virtue & intelligence of the great mass of their countrymen, in whose ranks they themselves also were to perform

AD, DLC (76).

Draft by Andrew Jackson on Indian removal

[The versions that follow by Donelson and Amos Kendall, and a subsequent reworking by Donelson, revised this initial Jackson draft toward its final form in the annual message (Richardson, 2:519–23).]

Indians—
It is a subject of pleasing reflection that the Indians within the states are manifesting a disposition to move from the places they at present occupy. Besides the prospect of increased happiness & benefit to themselves, the unpleasant controversies which may arise, as to state, and general government authority, will be avoided, and conflicts arising therefrom be prevented. Towards the aboriginies of ~~our~~ the country none feels a more lively or deep interest than myself, or would go farther in redeeming them from their present condition, and to render them a happy & prosperous people. I have said to them candidly what from the exercise of my best judgment I believed to be correct, that within the limits of a state, the general government, could not extend to them its fostering protection; that the superintending care of the government, could not ~~extend~~ be granted to the extent of inhibiting the states, to control & direct them, as other citizens of the states are controlled. The acts and laws of a state, within its limits must claim a paramount operation over these of the general government in all cases, except where having parted with the power, the exercise of it, is rightfully in the hands of the Federal authority. "To regulate trade among the several states, and with the Indian tribes," is the

authority upon this subject derived from the constitution. Under this grant of authority, it is not pretended, or rather should not be, that the states are precluded, from the exercise of a wholsome & equitable legislation over persons & property within their limits. The states are sovereign except to the extent only that they have parted with their sovereignty, "for the common defence & general welfare" of the country. I have been unable to perceive any sufficient reason, why the Red man more than the White, may claim exemption from the municipal laws of the state within which they reside; and governed by that belief, I have so declared, and so acted. With these impressions a removal appeared to me, to be the only means whereby to obtain for the Indians prosperity and happiness; and to place them in a situation, where relieved from the operation of state laws, the fostering care of the govt. could be extended to them to greater advantage, and where they must be happier

These things have been brought to the consideration of our Indian brothers and fully explained. Some of the tribes, the choctaws, & chickasaws, perceiving the force of these kind suggestions made to them, with great unanimity have determined to avail themselves of the liberal offers presented ~~to them~~ by the act of the last congress and to remove beyond the river Mississippi. Treaties have been entered into with them, which in due time will be submitted ~~to the Senate~~ for ~~their~~ consideration. In making these arrangements, reason & argument to convince, not threats, or force, to intimidate, have been the instruments employed. Nothing uncandid or unfair has been resorted to whereby to create an improper influence; to their judgment and sound reflection under all the circumstances with which they were surrounded, was the matter submitted to them. Being the last treaties ever to be made with them, a liberal & generous policy was deemed advisable to be pursued, to afford them an evidence of the justice of the government & the means of becoming an improved & prosperous people at their new homes.

When our fore fathers arrived upon these shores they found the Indians, the owners and occupants of the soil. As the white population increased, the Red man, yielding up his place, he gradually and peaceably retired, until now, in the distant forest only, does he find a resting place. Our sympathies should be arroused in their favour; and every kindness and good feeling exercised towards them; not by encouraging them to remain within the states, where it is impossible they can be contented and happy; but by giving them a new home, free from interruption, where they may dwell under their own laws, afford the only means by which they can be preserved, made happy, and perpetuated.

AD, DLC (76).

Draft by Andrew Jackson Donelson on Indian removal

It is a subject of pleasing reflection that the Indians within the limits of the States are manifesting a disposition to accept the provisions which are contained in the act of the last session of Congress for their removal. Besides the prospect of increased happiness and benefit to themselves inviting this step, its importance in terminating the conflict between the authority of the general and State Governments which the situation of the Indians in regard to each is so well calculated to create, has made the execution of that law an object of the deepest solicitude.

Towards the aborigines of the country no one can indulge a more friendly feeling than myself, or would go further to reclaim them from their wandering habits and make them a happy and prosperous people as far as they are susceptible of this change by the arts of civilization. I have stated to them candidly what my experience and best judgment have suggested to be the duty of the general Government, both in regard to their true interests and the power of the states within whose limits they are now located. They have been informed that the superintending care of this Government could not be so extended by Treaty as to operate as an inhibition of the right of those states to controul them as other citizens are within their territorial bounds; and that the benefits of the Treaty stipulations under which they had enjoyed the protection of the United States must be construed as subordinate to the right of the States, in contravention of which those Treaties could not, and were never designed to operate. In recognizing this principle, I feell pursuaded that I do but justice to those sovereign members of our union whose legislation over the persons and property within their chartered limits cannot be circumscribed by any other power than that which they have voluntarily transferred to the constitution and there defined with too much precision and care to make the reservation of this to themselves a question of doubt in my mind. "To regulate trade among the several states and with the Indian tribes" is the only authority over the subject which they have given to the United States. The concession that this authority contemplated the residence of the Indian tribes within the limits of the states, as a distinct people, independent of the power and jurisdiction of the states, would defeat the safeguard which another provision of the constitution contains in behalf of the state jurisdiction, and is in other respects so irreconcileable to the general spirit of the terms of union, that I could not think for a moment of admitting it in the views which I felt it my duty to present to the Indians. I have been unable to perceive any good reason why the Red man more than the White should claim exemption from the municipal laws of the States within whose limits they reside; and have accordingly in my intercourse with him rather endeavored to explain the justice of this obligation than to use it as a means of effecting his removal against his consent.

With a full understanding of this subject the Choctaw and chickasaw tribes have with great unanimity determined to avail themselves of the liberal offers presented by the act of the last session of congress, and have agreed to move beyond the Mississippi river. Treaties have been concluded with them which will be submitted to ~~the~~ your consideration ~~of the senate~~ in due time. In making these Treaties, reason and argument to convince, not threats nor force to intimidate them have been the instruments employed. To their judgment and best reflection under a full view of their true condition, were the terms of the Government submitted. As they are the last Treaties in all probability which will be made with them, they are characterised by great liberality, and while they afford evidence of the justice of the Government secure to them the means of future prosperity and improvement in a much higher degree than they could enjoy within the limits of the States of Alabama & Mississippi.

When our Forefathers became acquainted with the Indians, they were the owners and occupants of the soil; but a fate not the less just because it excites our sympathies has changed the relative condition of the desendents

[Endorsed by AJ:] reviewed & copied—These sheets to be preserved—

AD, DLC (76).

Draft by Amos Kendall on Indian removal

It gives me pleasure to announce to Congress, that the benevolent policy of the government, steadily pursued for ~~the last~~ nearly thirty years, in relation to the removal of the Indians beyond the white settlements, is approaching to a happy consummation. Two important tribes have accepted the provision made for their removal at the last session of Congress; and it is believed, that their example and the obvious advantages to themselves, will induce the remaining tribes also to seek new homes.

The consequences of a speedy removal will be important to the United States, to individual states, and to the Indians themselves. The pecuniary advantages which it promises to the government, are the least of its recommendations. It puts an end to all possible danger of collision between the authorities of the general and state governments on account of the Indians. It will place a dense and civilized population in large tracts of country now occupied by a few savage hunters. By opening the whole territory between Tennessee on the north and Louisiana on the south to the settlement of whites, it will incalculably strengthen the southwestern frontier and render the adjacent states strong enough to repel future invasion without aid from a distance. It will clear the whole state of Mississippi and the western part of Alabama of Indian occupancy and enable those states to advance rapidly in population, wealth and power. It will separate the Indians from immediate contact with settlements of whites, free them from the power of the states, enable them to pursue happiness in their own way under their own rude institutions, will retard the progress of decay which is lessening their numbers, and perhaps cause them gradually, under the protection of the government and through the influence of good men, to cast off their savage habits and become in time an interesting, civilized and Christian community. These consequences, some of them so certain and the rest so probable, make the complete execution of the plan sanctioned by Congress at their last session, an object of much solicitude.

Towards the aborigines of the country, no one can indulge a more kindly feeling than myself, or would go further in attempts to reclaim them from their wandering habits and make them a happy and prosperous people. I have endeavored to impress upon them my own solemn convictions of the duties and powers of the general government in relation to the state authorities and the Indians living within their borders. They have been informed, that the superintending care of this government could not be so extended by treaty as to exempt them from the legislative control of the states within which they reside, and that the treaty stipulations under which they have enjoyed its protection, must be construed as subordinate to the sovereign right of the states to subject all persons within their limits, of whatever race or complexion, to the control of their laws. In recognizing and enforcing this principle, I feel persuaded that I do but justice to the constitutional rights of the sovereign states which compose our confederacy. In the constitution can be found no relinquishment of the preexisting right of the states to fix the civil and political condition of all persons living within their borders and making them amenable to their tribunals, whether black, white or red. "To regulate ~~trade~~ commerce among the several states and with the Indian tribes" is the only power over the subject which the states have delegated to the general government. By sufferance of some of the states, several Indian tribes have been permitted to maintain a separate existence within their limits and exercise most of the attributes of sovreignty. But, as before the adoption of the federal constitution, so at this time, whenever a state chooses to extend its jurisdiction over those bodies of men, they cease to be separate tribes, and can be treated by the United States only as citizens of the state. They are no longer one of those "Indian Tribes" with which the Congress of the United States may "regulate ~~the trade and intercourse~~ the commerce." For the justice of the laws passed by the states ~~Legislatures~~ within the scope of their reserved powers, they are not responsible to this government. As individuals we may entertain and express our opinions of their acts; but as a government, we have as little right to control them as we have to prescribe laws to foreign nations. A state of things might indeed arise, in which it would be the duty of this government, in the performance of its constitutional obligations, to aid the states in maintaining and enforcing their laws and preventing their dismemberment.

With a full understanding of the subject, the Choctaw and Chickasaw Tribes, have, with great unanimity, determined to avail themselves of the liberal offers presented by the act of Congress, and have agreed to remove beyond the Mississippi river. Treaties have been made with them, which, in due season, will be submitted to your consideration. In making these treaties, reason and argument have been used to convince them, not threats or force to intimidate ~~them~~. They were made to understand their true condition in relation to the state and general governments, and they have preferred maintaining their savage independence in the western forests to submitting to the laws of the states in which they now reside. These treaties, being probably the last which will ever be made with them, are characterized by great liberality on the part of the government. They give the Indians a liberal sum in consideration of their removal, & secure to them not only an ample territory west of the Mississippi, but also the means of easy removal and comfortable subsistence on their arrival at their new homes. If it be their real interest ~~of~~ to maintain a separate existence, they will there be at liberty to do so without the inconveniences and vexations to which they would unavoidably have been subject in Mississippi and Alabama.

Humanity has often wept over the fate of the aborigines of this country, and Philanthropy has been busily employed for two centuries in devising means to avert it. But the progress of their decay has never been for a moment arrested, and one by one have many powerful tribes disappeared from the earth. To follow to the tomb the last of his race and tread on the graves of extinct nations, excites melancholy reflections. But true Philosophy reconciles the mind to these vicissitudes in nations as it does to the extinction of one generation to make room[1]

our confederacy.

May we not hope, therefore, that all good citizens, and none more zealously than those who think the Indians oppressed by subjection to the laws of the states, will unite with the government in attempting to open the eyes of those ~~Indians~~ children of the forest to their true condition, and, by a speedy removal, relieving them from all the evils, real or imaginary, present or prospective, which they feel or fear.

[Endorsed by AJ:] The Indians—This perfect & to be copied—

AD, DLC (76).
  1. A page or more is missing here.

Draft by Andrew Jackson on the tariff

[This sketch on the tariff and the customs by Jackson underwent several redraftings, including the three that follow, on its way to final form in the message (Richardson, 2:523–25).]

Among the numerous cause for gratitude to the Supreme being, and of congratulation to the nation, the prosperous state of our import revenues is not to be overlooked. It will not only afford the means more rapidly than was anticipated of absorbing the public debts, but it tends to shew that the Tariff has not been productive of these evils to our commerce which were so confidenly anticipated by its oponents—by the vigilence of our Custom House officers smuggling has been measurably kept down and the revenue laws well executed considering how great the temptations for violating them; The public debt secured to be paid I would recommend a judicious revision of the Tariff &c &c guarding the labour of our own country by vestal vigilence, by placing it on a fair competition with those of other countries, and by reducing the duty on all articles that do not come in competition with our own labour &c &c—
The public

AD, DLC (76).

Draft by Andrew Jackson Donelson on the tariff

With whatever pride and satisfaction we may justly contemplate our national character it must in candour be admitted that it is not intirely exempt from that weakness common to human nature which mingling feeling with interest is too apt to forget the just limits of both. It is this tendency of the public mind which makes it so difficult to restrain the measures of the Government in relation to the Tariff to that medium course by which ruinous revulsions in the affairs of our citizens can alone be avoided, and those conflicting interests inseparable from any state of society best reconciled.

The excesses to which this subject is exposed, arising from its practical effects upon private interests which have varied with circumstances, are, on the one hand, a disposition to oppose any encouragement of our manufactures by regulations of the commercial Tariff adopted to that end altho' a discreet exercise of that power has been repeatedly recommended by Washington, Jefferson, Madison, and Monroe, and acted upon by Congress in almost every stage of the Govt. and on the other hand, a temptation to lose sight of national objects and convert a measure which should be used alone with reference to the general good, to the promotion of private and local interests, regardless of its oppressive operation upon other quarters of the country equally entitled to the favor and protection of the Government; and what is perhaps worse than all to make this great subject so deeply affecting the private interests of every man in the community subservient to the sinister and short sighted views of faction.

I cannot, fellow citizens, too earnestly for my own feelings, or the common good of all, warn you against the blighting consequences of a course so exceptionable   The public voice must effectually discountenance it before the Tariff can be so adjusted as to prove satisfactory to the great body of the people and be accommodated to their general interests.

AD, DLC (76).

Draft by Amos Kendall on the tariff

and comforts of life except in cases of extreme necessity. It depresses every species of industry without benefit to any, and taxes alike poverty and wealth ~~for the support of government~~.

Such a modification of the Tariff as will abrogate or reduce the import duties on all articles which enter into the necessaries and comforts of life, I should view as peculiarly adapted to the promotion of every species of industry and of none more than manufacturing.

Perhaps the best criterion to determine whether a particular interest ought to be protected, is to submit it singly to the representatives of the people. If, after full consideration unbiassed by any extraneous matter, a majority decides that its protection will conduce to the general good, there is little danger of injury or wrong in so adjusting the Tariff as to produce that result. It is worthy of inquiry, whether, in the adjustment of the existing Tariff, two or more minor interests, neither of which singly it was the interest of the people or the will of Congress to protect, did not, by combination, secure a common protection at the expence of the general good. It is obvious that no union of minor interests can produce an aggregate greater than the same number of major interests; and each new interest added, instead of increasing the propriety of the measure, could only increase the balance against it. If portions of the Tariff were introduced by a combination of minorities in Congress, representing local and minor interests, it follows that injustice was done to the people which ought to be repaired.

It is also worthy of inquiry whether the agricultural interest would not be materially benefitted by a reduction of duties on such imported luxuries as are paid for abroad with our exported produce. If the merchant pays for the wine he drinks with produce purchased from the farmer, it is the farmer's interest that the importation and consumption of wine should increase, because his market will be enlarged in the same proportion.

The Tariff is a subject of much delicacy, and, on account of the interests involved, should be touched with caution. While an abandonment of the policy in which it originated, a policy coeval with our government and enforced through successive administrations, is neither to be expected nor desired, the people have a right to demand and a large portion of them do demand, that it shall be so modified as to correct abuses and obviate injustice. It must not be forgotten, that the only just object of the protecting policy is the general good. It is an abuse, when it is used as a means of laying a perpetual tax on one species of industry for the benefit of another. The abuse is glaring, when it is used to concentrate benefits on one section of the Union and burdens on another. It is an abuse, when it taxes the whole labor of the Union for the protection of minute and local interests. It is an abuse, when selfish combinations protect a mass of ~~minor~~ local interests at the expence of a double weight of general interests, taxing the whole people for the benefit of a few. The abuse will be fatal to the purity of our government and dangerous to the union, should the time come when the revenues thus raised ~~shall~~ will not be needed for any purpose of public utility; and members of the government, instead of economizing the public funds, shall seek new objects of expenditure as an apology for continuing unjust burdens upon the people. The public debt will soon be paid. Without a change in the Tariff ~~our revenue~~ it will then produce an annual surplus revenue of about ten millions of dollars. Unless Congress give it back to the states or fix on a general system of internal improvements, there is ground to fear that it will engender habits of profusion and practices of corruption unexampled in republican government. It behoves the people to consider, whether they will be taxed ten millions of dollars in the necessaries and comforts of life, merely that their government may have the power, by expending it at will, to administer to the cupidity of its favorites, and, in the manner of distribution, corrupt the very fountains of its authority.

AD, DLC (76).

Draft on the tariff

Among the numerous causes for gratitude to the Supreme Being and of congratulation to the Nation, the prosperous condition of our import revenues deserves particular remembrance. They promise the means of extinguishing the public debt more speedily than was anticipated and furnish a practical illustration of the effects of the existing Tariff upon our commercial interests. The present adjustment of the Tariff is objected to by some as unconstitutional, and in some of its parts by almost all as inexpedient.

The power to lay duties on imports originally belonged to each separate State. The right to adjust those duties with the view of giving protection and encouragement to manufactures, is so intirely an incident to that power that it cannot exist without it. The states delegated the power to the General Government without limitation or restriction. It is therefore, possessed by the General Government with all its incidents, in as full a manner as it was by the states.[1] One of these incidents is the right so to adjust the duties as to give protection and encouragement to domestic manufactures and other kinds of industry. If this right be not possessed by the General Government, it is extinct. The states do no possess it, because they have delegated to the general government the entire power to which it belongs. If it be not in the general Government, our political system presents the anomaly of a people voluntarily stripped of the right to foster their own industry by legislation and counteract by retaliatory measures the selfish policy of foreign nations. It is not extinct, because there is no constitutional inhibition of its exercise, it is vested in the general government, because the whole power to which it belongs was delegated by the States. In this conclusion I am confirmed by the recommendations of the first President under the constitution and each of his successors,[2] by the uniform practice of Congress; the continued acquiescence of the states and the general understanding of the people. In the inexpediency of the present adjustment of the Tariff, almost all agree. Some despair of a remedy without a resort to threats or resistance; others fear to touch the objectionable parts, lest those they approve, should be involved in the ruin. I am persuaded that both do injustice to the American people, and to their representatives in Congress. Our people are not unjust, nor are their representatives corrupt. The general interest is the interest of each. My confidence is entire, that to secure the adoption of such modifications of the Tariff as the general interests require, it is only necessary to make those interests understood.

It is an infirmity of our nature to mingle our interests and prejudices with the operation of our reasoning powers, and attribute to the object of our likes and dislikes, qualities they do not possess, and effects they do not produce. The effects of the present Tariff are doubtless over-estimated, both in its evils and its advantages. By one set of reasoners, the reduced prices of cotton, and other agricultural products is ascribed to this agent, and the reduced price of manufatured articles, by another. The truth probably is, that neither is at all affected, or but very slightly, by its operations. The depreciation of prices extends through the commercial world and embraces not only the raw material and manufatured article, but provisions and lands. The cause, therefore is deeper and more pervading than the Tariff of the United States. It may probably be found in the increased value of the precious metals produced by a reduction of the supply. While commerce has rapidly extended its dominion and population increased: The supply of gold and silver, the universal medium of exchange, has been greatly interrupted by civil convulsions in the mining countries. A partial effect has doubtless been produced upon the price of produce and manufatures, by an increase of operations and improvements in machinery. On the whole, there has not been so much a reduction in the value of lands, produce and manufatures as an appreciation in the standard of value. More value is represented by the dollar than formerly. The effect has been like making the yard longer or the bushel larger. It is not therefore, in the general depreciation of the price of produce that the evils of the Tariff are felt, nor are its benefits to be found in the diminished price of manufactured articles. Were it blotted out of existence, the former would not be greater while the latter would perhaps be the less.

The chief object of a Tariff should be revenue. Its exactions may be so adjusted as to encourage manufactures. In this adjustment, it is the duty of the Government to be directed by the general good. Objects of national importance only ought to be protected. Of these, the productions of our soil, of our mines and our workshops, essential to national defence occupy the first rank. Whatever other species of domestic manufature can with temporary protection compete with the foreign article on equal terms, merits also the attention of government in the adjustment of the Tariff. It is the interest of the farmer that the manufacturor shall be where he can furnish him with his raw material and provisions, if he do not have to pay too much for it.

The present Tariff taxes some of the comforts of life unnecessarily high, undertakes to protect interests too local and minute to justify a general tax for their protection, and attempts to force the establishment of some species of manufatures for which the country is not ripe.

Much relief will be felt from the measures of last session, but the same policy may be beneficially extended. Of all taxes next to a poll tax, a tax on the food and drink, and other necessaries & comforts of the citizens, is the most odious and unjust.

It falls upon men, not in proportion to their ability to pay, but in proportion to the comforts they enjoy. The rich do not feel it; but it sometimes obliges the poor to abridge their comforts. Whether it comes in the shape of an excise upon bread or beer or an import duty upon sugar and tea, it is the same in principle and effect. In other countries, it has been made to reach every article of food and drink, clothing and furniture, fire and light, until the profits of labour have been entirely absorbed, producing penury, wretchedness, vice and crime. A Government which consults the general happiness and prosperity, will never tax the necessaries and comforts of life except in cases of extreme necessity.

It depresses every species of industry without benefit to any, and taxes alike poverty and wealth. Such a modification of the Tariff as will abrogate or reduce the import duties on all articles which enter into the necessaries and comforts of life, I should view as peculiarly adapted to the promotion of every species of industry, and of none more than manufacturing.

Perhaps the best criterion to determine whether a particular interest ought to be protected, is to submit it singlly to the representatives of the people. If, after full consideration unbiassed by any extraneous matter, a majority decides that its protection will conduce to the general good, there is little danger of injury or wrong in so adjusting the Tariff as to produce that result. It is worthy of enquiry, whether in the adjustment of the existing Tariff, two or more minor interests, neither of which singly, it was the interest of the people or the will of Congress to protect, did not, by combination, secure a common protection at the expence of the general good. It is obvious that no union of minor interests can produce an aggregate greater than the same number of major interests; and each new interest added, instead of increasing the propriety of the measure, could only increase the ballance against it.[3] If portions of the Tariff were introduced by a combination of minorities in Congress representing local and minor interests, it follows that injustice was done to the people which ought to be repaired.

It is also worthy of enquiry whether the agricultural interests would not be materially benefitted by a reduction of duties on such imported luxuries as are paid for abroad with our exported produce. If the merchant pays for the wine[4] he drinks with produce purchased from the farmer, it is the farmers interest that the importation and consumption of wine should increase, his market will be enlarged in the same proportion.

The Tariff is a subject of much delicacy, and, on account of the interests involved, should be touched with caution. While an abandonment of the policy in which it originated, a policy coeval with our Government and enforced through successive administrations, is neither to be expected nor desired, the people have a right to demand and a large portion of them do demand, that it shall be so modified as to correct abuses and obviate injustice. It must not be forgotten, that the only just object of the protecting policy is the general good. It is an abuse, when it is used as a means of laying a perpetual tax on one species of industry for the benefit of another. The abuse is glaring, when it is used to concentrate benefits on one section of the union, and burdens on another. It is an abuse, when selfish combinations protect a mass of local interests at the expence of a double weight of general interests, taxing the whole people for the benefit of the few. It is an abuse when it taxes the whole labor of the union for the protection of minute and local interests. The abuse will be fatal to the purity of our government and dangerous to the union, should the time come when the revenues thus raised will not be needed for any purpose of public utility; and members of the Government, instead of economizing the public funds, shall seek new objects of expenditure as an apology for continuing unjust burdens upon the people. The public debt will soon be paid. Without a change in the Tariff, it will then produce an annual surplus revenue of about ten millions of dollars. Unless Congress give it back to the states, or fix on a general system of internal improvements, there is ground to fear that it will engender habits of profusion and practices of corruption unexampled in a republican government. It behoves the people to consider, whether they will be taxed ten millions of dollars in the necessaries and comforts of life, merely that their government may have the power, by expending it at will, to administer to the cupidity of its favorites, and in the manner of distribution, corrupt the very fountains of its authority.

D in AJ Jr.'s hand, DLC (76).
   1. Van Buren wrote here in the margin: "Qure whether a general affirmation of its constitutionality would not be preferable to an argument."
   2. Van Buren wrote here in the margin: "The elder Adams did not & the younger with qualifications."
   3. Van Buren wrote opposite this sentence: "not extremely intelligible though doubtless just."

4. Van Buren wrote opposite this word: "Quere as to taking *wine* for the purpose of illustration."

Draft by Andrew Jackson on national defense

[Donelson revised this passage toward its final form in the annual message (Richardson, 2:526).]

Respecting the army, and the general System of preparation and defence, under the superintendence of the War Department, I beg leave to refer you to the report of the Secretary of War which accompanies this communication. Some of the Fortifications intended for the defence and security of our maratime frontier being compleated, and others in a state of rapid progress, it becomes a matter worthy of consideration, if their necessary armaments should not be in readiness at an earlier period than can be effected under the present authorised appropriations. Happily for us, we are now at peace, and an earnest hope is entertained, that the blessings it affords may be long continued to us; but at what time the amicable relations of a country may be interrupted is beyond the ~~knowledge~~ view of human foresight to determine; to be prepared for such an emergency, to the extent our means will enable us is ~~matter of~~ an imperious duty, and should be of inclination with all who vallue the inestimable priviledges we enjoy.

AD, DLC (76).

Draft by William Taylor Barry on the post office

[This draft, subsequently polished by Donelson, closely prefigures the final text in the message (Richardson, 2:526–27).]

The Report of the Post Master General in like manner exhibits a satisfactory view of the important branch of the government under his charge. In addition to the benefits already extended by the operations of the Post Office Department, considerable improvements have been secured within the present year, by an increase in the accommodation of stage-coaches & in the frequency and celerity of the transportation of the mail between some of the most important points of the Union; ~~and~~ these improvements have been provided for, at an estimated saveing to the Department of upwards of seventy two thousand dollars. Notwithstanding the excess of expenditure beyond the current receits for a few years past, necessarily incured in the fulfillment of existing contracts, and in the additional expences, between the periods of contracting, ~~necessary~~ to meet the demands created by the rapid growth & extension of our flourishing country, yet the satisfactory assureance is given that the future revenue of the Department will be sufficient to meet its extensive engagements. The system which has been recently introduced, that subjects its receits & disbursements to strict regulation has in its operation entirely fulfilled its design. It gives full assureance of the certainty of account both of transmission and preservation of the funds of the Department. The efficiency and industry of its officers, and the ability and energy of ~~its~~ Contractors, justify an increased confidence in ~~the~~ its continued prosperity ~~of this valuable Department~~.

AD, DLC (76).

Draft by Andrew Jackson on the District of Columbia

[This passage was reworked by Donelson toward its final form in the message (Richardson, 2:528).]

The District of Columbia requires your consideration, and I ask your particular attention to its situation. A place of ten miles square placed by the constitution under the peculiar control of Congress, by whom exclusive jurisdiction is possessed, certainly demands to have extended to it greater care than has hitherto been ~~extended to it~~ bestowed. The inconsiderable interest that uniformly has been felt in relation to this subject, and the want of attention which has been manifested, is proof how little is to be expected from the legislation of Congress in reference to ordinary local details. Matters of high importance to ~~Congress~~ the country engross the attention of members, and hence but little time or even ~~attention~~ inclination is had to examine into those which are of minor local considerations, & in which none of the constituents of the representatives are immediately interested. For a class of citizens immediately under the view of Congress, to possess fewer advantages than are enjoyed by other portions of the union cannot fail by the contrast, in the end to be productive of injurious effects. Different laws with different penalties, are found to prevail within the District, so that at one side of the river Potomac imprisonment, & on the other side death is inflicted for the same cause of offence. Many laws which existed years ago remain unchanged, and without amelioration by the march of mind and improvement in the principles of Government. These things require immediate consideration and change, after some plan to be agreed upon by Congress. This District being under the immediate care & control of Congress, great care and caution should be taken that there should be afforded no cause of just complaint. As the people cannot participate in legislation before congress a mode of ascertaining their grievances & their wants should be afforded. A Delegate might answer this purpose, thro whom the wishes & wants of the community might be made known. Every citizen not in theory, but in practice, ought to understand the principles of our free government—the extent of representative authority, & dependence & responsibility to the people ~~elect~~ who elect. A mutual & proper relation & dependence between governors & governed, must necessarily be cherished to give efficiency & stability to any form of government, republican in its character. Here this is not the case. Something of limited local legislation, has heretofore been conceded while a more enlarged one resides in congress, where seldom time is found to give attention to matters, which altho local, are of high consideration to many of our citizens, & where none of them are permitted to be present to make known truly as they should be, those things which are necessary and proper to be acted upon for their benefit. That these evils may meet with a remedy I have thought it proper to present ~~their situation~~ them to Congress for their immediate action

The Penitentiary is ready for the reception of convicts, & only awaits the Legislation by Congress, necessary to put it into operation—upon this subject I beg leave to draw your attention to my communica- of last session.

AD, DLC (76).

Draft on the Bank of the United States and conclusion by Andrew Jackson Donelson

[This draft up to its closing paragraph derives from the passage inscribed by Jackson in his memorandum book (above, pp. 601–2) and sent to Van Buren on November 1. The final version closely follows this text (Richardson, 2:528–29).]

The importance of the principles involved in the enquiry whether it will be proper to recharter the Bank of the United States, requires that I should again call the attention of Congress to the subject. Nothing has occurred to lessen, in any degree, the dangers which ~~very~~ many of our ~~safest Statesmen~~ Citizens apprehend from that institution as at present organised~~, nor is the opinion of its unconstitutionality less extensive or less deeply impressed~~. In the spirit of improvement and compromise which distinguishes our country and its institutions, it becomes us to inquire, whether it be not ~~proper~~ possible to secure the advantages afforded by the present Bank, thro' the agency of ~~the~~ a Bank of the United States so modified in its principles and structure, as to obviate constitutional and other objections

It is thought practicable to organise such a Bank with the necessary officers as a Branch of the Treasury Department, based on the public and individual deposits, without[1]

with specie. In times of public emergency the capacities of such an institution might be enlarged by ~~act of Congress~~ legislative provision.

These suggestions are made, not so much as a recommendation, as with a view of calling the attention of Congress to the possible modifications of a system which cannot continue to exist in its present form, without occasional collisions with the local authorities, and perpetual apprehensions and discontents on the part of the States and the people.

In conclusion, Fellow citizens allow me to invoke in behalf of your deliberations that spirit of conciliation and disinterestedness which is the gift of Patriotism. ~~An~~ Under an overruling and merciful Providence ~~has thus far signalized its influence agency in advancing the prosperity and glory of our country. May we preserve its influence, and deserve its rewards~~ the agency of this spirit has thus far been signalized in ~~the advancement of~~ the prosperity and glory of our beloved country. May its influence be eternal.

AD, DLC (76).
    1. A page is missing here.

To Amos Kendall

[Private.]

DECBRE 6, 1830.

    The President, with his respects to Mr. Kendall, inquires when he can get a few of Mr. Blair's prospectus. He wishes to forward a few of them with the message. Could the p. get a few copies of the message, this evening—

Printed, *Cincinnati Commercial*, February 4, 1879, DLC (38). Francis Preston Blair's new Washington paper, *The Globe*, began publication December 7. Its prospectus, printed in the first issue, announced its support for AJ's principles and policies and for his election to a second term.

To John Coffee

Washington Decbr. 6th. 1830—

My Dr. Genl.

    I have not had a line from you since I shook you by the hand in Franklin. I have heard from you thro' our mutual friend Major Eaton to whom you have occasionally written; and am happy that you and your amiable family are well.

    We are here, going on very well, altho', loansome, still out of the way of the Gossips of the City—The faction are marshalling their forces, *in secrete*, but the imprudence of Genl Desha, has unmasked their views, rather early for the ~~views~~ benefit of his prompter; I can assure you the *pitt* dug for Eaton, in which they expected to plunge me into, will be the grave (political) of the movers, a party cannot flourish with such a tool as Doctor Boyd McNairy—he is the depraved wretch, the letter writer from Nashville—& it is only necessary to expose his name, which carries with it, nothing but infamy to convince the moral portion of the world, of the wicked designs, of the faction. Congress has not made a House today in consequence of the absence of the speaker who is sick, but expected tomorrow. I enclose you my message; I would like to hear your opinion of it.[1]

I have just recd. a long letter from my friend McLamore, upon the subject of my Cabinet, & Major & Mrs. Eaton   I fear he has been only conversant with those who profess friendship for me, but who would destroy Eaton however unjustly, to injure me. I intend to answer it the first leisure friendly & frankly.[2] I love my connections, but if it is believed, that I can ever abandon a friend, & that under circumstances with which my friend Eaton is surrounded, they know nothing of me—"a friend in need, is a friend indeed" & I loath the wretch that would abandon his friends, for the smiles of a faction, by me it never has or will be done—Ere long I will have my Cabinet as it ought to be, *a unit*. The double dealing of J. C. C. is perfectly unmasked—he is now as to myself perfectly harmless.

you will receive enclosed the prospectus of a paper to be published here; by Mr Blair, the former Editor of the K.y. argus, & aid of Mr Kendall. It is of the true faith, and I hope you & the Winstons will patronise it. Mr Blair arrived here five days ago, & tomorrow his first paper will appear. I will send it to you.[3]

Present me affectionately to your amiable family, to Miss Mary Easton & your daughter if with you & believe me Your friend

Andrew Jackson

ALS, THi (16-1343).
1. House Speaker Andrew Stevenson being absent from illness, Congress met and adjourned on December 6. The next day, December 7, both houses reconvened and received AJ's annual message of the day before.
2. AJ wrote McLemore on December 25 (below).
3. Anthony Winston (1782–1841) and John Jones Winston (1785–1850) lived in north Alabama.

To Samuel Jackson Hays

Washington Decbr. 7 1830—

My Dr Saml

I enclose you my message this day delivered. It is published in the *Globe*

I send for you Doctor Butler, Col S. D. Hays & my friend Chester, this Message is for you all, not having one for each, with the prospectus of the *Globe*—It is the true faith, no nulification *in the Globe*—patronise it—I will be happy to hear your opinion of the message, and expect you all to patronise the Globe—The Editor, is the late Editor of the Ky Argus, no nulifier—but of the true faith—I will be happy to see you, & your Dr wife here, with my namesake—Carolina is torn to pieces, I hope the steam will blow off without bursting a boiler & that our friend Hamilton will be elected Govr—but all is doubtful[1]—I would like to see Narcissa with you—salutations to all. yrs affectionately

A. J.

ALS, Samuel J. Hays (16-1348).
    1. The South Carolina legislature elected James Hamilton Jr. governor on December 9.

To Adam Huntsman

SIR:

I send you my Message, published in the Globe. Read the Message and let me have your strictures freely upon it. You see I have spoken freely as I ought. Let the people judge. If my opinions are not congenial with the true republican faith—let the people determine it. The Hermitage is my choice. Yours,

ANDREW JACKSON.

P.S. There in no Nullification in the Message, and perhaps it will not find a place in the Globe. A. J.

Printed, Washington *Globe*, June 15, 1831 (16-0911). On May 2, 1831, the *National Journal* accused AJ of demeaning his office and abusing his frank by distributing the *Globe* prospectus and soliciting subscriptions. It cited a letter to an unnamed Tennessee state senator as proof. In response, Adam Huntsman (1786–1849) of Jackson, Tenn., identified himself as the letter's recipient and published this text in the *Globe* to prove the accusations false.

From John A. Parker

Tappahannock 8th December 1830

Mr. R M Forbes, visited Washington a few days before the last congress ajourned; and on his return, he remarked to me, that he was a good deal surprised to find, that Wm. Robinson of Westmoreland, formerly secretary of the Westmd. Jackson meetings, had abandoned the support of Genl. Jackson and his administration, and was at the time he met with him one of the most thorough going oppositionists he had seen in his Travels, that he appeared to take pleasure in abuseing the President and his cabinet, said it was decidedly the weakest, most corrupt, and electioneering Administration that we had ever had—This is the substance, and I think as near the language as can be, which Mr Forbes represented Robinson as having used—whereever Mr. Forbes is known his word will be received, and I regret his absense prevents me from obtaining his certificate. I make this statement from no unkind feelings towards Robinson, but having been informed that the administration was about to confer office on him, and knowing him to be unworthy of its confidence; as a friend to the administration, I am prompted to do it.

John A. Parker

[Endorsed by AJ:] Confidential—Mr. Parker Statement of the abuse by Colo. Robinson of the present administration to be kept carefully on file—A. J

ADS, DLC (38). John A. Parker (1804–1894) of Westmoreland County, Va., had sought a territorial office earlier in the year (DNA-RG 59, M639-17). William Robinson (1782–1857), a prominent Virginia Jackson organizer in 1824 and 1828, had applied to AJ for various posts, most recently commissioner of the General Land Office on August 9. He was appointed a War Department clerk in 1833 (*Jackson Papers*, 7:214–16).

To James Monroe

Washington Decbr. 9th. 1830

My Dear Sir,

It gives me great pleasure to thank you for your favor of the 5th. inst enclosing the oration recently delivered by Mr. Gouverneur

Preserving the most lively recollection of your great public services and the many proofs they exhibit of sincere friendship to me, I offer you my most eanrest wishes for the recovery of your health and its happy enjoyment[.] With great respect yr. obt sert

Andrew Jackson

[In AJ's hand:] P.S. I enclose you a copy of my Message

A. J

LS in AJ Donelson's hand, THer (16-1359). Copy, DLC (38). Samuel Laurence Gouverneur (1799–1865) was New York City postmaster and Monroe's son-in-law. His speech, published as *Oration delivered by Samuel L. Gouverneur, Esq. on the 26th. November, 1830, at Washington Square, before the citizens of New-York*, celebrated the change of government in France.

To William Savin Fulton

Strictly confidential.

Washington Decbr. 10th. 1830—

Dr Sir

It has been stated to me that an extensive expedition against Texas is organising in the United States, with a view to the establishment of an independent government in that province, and that Genl Houston is to be at the head of it. From all the circumstances communicated to me upon this subject, and which have fallen under my observation, I am induced to believe, & I do hope, (notwithstanding the circumstancial manner in which it is related to me) that the information I have received is erroneous, and it is unnessary that I should add my sincere wish that it may be so. No movements have been made; nor have any facts been established, which would require, or would justify the adoption of official procedings against individuals implicated—yet so strong is the detestation of the criminal step alluded to, and such are my apprehensions of the extent to which the peace & honor of the country might be compromitted by it, as to make me anxious to do every thing short of it, which may serve to illicit the truth, and to furnish me with the necessary facts (if they exist) to lay the foundation of further measures. It is said that enlistments have been made for the enterprise in various parts of the Union—that confederates are to repair as travellers to different parts of the Missippi, where they have already chartered Steam Boats on which to embark—That the point of rendezvous is to be in the Arkansa Territory, & that the cooperation of the Indians is looked to by those engaged in the contemplated expedition.

I know of no one whose situation will better enable him to watch the course of things, & keep me truly and constantly advised of any movements which may serve to justify the suspicions which are entertained than yourself, and I know I can rely with confidence on your fidelity and activity. To secure your exertions in that regard, is the object of this letter, & it is because I wish it to be considered rather as a private than an official act, that it is addressed to you & not to the Governor, (who is understood to be now in Kentuckey).

The course to be pursued to effect the object in view, must of necessity be left to your discretion—enjoining only, that the utmost secrecy to be observed on your part. If in the performance of the duty required of you, any expences are necessarily incurred by you, I will see they are refunded. I am very respectfully yr friend

Andrew Jackson

ALS (at March 13, 1839), DNA-RG 59 (M179-88). Facsimile of ALS draft, Robert Mayo, *Political Sketches of Eight Years in Washington* (16-1365); Copy (at February 16, 1839), DLC (52). Mayo's facsimile included an AJ endorsement: "(Copy) Confidential Wm. Fulton Sec. of the T. of Florida—private & confidential—"

From Charles Rhind

Washington 10th. Decr. 1830

Sir

I think it proper to state to you, the circumstances under which I became possessed of the Arabian Horses landed from the Vessel in which I reached, the U. States from Turkey.

Finding, during my residence at Constantinople, that our Turkish Friends were far behind us in many improvements, I suggested to the Ministers several, which were of great use to them, and after closing the business of the Negotiation, much of my time was occupied in giving them Drafts, schemes, and elucidations. The Sultan, I understood, took great interest in these suggestions, and many enquiries were made of me by his request to all of which I afforded the best explanation in my power.[1]

It being customary at that Court, for the person who negotiates a Treaty to remain there until the ratifications are exchanged, or by express assent of the Porte to leave a person in his place, I was therefore under the necessity of appointing Mr. Navoni to that Station, and presented him in that capacity to the Reis Effendi.[2] I shortly thereafter took formal leave of the Turkish Ministers.

Finding that no Vessel would leave Turkey for the U. States prior to the 1st. of Septr. I determined instead of remaining idle at Constantinople to proceed to Odessa (a Voyage of three days) and make the necessary arrangements there for the reception of our Vessels, having accomplished this, I returned to Constantinople on my way to Smyrna, where I was to embark.

On reaching the Capital I had several interviews and communications with my former Turkish Friends, and suggested other improvements in their System, very gratifying to them.

Being informed by the Reis Effendi, that permission would be granted me to export one or more Arabian Horses, and conceiving, that whilst it would be a personal object to myself, it would also be a benefit to our Country, if I succeeded in conveying one to the U. States, I visited the Studs of many of the Nobility in order to select some, and was on the eve of closing for the purchase of two, when the circumstance coming to the knowledge of the Sultan, he, on the 31st. of August, directed Four horses to be sent me in his Name. Altho this was evidently not intended as a present to me in my official capacity since the Ministers were aware I could not accept them as such, still the gift, was one that could not be returned without giving Offence.[3] Being well informed that to refuse them would be considered an insult, to the Sultan, and would doubtless be attended with injury to the interests of the U. States, and Mr. Navoni, as well as others assured me that I must take them away from Constantinople, if I should cut their throats, and throw them overboard the next day. I was consequently obliged to take them and relinquish the purchase of those I had selected; I immediately had the Four horses appraised by competent judges on the spot, and took them with me to Smyrna.

Having no Funds of the U. States or the means of raising them to pay for their expenses and passage to America—I shipped them as a Commercial Adventure in the name of, and for account, of the Owners of the Vessel in which they came, and from whom I had received an individual credit on London, previous to leaving the U States. The Horses are consequently in their possession, but if the U. States have a claim for their value, I presume those Gentlemen will pay it over, should they sell for more than the expenses attending them—which of course are very considerable[4]

So far as regards myself I am ready to transfer to the U States, any right, title or interest I may have in them, should it be required. With great respect I have the honor to be Your ob. St.

Chas Rhind

ALS, DNA-RG 233 (16-1384). *HRRep* 107, 21st Cong., 2d sess., pp. 2–3 (Serial 210). AJ forwarded this letter to Congress on February 22, 1831, asking its direction on the disposition of the horses (Richardson, 2:536). They were claimed by the government and sold at auction in New York City in May 1831, though the proceeds fell short of expenses.

1. Mahmud II (1785–1839) was sultan of the Ottoman Empire.

2. Nicholas Navoni, an Italian, served as dragoman for U.S. diplomats at Constantinople.

3. Article 1 of the Constitution prohibits persons holding office under the United States from accepting "any present, Emolument, Office, or Title, of any kind whatever, from any King, Prince, or foreign State" without the consent of Congress.

4. The horses reached New York in November on the brig *Phebe Ann* and were held by the merchant firm G. G. & S. Howland.

To Martin Van Buren

Decbr 11th. 1830

My Dr Sir

I have had only time to glance over Govr. Popes letter, and it strikes me that the provisions of the act of Congress to prevent settlements being made on land ceded to the U. States, until authorised by law; approved 3d. of march 1807—gives the proper remedy; to which I would draw your attention. A proclamation by the President, founded on this law & particularly the 4th. section, would have the effect of quieting our citizens, & driving off those intruders, without bring into contact at present, the right of Mexico with that of the U.S. and how far Mexico can claim under her conquest from Spain, under our treaty with Spain

It is due to our national character to act promptly on this subject, protect the citizens under our known, & exercised jurisdiction, until the boundery is established by some act of the two governments. The proclamation proposed will have the desired effect a precedent will be found in the General Land office. If you concur with me, have the proclamation prepared, for my signature by the Commissioner of the General Land office, which I will have forwarded without delay to the marshal with instructions to the Governor if necessary to aid the marshal in its execution—

yrs respectfully

Andrew Jackson

ALS, DNA-RG 59 (M179-69). *TPUS*, 21:299–300. John Pope had reported to Van Buren on November 17 that Benjamin R. Milam's surveys within the disputed territory were continuing, apparently with Mexican approval. Pope proposed that AJ "quiet the fears of the people" by ordering the removal of illegal settlers (*TPUS*, 21:287–88). The law of March 3, 1807, prohibited unsanctioned occupancy of public lands and authorized the eviction and prosecution of offenders. On February 10, 1831, AJ issued a proclamation ordering unlawful settlers in Lafayette, Sevier, and Miller counties to remove or face expulsion by the marshal, backed by military force, beginning April 15 (Richardson, 2:543–44).

From John Coffee

(Private)

Coxes Creek near Florence
12th. Decr. 1830

Dear Genl.

I received your kind letter some time since, and before I would write you, I have been waiting the result of our senatorial election, in the Legislature of our State, but as yet the election has not taken place. You will no doubt recollect what took place at Franklin Ten, when Govr. Gabriel Moore was there, his conversation with you on the subject of Col. McKinleys course, in the appointment of Marshal for north Alabama—after which he requested me to say to Col. McKinley that you had satisfied him on that subject, and that he would not oppose him for the senate of the United States—but notwithstanding he has come out, and is now the promanent candidate against McKinley—all his other opponents having tried their strength and failed, they brought the Govr. out as their last resort. It is very doubtfull the result of the election, could McKinley have remained with the Legislature I have no doubt but he wd. have been elected, but in his absence they will have every advantage by lying and otherwise deceiving the members who are unacquainted with him, therefore the thing is doubtfull for the present. I have fears that Moore will not support you if elected, from the fact, that he complains of McKinley's not having opposed the nomination of Patterson for Marshal when before the senate for their approval, this proves how far he would support you, when you did not go precisely the way he and his friends wanted you to go—but if he is elected (and I hope in God he will not be) we will soon see in what ranks he will muster.[1] It is strange and unnatural to know the undoubted fact, that the people by a very large majority are decidedly in favour of you, and the course of your administration, yet that they will elect men of different principles, and such as they aught to know would not represent them correctly in the counsels of the nation, how long will the people be gulled in this way. We will expect in few days to receive your message to Congress—great anxiety is expressed to see it, yet there is no subject which we feel particularly interested in, that is at all doubtfull.

I hope you are getting along in your domestic department better than formerly, as you have no family that requires your particular notice at all—this leaves your whole and undivided attention to your public duties, which is no doubt very laborious—but the God of nature has endowed you with the qualifications for such great and trying events which every day pass in your review and under your controul, and I hope and trust in him, that he will support you untill you shall accomplish the great work of reformation, and settle our Govt. down on honest, and republican principles. I have nothing to say to you of any importance—our Crops are gathered in, and are short, I shall make only about 50 Bales of Cotton, and A. J. Hutchings about 60 Bales, we are not quite done Ginning yet, but so far that we can calculate nearly the Amt. made. The price is likely to be low, Louisiana and Missi. Cotton are now selling at New Orleans for 10 to 11 cents & dull at that—but sellers are not willing either to let it go at those low rates. If peace shall be restored, or rather continue in Europe, we expect better prices.

By a letter just recd. from Col. Edwd. Ward he informs me that he has sold his plantation where he lives to Mr. Baldwin who married Miss Dickson for $9.000 and stock, Crop, & farming utensils to amount of about $1500. This he remarks has more than paid his debt to the estate of Doctr. Dickson, but he looks to Col. Ben Jones's estate for the balance which will be coming to him. The Col. remarked in his letter, that this contract, had placed him with the proud feelings of a farmer out of debt, and more happy than he had been for many years, that in a few weeks he and Mrs. Ward would set out to their new home in the Western district, his first best choice, of all he ever owned. I mention this to shew you that Andrew J. Hutchings need not longer think of getting that plantation, which he had very much set his heart on, for I got alletter from him by the same mail which brought me Col. Wards letter.[2] But if Andw. keeps in the same notion of prefering to live in the neighbourhood of the Hermitage, to his place in Alabama, I think he can get some other place, that will suit as well. I have been of late a little chequered in health, by Rheumatism, otherwise pretty well my family are in good health. Polley requests to be presented to you affectionately, to which I add my own best wishes, for your health & happiness—your friend—

Jno. Coffee

ALS (at December 18), DLC (38). AJ replied on December 28 (below).

1. Gabriel Moore (1785–1845) was governor of Alabama and a candidate before the legislature against incumbent John McKinley for the latter's Senate seat. Moore's nephew Benjamin Tyson Moore (c1803–1870) had held temporary appointment as marshal in north Alabama in 1829 and sought the regular post in 1830. In May AJ had instead appointed Benjamin Patteson (1789–1862). Just before leaving for Washington, McKinley published addresses to the Alabama legislature on November 19 and 23. He accused Gabriel Moore of opposing him for the Senate, in violation of a previous pledge, because he had failed to procure Moore's nephew's appointment. McKinley claimed he had indeed pressed young Moore upon AJ, but that Moore blamed him for not opposing Patteson's confirmation in the Senate.

McKinley offered Coffee as witness to Moore's reversal. On November 30 Moore published two addresses in reply. He charged McKinley with secretly backing Patteson against his nephew, cited other objections to McKinley's public conduct, and denied promising not to run against him (Huntsville *Southern Advocate*, Dec 11, 1830).

On December 1 Coffee wrote McKinley confirming his account. Coffee related that he and AJ had met with Moore at Franklin in August. Moore there charged that McKinley had reneged on his pledge to support young Moore for marshal. Coffee and AJ assured him otherwise, and Moore, declaring himself satisfied, promised that he would not be a candidate for the Senate.

On December 13, the day after this letter, the Alabama legislature elected Moore senator over McKinley by 49 to 40 for the term beginning March 4, 1831.

2. Edward Ward (d. 1837), AJ's longtime neighbor, had purchased his Hunter's Hill plantation in 1804. On December 5 Ward wrote Coffee of its sale to Henry Baldwin Jr. (1803–1868), son of Supreme Court justice Henry Baldwin. Baldwin had just married Mary Florida Dickson (b. c1810), daughter of the late Nashville physician and congressman William Dickson (1770–1816). Edward Ward was her legal guardian and executor of Dickson's estate. Benjamin B. Jones (1792–1830) of Lawrence Co., Ala., had died in March. On December 4 Andrew J. Hutchings wrote Coffee from the Hermitage of his wish to purchase Hunter's Hill (Coffee Papers, THi).

From William Wyatt

NEAR TALLAHASSEE, December 13th 1830.

To the President of the United States.

SIR:—

Herewith you will receive a copy of a petition against the public conduct of Governor Duval, which was handed to me with a request that I would send it to your excellency. This petition, I am informed, was signed by many of the most respectable citizens of St. Augustine, and presented to Mr. Adams, of which fact the delegate can more fully inform you.

I am told that Governor Duval, is now *privately* getting certificates from some of the gentlemen, to whom I have referred as witnesses, in my charges against him. Some of those persons I knew at the time, to be personally friendly to the governor; and in fact, have aggrandised themselves under his patronage; and would, I have no doubt, to gratify him, give *privately* such statements as would not contain the whole facts, or as could easily be reconciled to his interest:—when on the other hand, if they were called upon by the government to state publicly in the presence of the parties, their evidence would be materially different.

It was with a view to avoid this difficulty, that I desired, and as I now most respectfully request of you, to appoint an agent to come into the Territory and take the evidence—allowing each party to propound such questions to the witnesses as they may think proper, touching the subject; and also, to collect the documentary evidence.

I think it due to me, and to the public interest, that every facility be afforded, by which a full development of the whole facts could be arrived at.

Should this course, or any similar one be adopted by you, I pledge myself to prove every material fact set forth in the charges. I would myself have obtained statements from many persons acquainted with the fact, had I not conceived any *exparie* investigations to be illiberal to Governor Duval.

I have been informed, by the delegate, that Mr. Donalson, your private secretary, told him that imputations against my private character, had been made to you, with a view to induce you, not to take any notice of those charges, or in other words not to investigate them, regardless of any imputations which Governor Duval could make or cause to be made to you, derogatory to my character.[1] I must remonstrate against such a course as being at war with the true principles of our government.

The private or public character of a petitioner, who seeks constitutional redress, or correction of a base power, I humbly conceive, have nothing to do with the guilt or innocence of the accused. It certainly would have been more proper for Governor Duval, to have himself insisted upon an investigation, than to have attempted to load me with false, and slanderous imputations. The one would have been some evidence of innocence, but the other is a convincing proof of his guilt.

I have attempted to repel this ungenerous attack upon me, in a letter addressed to Governor Duval, herewith inclosed, which I beg you to read.

I am, Sir, with High considerations of respect, Your obedient servant,

W. WYATT.

Printed, Tallahassee *Floridian*, October 23, 1832 (mAJs). Wyatt (c1787–1850) had served on the Florida Territory legislative council. Around March of 1830 he wrote AJ charging Governor William P. Duval with official oppression and fraud going back to 1824 (Tallahassee *Floridian*, Jan 5, 1833). Prompted by Duval, Robert W. Williams on April 26 and Isham G. Searcy on May 20 wrote AJ blasting Wyatt as a degraded character and attributing his charges to malice and spite (DNA-RG 46, 15-0816 & 15-1058). Wyatt in turn wrote Duval, accusing him of trying to shirk investigation of his official conduct by leveling personal attacks on himself and on territorial delegate Joseph M. White, who had presented Wyatt's charges to AJ (*Pensacola Gazette*, Jan 11, 1831). White wrote AJ on December 18 (below).

1. White wrote Wyatt to this effect on July 15, 1830 (*Pensacola Gazette*, Jan 11, 1831).

From John W. Quinney

Washington Dec 14th 1830

Great Father:

Your red children of the Stockbridge and Munsee Tribes, who have emigrated from the State of N.Y. to Green Bay, send thro' me their salutations to you & your wise men who are sitting around the Great Council fire to deliberate upon the welfare of your Nation, and have instructed me to make known to you their wishes and their wants.

We thank the Great Spirit who has given us a father, who always attends to the cries of his red children.

Difficulties and doubts have arisen in the minds of our people in regard to their true situation, which we wish to have settled this winter. We desire to understand our situation fully & to know what we have to depend upon. It was hoped when the late commission arrived at Green Bay, that all things would have been finally adjusted & an allotment of lands made suitable to our wishes & sufficient for agricultural purposes. This, Father, so far as our interests are concerned, has not been done. In the application now made it is intended to set forth the claims & wants of the Tribes which I represent, without any connection with our Brethren of the Six Nations; &, it may be necessary to explain the origin of our association with them in the negociations of 1821 & 22.

Many years ago, the Miami or Maumee & other Tribes granted to the Stockbridge, Munsee and Deleware Tribes a large tract of country on White River, in the now Indiana State, whither the Delewares & a portion of our Tribes immediately removed & our people remained there untill the late War, when they were obliged to return to the State of N.Y. At the restoration of peace, we contemplated a reunion of our people upon White River & a portion of the Stockbridge Tribe was accordingly fitted out in the Year 1818 to go on, in advance of the rest—but ere they arrived at the place of their destination, the Delewares alone had sold to the United States, at the Treaty of St Mary's (Ohio) all the lands which were owned jointly and equally by themselves & their Brethren the Stockbridge & Munsee Tribes.

In 1819 the Stockbridge made an application to the Government for redress—in 1820 they renewed their application and in 1821 they & the Munsee Tribe agreed to relinquish their claims upon the White River to the U.S. provided, that, besides the payment of three thousand dollars they should be assisted in procuring a Country some where to the westward & which was to be confirmed to them and their posterity forever.[1]

About this time, the Six Nations and others resident in the State of New York, under the auspices of the United States' Government were deeply engaged in securing a Country some where to the westward for their future residence; and the Stockbridge & Munsee Tribes having now the same object in view, cooperated with them and sent a Deputation to Green Bay the same year, supported & protected by an Agent from the Government, specially deputed for that purpose.

Thus, Father, has arisen a connection, which we have no other objections to, save that we are anxious to urge our stronger claims particularly and alone. Of the considerations paid to the Winnebagoes & Menominies for the sale of their lands in 1821 & 22, we contributed the one half; and we think it nothing but proper and fair, that whatever may be your opinion as to the quantity the New York Indians, as a whole, are entitled to, we should receive that proportion, rightfully to be expected from the pledges of the Govt. at the sale of the White River tract & from the amount of our contributions in the negociations with our Brethren of the west.

In the report of the late Commission we are set down for six thousand Acres at the Grand Kaccalin of Fox River, & were told that if this was insufficient for our wants, a portion of our Brethren might cross the River and reside on the tract there alotted to the Oneida & other Tribes. To this arrangement we have to oppose the strongest objections. Our Father is well aware of the inconvenience & injury a separation of this sort would produce, besides which, we are now settled on the East side of the River & have already made at great expense & hard labor extensive improvements in clearing lands, building houses, Mills &c. &c.[2]

We ask therefore, Father, to have alotted to us, the Stockbridge & Munsee Tribes All that portion of land, being a part of the tract the N. York Indians proposed to accept of the U.S. Commissioners in a final adjustment of their claims, Comprehended within the following boundaries viz. Beginning at the Southern boundary line of the purchase in 1821 from the Winnebagoes & Menominies, thence running down the Fox River to the upper or Southern line of the cession made by the New York Indians to the Brotherton Indians in 1825, thence running East with sd. line to a point fifteen Miles from the River; thence South to the upper or Southern boundary line of the purchase of 1821 aforesaid & from thence North West along sd. last mentioned line to the place of beginning, on Fox River.

We wish moreover to know if the decision of our Great Father in the case ~~would~~ will be final & prevent all further difficulties & by what tenure we are to hold these lands—this question involves all that is dear and valuable to us. We hope therefore that you will inform us certainly & fully. Father, we wish a home—give us that home. Let it be free from intrusion, violence & the Interests of strangers and we shall be content. We will bless you and teach our children to bless you and the Good Spirit will bless you.

Father: We understand a question has been made by interested white men in regard to the validity of our Treaty with the Menominies in 1822.

It is not necessary for us here to enter into a vindication of our proceedings & to establish the engagements of each party in that transaction as being fair & forever binding—the ratification of our Great Father President Munroe saves us in this. But we wish to lay fast hold of your good opinion & for this purpose desire that you will ascertain yourself of all circumstances connected with that transaction. To avoid difficulty with our western Brethren, we and our confederates the Six Nations proposed to the Commissioners to relinquish all the rest, provided a small part (which was then defined) was secured to us forever. The same overture is still made & your concurence most ardently desired.[3]

Great Father may you live long & rule this Nation in peace and happiness. For & in behalf of the Chiefs & Head Men of the Stockbridge & Munsee Tribes.

John W. Quinney

ADS, DNA-RG 75 (M234-315). Copy, DNA-RG 46 (16-1431). *SDoc* 512, 23d Cong., 1st sess., vol. 2, pp. 198–200 (Serial 245). Educated in New York state, Quinney (1797–1855) was a leading Stockbridge spokesman. He had represented them before the investigating commission in August at Green Bay and in the delegation of New York Indians that afterward came to Washington to protest the commissioners' report.

1. Delaware, Stockbridge (or Mohican), and Munsee Indians had settled before the Revolution on land obtained from the Miami Indians on White River in Indiana. By the Treaty of St. Mary's in October 1818, the Delawares, acting alone, ceded all their land in the state and agreed to move west of the Mississippi. The Stockbridges protested this dispossession of their joint domain to Congress in 1819 (*HRRep* 70, 16th Cong., 1st sess., Serial 40).

2. The Green Bay commission report made no specific provision for the Stockbridges or Munsees apart from the other New York Indians. It proposed allocating to all of them 275,000 acres on the west side of Fox River and 6,000 on the east, with the Indians living there to remove to the west side if the government paid for their improvements (*SDoc* 512, 23d Cong., 1st sess., vol. 2, pp. 127, 162–63, Serial 245).

3. On January 20, 1831, a delegation headed by Quinney petitioned AJ for a total settlement of 858,000 acres astride the Fox for the New York Indians, to be partitioned specifically among them (*SDoc* 512, 23d Cong., 1st sess., vol. 2, pp. 396–99, Serial 245). In 1832 a Menominee treaty instead secured to the Stockbridges and Munsees a new domicile of two townships (46,080 acres) east of Lake Winnebago, further upriver on the Fox.

To John Henry Eaton

Decbr. 14th. 1830—

The President with his respects, incloses to the secretary of war a memorial just presented to him by John W. Quinney delegate from the Stockbridge & Maumee tribes for his report thereon, that justice may be done to the memorialists, if it has not been extended to them.

The Sec. will, as soon as a report of the case can be made, see the President on this subject, so that a time may be set, when he will see the delegation and give them an answer to their memorial. The Secretary of

War will, for this purpose, say to Mr Quinney that he will notify him of the day when the President will be prepared to see them.

AN, DNA-RG 75 (M234-315). Copy, DNA-RG 46 (16-1423). *SDoc* 512, 23d Cong., 1st sess., vol. 2, p. 198 (Serial 245). The copy and print version corrected AJ's "Maumee" to Munsee.

From Charles Edward Dudley

Wednesday Evening
15th. December 1830

Mr Dudley's compliments to the President with a Bushel of Hickory nuts, which Mrs Dudley requests his acceptance of: they are from a tree in *Ulster* county—the only one known in the State of Newyork that bears nuts of this size and quality. Those now sent were lately receiv'd from an aged Aunt of Mrs. Dudleys, who has had a monopoly of all the fruit the tree yielded for more than forty years, excepting in one instance when a Bushel was procured by a connexion of the family & forwarded to President Jefferson during his first term of Office.

*[Endorsed by AJ:] [. . .]*desires his thanks to be presented to Mrs Duddley for this kind token of her respect, ~~for~~ in whose welfare, he will always take the most lively interest—

[Endorsed by AJ:] Col. Dudley of Newyork, presenting from Mrs. D. Hickory Nutts with the reply—Decbr 18th. 1830—

AN, DLC (38). The nuts came from Blandina Elmendorf Bruyn (1753–1832), an aunt of Dudley's wife in Kingston, N.Y.

From Samuel Houston

Wigwam Neosho
15th Decr 1830

Sir,
I have the honor to address you upon the subject of one of your old soldiers at the "Battle of Orleans." I allude to Capt Nathaniel Pryor, who has for several years past resided with the Osages as a sub agent, by appointment of Govr Clark but without any permanent appointment from Government. A vacancy has lately occured by the decease of Mr Carr, sub agent for the Osages; and I do most *earnestly*, solicit the appointment for him.[1] When you were elected President of the U States, I assured you,

that I would, not annoy you with recommendations in favor of persons who might wish to obtain office, or patronage from you: But as I regard the claims of capt Pryor, as peculiar, and paramount to those, of any man, within my knowledge, I can not withhold a just tribute of regard. He was the first man who volunteered, to accompany Lewis, and Clark, on their tour to the Pacific Ocean—He was then in the Army some four or five years—resigned, & at the commencement of the last war entered the Army again, and was a Captain in the 44th Regt, under you, at New Orleans; and a *braver* man, never fought under the wings, of your Eagles. He has done more to tame, and pacificate the dispositions of the Osages, to the whites, and surrounding Tribes of Indians than all other men; and has done more in promoting the authority of the U. States and compelling the Osages, to comply with demands from Colonel Arbuckle than any person could have supposed. Capt Pryor is a man of amiable character, and disposition—of fine sense, strict honor, perfectly temperate, in his habits—and unremiting in his attention to business. The Secy of War assured me when I was last at Washington, that his "claims should be considered of"—yet another was appointed, and he was passed by. He is poor, having been twice robbed by Indians of *Furs*, and merchandise some ten years since. For better information, in relation to Capt Pryor, I will beg leave to refer you to Genl Campbell, Colo Benton, and Gov Floyd of Va who is his first cousin.[2] With every wish for your Glory & Happiness, I have the honor, to be your most obt servt

Sam Houston

[Endorsed by AJ:] Refered to the Secretary of War   A. J.

ALS, DNA-RG 75 (M234-631). ALS photostat, TxU (14-1440). *Writings of Sam Houston*, 1:193–95. Nathaniel Hale Pryor (1772–1831) was an Army sergeant in the overland expedition of Meriwether Lewis (1774–1809) and William Clark in 1804–06. He left the Army as a Captain in 1815 and worked as a fur trader and merchant. Houston also wrote Eaton about Pryor this same day (*American Historical Review* 24 [Jan 1919]: 261–62). The War Department appointed Pryor subagent to the Osages in May 1831, just days before his death.

1. Anthony V. Carr, appointed Osage subagent in July, had just died.
2. John Floyd (1783–1837) was governor of Virginia. His father and Pryor's mother were siblings.

To Charles Edward Dudley

Decbr. 18th. 1830—

The President with kind salutations to Colo. Duddley, of New york, acknowledges the receipt of his note of the 15th. instant accompanied with the highly esteemed present from Mrs. Duddley of Hickory nutts, "from a tree in Ulster, the only one of the kind known in Newyork," which he accepts with peculiar pleasure. To perpetuate this memento of the kind regard of Mrs. & Mr Duddley, he has sent one Dozzen of those nuts, to be planted in his garden at the Hermitage, to encircle the Tomb of his departed wife, & to have the following inscription engraved on the marble—"*The Duddley Hickory of Ulster Newyork*, presented by Mrs. & Mr. Duddley to the President."

The President requests his sincere thanks to be presented to Mrs. Duddley for this kind token of her respect, in whose welfare he will always take the most lively interest.

AN draft, DLC (38).

From James Gwin

Nash. Dec 18 1830

Der. Genral

your Kind favour of the 25th Nov, is now before me the friendley attention you have given my Letter in which I soliseted a favour for my son, has strenthened all those Bonds of friendship which has bin Long nourshed in my heart towards you, I regret that I had not knowen the Rule in the department of admiting but one of a famley.[1] I therefore Bag leave to withdrw, with your permision my sons recomendation as a Clerk in the P.O.D as I highley approve of the Rule that is adopted in the department, and as I wish by no meains to gave your unprincibeld opponents a plea of complaint, on account of partiality, but as there will be a grate opening to young men of interprise & industry in the newly acquerd Indian Teritory If he could git som place in the Ginneral Survayors department that would help him to git a start in the world it would be most graitfully receved and never forgotten by your old & unwavering friend, my son has studed all the parts of survaying with doctor Thrustian and has had som practice, he is a stronge active young man in the prime of Life, and can go through aney kind of fiteage, but should aney araingement have taken place for him before this reaches you, it will be well and if not I hope you will pardon my solisitude for my childrens wellfare, I have spent the prime of my life in serving the church & state nerley gratiousley and have bin unfortunate in the things of this world I have obayd the call of my country from 14 years of age at which age I went with my elder brothers in to the armey of the revelution, 40 years ago I reached this country—I then found you hearr a young man full of strenth, and readey to meet danger. I can say with you I never shund danger in all the perilous scens of indean warfare that we was subject too in the setling this country and down to the close of perials on the plains of orlens. There are but few Left now to tell thaire children what the furst settelors of this country had to incounter, I have served the church about 30 years in my feabel manor, she has not bin abel to do aney for my help in my Last years, my country has never done aney thing for me untill your good heart noticed my unfourtinate Samuel—but I have no complaint againts my country nor the church, I carry my boun-tey with me, which is I have indeavoured to serve my genaration from pure motives for the genral good and am still readey & wiling to suffer and die for my country & her pure institutions which makes her children free men, I confes I have a grate desier to see my children placed in her servis, and near your purson, for thare is no men on Erth that I would soonor Trust your life with than my sons, perhaps you will conclude I am giting quite Vaine, be it so, no man Knowes how to mak alawence for exprseans of a warm heart better then yourself—

before this reaches you I presume you will have gotten a letter from our friend Cryer on the subject of the rencounter that took place between Genl Dashae & Col Burton, Cryer informd me he had ritin to you on that subject in detaile as he was an Eye witness to the hole afare but Lest that Letter should faile, I will gave you a few perticlers as cryer gave them to me—the court in Gallatin ajurnd to gave the gentelmen an oppertunitey of adresing the peopal, Deshae had in a prvious speach stated that he did not know what had given Col. Burton offenc at him unles it was in concequenc of advice he had gaven you on the subject of taken Maj Ettan into the cabbinet which he deshae opposed (on acount of his wife being a woman of bad fame, this subject was revived again in the court house in the course of which Col Burton gave deshae the D—d lye, deshae maid at him for battel. Burton presented his pistol at Deshas brest but the pistol mist fier he then thew the pistol at Desha and walked out of the house desha followed him Burton commenced Caining him & broke his cain to peaces on him—while this was going on Deshaes newphew struck Burton with a rock which brauht Burton to the ground. Deshae gumpt on him and gouged both his Eys badley so the fight ended—Deshae was find $37. Deshae after the tryal was over atacked Cryer (who was examend on the case in court) and thretned to whip him, but Cryer told him he did not intend to Let him whip him deshae turnd off and said he would see him at another time so the matter stands between them—deshae declined, being a candedate, and recommended Genl. Hall to whome he gave his intrest, Hall accepted and declard himself a candedate. the Race is now between Hall & Burton, deshaes conduct has so disgusted the peopal, that maney of Genl Halls friends will not suport him, because he is cald Deshas candi-date and I have no doubt but that he will Loose his alection in concequenc of it altho he was the most popler man in the district as you know[2]

now Sr. thairr is no Doubt with me that Genl deshae has ruiend his popelaratey by Meddeling with Mrs Ettans Caractor the feeling part of the Communatey feel indignent at the man that with out aney pravacation will attempt to Engur feemal Caractor, and if Mrs. Ettan does conduct herself fair & prudent (which I hope she will) and be patiant she may live to see her slanders put to shame and her & her beloved husband &

children Coverd with honer—but much depends on her prudent conduct   publick centement in this place is grately turned in her favour this
has bin prodused by reading the Docoment that was Left with me.

I hope Maj. Ettan will not pay aney attention to Deshaes remarks
about his wife. Let his friends settel that matter with deshae heare. desha
is a rash imprudent man, and is not governed by sound good reason
he had a faire oppertunity to have gotten out of the difficulty that he
brought himself into about Mrs. Ettan when the testemoney was so cleare
in her favour and to which he might have had (& perhaps had free acces
too) but his foolish vaine heart would not yield to honorabel concesion,
which would have saved his popelaraty, the time is past he must abide
his fate—our anuel conference unanimouly disaproved the conduct of
our Misionareys in the nation the prosedens of which you will see in the
publik prints[3]—May our most Holey & most indulgent Creator preserve
you & bring you safe through all your troubels to your grave in peace[.]
yours in the Bonds of true friendship

James Gwin

[Endorsed by AJ:] The Revd. James Gwin—to be answered. A. J.

ALS, DLC (38).
    1. Gwin's eldest son, Samuel Gwin (c1794–1838), had received a Post Office Department
clerkship at Washington in 1829. Another son, William McKendree Gwin (1805–1888), was
appointed federal marshal for Mississippi by AJ in 1833 and later became a U.S. senator
from California.
    2. Hall defeated Burton to succeed Desha in the August 1831 congressional election.
    3. On September 25, 1830, eight Methodist missionaries to the Cherokees adopted
resolutions protesting removal as ruinous to the Indians and calling on the Tennessee Annual
Conference for support. On November 12 the Conference approved resolutions reproving
the missionaries for interfering in political affairs.

From Sylvester Simmons Southworth

(Private & Confidential)

Providence R.I. December 18. 1830.

Sir,

I am the editor and joint proprietor of the paper, which I forward you
with this letter. I have uniformly opposed your election, to the Presidency,
with candor and temper, first because I never was an admirer of many
of your military acts, and Secondly, because I have always entertained
a warm political and personal friendship for Mr Clay. Your Message,
delivered to the present Congress, has had a tendency to alter my opinions
concerning you; and it has convinced me, that I have always been in error,
with reference to your political sentiments and views of policy.

If the recommendations, contained in your message, be followed, the
nation must be revived and benefitted, and a grateful people, will hail you

as their friend and benefactor. You have taken a bold stand to put down the profligacy and corruptions of former administrations, and I pray you may succeede.

I behold in your message, everything that the american people could ask or hope for. It is the ablest and most comprehensive State Paper that I have ever read, and as such it will be cherished by the good citizens of this country. By the paper, which I send you, you will see, that I have approved of parts of the Message, which are the most objectionable to your New England opposers.

I have the honor to be Dr Sir your fellow citizen and most obedient Humble servt.

Sylvester S. Southworth
Ed. Literary Subaltern

[Endorsed by AJ:] private—Mr. S. Southworth R.I. letter inclosing his paper with his strictures on the Message—to be carefully preserved A. J.

ALS, DLC (38; 16-1486). Southworth (1797–1872) had established the *Literary Subaltern* in Providence, R.I., in 1829.

From Joseph M. White

WASHINGTON, December 18th 1830.

SIR:—

I have had the honour to receive a note from your private secretary, stating that you had considered the answer of Governor Duval, to the charges against him satisfactory.

The individual who sent them, avers his readiness to prove them, & as they implicate the official conduct of an officer, holding an important, and responsible trust, it is due to him and to the territory that they should be investigated. To give authenticity to the testimony, and to afford to the governor an opportunity of cross examination; I am requested by Mr. Wyatt, to solicit the appointment of an agent, to receive the testimony, and to have Governor Duval notified of the fact. I was led to believe from a conversation I had with you, that representations had been made from sources deemed respectable, that the individual preferring the charges, was one of infamous character.

It is not my purpose to forestal the decision by giving weight to the accusations, nor is it proper that I should suffer charges of serious import to be overlooked by general denunciations against an individual who solicits an investigation into abuse of power.

It is proper, therefore, that your Excellency should be informed, that the person who sent them had been three times elected a member of the legislative council of the territory, from the largest district in it, and *could now out Poll the governor* for any office in the community in which they both live.

I have the honour to be, Your most obedient servant,

JOSEPH M. WHITE.

Printed, Tallahassee *Floridian*, October 23, 1832 (mAJs). In December 1831 AJ nominated Duval for a new four-year term as governor. White and others lodged protests against the nomination and renewed their charges against Duval. After investigation, the Senate confirmed Duval by 32 to 10 on April 30, 1832.

From Amos Kendall

It was stated to me in 1828, that the Branch of the United States Bank at Louisville in Kentucky, by the act of two of its directors, did, on the Sunday preceding the state election in 1825, *give* to Samuel Q. Richardson and others $250 of the funds of that Branch, to be applied in carrying the election in Jefferson county in favor of the party then called the Old Court Party; that two persons on the same day, went to Shippingsport and opened several grog-shops with a part of the money and collected together the boatmen and loose characters preparatory to next day's operations; that another party made similar arrangements and hired all the hacks in Louisville for the election, with the balance of the money; that on Monday, the first day of the election, the hacks so hired, with banners and mottoes, were constantly employed in carrying up the voters thus influenced and collected, from Shippingsport and other places: By which means the Old Court Party carried the election by about 400 majority.[1]

The next year, when this influence was not exerted, the New Court Party succeeded in that county by more than 400 majority.

[Endorsed by AJ:] James McGillycuddy, Louisville to be addressed upon the within subject—through the Secretary of State or Treasury

AD, DLC (38; 16-1505). Samuel Q. Richardson (1791–1835) was a Frankfort lawyer and James McGilly Cuddy was a Louisville businessman. Kendall had sent this same account to Treasury secretary Ingham a year earlier, on November 23, 1829, naming Richardson as his informant (Ingham Papers, PU).

1. In 1823 the Kentucky Court of Appeals voided a state debtor relief law opposed by the Bank of the United States. The legislature responded by supplanting the existing court with a new one. The two courts vied for legitimacy until 1826, when the Old Court prevailed. The contest prefigured later political alignments, with many Clay men backing the Old Court and future Jacksonians supporting the New. Kendall, then a Kentucky editor and a Clay man, was a leader of the New Court party.

To Samuel Delucenna Ingham

Decbr. 20th. 1830

Sir

A communication, of which the within is a copy, has reached me from a quarter entitled to credit, and I think it due as well to the public interest as the credit of the Bank that its truth or falshood should be established. you are therefore requested to send Mr. McGilleycuddy a copy of the enclosed memorandom and request him to say how far it is warranted by the facts in the case—to the end that if his statement corroborates the enclosed, it may be communicated to the Bank and steps taken to correct such abuses in future[.] I am very respectfully yr mo. ob. servt.

Andrew Jackson

[Endorsed by AJ:] Copy of letter to Mr S. D. Ingham dated 20th. Decbr 1830, with the copy of Mr. K.s memorandom within—A J.   this to be filed A.J

ALS draft, DLC (38).

Memorandum Book on the Nomination of Stockley Donelson Hays

[This entry, appearing out of sequence near the back of Jackson's memorandum book, was written some time later than the events of December 19 and 20 it describes, most likely during or after Senate action on Hays's nomination in February 1831.]

On the 19th. day of Decbr. 1830, an interview was had by the President with Mr Poindexter, Judge Ellis, Genl Hinds, and judge Grundy on the subject of nominating Col S. D. Hays for the Survayor Genl office State of M. after explaining the strong & respectable recommendations presented to the President, urging his public services, & the claims of his father & the father of his wife, his poverty, and his military services in last war in the defence of M. against the Indians &c &c—judge Ellis remarked, that he could not join in the recommendation of Col Hays as he had recommended another, but if I nominated him he would vote for him, Mr Poindexter, by his silence, acquiesced, and judge Grundy after the Gentlemen with himself passed out of room, returned & said to me, *now*, you will send up the nomination of Col. Hays—I replied I would tomorrow; & accordingly did so—the day after his nomination I recd.

a letter from Mr. P. objecting &c &c to the nomination—see letters & secrete journal.[1]

AN, DLC (64). George Poindexter (1779–1853) and Powhatan Ellis were Mississippi's two senators and Thomas Hinds was its sole congressman. Stockley D. Hays had been quarter-master of Tennessee troops in the War of 1812 and later an Army judge advocate. His father, AJ's brother-in-law Robert Hays, had fought in the Revolution and mustered Tennessee troops in the War of 1812. Stockley's father-in-law, Thomas Butler (1754–1805), was also a Revolutionary veteran and a career Army officer. AJ nominated Hays for surveyor of public lands south of Tennessee on December 20, and wrote Poindexter the same day (below).

1. A memorandum in AJ Donelson's hand records Senate proceedings in executive session on Hays's nomination from December 23, 1830, through February 3, 1831 (DLC-38).

To George Poindexter

December 20th. 1830

Dear Sir,

I have just received your note of this date in relation to the appointment of a surveyor for the district of public lands south of Tennessee. Your views correspond with mine and the practice of the Government in most cases heretofore: but they do not seem to have embraced the fact that the district in question included two states instead of one; and that therefore an appointment upon the principles stated by you would not necessarily fall to Mississippi. Seeing that Louisiana would remind me as forcibly of her claims as you have represented those of ~~Louisiana~~ Mississippi, it occurred to me that both not being able to obtain it, both would consent to relieve the President of the delicacy of a choice between them and allow him to offer them a citizen any way qualified from another state. Another consideration suggesting the propriety of this course may be found in the fact that the public interest had already been much neglected by the various removals and resignations to which that office had been lately subjected, and the consequent necessity for the appointment of one who would certainly devote his whole attention and time to its duties.[1] Col Hays combining all the necessary qualifications and having been on various occasions strongly recommended for office by many of the distinguished citizens of Tennessee, has been therefore selected and nominated for the one in question. I had hoped after the conversation between us on the evening to which you have alluded, that this step would not have been unsatisfactory

Should the land districts be seperated and Mississippi form an entire one the claims of the worthy gentleman you have named will not be overlooked.

I have expressed my concurrence with your views generally as those which must in the main regulate the practice of the Government in making appointments. You must be sensible however that they do not derive their force from any claim which the citizens of any state or states can urge as a matter of right strictly speaking. All such offices are created for the public good. I am very respectfully yr. obt svt

Andrew Jackson

LS in AJ Donelson's hand, Ms-Ar (16-1509). J. F. H. Claiborne, *Mississippi as a Province, Territory and State* (1880), pp. 398–99. On December 23 Poindexter moved in the Senate to refer Hays's nomination to a select committee to inquire whether he was a Mississippi resident and properly qualified for the post. On January 12, 1831, the Senate adopted a modified resolution referring Hays's nomination to the Public Lands Committee and dropping the query about his residency. The committee collected the recommendations sent for Hays and also, at Poindexter's prompting, canvassed the eleven members of Tennessee's congressional delegation on his competence and sobriety. All the replies except David Crockett's were noncommittal, disclaiming much knowledge of Hays. Crockett, in whose district Hays lived, declared him insolvent and unskilled, "notorious for intemperance—bordering on Sottishness," and "emphaticaly" unfit to serve (DNA-RG 46). The committee reported on January 31. On February 3, the Senate approved, 22 to 10, a resolution by Poindexter declaring it "inexpedient" to appoint a non-resident to office within a state "without some evident necessity for such appointment." On February 18, AJ withdrew Hays's nomination for surveyor and nominated him instead for register of the Clinton, Miss., land office. He was confirmed, 25 to 19, on February 21 (*Senate Executive Proceedings*, 4:135, 136, 145, 147, 150–51, 158, 161).

1. AJ had removed James P. Turner as surveyor in September 1829 for William S. Hamilton. After Hamilton declined, he appointed Joseph Dunbar in December 1829. Dunbar's resignation effective January 1, 1831, opened the vacancy for Hays.

To the Marquis de Lafayette

December 23rd. 1830—

My Dr Sir

I avail myself of the visit which Genl Bernard is about to pay to regenerated France to offer you my friendly salutations, and bespeak in his behalf that attention which no one so well as yourself will know how to apply to his peculiar destiny. Tho' unable to perform a part in the glorious struggle which has the honor of signalising more than all others the name of France; I can assure you, it had not a more sympathising observer in any country than Genl Bernard, or one who foresaw with more accuracy the great moral developments of which it was the fruit.

This visit therefore to his native land will be like that of a child to a Parent who were parted in adversity, but who have each outlived the shock, and regained under the auspices of a kind Providence and a noble relience on the principles of liberty, the happiness of meeting again, and of knowing that there is an altar around which they can now hear common worship, tho', a sea may roll between them.

I refer you to the Genl. for an account of such of the incidents of this Country as may interest you; and tender to you and the amiable family of

La Grange, the homage of my sincere regard, and my prayes for your long life, & happiness, both here & hereafter.[1]

Andrew Jackson

ALS, NIC (16-1549). LS draft in AJ Donelson's hand with closing by AJ, DLC (38). Simon Bernard (1779–1839) was a French-born military engineer. He served on Napoleon's staff and after Waterloo came to the U.S., where, on Lafayette's recommendation, he was appointed in 1816 to plan a system of coastal fortifications, with the pay and title of an Army general. In 1831 he resigned, returned to France, and reentered French military service under Louis Philippe.
    1. La Grange was Lafayette's estate outside Paris. AJ's word in the draft is "prayers."

From Joseph Kincaid and from Mushulatubbe et al.

December the 23d 1830 Chocktaw Nation

Dear Sir:

we are on the treaty Ground at the Dancing Rabbit in Council assembled few in number it was a Secret kept by them that we were to assemble and accede to any thing that they should propose there is several Traders has been in our Nation Trading with our people and has great acpts which has not been Recognised as Just acpts. I have no Education therefore it appears to me that you have taken all advantages of us—therefore we Request of you and Every Gentleman in Congress to Do all they can for us poor Red people as we are Distresed and oblidged to leave our Country and leave our Native land and go to the west I am but one Individual but I am athorised by our head men to write to you to Do the best and all you can for the poor Red people I am your most obednt. friend and humble Servant

Joseph Kincaid

Friends and brothers

the Honr. Andrew Jackson presid of the US we are oblidged to write to you that we as a comparison has been in a habbit of hireing men which if he performed we paid him well if not we turned him off without any pay we have Employd and payed those Yankee Missionarys for twelve years for which we have Recd. no compensationsation we have never Recd. a Scholar out of their Schools that was able to keep a grogshop Book when we found that we Could Get nothing from them we Established an acadamy in kentucky under the Direction of the presidendent and the Superintendence of R M Johnston from which we have Recd. a great number of first Rate Scholars, for the Misionaryes under the Direction of Cyrus Kingsberry they have six years of annuity Coming to them of the apropriation made to them for Servises that they promised to Render to us which they have not performed therefore we Request that they Should get no more of our money this is all that we have to say to you but we have lost all Confidence of the Missionarry and Humbly Request that they get no more of our money,[1] I am with Respect your mos obedent. Servt.

Mushuletubbe	his	X	mark
Joseph Kincaid	his	X	mark
Oklabbe	his	X	mark
Ispiah homah	his	X	mark
Hiram King			
Peter King			
Charles King			
James M. King			

Test M Mackey US Intr.

[Endorsed by John H. Eaton:] I wish to see the order of the choctaw chiefs setting out this fund to the Missories   E

LS and DS, DNA-RG 75 (M234-774). Copy, DNA-RG 46 (16-1548, 16-1381). *SDoc* 512, 23d Cong., 1st sess., vol. 2, pp. 205–6 (Serial 245). Kincaid was Mushulatubbe's nephew. The December 23 date on this document may be an error. The date on the address envelope, in the same hand, is December 3. AJ, in Washington, received and forwarded it on to Eaton on December 27 (below).
    1. In 1818 the American Board of Commissioners for Foreign Missions began a school establishment in the Choctaw Nation under Presbyterian missionary Cyrus Kingsbury (1786–1870). The Choctaws supported the system with appropriations from their annuity. In 1820 the three Choctaw districts had pledged $2,000 each, $6,000 all told, to the schools for the next sixteen years. By 1830, when the Board reported operating nine schools with 278 students, total annuity funding had reached $58,000.

To John Branch

Decbr. 24th. 1830—

The President with his respects to the secretary of the Navy, encloses him a letter just received from Commodore Barron, on the subject of the dry Dock at Gosport. The President desires that you should make known his ~~desire~~ solicitude to have this Dock compleated as early as possible, that our large vessels of war may be got in them for repair & prevented from that ruin that must ensue from their present condition—and urge upon the Superintendent the propriety of pushing the stonework to its completion, & in the mean time to attend to the other description of work, such as clearing the way for the Ships to enter the Dock &c &c &c—so that the whole may be compleated at the same time

AN, DNA-RG 45 (M124-125). Congress had authorized construction of a dry dock at the Gosport navy yard in 1827. Answering a query from AJ about progress, James Barron wrote him on November 30 predicting completion of the stonework within a year, and suggesting that AJ inform supervising engineer Loammi Baldwin Jr. (1780–1838) of his desire to have the whole finished by then. The Gosport dry dock opened in 1833.

James Alexander Hamilton
to William Berkeley Lewis

N.Y. Decr. 24' 1830

My dear Lewis

I have written a formal letter which is enclosed denying all fully the statement of the letter written to be used as you may please

It is difficult for *me* as you know to be responsible for what my brothers or friends may say but it is quite as impossible for me to restrain the Gossip & falsehood of the letters written in this city as it is for you there in Washington

I thank you for the attention to my friends the Hones which has been very great & I am sure quite satisfactory

My respects to all[.] your &

J A H

ALS, DLC (38).

[Enclosure: Hamilton to Lewis]

New York Decr. 24' 1830.

Dear Sir

Your letter of the 20' Inst. in which you state that letters have been received in Washington stating that one of my brothers has been heard to say that I had written the Presidents inaugural address and that Mr Van Buren wrote his last message & I corrected it was received yesterday and immediately communicated to my Brothers who all state most unequivocally that they have never said any thing of the kind and they authorise me to assure you that the statement is false in all its parts   Alexander has sent me a written statement to that effect & the other two are ready to do the same if required

This is a part of the tactics of the enemy   Their game is desperate & will be played in any way however unworthy—(You are authorised to use this letter as you please   I remain Your friend & Srt

James A Hamilton

[Endorsed by AJ:] Colo. J. A. Hamilton denying, positively the slang about the inagural address being written by him—to be kept on file— A. J. Decbr 26th. 1830—

ALS, DLC (38). AJ was frequently charged with not writing his own messages. On December 11 the *New York Daily Advertiser* printed an anonymous letter from Washington, dated December 6, stating that "the disjointed parts" of AJ's second annual message were "put together by Mr. Van Buren" and "smoothed over and varnished by Mr. Hamilton." Hamilton's brothers Alexander (1786–1875), John Church (1792–1882), and Philip (1802–1884) were attorneys in New York City.

To John Christmas McLemore

Washington Decbr. 25th. 1830—

My Dr Sir

The company having retired after the bustle of the day, at 9 oclock P. M. I sit down to reply to your private letter of the 17th ultimo agreable to the promise made you in my last—several attempts have been made by me to comply with this promise sooner, but always interrupted, & at this period of the night will not allow me to pay that full attention to it which it merits, and which I would wish to bestow upon it.

You are fully apprised of the causes that forced me from that retirement, which I had chosen, to repair a broken, and worn down constitution, in the service of my country; and with what reluctance I yielded to the wishes of my friends, and the solicitations of the people throughout the union. It was urged upon me, that the great principles of the constitution ~~that~~ upon which our republican government rests might be preserved, and our liberties perpetuated. My services being thus thought necessary, I yielded to the call of my country, & permitted my name to be presented to the nation. You will remember the torrents of abuse, with the vilest slanders that were heaped upon me; and ~~even~~ these tools of corruption could not spare female character, and my dear wife was made the victam of these fiends, & demons of slander and her life shortened, by the many unjust attacks upon her; she was indeed permitted to live to witness the triumph of virtue over the vilest slander, & detraction; for which, under the heavy bereavement by her death, I feel thankful to my god. I was elected—it became my duty then to form a Cabinet to aid me in the administration of the government, and carry into effect they great principles of reform called for by the people, and for which I had been drawn from my chosen retirement. In this selection, it behoved me to have one, at least, in whom I had from long experience, full confidence, and with whom I knew I could converse upon all subjects, without fear of that confidence being violated. Two men presented themselves to my mind; judge White & Major Eaton, either of whom I knew worthy of my confidence, & capable. My well tried friend, judge Overton, who I consulted agreed with me in opinion, and upon the receipt of the certain intelligence of my election I wrote judge White confidentially on the subject, requesting him to be one of my Cabinet, but on the event that he would not consent, to hand the letter to Major Eaton, adding that they both had an agency in drawing me from my retirement, and one, or the other, must aid me in the administration of the Government. You have been advised, that the first declined, and the latter with great reluctance agreed to comply with my request. Experience has taught me the wisdom of my course, and the propriety of my choice; Major Eaton has but one wish—the prosperity of my administration. He looks not for any other reward. The reasons why I had selected Major Eaton was made known to my friends. The moment this selection of Major Eaton was known, then the combination, & conspiracy commenced, and every abominable slander, that wickedness & slander falshood could invent, to coerce me to abandon him, was put into circulation about him & his wife—having a full knowledge of the purity of his character, I could not abandoned him, nay I ought not, justice & truth told me, that disgrace awaited me if I did, & if I had, I am sure a just god must have frowned upon the act. Under these circumstances, let me ask you, what ought to have been the conduct of my friends. The moral character of Major Eaton was known by every man acquainted with him to be without spot or blemish. My friendship for, & confidence in him, was known to all, he had taken to himself a wife of his own choice, and his moral character being without blemish, the very act of his marrying her was proof to every man of virtue, & honor, that he believed her to be virtuous, and it was anough for his friends to know that he had married her to put down the slang of the gossips of the city, and their duty to treat her as a virtuous woman, as Mrs. Eaton unless proof of her want of virtue was brought forth—but I happened to be here, when the slander began & knew the rise & cause of it, & I have always believed her as virtuous a woman as lives. But this is not all. To every one who knew the obligations of Masonry, and did know, that Major Eaton was a mason, Mr Timberlake a mason & Major Oneal, (the father) also a mason, was surely sufficient with all masons (unless indeed Major Eaton was viewed as one of the most wicked, depraved, & perjured villains on earth, it was proof positive of the fals-hood of the rumors & slanders circulated by this combination of gossips in this city for the most base, & wicked purposes; this you as a mason must concede. Under these circumstances, what was the course that friend-ship justice, & propriety pointed out, to be pursued by my friends, and my cabinet who, had been selected with a view to harmony, and who came together in the most cordial friendship; was it not the imperious duty of my cabinet that harmony & sociability between them & their families should exist, and be maintained, and that my Dr Emily, who represented me by filling the vacancy occasioned by the death of my Dr wife should know no one; should make no diference in the comity extended to any of the heads of departments & their families on all proper occasions, and repel by their conduct the vile slanders of the Gossips of this combination, by shewing by their conduct, that the despised the slanderer, by shewing to Major Eaton & his wife on all proper occasions a proper respect such as was due to his good moral character and my boosom & well tried friend. This appear to me to have been the course, of friendship to me, and justice to Major Eaton, who was my boosom friend, and not by their shunning Major Eaton & his family & associating with his violent enemies & traducers, giveing to the malicious & wicked an opportunity of saying "surely these rumors about Major Eaton & his family must be true, or the family of the President would associate with them as they do with the other heads of Departments, particularly as Major Eaton is known to be the boosom friend of the President." Therefore we will not associate with them as they do not." ¿was this not well calculated to drive Major Eaton out of my Cabinet? was it not calculated to weaken my administration, by given food to my enemies to attack me for having appointed a man with whom my family would not associate—nay it was an imputation upon me, that I would attempt to bring dishonor upon my family and my country by introducing them into dishonorable company & a base character in my cabinet—has this ever been the case, have I ever attempted to dishonour my connections by associating with bad characters? why then was it, that my family situated, as I was, departed from my council, & obayed that of strangers; became the associates of the greatest revilers of my friend some of whom rumor said as much about, as about Major & Mrs Eaton? was this treatment proper to me as President of the united States and by those representing me as such in the ~~stead~~ place of my departed wife—¿was this proper as the head of the family, & they in the ~~stead~~ place of my children to one they knew I was attached by the strongest ties of friendship & gratitude—one in whom I had the greatest confidence, and in consequence thereof, I had invited into my cabinet, and who I could not part from under existing circumstance without disgrace to myself, and great injustice to him. I am willing to ascribe all this to the inexperience of my family who were overreached by the secrete workings of the great political magician who works in darkness, is plausible, but cunning, and as deceitful as Satan. For political purposes, Major Eaton was to be driven from my cabinet, and compel me to submit to the disgrace & injury of such an event. It was known I loved my family, the eyes & arts therefore of the combination was turned to, & set upon ~~my family~~ them to bring about this object, it was believed I would yield Major Eaton, rather than have a split with them, or seperate from them. I saw their object admonished my family, & with tears ~~in my eyes~~, reiterated to them over, & over again, and assured them I could submit to any thing, but to disgrace, & the sacrafice of my friend; but all in vain, the arts & cunning of those gossips poured the rumors of slanders in their ears, they listened to them & were poisoned; would read nothing in vindication of Mrs. Eatons innocence, altho, *on my table & refered to*, abandoned my council, adhered to that of strangers and the result you know. I was prepared to sacrafice any thing but my honor & my friend, this I could not, nor never will—all that was necessary of my family, nay, all that I asked of them, was to extend to Major Eaton & his, the same comity that they extended to the other heads of departments. This was a moral duty, it was due to me, from my situation, it was due to justice, it was due to friendship, and that harmony that was necessary to be maintained in my Cabinet; & had it been yielded, every thing would have been well, harmony maintained, and my enemies disappointed & ~~disregarded~~ defeated; but alas, my advice was disregarded, that of strangers followed, and the harmony of my family destroyed, & my peace of mind unwarrantably disturbed.

How different has been the course of my true friends here, and else where; Major Barry & his lady, Genl Clark & his family, Major Smith, Col F. Preston & theirs, Mr Dudley & his, Mr Kendal, Major Smith & theirs, Doctor Jones & his, Genl D. Green & his, and hundreds more that could be named, pursued a course worthy of themselves, & just to Major Eaton and to myself. They never shunned the society of Major & Mrs. Eaton; *and have their characters suffered on that account*, and whilst Genl Gains, (agreable to his mission) is secretely associating with that *black hearted villain* Dr B. McNairy, and aiding in the secrete slander, & heading the unheard of combination against Major Eaton, & his lady, the family of Genl Leavensworth are, the inmates of Major Eatons family, and Mrs. Eatons companion every where.[1] Contrast this open magnanimous course, to the association with secrete slanderers, against female character, and which comports most with that justice & magnanimity due to female reputation, & to honor. Had the course adopted by judge Overton, Mr Randal McGavock, Genl John Coffee, Mr L Donelson and the citizens of Franklin been adopted, instead of the unjust & cruel course of some citizens of Nashville, I am sure it would have redounded more to their credit both, at home, & abroad, and more to their own peace of mind, when left free from bias, to calm reflection—for really there never was a more cruel unjust & unchristian combination than that, & what was adding to its wickedness, that all this was done on mere rumor, and before she was in the country, & before it was known that she would even stop in the village.

You have intimated to me that I might have recd. improper impressions from Major Eaton & Major Lewis. In this I assure you, that you are mistaken, Major & Mrs. Donelson never had, as far as I know, a better friends, like myself, ~~he~~ Major Lewis regretted the course that was adopted by my family, so grateful to my enemies, & unpleasant to my friends, when it was in the power of my family by a proper course towards all my Cabinet & their families, at once to put it down—and as to Major Eaton he never conversed with me on the subject but twice, and once was, on our return from Point Comfort on the cruel treatment on that trip, which was observed by all, and when the persecution was at its hight, and the attempt made to drive him from society, he made known to me his feelings, including the unjust conduct of my family on all public occasions keeping round them his open & inveterate enemies & Mrs Donelsons distant coolness to Mrs. Eaton Mrs. Barry & their associates, & the cruel conduct experienced from her, at the Dutch ministers. But on all occasions has manifested the most cordial wishes to harmonise with every branch of the family, and Major A. J. Donelson knew his goodness of heart. I had put him & Edward Butler under his charge when first sent to the military academy.[2] I can assure you, my family were overreached by the designing and artful cunning of the puppets of J. C. Calhoun, who in secrete, worked the wiers, and who dreaded the popularity of Eaton, & that he would not be his supporter, & it is only the second Edition of the secrete lunge in the dark against me in 1818, under the open & avowed declarations of friendship, & support. I pray you read the Documents in the case of Eaton, keeping in view the fact of Dr Ely's being the firm & decided friend of Eaton, and his note to me, *not to seperate from him*, and then, his course taken in his letter to me, against him, & his enquiry of me, if me & Major Eaton was not *opposed to Mr Calhoun*, and at once you will see, that all this originated in a political combination to put Major Eaton out of the Cabinet, & disgrace me, and weaken my administration for having appointed him. I say read the Documents & see who were the actors in this thing—apostate clergy, perjured masons &c &c, & you will understand how the combination was got up, & why it has extended itself to Nashville, and why the letter was written from there to Lexington Kentucky a combination unheard of before in any christian country against female character, & which has established a precedent by which the most innocent female, can be destroyed—on *rumour*, which can be set on foot by *a hired slave*, and propagated, by hired gossips—ought not every husband, father & mother shudder at such a precedent—and this is done in the case under review, and the evidence of her innocence refused to be read by those whose ears have been open to these rumors— justice & truth combined with charity must blush at, & condemn such a course.

The political view you present of late, of Nashville, is a further confirmation of the source of the combination and it being founded on political views. The conduct of Genl Desha is proof strong as holy writ. He is a strong Calhounite how can his course & inveterate hostility have arisen against me & Major Eaton but from this source, I had never lisped to a soul but to himself, a word of disatisfaction of his course against Eaton I was his constant friend & he professing to be mine, leaves my House in apparent friendship goes to Gallatine & there declares his intention of coming out against me & Major Eaton, an by way of excuse for himself for this sommerset, tells an *unfounded falshood* knowing it to be such. This combination can be traced into Alabama. The great author of the nullifying Doctrine J. C. Calhoun had often introduced to Colo. McKinley his views on the nulifying Doctrine. The Colo. possessing too much candor, openly told him he was in toto, against this Doctrine. Being thus informed, McKinley was secretely to be undermined & put down.

Calhoun having got Mr Lewis of Alabama into his crew & under his influence, a secrete course was adopted, the Govr. of Alabama, after his declarations of friendship towards McKinley, to Genl Coffee & myself & that his name should not be used in opposition to Colo. McKinley, has violated this pledge, his name is up, & it is supposed McKinley is beaten.[3] Thus the nulifying doctrine is to be introduced into alabama. Moor is to become my opposer & Calhouns supporter—look into the subscription to Tanneyhills paper, and who of my professed friends but those attached to Calhoun, has become subscribers.[4] I knew his treachery, I warned my family against it, but all to no purpose, Major Donelson was so much over-reached by his plausible pretences, that at one time, he like myself thought he was too honorable to have made the *secrete movement* in the *secrete cabinet* against me in 1818, when he was making the strongest declaration of support and approbation of my conduct. The scene will now I trust be changed when I have positive proof of his duplicity on that occasion, and the course of Mr McDuffie his satelite, in his report of the Bank last session, & his insulated report about the Presidential reform—this, leaving all other amendments recommended out of view, shews the cloven foot, & points directly to Mr Calhoon   If Calhoun could have got Eaton driven out of the Cabinet, by his secrete & wicked plans, he knew it would afford a channel of attack by him & my enemies, against me, by which my standing was to be destroyed, & his elevated, & the popularity of Eaton, which he calculated against him, destroyed. This was as well understood by me at the time, as it is now, and all I regretted that the good sense of my friends could not see it, and my admonitions to my family could not prevail to disappoint, and put down such a combination of wickedness, gotten up purely, that a base deceptive demagogue, might thereby be elevated, on the destruction of private worth, & female character. The conduct of Genl Desha in his speech refering to Judge McLean, shews the importance the Calhounites place upon the destruction of Eaton, and his popularity.

The judge is himself seeking after elevation, whether in conjunction with Mr C. or not is not material. He knows that Eaton will not support him therefore in a secrete way, with all his professions of religion, would secretely circulate slander against Major Eaton & his lady, altho he attended the wedding as an invited guest, and hailed the happy pair and took them into society as far as this religious judge could by his countenance. What a curse must heaven have in store for a man professing religion, that would thus act, I leave you to Judge. How far his honor is guilty of the conduct that has been ascribed to him by Desha I know not, I suppose in proper time Major Eaton will know. But one thing I do know he was endeavouring to injure me & Major Eaton by whispers to the Methodist Clergy—of this I have written proof.[5]

When you were first here, & before I ever set out for Nashville I gave you a full history of those things—made known to you my views &

wishes—and the objects of this wicked combination here, to destroy Eaton & his lady, drive them out of society & thereby injure me. You visited Major & Mrs. Eaton, was pleased with them, & expressed your concurrence in the view I had taken, an assured me that on your return to Nashville you would place all matters right there. Colo. Wilson[6] had given the same assurance, and fearing from the course of Mr Hill whilst here & knowing that his feelings were not good towards Major Eaton & his connections at Franklin, I was rejoiced to hear your declaration, for I knew if you did, I could with your & other friends restore harmony between my family & Major Eatons, for which I had struggled, & which would have been the first pleasure of my life—for it has become certain, that a friendly official course must be restored between my family and all the heads of departments and theres, or a seperation take place, an event of the most painful nature to me. you must remember when you met us & communicated to me the determination of a combination at Nashville, the pain I expressed, but the firmness of my course—when I got to the Springs & the whole combination exposed to me; & that my connections were countenancing it, I had feelings I hope never again to experience—they were still more accute, when Andrew told me, my family were not to continue such at the Hermitage, and when I reached my home found the angry feelings of my connections on this subject; the great injury that had been done to my friend, the constant & undeviating friend of my Dr. departed wife, it filled me with horror of the cruelty & wickedness of man, brought. fresh to my view the various wicked falshood levelled at the fair fame of her who was no more, & who never deserved it from any, I could not but feel for my friend, and deplore the errors of my connection, well calculated to disgrace & destroy me—my course was taken—you know the rest. A course that my calmn judgt. had fixed upon, to be proper & right, & my calm review has every day confirmed me in its justness and propriety, for I was willing to yield to my family, every thing, but the government of my House, and the abandonment of my friend without cause. I had often brought to their view, the old adage "that a House divided against itself could not stand"; and I did believe that those that Major Barry & his family, McLean & Rives—Duddly & hundreds others who had familiary associated with, and with whom I had as a boosom friend, could not disgracee my family, by extending to them the same comity as to the other heads of Departments. This was all that was required, and if it had been carried into effect, this wicked combination would have been put down, long since—& you may rest assured ~~they~~ my enemies will fall into the pitt that Calhoun & his wicked engines are preparing for me. But These things have gone by. The great delicacy is now how to restore harmony. I am taking a full view of the passing scenes, it must be restored, and my Cabinet a unite again, if this can be without seperating them, it will be a pleasure to me—and the moment a social intercourse due from my family to all the heads of departments can be restored, it will be the happiest moment of my life to see my Dr Emily and her two sweet little ones here, together with my sincere friend Mary Easton, but until that can be, I cannot have a female family here that will permit their names, & their conduct, to the heads of any departments, to be a source for my enemies to assail & destroy me. I must close this long & perhaps unconnected letter, but one founded in fact, & principle of justice to all. I shall write you again when I can see the course certain men take in congress. In the meantime I will be happy to hear from you & remember the adage "that a House divided against itself cannot stand"—and that I never will without cause abandon a friend. If any chooses to withdraw from me, however much I may regret it—They must go. Present me to your Lady & amiable family & to all my connections who may inquire for me—to old Mrs. D. to Emily & her two little ones, to Miss Mary Easton & say to her I have just recd. her kind letter which will be replied to as soon as I have leisure to William & his wife to Mr Martin & his to Stockly & his & believe your friend.[7]

Andrew Jackson

P.S. I have this moment recd a copy of a letter from Mr Crawford to Calhoun, in answer to Mr. _____ It is pointed & severe & proves Calhoun *a villain*.[8]

ALS, NHi (16-1562). Above the postscript AJ mistakenly wrote "Mr Jno. C. Calhoun" as the addressee. McLemore had been counseling Emily Donelson and Mary Ann Eastin on their replies to AJ. On November 10 he had written Donelson of his resolve to "risque *every thing*" by writing AJ about the Eaton affair. He would, "be the consequences what they may, tell our dear old friend the *whole truth and nothing but the truth*—that he is rong, and you right," that William B. Lewis was "the prime cause of all his misfortunes," and that AJ should "*get him out of his house*" and send Eaton abroad (Donelson Papers, DLC).

1. Henry Leavenworth (1783–1834) was an Army brevet brigadier general. His wife was Harriet Lovejoy Leavenworth.

2. AJ's ward Edward George Washington Butler (1800–1888) had entered West Point in 1816 and AJ Donelson in 1817, both graduating in 1820.

3. Dixon Hall Lewis (1802–1848) was an Alabama congressman.

4. Wilkins Tannehill (1787–1858) was a former mayor of Nashville. In November 1830 he issued a prospectus for a new pro-Clay paper, the *Nashville Herald*, to begin publishing in January 1831.

5. Supreme Court Justice John McLean was a prominent Methodist.

6. AJ's friend George Wilson (1778–1848) had published the *Nashville Gazette* from 1819 to 1827.

7. Catherine Donelson (1799–1836), the sister of William, Stockley, and Emily, was married to James Glasgow Martin (1791–1849).

8. On October 2 William H. Crawford had sent Calhoun a scathing letter assailing Calhoun's May 29 defense to AJ against the charges in Crawford's April 30 letter to John Forsyth. Branding Calhoun "a degraded and disgraced man, for whom no man of honor and character could feel any other than the most sovereign contempt," Crawford charged him with mounting quibbles and falsehoods in a vain and pathetic effort to exculpate his Cabinet treachery in 1818 (DLC-38; *Calhoun Papers*, 11:233–48).

From William Pitt Preble

(dup.)

The Hague, 25th. Decr. 1830

Sir

The Minister of Foreign Affairs informed the British Ambassador and myself last week, that we might expect to receive the decision of the King on the matter, referred to him as Arbiter, in the course of the month, provided nothing special intervened, which was not anticipated. Nothing has transpired in the sleightest degree indicative of what, that decision is to be.[1] Whatever it may be, I hope this is the last occasion, in which the Government of The United States will ever consent to refer a question of boundary to any Sovereign. Allow me also to assure you, that, whatever it may be, I have not been wanting in my earnest endeavors to watch over and protect the rights and interests of our country. It would I think be somewhat difficult to select a time, when the general course of events was less favorable, than that, during which the subject of our boundary has been pending before the King of this country. All possible jealousy had been awakened and prejudice excited against liberal principles. The present administration of the United States and its officers are regarded as the liberals of America, and more than suspected of sympathizing with the successful revolutionists of France and the liberals of Europe. There is in fact scarcely a foreign minister at this court, who has not given me distinctly to understand that all "the jacobinism" of Europe, as they call it, is to be traced to the example and institutions of America. In this state of feeling my views of propriety have led me to keep as far as possible aloof from the politics and excitement every where around me. This to me has not been a difficult task because the special interests and national faith and neutrality of my own country occupied a more important place in my estimation than even the spirit-stirring movements in Europe. At this Court such has been the King's feeling that two Ministers have been recalled at his request on suspicion of unfavorable leanings, as it is believed. My request now is that as early in the season as circumstances will admit, I may be permitted to return to The United States   It is believed that long before I can receive any answer from the U.S. the question of the future condition of Belgium will have been settled.[2] But I am not specially desirous that you should send me there though I am willing to go if The President wishes it. There is however a business which in case the King should decide in our favor I am desirous to have committed to me. By the seventh article of the Convention under which the King is now acting it is provided that the decision of the Arbiter "shall be carried without reserve into immediate effect *by commissioners* appointed for that purpose by the contracting parties" This subject has been pending many years. It is for the interest of Maine as well as of the U.S. that there should be an end of it and of the expense attending it. If the President will please to appoint me Commissioner on the part of the U.S. I will undertake that the business shall be finished promptly, effectually and well; and more over with all possible economy. *It shall not be a husbanded job.* It will be recollected by The President that the boundary to be established separating Maine from the British dominions will in length be not less than four hundred miles.

I am happy to see from the recent election in Maine that the popularity of the administration is firmly established there.[3] Private letters inform me that that popularity is still greater than the votes would seem to indicate. Of this I am sure that when the heat of personal and party animosity shall have passed away, the people of the U.S. will acknowledge the restoring and salutary influence of the present administration upon the movement and action of our National Government.

I have spoken of the form of granting a leave of absence rather than that of a recal. The Duke of Saxe Weimar, who is intimate with the King and high in his confidence has expressed to me a wish indicative of feeling that it was desired the government of the U.S. should keep a Minister here. But I am of the opinion that there is no occasion of keeping a Minister here either as a matter of interest or policy: at the same time it has appeared to me that a leave of absence might save appearances as well as feelings.[4]

With the highest respect and consideration I have the honor to be Sir your very obedient and humble servant.

Wm. P. Preble

ALS copy, DLC-Van Buren Papers (16-1579). Learning that the ship carrying the original of this letter had not yet sailed, Preble sent this copy to AJ on January 17, 1831, with a new letter again soliciting a leave of absence.

1. Unable to settle the boundary between Maine and Canada, the U.S. and Britain had agreed in an 1827 convention to refer the dispute to a friendly sovereign. King William I (1772–1843) of the Netherlands was chosen as arbiter, and in 1829 AJ appointed Preble minister to the Netherlands to present the American case. On January 10, 1831, William delivered a decision that awarded the U.S. somewhat over half the disputed territory. AJ submitted the settlement to the Senate, which refused it in 1832. Johan Gijsbert Verstolk van Soelen (1776–1845) was the Dutch foreign minister, and Charles Bagot (1781–1843) was the British ambassador.

2. Belgian provinces in the Netherlands had rebelled against Dutch rule and declared independence in October 1830, leading to the establishment of the Kingdom of Belgium in 1831.

3. In September elections Maine Jacksonians won the governorship, five of seven congressional seats, and majorities in the state legislature.

4. Before Preble's appointment in 1829 a chargé d'affaires rather than a full minister had represented the U.S. in the Netherlands. Karl Friedrich (1783–1853) was the Grand Duke of Saxe-Weimar-Eisenach.

To John Henry Eaton

Decbr. 27th. 1830—

The President with his respects to the Secretary of War encloses him a letter from Mushulatubby & other chiefs of the Choctaw Nation, & requests to be informed whether there has been any stipulation in the late treaty as it respects the annuity agreed to be given to the missionaries in the choctaw Nation for a school fund.[1]

The President intended to go to the office of the Sec. of War to day, but it is too bad; he has just received a copy of a letter from Mr Crawford to Mr. Calhoun, with extracts from Mr. A. & Crowningshields, which places Mr C. in a very unpleasant dilemma. The first clear day I will be over.[2]

AN, DNA-RG 107 (M222-27).
1. The Treaty of Dancing Rabbit Creek pledged the U.S. to continue all previous Choctaw annuities unchanged, to educate forty Choctaw youths for twenty years at its own expense, and to spend $10,000 erecting churches and schoolhouses and $50,000 over twenty years to support three teachers. It made no particular mention of missionary schools.
2. William H. Crawford had written Benjamin W. Crowninshield and John Q. Adams for their recollections of deliberations in Monroe's Cabinet. He appended extracts of their replies to his October 2 letter to Calhoun. Crowninshield, writing on July 25, 1830, recalled that Calhoun had been "severe" upon AJ's conduct in Florida. Adams wrote on July 30 that "it was urged" that AJ be brought to trial for taking St. Marks and Pensacola, but that he thought then, and still did, that AJ's conduct merited an even more "decided and unequivocal approbation" than it received (DLC-38; *Calhoun Papers*, 11:245, 247).

To John Coffee

Washington Decbr. 28th. 1830—

My Dr Genl

I have just received your letter of the 12th. instant, & in reply, well recollect the conversation that took place between Governor Moor & myself on the subject of Colo. McKinleys course in the appointment of Marshal for North Alabama, and also your communicating to me the conversation you had with him on this subject; viz, that my information had fully convinced him of the fair and upright course of Col McKinley in that case, and that he would not oppose him for the senate. Colo. McKinley & Col King the senators for Alabama, had presented young Mr Moor, brother of the Governor as a candidate for the Marshalsea of upper Alabama, they had waited upon me three times on this subject, & pressed Mr Moor upon me with great earnestness, for this appointment. I replied, I could not appoint him in preference to Mr Patterson who had fought & bled under my immediate command, & whose claims I could not overlook, and give it to a young man but a short time in the state & who had no claims upon the country more than other young men of equal merit.[1] They replied, that it was a subject Governor Moor had much at heart, & nothing they would say or do would convince him that they had done their duty, but his nomination. I observed to them, that, I at all times regretted in my nominations, to have to differ with the senators of a state, but in this instance, the duty I owed to the merit of Mr Patterson, and his real claims upon his country, was imperious, & compelled me as an act of duty, to nominate him to the senate, and that I would so write, to the governor. I did so right to Governor Moor; and when I met him at Franklin, I enquired of him if he had received my letter & his answer in the afirmative—and after a full conversation with him on the subject, he assured me that he was fully satisfied with the conduct of Col McKinley, & said it had been urged by some of his friends that he should be a candidate for the senate, of the U. States, but that he would not permit his name to be used in opposition to Col. McKinley—on the same day you communicated to me the conversation the Govr. had with you, & the request he had made that you should say to Col McKinley, that I had fully satisfied him, & that he would not oppose Col McKinley for the senate. I was pleased that he had thus instructed you to communicate to Col McKinley, knowing as I did how faithfully both the senators had urged the claims of young Mr Moor upon me. When I heard that the Govr. was the opposing candidate to Col McKinley I gave to it a contradiction, & my reasons therfor, that he had, said, both to you, & to me, that he would not permit his name to be run in opposition to Col McKinley, & if he did, after the pledge he had made, no one could have any confidence in him hereafter, and sure I am, if he has permitted it, that no honest man ever can have confidence in him again. If it be true that he is elected over, & in opposition to Col McKinley, the good people of Alabama has but one course to pursue, & that justice points to—elect Col McKinley Governor of the state, for I hesitate not in believing, that this has been a secrete intrigue of the great *nullifyer*, & after he had tried to convert McKinley, to his nullifying doctrines & could not, through his agent Mr. L[2] of Alabama, set to work this secrete conspiracy against Col McKinley, & the better to disguise it, Govern. Moor give you & me the assurance that he would not permit himself to be run against him, knowing you to be his friend, & knowing as he must, that it was only by silent intrigue, that McKinley could be beaten. That Moor if elected comes here an opposer of the present administration, and perfect nullifyer & supporter of the So. Carolina nullifying Doctrine—see to this.

I sent you the first copy of my message, two days in advance of others, by mail & I hope it reached you in due time—it has been well received by the great body of the nation, and my principles being candidly avowed upon which I will continue to act, I trust it will prevent much loggroling legislation, being assured, that I will negative all such, & put down the corrupting system of union with corporations; & appropriations for local objects.

I have been much pressed with business, & my domestic concerns have harried my feelings more than any other event of my life. My family were overreached by the hidden intrigues of the great Magician, who believed that the popularity of Eaton would be in the way of his ambition, & be bestowed upon another, therefore that it was necessary to coerce me to abandon him, by which, I must suffer in the public estimation for having appointed him, & that he might wield me to his views, or secretely use it to my destruction. A man who could secretely make the attempt, as he did in the cabinet in 1818, to destroy me, & that under the stongest professions of friendship, is base anough to do any thing—the attempt was on my family, believing if they could be enlisted against Major Eaton, my attachment to them, would compel me to yield Eaton to the fabricated slanders, rather than separate from them—I saw the evil, remonstrated & pursuaded my family against this *snare*, but without effect. I have the copy of a letter from Mr Crawford to Calhoun, in reply to the one written to me, a copy of which was furnished him, that proves that he, & he only, made a movement for my punishment & disgrace. This is supported by Crowningshield & Mr Adams ¿ What think you of such baseness under the warmest professions of friendship, & support. Such has been the prejudiced feelings of Major Donelson, that it was with some persuasion I could get him to read the copy of Mr Crawfords letter to Mr Calhoun— when read he admitted it was severe, but said no more. I never witnessed such infatuation before as took possession of Emily, and Andrew   The viewed me their worst, enemy, and really, that I wanted to disgrace them by associating with Major & Mrs. Eaton   This was urged upon them, and the ulogy pronounced, that they deserved golden medles for departing from my councils. Weak delusion, arising from a want of experience, and the corruption of this world—for those advisers, who under professions of friendship had endeavoured to destroy me, as soon as they had wielded my family to aid in the destruction of Major Eaton & his wife, would have employed the same wicked, & insidious arts, to destroy them.

I hope all things may come right again, but I have not yet ought to expect much from any change I have experienced in Major Donelson, his demeanor towards Major Eaton is more free, & pleasant, than formerly, but I have seen much of the old leven in the old junto—my *Cabinet must become a unit again*

I regret the shortness of your crop, altho mine is not more than a half crop. I hope peace will continue in Europe—still the speech of the King of England displays warmth on the subject of Belgium. I think Europe is not prepared for war, it has too much revolutionary combustible within itself, not to dread a war against France *now*.[3]

I am happy to learn that Col Ward is at length clear of debt. I wish him & his family happy, he has been perplexed very much by his kin, and it is time that he should be freed from his trouble. Hutchings, or no one for him, could have given, in justice, $9000 for it. Balden will I expect be soon tired of farming.[4]

When your leisure will permit I will thank you to remind William W. Crawford, that one half his note I expect he will pay soon, when you will deliver it up to him—when I can learn that this & Mr Griffins debt is in your hands I will be satisfied. I hope our friend Fulton will be able shortly to pay his debt.[5]

I regret to hear that your health of late has not been so good as formerly, your late exposure in the choctaw nation was well calculated to fill you with accumulated bile, & until you remove it by a potent dose of calomel, letting it lay upon your stomach 6 hours, & then working it off with an active dose of Epsom, or Herodsburgh salts—try this & I will ensure you good health for one year.

Present me kindly to Polly and your amiable family, and when you find leisure please write me—before I close I must remark how much I am crouded with business and company & how little time I have to write to a friend—you will see the hurry in which I commenced this hasty scrall to you, by beginning on the wrong side of the sheet, which I never discovered until I had wrote to the bottom. I had not time to write it over, & continued as you see, but you will I trust excuse it & believe me your friend.

Andrew Jackson

ALS, THi (17-0023).
1. Benjamin Patteson had served in AJ's personal guard in the Creek campaign. William Rufus de Vane King (1786–1853) was Alabama's other senator.
2. Likely Dixon H. Lewis.
3. British intervention to prevent an independent Belgium from falling under the sway of France appeared possible. In his speech to open Parliament on November 4, King William IV said he "witnessed, with deep regret, the state of affairs in the Low Countries" and would work "in concert with my Allies, to devise such means of restoring tranquillity as may be compatible with the welfare and good government of the Netherlands, and with the future security of other States" (*Hansard's Parliamentary Debates*, 3d ser., 1:8–9).
4. Balden was Henry Baldwin Jr.
5. William White Crawford, son of AJ's cousin James Crawford Jr., had signed a promissory note to AJ for $400 on January 30, 1827. William Griffin (c1780–c1839) owed AJ for the purchase of a slave named George in 1823. William S. Fulton owed AJ $400 plus interest for Florence, Ala., land purchases in 1826.

From the Marquis de Lafayette

Paris December 28th 1830

My dear Sir

I Have Had the pleasure to Receive your friendly answer to my Letter from the Hôtel de Ville, when, after the three great days I thought it a matter of duty and affection to Report myself to you. Now my own situation is changed but not so the success of the Revolution which, as you may see in the European papers, Has already contributed, By the force of example, to the liberties of some other parts of the Continent and to the overthrow of the Wellingtonian Ministry.[1] the new representative of france in the U.S. Mr. Serrurier will give you more particulars than could be comprehended within the compass of a Letter. He is an excellent man, most sincerely atached to America, and Having in the negotiation of the claims been zealous and well intentioned.[2] I much Lament it Has not yet been settled Beyond the principle which Has been freely recognised, But farther than that it is yet in the Hands of a committee and the minister of foreign affairs with the Hope and promise of a speedy conclusion. So I refer myself to Mr. Serrurier, observing By the By that in affairs of Government it shows that my influence is not so powerful as might be generally supposed. This However I must say that Both King and Minister are well disposed, and that the financeering situation, owing to the revolutionary times, is much embarassed. I hope Mr. Rives will be able to send more positive news during the session of Congress. My Resignation of the Command of the french National Guards will be explained to you by the papers, By my order of the day, my observations in the House, and By Mr. Serrurier; I shall only add the Best Wishes and Respects of Your affectionate friend

Lafayette

Mrs donaldson to whom I offer my Best Regards will find Mrs Serrurier a very amiable Lady

ALS (at December 28, 1836), DLC (49; 17-0031). Copy, DLC-Lafayette Papers (mAJs).

1. In December 1830 the French Chamber of Deputies reorganized the National Guard and ousted Lafayette from command. He declined a title as honorary commander of the new force. In England, agricultural riots in the summer of 1830 contributed to the fall of Wellington's Tory government, which suffered a Parliamentary vote of no confidence and gave way to a Whig ministry in November.

2. Louis Barbé Charles Sérurier (1775–1860), a French diplomat who had facilitated Rives's claims negotiation in Paris, was the new minister to the United States. He had served in the same post from 1811 to 1816, and married Louise Pageot (1795–1876) in New York in 1814.

From Martin Van Buren

Will the President have the goodness to inform the Secry. of State at what hour he will receive company on New-Years day & whether as has been usual it will be agreeable to him to receive the Foreign Ministers half an hour before the company assembles—

AN, DNA-RG 59 (M179-69).

To Martin Van Buren

Decbr. 29th. 1830—

The President returns his respects to the sec. of State, & informs him that the House of the P. will be opened, generally at 12—but half after 11. Specially, for the Foreighn ministers & heads of Departmts.

AN, DNA-RG 59 (M179-69).

From John Coffee

Coxes Creek, near Florence A
29th. Decr. 1830.

Dear Genl.

I am indebted to you two letters, since I wrote you, I would write oftener, but have nothing to write you which can interest you much, and I am unwilling to tax your time, with reading letters that have no interest in them—indeed such is the case at present, but having seen and read your Message to Congress, I feel it a duty to tell you, how much I am delighted with it—hereabouts, all approve it, and your friends are highly gratified to see the success you have had, in administering the Govt.—your political enemies admire it, and your *personal* enemies are silent, not one word has been utterd against it. I don't expect to hear anything more in opposition to you in this quarter, it is setled down that you are to be reelected, and without opposition—You have put the Indian question in so fair a view, that it will certainly stop the mouths of all honest opponents, and others we need not try to convince. A few days since I enclosed Major Eaton a letter which I recd. from George S. Gaines Esqr. traveling Agent with the Choctaws, which contains the latest information I have from the two exploring parties, I suppose Major Eaton will have informed you of its contents, I hope the two deligations, will meet in the western country, and make an agreement for the Chickasaws, to settle in the Choctaw Country, if they do not effect it before their return, no time aught to be lost when they return, in trying to effect such an arrangement[1]—Before this reaches you, you will have heard that Govr. Moore has been elected by our Legislature, to the senate of the United States, in place of Col. McKinley, this has been one of the most corrupt, and intrigueing elections, ever had in this state, or I hope in any other—and I am sorry to say that your long professed friend, David Hubbard has been one of the most promenent men in the dirty work[2]—and the Govr. himself has done his part in this low intrigueing business, in doing which, he has denied the conversation had between him and myself at Franklin last August when you were there—no doubt you will recollect, that I informed you and Major Eaton, and many others at the time, and immediately after the Govr. and myself conversed—that he the Govr. had said to me, that you had assured him that Col. McKinley had recommended his nephew to you, to be appointed Marshal of north Alabama, as McK. had promised him he would do which information from you, had satisfied him with McK. when he requested me to inform McKinley, when I returned home and saw him, that he Moore would not be a candidate in opposition to him, for the senate of the U States &c—now when he come out and offered, he addressed a handbill to the members of the legislature, after McKinley left Tuscaloosa, and too late for me to see it, and reply before the election come on, in which he denied having sent such message by me to McKinley, and if I had said so, I was greatly mistaken—Could I have seen it in time, I would have mounted my horse and gone immediately to Tuscaloosa to correct him, but it was too late—I wrote his Excly. tho, a pretty strong letter, calling on him to answer my written statement of his conversation with me at Franklin, and to put his answer in the hands of Judge Gale, and at the same time I requested Judge Gale, to place the whole correspondence before the members of the Legislature, and let them see the true character of the man they had just promoted to office & honor, over an able, honest, and intelligent public servant[3]—had the Legislature have elected Govr. Moore, over McKinley upon fair & honest principles, I would be the last man on earth, who would complain, for such was their privilege, & such they had a right to do—could McKinley have remained with them, he would have been elected, but the very moment he left there, to attend to his duty in Congress, they opened their false batteries, and no one to contradict them, they changed the votes of several members who were decidedly for McK. while he was present—I wish that Moore may support you, and your measures, he has promised to do so, but from the course he pursued in the election, your friends here are very doubtful time will show the result—more than three fourths of the voters of Lauderdale County, instructed James Jackson to vote for McKinley notwithstanding he voted for Moore, and did all he could to defeat the election of McK—I hope this act of his, will open the eyes of the people, and put him down, never more to rise politically—yet strange as it may seem, James voted for a resolution, complementing you, and approving of your administration, thus it seems he intends to try and keep up his popularity—

I will write you again in a week or ten days—

My family are all well—Polley and our little ones all unite with me in tendering our love to you, & the two Andrews, & Mr. Earl—respectfully yours—

Jno. Coffee

[Endorsed by AJ:] Genl Coffee recd. Janry 17th. 1831—

ALS, DLC (38).
1. The Chickasaw and Choctaw exploring parties met up in the west and returned in February 1831. The Chickasaws declined to settle among the Choctaws, and failure to find them a suitable country rendered void the treaty made at Franklin in August. Coffee and the Chickasaws negotiated another removal treaty in October 1832.
2. David Hubbard (1792–1874), a north Alabama lawyer, legislator, and later congressman, had published an address to the legislature attacking McKinley during the Senate campaign (Huntsville *Southern Advocate*, Dec 11, 1830).
3. Coffee wrote Moore contesting statements in his November 30 address to the legislature. Moore replied on January 4, 1831. He denied telling Coffee at Franklin that AJ's explanations had satisfied him about McKinley or that he had ever pledged not to run against him. John Gayle (1792–1859), state House speaker and later governor, delivered both letters.

From Graves W. Steele

Hermitage Dec 30th. 1830—

Dr Genl

I have recd your letter of the 9th of this instant as respects your picture and Mrs. Jacksons   I am trewley sorry that his unplesent circumstance has hapund thair is not a man Living that I have moore respect for the feelings of than yourself   I am not capable of making the necessary acknoledgements for this transgression—Some time befour you left home you told me that a artist who Resided in Nashville would come up and take a coppy of Mrs. Jacksons portrait this Gentleman came up sometime after you left home and informd me that it was out of his power to coppey this at your house and request me to let him take them to Nashville I objectied to this—this Gentlemans reply was that it was your wish and earnest desire for him to coppey them and send them on to you not nowing but this was your wish and by the influence of your friends who was present and under a solemn promise that it should be taken care of and returnd with out the least injurey which has been don   this my dear sir is the onley reason that I have to give you for this transgression—[1]

you request me to send you Doct Hoggs apt count their is two trunks In your Room one of them ar open the otheir is fast and I have not got the kee of the Large wone nor could not find it about the house—I examined all the papers that was in the small trunk but this apt count was not in it the otheir beaying fast and the kee not beaying with me there was know chance In making eney examination in that—If you wish me to open that trunk you must write to me and I will attend to it for you—

whilst you was at home you sent me to Nashville to make a settlement with Doct Hogg for his attendance after you left home   I went agreable to your request and had the apt count posted up from the time of Mrs Jacksons Death untueill the time of this settlement the apt count was about $127 dollars I had acp count against him for upwards of twenty dollars that with some Deductions for extrivagant charges redust it to about one hundred dollars you gave me a Letter to him and one directed to Cozzen John Coffee directing him to pay doct Hogg this is all the apt count that I have ever contracted with Doct Hogg I see som oald apt counts against you for part of the year 1825 & 26 & 2 and maid mention of it to you and you stated that you had paid up to the time that you left home   If he has presented aney otheir apt count that has bin contractted by me [it] is fauls I have not had him in the familey [since] you Left this place

Your familey ar all wel[l and] your stock of Brood horses Look as well [as] you can wish for I have only taken inn about thirty three thoussend pounds of se[ed] Cotten I maid application to Mr. Donelso[ns] overseer (after ginning your crop for his he faild to send I then gind for Nichol & Hill 20 Bales I then maid application to Wm Donelson for AJD crop he then informd me that it was a request of AJD by letter that he should Gin the crop but his beaying behind has since sent it to me which at this anusual time has bin the means of my Loosing wards crop and his mothiers which is and hundred and tenn thoussand lbs of seed cotten which would have bin worth upwards of $200—I am respectfuly your most Humble Servant

Graves Steele

ALS, DLC (38).
    1. Itinerant artist James Guild (1797–1841) made miniatures of AJ and Rachel. He wrote AJ on January 4, 1831.

Memorandum on Account with Samuel Hogg

In 1828 wishing to close my guardianship with the estate of A. J. Hutchings, and to transfer the duty to Genl Coffee—after an understanding with Doctor Hogg that it would be agreable to him, & he having furnished me with the amount of his medical attendance &c &c, as endorsed on the account current, I made out the account struck the ballance due me, and finding that fifteen hundred dollars, with other disbursments, would close the account with the estate of Hutchings I drew a note for that sum & sent to the Doctor for his execution—which was executed by him & sent to me, leaving a ballance due me of Eighty three dollars and seventy five cents, applicable to my medical account with him.[1] When in Tennessee I wrote to Doctor Hogg a note, that I wished him to furnish me with my medical account as I wished to close my accounts and particularly with Mr Steel—he sent me word he would be up & see me and a few days before I left home, sent Mr Steel down for the account—and agreable to Doctor Hoggs statement and receipt upon the account, I drew the order on General Coffee using his own words on the back of the account, "it being the amount due up to 21rst. july 1830,"—which will appear refference being had to said account on file in my trunk at the Hermitage therefore the mistake is with doctor Hogg and not with me if mistake exists. This however is immaterial, as if there were a thousand mistakes & as many receipts whenever made apparent, Doctor Hogg knows they would be rectified. As to the rumors—stated in his letter of M*[ay]* being offended when the account was presented, I have only & that he has forfeighted my confidence as a phician is utterly false, and they are like many other rumors that each have a hundred tongues, & every tongue a hundred lies. request Doctor Hogg to make out his whole account & forwarded to you for settlement. Steel set in January 1829, and it was sent up to 1rst July 1830 as will appear by the Doctors acpts sent by Steel A. J

ADS, DLC (73; 16-0909).
    1. Hogg had owed AJ $1583.75 in debts going back to 1823. In June 1828 AJ took a note from him for $1500, made payable to AJ as guardian of Andrew J. Hutchings.

To John Henry Eaton

The President requests that the sec. of war will have made out by one of the clerks in the Indian Bureau, a roster of the reserves for lands made to the cherokee chiefs in the Treaties made since 1812 and to what chiefs made. This is wanted to send to our private agent to produce to the chiefs of the old nation who have never got any, who now begin to enquire & see that all those officers of the judciary & cherokee legislators & principle chief have heretofor got reserves, have now moved into The old nation & are preventing those from treating who have never recd any benefit.

[Endorsed by Eaton:] Mr. Hamilton will have this attended to—J H E[1]

AD fragment, DNA-RG 75 (M234-74). The private agent was probably John Lowrey, dispatched by Eaton on September 1 to persuade the Cherokees to remove. In late October Lowrey reported the Cherokee government's refusal to consider his proposals, which included a reservation in fee simple for every Cherokee. However, he said many Cherokees now wanted reservations and were becoming restive and jealous under tribal officials who already had their own reservations and were getting rich off them (*SDoc* 512, 23d Cong., 1st sess., vol. 2, pp. 178–79, Serial 245).
    1. War Department clerk Samuel S. Hamilton (c1782–1832) replaced Thomas L. McKenney as head of the Indian bureau.

Memoranda

Mr Devereux—claim of the Brig osprey upon the Govt. of Lisbon—our charge de affairs to be instructed to push the payment of this claim—wrote a note to Sec of State calling his attention again to this claim A. J.[1]

Mc.Girk. receiver at Lexington M.o. Markum Fristoe is an applicant—apply for information to Mr Pettis & Col Benton &c &c[2]

Capt. P—reports from information, viz. West Point—*Public land*—wood cutt \$2. to 2.50 given for cutting & halling, and then charged to the Government at \$4 or \$4.50—enquire into this, & have the quartermasters accounts examined. There has been \$10,000 given for a tract of land to prevent tippling shops, or taverns near this establishment. The tavern being removed, & it is said, that a tippling house has been licensed to be established on the public property. Enquire into this matter.[3] Enquire of a Mr Patrick living near the Point at cole spring landing a merchant &c &c. Stoppages made for damages to books, how is this applied enquire—is there appropriations made to cover this, if so, to what use has the stoppages been applied.

ANS, DLC (38).

1. James Devereux (1766–1846) of Salem, Mass., was co-owner of the brig *Osprey*, whose cargo of jerked beef was seized by Portuguese military forces at Bahia for their use in 1823. The Portuguese government had acknowledged a minimal claim for the value of the cargo but not paid it despite repeated importunities. On September 24, 1830, Van Buren wrote Devereux with news that Portugal had agreed to settle the claim (DNA-RG 59, M40-21). Further delay ensued, and on March 1, 1831, Van Buren instructed chargé Thomas Ludwell Lee Brent (1784–1845) to "demand, in earnest but respectful terms, of the Portuguese Government, the immediate satisfaction of this long protracted affair" (DNA-RG 59, M77-8).

2. Markham Fristoe (1784–1868) was a Missouri sheriff and later legislator. On December 23 AJ appointed Edwin M. Ryland to replace Andrew S. McGirk as receiver of the Lexington land office.

3. In 1824 the U.S. had purchased the Oliver Gridley farm adjoining the Military Academy for \$10,000 and converted a tavern on the property into a cadet hospital.

Memorandum on Turkish Negotiations

[Jackson's second annual message on December 6 announced a favorable result to commercial negotiations with Turkey. On December 10 he sent the treaty signed by commissioners Charles Rhind, James Biddle, and David Offley to the Senate. The Senate requested copies of their instructions on December 16 and Jackson submitted them on December 20 (Richardson, 2:504–5, 530–31). This memorandum might have been drawn up about that time or as late as 1832. On May 29 and July 14, 1832, Jackson sent the House of Representatives, at its request, a full record of Turkish negotiations since 1819, including all the documents mentioned herein in nearly the same order (HRDoc 250, 22d Cong., 1st sess., Serial 221).]

Navoni relates the acts of Mr Bradish & the Port—the same obstacles existed until Sept. 1827, when enquiry was made, if any persons was authorised to treat with the Port—2nd. Janry 1828—The Port's enquiry where Bradish was—The Naval commander at Smyrna, cloathed with power to treat—as the Port suggested—The Port anxious to conclude a Treaty of commerce with america—was anxious to do so. and requested Navoni to make this wish to the Govrmt. of america—The proposition of the Port was for an alliance—This would be dificult &c &c. The Port said mercantile benefits would not do, he wanted political advantages.[1] Articles—a mere project, of a Treaty, about the commerce of the Black Sea—27th. 1827—with Spain, Denmark & Naples.[2] 7th. of Febry, 1828—The Port well disposed to treat—note by Mr Bradish—July 21rst. 1828—John Adams to Mr Ofley—full powers to treat to Ofley & Comdr. Crane—There report—failed in the negotiation—see report[3]—Rhind was appointed with Biddle & Offley—see instructions   succeeded—see Treaty—A. J.

[Endorsed by AJ:] Turkish negotiation Crane & Offley fails A. J. appoints Rhind Biddle & Offley & succeeds   A. J.

ANS, DLC (38).
    1. In 1820 the U.S. had sent Luther Bradish (1783–1863) as an unofficial emissary to Turkey. Receiving no answer from the Porte to his proposal for a commercial negotiation, Bradish departed for Europe, leaving matters at Constantinople to dragoman Nicholas Navoni. On January 24, 1828, Navoni wrote Secretary of Henry Clay that in September 1827 and again on January 2, 1828, a Turkish agent had approached him about a commercial negotiation, inquiring about Bradish's whereabouts and whether William Montgomery Crane (1784–1846), commander of the Navy's Mediterranean squadron, was clothed with diplomatic powers. At an audience on January 12 the Reis Effendi told Navoni that Turkey wanted not only a commercial treaty but "political advantages," especially a means to quickly replace warships lost at the battle of Navarino. Navoni told him this would be dificult (*HRDoc* 250, 22d Cong., 1st sess., pp. 3–12, 55–60, Serial 221).
    2. Treaties signed October 16, 1827 gave vessels of Denmark, Spain, and the Two Sicilies (Naples) the right of passage on the Black Sea. Navoni had sent Clay a generic text.
    3. On February 17, 1828, David Offley sent Clay a note from the Porte of February 7 announcing its readiness to conclude a commercial treaty. On July 21 President Adams formally commissioned Offley and Crane as negotiators. They reported to AJ on March 17, 1829, that their negotiations had reached impasse (*HRDoc* 250, 22d Cong., 1st sess., pp. 53–55, 63, Supplement p. 17, Serial 221).

Calendar, 1830

Jan 4   To the United States Senate. DS, DNA-RG 46 (14-1321). *SDoc* 12, 21st Cong., 1st sess., pp. 1–2 (Serial 192); Richardson, 2:464–65. Presents and recommends South Carolina's claim for reimbursement of War of 1812 expenses.

Jan 4   To the United States Senate. DS, DNA-RG 46 (14-1325). *Senate Executive Proceedings*, 4:35. Nominates government directors of the BUS for 1830.

Jan 4   To the United States Senate. DS, DNA-RG 46 (14-1327). *Senate Executive Proceedings*, 4:41. Nominates Henry Baldwin to the Supreme Court.

Jan 4   To the United States Senate. DS, DNA-RG 46; Draft, DLC (14-1329). *Senate Executive Proceedings*, 4:35. Nominates Army officers for appointment and promotion.

Jan 4   To the United States Senate. DS, DNA-RG 46 (14-1332). *Senate Executive Proceedings*, 4:41; Richardson, 2:465. Submits a Sep 1829 supplement to the 1818 Delaware Indian treaty for ratification.

Jan 4   From James Allen et al. DS, DNA-RG 59 (M639-21). Kentucky legislators and Francis P. Blair recommend George Shannon for governor of proposed Huron Territory.

Jan 4   From Samuel Delucenna Ingham. LS, DNA-RG 46 (14-1320). *SDoc* 11, 21st Cong., 1st sess., p. 1 (Serial 192). Submits data requested by the Senate in Dec 1828 on federal land and money appropriated for education and internal improvement.

Jan 5   To the United States House of Representatives. DS, DNA-RG 233 (14-1337). Richardson, 2:466. Transmits the Oct 29, 1829, memorial of Bernard Marigny et al., Spanish land claimants in West Florida.

Jan 5   To the United States Senate. DS, DNA-RG 46 (14-1339). *SDoc* 11, 21st Cong., 1st sess., p. 1 (Serial 192); Richardson, 2:466. Transmits the Jan 4 Treasury report on federal land and money appropriated for education and internal improvement.

Jan 5   To the United States Senate. DS, DNA-RG 46 (14-1342). *Senate Executive Proceedings*, 4:43. Amends his nomination of government directors of the BUS.

[Jan 5]   To the United States Senate. DS, DNA-RG 46 (14-1344). *Senate Executive Proceedings*, 4:41–42. Nominates attorneys, marshals, and a territorial secretary.

Jan 5   From Gerard Chittocque Brandon et al. DS, DNA-RG 59 (M639-3). Recommend William Briscoe for marshal in Mississippi.

Jan 5   From Joshua Young and Alexander Mills. LS, DNA-RG 45 (M124-122). Complain that the Navy has cheated them out of pay and rations. Referred by AJ to Branch for remedy "if Justice has been witheld."

Jan 5   James Laurie et al. to John Branch. LS, DNA-RG 45 (M124-122). Recommend John W. Anderson as assistant agent for settling recaptured Africans in Liberia. Approved by AJ.

Jan 6   To the United States Senate. DS, DNA-RG 46 (14-1349). *Senate Executive Proceedings*, 4:44. Nominates customs appraisers.

Jan 6   From John Branch. LC, DNA-RG 45 (M472-1). Submits the court-martial of Navy lieutenant Thomas W. Freelon, sentenced to suspension from duty for insubordination and disobedience.

Jan 6   From Moses Van Campen. ALS, DNA-RG 107 (M222-28). Describes his Revolutionary services and requests an officer's pension. Referred favorably by AJ to Eaton.

Jan 6   Appointment of John W. Anderson as assistant agent for settling recaptured Africans in Liberia. LC, DNA-RG 45 (M205-1).

Jan 6   Check to Andrew Jackson Donelson for $1,075. DS, DLC (37).

Jan 6   Receipted tailor's bill from Samuel Ditty to Andrew Jackson Jr. DS, DLC (38). Runs to Oct 19.

Jan 6   Peter Hagner to Isaac Hill. Copy, DNA-RG 107 (M222-27). Lists government officers delinquent in rendering quarterly accounts. Referred by AJ to Berrien querying his authority to remove delinquent BUS branch presidents.

Jan 7   To James Kirke Paulding. LS, CSt (14-1352). Forwards with pleasure Kendall's Jan 5 letter commending Paulding's integrity as navy agent.

Jan 7   To Unknown. LS, MeB (mAJs). Returns papers submitted in defense of Florida judge Joseph L. Smith.

Jan 7   From John Branch. Printed, *HRDoc* 115, 21st Cong., 1st sess., p. 6 (Serial 198) (14-1351). Submits a report from Amos Kendall on the accounts of former Norfolk navy agent Miles King.

Jan 7   From Henry Naylor et al. DS, DNA-RG 94 (M567-54). Recommend a reorganization of the District of Columbia militia. Referred approvingly by AJ to Eaton.

Jan 7   From John Pemberton. ALS, DNA-RG 59 (M639-11). Draft, PHi (14-1354). Complains of Michael Hogan, consul at Valparaiso, as unpatriotic and unfit.

Jan 7   Check to self for $50. DS, DLC (37).

Jan 7   Thomas Law to [Andrew Jackson Donelson]. ALS, DLC (37). Asks if AJ would like to be president of the Columbian Institute.

Jan 8   *From Alfred Balch.*   18

Jan 8   From Sylvester Beecher et al. and from Truman Enos et al. DSs, DNA-RG 59 (M639-14). Recommend Thomas T. Loomis for secretary of proposed Huron Territory.

Jan 8   From James Fenner. ALS, DLC (14-1356). Recommends continuing Samuel Brown as naval officer at Providence, R.I.

Jan 8   *From James Gadsden.*   21

Jan 8   From Silas Halsey. ADS, DNA-RG 107 (M222-27). Protests his dismissal as military storekeeper at Plattsburgh, N.Y.

Jan 8   *From Samuel Delucenna Ingham.*   22

Jan 8   Affidavit of John Anderson. ADS, DNA-RG 59 (14-1374).

	Attests that Edward Barneville, confined for debt to the U.S., is poor and unable to pay. AJ orders his release.
Jan 9	From Felix Grundy. ALS, DLC (14-1359). Encloses a letter from John B. Gibson approving AJ's conduct in office.
Jan 9	*From Persis Brown Goodrich Lovely.* 23
Jan 9	From James Mosher and from Joel Vickers. ALSs, DNA-RG 59 (M639-12). Recommend John Irwin for commercial agent at Port-au-Prince, Haiti.
Jan 9	From John F. Ryland. ALS, DNA-RG 46 (14-1363). Introduces and recommends Willis M. Green.
Jan 9	From Philip Evan Thomas. LS, DNA-RG 107 (M221-110). Baltimore & Ohio Rail Road president extends thanks for route surveys by Army engineers and other federal assistance.
Jan 9	Disapproval of Navy lieutenant Thomas W. Freelon's court-martial for procedural errors and substantive injustice, and order for him to return to duty. DS, DNA-RG 125 (M273-22). Copy, PPRF (mAJs).
Jan 10	*To Hardy Murfree Cryer.* 24
Jan 10	From William Wright. ALS, DNA-RG 46 (14-1370). Recommends Willis M. Green for office.
Jan 11	*From Estwick Evans.* 26
Jan 11	*From John Thomson.* 27
Jan 11	Discharge for jailed insolvent public debtor Edward Barneville. LC, DNA-RG 59 (14-1373; T967-1).
Jan 11	Order for release on payment of costs for the brig *Brutus*, libelled at New Orleans for carrying a slave of former Louisiana senator Dominique Bouligny home from Washington without the required manifest. ANS, DNA-RG 59 (14-1398).
Jan 11	Order to remit the $1000 penalty against Stephen Davenport, master of the brig *Brutus*, for carrying Dominique Bouligny's slave home to New Orleans without the required manifest. ANS, DNA-RG 59 (14-1407).
Jan 11	Account with Tucker & Thompson for clothing. DS, DLC (72). Runs to Feb 22.
Jan 11	Account of Andrew Jackson Jr. with Tucker & Thompson for clothing. DS, DLC (14-1382). Bassett, 4:221. Receipted Jan 3, 1831.
Jan 11	John Blair to Martin Van Buren. ALS, DNA-RG 59 (14-1411). Urges a release for pardoned mail thief Abram B. Fickle, still imprisoned for inability to pay costs. Approved by AJ.
Jan 12	*To Ezra Stiles Ely.* 28
Jan 12	*To Martin Van Buren.* 30
Jan 12	From Edward E. Brooks. ALS, THer (14-1385). Asks to be appointed Michigan Territory marshal.
Jan 12	From Elisabeth Petchaka. LS and Copy, DNA-RG 75 (14-1386). Asks permission to sell her reserved land under the Delaware treaty of 1818.
Jan 12	Nicholas Philip Trist to Andrew Jackson Donelson. ALS, DNA-RG 59 (M639-3). Reports on charges of misconduct against Pennsylvania district attorney Alexander Brackenridge.

Jan 13	To the United States Senate. DS, DNA-RG 46 (14-1414). *Senate Executive Proceedings*, 4:45–47. Nominates customs officers.
Jan 13	To the United States Senate. DS, DNA-RG 46 (14-1421). *Senate Executive Proceedings*, 4:48. Nominates Thomas Loomis for customs collector at Sackett's Harbor, N.Y.
Jan 13	To the United States Senate. DS, Gallery of History (mAJs). *Senate Executive Proceedings*, 4:48 (14-1423). Withdraws the premature renomination of Maryland marshal Thomas Finley, whose term is unexpired.
Jan 13	*From Caleb Atwater.* 31
[Jan 13]	From Ephraim Hubbard Foster et al. DS, DNA-RG 59 (15-0183). Tennessee legislators and federal prosecutors urge a pardon for young mail thief Baxter A. Powel. Approved by AJ Feb 16.
Jan 13	From Martin Gordon and John Slidell. LS, DNA-RG 59 (M639-4). Recommend Henry Carleton for federal judge if a new circuit to include Louisiana is added.
Jan 13	Release for the brig *Brutus* on payment of costs. LC, DNA-RG 59 (14-1391; T967-1).
Jan 13	Remission of penalties and discharge from arrest on payment of costs for Stephen Davenport, master of the brig *Brutus*. LC, DNA-RG 59 (14-1400; T967-1).
Jan 13	Remission of punishment and discharge from prison for mail thief Abram P. Fickle. LC, DNA-RG 59 (14-1409; T967-1).
Jan 13	John P. Sheldon to Martin Van Buren. ALS, DNA-RG 59 (M639-20). Accuses Michigan Territory marshal Thomas Rowland of defrauding the government. Endorsed by AJ to remove him if true.
Jan 14	*To John Henry Eaton.* 31
Jan 14	From John Henry Eaton. ALS, DNA-RG 233 (14-1424). *HRDoc* 24, 21st Cong., 1st sess., p. 2 (Serial 196). Submits estimates of appropriations needed to implement newly ratified Indian treaties.
Jan 14	To the United States Congress. DS, DNA-RG 233 (14-1431). *HRDoc* 24, 21st Cong., 1st sess., p. 1 (Serial 196); Richardson, 2:466. Transmits three newly ratified Indian treaties and estimates of appropriations needed to implement them.
[Jan 14]	From William Bartlett. ADS, DNA-RG 59 (14-1436). Convicted thief begs a pardon, pleading innocence, youth, and fear of shaming his father. Approved by AJ Jan 16.
Jan 14	From Clement Comer Clay. ALS, DNA-RG 59 (15-0604). Solicits a pardon for young David H. Dyer, sentenced to ten years for pilfering banknotes from the mail.
Jan 14	From David Corbin Ker. ALS, DNA-RG 59 (M639-4). Recommends Henry Carleton for federal judge if a new circuit to include Louisiana is added.
Jan 14	From Dom Miguel, King of Portugal. LS, Copy, and translation, DNA-RG 59 (14-1425). Announces the death of his mother.
Jan 14	From Jonah Thompson et al. DS, DNA-RG 59 (M639-10).

	John Q. Adams with political bias in rejecting him for midshipman, and asks to be appointed to West Point.
Jan 18	From Alfred Hennen. ALS, DNA-RG 59 (M639-4). Recommends Henry Carleton for federal judge if a new circuit is created for Louisiana and Mississippi.
Jan 18	From Samuel Delucenna Ingham. ANS, DNA-RG 217 (M235-610). Submits Morgan L. Martin's claim for pay as acting district attorney in Michigan Territory. Approved by AJ Jan 22.
Jan 18	From John Leonard. ALS, DNA-RG 59 (M639-14). Asks AJ's attention to his protest against removal as consul at Barcelona, complaint of official conspiracy, and request for reinstatement.
Jan 18	*From Young King et al.* 39
Jan 18	Pardon for petty thief Eliza Cowan. LC, DNA-RG 59 (14-1452; T967-1).
Jan 18	Samuel McKean and George Wolf to John Branch. ALS and ANS (Jan 27), DNA-RG 46 (14-1460). Recommend Sterrett Ramsey for naval purser. Endorsed favorably by AJ.
Jan 19	*To Stephen Pleasonton.* 41
Jan 19	To the United States Congress. DS, DNA-RG 233 (14-1470). *HRDoc* 31, 21st Cong., 1st sess., pp. 1–2 (Serial 196); Richardson, 2:466–67. Conveys a gold medal presented him by the Colombian government, hopes Bolívar will support liberal institutions, reports progress in settling American merchant claims, and praises minister Thomas P. Moore.
[cJan 19]	To Martin Van Buren. AN, Heritage Collectors' Society, Inc. (mAJs; 12-0400). Asks for the papers on the marshal's appointment at Key West.
Jan 19	To the United States Senate. DS, DNA-RG 46 (14-1476). *Senate Executive Proceedings*, 4:51. Nominates marshals, attorneys, and a territorial secretary.
Jan 19	To the United States Senate. ADS, DNA-RG 46 (14-1474). *Senate Executive Proceedings*, 4:51. Nominates Lackland M. Stone for marshal in Florida.
Jan [19]	From Moses M. Gove. DS, DNA-RG 59 (17-0871). Petitions for remission of his $1,000 fine for smuggling salt and release from imprisonment.
Jan 19	Pardon for Joseph Downing for assault. LC, DNA-RG 59 (14-1464; T967-1).
Jan 20	*To Sarah Bronaugh.* 41
Jan 20	From Samuel Delucenna Ingham. LS, DNA-RG 233 (14-1480). *HRDoc* 34, 21st Cong., 1st sess., pp. 1–2 (Serial 196). Asks AJ to request an appropriation for a $400 annuity to the United Society of Christian Indians, as promised them in 1823.
Jan 20	To the United States Congress. DS, DNA-RG 233 (14-1482). *HRDoc* 34, 21st Cong., 1st sess., p. 1 (Serial 196); Richardson, 2:468. Requests an appropriation for a $400 annuity to the United Society of Christian Indians.
Jan 20	To the United States Senate. DS, DNA-RG 46 (14-1484). *Senate Executive Proceedings*, 4:51. Nominates James Duncan for receiver at the Washington, Miss., land office.

Jan 20	To the United States Senate. DS, DNA-RG 46 (14-1486). *Senate Executive Proceedings*, 4:50. Nominates customs officers.
Jan 20	To the United States Senate. DS, DNA-RG 46 (14-1488). *Senate Executive Proceedings*, 4:49–50. Nominates land office registers and receivers.
Jan 20	*From John Caldwell Calhoun.* 42
Jan 20	From Nathan Morse. ALS, DNA-RG 59 (M639-4). Recommends Henry Carleton for federal judge if a new circuit is added to include Louisiana.
Jan 20	From Stephen Simpson. ALS, DLC (37). Names Henry Toland as the friend who intimated he would be appointed navy agent at Philadelphia.
Jan 20	*From Martin Van Buren.* 43
Jan 20	Account with tailor Christian Eckloff. DS, DLC (38). Receipted May 29.
Jan 20	Account of Andrew Jackson Jr. with tailor Christian Eckloff. DS, DLC (38). Receipted May 18.
Jan 21	*From Eneah Micco et al.* 43
Jan 21	From Eneah Micco et al. DS, DNA-RG 75 (M234-222). Deny to AJ and Eaton sanctioning complaints against Creek agent John Crowell, with whom they are well satisfied.
Jan 21	From Jean Baptiste Plauché. ALS, DNA-RG 59 (M639-4). Recommends Henry Carleton for federal judge if a new circuit to include Louisiana is added.
Jan 21	From Martin Van Buren. DSs, DNA-RG 46 and DNA-RG 233; LC, DNA-RG 59 (14-1494). *HRDoc* 38, 21st Cong., 1st sess., pp. 1–2 (Serial 196). Submits a report from Patent Office superintendent John D. Craig, charging past mismanagement and proposing improvements and reforms.
Jan 22	To Samuel Delucenna Ingham. LC, DNA-RG 75 (M21-6). Authorizes payments from the Treasury to the Choctaw, Creek, and Potawatomi education funds.
Jan 22	To the United States Senate. DS, DNA-RG 46 (15-0001). *Senate Executive Proceedings*, 4:51–53. Nominates diplomats and consuls.
Jan 22	From Anthony Dey. ALS, DLC (37). Calls on the U.S. if it acquires Texas to honor the validity of a large land grant in which he and other Americans hold interest.
Jan 22	*From Louis McLane.* 44
Jan 22	From David Porter. ALS, DNA-RG 59 (M179-68). Warns of Mexican plans to illegally commission privateers against Spain in the U.S.
Jan 22	From Robert G. Shaw et al. DS, DNA-RG 59 (M639-17). Recommend John H. Offley for consul at Trieste.
Jan 22	From Fleet Smith. ALS, DNA-RG 59 (M639-22). Asks to be appointed commissioner to settle American claims against Denmark.
Jan 22	James Gray to Martin Van Buren. ALS, DNA-RG 59 (M639-3). Asks the result of his charges of fraud against Pennsylvania district attorney Alexander Brackenridge. Endorsed by AJ.

Jan 23	*To John Branch.*	*45*
Jan 23	To Francis I, King of the Two Sicilies. LC, DNA-RG 59 (15-0007). Offers congratulations on his daughter's marriage to Ferdinand VII of Spain.	
Jan 23	To Pedro I, Emperor of Brazil. LC, DNA-RG 59 (15-0008). Offers congratulations on his marriage.	
Jan 23	*From John L. Allen.*	*46*
Jan 23	From Henry Carleton. ALS, DNA-RG 59 (M639-4). Asks to be appointed judge if a new circuit to include Louisiana is created.	
[Jan 23]	From Sebastian Hiriart et al. DS, DNA-RG 59 (M639-4). Louisiana legislators recommend Henry Carleton for judge if a circuit is added to include their state.	
Jan 23	From John Van Lear McMahon. ALS, DNA-RG 59 (M639-12). Recommends John Irwin for consul at Port-au-Prince, Haiti.	
Jan 24	*To Martin Van Buren.*	*49*
Jan 24	From William Robinson. ALS, TNJ (15-0011). Requests an office and recommends his son Edwin W. Robinson for cadet at West Point.	
[Jan 24]	*Memorandum book.*	*50*
Jan 24	John Biddle to Martin Van Buren. ALS, DNA-RG 59 (M639-14). *TPUS*, 12:112–14. Defends Michigan district attorney Daniel Le Roy against James D. Doty's 1826 charge, referred by AJ for inquiry (DNA-RG 59, M531-5), of refusing to attend court outside Detroit, and promises to inquire further. Endorsed by AJ to pursue.	
Jan 25	To the United States Senate. DS, DNA-RG 46 (15-0017). *Senate Executive Proceedings*, 4:53. Nominates customs appraisers.	
Jan 25	To the United States Senate. DS, DNA-RG 46 (15-0019). *Senate Executive Proceedings*, 4:53–54. Nominates customs officers for reappointment.	
Jan 25	To the United States Senate. DS, DNA-RG 46 (15-0022). *Senate Executive Proceedings*, 4:54. Nominates Alexandria, D.C., justices of the peace for reappointment.	
[cJan 25]	*To Martin Van Buren.*	*51*
Jan 25	From John Branch. LC, DNA-RG 45 (M472-1). Returns the complaint of former purser's steward Tobias Nock against Navy purser Edward N. Cox, with Cox's defense.	
Jan 25	From John Pope Oldham. ALS, DNA-RG 46 (15-0015). Recommends Willis M. Green for office.	
Jan 25	William Duane to John Henry Eaton or Samuel Delucenna Ingham. ALS, DLC (37). Censures John Q. Adams's conduct of the Florida negotiations and the narrow, spiteful New England character that produced Foot's resolution on the public lands and secret disunionism; proposes a topographical office in the War Department.	
Jan 26	*To John Branch.*	*51*
Jan 26	To the United States Congress. DSs, DNA-RG 46 and DNA-RG 233 (15-0030). *HRDoc* 38, 21st Cong., 1st sess., p. 1 (Serial	

196); Richardson, 2:468. Transmits the Patent Office report and
endorses its recommendations.

Jan 26   To the United States Congress. DSs, DNA-RG 46 and DNA-RG
233 (15-0036). *HRDoc* 37, 21st Cong., 1st sess., pp. 1–5 (Serial
196); Richardson, 2:468–72. Recommends revising and
clarifying the laws governing compensation for American
diplomats abroad.

Jan 26   To the United States Senate. DS, DNA-RG 46 (15-0056). *Senate
Executive Proceedings*, 4:54. Nominates Bernard Smith for
register of the Little Rock, Ark., land office.

Jan 26   From Ela Collins, Charles Dayan and Sylvester Miller. LS, DNA-
RG 59 (M639-15). *TPUS*, 12:115–16. Recommend Morgan L.
Martin for district attorney in Michigan Territory.

Jan 26   From William W. Gault et al. LS, DNA-RG 46 (15-0027). Ohio
legislators applaud Joseph H. Larwill's nomination as receiver of
the Tiffin land office and charge his opponents with partisan
malice.

[Jan 27]   From David Scott et al. DS, DNA-RG 59 (M639-22).
Recommend Francis A. Smith for bearer of dispatches to
Europe.

Jan 27   Andrew Jackson Donelson to John Branch. ALS, DNA-RG 45
(M124-122). Conveys AJ's directive for naval commanders to
collect sugar cane and other foreign crop and seed samples
suitable for domestic cultivation, pursuant to a House
resolution.

Jan 27   Memorandum by Andrew Jackson Donelson that the House
request to collect foreign crop and seed samples has been sent to
the State and Navy departments. ANS, DLC (60).

Jan 28   Check to Pishey Thompson for $56. DS, DLC (37).

Jan 29   To Campbell Patrick White. Photocopy of LS, William C. Cook
(mAJs). Gives his recollection that the steamboat *Vesuvius* was
not in public employ when it ran aground at New Orleans in
December 1814, contrary to the claim of Robert Fulton's heirs.

[cJan 29]   From Henry Ashton. ALS, DNA-RG 233 (15-0061). *HRDoc* 46,
21st Cong., 1st sess., p. 1 (Serial 196). Submits the annual report
of the District of Columbia penitentiary inspectors.

Jan 29   From Jonathan Kearsley et al. DSs, DNA-RG 59 (M639-27).
TPUS, 12:116–19. Request James Witherell's removal as
secretary of Michigan Territory.

Jan 30   To the United States Congress. DS, DNA-RG 233 (15-0079).
HRDoc 46, 21st Cong., 1st sess., p. 1 (Serial 196); Richardson,
2:473. Transmits the annual report of the District of Columbia
penitentiary inspectors and recommends compensating their
services.

	extra pay for performing Army recruitment duty in 1818–19. Referred skeptically by AJ to Eaton.
Feb 4	From Robert Lucas. ALS, DNA-RG 59 (M639-2). Recommends Walter M. Blake for a land office or Indian agency.
Feb 4	Order to include Marine with Army officers on the court-martial of Marine Brevet Lieutenant Colonel Samuel Miller. DS, DNA-RG 94 (M567-51).
Feb 4	Memorandum by Andrew Jackson Donelson of notifying the State and Treasury Departments of Senate confirmations of executive nominees. ANS, DLC (60).
Feb 5	From John Henry Eaton. ALS, DNA-RG 46 (15-0104). LC, DNA-RG 107 (M127-2). *SDoc* 46, 21st Cong., 1st sess., p. 1 (Serial 192). Submits a report on military protection for Santa Fe traders against Indian depredations.
Feb 5	To the United States Senate. DS, DNA-RG 46 (15-0106). *SDoc* 46, 21st Cong., 1st sess., p. 1 (Serial 192); Richardson, 2:473. Transmits the War Department report on protecting the Santa Fe trade.
Feb 5	To John Henry Eaton. Abstract, DNA-RG 75 (M18-2). Requests a report on a Wisconsin boundary dispute between the New York, Winnebago, and Menominee Indians, referred for presidential decision by the 1827 Chippewa treaty.
Feb 5	To the United States Senate. DS, DNA-RG 46 (15-0109). Draft, DNA-RG 75 (M234-433). *Senate Executive Proceedings*, 4:56. Nominates Indian agents.
Feb 5	To the United States Senate. DS, DNA-RG 46 (15-0111). *Senate Executive Proceedings*, 4:56. Nominates John G. Mawney for a new term as customs surveyor at East Greenwich, R.I.
Feb 5	From John Branch. LC, DNA-RG 45 (M472-1). Transmits further papers on the dispute between Navy purser Edward N. Cox and Tobias Nock over Nock's accounts.
Feb 6	*From Louis McLane.* 67
Feb 6	Check to Michael Anthony Giusta for $1,002. DS, DLC (37).
Feb 7	To John Henry Eaton. Abstract, DNA-RG 107 (M22-25). Recommends Samuel P. Walker Jr. for cadet at West Point.
Feb 7	From Gerard Chittocque Brandon et al. Copy, DNA-RG 59 (M639-19). Mississippi governor and legislators recommend Peter Randolph for the Supreme Court if a new judicial circuit is added. Endorsed by AJ.
Feb 7	From Mary Ann Townsend. ALS, DNA-RG 94 (M567-56). Requests an Army discharge for her underage son Edwin C. Townsend. Ordered by Eaton.
Feb 8	To the United States Congress. DSs, DNA-RG 46 and DNA-RG 233 (15-0113). *HRDoc* 56, 21st Cong., 1st sess., p. 1 (Serial 197). Transmits the annual report of the Mint for 1829.
Feb 8	From James Williams. Copy, DNA-RG 233 (mAJs). Praises Joseph L. Smith's excellence as Florida district judge and condemns his traducers.
Feb 9	*From Samuel Delucenna Ingham.* 68
[Feb 9]	*To Samuel Delucenna Ingham.* 68

Feb 17 From Littleton Waller Tazewell. ALS, DNA-RG 45 (M124-122). Copy, DNA-RG 233 (15-0166). Copy, Vi (mAJs). *HRDoc* 115, 21st Cong., 1st sess., pp. 7–8 (Serial 198). Requests a re-examination of the accounts of former Norfolk navy agent Miles King.

Feb 18 *To Samuel Delucenna Ingham.* 80

Feb 18 To the United States House of Representatives. DS, DNA-RG 233 (15-0192). *HRDoc* 66, 21st Cong., 1st sess., p. 1 (Serial 197); Richardson, 2:473. Transmits the report on William B. Lawrence's disputed salary as acting chargé d'affaires to Great Britain.

Feb 18 From Richmond Brown et al. DS, DNA-RG 59 (M639-21). Massachusetts legislators recommend Jonas L. Sibley for marshal.

Feb 18 From Samuel Delucenna Ingham. ALS, DNA-RG 59 (15-0229). Recommends a release for Samuel L. Valentine, imprisoned for debt to the U.S. Approved by AJ Feb 20.

Feb 18 From John Telemachus Johnson. ALS, DNA-RG 59 (M639-16). Recommends Abraham B. Morton for marshal of proposed Huron Territory.

Feb 18 From Jonas Sibley. ALS, DNA-RG 59 (M639-21). Recommends his son Jonas L. Sibley for marshal in Massachusetts.

Feb 18 Deed from Peter Guerrant Moseley for 151 acres in Wilson Co., Tenn., sold to AJ for $1812. Registered May 20. Copy, DLC (38). Copies, TLWil and TNDa (15-0176).

Feb 18 Pardon for juvenile mail thief Baxter A. Powel. LC, DNA-RG 59 (15-0181; T967-1).

Feb 18 Andrew Jackson Donelson to [Martin Van Buren]. ANS, DNA-RG 59 (M639-4). Transmits recommendations for Henry Carleton for federal circuit judge.

Feb 19 *To John Macpherson Berrien.* 81

Feb 19 To John Branch. Copy, DNA-RG 233 (15-0203). *HRDoc* 115, 21st Cong., 1st sess., p. 9 (Serial 198). Orders a re-examination of the accounts of former Norfolk navy agent Miles King.

Feb 19 *To William Ramsey and Thomas Hartley Crawford.* 82
Feb 19 *To Littleton Waller Tazewell.* 83

Feb 20 To Littleton Waller Tazewell. ALS, NjMoHP (15-0211). Encloses his Feb 19 letter, which he had neglected to send.

Feb 20 *From Littleton Waller Tazewell.* 83

Feb 20 To the United States Senate. ADS, DNA-RG 46 (15-0217). *Senate Executive Proceedings*, 4:62; Richardson, 2:474. Withdraws his Feb 5 nomination of John Campbell, just revealed as a public defaulter, for Creek agent.

Feb 20 To the United States Senate. DS, DNA-RG 46 (15-0219). *Senate Executive Proceedings*, 4:63. Nominates Daniel M. Durell for government director of the BUS.

Feb 20 To the United States Senate. DS, DNA-RG 46 (15-0221). *Senate Executive Proceedings*, 4:62–63. Nominates district attorneys for Mississippi and north Alabama.

Feb 26   From Frederick Hambright. ALS, DNA-RG 59 (M639-23).
             Recommends Samuel C. Stambaugh for marshal in Pennsylvania.
[Feb 26]   From Henry Logan et al. NS, DNA-RG 59 (M639-23).
             Pennsylvania state senators second Frederick Hambright's
             recommendation of Samuel C. Stambaugh for marshal.
Feb 26   From George Rahn. ALS, DNA-RG 59 (M639-23). Recommends
             Samuel C. Stambaugh for marshal in Pennsylvania.
Feb 27   To the United States Senate. DS, DNA-RG 46 (15-0260). *Senate
             Executive Proceedings*, 4:63. Nominates customs collectors for
             reappointment.
Feb 27   From John Branch. LC, DNA-RG 45 (M472-1). Submits reports
             by Amos Kendall and Isaac Hill on late naval purser John B.
             Timberlake's accounts, in answer to a Senate call of Feb 17.
Feb 27   From Nathaniel P. Fetterman et al. LS, DNA-RG 59 (M639-23).
             Pennsylvania legislators recommend Samuel C. Stambaugh for
             marshal.
[Feb 27]   From Joseph Hemphill et al. DS, DNA-RG 46 (14-1239).
             Charles Biddle, *Senator Grundy's Political Conduct Reviewed*
             (Nashville, 1832), p. 11. Pennsylvania congressmen recommend
             Charles Biddle for office.
Feb 27   From Roley McIntosh and Benjamin Hawkins. LS, DNA-RG 75
             (M234-236). Enclose and ask AJ's special attention to their
             appeal of Feb 25.
Feb 27   From Jesse Miller and Henry R. Welsh. LS, DNA-RG 59
             (M639-23). Recommend Samuel C. Stambaugh for office.
[Feb 27]   From Walter S. Franklin and Alexander Mahon. NS, DNA-RG
             59 (M639-23). Concur in recommending Samuel C. Stambaugh
             for office.
Feb 27   From Josiah Sheldon. DS, DNA-RG 59 (16-0744). Defaulted
             former U.S. internal revenue collector seeks release from
             confinement within gaol limits of Monroe County, N.Y.
Feb 27   From Addison Gardiner et al. DS, DNA-RG 59 (16-0748). Urge
             the release of defaulter Josiah Sheldon. Referred by AJ on Jun 2
             to U.S. district attorney Samuel Beardsley to report on Sheldon's
             ability to pay his debt and possible hidden assets.
Feb 27   From John S. Topp et al. DS, DNA-RG 59 (M639-1).
             Recommend William E. Anderson for judge if Congress creates a
             new circuit embracing Tennessee.
Feb 28   *To Hardy Murfree Cryer.*   *105*
Feb 28   *To Charles Jones Love.*   *106*
Feb 28   From Jesse R. Burden. ALS, DNA-RG 59 (M639-23).
             Recommends Samuel C. Stambaugh for office.
[Feb]   From William Henry Allen. ADS, DNA-RG 107 (M222-28).
             Requests authority to house the St. Augustine, Fla., land office in
             a disused government building.
[cFeb]   From Joshua Clarke et al. DS, DNA-RG 59 (M639-27).
             Recommend Micajah T. Williams for governor of proposed
             Huron Territory.
[cFeb]   From Benjamin Tappan. ALS, DNA-RG 59 (M639-27).

Mar 4	From Tandy Walker. ALS, DNA-RG 75 (M234-222). Asks AJ's help with his claim for services and losses in the Creek War.
Mar 5	To the United States Senate. DS, DNA-RG 46 (15-0300). *Senate Executive Proceedings*, 4:65. Nominates customs collectors.
Mar 5	To the United States Senate. DS, DNA-RG 46 (15-0302). *Senate Executive Proceedings*, 4:65. Nominates customs and land officers for reappointment.
Mar 5	*From George Graham.* 119
Mar 5	From Samuel Delucenna Ingham. LS, DLC (75). Recommends Stephen Cornell for revenue cutter warrant officer.
Mar 5	From Benjamin Jones Shain. ADS, DNA-RG 76 (15-0297). Asks AJ's aid in securing redress for his arrest and beating by Spanish officers at Havana in 1821.
[Mar 5]	Statement of pedigree for the horse Bolivar. Printed, *Nashville Republican and State Gazette*, Mar 5 (mAJs).
Mar 5	Receipt from John Lutz for purchase of a saddle. ADS, DLC (37).
Mar 6	*To Robert Young Hayne.* 122
Mar 6	*To Samuel Delucenna Ingham.* 123
Mar 6	*To Francis Preston.* 124
Mar 6	Proclamation ordering removal of public land intruders in the Huntsville, Ala., district. DS and draft, DNA-RG 59 (T1223-1). Copy, DNA-RG 59 (15-0305). Richardson, 2:494–95.
Mar 6	Approval of Navy lieutenant John H. Bell's court-martial for intemperance, with remission of his sentence to be cashiered from the service. DS, DNA-RG 125 (M273-22). Copy, DNA-RG 46 (15-0307).
Mar 6	Approval of Navy lieutenant Thomas S. Hamersley's court-martial and sentence of cashiering for insubordination, drunkenness, and fighting. DS, DNA-RG 125 (M273-25).
Mar 6	Approval of midshipman William M. A. Moore's court-martial for insulting fellow officers, with remission of his sentence to be cashiered from the service. DS, DNA-RG 125 (M273-22).
Mar 6	Check to Andrew Jackson Donelson for $50. DS, DLC (37).
Mar 6	Check to Andrew Jackson Donelson for $1,000. DS, DLC (37).
Mar 6	Andrew Jackson Donelson memorandum of the balance in AJ's BUS account. ANS, TNJ (15-0308).
Mar 8	*To Samuel Delucenna Ingham.* 124
Mar 8	William Henry Harrison to Martin Van Buren. LS, DNA-RG 59 (T33-5). Repels the Colombian government's charge of plotting its overthrow in 1829 and protests its mistreatment of him. Endorsed by AJ to Van Buren on Mar 20 to request proof from Colombian authorities.
Mar 9	*To Francis Preston.* 125
Mar 9	To the United States House of Representatives. DS, DNA-RG 233 (15-0319). *HRDoc* 94, 21st Cong., 1st sess., p. 1 (Serial 198); Richardson, 2:474. Transmits Virginia governor William B. Giles's communication of Mar 2 concerning the C & O Canal.

Mar 9   To the United States House of Representatives. Printed, *House Journal*, 21st Cong., 1st sess., p. 394 (Serial 194) (15-0321). Richardson, 2:474. Presents memorials from Francis H. Nicoll and from Pennsylvania U.S. marshal John Conard, the latter seeking protection from Nicoll's judgment against him incurred in performing his official duties.

Mar 9   To the United States Senate. DS, DNA-RG 46 (15-0322). *Senate Executive Proceedings*, 4:66. Nominates Thomas F. Knox for consul at Angostura, Colombia.

Mar 9   From Richard Keith Call. ALS, DLC (72). Recommends John Whitehead.

Mar 9   From John Kean Dayton. ALS, DNA-RG 59 (M639-6). Applies for a Navy Department clerkship.

Mar 9   *From Andrew Jackson Donelson.*   *126*

Mar 9   From Samuel Delucenna Ingham. LS, DNA-RG 46 (15-0315). Encloses a copy of Israel T. Canby's bond as receiver of the Crawfordsville, Ind., land office.

Mar 9   From Daniel H. Miller et al. DS, DNA-RG 59 (M639-11). Recommend Peter Hotz Jr. for consul at Valencia, Spain.

Mar 9   Receipted bill from Auguste Bernay for ice cream and fruit. DS, THer (15-0313). Runs to Apr 2.

Mar 10   To the United States Senate. DS, DNA-RG 46 (15-0335). *Senate Journal*, 21st Cong., 1st sess., p. 176 (Serial 191); Richardson, 2:474–75. Transmits Israel T. Canby's bond as receiver of the Crawfordsville, Ind., land office, requested by the Senate Mar 6.

Mar 10   To the United States Senate. Facsimile of LS, Gallery of History catalog, Mar 12, 1997 (mAJs). *Senate Executive Proceedings*, 4:67 (15-0337). Withdraws John M. Bowyer's nomination as consul at Guazacualco, Mexico.

Mar 10   From Joseph S. Boissiere. DS, DNA-RG 59 (15-0481). Master of the schooner *Argonaut* asks for relief of a $500 penalty for omitting to present his ship's papers to the consul at Cartagena on an 1826 voyage.

Mar 10   Approval of a reservation of public lands for an arsenal at Mount Vernon, Ala. DS, DNA-RG 49 (15-0328).

Mar 10   William Clew to Joel Barlow Sutherland. ALS, DNA-RG 59 (15-0697). Asks his help in obtaining a pardon for stealing from the BUS. Endorsed by AJ.

Mar 10   Amos Kendall to John Branch. LS, DNA-RG 233 (15-0324). Explains he cannot revisit late Alabama marshal Taliaferro Livingston's previously rejected claim for additional expenses in keeping captured Africans unless instructed by AJ. AJ declines to intervene Mar 17.

Mar 10   Receipted bill from F. Masi & Co. to Emily Tennessee Donelson for jewelry and sundries. DS, DLC (39). Runs to May 9, 1831. Paid by AJ.

Mar 11   *To Littleton Waller Tazewell.*   *128*

Mar 11   To the United States Senate. DS, DNA-RG 46 (15-0342). *Senate Executive Proceedings*, 4:68. Nominates Peter Hotz Jr. for consul at Valencia, Spain.

Mar 11	To the United States Senate. DS, DNA-RG 46 (15-0344). *Senate Executive Proceedings*, 4:68. Nominates customs officers for reappointment.
Mar 11	To the United States Senate. ADS, DNA-RG 46 (15-0346). *Senate Executive Proceedings*, 4:67. Nominates David Porter for consul general at Algiers and district attorneys for reappointment.
Mar 11	To the United States Senate. ADS, DNA-RG 46 (15-0348). *Senate Executive Proceedings*, 4:67. Nominates John Crowninshield for customs appraiser at Boston.
Mar 11	From James Nelson Barker. ALS, PHi (15-0338). Introduces Revolutionary pension claimant Moses Smith.
Mar 11	From Thomas W. Freelon. ALS, DNA-RG 125 (M273-25). Asks leniency for Navy lieutenant Thomas S. Hamersley, victim of undue severity and political persecution.
Mar 11	From [George Graham]. N, DNA-RG 59 (15-0526). Submits land patents for signature.
Mar 11	AJ endorsement noting Peter Hotz Jr.'s nomination as consul at Valencia. ANS, John F. Reed (15-0340).
Mar 11	Check to Ebenezer James Hume for $100. DS, DLC (37).
Mar 12	*To William Polk.* 128
Mar 12	To George D. Strong et al. Printed, *Morning Courier and New-York Enquirer*, Mar 22 (mAJs; 15-0351). Thanks them for a framed copy of his first annual message printed on satin.
Mar 12	To the United States Senate. DS, DNA-RG 46 (15-0352). *Senate Executive Proceedings*, 4:68. Nominates John Phagan for Seminole Indian agent.
[Mar 12]	From Felix Grundy et al. DS, DNA-RG 46 (14-1237). Biddle, *Senator Grundy's Political Conduct Reviewed* (Nashville, 1832), p. 12. Tennessee senator and congressmen recommend Charles Biddle for office.
Mar 12	From Charles Biddle. Printed, Biddle, *Senator Grundy's Political Conduct Reviewed* (Nashville, 1832), pp. 11–12 (mAJs). Requests an office and encloses his recommendation from Tennesseans in Congress.
Mar 12	From John Branch. LC, DNA-RG 45 (M472-1). Recommends renominating Marine lieutenant Charles F. Spering for promotion with a corrected date.
Mar 12	From John Mason. ALS, DNA-RG 125 (M273-25). Testifies to Thomas S. Hamersley's good character. Concurring note by George Graham.
Mar 12	Approval of midshipman Benjamin S. Slye's court-martial and sentence of dismissal for disobeying orders and unbecoming conduct. ANS, DNA-RG 125 (M273-22).
Mar 13	*To William Branch Giles.* 129
Mar 13	To the United States Senate. DS, DNA-RG 46 (15-0359). *Senate Executive Proceedings*, 4:69. Nominates Charles F. Morehouse for register of the Ouachita, La., land office.
Mar 13	From James Collinsworth. ALS, DNA-RG 59 (15-0421). States that defaulting former Indian agent Robert C. Nicholas, jailed at

	Nashville for his debt to the U.S., is wholly insolvent. AJ orders his release Mar 18.
Mar 13	From Samuel Delucenna Ingham. ALS, DNA-RG 59 (M639-3). LC, PU (mAJs). States his knowledge of the Alexander Brackenridge case, which he has communicated to Van Buren.
Mar 14	To Unknown. AL draft fragment, DLC (72). Responds to a letter of Feb 26.
Mar 14	From James Ewell. ALS, DNA-RG 59 (M639-7). Asks to be appointed distributor of the laws to help him vend his *Medical Companion*.
Mar 15	From Martin Van Buren. DS, DNA-RG 233; LC, DNA-RG 59 (15-0371). *HRDoc* 80, 21st Cong., 1st sess., pp. 1–2 (Serial 197). Reports on unavailing efforts to procure a record of the Florida/Georgia boundary line run pursuant to the Spanish treaty of 1795.
Mar 15	To the United States House of Representatives. DS, DNA-RG 233 (15-0368). *HRDoc* 80, 21st Cong., 1st sess., p. 1 (Serial 197); Richardson, 2:475. Transmits Van Buren's report on the Florida boundary.
Mar 15	From William Brent. ALS, DNA-RG 125 (M273-25). Defends Thomas S. Hamersley's character and pleads his cause. Concurring note by Daniel Brent.
Mar 15	From Frederick E. Bunker. ADS and ADS duplicate, DNA-RG 59 (M639-3). Asks to be appointed consul at Constantinople.
Mar 15	From Micajah Green Lewis Claiborne. ALS and ALS duplicate, DNA-RG 125 (M273-25). Defends Thomas S. Hamersley as a victim of personal and political persecution.
Mar 15	From George Mifflin Dallas et al. DS, DNA-RG 59 (M639-9). Recommend Thomas W. Gilpin for a consulate.
Mar 15	From James Harvey Hook. ALS, PHi (15-0364). Recommends needy Revolutionary veteran Moses Smith for caretaker at Fort Mifflin, Pa.
Mar 15	From William Morrison Oliver et al. DS, DNA-RG 59 (M639-13). New York legislators recommend Perley Keyes for governor of proposed Huron Territory.
Mar 15	*From Spencer Darwin Pettis.* *130*
Mar 15	From Nathaniel Williams. ALS, DNA-RG 59 (15-0486). Endorses *Argonaut* master Joseph S. Boissiere's plea of innocent intentions and request for leniency for his failure to report to the consul at Cartagena. AJ orders pardon Mar 26.
Mar 15	Check to Andrew Jackson Donelson for $412.50. DS, DLC (37).
Mar 15	Draft on AJ for $435.35, endorsed for payment Mar 17. Abstract, American Art Association catalog, 1926 (15-0370).
Mar 15	Andrew Jackson Donelson to Daniel Brent. ALS, DNA-RG 59 (M179-68). Instructs him to deliver David Porter's passport.
Mar 15	Andrew Jackson Donelson to Edward George Washington Butler. ALS, LNHiC (15-0362). Censures Congress's misdoings and encloses a paper. Franked by AJ.
Mar 16	To the United States Senate. ADS, DNA-RG 46 (15-0377).

	Senate Executive Proceedings, 4:69. Nominates Finis Ewing for register of the Lexington, Mo., land office.	
Mar 16	*To Samuel Delucenna Ingham.*	*130*
Mar 16	To the United States Senate. DS, DNA-RG 46 (15-0379). *Senate Executive Proceedings*, 4:70. Nominates Frederick R. Conway for recorder of land titles in Missouri.	
[Mar 16]	To the United States Senate. DS, DNA-RG 46 (15-0381). *Senate Executive Proceedings*, 4:69. Nominates George Black for consul at Santos, Brazil.	
Mar 16	*From James Alexander Hamilton.*	*131*
Mar 16	From William Brown Hodgson. ALS, DNA-RG 59 (M179-68). Suggests reducing the scope of presents to be distributed by the new U.S. consul general to Algiers.	
Mar 16	*From Francis Preston.*	*132*
Mar 16	From Martin Van Buren. LC, DNA-RG 59 (M40-21). Transmits a copy of the biennial *Register of Officers and Agents, Civil, Military, and Naval, in the Service of the United States.*	
Mar 16	Bill from Charles Polkinhorn for coach reins. DS, DLC (38). Receipted Jan 3, 1831.	
Mar 17	*To Louis McLane.*	*133*
Mar 17	From John Macpherson Berrien. LC, DNA-RG 60 (T412-3). *HRDoc* 123, 26th Cong., 2d sess., pp. 756–57 (Serial 387). Recommends pardoning Adelaide Adam, Asa Fairfield, and Adam Stone for unintentionally violating the ban on slave importations.	
Mar 17	From John Branch. LS, DNA-RG 233 (15-0383). LC, DNA-RG 45 (M472-1). Submits late Alabama marshal Taliaferro Livingston's previously rejected claim for expenses in keeping Africans and Kendall's Mar 10 report thereon.	
Mar 17	From John Henry Eaton. LS, DNA-RG 233; LC, DNA-RG 77 (15-0385). LC, DNA-RG 77 (M65-3). *HRDoc* 82, 21st Cong., 1st sess., p. 1 (Serial 197). Submits a report on a survey of the Penobscot River.	
Mar 17	Receipted bill from Charles W. Patterson for muffins. ADS, THer (15-0388).	
Mar 18	To the United States House of Representatives. DS, DNA-RG 233 (15-0395). *HRDoc* 82, 21st Cong., 1st sess., p. 1 (Serial 197); Richardson, 2:475. Transmits the report of the Penobscot River survey.	
Mar 18	To the United States Senate. DS, DNA-RG 46 (15-0397). *Senate Executive Proceedings*, 4:72. Nominates an Army paymaster and Indian agent.	
Mar 18	To the United States Senate. Printed, *Senate Executive Proceedings*, 4:75 (15-0399). Nominates James Davis for consul at Guazacualco, Mexico.	
[Mar 18]	From Joseph Ficklin et al. DS, DNA-RG 59 (M639-21). Recommend George Shannon for governor of proposed Huron Territory.	
Mar 18	From Joseph Ficklin. ALS, DNA-RG 59 (M639-21). Encloses the recommendation for George Shannon.	

	Executive Proceedings, 4:85. Nominates John Hamm for chargé d'affaires to Central America.
Mar 31	To the United States Senate. DS, DNA-RG 46 (15-0546). *Senate Executive Proceedings*, 4:85. Nominates James W. Exum for marshal in Florida.
Mar 31	To the United States Senate. DS, DNA-RG 46 (15-0548). *Senate Executive Proceedings*, 4:85. Nominates Willis M. Green for receiver of the Palmyra, Mo., land office.
Mar 31	*To Martin Van Buren.* 166
Mar 31	From Johnson Simonds. DS, DNA-RG 59 (15-0666). Asks remission of his fine and costs for fighting so he can be released from the D.C. jail. Approved by AJ Apr 9.
Mar 31	Approval of Navy purser William Paul Zantzinger's court-martial and sentence of cashiering. DS, DNA-RG 45 (M148-61).
[Mar]	From Henry Conwell et al. DS, DNA-RG 59 (M639-15). Recommend James McHenry for consul at Belfast.
[Mar]	From Harvey Cook et al. DS, DNA-RG 59 (M639-20). *TPUS*, 12:104–5. Oppose removing Thomas Rowland as marshal in Michigan Territory.
[Mar]	From Harrison Daniel et al. DS, DNA-RG 59 (M639-21). Recommend George Shannon for governor of proposed Huron Territory.
Mar	From John Milton Goodenow et al. LS, DNA-RG 59 (M639-2). Recommend Walter M. Blake for marshal of proposed Huron Territory.
[cMar]	From James T. Homans. ALS, DNA-RG 125 (M273-25). Defends cashiered Navy lieutenant Thomas S. Hamersley as the victim of Captain John O. Creighton's political persecution.
[cMar]	From Thomson Francis Mason. ALS, DNA-RG 125 (M273-25). Testifies to Thomas S. Hamersley's good character and asks for his reinstatement.
[cMar]	From John McNeil. ALS, DNA-RG 125 (M273-25). Testifies to Thomas S. Hamersley's sobriety and good character.
[Mar]	From David Meldrum et al. DS, DNA-RG 59 (M639-27). Extract (signature list), *TPUS*, 12:155. Oppose removing James Witherell as secretary of Michigan Territory.
[cMar]	From Thomas Robbins. AL draft, CtHi (mAJs). Protests Georgia's claim of authority over the Cherokees as a violation of justice, law, and treaties.
[Mar]	From Thomas Rowland et al. DSs, DNA-RG 59 (M639-27). *TPUS*, 12:151–55. Oppose removing James Witherell as secretary of Michigan Territory.
[cMar]	From Abraham Russel Smith. ALS, DNA-RG 59 (M639-22). Asks to be appointed consul at Pará, Brazil.
Mar	From Norman S. Sprague. ALS, DNA-RG 59 (M639-27). *TPUS*, 12:147–51. Opposes removing Michigan Territory secretary James Witherell and attacks his critics John Biddle and Thomas C. Sheldon.
[cMar]	From William Wyatt. Printed extract, Tallahassee *Floridian*,

	Executive Proceedings, 4:86. Nominates Daniel M. Durell for district attorney in New Hampshire.
Apr 5	To the United States Senate. DS, DNA-RG 46 (15-0586). *Senate Executive Proceedings*, 4:86. Nominates William Pickering for Portsmouth, N.H., customs collector.
Apr 5	From John Strode Barbour. ALS, DNA-RG 125 (M273-25). Praises Thomas S. Hamersley's character and asks his continuance in the Navy.
Apr 5	*From Ralph Eleazar Whitesides Earl.* 175
Apr 5	From Edward Livingston. ALS, DNA-RG 59 (M639-14). Recommends Craven P. Luckett for office.
Apr 5	*Order of pardon for David H. Dyer.* 177
Apr 6	From John Henry Eaton. ALS, DNA-RG 46 (15-0619). Submits documents requested by the Senate Apr 5 concerning Indian agent nominee Wharton Rector's fitness for office.
Apr 6	To the United States Senate. DS, DNA-RG 46 (15-0630). *Senate Executive Proceedings*, 4:88; Richardson, 2:476. Transmits the documents concerning Wharton Rector.
Apr 6	*To John Pitchlynn.* 178
Apr 6	From George Graham. LC, DNA-RG 49 (M25-25). Transmits an application to lease a reserved salt spring section in Michigan Territory.
Apr 6	From John Pemberton. ALS copy, PHi (15-0621). Thanks AJ for his appointment as naval officer at Philadelphia.
Apr 6	Pardon for mail thief David H. Dyer. LC, DNA-RG 59 (15-0588; T967-1).
Apr 6	James P. Turner to George Graham. ALS, DNA-RG 49 (M1329-4; 15-0625). Accuses James Allison and Thomas Butler of land frauds. AJ demands May 15 that Turner prove or retract the charges.
Apr 7	From Henry Eckford. ALS, DNA-RG 45 (M124-123). Offers the government cut naval timber at a bargain price.
Apr 7	*To John Branch.* 179
Apr 7	From John Henry Eaton. LS, DNA-RG 46 (15-0632). *Senate Executive Proceedings*, 4:96. Submits a list of Army paymasters for reappointment.
Apr 7	From Alexander Ogle. ALS, TNJ (15-0637). Recommends Michael Wilison for land office register in Indiana or Michigan Territory.
Apr 7	*From Hestor Lockhart Stevens et al.* 186
Apr 7	*From John Stevens.* 179
[cApr 7]	*From Martin Van Buren.* 181
Apr 7	Check to Andrew Jackson Donelson for $800. DS, DLC (38).
Apr 8	To Louis, Grand Duke of Baden. LC, DNA-RG 59 (15-0643). Offers congratulations on the birth of a nephew.
Apr 8	To Dom Miguel, King of Portugal. LC, DNA-RG 59 (15-0644). Offers condolences on the death of his mother.
Apr 8	To the United States Senate. DS, DNA-RG 46 (15-0645). *Senate Executive Proceedings*, 4:88. Nominates John B. Murphy for customs collector of Teche district, La.

Apr 8	From Robert Desha. ALS, DNA-RG 94 (M567-51). Recommends Benjamin Desha for Arkansas Territory militia general. Referred by AJ to Eaton.
Apr 8	Check to Samuel Jackson Hays for $150. DS, DLC (38).
Apr 8	Check to Andrew Jackson Hutchings for $185. DS, DLC (38).
Apr 8	*Clement Comer Clay and John McKinley to Martin Van Buren.* 182
Apr 8	Bill from William Thumlert to Andrew Jackson Jr. for footwear. DS, DLC (40). Receipted Jan 10, 1832.
Apr 9	To John Branch. ANS, DNA-RG 125 (M273-25). Refers the "strong testimonials" in behalf of Thomas S. Hamersley.
Apr 9	From John Branch. LS, DNA-RG 46 (15-0647). LC, DNA-RG 45 (M472-1). Submits navy agent nominations rephrased as required by the Senate to state the cause of the vacancy instead of the date of appointment, and recommends abolishing the posts at New Orleans and Lima, Peru.
Apr 9	To the United States Senate. DS, DNA-RG 46 (15-0654). LC, DNA-RG 45 (M472-1). *Senate Executive Proceedings*, 4:88. Nominates navy agents.
Apr 9	From John Henry Eaton. LS, DNA-RG 46 (15-0649). *Senate Executive Proceedings*, 4:91–92. Submits Army promotions.
Apr 9	From John Henry Eaton. LS, DNA-RG 46 (15-0651). *Senate Executive Proceedings*, 4:92. Submits Army brevet promotions.
Apr 9	From Chittenden Lyon et al. DS, DNA-RG 59 (M639-14). Congressmen recommend Craven P. Luckett for office.
Apr 10	*To John Coffee.* 183
Apr 10	To the United States Senate. DS, DNA-RG 46 (15-0669). *Senate Executive Proceedings*, 4:88. Withdraws nominations of navy agents at New Orleans and Lima, Peru.
Apr 10	*To Martin Van Buren.* 184
Apr 10	From Thomas Fowler. DS, DNA-RG 59 (15-0742). Convicted thief begs remission of his fine and costs and release from confinement. Approved by AJ Apr 14.
Apr 10	From Lawrence Kearny. ALS, DNA-RG 46 (15-0660). Urges reinstating Lieutenant Edmund Byrne, dismissed from the Navy for his connection to a duel.
Apr 10	From Daniel Todd Patterson. ALS, DNA-RG 46 (15-0663). Commends Edmund Byrne's character and recommends his reinstatement.
Apr 10	*From Hestor Lockhart Stevens.* 186
Apr 10	Remission of fine and costs and discharge for prisoner Johnson Simonds, convicted of fighting. LC, DNA-RG 59 (15-0665; T967-1).
Apr 11	From Edmund Pendleton Kennedy. ALS, DNA-RG 46 (15-0671). Commends dismissed Navy lieutenant Edmund Byrne.
Apr 11	*Daniel W. Wright to Powhatan Ellis.* 188
Apr 12	To the United States Senate. DS, DNA-RG 46 (15-0683). *Senate Executive Proceedings*, 4:90. Nominates Paul L. Chouteau for Osage Indian agent.
Apr 12	From John Gilmore. ALS, DNA-RG 59 (M639-3). Forwards a

Pittsburgh recommendation for George W. Buchanan as district
attorney in Pennsylvania.

Apr 12   From Andrew Marschalk. ALS, DNA-RG 49 (15-0679).
Complains of inadequate compensation for publishing
proclamations of federal land sales.

Apr 12   From Joel Barlow Sutherland. ALS, DNA-RG 59 (15-0699).
Encloses proofs that pardoned thief William Clew is unable to
pay fine and costs. AJ orders his release.

Apr 12   *From Nicholas Philip Trist.*   *190*

Apr 12   From Gulian Crommelin Verplanck. ALS, DNA-RG 76 (15-
0685). Encloses the Feb 24 memorial of Thomas R. Mercein et
al., claimants against Buenos Aires.

Apr 12   From Lewis Warrington. ALS, DNA-RG 46 (15-0687).
Commends dismissed Navy lieutenant Edmund Byrne.

Apr 13   From John Henry Eaton. DS, DNA-RG 233 (15-0688). *HRDoc*
91, 21st Cong., 1st sess., pp. 1–2 (Serial 198). Submits a report
on the expense and military force required for Indian removal.

Apr 13   To the United States House of Representatives. DS, DNA-RG
233 (15-0692). *HRDoc* 91, 21st Cong., 1st sess., p. 1 (Serial
198); Richardson, 2:476. Transmits Eaton's report on the
expense and military force required for Indian removal.

Apr 13   *Toast at Jefferson Birthday dinner.*   *190*

Apr 13   Approval of acting sailing master Alexander Gibson's Navy
court-martial and sentence of cashiering for misconduct and
drunkenness, with remission of his forfeiture of pay and
disbarment from future service. DS, DNA-RG 125 (M273-23).

Apr 13   Approval of Navy captain Beekman V. Hoffman's court-martial
for neglect of duty and disobedience, with remission of his
sentence of cashiering. DS, DNA-RG 125 (M273-23).

Apr 13   Order for release of prisoner William Clew. ADS, DNA-RG 59
(15-0704).

Apr 13   Andrew Jackson Donelson to Daniel Brent. ALS, DNA-RG 59
(M179-68). Asks if David H. Dyer's pardon, which Clement C.
Clay awaits, is ready.

Apr 14   To the United States Senate. ADS, DNA-RG 46 (15-0707).
Senate Executive Proceedings, 4:91. Nominates Army officers
for brevet and line promotions.

Apr 14   From Alexander Claxton and Isaac McKeever. LS, DNA-RG 46
(15-0694). Urge reinstating dismissed Navy lieutenant Edmund
Byrne.

Apr 14   Remission of fine and costs and discharge for prisoner William
Clew. LC, DNA-RG 59 (15-0696; T967-1).

Apr 15   To the United States Senate. DS, DNA-RG 46 (15-0725). *Senate
Executive Proceedings*, 4:93; Richardson, 2:476–77. Submits
evidence requested by the Senate on John Hamm's past conduct
as Ohio marshal, and asks to defer action on his nomination as
chargé d'affaires to Central America pending news of a
government change there.

Apr 15   *To Martin Van Buren.*   *191*

222). Creek chiefs reaffirm confidence in agent John Crowell and disavow purported calls for his removal.

Apr 20   From Daniel Van Voorhis. ALS, DNA-RG 45 (M124-123). Proposes to supply hardware to the Brooklyn navy yard.

Apr 20   From John Garrison, William W. Jackson, and Richard Cornwell. DS, DNA-RG 45 (M124-123). Recommend Daniel Van Voorhis for supplier to the Brooklyn navy yard.

Apr 20   From Campbell Patrick White. ALS, DLC (15-0763). Recommends James Kelly for a commission in the Marines.

Apr 20   George Mifflin Dallas to Martin Van Buren. ALS, DNA-RG 59 (M179-68). Transmits Spanish minister Francisco Tacon's request not to prosecute Joseph Vandegrift of Philadelphia for molesting his family and baggage in the street. Endorsed by AJ to Van Buren on Apr 22 to order the prosecution dropped and to conspicuously thank Tacon.

Apr 21   To the United States Senate. DS, DNA-RG 46 (15-0765). *Senate Executive Proceedings*, 4:94. Nominates Benjamin Evens for consul at Campeche, Mexico.

Apr 21   From Benjamin W. Didenhover. DS, DNA-RG 59 (15-0884). Indigent prisoner begs release and remission of his fine and costs for assault. Approved by AJ May 4.

Apr 22   From John Henry Eaton. LS, DNA-RG 233; LC, DNA-RG 77 (15-0767). LC, DNA-RG 107 (M127-2). LC, DNA-RG 77 (M65-3). *HRDoc* 93, 21st Cong., 1st sess., p. 1 (Serial 198). Submits an Army engineers' survey report on the harbor of St. Augustine, Fla.

Apr 22   To the United States House of Representatives. DS, DNA-RG 233 (15-0770). *HRDoc* 93, 21st Cong., 1st sess., p. 1 (Serial 198); Richardson, 2:477. Transmits the survey report on St. Augustine harbor.

Apr 22   To the United States Senate. DS, DNA-RG 46 (15-0772). *Senate Executive Proceedings*, 4:94 (dated Apr 23). Nominates Marine officers for promotion.

Apr 22   To the United States Senate. DS, DNA-RG 46 (15-0774). *Senate Executive Proceedings*, 4:94–95. Nominates Arkansas Territory militia generals.

Apr 22   From Lewis Clephane and John Gardiner. DS, DNA-RG 75 (M234-433). Ask permission to borrow and copy Indian portraits in the War Department. Referred by AJ to Eaton.

Apr 22   From John Henry Eaton. ALS, CSmH (15-0769). Submits an 1825 William Clark letter explaining his Osage and Kansas treaties, requested by the Senate Apr 20.

Apr 22   *From Edward Everett.*   *203*

Apr 22   From Thomas Norman. ALS, DNA-RG 45 (M124-123). Complains that Amos Kendall has refused his claim for usual expenses while giving evidence in the investigation of John B. Timberlake's accounts. Forwarded by AJ to Branch.

Apr 22   From John Usher. DS, DNA-RG 59 (15-0941). Begs remission of his fine for inadvertently selling liquor without a license. Approved by AJ May 5.

procure the release of captain William Taylor of the privateer *Federal*, arrested in Martinique. Referred by AJ to Van Buren.

Apr 30 | To *John Christmas McLemore*. | 219

Apr 30 | From James Fenner. Copy, RPB-JH (15-0861). Introduces and commends Benjamin Fry.

[cApr] | From Daniel Turner. LS, DNA-RG 46 (15-0555). Urges reinstating dismissed Navy lieutenant Edmund Byrne.

[Apr-May] | To *George Graham*. | 220

May 1 | From Samuel Delucenna Ingham. LS, DNA-RG 46 (15-0873). Reports that Mount Salus, Miss., land office receiver James C. Dickson is in default to the government.

May 1 | To the United States Senate. DS, DNA-RG 46 (15-0874). *Senate Executive Proceedings*, 4:99; Richardson, 2:477. Nominates Hiram G. Runnels in place of James C. Dickson as receiver of the Mount Salus, Miss., land office.

May 1 | From James Blair. AN, DLC (72). Submits a prospectus and solicits a subscription. Subscription purchased by AJ.

May 2 | From Ferdinand Fayette Pepin. ALS, DNA-RG 94 (M688-70). Asks to be appointed to West Point.

May 3 | To *James Alexander Hamilton*. | 221

[cMay 3] | To David Henshaw. N, MB (15-0877). Invitation to dinner.

May 3 | From John Atkinson. DS, DNA-RG 59 (15-0879). Begs release from jail and remission of his fine and costs for breach of the peace. Approved by AJ May 4.

May 3 | From James Carroll Jr. et al. DS, DNA-RG 59 (17-0138). Recommend mail robber John Amonheizer for pardon.

[cMay 3] | From D. W. Hudson. ADS, DNA-RG 59 (17-0142). Seconds the recommendation to pardon mail robber John Amonheizer.

May 3 | From Thomas Dulany. DS, DNA-RG 59 (15-0892). Begs release from jail and remission of his fine for rioting. Approved by AJ May 4.

May 3 | From Thomas Jones. DS, DNA-RG 59 (15-0898). Begs release from jail and remission of his fine for petty larceny. Approved by AJ May 4.

[May 4] | From *Martin Van Buren*. | 222

May 4 | To *Martin Van Buren*. | 223

May 4 | To *Martin Van Buren*. | 223

May 4 | From *Martin Van Buren*. | 224

May 4 | To the United States Senate. DS, DNA-RG 46 (15-0912). *Senate Executive Proceedings*, 4:99. Nominates Samuel Larned for chargé d'affaires to Peru.

May 4 | From John Anderson. ALS, DNA-RG 59 (15-0952). Requests another release for Edward Barneville, re-imprisoned on execution of his debt to the U.S. Referred by AJ to the State Department for report on how his debt arose.

May 4 | From John Branch. LC, DNA-RG 45 (M472-1). Submits a report on the marine railway at Philadelphia.

May 4 | From Tench Ringgold. ADS, DNA-RG 59 (15-0888). Confirms that D.C. pardon supplicants John Atkinson, Thomas Jones,

	Thomas Dulany, and Benjamin W. Didenhover are poor and unable to pay their fines and costs.	
May 4	Release for prisoner John Atkinson and remission of his fine and costs for breach of the peace. LC, DNA-RG 59 (15-0878; T967-1).	
May 4	Release for prisoner Benjamin W. Didenhover and remission of his fine and costs for assault. LC, DNA-RG 59 (15-0883; T967-1).	
May 4	Release for prisoner Thomas Dulany and remission of his fine for rioting. LC, DNA-RG 59 (15-0891; T967-1).	
May 4	Release for prisoner Thomas Jones and remission of his fine for petty larceny. LC, DNA-RG 59 (15-0896; T967-1).	
May 4	Release for prisoner Abraham Russell and remission of his fine and costs for assault. LC, DNA-RG 59 (15-0902; T967-1).	
May 4	Release for prisoner Judson Russell and remission of his fine and costs for assault. LC, DNA-RG 59 (15-0908; T967-1).	
May 5	*To John Branch.*	225
May 5	To the United States Senate. Printed, *Senate Executive Proceedings*, 4:99 (15-0924). Withdraws Benjamin Evens's nomination as consul at Campeche, Mexico.	
May 5	*From Samuel Jackson Hays.*	226
May 5	From Ross Wilkins. ALS, DLC (38). Asks to be appointed Army paymaster.	
May 5	Check to Andrew Jackson Donelson for $1,150. DS, DLC (38).	
May 5	Robert West to Henry Toland. D, DLC (38). Bill for twelve mahogany chairs.	
May 6	*To the United States Senate.*	228
May 6	To the United States Senate. DS, DNA-RG 46 (15-0933). *Senate Executive Proceedings*, 4:99. Nominates Benjamin Patteson for marshal in north Alabama.	
May 6	To the United States Senate. DS, DNA-RG 46 (15-0935). *Senate Executive Proceedings*, 4:100. Nominates Robert L. Crawford for marshal in South Carolina.	
May 6	To the United States Senate. DS, DNA-RG 46 (15-0937). *Senate Executive Proceedings*, 4:100. Nominates John T. Mason for secretary of Michigan Territory.	
May 6	From Baron de Mareuil. ALS and Copy, DNA-RG 59 (M53-8). Takes leave as French minister to the U.S.	
May 6	From John K. Smith. ALS, DNA-RG 46 (15-0925). Recommends Edward Chandler for district attorney in Florida.	
May 6	Remission of a fine against John Usher for selling liquor without a license. LC, DNA-RG 59 (15-0939; T967-1).	
May 6	Ross Wilkins to Harmar Denny. ALS, DLC (38). Urges his political service to AJ as qualification to be appointed Army paymaster.	
May 7	To John Henry Eaton. Abstract, DNA-RG 107 (M22-26). Appoints William Piatt Army paymaster.	
May 7	To the United States Senate. DS, DNA-RG 46 (15-0945). *Senate Executive Proceedings*, 4:100. Nominates William Piatt for Army paymaster.	

May 7   To the United States Senate. DS, DNA-RG 46 (15-0947). *Senate Executive Proceedings*, 4:100. Nominates Edward Chandler for district attorney in Florida.

May 7   From Rebecca Edwards. ALS, DNA-RG 94 (M567-51). Requests an Army discharge for her son Jordan Edwards, in frail health.

May 7   From John Floyd. Copy, DNA-RG 59 (M639-23). Recommends Samuel A. Storrow for chargé d'affaires to Brazil.

May 7   From John W. Simonton. ALS, DNA-RG 45 (M124-124). Asks the removal of decrepit government buildings in Key West, Fla. Endorsed favorably by AJ to Branch.

May 7   John Anderson to Martin Van Buren. ALS, DNA-RG 59 (15-0955). Reports that Edward Barneville's debt to the U.S. is from his unsettled balance as an Army captain in the War of 1812 and that he is now wholly destitute. AJ orders his release.

May 7   Andrew Jackson Donelson to John Branch. ALS, DNA-RG 45 (M124-124). Sends the papers for Army lieutenant Thomas Burke's exchange of rank with Marine lieutenant Constantine Smith.

May 8   From Albert Peebly. ALS, DNA-RG 59 (M179-68). Requests a patent for his improved plow.

May 8   From Samuel Hyde Saunders. ALS, DNA-RG 49 (15-0964). Asks AJ to process his warrants for land in Ohio's Virginia Military District.

May 8   Discharge from confinement for insolvent public debtor Edward Barneville. LC, DNA-RG 59 (15-0951; T967-1).

[May 10]   From Edward Johnson Etting et al. DS, DNA-RG 233 (15-0969). Complain of a tariff loophole allowing British manufacturers to evade the duty on imported bar iron. Referred by AJ to Congress via John Scott of Pennsylvania.

May 10   From Charles Rhind. LS, DNA-RG 59 (M46-3). Copy (extract), DNA-RG 11 (15-0973). *HRDoc* 250, 22d Cong., 1st sess., pp. 77–94 (Serial 221). Describes the negotiations leading to his conclusion on May 7 of a commercial treaty with Turkey.

May 10   Unconditional pardon and order for discharge of prisoner William Clew. LC, DNA-RG 59 (T967-1).

May 11   From John Branch. LS, DNA-RG 46 (15-0981). LC, DNA-RG 45 (M472-1). Submits and explains nominations of naval surgeons and assistant surgeons, pursers, and chaplains.

May 11   From James Alexander Hamilton. ALS, DNA-RG 59 (15-1023). Recommends dropping prosecution of William Dawes, master of the *Rebecca*, for his inadvertent failure to file a correct crew list for a foreign voyage as required by law. Approved by AJ May 13.

May 24	To the United States Senate. DS, DNA-RG 46 (15-1080). *Senate Executive Proceedings*, 4:107. Nominates diplomats abroad.
May 24	From Anthony Butler. ALS, DLC (38). Introduces Lorenzo de Zavala, on a visit to the U.S. Endorsed by AJ "To be treated with attention."
May 24	From John Henry Eaton. LS, DNA-RG 233 (15-1075). LC, DNA-RG 107 (M127-2). LC, DNA-RG 77 (M65-3). Submits an engineer's report on the harbors of Stamford and Norwalk, Conn.
May 24	From Thomas Hinds. ALS, DNA-RG 59 (M639-24). Recommends Robert T. Thompson for office. Endorsed by AJ for safekeeping.
May [24]	*From Mary Wilson.* 273
May 24	Edward Robinson to Elias Glenn. DS, DNA-RG 59 (15-1498). Master of the coastwise schooner *William F. Murray* begs remission of his $10,000 fine for landing eight slaves without delivering the required manifest. Approved by AJ Jun 16.
May 24	Check to William Berkeley Lewis for $1,848. DS, DLC (38).
[May 25]	From Benjamin Chew Howard. Extract, Gary Hendershott catalog 79, Mar 1993 (mAJs). Recommends Mr. Hollingsworth for Navy midshipman.
May 25	To John Branch. Facsimile of ANS, Gary Hendershott catalog 79, Mar 1993 (mAJs). Encloses and endorses Benjamin C. Howard's recommendation of Mr. Hollingsworth for Navy midshipman.
May 25	*To Martin Van Buren.* 275
May 25	Andrew Jackson Donelson to Daniel Brent. ALS, DNA-RG 59 (M179-73). Asks for William Lytle's nomination as surveyor general.
May 25	To the United States Senate. DS, DNA-RG 46 (15-1091). *Senate Executive Proceedings*, 4:108. Nominates William Lytle for surveyor general in Ohio, Indiana, and Michigan.
May 25	To Enoch Reynolds. LC, DNA-RG 59 (15-1088). Appoints him acting second comptroller in Isaac Hill's absence.
May 25	To the United States House of Representatives. DS, DNA-RG 233 (15-1089). *House Journal*, 21st Cong., 1st sess., p. 714 (Serial 194); Richardson, 2:480. Transmits the report of a survey of the harbors of Stamford and Norwalk, Conn.
May 25	To the United States Senate. ADS, DNA-RG 46 (15-1093). *Senate Executive Proceedings*, 4:109. Nominates James B. Thornton for second comptroller of the Treasury.
May 25	From Robert Desha. ALS, TNJ (15-1082). Recommends Benjamin Patton Jr. for a diplomatic post.
May 25	From Benjamin Patton Jr. ALS, TNJ (15-1085). Asks to be appointed secretary of legation.
May 26	To the United States Congress. DS, DNA-RG 233; DS, DLC (15-1097). *HRDoc* 110, 21st Cong., 1st sess., p. 1 (Serial 198); Richardson, 2:480–81. Asks for authority during the pending congressional recess to implement the anticipated agreement with Britain for reopening the West Indian colonial trade.

	Richardson, 2:482. Requests an appropriation to fund the continuation of Marine Corps pay and allowances stopped in 1829 because unsanctioned by law.
May 29	From John Branch. LS, DNA-RG 46 (15-1199). LC, DNA-RG 45 (M472-1). Recommends passed midshipman William W. Hunter for promotion.
May 29	To the United States Senate. DS, DNA-RG 46 (15-1218). LC, DNA-RG 45 (M472-1). *Senate Executive Proceedings*, 4:115. Nominates William W. Hunter for Navy lieutenant.
May 29	To the United States Senate. DS, DNA-RG 46 (15-1210). *SDoc* 145, 21st Cong., 1st sess., p. 1 (Serial 193); Richardson, 2:482. Transmits the Treasury report on appropriations of land and money within the states and the value of exports from them.
May 29	To the United States Senate. DS, DNA-RG 46 (15-1212). *Senate Executive Proceedings*, 4:115. Nominates John S. Langham for consul at Santa Fe, Mexico.
May 29	To the United States Senate. DS, DNA-RG 46 (15-1216). *Senate Executive Proceedings*, 4:115. Corrects John S. Langham's nomination to consul at Chihuahua, Mexico.
May 29	To the United States Senate. DS, DNA-RG 46 (15-1214). *Senate Executive Proceedings*, 4:115. Nominates Abraham B. Mead for New York City customs appraiser.
May 29	To the United States Senate. ADS, DNA-RG 46 (15-1220). *Senate Executive Proceedings*, 4:117. Nominates Richard W. Cummins for Shawnee and Delaware Indian agent.
May 29	To the United States Senate. DS, DNA-RG 46 (15-1222). *Senate Executive Proceedings*, 4:119. Nominates Virgil Maxcy for solicitor of the Treasury.
May 29	To the United States Senate. DS, DNA-RG 46 (15-1224). *Senate Executive Proceedings*, 4:117. Nominates justices of the peace for Washington, D.C.
May 29	From Edmund Byrne. ALS, DNA-RG 45 (M124-124). Solicits federal patronage for his new process for waterproofing ships.
May 29	*From John Caldwell Calhoun.* 305
May 29	From Mary Wilson. ADS, DNA-RG 59 (15-1418). Thomas Porter, *The Mail Robbers, or Evils Attendant on a Sinful Life* (Philadelphia, 1830), pp. 31–33. Begs AJ to spare her brother George Wilson, sentenced to death for robbing the mail.
May 29	Check to Andrew Jackson Donelson for $100. DS, DLC (38).
May 29	Christian Eckloff to Andrew Jackson Jr. ADS, DLC (38). Tailor's bill. Receipted Jan 3, 1831.
May 30	*To John Caldwell Calhoun.* 321
May 30	To the United States Senate. DS, DNA-RG 46 (15-1230). *Senate Executive Proceedings*, 4:121. Nominates Caleb Cloud for assistant naval surgeon.
May 31	To the United States Congress. DS (dated May 30), DNA-RG 46; DS, DNA-RG 233 (15-1226). *HRDoc* 123, 21st Cong., 1st sess. (Serial 198); Richardson, 2:483. Approves an internal improvement bill on the understanding that its appropriation for a road from Detroit to Chicago will be spent only within

	the safe return of crew from the *Eagle* accidentally left at Fernando de Noronha, and apologizes for his erroneous report of their detention there.
Jun 8	From William C. Nye. ALS, DNA-RG 59 (M179-68). Repeats his news and apology concerning the safe return of the *Eagle* seamen from Fernando de Noronha.
Jun 8	From Benjamin Phillips. ALS, DNA-RG 45 (M124-124). Urges discharging Philadelphia naval constructors Samuel Humphreys and James Keene for incompetence and political hostility.
Jun 8	*From John Randolph.* 356
Jun 8	From John Thornton et al. DS, DNA-RG 59 (15-1324). Ask AJ to commute the death sentence of mail robber James Porter.
Jun 8	Commission for James Sevier Conway as commissioner for the Arkansas-Louisiana boundary survey. Printed, *TPUS*, 21:232 (15-1322).
Jun 8	Commission for William Pelham as surveyor of the Arkansas-Louisiana boundary line. DS, DNA-RG 46 (15-1323). *TPUS*, 21:233.
Jun 8	Bill from Tucker & Thompson for clothing. DS, DLC (73). Receipted Jun 16.
Jun 9	*To Samuel Delucenna Ingham.* 356
Jun 9	To William Cabell Rives. LS, DLC (15-1335). Introduces L. A. Marshall, an American student in Paris.
Jun 9	From John Branch. LC, DNA-RG 45 (M472-1). Submits a roster of naval officers with their current duty and explains why those not on furlough all draw full pay.
Jun 9	*From Margaret O'Neale Timberlake Eaton.* 357
Jun 9	*From James Ronaldson.* 358
Jun 9	Check [to Mr. Huygens] for $250. DS, DLC (38).
Jun 10	From Henry Baldwin and Joseph Hopkinson. LS, DNA-RG 59 (15-1422). Inform that they have issued a warrant for the execution of James Porter and George Wilson on Jul 2.
Jun 10	From William D. Ferguson. Printed, *TPUS*, 21:235–36 (15-1336). Complains that judicial annulment of fraudulent Spanish land titles in Arkansas will dispossess many poor, innocent, and worthy settlers.
Jun 10	From James C. Haughey. DS, DNA-RG 59 (15-1361). Begs remission of his fine and costs for assault and battery and release from jail. Approved by AJ Jun 10.
Jun 11	To John Branch. LS, DNA-RG 46 (15-1338). Rescinds Lieutenant Francis S. Neville's dismissal from the Marines on the plea of his mother.
Jun 11	From Samuel Fisher Bradford. ALS, DNA-RG 59 (15-1424). Introduces nephew Vincent L. Bradford, on a "*visit of mercy*" for convicted mail robber George Wilson.
Jun 11	From John Kintzing Kane. ALS, DNA-RG 59 (15-1426). Asks AJ to commute the death sentence of his client George Wilson.
Jun 11	From John A. Kearney. ALS, DNA-RG 45 (M148-62). Naval surgeon thanks AJ for his leniency and confidence and asks to be stationed at the Washington navy yard.

	Complains that he was unfairly underbid for a contract to build the lightkeeper's house at St. Simons, Ga.	
Jun 14	Remission of forfeiture and relinquishment of prosecution against the sloop *Nun* for its unintentional violation of the slave-importation laws. DS, The Gilder Lehrman Institute of American History (mAJs). LC, DNA-RG 59 (15-1392; T967-1).	
Jun 14	*Order of Pardon for George Wilson.*	374
Jun 14	Pardon for George Wilson. LC, DNA-RG 59 (15-1412; T967-1).	
Jun 15	To John M. Moore. LC, DNA-RG 59; Copy, DNA-RG 217 (15-1461). Appoints him acting GLO commissioner in George Graham's absence or illness.	
Jun 15	*To Philip Grymes Randolph.*	375
Jun 15	From James Biddle. LS, DNA-RG 217 (15-1449). LS duplicate, DNA-RG 59 (M46-3). Renders an account of $21,136 expended in the Turkish treaty negotiation. Endorsed by AJ Nov 24 to approve paying the excess over the $20,000 authorized.	
Jun 15	From John Branch. LC, DNA-RG 45 (M472-1). Submits Charles Stewart's commission as a member of the Navy Board for signature.	
Jun 15	From Edward Lloyd. ALS, DNA-RG 45 (mAJs). Recommends Richard Lloyd Tilghman for midshipman.	
Jun 15	From Virgil Maxcy. ALS, DNA-RG 49 (15-1459). *TPUS*, 21:238–39. Asks authority to send original documents in GLO files to Arkansas as evidence to overturn fraudulent land titles.	
Jun 15	From John Archer Morton. Copy, DLC (mAJs). Asks to be appointed consul at Bordeaux.	
Jun 15	From Martin Van Buren. DS, DNA-RG 217 (15-1464). Recommends disallowing Thomas D. Anderson's disputed expense claims as late consul at Tunis except a single charge of $1,000. Approved by AJ.	
Jun 15	Temporary commission for Charles Barnet as consul at Venice. Copy, DNA-RG 59 (15-1448).	
Jun 15	Temporary commission for Paul Eynaud as consul at Malta. Copy, DNA-RG 59 (15-1457).	
Jun 15	Temporary commission for Thomas William Gilpin as consul at Belfast. Copy, DNA-RG 59 (15-1458).	
Jun 15	Andrew Jackson Donelson to Martin Van Buren. ALS, DNA-RG 59 (15-1455). Asks attention to the Jun 14 request of Louis Marchand, whom AJ greatly respects.	
Jun 16	*To John Macpherson Berrien.*	375
Jun 16	*To James Biddle.*	376
Jun 16	To James Eakin. LS, Hudson Rogue Co. (mAJs). LC, DNA-RG 59 (15-1470). Appoints him acting second auditor in William B. Lewis's absence or illness.	
Jun 16	To Nicholas I, Emperor of Russia. LC, DNA-RG 59 (15-1472). Announces Henry Middleton's recall as minister to Russia.	
Jun 16	*To Francis Preston.*	376
Jun 16	To Sylvanus Thayer. LS, NWM (15-1482). Introduces entering West Point cadet Thomas P. Giles.	

remission of his fine for smuggling salt and release from
confinement. Approved by AJ Oct 4.

General Land Office commissioner or superintendent of Indian affairs.

Sep 15	From William Shaler. ALS, DNA-RG 107 (16-0243). Requests a West Point cadetship for his nephew Elias M. Stilwell.	
Sep 15	From William I, King of the Netherlands. LS, DNA-RG 59 (16-0246). Announces the marriage of his daughter Princess Marianne to Prince Albert of Prussia.	
Sep 16	Check to Michael Anthony Giusta for $200. DS by William B. Lewis, DLC (38).	
Sep 17	From Rufus Sewall. ALS, DLC (38). Appeals for Moses M. Gove's release from prison.	

Sep 18	From José Francisco Morazán Quezada. LS, DNA-RG 59 (T34-1). Announces his accession to the presidency of Central America.	
Sep 18	Proclamation suspending discriminating duties on shipping from the Grand Duchy of Oldenburg. DS, DNA-RG 59 (T1223-1). LC, DNA-RG 59 (16-0252). Richardson, 2:496–97.	
Sep 20	From James McDowell Jr. et al. Printed, *Richmond Enquirer*, Oct 1 (mAJs). Welcome AJ to Lexington, Va., and invite him to a public dinner.	
Sep 20	To James McDowell Jr. et al. Printed, *Richmond Enquirer*, Oct 1 (mAJs). Returns greetings and declines a public dinner.	
Sep 20	From Philip Walker. ALS, DLC (38). Revolutionary veteran applauds AJ and presents two hickory brooms to sweep away the remnants of Federalism and national debt.	

Sep 24	From Lawrence Taliaferro Dade et al. Printed, *US Telegraph*, Sep 29 (16-0258). Invite AJ to a public dinner at Orange Court House, Va.	
Sep 24	To Lawrence Taliaferro Dade et al. Printed, *US Telegraph*, Sep 29 (16-0259). Thankfully declines a public dinner.	
Sep 24	From Stephen George Roszel et al. DS, DNA-RG 59 (M639-16). Recommend Benjamin K. Morsell for justice of the peace in Washington, D.C. Appointed by AJ Sep 29.	
Sep 26	From Joel Scott. ALS, DNA-RG 59 (16-0528). Kentucky penitentiary keeper recommends remission of the $100 fine and release for mail robber John Rees on imminent completion of his seven-year sentence. Approved by AJ Oct 22.	
Sep 27	To Louis Philippe, King of the French. LC, DNA-RG 59 (16-0260). Presents American minister William C. Rives.	
Sep 27	To Robert Oliver. Extract, Carnegie Book Shop catalog, 1966 (16-0261). Recommends John C. McLemore for a loan.	
Sep 27	From John Macpherson Berrien. ALS, DNA-RG 59 (M639-9). Encloses letters from Levi Woodbury (M639-27) disclaiming interest in the New Hampshire district judgeship and recommending Samuel Green.	
Sep 27	From Solomon G. Krepps, Thomas Sloan, and Henry J. Rigden. LS, DNA-RG 75 (M234-433). Renew their proposal to carry	

emigrating Indians by steamboat up the Arkansas River.
Referred by AJ to Eaton.

Sep 27 From Joseph L. Kuhn. ALS copy, DNA-RG 125 (M273-27).
Complains of continued Treasury persecution over his accounts
as Marine paymaster.

Sep 27 From Isaac McKim et al. Copy, DNA-RG 59 (M639-1).
Recommend Charles H. Appleton for consul or customs officer.

Sep 28 *To James Henry Handy.* 530

Sep 28 From Charles Richard Vaughan. ALS copy, DLC; AL copy,
UkOxU-As (mAJs). Presents his new credentials under William
IV and hopes for continued cordial relations.

[Sep 28] *To Charles Richard Vaughan.* 530

[cSep 28] From John H. Baker et al. DS, DNA-RG 59 (M639-25).
Recommend Nicholas B. Van Zandt for justice of the peace in
Washington, D.C. Appointed by AJ Sep 29.

Sep 28 From William Kidd. ALS, THer (16-0262). Asks AJ not to
pardon John King, murderer of his brother John Kidd. Endorsed
by AJ.

Sep 28 From Philip Grymes Randolph. ALS, DNA-RG 75 (M234-74).
LC, DNA-RG 107 (M127-2). Copy, DNA-RG 46 (16-0265).
SDoc 512, 23d Cong., 1st sess., vol. 2, pp. 212–13 (Serial 245).
Encloses a Sep 18 protest from George R. Gilmer against John
Coffee's report on the Cherokee boundary. Referred by AJ to
Eaton for a synopsis of evidence.

Sep 29 To William IV, King of Great Britain. LC, DNA-RG 59 (16-
0271). Offers condolences on the death of King George IV.

Sep 29 To William IV, King of Great Britain. LC, DNA-RG 59; Draft,
DLC (16-0272). Offers congratulations on his accession to the
throne.

Sep 29 *From John Coffee.* 531

Sep 29 *From John Randolph.* 532

Sep 29 From Lewis Sanders Jr. ALS, DNA-RG 59 (16-0531). Seconds
Joel Scott's Sep 26 recommendation to release prisoner John
Rees and remit his fine. Endorsed by AJ.

Sep 29 Temporary commission for Benjamin K. Morsell and Nicholas
Biddle Van Zandt as justices of the peace in Washington, D.C.
LC, DNA-RG 59 (16-0270).

Sep 30 *To John Overton.* 534

Sep 30 From Philip Grymes Randolph. ALS, DNA-RG 108 (16-0281).
Submits for approval Army lieutenant Ephraim K. Smith's court-
martial for whipping six soldiers.

Sep 30 From Leander J. Sharp. ALS, DNA-RG 59 (16-0534). Concurs
in Joel Scott's recommendation to release prisoner John Rees.

Sep 30 Temporary commission for William Findlay as treasurer of the
Mint. LC, DNA-RG 59 (16-0275).

Sep 30 Temporary commission for Elijah Hayward as commissioner of
the General Land Office. LC, DNA-RG 59 (16-0276).

[Sep] From John Baskerville. ALS, DLC (60; 14-1226). Salutes AJ and
recalls their service together at New Orleans.

[Sep]	From Ephraim Hubbard Foster et al. DS, DNA-RG 94 (M567-51). Recommend John Drennen for sutler at Cantonment Gibson.	
Oct 1	*To the Marquis de Lafayette.*	*537*
Oct 1	Continuation of John M. Moore's appointment as acting commissioner of the General Land Office. LC, DNA-RG 59 (16-0292).	
Oct 1	Approval of Lieutenant Ephraim Kirby Smith's court-martial and the sentence of dismissal from the service. DS, DNA-RG 153 (16-0293).	
Oct 2	*To Samuel Jackson Hays.*	*538*
Oct 2	From John Macpherson Berrien. LC, DNA-RG 60 (T412-3). *HRDoc* 123, 26th Cong., 2d sess., pp. 793–94 (Serial 387). Submits an opinion that Revolutionary colonel Robert H. Harrison's daughters are not entitled to interest on the five years' pay awarded them by Congress.	
Oct 2	From John Branch. LC, DNA-RG 45 (M472-1). Reports on his investigation into the unauthorized reconstruction of the sloop *John Adams* and condemns the Navy commissioners for surreptitiously building new ships under the guise of repairs.	
Oct 2	From Joseph Hemphill. ALS, DLC (16-0302). Recommends James Wiltbank for chaplain at the Philadelphia navy yard. Referred favorably by AJ to Branch.	
Oct 2	From George W. Palmer, Frederick Palmer, Thomas Palmer, and Lewis Palmer. DS, DNA-RG 59 (17-0846). Beg release from imprisonment and remission of their fine for smuggling rum. Refused by AJ Nov 15.	
Oct 2	Receipted carriagemaker's bill from Nelson Davidson. ADS, DLC (73). Runs to Nov 8.	
Oct 2	William Harris Crawford to John Caldwell Calhoun. Copy, DLC (38). *Calhoun Papers*, 11:233–48. Charges Calhoun with falsifying facts to exculpate himself in his May 29 account to AJ of the Cabinet controversy over the Seminole campaign.	
[Oct 3]	*To Martin Van Buren.*	*539*
Oct 3	*To John Coffee.*	*539*
[cOct 4]	*To Martin Van Buren.*	*540*
[Oct 4]	From John Pope. ALS and Copy, DNA-RG 59 (M179-69). *TPUS*, 21:277–78. Warns of Mexican border encroachments and urges immediate settlement of the boundary.	
Oct 4	Release for prisoner Stephen Harding and remission of his fine for smuggling salt. LC, DNA-RG 59 (16-0308).	
Oct 5	*To James Alexander Hamilton.*	*541*
Oct 5	From John Branch. LC, DNA-RG 45 (M472-1). Encloses midshipmen's warrants for signature.	
Oct 5	From William H. Dingee. ALS, DNA-RG 59 (M639-6). Asks to be appointed vice-consul at Santa Catarina, Brazil.	
Oct 5	From Edward McLaughlin. ALS, DNA-RG 45 (M148-64). Dismissed naval chaplain seeks a new appointment.	
Oct 5	Proclamation opening American ports to British colonial shipping. DS, DNA-RG 59 (T1223-1). LC, DNA-RG 56	

Oct 15	From Stephen Chapin. ALS, DNA-RG 46 (16-0386). Recommends Walter Colton for naval chaplain.	
[Oct 15]	From Ferdinand VII, King of Spain. LS, DNA-RG 59 (16-0388). Announces the birth of his daughter Isabella.	
Oct 15	From Thomas Janvier. DS, DNA-RG 59 (16-0593). Petitions for release from custody and remission of his $200 forfeited recognizance for non-appearance as a witness, due to illness, in the prosecution of John Gooding for illegal slave trading.	
Oct 15	From Virgil Maxcy. LS, DNA-RG 206 (16-0391). ALS draft, DNA-RG 206 (mAJs). Asks approval to carry the case of *U.S. v. Eleazar W. Ripley* to the Supreme Court. Approved by AJ.	

Oct 16	From Adam Lindsay et al. DS, DNA-RG 59 (M639-3). Recommend Nathaniel Brady for justice of the peace in Washington, D.C. Appointed by AJ Nov 5.	
Oct 16	From Nathaniel Williams. ALS, DNA-RG 59 (16-0596). Supports Thomas Janvier's Oct 15 petition despite his deliberately shirking testifying against John Gooding.	
Oct 16	Release for prisoner François Eugène Malibran on payment of costs. LC, DNA-RG 59 (16-0401; T967-1).	
Oct 16	Charles Davies to Andrew Jackson Donelson. ALS, DNA-RG 107 (M222-27). Urges asking the West Point faculty's recommendation on a new professor of engineering. Referred by AJ to Eaton to do so.	
Oct 17	To Unknown. Printed extract, *New Orleans Times*, Apr 21, 1878 (mAJs). Declares himself Eaton's undeviating friend.	
Oct 17	From Leopold, Grand Duke of Baden. LS, DNA-RG 59 (16-0430). Announces his brother Wilhelm's marriage to Elisabeth of Württemberg.	
Oct 17	From John Peter Van Ness. Abstract, DNA-RG 107 (M22-27). Recommends Stephen W. Roszel for assistant Army surgeon.	

Oct 18	From William Gracie. LS, DNA-RG 59 (M639-9). Asks to be appointed secretary of legation at Paris.	
Oct 18	From John Pemberton. ALS copy, PHi (16-0436). Introduces Abiah Sharpe.	

[Oct 19]	From Leonard Ellis. DS, DNA-RG 59 (16-0444). Asks remission of his fine and costs for assault and battery, which he is unable to pay, and release from prison after having served more than double his sentence. Approved by AJ.	
Oct 19	Remission of fine and costs and release for prisoner Leonard Ellis. LC, DNA-RG 59 (16-0443; T967-1).	
[Oct 19]	From W. G. Ewing et al. DS, DNA-RG 75 (16-0448). Creditors	

of deceased Potawatomi chief George Cicott ask AJ not to
approve a transfer of his 1826 treaty reservation lands to his
brother Zachariah Cicott until his estate is settled.

Oct 19   From Robert Oliver. ALS, DNA-RG 59 (M639-10).
Recommends Charles C. Harper for commissioner to settle
French spoliation claims.

Oct 19   From Jose Aranero Ruiz. LS, DLC (73). Asks for money so he
can return to Spain and fight for liberty.

Oct 19   Check to Andrew Jackson Jr. for $90.87. DS, DLC (38).

Oct 20   From Charles Cassedy. ALS, DLC (38; 16-0454). Accuses his
publisher John C. Gunn of duplicity and fraud, and explains
that his pending vindication of General James Winchester's
conduct in the War of 1812 is wholly unconnected to present
politics.

Oct 20   From James Gadsden. ALS, DNA-RG 233 (16-0460). Supports
Solomon D. Betton's appeal of his accounts as commissioner to
purchase Creek improvements.

Oct 20   From Robert Oliver. ALS, DNA-RG 59 (M639-26).
Recommends Henry Wheaton for a diplomatic appointment.

[Oct 21]   To Jules de Menon. N, CLjC (mAJs). Invitation to dinner.

Oct 22   To John Peter Van Ness. N, DLC (16-0468). Accepts an
invitation to a Washington celebration of the revolution in
France.

Oct 22   From John Van Lear McMahon. ALS, DNA-RG 59 (16-0604).
Supports Thomas Janvier's Oct 15 petition and explains
Janvier's reluctance to testify against his benefactor and
employer John Gooding. Remission and release approved
by AJ Oct 28.

Oct 22   From Ebenezer Prentis and John Prentis. LS, DNA-RG 156
(16-0465). Offer a secret invention for the Army.

Oct 23   To Addison Powell. Copy, DNA-RG 46 (16-0495). Asks the
name of the postal clerk who divulged information to James
Reeside about a competing mail contract bid.

Oct 23   From Addison Powell. Copy, DNA-RG 46 (16-0499). Replies
that mail contractor Caleb Leonard, now absent from
Washington, can identify the guilty postal clerk by sight.

Oct 23   From John Branch. LS and Copy, DNA-RG 49; Copy, DNA-RG
45 (16-0475). LC, DNA-RG 45 (M472-1). Recommends Florida
timberlands for designation as naval reserves.

Oct 23   To John Branch. AN, DNA-RG 45 (M124-125). Approves
Florida timberlands for designation as naval reserves.

[Oct 23]   To Martin Van Buren. ANS, DNA-RG 59 (M179-69). LC,
DNA-RG 59 (M40-21). Explains that prisoner Eugène Malibran

need pay only legal costs, not his penalty or interest, to obtain release.

Nov 2   From James G. Ringgold. ALS, DNA-RG 217 (M235-648). Claims $700 for his work in preparing the U.S. case against Florida land claimants holding purported Spanish grants. Referred by AJ to Ingham.

Nov 2   From John Robb. Abstract, DNA-RG 107 (M22-27). Recommends Stephen W. Roszel for assistant Army surgeon.

Nov 2   Temporary commission for Matthew Harvey as district judge in New Hampshire. LC, DNA-RG 59 (16-0642).

Nov 2   John Moore McCalla to Daniel Brent. ALS, DNA-RG 59 (16-0724). Reports that pardoned mail robber John Rees is unable to pay the $258.75 in costs to procure his release. AJ orders remission of costs, Nov 13.

Nov 3   From John Branch. LC, DNA-RG 45 (M472-1). Submits Marine lieutenant Francis S. Neville's commission for signature.

Nov 3   From Robert Wortham. Abstract, DNA-RG 107 (M22-27). Submits a recommendation for his appointment as Indian agent.

Nov 4   From Thomas S. Hayes. DS, DNA-RG 59 (16-0965). Petitions for release from custody and remission of his forfeited recognizance for not appearing as a witness at the prosecution of John Gooding, being then away at sea. Endorsed by AJ on Dec 1: "Humanity dictates the liberation of the prisoner."

Nov 4   From Benjamin Wood Richards. Copy, DNA-RG 60 (mAJs). Resigns as government director of the BUS.

Nov 4   From Rufus Sewall et al. Copy, DNA-RG 49 (16-0644). Appeal for protection from persecuting officials of their right to cut timber on their Florida pre-emption claims.

Nov 6   To Virgil Maxcy. AN, DNA-RG 206 (16-0655). Asks for the district attorney's report on *U.S. v. Peter B. Porter*, concerning Porter's disputed salary as Canadian boundary commissioner.

Nov 6   To Virgil Maxcy. DS, DNA-RG 206 (16-0657). Orders an appeal of the district court's ruling against the government in *U.S. v. Peter B. Porter*.

Nov 6   From John Branch. LC, DNA-RG 45 (M472-1). Recommends reinstating dismissed midshipman Robert E. Hooe.

Nov 6   From John Branch. LC, DNA-RG 45 (M472-1). Submits naval chaplain Walter Colton's commission for signature.

Nov 6   From Elizabeth Frost. ALS, DNA-RG 45 (M124-125). Begs AJ to discharge her husband Andrew Frost from the Marines.

Nov 6   From George Mason Graham. ALS, ViHi (mAJs). Appeals for compensation for his late father George Graham's service as agent to wind up the government's Indian trading establishment.

[cNov 6]   From Hugh McElderry. ALS, DNA-RG 59 (M639-12). Recommends Louis W. Jenkins for secretary of legation at Paris.

Nov 6   From John Van Lear McMahon. ALS, DNA-RG 59 (M639-12). Touts Louis W. Jenkins for secretary of legation at Paris and brands applicant Peter H. Cruse as a foe of the administration.

Nov 6	From James Mosher. ALS, DNA-RG 59 (M639-12). Recommends Louis W. Jenkins for secretary of legation at Paris.	
Nov 6	From George H. Steuart. ALS, THer (16-0660). Warns AJ not to appoint Peter H. Cruse secretary of legation at Paris.	
Nov 6	Check [for Michael Anthony Giusta] for $850. DS, DLC (38).	
Nov 7	*To Robert Johnstone Chester.*	611
Nov 7	To Henry Middleton Rutledge. Printed extract and ALS facsimile fragment, Harmers of New York catalog, sale 2858 (mAJs). Remarks on his health and promises to consider Rutledge's friend for a surveyor's appointment.	
Nov 7	From James Gordon Brooks. ALS, DNA-RG 15 (16-0665). Accuses the Treasury of deliberately withholding the Revolutionary pension due his father David Brooks.	
Nov 7	From Isaac McKeever. LS, DNA-RG 46 (16-0675). Recommends Benjamin J. Cahoon for naval purser.	
Nov 7	From Edward Worrell. ALS, DNA-RG 107 (M222-28). Demands that AJ fulfill his promise to appoint him an Army surgeon.	
[cNov 8]	From Horace Bassett et al. Copies, DNA-RG 46; Copy, DNA-RG 233 (16-0679). *HRDoc* 85, 21st Cong., 2d sess., pp. 8–9 (Serial 208). Protest the GLO's rejection of Indiana's selection of ceded Potawatomi lands to be sold to fund construction of a road.	
Nov 8	*From Robert Butler.*	612
Nov 8	*From Preserved Fish et al.*	613
Nov 8	From Samuel Delucenna Ingham. Ds, DNA-RG 233 (16-0693). *SDoc* 1, 21st Cong., 2d sess., p. 28 (Serial 203). Recommends asking Congress to give the attorney general authority to prosecute fraudulent land and pension claimants.	
Nov 8	Receipted bill from Thompson & Homans for purchase of the *Encyclopedia Americana.* DS, DLC (39). Runs to Jun 23, 1831.	
Nov 8	Temporary commission for Friedrich List as consul at Hamburg. Copies, DNA-RG 59 (16-0699).	
Nov 8	George Bomford to John Henry Eaton. ALS, DNA-RG 94 (M567-56). Reports that Lieutenant Martin Thomas is behind in his accounts as late commander of the St. Louis arsenal. AJ orders his arrest and court-martial Nov 23.	
Nov 9	To John Henry Eaton. AN, DNA-RG 107 (M221-111). Asks him to make a "respectful answer" to George R. Gilmer's Oct 29 letter, informing him of orders to Major Philip Wager to withdraw federal troops from Cherokee country.	
Nov 9	*From Andrew Jackson Donelson.*	615
Nov 9	From Ferdinand II, King of the Two Sicilies. LS, DNA-RG 59 (16-0701). Copy, DNA-RG 59 (M55-1). Announces the death of his father Francis I and his succession to the throne.	
Nov 9	*From James Alexander Hamilton.*	615
Nov 9	Appointment of Joshua Nelson as justice of the peace in Washington, D.C. ANS, DNA-RG 59 (M639-17).	
Nov 9	Temporary commission for Nathaniel Niles as secretary of legation at Paris. LC, DNA-RG 59 (16-0704).	

	copy of his Sep 1 instructions to special agent John Lowrey (*SDoc* 512, 23d Cong., 1st sess., vol. 2, pp. 98–99, Serial 245), inviting the Cherokees to reconsider their refusal to remove.	
Nov 15	From George R. Montague. ALS fragment, DLC (38). Begs aid for young Livingston from Cincinnati. Endorsed by AJ that he gave five dollars: "I hope it may be useful & learn him proper oconomy—& to live within his means—he is a pretty youth."	
Nov 15	From Nathaniel Silsbee. ALS, DNA-RG 59 (M179-69). Encloses the Oct 29 memorial of Joseph Peabody et al.	
Nov 15	From Sarah Ann Weathers. ALS, DNA-RG 107 (M221-111). Complains she has never received the back pay due her as daughter of Revolutionary Major Thomas H. Boyle.	
Nov 16	*To Andrew Jackson Donelson.*	628
Nov 16	*To Nathan Reid.*	629
Nov 16	From Richard Keith Call et al. LS, DNA-RG 59 (M639-1). Recommend reappointing Florida marshal Alexander Adair.	
Nov 16	*From William Craig.*	630
Nov 16	Release from confinement, on payment of costs, for defaulted former U.S. internal revenue collector Josiah Sheldon. LC, DNA-RG 59 (16-0742; T967-1).	
Nov 17	*To John Henry Eaton.*	630
Nov 17	*From Stephen Simpson.*	631
Nov 18	*To John Henry Eaton.*	631
Nov 18	*To Martin Van Buren.*	632
Nov 18	To William I, King of the Netherlands. LC, DNA-RG 59; Draft, DLC (16-0804). Offers congratulations on his daughter's marriage.	
Nov 18	From John Branch. LC, DNA-RG 45 (M472-1). Submits naval purser Sterrett Ramsey's commission for signature.	
Nov 18	From James Gettys et al. DS, DNA-RG 59 (16-0888). Recommend releasing prisoner Naylor Webster and remitting his fine and costs for assault and battery. Approved by AJ Nov 26.	
[Nov 19]	From John Major, William Downes, and Edward Miles. D, DNA-RG 59 (16-0820). Appeal for release from imprisonment and remission of their fine and costs for making a riot. Approved by AJ Nov 20.	
Nov 20	*To Louis Philippe, King of the French.*	632
Nov 20	To Louis Philippe, King of the French. LC, DNA-RG 59; Draft, DLC (16-0815). Offers condolences on the death of Louis Henry, Duke of Bourbon and Prince of Condé.	
Nov 20	To Isaac Sanderson. LS, MMHi (mAJs). Thanks him for a sample of machine-made paper and compliments its quality.	
Nov 20	From John Branch. LC, DNA-RG 45 (M472-1). Submits Thomas Burke's commission as Marine lieutenant for signature.	
Nov 20	Remission of fine and costs and release for prisoners John Major, William Downes, and Edward Miles. LC, DNA-RG 59 (16-0818; T967-1).	
Nov 20	Check for $31.50. DS, DLC (38).	
Nov 20	Atlas Jones to John Henry Eaton. ALS, DNA-RG 46 (16-0809).	

Recommends Stockley D. Hays for surveyor general of public lands south of Tennessee. Endorsed by AJ.

Nov 21   *To Samuel Jackson Hays.*   *633*

Nov 21   From George Vashon. ALS, DNA-RG 75 (M234-77). Copy, DNA-RG 46 (16-0828). *SDoc* 512, 23d Cong., 1st sess., vol. 2, pp. 187–89 (Serial 245). Proposes boundaries for the western Creek, Cherokee, Chickasaw, Choctaw, and Osage domains.

Nov 21   John Randolph to Martin Van Buren. ALS, DLC (38). Explains his declining to deliver Henry Middleton his notice of recall and says that Middleton has underestimated Prince Lieven.

Nov 22   From Michael Mellon. DS, DNA-RG 59 (16-1399). Requests a pardon for stealing from a found mail bag, a crime of temptation rather than wickedness.

Nov 22   From Franklin Lee et al. DS, DNA-RG 59 (16-1401). Jurors at Michael Mellon's trial for mail larceny support his plea for pardon. Seconded by George M. Dallas.

Nov 22   From Henry Baldwin and Joseph Hopkinson. DNA-RG 59 (16-1404). Judges at Michael Mellon's trial recommend him for pardon. Approved by AJ Dec 10.

Nov 22   From Robert Oliver. ALS, DNA-RG 76 (16-0832). Forwards the opinion of an American in Paris that the moment is ripe to press spoliation claims against France and Naples.

Nov 23   *To John Branch.*   *634*

[Nov 23]   Memorandum summarizing the court-martial record of Master Commandant John Henry Clack. AN, DLC (72; 16-0841).

Nov 23   *Approval of John Henry Clack's court-martial.*   *635*

Nov 23   Approval of Navy lieutenant Charles Ellery's court-martial and sentence of dismissal from the service for intemperance and sleeping on watch. ADS, DNA-RG 46 (16-0843).

Nov 23   John M. Buchanan to Andrew Jackson Donelson. ALS, DLC (16-0838). Bills AJ for subscription to the Cumberland *Maryland Advocate* and urges him to accept a second term.

Nov 24   *From Stephen Simpson.*   *635*

Nov 25   *To Robert Johnstone Chester.*   *636*

[cNov 25]   From Adam Huntsman et al. DS, DNA-RG 46 (16-0872). Urge Stockley D. Hays's claim to appointment as surveyor general of public lands.

Nov 25   From Dunning D. McNair. Abstract, DNA-RG 107 (M22-27). Asks to be appointed Indian agent.

Nov 25   John P. Moore to Andrew Jackson Jr. ALS, DLC (38). Reports progress in making his special rifle.

Nov 26   From John Branch. LS, DNA-RG 49 (16-0877). LC, DNA-RG 45 (M472-1). *TPUS*, 24:457. Recommends Florida timberlands for designation as naval reserves. Approved by AJ.

Nov 26   From Elijah Hayward. LC, DNA-RG 49 (M25-26). *TPUS*, 24:458. Reports against the Nov 4 petition of Rufus Sewall and others, questioning their pre-emption claims and denying their right to cut timber on public land.

Nov 26   Release for prisoner Naylor Webster and remission of his fine and costs for assault and battery. LC, DNA-RG 59 (16-0887; T967-1).

Dec 6	*To Amos Kendall.*	*680*
Dec 6	*To John Coffee.*	*680*
Dec 6	From Benjamin Johnson. ALS, DNA-RG 59 (M639-19). *TPUS*, 21:295–96. Recommends Elias Rector for marshal in Arkansas Territory.	
Dec 6	From James Van Horne. ALS, DNA-RG 59 (M639-25). Applies for a clerkship or other office.	
Dec 7	*To Samuel Jackson Hays.*	*681*
[cDec 7]	*To Adam Huntsman.*	*682*
[Dec 7]	Check to William Berkeley Lewis for $120. DS, DLC (58; 16-1351).	
Dec 7	Check [for Michael Anthony Giusta] for $620. DS, DLC (38).	
Dec 8	From Thomas Green Davidson and Alexander Gordon Penn. LS, DNA-RG 49 (16-1352). St. Helena, La., district land officers complain that burdensome GLO rules impede the settlement of land claims derived from foreign grants. Endorsed by AJ that present procedures prevent fraud and cannot be changed without legislation.	
Dec 8	*From John A. Parker.*	*682*
Dec 8	From Henry Simpson et al. DS, DNA-RG 59 (M639-11). Pennsylvania legislators recommend Horatio Hubbell for consul at Constantinople.	
Dec 9	*To James Monroe.*	*683*
Dec 9	To the United States Senate. DS, DNA-RG 46 (16-1361). *Senate Journal*, 21st Cong., 2d sess., p. 233 (Serial 202); *Senate Executive Proceedings*, 4:126; Richardson, 2:529. Submits the Choctaw removal treaty of Dancing Rabbit Creek for ratification.	
Dec 9	To the United States Senate. DS, DNA-RG 46 (16-1363). *Senate Executive Proceedings*, 4:127. Nominates claims commissioners under the convention with Denmark.	
Dec 9	Check [for Samuel Hogg] for $64.75. DS, DLC (38).	
Dec 10	*To William Savin Fulton.*	*683*
Dec 10	To the United States Congress. DS, DNA-RG 46; DS, DNA-RG 233 (16-1388). *HRDoc* 3, 21st Cong., 2d sess., p. 1 (Serial 206); Richardson, 2:530. Transmits copies of the ratified claims convention with Denmark.	
Dec 10	To the United States Senate. Draft, DNA-RG 11 (16-1392). *Senate Executive Proceedings*, 4:126; Richardson, 2:530. Submits the commercial treaty with Turkey.	
Dec 10	From Cyrenius Chapin. ALS, DNA-RG 75 (M234-433). Asks AJ to restore Henry B. Brevoort as Indian agent at Green Bay; seconded by Oliver Forward.	
Dec 10	From Ephraim Hubbard Foster. ALS, DLC (38). Recommends John W. Campbell for an office in the newly ceded southern Indian lands.	
Dec 10	From Elijah Hayward. LS, DNA-RG 49 (16-1369). LC, DNA-RG 49 (M25-26). Submits the War Department's request to reserve land for Cantonment Brooke in Florida, refused by him	

because it will overlap existing private claims. Reservation approved by AJ.

Dec 10   Elijah Hayward to John Henry Eaton. LS, DNA-RG 49 (16-1377). Encloses AJ's approval of the military land reservation at Cantonment Brooke.

Dec 10   From Richard Mentor Johnson. ALS, DLC (16-1380). Recommends Edward J. Mallett for secretary to the Danish claims commissioners.

Dec 10   From Christopher Vandeventer. Abstract, DNA-RG 107 (M22-27). Asks for his son Eugene to be appointed cadet at West Point.

Dec 10   Approval of midshipman Francis G. Beatty's court-martial and sentence of dismissal for fraud and scandalous conduct. ADS, DNA-RG 125 (M273-25).

Dec 10   Approval of midshipman Timothy B. Field's court-martial and sentence of dismissal for disobeying orders and unbecoming conduct. ADS, DNA-RG 125 (M273-25).

Dec 10   Approval of midshipman Amedeus B. Marrast's court-martial and sentence of dismissal for contempt to superiors, scandalous conduct, and disobeying orders. ADS, DNA-RG 125 (M273-25).

Dec 10   Approval of midshipman William R. O'Sullivan's court-martial and sentence of dismissal for disobeying orders, fraud, and scandalous conduct. ADS, DNA-RG 125 (M273-25).

Dec 10   Approval of midshipman Zebulon P. Wardell's court-martial and sentence of cashiering for contempt to superiors and disobeying orders. ANS, DNA-RG 125 (M273-25).

Dec 11   To the United States Senate. DS, DNA-RG 46 (16-1408). *Senate Executive Proceedings*, 4:128. Nominates customs officers.

[cDec 11] From Charles L. Fearson. ADS, DNA-RG 59 (16-1416). Appeals for remission of his fine and costs for assault and battery and release from jail. Approved by AJ Dec 11.

Dec 11   Pardon of Michael Mellon for larceny of the mail. LC, DNA-RG 59 (16-1398; T967-1).

Dec 13   From John DeRossett Toomer et al. Printed, Fayetteville *Carolina Observer*, Feb 3, 1831 (mAJs). *US Telegraph*, Mar 3, 1831 (16-1420). Invite AJ to visit Fayetteville, N.C.

Dec 13   Release for prisoner Charles L. Fearson and remission of his fine and costs for assault and battery. LC, DNA-RG 59 (16-1414; T967-1).

[Dec 14]   To the United States Senate. DS, DNA-RG 46 (16-1435). *Senate Executive Proceedings*, 4:127–28. Nominates judges and civil and diplomatic officers.

Dec 14   To the United States Senate. DS, DNA-RG 46 (16-1438). *Senate*

	Executive Proceedings, 4:129. Nominates Navy and Marine officers.
Dec 14	From John Biddle. ALS, DNA-RG 77 (16-1421). Encloses the Michigan Territory Legislative Council memorial of Jul 30.
Dec 14	From John Henry Eaton. LS, DNA-RG 46 (16-1425). *Senate Executive Proceedings*, 4:131–33. Submits Army appointments and promotions for Senate confirmation.
Dec 14	From George Poindexter. Abstract, DNA-RG 107 (M22-27). Recommends Burgess B. Long for an Indian appointment.
Dec 14	Bill from John P. Carter to Andrew Jackson Jr. for clothing. DS, DLC (38). Receipted Apr 26, 1831.
Dec 15	To the United States Congress. DS, DNA-RG 46; DS, DNA-RG 233 (16-1446). *HRDoc* 8, 21st Cong., 2d sess. (Serial 206); Richardson, 2:530. Requests legislation giving further time to complete the census.
Dec 15	To the United States Senate. DS, DNA-RG 46 (16-1450). *Senate Executive Proceedings*, 4:129. Nominates customs officers.
Dec 15	To the United States Senate. DS, DNA-RG 46 (16-1452). *Senate Executive Proceedings*, 4:129. Nominates Arthur Taylor Jr. for customs surveyor at Norfolk, Va.
Dec 15	To the United States Senate. DS, DNA-RG 46 (16-1454). *Senate Executive Proceedings*, 4:129–30. Nominates land office receivers.
Dec 15	From J. Brasseur. ALS, DNA-RG 59 (M639-3). Asks to be appointed consul at Ostend, Belgium.

Dec 15	From Jacob Keiper. Abstract, DNA-RG 107 (M22-27). Applies for an Army pension.
Dec 15	From Louis Philippe, King of the French. DS, DNA-RG 59 (16-1444). Presents Louis Sérurier, French minister to the U.S.
Dec 15	From Walter Oliver et al. Abstract, DNA-RG 107 (M22-27). Recommend Jacob Harrington for Indian agent.
Dec 16	To John Branch. Abstract, B. Altman & Co., *New York Times*, Jul 9, 1978, p. 14 (mAJs). Refers an application.
Dec 16	From John Amonheizer. DS, DNA-RG 59 (17-0159). Affirms in support of his petition for pardon for mail robbery that he has no property and cannot pay court costs. Pardoned by AJ, Jan 3, 1831.
Dec 16	From John Henry Eaton. LS, DNA-RG 46 (16-1461). LC, DNA-RG 107 (M127-2). *Senate Executive Proceedings*, 4:138–39. Submits Indian agent appointments for Senate confirmation.
Dec 16	From Henry Lee. ALS, DLC (38). Reports on his travels in Italy.
Dec 16	From William Russell. Abstract, DNA-RG 107 (M22-27). Asks for an Indian appointment.
Dec 16	AJ affidavit confirming that he met the mother of Joseph Brown, now a claimant before Congress, on her escape from Cherokee captivity after the killing of her husband James Brown and seizure of his property in 1788. ADS, DNA-RG 46 (16-1456).

Dec 17	To the United States Senate. DS, DNA-RG 46 (16-1481). *Senate Executive Proceedings*, 4:130. Nominates Army officers for appointment and promotion.
Dec 17	To the United States Senate. DS, DNA-RG 46 (16-1483). *Senate Executive Proceedings*, 4:133–34. Nominates customs officers.
Dec 17	From John Henry Eaton. LS, DNA-RG 46 (16-1464). LC, DNA-RG 107 (M127-2). Printed, DNA-RG 46. Submits information requested by the Senate on the Choctaws' response to the Treaty of Dancing Rabbit Creek.
[Dec 17]	From Thomas Patton et al. DS, DNA-RG 59 (M639-12). Recommend Matthew Irwin for office.
Dec 17	From William Snodgrass et al. Abstract, DNA-RG 107 (M22-27). Recommend William K. Blair for assessor of Indian improvements.
Dec 17	From John Peter Van Ness. ALS, DNA-RG 59 (M639-8). Recommends John E. Frost for secretary to the Danish claims commissioners.
Dec 17	Order to drop the prosecution of John T. Smith and pardon him for carrying slaves across Chesapeake Bay in inadvertent violation of the revenue laws. ADS, DNA-RG 59 (16-1467).

Dec 18	*To Charles Edward Dudley.*	*695*
Dec 18	To the United States Senate. DS, DNA-RG 46 (16-1490). *Senate Executive Proceedings*, 4:135. Nominates Thomas Mussey for customs collector at New London, Conn.	
Dec 18	To the United States Senate. DS, DNA-RG 46 (16-1492). *Senate Executive Proceedings*, 4:135. Nominates land office registers and receivers.	
Dec 18	*From James Gwin.*	*696*
Dec 18	*From Sylvester Simmons Southworth.*	*698*
Dec 18	*From Joseph M. White.*	*699*
Dec 18	From Martin Van Buren. DS, DNA-RG 46; LC, DNA-RG 59 (16-1494). Submits papers requested by the Senate documenting the commercial negotiations with Turkey.	
Dec 18	From Andrew Wilson. Abstract, DNA-RG 156 (16-1501). Requests an appointment in the ordnance corps.	
Dec 18	Check to Andrew Jackson Jr. for $100. DS, DLC (38).	
Dec 18	Andrew Jackson Donelson to John Henry Eaton. ALS, DNA-RG 107 (M221-111). Transmits a House call for information on federal internal improvement expenditures.	
Dec 18	Andrew Jackson Donelson to Martin Van Buren. ALS, DNA-RG 59 (M179-69). Requests a commission for Philip P. Barbour, confirmed by the Senate as district judge in Virginia.	
Dec 19	From James Barron. ALS, DNA-RG 45 (M124-125). Recommends James Cornick.	
[Dec 20]	To Edward Everett. N, MHi (mAJs). Invitation to dinner.	
[Dec 20]	*From Amos Kendall.*	*700*
Dec 20	*To Samuel Delucenna Ingham.*	*701*
Dec 20	To the United States Senate. DS, DNA-RG 46 (16-1517). *Senate Executive Proceedings*, 4:135. Nominates Stockley D. Hays for surveyor general of public lands south of Tennessee.	

Dec 23	From John Henry Eaton. LS, DNA-RG 46 (16-1545). *Senate Executive Proceedings*, 4:138. Submits Army engineer promotions for Senate confirmation.	
Dec 23	*From Joseph Kincaid and from Mushulatubbe et al.*	704
Dec 23	Copy by AJ Donelson of Senate proceedings on the nomination of Stockley Donelson Hays through Feb 3, 1831. D, DLC (38).	
Dec 24	*To John Branch.*	705
Dec 24	To James Reid Pringle. Printed, Columbia, S.C., *Southern Times & State Gazette*, Jan 15, 1831 (mAJs). *Niles*, Jan 29, 1831 (16-1556). Thanks him for an official invitation to visit Charleston, S.C.	
Dec 24	From Henry Lee. ALS, DLC (38). Describes his Italian travels, including a visit to the Cannae battlefield and an interview with Napoleon's mother in Rome.	
Dec 24	*James Alexander Hamilton to William Berkeley Lewis.*	706
Dec 25	*To John Christmas McLemore.*	707
Dec 25	From George Gredy. ALS, DNA-RG 45 (16-1558). Requests a certificate of his volunteer service with Oliver H. Perry at Lake Erie in 1813, entitling him to a silver medal.	
Dec 25	From William McCoy. Abstract, DNA-RG 107 (M22-27). Transmits James Clark's recommendation of his son Michael M. Clark for assistant quartermaster.	
Dec 25	*From William Pitt Preble.*	715
Dec 25	From J. W. L. Robarts et al. DS, DNA-RG 46 (16-1584). *TPUS*, 24:477–78. Defend William P. Duval's character and urge his retention as Florida governor.	
Dec 26	From James Penn et al. LS, DNA-RG 59 (M639-5). Alabama legislators recommend federal district judge William Crawford for Supreme Court justice.	
Dec 27	*To John Henry Eaton.*	717
Dec 27	To the United States Senate. DS, DNA-RG 46 (17-0018). *Senate Executive Proceedings*, 4:137. Nominates government directors of the BUS for 1831.	
Dec 27	From Randal Abner et al. DS, DNA-RG 75 (M234-832). Copy, WHi; Copy, DNA-RG 46 (17-0002). *SDoc* 512, 23d Cong., 1st sess., vol. 2, pp. 206–9 (Serial 245). Brothertown Indians request a larger reservation on the Fox River in Wisconsin.	
Dec 27	From John Henry Eaton. LS, DNA-RG 46 (17-0016). LC, DNA-RG 75 (M21-7). Copy, DNA-RG 75 (M234-433). Submits the Sac and Fox and Sioux treaties of Prairie du Chien for Senate approval.	
Dec 27	From Samuel Delucenna Ingham. LS, DNA-RG 233 (17-0017). *HRDoc* 30, 21st Cong., 2d sess., p. 20 (Serial 206). Submits a list of Treasury payments for internal improvements since 1789.	
Dec 27	Check to self for $100. DS, DLC (38).	
Dec 28	*To John Coffee.*	717
Dec 28	To the United States Senate. DS, DNA-RG 46 (17-0032). *Senate Executive Proceedings*, 4:138. Nominates Army engineers for promotion.	

Dec 28	To the United States Senate. DS, DNA-RG 46 (17-0034). *Senate Executive Proceedings*, 4:138. Nominates Indian agents.
Dec 28	From William Drayton and Robert Young Hayne. LS, DNA-RG 45 (M124-125). Present Robert D. Wainwright's claim to backdate his brevet promotion to Marine lieutenant colonel.
Dec 28	From Henry Williams Dwight. ALS, DNA-RG 45 (M124-125). Appeals for the restoration of Navy midshipman Timothy B. Field, dismissed for going ashore without leave. Referred by AJ to Branch to beware of injurious precedent, but perhaps to reappoint with loss of grade if this was Field's only offense.
Dec 28	*From the Marquis de Lafayette.* 720
Dec 29	To the United States Senate. DS, DNA-RG 46 (17-0038). *Senate Executive Proceedings*, 4:140; Richardson, 2:531. Submits the July 1830 Sac and Fox and Sioux treaties of Prairie du Chien for Senate approval.
Dec 29	To the United States Senate. DS, DNA-RG 46 (17-0040). *Senate Executive Proceedings*, 4:140. Nominates justices of the peace for Washington, D.C.
[Dec 29]	*From Martin Van Buren.* 721
Dec 29	*To Martin Van Buren.* 722
Dec 29	*From John Coffee.* 722
Dec 29	From William Cabell Rives. AL abstract, DLC (17-0037). Introduces French minister Louis Sérurier.
Dec 30	To the United States Senate. DS, DNA-RG 46 (17-0042). *Senate Executive Proceedings*, 4:141; Richardson, 2:531. Corrects his error of Apr 22 to show that John Nicks had resigned, not been removed, as Arkansas Territory militia brigadier.
Dec 30	To the United States Senate. DS, DNA-RG 46 (17-0044). *Senate Executive Proceedings*, 4:142. Nominates Thomas Finley for marshal in Maryland.
Dec 30	*From Graves W. Steele.* 724
Dec 30	Check to Andrew Jackson Jr. for $100. DS, DLC (38).
Dec 31	To the United States Congress. DS, DNA-RG 46; DS, DNA-RG 233; Draft, DNA-RG 59 (17-0051). *SDoc* 21, 21st Cong., 2d sess., p. 1 (Serial 203); Richardson, 2:531–32. Transmits Van Buren's correspondence with envoy Peter von Scholten over relieving restrictions on trade with the Danish West Indies.
Dec 31	To the United States Senate. DS, DNA-RG 46 (17-0057). *Senate Executive Proceedings*, 4:141. Nominates Edward Pescud for customs surveyor at Petersburg, Va.
Dec 31	To the United States Senate. DS, DNA-RG 46 (17-0059). *Senate Executive Proceedings*, 4:141. Nominates Gilbert Dennison for consul at Panama.
Dec 31	To Martin Van Buren. AN, DNA-RG 59 (M639-7). Returns Silas K. Everett's recommendation of Gilbert Dennison to succeed him as consul at Panama.
Dec 31	From John Branch. LC, DNA-RG 45 (M472-1). Proposes Marine second lieutenant Joseph L. C. Hardy for promotion.
Dec 31	To the United States Senate. DS, DNA-RG 46 (17-0061); LC, DNA-RG 45 (M472-1). *Senate Executive Proceedings*, 4:141.

Nominates Joseph L. C. Hardy for promotion to Marine first lieutenant.

Dec 31   From David Jewett Baker. ALS, DNA-RG 107 (17-0047). Transmits a recommendation for Francis Prince.

[cDec]   From C. A. Norton et al. DS, DNA-RG 46 (16-0912). Recommend Thomas Irwin for Pennsylvania district judge.

[cDec]   From Thomas Ringland et al. DS, DNA-RG 46 (16-0915). Pennsylvania legislators recommend Thomas Irwin for district judge.

[cDec]   From Andrew Stewart et al. DS, DNA-RG 46 (16-0918). Recommend Thomas Irwin for Pennsylvania district judge.

[c1830]   To George Gray Leiper and Joseph Hemphill. Draft (at 1831), DLC (40). Thanks Mrs. Linde for the gift of a handmade silk purse.

[1830]   From Joseph S. Cabot et al. LS, DNA-RG 59 (M639-6). Recommend John Davis for chargé d'affaires to Buenos Aires.

1830   From John Milton Goodenow. AD, THer (14-1235). Presents a copy of his *Historical Sketches of the Principles and Maxims of American Jurisprudence* (1819) once owned by Thomas Jefferson.

[c1830]   To Samuel Delucenna Ingham. ANS, PU (12-0371). Note to await further word from the consul while ascertaining facts from confidential sources.

[c1830]   From Samuel Delucenna Ingham. AN, DLC (38). Statement of Treasury receipts for 1829 and 1830.

[1830]   Drafts by AJ Donelson for a publication refuting the claim in *Biographical Sketch of General John Adair* (Washington, 1830) that it was Adair's idea to place the Kentucky militia in ready reserve at New Orleans. D, DLC (72).

[c1830] Feb 19   From George Corbin Washington. ALS, THer (15-0210). Encloses a letter from Thomas G. Plummer of Mt. Vernon, Ohio.

[c1830] May 2   From George Washington Keeton. ALS, TNJ (13-0240). Asks for a government clerkship.

Index

Page numbers between 729 and 810 refer to the Calendar. An index reference to a single page of the Calendar may represent more than one item on that page. **Bolded italic** page numbers following a proper name represent documents printed in the volume written to or by that person or group.

Maria (Hermitage slave child), 611–12, 636
Maria Christina of the Two Sicilies, 752
Marianne, Princess of the Netherlands, 787
Marigny, Bernard, 730
Marine corps: court-martials, 740, 744; in annual message, 651; officer appointments, promotions, and dismissals, 729, 749, 752, 756, 760–62, 766, 768, 774–76, 782, 791, 796, 799, 805, 809–10; pay and allowances, 769, 772; paymaster, 788, 790–91; soldier discharge, 796
Marks, William, 251
Marrast, Amedeus B., 804
Marschalk, Andrew, 759
Marshall, Benjamin (Creek), 202–3, 207
Marshall, John, 212, 388
Marshall, Joseph (Creek), 202–3
Marshall, L. A., 776
Marshals, U.S. *See under names and states*
Martin, Catherine Donelson, 714
Martin, George Montgomery, 782
Martin, George Washington, 549, 551
Martin, James Glasgow, 714
Martin, John (Cherokee), 160–61
Martin, Morgan Lewis, 735, 738
Maryland: and Cumberland Road, 286, 295; penitentiary, 762; politics, 69, 335–36, 348, 398–99, 442, 458, 746; U.S. marshal, 733, 809
Maryland Advocate (Cumberland), 800
Maryland Gazette (Annapolis), 398–99
Masi, F. & Co., 748
Mason, John, 749
Mason, John Thomson, 166–67, 181, 206, 526–27, 765
Mason, Richard Chichester, 754
Mason, Stevens Thomson, 167
Mason, Thomson Francis, 755
Masonry, 161–62; in Eaton affair, 708, 711. *See also* Anti-Masonry
Massachusetts: politics and appointments, 85–88, 126–28, 167–68, 442, 471–72, 742–44
Mattingly, George, 777
Maury, ____, 645, 647
Maury, Abram Poindexter, 769
Maury, William Henry, 769
Mawney, John G., 740
Maxcy, Virgil: solicitor of the Treasury, 337, 772, 778, 792, 796
Mayo, Robert: *643–47;* 684
Mayrant, Robert P., 753

Mayson, Charles C., 782
Maysville Road veto: *279–300;* preparation, 223–25, 261, 264–66; AJ on, 300, 303, 305, 332, 367, 388, 396–98, 400, 402, 422–24, 546; invoked in lighthouse bill veto, 323–24, 326–28, 331; acclaimed, 302, 335, 348, 355, 395, 398–401, 411, 417, 442, 448–49, 458, 512–13, 557, 612, 783, 786; opposed, 396, 403, 459, 624; precedent feared, 359–60
McAfee, Robert Breckinridge, 417–18, 784
McArthur, Duncan, 61–62
McBee, Silas, 453–54
McCall, James, 526–27
McCalla, John Moore: *552;* 486–87, 552, 796
McCarty, Elizabeth, 212
McClain, George, 550
McClintock, John, 801
McClung, Charles, 637
McClure, Richard, 396–97, 409–10, 412
McCoy, William, 808
McDonald, James L. (Choctaw), 156, 158, 238, 247
McDowell, James, Jr., 787
McDuffie, George: and Decatur claim, 136; and diplomatic appropriations, 225, 493; and electoral college reform, 183–84, 712; and nullification, 577; and Seminole controversy, 312–14, 321; BUS report, 221, 266, 305, 343–48, 352, 396–97, 403, 410, 456–57, 493–94, 712
McElderry, Hugh, 796
McElvain, John, 61–62, 529
McFarland, Samuel, 780
McGavock, Randal, 580–81, 710
McGillivray, William (Chickasaw), 511–12
McGilvery, William (Creek), 419–20
McGirk, Andrew Stephen, 162, 727
McHenry, James, 755
McIntire, Rufus, 431–32
McIntosh Creeks. *See* Creek Indians, Western
McIntosh, Roley (Creek): *98–105, 146–50, 214–18;* 202–3, 405, 745
McIntosh, William (Creek), 98, 100–102, 104, 146–48, 150
McKean, Samuel, 735
McKeever, Isaac, 759, 797
McKenney, Thomas Loraine, superintendent of Indian affairs, 24, 77, 210; and annuities, 62, 228, 241, 462; and Cherokees, 115, 195; and